World Scientific Handbook in Financial Economics Series — Vol.6

WORLD SCIENTIFIC REFERENCE ON

HANDBOOK OF THE ECONOMICS OF WINE

❶ Prices, Finance, and Expert Opinion

World Scientific Handbook in Financial Economics Series

(ISSN: 2010-1732)

The Handbooks in Financial Economics (HIFE) are intended to be a definitive source for comprehensive and accessible information in the field of finance. Each individual volume in the series presents an accurate self-contained survey of a sub-field of finance, suitable for use by finance, economics and financial engineering professors and lecturers, professional researchers, investments, pension fund and insurance portfolio mangers, risk managers, graduate students and as a teaching supplement.

The HIFE series will broadly cover various areas of finance in a multi-handbook series. The HIFE series has its own web page that include detailed information such as the introductory chapter to each volume, an abstract of each chapter and biographies of editors. The series will be promoted by the publisher at major academic meetings and through other sources. There will be links with research articles in major journals.

The goal is to have a broad group of outstanding volumes in various areas of financial economics. The evidence is that acceptance of all the books is strengthened over time and by the presence of other strong volumes. Sales, citations, royalties and recognition tend to grow over time faster than the number of volumes published.

Published

Vol. 6 *Handbook of the Economics of Wine (In 2 Volumes)*
Volume 1: Prices, Finance, and Expert Opinion
Volume 2: Reputation, Regulation, and Market Organization
edited by Orley Ashenfelter, Olivier Gergaud, Karl Storchmann & William T. Ziemba

Vol. 5 *The World Scientific Handbook of Futures Markets*
edited by Anastasios G. Malliaris & William T. Ziemba

Vol. 4 *Handbook of the Fundamentals of Financial Decision Making (In 2 Parts)*
edited by Leonard C. MacLean & William T. Ziemba

Vol. 3 *The Kelly Capital Growth Investment Criterion: Theory and Practice*
edited by Leonard C. MacLean, Edward O. Thorp & William T. Ziemba

Vol. 2 *Efficiency of Racetrack Betting Markets (2008 Edition)*
edited by Donald B. Hausch, Victor S. Y. Lo & William T. Ziemba

Forthcoming

The World Scientific Handbook of Insurance (To be announced)

More information on this series can also be found at http://www.worldscientific.com/series/wshfes

World Scientific Handbook in Financial Economics Series — Vol.6

WORLD SCIENTIFIC REFERENCE ON HANDBOOK OF THE ECONOMICS OF WINE

❶ Prices, Finance, and Expert Opinion

Orley Ashenfelter, Olivier Gergaud, Karl Storchmann and **William Ziemba**

Editors

World Scientific

NEW JERSEY • LONDON • SINGAPORE • BEIJING • SHANGHAI • HONG KONG • TAIPEI • CHENNAI • TOKYO

Published by

World Scientific Publishing Co. Pte. Ltd.
5 Toh Tuck Link, Singapore 596224
USA office: 27 Warren Street, Suite 401-402, Hackensack, NJ 07601
UK office: 57 Shelton Street, Covent Garden, London WC2H 9HE

Library of Congress Cataloging-in-Publication Data
Names: Ashenfelter, Orley, 1942– editor.
Title: Handbook of the economics of wine / edited by Orley Ashenfelter (Princeton) [and three others].
Description: New Jersey : World Scientific, [2018] | Series: World Scientific handbook in financial economics series ; volume 6 Contents: Volume 1. Prices, finance, and expert opinion -- Volume 2. Reputation, regulation, and market organization.
Identifiers: LCCN 2017044682| ISBN 9789814740579 (hc set : alk. paper) | ISBN 9789814740586 (hc: v.1 : alk. paper) | ISBN 9789814740593 (hc: v.2 : alk. paper)
Subjects: LCSH: Wine industry. | Wine and wine making--Economic aspects.
Classification: LCC HD9370.5 .H36 2018 | DDC 338.4/76632--dc23
LC record available at https://lccn.loc.gov/2017044682

British Library Cataloguing-in-Publication Data
A catalogue record for this book is available from the British Library.

ISBN: 978-981-3270-35-0 (pbk set) For special sales only
ISBN: 978-981-3270-36-7 (pbk: v.1) For special sales only
ISBN: 978-981-3270-37-4 (pbk: v.2) For special sales only

For any available supplementary material, please visit
http://www.worldscientific.com/worldscibooks/10.1142/9834#t=suppl

Desk Editors: Herbert Moses/Lum Pui Yee

Typeset by Stallion Press
Email: enquiries@stallionpress.com

Printed in Singapore

About the Editors

Ashenfelter Orley is Joseph Douglas Green 1895 Professor of Economics and former Director of the Industrial Relations Section at Princeton University. He has been the President of the American Economic Association, the American Law and Economics Association, and the Society of Labor Economics. He is currently the President of the Western Economic Association International and the American Association of Wine Economists. He edited the *American Economic Review* and founded and edited the *American Law and Economics Review.* As Director of the Office of Evaluation of the US Department of Labor in 1972, he began the work that is now widely recognized as the separate field of "quantitative social program evaluation." He is also regarded as the originator of the use of so-called "natural experiments" to infer causality about economic relationships. He has also been the leader in the recent emphasis in quantitative economic analysis on the use of creative methods of data collection.

Gergaud Olivier is Professor of Economics at KEDGE Business School in Bordeaux and Affiliate Researcher at LIEPP in Sciences Po. He holds a Ph.D. from the University of Reims and an accreditation to supervise research from Sciences Po. His research areas are Cultural Economics, Wine Economics, Sports Economics, and Restaurant Economics. He has been a visiting professor at different European (Sciences Po, Université Libre de Bruxelles) and North American universities

(HEC Montréal, NYU, and UCLA). He has published several papers in international journals such as *Economic Journal*, *Economic Inquiry*, *Journal of Economic Behavior and Organization*, *Journal of Wine Economics*, and *Oxford Bulletin of Economics and Statistics*. He currently serves on the Editorial Advisory Board of the *Journal of Wine Economics* and on the Editorial Board of the *Journal of Prediction Markets*.

Storchmann Karl is Clinical Professor of Economics at the New York University, a Co-Founder and the Managing Editor of the *Journal of Wine Economics*, and Vice President of the American Association of Wine Economists (AAWE). He has taught or held permanent or visiting positions in many universities, including Yale University, UCLA, University of Paris II Panthéon-Assas, University of Bordeaux, and Whitman College. His research interests encompass agricultural, energy, and environmental economics. His most recent research focuses on the impact of climate change on the wine industry, particularly on wine prices and vineyard land profitability. He has published in various journals including *American Economic Review*, *Review of Economics and Statistics*, and the *Journal of Wine Economics*.

Ziemba T. William is the Alumni Professor (Emeritus) of Financial Modeling and Stochastic Optimization in the Sauder School of Business, University of British Columbia where he taught from 1968–2006. His Ph.D. is from the University of California, Berkeley. He has been a visiting professor at Cambridge, Oxford, London School of Economics, University of Reading and Warwick in the UK, at Stanford, UCLA, Berkeley, MIT, University of Washington and Chicago in the US, Universities of Bergamo, Venice and Luiss in Italy, the Universities of Zurich, Cyprus, Tsukuba (Japan), Sabanci (Turkey), EDHEC (France), KAIST (Korea), and the National University and the National Technological University of Singapore. His research is in asset-liability management, portfolio theory and practice, security market imperfections, Japanese and Asian financial markets, hedge fund strategies, risk management, sports and lottery investments, and applied stochastic programming. His co-written practitioner paper on the Russell–Yasuda model won second prize in the 1993 Edelman Practice of Management Science Competition. In 2015, he won the futures part of the Battle of the Quants Trading Contest and beat the equity winner as well. He has published widely in journals such as *Operations Research, Management Science, Mathematics of OR, Mathematical Programming, American Economic Review, Journal of Economic Perspectives, Journal of Finance, Journal of Economic Dynamics and Control, JFQA, Quantitative Finance, Journal of Portfolio Management* and *Journal of Banking and Finance* and in many books and special journal issues. He is the series editor for North Holland's Handbooks in Finance, World Scientific Handbooks in Financial Economics and Books in Finance, and previously was the CORS editor of INFOR and the department of finance editor of *Management Science*, 1982–1992. He has continued his columns in *Wilmott* and his 2013 book with Rachel Ziemba have the 2007–2013 columns updated with new material published by World Scientific.

List of Contributors

Almenberg Johan
Department of Economics, Stockholm School of Economics, and the Research Institute of Industrial Economics, Sveriges Riksbank, SE-103 37 Stockholm, Sweden

Alston M. Julian
Department of Agricultural and Resource Economics at the University of California, Davis, One Shields Avenue, Davis, CA 95616, USA
Robert Mondavi Institute Center for Wine Economics at the University of California, USA

Ashenfelter Orley
Department of Economics, Princeton University, Princeton, NJ 08540, USA
Economics Department, Firestone Library, Princeton University, Princeton, NJ 08544, USA

Ashton H. Robert
L. Palmer Fox Professor, Fuqua School of Business, Duke University, USA

Burton J. Benjamin
Associate, Lehman Brothers, 3 World Trade Center, 19th Ave., New York, NY l0285, USA

Cicchetti V. Domenic
Yale Home Office, 94 Linsley Lake Road, North Branford, CT 06471, USA

Combris Pierre
INRA, UR1303, ALISS Alimentation et Sciences Sociales, F-94205 Ivry-sur-Seine, France

Costanigro Marco
Department of Agricultural and Resource Economics, Colorado State University, Fort Collins, CO 80523, USA

Cross Robin
Department of Agricultural and Resource Economics, Oregon State University, Corvallis, OR 97331, USA

Dreber Anna
Department of Economics, Stockholm School of Economics, and Program for Evolutionary Dynamics, P.O. Box 6501, 113 83 Stockholm, Sweden

Dubois Pierre
Toulouse School of Economics, Université de Toulouse 1 Capitole, Toulouse 21 Allée de Brienne 31000 Toulouse, France

Emerson W. John
Department of Statistics, Yale University, USA

Fogarty J. James
School of Agricultural and Resource Economics, University of Western Australia, 35 Stirling Hwy, Crawley 6009, Australia

Fuller B. Kate
Department of Agricultural Economics and Economics Montana State University, PO Box 172920, Bozeman, MT 59717, USA

Gergaud Olivier
KEDGE Business School and LIEPP — Sciences Po, Paris, France

Ginsburgh Victor
ECARES, Université Libre de Bruxelles and CORE, Université Catholique de Louvain, Belgium

Goldstein Robin
Fearless Critic Media, 2011 B Bouldin Avenue, Austin, TX 78704, USA

Hadj Ali Héla
Research Fellow at INRA (National Institute for Research in Agriculture), Toulouse, France

Henderson Caroline
Ecole hôtelière de Lausanne, HES-SO University of Applied Sciences Western Switzerland Route de Cojonnex 18, 1000 Lausanne 25, Switzerland

Herschkowitsch Alexis
Fearless Critic Media, 2011 B Bouldin Avenue, Austin, TX 78704, USA

Hodgson T. Robert
Professor Emeritus, Department of Oceanography, Humboldt State University, Arcata, CA 95521, USA

Issanchou Sylvie
Centre des Sciences du Goût et de lálimentation, AgroSup Dijon, CNRS, INRA, Université Bourgogne Franche Comté, F-21000 Dijon, France

Jacobsen P. Joyce
Professor of Economics, Economics Department, Public Affairs Center, Wesleyan University, Middletown, CT 06459, USA

Katz Jacob
Fearless Critic Media, 2011 B Bouldin Avenue, Austin, TX 78704, USA

Lange Christine
Centre des Sciences du Goût et de l'alimentation, AgroSup Dijon, CNRS, INRA, Université Bourgogne Franche Comté, F-21000 Dijon, France

Lapsley T. James
Department of Viticulture & Enology at the University of California, Davis and UC Agricultural Issues Center, One Shields Avenue, Davis, CA 95616, USA

Lecocq Sébastien
INRA, UR1303 ALISS, Alimentation et Sciences Sociales, F-94205 Ivry-sur-Seine, France

Masset Philippe
Ecole hôtelière de Lausanne, HES-SO University of Applied Sciences, Western Switzerland

McCluskey J. Jill
School of Economic Sciences and Food Policy Fellow, International Marketing Program for Agricultural Commodities and Trade (IMPACT) Center, Washington State University, Pullman, WA 99164-6210, USA

Mittelhammer C. Ron
School of Economic Sciences and Department of Statistics, Washington State University, Pullman, WA 99164-6210, USA

Nauges Céline
Toulouse School of Economics, INRA, Université de Toulouse 1 Capitole, Senior Research Fellow at Toulouse School of Economics, INRA, University of Toulouse, Toulouse, France

Plantinga J. Andrew
Bren School of Environmental Science & Management, University of California, Santa Barbara, CA 93106-5131, USA

Quandt Richard
Department of Economics, Princeton University, Emeritus Princeton, NJ 08544, USA

Reagans Ray
MIT Sloan School of Management, Cambridge, MA 02142, USA

Roberts W. Peter
Goizueta Business School, Emory University, Atlanta, GA 30306, USA

Sanning W. Lee
Department of Economics and Finance, University of Wyoming, 1000 East University Ave., Laramie, WY 82071, USA

Shaffer Sherrill
Department of Economics and Finance, University of Wyoming, 1000 East University Ave., Laramie, WY 82071, USA

Sharratt Jo Marie
Department of Economics and Finance, University of Wyoming, 1000 East University Ave., Laramie, WY 82071, USA

Soleas George
Quality Assurance and Specialty Services, Liquor Control Board of Ontario, 1 Yonge Street, Suite 1401, Toronto, Ontario, M5E 1E5, Canada

Stavins N. Robert
John F. Kennedy School of Government, Harvard University, 79 John F. Kennedy Street, Cambridge, MA 02138, National Bureau of Economic Research and Resources of the Future, USA

Storchmann Karl
Economics Department, New York University, 19 West Fourth Street, New York, NY 10012, USA

Visser Michael
CREST, CNRS, ENSAE, University of Paris-Saclay and CRED, University of Paris 2, France

Weil L. Roman
Graduate School of Business, University of Chicago, 5807 S. Woodlawn Avenue, Chicago, IL 60637, USA

Contents

Part I

Introduction

Chapter 1

Wine Economics*

Karl Storchmann

Economics Department, New York University,
19 West Fourth Street, New York, NY 10012, USA
karl.storchmann@nyu.edu

Fine wine has a few characteristics that differentiate it from other agricultural commodities and beverages, rendering it an interesting topic for economists. Fine wine can regularly fetch bottle prices that exceed several thousand dollars. It can be stored a long time and can increase in value with age. Fine-wine quality and prices are extraordinarily sensitive to fluctuations in the weather the year in which the grapes were grown. Wine is an experience good, that is, its quality cannot be ascertained before consumption. As a result, consumers often rely on "expert opinion" regarding quality and maturation prospects. This chapter describes the emergence and the unparalleled rise of wine economics from the 1980s to the present and sheds light on its three main topics: finance, climate change, and the role of expert opinion.

1. Introduction

Humans have cultivated vines for the production of wine for thousands of years. According to Unwin (1991), the origins of viticulture lie in the region between the Black Sea and the Caspian Sea and date back to 4000 B.C.E., possibly even 6000 B.C.E. Only a few products have such a long history with a production process that has remained more or less unchanged.

Accordingly, over the past millennia, a large body of viticultural and enological literature has accumulated. Early examples date back more than 2,000 years (Robinson, 2006). The Roman statesman Marcus Cato, also known as Cato the Elder (234–149 B.C.E.), in his book *De agri cultura* provides detailed practical advice on how to profitably run a wine farm. Among other

*This article originally appeared in *Journal of Wine Economics* (2012), 7(1), 1–33.

topics, he stresses that grapes should be fully ripe when harvested and that all vats need to be perfectly clean to prevent wine from turning into vinegar. Another Roman, Lucius Columella, discusses many technical aspects of Roman viticulture in his treatise on farming, *De re rustica* (60 C.E.). In two books, he elaborates on topics such as which grape variety grows best on which soil type. He lays out many elements of modern vine training and trellising. For instance, he recommends a vine spacing of a double pace (about 1.50 m), vines to be trained on chestnut stakes as high as a man, and willow shoots to fasten the vines (a natural fastener that is still being used in the Mosel Valley).

Economists have taken notice of wine and the vine as well. Adam Smith, David Ricardo, John Stuart Mill, Karl Marx, and Leon Walras all wrote, to some extent, about wine (see, e.g., Chaikind, 2010). Although these early writings are on topics such as the value of vineyard land or trade, they mostly touch on wine only in passing or refer to it as an example. In addition, these references are too scattered over more than a century for them to constitute wine economics as an independent economic discipline.

Wine economics as a discipline that analyses wine-related issues as its main focus entered the scene much later. Over the past two decades, wine economics has emerged as a growing field, not only within agricultural economics but in adjacent fields such as finance, trade, growth, and environmental economics as well. Several academic associations are devoted to furthering the economics of wine. At the annual conferences of the largest one, namely, the American Association of Wine Economists (AAWE), more than 200 wine economists from all over the world regularly meet and present the results of their research. For example, at the 2011 annual AAWE meetings in Bolzano, Italy, 130 papers were presented on wine economics. Since 2006, and in addition to the agricultural economics journals, one academic journal is devoted to wine and economics, the *Journal of Wine Economics*.[1] Furthermore, wine economics research has been increasingly recognized by general economics journals.

In what respect is wine different from milk, coffee, tea, or beer? This chapter aims to sketch the emergence of wine economics and recent developments in the economics literature. Furthermore, I want to shed some light

[1]Apart from the *Journal of Wine Economics* of the AAWE, there are several journals that, although not purely economics-oriented, also publish economic wine-related analyses; these journals are the *International Journal of Wine Business Research* of the Academy of Wine Business Research, the *Journal of Wine Research* of the Institute of the Masters of Wine and the *International Journal of Wine Research.*

on the three main research issues of wine economics, namely: wine as an investment, environmental issues, and the role of experts. The remainder of the chapter is organized as follows: Section 2 provides some data on the development of wine in the scholarly literature over the past few decades; Section 3 describes the emergence of wine economics; the central topics of wine economics are introduced in Sections 4–6, and Section 7 concludes and provides an outlook.

2. Developments

Although wine is not the most talked-about subject in the world, it may still be important compared to other beverages. In order to get an idea of the general relevance of a topic, I conducted a simple Google search for words such as "wine" or "beer." Certainly, counting Google hits as a measure of general relevance is not without problems. First, some topics might be discussed on the Internet a lot while others are more offline topics, that is, online publications and bloggers focus their Internet chatter on some topics more than others. Second, counting Google hits of single words can result in an exaggerated count when unrelated terms contain this word. For instance, all searches for "tea" will also contain references to "tea party," which has little relation to the beverage. Third, the search is confined to the English language, which can disadvantage certain topics. For instance, "wine" might have resulted in relatively more results if the French word (*vin*) had been included. Notwithstanding these issues, a Google search can still lead to insightful results.

Figure 1 reports the results of this Google search, done on September 5, 2010, for beverage words, such as "coffee," "milk," "tea," "water," and "wine." At 343 million results, the word "wine" yields more hits than any other beverage, except for water. However, compared to words, such as "bread" (450 million), "sport" (548 million), "sex" (586 million), "apple" (705 million), "money" (4.7 billion) or "car" (5.57 billion), the number of Google results for "wine" appears to be rather small.

Figure 2 provides the number of Google Scholar hits, that is, hits in scholarly publications, for the same subjects from 1940 to 2010. Because Google Scholar allows users to search by discipline, I confined the search to "business," "administration," "finance," and "economics." Surprisingly, the general Internet chatter by online publications, bloggers, and so on is inadequately reflected in scholarly relevance. First, of the considered beverages, "wine," with 26,600 hits, has the least scholarly coverage while — apart from

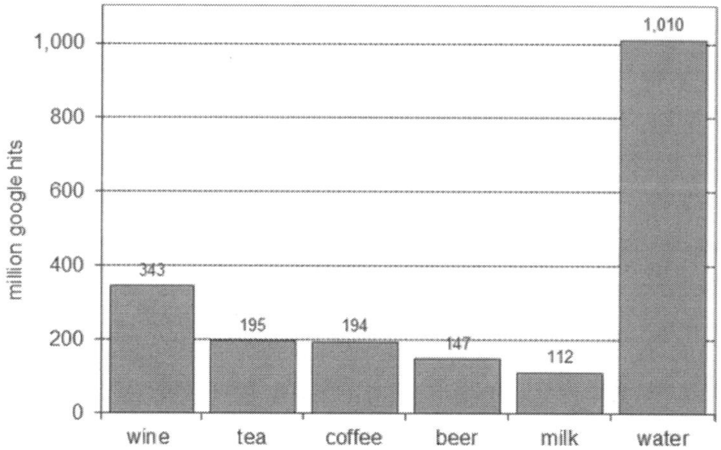

Figure 1. Google Hits for Selected Beverages (million hits, September 2010)

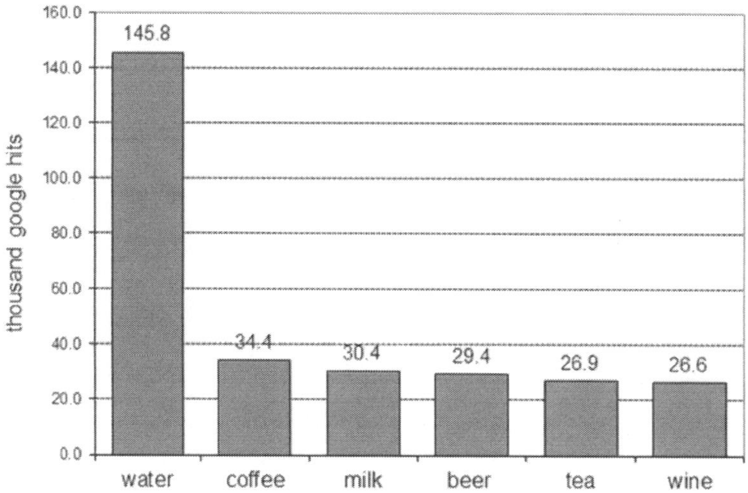

Figure 2. Google Scholar Hits for Selected Beverages in Business, Administration Finance and Economics, 1940–2010 (September 5, 2010)

"water" — "coffee" exhibits the highest coverage (34,000 hits). Second, and unsurprisingly, scholarly hits amount to only a very small fraction of all general hits. However, the range of the ratio "all Google hits to Google Scholar hits" is astoundingly high. Although "milk" generates less than 3,700 general Google hits per Google Scholar hit, the same metric is almost 13,000 for wine (Table 1). In fact, of all beverages, wine has by far the most nonscholarly hits per scholarly hit. Clearly, more people have opinions about wine and write

Table 1. Scholarly Ratio of Selected Beverages

Beverage	All Google hits (in million)	Google Scholar hits	All Google hits per Google Scholar hit
Wine	343	26,600	12,895
Tea	195	26,900	7,249
Water	1,010	145,800	6,927
Coffee	194	34,000	5,706
Beer	147	29,400	5,000
Milk	112	30,400	3,684

Note: Google hits and Google Scholar hits from 1940 to 2010 as of September 5, 2010.

about them than they do about milk. This appears to square with Richard Quandt's statement in his article "On Wine Bullshit" in the *Journal of Wine Economics*: "I think the wine trade is intrinsically bullshit-prone and therefore attracts bullshit artists" (2007, p. 135).

These results are apparently not in line with the emergence of a new academic field called *Wine Economics*. However, two facts change the picture again: the scholarly growth rate and the quality of the publications.

Figure 3 depicts the decennial changes in Google Scholar hits. Compared to the other beverages, "wine" has consistently exhibited the largest scholarly growth rates since the 1980. In contrast, "milk," the beverage with the highest scholarly ratio (see Table 1), has experienced its largest growth rates in the 1960s and has lagged behind ever since.

In addition, when considering the scholarly hits in the top (applied) economics journals only,[2] "Wine" exhibits the fewest hits for the 1980s but is first in the 2000s (Figure 4).[3] Figure 5 shows the corresponding growth rate from the 1980s to the present. Among the six beverages, the growth rate of "wine" citations in top general economic journals is second to none. In fact, the growth rate of "wine" is higher than all the other five beverages combined.

The findings of the Google analysis can be summarized as follows: (i) Compared to other beverages, "wine" exhibits a lively online presence, suggesting that wine is a topic that people want to talk about. (ii) However,

[2]These figures refer to *American Economic Review, Journal of Political Economy, Quarterly Journal of Economics, Review of Economics and Statistics*, and *The Economic Journal.*

[3]The word "wine" must be mentioned in either the title or the abstract of the article.

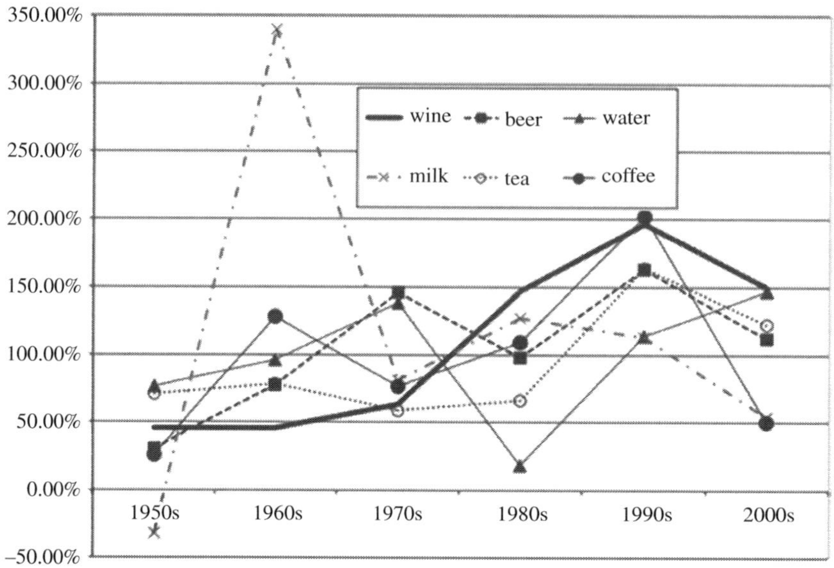

Figure 3. Growth Rates of Google Scholar Hits in Business, Economics and Finance for Selected Beverages by Decade, 1950–2010

not all of this Internet chatter is scholarly. Of all beverages, "wine" has the highest "nonscholarly rate" (general Google hits per Google Scholar hit). (iii) Despite (or because of) the fact that "wine" is prone to attract nonscholarly Internet hits, "wine" has experienced extraordinary growth in the scholarly literature over the past two decades and (iv) When considering the journal quality of scholarly hits, "wine" has risen from the bottom in the 1980s to the top in the 2000s. Its citation growth rate over this period is higher than for all the other beverages combined.

What has caused this enormous interest in wine over the past two decades, especially in the high-end general economic literature?

3. The Emergence

Fine wine has a few characteristics that differentiate it from other agricultural commodities and beverages, rendering it an interesting topic for economists. First, fine wine can regularly fetch bottle prices that exceed several thousand dollars. In fact, the world's most expensive bottle, a 1787 Château Lafite, purportedly formerly owned by Thomas Jefferson, was auctioned off by Christie's of London in 1985 and sold for £105,000, which was equivalent to approximately $322,000 in 2011. Second, fine wine can be stored a long time and can increase in value with age. Third, fine wine quality and

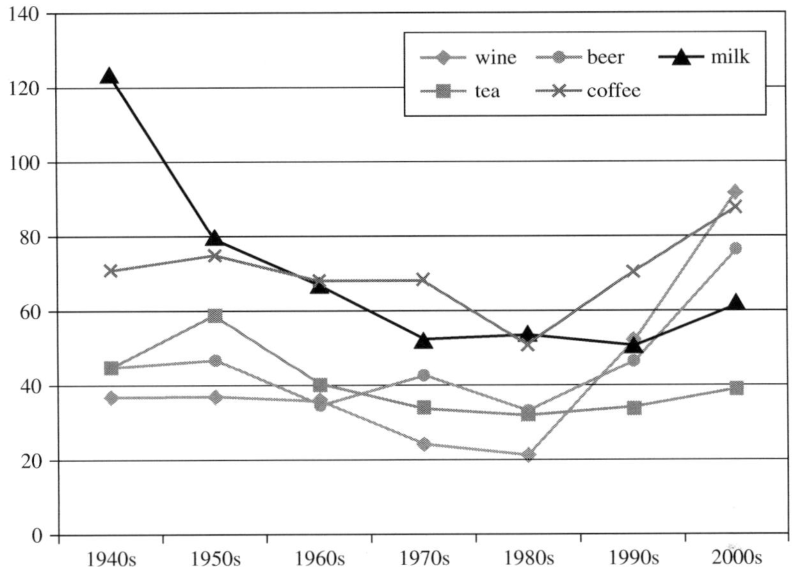

Figure 4. Google Scholar Hits in Top General Economics Journals (*American Economic Review, Economic Journal, Journal of Political Economy, Quarterly Journal of Economics, Review of Economics and Statistics*) by Decade from the 1940s to the 2000s

prices are extraordinarily sensitive to fluctuations in the weather the year in which the grapes were grown. Fourth, wine is an experience good, that is, a good for which it is difficult to ascertain its quality before consumption. As a result, consumers often rely heavily on "expert opinion" regarding quality and maturation prospects.

In 1986, Princeton economics professor Orley Ashenfelter launched a newsletter called *Liquid Assets — The International Guide to Fine Wines.* As the first publication of its kind and in stark contrast to the prevailing glossy wine literature, *Liquid Assets* was devoted to the quantitative analysis of the fine-wine market. Ashenfelter published auction prices and provided numerous economic analyses, such as an updated "new objective ranking of the châteaux of Bordeaux." Like the original classification of 1855, Ashenfelter's ranking was completely empirical and based on wine auction prices and not — as might be thought — on "expert opinion" (1988, 1997).[4] Other articles have tackled issues such as the impact of wine critics on wine prices (Ashenfelter, 1992). *Liquid Assets* ran a successful campaign to allow

[4]Historically, all vineyard classifications were based on wine prices, land prices, or land profits. The existence of professional "wine critics" is a fairly recent phenomenon from no earlier than the 1970s.

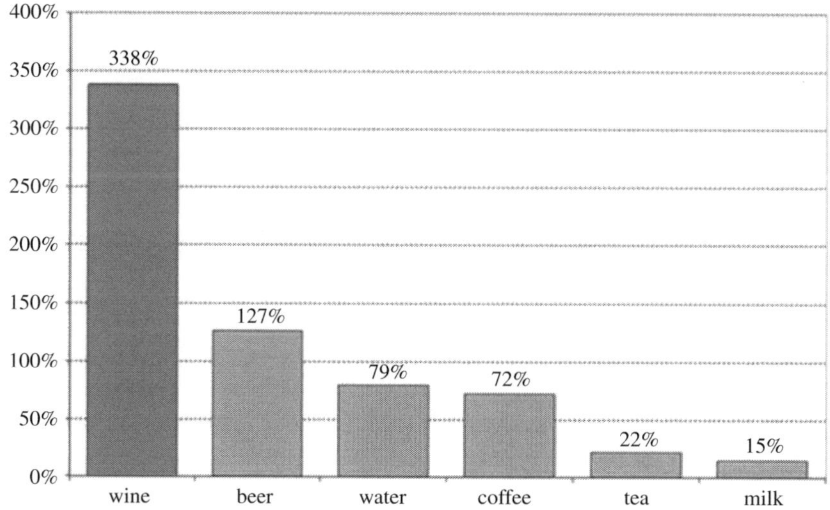

Figure 5. Growth Rates of Google Scholar Hits in Top General Economics Journals (*American Economic Review, Economic Journal, Journal of Political Economy, Quarterly Journal of Economics, Review of Economics and Statistics*) from the 1980s to the 2000s

wine drinkers to bring their own wine to New York City restaurants (e.g., Ashenfelter, 1991). Another campaign focused on fine wine auctions and their legality in some states (Ashenfelter, 1987b).

However, the central theme of Ashenfelter's research published in *Liquid Assets* has always been the assessment of vintage quality for wines from various regions (e.g., Ashenfelter, 1986, 1987c, 1987d). Essentially, Ashenfelter devised an econometric model that explains auction prices of mature wines by referring to the wine's age and the weather in the year during which the grapes were grown. This model has proven surprisingly effective at assessing the quality of Bordeaux vintages and predicting prices of mature wines.

Given that Ashenfelter was the editor of the prestigious *American Economic Review*,[5] his wine-related works received considerable attention from economists and the general public alike. The *New York Times* has published numerous articles on Ashenfelter's wine economics research in its Wine and Food Section, in the Business Section, and on the front page (e.g., Goldberg, 1987; Passell, 1990a, 1990b; Prial, 1990). TV channels, such as ABC, CNN, CNBC, and Bloomberg, have aired special reports on his econometric wine models. The wine trade and wine critics, however, have

[5]In fact, he edited the *AER* from 1985 to 2001, having had the longest tenure of all editors, second only to the founding editor, Davis Dewey (1911–1940).

been less intrigued. The New York wine merchant William Sokolin calls Ashenfelter's equation "somewhere between violent and hysterical" (Ayres, 2007). Robert Parker, the world's most influential wine critic, deems Ashenfelter's empirical approach "really a Neanderthal way of looking at wine. It is so absurd as to be laughable," in short, "an absolute total sham" (Ayres, 2007).

Why is the wine world up in arms against an empirical approach to wine? Frank Prial of the *New York Times* writes:

> Two reasons. Some elements of the wine trade are angry because the Ashenfelter equation could be helpful in identifying lesser vintages they have promoted. For example, he is down on 1986, a year praised by more conventional commentators. Mr. Ashenfelter, or at least his numbers, say the vintage will be the worst of the 1980's. Secondly, and more seriously, he is accused of relegating the whole wine-tasting mystique to a minor role. Supposedly, the sipping, spitting, sniffing and note-taking so dear to wine romantics have all been rendered obsolete by mathematics. (1990)

Ashenfelter *et al.* (1995) published an updated version of the "Bordeaux equation" and later, in 2008, in *The Economic Journal* (Ashenfelter, 2008). The Bordeaux model is a cross-sectional model with the (natural logarithm of) price index of a Bordeaux wine portfolio as dependent variable and the wine's age and various weather data as independent variables. Table 2 shows the results of three different variants. Column (1) reports the results when only age is used as explanatory variable, and columns (2) and (3) also include weather variables. The equation in column (2) is most commonly referred to as the "Bordeaux equation." It contains the main seeds of wine economics and its major research topics: (1) the value of wine as an alternative financial asset, (2) wine and climate change, and (3) wine and expert opinion.

First, the Bordeaux equation laid the foundation for a large body of research in wine's role as an alternative financial asset. The age coefficient of 0.0238 (Table 2, column (2)) represents the real rate of return to holding Bordeaux wine.[6] One more year of age adds 2.38% to the wine portfolio's value. Does that justify holding wine as an alternative asset in lieu of stock?

In addition to storing wine, consumers might also invest in Bordeaux wine futures one year after the harvest. The future prices are set by the producers and might not reflect the true market value of the wine. The true market is not known before the wine is finally released and traded, which normally happens three years after the harvest. Young Bordeaux *grands crus*

[6]Note that "real" does not refer to the CPI basket of consumer goods but, rather, to wine only.

Table 2. Bordeaux Wine Prices and the Weather

Independent variable	Dependent variable logarithm of London auction prices for mature red Bordeaux wines (1)	(2)	(3)
Age of vintage	0.0354	0.0238	0.240
	(0.0137)	(0.00717)	(0.00747)
Average temperature over growing season (April–September)		0.616	0.608
		(0.0952)	(0.116)
Rain in August		−0.00386	−0.00380
		(0.00081)	(0.000950)
Rain in the months preceding the vintage (October–March)		0.001173	0.00115
		(0.000482)	(0.000505)
Average temperature in September			0.00765
			(0.0565)
R^2	0.212	0.828	0.828
Root mean squared error	0.575	0.287	0.293

Notes: All regressions are of the (natural logarithm of) price of different vintages of a portfolio of Bordeaux chateau wines on climate variables, using as data the vintages of 1952–1980, excluding the 1954 and 1956 vintages, which are now rarely sold; all regressions contain an intercept, which is not reported. Standard errors are in parentheses.

Source: Ashenfelter (2008).

are typically very tannic and need a maturation period of eight to 10 years to be drinkable. Ashenfelter shows that, as the wines approach their drinkable age, the auction prices slowly converge toward their predicted price. Therefore, consumers can arbitrage if the initial future price is sufficiently lower than the expected market price from the Bordeaux equation. (However, this is almost never the case.) In this way, the Ashenfelter equation has paved the way for a new strain of research in wine and finance.

Second, Ashenfelter finds that weather is crucial in producing a good vintage. In particular, a warm growing season, a dry harvest, and plenty of rainfall in the winter preceding the growing season create ideal conditions for high-quality wine in the Bordeaux region. Of course, the relationship between wine quality and weather has been known to wine producers for thousands of years, but consumers seem to have forgotten this and prefer to listen to "experts." The Ashenfelter equation does not only repeat already known facts, but exactly quantifies the relationship between wine prices and weather. In addition, and this has become increasingly important, it can assess the effect of global warming on wine prices (and thus on land values).

Table 3. Annualized Nominal Rates of Return for Various Wine Portfolios, 1986–1996

Aggregate	7.9%
First growth	6.7%
1961 vintage	
All	8.3%
First growths	9.6%
1982 vintage	13.9%
Parker's top 15	
All vintages	7.8%
1961 vintage	9.9%
1982 vintage	16.2%
Sokolin's 1985 investment grades	
Grade one	7.7%
Grade two	7.2%
Grade three	5.3%
Sokolin's 1985 portfolio	
Average prices	9.4%
Maximum prices	11.8%
Dow Jones	13.5%
T-Bills (1 year)	5.8%

Source: Burton and Jacobson (2001).

The equations in Table 2 show the positive effect of warming on Bordeaux wine prices, a result that has been confirmed for several northern European wine-growing regions. The opposite might be true for wine regions that are already at their optimal growing-season temperature. The Bordeaux equation, therefore, also contains the seeds for many future articles on wine and climate change.

Third, the Bordeaux equation shows that wine experts are less reliable than quantitative methods in predicting a wine's quality. Because Bordeaux wines are not ready to be consumed before an age of about eight to 10 years, vintage assessments need to forecast a vintage's quality. Although the Bordeaux equation's predictions with an R^2 of 0.828 are fairly accurate, experts steadily adjust their ratings as more information about a wine's drinkability becomes available. Particularly mediocre vintages are often rated too highly. For instance, in 1983, Parker deemed the 1975 vintage in Pomerol and St. Emilion (subappellations within the Bordeaux winegrowing region) outstanding and awarded it 95 out of 100 points. He also added that the wines were too tannic to be drunk and should be stored for a long time (a sign of a great vintage). However, as these wines matured, Parker dramatically adjusted his rating. In 1989, he awarded this very vintage only 88 points and recommended that the wines be consumed immediately rather than stored. That is, within six years, Parker's 1975 vintage rating dropped from outstanding to below average. In contrast, the Bordeaux equation had already predicted the mediocre quality of this vintage in 1975, immediately after the harvest. In addition, expert opinion is not free. In order to obtain vintage ratings, consumers must subscribe to Parker's newsletter or buy similar wine magazines. Whether data, by contrast, are freely available online.[7]

4. Wine and Finance

Only a very small minority of wines will gain in quality and price when properly stored. The overwhelming majority of wines produced will not benefit from being stored for more than two or three years. Wine investors concentrate mainly on the finest growths from Bordeaux and Burgundy and selected wines from California and Australia. In the past 25 years, these wines have become the focus of an increasing number of investors and a large "wine-investing industry" has evolved around this phenomenon. Like stock market indices, such as the Dow Jones Industrial Average, the London International Vintners Exchange (Liv-ex), a market for wine merchants established in 1999, tracks wine prices and reports the development of several wine price indices.[8]

Expectedly, the wine trade declares wine the ultimate asset. Wine generates above-average returns, helps to diversity an investor's portfolio, and thus lowers the risk and — if all fails — they can still drink it. Zachy's, a major New York wine retailer and wine auction house, states that "top Bordeaux prices have increased in the auction market 25–50% per year for the last several years" (Burton and Jacobsen, 2001, p. 338). In 1998, Peter Meltzer, the auction correspondent of the *Wine Spectator*, the world's largest wine magazine, wrote that "throughout the 1990s, the wine market has outpaced

[7]The Royal Netherlands Meteorological Institute provides numerous long time-series data from weather stations all over the world at no charge (Koninklijk Nederlands Meteorologisch Instituut, 2011).

[8]The Liv-ex indices are Liv-ex Fine Wine 50, Liv-ex Fine Wine 100, Liv-ex Fine Claret Chip, Liv-ex Wine Investible Index, and Liv-ex Fine Wine 500 (Liv-ex, 2012).

Table 4. Nominal Annual Rates of Return for Wine and Other Assets, 1986–1996

	All	First growths	1961	1982	Dow Jones	T-bills
Annual return	7.9%	6.7%	8.3%	13.9%	13.5%	5.8%
Standard deviation	0.133	0.261	0.290	0.134	0.079	0.008

Source: Burton and Jacobson (2001).

the Dow Jones" (Burton and Jacobsen, 2001, p. 338). More spectacular profit margins for selected wines were reported by Sokolin (1998).

The rapid increase in public attention has been accompanied by a growing body of economic literature that assesses the return as well as the risk of investing in wine. Broadly, cross-section models can be distinguished from time-series models.

The studies by Ashenfelter (Ashenfelter, 2008; Ashenfelter *et al.*, 1995) mentioned in Section 3 are based on prior work published in *Liquid Assets* (e.g., Ashenfelter, 1987a) and are cross-section analyses. Therefore, the coefficient of the age variable of the Bordeaux equation in Table 2 reflects the effect of age at one point in time and reports the real, rather than the nominal, rate of return. Given that the Dow Jones index grew by 30.2% (nominal) in 1991 (see Table 5), a 2.4% real wine return is fairly low. It should be noted that equities would also have yielded dividends while the only financial returns to wine are due to capital gains and also incur storage cost.

In a similar fashion, Haeger and Storchmann (2006) and Jones and Storchmann (2001) report cross-sectional real rate of returns for selected châteaux of Bordeaux wines and California pinot noirs, respectively, that are significantly below those for common stock (see Table 5).

In a pooled SUR (Seemingly Unrelated Regression) model for Australian Grange, one of Australia's icon wines, traded in 1991–1993 auctions, Ashenfelter and Byron (1995) find nominal annual returns of between 12% and 18%. They find market inefficiencies, with many young wines being significantly underpriced.

Similarly, Wood and Anderson analyzed three Australian icon wines, Grange, St. Henri, and Hill of Grace. They also employed an SUR approach but modeled age as a cubic function; prices rise "when the wine is young, plateauing out around optimal drinking time, before increasing again in value as the wine becomes an 'antique' wine" (Wood and Anderson, 2006, p. 146). Due to the cubic specification, the real rate of return is dependent on the wine's age. For instance, Hill of Grace yielded a real return of 14.8% in its second year, 0% in year 20, and 10.4% in year 30. In the first 20 years of the

Table 5. Rate of Return to Holding Wine: Selected Empirical Results

Source	Wine (model)[a]	Period	Rate of return (nominal p.a.)	Comparison (nominal p.a.)[b]
Krasker (1979)	Bordeaux and California (TS)	1973–1977	No statistical difference from T-bills	Dow Jones: −0.8% T-bills: 6.9%
Jaeger (1981)	Bordeaux and California (TS)	1969–1977	8.5–16.6% above T-bills (depending on storage cost)	Dow Jones: 0.3% T-bills: 6.5%
Weil (1993)	Bordeaux, Burgundy, Rhone (TS)	1976–1992	6.5% (portfolio of a particular investor)	Dow Jones: 19.3% T-bills: 8.6%
Ashenfelter *et al.* (1995)	Bordeaux (CS)	1990–1991	2.4% (real rate of return)	Dow Jones: 30.2% T-Bills: 5.9%
Ashenfelter and Byron (1995)	Australian Grange (Pooled)	1991–1994	12.0–18.0%	Dow Jones: 6.2% T-bills: 4.4%
Burton and Jacobson (2001)	Bordeaux (TS)	1986–1996	Average 7.9% (range from 5.3% to 16.2%)	Dow Jones: 13.5% T-bills: 6.1%
Jones and Storchmann (2001)	Bordeaux (CS)	1996–1997	1.2–9.6% (real rate of return, varies by chateau)	Dow Jones: 31.9% T-bills: 5.1%
Haeger and Storchmann (2006)	U.S. Pinot Noir (CS)	1998–2003	8.0% (real rate of return)	Dow Jones: 13.3% T-bills: 3.6%

Wood and Anderson (2006)	Australian icon wines (Pooled)	1992–2000	Dependent on age, for first 20 years 2.2–4.3% (real rate)	Dow Jones: 14.4% T-bills: 5.1%
Sanning *et al.* (2008)	Bordeaux (TS)	1996–2003	Wide range depending on wine/vintage Avg. first growths: 8.4% (SD 7.8%)	Dow Jones: 8.6% (SD 18.7%), T-bills: 4.3%
Masset and Henderson (2010)	Bordeaux (TS)	1996–2007	4.1–6.0% (SD 5.3–9.4%) depending on portfolio	Dow Jones: 7.8% (SD 19.7%), T-bills: 4.1%; [reference portfolio: 7.4% (SD 14.1%)]
Masset and Weisskopf (2010)	Bordeaux (TS)	1996–2009	Various wines and periods [e.g., Bordeaux 1996–2009: 8.1% (SD 10.3%)]	Dow Jones: 4.8% (SD 19.4%) T-bills: 3.7%
Fogarty (2010)	Australian wine (TS)	1990–2000	8.2% (SD 3.9%)	Australian shares: 10.7% (SD 5.8%), U.S. shares: 19.2% (SD 8.7%). T-bills: 5.6%

Notes: [a]TS = time series, CS = cross-section, [b]T-bills = Treasury bills with a one-year maturity (Federal Reserve Bank, 2011), SD = standard deviation in %.

wine's age, the average annual return equaled 4.3%, which was significantly below the annualized 14.4% growth rate of the Dow Jones (Table 5).

Krasker (1979) conducted the first economic time-series analyses of the rate of return on storing wine. Drawing on 137 observations of red Bordeaux and California Cabernet Sauvignon for the period from 1973 to 1977, he found that the rate of return on holding wine was not significantly different from that for risk-free U.S. Treasury bills. In contrast, Jaeger (1981) found that, for a wine portfolio similar to Krasker's (1979), wine outperformed Treasury bills by 16.6%. Although Krasker's (1979) storage cost was endogenous and was estimated at \$16.60 per case and year, Jaeger assumed a substantially lower exogenous annual storage cost of \$0.45. In addition, she used a longer time period, from 1969 to 1977 — potentially lowering the dampening effect of the 1973–1975 recession. As Jaeger has shown in several variants of her model (Jaeger, 1981, p. 589), the higher returns compared to Krasker's (1979) result were equally due to the different time period (+8.5%) and the lower storage cost (+8.1%).

Weil (1993) analyzed the actual portfolio of a specific wine investor and tracked each of his purchases and sales from 1976 to 1992. The portfolio consisted of various Bordeaux, Burgundy, and Northern Rhône wines. Overall, Weil (1993) analyzed 68 transactions and accounts for actual storage costs and all clearing fees and sales commissions. For each transaction, he compared the rate of return with a hypothetical return if the investor had invested in the Dow Jones during the same time period. As a result, although an investment in stock would have yielded an annualized rate of return of 19.3% (Table 5), the actual wine transactions resulted in only 6.5% (all nominal and before tax).

Burton and Jacobsen (2001) analyzed the returns from storing Bordeaux wines for the time period from 1986 to 1996, using repeat-sales regressions. They compared the semiannual returns of various wine portfolios against those of financial assets. As reported in Table 3, Burton and Jacobsen found that a portfolio of first growths (6.7% p.a.) barely outperformed Treasury bills (5.8%), let alone the Dow Jones index (13.2%). Even a portfolio of Sokolin's (1998) first investment-grade wines did not yield more than 9.4% at average auction prices or 11.4% at maximum prices.[9] In fact, only top Parker-rated wines of the 1982 vintage outperformed the Dow Jones during the observed time frame. When sales commission, insurance, and storage

[9]When considering sales commission, insurance and storage these return rates fall to 5.7% for average prices and 8.4% for maximum prices, respectively (Burton and Jacobsen, 2001).

were subtracted, however, the returns on 1982 wines were not different from those on equities (which, in addition, provided dividends).

As Burton and Jacobsen (2001) reported in Table 4, not only does wine generally yield lower returns than stock but wine investment is also riskier. The standard deviation of a portfolio consisting of all *grands crus* is more than twice as high as that of the Dow Jones. Portfolios that focus on First Growths or the 1961 vintage only exhibit an even larger price variation.

More recently, Sanning *et al.* (2008) analyzed Bordeaux auction prices from 1996 to 2003 using the Fama–French-Three-Factor Model and the capital asset pricing model (CAPM). They found a wide range of annualized risk-adjusted returns averaging at approximately 8.5%; the standard deviations were similar to those found by Burton and Jacobsen (2001). However, Sanning *et al.* (2008) also found that the covariance between wine and equity market returns was close to zero, rendering wine a potential hedging asset that might offset or protect against stock market risks. Similarly, in a recent analysis of Australian wines, Fogarty found "that despite the return to Australian wine being lower than the return to standard financial assets, wine does provide a modest diversification benefit" (2010, p. 119).

These findings found additional support from Masset and Henderson (2010), who analyzed a 1996–2007 sample of Bordeaux wine prices. They found that wine can provide diversification risk-reduction benefits and calculate optimal portfolio shares for equity, wine, and art for investors with different preferences with respect to expected returns, variance, skewness, and kurtosis. Although it may be advisable for investors to hold a fraction of their portfolio in wine, Masset and Henderson (2010) also call for caution. First, wine is less liquid than stock. Second, diversification advantages may change over time. They computed a moving 24-month window correlation between the Standard & Poor's 500 Index and two wine indices and showed that the correlation between equities and wine varies. Although there was no correlation from 2000 until the financial crisis began in October 2008, that changed significantly thereafter. Masset and Henderson (2010) suspected the flight to more liquid assets to be the likely cause. Positive correlations between equities and wine will, however, potentially thwart any diversification strategy.

Masset and Weisskopf (2010) studied the profitability of wine investments during the financial crisis of 2008. Analyzing different portfolios for five investor types (from conservative to aggressive) and taking risk aversion, different financial assets, and various wine indices into consideration, they showed that the addition of wine to a portfolio is beneficial for private

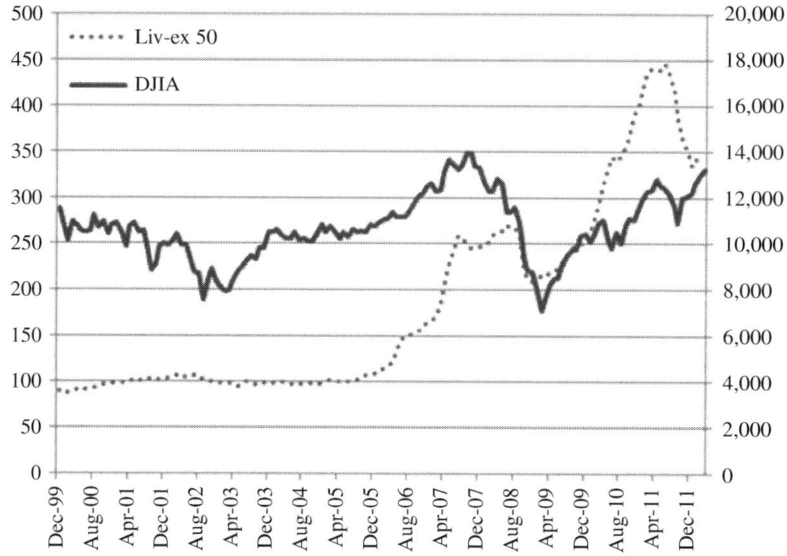

Figure 6. Liv-ex 50 and Dow Jones Industrial Index December 1999 to March 2012

investors. Adding wine to a portfolio improves returns as well as skewness and kurtosis. Employing a conditional CAPM, Masset and Weisskopf (2010) found that both alphas and betas vary over time.[10] Wine returns appear to be unrelated to market risk but behave cyclically with the economy and the dollar-to-euro exchange rate. Di Vittorio and Ginsburgh (1996) reported similar findings for Medoc wine auctions at Christie's.

Figure 6 shows the developments of the Liv-ex 50 and the Dow Jones Industrial Average from December 1999 to March 2012. First, the graph depicts the covariance between wine market and stock market since 2008 (betas). The wine market follows the stock market. Second, the figure also displays the extraordinary growth in wine prices since about 2005 (alphas). This trend was temporarily interrupted by the financial crisis. However, since the spring of 2011, the Liv-ex 50 index has experienced a major correction. From June 2001 to March 2012, the wine index declined by more than 22% while the Dow Jones increased by 6%.

Jovanovic (2008) studied the prices of selected older Bordeaux wines (e.g., Lafite, 1865, 1875, 1900; Margaux, 1900; Yquem, 1900) at auctions, on restaurant wine lists and at retail outlets over the past 100 years. Based

[10]Alpha is a risk-adjusted measure of the so-called active return on an investment. Beta describes the relation of an asset's return compared to the whole market.

on the works of Hotelling (1931), Jovanovic shows theoretically how bubble equilibria can form for exhaustible resources, such as wine. In most equilibria, the price of a resource rises at the rate of interest. "In a bubble equilibrium, however, the consumption of the resource peters out, and a positive fraction of the original stock continues to be traded forever. And that may well be happening in the market for high-end Bordeaux wines" (Jovanovic, 2008, p. 1).

5. Wine and Climate Change

It has been known for more than 2,000 years that the quality of any fruit, and wine grapes in particular, depends on the weather during its growing season. For instance, the Roman naturalist Pliny the Elder (23–79 C.E.) noticed that grape quality varies across vineyards due to (micro)climatic factors (Pliny, 77/2007). Some of the earliest work that evaluates the relationship between wine and climate dates back to the pioneering University of California at Davis viticulturalists Amerine and Winkler (1944), who mapped the nascent grape-growing regions of California. More recently, Gladstones (1992) provides a detailed reference of environmental factors that affect viticulture. The close relationship between weather and wine has also been exploited for reverse inferences. Historical climatologists use data on harvest dates and phenological stages to generate medieval weather data (see, e.g., Brázdil *et al.*, 2005; Garcia de Cortázar-Atauri *et al.*, 2010).

Given that fine-wine quality and prices are very responsive to weather variables, such as temperature and rainfall, any variation in weather results in equivalent price variations. Although some regions, such as California, exhibit little year-to-year weather variation, most European wine-growing regions, including the Bordeaux region, have experienced substantially higher annual weather volatility. Accordingly, vintage-related price variations for Bordeaux wines are significantly higher than those for Napa wines. Ashenfelter (2008) reports that, depending on the vintage, auction prices for Bordeaux grand cru wines can differ by a factor 10 or more.

The first empirical evaluations of the effect of weather on wine prices were carried out by Ashenfelter and were published in *Liquid Asset* in the late 1980s (e.g., Ashenfelter, 1986, 1987c, 1987d, 1990). The Bordeaux equation in column (2) of Table 2 reports a growing season temperature coefficient of 0.616, that is, a growing-season temperature increase of 1°C results in a 61.6% price increase. Given that, since 1945, average Bordeaux growing-season temperatures have ranged between 14.98°C (1972) and 19.83°C

(2003) large price variations are hardly surprising. Predicted temperature increases for the European wine-growing regions for this century are between 1.5°C and 5°C (e.g., European Commission, 2009; IPCC, 2007), that is, an extent of variation that is within the already experienced range of regular annual weather fluctuations. Predictions for precipitation are less reliable and generally conclude that precipitation will increase in Scandinavia and decrease in Southern Europe; the direction of changes and their extent in the heart of Europe, including France, are uncertain (European Commission, 2009). Assuming future temperature increases and no changes in precipitation, Ashenfelter's Bordeaux equation, therefore, predicts substantial price increases for Bordeaux *grands crus*.

Jones and Storchmann (2001) confirmed the positive effect of global warming on the Bordeaux wine region. They modeled the effect of weather by estimating cross-sectional equations for each of 21 selected *premiers crus* châteaux. Given that each château's wine is a unique blend that is either dominated by Cabernet Sauvignon or Merlot or is a blend of both,[11] Jones and Storchmann (2001) first computed the weather's impact on the sugar and acid level of each of these grape varieties. Taking into account the respective blend proportions, they then proceeded with a price equation. They found that Merlot is more responsive to weather than Cabernet Sauvignon. That is, in a scenario of global warming, Merlot-dominated wines, such as Château Petrus, would disproportionally benefit.

Ashenfelter and Storchmann (2010b) employed three different models to evaluate the effect of warming on Mosel vineyards in Germany. In the first model, they explained the Prussian vineyard classification from 1868. Based on land profits for the period from 1837 to 1860,[12] the Prussian government assigned one of eight ranks to each vineyard; rank 1 vineyards commanded the highest wine prices and were highly profitable, while rank 8 vineyards yielded the lowest profits (if any). This vineyard classification was not carried out as an orientation guide for wine aficionados but, rather, as a basis for fair and just taxes; high-profit land was taxed more than low-profit land. Using an ordered-probit model, Ashenfelter and Storchmann (2010b) showed that the Prussian ranking (and thus the willingness to pay for wine) could be explained by referring to the main vineyard characteristics, namely, soil type

[11]Many châteaux add smaller quantities of Cabernet Franc, Petit Verdot, Malbec, or Carménére. For Château Cheval Blanc, however, Cabernet Franc is the dominant variety.
[12]The profit was calculated as the product of wine price and crop yield minus cost of growing. A detailed description is provided by Beck (1869). Karl Marx (1843) published some critical comments about the calculation method in 1843.

and the land's potential ability to capture incoming solar radiation, that is, energy. The darker the soil (mainly dark slate that can store the heat) and the higher the potential solar energy of a vineyard, the better is its rank. The amount of solar radiation that a plot of land can capture can be calculated in a fashion similar to that of a solar panel and depends on its latitude, slope, and orientation. For the German Mosel, which is located at the northern frontier of professional viticulture, energy is a scarce resource and the best vineyards are south-facing and exhibit a 45-degree slope. In the next step, Ashenfelter and Storchmann (2010b) employed the Boltzmann equation to link solar radiation to temperature. Higher temperatures require more solar radiation. Higher solar radiation, in turn, will change the likelihood that a certain vineyard will have a high-quality rank. As a result, further warming will shift the rank distribution of all Mosel vineyards from low to high quality and will thus increase land prices. Under a warming scenario of 3°C, the value of vineyards in the Mosel might double.

Ashenfelter and Storchmann (2010b) compared these results with two different time-series models. In one model, they regressed the accountancy data of wineries from various West German wine-growing regions on weather. Table 6 shows that the marginal effect of temperature on winery profits (excluding subsidies, column 1) is approximately 0.309. A growing-season temperature increase of 3°C might raise profits by about 150%. Interestingly, temperatures do not alter production costs; column (3) of Table 6 reports only insignificant effects, that is, profit increases are virtually identical to revenue increases.

In their third model, Ashenfelter and Storchmann (2010b) regressed Mosel wine revenue on temperatures. They showed that crop yields as well as prices respond positively to higher growing-season temperatures. This model suggests that a warming of 3°C might raise revenue by approximately 180%. Figure 7 depicts the suggested temperature impact of all three models, which all show a positive relationship between growing-season temperatures and profits, revenues, or land values. Given the entirely different nature of the models, the results are remarkably consistent.

In a different article, Ashenfelter and Storchmann (2010a) showed that, depending on the wine sample considered, regressing price on temperature might result in biased results. Comparing auction, retail, and wholesale prices yielded the strongest positive temperature effects for wines sold at auction and much smaller effects for the wholesale sample. Given that only a tiny fraction of the wines produced are sold at auction (e.g., only those of the highest quality) referring to auction prices can overstate the effect of warming.

Table 6. Weather and Real per Hectare Profits and Costs

	(1) ln(profits − subsidies)	(2) ln(profits incl. subsidies)	(3) ln(costs)
Temperature growing season[a]	0.309*** (5.17)[5.25]	0.305*** (4.71)[5.11]	0.026 (0.18)[0.19]
Rainfall winter[b]	−0.0034*** (−9.77)[−9.90]	−0.0031*** (−3.23)[−8.51]	−0.0003 (−0.29)[−0.29]
Rainfall growing season[c]	−0.0009*** (−4.62)[−4.68]	−0.0009*** (−1.75)[−5.67]	−0.0001 (−0.51)[−0.52]
Trend	−0.074*** (−8.79)[−8.91]	−0.072*** (−8.37)[−7.98]	−0.029 (−1.40)[−1.42]
Fixed effects			
Mosel	8.09	8.14	10.33
Rheinhessen	7.55	7.52	10.14
Rheingau	8.28	8.14	10.35
Pfalz	7.79	7.75	9.86
Baden–Württemberg	8.48	8.43	10.18
Franken	8.11	8.10	10.41
R^2	0.663	0.644	0.538
F statistic	9.17	11.25	8.26
N	52	52	57

Note: [a]February to October, in degrees Celsius. [b]December to February prior to growing season, in milliliters. [c]April to October, in milliliters. All weather data are from the station in Trier (Mosel); ***significance level of 1%; Newey–West robust t-values in parentheses; t-values based on year clustered standard errors in brackets.

Source: Ashenfelter and Storchmann (2010a).

In a long-run time-series analysis covering the period from 1800 to 2009, Chevet *et al.* (2011) studied prices and yields of a *premier cru* château in the Bordeaux region. They found a positive impact of temperature on both yields and prices. However, while the temperature responsiveness of crop yields has fallen dramatically over time, prices have become substantially more sensitive to growing-season temperature changes.[13] Apparently, technological improvements have helped wine growers to lower the weather's impact on crop levels. However, the findings also suggest that prices are not driven by quantity produced alone. Quality effects

[13]While the yield coefficient has fallen from 0.31 (1847–1900) to 0.08 (1961–2009), the price coefficient has increased from 0.004 (1839–1900) to 0.45 (1961–2009) (Chevet *et al.*, 2011).

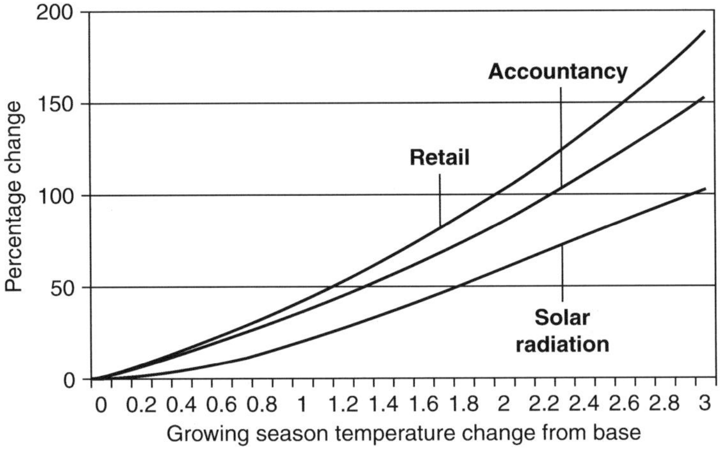

Figure 7. Temperature Changes and Percentage Changes in Land Value
Source: Ashenfelter and Storchmann (2010a).

and growing market demand must more than offset the price declining effect of yield increases due to warmer growing seasons.

All the articles mentioned above employ linear temperature specifications, that is, the marginal effect of temperature on wine prices is implicitly assumed to be constant. That might be justified for regions in cooler climates, such as Bordeaux and Germany, or when drawing on data from colder periods such as the "Little Ice Age" of the early and mid-nineteenth century. For warmer regions, especially in the New World, nonlinear specifications might be more appropriate. Byron and Ashenfelter (1995), in their analysis of Australian Grange (see Section 4), regressed a squared function in which wine prices grow with increasing temperatures but at a decreasing rate. Wood and Anderson (2006) also employed a squared temperature specification for Australian icon-wine prices. Similarly, Haeger and Storchmann (2006) estimated a squared function for U.S. pinot noirs that have their price-maximizing peak at a growing-season temperature of 22.2°C (from April to September). Many U.S. growing regions are already above the optimal temperature (Salem, Oregon: 23.2°C; Napa, California: 26.2°C; Paso Robles, California: 30.3°C). Further warming might thus have detrimental effects on Pinot Noir prices. In contrast, Burgundy (Dijon: 22.0°C) as well as German wine regions (Karlsruhe, Pfalz: 21.3°C) are still benefiting from further warming.

Some studies focused on wine quality rather than on wine prices or winery profits. Jones *et al.* (2005) analyzed the effect of temperature on

Sotheby's vintage ratings from 1950 to 1999 for all major wine regions worldwide. They employed nonlinear squared time-series models for each region and show that there are winners and losers in global warming. In general, although wine-growing regions in northern France and Germany will produce better wine quality with increasing temperatures, wine-growing regions in Spain (Rioja), California, and South Australia (Barossa Valley) might suffer from any further warming.

Storchmann (2005) examined the weather determinants of the quality of Schloss Johannisberg wine in the German Rheingau region from 1700 to 2003 employing an ordered-probit model. He drew on documented vintage classifications (such as "top wine," "sour," "lesser vintage") in historical harvest books, grouped them into five quality ranks, and regressed these ranks on various weather data. Because instrumental weather data for the covered period are available only from weather stations in England and, with some restrictions, in the Netherlands, he also referred to monthly index data. The results showed that (1) English weather data are a good proxy variable for the actual weather conditions in the Johannisberg vineyards[14] and (2) that moderate warming will improve the quality of Rheingau wines.

It is clear from these analyses that, in the wine industry as in many other industries, there are winners and losers in global warming. Changing climate requires many technological adjustments and varietal substitutions. In addition, in order to mitigate the deteriorating effects of temperature increases, viticultural regions tend to move toward the poles, to higher elevations or, for example, in California, closer to the coast.

6. Wine and Expert Opinion

6.1. *Expert ratings and price impact*

Because wine is an experience good, and its characteristics are not known to most wine drinkers before consumption, experts and their critical reviews can help to fill an information void.

Accordingly, the market for expert opinion on wine is large. The seven major U.S. wine magazines have a combined subscribership of more than

[14]This squares with the results of an analysis by Lecocq and Visser (2006), who analyzed Bordeaux wine prices. They compared the results when drawing on data from only one weather station to those from numerous local stations. They conclude that using localized data does not improve the models' explanatory power.

Table 7. Subscriptions to Selected U.S. Wine Magazines in 2010

Magazine title	Founded	Subscriptions	Single copies sold	Subscription price[a] ($)	Single-copy price ($)	Sales revenue ($1,000)
California Grapevine	1973	3,000[b]	n.a.	32.00		96.0
Connoisseurs' Guide to California Wine	1974	7,000[b]	n.a.	90.00		630.0
Wine Spectator	1976	368,522	32,030	49.95	4.95	18,887.0
Wine Advocate	1978	50,000	0	75.00		3,750.0
Wine Enthusiast	1979	108,000	4,653	29.95	4.95	3,257.6
Wine and Spirits	1981	23,000	48,000	29.95	5.99	976.4
The Wine News[c]	1985	30,250[b]	24,750	25.00	5.00	880.0

Note: [a]For 2010, [b]as of 1999, online only, a hardcopy subscription costs $120/year, [c]discontinued in 2010.
Sources: Association of Magazine Media (2011), Pitcher (2003), and the websites of the respective magazines.

500,000 (Table 7), with 350,000 alone for the *Wine Spectator*; wine magazine sales total more than $25 million. In addition, there are a few foreign magazines (e.g., *Decanter*) and numerous smaller publications, online services (e.g., JancisRobinson.com), and wine blogs.

Another remarkable fact shown in Table 7 is the sudden and rapidly growing interest in expert opinion. The first U.S. wine magazines started in California in the mid-1970s. Even *Wine Spectator* was originally launched in San Diego and moved to New York only after Marvin Shanken bought the publication from founder Bob Morrisey in 1981. Considering that there was no national wine magazine before the mid-1970s, this sudden and rapidly growing demand for expert opinion is fairly amazing.

Wine consumers and investors rely on experts in many ways. Experts predict the quality of particular (especially Bordeaux) vintages that have not been traded yet in order to help wine investors and connoisseurs to decide whether to buy futures. They describe a wine's taste and smell and rate wines or award gold medals to help consumers make a choice.

Ashenfelter (e.g., Ashenfelter, 1987d, 1990, 1992, 2008; Ashenfelter *et al.*, 1995) has shown that expert opinion regarding Bordeaux vintage qualities can be seriously flawed. Relying on publicly available information, such as weather data, yields more reliable results. Furthermore, weather data about a certain vintage are available directly after the harvest, that is, about half a year before the first experts have tasted and rated the vintage. In addition, weather information is available at no cost.

Ashenfelter (2008) has also shown that the Bordeaux wine market exhibits considerable inefficiencies. Directly after their release, many young wines have prices that deviate substantially from the predicted price based on weather. In fact, most vintages are overpriced. However, after about 10 years, when the wines enter the drinkable stage, wine prices converge on the predicted price based on the weather. According to Ashenfelter (2008), the overpricing during the wines' early life is especially pronounced for vintages that are predicted to be the worst. For instance, prices for the 1969 vintage decreased by 76% within the first 15 years after its release: "This suggests that, in large measure, the ability of the weather to predict the quality of the wines is either unknown or ignored by the early purchasers and sellers of the wines" (Ashenfelter, 2008, p. F183).

One reverse anomaly is the 1982 Bordeaux vintage whose prices soared above the weather-predicted price and even 30 years after its release have not converged at the expected price (Ashenfelter, 2008). The main reason for this phenomenon could be the high praise for this vintage by wine critics, in particular by Parker, who is widely considered the most influential wine critic. For the 1982 vintage, Parker awarded a perfect score of 100 points to seven Bordeaux *grands crus*, more than for any vintage before.[15]

This raises the question of whether and to what extent wine critics influence wine prices. Based on prior analyses by Ashenfelter (1990), Ashenfelter and Jones (2013) examined the efficiency and the price influence of expert ratings for Bordeaux wines. They contrasted the explanatory value of ordered vintage quality indicators by well-known experts, namely, the University of Bordeaux enology professors Riberau-Gayon and Guimberteau, with publicly available weather data to examine whether the experts' opinion contains any private information beyond what is already publicly known. In two models, they regressed wine prices first on expert ratings only and then on weather data only and found that both kind of variables are good price predictors. In the following step, they added the experts' ratings to the weather data equation. As a result, expert ratings become inconsistent and insignificant, suggesting that they do not contain any private information. This result finds further support from the fact that weather data are excellent predictors of the

[15]Other outstanding Parker-rated Bordeaux vintages are (number of 100-point wines in parenthesis): 2000 (7), 1961 (4), 1945 (3), 1989 (3), and 1990 (3).

experts' ratings. Haeger and Storchmann (2006) pursued a similar sequential approach and found that *Wine Spectator* points only marginally improve weather-based models of U.S. pinot noir wine prices. Jones and Storchmann (2001) differentiated this approach by château and reported that prices of smaller châteaux, those that make Cabernet Sauvignon-dominated wines and those that have been rated highly in the past, are more sensitive to Parker points than others.

Hadj Ali and Nauges (2007) examined Bordeaux *en primeur* prices, that is, wine future prices that are set by the châteaux in the spring after the harvest. Using a hedonic approach, they found a statistically significant but small effect of critical points by *Wine Spectator* as well as by Parker in addition to fundamentals. Hadj Ali and Nauges (2007) found that Parker's impact on future prices is fairly small: one additional Parker point results in an average price increase of 1.01%.

Hadj Ali *et al.* (2008) referred to a natural experiment in order to disentangle the public and the private information content of expert ratings. They analyzed the influence of Parker ratings on Bordeaux *en primeur* prices by drawing on a natural experiment. Normally, the Bordeaux châteaux set their *en primeur* prices in the spring following the harvest — after Parker has tasted and rated the wines. The châteaux, therefore, have the opportunity to incorporate any possible private information contained in Parker's rating into the price. However, in the spring of 2003, Parker did not visit the region and did not publish his assessment of the 2002 vintage before the fall of 2003. Thus, the châteaux set their 2002 *en primeur* prices without Parker's rating. The authors confirmed the small price relevance of critical points already found by Hadj Ali and Nauges (2007). The fact that Parker visits the Bordeaux region and tastes and rates *en primeur* wines has an average value of approximately €2.80 per bottle, that is, less than 2% of the average *en primeur* price for *premier cru*.

6.2. *Experts and wine words*

Wine critics and experts not only convey private information about a wine's quality by assigning grades or points but also provide verbal descriptions of the smell and taste. Parker alone has evaluated and described the appearance, smell, and taste of more than 180,000 wines in his newsletter *The Wine Advocate; Wine Spectator* lists over 240,000 wine reviews on its website. Over the past 40 years, a rich wine vocabulary has evolved.

According to Parker's *A Glossary of Wine Terms*, wine descriptors include terms such as "angular," "austere," "backward," "chewy," "decadent," "dumb," "precocious," and "unctuous" (Parker, 2011). For instance, Parker describes a Rhône wine as follows: "Deep ruby color includes purpose nuances. Closed aromatically, hints of creme de cassis and black cherries. Cuts broad swath across the palate with considerable depth and concentration. Tannic as well as broodingly backward" (Weil, 2007, p. 140).

What is the informational value of wine words? In one of the first studies, the linguist Lehrer (1975) examined the function and value of the wine language. She ran several experiments to assess the degree of useful communication about wine flavors. In one experiment, she let people first describe three distinctly different wines. In subsequent blind tastings, she then asked the subjects to match the description with the wine. Surprisingly, the subjects were unable to produce a better than chance match, thus casting doubts on the informational value of wine words.

Lawless (1984) compared the matching ability of wine experts and non-experts when drawing on descriptions by either group. In his experiments, only expert tasters using expert descriptions performed slightly better than random. All other combinations, such as *expert descriptions and amateur tasters* or *amateur descriptions and amateur tasters*, resulted in outcomes that were no better than chance.

More recently, Weil (2007) analyzed the value of wine words. He drew on published wine descriptions in *Wine Spectator* and Parker's *Wine Advocate* and asked subjects to match three wines with the corresponding description. The overall matching performance was random.

Why do wine consumers rely on expert opinion if they do not provide any practical use?

Quandt (2007) analyzed the wine market by referring to a book by Princeton philosophy professor Harry G. Frankfurt called *On Bullshit* (2005). He concluded: "I think the wine trade is intrinsically bullshit-prone and therefore attracts bullshit artists" (Quandt, 2007, p. 135). This seems to be confirmed by the relatively high nonscholarly Google hit ratio reported in Table 1.

However, according to Ramirez (2010), wine descriptions appear to exert influence not only on wine critics but also on producers. Analyzing 2,700 *Wine Spectator* reviews of recent Napa Cabernet Sauvignon and employing a dynamic price model, Ramirez found that the length of the review (measured by the number of characters) has a significant positive price effect — even after controlling for quality. In addition, he found that the price effect does not result from "purely analytical" words but, rather, from metaphorical language. This suggests that consumers find prose more persuasive than neutral descriptions, that is, wine descriptions might meet needs other than the mere transmission of information.

6.3. *Expert failure*

Not only can expert opinion be of little informational value, but it can also be downright flawed. Hodgson (2008) analyzed the performance of wine judges at a major U.S. wine competition from 2005 to 2008. At these wine competitions, panels of four wine judges assess samples of 30 wines and award medals (Gold, Silver, Bronze) to excellent wines. Unknown to the judges, Hodgson inserted triplet pourings of one bottle into the sample, that is, three of the 30 wines within one flight were identical. Only 10% of the judges were able to rank these wines within the same medal rank; another 10% assessed the triplet wines within a two-medal range, that is, 80% of the examined judges ranked identical wine more than two medal ranks apart. In addition, even the 10% of judges who assigned the same quality rank to identical wines were unable to repeat this performance the following year. These results suggest that experts award medals at random.

This conclusion finds further support in a second study by Hodgson (2009). Hodgson, a wine maker himself, observed that wines entered into several competitions rarely received identical evaluations in each of them. A wine might obtain a Gold medal in one competition and nothing in another. If a Gold medal were a good predictor for quality, then the probability of receiving a Gold medal at competition B should *not* be independent of whether this wine already obtained a Gold at competition A. In fact, a wine that receives a Gold at competition A should have a higher than random chance of obtaining a Gold at competition B.

However, Hodgson (2009) found that this is not the case. The probability of obtaining a Gold medal at competition B is stochastically independent and follows the binomial probability distribution. For instance, if the chance of receiving a Gold at any competition were 10% and if the distribution of Gold medals were random (i.e., independent of quality) the chance of receiving two Gold medals would equal $0.1 * 0.1 = 0.01$. Hodgson found that this is the case for wine competitions and states “that chance alone may account for the number of Gold medals that a wine receives” (2009, p. 8).

Expert opinion does not suffer only from a lack of expertise, however. Sometimes conflicts of interest can result in biased outcomes. Reuter (2009) examined whether wineries that advertise in *Wine Spectator* receive better critical evaluations of their wines. He exploited the fact that the other large wine magazine, *Wine Advocate*, does not accept winery advertising.

Although advertisers and nonadvertisers obtain similar ratings, when he controlled for quality by referring to *Wine Advocate* ratings, Reuter (2009) found that advertisers receive almost one more critical point than do nonadvertisers. The effect seems largely due to a higher chance of being "retasted." When a blind tasting yields unexpected results, *Wine Spectator* allows a retasting, that is, the wine will be added to the next flight and thus "gets a second chance." It appears that advertisers obtain this opportunity more frequently than non-advertisers.

But, even worse, Goldstein (2008) reported that, in addition to being flawed or biased, expert opinion can be entirely made up. Goldstein applied for the Wine Spectator Award of Excellence, that is regularly given to restaurants with an outstanding wine list. However, Goldstein has never owned nor managed a restaurant. Instead, he launched a website for a fictitious restaurant in Milan, Italy; he posted menus and two wine lists — a regular list and a reserve list. For the expensive reserve list, he mostly selected wines that received only between 50 and 70 *Wine Spectator* points. *Wine Spectator* deems wines in the 50–74-point range "not recommended" and wines in the 75–79-point rage "mediocre: a drinkable wine that may have minor flaws." In order to add some credibility to his made-up restaurant, Goldstein also obtained an Italian telephone and fax number. He submitted his application, a letter and a $250 fee — and after an evaluation phase of a few weeks, he indeed received the Wine Spectator Award of Excellence.

This means that *Wine Spectator* granted an award of distinction to a nonexistent restaurant. The expert's service, namely, conveying information about an experience good, has become an experience good (or even a credence good) itself. Ashenfelter *et al.* (2011) showed in a theoretical and empirical model that earning a *Wine Spectator* Award of Excellence is meaningless for the quality of the wine list. Only restaurants that can charge their customers for the cost incurred will apply for the award. Thus, after controlling for the quality of food, service and décor, Ashenfelter *et al.* (2011) found that applying for (and receiving) a *Wine Spectator* Award of Excellence only results in higher prices.

However, the issue of flawed or even fraudulent expert opinion is not unique to the wine industry. A recent *ABC News* report on the Better Business Bureau (BBB), an institution that evaluates and rates businesses in the United States, showed that numerous nonexistent businesses, such as a fictitious firm named Hamas, received impeccable ratings as long as they paid the evaluation fee. Others that declined to pay, such as Disneyland or some of Wolfgang Puck's restaurants, received an F (Rhee and Ross, 2010).

Clearly, inherent issues arise when the evaluate pays the expert who evaluates him. There has long been a suspicion that the evaluations of business rating companies such as Moody's, Fitch, or Standard & Poor's may be equally flawed.

7. Summary

Compared to other beverages, wine enjoys a lively Internet presence; wine writers, critics, bloggers, consumers, winegrowers, and merchants all write about wine. In contrast, significantly less scholarly work has been conducted on wine than on any other beverage. As a result, a Google search shows that the general Internet chatter on wine per Google Scholar hit is second to none among all beverages. Although milk generates less than 4,000 general Google hits per scholarly citation, wine generates almost 13,000. Clearly, more people have opinions about wine and write about them than they do about milk.

However, the scholarly economics work on wine has grown substantially since the mid-1980s. Meanwhile, wine has become the leading beverage cited particularly in high-end general economics journals. In 2006, the AAWE was founded and the association's publication, the *Journal of Wine Economics*, is entirely devoted to economic issues related to wine.

The origins of wine economics can be found in the newsletter *Liquid Assets*, which was launched by Ashenfelter in 1986. *Liquid Assets* has been devoted to a quantitative way of looking at the wine market. Although Ashenfelter has published many ground-breaking wine papers in his newsletter, the most influential one was arguably his analysis of Bordeaux wine prices and the weather, for it contains the seeds of the three major research topics in wine economics: finance, climate, and experts.

More than 25 years after the launch of *Liquid Assets*, consumers can look back on a substantial and increasing body of high-end economic literature in all three fields. It appears to be typical for wine economics that the findings of many analyses have implications that go beyond the wine market. Financial wine studies not only analyze the effects of portfolio diversification and risk control but also contribute to general research on the development of asset bubbles. Analyses of wine and weather provide a complex picture of winners and losers from climate change. Wine-related research on the role and value of expert opinion can be applied to seemingly wine-distant issues such as business rating agencies like Standard & Poor's or Moody's.

In the past decade, the research into wine economics has diversified and gone beyond finance, climate, and experts. In particular, research interest has grown on issues related to market regulation, quality signaling and consumer search.

The repeal of Prohibition in the United States, in 1933, granted states the authority to regulate the production, distribution, and consumption of alcohol, resulting in a wide range of rules and standards across the country; for instance, many states prohibited direct interstate wine shipping. Riekhof and Sykuta (2005) analyzed the political economy of interstate shipment regulations and showed that wine distributors are the driving force behind shipping restrictions; the higher the distributors' market concentration within a given state, the more likely it is that this state will prohibit direct shipments. In addition, Gokcekus and Nottebaum (2012) find that states with little tax revenue, proxied by the fraction of federal aid received, tend to prohibit direct wine shipments.

Wiseman and Ellig (2004) investigated wine prices in Virginia and concluded that the prohibition of out-of-state online sales has resulted in a 10% increase in prices. When the state of Virginia legalized direct wine shipping to consumers from out-of-state sellers in 2003, not only the price level but also the retail price variance among retail outlets decreased dramatically (Wiseman and Ellig, 2007). Sharma (2010) analyzed whether direct shipping restrictions impair smaller firms more than larger ones. Jaeger and Storchmann (2011) examined the impact of various wine market regulations in the United States on consumer search and retail price variations.

The available literature on asymmetric information and quality signaling is especially rich. Various articles have analyzed the effect of reputation on wine prices and decomposed the effect into the components product, firm, and regional reputation (e.g., Costanigro *et al.*, 2010; Frick *et al.*, 2011; Landon and Smith, 1998; Schamel, 2009). Cross *et al.* (2011) analyzed the impact of regional reputation on Oregon vineyard prices. Schnabel and Storchmann (2010) assessed the role of prices as quality signals in the German wine market. Roberts *et al.* (2011) examined whether a winery can signal quality and command higher prices by hiring a well-known winemaker from a prominent competitor.

Certainly, wine economics research has reached well beyond the issues described and will not stop here. In addition to further analyses of the topics mentioned above, wine economists will open new research avenues. One apparent new impetus might come from the rise of Asian wine markets and the resulting dramatic increase in fine wine prices. On the one hand, wine can provide valuable insights in the forming of bubbles. On the other hand, and given that soaring wine prices have been accompanied by a soaring number of counterfeits, wine economics can give forensic economics new impetus.

Acknowledgments

This chapter is based on the Simon Brandt Memorial Address I presented at the joint Annual Conference of the African Association of Agricultural Economists and the Agricultural Economics Association of South Africa, Cape Town, September 20, 2010. I am grateful to Nick Vink, University of Stellenbosch, and Orley Ashenfelter, Princeton University, for many helpful comments. A shorter version of this chapter appeared in *Agrekon* (Storchmann, 2011).

References

Amerine, M., and Winkler, M. (1944). Composition and quality of musts and wines of California grapes. *Hilgardia*, 15, 493–675.

Ashenfelter, O. (1986). Why we do it. *Liquid Assets*, 1, 1–7.

Ashenfelter, O. (1987a). Fine wine trading tips: California Cabernet wine-aging mutual find. *Liquid Assets*, 2, 11–14.

Ashenfelter, O. (1987b). How to sell your wines easily and legally in the U.S. (Why didn't anybody tell us this before?). *Liquid Assets*, 3, 1–7.

Ashenfelter, O. (1987c). Objective vintage charts: Red Bordeaux and California Cabernet Sauvignon. *Liquid Assets*, 3, 8–13.

Ashenfelter, O. (1987d). Vintage advice: Is 1986 another outstanding Bordeaux vintage? (No! And you heard it here first). *Liquid Assets*, 2, 1–7.

Ashenfelter, O. (1988). A new objective ranking of the chateaux of Bordeaux (Based on auction prices, of course!). *Liquid Assets*, 5, 1–6.

Ashenfelter, O. (1990). Just how good are wine writers' predictions? (Surprise! The recent vintages are rated highest!). *Liquid Assets*, 7, 1–9.

Ashenfelter, O. (1991). Restaurants: New York and suburbs, things are changing. (The best restaurants where you can bring your own wine — No. 2 of a series). *Liquid Assets*, 8, 1–11.

Ashenfelter, O. (1992). Critiquing the wine critics: Broadbent versus Parker (A review of two most influential books on Bordeaux wines). *Liquid Assets*, 9, 1–11.

Ashenfelter, O. (1997). A new objective ranking of the chateaux of Bordeaux. *Liquid Assets*, 13, 1–6.

Ashenfelter, O. (2008). Predicting the prices and quality of Bordeaux wines. *Economic Journal*, 118, 40–53.

Ashenfelter, O., and Jones, G. (2013). The demand for expert opinion: Bordeaux wine. *Journal of Wine Economics*, 8(3), 285–293.

Ashenfelter, O., and Storchmann, K. (2010a). Measuring the economic effect of global warming on viticulture using auction, retail and wholesale prices. *Review of Industrial Organization*, 37, 51–64.

Ashenfelter, O., and Storchmann, K. (2010b). Using a hedonic model of solar radiation to assess the economic effect of climate change: The case of Mosel valley vineyards. *Review of Economics and Statistics*, 92(2), 333–349.

Ashenfelter, O., Ashmore, D., and Lalonde, R. (1995). Bordeaux wine vintage quality and the weather. *Chance*, 8, 7–13.

Ashenfelter, O., Goldstein, R., and Riddell, C. (2011). Do expert ratings measure quality? The case of restaurant wine lists. *Paper presented at the 4th Annual AAWE Conference at the University of California at Davis*, June 2010.

Association of Magazine Media (2011). Facts and figures. http://magazine.org/consumer_marketing/circ_trends/index.aspx (accessed June 20, 2011).

Ayres, I. (2007). *Super Crunchers: Why Thinking-by-Numbers is the New Way to be Smart.* New York: Bantam Books.

Beck, O. (1869). *Der Weinbau an der Mosel und Saar. Nebst einer vom koniglichen Katasterinspekteur Steuerrath Clotten zu Trier angefertigten Weinbaukarte.* Trier: Selbstverlag der königlichen Regierung zu Trier.

Brázdil, R., Pfister, C., Wanner, H., Storch, H. von., and Luterbacher, J. (2005). Historical climatology in Europe: State of the art. *Climatic Change*, 70(3), 363–430.

Burton, B.J., and Jacobsen, J.P. (2001). The rate of return on investment in wine. *Economic Inquiry*, 39, 337–350.

Byron, R.P., and Ashenfelter, O. (1995). Predicting the quality of an unborn Grange. *Economic Record*, 71, 40–53.

Chaikind, S. (2010). The role of viticulture and enology in the development of economic thought. How wine contributed to modern economic theory. American Association of Wine Economists AAWE, Working Paper, No. 74.

Chevet, J.-M., Lecocq, S., and Visser, M. (2011). Climate, grapevine phenology, wine production, and prices: Pauillac (1800–2009). *American Economic Review: Papers and Proceedings*, 101, 142–146.

Costanigro, M., McCluskey, J.J., and Goemans, C. (2010). The economics of nested names: Name specificity, reputations, and price premia. *American Journal of Agricultural Economics*, 92, 1339–1350.

Cross, R., Plantinga, A.J., and Stavins, R.N. (2011). What is the value of terroir? *American Economic Review: Papers and Proceedings*, 101, 152–156.

Di Vittorio, A., and Ginsburgh, V. (1996). Pricing red wines of Medoc vintages from 1949 to 1989 at Christie's auctions. *Journal de la Société Statistique de Paris*, 137, 19–49.

European Commission (2009). Regions 2020. The climate change challenge for European regions. Directorate General for Regional Policy. Background document to commission staff working document SEC (2008) 2868 Final, Brussels: European Commission.

Federal Reserve Bank (2011). Selected interest rates: historical data. www.federalreserve.gov/releases/h15/data.htm (accessed June 20, 2011).

Fogarty, J.J. (2010). Wine investment and portfolio diversification gains. *Journal of Wine Economics*, 5(1), 119–131.

Frankfurt, H.G. (2005). *On Bullshit.* Princeton: Princeton University Press.

Frick, B., Eggert, A., and Hogreve, A. (2011). The returns to reputation: Empirical evidence from German wine auctions. *Paper presented at the 4th Annual AAWE Conference at the University of California at Davis*, June 2010.

Garcia de Cortázar-Atauri, I., Daux, V., Garnier, E., Yiou, P., Viovy, N., Seguin, B., Boursiquot, J.M., Parker, A.K., Van Leeuwen, C., and Chuine, I. (2010). Climate reconstructions from grape harvest dates: Methodology and uncertainties. *The Holocene,* 20, 599–608.

Gladstones, J. (1992). *Viticulture and Environment.* Adelaide, South Australia: Winetitles.

Goldberg, H.G. (1987). Wine talk. *New York Times*, October 28.

Gokcekus, O., and Nottebaum, D. (2012). Public finance, special interests, and direct wine shipping laws in the United States. *Journal of Wine Economics*, 7(1), 35–48.

Goldstein, R. (2008). What does it take to get a Wine Spectator Award of Excellence? Blindtaste, August 15. http://blindtaste.com/2008/08/15/what-does-it-take-to-get-a-wine-spectator-award-of-excellence/ (accessed June 20, 2011).

Hadj Ali, H., and Nauges, C. (2007). Reputation and quality effects in the pricing of experience goods: The case of *en primeur* wine. *American Journal of Agricultural Economics*, 89, 91–103.

Hadj Ali, H., Lecocq, S., and Visser, M. (2008). The impact of gurus: Parker grades and *en primeur* wine prices. *Economic Journal*, 118, F158–F173.

Haeger, J.W., and Storchmann, K. (2006). Prices of American pinot noir wines: Climate, craftsmanship, critics. *Agricultural Economics*, 35, 67–78.

Hodgson, R.T. (2008). An examination of judge reliability at a major U.S. wine competition. *Journal of Wine Economics*, 3, 105–113.

Hodgson, R.T. (2009). An analysis of the concordance among 13 U.S. wine competitions. *Journal of Wine Economics*, 4, 1–9.

Hotelling, H. (1931). The economics of exhaustible resources. *Journal of Political Economy*, 39, 137–175.

Intergovernmental Panel on Climate Change (IPCC) (2007). *Climatic change 2007: Impacts, adaptation and vulnerability.* Contribution of Working Group II to the Fourth Assessment Report of the Intergovernmental Panel on Climate Change, edited by M.L. Parry, O.F. Canziani, J.P. Palutikof, P.J. van der Linden, and C.E. Hanson. Cambridge: Cambridge University Press.

Jaeger, D.A., and Storchmann, K. (2011). Wine retail price dispersion in the United States: searching for expensive wines? *American Economic Review: Papers and Proceedings*, 101(3), 136–141.

Jaeger, E. (1981). To save or savor: The rate of return to storing wine. *Journal of Political Economy*, 89(3), 584–592.

Jones, G.V., and Storchmann, K. (2001). Wine market prices and investment under uncertainty: An econometric model for Bordeaux *crus classés. Agricultural Economics*, 26(2), 115–133.

Jones, G.V., White, M.A., Cooper, O.R., and Storchmann, K. (2005). Climate change and global wine quality. *Climatic Change*, 73(3), 319–343.

Jovanovic, B. (2008). Bubbles in the prices of exhaustible resources. American Association of Wine Economists, AAWE Working Paper No. 32.

Koninklijk Nederlands Meteorologisch Instituut (2011). KNMI Climate Explorer. De Bilt, Netherlands. http://climexp.knmi.nl/start.cgi?someone@somewhere/ (accessed June 20, 2011).

Krasker, W.S. (1979). The rate of return to storing wines. *Journal of Political Economy*, 87(6), 1363–1367.

Landon, S., and Smith, C.E. (1998). Quality expectations, reputation, and price. *Southern Economic Journal*, 64(3), 628–647.

Lawless, H. (1984). Flavor description of white wine by "expert" and nonexpert wine consumers. *Journal of Food Science*, 49(1), 120–123.

Lecocq, S., and Visser, M. (2006). Spatial variations in weather conditions and wine prices in Bordeaux. *Journal of Wine Economics*, 1(2), 114–124.

Lehrer, A. (1975). Talking about wine. *Language*, 51(4), 901–923.

Liv-ex (2012). www.liv-ex.com (accessed April 13, 2012).

Marx, K. (1843). Rechtfertigung des ++−Korrespondenten von der Mosel. *Rheinische Zeitung*, No. 15, 17, 18, 19 and 20 (of January 15, 17, 18, 19, and 20, 1843). (English translation: Justification of the Correspondent from the Mosel. www.marxists.org/archive/marx/works/1843/01/15.htm (accessed June 20, 2011).

Masset, P., and Henderson, C. (2010). Wine as an alternative asset class. *Journal of Wine Economics*, 5(1), 87–118.

Masset, P., and Weisskopf, J.-P. (2010). Raise your glass: Wine investment and the financial crisis. American Association of Wine Economists, AAWE Working Paper No. 57.

Parker, R. (2011). A glossary of wine terms. https://www.erobertparker.com/info/glossary.asp (accessed June 20, 2011).

Passell, P. (1990a). Economic scene: More great wine before its time. *New York Times*, December 12.

Passell, P. (1990b). Wine equation puts some noses out of joint. *New York Times*, March 4.

Pitcher, S. (2003). A critical survey of major wine review publications. www.winepros.org/aftertaste/pub-survey.htm (accessed June 20, 2011).

Pliny the Elder (77/2007). *Pliny's Natural History in Thirty-Seven Books.* Whitefish, MT: Kessinger.

Prial, F. (1990). Wine talk. *New York Times*, May 23.

Quandt, R.E. (2007). On wine bullshit: Some new software. *Journal of Wine Economics*, 2(2), 129–135.

Ramirez, C. (2010). Do tasting notes add value? Evidence from Napa wines. *Journal of Wine Economics*, 5(1), 143–163.

Reuter, J. (2009). Does advertising bias product reviews? An analysis of wine ratings. *Journal of Wine Economics*, 4(2), 125–151.

Rhee, J., and Ross, B. (2010). Terror group gets 'A' rating from Better Business Bureau. *ABC News*, November 12. http://abcnews.go.com/Blotter/business-bureau-best-ratings-money-buy/story?id=12123843/ (accessed June 20, 2011).

Riekhof, G.M., and Sykuta, M.E. (2005). Politics, economics, and the regulation of direct interstate shipment in the wine industry. *American Journal of Agricultural Economics*, 87(2), 439–452.

Roberts, P.W., Khaire, M., and Rider, C. (2011). Isolating the symbolic implications of employee mobility: Price increases after hiring winemakers from prominent wineries. *American Economic Review: Papers and Proceedings*, 101(3), 147–151.

Robinson, J. (2006). *The Oxford Companion to Wine.* 2nd ed. Oxford: Oxford University Press.

Sanning, L.W., Shaffer, S., and Sharratt, J.M. (2008). Bordeaux wine as a financial investment. *Journal of Wine Economics*, 3(1), 51–71.

Schamel, G. (2009). Dynamic analysis of brand and regional reputation: The case of wine. *Journal of Wine Economics*, 4(1), 62–80.

Schnabel, H., and Storchmann, K. (2010). Prices as quality signals: Evidence from the wine market. *Journal of Agricultural and Food Industrial Organization* 8, Article 2.

Sharma, R. (2010). Stock market reaction to court decisions related to differential treatment of in-state and out-of-state internet wine sales. *Journal of Wine Economics*, 5(1), 69–86.

Sokolin, W. (1998). *The Complete Wine Investor. Collecting Wine for Pleasure and Profit.* Rocklin, CA: Prima.

Storchmann, K. (2005). English weather and Rhine wine quality: An ordered probit model. *Journal of Wine Research*, 16(2), 105–119.

Storchmann, K. (2011). Wine economics: Emergence, developments, and topics. *Agrekon*, 50(3), 1–28.

Unwin, T. (1991). *Wine and the Vine. A Historical Geography of Viticulture and the Wine Trade.* London and New York: Routledge.

Weil, R. (1993). Do not invest in wine, at least in the U.S., unless you plan to drink it, and maybe not even then. Or: As an investment wine is a no corker. Mimeo, University of Chicago.

Weil, R. (2007). Debunking critics' wine words: Can amateurs distinguish the smell of asphalt from the taste of cherries? *Journal of Wine Economics*, 2(2), 136–144.

Wiseman, A.E., and Ellig, J. (2004). Market and nonmarket barriers to internet wine sales: The case of Virginia. *Business and Politics*, 6(2), Article 4.

Wiseman, A.E., and Ellig, J. (2007). The politics of wine: Trade barriers, interest groups, and the commerce clause. *Journal of Politics*, 69(3), 859–875.

Wood, D., and Anderson, K. (2006). What determines the future value of an icon wine? New evidence from Australia. *Journal of Wine Economics*, 1(2), 141–161.

Part II

Wine and Natural Environment

Chapter 2

Predicting the Quality and Prices of Bordeaux Wine*

Orley Ashenfelter

Department of Economics, Princeton University,
Princeton, NJ 08540, USA
c6789@princeton.edu

Bordeaux wines have been made in much the same way for centuries. This chapter shows that the variability in the quality and prices of Bordeaux vintages is predicted by the weather that created the grapes. The price equation provides a measure of the real rate of return to holding wines (about 2–3% per annum) and implies far greater variability in the early or "en primeur" wine prices than is observed. The analysis provides a useful basis for assessing market inefficiency, the effect of climate change on the wine industry and the role of expert opinion in determining wine prices.

1. Introduction

Red wines have been produced in the Bordeaux region of France in much the same way, for hundreds of years. Yet, there are differences in quality and price from year to year that can sometimes be quite large. Until very recently, these quality differences have been considered a great mystery. In this chapter, I show that the factors that affect fluctuations in wine vintage quality can be explained in a simple quantitative way. In short, I show that a simple statistical analysis predicts the quality of a vintage, and hence its price, from the weather during its growing season. Along the way, I show how the aging of wine affects its price, and under what circumstances it pays to buy wines before they are at their best for drinking. Since this procedure for predicting wine quality has now been in use for over a decade, I also provide

*This article originally appeared in *The Economic Journal* (2008), 118, F174–F184. Published by Blackwell Publishing, 9600 Garsington Road, Oxford OX4 2DQ, UK and 350 Main Street, Malden, MA 02148, USA.

an appraisal of its successes (and failures) and a discussion of the role this information has played in the evolution of the wine trade.

When a red Bordeaux wine is young it is astringent and most people will find it unpleasant to drink. As a wine ages it loses its astringency. Because Bordeaux wines taste better when they are older, there is an obvious incentive to store them until they have come of age. As a result, there is an active market for both younger and older wines. Traditionally, what has not been so obvious is exactly how good a wine will be when it matures. This ambiguity leaves room for speculation and, as a result, the price of the wine when it is first offered in its youth will often not match the price of the wine when it matures. The primary goal in this chapter is to study how the price of mature wines may be predicted from data available when the grapes are picked, and then to explore the effect that this has on the initial and final prices of the wines. A secondary goal is to show how this straightforward hedonic method has now been used in many other grape growing regions to quantify the role the weather plays in determining the quality of wine vintages.

The study of how wine vintages are priced provides a fascinating window on the operation of a market that has high visibility in many countries. In more recent years, as concerns and evidence regarding global warming have mounted, the role of the weather in determining wine quality and prices has taken on greater urgency. Climate change will no doubt affect wine production with, as Jones *et al.* (2005) show, winners and losers. The evidence on wine prices and weather provides one avenue for calibrating who the winners and losers are likely to be and how much they may win or lose.

2. Vineyards and Vintages

The best wines of Bordeaux are made from grapes (typically cabernet sauvignon and merlot) grown on specific vineyard properties and the wine is named after the property, or chateau, that controls where the grapes are grown. In fact, knowledge of the chateau (essentially the vineyard) and vintage provides most of the information needed to know the quality of the wine. That is, if there are ten vintages and six châteaux, there are, in principle, 60 different wines of different quality. It might seem a daunting task to determine the quality of each wine. However, knowing the reputations of the six châteaux and the ten vintages gives sufficient data to determine the quality of all 60. In other words, good vintages produce good wines in all vineyards and the best wines are produced in the best vineyards in all vintages.

Table 1. London Auction Prices for Mature Red Bordeaux Wines

	Châteaux (Vineyards)						
Vintage	Lafite	Latour	Cheval Blanc	Cos d'Estournel	Montrose	Pichon Lalande	Average
1960	494	464	486				479
1961	4,335	5,432	3,534	1,170	1,125	1,579	4,884
1962	889	1,064	821	521	456	281	977
1963	340	471		251			406
1964	649	1,114	1,125	315	350	410	882
1965	190	424				258	307
1966	1,274	1,537	1,260	546	482	734	1,406
1967	374	530	441	213	236	243	452
1968	223	365	274				294
1969	251	319		123	84	152	285
Average	1,504	1,935	1,436	553	530	649	

Notes: Prices are for wines auctioned in 1990 to 1991, and are shown in $US per dozen bottles.

Although this point is sometimes denied by those who produce the wines, and especially by the sellers of young wines, it is easy to establish its truth by reference to the prices of the mature wines. To demonstrate the point, Table 1 indicates the market price in the early 1990s in London of six Bordeaux châteaux from the ten vintages from 1960 to 1969.

These châteaux were selected because they are large producers and their wines are sold very frequently. A blank in the table indicates that the wine had not appeared in the market in some time. (Lower quality vintages are typically the first to leave the market.) The vintages from 1960 to 1969 are selected because by now these wines are fully mature and there is no remaining uncertainty about their quality.

From Table 1, one can see that knowledge of the average price of the vintage (shown in the last column) and knowledge of the average chateau price (shown in the last row) tells much about the price of each wine. For example, by examining the last column of Table 1 it is clear that 1961 was the best year in this decade and that it was followed by 1966, and then 1962 and 1964 in quality (and price). There would be no dispute about this ranking from wine lovers anywhere in the world. Likewise, in the bottom row the average prices by chateau indicate that Latour is the most outstanding chateau in the group. Finding the 1961 Latour entry in the Table 1, reveals that indeed, this is the best wine of the decade in this group. In fact, a more advanced statistical analysis reveals that information on chateau and vintage alone explain over 90% of the variation in the prices. In short, there is not much room for other factors to play a very big role in price determination.

A ranking of the châteaux in order of quality based on their prices would be Latour, Lafite, Cheval Blanc, Pichon-Lalande, Cos d'Estournel, and Montrose. In fact, as Edmund Penning-Rowsell (1985) points out in his classic book *The Wines of Bordeaux*, the famous 1855 classification of the châteaux of Bordeaux into quality grades was based on a similar assessment by price alone. Surprisingly, the 1855 classification ranks these châteaux in only a slightly different order: Lafite, Latour, Pichon-Lalande, Cos d'Estournel, and Montrose.[1] Likewise, a ranking of the quality of the vintages based on price alone would be 1961, 1966, 1962, 1964, and 1967. The remaining vintages (1960, 1963, 1965, 1968, and 1969) would be ranked inferior to these five, and perhaps because of this fact, many of the wines from these inferior vintages are no longer sold in the secondary market.

As is apparent from Table 1, there are two natural dimensions on which to search for hedonic determinants of wine quality: The vintage and the vineyard. In climatological terms it is natural to associate the first with "weather" variability from year to year and the second with "climate" variability across vineyards. In what follows, I focus on the weather and thus on the factors that determine the nature and quality of the wines from particular vintages in Bordeaux. However, there is now considerable research on the climate factors that are the determinants of vineyard quality. Some of the earliest work dates back to the pioneering viticulturalists Amerine and Winkler (1944), who mapped the nascent grape growing regions of California. Gladstones (1992) provided a more nuanced analysis for key Australian vineyards. Econometric analyses using data from vineyards in France (Combris *et al.*, 1997; Jones and Storchmann, 2001), California (Haeger and Storchmann, 2006) and Germany (Ashenfelter and Storchmann, 2006) all show that heat retention and drainage (to remove excess water when it exists) are key determinants of vineyards' prices and wine quality. Typically, the cooler sites in hot regions and the warmer sites in cool regions are the best but the ideal conditions vary according to the type of grape.

3. Returns to Holding Bordeaux Wine

It is natural to wonder why wines from the same chateau, made by the same winemaker, and made in the same manner could have such varying prices as

[1]Cheval Blanc was not ranked in 1855.

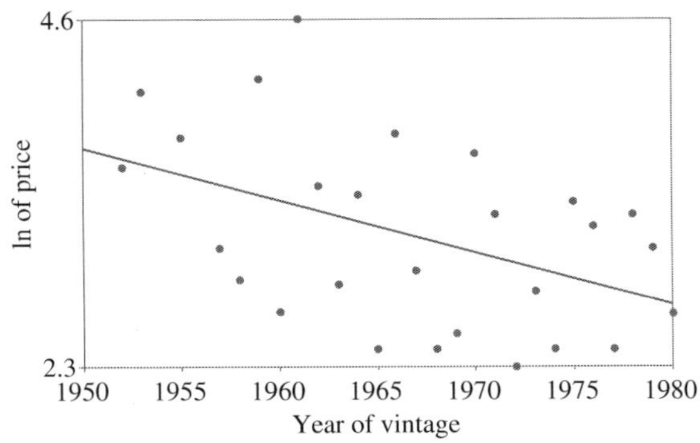

Figure 1. Red Bordeaux Wine Prices, Relative to 1961 Vintage

indicated by Table 1. Apparently, there must be some difference generated by the different vintages in which the wines were made. There are two natural explanations. First, the older wines have been held longer and this requires a payoff to the investment that has been made in foregoing the consumption of the wines.

To test this hypothesis, I have constructed an index of the price of a portfolio of wines from each vintage displayed in Figure 1.[2] Figure 1 provides a graphical representation of the results. Since these points represent the average across many châteaux in a given year, the price differences represent differences that are due only to the vintage in which the wines were produced.

Figure 1 is a scatter diagram of the price of the wines of a vintage against the vintage year. Examining either the data points or the "best-fit-line," it is apparent that there is a negative relationship between the two variables. The slope of the best-fit-line line is -0.035 and, as I have learned from further experimentation, as long as the sample includes at least 20 vintages, a slope of around -0.03 is invariably obtained. This means that the older a wine, the greater is its value. However, as can be seen in Figure 1, this also clearly leaves much variation in average prices across vintages that is unexplained.

[2]In the remainder of the article I use an index based on the wines of several châteaux as a measure of the price. See Ashenfelter *et al.* (1995). The châteaux are deliberately selected to represent the most expensive wines (Lafite, Latour, Margaux, and Cheval Blanc) as well as a selection of wines that are less expensive (Ducru Beaucaillou, Leoville Las Cases, Palmer, Pichon Lalande, Beychevelle, Cos d'Estournel, Giscours, Gruaud-Larose, and Lynch-Bages). A different selection of châteaux for the portfolio would have very little effect on the results.

4. Vintages and the Weather

It is well known that the quality of any fruit, in general, depends on the weather during the growing season that produced the fruit. What is not so widely understood is that in some localities the weather will vary dramatically from one year to the next. In California, for example, it never rains in the summer and it is always warm in the summer. There is a simple reason for this. In California, a high-pressure weather system settles each summer over the California coast and produces a warm, dry growing season for the grapes planted there. In Bordeaux this sometimes happens — but sometimes it does not. Australia is an intermediate case, where summers are usually dry, though not always. Summers in Bordeaux can be hot and dry, hot and wet, cool and dry, most unpleasant of all, and cool and wet. In general, high quality vintages for Bordeaux wines correspond to the years in which August and September are dry, the growing season is warm, and the previous winter has been wet. Except in places where irrigation is common to make up for low winter rainfalls, this finding will not surprise winemakers anywhere in the world.

Figure 2 establishes that it is hot, dry summers that produce the vintages in which the mature wines obtain the higher prices. This figure displays for each vintage the summer temperature from low to high as you move from left to right, and the harvest rain from low to high as you move from top to bottom. Vintages that sell for an above average price are displayed with dark points, and vintages that sell for a below average price are displayed with light points.

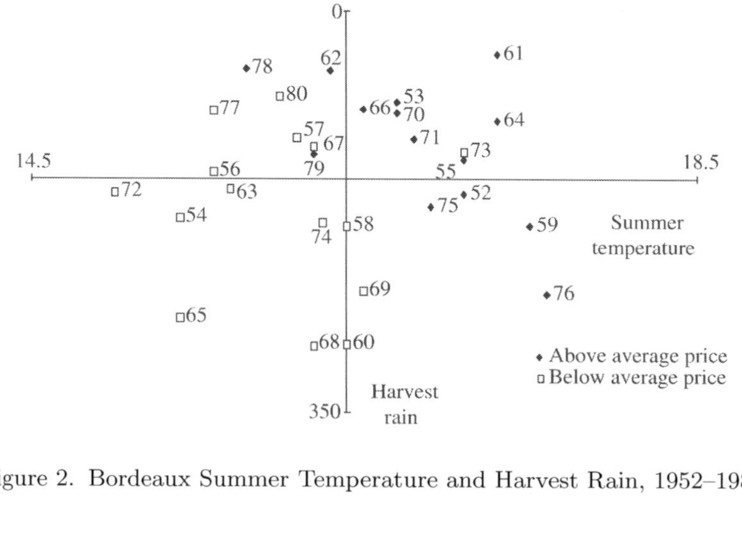

Figure 2. Bordeaux Summer Temperature and Harvest Rain, 1952–1980

If the weather is the key determinant of wine quality, then the dark points should be in the northeast quadrant of the diagram and the light points should be in the southwest quadrant of the diagram, and the other two quadrants should have a mixture of dark and light points. It is apparent that this is precisely the case. Even anomalies, like the 1973 vintage, tend to corroborate the fact that the weather determines the quality of the wines, because although the wines of this vintage, which are of somewhat above average quality, have always sold at relatively low prices, insiders know that they are often bargains (and indeed I have bought and consumed a lot of them!)

Ideally, the weather's effect on wine quality and price could be tested with a controlled laboratory experiment. However, this is obviously not feasible as there is no way to control the weather in France (yet!). This inability to create a controlled experiment leads to the use of so called "natural experiments." A natural experiment is a set of circumstances that occurs naturally (or at least is external to our control) and exhibits sufficient variation to identify the causal effects of interest. The case of weather in Bordeaux presents a very nice natural experiment. The weather differs sufficiently from year to year and the quality of the grapes is recorded sufficiently (through wine prices) to measure weather's true effects on quality.

The result of a regression of the prices of the wines on the weather variables is reported in Table 2.[3] Although the weather data are taken from a single station in Merignac, a part of the Bordeaux region, Lecocq and Visser (2006) have shown that the weather variability across components of the small Bordeaux region are so similar that more detailed data add little to the analysis. The results indicate that in a model that includes four variables, the age of the vintage, the average temperature over the growing season (April–September), the amount of rain in September and August, and the amount of rain in the months preceding the vintage (October–March) about 80% of the variation in the average price of Bordeaux wine vintages is explained. Analysis of the effects of age alone produces a model that explains only slightly more than 20%, suggesting that the weather is an extremely important determinant of the quality of a wine vintage and its price at maturation.

With this model, it is possible to predict the relative price at which the new vintage should be sold as soon as the growing season is complete. The

[3]All analyses use as data the vintages of 1952–1980, excluding the 1954 and 1956 vintages, which are now rarely sold.

Table 2. Regressions of Log Wine Price on Climate Variables

Independent variables	(1)		(2)		(3)	
Age of vintage	0.0354	(0.0137)	0.0238	(0.0072)	0.2400	(0.0075)
Average temperature over growing season (April–September)	—		0.6160	(0.0952)	0.6080	(0.1160)
Rain in August	—		−0.00386	(0.00081)	−0.00380	(0.00095)
Rain in the months preceding the vintage (October–March)	—		0.00117	(0.00048)	0.00115	(0.00051)
Average temperature in September	—		—		0.0077	(0.0565)
R-squared	0.212		0.828		0.828	
Root mean Square error	0.575		0.287		0.293	

Notes: All regressions are of the (logarithm of) the price of different vintages of a portfolio of Bordeaux chateau wines on climate variables, using as data the vintages of 1952–1980, excluding the 1954 and 1956 vintages, which are now rarely sold; all regressions contain an intercept, which is not reported. Standard errors are in parentheses.

basic idea for these predictions is displayed in Figure 3. This figure adds to Figure 2 the data for the vintages from 1981–2003 but keeps the axes in the same place, based on the historical normal rainfall and temperature data.

Two things are immediately apparent from Figure 3. First, all but one of these recent vintages (1986) was produced by a growing season that was warmer than what is historically "normal." Indeed a test of whether the mean temperature in the later period is different from the mean temperature in the earlier period strongly rejects equality in favor of warmer temperatures in the later period. On the other hand, the average rainfall during the harvest in later period shows no difference from "normal." Indeed, the prevalence of such warm weather in the summer in the last two decades no doubt accounts, in part, for the deeply held conviction that many Europeans hold that global warming is already upon us. This unusual run of extraordinary weather has resulted in a huge quantity of excellent red Bordeaux wines. Although it is rarely remarked upon by anyone but economists, global warming creates both winners and losers.

Second, the weather that created the vintages of 1989, 1990, 2000, and 2003 appears to be quite exceptional by any standard. Indeed, the question must be asked, is it appropriate to predict that the wines of these vintages

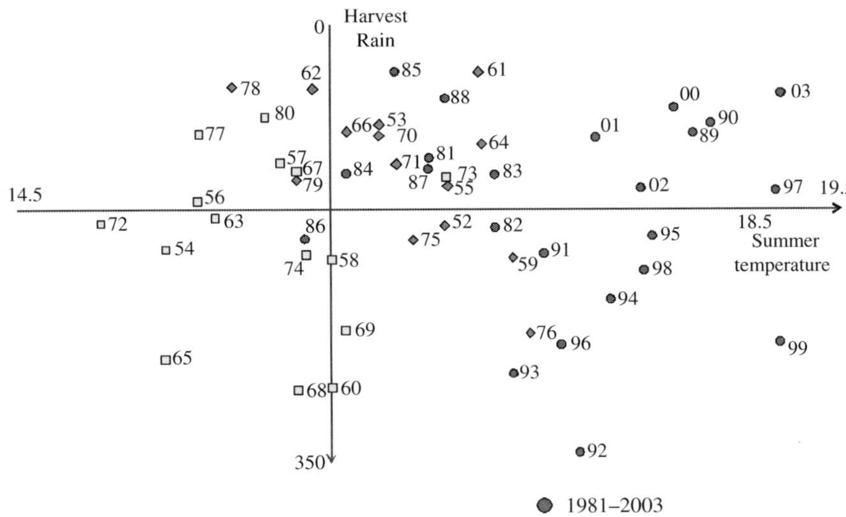

Figure 3. Rainfall and Temperature in Bordeaux: 1952–2003

will be of outstanding quality when the temperature that produced them is so far outside the normal range?

Before making the predictions for 1989 or 1990, I asked the late Lincoln Moses, a distinguished Stanford statistician, for advice. Moses suggested two informal tests.

(*a*) Would the last major "out of sample" prediction have been correct? The idea here is to use the past to indirectly test the ability of the relationship to stretch beyond the available data. In fact, the last major "out of sample" prediction for which all uncertainty had been resolved was the vintage of 1961, which had the lowest August–September rainfall in Bordeaux history. Just as the unusual weather predicted, the market (see Table 1), and most wine lovers, have come to consider this an outstanding vintage.

(*b*) Was the warmth of the 1989 and 1990 growing seasons in Bordeaux greater than the normal warmth in other places where similar grapes are grown? The idea here is to determine whether the temperature in Bordeaux is abnormal by comparison with grape growing regions that may be even warmer. In fact, the temperature in 1989 or 1990 in Bordeaux was no higher than the average temperature in the Barossa Valley of South Australia or the Napa Valley in California, places where high quality red wines are made from similar grape types.

Based on these two informal tests, I decided in 1991 to predict that both the 1989 and 1990 vintages in Bordeaux were likely to be outstanding. Ironically, many professional wine writers did not concur with this prediction at the time. In the years that have followed minds have been changed; and there is now virtually unanimous agreement that 1989 and 1990 are two of the outstanding vintages of the last 50 years.

Among current vintages, Figure 3 indicates that the 2000 and 2003 vintages are in a league similar to the outstanding vintages of 1989 and 1990. And what does the wine press say about these vintages? It is not hard to find out, as these wines have been advertised for sale over the last several years using the fantastic praise heaped upon them. For example, Robert Parker widely considered the most influential taster says, "2000 is the greatest vintage Bordeaux has ever produced. Remarkably consistent from top to bottom, there has never been a year where so many exceptional wines were produced." He is no less ecstatic about the 2003 vintage. And yet we learned this without tasting a single drop of wine.

In recent years, the hedonic approach to analyzing wine vintages has been applied in several other areas, including Australia (Ashenfelter and Byron, 1995; Wood and Anderson, 2006) and Italy (Corsi and Ashenfelter, 2001). Fair (2002) even reports a series of independent tests of the *ex post* forecasting ability of the weather model for Bordeaux, concluding that it provides accurate predictions so long as the purpose is to drink (as opposed to collect) the wines.

One of the most interesting issues raised by the study of these hedonic models of vintage quality is the role it implies for expert opinion in the determination of wine prices. Ian Ayes recent book, *Super Crunchers* (2007), is an exploration of this topic using examples from several fields of economics including the study of wine pricing. Related papers include those by Ashenfelter and Jones (2000) and Ali *et al.* (2008). Although it is difficult to summarize the conclusions of this ongoing area of research, there is evidence that "expert" opinion that is unrelated (i.e., orthogonal) to the fundamental determinants of wine quality plays a role in determining wine prices, at least in the short run. This naturally raises the unresolved question of just what determines the "demand" for expert opinion.

5. Market Inefficiency

Given that the weather plays such a large role in determining the quality and prices of the mature wines of a vintage, does the market take account of this information when the young wines are priced? In short, were the relative prices of the vintages when they were first sold at market good forecasts of the relative prices of the wines when they matured, and if so, were these forecasts as good as the predictions made using the data on weather alone?

Table 3 reveals the answer to both of these questions. The entries for each of the vintages in Table 3 are index prices of the wines in the market in each calendar year from 1971 to 1989. The index method used here is to simply put the price of the wine relative to the "benchmark portfolio" listed in column 1 of Table 3.[4] For example, in Table 3 an entry of 1.0 would represent a vintage with equal value to the benchmark portfolio in a given year and an entry of 0.5 would be a vintage with half the value of the benchmark portfolio. In the bottom row of Table 3 is listed the predicted relative price of the vintage as taken from the model created earlier using weather and age to predict the price at maturation.

The data in Table 3 confirm two remarkable facts. First, most of these older vintages began their lives in the auction markets at prices that are far above what they will ultimately fetch. For instance, the bottom row of Table 3 indicates that, based on the weather, the wines of a vintage like 1967 would have been expected to sell for about one-half the price of an average of the wines from the 1961, 1962, 1964, and 1966 vintages (the benchmark portfolio). But in fact, the wines entered the auction markets in 1972 at about 50% more than expected, and slowly drifted down in relative price over the years. Second, Table 3 confirms that the prices predicted by our model are remarkably good indicators of the prices at which the mature wines will ultimately trade. Additionally, it should be mentioned that the model was fit from an entirely different set of data than the set presented above. This eliminates the possibility that this model only performs well because it simply predicts information that it essentially already knows.

One interesting way to see the inefficiency in the wine market is to compare the prices of the vintages of 1962, 1964, 1967, and 1969 in calendar year 1972. As the weather data in Figure 2 indicate, and the prediction in the bottom row of Table 3 confirms, in 1972 one should have expected that the 1962 and 1964 vintages would sell for considerably more than the vintages of both 1967 and 1969. In fact, in 1972 these four vintages fetched nearly identical prices, in sharp contrast to what the weather would have indicated.

[4] The benchmark portfolio is the average price of the wines from the 1961, 1962, 1964, and 1966 vintages. This is done for statistical ease, and these vintages were chosen for their superior quality.

Table 3. Relative Prices per Case of Wines from a Portfolio of Bordeaux Châteaux

Year of sale	Benchmark portfolio[a]	Vintage 1961	1962	1963	1964	1965	1966	1967	1968	1969	1970	1971	1972
1971	€54	1.68	0.79	0.41	0.76		0.79						
1972	€97	1.58	0.76	0.26	0.70	0.27	0.96	0.77		0.75			
1973	€119	1.62	0.71	0.28	0.74	0.24	0.93	0.62	0.28	0.70	0.83		
1974	€85	1.31	0.77	0.39	0.84		1.08	0.78	0.30	0.70	0.88		0.30
1975	€76	1.65	0.77	0.29	0.78	0.35	0.60	0.57	0.31	0.41	0.84	0.61	0.44
1976	€109	1.67	0.83	0.30	0.66	0.29	0.65	0.51	0.23	0.36	0.69	0.54	
1977	€165	1.67	0.83	0.26	0.63	0.26	0.87	0.50	0.23	0.36	0.70	0.51	0.32
1978	€215	1.67	0.76	0.26	0.65	0.18	0.91	0.45	0.25	0.31	0.70	0.53	0.25
1979	€274	1.61	0.73	0.20	0.66	0.23	1.00	0.49	0.24	0.29	0.71	0.50	0.23
1981	€296	1.75	0.62	0.22	0.70	0.04	0.93	0.47	0.25	0.29	0.82	0.52	0.22
1982	€420	1.80	0.71	0.15	0.60	0.18	0.89	0.39	0.17	0.24	0.77	0.55	0.19
1983	€586	1.77	0.53	0.10	0.59	0.18	1.11	0.36	0.18	0.21	0.91	0.48	0.20
1985	€952	2.19	0.53	0.12	0.50	0.21	0.78	0.30	0.11	0.14	0.68	0.46	0.13
1986	€888	2.10	0.56	0.25	0.54	0.17	0.80	0.30	0.15	0.19	0.65	0.46	0.14
1987	€901	2.11	0.56		0.53		0.80	0.32	0.19	0.20	0.64	0.49	0.18
1988	€854	2.01	0.56	0.21	0.61	0.14	0.82	0.34	0.23	0.20	0.67	0.58	0.17
1989	€1,048	2.09	0.61	0.28	0.53	0.19	0.77	0.27	0.24	0.18	0.66	0.43	0.15
Predicted price[b]		1.74	0.72	0.29	0.76	0.16	0.78	0.49	0.21	0.29	0.6	0.53	0.014

Notes: [a]Prices are per case of a portfolio of Bordeaux châteaux relative to the price of a "benchmark" portfolio of wines for the vintages of 1961, 1962, 1964, and 1966. [b]Predicted prices are fitted from the earlier regression of prices on age and weather.

However, by around 1979 the prices of the 1969s and 1967s had fallen to around what would have been predicted by the weather.

It is apparent from Table 3 and from the above example that most vintages are over-priced when the wines are first offered on the auction market and that this state of affairs often persists for ten years or more following the year of the vintage. Remarkably, the over-pricing of the vintages is especially apparent for those vintages that, from the weather, we would predict to be the poorest. This suggests that, in large measure, the ability of the weather to predict the quality of the wines is either unknown or ignored by the early purchasers and sellers of the wines.

One of the most fascinating surprises with respect to vintage pricing is provided by the 1982 vintage. As the data in Figure 3 indicate, this was a warm year, although not especially a dry one and the wines should be good. However, what has happened to these wines is quite remarkable, with their prices virtually taking on a life of their own. Today, the wines from this vintage are priced at double and triple the prices of the superior 1989 and 1990 vintages, and there is no indication — yet — that there will be any correction soon. That there is something odd about the vintage is attested to by the current state of the auction markets, where huge quantities of 1982s are put up for sale at current prices but where no one wants to part with their 1983s or 1985s. This suggests that the auction market may have evolved to include two classes of buyers, those who buy for the wine and those simply looking for a status symbol. The sellers of the 1982s are the former, while the buyers are the latter.

The 1982 vintage phenomenon raises serious problems for those who would like to invest in wine but not consume it. How does one predict that a vintage will become a status symbol? For those who consume their wines, anomalies like 1982 cause no problem — they simply buy the wines based on fundamentals and then drink the wines that do not appreciate in price and sell those that do. Wine investors do not, sadly, have the more pleasant half of these two options.

6. Conclusions

There is much variability in the prices of mature Bordeaux wines but, as shown, much of it can be explained. First, much of this variability can be explained once the vintage of the wine and its producer is known. Second, a straightforward statistical analysis of the weather in which a vintage is grown and consideration of its age can be used to describe much of the variability in prices across vintages. Finally, the historical reputation of the chateau that produced the wine explains much of the remaining variability in prices. But why does the market for immature red Bordeaux wines appear to be so inefficient when the market for mature wines appears to be so efficient? There may be several related explanations. The current Bordeaux marketing system has the character of an agricultural income stabilization system and this may be its purpose. For growers to maintain the same income from year to year the price of the young wines must be inversely related to the quantity produced and independent of the quality. In other words, the fewer grapes they produce, the more money they need per grape to maintain the same income; quality must be kept independent of the price or their income would be subject to volatility. Although the actual pricing of young Bordeaux wines falls short of this ideal, it is clearly closer to it than would occur if purchasers used the information available from the weather for determining the quality of the wines. The producers do attempt to raise prices when crops are small, despite the evidence that the quantity of the wines (determined by the weather in the spring) is generally unrelated to the quality of the wines (determined mainly by weather in the remainder of the year). Moreover, it is common for the proprietors to claim that each vintage is a good one, independent of the weather that produced it. Indeed, there is no obvious incentive for an individual proprietor to ever claim anything else!

A more fundamental question arises about the motives of the early purchasers of the wines. Why have they ignored the evidence that the weather during a grape growing season is a fundamental and easily measured determinant of the quality of the mature wines? And will they continue to do so as the evidence for the predictability of the quality of new vintages accumulates?[5]

Acknowledgments

The author thanks the Editor of this Journal and an anonymous referee for helpful comments. All interpretations and any errors are the author's sole responsibility.

---

[5]There is some slowly accumulating evidence that today wine critics make fewer prognostications that are as wildly inaccurate as used to be the case. That is, their prognostications about "important" vintages may be less wildly inaccurate today. Still, there are exceptions, such as the 1997 vintage — which is probably the only seriously under-priced vintage currently available. An even greater puzzle is posed by how one explains why, if wine critics simply do as well as those who read the weather, there is a demand for their services.

References

Ali, H., Lecocq, S., and Visser, M. (2008). The impact of gurus: Parker grades and "en primeur" wine prices. *Economic Journal*, 118(529), F174–F184.

Amerine, M., and Winkler, M. (1944). Composition and quality of musts and wines of California grapes. *Hilgardia*, 15, 493–675.

Ashenfelter, O., Ashmore, D., and Lalonde, R. (1995). Bordeaux wine vintage quality and the weather. *Chance*, 8(4), 7–13.

Ashenfelter, O., and Byron, R.P. (1995). Predicting the quality of an unborn Grange. *Economic Record*, 71, 40–53.

Ashenfelter, O., and Jones, G. (2000). The demand for expert opinions: Bordeaux wine. *Cahier Scientifique de l'Observatoire des Conjonctures Vincoles Europeenenes*, 3 (March), 1–17.

Ashenfelter, O., and Storchmann, K. (2006). Using a hedonic model of solar radiation to assess the economic effect of climate change: The case of Mosel valley vineyards, NBER Working Paper No. 12380 (July).

Combris, P., Lecocq, S., and Visser, M. (1997). Estimation of a hedonic price equation for Bordeaux wine: Does quality matter? *Economic Journal*, 107, 390–402.

Corsi, A., and Ashenfelter, O. (2001). Predicting Italian wine quality from weather data and expert's ratings. In: Pichery, M. and Terraza, M. (eds.), *Oenometrie IX. 9th Annual Meeting of the Vineyard Data Quantification Society in Montpellier*, Cahier Scientific No. 4, Montpellier.

Fair, R. (2002). *Predicting Presidential Elections and Other Things.* Stanford, CA: Stanford University Press.

Gladstones, J. (1992). *Viticulture and Environment.* Adelaide, South Australia: Winetitles.

Haeger, J., and Storchmann, K. (2006). Prices of American pinot noir wines: climate, craftsmanship, critics. *Agricultural Economics*, 35, 67–78.

Jones, G., and Storchmann, K. (2001). Wine market prices and investment under uncertainty: An econometric model for Bordeaux Cru classes. *Agricultural Economics*, 26, 114–133.

Jones, G.V., White, M.A., Cooper, O.R., and Storchmann, K. (2005). Climate change and global wine quality. *Climatic Change*, 73(3), 319–343.

Lecocq, S., and Visser, M. (2006). Spatial variations in weather conditions and wine prices in Bordeaux. *Journal of Wine Economics*, 1, 114–124.

Penning-Rowsell, E. (1985). *The Wines of Bordeaux.* San Francisco, CA: The Wine Appreciation Guild.

Wood, D., and Anderson, K. (2006). What determines the future value of an icon wine? New evidence from Australia. *Journal of Wine Economics*, 1(2), 141–161.

Chapter 3

Using Hedonic Models of Solar Radiation and Weather to Assess the Economic Effect of Climate Change: The Case of Mosel Valley Vineyards*

Orley Ashenfelter[†] **and Karl Storchmann**[‡]

[†]*Economics Department, Firestone Library,*
Princeton University, Princeton, NJ 08544, USA
c6789@princeton.edu

[‡]*Economics Department, New York University,*
19 W 4th Street, New York, NY 10012, USA
karl.storchmann@nyu.du

In this chapter, we use two alternative methods to assess the effects of climate change on the quality of wines from the vineyards of the Mosel Valley in Germany. In the first, structural approach we use a physical model of solar radiation to measure the amount of energy collected by a vineyard and then to establish the econometric relation between energy and vineyard quality. Coupling this hedonic function with the physics of heat and energy permits a calculation of the impact of any temperature change on vineyard quality (and prices). In a second approach, we measure the effect of year-to-year changes in the weather on land or crop values in the same region and use the estimated hedonic equation to measure the effect of temperature change on prices. The empirical results of both analyses indicate that the vineyards of the Mosel Valley will increase in value under a scenario of global warming, and perhaps by a considerable amount.

1. Introduction

In this chapter, we provide and compare the results of two methods for assessing the effects of climate change on the quality of agricultural land using a

*This article originally appeared in *The Review of Economics and Statistics* (2010), 92(2), 333–349.

rich set of data on the vineyards of the Mosel Valley in Germany. The first method uses a structural model of solar radiation to measure the amount of energy collected by a vineyard and then to establish the econometric relation between energy and vineyard quality. Coupling this hedonic function with the elementary physics of heat and energy permits a calculation of the impact of any temperature change on vineyard quality (and prices). Although we show that this approach can, in principle, be applied to any crop grown on any land, the vineyards of the Mosel are a particularly attractive place to assess this method for measuring the effect that expected climate changes may have on quality and relative prices. Since the vineyards of this valley are situated near the far northern boundary feasible for grape production, they differ enormously in their suitability for grape growing. We show that this variability is due primarily to the extent to which each vineyard is able to capture radiant solar energy, so that these data provide a particularly credible experiment for identifying and measuring the appropriate hedonic equation.

The second method uses the so-called Ricardian approach applied by Mendelsohn, Nordhaus, and Shaw (1994) to the study of effects of climate change on agriculture. Their empirical research, based as it is on hedonic models from highly aggregated data, has been critiqued and extended to consider difficult issues of functional form and specification by Schlenker, Hanemann, and Fisher (2005, 2006) and Deschênes and Greenstone (2006). These more recent studies generally find considerable heterogeneity in the expected effects of climate change. Depending on the region considered, climate change may lead to either positive or negative effects on land values, with considerable uncertainty about the aggregate effect. Our approach follows this more recent work by studying a very specific area and type of crop and by establishing the economic relation using time-series variation in the weather.

As is well known, there are likely to be winners and losers from any potential climate change. The empirical results of both analyses are broadly similar and indicate that the vineyards of the Mosel Valley will increase in value under a scenario of global warming, and perhaps by a considerable amount. Vineyard and grape prices increase more than proportionally with greater ripeness, so that we estimate a 3°C increase in temperature would more than double the value of this vineyard area, while a 1°C increase would increase prices by more than 20%.

The chapter is structured as follows. In Section 2, we explain how solar radiation is captured by a vineyard and how an energy value can be calculated for each vineyard site using the basic physics of solar panel construction. Section 3 discusses the data we use for the analysis, including the data on vineyard quality that we have constructed and the hedonic characteristics of the vineyards we study. In Section 4, we present the estimates of our hedonic model of vineyard site quality, while Section 5 contains our calculations of the impact of possible climate change on the quality distribution of vineyard sites. In Section 6, we report estimates of the effect of time-series variation in the weather on wine prices and accounting profits and compare the implied estimated effects of climate change on land prices with those we obtain from the cross-section model of vineyard quality determination. We summarize our findings in Section 7.

2. Radiation Use Efficiency, Solar Panels, and Vineyards

Commercial viticulture is found only between 35° and 50° latitude. Located between 49.61° and 50.34° latitude, the vineyards of Germany's Mosel region are thus at the cold limit for grape growing. As a result, all Mosel vineyards depend on special site characteristics to ensure winter survival and ripening (Gladstones, 1992). As we will show, with these growing conditions, a good vineyard site must be, among other things, a natural solar panel, maximizing the incoming solar radiation with its angle of incidence and orientation.

2.1. *Radiation use efficiency*

Surprisingly, formal research on the influence of light on crop growth dates primarily from the late 1950s (De Wit, 1959). Some twenty years later, Monteith (1977) provided the basis for calculating the quantitative relationship between intercepted solar radiation (energy) and the amount of dry biomass produced. This relationship is expressed by the term *radiation use efficiency* (RUE), and it measures the mass accumulation in gram dry matter per $MJ^{-1}m^{-2}$ of intercepted solar radiation. It is this biomass that represents the economically valuable output of a plant.

Subsequent studies have estimated RUE for different crops (Sinclair and Muchow, 1999), and this research continues today. It is likely that the RUE is fairly similar for the members of a specific crop but varies significantly among crop species. As shown in Table 1, C_4 species such as maize, sorghum, and sugarcane have significantly higher RUE than do the C_3 species, such as potatoes, wheat, barley, rice, soybeans, and sunflowers.[1] The only study of the RUE of grapevines (*Vitis vinifera*) of which we are aware is for the Merlot variety (Castelan-Estrada, 2001). With a radiation use efficiency between

[1] C_4 crops produce less complicated nutrients like sugar and starch, whereas C_3 crops produce more complex and higher-quality nutrients like oil and protein.

Table 1. Solar Radiation Efficiency of Selected Crops

	Crop	RUE_{max}[a]
C_4 species	Sugarcane	2.0
	Maize	1.8
	Grain sorghum	1.7
C_3 species	Potato	1.7
	Wheat	1.6
	Sunflower	1.6
	Rice	1.4
	Soybean	1.3
Other	Tomato	1.5
	Cauliflower	1.1
	Apple	0.8
	Grapevine (merlot)	0.7

Note: [a]Maximum RUE in gram dry matter $MJ^{-1}m^{-2}$ of intercepted solar radiation.
Sources: Sinclair and Muchow (1999), Environmental Protection Agency (2002), and Castelan-Estrada (2001).

0.57 and 0.70 g $MJ^{-1}m^{-2}$, this study indicates that in terms of RUE, *Vitis vinifera* belong to the least efficient plants. It follows that the energy intensity of a particular site is far more important for grapevines than it is for wheat or cauliflower.

2.2. *Vineyards as solar panels*

Only a part of solar radiation reaches the surface of the earth directly (*beam radiation*). Another part is scattered by the atmosphere and reaches the surface as so-called *diffuse radiation*. The sum of both is referred to as *total solar radiation*. However, it is apparent that total solar radiation is highly dependent on the amount, kind, and density of clouds, and it varies with time and place. For simplicity, engineers often calculate the so-called extraterrestrial radiation, that is, the radiation that would be available if there were no atmosphere (Duffie and Beckman, 1991). This is the simplification we will use to construct a measure of the differences in solar radiation input provided by the different vineyards of the Mosel Valley. Since all these vineyards lie in a very small geographical region, we know that differences across vineyards in total radiation are due primarily to differences in site characteristics, not to differences in the weather.

Figure 1 shows the extraterrestrial radiation on a horizontal surface for different geographical latitudes in the Northern Hemisphere. It is apparent

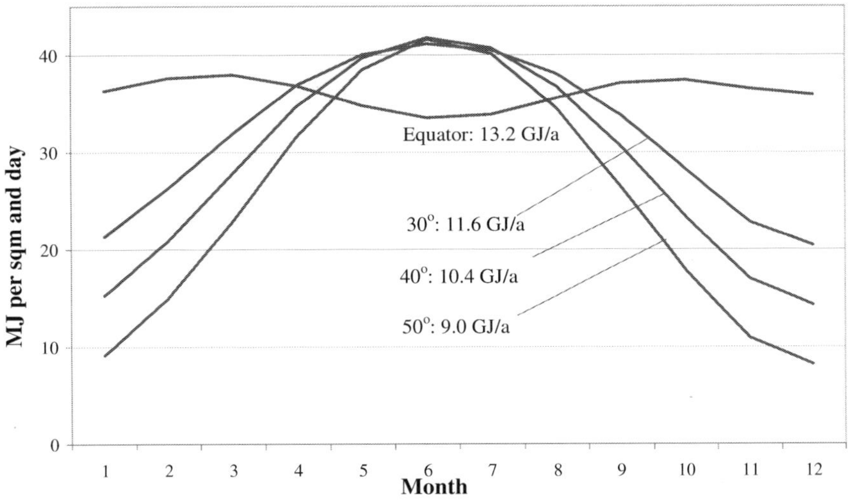

Figure 1. Solar Radiation by Latitude on a Horizontal Surface in the Northern Hemisphere

that there is a large difference in both the total amount of energy as well as its distribution over the year. While a plane at the equator receives the maximum energy amount of about 13.2 $GJm^{-2}a^{-1}$, the incoming radiation decreases with increasing latitude. With an energy level of 9.1 $GJm^{-2}a^{-1}$ the Mosel-Saar-Ruwer region obtains only two-thirds of the total maximum energy amount. Moreover, whereas the energy flux at the equator is comparatively evenly distributed, the radiation pattern becomes increasingly focused on June 21 the farther north one gets. Daily solar radiation in the North is even greater in the summer than at equatorial latitudes because of the North's long summer days. As Figure 1 indicates, the farther north one goes, the less energy there is available during off-peak times in late spring and late summer. For instance, at the end of October, the main harvest time for Riesling grapes in the Mosel valley, there is only a photon flux of 13 $MJm^{-2}day^{-1}$ compared to 37 $MJm^{-2}day^{-1}$ at the equator, that is, only one-third of the maximal achievable amount.

This energy deficit at high latitudes can be remedied by the right slope. Figure 2 shows the solar radiation for the Mosel city of Trier (49.8° north) by inclination (assuming a southern orientation). Although a plane surface receives only 9.1 $GJm^{-2}a^{-1}$ (as already shown in figure 1), increasing inclination enhances the energy level significantly. A tilt of 45° provides more than 40% more energy (12.8 $GJm^{-2}a^{-1}$) and only 3% less than the maximum amount achievable at the equator. Moreover, the distribution over the year strikingly resembles that of the equator; the energy flow from March

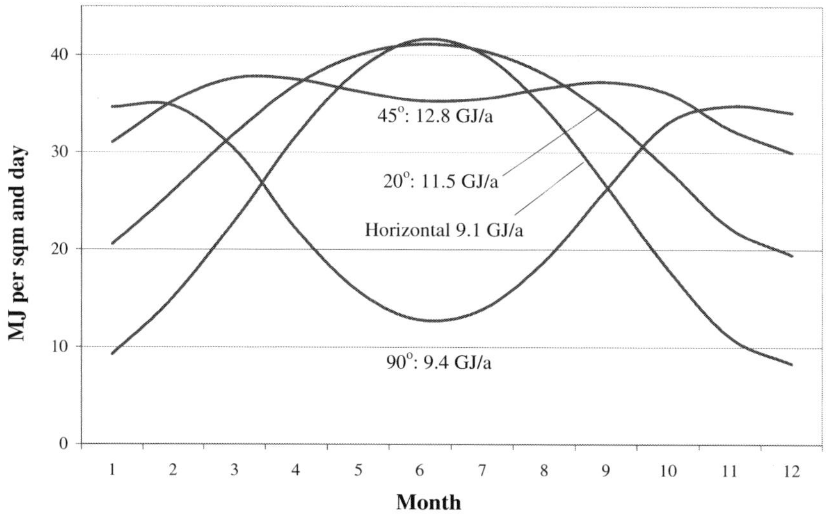

Figure 2. Solar Radiation by Inclination on a Southward-Oriented Surface in Trier (49.8° North)

to October is almost the same. Hence, a vineyard's inclination can almost perfectly offset its unfavorable latitude. However, this does not mean that the steeper vineyards are always better. Vineyards that are tilted more than 45° receive less energy than those with less inclination (at this latitude), and the energy received is also more unequally distributed over the course of the year. For example, an inclination of 90° yields only slightly more solar radiation than a horizontal surface does. The optimal inclination is dependent on the latitude: the farther north, the steeper the optimal site must be. With respect to the Mosel Valley the optimal tilt is about 45°.

The calculations thus far are based on the assumption that the tilted vineyard has a southern orientation. Figure 3 shows the impact of a different orientation for the vineyard on solar energy, holding the latitude constant (at Trier's) and holding the inclination at its optimal level for this latitude: 45°. A southern aspect is the ideal, and with increasing deviation from a southern aspect, the energy yield falls dramatically. If the tilted vineyard is west facing, the yearly solar radiation is less than on a horizontal surface (8.9 compared to 9.1 $\mathrm{GJm^{-2}a^{-1}}$ given in Figure 2). A sloping vineyard with a northwestern aspect receives only 4.7 $\mathrm{GJm^{-2}a^{-1}}$, less than a horizontal plane in the Arctic Circle.[2]

[2]This raises the question of why there are steep vineyards with unfavorable orientations at all. The energy yield is lower than on a plane surface, while the labor costs are considerably higher. It seems likely that these vineyard sites were selected for noneconomic reasons, such as their nearness to a cloister.

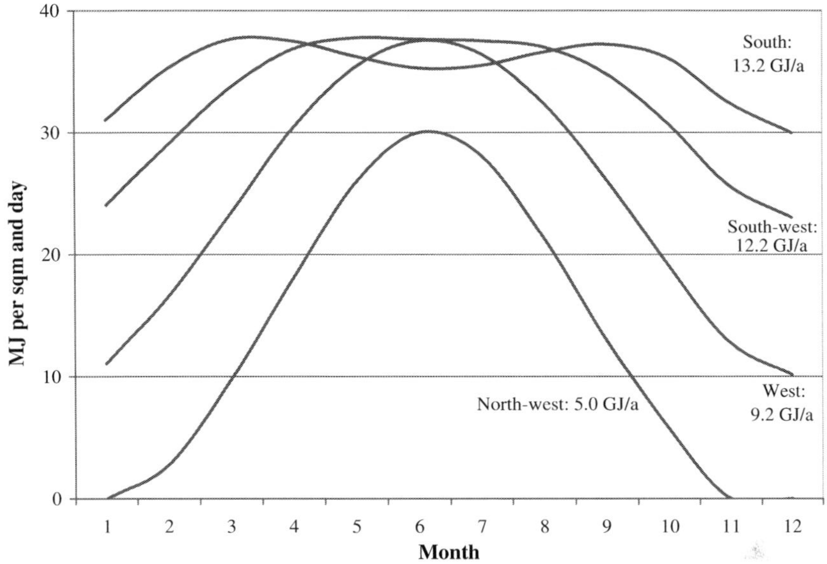

Figure 3. Solar Radiation by Orientation on a 45° Tilted Surface in Trier (49.8° North)

2.3. *Calculation of solar radiation*

Given data on the latitude (φ), slope (β), and orientation (γ) for any vineyard or agricultural site, we show in the appendix how to calculate a single measure of solar radiation for each month of the year. We aggregated these monthly figures for the vineyards of the Mosel to obtain measures of solar radiation during both the critical ripening period for grapes (September and October) and the full year. These are the data we use in our hedonic analysis.[3] Summary statistics of these measures are contained in the bottom two rows of Table 4. The data indicate remarkable variability among the vineyards. For example, the annual energy yield ranges from a high of 12.802 GJm^{-2} to a low of 5.568 GJm^{-2}, or nearly a 130% difference. The total variability in our measure of solar radiation in the crucial ripening period for grapes is even greater and spans the range from 2.237 GJm^{-2} to 0.695 GJm^{-2}, or nearly a 220% difference.

2.4. *Other factors that affect vineyard sites*

Gladstones (1992) provides a detailed analysis of several other factors that make specific geographic sites more or less suitable for the production of high-quality grapes. Important factors include those that reduce diurnal

[3]Detailed calculations for individual vineyards are available from the authors on request.

(night–day) temperature differences. Nearness to a body of water and, especially, soil type are important determinants of diurnal fluctuations. Thus, the heat storage capacity and solar reflectivity (measured by its albedo number, α) of some soils is of considerable potential importance in determining the quality of a vineyard site, and we also measure these factors in the empirical analysis below.

3. Data

Our analysis makes use of data from two different sources on very specific vineyard sites.[4] Unfortunately the definition of these distinct vineyard sites has changed at times so that our two key sources are not based on precisely the same vineyard definitions. Stöhr, Cüppers, and Fass (1981) provide a comprehensive description of all the geographic characteristics of the Mosel-Saar-Ruwer vineyard sites as they were defined in 1971.[5] These data were taken as the baseline for our calculations. We supplemented these data on the geographic characteristics of the vineyards with measures of the historical prices of the vineyards based on taxation records, primarily from the nineteenth century. Since the latter data were based on finer divisions of vineyards, that is, smaller vineyard sites, we lose some information by aggregating to the 1971 benchmark.[6]

3.1. *Vineyard price and quality*

The most difficult aspect of our data construction is the ranking by price of the respective vineyards. Prices of vineyard sites have been assessed for taxation purposes in the Mosel since the seventeenth century. An early example of such a ranking that was made by the French, who controlled the Mosel area in the early part of the nineteenth century, is contained in Table 2.

[4]German vineyard sites have precise names to avoid duplication. A vineyard in the town of Berncastel is a "Berncasteler." The "Doctor" vineyard in the town of Berncastel is thus known as the "Berncasteler Doctor" to distinguish it from any other vineyard named "Doctor."

[5]The Mosel River is the largest tributary of the Rhine. The grapegrowing region known as the Mosel, which runs with the river roughly 206 kilometers northeast from Trier to Koblenz, actually consists of a system of river valleys that includes the tributaries the Saar and the Ruwer. Thus, the official term for this wine area is "Mosel-Saar-Ruwer."

[6]For instance, in 1910 there were about 4,550 defined vineyard sites within a demarcated area of 6,800 hectares (Goldschmidt, 1925). The German wine law of 1971 defines only 523 vineyard sites within an area of 11,985 hectares (Stöhr *et al.*, 1981; Statistisches Bundesamt, 1998).

Table 2. French Ranking of Mosel Vineyards in 1804 Grades by Village and Repurchase Price

Grade	Village	Repurchase price in Francs/1,000 Liter
1	Dusemond (Brauneberg)	172
2	Piesport, Wehlen, Machern, Graach, Zeltingen, Erden, Lösenich	150
3	Niederremmel, Müstert, Reinsport, Berncastel, Grünhaus, Kesten, Oberremmel, Minheim	140
4	Kous (Cues), Lieser, Winterich, Ürzig, Kröf, Köwerich, Mülheim, Thron, Kinheim, Kindel, Wolf, Kasel, St. Matthias, Okfen, Kastel, Staadt, Neumagen	129
5	Trittenheim, Mehring, Monzel, Waltrach, Isselbach, Konz	118
6	Rachtig, Awelsbach, Mertesdorf, Veldenz, Thörnich, Reul, Maring, Burgen, Olewig, Krutweiler, Ayl, Bibelhausen, Irsch/Saar	107
7	Pfalzel, Pichter, Merzlich, Niederleuken, Klüsserath, Wawern, Pölich, Köwerich, Platten, Filzen/Mosel, Neudorf, Trier, Hamm, Komlingen, Nennig, Mies, Helfand, Detzem, Schweich, Longen, Lörsch, Ensch, Longuich, Osan	96
8	Niedermennig, Leiwen, Schleich, Fell, Löwenbrück, Kreutz, Kürenz, Feyen, Palzem, Rölingen, Fasterau, Beurig, Perl, Sendorf	86
9	Wittlich, Andel, Pallien, Erang, Metzdorf, Euren, Zewen, Oberkirch, Monaise, Niederkirch, Ruwer, Pellingen, Irsch-Olewig, Kenn, Feilz, Plein, Luxem, Kernscheid, Issel, Bekond, Hetzrath, Rivenich, Riol	75
10	Bengel, Springirsbach, Korlingen, Drees, Bergweiler, Hupperat, Flusbach, Bausendorf, Olkenbach	64

Source: According to Le Ministre des Finances de la France (1811) and Heger (1905).

A "repurchase price" was set for the wines of each vineyard, and this formed the basis for its taxation.[7] However, we rely primarily on the work of the Prussian tax administration during the mid-nineteenth century for our ranking of vineyards by price. Using the work started by the French, the Prussians completed a meticulously detailed land register in the 1830s in order to tax the land according to the value of its production. Using the method

[7]The Napoleonic administration promoted the self-reliability and independence of vintners from church and nobility and allowed vintners to pay their rent in money. The "repurchase price" was the price a vintner had to pay if he wanted to repurchase his in-kind rent (i.e., grapes) to market himself.

very similar to that used for the classification of Bordeaux wines in 1855 (Penning-Roswell, 1986; Markham, 1998), the value of vineyard sites was taken as proportional to the average prices for the wines of each vineyard over a 24-year period from 1837 to 1860 (Beck, 1869).[8] The Prussian tax administration distinguished eight different net yield grades, and in 1869, this ranking was published by the Government of the King of Prussia (Beck, 1869). This list distinguishes the different vineyards within the various villages. To provide the detailed location of the vineyard sites, the government also published a map of these sites for the administrative district of Trier (the upper Mosel) in 1868 (Clotten, 1868) and a similar map for the lower Mosel (for the district of Koblenz) in 1897 (Lintz, 1897).

We use these maps to construct a price-based ranking of the vineyards. Unfortunately the vineyard sites ranked by price in Beck (1869) are not necessarily identical to those used by Stöhr *et al.* (1981) to provide vineyard site characteristics. Accordingly, the maps of 1868 and 1897, respectively, as well as the maps provided by Stöhr *et al.* were used to apply the Prussian ranking to contemporary vineyard sites.

The estimates we obtained were compared to the vineyard-size figures published by the Prussian government (Beck, 1869). The comparison of these figures as well as the maps ensures a certain degree of consistency. In addition, any "new vineyards" that did not exist during the period of the 1869 ranking were excluded from the analysis. As a result, of the 523 currently recognized vineyards, only 344 vineyard sites are included in our analysis. Finally, the results of our analysis were cross-checked with the "new" vineyard classification constructed by Stuart Pigott (1995), which is also based on the older Prussian ranking. Our ranking, like those before, distinguishes eight ordinal grades of vineyard quality, where rank 1 denotes the highest quality and rank 8 denotes the lowest quality.

Table 3 provides the frequency distribution of our rankings. It is obvious that the larger average vineyard site size in the current definitions leads to a leveling out of the quality distribution compared to older definitions. While the Prussian ranking had 60 vineyards comprising 44 hectares ranked in the top-quality group, the application of the Prussian ranking to current vineyard sites shows that only one, the Berncasteler Doctor, is ranked wholly

[8] In order to avoid distortions caused by differences in prices across different vintages, the optimal estimation period and the appropriate computational method were discussed in great detail at the time (e.g., Daezel, 1815; Flotow, 1820; Gebhard, 1824; Schimmelfennig, 1831).

Table 3. Distribution of Vineyard Site Ranking

Rank	Percent	Number
1	1	0.29
2	11	3.20
3	23	6.69
4	59	17.15
5	63	18.31
6	85	24.71
7	69	20.06
8	33	9.59
Total	344	100.00

Source: Own calculations.

in the top-quality category.[9] With today's list of vineyard sites, only 10% of all vineyard sites belong to even the first three ranks, while most fall into ranks 6 and 7.

3.2. *Physical vineyard site characteristics*

Data on physical vineyard attributes were taken from Stöhr *et al.* (1981). For each site, they report the latitude, slope, altitude, orientation, depth of soil, type of soil, and size of the vineyard. The slope is given as a fraction of the vineyard that is steep, middle, or flat. We constructed the variable "slope" as a weighted average of these slope measures, where 45° is take as steep, 22.5° is middle, and 0° is flat. Table 4 shows the basic results of our calculations. The average slope of a Mosel vineyard is very steep, at 38°, which is not far from the optimum of 45°, although at least one vineyard is entirely flat.

Stöhr *et al.* (1981) provide the "prevailing orientation" of the vineyards in twelve categories according to the entries on a compass. These are, for example, south or southwest. We assigned a value to the variable "orientation" by the degrees of deviation of the vineyard from south: 0° for southern orientation, 90° for west or east, and 180° for north. For instance, an aspect given as south-southwest (SSW) would be measured as 30°, which we assume is the average orientation of the vineyard. When a vineyard had a compound orientation measure, such as "south and west," we simply assumed a 50/50

[9]The size of this vineyard is only 1.0 hectare, which is much smaller than the average vineyard size of 21.2 hectares.

Table 4. Descriptive Statistics of Variables

Variable	Mean	S.D.	Minimum	Maximum
Rank	5.52	1.56	1	8
Slope (degree)	38.28	7.97	0	45
Orientation[a]	46.71	28.68	0	135
Latitude (degree)	49.95	0.20	49.61	50.34
Altitude (in meters)	120.02	43.83	22	226
Hectare	26.31	37.99	0.2	420
Energy (GJm^{-2} per year)	11.27	1.47	5.57	12.8
Energy (MJm^{-2} in Sept/Oct)	1,872.3	318.0	694.6	2,237.4

Notes: [a]Deviation from southern orientation in degrees.

relation and defined the deviation from south as 45°. Overall, the data in Table 4 show that while a south-southwest orientation is the average, there is considerable variation, with at least one vineyard facing northwest (135°).

The altitude of a vineyard is given in meters at its lowest and its highest point. The altitude of these Mosel vineyards ranges between 320 m in the Saar valley and 65 m near the Rhine River. Altitude alone seems unlikely to affect a Mosel vineyard's quality given that all these vineyards are well below 500 meters (Gladstones, 1992). However, since the impact of large water bodies on diurnal air circulation is considered important for quality (Gladstones, 1992), we used data on the altitude of the Mosel River to calculate the altitude difference between the vineyard and the water body. We expect a large difference to have a negative effect on wine quality and a vineyard's ranking.

Stöhr *et al.* provide measures of the soil's depth as deep, moderate, and flat. We calculated the depth of the soil as a single variable ranging from 0 to 1, where 1 is deep and 0 is flat. For instance, a vineyard like the Erdener Praelat, which is described as deep to moderately deep, was assigned the value 0.75. The impact of soil depth on wine quality is not well understood. On the one hand, shallow and rocky soils limit potential vine rooting depth and provide only restricted water storage capacity. On the other hand, shallow and rocky soils provide fine drainage and resistance to soil erosion, which is particularly important on slopes. Since the Mosel region is not characterized as a particularly dry climate, the latter may be the more important effect (Gladstones, 1992).

Besides the depth of the soil, we also have measures of the kind of soil. This is particularly important because of the heat storage capacity of certain soils. Heat is absorbed during the day, which is followed by marked and prolonged re-radiation of warmth at night. Slate is one of the most heat-absorbent soils.[10] In fact, the entire Mosel-Saar-Ruwer region is characterized primarily by different forms of slate, although other soils prevail in the valley around Trier (sandstone) and between Trier and the border with Luxembourg (limestone). However, single vineyards often contain many alternative soil types. We distinguish twelve kinds of soil: weathered slate, slate quartzite, clay slate, greywacke, quartzite, sandstone, limestone, gravel, finesoil, alluvial soil, sand, and clay/loam. We constructed a set of dummy variables for these soil types, where the variable takes a 1 if this soil type exists in the vineyard and 0 otherwise.

All of these variables are assumed to reflect the average characteristics of the vineyard. However, within a single vineyard, conditions can deviate substantially from this average, and the deviation is likely to be larger the larger the size of the vineyard. We therefore also included in our hedonic analyses a measure of the total size of the vineyard. If the uncertainty associated with vineyard quality leads to lower quality and prices, then we expect larger vineyards to, other things the same, be of lower quality.

Though most of the vineyards of the Mosel-Saar-Ruwer region are near one of the rivers for which they are named, a small number of remote vineyards are located near castles or cloisters. Since these vineyards do not benefit from the smaller diurnal temperature fluctuations due to proximity to a large water body, we also introduced a dummy variable that takes on the value unity when a vineyard is remote and 0 otherwise. We expect it to have a negative effect on vineyard quality.

4. Hedonic Model of Vineyard Quality

Given the discrete natural order of the dependent variable and the fact that the differences between the ranks are not necessarily equivalent, we fit our hedonic model using an ordered probit function.[11] In this setup, the observed response is taken to depend on a latent variable y_i^*, which depends linearly on the explanatory variables $\mathbf{X_i}$:

$$y_i^* = \mathbf{X_i}\boldsymbol{\beta} + \varepsilon_i, \quad \text{with } \varepsilon_i \sim N(0,1). \tag{1}$$

[10]Because of its low reflectivity of solar radiation (measured by its albedo value), slate is also considered an important building material for the passive usage of solar energy. Common albedo values are: slate 0.10, wet sand 0.15, dry sand 0.25, concrete 0.30, and limestone 0.40 (SolVent, 2001).

[11]See, for example, Davidson and MacKinnon (1993) or Greene (2003).

The observed category of y_i is based on y_i^* and can take on eight values:

$$y_i = \begin{Bmatrix} 1 & \text{if } y_i^* \leq \gamma_1 \\ j & \text{if } \gamma_{j-1} \leq y_i^* < \gamma_j \\ 8 & \text{if } \gamma_7 \leq y_i^* \end{Bmatrix}. \tag{2}$$

The probability of y_i being in a particular rank is

$$\begin{aligned} \Pr(y_i = 1) &= \Pr(y_i^* < \gamma_1) = \Pr(\mathbf{X_i}\boldsymbol{\beta} + \varepsilon_i < \gamma_1) \\ &= \Pr(\varepsilon_i < \gamma_1 - \mathbf{X_i}\boldsymbol{\beta}) = \Phi(\gamma_1 - \mathbf{X_i}\boldsymbol{\beta}) \\ \Pr(y_i = 2) &= \Pr(\gamma_1 \leq y_i^* < \gamma_2) \\ &= \Pr(\gamma_1 \leq \mathbf{X_i}\boldsymbol{\beta} + \varepsilon_i < \gamma_2) \\ &= \Pr(\varepsilon_i < \gamma_2 - \mathbf{X_i}\boldsymbol{\beta}) - (\varepsilon_i \leq \gamma_1 - \mathbf{X_i}\boldsymbol{\beta}) \\ &= \Phi(\gamma_2 - \mathbf{X_i}\boldsymbol{\beta}) - \Phi(\gamma_1 - \mathbf{X_i}\boldsymbol{\beta}) \\ &\cdots \\ \Pr(y_i = 8) &= \Pr(y_i^* \geq \gamma_7) = \Pr(\mathbf{X_i}\boldsymbol{\beta} + \varepsilon_i \geq \gamma_7) \\ &= \Pr(\varepsilon_i \geq \gamma_7 - \mathbf{X_i}\boldsymbol{\beta}) = \Phi(\mathbf{X_i}\boldsymbol{\beta} - \gamma_7), \end{aligned} \tag{3}$$

where $\Phi\cdot$ denotes the cumulative normal distribution function.

The results of the estimation are contained in Table 5 for several specifications of the basic set of independent variables ($\mathbf{X}$) that determine quality. These vineyard quality variables, discussed earlier, are listed as the row labels in Table 5. In a first specification (column 1), we include variables related to soil characteristics and include as separate variables the three determinants (slope, orientation, and latitude) of our measure of the solar energy captured by the vineyard. This is a reduced-form regression that we use to test the basic predictions of our model of energy retention. In order to extrapolate the impact of a change in climate on vineyard quality, it is essential that this model of energy retention provides a reasonable approximation of how radiant energy affects vineyard site quality.

The results in columns 2 and 3 reflect the imposition of the constraint that the three energy variables are captured by the specific formula contained in the appendix. Comparing the unconstrained results in column 1 to the results in columns 2 and 3 provides a basic empirical test of the accuracy of this formula for predicting how solar energy affects vineyard prices.

In fitting the constrained model, we aggregated the variables slope, orientation, and latitude in two ways to determine a measure of potential energy. In column 2 we use a formula that assumes that the energy the plant receives

Table 5. Determinants of the Vineyard Site Ranking Results of the Ordered Probit Model

Variable	(1)	(2) (Annual energy)	(3) (Fall energy)
Slope	-3.13^{***}		
	(−6.44)		
Orientation	0.04^{***}		
	(12.71)		
Latitude	0.29		
	(0.57)		
Energy (KJm^{-2})		-0.86^{***}	-4.10^{***}
		(−11.50)	(−11.53)
Clay slate	-2.35^{***}	-2.09^{***}	-2.13^{***}
	(−7.21)	(−6.79)	(−6.89)
Weathered slate	-1.59^{***}	-1.32^{***}	-1.35^{***}
	(−5.92)	(−5.10)	(−5.20)
Slate quartzite	-0.72^{*}	-0.53^{+}	-0.57^{+}
	(−2.23)	(−1.71)	(−1.86)
Sandstone	−0.38	−0.17	−0.20
	(−0.97)	(−0.32)	(−0.41)
Finesoil	−0.11	−0.27	−0.26
	(−0.41)	(−1.19)	(−1.15)
Sand	1.05^{***}	1.12^{***}	1.08^{***}
	(3.48)	(4.38)	(4.21)
Clay, loam	0.86^{***}	0.91^{***}	0.89^{***}
	(3.88)	(4.10)	(4.04)
Quartzite	0.65^{+}	0.81^{*}	0.80^{*}
	(1.70)	(2.15)	(2.14)
Gravel	−0.04	0.17	0.12
	(−0.08)	(0.37)	(0.25)
Graywacke	−0.03	0.13	0.10
	(−0.12)	(0.88)	(0.68)
Limestone	−0.20	0.17	0.06
	(−0.31)	(0.25)	(0.09)
Alluvial soil	−0.08	0.02	−0.04
	(−0.20)	(0.07)	(−0.13)
Depth of soil	1.70^{***}	1.94^{***}	1.91^{***}
	(6.06)	(6.97)	(6.87)
Altitude difference[a]	0.01^{***}	0.01^{***}	0.01^{***}
	(3.57)	(2.83)	(2.88)
Vineyard size	0.01^{***}	0.01^{***}	0.01^{***}
	(5.39)	(6.71)	(6.61)
Remote vineyard	1.36^{***}	1.41^{***}	1.29^{***}
	(3.98)	(4.31)	(3.80)
γ_1	8.48	-13.63^{***}	-11.84^{***}
	(0.35)	(−11.65)	(−11.60)

(*Continued*)

Table 5. (*Continued*)

Variable	(1)	(2) (Annual energy)	(3) (Fall energy)
γ_2	9.98	−12.19***	−10.38***
	(0.41)	(−11.06)	(−11.00)
γ_3	10.80	−11.38***	−9.56***
	(0.45)	(−10.81)	(11.00)
γ_4	11.97	−10.31***	−8.46***
	(0.50)	(−10.06)	(9.83)
γ_5	13.05	−9.34***	−7.47***
	(0.54)	(−9.34)	(8.96)
γ_6	14.65	−7.846***	−5.926***
	(0.61)	(−8.28)	(−7.59)
γ_7	16.81	−5.782***	−3.826***
	(0.70)	(−6.56)	(−5.31)
Log likelihood	−376.0	−397.3	−393.5
Pseudo-R^2 (in %)	39.7	36.3	36.9

Note: Huber-White robust z-statistics in parentheses.
[a]Altitude difference between vineyard and Mosel river.
Significance level of 1% (***), 5% (*), 10% (+).

throughout the entire year is the appropriate measure, while in column 3, we assume that the energy the plant receives in the fall is the appropriate measure. Neither of these measures is likely to be ideal, but they are very highly correlated in any event. Moreover, these two extreme cases span all the reasonable alternatives.

A comparison of the results indicates that the constrained measure of "fall energy" in column 3 provides a slightly better fit to the data (judging from the maximized likelihood ratio) than the measure of "annual energy," and so we rely on it for further analyses. A straightforward way to assess the goodness-of-fit qualities of an ordered probit model is a comparison of predicted and actual results. In Table 6 we use the results of column 3 of Table 5 to assess the model's predictive quality. Predicted quality ranks are listed in the first column, and the distribution of the deviations of the actual from the predicted ranks is listed in the remaining columns for each predicted rank. For example, 85 vineyards are predicted to be in the largest category, rank 6, of which 54 predictions are correct, 28 are off by one rank, and 3 are off by two ranks. Overall, the ranks of 50.9% of all vineyards are predicted correctly, while 42.2% of the predictions are off by a deviation of one rank. Taken together, the average deviation is only 0.57 quality ranks.

A test of the constraint that energy determines vineyard quality in the precise form we have assumed may be based on a comparison of twice the

Table 6. Prediction and Deviation by Rank

	Deviation by number of ranks								
Rank	0	1	2	3	4	5	6	7	Sum
1	0	0	1	0	0	0	0	0	1
2	**5**	0	4	1	1	0	0	—	11
3	0	19	3	1	0	0	—	—	23
4	33	20	6	0	0	—	—	—	59
5	24	35	4	0	0	—	—	—	63
6	54	28	3	0	0	0	—	—	85
7	41	28	0	0	0	0	0	—	69
8	18	15	0	0	0	0	0	0	33
Sum	175	145	21	2	1	0	0	0	344
in %	50.9	42.2	6.1	0.6	0.3	0.0	0.0	0.0	100.0

Source: Own calculations.

difference in the log likelihood between columns 1 and 3 of Table 5. This test rejects the precise constraint at any reasonable level of statistical significance, but it is apparent from Table 6 that the constrained measure captures the major variability in the data. As a result, we use the basic results in column 3 of Table 5 in simulating the effects of climate change in the analysis below.

Since the vineyard ranking is defined as 1 being best and 8 being worst, a positive influence of an independent variable on the quality of the vineyard is indicated by a negative sign. It is apparent that the potential solar radiation variable has a significant effect on the rating of a vineyard site. In addition, slate of any type increases the quality of the vineyard, especially weathered slate and clay slate. As expected, sand, gravel, and loam have a far lower ability to store heat and are, by comparison with slate, less advantageous for the vineyard's quality.

The results in Table 5 also provide evidence for the importance of a water body close to the vineyard. Vineyards that are remote from the Mosel River and those that are far above the river suffer from these features. Both of these factors lead to larger diurnal temperature fluctuations and thus to lower-quality vineyard sites.

Finally, the estimates confirm the hypothesis that larger-sized vineyards, given our measurements of the other measures of a vineyard's qualities, do suffer a disadvantage in quality.

The estimated coefficients of an ordered probit model must be interpreted with some care. The sign of $\hat{\boldsymbol{\beta}}$ shows the direction of the change in the probability of falling in the end point rankings ($y_i = 1$) and ($y_i = 8$) when $\mathbf{X}$

Table 7. Marginal Effects of Model Using Fall Solar Radiation

	Probability (in %)							
	Rank 1	Rank 2	Rank 3	Rank 4	Rank 5	Rank 6	Rank 7	Rank 8
Baseline	0.27	3.32	6.52	16.79	18.95	24.61	19.65	9.74
	Change in Probability (in %)							
Continuous variables[a]								
Fall energy	1.19	5.96	5.17	3.35	−2.07	−5.06	−5.45	−3.09
Depth of soil	−0.02	−0.25	−0.44	−0.71	−0.21	0.24	0.60	0.78
Altitude[b]	−0.02	−0.24	−0.34	−0.44	−0.04	0.32	0.42	0.36
Vineyard size	−0.01	−0.08	−0.12	−0.19	−0.04	0.23	0.05	0.15
Dummy variables[c]								
Clay slate	4.46	14.90	9.68	7.42	−0.38	−9.69	−15.92	−10.48
Weathered slate	1.85	6.02	5.98	8.31	2.46	−5.36	−10.60	−8.66
Slate quartzite	0.56	3.41	3.59	3.30	−0.65	−3.27	−3.91	−3.04
Sand	−0.26	−2.87	−4.83	−9.13	−4.14	4.38	8.60	8.26
Clay, loam	−0.24	−2.67	−4.44	−7.78	−2.82	4.17	8.13	5.65
Quartzite	−0.23	−2.44	−3.99	−7.01	−2.35	3.99	6.29	5.74
Remote	−0.26	−3.13	−5.64	−11.66	−6.44	5.29	10.99	10.86

Notes: [a]Effect of a 10% increase, [b]difference in altitude between vineyard and Mosel River, [c]difference between the values 0 and 1.

changes. $\Pr(y_i = 1)$ changes in the opposite direction of the sign of $\hat{\boldsymbol{\beta}}$, and $\Pr(y_i = 8)$ changes in the same direction as the sign of $\hat{\boldsymbol{\beta}}$. The effects on the probability of falling in any of the middle rankings are unclear, a priori.

Table 7 reports the marginal effects of the significant variables of the model listed in column 3 of Table 5 that uses the fall radiation variable. Marginal effects are measured relative to the baseline probabilities given in the first line. As the table shows, the percentage of vineyard sites expected to be ranked 1 is 0.27%, while the percentage for rank 2 is 3.32%. The following set of rows reports the effect of a change of 10% in the value of an independent variable on these percentages. Thus, an increase in potential solar radiation by 10% will increase the vineyard's probability of being ranked 1 by 1.19% to 1.46%. Similarly, the probability of being ranked 2 will increase from 3.34% to 9.33%. Since the changes sum up to 0, energy increases entail a drop in the likelihood of being in rank 6, 7, or 8. Similarly, deeper soil, a greater altitude difference between the vineyard and the Mosel River, and a larger vineyard size decrease the probabilities of being in the high-quality ranks. However, it is apparent that the marginal effect of the solar radiation variable is substantial compared to the effects of each of these other variables.

The marginal effects of the dummy variables were calculated as the effect of the difference between the values 0 and 1 while holding the other variables at their mean values. The marginal effects of these variables show the great importance of soil type on vineyard quality and also the great importance of having a vineyard site that is influenced by proximity to the Mosel River.

5. Solar Radiation and Global Warming

Since vineyard quality is dependent on solar energy absorption, it follows that in a place like the Mosel Valley, climate change that leads to warmer temperatures will lead to higher-quality wines and prices. Land prices, which represent the capitalized value of these wine prices, less other costs of production, should therefore also increase. It follows that the many recent studies that predict that climate change is leading to warmer temperatures also predict increased land values in areas like the Mosel Valley. In what follows, we set out a simple model that permits us to estimate the effect of climate change on the overall quality of the Mosel's vineyards and thus on their prices.

Most scenarios about global temperature change[12] provide a summary measure of expected temperature changes, whereas we have established the connection between solar energy reception and vineyard quality. Although there is, of course, a relationship between solar energy and the earth's temperature, the relationship involves a comparison of energy inflow and outflow. Absorbed energy from the sun is converted to heat, which causes the earth to warm up. However, the temperature maximum occurs not at the time of maximum solar energy input but later. This lag is the result of the energy storage system and the resistance to energy flows. Figure 4 shows that in a simple model, temperature is the result of the influx of solar energy and the energy radiated by the earth. Thus, as long as the net influx is positive, temperatures will rise and vice versa. The result is that the temperature maximum is attained after the influx maximum.

We use the following simplified model to establish the interrelations between solar radiation and temperature (see Hartmann, 1994; Andrews, 2000) for the purpose of simulating the effect of various global warming scenarios on vineyard quality and prices.

With radius R and the earth's receptive surface πR^2, the energy absorbed by the planet is equal to

$$(1 - \alpha)\pi R^2 S = (\text{energy absorbed by the earth}), \tag{4}$$

[12]See Johns *et al.* (1997).

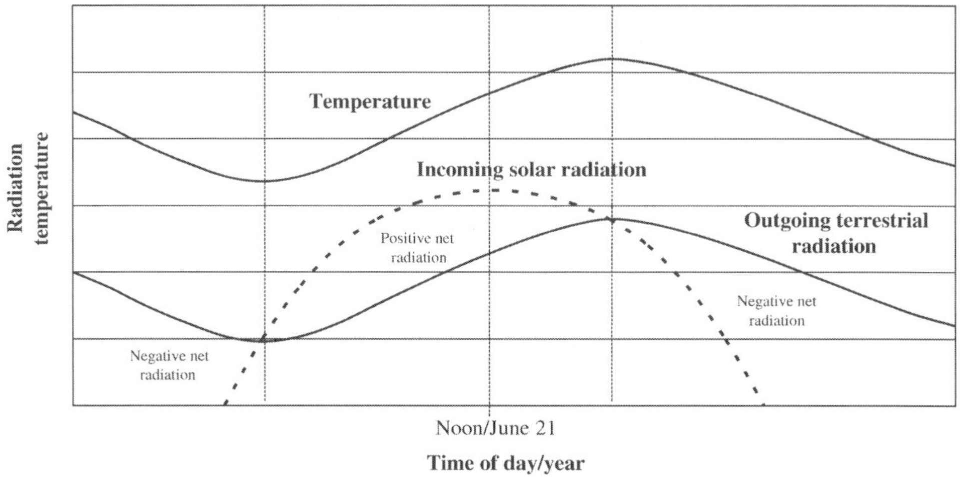

Figure 4. Solar Radiation and Temperature

where α is the albedo number of the earth's atmosphere and S is the solar constant. We assume that $\alpha = 0.3$, which implies that the earth reflects 30% of the incoming solar energy back to space.

If the earth is assumed to emit like a blackbody,[13] the energy radiated from our planet is, according to the Stefan-Boltzmann law, equal to

$$(4\pi R^2)\sigma T_s^4 = \text{(energy radiated from the earth)}, \tag{5}$$

where T_s is the planet's surface temperature and σ is the Stefan-Boltzmann constant.[14]

Setting equations (4) and (5) equal and solving for the equilibrium temperature yields

$$T_s = \sqrt[4]{(1-\alpha)S/4\sigma}. \tag{6}$$

According to equation (6), the earth's surface temperature is equal to 255 K (or $-18°$C) which is well below the measured average temperature of approximately 288 K (or 15°C).

To make this model more realistic, it is necessary to incorporate the atmospheric effects that are associated with the earth and act like a greenhouse. If we assume an atmosphere that absorbs all long-wave terrestrial

[13] A *blackbody* absorbs all the radiant energy it receives, regardless of the wavelength.
[14] The Stefan-Boltzmann constant is equal to $5.67 * 10^{-8}\ \mathrm{JK}^{-1}$.

radiation but is transparent to short-wave solar radiation, at the top of this atmospheric layer the energy balance remains the same with

$$\sigma T_a^4 = (1-\alpha)S/4, \tag{7}$$

where T_a is the atmospheric temperature. Assuming further that $\alpha T_s^4 = 2\sigma T_a^4$, that is, half of the energy absorbed by the atmosphere is reflected back to the earth, we get

$$T_s = \sqrt[4]{(1-\alpha)S/2\sigma}. \tag{8}$$

Equation (8) predicts an average temperature of 303 K (or 30°C) for the earth, which is much closer to the observed value.

Equation (8) allows us to compute changes in radiant energy associated with any given temperature variation. Accordingly, a temperature increase of 1°C is associated with additional radiation energy of 47.43 MJ/month. Similarly, a temperature increase of 2°C or 3°C translates into radiation energy increases of 94.87 and 142.82 MJ/month, respectively.

Table 8 reports the changes in a vineyard's probability of being in a certain rank using the results in Table 7 and various assumptions about the likely magnitude of climate change. For example, a temperature increase of 1°C corresponds to an increase in potential solar radiation of 47.43 MJ/month, which changes the likelihood of an average vineyard being

Table 8. Global Warming and Vineyard Ranking

		Probability (in %)							
		Rank 1	Rank 2	Rank 3	Rank 4	Rank 5	Rank 6	Rank 7	Rank 8
Baseline		0.27	3.32	6.52	16.79	18.95	24.61	19.65	9.74
		Change in Probability (in %)							
Temperature increase	Energy increase (MJ/month)								
1°C	47.43	0.32	2.19	2.46	2.45	−0.29	−2.21	−2.79	−2.13
2°C	94.87	0.95	5.21	4.95	3.88	−1.23	−4.50	−5.44	−3.82
3°C	142.82	2.06	9.02	7.10	4.22	−2.54	−6.80	−7.93	−5.24
		Number of Vineyards							
Baseline		0	6	4	79	64	94	69	28
1°C increase		0	13	5	111	43	91	62	19
2°C increase		0	30	11	121	37	83	47	15
3°C increase		2	56	10	115	39	73	36	13

rated number 1 by 0.32%, that is, from 0.27% to 0.59%. Similarly, the likelihood of being rated number 8 will decrease by 2.13%, that is, from 9.74% to 7.61%. Predicted temperature increases in the Mosel area for the near term are around 2°C for moderate warming scenarios, with higher predicted temperature increases in the longer term. These three scenarios should provide a general indication of magnitudes to be expected.[15]

As also reported in Table 8, the number of vineyards in each category will change with increased warming. While in the base scenario only 10 vineyards were rated quality 1, 2, or 3, a temperature increase of 1°C will lift this number to 18. In comparison, if temperatures increased by 3°C, 68 vineyards would be rated within the best three categories.

In order to convert these changes in vineyard quality ranking into changes in vineyard prices, we weight land values in each quality category by the size of the respective vineyards. While the size of each vineyard is given in Stöhr *et al.* (1981), the land value of each quality class was taken from land sales surveys provided by the governments of the four counties that cover the Mosel area (Landkreis Bernkastel-Wittlich, 2004; Landkreis Cochem-Zell, 2004; Landkreis Mayen-Koblenz, 2004; Landkreis Trier, 2004). The surveys provide average sales prices of vineyard land in 2003, differentiated by municipality and vineyard quality level. This permits us to estimate vineyard-specific market prices.[16] From these data, we calculated average land values for each quality category. The land values range from 0.50 euros per m^2 for vineyards in quality category 8 to 130 euros per m^2 for vineyards in quality category 1.[17]

Table 9 reports the hectares of vineyards in each quality category and in each scenario. While in the baseline scenario only 30 hectares of vineyards are within the top three quality ranks, a temperature increase of 1°C would put more than 100 hectares in these categories. These temperature increases also lead to higher predicted land values. In fact, because of the steeply increasing land prices as we move from lower- to higher-quality vineyards, the change in land values is proportionally greater than the mere increase in temperatures. While a 1°C increase results in an increase in the total

[15] See, for example, the Hadley Center's work in Johns *et al.* (1997).

[16] The reported sales prices reflect only the land value and do not include the value of vines that might be planted on it.

[17] Our calculations are based on the following land values per m^2: 130 euros (rank 1), 20 euros (rank 2), 10 euros (rank 3), 7 euros (rank 4), 4 euros (rank 5), 2 euros (rank 6), 1 euro (rank 7), and 0.50 euro (rank 8). It is apparent that the prices drop dramatically with quality.

Table 9. Global Warming and Land Values, in 2003 Prices

	Baseline	Simulation 1°C	Simulation 2°C	Simulation 3°C
Hectares				
Rank 1	0.0	0.0	0.0	7.8
Rank 2	19.3	71.1	375.5	851.6
Rank 3	10.8	32.1	212.8	134.6
Rank 4	1,283.4	1,958.2	2,317.2	2,338.0
Rank 5	1,365.5	995.8	965.2	1,086.4
Rank 6	2,384.9	2,640.6	2,582.7	2,366.2
Rank 7	2,851.1	2,431.9	1,843.7	1,550.5
Rank 8	1,134.6	919.9	752.5	714.5
Total	9,049.6	9,049.6	9,049.6	9,049.6
Value in million €	231.3	276.1	371.0	467.4

vineyard land value of 20% (from 231 million euros to 276 million euros), a 3°C increase in temperature will double the overall land value.

6. Effects of Annual Weather Changes on Prices, Profits, and Quantities

Our analysis of the effect of the role of solar radiation in determining wine and vineyard quality can be compared to a direct analysis of the effect of year-to-year fluctuations in the weather on agricultural prices and profits. Each approach has its advantages, but in principle, if accurately measured, they should provide similar evidence.

We have two sources of data with which to provide time-series estimates: (a) data from accounting records of vineyard profits and (b) data on retail and auction prices of wine. Each of these data sources has advantages and disadvantages.

6.1. *Weather and accounting profits*

Our data on accounting profits come from a set of test wineries in six German viticultural areas that include the Mosel and some nearby regions. Beginning with the agricultural year 1971–1972, the German Department of Agriculture annually has reported aggregate balance sheet and accounting results for a number of sample wineries in the regions known as Mosel-Saar-Ruwer, Rheinhessen, Rheinpfalz, and Baden-Wuerttemberg. For a shorter period starting in 1982, data are also available for the additional regions of Rheingau

(1982–2000) and Franken (1986–present). These viticultural regions all lie in the valley of the Rhine River and its tributaries, the Mosel and the Main. They stretch from Freiburg in the south (47.6° N) to Koblenz in the north (50.2° N), a distance of approximately 180 miles, similar to the length of California's major wine-growing region, the San Joaquin valley. These vineyard areas are not identical, and we use separate fixed effects in the empirical analysis for each of them. However, the wines from these regions have many common features, and we expect the effect of growing season temperature changes on profits to be similar across the regions.

The number of test wineries varies by wine region and changes slightly from year to year. There are currently data for about 165 reporting test wineries in the Mosel regions, covering approximately 20% of the bearing acreage. Data for the individual firms are proprietary, and only regionally aggregated figures are published in the annual agricultural reports of the German Department of Agriculture (Federal Ministry of Food, Agriculture and Consumer Protection, 1973–2007).

A potential complication for the analysis is that in all six wine regions, vintners receive considerable subsidies. In 2006, the European Union spent approximately 1.5 billion euros on measures such as wine distillation, storage of wine, and grubbing-up and restructuring schemes (see European Commission, 2006). In addition, there are substantial financial aids provided by the German federal government and the respective state governments for tax-exempt diesel fuels, social insurance, and the maintenance of steep-slope vineyards. It is likely that some of these subsidies are not independent of annual changes in the weather variables. As a result, we report separate analyses of gross profit data (including subsidies) and net profit data (excluding subsidies).

In Table 10, we report the results of regressions of profit and costs on some key weather variables. We report the results using the data from a single weather station (Trier) in view of the geographical proximity of the viticultural regions we study. Drawing on data from regional weather stations did not change or improve the precision of the estimates, a result similar to that reported by Lecocq and Visser (2006) for an analysis of the Bordeaux region in France.[18]

[18]Lecocq and Visser (2006) show for the Bordeaux region that using data on the local weather within a homogenous wine region yields little additional explanatory power over using data from only one weather station. In either case, the weather station data serve only as approximations for the time-series variation in the weather within each vineyard.

Table 10. Weather and Real per Hectare Profits, Subsidies, and Costs of German Wineries

	(1) In (Profits − Subsidies)	(2) In (Profits including subsidies)	(3) In (costs)
Temperature growing season[a]	0.309*** (5.17)[5.25]	0.305*** (4.71)[5.11]	0.026 (0.18)[0.19]
Rainfall winter[b]	−0.0034*** (−9.77)[−9.90]	−0.0031*** (−3.23)[−8.51]	−0.0003 (−0.29)[−0.29]
Rainfall growing season[c]	−0.0009*** (−4.62)[−4.68]	−0.0009*** (−1.75)[−5.67]	−0.0001 (−0.51)[−0.52]
Trend	−0.074*** (−8.79)[−8.91]	−0.072*** (−8.37)[−7.98]	−0.029 (−1.40)[−1.42]
Fixed effects			
Mosel	8.09	8.14	10.33
Rheinhessen	7.55	7.52	10.14
Rheingau	8.28	8.14	10.35
Pfalz	7.79	7.75	9.86
Baden-Württemberg	8.48	8.43	10.18
Franken	8.11	8.10	10.41
R^2	0.663	0.644	0.538
F statistic	9.17	11.25	8.26
N	52	52	57

Notes: [a]February to October, in degrees Celsius, [b]December to February prior to growing season in ml, [c]April to October in ml.
Significance level of 1% (***); Newey-West robust t-values in parentheses; t-values based on year clustered standard errors in brackets.

The weather variables we include in the regressions are (a) the average temperature over the growing season (in Centigrade degrees), (b) the total rainfall (in millimeters) in the growing season, and (c) the total rainfall in the winter preceding the growing season. In northern latitudes, warmer and drier growing seasons are expected to lead to higher fruit quality. The precise relation varies with the grape type, but this relation has been quantified in many viticultural areas.[19] Winter rainfall has also been shown to have a positive effect on fruit and wine quality, although this result has not been

[19]See, for example, Ashenfelter (2008), Haeger and Storchmann (2006), Jones and Storchmann (2001), and Ashenfelter and Byron (1995).

found for all the viticultural areas where it has been studied. Our primary interest is in the effect of temperature on vineyard profits, but to the extent that rainfall and temperatures are correlated, it is essential to control for these other aspects of the weather in the regressions.

The results in columns 1 and 2 of Table 10 indicate a positive and statistically significant effect of growing season temperatures on profits, whereas the effect of both rainfall variables is negative. Both net (market) profits, that is, profits excluding subsidies, and gross profits (including subsidies), exhibit almost identical sensitivities with respect to all the weather variables. The estimates suggest that a temperature increase of 3°C results in profit increases of approximately 150%, which is larger than we found for the structural hedonic model of solar radiation. A more detailed discussion and comparison of the results may be found below.

The results in column 2 indicate that proportional profit changes are not affected by the various subsidies that vintners receive. However, this may be a result of the fact that support measures for German vintners are comparatively small, at least by European standards. Between 1995 and 2005, the Mosel test wineries received direct annual subsidies worth between 800 and 1,200 euros per hectare, which is between 10% and 23% of their respective profits. According to the Farm Accountancy Data Network of the European Union, direct payments for many southern European wineries, especially in Toscana, Umbria, and Midi-Pyrénées, regularly exceed 10,000 euros per hectare (European Commission, 2007).

As reported in column 3, there is no significant relationship between total per hectare cost and the weather variables for these German wineries. In results that are not reported in the table, we found that also to be true for overall costs, as well as for the component costs of personnel, material, depreciation, and other miscellaneous costs.

6.2. *Weather and revenues using retail and auction prices*

In a second time-series analysis, we make use of retail and auction price data. Each data set has advantages and disadvantages. A disadvantage of the retail price data is that they refer to posted prices, which may not be transaction prices. An advantage of these data is that they cover a wide range of Mosel wine producers. The auction prices refer to actual transaction prices, but only a tiny fraction of the very finest Mosel wines are sold at auction. As a result, the auction prices may not be representative of the region more generally.

We confine our analysis to the Mosel Valley and its five viticultural districts (called Bereich): the Upper Mosel (from Luxemburg to the City of Trier), the Middle Mosel (from Trier to the village of Pünderich), the Lower Mosel (from Zell to the Rhine River), and the two Mosel tributaries, the Saar and the Ruwer Valley.

There is an added complexity in the study of the prices of German wines that results from the way the wines are labeled and marketed. German wines are classified (and labeled) according to the natural sugar content of the must (freshly pressed grapes) measured on the Oechsle scale.[20] In ascending order, the quality levels and Oechsle thresholds for Mosel wines are Quality Wine (no °Oe requirement), Kabinett (70°Oe), Spätlese (76°Oe), Auslese (83°Oe), Beerenauslese and Eiswein (110°Oe), and Trockenbeerenauslese (150°Oe). A primary quality distinction is that with the exception of Quality Wine, it is illegal to add sugar to the must. As a result, wine prices are distinguished by the vineyard where the grapes are grown and by the quality level.

Our retail price data come from the 1994–2006 issues of the Gault Millau Wine Guide for Germany (Diel and Payne, 1994–2006). The wine guide provides detailed information about the wines' characteristics such as age, geographical origin (vineyard and wine district), and quality classification, and the data permit us to calculate wine prices for each wine district and quality level accounting for other characteristics.

Our auction price data come from the period 1992–2006 from the wine associations VDP Grosser Ring and Bernkasteler Ring. These groups of wineries annually present and sell the latest vintage of their wines. The auctions focus on the upper end of the quality scale, and there are rarely any Kabinett quality wines sold. Less than 0.5% of all wine put up for auction is Quality Wine. This quality selection, and the fact that only 0.02% of all Mosel wines (0.08% of the corresponding values) are sold in auctions, implies that these data are not likely to be representative of the regional average response to our weather variables. As we shall see, the response of prices to the average temperature during the growing season is very sensitive to the

[20]Degrees Oechsle (°Oe) is used in Germany and Switzerland and denotes the specific weight of the must compared to the weight of water at a temperature of 20°C, while much of the English-speaking world uses a measure called brix. One liter of water weighs 1,000 g, which equals 0 degrees Oechsle. Accordingly, grape must with a mass of 1,084 grams per liter has 84°Oe. Since the mass difference between equivalent volumes of must and water is almost entirely due to the dissolved sugar in the must, degrees Oechsle measures the relative sweetness of the grape juice. Approximately, 1 brix is equal to 1 degree Oechsle divided by 4.35 (Peynaud, 1984).

particular type of wine quality being studied, making it likely that these data may suffer from selection bias. In particular, since the prices of the higher-quality wine types are much more responsive to temperature increases, the auction price data are likely to dramatically overstate the average effect of a temperature change on prices. Although we report the results using these data for completeness, we do not rely on them for our primary analysis.

Although revenue per hectare data are not readily available, they can be computed by multiplying crop yield data by the average prices for each district and each wine quality level. Let R_{idt}, P_{idt}, and Q_{idt} denote per hectare revenue, price, and quantity produced of wine quality level i in district d and at time t; then

$$R_{idt} = \sum_{i=1}^{7} \sum_{d=1}^{5} (P_{idt} \cdot Q_{idt}). \tag{9}$$

Total revenue in wine district d will be determined by prices and quantities produced in each quality category.

Wine production data by district and quality category for the years 1997 to 2006 were prepared and provided by the Statistical Office of the State of Rheinland-Pfalz and its agricultural commission (Landwirtschaftskammer).[21] Detailed production data for the time period before 1997 are not available.

Column 1 of Table 11 contains the results of the price equation drawing on retail prices. Since wines are labeled by their (a) quality level (TBA/BA/Eiswein — the highest quality group; and, in decreasing order of quality, Auslese, Spätlese, Kabinett, Quality Wine), and (b) their regions, we have interacted the temperature variable with each of these categories in order to produce quality- and region-specific temperature coefficient estimates. Quality Wine from the Upper Mosel serves as reference. It is apparent that warmer weather has a significantly positive effect on prices. Higher wine qualities, such as Beerenauslese, Trockenbeerenauslese, and Eiswein, benefit from a warmer growing season more than lower qualities do. In addition, the marginal effect of temperature increases is the highest in the districts of the Mosel tributaries Saar and Ruwer.

The results in column 2 indicate that auction prices are even more responsive to temperature changes than retail prices, as we expected.

To obtain an overall estimate of temperatures on gross revenue per hectare, we must combine the information on crop yields by region and

[21] These data are available, by request, from the authors.

Table 11. Weather, Wine Prices, and Revenue

	Dependent variable		
	(1) In (Retail prices)[d]	(2) In (Auction prices)[d]	(3) Retail price revenue per hectare[d]
Constant	1.610***	−4.952***	
	(6.62)	(−10.55)	
Growing season temperature[a]	−0.019	0.349***	0.354**
	(−0.85)	(3.86)	[2.37]
BA/TBA/Eiswein × growing season temperature[a]	0.232***	0.217***	
	(36.32)	(5.11)	
Auslese × growing season temperature[a]	0.108***	0.015	
	(39.43)	(0.37)	
Spätlese × growing season temperature[a]	0.036***	−0.069***	
	(15.68)	(−1.68)	
Kabinett × growing season temperature[a]	0.004	−0.112***	
	(1.82)	(−2.71)	
Middle Mosel × growing season temperature[a]	0.017***	−0.002	
	(5.50)	(−0.05)	
Lower Mosel × growing season temperature[a]	0.021***	0.034	
	(4.23)	(0.34)	
Saar × growing season temperature[a]	0.030***	0.008*	
	(8.10)	(0.25)	
Ruwer × growing season temperature[a]	0.023***	0.004*	
	(5.89)	(0.14)	
Rain winter[b]	−0.000	−0.002***	−0.0003***
	(−1.89)	(−2.95)	[−3.42]
Rain growing season[c]	0.000***	0.002***	0.0002
	(2.58)	(7.46)	[3.66]
In (age)	0.219***	−0.303***	
	(3.39)	(−4.15)	
Trend			−0.028*
			[−2.29]
R^2	0.635	0.721	0.512
F statistic	761.02	517.38	10.09
n	5,263	2,413	50

Notes: [a]February to October, [b]December to February, [c]April to October, [d]In real prices.
Significance level of 1% (***), 2% (**), 5% (*); Newey-West robust t-values in parentheses; t-values based on year clustered standard errors in brackets. Although not reported here, all equations include district-fixed effects.

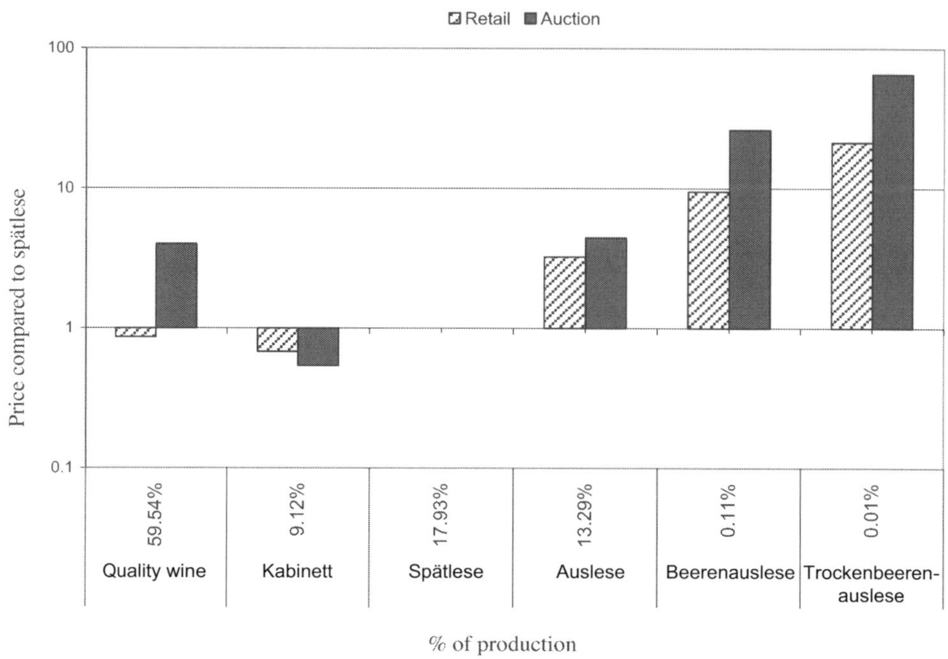

Figure 5. Wine Quality and Prices (Price of Spätlese = 1)

quality level with the average prices by region and quality level. Figure 5 shows the relative prices of wines in the various categories. The price differences are enormous, with wines in the highest-quality category, Trockenbeerenauslese, being priced 20 times higher than in the Spätlese category. (At auctions, this ratio is higher, sometimes exceeding 60.) At the same time, the production of high-quality wines is very small.

Figure 6 shows the fraction of wines of Auslese and higher qualities as part of the entire production in selected districts and the Mosel region as a whole over the period 1997–2006. The Ruwer region exhibits the highest variance, with a range from 1% in 1998 to 52% in 2003. Figure 6 also shows the average growing season temperature over the same period, and it is apparent that more high-quality wines are produced in warmer years. The result is that increases in temperatures result in increases in wine prices within each quality segment and that increases in temperatures also shift the quality structure of wines produced upward.

Another interesting feature of Figure 6 is the apparent upward trend in temperatures.[22] At the same time, there is also an apparent upward trend

[22]Using data over the longer period from 1960 to 2006, a regression of average temperature on a trend variable (and a constant term) yields a coefficient of 0.034 at the 0.01%

Figure 6. Growing Season Temperatures and High-End Wine Production Percentage Production of Auslese + Wines in Selected Mosel Districts

in the amount of higherquality wine being produced. This has led many observers to remark on the increased prosperity of the Mosel wine region in recent years. It is unclear, of course, whether this is a result of permanent climate change or something more transitory.

Column 3 of Table 11 indicates that revenue (based on retail prices) and using equation (9) significantly increase with warmer weather, as expected. The rainfall variables are either insignificant or have unexpected signs. Assuming that cost and temperature changes are not correlated (as the accounting data indicated above), these revenue changes will translate directly into changes in profits and land values.

6.3. *Comparison of the effects of climate change on land values*

Figure 7 summarizes the findings of the two different times series analyses and contrasts them with the hedonic cross-sectional model of solar radiation. Since we compute percentage changes in revenue or profits, respectively, the

significance level. Thus, since 1960, average growing season temperatures in the Mosel valley have increased by 1.6°C.

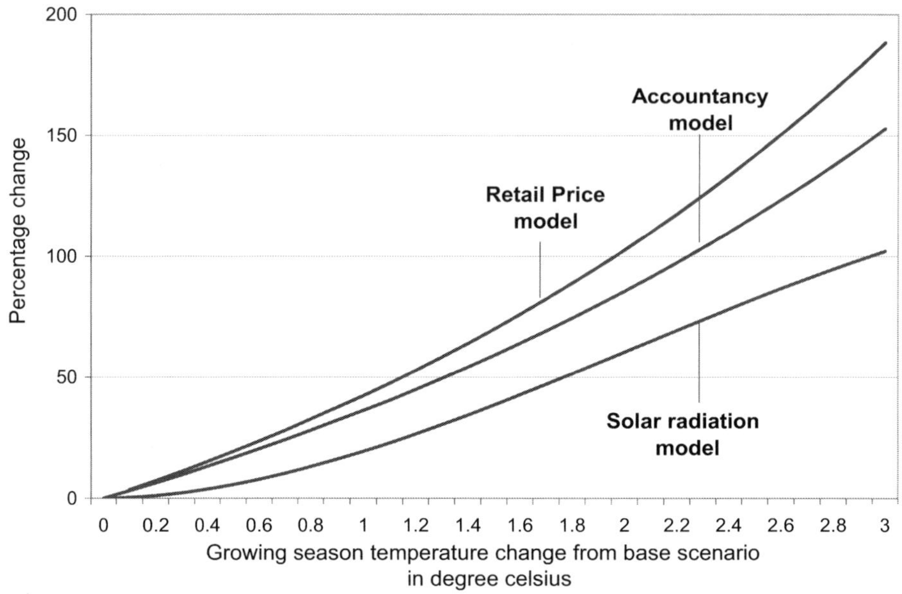

Figure 7. Temperature Changes and Percentage Changes in Land Values

figures translate directly into comparisons of percentage changes in land values.

All three models show a positive relationship between growing season temperatures and profits or land values. They also show that in the range of data we study, prices increase more than proportionately with temperatures. Given the entirely different nature of the models, the results are remarkably consistent. The models predict that a 3°C annual temperature increase will lead to an increase in vineyard values by 102% (solar radiation model), 152% (accounting profits model), or 188% (revenue model). It is apparent that the more structural cross-section model indicates a smaller sensitivity of land prices to temperature changes than the time-series model. It is unclear precisely why this occurs, but the cross-section analysis may be providing estimates that are more appropriate for the analysis of long-term equilibria, while the time-series estimates may be more appropriate for the analysis of short-term effects.

7. Conclusions

The basic results in this chapter show how the link between temperature and solar radiation can be used to construct a structural model to predict changes in agricultural land prices and crop values associated with climate change. The key to building this relationship is to establish the hedonic relation between the determinants of solar radiation received by an area and land values. For vineyard areas, many of the key hedonic characteristics of the vineyard are related to energy absorption, which leads to an important effect of climate change on crop quality. Grapevines have very low radiation use efficiency (RUE), and no doubt the hedonic relationship we estimate is related to this fact. It seems that further research might be usefully guided by measuring the hedonic relationship of solar energy received for crops with different RUEs.

Although our purpose here has been to use this hedonic relationship to evaluate the effect of climate change on land values, it should be clear that to the extent other undeveloped vineyard areas may exist in the world, this relationship could be used to evaluate the economic viability of new plantings. In short, this hedonic relationship could be used for determining vineyard site selection in undeveloped areas.

We have also computed estimates of the effect of annual time-series weather changes on vineyard profitability and wine prices. This provides a check on both methods of analysis. It appears that although the results are far from identical, they do provide estimates of roughly the same orders of magnitude. This suggests that the direct measurement of changes in the weather from year to year may be a useful shorthand method for calculating the order of magnitude of longer-term effects.

As is well known, there are likely to be winners and losers from any potential climate change. Our empirical results indicate that climate change may result in considerable increases in the value of the Mosel vineyard region because of increasing wine quality. A moderate 1°C temperature increase would lead to an aggregate increase in land value of 20% or more, while an increase of 3°C would more than double the land value.

These results have several limitations. First, our empirical analysis does not take account of general equilibrium effects that might result in a restructuring of land prices. The Mosel Valley is suited primarily for grape growing only, so a change in the relative price of vineyards of different quality induced by climate change could have a dramatic effect on our calculations. Second, our results provide only a small part of an overall appraisal of the role of climate change on agricultural values. There are no doubt places where increased temperatures will decrease the quality of wine grapes because of excessive heat. Only additional research will provide the evidence to evaluate these issues more completely.

Acknowledgments

We are indebted to many people in the Mosel Valley for assistance with our research, but particularly to Rita and Clemens Busch of Pünderich. We are indebted to Kym Anderson, Victor Ginsburgh, Robert Stavins, and especially Michael Greenstone for helpful comments on an earlier draft of this chapter. We also thank two anonymous referees whose comments helped to substantially improve this chapter.

References

Andrews, D.G. (2000). *An Introduction to Atmospheric Physics.* Cambridge: Cambridge University Press.

Ashenfelter, O. (2008). Predicting the prices and quality of Bordeaux wines. *Economic Journal*, 118, F174–F184.

Ashenfelter, O., and Byron, R.P. (1995). Predicting the quality of an unborn grange. *Economic Record*, 71, 40–53.

Beck, O. (1869). *Der Weinbau an der Mosel und Saar. Nebst einer vom königlichen Katasterinspekteur Steuerrath Clotten zu Trier angefertigten Weinbaukarte.* Trier: Selbstverlag der königlichen Regierung zu Trier.

Bernkasteler Ring (1992–2006). *Auktionsergebnisse.* Annual Reports. Bernkasteler Ring, Bernkastel-Kues.

Bernkasteler Ring (1999). *100 Jahre Bernkasteler Ring 1899–1999.* Bernkastel-Kues: Krämer-Druck.

Castelan-Estrada, M. (2001). Répartition de la biomasse chez Vitis vinifera; rendement de conversion du rayonnement solaire global et coûts energétiques, doctoral dissertation, Institut National Agronomique Paris-Grignon, INRA Bordeaux. http://www.bordeaux.inra.fr/ECAV/doc/castelan.pdf.

Clotten, F.J. (1868). *Saar and Mosel Weinbaukarte für den Regierungsbezirk Trier.* Trier: Lintz Verlag.

Daezel, G.A. (1815). *Beweis, dass die in acht Procenten des Rohertrages ausgesprochene Grundsteuer gerecht und national-ökonomisch sey. Und: dass der Rohertrag der Grundstücke zur Grundlage ihrer Werthes-Schätzung angenommen werden könne.* München: Lindauer.

Davidson, R., and MacKinnon, J. (1993). *Estimation and Inference in Econometrics.* New York: Oxford University Press.

Deschênes, O., and Greenstone, M. (2006). The Economic Impacts of Climate Change: Evidence from Agricultural Profits and Random Fluctuations in Weather, MIT Department of Economics research paper no. 04-25.

de Wit, C.T. (1959). Potential photosynthesis of crop surfaces. *Netherlands Journal of Agricultural Science*, 7, 141–149.

Diel, A., and Payne, J. (1994–2006). *Weine Guide Deutschland.* Munich: Wilhelm Heyne.

Duffie, J.A. and Beckman, W.A. (1991). *Solar Engineering of Thermal Processes*, 2nd ed. New York: Wiley.

Environmental Protection Agency (2002). *The Soil and Water Assessment Tool SWAT 2000.* Temple, TX: Texas Water Resources Institute.

European Commission (2007). Farm Accountancy Data Network FADN Public Database. http://ec.europa.eu/agriculture/rica/.

European Commission (2006). *Directorate-General for Agriculture and Rural Development*, Wine — Common Market Organization, Working paper.

Federal Ministry of Food (1973–2007). Agriculture and Consumer Protection. Bonn and Berlin: Agrarbericht, Bundestagsdrucksache.

Flotow, G. Von (1820). *Versuch einer Anleitung zu Abschätzung der Grundstücke nach Classen, besonders zu Behufe einer Grundsteuer-Rectification.* Leipzig: Hartmann.

Gebhard, G. (1824). *Grundsteuer-Kataster aus der Messung und dem Reinertrage der einzelnen Grundstücke entwickelt.* München: Finsterlin.

Gladstones, J. (1992). *Viticulture and Environment.* Adelaide: Winetitles.

Goldschmidt, F. (1925). *Deutschlands Weinbauorte und Weinbergslagen*, 3rd ed. Mainz: Verlag der Deutschen Wein-Zeitung.

Greene, W. (2003). *Econometrics Analysis*, 5th ed. Upper Saddle River, NJ: Prentice Hall.

Haeger, J.W., and Storchmann, K. (2006). Prices of American pinot noir wines: Climate, craftsmanship, critics. *Agricultural Economics*, 35, 67–78.

Hartmann, D.L. (1994). *Global Physical Climatology.* San Diego: Academic Press.

Heger, J.P. (1905). Die Klassifikation der Moselweine in alter und neuer Zeit. *Trierische Chronik*, 1(6), 81–89.

Iqbal, M. (1983). *An Introduction to Solar Radiation.* San Diego: Academic Press.

Johns, T.C., Carnell, R.E., Gregory, J.F., Mitchell, J., Senior, C., Test, S., and Wood, R.A. (1997). The second hadley centre coupled ocean-atmosphere GCM: Model description, spinup and validation. *Climate Dynamics* 13, 103–134.

Jones, G., and Storchmann, K. (2001). Wine market prices and investment under uncertainty: An econometric model for Bordeaux Crus classés. *Agricultural Economics*, 26, 115–133.

Klein, S.A. (1977). Calculation of monthly average insolation on tilted surfaces. *Solar Energy* 19, 325–329; 20, 441 (erratum), and 25, 287 (comment).

Landkreis Bernkastel-Wittlich (2004). *Bericht über den Grundstücksmarkt im Landkreis Bernkastel-Wittlich.* Bernkastel: Vermessungs- and Katasteramt.

Landkreis Cochem-Zell (2004). *Bericht über den Grundstücksmarkt im Landkreis Cochem-Zell.* Cochem: Vermessungs- und Katasteramt.

Landkreis Mayen-Koblenz (2004). *Bericht über den Grundstücksmarkt im Landkreis Mayen-Koblenz.* Koblenz: Vermessungs- and Katasteramt.

Landkreis Trier (2004). *Bericht über den Grundstücksmarkt im Landkreis Trier.* Trier: Vermessungs- and Katasteramt.

Lecocq, S., and Visser, M. (2006). Spatial variations in weather conditions and wine prices in Bordeaux. *Journal of Wine Economics*, 1, 114–124.

Le Ministre des Finances de la France (1811). *Recueil méthodique des lois, décrets, réglements, instructions et decisions sur le cadastre de la France.* Paris.

Lintz, F. (Ed.). (1897). *Mosel Weinbaukarte für den Regierungsbezirk Coblenz.* Trier: Lintz Verlag.

Markham, D. (1998). *1855: A History of the Bordeaux Classification.* New York: McGraw-Hill.

Mendelsohn, R., Nordhaus, W.D., and Shaw, D. (1994). The impact of global warming on agriculture: A Ricardian analysis. *American Economic Review*, 84, 753–771.

Monteith, J.L. (1977). Climate and the efficiency of crop production in Britain. *Philosophical Transactions of the Royal Society of London Series B — Biological Sciences*, 281, 277–294.

Penning-Roswell, E. (1986). *Wines of Bordeaux*, 6th ed. New York: Penguin Books.
Peynaud, E. (1984). *Knowing and Making Wine*. New York: Wiley.
Pigott, S. (1995). *The Wine Atlas of Germany and Traveler's Guide to the Vineyards*. London: Mitchell Beazley.
Schimmelfennig, F.G. (1831). *Historische Darstellung der Grundsteuer-Verfassungen in den Preuischen Staaten*. Berlin: Logier.
Schlenker, W., Hanemann, W.M., and Fisher, A. (2005). Will U.S. Agriculture really benefit from global warming? Accounting for irrigation in the Hedonic approach. *American Economic Review*, 95, 395–406.
Schlenker, W., Hanemann, W.M., and Fisher, A. (2006). The impact of global warming on U.S. agriculture: An econometric analysis of optimal growing conditions. *Review of Economics and Statistics*, 88, 113–125.
Sinclair, T.R., and Muchow, R.C. (1999). Radiation use efficiency. *Advances in Agronomy*, 65, 215–265.
SolVent (2001). http://www.brunel.ac.uk/research/solvent/pdf/climate.pdf.
Statistisches Bundesamt (1998). *Fachserie 3, Land- und Fortstwirtschaft, Fischerei, Reihe 3.1.5 Landwirtschaftliche Bodennutzung*. Stuttgart: Metzler-Poeschel.
Stöhr, W., Cüppers, H., and Fass, K.-H. (1981). *Mosel-Saar-Ruwer*. Stuttgart: Seewald.
VDP Grosser Ring (1992–2006). *Auktionsergebnisse*. Annual Reports. Trier: VDP.

Appendix

According to Duffie and Beckman (1991) and Iqbal (1983), we calculate the daily extraterrestrial solar radiation $H_{O\beta\gamma}$ as

$$\begin{aligned} H_{O\beta\gamma} = (12/\pi) I_{SC} E_O (&\cos\beta \sin\delta \sin\phi |\omega_{ss} \\ &- \omega_{sr}|\pi/180 - \sin\delta\cos\phi\sin\beta\cos\gamma|\omega_{ss} \\ &- \omega_{sr}| + \cos\phi\cos\delta\cos\beta|\sin\omega_{ss} - \sin\omega_{sr}| \\ &+ \cos\delta\cos\gamma\sin\phi\sin\beta|\sin\omega_{ss} - \omega_{sr}| \\ &+ \cos\delta\sin\beta\sin\gamma|\cos\omega_{ss} - \cos\omega_{sr}|) \end{aligned}$$

with

$$\omega_{sr} = \min\left[w_s, \cos^{-1}\left(\frac{-xy - \sqrt{x^2 - y^2 + 1}}{x^2 + 1}\right)\right]$$

$$\omega_{ss} = -\min\left[w_s, \cos^{-1}\left(\frac{-xy + \sqrt{x^2 - y^2 + 1}}{x^2 + 1}\right)\right]$$

for $\gamma > 0$ (the surface is oriented toward the east) and

$$\omega_{sr} = \min\left[w_s, \cos^{-1}\left(\frac{-xy + \sqrt{x^2 - y^2 + 1}}{x^2 + 1}\right)\right]$$

$$\omega_{ss} = -\min\left[w_s, \cos^{-1}\left(\frac{-xy - \sqrt{x^2 - y^2 + 1}}{x^2 + 1}\right)\right]$$

for $\gamma < 0$ (the surface is oriented toward the west), where

$$x = \frac{\cos\phi}{\sin\gamma\tan\beta} + \frac{\sin\phi}{\tan\gamma}$$

$$y = \tan\delta\left(\frac{\sin\phi}{\sin\gamma\tan\beta} - \frac{\cos\phi}{\tan\gamma}\right)$$

$$\omega_s = \cos^{-1}(-\tan\phi\tan\delta).$$

with

I_{SC} Solar constant (4.921 MJ/m^2 hr).

E_O Eccentricity correction factor (tables for each day of the year).

β Slope the angle between the plane of the surface and the horizontal, $0^\circ \leq \beta \leq 180^\circ$, ($\beta > 90^\circ$ implies that the surface is downward facing).

δ Declination, the angular position of the sun at solar noon (when the sun is on the local meridian) with respect to the plane of the equator, north positive, $-23.34^\circ \leq \delta \leq 23.45^\circ$ (tables for each day of the year).

ϕ Latitude, the angular location north or south of the equator, north positive $-90^\circ \leq \phi \leq 90^\circ$.

γ Surface azimuth angle, the deviation of the projection on a horizontal plane of the normal to the surface from the local meridian, with zero due south, east positive, and west negative; $-180^\circ \leq \gamma \leq 180^\circ$.

ω_{ss} Sunset hour angle for a tilted surface.

ω_{sr} Sunrise hour angle for a tilted surface.

ω_s Sunrise hour angle for a horizontal surface.

The daily extraterrestrial solar radiation was multiplied by the number of days of the respective month in order to obtain the monthly value. Data for the characteristic average day for each month are provided by Klein (1977), and values for the eccentricity correction factor, E_O, and the declination, δ, respectively, are given in Table A1.

Table A1. Characteristic Eccentricity Correction Factor and Declination

Month	Day of the month	Day of the year	E_o	δ
January	17	17	1.0340	−20.88
February	16	47	1.0251	−12.53
March	16	75	1.0108	−1.93
April	15	105	0.9932	9.60
May	15	135	0.9780	18.77
June	11	162	0.9692	23.09
July	17	198	0.9673	21.34
August	16	228	0.9746	13.94
September	15	258	0.9885	3.27
October	15	288	1.0058	−8.30
November	14	318	1.0222	−18.11
December	10	344	1.0319	−22.28

Source: According to Klein (1977) and Duffie and Beckman (1991).

Chapter 4

Natural Endowments, Production Technologies and the Quality of Wines in Bordeaux. Does Terroir Matter?*

Olivier Gergaud[†] **and Victor Ginsburgh**[‡]

[†]*KEDGE Business School and LIEPP – Sciences Po, Paris, France*
olivier.gergaud@kedgebs.com

[‡]*ECARES, Université Libre de Bruxelles and CORE,*
Université Catholique de Louvain, Belgium
vginsbur@ulb.ac.be

We study whether quality assessments made by wine experts and by consumers (based on prices obtained at auction between 1980 and 1992) can be explained by variables describing endowments (land characteristics, exposures of vineyards) and technologies (from grape varieties and picking, to bottled wines). However, since technological choices are likely to depend on endowments, the effects can only be identified using an instrumental variables approach. We show that technological choices affect quality much more than natural endowments, the effect of which is negligible.

1. Introduction

Winemaking cannot be envisaged unless very specific weather conditions prevail. But this is obviously not sufficient, since winemaking also involves a complex technology that needs natural endowments which can hardly be modified (land, slopes' exposure, other endowments, summarized by what is often called "terroir"), inputs that take 20 to 30 years before producing good quality outputs (vines), manual operations (picking), mechanical operations (crushing, racking), chemical processes (during fermentation) and specific

*This article originally appeared in *The Economic Journal* (2008), 118, 142–157.

storage conditions once the wine is bottled. There is little that can be done to correct an error in one of the various and delicate steps which extend over several years for every vintage, though nowadays it is said that a good chemist can make miracles. Wine is also the subject of many legends and production secrets. Wine tasting adds to this aura of mystery with its esoteric vocabulary describing perfumes and the harmony of a wine.

The influence of weather has been the subject of several studies, which consistently show that rain is needed during the winter season, while dry weather is good during the growing season and when grapes are picked. Warm weather has also a positive effect during the whole growing season.[1] An important question is whether good climatic conditions and specific choices of vines are sufficient to produce quality wines or whether, as the French have often claimed and still do, there is no good substitute for terroir. Thus goes Madame Denise Capbern Gasqueton, owner of Château Calon-Ségur, a third-growth Saint-Estèphe:

> I drink [foreign] wines. Very good wines are produced in Chile, for example, but they lack terroir, and terroir is what makes everything. A wine that is well-produced is a good wine, but lacks complexity and other elements to which we are used. (Interview, 2003)

At best, this looks highly exaggerated. At worst, terroir has no influence at all, and the right combination of weather, vines, technology and chemistry are sufficient. This was already the opinion of Johan Joseph Krug (1800–1866), a famous champagne producer, who pointed out that

> a good wine comes from a good grape, good vats, a good cellar and a gentleman who is able to coordinate the various ingredients. (quoted in Krug and Krug, 1979)

and indeed, highly appreciated wines are now produced in California, South Africa, Australia, South America,[2] as well as in some regions, such as Languedoc-Roussillon in Southern France that were thought, 20 or 30 years ago, to be good enough for "table wines" only.

Wine can be viewed as a commodity endowed with characteristics that make it both vertically and horizontally differentiated. Though wines from a given region differ, good weather benefits equally to all of them.[3] Weather seems to generate vertical differentiation — all the wines produced in a region benefit to the same extent from good weather conditions, and experts

---

[1]See among others Ashenfelter *et al.* (1995) or Di Vittorio and Ginsburgh (1996).
[2]Including northeastern Brazil. See Andrew Downie, "Napa Valley? Bordeaux? No, but still wine country," *The New York Times*, May 15, 2007.
[3]See Ashenfelter *et al.* (1995).

as well as experienced consumers can recognize this, while it may be terroir and technological choices that make for horizontal differentiation — some consumers prefer Château Mouton, a wine from the Pauillac region, others prefer Château Lafite, also a Pauillac. At least this is suggested by looking at the opinions of wine experts who agree more on classifying vintages than on classifying châteaux. The (Spearman rank) correlation coefficient between rankings by Michael Broadbent (Christie's well-known wine expert) and Robert Parker is equal to 0.75 for the 30 Haut-Médoc vintages from 1961 to 1990, while it is equal to 0.47 only when they come to rank 48 châteaux of the same region, over the same years.

As was pointed out before, the relation between climate and wine quality is reasonably well documented. There is much less evidence on whether and how terroir and production technologies influence quality.[4] We are interested in trying to quantify the impact of each of the many inputs and steps used in producing wine in one of the most renowned wine producing regions of France, Haut-Médoc with its celebrated châteaux, such as Mouton-Rothschild, Latour, Lafite-Rothschild and Margaux.

We use a database on terroir characteristics and techniques in some 100 vineyards in 1990, to describe and quantify the wine-processing technology and to separate its effects on quality from legend on the one hand, and from reputation effects on the other.

The chapter is organized as follows. Section 2 clarifies what we call "terroir" in this chapter. Section 3 is devoted to the description of the database (land characteristics and technologies). In Section 4, we try to disentangle the effects that terroir and technologies are supposed to have on the quality of wines, proxied by classifications made by three wine experts (Parker, Bettane and Desseauve, and Broadbent) and indirectly, by consumers, through the prices that they are ready to pay at auction. Section 5 draws some conclusions.

2. Terroir and Technology: General Considerations

Terroir is a French word that has many interpretations. Here is what Robert Tinlot (2001, p. 9) a former Director General of the Organisation Internationale de la Vigne et du Vin (OIV) writes in a paper entitled "Terroir: A concept that wins over the world":

> There is no wine region in our world that does not try to value its vineyards and their output without reference to the character that they inherit from the

[4]See however Ashenfelter and Storchmann (2006), Ginsburgh *et al.* (1994).

> place where the wine is produced. Consumers who visit producers are particularly sensitive to the beauty of the landscape, to the architecture of the villages and to any other element that belongs to the region of production.

Thus terroir includes even the landscape, as if it affected the quality and the taste of the wine. Tinlot (2001, p. 10) becomes a bit more reasonable in the next pages, suggesting that an objective definition of terroir should be restricted to "natural endowments of a region, such as soil, subsoil, slopes and exposure of the vineyards, climate." But he adds that more recently, there is a

> tendency to extend the notion to human factors, such as know-how and local traditions of the local population, that are influenced by the natural, social, political and, why not, religious conditions that prevail in the region ... which leads quite naturally to the French notion of *appellation d'origine contrôlée.*

This is essentially the same as what is described by Wilson (1998, p. 55):[5]

> Terroir has become a buzz word in English wine literature. The lighthearted use disregards reverence for the land which is a critical, invisible element of the term. The true concept is not easily grasped but includes physical elements of the vineyard habitat — the vine, subsoil, siting, drainage, and microclimate. Beyond the measurable ecosystem, there is an additional dimension — the spiritual aspect that recognises the joys, the heartbreaks, the pride, the sweat, and the frustrations of its history.

In this chapter, we restrict the notion of terroir to natural endowments which are non-transferable, and which are likely to really influence in a measurable way both the quality and the taste of a wine: soil, subsoil, slopes and exposure of vineyards. All the other elements are either not quantifiable (e.g., the influence of social relations for instance) or can be reproduced elsewhere, taking into account adjustments due to local conditions. Clearly not all grapes grow in every region because of soil, slopes and climate but enough experimentation exists and winemakers know how this should be handled. All the rest, including the choice of grapes, is technological.[6]

3. Terroir and Technology in the Haut-Médoc Region

Data on the Haut-Médoc region were collected during the winter and spring of 1990–1991 by Andras and Muriel Monzak[7] who conducted interviews in

[5]Quoted in Barham (2003, p. 131).

[6]Note that it may sometimes be difficult to distinguish terroir and weather. Terroir can be used to offset unfavorable weather conditions. In the Mosel valley, for instance, steep slopes help to capture more solar energy and dark slate stores more heat. See Ashenfelter and Storchmann (2006).

[7]See Ginsburgh *et al.* (1994).

102 châteaux. Each château was visited and a questionnaire was handed out with some thirty questions on types of soil, exposure of the vineyards, grape varieties, age of vines, picking techniques, wine-making and "élevage." The questions were set up to make quantification easy. Some answers are represented by continuous variables, such as the proportions of grape varieties, but most are categorical (and represented by dummy variables), since they describe the types of production techniques used.

In Table 1, we give a very concise description of the various elements, which are usually thought to produce a good wine. These can be classified

Table 1. Description of Endowments and Technologies

Variables used	Type of variable	Short description
Endowments		
Soil	4 dummies	(presence of) clay-chalk, gravel, gravel-sand, sand
	5 dummies	(presence of) nitrogen, phosphoric acid, lime, potassium, magnesia
Slopes	5 dummies	(presence of) East, South, West, Southeast, Southwest-oriented slopes
	1 dummy	(presence of) higher altitude slopes
Grape varieties	4 continuous	(proportions of) Cabernet Sauvignon, Merlot, Cabernet Franc, Petit Verdot
Age of vines	3 dummies	(presence of) 5–20 years old, 20–40 years old and more than 40 years old vines.
Wine-making		
Picking grapes	1 dummy	if manual picking of grapes only
Selecting grapes	1 dummy	if manual sorting only
Destemming-Crushing	1 dummy	if crushing before de-stemming
Pumping into fermentation vats		all châteaux proceed in the same way
Fermentation (types of vats)		most châteaux use stainless steel (together with other vats)
Heating the must	1 dummy	if heating is used
Pumping the wine juice over the cap	3 dummies	three techniques used: open tank with floating marc; closed tank; open tank with submerged marc
Maceration		all châteaux proceed in the same way
Pressing	number of pressings	
Ageing in barrels	1 dummy	if oak barrels are used
Racking the wine	number of rackings	
Fining the wine	1 dummy	if fresh egg whites are used
Filtering the wine	3 dummies	three techniques used: kieselguhr; cellulosic components; adsorption

as follows: soil, exposure of the slopes, grape varieties, age of vines and wine-making. Clearly, weather conditions and age of the wine are also important characteristics but, since we are only interested in differentiating between châteaux and not vintages, this should not concern us here.[8] Appendix 1 describes technologies and the variables used in some more detail.

4. Disentangling the Effects of Natural Endowments and Technology

The simplest idea which comes to mind is to regress "quality" (represented by the three alternative classifications produced by wine experts, or by prices obtained at auction) on the variables defined in Section 3, which measure natural endowments and technologies. The problem is that correlation between technological variables and quality does not necessarily mean that the former have an effect on the latter, since production choices may have been influenced by natural endowment characteristics, to correct for their possible negative effects. We are thus faced with a simultaneous equations model in which quality depends on endowments and technological choices, and technological choices depend on endowments. To determine the effect of technologies, instrumental variables which affect production technologies but have no (or hopefully little) effect on endowments[9] should be used. The model can be written:

$$\mathcal{Q} = \mathbf{E}\boldsymbol{\alpha} + \mathbf{T}\boldsymbol{\beta} + u \qquad (1)$$

$$\mathbf{T} = \mathbf{E}\boldsymbol{\gamma} + \mathbf{W}\boldsymbol{\delta} + v, \qquad (2)$$

where Q represents quality, $\mathbf{E}$ is a vector of endowments, $\mathbf{T}$ a vector of technological variables, and $\mathbf{W}$ a vector of instruments; $\boldsymbol{\alpha}$, $\boldsymbol{\beta}$, $\boldsymbol{\gamma}$, and $\boldsymbol{\delta}$ are vectors of parameters, and u and v are error terms. Note that (1) represents a single equation, while (2) contains one equation for each technological variable.

The instruments $\mathbf{W}$ consist of dummies representing the 1855 classification (First to Fifth Growth wines[10] and Other) and the cultivated area

[8]Most studies on the impact of weather on Bordeaux wines consider conditions in one central weather station (Mérignac). Lecocq and Visser (2006) show that a finer grid of stations that are closer to vineyards leads to comparable results.
[9]Endowments can be changed to some extent, by adding chemicals, dropping unfavorable slopes, etc. But this remains marginal.
[10]In 1855, the wines of Médoc were classified. At that time, 60 châteaux were selected and classified as First to Fifth-Growth on the basis of their quality (actually, on the basis of

(and its square) expressed in hectares — as a proxy for the wealth of the vineyard. The 1855 classification seems a reasonable instrument. It is likely to be correlated with today's technologies (a vineyard classified in 1855 should have had incentives to make good technological choices in order to fulfill the promise made by the label).

Quality is represented by three recent ratings, and by auction prices obtained at Christie's London. The first rating is due to Robert Parker (1985), who classifies wines into nine categories: First to Fifth-Growth, Cru Grand Bourgeois Exceptionnel, Cru Grand Bourgeois, Cru Bourgeois and Other. We grouped all wines from Cru Grand Bourgeois Exceptionnel to Other into a single category, which leaves us with six categories. The second rating is due to Bettane and Desseauve (2000), editors of the Revue *du Vin de France*, who classify wines into five groups (3, 2, 1, and 0 stars, and unclassified). The third rating is obtained by calculations based on Michael Broadbent (1991), Christie's well-known wine expert. Broadbent gives zero to five stars to wines but does not taste systematically all the vintages of the various châteaux. As a result, while some of them are tasted and graded more than 20 times over the period 1961–1990, others do not appear in the tasting list. We decided to compute average ratings for the 63 wines that Broadbent assessed at least three times.

For prices, we use the coefficients associated with château dummies obtained in a hedonic price regression ran by Di Vittorio and Ginsburgh (1996). This regression is based on some 30,000 lots (that include vintages from 1949 to 1989 for 51 Haut-Médoc vineyards) sold by Christie's London between 1980 and 1992.

4.1. *Estimation results*

Since there is little, if any, theory concerning the impact of endowments and of the various steps of the production process, we were led to select variables using OLS backward and forward stepwise procedures as a first step. More precisely, we ran two distinct stepwise procedures: one in which quality (or price) is regressed on endowments and another one where the regressors are technologies,[11] to give each group of variables their chance to

their prices). The only change since 1855 was made in 1973, when Mouton-Rothschild was elevated to a First-Growth wine.

[11]Technologies are the values predicted by an equation $\mathbf{T} = \mathbf{E}\gamma + \mathbf{W}\delta$ for the variables representing technological choices, where γ and δ are estimated by OLS. Technologies are mainly represented by dummies and not by continuous variables, which may suggest using logit or probit regressions. See however Angrist and Krueger (2001, p. 80) who suggest

pass the statistical procedure. All the variables selected by either procedure were included.[12] Our first group of results, presented in Appendix Table A.1, is obtained by two-stage least squares. These lead to the following three observations:

(a) Though the variables that enter the four quality equations (Parker, Bettane and Desseauve, Broadbent and Prices) were selected as contributing to explain quality (or prices) in the stepwise procedures, the number of coefficients that are significantly different from zero is small, particularly for endowments. We do not discuss individual coefficients, since the hypotheses that we want to test is whether endowments (as a group) or technologies (as a group) have an effect on quality.
(b) Durbin-Wu-Hausman tests are used to check whether technologies are exogenous and whether we could have run ordinary least squares to estimate our quality equations (1). Intuitively, this test calculates the "distance" between parameters obtained by OLS and by TSLS. If the distance (a χ^2-statistic) is small, there is no difference between OLS and TSLS, and technologies could be considered exogenous. The calculated values that appear in the upper part of Appendix Table A.2 clearly indicate that OLS would lead to inconsistent estimates for the Parker and the Bettane and Dessauve equations: technologies are endogenous. OLS estimation is acceptable for the two other equations (Broadbent and auction prices).[13]
(c) The results that are reproduced in the lower part of Table 2 deal with our main concern. What, if any, is the effect on quality of terroir and of technology. The hypotheses that are tested here are H_{0E}: endowments have no effect and H_{0T}: technologies have no effect. The results show that endowments do hardly matter in the Parker, the B&D and the Price equations:[14] removing endowment variables does not significantly change the results. This is far from being the case for technologies. Endowments do not seem to matter, whereas technologies do.

using OLS instead. The correlation coefficients obtained in this step vary between 0.24 and 0.43. The distribution is as follows: $R^2 < 0.30$: 8 instances; R^2 between 0.30 and 0.40: 7; $R^2 > 0.40$: 2.

[12]The significance level considered for adding in the forward procedure (removing in the backward procedure) a variable to (from) the model is 5% (10%).

[13]Note that, as suggested by Professor Peter Spencer, we also ran one-stage OLS (and ordered probits where needed) regressions of quality (and prices) on the endowments and on the instruments directly. This also showed that endowments hardly contribute to quality.

[14]This is not so in the Broadbent equation. Note, however, that there is only one (significant) endowment variable that appears in this equation (altitude).

Table 2. Testing for Exogeneity of Technologies and for the Contribution of Endowments and Technologies on Quality and Prices

	Parker	B&D	Broadbent	Prices
Testing for exogeneity of technologies (Durbin-Wu-Hausman test)				
χ^2-test	21.99	27.25	2.61	4.18
Degrees of freedom	5	7	5	4
Significance	(0.000)	(0.000)	(0.760)	(0.383)
Testing for the contribution of endowments and technologies				
H_{0E}: *Endowments have no effect*				
F-test	0.79	2.34	11.54	1.70
Degrees of freedom	4, 92	3, 91	1, 56	5, 41
Significance level	(0.537)	(0.079)	(0.001)	(0.157)
H_{0T}: *Technologies have no effect*				
F-test	8.01	6.83	4.53	4.82
Degrees of freedom	5, 92	7, 91	5, 56	4, 41
Significance level	(0.000)	(0.000)	(0.002)	(0.003)

Notes: All estimation is by two-stage least squares.

Recall that Parker and Bettane and Dessauve express their quality ratings by integers (1 to 5) or number of stars (1 to 4). Therefore, using ordered probit maximum likelihood methods to estimate (1) is more appropriate than the linear method used by TSLS. This generates two difficulties.

First, given the number of endogenous variables and equations,[15] it is unlikely that a full information maximum likelihood simultaneous estimation of the system (1)–(2) is feasible.[16] This prompted us to use a two-step procedure, in which the first step consists in constructing instrumented technologies, the second in using endowments and instrumented technologies to estimate the quality (or price) equation by ordered probit.

This leads to the second difficulty, since the standard errors of the parameters estimated in the second step are biased.[17] To correct for this, we ran 200 bootstrap replications for each equation and used these to estimate unbiased standard errors. Regression results appear in Appendix Table A.2. The

[15]One quality equation (1) plus as many equations of type (2) as there are endogenous technological variables that enter (1).

[16]As pointed out by Maddala (1985, p. 221), if the model contains a large number of truncated variables, estimation by maximum likelihood may be infeasible, because it involves the evaluation of multiple integrals. Though computing possibilities have increased tremendously since Maddala's writing, making the computations converge remains problematic.

[17]See Maddala (1985, pp. 234 and ff).

Table 3. Testing for the Contribution of Endowments and Technologies on Quality and Prices

	Parker	B&D
H_{0E}: *Endowments have no effect*		
χ^2-test	6.60	11.98
Degrees of freedom	4	3
Tabulated significance levels		
1%	13.23	11.34
5%	9.49	7.81
10%	7.78	6.25
Simulated significance levels		
1%	23.37	16.39
5%	18.11	11.77
10%	16.66	8.87
H_{0E}: *Technologies have no effect*		
χ^2-test	41.50	56.5
Degrees of freedom	5	7
Tabulated significance levels		
1%	15.09	18.48
5%	11.07	14.07
10%	9.24	12.02
Simulated significance levels		
1%	36.15	31.84
5%	27.04	23.35
10%	23.86	21.05

Notes: Two-step estimation; second step is an ML ordered probit.

more interesting results on whether endowments and technologies have an effect can be found in Table 3. Usual tabulated significance levels would reject both H_{0E}: endowments have no effect (in the case of B&D) and H_{0T}: technologies have no effect (Parker and B&D), though H_{0T} is rejected at a much lower confidence level than H_{0E}. Simulated significance levels, which have to be used here,[18] do not reject the hypothesis that endowments have no effect on quality but reject this hypothesis for technologies.

[18]See Appendix 2.

5. Concluding Comments

It may be tempting to conclude that the wine-making technology has become so sophisticated that it can completely shade the effect of terroir and that vines can be grown in almost any place, as long as weather permits and the right combination of vines is made.[19] The French terroir legend obviously does not hold, at least in the Haut-Médoc region, which is probably one of the most famous in the world. Nowadays, high quality wines are produced in many different environments, including Languedoc in the South of France, a region which was supposed to be able to grow table wines only.

Old-world producers — Italy, Spain and more specifically France — use a terroir-based strategy intensively to convince consumers that they produce top-quality wines (good wines, best terroir and old-world are synonymous). Conversely, new-world producers have favored a brand-based strategy (sun, good oenologists and sophisticated wineries are key ingredients to make top-of-the-range wines; terroir is not considered a crucial factor). Nevertheless, none of the two strategies seems satisfactory in the very competitive world market that prevails nowadays. Indeed, in order to improve market shares, some new-world producers are intending to develop a certification system, that is a terroir-based strategy. The Napa Valley example is interesting and illustrative. In this region, several producers like Dominus Estate are currently applying to get an official appellation from the Bureau of Alcohol, Tobacco and Firearms. On the other hand, old-world producers (Bordeaux and Burgundy essentially) have decided to advertise more to develop their generic brands. In doing so, French producers try to mitigate the numerous drawbacks of their "Appellation d'Origine Contrôleé" (AOC) system[20] in order to recover their lost market shares. AOC laws are now much too strict. Many exceptional wines such as Daumas-Gassac, for example, are unable to obtain an AOC label essentially because they use vines that are not in conformity with the AOC rule. Daumas-Gassac sells at prices comparable to Second-Growth Pauillacs or Margaux. As a result, producers are forced to sell under the appellation "vin de pays," a low grade for a wine.[21] On the contrary, discovering the

[19] On this issue, see Ashenfelter (1998).

[20] For Barham (2003), the AOC label of origin may be seen as an application of the concept of terroir. It is conceived "to make the transition from produit de terroir as a concept to the 'qualified' agro-food entity that becomes an AOC label product."

[21] French wines are classified into four categories, "Appellation d'origine contrôlée (AOC)," "Appellation d'origine vin délimité de qualité supérieure (AOVDQS)," "Vin de pays," and "Vin de table."

holy grail is apparently not very difficult: Didier Daguenau, who is known to produce outstanding Pouilly-Fumé wines, obtained an AOC label for his worst production, a lemon he calls "quintessence of my balls" (sic), produced with bad quality grapes that are however in conformity with the AOC tradition. In its current version, the complex and costly French AOC system seems unable to produce more than just horizontal differentiation (typicity). As a matter of fact, it cannot guarantee a high level of quality (vertical differentiation).

This does not mean that a wine with a Saint Estèphe taste can be grown in Napa Valley or in Chile, but that wines of comparable quality can be. Since the taste of a wine is a horizontal quality, some consumers will prefer the Saint Esthèphe, others will prefer a wine from Chile but they will agree that both are good wines.

Acknowledgments

We are grateful to Orley Ashenfelter for his suggestion to rework the Ginsburgh *et al.* (1994) paper, as well as to Christophe Croux, Marcelo Fernandez, Abdul Noury, Loic Sadoulet, Peter Spencer, Etienne Wasmer and especially Catherine Dehon, for fruitful discussions on instrumental and less instrumental variables and for comments on a previous version. Comments and suggestions by two referees and by Alan Duncan are also very gratefully acknowledged.

References

Angrist, Joshua and Krueger, Alan (2001). Instrumental variables and the search for identification: From supply and demand to natural experiments. *Journal of Economic Perspectives*, 15, 69–85.

Ashenfelter, Orley, Ashmore, David and Lalonde, Robert (1995). Bordeaux wine vintage quality and the weather. *Chance*, 8, 7–14.

Ashenfelter, Orley (2017). The hedonic approach to vineyard site selection: Adaptation to climate change and grape growing in emerging markets. *Journal of Wine Econonmics*, 12, 3–15.

Ashenfelter, Orley and Storchmann, Karl (2006). Using a hedonic model of solar radiation to assess the economic effect of climate change: The case of the Mosel valley vineyards. Working Paper 12380, National Bureau of Economic Research.

Barham, Elizabeth (2003). Translating terroir: The global challenge of French AOC labelling. *Journal of Rural Studies*, 19, 127–138.

Bettane, Michel and Desseauve, Thierry (2000). *Le Classement des Vins et Domaines en France 2001*, Paris: Editions de la Revue du Vin de France.

Broadbent, Michael (1991). *The New Great Vintage Wine Book*, New York: Alfred A. Knopf.

Di Vittorio, Albert and Ginsburgh, Victor (1996). Des enchères comme révélateurs du classement des vins. *Journal de la Société Statistique de Paris*, 137, 19–49.

Efron, Bradley and Tibshirani, Robert J. (1998). *An Introduction to the Bootstrap*, London: Chapman & Hall/CRC.
Ginsburgh, Victor, Monzak, Muriel and Monzak, Andras (2013). Red wines of Médoc: What is wine tasting worth? *Journal of Wine Economics*, 8, 159–188.
Krug, Henri and Krug, Rémi (1979). *L'art du Champagne*, Paris: R. Laffont.
Lecocq, Sébastien and Visser, Michael (2006). Spatial variations in weather conditions and wine prices in Bordeaux. *Journal of Wine Economics*, 2, 114–124.
Maddala, G.S. (1985). *Limited-Dependent and Qualitative Variables in Econometrics*, Cambridge: Cambridge University Press.
Parker, Robert, M. (1985). *Bordeaux, The Definitive Guide for the Wines Produced since 1961*, New-York: Simon and Schuster.
Parker, Robert, M. (1990). *Les Vins de Bordeaux*, Paris: Solar.
Tinlot, Robert (2001). Le terroir: Un concept à la conquête du monde. *Revue des Œnologues et des Techniques Vitivinicoles et Œnologiques*, 101, 9–11.
Wilson, James (1998). Terroir: *The Role of Geology, Climate and Culture in the Making of French Wines*, Berkeley: University of California Press.

Appendix 1. Description of Endowments and Technologies

A.1.1. *Soil*

In the Haut-Médoc region, soil ranges from heavy clay to light gravels. One usually distinguishes four types of soil, present in various proportions: clay-chalky, gravely, gravel-sandy and sandy. Some soils are better than others and deep gravel beds (like in Pauillac) seem to be the best, though there are outstanding wines produced in the much poorer gravel-sandy region of Margaux. Subtle differences in soil may lead to very different styles. However, "(soil) is not, as the Bordelais would have one believe, the only element necessary to make a great wine." (Parker, 1985, p. 505).

In addition to soil density, chemical composition is also thought to play an important role. The database singles out five (non-exclusive) chemical components: nitrogen, phosphoric acid, potassium, lime and magnesia. Though fertilizer is kept to a minimum, it is used to maintain the complex mineral and chemical equilibrium.

These various characteristics are measured by four dummy soil variables (clay-chalk, gravel, gravel-sand and sand, which take the value 1 if the type is present, 0 otherwise), and five dummy chemical components variables (nitrogen, phosphoric acid, lime, potassium and magnesia).

A.1.2. *Slope exposure*

Slopes exposed to the East and the Southeast are protected from western winds, dominant in the region. The rising sun quickly dries the dew and reduces the risk of grapes going rotten. Western slopes are usually closer to the river Garonne and are more likely to have a gravelly soil; they also benefit from some light reflection thanks to the river. These characteristics are represented by five dummy variables (Eastern, Southeastern, Southern, Southwestern and Western exposures), which take the value 1, if the château possesses slopes with a given exposure.[22] Slopes can be of low or higher altitude. A dummy is included and takes the value 1, if the château grows vines on higher altitude lots.

A.1.3. *Grape varieties*

Haut-Médoc wines result from a combination of five varieties of grapes used in varying proportions: Cabernet Sauvignon (40 to 85%), Merlot (5 to 45%), Cabernet Franc (0 to 30%), Petit Verdot (3 to 8%) and Malbec, in small proportions (less than 2%). These varieties ripen and are harvested at different times and weather conditions at certain moments may thus influence some vineyards more than others, in accordance with the grape varieties used. Each variety has its own influence on the characteristics of wines. Cabernet Sauvignon is poor in sugar, rich in tannin and allows wines to age. Merlot is the first to ripen, is less tannic and richer in sugar than Cabernet Sauvignon. This makes the association of both varieties very attractive. Cabernet Franc ripens earlier than Cabernet Sauvignon, adds bouquet and tends to produce lighter wines. Petit Verdot ripens late (and is therefore used only in small proportions), is very tannic and rich in sugar, adding alcohol to the wine. Malbec is being replaced more and more by Merlot, with which it shares the same qualities. It is worth noting that grape varieties may lead to different outcomes according to the type of soil on which they are grown. Grape varieties are represented by four variables which represent the proportions used by every château.

A.1.4. *Age of vines*

Old vines produce less but a wine of better quality. Mouton-Rothschild vines for instance are, on average, 43 years old. So are the vines at Lafite-Rothschild, another Pauillac First-Growth. Age, however, does not seem to be necessary. Pichon Lalande, classified as a First-Growth by Parker, has

[22]For a given château, several of the variables may be equal to 1, if vines are grown on different types of slopes. Since the final product results from blending, this definition looks reasonable.

vines the average age of which is 22 years only. Vines are classified into three age categories, represented by three dummy varaibles.[23,24]

A.1.5. *Wine-making*

We now follow the production process through the eight steps distinguished by Parker (1985), and on which the questionnaire was based: (1) picking and selecting, (2) de-stemming and crushing, (3) pumping into fermentation tanks, (4) fermenting of grape sugar into alcohol, (5) macerating or keeping the grape skins and pips in contact with the grape juice for additional extract and color, (6) pressing and racking or transferring the wine to small barrels (or tanks) for the secondary (malolactic) fermentation to be completed, (7) putting the wine in oak barrels and letting it age, and (8) bottling the wine.

(1) *Picking and selecting*

Harvesting usually starts after September 15 and may take as long as three weeks. Manual picking is disappearing, since it costs more and may take too much time. Automatic picking is faster, allowing thus to harvest at the right maturity but may damage grapes and mix more stems than needed. In most cases, both methods are used but some châteaux still resort to manual picking exclusively. A dummy variable is defined which takes the value 1, if only manual picking is used.

Whether the picking is manual or not, grapes must be selected: damaged, unripe or rotten berries must be eliminated, before crushing starts. Most châteaux instruct their pickers to eliminate unhealthy grapes and some châteaux still sort grapes by hand, after the picking. In such cases, a dummy variable (manual sorting) takes the value 1.

(2) *De-stemming and crushing*

In most châteaux, crushing the berries and de-stemming[25] is done simultaneously. Some vine-yards still use the older technique of crushing before

[23]Age 1 = 1 for 5 to 20 years old vines; Age 2 = 1 for 20 to 40 years old vines; Age 3 = 1 for vines older than 40 years. In general, there will thus be several variables equal to 1 for a château.

[24]An alternative would have been to compute an average age of vines for every château; our questionnaire was not put up under that form and Parker (1985) does not provide this information for all the châteaux.

[25]De-stemming may be total or partial, since stems and pips add tannin. Most châteaux de-stem fully.

de-stemming. A dummy variable (crushing) takes the value 1 when this is the case.

(3) *Pumping into fermentation vats*

The partially crushed berries are then pumped into vats and fermentation can start. Several chemical decisions have to be made at this point. These consist in: adding sulfite (which has many complex effects and is practiced by all châteaux); chaptalizing (adding sugar, increases the alcohol content and is used by most châteaux, when needed); acidifying or de-acidifying (are not practised and only seldom allowed; adding yeast is used to start fermentation unless the process starts spontaneously; used by all châteaux). Since all vineyards proceed similarly, it is not possible to capture the possible effects of these chemical steps.

(4) *Fermenting of grape sugar into alcohol*

Several types of vats are used: oak, cement and stainless steel. During fermentation, temperature has to stay within tight bounds, usually between 25°C and 30°C. Fermentation does not start if the temperature is too low, while acetic bacteria may grow and natural yeasts will be destroyed (and stop fermentation) if temperature increases too much. This severe monitoring is easier to achieve in stainless steel tanks, by running cool water over the outside of the tanks. In the two other cases (oak and concrete tanks), wine must be run through cooling tubes. Oak vats, on the other hand, are more natural and allow wood components to mix with the wine. Since most châteaux use stainless steel, we did not include the possible choices in our regressions.

The crushed grapes are in some cases mixed with heated must. This step, represented by a dummy, which takes the value 1 if heating is used, is supposed to free coloring and some other components.

During fermentation, skins, stems, and pips rise to the top of the tank and form a solid cap (the "chapeau"), which must be kept moist by pumping the wine juice over it (remontage). Three techniques are available to achieve this: open tank with floating marc; closed tank; open tank with submerged marc. The first technique allows a contact with air. This may oxidize (and infect) the wine, and needs a remontage. Both these drawbacks are avoided in the third technique. Oxidation is also avoided in the second technique but since temperature may increase too much, a remontage (and thus, a contact with air) may be needed. The techniques are represented by three dummies.

(5) *Maceration*

After the alcoholic fermentation is completed, the wine is macerated with the skins for one to two weeks. The length of this period is crucial for the wine but since most châteaux proceed in the same way we included no control variable.

(6) *Pressing*

After steps (4) and (5) which constitute the *cuvaison*, the wine is separated from its lees. The free-run juice is the wine of better quality, while the remainder is pressed one or several times, resulting in press-wine which is more pigmented and tannic than the free-run juice. Some press-wine (the proportion depends on the year and the château) is then blended with the free-juice to adjust for color and tannin. Several types of presses exist but are said to have no influence on quality, which may, however, be negatively influenced by the number of pressings.

(7) *Ageing in barrels and racking*

The wine is then transferred to 225-liter barrels (where the alcoholic fermentation may be pursued) and the secondary (or malolactic) fermentation, which adds roundness and character, starts and lasts for three to five months. Most châteaux use (a mix of old and new[26]) oak barrels. Some Crus Bourgeois use both oak barrels and tanks. A dummy variable takes the value 1, if oak barrels are used, in isolation or in conjunction with other.

The ageing in barrels varies between 12 and 24 months (depending on the vintage), during which a number of steps have to be taken. First, the wine evaporates and produces carbon dioxide; this empties the casks, which have to be refilled every week; all châteaux carry out this step. Secondly, the wine is racked several times during the first year, to separate the clear wine from the lees which have fallen to the bottom of the cask. We introduced a variable representing the number of rackings. Thirdly, all châteaux carry out a procedure which cleans the wine from suspended matter. This is the

[26]Whether the barrels have to be new or old is a hotly debated issue; we had little information on this and could not take it into account in our regressions.

fining of the wine, achieved with egg whites, fresh or not. A variable which takes the value 1, if fresh egg whites are used, captures the influence.[27]

(8) *Bottling the wine*

In January following the vintage, most châteaux select the wine which is going to be bottled under the château's name, while the remainder will be sold under secondary labels, or in other ways. At the same time, wines resulting from different vines are blended. Since these two steps are impossible to quantify and are used in most places, they are not included in our analysis.

Before bottling takes place, wines are filtered,[28] in order to remove solid matters. There are two filtering techniques which proceed mechanically (one uses kieselguhr, the other cellulosic-asbestos filtering components); a third process is adsorption. The particularity is that adsorption needs one of the two other processes, while each of the mechanical processes can be used on its own. To represent this technology, we introduce three dummy variables which take the value 1, if the technique is used, 0 otherwise.[29]

Appendix 2. Deriving the Quantiles of the Likelihood Ratio Statistic

The asymptotic distribution of the likelihood ratio statistic under the null hypothesis is not known *a priori*. Therefore, one has to simulate this distribution for each hypothesis that needs to be tested. For this, we first regress (using ordered probit maximum likelihood) each quality equation under the null hypothesis. For example, if we want to test "H_{0E}: Endowments have no effect," we regress quality on technical variables, ignoring endowments:

$$Q = \mathbf{T}\boldsymbol{\beta} + u. \tag{A1}$$

The estimated parameters are used to construct a prediction for the latent variable, Q_h, to which one adds a random error w.[30] This generates simulated quality, say Q_{hw}, under H_{0E}. Recall that the original observations for quality are integer-valued. The values generated by this procedure can take any

[27] Fining can also be achieved with bentonite or gelatine. This was the case only once or twice in our sample.

[28] Note that some châteaux start to filter in earlier stages.

[29] Note that First-Growths never filter their wine, and only 3 Second-Growths do so; other Growth-wines use asbestos filtering, with or without adsorption; Crus Bourgeois use kieselguhr filters exclusively.

[30] We experimented with a normal distribution and a student distribution with five degrees of freedom. Results were insensitive to the choice of the distribution.

value, and have to be made discrete by rounding. The simulated rounded values are then used as a dependent variable to estimate parameters of both the unconstrained and the constrained models (A2) and (A3):[31]

$$Q_{hw} = \mathbf{E}\boldsymbol{\alpha} + \mathbf{T}\boldsymbol{\beta} + u \tag{A2}$$

$$Q_{hw} = \mathbf{T}\boldsymbol{\beta} + u. \tag{A3}$$

The two regressions are bootstrapped 200 times in order to construct simulated values for the likelihoods of both equations, and this leads to 200 likelihood ratio statistics. Since the likelihood ratio statistic distributions derived from this procedure did not match with the chi-square distribution, we extracted and used the appropriate empirical quantiles (1%, 5%, and 10%) for inference purposes.[32]

Table A.1. Effects of Natural Endowments and Technologies on Quality

	Parker		B&D		Broadbent		Prices	
	Coeff.	St. err.	Coeff.	St. err.	Coeff.	St. err.	Coeff.	St. err.
Natural endowments								
Soil								
Clay-chalk	0.317	0.485	0.263	0.303				
Gravel								
Gravel-sand								
Sand								
Nitrogen							−0.121	0.123
Phosphoric acid								
Potassium								
Lime (CaO)								
Magnesia (MgO)			0.568	0.511				
Exposure								
Altitude ('high')					0.336	0.099		
East	0.542	0.341	0.521	0.245			0.490	0.186
South-East								
South	0.122	0.440					0.209	0.130
South-West	0.225	0.378					−0.032	0.149
West							−0.363	0.187

(Continued)

[31] Note here that adding a small noise differentiates (A3) from (A1) randomly.
[32] Changing the number of replications did not change the results.

Table A.1. (*Continued*)

	Parker		B&D		Broadbent		Prices	
	Coeff.	St. err.	Coeff.	St. err.	Coeff.	St. err.	Coeff.	St. err.
Technologies								
Age of vines								
5–20 years old								
20–40 years old			1.492	0.798				
More than 40			0.853	0.797				
Grape varieties								
Cabernet Sauvignon								
Merlot	−0.129	0.042	−0.061	0.030				
Cabernet franc					−0.008	0.008		
Petit Verdot								
Vinification								
Manual picking	0.955	0.955	1.176	0.590	0.492	0.168	0.026	0.264
Manual sorting	0.946	1.687						
Crushing								
Heating								
Open float	−0.737	0.694	−0.674	0.464	−0.119	0.116	−0.285	0.196
Closed								
O sub								
No. of pressings					−0.116	0.071		
Oak barrels	1.913	1.206	1.522	0.722	0.133	0.126	0.632	0.286
Kieselguhr filtration			−1.815	0.854				
Asbestos								
Adsorption								
Fresh eggs							0.108	0.267
Intercept	3.569	1.348	0.422	1.236	0.433	0.245	4.551	0.368
R-square	0.168		0.233		0.420		0.425	
No. of observations	102		102		63		51	

Notes: Two-stage least squares estimation. Variables selected (among 15 variables representing endowments and 21 representing technological choices) by stepwise regressions. See text for further explanation of results.

Table A.2. Effects of Natural Endowments and Technologies on Quality

	Parker			B&D		
	Coeff.	St. err.	B. st. err.*	Coeff.	St. err.	B. st. err.*
Natural endowments						
Soil						
Clay-chalk	0.284	0.394	0.467	0.338	0.336	0.455
Gravel						
Gravel-sand						
Sand						
Nitrogen						
Phosphoric acid						
Potassium						
Lime (CaO)						
Magnesia (MgO)				0.765	0.574	0.719
Exposure						
Altitude ('high')						
East	0.559	0.259	0.272[w]	0.747	0.256	0.307[w]
South-East						
South	0.106	0.338	0.457			
South-West	0.340	0.304	0.366			
West						
Technologies						
Age of vines						
5–20 years old						
20–40 years old				2.340	0.902	0.875[w]
More than 40				1.483	0.848	0.981
Grape varieties						
Cabernet Sauvignon						
Merlot	−0.147	0.034	0.044[w]	−0.100	0.033	0.045[n,p]
Cabernet franc						
Petit Verdot						
Vinification						
Manual picking	1.261	0.752	0.785	1.694	0.645	0.703[n,p]
Manual sorting	1.095	1.259	1.947			
Crushing						
Heating						
Open float	−1.047	0.548	0.687	−1.072	0.486	0.677[p,b]
Closed						
O sub						
No. of pressings						
Oak barrels	1.119	0.907	1.062	2.091	0.791	0.803[w]
Kieselguhr filtration				−2.664	1.002	1.295[n,p]
Asbestos						
Absorption						
Fresh eggs						
Yield						

(*Continued*)

Table A.2. (*Continued*)

	Parker			B&D		
	Coeff.	St. err.	B. st. err.*	Coeff.	St. err.	B. st. err.*
Ordered Probit cut-off values						
1	−3.013	1.072	1.337[w]	0.234	1.274	1.379
2	−2.024	1.058	1.266	1.465	1.275	1.334
3	−1.593	1.057	1.278	2.456	1.305	1.297[p]
4	−0.969	1.059	1.266	4.010	1.378	1.392[w]
5	−0.672	1.063	1.280			
Pseudo R-square	0.234			0.314		
No. of observations	102			102		

Notes: Two-step estimation; second step is an ML ordered probit. *Standard error obtained from 200 bootstrap replications. n, p, b and w indicate that the coefficient is significantly different from zero at the 5% level according to the confidence intervals using three different approaches: normal approximation (n), percentile (p) and bias corrected bootstrap (b); w is used if all methods point to significance at the 5% level. See Efron and Tibshirani (1998, ch.1–4).

Chapter 5

The Value of Terroir: Hedonic Estimation of Vineyard Sale Prices*

Robin Cross[†], Andrew J. Plantinga[‡], and Robert N. Stavins[§]

[†]*Department of Agricultural and Resource Economics,*
Oregon State University, Corvallis, OR 97331, USA
robin.cross@oregonstate.edu

[‡]*Bren School of Environmental Science & Management,*
University of California, Santa Barbara, CA 93106-5131, USA
plantinga@oregonstate.edu

[§]*John F. Kennedy School of Government,*
Harvard University, 79 John F. Kennedy Street,
Cambridge, MA 02138,
National Bureau of Economic Research
and Resources for the Future, USA
robert_stavins@harvard.edu

We examine the value of terroir, which refers to the special characteristics of a place that impart unique qualities to the wine produced. We do this by conducting a hedonic analysis of vineyard sales in the Willamette Valley of Oregon to ascertain whether site attributes, such as slope, aspect, elevation, and soil types, or designated appellations are more important determinants of price. We find that prices are strongly determined by sub-AVA appellation designations, but not by specific site attributes. These results indicate that the concept of terroir matters economically, although the reality of terroir — as proxied for by locational attributes — is not significant.

1. Introduction

Wine producers and enthusiasts use the term "terroir," from the French *terre* (meaning land), to refer to the special characteristics of a place that

*This article originally appeared in *Journal of Wine Economics* (2011), 6(1), 1–14.

impart unique qualities to the wine produced. The Appellation d'Origine Contrôlée (AOC) system in France, and similar systems adopted in other major wine-producing countries, are based upon the geographic location of grape production, and are therefore predicated on this notion of terroir. Under a parallel U.S. system, production regions are designated as American Viticultural Areas (AVAs), with finer geographical designations known as sub-AVAs. Such designations allow wineries to identify the geographical origin of the grapes used in producing their wines, and — equally important — seek to prevent producers outside the AVA from making false claims about the nature and origin of their wines.

What is the value of terroir in the American context? Does the "reality of terroir" — the location-specific geology and geography (including climate) — predominate in determining the quality of wine? Does the "concept of terroir" — the location within an officially named appellation — impart additional value to grapes and wine? More to the point, does location within such an appellation impart additional value to vineyards?

The central question we address is whether measurable site attributes — such as slope, aspect, elevation, and soil type — or appellation designations are more important determinants of vineyard prices.[1] We do this by conducting a hedonic price analysis to investigate sales of vineyards in Oregon's Willamette Valley, one of the most important wine-producing regions in the United States.[2]

How should site attributes and sub-AVA designations influence vineyard prices? If site attributes significantly affect wine quality and if consumers are able to discriminate such quality, then vineyard prices would depend on site attributes alone,[3] and AVA designations would be redundant. Alternatively, consumers might not be able to discriminate among wines perfectly and might use AVA designations as signals of average quality of wines from respective areas, and/or might derive utility directly from drinking wines which they know to be of particular pedigree. In this intermediate case, site attributes and AVA designations would influence vineyard prices, with the

[1]The notion of terroir sometimes extends beyond natural endowments to encompass the history and culture of a place, but we use a narrower and more common definition of terroir focused on physical attributes of the location (Gergaud and Ginsburgh, 2008).
[2]The Willamette Valley is designated as an AVA. Within the valley, there are six sub-AVAs: Chehalem Mountains, Yamhill-Carlton District, Ribbon Ridge, Dundee Hills, McMinnville, and Eola-Amity Hills (Figure 1).
[3]Wine quality is affected not only by site attributes, but also by the quality of growing stock, as well as vineyard management, and the skills and resources of the winemaker.

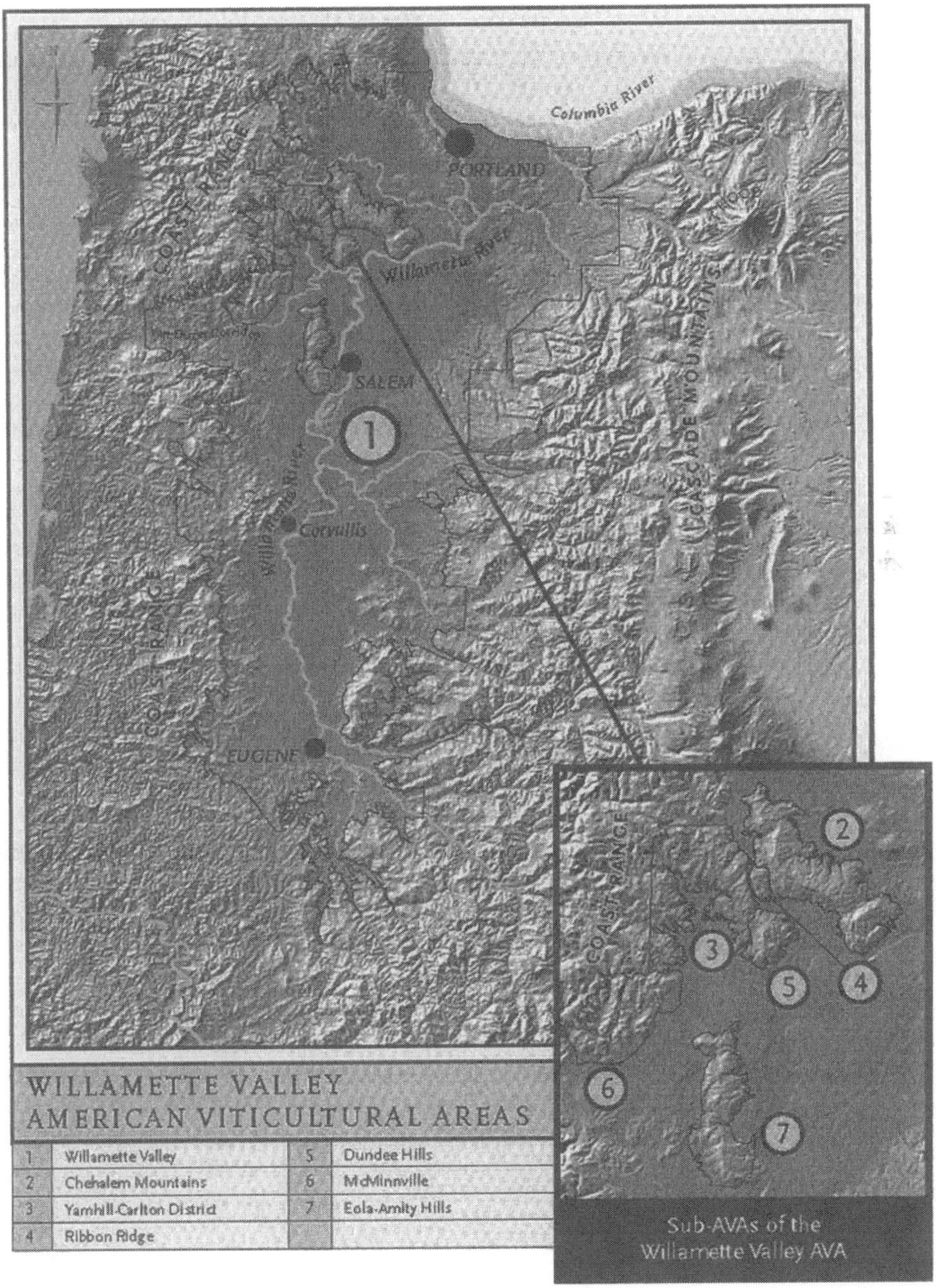

Figure 1. The Sub-AVAs of the Willamette Valley, Oregon
Source: Oregon Wine Board. Used with permission.

variables for site attributes measuring how producers value intra-AVA differences in vineyard characteristics. Presumably, producers attach premiums to site attributes that enhance wine quality, provided that consumers can perceive and are willing to pay for such quality differences.

What if, at the extreme, variation in vineyard prices is explained completely by AVA designations (i.e., site attributes are irrelevant)? This would indicate that terroir matters economically — as a concept, though not as a fundamental reality. Producers might recognize the value of the AVA designation because they know that consumers will pay more for the experience of drinking wine from designated areas.[4] But the fact that site attributes are unimportant suggests that consumers cannot discern quality differences. Any appreciation they might express for an area's terroir would essentially be founded on reputation, not reality.

In the next part of the chapter, we discuss some related research from the wine economics literature. Then, in Section 3, we describe the data we employ, as well as our estimation strategy. In Section 4, we present our results plus some robustness checks. Section 5 concludes.

2. Previous Literature

Our analysis is related to and builds upon previous work by others. In one recent study, Gergaud and Ginsburgh (2008) find that site attributes of vineyards in the Haut-Médoc appellation in Bordeaux have no effect on wine prices or ratings, after controlling for producer differences in wine-making technology. Our study builds on this work by examining — in addition to site characteristics — the value assigned to appellation designations. Further, we are able to measure site characteristics more precisely than Gergaud and Ginsburgh by using GIS-based information to develop highly detailed physiographic profiles of each parcel.

In another recent study, Ashenfelter and Storchmann (2010) investigate the effects of climate on vineyards in the Mosel Valley. As in our study, the authors have fine-scale data on vineyard characteristics. They find that site characteristics — including slope, orientation, soil types, soil depth, and altitude — as well as solar radiation are significant determinants of vineyard quality. We do not include climate variables in our analysis, because of trivial

[4]Alternatively, buyers might be less informed than sellers about how vineyard attributes affect wine quality, and, therefore, use the AVA designation as a signal of quality. Or producers may bid up the value of vineyards located in designated appellations because there is prestige associated with owning vineyards in such areas.

variation in rainfall, humidity, and wind across the relevant portion of the Willamette Valley, but our site attribute variables proxy for the amount of solar radiation received by vineyards.

An important similarity and difference with our study concerns respective dependent variables. Gergaud and Ginsburgh (2008) and Ashenfelter and Storchmann (2010) employ measures that are based on wine prices or ratings. Our dependent variable, vineyard sale prices, is preferable in the context of our investigation into the value of terroir, because it avoids potentially confounding influences on our results of non-vineyards inputs into wine production (such as labor and wine-making techniques). Provided that these inputs are variable and reproducible, profit-maximization implies that the optimal levels of these inputs are implicit functions of fixed and non-reproducible vineyard attributes and input and output prices that are constant across the vineyards in our sample. As such, we can estimate the implicit prices of vineyard attributes using a simple hedonic equation for vineyard sales. Previous authors have estimated similar models in order to study the effects of climate change on U.S. agriculture (e.g., Mendelsohn *et al.*, 1994).

As we suggest above, if consumers have limited information about specific vineyards or are unable to judge differences in quality among wines, then they might use appellation designations as signals of quality of wines from respective areas. In fact, the results of many blind taste tests indicate that wine consumers have very limited ability to distinguish intrinsic qualities of wine (sweetness, acidity, tannins, etc.), and instead judge quality by relying on extrinsic signals, such as price, origin, and wine-maker reputation.

For example, Veale and Quester (2008) found that tasters' perceptions of quality were strongly correlated with price and country of origin, but not with intrinsic qualities related to taste. Similarly, Goldstein *et al.* (2008) found that when price information is withheld, non-expert tasters show no preference for more expensive wines and even show a slight preference for less expensive wines.[5]

[5]Tasters with some wine training demonstrated a non-negative relationship between price and enjoyment. However, Hodgson (2009a, 2009b) has found that even wine judges have difficulty consistently evaluating wines. Using data on over 4,000 wines entered in 13 competitions, Hodgson (2009a) found that the probability of winning a Gold medal in one competition was statistically independent of winning a Gold medal in another competition. Further, Hodgson (2009b) found that judges at the 2009 California State Fair commercial wine competition were inconsistent in their evaluations.

3. Data and Estimation Strategy

3.1. *Dependent variable for hedonic estimation: Vineyard value*

In order to investigate the relationship between vineyard sales prices, site attributes, and appellation designation, we employ a new data set on vineyard sales provided by Northwest Farm Credit Services, a lending institution specializing in agriculture. The database includes the universe of 104 sales between 1995 and 2007 of properties in the Willamette Valley that included vineyards and vinelands.[6] In addition to total sale price, size, and location of property, sales records include an appraiser's estimate of the value of non-vineyard assets, such as dwellings and other buildings, winery equipment, and non-vineyard land. We subtract the estimated values of these non-vineyard assets from the total sale price to obtain the value of vineyards in each sale.

A remaining complication is that vineyards differ in terms of grape varietals planted, whether rootstocks are resistant to phylloxera, and type of trellis system in place. This heterogeneity accounts for some portion of the difference in sale prices. Because terroir relates exclusively to non-transferable attributes of vineyards, such as soils, elevation, slope, and climate, we also subtract from the vineyard value the appraiser's estimate of the value of all vineyard enhancements. This leaves us with the estimated price of bare land for vineyards. After converting these values to 2007 dollars using the Consumer Price Index, and dividing by the area of vineyards, we obtain the real per-acre vineyard value for each property, denoted *vinevalue*. The log of this variable is the dependent variable in our hedonic model.

3.2. *Vineyard attributes*

The sales records from Northwest Farm Credit Services provide information about average characteristics of vineyards included in each sale. We develop more precise measures, using GIS-based information on slope, aspect, elevation, and soils. The location of each parcel is determined from tax lot boundaries and matched to GIS maps of physiographic variables.[7]

---

[6]Vinelands are areas that can be developed for vineyards. We use the term "vineyards" to refer collectively to vineyards and vinelands.

[7]The tax lot information was obtained from county tax assessors' offices. Contour information was derived from USGS National Elevation Dataset data at 10 and 30 meter scales

Parcels are divided into 10-meter pixels and each pixel is classified according to 14 slope, 16 aspect, 86 elevation, and 8 soil group categories. For example, slope categories are 2–4 degrees, 4–6 degrees, and so forth. Elevation categories are 150–159 feet, 160–169 feet, and so on. Because the number of categories exceeds the number of observed sales, we combine them following conventional wisdom about which vineyard attributes are most favorable or unfavorable.[8] We then compute the percentages of each parcel in each of these aggregated categories, and use these as independent variables in our hedonic regressions. The definitions of all variables are found in Table 1.

As discussed above, the elevation, slope, and aspect variables determine the amount of solar radiation received at each site and, thus, are proxies for one important component of climate. We did not include additional controls for rainfall, humidity, and wind because these factors exhibit little variation within the Willamette Valley.

We conducted sensitivity analyses on the site attribute variables. Because there are other reasonable ways to specify the categories discussed above, we explored alternative definitions, and found that our results were not sensitive to these changes. Another issue with the site attribute variables is that they are defined for the entire property, not only the vineyard portion of the parcel. Unfortunately, we cannot refine these measures, because we do not know exactly where vineyards are located within parcels. Instead, we conduct two robustness tests, discussed below, to explore whether our results are affected by this measurement error. For this purpose, we construct a variable, denoted *percentvine*, measuring the percentage of the parcel in vineyards.

In addition to the site attribute variables, we construct a variable for the area of the vineyards (*vineacres*) and indicator variables for the location of a parcel within a sub-AVA (*eola* for Eola-Amity Hills, *mcminnville* for

(http://seamless.usgs.gov/ned1.php). Soil information came from the USDA/NRCS Soil Data Mart (http://soildatamart.nrcs.usda.gov/).

[8]We define three elevation variables: best (250–450 feet), possible (200–250 feet, 450–650 feet), and too low or too high (<200 feet, >650 feet), denoted *bestelev*, *posselev*, and *lowhighelev*, respectively. Vineyards that are too high or too low face greater risk of frost and low temperatures that inhibit ripening. South-facing slopes are regarded as preferable. We define the aspect variables as south (*south*), southeast or southwest (*southew*), east or west (*eastwest*), and north (*north*). Jory-Nekiah and Willakenzie-Hazelair are considered the best soils for producing pinot noir, and so we define *bestsoil* as the share of the parcel with either of these soils. The two other soil variables are *goodsoil* (Amity-Dayton, Bellpine, Laurelwood, or Yamhill soils) and *poorsoil* (Willamette-Woodburn and other soils). Finally, vineyards that are too flat (<2 degrees) tend to be poorly drained and those that are too steep (>12 degrees) are difficult to harvest. We define *bestslope* as the percentage of the parcel with slopes between 2 and 12 degrees and *flatsteep* as the residual.

Table 1. Variable Definitions

Variable	Definition
vinevalue	real per-acre vineyard value
vineacres	area of the parcel in vineyards, in acres
bestelev	share of the parcel with best elevation (250–450 feet)
posselev	share of the parcel with possible elevation (200–250 feet, 450–650 feet)
lowhighelev	share of the parcel with low (<200 feet) or high (>650 feet) elevation
south	share of the parcel with south aspect
southew	share of the parcel with southeast or southwest aspect
eastwest	share of the parcel with east or west aspect
north	share of the parcel with north aspect
bestsoil	share of the parcel with best soils (Jory-Nekiah, Willakenzie-Hazelair)
goodsoil	share of the parcel with good soils (Amity-Dayton, Bellpine, Laurelwood, Yamhill)
poorsoil	share of the parcel with poor soils (Willamette-Woodburn, others)
bestslope	share of the parcel with the best slope (2–12 degrees)
flatsteep	share of the parcel that is flat (<2 degrees) or steep (>12 degrees)
percentvine	share of the parcel that is in vineyards
eola	indicator variable equal to 1 if the parcel is in Eola-Amity Hills sub-AVA; 0 otherwise
mcminnville	indicator variable equal to 1 if the parcel is in McMinnville sub-AVA; 0 otherwise
yamhill	indicator variable equal to 1 if the parcel is in Yamhill-Carlton sub-AVA; 0 otherwise
dundee	indicator variable equal to 1 if the parcel is in Dundee Hills sub-AVA; 0 otherwise
chehalem	indicator variable equal to 1 if the parcel is in Chehalem Hills sub-AVA; 0 otherwise
nosub	indicator variable equal to 1 if the parcel is not in a sub-AVA; 0 otherwise
saledate	indicator variable equal to 1 if sale occurred after the official designation of the sub-AVA; 0 otherwise
distancesub	distance to nearest sub-appellation, in feet; 0 for parcels in a sub-AVA

McMinnville, *yamhill* for Yamhill-Carlton, *dundee* for Dundee Hills, *chehalem* for Chehalem Hills, and *nosub* if the parcel is outside these sub-AVAs).[9] Parcels outside of sub-AVAs are demarcated as being in the Willamette Valley AVA. It is important to acknowledge that, although the Willamette Valley AVA was established in 1984, the sub-AVA designations were not officially adopted until 2005 and 2006. Prior to this time, the areas that would later be designated as sub-AVAs were well recognized by wine producers, and it was common practice to label the origin of wines using the same

[9]We have no observations of sales within the Ribbon Ridge sub-AVA.

Table 2. Summary Statistics

Variable	Mean	Standard error	Minimum	Maximum
vinevalue	101,49	5,917	2,500	42,000
vineacres	43.48	46.53	7	400
bestelev	0.470	0.392	0	1
posselev	0.372	0.330	0	1
lowhighelev	0.158	0.312	0	1
south	0.313	0.226	0	0.994
southew	0.338	0.161	0.006	0.995
eastwest	0.181	0.123	0	0.560
north	0.168	0.176	0	0.707
bestsoil	0.345	0.418	0	1
goodsoil	0.305	0.377	0	1
poorsoil	0.350	0.374	0	1
bestslope	0.873	0.141	0	1
flatsteep	0.127	0.141	0	1
percentvine	0.681	0.214	0.162	1
eola	0.125	0.332	0	1
mcminnville	0.029	0.168	0	1
yamhill	0.163	0.372	0	1
dundee	0.231	0.423	0	1
chehalem	0.144	0.353	0	1
nosub	0.308	0.464	0	1
saledate	0.171	0.379	0	1
distancesub	36,430	86,750	0	355,833

Number of observations = 104

geographical terms.[10] We construct a variable, *saledate*, equal to 1 if the sale occurred after the respective sub-AVA designation became official and 0 otherwise, and use it to test for changes in the effects of the sub-AVA designation.

Finally, for use in robustness tests, we computed the straight-line distance from each parcel to the nearest sub-AVA. This variable, denoted *distancesub*, equals 0 if the parcel is within a sub-AVA.

Summary statistics for all variables are presented in Table 2. The average unlogged price for vineyards (*vinevalue*) is about $10,000 per acre, with prices ranging from $2,500 to $42,000 per acre. Given that our sample includes only parcels with vineyards, we must have within-sample variation in site attributes if we hope to measure effects of terroir. The statistics in Table 2

[10]For example, in 2004, Archery Summit labeled their Red Hills Estate wine "Dundee Hills Pinot Noir."

reveal that 31.3, 47.0, 34.5, and 87.3% of the land within our sample of parcels, respectively, faces directly south, and has the best elevation, soils, and slopes. At the other extreme, 16.8, 15.8, 35.0, and 12.7% of the land, respectively, is in the least desirable categories for aspect, elevation, soils, and slope. With the possible exception of the slope variable, these statistics suggest that our sample reflects a significant range of physiographic conditions.

4. Results and Robustness Tests

For our basic model, we regress the log of *vinevalue* on *vineacres*, the square of *vineacres* (*sqvineacres*), site attributes, sub-AVA designations, and a constant term. The omitted variables are *lowhighelev*, *north*, *poorsoil*, *flatsteep*, and *nosub*. Because these are the least desirable categories, we expect the coefficients on the included site attribute and sub-AVA variables to be positive.

The results, in Table 3, reveal that most of the estimated coefficients on the site attribute variables are positive, but none are significantly different from zero. The smallest *p*-value is 0.311, and none of the estimates are even

Table 3. Estimation Results: Basic Model

Variable	Estimate	Standard error	*p*-value
constant	8.582	0.3328	0.000
vineacres	−0.005	0.0021	0.013
sqvineacres	0.000014	0.000006	0.016
bestelev	0.157	0.1539	0.311
posselev	0.130	0.1641	0.430
south	0.202	0.2684	0.453
southew	−0.088	0.2673	0.743
eastwest	0.270	0.4710	0.567
bestsoil	−0.030	0.1565	0.850
goodsoil	0.048	0.1369	0.725
bestslope	0.075	0.2856	0.792
eola	0.438	0.1382	0.002
mcminnville	0.154	0.2303	0.504
yamhill	0.529	0.1350	0.000
dundee	0.852	0.1425	0.000
chehalem	0.482	0.1246	0.000

Dependent variable = log of vinevalue
Number of observations = 104
Adj. R-squared = 0.422

marginally significant.[11] In contrast, four of the five estimated coefficients for sub-AVA are significantly different from zero at better than the 1% level. Parcels within the Eola-Amity Hills, Yamhill-Carlton, Dundee Hills, and Chehalem Hills sub-AVA sell for significantly more than parcels without a sub-AVA designation. In 2007 dollars, the premiums associated with location within these sub-AVAs were, respectively, $2,933, $3,721, $7,163, and $3,306 per acre.

Pairwise F-tests indicate that the coefficient on *dundee* is different from those on *eola*, *yamhill*, and *chehalem*, but that the coefficients on *eola*, *yamhill*, and *chehalem* are statistically indistinguishable from one another. The coefficients on parcel size indicate that the per-acre price falls as the parcel size increases, but at a diminishing rate. Finally, the adjusted R^2 is 0.422, reasonably high for cross-section data.

As mentioned above, the sub-AVA designations did not become official until 2005 and 2006. For the Eola-Amity Hills, Yamhill-Carlton, and Dundee Hills sub-AVAs, our sample includes sales that occurred before and after the official designation. To test for a corresponding shift in the sub-AVA premium in these cases, we interact *eola*, *yamhill*, and *dundee* with *saledate* and add these variables to the basic model. We find that the coefficient estimates are positive and significant in all cases, indicating a rise in the premiums following the official adoption of the sub-AVAs.[12]

Why are the impacts of site attributes on sales price insignificant? As mentioned above, the site attribute variables are measured over the entire parcel, not just the vineyard portion, which may decrease the precision of these variables and explain why the estimated coefficients are not significantly different from zero. To explore this possibility, we restrict the sample to parcels that are at least 50% vineyards ($percentvine \geq 0.50$). For the entire sample, an average of 68% of the parcel area is vineyards, with a minimum of 16 and a maximum of 100% (Table 2). With a 50% cut-off, we still have 83 observations with which to estimate the model. The results (not reported, but available upon request) show little change from the basic model. None of the coefficient estimates for site attributes are significantly different from zero, and the estimates for sub-AVAs have similar magnitude and significance level. Qualitatively, the findings remain the same for cut-off values of 68%

[11]The results do not change appreciably if we use robust standard error estimates.

[12]The Eola-Amity Hills premium increases from $590 to $5,621 per acre, the Yamhill-Carlton premium increases from $2,186 to $7,064 per acre, and the Dundee Hills premium increases from $4,440 to $15,474 per acre. The full set of results is available from the corresponding author upon request.

Table 4. Estimation Results: No Sub-AVA Variables

Variable	Estimate	Standard error	p-value
constant	8.822	0.3842	0.000
vineacres	−0.008	0.0024	0.001
sqvineacres	0.000018	0.000007	0.009
bestelev	0.255	0.1766	0.152
posselev	−0.009	0.1933	0.961
south	0.102	0.3101	0.743
southew	−0.189	0.3104	0.544
eastwest	0.337	0.5298	0.526
bestsoil	0.494	0.1443	0.001
goodsoil	0.242	0.1422	0.093
bestslope	0.192	0.3370	0.571

Dependent variable = log of vinevalue
Number of observations = 104
Adj. R-squared = 0.165

and 75%. We also re-estimate the basic model with *percentvine* entered as an independent variable in the basic model. The associated coefficient is not significantly different from zero.

Another possible explanation for the insignificance of the site attribute variables is that their effects could be masked by the sub-AVA designations. The sub-AVA designations are supposed to be based on the area's terroir. In this case, the subAVA variables would measure the average effect of the site attributes of parcels within the sub-AVA, and dropping the sub-AVA variables would increase the explanatory power of the site attributes. We find this result in the case of the *bestsoil* variable, which has a positive and significant (5% level) coefficient when we omit the sub-AVA variables (Table 4).

Further investigation reveals that the *bestsoil* variable is highly correlated with the indicator variable for the Dundee Hills sub-AVA (*dundee*) but not with the other sub-AVA variables.[13] Thus, the model in Table 4 does not identify whether higher vineyard prices are the result of soils or location within the Dundee Hills sub-AVA. We split the sample into two groups — parcels inside and outside the Dundee Hills sub-AVA — and estimate separate models with only the site attribute variables. In both cases, the coefficient on the *bestsoil* variable is insignificant, suggesting that it is the Dundee Hills location, and not better soils, that raises vineyard prices.[14]

[13]The simple correlation coefficient for *bestsoil* and *dundee* is 0.69.

[14]There are 24 parcels inside the Dundee Hills sub-AVA and 80 parcels outside. With these sub-samples, the p-values for the *bestsoil* variable are, respectively, 0.81 and 0.90. Although

Table 5. Standard Deviation of Site Attributes by Sub-AVA

Variable	All	Eola	McMinnville	Yamhill	Dundee	Chehalem	Nosub
bestelev	0.392	0.287	0.405	0.249	0.370	0.416	0.390
posselev	0.330	0.267	0.306	0.159	0.360	0.330	0.374
lowhighelev	0.312	0.031	0.166	0.166	0.424	0.259	0.305
south	0.226	0.138	0.249	0.209	0.335	0.169	0.185
southew	0.161	0.095	0.078	0.172	0.221	0.093	0.154
eastwest	0.123	0.104	0.102	0.084	0.144	0.141	0.113
north	0.176	0.190	0.097	0.224	0.145	0.143	0.170
bestsoil	0.418	0.305	0.007	0.213	0.292	0.311	0.313
goodsoil	0.377	0.162	0.425	0.314	0.133	0.433	0.344
poorsoil	0.374	0.326	0.432	0.215	0.218	0.461	0.372
bestslope	0.141	0.077	0.019	0.131	0.115	0.109	0.188
flatsteep	0.141	0.077	0.019	0.131	0.115	0.109	0.188

Number of observations = 104

A further check is to see if there is variation in the site attributes within sub-AVAs. If not, then the effects of the site attributes will be captured by the sub-AVA variables. Table 5 reports the standard deviation of the site attributes for the whole sample and for parcels within each sub-AVA. The statistics indicate similar variation in site attributes within and across sub-AVAs.

Finally, if the terroir of a sub-AVA has important influences on wine quality, then parcels that are outside, but close to, sub-AVAs should be valued more than parcels that are farther away. We re-estimate the basic model with the variable *distancesub* included. This corresponding *p*-value is 0.45.[15]

Our results indicate that the significant premiums associated with sub-AVA designations are unrelated to observable site attributes. An alternative explanation is that bottle prices for wines from sub-AVAs command higher prices (for reputational reasons), which bids up the prices of sub-AVA vineyards. To examine this possibility, we summarized data on 2006 Pinot Noir bottle prices for the Willamette Valley AVA and for each sub-AVA. From

the mean of *bestsoil* is higher for parcels inside the Dundee Hills sub-AVA (0.87 compared to 0.19), there is considerable variation in the *bestsoil* variable within the sub-samples. In both cases, *bestsoil* has a standard deviation of about 0.30 and minimum and maximum values of 0 and 1, respectively.

[15] A similar result is obtained when we drop two observations for parcels that are outside but closest to the McMinnville sub-AVA. There is no premium associated with being inside this sub-AVA. Full results are available from the corresponding author upon request.

Table 6. External Evidence on Sub-AVA Rankings

Our results		Wine spectator		Robert Parker	
sub-AVA	Vineyard premium	sub-AVA	Avg. bottle price	sub-AVA	Avg. bottle price
Willamette Valley	$0	McMinnville	$40.40	McMinnville	$42.60
McMinnville	$0	Willamette Valley	$46.30	Willamette Valley	$47.40
Eola-Amity Hills	$2,933	Yamhill-Carlton	$48.50	Yamhill-Carlton	$48.20
Chehalem Mountains	$3,306	Eola-Amity Hills	$51.30	Eola-Amity Hills	$49.90
Yamhill-Carlton	$3,721	Chehalem Mountains	$52.00	Dundee Hills	$54.20
Dundee Hills	$7,163	Dundee Hills	$58.70	Chehalem Mountains	$54.60

Note: The vineyard premium is the increment in sale price (in 2007 dollars per acre) resulting from location inside a sub-AVA.

the *Wine Spectator* database, we obtained 243 observations, and from the *Wine Advocate* (Robert Parker) database 310 observations. In Table 6, we report the vineyard premiums (in 2007 dollars), based on the results from Table 3, plus the average bottle prices (in 2007 dollars) from our two wine data sources. The rankings of vineyard premiums are broadly consistent with bottle rankings. McMinnville and Willamette Valley are at the bottom in all rankings and Dundee Hills is at or second from the top. Of course, the bottle prices are also affected by the skills and reputations of winemakers, and so these results are, at most, suggestive of correlation between vineyard and bottle prices.[16]

5. Conclusions

We have estimated a hedonic model of vineyard prices in Oregon to examine whether they vary systematically with designated appellation, after controlling for site attributes. Despite using precise measures of site attributes, we do not find evidence of a significant effect of these variables on vineyard prices, and a series of robustness tests does not alter this finding. But, we do

[16]Because there is considerable variation in bottle prices within sub-AVAs, we cannot reject the null hypothesis that average bottle prices are the same across sub-AVAs.

find that vineyard prices are strongly determined by whether or not parcels are inside specific sub-AVAs. The delineation of sub-AVAs is intended to capture the unique characteristics of a geographical area as they relate to grape production.[17] That is, sub-AVAs are supposed to reflect the area's terroir. Our finding that the physical characteristics of vineyards are not priced implicitly in the land market raises questions about whether sub-AVA designations have a meaningful connection — in reality — with terroir.

Nevertheless, our results make clear that the concept of terroir matters economically. Buyers and sellers of vineyard parcels in the Willamette Valley of Oregon attach a significant premium to the sub-AVA designations, ranging from about $3,000 per acre for Eola-Amity Hills, Chehalem Mountains, and Yamhill-Carlton, to over $7,000 per acre for Dundee Hills. One possibility is that buyers are less informed than sellers about how the attributes of a vineyard will affect wine quality and, therefore, rely on sub-AVA designations as quality signals. Either way, consumers are evidently willing to pay more for the experience of drinking wines from these areas. While they may not discriminate among wines in terms of their intrinsic qualities, consumers are responding to extrinsic qualities of wines, such as price and area of origin.

Acknowledgments

The authors are grateful to Charles Mason, Larry Lev, an anonymous referee, session participants at the 2009 American Association of Wine Economics and 2011 Allied Social Science Association meetings, and seminar participants at Oregon State University, the Oregon Wine Research Institute, and the University of Puget Sound for helpful comments on a previous version of this chapter (Cross *et al.*, 2011), but all remaining errors are their own.

References

Ashenfelter, O., and Storchmann, K. (2010). Using hedonic models of solar radiation and weather to assess the economic effect of climate change: The case of Mosel valley vineyards. *Review of Economics and Statistics*, 92(2), 333–349.

Cross, R., Plantinga, A.J., and Stavins, R.N. (2011). What is the value of terroir? *American Economic Review, Papers and Proceedings*, 101(3), 152–156.

[17] The Bureau of Alcohol, Tobacco, and Firearms, which designates AVAs in the United States, defines a viticultural area as, "a delimited, grape-growing region distinguishable by geographical features."

Gergaud, O., and Ginsburgh, V. (2008). Natural endowments, production technologies and the quality of wines in Bordeaux. Does terroir matter? *The Economic Journal*, 118 (June), F142–F157.

Goldstein, R., Almenberg, J., Dreher, A., Emerson, J.W., Herschkowitsch, A., and Katz, J. (2008). Do more expensive wines taste better? Evidence from a large sample of blind tastings. *Journal of Wine Economics*, 3(1), 1–9.

Hodgson, R.T. (2009a). An analysis of the concordance among 13 U.S. wine competitions. *Journal of Wine Economics*, 4(1), 1–9.

Hodgson, R.T. (2009b). How expert are "expert" wine judges? *Journal of Wine Economics*, 4(2), 233–241.

Mendelsohn, R., Nordhaus, W.D., and Shaw, D. (1994). The impact of global warming on agriculture: A Ricardian analysis. *American Economic Review*, 84(4), 753–771.

Veale, R., and Quester, P. (2008). Consumer sensory evaluations of wine quality: The respective influence of price and country of origin. *Journal of Wine Economics*, 3(1), 10–29.

Chapter 6

Too Much of a Good Thing? Causes and Consequences of Increases in Sugar Content of California Wine Grapes*

Julian M. Alston[†], Kate B. Fuller[‡], James T. Lapsley[§], and George Soleas[¶]

[†]*Department of Agricultural and Resource Economics at the University of California, Davis, One Shields Avenue, Davis, CA 95616, USA and Robert Mondavi Institute Center for Wine Economics at the University of California, USA*
julian@primal.ucdavis.edu

[‡]*Department of Agricultural Economics and Economics Montana State University, PO Box 172920, Bozeman, MT 59717, USA*
kate.fuller@montana.edu

[§]*Department of Viticulture & Enology at the University of California, Davis and UC Agricultural Issues Center, One Shields Avenue, Davis, CA 95616, USA*
jtlapsley@ucdavis.edu

[¶]*Quality Assurance and Specialty Services, Liquor Control Board of Ontario, 1 Yonge Street, Suite 1401, Toronto, Ontario, M5E 1E5, Canada*
george.soleas@lcbo.com

*This article originally appeared in *Journal of Wine Economics* (2011), 6(2), 135–159.

Too Much of a Good Thing?
Some wine writers express their dismay
Over high alcohol cabernet
Burning coal, says Al Gore
Not the high Parker score
Is the cause of the rising baumé

Still a 15 percent chardonnay
Will be too hot to drink most would say
Lower Brix on the vine
Spinning tricks with the wine
Or a lie on the label might pay

The sugar content of California wine grapes has increased significantly over the past 10–20 years, and this implies a corresponding increase in the alcohol content of wine made with those grapes. In this chapter, we develop a simple model of winegrape production and quality, including sugar content and other characteristics as choice variables along with yield. Using this model we derive hypotheses about alternative theoretical explanations for the phenomenon of rising sugar content of grapes, including effects of changes in climate and producer responses to changes in consumer demand. We analyze detailed data on changes in the sugar content of California wine grapes at crush to obtain insight into the relative importance of the different influences. We buttress this analysis of sugar content of wine grapes with data on the alcohol content of wine.

1. Introduction

The sugar content of California wine grapes has increased significantly over the past 10–20 years, and this implies a corresponding increase in the alcohol content of wine made with those grapes. The sugar content of California wine grapes at harvest increased from 21.4 degrees Brix in 1980 (average across all wines and all districts) to 21.8 degrees Brix in 1990 and 23.3 degrees Brix in 2008.[1] Relative to the average sugar content in 1980 this amounts to an increase of almost 7% over the most recent 18 years and 9% over 28 years. Since sugar converts essentially directly into alcohol, a 9% increase in the average sugar content of wine grapes implies a corresponding 9% increase in the average alcohol content of wine. These changes might have resulted from changes in climate (e.g., generally hotter weather), cultural changes in the vineyard (e.g., later harvest dates) either in response to perceived demand

[1]Degrees Brix (°Bx) is a measurement of the relative density of dissolved sucrose in unfermented grape juice, in grams per 100 milliliters. A 25 °Bx solution has 25 grams of sucrose sugar per 100 milliliters of liquid. The percentage of alcohol by volume of the finished wine is estimated to be 0.55 times the °Bx of the grape juice.

for more-intense or riper-flavored wines (e.g., as reflected in higher "Parker" scores) or to mitigate the effects of climate change, or some combination of the two.

In this chapter, we document the increases in the sugar content of wine grapes and their implications for the alcohol content of wine in California, and evaluate the roles of exogenous changes in climate versus human responses (both in the vineyard and the winery) to climate change and other influences in determining the changing sugar content of wine grapes. Our main statistical analysis uses annual data, by variety of grapes and crush district, on the average sugar content of wine grapes at crush, for 1980 through 2008, along with other data on yield, acreage, and production of wine grapes by variety and county. This analysis is buttressed by an analysis of the changes over time in the alcohol content of California wine tested by the Liquor Control Board of Ontario (LCBO), Canada.

2. Evolution of California Winegrape Production

The primary motivation for this work came from the observation of rising sugar content of California wine grapes at harvest. The extent of change varied by variety and growing region, as well as over time, but it is clear that a shift towards higher sugar at harvest became evident in the mid 1990s and through the first decade of the 21st century. In the case of white varieties, which are generally picked at lower sugar than are red grapes, sugar at harvest increased by just under 12%, moving from an average sugar at harvest of 20.7 degrees Brix in the years 1980–1984, to 23.2 degrees Brix for the period 2005–2007. Red grapes increased from 22.2 to 24.3 degrees Brix for the same time period. Average degrees Brix at harvest for red varieties, as a single category, was reduced by the inclusion of Zinfandel, a red variety that is generally harvested at low sugar for the production of white Zinfandel. Indeed, average sugar at harvest barely changed for Zinfandel, rising from 22.0 only to 22.6 degrees Brix between 1980–1984 and 2005–2007. In contrast, Cabernet Sauvignon increased from 22.8 degrees Brix in 1980–1984 to 25.0 in 2005–2007. Figure 1 charts the rise of sugar at harvest for California as a whole.

Various other changes in the California wine and winegrape industry may have had some influence on the changes in the sugar content of winegrapes that are the focus of this chapter. During the 30 years between 1980 and 2010, California's winegrape vineyards changed dramatically. The most obvious difference was the physical expansion in total acreage and shift in the location

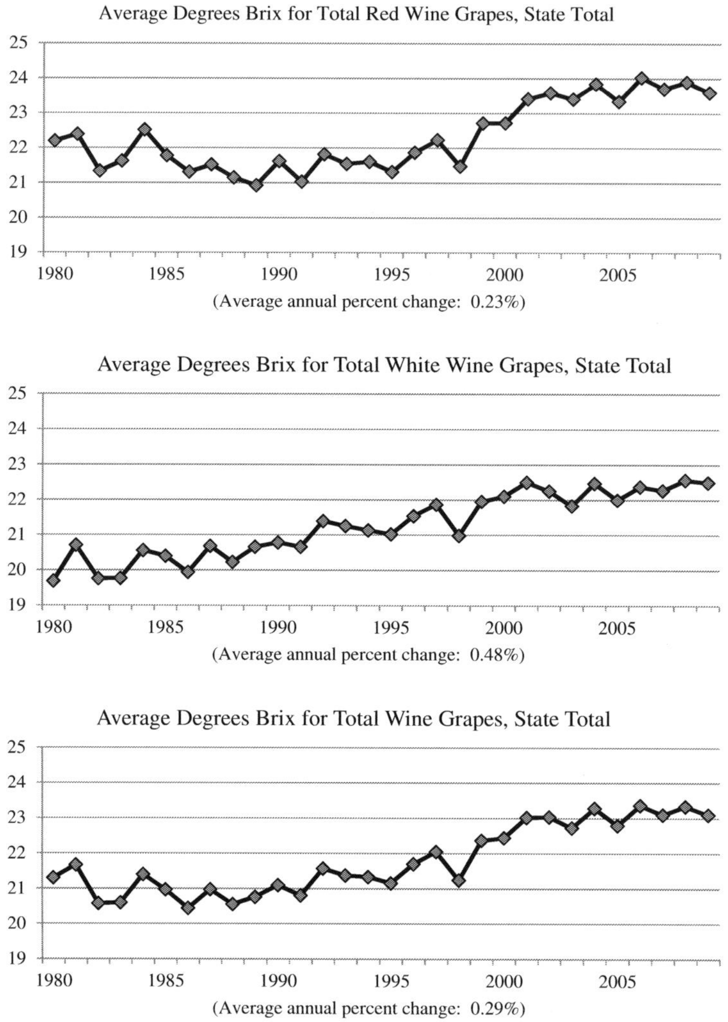

Figure 1. Trends in Sugar Content (Degrees Brix) of California Wine Grapes, 1980–2008
Source: Created by the authors using data from NASS/CDFA Grape Crush Reports, 1981–2010.

of production. Bearing acreage increased by 60%, from 278,935 acres in 1981 to 445,472 acres in 2007.[2] Much of this increase was in the premium regions. Less obvious were the changes in the varietal composition of California's

[2]Acreage figures are derived from the NASS/CDFA (1980–2010b) Grape Acreage Report. Figures for tonnage are derived from the NASS/CDFA (1980–2010a) Grape Crush Report.

vineyards, with a shift over time to premium varieties used increasingly to produce wine with varietal labels.

Changes in the structure of the bearing and nonbearing age structure of the vineyard give some indication of the trends and cycles in production. Assuming an economic life of 30 years for a vineyard, and allowing that vineyards do not become productive until the fourth year, at any given time non-bearing acreage equal to approximately 10% of bearing acreage is required to replace aging vineyards that are soon to be grubbed out.[3] Figure 2, Panel *a* shows white and red non-bearing acreage as a percentage of total bearing acreage of white and red wine grapes, respectively, and the average price per ton of wine grapes in California.[4] Several points stand out. First, boom and bust cycles are evident, with nonbearing acreage well above 10% of bearing acreage in some periods, but well below in other periods. Second, red and white varieties were not replaced at the same rate.[5] In 1981, white varieties accounted for approximately 38% of the 278,935 bearing acres of wine grapes in California. By 1984, white varieties represented more than 50% of all acreage, and white varieties remained dominant until 1998, when red varieties accounted for 50.7%. The trend toward red varieties has continued and in 2007 red varieties claimed just under 62% of all California winegrape acreage.

The state aggregate figures mask significant spatial variation. As can be seen in Figure 2, Panel *b*, in most years during the two decades from 1985 to 2005, Napa and Sonoma counties had a higher percentage of non-bearing acreage than did the state as a whole. These counties suffered a phylloxera infestation in the 1980s and 1990s, necessitating replanting of existing vineyards as well as new vineyard plantings to meet increased demand. During this period, wine consumers in the United States increasingly chose varietally labeled wine, leading to the dominance of "premium" varieties such as Chardonnay, Cabernet Sauvignon, Zinfandel, and Merlot. In 1985, only 19% of California table wine carried a varietal label, but within 15 years, by 2000, varietally labeled wine accounted for 71% of all California table wine

[3]Vineyards can certainly be productive for more than 30 years, but by that age, productivity declines and vineyards are often replanted. Because vineyards are often planted in cycles, vineyard age is not uniform over time and the 10% non-bearing acreage is merely a useful guideline rather than a precise figure.

[4]These prices were deflated using the price deflator for GDP, based in 2008.

[5]These figures treat Zinfandel as a red grape variety, although the vast majority of its fruit has been used to produce white Zinfandel, so it perhaps should be classified as a "white" grape variety.

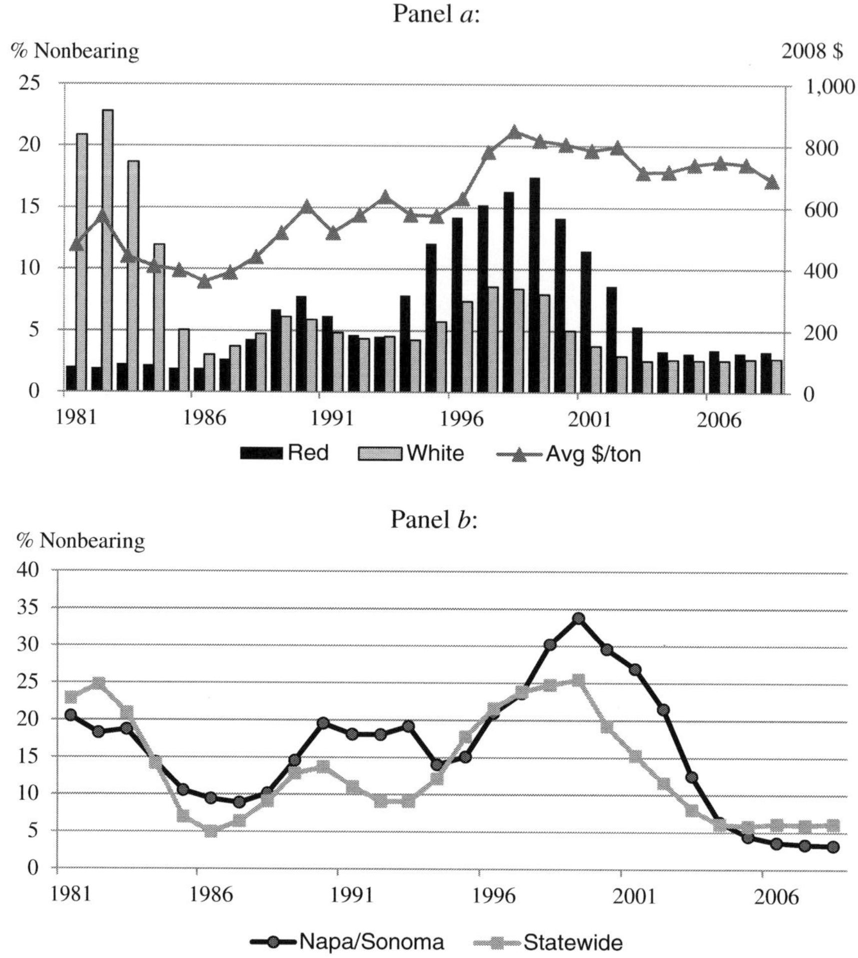

Figure 2. Nonbearing Acreage of Wine Grapes as a Percentage of Bearing Acreage
Source: Created by the authors using data from NASS/CDFA Grape Acreage Reports, 1982–2010.

by volume (Shanken, 2001, p. 97).[6] Although costly in materials and lost harvest revenue, the replanting in Napa and Sonoma roughly coincided with a market swing to red wine in the 1990s, and allowed vineyard owners to convert their vineyards to red varieties, especially Cabernet Sauvignon and Merlot, while adopting higher planting densities and new trellising systems.

The trend to grow premium varieties of red wine was accompanied by a shift to produce a greater share of production in the premium regions. In

[6]Under U.S. law, varietally labeled wine must contain at least 75% of the named variety.

1981, slightly more than 50% of California's winegrape acreage was located in the southern San Joaquin Valley but by 2008, this percentage had fallen to slightly more than 33% of acreage. While total California winegrape vineyard acreage had expanded by 164,756 acres (a 59% increase), San Joaquin Valley acreage had increased by only 12,422 acres, or 8.5%. As can be seen in Figure 3, the areas experiencing the greatest percentage growth in acreage were the Delta, which grew by 185% from 17,355 acres in 1981 to 49,558 acres in 2008; the North Coast, which expanded by 128% from 55,474 acres in 1981 to 126,455 acres in 2008; and the Central Coast, which doubled in size from 41,015 acres in 1981 to 82,600 acres in 2008.[7]

California's vineyard regions differ significantly in yield and in perceived quality, which is reflected in the average price per ton paid for grapes from different regions. Figure 4 shows the average price per ton for Cabernet Sauvignon and Chardonnay wine grapes for five California viticultural areas in 2008. The price ranged from an average price of $4,648 a ton for Cabernet Sauvignon grown in Napa County, to a low of $363 a ton for the same variety grown in district 14, which is located at the southern end of the San Joaquin Valley. The higher prices paid for Cabernet from Napa and Sonoma counties reflect the very real compositional differences, such as higher acidity, deeper color, and greater intensity, relative to grapes grown in California's warm interior valley. To some extent the prices also are indicative of yield. In 2008, Napa County vineyards delivered 2.4 tons of Cabernet per acre, and neighboring Sonoma County yields were only a bit higher at 2.8 tons. In the warm interior valley, Delta vineyards produced 7.6 tons per acre of Cabernet while district 14 yielded 15.1 tons per acre. Monterey and San Benito counties in California's Central Coast, yielded 4.4 tons per acre.

In Figure 5, Panel *a* shows the percentage of tons by region while Panel *b* displays the percentage of value by region in 2008. The North Coast, which accounted for just less than 10% of all grapes crushed, commanded over

[7]For the present purpose, we have divided California into five viticultural areas: (1) the "North Coast," including Napa, Sonoma, Mendocino, Lake and Marin counties; (2) the "Central Coast," including Monterey, San Benito, San Luis Obispo, and Santa Barbara counties; (3) the "Delta," which includes the northern portion of San Joaquin County and southern portions of Yolo and Sacramento counties adjacent to California's delta; (4) the "San Joaquin Valley," comprising southern San Joaquin County, Stanislaus, Merced, Madera, Fresno, Tulare, Kings and Kern counties; and "Other" which includes the Sierra foothills, southern California, and the northern Sacramento Valley (in aggregate the "Other" area comprises approximately 6% of vineyard acreage and 3.5% of total tonnage).

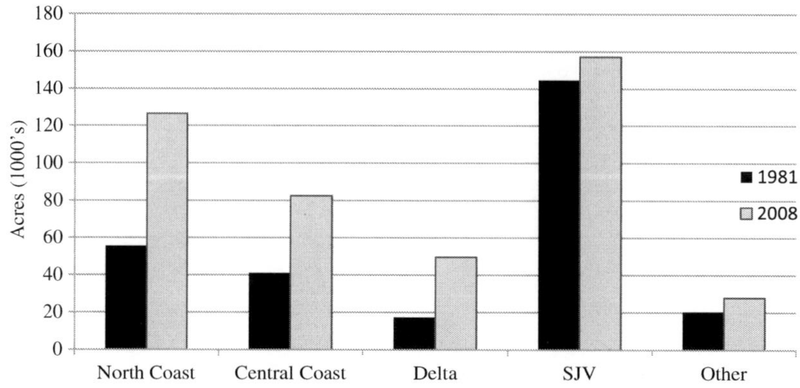

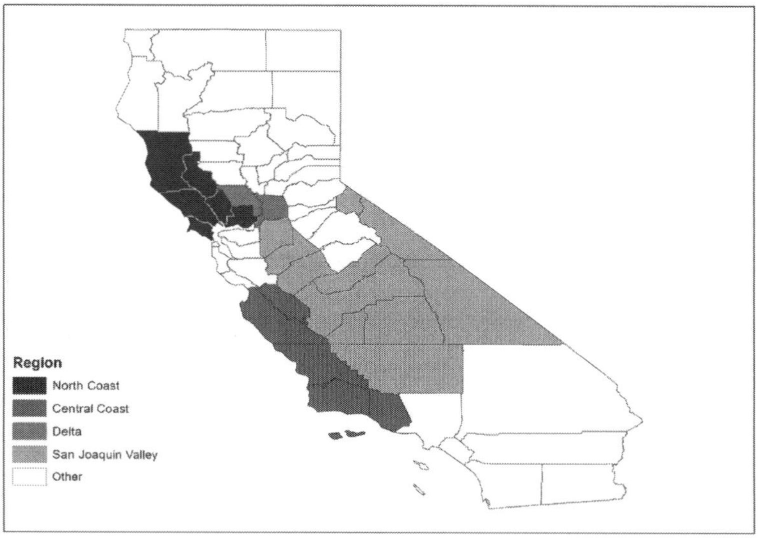

Figure 3. Regional Distribution of California Winegrape Acreage, 1981 and 2008
Source: Created by the authors using data from NASS/CDFA Grape Acreage Reports, 1982–2010.

38% of all revenue. It is followed by the Central Coast, which grew 9.4% of all tons crushed and claimed 18.8% of revenue. The Delta, the coolest area of California's interior valley, delivered 17.1% of all grapes crushed, and received 13.5% of the revenue. The southern San Joaquin Valley, responsible for producing 61% of California's harvest, received just under 27% of the revenue. Clearly growing grapes is a significantly different business in Napa than in the San Joaquin Valley.

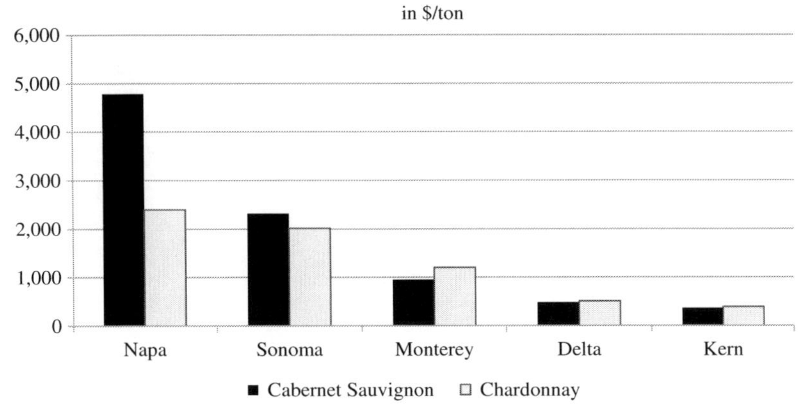

Figure 4. Price of Cabernet Sauvignon and Chardonnay in Various Places, 2008

Source: Created by the authors using data from NASS/CDFA Grape Crush Reports, 1981–2010.

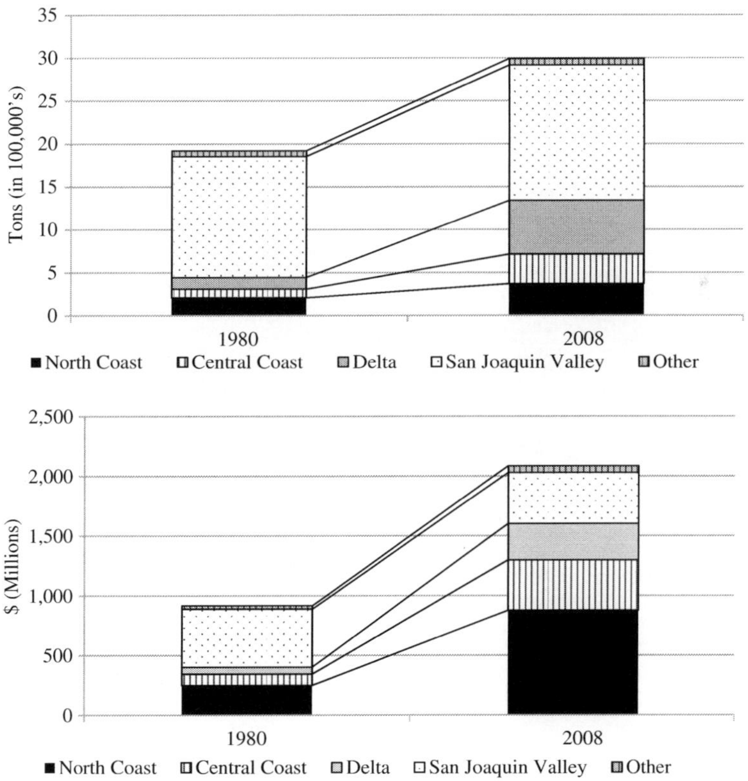

Figure 5. Total Tons Harvested and Value in 1980 and 2008, by Region

Source: Created by the authors using data from NASS/CDFA Grape Crush Reports, 1981–2010.

3. A Simple Model of Determinants of Sugar in Wine Grapes

It is unclear why sugar has increased at harvest but several contributing factors have been suggested. Global warming is often mentioned. For instance, average minimum temperatures in the San Joaquin Valley rose by about 2.5 degrees Fahrenheit (almost 1.4°C) from the 1930s to the first years of the 21st century, and most of that increase became apparent during the most recent 20–30 years (Bar-Am, 2012, in process; see also Weare, 2009). Denser coastal vineyard plantings and new trellising systems are also often cited. Some wine makers point to the new rootstock/scion interactions that were introduced following the collapse of the rootstock, AXR to phylloxera, indicating that these new vineyards achieve sugar ripeness prior to reaching phenolic maturity, making it necessary for the grapes to "hang" longer than in the past. Still others claim that higher sugar at harvest is simply a style choice, with no underlying physiological reason to be found in the vineyard.

Whatever, the case, it is clear that higher sugar grapes, if fermented to dryness, result in higher alcohol wines. Higher alcohol in wines may or may not be a desired outcome. The presence of more alcohol can contribute to a perception of "hotness" for some consumers, while for others higher alcohol may add a sense of sweetness to the wine. However, under the United States tax system, wines above 14% alcohol by volume are taxed at $0.50 a gallon more than are wines with less than 14% alcohol by volume.[8] The demand to reduce alcohol concentrations has given rise to a new business in California, alcohol reduction. Currently two firms, Wine Secrets and ConeTech, specialize in alcohol removal. Use of such technology indicates a demand to reduce the alcohol content of wine.[9]

In this section, we develop a model of winegrape production and quality, including sugar content and other characteristics as choice variables along with yield, which we can use to derive hypotheses about alternative

[8]Federal tax rates are $1.07 per gallon for wine having 7 to 14% alcohol and $1.57 per gallon for wine between 14 and 21% alcohol by volume. See http://www.ttb.gov/tax_audit/atftaxes.shtml.

[9]Based on its production of "proof gallons," we estimate that ConeTech alone treated roughly 3.3 million gallons of wine per year for the four years 2005–2008, which represents a finished amount of approximately 16.5 million gallons (assuming 20% of a lot would be treated), or about 3% of California's annual wine production. ConeTech indicates that they have sold their technology to several large California wineries, but declined to name their clients.

theoretical explanations for the phenomenon of rising sugar content of grapes. Growers' variable profit per acre of wine grapes of variety ν grown in crush district d in year t is equal to gross revenue per acre (yield in tons per acre, $Y_{\nu dt}$ times the price per ton, $P_{\nu dt}$) minus variable costs (the quantity of variable inputs used per acre, $X_{\nu dt}$ times the price per unit of inputs, ν_t). That is:

$$\pi^G_{d\nu t} = P_{d\nu t} Y_{d\nu t} - \nu_t X_{d\nu t}. \tag{1}$$

The price of wine grapes varies, depending on their sugar content, B (in degrees Brix) and other physical quality characteristics, Q (such as acidity), as well as the variety, V, the district, D, and the year, Y (reflecting market conditions). Thus:

$$P_{d\nu t} = \mathrm{p}(B_{d\nu t}, Q_{d\nu t}, D_d, V_\nu, T_t). \tag{2}$$

The yield of wine grapes varies among crush districts, varieties, and years, and with changes in the quantity of variable inputs, X; it also depends on weather conditions during the growing season in the crush district, W_{dt} (a complex of rainfall and temperature variables), and management practices applied to the particular variety, $M_{d\nu t}$. The yield relationship may also vary over time reflecting year-to-year and secular changes in technology that are not captured in the weather and management variables (e.g., because of changes in climate, rootstocks, pest and disease prevalence, or other factors), and the variable T_t is included to represent these aspects.

$$Y_{d\nu t} = \mathrm{p}(X_{d\nu t}, W_{dt}, M_{d\nu t}, D_d, V_\nu, T_t). \tag{3}$$

The sugar content of wine grapes (B) and other quality characteristics (Q) depend on the same factors that affect yield.

$$B_{d\nu t} = \mathrm{b}(X_{d\nu t}, W_{dt}, M_{d\nu t}, D_d, V_\nu, T_t). \tag{4}$$

$$Q_{d\nu t} = \mathrm{q}(X_{d\nu t}, W_{dt}, M_{d\nu t}, D_d, V_\nu, T_t). \tag{5}$$

Winemakers' variable profit per gallon of bulk wine (or equivalent quantity of wine grapes) produced using variety v grown in crush district d in year t is equal to gross revenue per gallon, $G_{d\nu t}$ minus (a) the cost of excise taxes per gallon, E, which depend on the alcohol content of the wine, $A_{d\nu t}$, (b) the cost of the wine grapes, (c) variable costs of winemaking (the quantity of variable inputs used per gallon, $Z_{\nu dt}$ times the price per unit of inputs, r_t), and (d) expenditure on removal of alcohol from wine, $S_{\nu dt}$.[10] That is:

$$\pi^W_{d\nu t} = G_{d\nu t} - E(A_{d\nu}) - P_{d\nu t}Y_{d\nu t} - r_t Z_{d\nu t} - S_{d\nu t}. \tag{6}$$

The value of wine per gallon depends on its alcohol content, A, other physical quality characteristics, K, as well as the variety, V, the district, D, and the year, Y.

$$G_{d\nu t} = \mathrm{g}(A_{d\nu t}, K_{d\nu t}, D_d, V_\nu, T_t). \tag{7}$$

The alcohol content of the wine depends on the sugar content of the wine grapes, but can be modified by the expenditure of effort, S.

$$A_{d\nu t} = \mathrm{a}(B_{d\nu t}, S_{d\nu t}). \tag{8}$$

Other quality characteristics of the wine depend on the same variables, as well as the quality characteristics of the wine grapes, Q, the quantity of wine-making inputs, Z, and oenological management practices in the winery, O.

$$K_{d\nu t} = \mathrm{k}(Q_{d\nu t}, O_{d\nu t}, B_{d\nu t}, S_{d\nu t}, A_{d\nu t}, D_d, V_\nu, T_t). \tag{9}$$

We draw informally on this model in proposing two hypotheses about the sources of the rise in sugar content of California winegrapes. In each case the increase in sugar content of grapes is seen as an unsought consequence of other factors. The first hypothesis is that exogenous changes in the weather, with generally rising average temperatures, imply increases in sugar content of grapes even without any changes in management of the vineyard.[11] Profit-maximizing responses of growers and wineries to such changes could mitigate the implications for sugar content of grapes but should not be expected entirely to eliminate their impact.

The second hypothesis is that the trend was caused by a market demand (perceived or real) for wines with ripe flavors and lower tannin levels, attributes associated with grapes that are picked at higher degrees Brix.

[10] It might be useful to disaggregate into several categories of winemaking inputs for some purposes but for now we treat Z as a scalar aggregate, as we did with X for grape production.

[11] A literature is developing on the implications of climate and climate change for the wine industry, and some of that specific to California. Examples include Nemani *et al.* (2001), Tate (2001), Jones (2005, 2006, 2007), Jones *et al.* (2005), Webb *et al.* (2005), White *et al.* (2006), and Jones and Goodrich (2008). Issues addressed include various aspects of wine quality, yield, and the optimal location of production. Published work to date has not quantified the impacts on sugar content of grapes that are the subject of our work.

Under this hypothesis, profit-maximizing responses of wineries and growers to changes in demand for quality characteristics of wine required changes in viticultural practices that resulted in unsought increases in sugar content of grapes. For instance, extending the "hang time" and picking the grapes later than they would do otherwise is likely to result in higher sugar content, if only because the grapes are more dehydrated.[12] To some extent *vignerons* can independently manage the sugar content of grapes and other quality characteristics, but an increase in intensity and ripeness of fruit is likely to come to some extent at the expense of a reduction in tons per hectare and an increase in degrees Brix.[13]

4. Changing Sugar Content of California Wine Grapes

We assembled a very detailed data set (from annual crush reports and various other sources) that includes (a) annual data by variety of grapes and crush district on the average sugar content of wine grapes at crush, extending from 1980 through 2008, (b) other data on yield, acreage, and production of wine grapes by variety and county, and (c) daily data on temperatures by crush district. Using these data, we estimated variants of the following model to examine the extent of changes in degrees Brix (*BRIX*) over time among crush districts and varieties and the role of climate as represented by a heat index:

$$\begin{aligned} BRIX_{d\nu t} = \beta_0 + \beta_h H_{dt} + \sum_{j=1}^{V} \nu_j\, VAR_{\nu j} + \sum_{i=1}^{D} \delta_d DIST_{di} + \tau_0 T_t \\ + \sum_{j=1}^{V} \tau_j^{\nu} (VAR_{\nu j} \times T_t) + \sum_{i=1}^{D} \tau_i^{d} (DIST_{di} \times T_t) + \epsilon_{d\nu t} \end{aligned} \qquad (10)$$

---

[12] More-specifically, influential wine writers, such as Robert Parker of the *Wine Advocate* or James Laube of the *Wine Spectator*, may have encouraged the production of wines with strong, intense, riper fruit flavors, by giving very favorable ratings for such wines. This argument applies more directly to ultra-premium wines than to the large volume end of the market that is not subject to wine ratings, and probably more to red wines than white wines. However, changes in the ultra-premium end of the market might have led to similar subsequent movements in wines in the lower price categories. In addition, some of the market growth of moderately priced wines might have been facilitated by an emphasis on similar styles of wine that are attractive to less experienced wine consumers.

[13] A literature on the economic effects of weather and climate on wine quality has developed over the past 20 years, with contributions such as Ashenfelter, Ashmore and Lalonde (1995), Ashenfelter and Byron (1995), Ashenfelter (2008), Ashenfelter and Storchmann (2010), Jones *et al.* (2005), and Storchmann (2005).

In this model, H_{dt} is a weather variable, the "heat index" for crush district d during the growing season in year t. The other variables are dichotomous dummy (or indicator) variables such that $VAR_{\nu j} = 1$ if $j = v$, 0 otherwise, and $DIST_{di} = 1$ if $i = d$, 0 otherwise, and a time trend, T_t.

4.1. *Definitions of variables and data for the analysis*

We have data for the years 1980–2008 on average degrees Brix for over 200 varieties in 17 crush districts. (The number of varieties reported changes from year to year and from district to district. Varieties include wine, table, and raisin grapes.)[14] Table 1 reports average annual growth rates over the longer period 1980–2008 as well as 1990–2008, for a selection of important varieties, as well as for all red, all white, and all varieties, in each of the main production regions and for California as a whole. The data in the table are suggestive of the possibility that growth rates may have differed systematically among regions and varieties, an issue that we examine next. The statistical analysis that follows uses only the data for the more recent period, 1990–2008, for which the data are more consistent and more complete, and the estimated relationships are more likely to be stable and meaningful.

The daily measure of growing degrees (GDs) is equal to the average of the daily minimum and daily maximum temperature minus a base temperature of 50°F. The growing season for wine grapes is defined as extending over the six months, April through September. The accumulated total of growing degree units (GDUs) is the sum of GDs accumulated during the season. We use a growing season heat index, H defined as the average daily GDs during the growing season, equal to the accumulated GDUs divided by the total number of days.[15] We also experimented with the same variable applied to different periods (e.g., the entire year or particular months).

The data on monthly temperature averages were obtained from NOAA's National Climatic Data Center (NOAA, 2010). From hundreds of NOAA stations within California, we chose one weather station for each of the 17 crush districts. While more localized data would have been preferred, none were available. However, Lecocq and Visser (2006) showed that while highly

[14]These data were compiled from the Annual Grape Crush Reports, published by NASS/CDFA, various issues.

[15]We thank Professor Andrew Walker from the Department of Viticulture and Enology at UC Davis for advising us about the appropriate choice of a heat index for our purpose.

Table 1. Trends in Sugar Content of California Wine Grapes (Degrees Brix), by Variety and Region

Variety	Region					
	North Coast	Central Coast	Delta	San Joaquin Valley	Southern California	California
			(a) 1980–2008			
Average annual percentage change						
Sauvignon Blanc	−0.02	0.11	0.05	0.51	0.20	0.16
French Colombard	−0.12	—	0.25	0.22	—	0.20
Chardonnay	0.18	0.32	0.29	0.37	0.19	0.18
Chenin Blanc	0.05	0.29	0.30	0.33	−0.11	0.29
All White Varieties	0.30	0.42	0.68	0.40	0.61	0.47
Cabernet Sauvignon	0.30	0.25	0.33	0.23	0.38	0.25
Merlot	0.15	0.32	0.38	0.10	—	0.19
Zinfandel	0.37	0.17	0.07	−0.29	0.07	−0.16
Pinot Noir	0.39	0.30	—	0.72	—	0.42
All Red Varieties	0.36	0.35	0.27	0.17	0.18	0.26
All Varieties	0.34	0.38	0.34	0.22	0.30	0.31
			(b) 1990–2008			
Average annual percentage change						
Sauvignon Blanc	0.18	0.39	0.08	0.37	0.42	0.21
French Colombard	−0.05	—	0.19	0.04	—	0.04
Chardonnay	0.35	0.49	0.39	0.22	0.00	0.32
Chenin Blanc	0.12	0.72	0.23	0.16	0.07	0.20
All White Varieties	0.36	0.63	0.69	0.26	0.25	0.43
Cabernet Sauvignon	0.50	0.49	0.46	0.29	0.53	0.42
Merlot	0.44	0.55	0.44	0.18	0.35	0.40
Zinfandel	1.11	1.01	1.02	0.33	0.60	0.55
Pinot Noir	0.88	0.63	0.75	1.49	0.26	0.87
All Red Varieties	0.72	0.75	0.96	0.31	0.49	0.53
All Varieties	0.57	0.69	0.85	0.36	0.43	0.53

Notes: Entries in this table are average annual percentage changes, computed as ln (final value) − ln (initial value) divided by the number of years and multiplied by 100. For some years and some varieties, records are unavailable. In the table, this is indicated by "—."

Source: Created by the authors using data from NASS/CDFA Grape Crush Reports, 1981–2010.

localized data make for better-fitting models, weather station data approximate the disaggregated data quite well (see also, Haeger and Storchmann, 2006). We attempted to find stations that were geographically central to wine-growing areas within each district, while making sure that the station locations were not at higher altitudes, or were otherwise different from the areas where winegrapes are grown. In some instances, it was difficult to find a well-located station for which data were available for each month in the entire span of time we are examining. Some stations are relatively new, and so do not have historical data reaching more than several years back. Other stations have been shut down or have large gaps in reporting. As a result, we used some data from stations that were not ideal for our purposes, and we used the same weather station for districts 11 and 12.[16] Faced with a similar problem, Storchmann (2005) regressed Rhine wine quality on English weather from 1700 to 2003.

We tried the model in equation (11) with different aggregations of varieties and districts in preliminary analysis. To reduce the dimensions of the problem of reporting and interpreting results we opted to aggregate crush districts into four larger regions based on the average price of wine grapes in 2008. Table 2 shows the districts as classified. Similarly, rather than model individually every winegrape variety we included various aggregates such as "red" versus "white," and "premium" versus "non-premium" varieties, where "premium" included Cabernet Sauvignon, Merlot, and Chardonnay (we tried including Pinot Noir as well, but the results were not affected much).

---

[16]We were able to obtain data from the NOAA website for a number of weather stations in the Napa Valley on monthly average temperatures for the years 1990 through 2007, that we could use to compute our growing season heat index. None of these stations is located in the center of the vineyard area in the Napa Valley, and away from urban and other influences, as would be ideal for the purpose. Temperatures vary significantly within the valley, tending to increase as you go North and East, and consequently particular locations may not be fully representative of the Valley as a whole. In our initial analysis we used data from Markley Cove, which is at a higher altitude on the Eastern edge of Napa County, and somewhat warmer than locations in the Valley floor, especially at the Southern end. Data from Napa City Hospital, at the Southern end of the Valley, reflect a combination of urban influence and generally cooler conditions. Data from Healdsburg, which we used for Sonoma county, are more likely to be representative of the Napa Valley as a whole, because Healdsburg has temperature patterns quite similar to those of St Helena, which is somewhat warmer than the city of Napa, at the Southern end of the Valley. When we tried using data for Healdsburg instead of Markley Cove, the results were essentially identical. Based on this analysis we concluded that the results were not sensitive to the choice, and we report the results we obtained in the first instance, using data from Markley Cove to represent the Napa crush district.

Table 2. Definitions of Regions

Region (average winegrape price in 2008)	Includes crush districts
Ultra-premium (>$2,000/ton)	3 (Sonoma) 4 (Napa)
Premium ($1,000–$2,000/ton)	1 (Mendocino) 2 (Lake) 6 (San Francisco area) 7 (Monterey, San Benito) 8 (Santa Barbara area) 10 (Sierra Foothills area) 15 (Los Angeles, San Bernardino) 16 (San Diego area)
Fine ($500–$1,000/ton)	5 (Solano) 9 (Northern California area) 11 (San Joaquin, part of Sacramento) 17 (parts of Yolo, Sacramento)
Ordinary (<$500/ton)	12 (Merced area) 13 (Fresno area) 14 (Kern, parts of Kings, Tulare)

4.2. *Regression results for model of changes in Brix in California, 1990–2008*

Each of the four columns in Table 3 refers to a different variant of the model in equation (12). We estimated each model by ordinary least squares (OLS) but where possible we used Newey-West robust standard errors for hypothesis testing rather than the conventional OLS robust standard errors. We also ran the model with cluster-robust standard errors, but the effect on the results was very small. As well as estimating each model using conventional OLS we also estimated each model using weighted regression, where the data from each crush district were weighted according to shares of California's total production.[17] The rationale for using a weighted regression is that the data we are using are themselves annual averages for particular varieties within individual crush districts, with very different numbers of observations contributing to the average, depending on the volume of the crush. We prefer the estimates from the model using weighted regression, as reported in

[17] The weights were calculated using STATA's "aweight" option, with the weights for particular observations equal to the corresponding observation-specific tons crushed as a share of total California tonnage in the same year.

Table 3. Brix Regression Results, Annual Observations 1990–2008

Regressor	(1)	(2)	(3)	(4)
		(a) Weighted Observations		
Constant	20.91**	18.79**	19.25**	0.58**
	(0.107)	(0.447)	(0.418)	(0.424)
	[0.187]	[0.649]	[0.616]	
Trend	0.14**	0.10**	0.02	0.01**
	(0.011)	(0.009)	(0.011)	(0.007)
	[0.020]	[0.015]	[0.018]	
Variety				
Red		0.96**	0.22	0.19**
		(0.087)	(0.158)	(0.091)
		[0.156]	[0.274]	
Premium		1.89**	2.25**	0.36**
		(0.072)	(0.119)	(0.100)
		[0.123]	[0.200]	
Region				
Ultra-premium		1.34**	0.48	0.40**
		(0.121)	(0.176)	(0.116)
		[0.189]	[0.290]	
Premium		1.71**	0.80*	0.50**
		(0.206)	(0.215)	(0.140)
		[0.302]	[0.336]	
Fine		0.28	−0.91*	0.18**
		(0.137)	(0.265)	(0.154)
		[0.241]	[0.463]	
Heat Index		0.04*	0.05*	0.03**
(Growing Season		(0.018)	(0.017)	(0.010)
Average Degree Days)		[0.027]	[0.025]	
Trend × Region				
Ultra-premium			0.09**	−0.01
			(0.014)	(0.009)
			[0.023]	
Premium			0.09**	−0.00
			(0.013)	(0.009)
			[0.021]	
Fine			0.10**	0.00
			(0.023)	(0.013)
			[0.040]	
Trend × Variety				
Red			0.08**	0.00
			(0.005)	(0.008)
			[0.025]	

(Continued)

Table 3. (*Continued*)

Regressor	(1)	(2)	(3)	(4)
	(a) Weighted Observations			
Premium			−0.03**	−0.02**
			(0.0051)	(0.008)
			[0.019]	
Brix (Year-1)				0.35**
				(0.030)
Brix (Year-2)				0.41**
				(0.029)
Brix (Year-3)				0.17**
				(0.033)
Adjusted R^2	0.14	0.49	0.52	0.91
RMSE	1.94	1.49	1.45	0.63
	(b) Unweighted Observations			
Constant	21.87**	19.97**	20.35**	3.69**
	(0.032)	(0.121)	(0.140)	(0.371)
	[0.049]	[0.173]	[0.206]	
Trend	0.14**	0.13**	0.09**	0.03**
	(0.003)	(0.003)	(0.008)	(0.007)
	[0.004]	[0.004]	[0.013]	
Variety				
Red		1.05**	0.77**	0.21**
		(0.031)	(0.063)	(0.078)
		[0.048]	[0.093]	
Premium		0.70**	0.90**	0.18**
		(0.026)	(0.049)	(0.059)
		[0.039]	[0.072]	
Region				
Ultra-premium		1.28**	1.00**	0.50**
		(0.060)	(0.117)	(0.127)
		[0.091]	[0.174]	
Premium		1.25**	0.97**	0.58**
		(0.057)	(0.091)	(0.088)
		[0.085]	[0.139]	
Fine		0.74**	0.38*	0.41**
		(0.057)	(0.107)	(0.104)
		[0.090)	[0.166]	
Heat Index		0.02**	0.02**	0.02**
(Growing Season		(0.005)	(0.005)	(0.004)
Average Degree Days)		[0.006]	[0.006]	

(*Continued*)

Table 3. (*Continued*)

Regressor	(1)	(2)	(3)	(4)
(b) Unweighted Observations				
Trend × Region				
Ultra-premium			0.03	−0.01
			(0.010)	(0.010)
			[0.015]	
Premium			0.03*	−0.01
			(0.008)	(0.007)
			[0.012]	
Fine			0.03*	−0.01
			(0.010)	(0.009)
			[0.015]	
Trend × Variety				
Red			0.03**	0.01
			(0.006)	(0.006)
			[0.008]	
Premium			−0.02**	−0.00
			(0.005)	(0.005)
			[0.006]	
Brix (Year-1)				0.35**
				(0.032)
Brix (Year-2)				0.28**
				(0.036)
Brix (Year-3)				0.17**
				(0.020)
Adjusted R^2	0.14	0.26	0.27	0.61
RMSE	1.83	1.69	1.68	1.20

Notes: OLS robust standard error in parentheses. Newey-West robust standard error in square brackets. **, * Significant at the 1% and 5% levels, respectively, using Newey-West except in column (4). 13,379 observations.

Panel *a* of Table 3. The results from the same models using the unweighted data are also presented for comparison in Panel *b* of Table 3.

In Table 3, Panel *a*, column (1) includes the results from a regression of Brix against trend for all varieties and regions. The model predicts that on average, sugar content of California wine grapes increased by 0.14 degrees Brix per year over the years 1990–2008 from a base of 21.7 in 1989, a predicted increase of 2.5 degrees Brix, or 11.6% over the period. In column (2) the model is augmented with a weather variable (the heat index for the growing season), and various dummy variables for Variety and Region, retaining the assumption of a single trend growth rate applying to all varieties and regions. The trend growth rate in this model is slightly lower, 0.10 rather than 0.14 degrees Brix per year.

The coefficient on the heat index is positive and statistically significant indicating that a 1 degree increase in the index would result in a 0.04 degrees Brix increase in the sugar content of wine grapes. This is a comparatively small effect, since a 1 degree increase in the heat index requires a large temperature increase.[18] The first Variety dummy is set equal to 1 for "red" varieties (including Zinfandel, although significant quantities of Zinfandel are used to make White Zinfandel). The second Variety dummy is set equal to 1 for "premium" varieties (Cabernet Sauvignon, Merlot, or Chardonnay). Regional dummies represent the "fine," "premium," and "ultra premium" regions as defined in Table 2 such that the default region is "ordinary." The coefficients on all of the dummy variables for Varieties and Regions are positive and statistically significant (with the marginal exception of the "fine" region), indicating that red varieties, and premium varieties, and grapes from districts commanding price premia could be expected to have higher sugar content at crush compared with the default category.

In this case we interpret the intercept (18.79) as applying to the default category of "non-premium," "white" varieties from the "ordinary" region (crush districts 12, 13, and 14 in the southern San Joaquin Valley). The counterpart for red varieties is higher by 0.96 degrees Brix, the estimated dummy variable coefficient, and the counterpart for premium varieties is higher by 1.89 degrees Brix. It can be seen that compared with the default region ("ordinary") the other regions have higher degrees Brix associated with higher prices for wine grapes: by 0.28 degrees Brix for the "fine" region, 1.71 degrees Brix for the "premium" region and 1.34 degrees Brix for the "ultra premium" region. These results are consistent with the idea that higher sugar content and higher alcohol content are less desirable in lower-priced wine grapes, possibly because of the additional $0.50 cents per gallon tax on wine with more than 14% alcohol by volume.

The model in column (3) augments the model in column (2) with variables that interact the time trend with the dummy variables for varieties and regions. In this model the coefficient on the heat index indicates that a 1 degree increase in the index would result in a 0.05 degrees Brix increase

[18]For instance, an increase by 1 degree Fahrenheit in both the average daily minimum and the average daily maximum temperature throughout the six-month growing period would imply 1 degree increase in the index.

in the sugar content of wine grapes, slightly higher than that in the model without interaction terms, but the coefficient on the time trend (the growth rate for the default category) and several of the coefficients on the dummy variables for Varieties and Regions are no longer statistically significant. Still, premium varieties (but no longer red varieties) and grapes from the premium and fine districts (but not the ultra-premium district) could be expected to have higher sugar content at crush compared with the default category.

The interaction terms indicate significantly faster growth rates in sugar content for red varieties and premium varieties, and for grapes from the premium and fine regions, compared with the default; they indicate a slower growth rate for the ultra-premium region. The coefficients on the interaction terms represent the additional growth in degrees Brix per year for the dummy category relative to the default. The default category is non-premium, white varieties in the ordinary wine region, for which the trend growth rate is 0.02 degrees Brix per year from a base of 19.25 degrees Brix. Thus, for instance, for a premium white variety in the premium region, the corresponding estimate is a trend growth rate of 0.14 (0.02 + 0.09 + 0.03) degrees Brix per year from a base of 22.30 (19.25 + 2.25 + 0.80) degrees Brix.

Column (4) of Table 3 represents the same model as in column (3) augmented with lagged values of the dependent variable. We experimented with the number of lags of the dependent variable to include. The adjusted R-squared is maximized and the Akaike Information Criterion (AIC) is minimized when three lags are included, so that is the model we are reporting. In models with lagged dependent variables we could not compute Newey-West measures and so we report the OLS robust standard errors. Notably the coefficients on all three lagged-dependent variables are individually statistically significant, and diminishing with lag length, and they sum to 0.93, which means that in this model shocks have very persistent effects on the dependent variable. In addition, the long-run impact of a shock is on the order of 10–20 times its initial impact.[19] This implication of the model might not be equally plausible for all types of shocks. Otherwise, this model is to be preferred, on grounds of its superior statistical performance, to the one in column (3) that omits the lagged values of the dependent variable.

The coefficients for this model are generally plausible, and they are largely consistent with those of the variant in column (3). The coefficient

[19]The long-run multiplier for a permanent increase is equal to the short-run multiplier, divided by one minus the sum of the coefficients on the lagged dependent variable: $1/(1-0.93) = 14.3$.

on the heat index indicates that a 1 degree increase in the average heat index would result in a 0.03 degrees Brix increase in the sugar content of wine grapes in the current year. Taking the lagged dependent variables into account, a permanent increase in the heat index by 1 degree Fahrenheit would imply a 0.43 degrees Brix increase in the sugar content of wine grapes in the ultimate long run. Compared with the default variety, non-premium white, for red varieties sugar content is higher by 0.19 degrees Brix and for premium varieties it is higher by 0.36 degrees Brix. As in the other models, compared with the default region ("ordinary") the other regions have higher degrees Brix associated with higher prices for wine grapes: by 0.18 degrees Brix for the "fine" region, 0.50 degrees Brix for the "premium" region and 0.40 degrees Brix for the "ultra premium" region. Importantly, none of the coefficients on interactions of trend with region, or trend with red varieties, is statistically significant. For these categories the coefficient on the trend is the same as for the default category, 0.01 degrees Brix per year. Only for premium varieties is the trend growth rate significantly different: it is lower by 0.02 degrees Brix per year.

Of particular interest here is the relative importance of the heat index as an explanation of the rise in Brix. Across all the models, the results suggest that even a substantial rise in average temperature (or the average of the daily maximum and minimum temperatures) during the growing season would have had only modest effects on the sugar content of wine grapes. In fact, however, our data do not show a substantial rise in temperature between 1990 and 2007, as measured by the heat index. Table 4 includes two measures of the average trend rate in the index for each crush district: (a) the simple average of the annual proportional growth rates as measured by the logarithmic difference, and (b) the trend growth rate, from a regression of the logarithm of the index against a time trend. The estimates are expressed as annual percentage growth rates, and they include a mixture of small positive and negative numbers, none of which is statistically significantly different from zero. This outcome reflects the fact that the year-to-year movements in the index are large relative to any underlying trend that can be discerned. This aspect is revealed clearly in Figure 6, which represents the weighted heat index for California, in which the district-specific indexes are weighted according to the district shares of the total tonnage produced.

Combining the negligible trend in the heat index with its low coefficient in the model, our results imply that warming average temperatures in the growing season did not contribute substantially or significantly to the increase in sugar content of California's wine grapes during the almost

Table 4. Trends in the Heat Index by Crush District and for California, 1990–2008

Crush district	Annualized average change (%)	100*Slope from regression of Ln (Heat) on trend
	Percent per year	
1	−0.30	−0.23 (0.357)
2	−0.18	0.11 (0.722)
3	0.58	0.75 (0.007)
4	0.01	0.20 (0.374)
5	0.03	−0.01 (0.979)
6	−0.50	−0.16 (0.600)
7	−0.69	−0.55 (0.271)
8	−0.60	−0.05 (0.919)
9	0.02	0.14 (0.445)
10	0.85	1.01 (0.004)
11	−0.19	−0.09 (0.725)
12	−0.19	−0.09 (0.725)
13	0.22	0.25 (0.224)
14	0.22	0.26 (0.312)
15	0.04	0.27 (0.249)
16	−0.31	−0.83 (0.033)
17	0.07	0.28 (0.195)
State average (Weighted)	0.06	0.12 (0.405)

Notes: The weather station is the same for Districts 11 and 12. The annual heat index is a weighted average across crush districts, where the weights are tons crushed in the respective districts as a share of the total California tonnage. Standard errors in parentheses.

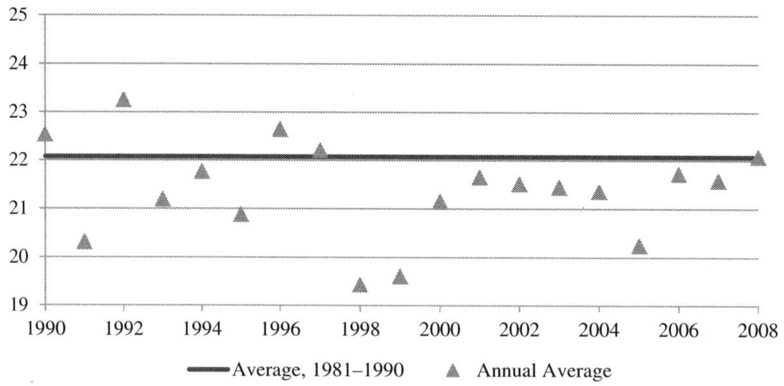

Figure 6. Growing Season Heat Index, California Weighted Average, 1990–2008

Notes: The annual heat index is a weighted average across crush districts where the weights are tons crushed in the respective districts as a share of the total California tonnage.

Source: Created by the authors using data from NOAA NCDC Climate Radar Data Inventories, 1980–2009.

twenty-year period 1990–2008. Other factors in the model do account for much of the rise in sugar content, including changes in the varietal mix and location of production. Some is attributed statistically to underlying trends that are not captured by specific variables in the model and might reflect elements of climate change not well represented by our heat index. Regardless of the cause, the rise in sugar content of grapes implies increases in alcohol content of wine that might not be desired by winemakers or consumers.

5. Changes in Alcohol Content of Wine: Too Much of a Good Thing?

Detailed data on the alcohol content of California wines are not available. While every wine bottle reports a figure for alcohol content on the label, the tolerances are wide and the information content is therefore limited. Specifically, U.S. law allows a range of plus or minus 1.5% for wine with 14% alcohol by volume or less, and plus or minus 1.0% for wine with more than 14% alcohol by volume. Wineries may have incentives to deliberately distort the information because the tax rate is higher for higher alcohol wine or for marketing reasons, if consumers prefer particular alcohol percentages. Consequently, label claims concerning alcohol content may be misleading. However, the Liquor Control Board of Ontario (LCBO), which has a monopoly on the importation of wine for sale in the province of Ontario, Canada, tests every wine it imports and records a number of characteristics including the alcohol content. We have obtained access to 18 years of LCBO data comprising information on a total of 129,123 samples composed of 80,421 red wines and 46,985 white wines. For each sample a number of measures are reported including the label claim of alcohol content and the actual alcohol content.

Here we report some preliminary analysis. Table 5 shows the average alcohol content of red wine, white wine, and both red and white wine from California tested by the LCBO in 1990 and in 2008. The data show that the average alcohol percentage increased by 0.30%, with a larger increase for white wine (0.38%) than for red wine (0.25%). This increase in alcohol percentage is consistent with an increase in the sugar content of the grapes used to make that wine of 0.55 degrees Brix, on average. Such an increase in degrees Brix over a 10 year period, while substantial, implies a relatively small growth rate compared with the actual growth. Further work remains to be done to examine the other characteristics of the wine tested.

The LCBO also records the alcohol percentage claimed on the wine label. We compared the true alcohol percentage and the label claims and found

Table 5. Alcohol Percentage of California Wine Measured by the LCBO: 1990 versus 2000

		Red wine	White wine	All wine
1990	Number of observations	329	152	481
	Mean (Standard deviation)	13.14 (0.65)	13.04 (0.96)	13.10 (0.77)
2000	Number of observations	115	171	286
	Mean (Standard deviation)	13.39 (1.44)	13.41 (0.84)	13.40 (1.12)
	Average difference in means (Standard error)	0.25 (0.10)	0.38 (0.10)	0.30 (0.07)
	t_1 (equal variances)	-2.51^{**}	-3.83^{**}	-4.36^{**}
	t_2 (unequal variances)	-1.81^{*}	-3.79^{**}	-3.97^{**}
	F	0.21^{**}	1.32^{*}	0.47^{**}

Notes: **, * Significant at the 1% and 10% levels of significance, respectively. t_1 and t_2 report the results of t-tests for a paired comparison under assumptions of equal and unequal variances, respectively. F is the F-value for a test of equal variances.

some remarkable discrepancies. On average across 7,920 observations of California wines, the actual alcohol percentage (13.35% by volume) exceeded the declared alcohol percentage (12.63% by volume) by 0.72% by volume. Further work is needed to examine more fully the nature of this discrepancy before we can evaluate causes. It seems unlikely that wineries are making consistent errors of this magnitude in measuring the true alcohol content of the wine. One possibility is that wine producers may be attempting to avoid tax, given that tax rates vary with alcohol percentage; another is that there may be marketing advantages from having label claims of alcohol percentages that are consistent with consumers' expectations for given types of wine; a third is that they simply cannot be bothered getting it right.

6. Conclusions

The work in this chapter has documented a substantial rise in the sugar content of wine grapes in California since 1980, and we have analyzed in detail patterns since 1990. All regions of production and all varieties grown have experienced some increase. We investigated the patterns among varieties and regions to try to shed light on the role of nurture, in terms of management choices by vignerons, versus nature, in terms of climate change as factors contributing to this growth. It is difficult to devise clean, definitive tests of these competing possibilities, given the complex relationships involved and the many dimensions for responses and interactions. However, we were able to distinguish some interesting patterns.

Previous studies have shown some increase in measures of temperature in California over the longer term, which may have contributed to changes in winegrape characteristics including sugar content at harvest. We used a measure of heat during the growing season for wine grapes to attempt to account for any direct effect of climate change. This measure itself exhibits large year-to-year swings making it difficult to discern clear trends in it. The variable contributed statistically significantly to the models, and showed that an increase in heat during the growing season would contribute to an increase in the sugar content of grapes. However, the heat index did not exhibit any statistically significant growth during the growing season and, in any event, its coefficient was small. Hence, this variable did not account for much of the growth of the average sugar content of grapes, compared with the other variables in the model.

Sugar content of grapes at harvest was relatively high for red varieties and premium varieties, and for grapes from ultra-premium and premium regions. The same categories tended to show evidence of faster growth rates in sugar content as well, but here the story is a little mixed, depending on the details of the model. In all of the models, however, the analysis shows a higher propensity for growth in sugar content for premium varieties, compared with non-premium varieties, even though premium varieties had higher sugar content to begin with. This feature and the patterns of the level of sugar content among regions and varieties could be consistent with a "Parker effect" where higher sugar content is an unintended consequence of wineries responding to market demand and seeking riper flavored, more-intense wines through longer hang times. A similar story holds for red (versus white varieties) in the models without lagged dependent variables, but not in the models with lagged dependent variables.

Regional patterns are important in relation to the average sugar content of grapes, but less so with regard to trends in sugar content. Using a definition of regions based on the average price of wine grapes, we found that the region with the lowest price of wine grapes (under $500 per ton) had significantly lower average degrees Brix at crush compared with all other regions. This finding could reflect the fact that sugar content is being managed in the vineyard, perhaps with a view to avoiding taxes that are disproportionately high on lower-valued wine. But independent of tax effects it may also be profitable, in producing lower-priced wines, to opt for a higher yield of wine per ton of grapes in exchange for lower Brix.

Preliminary analysis of data from the LCBO indicates that the alcohol content of California wine has risen in concert with the rise in sugar content of wine grapes, although possibly not to the same extent. This result is consistent with the fact that significant effort is being spent in wineries to remove alcohol from wine, which suggests that to some extent at least alcohol is a nuisance by-product in some wines; possibly because of tax implications. The finding that label claims appear systematically to understate the alcohol content of California wine sampled by the LCBO may reflect a perception that higher alcohol content diminishes the consumer value of certain wines.

Acknowledgments

We are grateful for data provided by the Liquor Control Board of Ontario and Calanit Bar-Am. The work for this project was partly supported by the University of California Agricultural Issues Center. Authorship is alphabetical. We thank the editor and a referee for helpful comments and suggestions.

References

Ashenfelter, O., Ashmore, D., and Lalonde, R. (1995). Bordeaux wine vintage quality and the weather. *Chance*, 8, 7–13.

Ashenfelter, O., and Byron, R.P. (1995). Predicting the quality of an unborn Grange. *The Economic Record*, 7(212), 40–53.

Ashenfelter, O. (2008). Predicting the prices and quality of Bordeaux wines. *The Economic Journal*, 118, 40–53.

Ashenfelter, O., and Storchmann, K. (2010). Using a hedonic model of solar radiation to assess the economic effect of climate change: The case of Mosel valley vineyards. *The Review of Economics and Statistics*, 92(2), 333–349.

Bar-Am, C. (2012). The economic effects of climate change of the California wine-grape industry. Unpublished doctoral dissertation, University of California, Davis (in process).

Haeger, J.W., and Storchmann, K. (2006). Prices of American Pinot Noir wines: Climate, craftsmanship, critics. *Agricultural Economics*, 35, 76–78.

Jones, G.V. (2005). Climate change in the western United States grape growing regions. *Acta Horticulturae* (ISHS), 689, 41–60.

Jones, G.V. (2006). Climate and terroir: Impacts of climate variability and change on wine. In: Macqueen, R.W. and Meinert, L.D. (eds.), *Fine Wine and Terroir — The Geoscience Perspective*, Geological Association of Canada, St. John's, Newfoundland, 203–216.

Jones, G.V. (2007). Climate change: Observations, projections, and general implications for viticulture and wine production. *Economics Department Working Paper* No. 7, Whitman College, Walla Walla, WA (online: http://hdl.handle.net/10349/593).

Jones, G.V., and Goodrich, G.B. (2008). Influence of climate variability on wine regions in the western USA and on wine quality in the Napa Valley. *Climate Research*, 35, 241–254.

Jones, G.V., White, M.A., Cooper, O.R., and Storchmann, K. (2005). Climate change and global wine quality. *Climatic Change*, 73(3), 319–343.

Lecocq, S., and Visser, M. (2006). Spatial variations in weather conditions and wine prices in Bordeaux. *Journal of Wine Economics*, 1(2), 114–124.

NASS/CDFA (1980–2010a). Final grape crush report. Various years. Sacramento, CA: California Department of Food and Agriculture (CDFA) and U.S. Department of Agriculture, National Agricultural Statistics Service (NASS) California Field Office. Sacramento, CA. http://www.cdfa.ca.gov/statistics/files/CDFA_Sec7.pdf.

NASS/CDFA (1980–2010b). Final grape acreage report. Various years. Sacramento, CA. http://www.nass.usda.gov/Statistics_by_State/California/Publications/Grape_Acreage/200804gabtb01.pdf.

Nemani, R.R., White, M.A., Cayan, D.R., Jones, G.V., Running, S.W., and Coughlan, J.C. (2001). Asymmetric climatic warming improves California vintages. *Climate Research*, 19(1), 25–34.

NOAA/NCDC (2010). Climate Radar Data Inventories. Available from http://lwf.ncdc.noaa.gov/oa/climate/stationlocator.html. Accessed January 2011.

Shanken, M. (2001). *The U.S. Wine Market, 2001 Edition.* New York: M. Shanken Communications.

Storchmann, K. (2005). English weather and Rhine wine quality: An ordered probit model. *Journal of Wine Research*, 16(2), 105–119.

Tate, A.B. (2001). Global warming's impact on wine. *Journal of Wine Research*, 12, 95–109.

Weare, B.C. (2009). How will changes in global climate influence California? *California Agriculture*, 63(2)(April–June), 59–66. Available at: http://ucanr.org/repository/CAO/issue.cfm?volume=63&issue=2.

Webb, L.B., Whetton, P.H., and Barlow, E.W.R. (2005). Impact on Australian viticulture from greenhouse induced temperature change. In: Zerger, A. and Argent, R.M. (eds.), *MODSIM 2005 International Congress on Modelling and Simulation.* Modelling and Simulation Society of Australia and New Zealand, December 2005, Melbourne, pp. 170–176.

White, M.A., Diffenbaugh, N.S., Jones, G.V., Pal, J.S., and Giorgi, F. (2006). Extreme heat reduces and shifts United States premium wine production in the 21st century. *Proceedings of the National Academy of Sciences*, 103(30), 11217–11222.

Part III

Hedonic Analysis of Wine Prices

Chapter 7

Estimation of a Hedonic Price Equation for Bordeaux Wine: Does Quality Matter*

Pierre Combris[†], Sébastien Lecocq[†], and Michael Visser[‡]

[†]*INRA, UR1303 ALISS Alimentation et Sciences Sociales,*
F-94205 Ivry-sur-Seine, France
Pierre.Combris@inra.fr
Sebastien.Lecocq@inra.fr

[‡]*CREST, CNRS, ENSAE, University of Paris-Saclay and CRED,*
University of Paris 2, France
Michael.Visser@ensae.fr

In this chapter the hedonic price technique is applied to Bordeaux wine. In the hedonic price function we include not only the "objective" characteristics appearing on the label of the bottle, but also the sensory characteristics of the wine. Our data come from an experimental study in which juries have evaluated and graded a sample of Bordeaux wines. The estimation of the hedonic price equation shows that the market price is essentially determined by the objective characteristics. The estimation of a jury grade equation shows that quality, unlike the market price, is essentially determined by the sensory characteristics.

1. Introduction

Covering an area of more than 100,000 hectares, the Bordeaux wine region is undoubtedly the world's largest wine region. It produces more than 660 million bottles per year, varying from simple and plain table wines to the most prestigious wines such as Pétrus, Margaux, Lafite-Rothschild, Latour, Yquem, Haut-Brion and others. The Bordeaux wine region produces bottles that can cost just FFr10 but also more than ten thousand francs, young wines that are ready to drink as well as wines that improve even after decades of keeping, wines that are made from different combinations and proportions of

*This article originally appeared in *The Economic Journal* (1997), 107, 390–402.

grape varieties, and wines that originate from various sorts of soils. Clearly, Bordeaux wines are not the same, but possess different characteristics and vary in quality. This makes Bordeaux wine a suitable product for a hedonic price analysis.

The hedonic price method is a useful approach to study the price–quality relationship of a product. The method amounts to a (possibly nonlinear) regression analysis of the price on the characteristics of the product. The implicit price of a characteristic is defined as the derivative of the price with respect to the product attribute. Rosen (1974) has shown under which market conditions the implicit price can be interpreted as the value consumers place on an additional unit of the characteristic. If the estimated implicit price turns out to be not significantly different from zero, then the characteristic is not valued by consumers, or the characteristic is not considered important or relevant in connection with the product.

The earliest reference to this literature seems to be Waugh (1928). He observed that prices of certain fresh vegetables varied considerably on the Boston wholesale market, and regressed the price on various physical characteristics of the vegetables. The notion "hedonic pricing method" is generally attributed to Court (1939). He applied the method to automobiles, and included several technical characteristics of the car in the hedonic price equation. It was not until Griliches (1961) that Court's work was really revived. Griliches' work on the hedonic price method had an important impact and immediately initiated a vast body of empirical work, with applications to the automobile industry (some recent references are Atkinson and Halverson (1984), Arguea and Hsiao (1993), and Couton *et al.* (1996)), the computer industry (Chow, 1967; Triplett, 1989), and the housing market (Witte *et al.*, 1979; Palmquist, 1984; Bartik, 1987).

As this list of applications shows, the hedonic price method has been applied mainly to durable goods. The application that we consider in this chapter is different in two respects. The first obvious difference is that Bordeaux wine is not a durable good, but a food product.[1] The second difference is that, unlike durable goods, not all the relevant characteristics of wine are easy to identify and to measure.[2] Although the label on the wine bottle gives important information about the vintage year, the name of the château, the

[1]Other applications of the hedonic price technique to food products are Ladd and Suvannunt (1976), Stanley and Tschirhart (1991), and the references in these two papers.
[2]Waugh also considered food products, but the relevant product characteristics were measurable physical properties that were readily available to all consumers by simple observation.

eventual ranking of the wine, etc..., this is only part of the story. Indeed, labels do not in general provide information on the sensory characteristics (taste, texture, or odor) of a wine. The purpose of this chapter is to estimate a hedonic price function for Bordeaux wine that includes both the label characteristics and the sensory characteristics. This will allow us to assess how much value consumers implicitly place on the label and sensory characteristics. It will also allow us to answer the intriguing question posed in the title of this chapter: does quality matter? As will be shown in the chapter, there is strong evidence that, at least in our data, quality is mainly determined by the sensory characteristics of a wine. By examining the estimates of the parameters associated with the sensory characteristics, we are able to tell to what extent quality matters in explaining market prices.

As far as we know, there are two other studies on the hedonic pricing of wine. In Nerlove (1995), which came to our attention while the present chapter was being revised, a hedonic price function is estimated using Swedish data. He argues that the Swedish wine market is not competitive (it is argued that the market prices and the product characteristics can be taken as exogenous to the Swedish consumer), and that a standard hedonic regression is not appropriate. The author proposes therefore an alternative method to draw inferences about consumer preferences. In Oczkowski (1994) the method is applied to Australian table wine. The main difference with the present study is that he essentially considers objective and easily observable characteristics (vintage year, vineyard region, grape variety, etc...). The sensory characteristics are lacking in his data set. Our data source, in contrast, contains detailed information about the sensory characteristics of wines, and has a number of other advantages over the sort of information one can find in wine guides.

The chapter is organized as follows. In Section 2, the data are presented. In Section 3, we present the empirical results. Section 4 contains some concluding remarks.

2. The Data

Natural candidates for our data source are the widely published and easily accessible wine guides. We feel, however, that most of these sources are inappropriate for estimating hedonic price equations. Indeed, wine guides do not in general verify the following conditions. First, all the wines that are tasted should be included in the sample, regardless of whether the wine is considered good or bad. In wine guides the wines of inferior quality are often deliberately under-represented for commercial reasons. High-quality wines, and in particular the well-known *cru classé* wines (like Lafite-Rothschild, Margaux, Latour, Haut-Brion, etc...), are the wines in which many wine fans are simply most interested.[3] Second, bottles that are specially prepared to participate in a wine contest must be avoided, as they are not, in general, representative for the overall production of the château. Third, in a concern for objectivity, the bottles must be evaluated and tasted by independent experts. In wine guides it is often the author, possibly assisted by a team of colleagues, who evaluates the wines. If at the same time the guide is sponsored by wine producers (which is often the case), then some objectivity may be lacking. Fourth, tasting must occur blindly. In evaluating a wine, the members of a jury must not be influenced in advance by the name of the château, the appellation, the ranking or the vintage. Fifth, all the wines in the sample must be bought under the same conditions. Differences in price levels between bottles of wine should reflect differences in wine characteristics, and not differences in purchase circumstances. This means that one should for instance avoid a sampling scheme in which part of the bottles are bought directly at the château, and another part at say the wine grocery.

To the best of our knowledge, the only data source satisfying these five conditions comes from an experimental study held by the *Institut National de la Consommation* (INC). The results from this study are published in the December 1992 issue of a French review called *50 Millions de Consommateurs*. We have extracted our data from this review.

Between 15 and 26 June 1992, about twenty collaborators of the INC and members of the *Confédération Syndicale du Cadre de Vie Aquitaine* visited at random 600 Bordeaux wine cultivators. In an effort to reproduce the environment in which an ordinary customer buys wine, no prior rendezvous was made with the wine cultivators. Fifty-nine cultivators were not present at the time of the visit. All the remaining 541 wine producers decided to participate in the study. At each participating château two bottles were purchased. The second bottle was purchased in case the first bottle had some defect. In most cases the buyers themselves have chosen the samples, in order to avoid the contest bottles. All the purchased wines were brought to the *Institut National de la Recherche Agronomique* (INRA) in Toulouse (France).

The tasting took place between 29 June and 4 July, in the tasting room of INRA. The experiment was organized by the oenology center of the Paul-Sabatier University of Toulouse. Three juries took part in the test. Each jury

[3]This is for instance the case with Bradfer *et al.* (1992), which is a guide on the best wines in France.

consisted of four persons: a professor of oenology from the Paul-Sabatier University, a recently graduated oenologist, a practicing oenologist, and a wine waiter. Although we know that each wine in the sample is evaluated by one jury, we cannot tell from our data which jury tasted which wine. Therefore, we cannot identify jury specific effects, and we will implicitly assume that the three juries are identical.

The evaluation of a wine generally consists of three parts: a visual examination, an olfactory examination, and a gustatory examination. The visual examination reveals the color of the wine, its brilliance, and its limpidity. It allows the jury members to make a judgment about the maturation of a wine. The visual examination can influence the jury before the actual tasting (olfactory and gustatory examination) starts. For this reason it was decided by the INC to omit the visual examination from the experiment.

After the tasting the jury is requested to write a technical comment on the wine. In the comment, that is published by the review *50 Millions de Consommateurs*, the jury members report their olfactory findings (the aromatic intensity of the wine, the finesse of the aromas, the complexity of the aromas), their gustatory findings (the firmness of the attack, the suppleness of the wine, the flatness, whether the wine is considered fat, the harmony between the components, the finish, etc...), and they make some general remarks about the wine (about the alcohol level in the wine, whether the wine needs further keeping or not, etc...). In the sequel of the chapter we shall refer to the above variables as the sensory characteristics of the wine. Each jury member also assigns a grade (between 0 and 20) to the wine. The review has published the average of the four grades, rounded off to the nearest quarter of a point (e.g., an average of 12.68 becomes 12.75).

For each wine, the review also gives information about the name of the château, the ranking of the wine (*grand cru classé* or *cru classé*, *cru bourgeois*, or *cru non classé*), the color of the wine (red or white; there are no rosé wines in the sample), the vintage (1989, 1990, or 1991), and the appellation (all the 54 Bordeaux appellations are represented in our sample; for practical reasons, these 54 appellations are regrouped into six larger appellations according to criteria proposed by the *Conseil Interprofessionnel du Vin de Bordeaux*). We shall refer to these variables as the objective characteristics of the wine. Recall that the objective characteristics are not known by the jury. Finally, the review gives for each wine the price level at which the bottle is purchased.

From the original sample of 541 observations we retain 519 wine bottles. Three bottles were eliminated because they were not evaluated (two samples were defective, and one was corked). The remaining observations were dropped because they were purchased at the wine merchant and not at the château (violation of condition five), or because the wine was extracted from the cask or the vat. Table 1 contains the complete list of the available variables in the sample, together with their abbreviations and some simple descriptive statistics.

Before turning to the model and the empirical results we need to give some further details about the sensory characteristics. Ideally, the sensory characteristics are determined from standard predefined forms in which the jury evaluates the different characteristics of the wine by ticking appropriate boxes. As outlined above, this is unfortunately not the way our sensory characteristics are defined. Instead, they come from the technical comment provided by the jury. To a certain extent it is up to the jury to decide how to write and what to include in its comment. Although the 519 comments in the sample show much resemblance (remember that there are only three juries), there is some heterogeneity, and in particular in a considerable number of technical comments some subjective characteristics are missing. To solve this missing variable problem we have to make some working hypotheses.

First we consider the case when the sensory characteristic is a dichotomous variable. If the characteristic is not mentioned in the comment we then assume that the wine does not possess this characteristic. The assumption we have made here does not appear very strong in the sense that *the absence* of a characteristic is never mentioned. Hence it is very likely that juries indeed only mention a sensory characteristic if the wine actually possesses it.

Next we consider the case when the sensory characteristic is a polytomous variable. For the FAT variable, the medium modality is never mentioned. Only the plump and lean modalities appear in the comments, the former indicating a quality and the latter a default. Following the same kind of reasoning as for the dichotomous variables, we assume that if the FAT variable is missing then the wine is medium fat. For the $HARM$ variable, we can infer the missing observations from other characteristics or other indications available in the jury's comment. Details can be obtained from the authors upon request. For the two remaining polytomous variables, $INTE$ and $FINI$, we cannot rely on the hypothesis made in the case of the FAT variable, because the medium modality appears relatively often. Therefore, if $INTE$ or $FINI$ are missing we cannot assume that they are equal to the medium modality. Furthermore, contrary to the $HARM$ variable, if $INTE$ or $FINI$ are missing they cannot be inferred from other indications in the comments. The variables $INTE$ and/or $FINI$ are missing for 326 observations. Hence there are 193 observations for which all characteristics are available.

Table 1. Descriptive Statistics

Variables	Abbreviations	Modalities	Descriptive statistics
Price	*PRICE*	Continuous	Mean = 52.78 Standard deviation = 31.05
Jury grade	*GRADE*	Continuous	Mean = 11.21 Standard deviation = 2.41
Sensory characteristics			
Olfactory examination			
Aromatic intensity	*INTE*	Strong = 3; Classic = 2; Discreet = 1	45.08; 32.64; 22.28
Finesse of aromas	*FINE*	Yes = 2; No = 1	15.61; 84.39
Complexity of aromas	*COMP*	Yes = 2; No = 1	23.70; 76.30
Gustatory examination			
Firmness of attack	*FIRM*	Yes = 2; No = 1	19.85; 80.15
Excessive acidity	*ACID*	Yes = 2; No = 1	13.87; 86.13
Suppleness	*SUPP*	Yes = 2; No = 1	28.90; 71.10
Flatness	*FLAT*	Yes = 2; No = 1	8.29; 91.71
Fat	*FAT*	Plump = 3; Medium = 2; Lean = 1	17.34; 79.19; 3.47
Well-concentrated	*WCON*	Yes = 2; No = 1	19.08; 80.92
Harmony between the components	*HARM*	Well balanced = 3; Balanced = 2; Unbalanced = 1	18.69; 50.29; 31.02
Presence of fine tannins	*TANI*	Yes = 2; No = 1	19.08; 80.92
Finish	*FINI*	Long = 3; Medium = 2; Short = 1	34.20; 50.78; 15.02
General remarks			
Alcohol excess	*ALCO*	Yes = 2; No = 1	15.41; 84.59
Traces of staleness	*STAL*	Yes = 2; No = 1	10.60; 89.40
Touch of reduction	*REDU*	Yes = 2; No = 1	3.47; 96.53
Keeping in vault needed	*KEEP*	Yes = 2; No = 1	29.87; 70.13
Objective characteristics Ranking	*RANK*	Cru or grand cru classé = 3; Cru bourgeois = 2; Cru non classé = 1	6.74; 9.25; 84.01
Red wine	*RED*	Yes = 2; No = 1	82.08; 17.92
White wine	*WHIT*	Yes = 2; No = 1	17.92; 82.08

(*Continued*)

Table 1. (*Continued*)

Variables	Abbreviations	Modalities	Descriptive statistics
1989 vintage	*AN*89	Yes = 2; No = 1	61.66; 38.34
1990 vintage	*AN*90	Yes = 2; No = 1	33.33; 66.67
1991 vintage	*AN*91	Yes = 2; No = 1	5.01; 94.99
Bordeaux group	*BORD*	Yes = 2; No = 1	15.99; 84.01
Côtes group	*COTE*	Yes = 2; No = 1	15.22; 84.78
Médoc and Graves group	*MEGR*	Yes = 2; No = 1	20.81; 79.19
Saint-Emilion Pomerol Fronsac group	*SEPF*	Yes = 2; No = 1	30.06; 69.94
Blancs Secs group	*BLSE*	Yes = 2; No = 1	12.91; 87.09
Blancs Doux group	*BLDO*	Yes = 2; No = 1	5.01; 94.99

Notes: The descriptive statistics are based on the complete sample of 519 wines; for the continuous variables we give the mean and standard deviation; for the discrete variables we give the percentage of observations that is equal to the relevant modality; for *INTE* and *FINI* the descriptive statistics are based on the subsample of 193 wines.

3. Empirical Results

3.1. *A preliminary analysis*

In our hedonic price equation the dependent variable is the logarithm of the price of Bordeaux wine, and in the explanatory variables we include all the characteristics of the bottle (the objective and the sensory variables defined in Section 2). It is tempting here to include also the jury grade in the vector of explanatory variables. This, however, would not be correct for two reasons. First, the jury grade is not really a characteristic of the wine, but rather a quality index that depends on the attributes of this wine. In Rosen's (1974) pure competition framework a hedonic price equation is supposed to be a function of intrinsic characteristics alone, and so the jury grade should not be included. Second, since the bottles are purchased *before* tasting takes place, the jury grade cannot, logically speaking, have any influence on the price level.[4]

In Table 2, column (1), we present the OLS estimates of the hedonic price equation based on the 193 observations for which all the characteristics are

[4]The jury grade can have an impact on future prices. In fact, following the publication of the *50 Millions de Consommateurs* review, many châteaux that received a good grade saw the demand for their wine augment considerably (personal communication with the INC). It is likely that these châteaux have responded by augmenting the price of their bottles. Unfortunately, we do not have the data to study this interesting phenomenon.

Table 2. Hedonic Price Equation

	(1)	(2)
Sensory variables		
WCON	0.163 (0.072)	
KEEP	0.207 (0.073)	0.158 (0.037)
Objective variables		
RANK	0.307 (0.051)	0.309 (0.030)
AN89	0.664 (0.111)	0.654 (0.075)
AN90	0.506 (0.112)	0.488 (0.077)
BORD	−0.418 (0.085)	−0.484 (0.052)
COTE	−0.204 (0.088)	−0.314 (0.050)
SEPF	0.260 (0.079)	0.162 (0.042)
BLDO	0.261 (0.096)	0.308 (0.073)
Constant	1.352 (0.327)	1.912 (0.225)
Number of observations	193	519
$\bar{R}^2$	0.662	0.631

Notes: Standard errors in parentheses; (1) results based on the subsample of 193 wines; (2) results based on the complete sample of 519 wines.

available.[5] The $\bar{R}^2$ is equal to 0.662, indicating that the overall fit of the hedonic price equation is relatively good. Given the large number of explanatory variables, we have used a stepwise procedure to select the regressors that are significant at the 5% level. It does not matter here whether we use a backward procedure or a forward procedure. In both cases the final set of selected explanatory variables is the same. In this sense the results are thus very robust. There are nine selected variables (and a constant).

The parameters corresponding to the first five variables in Table 2 take the expected sign: the price level increases if the wine is well concentrated, if the wine needs keeping, and if the wine is well ranked; the price level is also higher for the 1989 and 1990 vintages (the vintages of 1989 and 1990 are generally considered good compared to the 1991 vintage, see, for example, Johnson (1994)). Not much can be said in advance about the signs of the parameters associated with the remaining variables in Table 2. The outcome is essentially an empirical matter. It appears from Table 2 that the price level decreases when the wine originates from the Bordeaux or the Côtes appellation group; the price level increases when the wine originates from the Saint-Emilion Pomeral Fronsac or the Blancs Doux appellation group.

[5]The estimation results in this chapter are obtained with the Stata (version 4.0) software package.

It is remarkable that among the nine variables in Table 2, only two belong to the set of sensory variables.[6] This suggests that the price of a wine is essentially determined by the objective characteristics of the bottle, that is, the characteristics that are easily identifiable and identically perceived by all consumers.

We have given two arguments why it would not be appropriate to include the jury grade as an independent variable in the hedonic price equation. Instead, it seems of interest to consider the logarithm of this variable as a dependent variable, in an equation where the explanatory variables are the characteristics of the wine. In Table 3, column (1), we present the OLS estimates of this jury grade equation, based on the same sample of 193 bottles. For the jury grade equation the $\bar{R}^2$ is equal to 0.658, again indicating a relatively good overall fit. We use a stepwise procedure to select the regressors that are significant at the 5% level. Again, it does not matter whether we use a backward procedure or a forward procedure. There are ten selected variables (and a constant).

The parameters take the expected sign: the jury grade increases if the aromatic intensity of the wine is strong, if the wine has a complex nose, if the wine is considered fat, if the wine is well concentrated, if the harmony between the components is well balanced, if the finish is long, and if the wine needs keeping; the jury grade decreases if the alcohol level in the wine is too high, and if it concerns a 1991 vintage. Not much can be said in advance about the sign of *BLDO*. Table 3 shows that wines from the Blancs Doux group are generally not appreciated by the jury members. Whereas in the hedonic price equation the majority of significant variables are the objective characteristics, the opposite is true for the jury grade equation. Among the ten significant variables in Table 3, eight are sensory variables. This result, together with the fact that all the coefficients of the sensory variables take the expected sign, seems to justify (*ex post*) our codification of the sensory variables. Notice that, contrary to the hedonic price equation, *RANK* does not have a significant effect in the jury grade equation. This result is in support of the widely heard criticism that the ranking system is too old (the Médoc ranking system dates from 1855; the Graves ranking system dates from 1959; the Saint-Emilion ranking system dates from 1954,

[6]One might argue that since the objective variables are highly correlated with the sensory variables, the presence of the former variables prevents the latter to enter the hedonic price equation. To verify this possibility, we have regressed the logarithm of the price on the sensory variables alone. This time again only *WCON* and *KEEP* are the significant variables.

Table 3. Jury Grade Equation

	(1)	(2)
Sensory variables		
INTE	0.034 (0.010)	0.034 (0.006)
FINE		0.076 (0.019)
COMP	0.105 (0.018)	0.075 (0.018)
ACID		0.056 (0.021)
FIRM		0.044 (0.018)
SUPP		0.051 (0.016)
FAT	0.055 (0.017)	0.070 (0.016)
WCON	0.051 (0.022)	0.061 (0.021)
REDU		−0.078 (0.038)
ALCO	−0.085 (0.030)	
HARM	0.044 (0.012)	0.100 (0.011)
TANI		0.040 (0.018)
FINI	0.066 (0.013)	0.061 (0.015)
KEEP	0.059 (0.021)	0.110 (0.018)
Objective variables		
AN91	−0.095 (0.030)	
AN90		0.041 (0.017)
BLDO	−0.055 (0.026)	
WHIT		−0.067 (0.020)
SEPF		0.075 (0.018)
Constant	2.007 (0.081)	1.284 (0.099)
Number of observations	193	519
$\bar{R}^2$	0.658	0.597

Notes: Standard errors in parentheses; (1) results based on the subsample of 193 wines; (2) results based on the complete sample of 519 wines.

but is revised every 10 years, the last time in 1986), often irrelevant and needs to be updated. Our result appears in accordance with the conclusions drawn from a wine-tasting session held in January 1995, in San Francisco (as far as we know, the results of this study were only reported in the press). On the initiative of G. Getty, an American billionaire and a fan of Bordeaux wine, ten of the most famous wine tasters in the world were reunited in San Francisco to taste blindly a sample of Bordeaux wines. The sample contained all the Médoc wines with a ranking (some Graves were also included, but the results regarding these wines were not published). In 1855, 61 Médocs were ranked in five categories, and the jury members in Getty's study were requested to establish a new classification (from 1 to 61). Although the reshuffling did not turn out to be dramatic (for instance, the four first-category wines are still in the top 15), the 1855 and 1995 classifications were certainly not identical (for instance, one fifth-category wine can be found in the top 10). The fact that the hierarchy in the Médoc ranking system is somewhat challenged here is of course not very surprising. Since 1855 a lot of things have changed. Many châteaux have changed ownership, certain châteaux have doubled or even tripled their cultivation surface, new vinification methods have been introduced, etc...

Until now the hedonic price and jury grade equations have been estimated separately. However, the coefficient of correlation between the price level and jury grade is 0.443. It is therefore not unlikely that, conditionally on the explanatory variables, there is dependence as well. Hence, it is not unlikely that the error terms in the hedonic price level and jury grade equations are dependent. For this reason we perform a seemingly unrelated regression of the two equations. The estimated standard errors remain practically unchanged, and the Breusch–Pagan test rejects the hypothesis of dependence between the error terms. This means that, conditionally on the explanatory variables, the price level and jury grade are independent variables.

3.2. *Results based on the complete sample*

The estimations presented in Section 3.1 are based on 193 observations. They come from an initial sample of 519 wine bottles, from which 326 are discarded because one or two explanatory variables are missing. This is a drastic sample reduction, and one might wonder therefore whether the results presented in Section 3.1 are (partly) due to the relatively small size of the sample. To answer this question we perform OLS regressions of the hedonic price equation and jury grade equation on the complete sample of 519 observations, by adding in both equations two dummy variables that indicate if the variables $INTE$ or $FINI$ are missing. The first dummy equals 1 if $INTE$ is missing and is equal to 0 otherwise, the second dummy equals 1 if $FINI$ is missing and is equal to 0 otherwise. If $INTE$ or $FINI$ are missing we set these variables equal to 0. The estimates we obtain via the stepwise procedure (again it does not matter whether we use a backward procedure or forward procedure: the set of selected variables is exactly the same in both cases) suggest that the parameters associated with the two dummies are not significantly different from zero in the hedonic price equation. This in turn suggests that for the hedonic price equation it is not important to control for the fact that $INTE$ and $FINI$ can be missing. In the jury grade equation the parameter associated with the first dummy is also insignificant, but the parameter corresponding to the second dummy is significantly different from zero. Furthermore, as in Section 3.1, the parameter corresponding to $FINI$ is significant. As far as the jury grade equation is concerned it appears important, therefore, to control for the fact that the variable $FINI$ can be missing. In summary, we present the estimates of the following hedonic price and jury grade equations

$$\ln PRICE_i = \mathbf{X}_i\boldsymbol{\alpha} + u_i, \quad i = 1, \dots, n, \tag{1}$$

$$\ln GRADE_i = \mathbf{Z}_i\boldsymbol{\beta} + D_i\gamma + v_i, \quad i = 1, \dots, n, \tag{2}$$

where $\boldsymbol{X}_i$ and $\mathbf{Z}_i$ are the vectors of significant explanatory variables for observation i in the hedonic price equation and jury grade equation respectively, D_i is the dummy variable that is equal to 1 if $FINI_i$ is missing and 0 otherwise, $\boldsymbol{\alpha}$, $\boldsymbol{\beta}$ and γ are unknown parameters ($\boldsymbol{\alpha}$ and $\boldsymbol{\beta}$ are vectors and γ is a scalar), u_i and v_i are error terms with the usual properties, and n represents the total number of observations.

Before discussing the results we want to address the following issue. The jury reports, from which we extract the sensory variables, vary in length. In general, long reports are associated with high-quality wines (i.e., high grades), and *vice versa.*[7] This simply reflects the fact that jury members tend to be more enthusiastic as the tasted wine gets better. The variable $FINI$ is more likely to be missing if the jury report is short. As a consequence, the subsample containing the observations with known $FINI$ consists of wine bottles with comparatively high jury grades. This in turn might imply that a wine with a large error term is more likely to be in the subsample of wines with known $FINI$, and *vice versa.* In terms of (2), this can be interpreted as a negative correlation between the variable D_i and the error term v_i. It is well known that OLS estimation of (2) leads to inconsistent estimates if an explanatory variable is correlated with the error term. We must therefore test whether $\mathrm{E}(D_iv_i) = 0$. To do this we apply the Hausman (1978) test, which in the present context amounts to adding in (2) a variable $\hat{D}_i$, and testing whether the associated parameter of this variable is equal to zero. Here $\hat{D}_i$ denotes the fitted value in a regression of D_i upon a vector of instrumental variables $\mathbf{W}_i$, that is, $\hat{D}_i = \mathbf{W}_i\hat{\boldsymbol{\delta}}$, where $\hat{\boldsymbol{\delta}}$ is the OLS estimate. The vector of instrumental variables $\mathbf{W}_i$ includes $\mathbf{Z}_i$ and all other objective and sensory variables that do not have a significant effect on the jury grade. Since D_i is a binary variable it may be more appropriate to perform the Hausman test

[7] Whereas a high-quality wine is in most cases described by a report of six or seven lines, the report of a low-quality wine rarely exceeds three lines.

by considering $\hat{D}_i = \Phi(\mathbf{W}_i\hat{\boldsymbol{\delta}})$, where $\Phi(.)$ is the distribution function of a standard normal random variable, and $\hat{\boldsymbol{\delta}}$ is the ML estimate obtained from a probit analysis (in this case $\hat{D}_i$ is sometimes called a probability instrument, see Bowden and Turkington (1984)). In both cases the Hausman test does not reject the null hypothesis, and we thus conclude that OLS estimation of (2) leads to consistent estimates of the parameters of interest.

Table 2, column (2), gives the estimates of the hedonic price equation based on the complete sample. A comparison with column (1) shows that the variable $WCON$ is no longer significant, but that otherwise the set of significant variables is exactly the same. The signs of the parameters are also identical, and their magnitudes are of comparable order. Table 3, column (2), gives the estimates of the jury grade equation, in which we control for the fact that the variable $FINI$ can be missing. The estimate of γ is 0.070, and the standard error is 0.034. The estimate of this parameter takes the wrong sign, since we expect that $FINI$ is missing when wines are of lower quality. Since D is found to be exogenous, this unanticipated result is apparently not due to endogeneity problems. Let us first look at the results for the sensory variables. Comparing column (2) with column (1) we see that $ALCO$ is no longer significant, but that otherwise the effect of a larger sample size is to increase the number of significant sensory variables. We only discuss the effects of the newly entered sensory variables (since the parameters corresponding to the variables already present in column (1) take the same sign). The jury grade increases if the wine has a fine nose, if the attack of the wine is considered firm, if the wine is supple, and if the wine contains fine tannins; the jury grade decreases if there is a touch of reduction (bad smell or bad taste due to the presence of sulfur). The only sensory variable that does not have the expected effect is $ACID$: the jury grade increases if the wine is considered too acid. As far as the objective variables are concerned, we see that the variables $AN91$ and $BLDO$ are no longer significant. The newly entered variables are $AN90$ and $SEPF$ (positive effects), and $WHIT$ (negative effect).

Summarizing the results,[8] we see that the general picture that emerged from Section 3.1 is confirmed here, and even reinforced: the hedonic price equation is essentially determined by the objective variables and the jury

[8] A seemingly unrelated regression of (1) and (2) leads to the same conclusion as in Section 3.1: the estimated standard errors remain practically unchanged, and the Breusch–Pagan test rejects the hypothesis of dependence between the error terms.

equation is essentially determined by the sensory variables. We will comment more in detail on these findings in the conclusion.

4. Conclusions

The empirical results in this chapter indicate that the market price of Bordeaux wine can be explained primarily by the objective characteristics appearing on the label of the bottle. On the other hand, the quality of Bordeaux wine, as measured by a jury grade assigned by professional wine tasters, can be explained primarily by the sensory characteristics of the wine. Many variables that are important in explaining quality apparently do not play a role in the determination of the market price. We have two explanations for this conclusion. First, one might argue that tastes are not similar among jury members and consumers, and that they even differ between consumers. Some consumers may have a preference for say tannic wines, while others may prefer non-tannic wines. The effect of the first group of consumers would then be offset by the effect of the second group. In this case, the sensory characteristic would have no effect on the price of wine. This explanation is perhaps not so convincing for economists, since they rarely make the assumption that tastes are heterogeneous. For example, Stigler and Becker (1977) argue that "tastes neither change capriciously nor differ importantly among people."

The second explanation is in terms of imperfect information. In Rosen's pure competition framework, consumers are supposed to make their decisions on the basis of perfect information: all information is available for all consumers without any cost. This assumption is obviously unrealistic for certain products. Some characteristics may simply be easier to identify or perceive than others. In the case of Bordeaux wine, the objective characteristics (those mentioned on the label) are much easier to identify by consumers than the sensory characteristics. Therefore, it is more difficult, and thus more expensive, to obtain information about the latter than about the former. According to Lévy-Garboua (1976), if information is imperfect, rational consumers gather information about a characteristic if the marginal cost of obtaining the information is smaller than or equal to the marginal utility it generates. As it is expensive to obtain information about the sensory characteristics (only available through tasting, learning, and reading wine guides), consumers may decide to make their (wine) choice primarily on the basis of the objective characteristics, thus explaining the absence of almost all sensory characteristics in the hedonic price function.

Acknowledgments

We would like to thank O. Ashenfelter, F. Gardes, V. Lechene, L. Lévy-Garboua, T. Magnac, S. Rosen, and a referee for their comments.

References

Arguea, N.M., and Hsiao, C. (1993). Econometric issues of estimating hedonic price functions, with an application to the U.S. market for automobiles. *Journal of Econometrics*, 56, 243–267.

Atkinson, S.E., and Halverson, R. (1984). A new hedonic technique for estimating attribute demand: An application to the demand for automobile fuel efficiency. *Review of Economics and Statistics*, 66, 417–426.

Bartik, T.J. (1987). The estimation of demand parameters in hedonic price models. *Journal of Political Economy*, 95, 81–88.

Bowden, R.J., and Turkington, D.A. (1984). *Instrumental Variables.* Cambridge: Cambridge University Press.

Bradfer, A., de Clouet, A., and Maratier, C. (1992). *La cote des meilleurs vins de France.* Luçon: Editions Solar.

Chow, G.C. (1967). Technological change and the demand for computers. *American Economic Review*, 57, 1117–1130.

Court, A.T. (1939). Hedonic price indexes with automotive examples. In *The Dynamics of Automobile Demand.* New York: The General Motors Corporation.

Couton, C., Gardes, F., and Thépaut, Y. (1996). Hedonic prices for environmental characteristics in the French car market. *Applied Economics Letters*, 3, 435–440.

Griliches, Z. (1961). Hedonic price indexes for automobiles: An econometric analysis of quality change. In *The Price Statistics of the Federal Government.* New York: Columbia University Press.

Hausman, J.A. (1978). Specification tests in econometrics. *Econometrica*, 46, 1251–1270.

Johnson, H. (1994). *Hugh Johnson's Pocket Wine Book.* London: Mitchell Beazley.

Ladd, G.W., and Suvannunt, V. (1976). A model of consumer goods characteristics. *American Journal of Agricultural Economics*, 58, 504–510.

Lévy-Garboua, L. (1976). La nouvelle théorie du consommateur et la formation des choix. *Consommation*, 3, 83–99.

Nerlove, M. (1995). Hedonic price functions and the measurement of preferences: The case of Swedish wine consumers. *European Economic Review*, 39, 1697–1716.

Oczkowski, E. (1994). A hedonic price function for Australian premium wine. *Australian Journal of Agricultural Economics*, 38, 93–110.

Palmquist, R.B. (1984). Estimating demand for the characteristics of housing. *Review of Economics and Statistics*, 66, 394–404.

Rosen, S.M. (1974). Hedonic prices and implicit markets: Product differentiation in pure competition. *Journal of Political Economy*, 82, 34–55.

Stanley, L.R., and Tschirhart, J. (1991). Hedonic prices for a nondurable good: The case of breakfast cereals. *Review of Economics and Statistics*, 73, 537–541.

Stigler, G.J., and Becker, G.S. (1977). De gustibus non est disputandum. *American Economic Review*, 67, 76–90.

Triplett, J.E. (1989). Price and technological change in a capital good: A survey of research on computers. In *Technology and Capital Formation* (ed. D.W. Jorgenson and R. Landau). Cambridge: MIT Press.

Waugh, F.V. (1928). Quality factors influencing vegetable prices. *Journal of Farm Economics*, 10, 185–196.

Witte, A.D., Sumka, H.J., and Erekson, O.H. (1979). An estimate of a structural hedonic price model of the housing market: An application of Rosen's theory of implicit markets. *Econometrica*, 47, 1151–1173.

Chapter 8

Segmenting the Wine Market Based on Price: Hedonic Regression when Different Prices Mean Different Products*

Marco Costanigro[†], Jill J. McCluskey[‡], and Ron C. Mittelhammer[§]

[†]*Department of Agricultural and Resource Economics, Colorado State University, Fort Collins, CO 80523, USA*
marco.costanigro@colostate.edu

[‡]*School of Economic Sciences and Food Policy Fellow, International Marketing Program for Agricultural Commodities and Trade (IMPACT) Center, Washington State University, Pullman, WA 99164-6210, USA*
mccluskey@wsu.edu

[§]*School of Economic Sciences and Department of Statistics, Washington State University, Pullman, WA 99164-6210, USA*
mittelha@wsu.edu

Many economists have estimated hedonic price functions for red and white wine. However, estimating a single hedonic price function imposes the assumption that the implicit prices of the attributes are the same for any red or white wine. We argue that even within these two categories, wines are differentiated, and disregarding this heterogeneity causes an aggregation bias in the estimated implicit prices. By estimating hedonic functions specific to price ranges, we show that the wine market is segmented into several product classes or market segments. We find that a model accounting for the existence of wine classes has greater ability to explain the variability in the data and produces more accurate and interpretable results regarding the implicit prices of the attributes.

*This article originally appeared in *Journal of Agricultural Economics* (2007), 58(3), 454–466.

1. Introduction

Numerous authors have estimated hedonic functions for wine. Although part of this body of research focuses attention on a single type of wine such as Bordeaux, many studies estimate hedonic functions broadly applied to either red or white wine and in some cases to both. The implicit assumption in these studies is that the hedonic relationship between prices and attributes is unique and little variation in that hedonic relationship exists between or within the red and white wine classification. Using data on red wine, we investigate the possibilities that multiple wine classes or market segments exist and that separate hedonic functions should be estimated for each wine class.

The chapter proceeds as follows: first, a brief review of the existing hedonic literature is presented, and the case for the existence of differentiated wine classes is made. Then, the hedonic model is introduced as the theoretical basis of the analysis, the dataset presented and the empirical specification discussed. A methodology to identify market segments is then developed and applied, and class-specific hedonic models are estimated. Finally, the results are presented, and their implications discussed in the light of a comparison between the class-specific (or segmented) modeling approach vs. the traditional pooled approach.

2. Literature Review

The literature seeking to identify the determinants of wine prices using hedonic techniques is well established. A considerable number of studies have been carried out to determine which wine attributes significantly affect wine prices: Combris *et al.* (1997, 2000) showed that when regressing objective and sensory characteristics on wine price, the objective cues (such as expert rating score and vintage) are significant, whereas sensory variables (such as tannin content and other measurable chemicals) are not. Much of the literature (Oczkowski, 1994; Landon and Smith, 1997; Angulo *et al.*, 2000; Schamel and Anderson, 2003) indicates that ratings by specialized magazines are significant and should be included while modeling wine prices. Possible explanations for the insignificance of sensory cues are the difficulty of isolating the effect of each chemical on the final flavor and smell, and that only a small percentage of wine purchasers are connoisseurs. Therefore, expert ratings act as a signal to the consumer. It is uncertain whether expert ratings influence prices because they are good proxies for quality of the wine or because of their marketing effect. Oczkowski (2001) finds that tasting scores are only proxies for quality, and uses two-stage ordinary least squares and factor analysis to correct for measurement error in the independent variables. On the other hand, Schamel and Anderson (2003) find no evidence of such a problem in their sample. The region of production, capturing production cost differentials and the effects of the collective reputation of the district, and the vintage are often reported as significant variables (Angulo *et al.*, 2000; Schamel and Anderson, 2003). Steiner (2004) finds a declining valuation of French wines with geographical appellation in the British market.

3. Market Segmentation

Although various concerns regarding econometric pathologies endemic to the hedonic wine literature appear to be legitimate (see Oczkowski, 2001, regarding measurement error and Unwin, 1999, on heteroskedasticity, collinearity and an extensive critique of the field), we argue that the extreme heterogeneity of wine as a product class is a *prima facie* reason why fundamental model specification issues should be of principal concern to market analysts. Related to this issue, Thrane (2004) pointed out that it is unlikely that the same hedonic function will be applicable for red and white wines. That is, whether wine attributes affect red and white wines in the same way is a matter that should be tested empirically. In our opinion, the question can be posed on *a priori* grounds. For example, as the ageing potential of red and white wines differs considerably, it seems reasonable to expect that the implicit price of ageing will also be distinct.

Although estimating separate hedonic functions for red and white wines appears advisable at a minimum, the approach might not go far enough in reducing sample heterogeneity and may not produce the most meaningful or accurate comparisons of attribute values. The question of how else the market is segmented remains. Consider an example from the real estate literature to illustrate this issue. Researchers routinely estimate separate hedonic functions for single-family houses, duplexes, apartments and commercial buildings. It is recognized that the same attributes (say, squared footage) can affect prices in substantially different ways across property types. On the other hand, these product classes are believed to include properties that are, although heterogeneous, relatively similar. Therefore, consumers see them as variations on the same basic product. However, Straszheim (1974) argued further that market segmentation is present in the housing market even within such categorizations. He showed that by estimating separate hedonic price functions for different geographic areas of the San Francisco Bay area, the sum of squared errors (SSE) in predicting prices across the entire sample were significantly reduced. Freeman (1993) analyzed the conditions under which undifferentiated products are traded in segmented markets.

The objective of this study was to investigate whether the wine market should be segmented into differentiated markets or product classes. A major empirical challenge is the identification of such classes, as there are many possible ways to segment the wine market. Both the wine industry (Ernst and Young Entrepreneurs, 1999) and typical wine consumers (Hall *et al.*, 2001) use price categories to define product-class categories, which provides a rationale for one approach to identifying product classes: segment the wine market by price. The market analysis by Ernst and Young Entrepreneurs (1999), which aimed at providing tailored marketing strategies for the Australian wine industry, divided wines into commercial, semi-premium, premium and ultra-premium categories on the basis of retail price ranges[1] and analyzed each category. The wine industry tends to self-select into product-class categories. Scott Morton and Podolny (2002) analyzed the motivations of California winery owners and their effects on price and quality. They found that the owners who derive strong non-financial returns charge more for their product and placed themselves on the high-quality end of the spectrum. The owners whose focus was mostly financial were less likely to produce high-quality wines.

On the consumer side, Hall *et al.* (2001) found that price is used as a quality cue and that consumers look for different attributes, or value the same attributes differently, depending on the occasion the wine is meant to be consumed. One could argue that most consumers have a price range in mind before purchase, which depends on the occasion of consumption, and also look for different attributes depending on the occasion: a wine that works well enough for a casual dinner with friends might not be perceived as appropriate for a gala anniversary celebration. In other words, not all wines are fungible across occasions of consumption, and when deciding which wine to buy, the typical consumer compares alternatives within the chosen price range. Consequently, the same attributes can have different relevance across price categories and therefore different estimated coefficients.

[1]The authors specify that the price ranges for commercial, semi-premium, premium and ultra-premium are, respectively: less than A$8 or A$10, between A$10 and A$15 or A$20, between A$20 and A$30 or A$50, and more than A$30 or A$50.

Following the Ernst and Young Entrepreneurs (1999) analysis, we assume that four market segments are also applicable to the US red wine market but leave the identification of the classes' boundaries to empirical estimation. Hedonic regressions specific to each wine class are then estimated. Although the literature on wine valuation is extensive, to our knowledge, segmentation of the US red wine market has not been investigated and an analysis of the potentially different effects of product attributes across price segments has not been accomplished.

4. Theoretical Context

Following the standard hedonic price model (Rosen, 1974), the price of wine, P, is assumed to be described by a hedonic price function, $P = P(z)$, where z is a vector of attributes. The hedonic price of an additional unit of a particular attribute is determined as the partial derivative of the hedonic price function with respect to that particular attribute. Each consumer chooses an optimal bundle of attributes and all other goods in order to maximize utility subject to a budget constraint. For continuously varying attributes, the chosen bundle will place the consumer so that his or her indifference curve is tangent to the price gradient, $\partial P/\partial z_j$ for each attribute. Therefore, the marginal willingness to pay for a change in a wine attribute is equal to the derivative of the hedonic price function with respect to that attribute. Finite differences $\Delta P/\Delta z_j$ represent marginal willingness to pay for discretely varying attributes. Given that the market is segmented by price categories, the hedonic analysis is then represented by a set of hedonic price functions of the general form $P = P_m(Z)$ for $P \in (\ell_m, h_m)$, $m = 1, \ldots, s$, where s denotes the number of segments, and ℓ_m and h_m the lower and upper price boundaries of market segment m, respectively, with corresponding marginal willingness to pay for attributes given by $\partial P_m/\partial z_j$ or $\Delta P_m/\Delta Z_j$ for market segment m.

5. Data

The dataset is composed of 13,024 observations derived from 10 years (1991–2000) of ratings scores reported in the *Wine Spectator* magazine (online version) for California and Washington red wines. Four of the variables are non-binary: (i) price of the wine adjusted to 2,000 values by a consumer price index (CPI) for alcohol, (ii) score obtained in expert sensory evaluation by the *Wine Spectator*'s experts, (iii) the number of cases produced and (iv) the years of ageing before commercialization. Descriptive statistics

Table 1. Descriptive Statistics of Quantitative Explanatory Variables

State	Variable	Mean	Median	Minimum	Maximum
California[a]	Price[c]	31.1	22	3	2,000
	Cases	6,719	1,467	16	950,000
	Score	86.1	87	60	99
	Age	2.8	3	1	9
Washington[b]	Price[c]	23.3	20	5	144
	Cases	6,720	1,000	45	550,000
	Score	86.8	87	67	96
	Age	2.8	3	1	7

Notes: [a]11,774 observations; [b]1,250 observations; [c]Adjusted to year 2000 by a CPI index for alcohol.

for these variables are reported in Table 1. Note that wine prices have a positively skewed distribution, but the majority of the observations fall in the \$10 to \$50 range. California has more wines in the "expensive" category than Washington, with few Washington wines exceeding \$100.

Indicator variables were used to denote regions of production, wine varieties and the presence of label information. The regions of production for California wines include Napa Valley, Bay Area, Sonoma, South Coast, Carneros, Sierra-Foothills, and Mendocino, while Washington wines were not separated by regions. These geographical partitions are those adopted by the *Wine Spectator* to categorize the wines, often pooling several American Viticultural Areas (AVAs) in the same region. Varieties include Zinfandel, Pinot Noir, Cabernet Sauvignon, Merlot and Syrah grapes, as well as wines made from blending of different varieties (non-varietals). The vintage year is available for each wine along with other label information such as "reserve" and "estate produced." Table 2 reports all variables and abbreviations used throughout the chapter together with a brief description.

6. Specification

Economic theory often suggests the expected sign of the partial derivatives of price with respect to specific attributes but does not restrict functional form. Nevertheless, the choice of the functional form of the hedonic model is fundamental because it determines how the marginal prices will be functionally related to the attributes. Triplett (2004) argued that model specification is ultimately an empirical matter. Given the uncertainty surrounding the correct specification, a flexible functional form is arguably a prudent empirical

Table 2. Descriptions of the Abbreviations Used for the Explanatory Variables

Predictor	Short description
Score	Rating score from the *Wine Spectator*
Scscore	Score centered by subtracting its mean
Scscore^2	Scscore squared
Age	Years of ageing before commercialization
Agesc	Age centered by subtracting its mean
Agesc^2	Agesc squared
Cases	Number of cases produced
Lncas	Natural log of hundreds of cases produced
Napa Bay Area Sonoma South Coast Carneros Sierra Foothills Mendocino Washington	Region of production
Non-varietal Pinot Noir Cabernet Merlot Syrah	Grape variety
Reserve	"Reserve" was reported on the label
Vineyard	Specific name of the vineyard on the label
Estate	"Estate" produced wine
91, ..., 99	Vintage
Wa	Washington State wines

modeling strategy. A series of possible transformations of the dependent variable were considered and evaluated on the basis of variance stabilization, normality of the residuals and misspecification.[2] As in Landon and Smith (1997), we find that the inverse square root is the best performing transformation. The final specification of the independent variables was also determined by screening possible transformations of the non-binary variables and examining excluded variable residual plots. Furthermore, intercept and slope shifters are used to allow separate regression functions for Washington

[2]The Goldfeldt–Quandt test was used to detect heteroskedasticity proportional to predicted values and the RESET test for misspecification. For the normality of the residuals, we employed three different tests: Anderson–Darling, Kolmogorov–Smirnoff and Ryan–Joiner.

and California wines. The functional form ultimately selected is the following:

$$\begin{aligned}\text{Price}^{-0.5} &= \beta_0 + \beta_0^w + (\beta_1 + \beta_1^w \text{WA})(\text{Score}) + (\beta_2 + \beta_2^w \text{WA})(\text{Score})^2 \\ &\quad + (\beta_3 + \beta_3^w \text{WA})(\text{Age}) + (\beta_4 + \beta_4^w \text{WA})(\text{Age})^2 \\ &\quad + (\beta_5 + \beta_5^w \text{WA}) \ln(\text{Cases}) + \sum_{i=1}^{5} (\beta_{5+i} + \beta_{5+i}^w \text{WA})(\text{Variety}_i) \\ &\quad + \sum_{i=1}^{9} (\beta_{10+i} + \beta_{10+i}^w \text{WA})(\text{Vintage}_i) \\ &\quad + \sum_{i=1}^{3} (\beta_{19+i} + \beta_{19+i}^w \text{WA})(\text{Label}_i) + \sum_{i=1}^{7} \beta_{22+i}(\text{Region}_i) + \varepsilon_i \end{aligned} \tag{1}$$

where WA denotes an indicator variable for Washington State.

The model in equation (1) was estimated using ordinary least square (OLS). Formal testing detected a moderate degree of heteroskedasticity,[3] but the possible gains in estimation efficiency that might be achieved by adjusting the estimator for an appropriate heteroskedastic process were muted by the consistency of the OLS estimator and the large sample size on which the estimates are based.[4] Nevertheless, as a matter of caution the covariance matrix of the parameters was estimated using White's consistent heteroskedasticity-robust estimator.

7. Structural Breaks in Prices

Conceptually, the problem of partitioning the data by price is one of locating a set of n breakpoints that represent the price ranges that demarcate $n + 1$ market segments. We assume that four differentiated market segments exist, thereby setting the number of structural breaks, n, to three. To estimate the optimal location of the structural breaks, the criterion of maximizing goodness of fit to the data was adopted. In particular, the set of breakpoints were chosen that minimized the SSE across the four models (one for each

[3]It should be noticed that the power of a test increases as the sample size grows larger. In the limit, if the sample is large enough, a formal test will reject virtually *any* hypothesis stated in the form of strict equality.

[4]There is also the mitigating issue of the need to discover the correct heteroskedastic structure of the error process.

price segment) over all the possible different market partitions. The combinatorial nature of the search problem is clear: the number of alternative possible market segmentations is large, and for each of them four vectors of OLS coefficients are needed to calculate the test statistics. In order to reduce the number of calculations, 36 possible breakpoints located over the range from \$10 to \$70 were set. The grid commenced with increments of \$1 in the lower range of prices, from \$10 to \$35, where most of the data lie; then with steps of \$2 in the range from \$35 to \$45, but \$40 was also included; and finally with steps of \$5 from \$45 to \$70. An algorithm was written in GAUSS to estimate the statistics for all combinations of three breakpoints yielding calculable parameter estimates (i.e., for non-singular explanatory variable matrices). Once the optimal price breakpoints were located, price range-specific hedonic regressions were estimated using OLS.

8. Results and Discussion

The price breakpoints minimizing the SSE identified four price categories corresponding to the four hypothesized market segments: commercial wines (price less than \$13), semi-premium (between \$13 and \$21), premium (between \$21 and \$40) and ultra-premium ($\geqslant$\$40).[5] The sample sizes associated with these market segments are 1,635, 4,114, 4,809, and 2,475 observations, respectively.

Estimated coefficients of model (1) for the pooled (estimating a single hedonic function) and the segmented models are reported in Tables 3 and 4. Coefficients relative to the Washington slope shifters were mostly insignificant in the segmented model and are not included in the tables. Comparing the pooled to the segmented approach, the value of adjusted R^2 increases from 0.67 to 0.91. As in Straszheim (1974), the greater flexibility of the segmented approach allows us to capture the specifics of each wine class, resulting in substantially greater explanatory power.

The hypothesis that OLS regression coefficients are equal across the price categories was tested via a Wald statistic. The test statistic was framed analogous to a Chow-type test, whereby parameters associated with like variables across each of the price-segmented models were hypothesized to be equal. White's heteroskedasticity robust estimator was used in the test

[5]A reasonable concern is that the price breakpoints might not be the same for California and Washington. To investigate this hypothesis, we run the GAUSS algorithm on the two separated datasets. Interestingly, we find that the price categories minimizing SSE are the same for WA, CA and the pooled dataset.

Table 3. Ordinary Least Square Estimates for Pooled and Segmented Hedonic Functions (First Set)

	Pooled	Segmented			
Adjusted R^2	0.67	0.91[a]			
		Commercial 0.29	Semi-premium 0.21	Premium 0.19	Ultra-premium 0.33
No.	13,024	1,635	4,114	4,809	2,475
Covariate	Coefficient × 10^2 (t-ratio)				
Constant	21.999	29.233	23.943	18.794	14.543
	(104.7)	(56.66)	(140.3)	(116.6)	(50.2)
Scscore	−0.620	−0.275	−0.158	−0.145	−0.168
	(−61.29)	(−6.36)	(−15.86)	(−18.69)	(−10.79)
Scscore^2	−0.022	−0.005	−0.008	−0.007	−0.027
	(−16.47)	(−1.25)	(−6.61)	(−6.01)	(−10.35)
Agesc	−1.302	−0.572	−0.185	−0.185	−0.175
	(−23.69)	(−4.62)	(−4.62)	(−4.5)	(−1.83)
Agesc^2	0.108	0.334	0.078	0.038	−0.109
	(2.63)	(2.71)	(2.06)	(1.24)	(−2.01)
Lncas	1.004	0.486	0.292	0.290	0.185
	(41.75)	(7.82)	(15.82)	(16.28)	(5.51)
Napa[b]	−5.483	−1.602	−1.406	−0.478	0.188
	(−36.77)	(−5.78)	(−13.64)	(−3.51)	(0.83)
Bay Area[b]	−3.437	−1.266	−0.746	−0.135	0.364
	(−17.34)	(−3.67)	(−5.47)	(−0.84)	(1.41)
Sonoma[b]	−4.053	−2.251	−1.034	−0.110	0.573
	(−28.31)	(−10.38)	(−11.18)	(−0.82)	(2.55)
South Coast[b]	−3.222	−2.491	−0.809	0.147	1.246
	(−20.46)	(−8.81)	(−7.47)	(1.02)	(4.89)
Carneros[b]	−4.291	−2.899	−1.537	−0.086	0.423
	(−23.74)	(−6.28)	(−11.76)	(−0.56)	(1.69)
Sierra Foothills[b]	−2.327	−1.634	−0.296	−0.037	1.440
	(−10.3)	(−5.26)	(−2.02)	(−0.18)	(4.61)
Mendocino[b]	−2.406	−1.555	−0.538	0.196	1.183
	(−12.64)	(−5.24)	(−4.22)	(1.18)	(3.91)
Wa[b]	−0.652	1.178	−0.904	1.001	1.817
	(−0.95)	(1.44)	(−1.38)	(3.91)	(3.74)

Notes: [a]Calculated stacking the segmented datasets in a single (block diagonal) design matrix and estimating the segmented hedonic model all at once, with a single constant.
[b]Omitted variable: generic California.

Table 4. Ordinary Least Square Estimates for Pooled and Segmented Hedonic Functions (Second Set)

	Pooled	Segmented			
		Commercial	Semi-premium	Premium	Ultra-premium
Covariate		Coefficient × 10^2 (t-ratio)			
Nonvarietal[a]	−4.319	−0.910	−0.926	−1.207	−2.096
	(−27.29)	(−1.98)	(−5.93)	(−10.82)	(−9.05)
Pinot Noir[a]	−3.252	−0.588	−0.727	−1.122	−0.839
	(−32.16)	(−2.04)	(−9.13)	(−15.68)	(−4.01)
Cabernet[a]	−2.479	−0.684	−0.512	−1.060	−1.333
	(−24.4)	(−3.3)	(−6.7)	(−13.34)	(−6.33)
Merlot[a]	−2.200	−1.069	−0.759	−0.770	−0.653
	(−21.79)	(−4.77)	(−10.06)	(−9.751)	(−2.95)
Syrah[a]	−0.582	0.003	−0.392	−0.186	−0.029
	(−4.26)	(0.01)	(−3.8)	(−1.932)	(−0.11)
Reserve[b]	−1.105	0.690	−0.143	−0.512	0.438
	(−10.89)	(2.36)	(−1.5)	(−7.56)	(4.30)
Vineyard[b]	−0.858	−1.407	−0.151	−0.281	−0.171
	(−11.46)	(−5.99)	(−2.14)	(−5.25)	(−1.77)
Estate[b]	−0.601	−2.483	0.171	−0.261	−0.022
	(−2.88)	(−4.72)	(1.01)	(−1.62)	(−0.1)
91[c]	5.353	1.590	1.195	1.231	—
	(31.78)	(3.57)	(8.2)	(9.27)	—
92[c]	5.339	1.977	1.236	1.190	−0.021
	(31.38)	(4.37)	(8.6)	(9.38)	(−0.06)
93[c]	4.372	1.679	1.096	1.156	0.307
	(27.24)	(3.62)	(7.61)	(9.84)	(1.13)
94[c]	4.097	0.915	0.824	1.176	0.498
	(27.8)	(2.01)	(5.82)	(10.82)	(2.23)
95[c]	3.311	0.333	0.477	0.926	0.657
	(23.24)	(0.75)	(3.41)	(9.00)	(3.48)
96[c]	2.397	−0.001	0.236	0.699	0.646
	(17.75)	(−0.003)	(1.7)	(7.06)	(3.52)
97[c]	1.749	−0.209	0.225	0.696	0.383
	(13.07)	(−0.45)	(1.58)	(7.3)	(2.38)
98[c]	0.393	0.090	0.171	0.408	−0.385
	(2.77)	(0.181)	(1.12)	(4.03)	(−2.4)
99[c]	0.668	−0.346	0.170	0.294	0.050
	(5.02)	(−0.72)	(1.1)	(3.08)	(0.34)

Notes: [a]Omitted variable: Zinfandel; [b]Omitted variable: no additional label information; [c]Omitted variable: year 2000.
—,Variable not present in market segment.

Table 5. Wald Statistics (*P*-values) Testing the Hypothesis of Parameters' Equality Across Market Segment

	Semi-premium	Premium	Ultra-premium
Commercial	7,866	19,112	11,118
	(0.000)	(0.000)	(0.000)
Semi-premium		15,702	20,600
		(0.000)	(0.000)
Premium			9,838
			(0.000)

to represent the covariance matrix of the parameter estimates, and a value of the Wald statistic was then calculated to test the equality of all coefficients across classes. All test results strongly reject the null hypothesis (see Table 5).

In interpreting the results in Tables 3 and 4, it is important to note that because of the transformation of the dependent variable, coefficients with a negative sign signify a positive impact of the wine attribute on price, and vice versa. Empirical results conformed to *a priori* expectations: for all estimated models, price increases in ageing and rating score over the range of the data and decreases in the number of cases produced. Confirming previously published results, regional appellations command price premia relative to a generic California wine, with "Napa Valley" bringing the largest premium. The coefficients associated with the variety variables capture the difference in price relative to Zinfandel grapes and the coefficients for vintages refer to price differences relative to the excluded year 2000. Interestingly, all price impacts are negative and show a very clear pattern: the 1991 and 1992 vintages were the largest in magnitude, and then slowly decreased year by year. This suggests that these indicator variables may not only be representing a vintage effect (e.g., good or bad climatic conditions that can affect wine production) but may also be confounded by a temporal trend of the prices not accounted for by the CPI scaling.[6]

Examination of additional estimated hedonic function coefficients and corresponding implicit prices serves to further characterize each wine class

[6]Several authors (Pakes, 2003; Triplett, 2004) suggested the use of hedonic models to calculate CPI indexes as an alternative to the currently used matched models. The model specification of this research fits the "time dummy variable" method described by Triplett (2004, p. 48) to calculate CPI indexes. The fact that a time trend is still present despite the fact that prices had already been CPI-adjusted suggests that, as many authors observed, the two methods yield considerably different results.

and provide for a further contrast between the approach we propose in this chapter and the traditional pooled approach. We emphasize that, because of the transformation of the dependent variable, implicit prices are functions of both estimated coefficients and prices. Average implicit prices for each of the attributes were calculated using market segment-specific price averages and results and figures refer to the appropriate ranges of the data.[7]

The derivative of price with respect to the number of cases produced is strictly negative for all market segments and approaches zero as the number of cases increases. As for the quantitative difference across market segments, increasing total production decreases the market price of wines only slightly in the commercial market segment. The decrease is more pronounced in the two middle segments and is quite substantial in the ultra-premium wine segment (more than five times the estimate relative to the commercial segment). By estimating separated models, we are able to segregate wines that have a "collectible" or "cult wine" value from the "consumption"-type wines. The value of an additional point in the *Wine Spectator* tasting score shows an analogous effect: better scores in the tasting review increase the price of the wine significantly. This effect is increasingly important in order of the commercial, to semi-premium and premium market segments, and becomes highly relevant for the ultra-premium wines.

Differences across market segments regarding the impact of cellaring on wine price are even more pronounced (Figure 1). As expected, wine ageing for the commercial, semi-premium and premium classes exhibits decreasing marginal returns over time. In contrast, ultra-premium wines show different pricing dynamics: the implicit price of ageing increases over the full range of the data. The pooled regression approach does not account for qualitative differences (different signs or slopes across price segments), as only one coefficient (or, for the case of polynomials, one set) is estimated for each attribute. On the other hand, marginal prices are weighted by price, so that quantitative differences are embedded in the regression even in the pooled approach.

Examples of wine class-specific peculiarities in the estimated implicit prices are multiple. Washington wines sell for a discount in the premium and ultra-premium classes, but are no different from California wines in the

[7]We limit the number of figures presented in this chapter. Remaining figures and tables are available from the authors upon request. For the sake of reproducibility, the average prices relative to each market segment (commercial, semi-premium, premium, and ultra-premium) are \$10.01, \$17.11, \$28.38, and \$73.90, respectively.

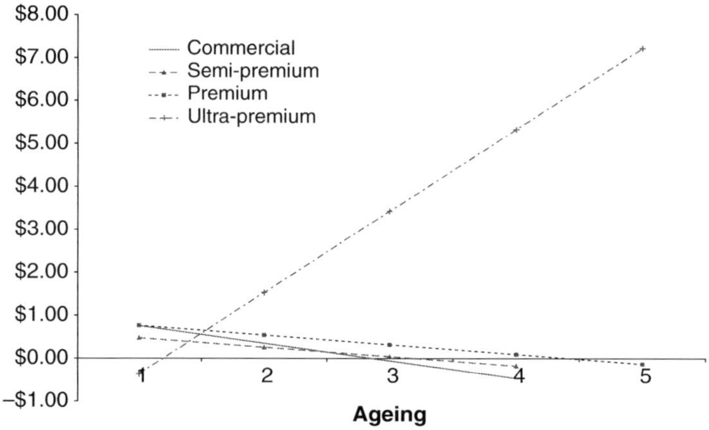

Figure 1. Implicit price of ageing for commercial, semi-premium, premium, and ultra-premium wines; calculated using estimates from the segmented model and class-specific price averages

commercial and semi-premium markets. Blended wines sell for a high premium in the fine wines segment, while they are not different from Zinfandel wines in the inexpensive price segment.[8]

Among the varietals, Merlots have the highest associated price premium in the commercial segment, while Cabernets and Pinot Noirs are the most expensive ultra-premium varietal wines. In general, we find that the segmented model produces a much richer and detailed amount of information relating to the character of wine markets.

Finally, we emphasize that estimated price premia from the pooled approach are consistently higher than those from the segmented approach. This can be explained in the context of the different interpretation of the estimates: the price premia associated with the pooled data refer to the mean value of the excluded variable for the *entire* price range, while the segmented price premia refer to the mean value of the excluded variable *within* the price category. The difference is not merely semantic. If wines in different classes are actually different products, this effect can result in false significance of the explanatory variables.

[8]Blended wines are a heterogeneous category. They range from "table wines" made from several grape varieties mixed in unknown percentages to high-quality, finely balanced wines, such as Meritage. In this instance, the segmented approach allows differentiating between these attributes that share a common denomination, but are inherently different.

9. Conclusions

We provide empirical evidence that the wine market is differentiated into multiple segments or wine classes. We find that a model considering market segmentation has greater ability to explain the variability of the data and, just as importantly, produces more defensible and informative estimates of the hedonic relationship between prices and wine attributes. The analysis identifies wine classes based on price ranges as well as out-of-sample information relating to the existence of different wine segments. By specifying hedonic functions for different product-class categories, we find evidence that consumers value the same wine attributes differently across categories.

There are many possible ways to segment the wine market. Although the current approach produced reasonable results, the matter of how best to identify segments in the wine market remains an open question. Research is on-going to develop methods that identify wine classes using information in addition to price and that endogenously determine the number of price segments.

Acknowledgments

The authors wish to acknowledge IMPACT for funding and thank without implicating Orley Ashenfelter, Wade Brorsen, Jayson Lusk, Jon Yoder, two anonymous reviewers and the editors for helpful comments and/or discussions.

References

Angulo, A.M., Gil, J.M., Gracia, A., and Sanchez, M. (2000). Hedonic prices for Spanish red quality wine. *British Food Journal*, 102, 481–493.

Combris, P., Sebastien, L., and Visser, M. (1997). Estimation of a hedonic price equation for Bordeaux wine: Does quality matter? *Economic Journal*, 107, 390–403.

Combris, P., Lecocq, S., and Visser, M. (2000). Estimation of a hedonic price equation for Burgundy wine. *Applied Economics*, 32, 961–967.

Ernst and Young Entrepreneurs (1999). *Etude des Filieres et des Strategies de Développement des Pays Producteurs de Vins dans le Monde: Analyse de la Filiere Viticole Australienne.* Paris: ONIVINS (Office National Interprofessionnel des Vins).

Freeman, A.M. (1993). *The Measurement of Environmental and Resource Values: Theory and Methods.* Washington, DC: Resources for the Future.

Hall, J., Lockshin, L., and O'Mahony, G.B. (2001). Exploring the links between the choice and dining occasion: Factors of influence. *International Journal of Wine Marketing*, 13, 36–53.

Landon, S., and Smith, C.E. (1997). The use of quality and reputation indicators by the consumers: The case of Bordeaux wine. *Journal of Consumer Policy*, 20, 289–323.

Oczkowski, E. (1994). Hedonic wine price function for Australian premium table wine. *Australian Journal of Agricultural Economics*, 38, 93–110.

Oczkowski, E. (2001). Hedonic wine price functions and measurement error. *Economic Record*, 77, 374–382.

Pakes, A. (2003). A reconsideration of hedonic price indexes with an application to PC's. *The American Economic Review*, 93, 1578–1596.

Rosen, S. (1974). Hedonic prices and implicit markets: Product differentiation in pure competition. *Journal of Political Economy*, 82, 34–55.

Schamel, G., and Anderson, K. (2003). Wine quality and varietal, regional and winery reputations: Hedonic prices for Australia and New Zealand. *Economic Record*, 79, 357–369.

Scott Morton, F.M., and Podolny, J.M. (2002). Love or money? The effects of owner motivation in the California wine industry. *Journal of Industrial Economics*, 40, 431–456.

Steiner, B. (2004). French wines on the decline? Econometric evidence from Britain. *Journal of Agricultural Economics*, 55, 267–288.

Straszheim, M. (1974). Hedonic estimation of housing market prices: A further comment. *Review of Economics and Statistics*, 56, 404–406.

Thrane, C. (2004). In defense of the price hedonic model in wine research. *Journal of Wine Research*, 15, 123–134.

Triplett, J. (2004). *Handbook on Hedonic Indexes and Quality Adjustments in Price Indexes: Special Application to Information Technology Products* OECD Science, Technology and Industry Working Papers. 2004/9. Paris: OECD Publishing.

Unwin, T. (1999). Hedonic price indexes and the qualities of wine. *Journal of Wine Research*, 10, 95–104.

Chapter 9

The Pricing of Experience Goods: The Example of *EN PRIMEUR* Wine*

Héla Hadj Ali† **and Céline Nauges**‡

†*Research Fellow at INRA*
(National Institute for Research in Agriculture)
Toulouse, France

‡*Senior Research Fellow at Toulouse School of Economics,*
INRA, University of Toulouse, Toulouse, France
celine.nauges@inra.fr

The market for "primeur" wine in the Bordeaux region allows producers to sell wine that is still in barrels. As with all experience goods, producers send quality signals to uninformed buyers. Using original data on Bordeaux wines, we show that the pricing behavior of producers depends to a large extent on their reputation, and much less on short-term changes in quality (as measured by experts' grades). We also find that the primeur price has an informative role, since a 10% increase in primeur price leads to a 3% increase in prices on the market for bottled wine.

1. Introduction

Most food products can be classified as experience goods (Nelson, 1970, 1974) because their quality can rarely be ascertained before actual consumption.[1] A substantial part of the theoretical literature dealing with experience goods has focused on sellers' activity to inform consumers in their purchases,

*This article originally appeared in *American Journal of Agricultural Economics* (2007), 89(1), 91–103.

[1]Food products are sometimes described as credence goods in the sense of Darby and Karni (1973) (i.e., some product attributes cannot be accurately evaluated even after consumption), for instance, when the production process involves environment-friendly practices.

particularly on the role of signaling and reputation. Prices, advertising expenditure (Milgrom and Roberts, 1986), and warranties (Grossman, 1981) are textbook illustrations of how a monopolist can signal the high quality of his product in a game with asymmetric information. Shapiro (1983) emphasized the role of reputation in a perfectly competitive environment by describing how consumers form rational expectations on the quality of experience goods based on the quality of goods produced in the past.

In the particular case of food products, producers often choose labeling as a signal of quality. Bureau and Valceschini (2003) showed that labeling helps promote differentiated products and allows small producers to benefit from a well-established collective reputation. More generally, the use of food labels is said to create the potential for price premia (Henneberry and Armbruster, 2003).

Quantitative measures of these "price premia" are quite rare, as well as, more generally, analyses of the pricing strategy and signaling activity of producers in markets for food products. This is especially the case when compared with hedonic studies that measure the consumers' assessment of food product attributes (see McCluskey and Loureiro, 2003, for a review). This chapter contributes to the empirical literature on experience goods by analyzing the pricing behavior of wine producers from the well-known Bordeaux region in France.

Original data on two markets (for "primeur" wine and for bottled wine) provide a unique opportunity to obtain new insights on the pricing strategy of producers. Primeur sales refer to a wine sold several months after the harvest, while it is still in barrels.[2] At the time of primeur sales, the price of the wine (produced by the *château* for a particular vintage) is chosen by each individual producer. We assume that this primeur price depends on the reputation of the *château* as well as on short-term changes in quality due to the climatic conditions that prevailed during the grape-growing season. Reputation involves the wine maker's know-how, which is measured, according to Shapiro (1983) and Tirole (1996), by the quality of the wine produced by the *château* in the past. It is still an open question how much of the producers' market power is driven by reputation rather than short-term changes in quality.

[2]The primeur market takes place every year in Spring, and represents one of the most important events on the Bordeaux market place. This type of sale allows producers to gain "cash-in-hand" before the wine is bottled. At the same time, it enables buyers to acquire rare wine at potential bargain prices, hence attracting more and more financial speculators (see Hadj Ali and Nauges, 2003).

The wine sold "*en primeur*" is released onto the market for bottled wines a few months after the primeur sales. We might argue that primeur price could be used by the producers as a signal of wine quality on the market for bottled wine. If this hypothesis was correct, that is, if consumers are expected to look for a signal on wine quality through primeur pricing, then producers might set wine prices accordingly.

In this study, we first separate the effects of reputation and short-term changes in quality, using an analysis of primeur prices to assess their respective impacts on the pricing strategy of producers. Secondly, we estimate the effect of the information content of the primeur price on the price of bottled wine. We distinguish between reputation based on expert grading of wine from previous vintages and "rank" reputation derived from the quality-based rank of the wine itself. The quality-based classification for Bordeaux wines, which is region-specific, provides information both on the geographical origin and the rank of the wine inside the region.[3] The labeling system aims to allow producers to certify certain claims about the wine production process. Among other things, it guarantees that the grapes are produced in a delimited region and sets the maximum yield allowed per unit area of land.

Using an unbalanced panel data set of 1,153 wines produced by 132 Bordeaux *châteaux* over fifteen vintages, we find evidence of a large and significant "reputation premium" mainly driven by the rank of the *château* in the classification system. In other words, the pricing behavior of the *châteaux* during primeur sales, and hence their relative market power, depends largely on the reputation driven by the quality-based rank, and to a much lesser extent on the reputation driven by past quality scores. We also find that short-term changes in wine quality had a very limited influence on the price set by the producers. The analysis showed that a 10% increase in primeur prices increases subsequent prices on the market for bottled wine by around 3%.

The high-reputation premium that we estimate on the subsample of Bordeaux producers provides empirical evidence that the use of food labels may give rise to price premia (Henneberry and Armbruster, 2003). It also provides empirical support to the statement that the labeling system in European wine markets "has proven successful in guaranteeing a good reputation for many European wines and relatively high profits for the producers" (Giraud-Héraud *et al.*, 2002; Marette and Zago, 2003). Our results also

[3]Bordeaux wines have been ranked in terms of quality-based classifications since the nineteenth century.

help understand why European wine producers from famous regions such as Bordeaux are against the idea of moving from the current system of wine labeling to a differentiation system based on grape variety as carried out in countries such as Australia, Chile, South Africa, and the United States. If there were no longer any labeling system promoting reputation, then producers would have to engage in costly marketing policies in order to be able to compete with (much larger) producers from the New World wine countries (Giraud-Héraud *et al.*, 2002).[4]

Our study also contributes to the literature on wine markets. Existing studies are mostly concerned with hedonic analyses on bottled wine (for a review, see Lecocq and Visser [2006]). The main findings of these previous studies are qualitatively very similar to the results obtained here. Previous authors agree on the larger impact of objective characteristics (vintage and region) and reputation (as measured by rank) on wine price. However, they also find a moderate influence of current quality (as measured by expert grading or sensory characteristics).

2. Reputation and Quality in the Pricing of Primeur Wine

Wine prices are set by producers before the opening of the primeur market. We assume that sellers know the future quality of their wine at the time of primeur sales and that market conditions are such that primeur prices truly reflect information on quality, that is, the market is not susceptible to the "lemons" problem as discussed by Akerlof (1970). A sufficiently high fraction of informed buyers acting in the market eliminates the lemons problem (Mahenc, 2004), which we assume to be the case for the Bordeaux primeur market. Furthermore, potential buyers are assumed not to be fully informed about wine quality, since wine is not yet finished at the time of primeur sales. Potential buyers are thus supposed to form quality expectations using information such as the climatic conditions that prevailed during the grape-growing season and the reputation of the *château*. Reputation is defined as the quality of the wine produced in the past (see Shapiro [1983] and Tirole [1996]), which we measure by grades attributed to the *château* for previous vintages and the quality-based rank of the wine. Grades are publicly available through numerous guides and reviews such as the *Revue du Vin de France*

[4]The European wine industry is highly fragmented. For instance, the average vineyard size in France is less than 2 hectares, compared with 111 hectares in Australia (Marette and Zago, 2003).

Table 1. The Three Ranking Systems for Bordeaux Reds

Médoc	Saint Emilion	Graves
ME-1 (5)	SE-1 (2)	GR (21)
ME-2 (14)	SE-2 (11)	
ME-3 (14)	SE-3 (55)	
ME-4 (10)		
ME-5 (18)		
ME-6 (117)		

Note: the number of classified *châteaux* is given in brackets.

or the annual "Bordeaux" issue of *Wine Spectator*, the U.S. wine magazine, having the largest circulation.

Bordeaux wine has been ranked since the nineteenth century within defined geographical areas (so-called regions). There are three ranking systems currently in use for Bordeaux reds (for a summary, see Table 1).

(1) The first ranking for wines from the *Médoc* dates back to 1855, and is largely unchanged to this day.[5] Wines were classified following a five-tier classification system ranging from top-quality *Premiers Crus* or First Growth (denoted here as ME-1) to *Cinquièmes Crus* or Fifth Growth (ME-5). Later on, in 1920, some of the nonranked *châteaux* were classified in a sixth group called *Crus Bourgeois* (ME-6).
(2) *Saint Emilion* wines, formally classified in 1955 (subsequently revised every ten years), follow a three-tier ranking system: *Premiers Grands Crus Classés A* (SE-1), *Premiers Grands Crus Classés B* (SE-2), and *Grands Crus Classés* (SE-3).
(3) Wine from the *Graves* (GR) was officially classified from the beginning of 1953.

Our database also contains *châteaux* belonging to the *Pomerol* area, which has always refused to rank its own wines.

This region-specific quality-based ranking allows producers to certify that the grapes come from a delimited region and that the yield does not exceed a predetermined level. The quality-based classification thus enhances wine differentiation, which, combined with heterogeneity in wine taste and possible barriers to entry, may drive monopolistic positions and thus provide market power especially to the foremost *châteaux* (Mahenc and Meunier,

[5]Except for one: the *château Haut-Brion*, which belongs to the *Graves* area.

2006). In addition to potential market failure due to imperfect competition, the asymmetric information between sellers and buyers is likely to create price distortion. This is because high-quality producers have an incentive to signal the high quality of their wine through the choice of a primeur price (see Shapiro, 1983; Mahenc and Meunier, 2003; Mahenc, 2004). Using theoretical arguments, Mahenc and Meunier (2003) have shown that only high primeur prices can provide an effective signal of high quality since it is more costly to produce high-quality than low-quality wine.

Hence, the "primeur" price function should incorporate "current" quality as well as reputation effects, along with some measures of market power and signaling costs. It is important to understand that a price function incorporating quality and reputation effects is theoretically consistent with the oligopolistic paradigm, as shown by Shaked and Sutton (1982), Tirole (1996), and Mahenc (2004), among others. The Bordeaux *grands crus* industry was indeed chosen as an illustration of an oligopolistic market, with two differentiated goods that differ in taste and quality, in Mahenc (2004).

The primeur price function used here for the empirical analysis incorporates measures of quality and reputation, and can be written as

$$P_{it} = P(VQ_t, WQ_{it}, LQ_{it}, R_i, POM_i, VINT_t) + \mu_i + v_{it} \tag{1}$$

where i and t are the index for *château* and vintage, respectively (the observation unit is the wine produced by *château* i for vintage t).

Current wine quality is measured by the two variables VQ_t and WQ_{it}. The overall vintage quality, as judged by *Wine Spectator* (see Table A1 in the Appendix for more details on this particular grade), is denoted as VQ_t, while wine quality, WQ_{it}, is the grade attributed by Robert Parker (a famous wine expert and editor of *The Wine Advocate*) to the bottled wine, long after its primeur sales.[6] The vintage grade from *Wine Spectator* provides a good approximation of the information on current vintage quality available to consumers during primeur sales. Ashenfelter, Ashmore, and Lalonde (1995) showed that the overall vintage quality was highly correlated with the climatic conditions that prevailed during the growing season. The scores attributed by Robert Parker to each wine measure the expected wine quality at maturity, an item of information that is assumed to be known by the seller at the time of primeur sales.[7]

[6]Both quality indices rise by unit intervals from a minimum of 50 to a maximum of 100.

[7]In hedonic studies of wine, quality grades given by experts are the most common measure of wine quality, see Oczkowski (1994, 2001), Jones and Storchmann (2001), Schamel and Anderson (2003), or Lecocq and Visser (2006) for a review. In their hedonic analyses of Bordeaux and Burgundy wines, Combris, Lecocq, and Visser (1997 and 2000) have shown

Reputation is measured by two variables (LQ and R), both of which are highly correlated with the quality of the wine produced in the past. LQ_{it} is the average of lagged quality scores, computed for each wine using all the available data.[8] We tried different model specifications, in particular the quality score given to the wine produced by the *château* during the last vintage, and an interaction effect between the mean of past quality scores and the rank. The model presented here produces the best-fit to our data. R_i is a vector of 0/1 variables, which is used to take account of the rank attributed to the wine in the quality-based classification system. We also include a dummy variable for the nonclassified wines, which groups together both wines from the *Pomerol* area and nonclassified wines from the *Médoc*, *Saint Emilion*, and *Graves*. As discussed above, the rank effect may incorporate both the degree of market power of the *château* and the signaling cost for high quality. Because of data limitations, we are unable to separate these effects. Indeed, we have no information on the number of bottles sold by each *château* at primeur sales, which could have been used to build a proxy for the Lerner index. POM_i is a dummy variable indicating whether or not the *château* belongs to the *Pomerol* region, which is the only area without any ranking system.

Finally, we take advantage of the panel form of the data to specify vintage dummies, $VINT_t$, and unobserved *château*-specific effects, μ_i. Since we use the *Wine Spectator*'s grade to take account of overall vintage quality, the vintage dummies allow us to check for any time-specific effect or market trends that would have affected the pricing behavior of all producers at the same time. The *château*-specific effect would reflect some "individual reputation" premium or, equivalently, market power based on the *château*'s name. In particular, we would expect the unobservable *château* effect to be larger for famous wines belonging to regions without any ranking system (*Pomerol* in our sample).

We assume a linear relationship between the primeur price and the explanatory variables. The random *château* effect, μ_i, and the usual idiosyncratic error term, v_{it}, are assumed to be uncorrelated, while being independently and identically distributed (i.i.d.) with a normal distribution centered on zero.[9]

sensory attributes (such as aroma, body, firmness, etc.) and chemical characteristics (such as acid and sugar levels) to be statistically insignificant.

[8]See also Landon and Smith (1997 and 1998) and Oczkowski (2001), who measure reputation through lagged quality scores in their hedonic analyses of bottled wine.

[9]The normal distribution of unobservable *château* effects is tested graphically in the empirical section.

3. Data and Estimation Results

In this study, we use a sample of 132 Bordeaux *châteaux* that produced red wine between 1983 and 1998, except for the 1984 vintage.[10] Overall, 1,153 wines are represented in the sample. As the data were provided by one of the most famous broker houses in Bordeaux, they can be considered as fairly representative of the market for Bordeaux wines. Primeur price is defined as the price of a 75-cl bottle in euro equivalent (base 1990).

Prices vary considerably across wines in the data set. Figure 1 shows that the trend in average primeur price matches the experts' judgment up until 1995. This seems to be no longer the case toward the end of the studied period, particularly for the 1997 vintage, which was sold at the highest primeur price despite not being recognized by *Wine Spectator* as a "good" wine.

Table 2 presents some simple statistics showing that average primeur prices match the ranking hierarchy: within each ranking, the better the rank, the higher the primeur price. In the *Médoc* classification, for example, the prices of wine belonging to the first-quality group (ME-1) are situated largely above the price of wine classified as lower quality, coming from ME-2 to ME-6. The last column, NC, groups the nonclassified wines from the three

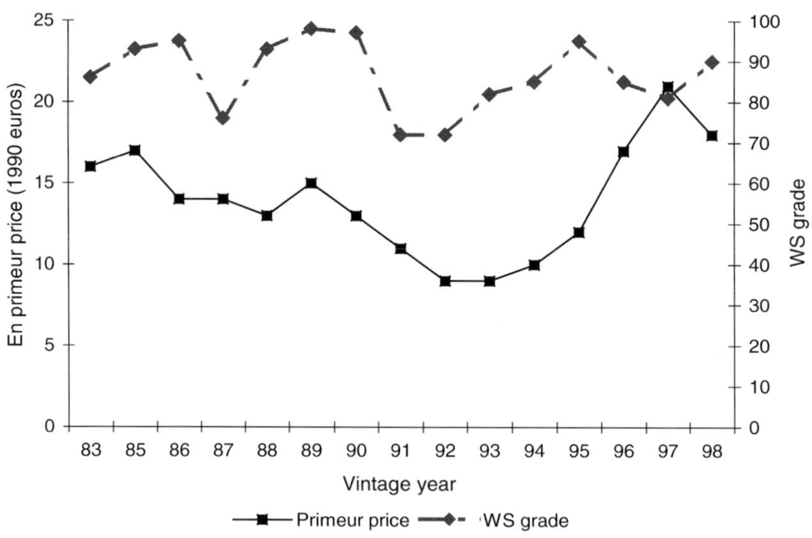

Figure 1. En Primeur Price and *Wine Spectator*'s Grade for 1983 to 1998 Vintages

[10]This vintage was removed from the catalog by the broker.

Table 2. Average Primeur Price by Rank (Prices in 1990 Euros Equivalent)

	Médoc						Saint Emilion			Graves	
	[ME-1	ME-2	ME-3	ME-4	ME-5	ME-6]	[SE-1	SE-2	SE-3]	[GR]	NC
Mean	34	15	10	10	9	7	40	16	11	15	16
St. Dev.	12	8	2	3	4	2	17	7	5	9	10
Number of wines	74	150	75	94	125	136	26	85	133	117	138

Note: *NC is for nonclassified. Number of wines: 1,153. Number of *châteaux*: 132.

regions that have adopted a ranking system (*Médoc*, *Saint Emilion*, and *Graves*), and the wines from the *Pomerol* region where no ranking system exists.

The model fitting the logarithm of the primeur price is estimated using the generalized least squares (GLS) method. We choose the *Premiers Grands Crus Classés A* from *Saint Emilion* (SE-1) as the reference for the rank dummies, and 1990 as the baseline vintage year. Table 3 presents the results of this model specification. In addition to estimated coefficients, standard errors, and probability, this table also reports — in the last two columns — the 95% confidence interval for the "multiplicative" marginal effects of each variable. Since the primeur price is expressed as a logarithm, taking the exponential of each estimated coefficient gives the multiplicative marginal effect of the corresponding variable (relative to the baseline case when considering dummy variables). For example, the marginal effect of not being classified has a 95% probability of lying in the [0.17, 0.35] interval, which means that, all other characteristics being equal, a nonclassified wine will be priced between 0.17 and 0.35 times the price of a wine ranked as a *Premiers Grands Crus Classés A* from *Saint Emilion.*

The overall fit of the model is good, since the overall R^2 value is 0.76 and most of the variables are significant at the 99% level. Although the two measures of current quality (Robert Parker's wine grade and *Wine Spectator*'s grade) prove to be highly significant, their impact on price is nevertheless rather limited as shown by the multiplicative marginal effect, which ranges between 1.00 and 1.02, that is, a one-point increase in grade has almost no effect on the price set by producers.[11] The average of past quality scores has an expected positive sign, but its influence on price is also very small.

[11]Robert Parker's grade has a small effect on the price chosen by producers, which might seem surprising to wine specialists (since Robert Parker is known to be highly influential on the Bordeaux wine markets). However, we should bear in mind that this coefficient

Table 3. GLS Estimation of Parameters in the Primeur Price Model

Dependent variable: Primeur price (log)	Coef.	Std. Err.	p-value	Marginal effects [95% conf. int.]	
Vintage Quality (*VQ*) — *Wine Spectator*'s grade	0.019	0.003	0.000	1.01	1.02
Wine Quality (*WQ*) — Parker's grade	0.006	0.001	0.000	1.00	1.01
Past Wine Quality (*LQ*)	0.013	0.002	0.000	1.01	1.02
Ranking (*R*)					
ME-*1*	−0.169	0.186	0.364	0.59	1.22
ME-2	−1.005	0.168	0.000	0.26	0.51
ME-3	−1.333	0.177	0.000	0.19	0.37
ME-4	−1.351	0.174	0.000	0.18	0.36
ME-5	−1.457	0.169	0.000	0.17	0.32
ME-6	−1.719	0.165	0.000	0.13	0.25
SE-1	—	—	—	1.00	1.00
SE-2	−0.889	0.178	0.000	0.29	0.58
SE-3	−1.326	0.166	0.000	0.19	0.37
GR	−1.067	0.170	0.000	0.25	0.48
Nonclassified	−1.406	0.176	0.000	0.17	0.35
Pomerol Designation (*POM*)	0.430	0.101	0.000	1.26	1.87
Vintage Effects (*VINT*)					
VINT83	0.244	0.042	0.000	1.17	1.39
VINT85	0.245	0.028	0.000	1.21	1.35
VINT86	0.045	0.026	0.077	1.00	1.10
VINT87	0.125	0.071	0.081	0.98	1.30
VINT88	0.091	0.026	0.001	1.04	1.15
VINT89	0.148	0.024	0.000	1.11	1.22
VINT90	—	—	—	1.00	1.00
VINT91	0.181	0.076	0.017	1.03	1.39
VINT92	0.081	0.072	0.264	0.94	1.25
VINT93	0.051	0.045	0.257	0.96	1.15
VINT94	0.134	0.037	0.000	1.06	1.23
VINT95	0.125	0.022	0.000	1.08	1.18
VINT96	0.590	0.039	0.000	1.67	1.95
VINT97	0.854	0.048	0.000	2.14	2.58
VINT98	0.590	0.028	0.000	1.71	1.91

R^2: 0.76.

Fraction of variance due to unobservable effects:	0.69
Total number of observations:	1,153
Total number of *châteaux*:	132

measures the impact of a one-point increase in Parker's grade, all other wine characteristics (vintage and rank) being equal.

Rank-reputation is found to influence significantly the pricing behavior of producers: wines belonging to all other ranks apart from the first rank in the *Médoc* area are priced significantly below wines from rank SE-1 (the baseline rank), according to the hierarchy of ranking in each area (i.e., the estimated effects tend to decrease from ME-2 to ME-6). The multiplicative effects range from 0.13 (ME-6) to 1.22 (ME-1), the latter being nonsignificant. In other words, if two wines from the same vintage obtain the same grade in Robert Parker's records, one belonging to the top-group of *Saint Emilion* (SE-1) and the other belonging to the lowest group of *Médoc* (ME-6), the former will still be priced on the primeur market between five and six times the price of the latter. These results indicate that there is a high reputation premium attached to the famous top ranks in the *Médoc* and *Saint Emilion* areas, which could be due to the exercise of market power combined with a signaling cost for high quality.

The decision of the *Pomerol châteaux* not to establish a quality-based classification explains the high significance of the corresponding dummy variable. The strong positive effect of the *Pomerol* indicator (the multiplicative marginal effect ranges between 1.26 and 1.87) on the primeur price reflects the market power attached to the name of an area (designation) that produces famous wine such as *Château Petrus*.

Most of the vintage dummies are highly significant with respect to the 1990 base vintage. All coefficients are positive, showing that the 1990 vintage, even if judged of very good quality, has been priced significantly below vintages of lower quality (see *Wine Spectator*'s grades in Table A1 of the Appendix). This last result indicates that market trends significantly influence the choice of primeur prices. In particular, we should note the high coefficients of the 1996 to 1998 dummies (multiplicative effects range from 1.67 to 2.58) when the wine market was flourishing because of the combined effects of the "French Paradox," the assessment of health benefits from wine consumption, and the emergence of new buyers from Asian countries.

Finally, estimation results show that 69% of the unexplained model variance is due to unobservable *château* effects. The *château* effect represents the pricing behavior of a *château* over and above the influence of current quality and rank-reputation (or collective reputation). A positive *château* effect indicates that the *château* has some market power provided by its name (individual reputation) and/or is willing to signal high quality by choosing high prices. Unobservable *château* effects can be identified in this model, while the statistical description may provide some insights about the heterogeneity in the sampled population of *châteaux*. Analysis of the 132 *château* effects yields

Table 4. *Château* Effects Estimated from Primeur Price Model

			Quartiles				
	Mean	Std. Dev.	25%	50%	75%	Min.	Max.
Overall	0.000 (1.00)	0.234 (1.26)	−0.147 (0.86)	−0.006 (0.99)	0.143 (1.15)	−0.537 (0.58)	0.699 (2.01)
ME-1	0.000 (1.00)	0.012 (1.01)	−0.009 (0.99)	−0.005 (0.99)	0.003 (1.00)	−0.009 (0.99)	0.020 (1.02)

Note: Multiplicative effects in brackets.

a close-to-normal distribution centered on 0 (see Figure A1 in Appendix). Table 4 reports some simple statistics on the *château*-specific effects.

We show that, for some of the *châteaux*, the unobserved *château* effect has a large impact on primeur prices. The multiplicative effect is found to range between 0.58 and 2.01, and between 0.86 and 1.15 for 50% of the *châteaux*. On the one hand, the estimated *château* effects for the five wines belonging to the first-quality ranking in the *Médoc* area (ME-1) are almost zero, which means that their market power is almost completely captured by the rank dummy. On the other hand, the highest estimated *château* effects very often correspond to wines produced by famous nonclassified *châteaux* (in particular, famous *châteaux* from the *Pomerol* area). These *châteaux* have some market power driven by their own name (individual reputation), rather than the quality-based rank.

4. The Informative Role of Primeur Price on Spot Price

Almost a year after the primeur sales, the wine is bottled and released onto the market. The price of bottled wine, or spot price, is determined by an interaction between producer supply and consumer demand. Consumers' willingness to pay depends on their expectations about wine quality. The primeur price, which is assumed to be known by the consumer, might play the role of a quality signal.[12]

[12]We do not discuss further consumers' perception of quality. It is now common knowledge that consumer's perception of quality is a blend formed by information from multiple sources (certification, labeling, brand names, packaging, price, etc.), see Zeithaml (1988) or Rao and Monroe (1988) for related discussions.

In this section, we measure the impact of primeur price on subsequent bottled wine prices,[13] while checking for the effects of current quality and reputation. If this impact is significant, then it will add to the previous analysis by explaining partly the pricing behavior of the *châteaux* at the time of primeur sales. In particular, we attempt to demonstrate that producers might be willing to signal quality on the market for bottled wine through the primeur price.

We use the same panel of 132 *châteaux* for which we have a five-year series of quarterly spot prices (from June 1996 to July 2000).[14] Because of large market fluctuations, we consider a de-trended spot price.[15] We include current quality, as measured by Robert Parker's grade, along with collective reputation through rank dummies and wine age. We specify an age-vintage interaction in the model because the relationship between age and price of bottled wine is found to be nonlinear and vary across vintages. The average lagged quality scores are removed from the model as they prove to be non-significant. We specify a *château*-specific effect and use GLS to estimate the model. The total number of observations is 11,841. Estimation results are presented in Table 5.

The "goodness-of-fit" of the model (R^2) is 0.86, which means that most of the variation in the price of bottled wine is explained by the selected explanatory variables. The introduction of the primeur price leads to a significant increase in the predictability of spot prices. We show that a 10% increase in the primeur price increases the subsequent prices of bottled wine by 3%. Taken along with the finding that current quality as measured by Robert Parker's ratings also has a very small impact on bottled wine prices, this result reinforces the hypothesis that the primeur price acts as a quality signal for consumers. Moreover, this confirms the general findings of empirical studies on commodity futures markets (see Cox [1976] or Carter [1999], for a review), which show that the forward price conveys some information that increases the predictability of spot prices. However, we should note

[13]Primeur price and spot price are clearly linked via arbitrage, which is due to the compensation given by the producers to buyers for accepting the price risk of holding primeur wine of uncertain quality. From our data, there is only one case where the spot price was less than the primeur price, which would be compatible with the Keynesian theory of normal backwardation (Keynes 1930).

[14]The broker's catalog contains market values for wine computed from the prices listed by wholesale wine merchants on the Bordeaux market.

[15]We use a quarterly price index calculated from the regression of the logarithm of price on quarter dummies in order to detrend prices.

Table 5. GLS Estimation of the Relationship between Primeur Price and Price of Bottled Wine

Dependent variable: price of bottled wine (log)	Coef.	Std. Err.	p-value	Marginal effects [95% conf. int.]	
Constant	0.605	0.123	0.000	1.44	2.33
Primeur price (log)	0.309	0.013	0.000	*0.28*	*0.33*
Wine quality (Parker's grade)	0.025	0.001	0.000	1.02	1.03
Ranking					
ME-1	−0.001	0.124	0.995	0.78	1.28
ME-2	−0.823	0.113	0.000	0.35	0.55
ME-3	−1.077	0.119	0.000	0.27	0.43
ME-4	−1.147	0.118	0.000	0.25	0.40
ME-5	−1.189	0.115	0.000	0.24	0.38
ME-6	−1.417	0.112	0.000	0.19	0.30
SE-1	—	—	—	1.00	1.00
SE-2	−0.860	0.120	0.000	0.33	0.54
SE-3	−1.257	0.112	0.000	0.23	0.35
GR	−1.081	0.114	0.000	0.27	0.42
Nonclassified	−1.223	0.119	0.000	0.23	0.37
Pomerol Designation	0.302	0.067	0.000	1.19	1.54
Age					
Age × *VINT83*	0.022	0.001	0.000	1.02	1.03
Age × *VINT85*	0.025	0.001	0.000	1.02	1.03
Age × *VINT86*	0.025	0.001	0.000	1.02	1.03
Age × *VINT87*	0.013	0.001	0.000	1.01	1.02
Age × *VINT88*	0.024	0.001	0.000	1.02	1.03
Age × *VINT89*	0.027	0.001	0.000	1.03	1.03
Age × *VINT90*	0.032	0.001	0.000	1.03	1.03
Age × *VINT91*	0.010	0.001	0.000	1.01	1.01
Age × *VINT92*	0.006	0.001	0.000	1.00	1.01
Age × *VINT93*	0.014	0.001	0.000	1.01	1.02
Age × *VINT94*	0.013	0.001	0.000	1.01	1.02
Age × *VINT95*	0.019	0.001	0.000	1.02	1.02
Age × *VINT96*	0.001	0.001	0.159	1.00	1.00
Age × *VINT97*	−0.022	0.001	0.000	0.98	0.98
Age × *VINT98*	−0.020	0.002	0.000	0.98	0.98
Age × *Age*	0.000	0.000	0.000	1.00	1.00
Fraction of variance due to unobservable effects:	0.38				
Total number of observations:	11,841				
Total number of *châteaux*:	132				
R-squared:	0.86				

Note: the numbers in italics in the last two columns represent elasticities and not multiplicative effects.

Table 6. *Château* Effects Estimated from Spot Price Model

			Quartiles				
	Mean	Std. Dev.	25%	50%	75%	Min.	Max.
Overall	0.000	0.235	−0.159	−0.15	0.136	−0.476	0.719
	(1.00)	(1.26)	(0.85)	(0.98)	(1.15)	(0.62)	(2.05)
ME-1	0.000	0.133	−0.039	−0.023	0.003	−0.153	0.213
	(1.00)	(1.14)	(0.96)	(0.98)	(1.00)	(0.86)	(1.24)

Note: Multiplicative effects in brackets.

that primeur sales do not have all the typical features of forward contracts, since there is no guarantee on the quality of the wine that is going to be delivered.[16]

Finally, the impact of ranking is found to be strong, with multiplicative effects ranging from 0.19 (lower bound of the interval for ME-6) to 1.28 (upper bound for ME-1). The chi-square test of equality of the age effect across vintages is rejected at the 1% level, indicating that the age premium is not the same across vintages of different quality. However, the impact of age on the price of bottled wine is somewhat limited, in the same range as the impact of quality. Hence, in the case of bottled wine as well, the ranking proves to have the strongest impact on price. This latter result highlights the role of labeling, in contrast with some published studies measuring the impact of food product labeling on consumers' behavior. Indeed, Van der Lans *et al.* (2001) employed a conjoint analysis to show that Protected Designation of Origin (PDO) labels have no direct effect on consumer preferences in the case of olive oil. Bonnet and Simioni (2001), using a mixed logit model of demand to reflect the distribution of consumers' willingness to pay for labeled cheese (Camembert), demonstrated that consumers did not value the quality signal provided by PDO labels for these French cheeses.

The fraction of unexplained variance due to *château*-specific effects is now reduced to 38%, compared to 69% in the primeur price model. The unobserved *château* effects are almost normally distributed (see Figure A2 in the Appendix). Simple statistics show that the range of multiplicative effects is very close to that reported in the case of primeur price (see Table 6). In this

[16]There has been an attempt to create a futures market for fine Bordeaux wines. In September 2001, *Euronext*, a privately owned stock exchange created by the merger of the Paris, Brussels, and Amsterdam stock markets in 2000, launched *WineFex*, the first futures market for first-quality Bordeaux wines. *Winefex* did not manage to attract liquidity and was canceled in November 2003.

model, the random *château* effect should be interpreted as the consumer's valuation of the name of the *château*.

5. Conclusions

Using a large and representative sample of Bordeaux wines, we show that the pricing behavior of producers during primeur sales depends largely on their reputation, and particularly on their ranking in the old quality-based classification system. We find that the few *Médoc* and *Saint Emilion châteaux* belonging to the top ranks set their primeur wine price significantly above *châteaux* belonging to the lower ranks. This high premium may be the result of strong market power and/or a high signaling cost. Separate identification of these two effects remains an open area for future research. Previous and current wine quality is found to have a very limited but significant impact on primeur price. Producers also appear to increase primeur prices when the expected demand is high because of a booming wine market.

The second part of the analysis looks at the relationship between spot price and primeur price, with reference to the literature on commodity futures markets. However, we should be cautious about generalizing our results to other futures markets, since primeur sales are informal and there is no guarantee on the quality of wine to be delivered. Nevertheless, our study supports the hypothesis that including primeur price in the spot-price function increases the predictability of spot prices.

Together with the low impact of current quality (and the nil impact of past quality as measured by grades attributed in the past), this result suggests that the consumers' belief about quality is influenced by primeur prices. The price of bottled wine in the spot price model, which here represents the valuation of wine by consumers, appears to be significantly driven by rank issues. These results contradict the findings of previous empirical studies on the impact of food product labeling on consumers' willingness to pay.

In general, the present study provides some empirical evidence that producers can gain price premia by using food labels (Henneberry and Armbruster, 2003). We find that the reputation premium — driven by quality-based ranking — is very high in an area such as Bordeaux, which benefits from a long-established reputation in wine making. The "reputation premium" driven by the quality-based classification significantly outweighs any effect driven by objective measures of past quality or the premium associated with short-term changes in current quality. These findings help in understanding why most European producers from famous regions such as Bordeaux are against the idea of abandoning the current labeling system.

It is somewhat surprising that the New World Wine countries choose product differentiation strategies based on names referring to the grape variety used in the production of each particular wine, instead of adopting labeling systems based on place of origin and quality ranks, which have proved to be successful in Europe. However, we argue that a region-specific and quality-based classification will allow producers to gain some reputation premium only in areas (e.g., in Europe) where a long-term reputation for wine making already exists. This argument is reinforced by the current situation observed in the United States: in places where recognition and reputation of a certain quality have increased (e.g., Sonoma County or Napa Valley), wineries have started changing their marketing strategies by placing more emphasis on the origin of the product (Loureiro, 2003).

This analysis was conducted using data covering vintages from 1983 to 1998, a period during which the French wine market was steadily growing. French wine is now facing more and more competition, especially from New World Wine countries. It would be interesting to conduct a similar analysis on the market for Bordeaux primeur wine using recent data. We could then measure whether the pricing strategy of Bordeaux producers has changed, and if the price premium driven by reputation is still high in the Bordeaux region

Acknowledgments

The authors wish to thank Pierre Dubois, Valérie Meunier, Katrin Millock, Michel Simioni, Alban Thomas, Ian M. Sheldon (the editor), Michael Visser, and two anonymous reviewers for their useful comments and suggestions that materially improved the chapter. The usual caveats apply.

References

Akerlof, G.A. (1970). The market for "Lemons": Quality uncertainty and the market mechanism. *Quarterly Journal of Economics*, 84, 488–500.

Ashenfelter, O., Ashmore, D., and Lalonde, R. (1995). Bordeaux wine vintage quality and the weather. *Chance*, 8, 7–14.

Bonnet, C., and Simioni, M. (2001). Assessing consumer response to protected designation of origin labeling: A mixed multinomial logit approach. *European Review of Agricultural Economics*, 28, 433–449.

Bureau, J.C., and Valceschini, E. (2003). European food-labeling policy: Successes and limitations. *Journal of Food Distribution Research*, 34(3), 70–76.

Carter, C.A. (1999). Commodity futures markets: A survey. *Australian Journal of Agricultural and Resource Economics*, 43, 209–247.

Combris, P., Lecocq, S., and Visser, M. (1997). Estimation of a hedonic price equation for bordeaux wine: Does quality matter? *Economic Journal*, 107, 390–402.

Combris, P., Lecocq, S., and Visser, M. (2000). Estimation of a hedonic price equation for burgundy wine. *Applied Economics*, 32, 961–967.

Cox, C. (1976). Futures trading and market information. *Journal of Political Economy*, 84, 1215–1237.

Darby, M., and Karni, E. (1973). Free competition and the optimal amount of fraud. *Journal of Law and Economics*, 16, 67–88.

Giraud-Héraud, E., Soler, G., and Tanguy, H. (2002). Concurrence Internationale dans le Secteur Viticole: Quel Avenir au Modèle d'Appellation d'Origine Contrôlée? *INRA Sciences Sociales*, 5–6/01.

Grossman, S.J. (1981). The informational role of warranties and private disclosure about product quality. *Journal of Law and Economics*, 24, 461–483.

Hadj Ali, H., and Nauges, C. (2003). Vente en primeur et investissement: une Etude sur les grands crus de bordeaux. *Economie et Prévision*, 159, 93–103.

Henneberry, S.R., and Armbruster, W.J. (2003). Emerging roles for food labels: Inform, protect, persuade. *Journal of Food Distribution Research*, 34(3), 62–69.

Jones, G.V., and Storchmann, K.H. (2001). Wine market prices and investment under uncertainty: An econometric model for Bordeaux crus classés. *Agricultural Economics*, 26, 115–133.

Keynes, J.M. (1930). *A Treatise on Money*. London: Macmillan.

Landon, S., and Smith, C.E. (1997). The use of quality and reputation indicators by consumers: The case of bordeaux wine. *Journal of Consumer Policy*, 20, 289–323.

Landon, S., and Smith, C.E. (1998). Quality expectations, reputation and price. *Southern Economic Journal*, 64, 628–647.

Lecocq, S., and Visser, M. (2006). What determines wine prices: Objective vs. sensory characteristics. *Journal of Wine Economics*, 1, 42–56.

Loureiro, M.L. (2003). Rethinking new wines: Implications of local and environmentally friendly labels. *Food Policy*, 28, 547–560.

Mahenc, P. (2004). The influence of informed buyers in markets susceptible to the lemons problem. *American Journal of Agricultural Economics*, 86(3), 649–659.

Mahenc, P., and Meunier, V. (2003). Forward markets and signals of quality. *Rand Journal of Economics*, 34, 478–494.

Mahenc, P., and Meunier, V. (2006). Early sales of bordeaux *grands crus*. *Journal of Wine Economics*, 1, 57–74.

Marette, S., and Zago, A. (2003). Advertising, collective action, and labeling in the European wine markets. *Journal of Food Distribution Research*, 34(3), 117–126.

McCluskey, J.J., and Loureiro, L. (2003). Consumer preferences and willingness to pay for food labeling: A discussion of empirical studies. *Journal of Food Distribution Research*, 34(3), 95–102.

Milgrom, P., and Roberts, J. (1986). Price and advertising signals of product quality. *Journal of Political Economy*, 94, 796–821.

Nelson, P. (1970). Information and consumer behavior. *Journal of Political Economy*, 78, 311–329.

Nelson, P. (1974). Advertising as information. *Journal of Political Economy*, 81, 729–754.

Oczkowski, E. (1994). A hedonic price function for Australian premium table wine. *Australian Journal of Agricultural Economics*, 38, 93–110.

Oczkowski, E. (2001). Hedonic wine price functions and measurement error. *Economic Record*, 77, 374–382.

Rao, A., and Monroe, K.B. (1988). The moderating effect of prior knowledge on cue utilization in product evaluations. *Journal of Consumer Research*, 15, 253–264.

Schamel, G., and Anderson, K. (2003). Wine quality and varietal, regional and winery reputations: Hedonic prices for Australia and New Zealand. *Economic Record*, 79, 357–369.

Shaked, A., and Sutton, J. (1982). Relaxing price competition through product differentiation. *Review of Economic Studies*, 49, 3–13.

Shapiro, C. (1983). Premiums for high quality products as rents to reputation. *Quarterly Journal of Economics*, 98, 659–680.

Tirole, J. (1996). A theory of collective reputations (with applications to the persistence of corruption and to firm quality). *Review of Economic Studies*, 63, 1–22.

Van der Lans, I.A., Van Ittersum, K., De Cicco, A., and Loseby, M. (2001). The role of the region of origin and EU certificates of origin in consumer evaluation of food products. *European Review of Agricultural Economics*, 28, 451–477.

Zeithaml, V.A. (1988). Consumer perceptions of price, quality, and value: A means-end model and synthesis of evidence. *Journal of Marketing*, 52, 2–22.

Appendix

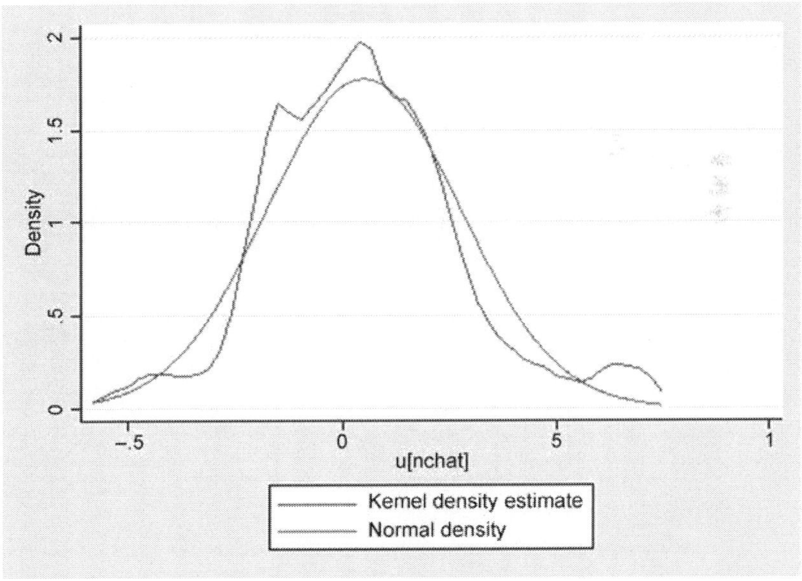

Figure A1. Distribution of Estimated *Château* Effects — Primeur Price Model

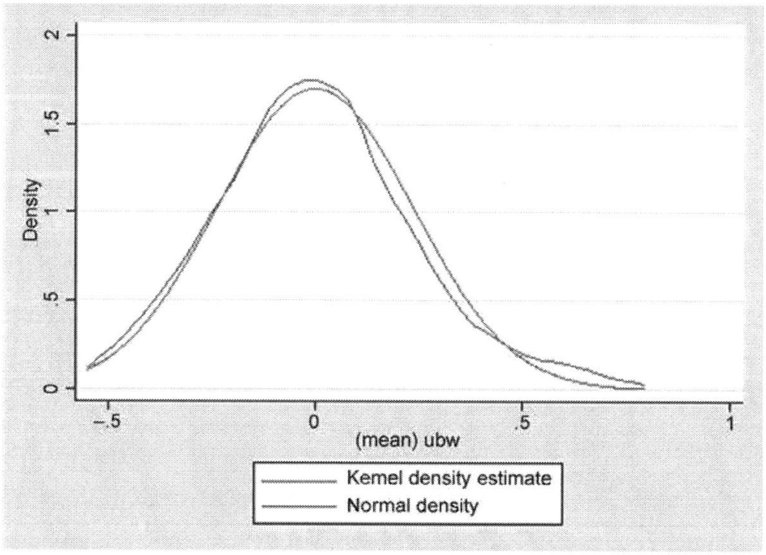

Figure A2. Distribution of Estimated *Château* Effects — Spot Price Model

Table A1. *Wine Spectator*'s Grades for Vintage Overall Quality

Vintage year	Ratings	
1983	86	(Good to very good)
1985	93	(Outstanding)
1986	95	(Classic)
1987	76	(Average)
1988	93	(Outstanding)
1989	98	(Classic)
1990	97	(Classic)
1991	72	(Average)
1992	72	(Average)
1993	82	(Good to very good)
1994	85	(Good to very good)
1995	95	(Classic)
1996	85	(Good to very good)
1997	81	(Good to very good)
1998	90	(Outstanding)

Part IV

Wine and Finance

Chapter 10

Bordeaux Wine as a Financial Investment*

Lee W. Sanning[†], Sherrill Shaffer[‡], and Jo Marie Sharratt[§]

[†]*Department of Economics and Finance, University of Wyoming, 1000 East University Ave., Laramie, WY 82071, USA, phone (307) 766-3848, lsanning@uwyo.edu*

[‡]*Department of Economics and Finance, University of Wyoming, 1000 East University Ave., Laramie, WY 82071, USA, phone (307) 766-2173, shaffer@uwyo.edu*

[§]*Department of Economics and Finance, University of Wyoming, 1000 East University Ave., Laramie, WY 82071, USA, phone (970) 225-1275, jo_mcgu ire@msn.com*

For repeat transactions data from monthly auction hammer prices, we analyze the level and quality of Bordeaux wine returns using the Fama-French Three-Factor Model and the Capital Asset Pricing Model. Returns average up to 0.75% per month above those predicted by these models. Further, investment grade wines benefit from low exposure to market risk factors, thus offering a valuable dimension of portfolio diversification. These findings are consistent with simple theoretical considerations and support a documented growing interest in wine investments.

1. Introduction

While many people consider buying wine and aging it for future consumption, few have historically viewed wine strictly as a financial investment. Yet

*This article originally appeared in *Journal of Wine Economics* (2008), 3(1), 51–71.

wine possesses characteristics that allow it to be considered and analyzed as an investment vehicle. Most important among these is an active trading market; monthly wine auctions at the top six auction houses frequently exceed $15 million. In recent years, at least two mutual funds have formed to invest specifically in wine: the Ascot Wine Management Fine Wine Fund, founded in 1999 by a Bahamian company, has exhibited annual gains ranging from 10.9% to 13%; and the Orange Wine Fund, founded in 2001, is listed on the Euronext Stock Exchange in Amsterdam. Information published by these funds indicates that they are managed with an approach similar to that of hedge funds (*International Herald Tribune*, 2001).

Additional evidence that wines are increasingly viewed as investment vehicles comes from recent proposed changes to British pension tax law. UK self-invested pension plans (SIPPs) are similar to some US individual retirement accounts (IRAs) which allow individual to invest virtually tax free. The proposed changes would have broadened the allowable assets to include "residential property and certain other assets such as fine wines" (HM Treasury, 2005). Chancellor of the Exchequer, at the time Gordon Brown, subsequently modified his position and ultimately classified these assets such that wine and other assets can be put into SIPPs but are ineligible for tax relief.[1]

Given these recent trends in viewing wine as an investment vehicle, an open question therefore is whether wine returns compare favorably with historical financial returns on other assets, both in mean value and in volatility or covariance. This chapter addresses that question, first by developing a simple conceptual framework to formulate specific hypotheses, and then by using both the Capital Asset Pricing Model (CAPM) and the Fama-French Three-Factor Model to test the hypotheses empirically (Fama and French, 1993). Our sample is formed from monthly repeat transactions data for individual wine-asset sales, which yields a time series of monthly returns. Consistent with our predictions, we find that the wines in our sample exhibit large, positive excess returns along with low exposure to commonly recognized market risk factors. These findings provide quantitative evidence that wine may be a viable investment asset, both alone and as part of a well diversified portfolio.

The remainder of this chapter is organized as follows. Section 2 summarizes related literature, Section 3 presents key concepts and hypotheses,

[1]For a summary specific to wine-assets and SIPPs, see *The Decanter.Com Guide to Wine and Sipps* (www.decanter.com/specials/71476.html).

Section 4 describes the data, Section 5 presents the empirical model, Section 6 reports the results, and Section 7 concludes.

2. Related Literature

Wine exhibits unique characteristics relative to traditional financial assets. Some of these characteristics are similar to those exhibited by other tangible assets such as collectible art. Wine does not pay a dividend; investors must pay for its storage, and the time required to liquidate a collection of wine can extend to four or five months. Further, a bottle of wine may break or may be otherwise deemed worthless if stored improperly.

While the subject of wine as an investment has been sparsely studied relative to traditional financial assets like stocks, mutual funds, bonds, etc., extant results and recommendations are mixed. Krasker (1979) analyzed returns over the period of 1973–1977 and found no risk premium for storing red Bordeaux and California Cabernet Sauvignon wines produced since 1950. Jaeger (1981), by contrast, established risk premiums in excess of 12% using Krasker's methodology but extending the sample period to eight years beginning in 1969 and incorporating a significantly lower measure of wine storage costs. Jaeger argued that the four-year period studied by Krasker biased his procedure toward finding a subnormal rate of return. Additionally, the different assumptions about storage costs affect the premiums measured. Jaeger's estimate of storage cost was approximately $0.50 per case annually while Krasker's estimate was over $16 per case for annual storage.

Weil (1993) calculated the returns to an individual wine portfolio using detailed information across a 13 year (1980–1992) acquisition and holding period. His results suggest that the return to wine assets is approximately 9.5% and increases to 11% if the portfolio is limited to Bordeaux wines. Weil concluded that these returns were much less than rates of return to NYSE stocks over the same period. Interestingly, the Bordeaux wines in the investor's portfolio exhibit lower return variation than other wines. Weil noted that this is not efficient since Bordeaux wines have a higher return and less risk. We extend this finding by calculating the excess returns of wine, returns over (or under) a risk-adjusted market return.

More recently, Burton and Jacobsen (2001) used a repeat-sale regression — an approach also used by Goetzmann (1993) to value the art market — to estimate the rate of return for Bordeaux wines during 1986–1996. Their findings include an annual nominal rate of return of almost 14% for a portfolio of 1982 wine but only 8.3% for a portfolio of 1961 wines. An aggregate portfolio of wines earned a nominal rate of 7.9% annually while a portfolio consisting of only those classified as "First Growth" earned 6.7%.[2] Of particular interest is the comparison to the Dow Jones Industrial Average: only the 1982 vintage portfolio outperforms the index over the period in question.

While these studies focused on establishing wine asset returns either in absolute terms or relative to a simple market return, they did not explicitly account for the financial risk of wine assets.[3] This chapter enhances this literature by both determining wine returns over a more recent time period and by investigating the degree of exposure and covariance between wine returns and common financial risk factors.

Other studies have focused on the determinants of wine prices. Combris, Lecocq, and Visser (1997 and 2000) explored whether market prices respond to various measures of quality. Objective characteristics, including the name of the producer, ranking of the wine (growth classification), color of the wine, and vintage, were found to be significantly associated with the variation in prices. By contrast, a majority of the subjective characteristics, including visual and olfactory findings, gustatory findings, and grade as determined by a "jury" of four persons, were found not to be significantly associated with market prices. Jones and Storchmann (2001), on the other hand, found wine ratings ("Parker points") to be a significant determinant of Bordeaux prices, along with sugar levels, acidity, and aging. Similarly, Cardebat and Figuet (2004) found sensory variables to be a significant determinant of Bordeaux prices for 1996–1999 vintages. While it is not surprising that some of these non-financial factors have been found to help explain or predict prices of specific wines, our empirical model does not include them because, from the perspective of a diversified investor, such factors correspond to firm-specific risk and the relevant financial question is to what extent such risk can be mitigated in a diversified portfolio.

Another set of literature addresses the hypothesis that collectibles act as a hedge against stock market risk by exhibiting a negative covariance with market returns or with inflation. Burton and Jacobsen (1999) summarized

---

[2]In most of the Bordeaux region, it is the wine producer (chateau) and not the land that is classified by growth. The five growth classifications were originally established to distinguish among the quality of the wines produced in the area (where First Growth represents the highest quality).

[3]Jaeger (1981) discusses risk as an important factor in wine investments, but does not incorporate an explicit measure of risk in the empirical model.

the research in this area. Specifically, they stated that while research has shown that returns on collectibles may be negatively correlated with stock market returns (for items including coins, stamps, and art), there is no evidence that collectibles are a hedge against stock market declines since returns on collectibles have been historically flat during the periods examined. Wines were not studied in this context. This chapter contributes to the literature by specifically measuring the covariance of wine returns with stock market returns.

3. Background Concepts and Hypotheses

One key issue that previous studies appear to have neglected is a formal comparison of fundamental sources of value across equities, wine assets, and other collectibles such as art. A standard and long-established approach to estimating the market value of an equity relies on the discounted present value of its dividend payouts (Gordon, 1962). In this approach, cash payouts to investors comprise the ultimate source of investment value. Under the simplifying assumption that dividends grow at a constant rate g, and discounting at a constant rate r_e, the discounted present value at time t of an infinite stream of dividends can be explicitly expressed in a simple form. The exact valuation and the corresponding rate of return on the investment will depend on details of timing and whether or not dividends are reinvested. For purposes of comparison, we calculate the valuation P_t as of the beginning of period t, assuming that the dividend D_t is paid at the end of period t. Under these assumptions, the value of the equity is:

$$P_t = D_t/(r_e - g), \tag{1}$$

in the discrete-time case.[4] A basic prediction of this model and an immediate consequence of equation (1) is that the value of an equity grows at the rate g. The total nominal annual net rate of return earned by an equity investor is the sum of this capital appreciation rate g plus the dividend rate implied by equation (1), which equals:

$$\text{equity return} = D/P_t + g = (r_e - g) + g = r_e. \tag{2}$$

This simplified and standard analysis incorporates uncertainty only implicitly; g is typically interpreted as an expected value while r_e is set

[4]Alternate assumptions about the timing of cash flows, or alternate notation, will yield a slightly different expression for valuation.

at a level that incorporates an appropriate risk premium. Thus, in general, $g < r_e$, a condition also needed as a technical requirement of the model to ensure a positive and finite valuation. Further, as a practical matter, the principle of opportunity costs suggests that the long-run growth rate of the aggregate economy constitutes a lower bound on values of r_e that are relevant to investors, and any risk premium would drive r_e above that bound. Combined with the accounting identity that no individual company can grow faster than the entire economy forever, this logic also ensures $g < r_e$.

The source of financial value of collectible artwork, by contrast, is ultimately derived from the consumption value of viewing the item. While the value of viewing a particular piece of art may vary over time and will typically vary from one individual to the next, any single painting or sculpture is a unique object that (apart from accidental damage or depreciation) will not change over time. Thus, at least in real terms, it is difficult to identify any reason why the consumption value of viewing any individual piece of art should be expected to increase over time, except possibly to the extent that close substitutes (such as other paintings by the same artist) may grow scarcer due to damage or loss. Further, this consumption value exists as a continuous stream, in that each owner has a constant opportunity to view the artwork while it remains in his possession.

This line of thought suggests that the pattern of returns to artwork resembles that of a perpetuity or consol, namely a (roughly) constant expected value of consumption in each period. If C denotes the value of viewing the artwork in each period, then the well-known perpetuity formula gives the present value of the artwork as $PV = C/r_a$ for an appropriate discount rate r_a, which need not be the same value as r_e applied to equity in equation (1). A notable property of this valuation is a complete absence of capital appreciation in equilibrium, at least in real terms. The total rate of return to an investor in art is then the stream of consumption value alone, which accrues in the form of viewing pleasure but not in any measurable financial form.[5]

[5]This prediction is broadly consistent with many previous empirical findings: nominal returns to art investments have been found to be lower than for either equity or bond investments by Baumol (1986), Buelens and Ginsburgh (1993), Goetzmann (1993), Candela and Scorcu (1997), and Agnello and Pierce (1998) for paintings, and by Pesando (1993) for prints. Some negative real returns were reported by Agnello and Pierce (1998) while real annual returns of less than 1% were reported by Baumol (1986), Buelens and Ginsburgh (1993), and Candela and Scorcu (1997).

One might similarly postulate that the fundamental source of financial value for wine likewise derives from its eventual consumption value. A crucial difference is that a bottle of wine must be consumed at a single point in time, rather than conferring a continuous and readily accessible stream of consumption benefits as is true of artwork.[6]

Further, the owner chooses the time of consumption. As Jaeger (1981) notes, wines typically exhibit an optimal storage period after which the gustatory experience is maximized and, while there is uncertainty regarding the optimal consumption date, rational behavior would suggest that most bottles (especially those purchased for investment purposes) would tend to be opened and their contents consumed near the expected optimal date. Thus, the nature of the financial returns to wine revolves around a single consumption event. If the optimal consumption value is C, then the present value of a bottle of wine is given by $PV = C/(1+r_w)^T$ where the optimal consumption date occurs T periods in the future, and this present value grows at the rate r_w in each period. The rate of return to a wine investment is thus r_w.

Although this simple framework abstracts from explicit representation of uncertainty, it not only captures important financial features of equity, art, and wine assets, but also — as a first-order approximation — it implies two key hypotheses or predictions. First, although the discount rate r_w applied to wine valuation need not be the same as that applied to equity valuation, both will typically be established as the risk-free rate of interest plus some risk premium, and hence will be of similar orders of magnitude. Because the quality of wine is subject to several sources of uncertainty not shared by equities, including the optimal time of consumption, possibility of spoilage among some bottles, and uncertainty over how well a particular vintage will age, it is plausible that $r_w > r_e$ in many cases. Since the analysis above shows that the equilibrium return to investment equals r_e for equity and r_w for wine, one prediction is that, unlike the return to art, *the rate of return to wine investments should be similar to that of equities, and may even exceed them.* This prediction is consistent with the findings of Jaeger (1981) and Weil (1993), though not with those of Krasker (1989), and will be further tested below.

A second prediction follows from the observation that the fundamental source of financial value for wine derives from a consumption experience

[6]We assume that non-gustatory consumption benefits of wine, such as any collectible value of wine labels or the consumption value of viewing a well-stocked wine cellar, ultimately derive from drinking the wine and are thus secondary in their financial impact.

unique to each variety and vintage of wine. The economic value of that consumption experience will typically be an increasing function of an investor's financial wealth, which in turn is affected by the aggregate performance of equity markets to the extent that equity holdings comprise a significant share of the investor's total wealth. However, this is a second-order effect as the idiosyncratic risk of wines will typically overwhelm this correlated component of risk. An implication is thus that *the financial returns to wine should exhibit low correlations with returns on purely financial assets such as equities.* This property, if true, would make wine an attractive investment as a means of diversifying purely financial portfolios, especially if the first prediction is also true. We present the first empirical test of this second hypothesis below.

4. Sample and Descriptive Statistics

The wine returns data in our sample are derived from an eight-year series of monthly auction "hammer price"[7] data from The Chicago Wine Company on red Bordeaux[8] vintages ranging from 1893 to 1998.[9] Founded by Philip H. Tenenbaum in May 1974, The Chicago Wine Company (TCWC) conducted its first fine wine auction in April 1977, making it the second company to conduct wine auctions in the U.S. TCWC represents one of the largest trading markets for wine assets. TCWC now conducts at least one live auction and one silent auction per month, significantly more annually than any other wine auction company in Chicago or the U.S. It should be noted that these open auctions constitute secondary-market transactions. Some wines sell as futures or are allocated on a limited basis and thus represent primary-market transactions. These are similar to equity IPOs and not accessible to most investors. While the returns to investing in wine futures are an interesting area, we leave this to future research.

We use data on red Bordeaux wines, a choice based on several features of this wine. First, red Bordeaux wines have been determined to benefit

[7]A hammer price refers to the price at which the bidding stops and the item for sale is said to be "hammered down" (Ashenfelter, 1989).

[8]Bordeaux refers to a wine-making area of France that straddles the Garonne and Dordogne Rivers. This area is world-famous for its reputation of being home to the finest red wine producers. The area benefits from a long and warm growing season as well as soil composition, made up of topsoil poor in nutrients and subsoil rich in minerals (Clarke, 1996).

[9]These data are readily available on The Chicago Wine Company's webpage of past auction hammer prices (http://www.tcwc.com/pauct.htm).

from extended aging (Jaeger, 1981). Perhaps related to this property, red Bordeaux wines are purchased more often for investment purposes than for consumption relative to white wines and wines from other regions. Consequently, French wines, and in particular those from Bordeaux, comprise the greater part of the wine auction market (Burton and Jacobsen, 2001). Annual classified growth Bordeaux sales are approximately $7 billion as of 2005.

Returns data are calculated for each month from repeat transactions. The returns are calculated for every vintage,[10] or year of production, and for every individual wine producer.[11] The calculation of monthly returns by vintage and producer is a three-step process. First, an average price per bottle is calculated for each year and month of trade by the vintage and producer.[12] Next, the average return for each vintage and producer is calculated by the difference in the log of the average price for the month of trade and the log of the average price for the prior month of trade. If a trade did not occur in the prior month, the return is designated as missing.[13] In the third step, a modified mean is calculated by winsorizing the sample as in Nissim and Ziv (2001), Dittmar (2004), and others.[14] For those portions of the analyses that require average returns by vintage and growth classification,[15] the data are categorized by classification and then averages are calculated for every

[10]Vintage refers to a particular year's grape harvest and may also refer to the wine of a single year (Oz Clarke, 1986)

[11]The sample is limited to wines with non-inferior bottle conditions. Wines with label conditions (stains, tears) as well as less than full shoulder fills are eliminated. The resulting data set therefore has consistent bottle conditions. This reduces return variance due to varying asset quality.

[12]The prices used to calculate returns are the hammer prices as reported by TCWC. As is standard with calculation of traditional asset returns, brokerage costs, account fees, or other forms of transactions costs are not accounted for since they vary across investors, investment horizon, and investment scale.

[13]To maximize sample size while maintaining econometric precision, we require a minimum of 15 observations for any given vintage producer or vintage growth portfolio.

[14]This method replaces extreme values in the sample with limits. In this study, the entire sample is divided into groups; the groups representing the highest 2.5% and the lowest 2.5% return values are replaced. The replacement values are those maximum and minimum values as calculated by respective vintage and producer. For example, if a return for a 1982 Latour falls within the bottom 2.5% of the entire sample of returns, the value is replaced with the minimum average return for the sample of 1982 Latou returns. This process resolves the problem of inconsistent outliers resulting from data entry errors and lack of data cleaning. Our choice of a 2.5% threshold lies between the 5% value used by Dittmar (2004) and the 0.1% value selected by Nissim and Ziv (2001).

[15]These are for First through Fifth Growth and for unclassified wines (*No Growth*).

year and month of trade by vintage and growth. Calculating averages as outlined above allows for a degree of smoothing of the returns data, which has been shown to exhibit a wide range of values. In addition, it mitigates the "declining price anomaly," a phenomenon in which identical lots of wine sold at a later time in a single auction are likely to sell for a lower price than those purchased earlier in the day (Ashenfelter, 1989).

The wine returns data are based on approximately 90 producers and include vintage years from 1893 through 1998. In total, the data include 13,662 wine asset returns recognized over the eight-year period 1996–2003. For the purpose of evaluating investment potential relative to equities, this period is fairly short; on the other hand, it includes a period of exceptionally high returns in the U.S. stock market, thereby providing a stringent benchmark for identifying excess returns. Of the 90 producers present in the sample, 47 belong to a growth classification.[16] Within the data set, there are 276 unique vintage and producer combinations and 83 unique vintage and growth groupings.

The three variables comprising the Fama-French Three-Factor Model, described below, are published monthly by Kenneth French and may be downloaded directly from his website.[17] The three factors consist of Rm-Rf, a measure of the value-weighted return on all NYSE, AMEX and NASDAQ stocks (from CRSP) net of the one-month Treasury bill rate, SMB (Small Minus Big), a measure of the difference in the average return on small and large market equity firms, and HML (High Minus Low), a measure of the difference in average return between high and low book-to-market equity firms.[18] Other data required to estimate the model include monthly U.S. Treasury returns, obtained from the CRSP government bond file.

4.1. *Descriptive statistics*

Table 1 presents descriptive statistics. Average monthly returns by vintage and producer range from −4.38% (1961 Petrus)[19] to 7.48% (1966 Haut Brion), with the average of all monthly returns at a respectable 0.51%. When only those wines that are classified in the growth categories are analyzed, the

[16]It should be noted that only five wines comprise the First Growth classification (Haut Brion, Lafite Rothschild, Latour, Margaux and Mouton Rothschild).

[17]http://mba.tuck.dartmouth.edu/pages/faculty/ken.french/data_library.html

[18]For a detailed description of the estimation of the factor returns, see Fama and French (1993).

[19]This number indicates that over the eight year trading period, 1961 Petrus has an average monthly return of −4.38%.

Table 1. Descriptive Statistics — Monthly Wine Returns

	Avg # monthly returns	Avg monthly % return	Std dev monthly % return	Min avg monthly % return	Max avg monthly % return	Avg min monthly % return	Avg max monthly % return
Vintage & Producer	37	0.51	6.05	−4.38	7.48	−11.26	13.98
Vintage & Producer[a]	39	0.78	7.20	−2.71	7.48	−12.45	16.07
Vintage & Growth	49	0.88	7.08	−2.86	4.18	−13.19	17.54
Vintage & Growth[a]	47	1.03	7.29	−2.39	4.03	−13.10	17.99
First Growth	49	0.70	7.81	−2.39	2.65	−13.85	18.58
Second Growth	58	1.45	7.12	−0.22	3.85	−12.88	17.66
Third Growth	53	1.08	7.16	0.26	2.29	−12.15	18.91
Fourth Growth	33	0.91	6.84	−0.83	4.03	−12.57	16.73
Fifth Growth	44	1.07	6.50	−1.25	3.85	−13.36	16.45
No Growth	55	0.45	6.45	−2.86	4.18	−13.46	16.23

Notes: [a]includes only those wines classified in one of the five growth classifications.
Avg # Monthly Returns is the average number of observations for the vintage-producer assets or vintage-growth asset.
For example, the average vintage producer return series has 37 monthly observations with an average monthly return of 0.51%.

average increases to 0.78%. Perhaps not that surprising to advocates of wine investment, more than 75 wines averaged 1% or more in monthly returns (see Table 2). The average minimum monthly return for all returns by vintage and producer is approximately −11%,[20] with an average maximum return of 14% (see Table 1). The standard deviation of all monthly returns by vintage and producer is 6%.

The average monthly returns as calculated by vintage and growth are similar though somewhat greater due to the difference in the weighting structure. When calculating averages by vintage and producer, each producer's average monthly return is given a weight of one. When calculating average returns by vintage and growth classification, the returns represent a

[20]This number is calculated by observing the lowest return for each wine (vintage-producer), and averaging these minimum returns across all wines (vintage-producer).

Table 2. Top 75 Wine Assets by Average Monthly Return

Vintage	Producer	Avg monthly % return	Vintage	Producer	Avg monthly % return
1966	Haut Brion	7.48	1989	Trotte Vieille	1.76
1982	Lynch Bages	4.95	1983	Pichon Lalande	1.74
1990	Pichon Lalande	4.39	1988	Mouton Rotschild	1.72
1989	L'Enclos	4.32	1989	Lynch Bages	1.72
1989	Canon La Gaffelière	4.07	1994	Margaux	1.70
1961	Latour	3.68	1990	Pichon Baron	1.69
1982	Petit Village	3.25	1986	Pichon Lalande	1.66
1988	Lafite Rothschild	3.18	1995	Meyney	1.53
1995	Pavillon Rouge du Margaux	2.77	1961	Lynch Bages	1.50
1970	Haut Brion	2.75	1989	L'Evangile	1.49
1989	Mouton Rothschild	2.73	1959	Haut Brion	1.48
1985	Margaux	2.72	1945	Mouton Rothschild	1.46
1986	Gruaud Larose	2.69	1986	Haut Brion	1.46
1990	Gruaud Larose	2.66	1995	Calon Ségur	1.45
1995	Lynch Bages	2.59	1982	La Mission Haut Brion	1.44
1970	Ducru Beaucaillou	2.51	1995	La Mission Haut Brion	1.38
1986	Cheval Blanc	2.49	1996	Bellefont-Belcier	1.36
1986	Talbot	2.49	1989	Pichon Lalande	1.33
1996	Léoville Poyferré	2.47	1989	Gruaud Larose	1.32
1996	Pape Clement	2.44	1982	Pavie	1.32
1990	Mouton Rothschild	2.29	1989	Belair	1.32
1989	Pichon Baron	2.24	1982	Gruaud Larose	1.28
1983	Léoville Las Cases	2.23	1986	Margaux	1.27
1985	Cos d'Estournel	2.20	1995	Ducru Beaucaillou	1.26
1990	Certan De May	2.12	1995	Léoville Las Cases	1.22
1988	La Mission Haut Brion	2.11	1982	Léoville Las Cases	1.22
1982	Cos d'Estournel	2.10	1996	Margaux	1.20
1990	Haut Brion	2.07	1989	Palmer	1.19
1982	Calon Ségur	2.00	1989	Fieuzal	1.17
1989	Figeac	2.00	1990	Troplong Mondot	1.17
1982	Lafite Rothschild	2.00	1990	L'Evangile	1.11
1989	Ducru Beaucaillou	1.91	1970	La Mission Haut Brion	1.10
1970	Lafite Rothschild	1.90	1986	Lafite Rothschild	1.08
1982	Pétrus	1.88	1970	Latour	1.06
1983	Margaux	1.87	1995	Grand Puy Lacoste	1.05
1998	Cheval Blanc	1.84	1998	Haut Brion	1.04
1989	Léoville Las Cases	1.81	1990	Calon Ségur	1.03
1990	Rauzan-Ségla	1.78			

mean of the average returns for all applicable producers in a given month. The monthly averages by vintage and growth range from −2.9% (1961 "no growth") to 4.2% (1979 "no growth"). The average for all returns by vintage and growth is 0.88% per month, with an average minimum of −13.2% and a maximum of 17.5%. When the sample is reduced to those wines categorized in one of the five growth classifications, the average monthly return is over 1%. When analyzed further by growth classification, Second Growth outperforms the other classifications on average monthly return with 1.45% (see Table 1).

These monthly returns are similar to those found in prior studies. For the years 1986 to 1996, the annual nominal rate of return for an aggregate portfolio of red Bordeaux was found to be 7.9% (Burton and Jacobsen, 2001). An average monthly return of 0.51 to 0.88% (6.2 to 11.1% annualized) occurs for all wines, while 0.78 to 1.03% (9.7 to 13.1% annualized) occurs for classified wines over the eight-year period from 1996 to 2003, which includes several depressed years in the equity market. Thus, relative to other asset classes, wine exhibits a strong positive return over the period.

There has been some debate over the extent to which additional nonpecuniary benefits associated with wine investment add to the monetary rate of return. Specifically, to what extent should investors consider the potential benefit of consumption? Strict economic theory maintains that the prices observed have already accounted for this option. Moreover, if markets are well functioning and complete, the rate of return on wine assets (net of costs and consumption benefits) should equal the rate of return on competing assets with identical risk (Burton and Jacobsen, 2001).

4.2. *Trading frequency*

Unreported results reveal a number of interesting patterns in trading frequency of the wines.[21] Of particular importance is the percentage of total returns accounted for by each growth classification. While the First Growth wines only account for 5.6% of the number of producers in the data, they account for approximately 20% of the trading volume. Another 20% of the trading activity comes from the trading of Second Growth wines. Third, Fourth, and Fifth Growth wines, in total, account for only 9.4% of total returns although they represent 30% of the producers in the sample. The

[21] Available from the authors upon request.

No Growth wines represent about 50% of both the number of producers and returns.

There also exist interesting patterns in monthly trading activity. For all growth classifications, wine trading volumes decline in February and March, increase in April and May, and decline again in June and July. Trading increases again in August, then declines in September and October. November, December, and January represent three consecutive months of substantial percentage increases. On average, the number of trades increases approximately 20% in November and another 20% in December. While beyond the scope of this study, future research may uncover seasonal trading strategies with arbitrage opportunities.

5. Regression Model

The Fama-French Three-Factor Model (TFM) (Fama and French, 1993) was developed in response to the research of the 1980s that revealed many empirical contradictions to the central CAPM. The CAPM predicts that expected returns are a function of their market βs and that the market βs suffice to describe the cross-section of expected returns on U.S. equities. Specifically, Fama and French (1992) confirm that, unlike the relationship between average return and β, there exists a strong negative relationship between firm size and average return and an even stronger positive relationship between book-to-market equity and average return, and that these two relationships persist in competition with other variables. Fama and French demonstrate that while the CAPM predictions hold for the pre-1969 period, they disappear for the 1963–1990 period. Thus, they augment the CAPM by including two additional variables, HML and SMB, as described above. The TFM has been shown to absorb common time-series variation in equity returns by producing intercepts closer to zero and increased R squared values. The empirical model is as follows:

$$R_{it} - RF_t = \alpha_i + \beta_{li}(RM_t - RF_t) + \beta_{2i}(SMB_t) + \beta_{3i}(HML_t) + \varepsilon_{it}, \quad (3)$$

where R_{it} is the return on a wine asset i (wine or wine portfolio) during month t, RF_t represents the risk-free rate (one month bill rate), RM_t represents the month t value-weighted return on all NYSE, AMEX, and NASDAQ stocks, SMB_t is the month t size factor HML_t is the month t book-to-market related factor.

Under this model, evaluating the financial performance of a wine asset is straightforward. The regression intercept represents the average abnormal return (positive or negative) and thus indicates whether an asset provides return in excess of the risk-adjusted return. A positive intercept indicates that, on average, the asset earned a return higher than suggested by the exposure to market risk factors.[22]

The regression analysis in this chapter includes both the TFM and CAPM. We include the CAPM, despite its relatively lower performance in explaining variations in asset returns, in order to estimate single-factor βs and to facilitate more traditional risk benchmarking of wine to other asset classes.[23]

The regression analyses include results based on average returns by vintage and producer, and by vintage and growth classification. The justification for separate regressions based on vintage comes from prior research on wine prices and returns. Vintage refers to a particular year's grape harvest and may also refer to the wine of a single year (Clarke, 1986). Research has shown that weather conditions during the growing season and the period of harvest play a significant role in forecasting long-run prices for wines (Corsi and Ashenfelter, 2003). Burton and Jacobsen show striking differences in returns based on vintage for red Bordeaux wines, with 1961 and 1982 vintage portfolios beating the market return. These results correspond well with published data regarding the ranking of wine quality by vintage. For example, 1982 is only one of two vintages rated as "exceptional" while 1961 rated as "excellent" for vintages since 1960 (Conseil Interprofessionnel du Vin de Bordeaux, 2004).

Growth classification of a particular wine has also been shown in prior studies to contribute significantly to its price. We confirm this by testing the significance of growth classifications using our auction data and the TFM. F-tests (unreported) support fixed differences in excess returns (alphas) and differences in beta coefficients (risk exposures) across the six growth categories (five classifies growths and one "no growth").[24] Based on these unreported results, individual regressions are estimated in the TFM and CAPM analyses for each of the unique vintage and growth groupings. Further, given

[22]The goal of this research is to use established models to analyze the quality of the returns that wines exhibit. This goal is different from developing a model to best *explain* wine returns, which we defer to future research. Our approach compares the financial returns of wines to those of equities, thus addressing the benefits of adding wine assets to an otherwise diversified portfolio.

[23]Single factor βs are universally used by practitioners while multi factor βs are used less commonly.

[24]Detailed results available from the authors upon request.

that the growth classifications are simply groupings of producers, individual regressions based on vintage and producer are analyzed as well.

6. Results

The results of our several hundred TFM regressions are summarized in Panel 1 of Table 3. As shown, the average regression intercepts (Jensen's alpha[25]) are positive. The average intercept over the time period analyzed here for the 276 regressions by vintage and producer is 0.186. Omitting the non-growth classification, the average excess return (regression intercept) for the 122 vintage-producer regressions increases to 0.419. *Average Rm-Rf* provides the average of the beta coefficients on the market factor. *Average SMB* provides the average of the beta coefficients on the size factor. *Average HML* provides the average of the beta coefficients on the book-to-market factor. The average coefficients for these three risk exposures are small relative to traditional equities, and many are in fact negative.

The results from the regression analysis establish two key findings. First, average wine returns are positive and in excess of risk-adjusted returns. Second, as indicated by the small risk factor loadings, wine returns covary minimally with market returns and other commonly accepted risk factors.[26] These results hold for regressions based on vintage and producer as well as on vintage and growth, and are consistent with the predictions of the theoretical framework presented above.

The results of the analysis by vintage and growth classification are largely equivalent, though somewhat greater due to the weighting structure discussed earlier. The average intercept for the 83 regressions by vintage and growth is 0.606. Again, if only the wines categorized within the five growth classifications are analyzed, the average of the 62 vintage-growth regression intercepts increases to 0.759. The significance of these results cannot be overstated. Investment grade wines provide, on average, substantially large, positive returns in excess of those forecasted by the Fama-French market risk factors. Specifically, these wines experienced monthly returns of 0.61 to

[25]This is a risk-adjusted performance measure that is the average return on a portfolio over and above that predicted, given the portfolio's beta and the average market return. This is the portfolio's alpha. In fact, the term is sometimes described as "Jensen's alpha."
[26]Because the covariance between wine returns and equity market returns is near zero, these standard financial models explain only a small portion of the total variation in wine returns (i.e., the R-squared values are low). On the other hand, these same models have been found to generate similar R-squared values of 0.03 (CAPM) to 0.05 (Fama-French) for individual monthly stock returns (Bartholdy and Peare, 2005).

Table 3. Average Regression Results

	# Regressions[b]	Average intercept	Average Rm-Rf	Average SMB	Average HML	Average R squared
Panel 1: Fama French 3 Factor Model						
Vintage & Producer	276	0.186	−0.008	−0.012	−0.066	0.095
Vintage & Producer[a]	122	0.419	−0.033	−0.049	−0.071	0.097
Vintage & Growth	83	0.606	−0.006	−0.034	−0.042	0.092
Vintage & Growth[a]	62	0.759	−0.020	0.037	−0.035	0.100
First Growth	22	0.478	−0.104	0.106	−0.030	0.094
Second Growth	18	1.330	−0.040	−0.149	−0.036	0.128
Third Growth	10	0.716	−0.049	0.037	−0.073	0.049
Fourth Growth	8	0.459	0.126	−0.264	−0.013	0.127
Fifth Growth	4	0.450	0.305	−0.053	−0.008	0.088
No Growth	21	0.154	0.037	−0.023	0.063	0.067
Panel 2: CAPM Model						
Vintage & Producer	276	0.168	−0.005			0.031
Vintage & Producer[a]	122	0.389	−0.019			0.030
Vintage & Growth	83	0.880	0.007			0.038
Vintage & Growth[a]	62	1.046	−0.002			0.041
First Growth	22	0.775	−0.074			0.052
Second Growth	18	1.532	−0.045			0.032
Third Growth	10	1.027	−0.018			0.027
Fourth Growth	8	0.750	0.107			0.024
Fifth Growth	4	0.727	0.310			0.035
No Growth	21	0.439	0.053			0.026

Notes: [a]Includes only those wines classified in one of the five growth classifications. [b]Because these are averages of numerous regression coefficients, t-statistics or p-values do not appear, but are discussed in the text and reflected in Figures 1(a)–2(b).

0.76% higher than those predicted by the Fama-French risk factors. On an annual basis, these compound to an excess return of 7.6 to 9.5%.

Figures 1(a) and 1(b) present the distributions of excess returns (intercept values) for the two sets of TFM regressions and their statistical significance. Approximately one-fourth of the intercepts for the regressions by vintage and growth are significant, indicated by the crosshatched portion of the bar graphs. Figure 1(b) indicates that the majority of the excess returns are positive.

Other regression results presented in Panel 1 of Table 3 provide evidence that wine assets covary minimally with commonly accepted market risk factors and thus provide a valuable source of diversification. The results show that there exists either a negative relationship between the wine asset returns and the Fama-French factors or an absence of a relationship (βs not significantly different from zero). For the 83 regressions based on returns by vintage and growth, the risk premium coefficient returned a significantly positive value in only six of the regressions. The remaining coefficients are either significantly negative (nine) or not significantly different from zero (68), with an overall average of -0.006. Results are similar for the coefficients for SMB, found to be significantly positive in five cases, significantly negative in five cases and not significantly different from zero in the remaining 73 regressions (average of -0.034). Results are similar for the HML coefficients, significantly positive in only two cases, significantly negative in eight cases and essentially zero in the remaining 73 (average of -0.042).

Further evidence that there exists a weak relationship between wine returns and the market risk factors is evident in the average R squared value of 0.09. The Fama-French factors, which have been shown to account for approximately 90% of the variation in stock returns, explain only 9% of the variation in wine returns on average. These results continue to hold in the regressions by vintage and producer. A mere 10% of the risk premium coefficients are significant with the majority significantly negative. With respect to the factor SMB, just over 8% of the coefficients are significant, and again, the majority is negative; 10% of the HML coefficients are significant and 87% of those are negative.

The CAPM regression results presented in Panel 2 of Table 3 are comparable to those of the TFM. The average intercepts for both sets of regressions are positive, indicating excess returns exist. The average intercept is 0.168 for the regressions by vintage and producer and 0.880 for those regressions by vintage and growth classification. The average coefficients on the market factor are both effectively zero (0.007 by vintage and growth and -0.005

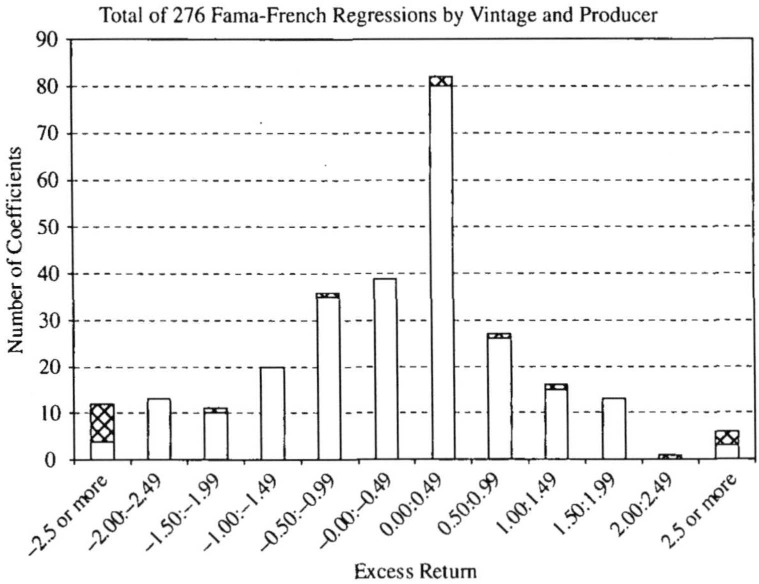

(a)

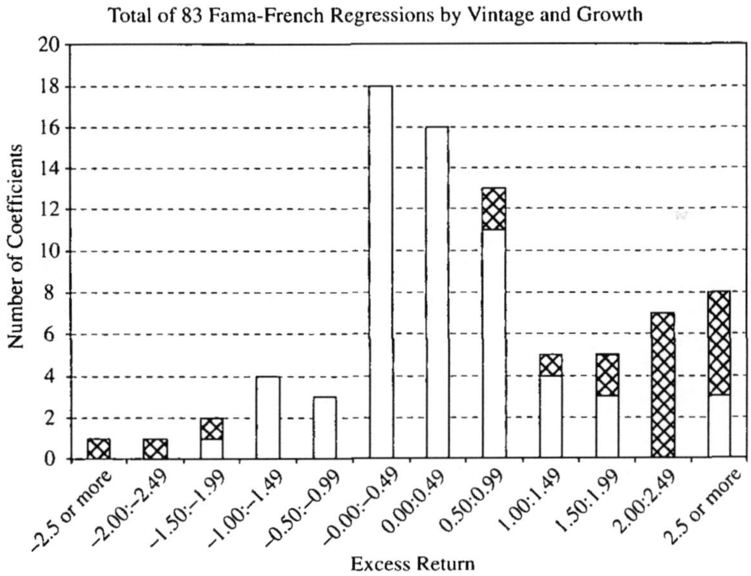

(b)

Figure 1. (a) Excess Return by Vintage and Producer. (b) Excess Return by Vintage and Growth. Figure 1(a) displays the distribution of the intercept values (excess returns) from the 276 TFM regressions by vintage and producer. Figure 1(b) displays the distribution of the intercept values from the 83 TFM regressions by vintage and growth. Statistically significant excess returns are displayed in the crosshatched areas. The majority of the statistically significant excess returns are positive.

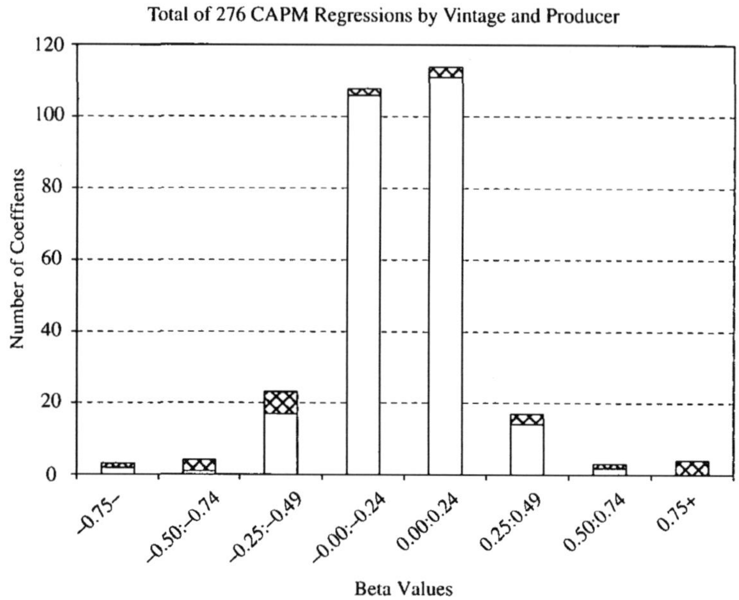

(a)

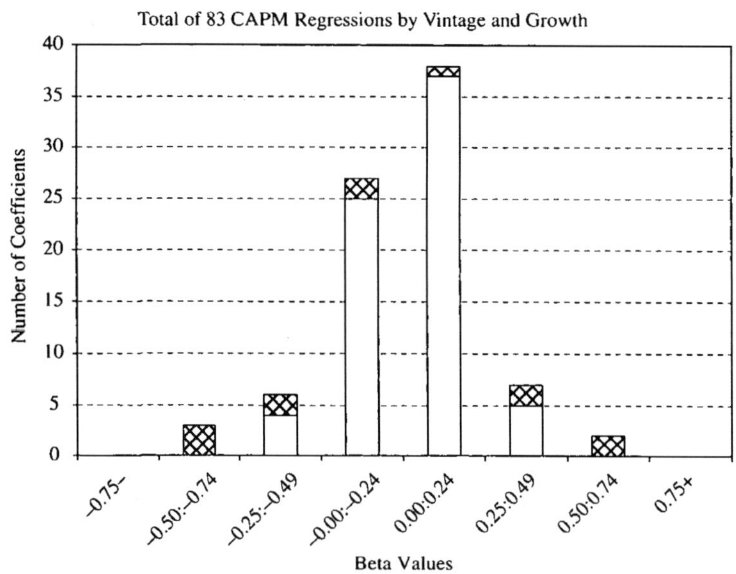

(b)

Figure 2. (a) Betas by Vintage and Producer. (b) Betas by Vintage and Growth. Figure 2(a) displays the distribution of the CAPM Beta values (market risk) from the 276 CAPM regressions by vintage and producer. Figure 2(b) displays the distribution of the CAPM Beta values from the 83 CAPM regressions by vintage and growth. Statistically significant betas are displayed in the crosshatched areas by vintage and producer) supporting the previous finding of low exposure to market return risk. Approximately 30% of the vintage and growth regression intercepts are significantly positive with the balance unable to reject the null hypothesis of $\alpha = 0$. In both sets of regressions (by vintage and growth and by vintage and producer) only 10% of the coefficients on the risk premiums are significant, indicated by the crosshatched portion of Figures 2(a) and 2(b).

7. Conclusions

The research presented here provides new insights into the returns and risks associated with wine as an investment vehicle. This study reveals two notable characteristics of investment grade wine, both predicted by simple theoretical analysis. First, investment grade wine assets provide, on average, positive returns in excess of those forecasted by well accepted models that have been shown to explain much of the variation in average stock returns. This result is consistent with previous findings by Jaeger (1981), but contrasts strongly with earlier findings by Krasker (1979). Although our sample period is fairly short, it includes a period of exceptionally high equity returns which provide a stringent test of excess returns for alternative investments. Second, investment grade wine assets benefit from low exposure to market risk factors and, as a result, provide a valuable source of diversification for investors seeking hedge investments. This property has not been previously studied in the case of wine.

Using a well-documented investment analysis tool, we show that wines on average provide large, positive excess returns. Specifically, using the Fama-French three-factor model, we document average excess returns of more than 0.60–0.75% per month and 7.5–9.5% per year over returns predicted by factors shown to account for risk. Furthermore, our results suggest that wines have very little exposure to common market risk factors and have effectively zero betas. The simple conceptual framework that we used to predict these two properties appears not to have been developed elsewhere in the context of collectible investments. The same framework also predicts roughly zero real financial returns to artwork, consistent with many previous empirical studies. The theoretical analysis indicates that the contrasting empirical findings for art and wine represent rational patterns rather than market anomalies.

Future research could usefully expand on this systematic distinction in at least two ways. First, the investor's decision regarding the optimal time at which to consume a particular bottle of wine is a dynamic programming problem under uncertainty, similar to the problem of optimal harvesting and related problems that have been extensively studied elsewhere. Applying dynamic analysis to the optimization of wine investment and consumption decisions may yield further testable empirical predictions.[27] Second, because consumption reduces the remaining stock of any particular vintage, the possibility of strategic consumption arises as a way of driving up the price of remaining units. Again, incorporating this feature could generate additional testable implications.

Another interesting extension would be to estimate the optimal share of wine in a diversified investment portfolio, taking account of the empirical pattern of wine returns (specifically, their mean, variance, and correlation with equity returns). We defer this task to future research for several reasons. First, the large number of wine varieties, vintages, and labels raises the issue of the appropriate method for computing such a share: should it be calculated for each individual wine, or for some diversified basket of wines? If the latter, what is the optimal share of each wine within the wine basket? Either way, such calculations would be a highly computationally intensive task. Second, the empirical results reported here raise the possibility that such an optimal share might turn out to be so large as to be infeasible in aggregate due to constraints in the supply of wine. That is, while a few small investors might be able to implement the optimal strategy, any systematic attempt by large numbers of institutional investors to follow the same strategy might bid up the market price of wine far above the levels observed under the current mix of investment and consumption objectives among wine buyers, ultimately arbitraging away any risk-adjusted excess returns.

Previous research on wine investments has pointed out many negative aspects of such investments. Investing in wine can be risky and the range of returns is quite wide. These characteristics have not changed. However, this chapter provides alternative research that supports the argument for investment in wine assets under current market conditions. Since a hedging strategy is one that offsets or protects against risk, and since wine assets do not fluctuate according to market risk factors, investors committed to researching those wine assets expected to deliver strong returns can construct a credible case for assembling a wine cellar, and, if by some chance one of your wine assets declines substantially in economic value, you can always exercise the implicit option to consume, and drink your Bordeaux.

---

[27] The authors are grateful to Kirk Vandezande for raising this point.

Acknowledgments

The authors are grateful for helpful comments from Jim Gunderson, Ivo Ph. Jansen, Fred Sterbenz, Kirk Vandezande and an anonymous referee.

References

Agnello, R.J., and Pierce, R.K. (1998). Disaggregated returns and risk in art purchases: The case of American paintings sold at auction from 1971–1996. *Tenth International Conference on Cultural Economics*, Barcelona.

Ashenfelter, O. (1989). How auctions work for wine and art. *Journal of Economic Perspectives*, 3(3), 23–26.

Bartholdy, J., and Peare, P. (2005). Estimation of expected return: CAPM vs. Fama and French. *International Review of Financial Analysis*, 14, 407–427.

Baumol, W.J. (1986). Unnatural value: Or art investment as floating crap game. *American Economic Review*, 76(2), 10–15.

Buelens, N., and Ginsburgh, V. (1993). Revisiting Baumol's "art as floating crap game." *European Economic Review*, 37(7), 1351–1371.

Burton, B.J., and Jacobsen, J.P. (1999). Measuring returns on investments in collectibles. *Journal of Economic Perspectives*, 13(4), 193–212.

Burton, B.J., and Jacobsen, J.P. (2001). The rate of return on investment in wine. *Economic Inquiry*, 39(3), 337–350.

Candela, G., and Scorcu, A.E. (1997). A price index for art market auctions: An application to the Italian market of modern and contemporary oil paintings. *Journal of Cultural Economics*, 21(3), 175–196.

Cardebat, J., and Figuet, J. (2004). What explains Bordeaux wine prices? *Applied Economics Letters*, 11, 293–296.

Clarke, O. (1996). *The Essential Wine Book.* New York: Simon & Schuster.

Combris, P., Lecocq, S., and Visser, M. (1997). Estimation of a hedonic price equation for Bordeaux wine: Does quality matter? *The Economic Journal*, 107(441), 390–402.

Combris, P., Lecocq, S., and Visser, M. (2000). Estimation of a hedonic price equation for Burgundy wine. *Applied Economics*, 32(8), 961–967.

Conseil Interprofessionnel du Vin de Bordeaux (2004). *Vintage Chart*, http://www.bordeaux.com/r_vi ntage.html, Bordeaux, France.

Corsi, A., and Ashenfelter, O. (2003). Predicting Italian wine quality from weather data and experts' ratings. Working Paper, Industrial Relations Section, Firestone Library, Princeton University.

Dittmar, A. (2004). Capital structure in corporate spin-offs. *Journal of Business*, 77(1), 9–43.

Fama, E.F., and French, K.R. (1992). The cross-section of expected stock returns. *Journal of Finance*, 47(2), 427–465.

Fama, E.F., and French, K.R. (1993). Common risk factors in the returns on stocks and bonds. *Journal of Financial Economics*, 33(1), 3–56.

Goetzmann, W.N. (1993). Accounting for taste: Art and the financial markets over three centuries. *American Economic Review*, 83(5), 1370–1376.

Gordon, M.J. (1962). *The Investment, Financing, and Valuation of the Corporation.* Homewood, IL: Irwin.

HM Treasury (2005). *Pre-Budget Report.* December (www.hm-treasury.gov.uk).

International Herald Tribune (2001). Mutual funds fill wine niche; investors can drink some distributions. June 16, http://www.iht.com/articles/23072.html.

Jaeger, E. (1981). To save or savor: The rate of return to storing wine. *Journal of Political Economy,* 89(3), 584–592.

Jones, G.V., and Storchmann, K. (2001). Wine market prices and investment under uncertainty: An econometric model for Bordeaux crus classés. *Agricultural Economics,* 26(2), 115–133.

Krasker, W. (1979). The rate of return to storing wines. *Journal of Political Economy,* 87(6), 1363–1367.

Nissim, D., and Ziv, A. (2001). Dividend changes and future profitability. *Journal of Finance,* 56(6), 2111–2133.

Pesando, J.E. (1993). Art as an investment: The market for modern prints. *American Economic Review,* 83(5), 1075–1089.

Weil, R. (1993). Do not invest in wine, at least in the U.S. unless you plan to drink it, and maybe not even then. *Paper presented at the 2nd International Conference of the Vineyard Data Quantification Society,* Verona, February.

Chapter 11

The Rate of Return on Investment in Wine*

Benjamin J. Burton† and Joyce P. Jacobsen‡

†*Associate, Lehman Brothers,*
3 World Trade Center, 19th Ave.,
New York, NY l0285, USA
bburton@lehman.com

‡*Professor of Economics,*
Economics Department, Public Affairs Center,
Wesleyan University, Middletown, CT 06459, USA
jjacobsen@weslcyan.edu

Is wine an investment alternative to stocks and bonds? First, we review prior studies regarding the pecuniary rate of return to wine and other alternatives to financial assets. Next, we calculate the rate of return to holding red Bordeaux wine from 1986 to 1996 using a repeat-sale regression. Finally, we contrast the financial performance of wine, both on an aggregate basis and for various portfolios, to that of other asset classes. We conclude that wine does 1986 yield greater returns than financial assets, especially when the volatility of returns and transaction costs are taken into account.

1. Introduction

Investments in art and other collectibles are generally deemed profitable, but empirical examinations of the relative attractiveness of noncapital good tangible assets relative to financial instruments have shown that art and other collectibles are not sound investments from a financial point of view. There is a large body of literature that calculates the rate of return on alternative asset classes and concludes with few exceptions that nonfinancial assets are *not* good financial investments. However, in the case of wine, the evidence is mixed: Collectors often maintain that the pecuniary rate of return on investments in wine is comparable to or exceeds investments in stocks and

*This article originally appeared in *Economic Inquiry* 2001, 39(3), 337–350.

bonds, and economists have not reached a consensus vis-à-vis the relative attractiveness of wine.

In this chapter we consider (1) how investment-grade wine compares to other alternative asset classes and (2) whether wine might be a viable investment alternative to stocks or bonds. First, we consider the results drawn from empirical investigations regarding the relative attractiveness of paintings and other collectibles as investments. Next, we review prior econometric evidence regarding the pecuniary rate of return to wine. Finally, we calculate the return on wine from 1986 to 1996 using a repeat-sale regression and contrast wine's financial performance, both for an aggregate portfolio and for selected submarkets, to that of other asset classes.

2. Most Investments in Collectibles Cannot be Justified as Purely Monetary

There is a virtual consensus in the economic literature of the arts that financial assets dominate less traditional tangible assets as investments, because art and other collectibles embody a compensating differential in the form of a "user benefit." Burton and Jacobsen (1999) offer a survey of this literature that finds that most quantitative examinations of the markets for art and other collectibles have concluded that the high risk-low return characteristics of noncapital good tangible assets effectively proscribe retaining them as financial investments.

A seminal study by Baumol (1986), for example, estimated the real annual rate of return on paintings over the period 1652 to 1961 to be only 0.55%. Frey and Pommerehne (1989), who subsequently extended Baumol's data set up through 1987 and expanded it by including sales from more countries, also concluded that paintings were relatively unattractive investment instruments, yielding only about 1.4% between 1635 and 1949 and 1.6% between 1950 and 1987 on an annual, inflation-adjusted basis.

More recent studies have only confirmed that investments in other forms of art and collectibles compare unfavorably to investments in traditional financial assets, especially when the rate of return is risk-adjusted.[1] Pesando (1993), for example, constructed a price index of modern prints over 1977

[1]See, for example, Graeser (1993), Dickie *et al.* (1994) and Pompe (1996). One notable exception to this tendency has been noted by Goetzmann (1993), who estimates the long-run annual nominal rate of return on paintings to be as high as 6.2% annually between 1850 and 1986. See Burton and Jacobsen (1999) for a full discussion of returns to collectibles.

to 1992 and estimated that the average real annual rate of return on an aggregate print portfolio was only 1.51% — well below the concomitant real return on stocks. Moreover, Pesando noted that the risk (as measured by the standard deviation of real returns) associated with investing in prints was comparable to or even exceeded investments in stocks or long-term bonds.

3. But What about Wine?

Wine has recently been proposed as an exception to this apparent rule, with casual observers submitting that wine has out-performed the Dow throughout the 1990s (Thomas, 1998). For example, Graeser (1993) has asserted that although collectibles are generally "a poor long-term investment," fine wine constitutes "a possible exception to this negative assessment." Clearly, the question of what is the rate of return on wine remains a fermenting issue: Anecdotal examples of extraordinary returns are by no means limited to wine, and few people would invest solely on the basis of the performance of a few cases. Nonetheless, wine could potentially yield systematic excess returns over similarly risky financial instruments and/or other noncapital good tangible assets.

In a parallel to the popular press coverage of the art market of the 1960s and 1970s, anecdotal instances in which particular wines and/or vintages have yielded above average returns have been used to suggest that wine might constitute a profitable investment instrument.[2] For example, Hugh Johnson (1971, 38) a leading wine writer, has noted: "Given the space, there is every argument for buying wine young, at its opening price, and 'laying it down' in a cellar or cupboard until it reaches maturity. Wine merchants are not slow to point out that it appreciates in monetary, as well as gastronomic, value out of proportion to the outlay."[3] Frank Prial, another wine writer who has frequently commented on the seemingly unbelievable price appreciation of recent wine vintages in his weekly *New York Times* column, recently submitted that "many wines that were priced $8 a few years ago are $12, and the $12 wines are $18 or $20" (Prial, 1997).[4] Still others are even more unabashed in their assessments: Peter Meltzer, auction correspondent

[2]See Spurrier (1997), Prial (1997), Tanzer (1997), and Ensrud (1997). However, popular sentiment may be turning against wine as an investment; see the pessimistic outlook for wine investment in Palmer (1998b).
[3]For additional evidence, see Grimond (1998), Peers (1997), Tanzer (1997), and Ensrud (1997).
[4]Also see Prial (1998) and Palmer (1998a).

for *Wine Spectator*, was recently quoted as saying that over the last several years, "The wine market has outpaced the Dow Jones" (Thomas 1998).[5] And wine expert Steven Spurrier (1997) has even described the current state of the market as "auction fever," intimating that the wine market is at present best characterized as a speculative bubble in the tradition of tulip-mania.

Others have noted that the apparent price appreciation has been especially rampant for particular high-end vineyards like first-growth Bordeaux.[6] A recent article in the *Wall Street Journal*, for example, encouraged investors to include wine in their investment portfolios by noting that the price of a case of 1982 Château Latour jumped 45% in the fourth quarter of 1996 (Peers, 1997). More generally, the "Zachys Gazette," a leading wine retailer's advertising feature published every other week in the *New York Times*, recently noted that "top Bordeaux prices have increased in the auction market 25% to 50% a year for the last several years" (Zachys Wine and Liquor, 1997).

It is ambiguous a priori whether wine should enjoy a pecuniary rate of return that is larger than that of financial assets and/or other noncapital good tangible assets. In well-functioning capital markets, risk-adjusted rates of return on different assets should be equilibrated through arbitrage. The equilibrium rate of return on an asset, net of insurance and storage costs and any flow of consumption services, should equal the net equilibrium return on competing assets with identical risk. Thus, given the substantial user benefits associated with owning wine (e.g., pride of cellar), one might expect the monetary rate of return on wine to be below that of financial assets. However, one might expect wine to yield a higher rate of return than those collectibles that do not generally require actual physical destruction (e.g., drinking) to be fully enjoyed and are therefore potentially subject to lower "depreciation" rates.

However, given the significant transaction and storage costs associated with trading and holding wine, it is unclear whether the rate of return on wine should be less than the return on similarly risky instrument in financial

[5]Alternatively, see Meltzer (1997).

[6]In 1855, the Bordeaux Syndicate of Brokers classified Bordeaux's vineyards according to price, designating each vineyard Premier Cru, Deuxièmc Cru, Troisième Cru, Quatrième Cru, or Cinquième Cru. First growths initially consisted of Château Lafite-Rothschild, Château Margaux, Château Latour, and Château Haut-Brion; in 1973, the syndicate added Château Mouton-Rothschild. We use the five first growths as designated in 1973 in our calculations related to first growths below.

markets. The nature and size of these costs will be considered in section V. The substantially less "liquid" nature of wine should also push the rate of return upward; it usually takes four to five months to liquidate a collection of wine. Unless one makes private arrangements for sale, the wine has to be put under contract with an auction house, shipped to the auctioneer's premises, inventoried at the auctioneer's warehouse, and manuscript written for the auction's catalog. Sales are held relatively infrequently (Christie's and Sotheby's each hold about 36 wine auctions worldwide per annum; there are about 300 wine auctions in total worldwide, but only about 90 of consequence) and are conducted only during the auction seasons of spring and fall.[7] Finally, the market is relatively thin: In a given auction there are usually 30 to 40 consignors selling wine to between 100 and 150 buyers,[8] making the sale price of a particular wine subject to the vagaries of a given auction.[9]

Pundits can easily argue that wine experts, like collectors themselves, are probably biased by their own interests, but existing econometric studies provide mixed evidence as to whether wine offers comparable returns to financial assets. Krasker (1979) conducted an early empirical investigation of the return to storing wine and concluded that the actual return to storing wine was "not nearly as large as was generally believed" (1366). Although Krasker's study was limited to four years and based on only 137 observations, he argued that wine is not a good investment instrument because the estimated return to investing in wine between 1973 and 1977 was not statistically different from zero, yielding 5.9% less than an average of the U.S. Treasury bill rate at the time. More recently, Weil (1993) analyzed a single investor's wine portfolio transactions from the mid-1970s through 1992 and calculated a nominal internal rate of return of around 8% per annum over a 15-year period, well below the nominal New York Stock Exchange return, which averaged 15%.

However, other empirical inquiries as to the relative attractiveness of wine have argued that wine can generate impressive capital gains. Jaeger

[7]The existence of this many wine auctions per year at multiple locations is a recent development; before 1992, Chicago was the only place where one could buy and sell wine in auction in the United States, the Chicago Wine Company having begun its auction in 1978.

[8]Auctions can be single-owner sales or have as many as 80 sellers; well-attended auctions can have well over 150 buyers, including commission bids and phone bids.

[9]Indeed, not all lots are sold (see Ashenfelter [1989], 24), although the percentage of unsold lot is generally less than 10% and in recent sales at Christie's has been below 1%.

(1981), for example, writing in part in reaction to Krasker's earlier contribution, concluded that from 1969 to 1977, wine actually yielded impressive positive returns. After modifying Krasker's storage cost estimate and using a longer time period that bridged recessions, Jaeger demonstrated that wine yielded a substantial premium over the risk-free rate. Specifically, she concluded that the financial performance of wine outperformed U.S. Treasury bill by 16.6%. Additionally, Byron and Ashenfelter (1995) found that Grange Hermitage, Australia's premier wine, has yielded a reasonable real rate of return of between 3.3% and 4.6% for various specifications over the period 1966–1991.[10]

4. Calculating the Rate of Return to Investment in Wine

4.1. *Methodology*

To update and expand on Krasker's and Jaeger's work, we use a more recent time period that spans both recessionary and expansionary periods and a price index construction method — the repeat-sale regression method — that allows for within-period return calculations as well as full-period return calculation. A generalization of the chain index method, the repeat-sale regression method yields an estimate as well as a standard error for each value of a log-price index, which can then be used to calculate the rate of price appreciation for wine. First advanced by Bailey *et al.* (1963) as an effective means for generating price indexes for real estate markets, the repeat-sale regression has been adapted to the art market by several authors. For example, Pesando (1993) used the repeat-sale regression method to estimate the return on modern prints, using selling prices of multiple prints to estimate changes in the value of an average print over a specified period.[11]

[10]There is a related strand of literature that attempts to explain the price of wine as a function of its characteristics in a cross-sectional hedonic regression framework; see Combris *et al.* (1997) for a recent case and some references. This literature does not generally broach the issue of wine as a potential investment instrument. Ashenfelter *et al.* (1993), who consider a set of 13 Bordeaux châteaux prices for vintage from 1952 to 1980, do find that it costs on average 2.4% more to buy a wine that is one year older than another wine, holding quality constant (as measured by temperature and rainfall in the vintage year). However, this docs not tell us how much wine prices have risen relative to money, which is what we and the other studies cited in the main text attempt to measure.

[11]Another author who has applied the repeat-sale regression method to the art market is Goetzmann (1993); he discusses both selection bias issues in using auction data and potential biases from using repeat-sale regression. He is particularly concerned with bias

The repeat-sale regression application to wine is obvious, even though it has not been used before to generate a price index for wine. A repeat-sale occurs whenever an "identical" bottle of wine — one of the same vineyard, vintage, and producer — is sold on two different occasions. For each pair of sales, a log-price relative is calculated by subtracting the log of the price on the earlier date from the log of the price on the later date. The log-price relatives are then regressed on a set of dummy variables which, for each observation of the dependent variable, are set equal to +1 at the time of the second sale, −1 at the time of the initial sale, and 0 at all other times. Thus, an observation is described as $r_{itt'} = \sum_{j=1}^{T} b_j x_{ij} + u_{itt'}$, where $r_{itt'} = \ln p_{it'} - \ln p_{it}$, with initial sale at time $t = 0, 1, \ldots, T-1$ and final sale at $t' = 1, \ldots, T; x_{ij}$ is a dummy variable that, as explained above, equals +1 at the time of the final sale, −1 at the time of the initial sale, and 0 otherwise; b_j is the value of the log-price index in period j; and $u_{itt'}$ is a disturbance term.

Putting together all the observations, in matrix notation, $r = x\beta + u$, where r and u are n-dimensional column vectors, where n is the number of pairs of transactions; β is a T-dimensional column vector of unknown logarithms of the index numbers to be estimated; and x is an $n \times T$ matrix. Given a pair of transactions with an initial period other than the base period (i.e., $t = 1, \ldots, T-1$), the associated row of x has −1 in the tth column and +1 in the t'th column, and all other elements of the row are zero. Note that the logs of the initial value of the index (β_0 at 1986.2) is normalized at zero (there is no constant term in the regression[12]), and the $T-1$ subsequent

caused by a small number of assets and fewer assets at the beginning of the series; these problems appear less serious for our application than for paintings.

[12]Estimation of a constant term for this equation would provide a measure of the nontemporal component of price change. For instance, Goetzmann and Spiegel (1995) calculate a positive constant for their house price index and interpret it as indicating the amount of improvement in a house between sales. Steele and Goy (1997) advise against use of a constant term in a repeat sale regression because they find that it overestimates the extra return of insiders. We estimated our regressions with a constant term for comparison and found a negative coefficient. Though a potential explanation for this is that in general disappointing wines are sold at auction, this does not appear to jibe with the noted preponderance of good vintage and châteaux in the market (This is found in our sample — for example, 27% of the repeat sales come from wine expert Parker's top 15 châteaux. However, although the 1961 and 1982 vintages together comprise some 15% of our repeat-sale data, other years that are less illustrious also appear with regularity such as 1970 — with 9% or the data — and 1985, with 6%); indeed wine market insiders would argue for the opposite. An alternative explanation suggested by one referee is a rarity/thinness hypothesis, by which wines sold more frequently have smaller price rises because they can be easily purchased at any point.

values of the log-price index are estimated by the regression. Assuming that the disturbances have zero means, constant variances, and that they are uncorrelated with each other, then the ordinary least squares (OLS) estimator, $b = (x'x)^{-1}(x'r)$, is the best linear unbiased estimator of the true parameter vector β.

The repeat-sale regression has the further attractive attribute that because the change in the value of the same wine is measured, no adjustment for quality differences between various wines is required. Thus, the quality-invariant price changes can be used to generate a quality-adjusted price index, calculated by taking the inverse log of the coefficients. Additionally, first-differencing the estimated coefficients yields a nominal rate of return between consecutive periods — in this case a semi-annual rate for wine.

The repeat-sale regression also facilitates comparisons with financial assets because it takes advantage of the information that is lodged in intermediate sales. Rather than calculating the rate of return based on two endpoints — as is the case in simple compounding formulas — and then imputing, say, particular annual rates of return within the period, the repeat-sales regression generates a unique estimate for each period. Indeed, in this sense, it maximizes the information in the longitudinal data, in which observations are a combination of time series and cross-sectional format. This overcomes one major obstacle to testing the economic efficiency of collectibles markets, which has been the difficulty associated with tracking the prices of individual objects over time.[13]

Studying an investment instrument like wine or prints further circumvents this problem, because these instruments are effectively produced in multiples. A first-growth vineyard, for example, might produce 15,000–20,000 cases of the same wine in a given vintage, all of which can be regarded as multiples in the sense that they are the same impression of one work. As a result, the increase in the number of repeat sales relative to those found for unique objects is quite dramatic. For example, Baumol's investigation of the return on paintings used the auction data recorded by Reitlinger (1961) to study the return on paintings that sold two or more times between 1652–1961. His data set, covering a period of more than three centuries, contains

[13]Note that the general thinness of the markets makes sales subject to the vagaries of a particular auction, thereby producing noise. The repeat-sale regression technique does little to rectify the latter problem and R^2 coefficients in repeat-sale regressions for the art market are frequently less than 0.30.

only 640 multiple sales. Pesando's study of prints, on the other hand, calculates a rate of return based on 27,691 repeat sales, even though the period of interest only covers 16 years.

4.2. *Data*

Wine auction data are available from various sources, but William Edgerton compiles one of the most comprehensive collections. His *Wine Price File*, which has been published semi-annually from 1989 to 1992 and annually thereafter, contains a record of the wines sold at the world's major auction houses (Christie's, Sotheby's, Davis & Company, etc.), since 1986. Compiled from the catalogs prepared in advance of the sales and the price lists that are released thereafter, the 1997 edition of the *Wine Price File* (Edgerton, 1997) contains over 75,000 entries. Each sale entry includes the wine's name, vintage, bottle size, producer, color, auction location and date, and hammer price (expressed in dollars regardless of locale). In addition, the level of the wine — the ullage, taken as an indicator of provenance — is recorded for some wines. We used the computer-readable advance version of this edition as the basis for our project and augmented this file with data entered by hand from the first edition of the *Wine Price File*, as Edgerton had discarded some data on earlier sales from the later editions.[14] No data were available from this source for auctions before 1986.

Repeat sales, as described above, occur whenever a distinct wine made in a particular vintage by the same vineyard or producer is sold on two different occasions. To simplify quantifying the return on wine and make the data manageable, only red Bordeaux are included in the regression. Red Bordeaux are most often bought strictly as an investment (though it is of course true that they are also bought for relatively immediate consumption), whereas wines from other regions, especially white wines, are bought primarily for immediate or relatively immediate consumption. French wines, the vast majority of which were Bordeaux, comprised more than 88% of the 1996–1997 wine auction market, in which approximately 1 million bottles of wine were auctioned worldwide (Blättel and Stainless, 1997).[15]

[14]Edgerton described his data-discarding method as random with regard to the magnitude of the recorded price, so no obvious bias upward or downward occurs from this selection method. Similarly, we randomly entered in prices from the earlier edition.

[15]Specifically, in the 1996–1997 auction season, French wines made up 88.1% of the $70 million turnover. Of course, some of these French wines were not Bordeaux, but Burgundies, Rhônes, and so on.

Furthermore, we only include wines that have been produced since 1960 in the regression. Eliminating wines that are older than 1960 minimizes the exogenous but time-varying factor of the "antique effect," which serves to confound the fundamental monetary return on wine.[16] In fact, both Jaeger (1981) and Krasker (1979) implemented similar restrictions in their analyses, limiting their econometric work to red Bordeaux and California younger than 1969. Krasker and Jaeger both argued that relatively young red Bordeaux and California wines are bought mostly for investment purposes because they will benefit the most from aging (and thus promise the greatest potential total capital gains).

Limiting the data to relatively young Bordeaux is also appealing because it negates the necessity of having an additional matrix in the regression to control for time-varying characteristics. As Steele and Goy (1997) have demonstrated, it is necessary to control for changes in the time-varying characteristics of the asset in question from one sale to the next. In the instance of wine, one would ostensibly like to include a hedonic specification in the repeat-sale regression to control for such characteristics as ullage, condition of the labels, whether the original wooden case is present, how much of the wine is offered in a given auction, and in which auction house the wine is sold.[17] Although such data are available for certain sales, auction houses and compilations of auction prices do not systematically report such details. But imposing the data restrictions mentioned above has the attractive effect of minimizing the magnitude of the time-varying characteristics of wine, thus generating a "purer" price index.[18]

---

[16]Wines usually mature for a given period of time and then subsequently start to turn bad. A red Bordeaux, for example, will (depending on the vintage) keep getting better (therefore more expensive) for 15–25 years, after which it will diminish both in terms of gastronomic appeal and monetary worth . At a certain point, however, the wine will become an antique, and its value will begin to increase once again. For example, in December 1997, Zachys/Christie's sold a bottle of 1811 Château d'Yquem for more than $20,000, even though the Sauterne had in all likelihood turned to vinegar.

[17]The presence of an original wooden case often commands a premium, and Ashenfelter (1989) discusses how the prices that a given wine realizes vary systematically from house to house and from locale to locale, although there is some evidence in his data (circa 1987) that differentials are decreasing, at least between London and New York.

[18]One example of the way in which this is true has to do with the ullage, or level of the wine. When wine that was produced before approximately 1960 is sold at auction, the ullage has a considerable effect on the price. Indeed, the ullage varies from bottle to bottle, depending on the provenance of the wine. Moreover, the ullage of a particular bottle of wine tends to change from one sale to the next as the wine ages. Limiting this investigation to wines that have been produced since 1960 effectively diminishes the magnitude of this

Next, we adopt the simplifying assumption that sales occur at the end of each auction season instead of at the actual date. Because auction sales are defined by seasons, it is easier to work with semi-annual observations, and doing so makes the data set somewhat more manageable. A calculation of the frequency distribution of wine sales in Edgerton's *Wine Price File* (1997) indicates that the majority of wine is sold in February–March and September–December, with each month within those seasons getting about equal attention. Wine is sold relatively infrequently during the rest of the year. If a particular bottle of wine is sold more than once in an observation period, its average price is used to calculate the dependent variable.[19] Although calculating the return on wine based on average prices over a given season blunts the impact of outliers, it is a necessary restriction given that even for the relatively short period of ten years the data set would otherwise approach an unmanageable size due to the combinatorial effect of adding additional observations. Even after implementing these various restrictions to our data, 315 different châteaux had repeat sales for one or more vintages. These sales data yielded 10,558 repeat-sales observations between the second half of 1986 (1986.2) and the second half of 1996 (1996.2).[20]

4.3. *Results*

Running the repeat-sale regression OLS for an aggregate portfolio of wine as described above yields the results shown in the first set of columns in Table 1. Table 1 shows each time period's coefficient plus its standard error for several different model specifications. As the table indicates, all coefficients are statistically significant at a high level of confidence, but the adjusted R^2 for the aggregate OLS index is only 0.173.

The relatively low R^2 reflects, at least in part, the substantial "noise" that is intrinsic in auction prices. In fact, other return-to-art studies that use auction data have embodied similar diagnostic results, and all of these studies have dismissed the low R^2. Pesando's (1993) study of the modern print market, for example, justified an R^2 of 0.239 by noting that "prices of identical prints that are sold within relatively narrow windows often vary

factor, by minimizing the importance of levels. This is obvious if one considers that auction houses generally do not even publish the ullage of a given wine in their catalog unless the wine was produced before 1978. For wines produced between 1978 and 1995, Christie's mentions ullage if it is below "top shoulder."

[19]Edgerton also had already averaged some prices before entering them into the database.

[20]There were only 8 surviving price points for the first half of 1986; these are grouped with the 79 price points for 1986.2.

Table 1. Wine Indexes Based on Repeat-Sales Regressions, 1986–1996

	All wines			First growths			1961 vintage			1982 vintage		
Period	Coefficient	Index	Return	Coefficient	Index	Return	Coefficient	Index	Return	Coefficient	Index	Return
1987.1	0.2850	1.3298	0.2850	0.4037	1.4974	0.4037	0.1283	1.1369	0.1283	0.2337	1.2632	0.2337
	(0.0268)		(0.0268)	(0.0531)		(0.0531)	(0.1259)		(0.1259)	(0.0538)		(0.0538)
1987.2	0.3918	1.4797	0.1068	0.3294	1.3902	−0.0743	0.3719	1.4505	0.2436	0.3448	1.4117	0.1111
	(0.0280)		(0.0227)	(0.0533)		(0.0449)	(0.1308)		(0.0908)	(0.0603)		(0.0503)
1988.1	0.4134	1.5120	0.0216	0.3149	1.3701	−0.0145	0.7259	2.0667	0.3540	0.5277	1.6950	0.1829
	(0.0256)		(0.0213)	(0.0512)	(0.0426)	(0.1226)		(0.0855)	(0.0539)		(0.0501)	
1988.2	0.5328	1.7037	0.1194	0.5674	1.7636	0.2525	0.6863	1.9863	−0.0397	0.5259	1.6920	−0.0018
	(0.0257)		(0.0181)	(0.0523)	(0.0415)	(0.1223)		(0.0696)	(0.0534)		(0.0414)	
1989.1	0.5575	1.7463	0.0247	0.4855	1.6249	−0.0819	0.7853	2.1931	0.0991	0.6980	2.0097	0.1721
	(0.0261)		(0.0186)	(0.0540)		(0.0451)	(0.1230)		(0.0707)	(0.0542)		(0.0412)
1989.2	0.3304	1.3915	−0.2271	0.8471	2.3329	0.3616	0.7715	2.1631	−0.0138	0.6929	1.9994	−0.0051
	(0.0386)		(0.0340)	(0.5012)		(0.5005)	(0.3072)		(0.2873)	(0.1382)		(0.1340)
1990.1	0.5184	1.6794	0.1880	0.7314	2.0780	−0.1157	0.9100	2.4844	0.1385	0.7657	2.1504	0.0728
	(0.0275)		(0.0342)	(0.0988)	(0.4914)	(0.1392)		(0.2965)	(0.0745)		(0.1425)	
1990.2	0.5315	1.7016	0.0131	0.7882	2.1944	0.0567	0.5303	1.6995	−0.3797	1.0066	2.7364	0.2410
	(0.0312)		(0.0255)	(0.2248)		(0.2374)	(0.1565)		(0.1280)	(0.0984)		(0.0968)
1991.1	0.5678	1.7643	0.0362	0.9094	2.4828	0.1212	0.8726	2.3931	0.3423	0.8113	2.2509	−0.1953
	(0.0276)		(0.0258)	(0.0884)		(0.2332)	(0.1482)		(0.1353)	(0.0662)		(0.0967)
1991.2	0.4260	1.5311	−0.1418	0.4789	1.6142	−0.4305	0.6454	1.9068	−0.2271	0.6503	1.9161	−0.1610
	(0.0302)		(0.0246)	(0.1156)		(0.1256)	(0.1687)		(0.1512)	(0.0729)		(0.0702)
1992.1	0.3836	1.4676	−0.0424	0.5879	1.8001	−0.1090	0.4481	1.5654	−0.1973	0.9322	2.5401	0.2819
	(0.0310)		(0.0284)	(0.1185)		(0.1500)	(0.1703)		(0.1813)	(0.0853)		(0.0886)

1992.2	0.4488	1.5664	0.0652	0.1905	1.2099	−0.3973	0.6066	1.8341	0.1584	0.8270	2.2865	−0.1052
	(0.0292)		(0.0271)	(0.1028)		(0.1447)	(0.1584)		(0.1667)	(0.0745)		(0.0914)
1993.1	0.2701	1.3101	−0.1787	0.1306	1.1395	−0.0600	0.2258	1.2533	−0.3808	0.8172	2.2641	−0.0098
	(0.0269)		(0.0228)	(0.0726)		(0.1064)	(0.1342)		(0.1256)	(0.0606)		(0.0714)
1993.2	0.4797	1.6156	0.2096	0.7070	2.0279	0.5765	0.8920	2.4399	0.6662	0.8200	2.2705	0.0028
	(0.0276)		(0.0209)	(0.1252)		(0.1270)	(0.1353)		(0.0990)	(0.0715)		(0.0648)
1994.1	0.3374	1.4014	−0.1423	0.2934	1.3410	−0.4136	0.3247	1.3836	−0.5673	0.8695	2.3856	0.0495
	(0.0249)		(0.0180)	(0.0677)		(0.1262)	(0.1256)		(0.0862)	(0.0516)		(0.0579)
1994.2	0.3889	1.4754	0.0515	0.3025	1.3533	0.0091	0.5350	1.7075	0.2104	0.8282	2.2892	−0.0413
	(0.0258)		(0.0151)	(0.0720)		(0.0726)	(0.1250)		(0.0673)	(0.0529)		(0.0320)
1995.1	0.4534	1.5736	0.0644	0.3997	1.4914	0.0972	0.6239	1.8662	0.0889	1.0037	2.7285	0.1755
	(0.0250)		(0.0156)	(0.0627)		(0.0692)	(0.1234)		(0.0648)	(0.0507)		(0.0314)
1995.2	0.5681	1.7648	0.1147	0.5998	1.8217	0.2001	0.6326	1.8825	0.0087	1.1736	3.2335	0.1698
	(0.0250)		(0.0141)	(0.0632)		(0.0613)	(0.1239)		(0.0675)	(0.0517)		(0.0302)
1996.1	0.6349	1.8868	0.0668	0.6016	1.8250	0.0018	0.8696	2.3859	0.2370	1.2307	3.4235	0.0571
	(0.0239)		(0.0124)	(0.0493)		(0.0497)	(0.1187)		(0.0626)	(0.0494)		(0.0287)
1996.2	0.7925	2.2088	0.1576	0.6671	1.9486	0.0656	0.8332	2.3008	−0.0363	1.3861	3.9991	0.1554
	(0.0260)		(0.0143)	(0.0516)		(0.0344)	(0.1279)		(0.0717)	(0.0518)		(0.0280)
Adj. R^2	0.1728			0.2187			11.3096			0.6557		
n	10558			1277			620			989		

Note: Standard errors are in parentheses.

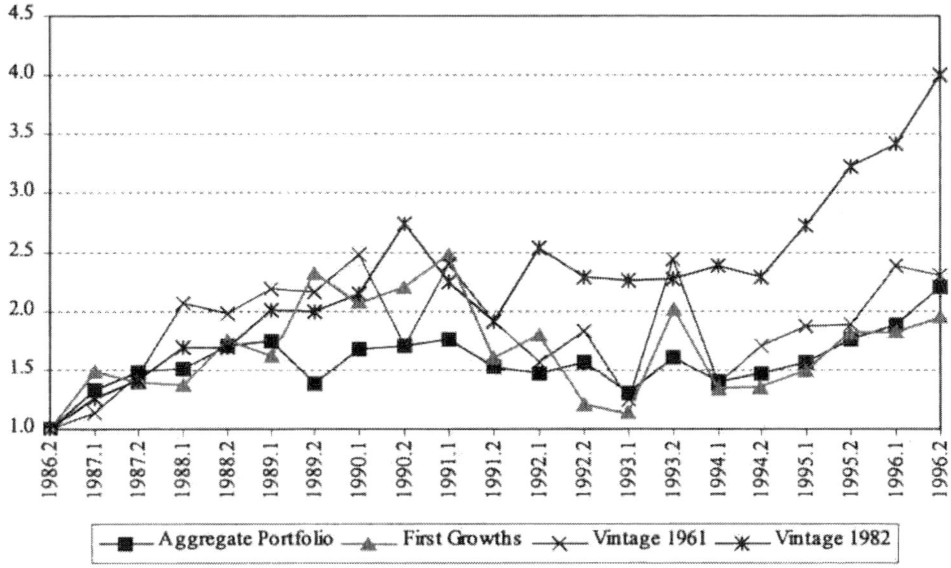

Figure 1. Price Indexes for Different Wine Portfolios, 1986–1996

substantially" (1077). Indeed, wine prices often vary substantially, depending on the wine's provenance and several other factors. For example, wine frequently sells for less late in the day — a phenomenon referred to as the "declining price anomaly" — due primarily to the overall thinness of the market (Ashenfelter, 1989).[21] Indeed, given the rather subjective nature of determinations of the quality of wine, it should not be surprising that wine prices are highly stochastic.

The coefficients generated by the repeat-sale regression can readily be used to construct a quality-adjusted price index over the period 1986.2 to 1996.2. The aggregate price index, along with some alternative specifications that are discussed below, is presented in Table 1 and graphed in Figure 1. The price index and its corresponding graph illustrate the well-documented wine depression of the late 1980s and early 1990s, for example, and the index allows us to identify the precise time when prices started to drop precipitously: 1989.1. Although prices continued to be depressed until the first half of 1994, it appears that the wine market — like the market for equity — has subsequently been bullish.

[21]See Ginsburgh (1998) for additional discussion of this anomaly in the wine auction context.

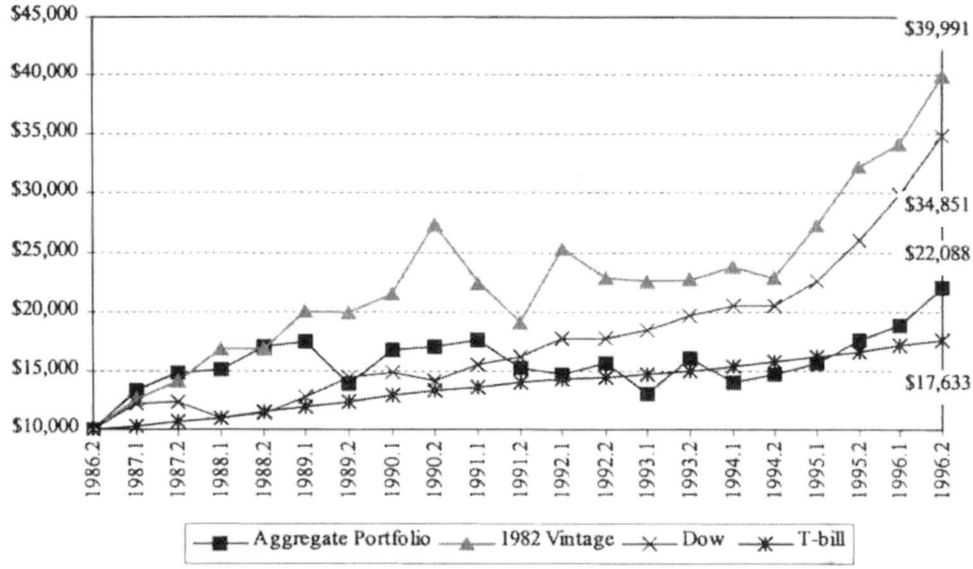

Figure 2. How $10,000 Would Have Performed for Different Asset Classes, 1986–1996

First-differencing the coefficients gives us a quality-invariant nominal semi-annual rate of return, and real rates of return can then readily be calculated by subtracting out inflation.[22] The average annual nominal rate of return between 1986.2 and 1996.2 for our sample was 7.9%, and the corresponding real rate of return was 3.1%. Notably, during the same period, the Dow Jones Industrial Average rose an average of 13.5% per year, *not* including dividends that were paid out, and the one-year Treasury bill yielded a nominal annual rate of 5.8%. As Figure 2 shows, $10,000 invested in an index fund that mirrored the Dow would have grown to over $34,000 by the end of the ten-year period. A diversified portfolio of wine, however, would have only been worth approximately $22,000. Again, this disparity only increases if one considers that equity would have also yielded dividends, whereas the only pecuniary return to wine comes from capital gains.

Though the wine portfolio ends up beating a pure debt portfolio, its value wavers substantially around the T-bill portfolio and only pulls substantially ahead during the 1990s in the second half of 1996. This aspect of Figure 2 underscores the importance of considering the variability of returns. As shown in Table 2, the variability of returns for wine compares unfavorably

[22]The Consumer Price Index was used to calculate the annual rate of inflation.

Table 2. Nominal Semi-Annual Rates of Return for Wine and Financial Assets, 1986–1996

	Wine				Financial Assets	
	All	First growths	1961 Vintage	1982 Vintage	Dow	1-Year T-bill
Semi-annual rate of return	0.0396	0.0334	0.0417	0.0693	0.0673	0.0289
Standard deviation	0.1331	0.2611	0.2897	0.1344	0.0791	0.0078
Coefficient of variation	3.3587	7.8264	6.9532	1.9396	1.1764	0.2699

to variability of standard financial assets between 1986 and 1996. The standard deviation of semi-annual returns for wine was 0.133 over the period, while the standard deviations for the Dow and one-year T-bills over the same period were only 0.079 and 0.008, respectively, and correspondingly the coefficient of variation for wine is notably higher. It is quite striking that the rate of return on wine is so volatile; considerable negative returns are frequently followed by significant positive returns.

Skeptics might contend that the reported return to wine is specific to the time period that is being studied and that it is artificially low due to the wine depression of the late 1980s. Indeed, Jaeger shows that the return on wine is relatively sensitive to the period that is being examined, as wine is a luxury good that is fairly demand elastic.[23] But even if the relevant holding period is restricted to the period that experts have often described as "auction fever," the return on wine is still subpar (Spurrier, 1997). Since 1993.2, investments in wine have yielded 15.5% nominally per year, well below the concurrent nominal performance of equity at 19.3%.[24]

So although it is true that financial assets have recently outperformed their historical average rates, it appears from these data that wine *does not* constitute a profitable investment alternative to equity. Moreover, it is not clear if wine is a "better" investment instrument than other noncapital goods, as there are collectibles with both higher and lower measured rates

[23]Notably, in contrast to Goetzmann's (1993) finding that the stock market index Granger-causes his art market index, we find no evidence of Granger-causation in either direction for either our aggregate index, or vintage-specific indexes, or our index of first growths in relation to the stock market.

[24]Indeed, to the extent that auction price data systematically selects wines with higher appreciation (i.e., owners Would be less likely to put wine up for auction that was unlikely to deliver positive returns), the index actually overestimate the true return to investing in wine.

of return (see Burton and Jacobsen [1999]). The evidence *does* suggest that wine is an alternative, albeit a risky one, to fixed income securities.

5. Comparison of Returns in Wine Submarkets

When confronted with the prospect that financial assets dominate less traditional noncapital tangible goods, experts often counter that particular segments of the market outperform others. Although this claim is syllogistic and generally backed only by anecdotal evidence, wine experts frequently use similar arguments to persuade collectors to hold portfolios of wine consisting of "blue chip" châteaux, good vintages, and/or trendy wines (Grimond, 1998). Instead of holding a widely diversified collection of wine, the argument goes, collectors should try to anticipate which wines are going to be hot in the near future and then overweight those wines in their portfolios accordingly.

We test this hypothesis that specific sub-markets could outperform the aggregate index using a number of approaches. First, we considered whether a portfolio consisting of only the arguably best, most desirable wines in the world — the Premier Crus of Bordeaux, also known as first growths — could beat the overall wine market. The resulting index is shown in the second section of Tables 1 and 2 and plotted in Figure 1. It turns out that the calculated nominal return on the first growth portfolio is slightly lower than for the aggregate portfolio (6.7% annual return, versus 7.9 % for the aggregate portfolio). The relative undesirability of the first growth portfolio is all the more evident if one considers the risk that is inherent in such an investment strategy. Indeed, from Figure 1 and Table 2, it is clear that the returns on the first growth portfolio are extremely volatile.

We next tested to see if the return on a broad portfolio consisting only of a given "good" vintage would exceed that of the aggregate portfolio. We ran regressions separately by vintage and discovered that two years in our sample that are considered especially good vintages — 1961 and 1982 — would in fact have yielded significant monetary returns. The results for the 1961 and 1982 vintages are shown in the third and fourth sections, respectively, of Tables 1 and 2, and the resultant price indexes are also plotted in Figure 1. If a collector were to have retained a portfolio of nothing but wines from the 1982 vintage, he or she would have earned a nominal annual rate of return of 13.9% and a real return of 9.1%. A portfolio consisting of wines produced in 1961 would have yielded a nominal rate of return of 8.3% and a real return of 3.5%. In addition, as shown in Table 2, the investor in 1982 vintage wines would have experienced lower volatility (as measured by the coefficient of variation) than that experienced by the aggregate wine portfolio (although still above the Dow). Wine from 1961, however, was significantly more volatile than the aggregate portfolio. All other vintage years for which there were sufficient observations to estimate an index yielded returns below the aggregate portfolio.

Ignoring risk for the moment, note that despite the exceptional performance of these two vintages, this does not mean one would necessarily have known in advance which vintage to invest in. Indeed, though wine buyers may have become more informed over time about the quality of successive vintages, this would tend to drive up the initial purchase price for good vintages and reduce subsequent price appreciation due to reduction of the revelation effect. Hence the highlighted performance of singular vintages *ex post* may provide little help in revealing future investment strategies.

One might still argue that our subsector portfolios are still not selective enough and that an informed investor would know exactly which wines to choose. Edgerton suggested we look at first growths only in the hot vintage years to find the highest returns. In addition, we calculated the return on suggestions made by two wine experts writing at the beginning of our sample period. Based on Robert Parker's list (1985, 494) of 15 châteaux that he considers worthy of the first-growth designation (not with regard to investment potential but with regard to quality), we estimate the return to three different portfolios — one for all vintage years, and for the 1961 and 1982 vintages separately.[25] Sokolin (1987, 29–31) specifically considers wines' investment potential in creating three classes of investment-grade wine and suggests one should buy a range of vintage years from these wineries for diversification; we consider the selected Bordeaux in each of these portfolios.[26] The three classes represent, in his view, different degrees of risk, name recognition, and expense (i.e., up-front costs of purchasing cases of the selected wines); grade one wines are supposed to offer higher returns and lower risk compared to grades two and three.

[25]The 15 châteaux are: Ausone, Cheval Blanc, Ducru-Beaucaillou, Gruaud-Larose, Haut-Brion, Lafite-Rothschild, Latour, Léoville-Las Cases, Margaux, La Mission-Haut-Brion, Mouton-Rothschild, Palmer, Pétrus, Pichon Lalande, and Trotanoy.

[26]The grade one portfolio contains 11 châteaux: Ausone, Cheval Blanc, Haut-Brion, Lafite-Rothschild, Latour, Lêoville-Las Cases, Margaux, La Mission-Haut-Brion, Mouton-Rothschild, Pétrus, and Pichon-Lalande. The grade two portfolio contains ten wines: Châteaux Beychevelle, Cantemerle, Cos d'Estournel, Ducru-Beaucaillou, Figeac, La Lagune, Lynch-Bages, Palmer, Trotanoy, and Domaine de Chevalier. The grade three portfolio contains seven châteaux: Canon, La Gaffeliére, Gloria, Grand-Puy-Lacoste, La Grave-Trigant de Boisset, Gruaud-Larose, and Rausan-Ségla.

Table 3. Annualized Nominal Rates of Return for Various Wine Portfolios, 1986–1996

Aggregate	7.9%
First growths	6.7%
1961 vintage	
all	8.3%
first growths	9.6%
1982 vintage	13.9%
Parker's 15	
all vintages	7.8%
1961 vintage	9.9%
1982 vintage	16.2%
Sokolin's investment grades	
grade one	7.7%
grade two	7.2%
grade three	5.3%
Sokolin's 1985 portfolio	
average prices	9.4%
maximum prices	11.8%

For these subsets of wines, we generally did not have enough observations in the middle of the time span to calculate a full repeat regression index, so we only show the endpoint index value. The resulting annualized nominal returns over the 1986–1996 period for these various portfolios are shown in Table 3 and are compared to the returns (now annualized) reported in Table 2. Following Edgerton's suggestion, we calculated the return on 1961 first growths; unfortunately, we had insufficient data to calculate the return on 1982 first growths. This rate (9.6%) turned out to indeed be higher than for either first growths taken as a whole (6.7%) or the 1961 vintage taken as a whole (8.3%). Parker's suggestion turns out to provide winners only if applied to the star vintages; the nominal growth for all vintages for these 15 châteaux is 7.8% per annum, which mirrors the aggregate portfolio. The high returns come for those who buy only 1961 or 1982 vintages from these châteaux, yielding nominal returns of 9.9% for the 1961 vintage and 16.2% for the 1982 vintage. Sokolin's portfolios perform less spectacularly and yield diminishing rates of return as he had predicted, with only the grade one suggestions yielding a nominal rate (7.7%) comparable to that for the aggregate portfolio; nominal returns on grades two and three, at 7.2% and 5.3%. respectively, leave some-thing to be desired.

Table 4. Returns on Sokolin's 1985 Wine Portfolio

		1996	
	1985 Futures price	Average auction price	Maximum auction price
5 cases Mouton-Rothschild	\$3,000	\$8,513	\$11,494
5 cases Lafite-Rothschild	\$3,150	\$5,767	\$6,900
5 cases Latour	\$3,000	\$5,784	\$8,050
5 cases Haut-Brion	\$2,500	\$6,098	\$7,527
5 cases Cheval Blanc	\$3,000	\$8,216	\$9,200
5 cases La Grave-Trigant-de-Boisset	\$1,250	\$1,670	\$1,670
5 cases Margaux	\$3,000	\$8,253	\$9,350
1 case Pétrus	\$1,200	\$4,910	\$6,900
Total	\$20,100	\$49,211	\$61,091
Annual rate of return		9.4%	11.8%
Minus 15% sales commission		41,829	\$51,927
Rate of return net of commission		7.6%	10.0%
Minus 1% insurance		\$41,337	\$51,316
Rate of return net of commission and insurance		7.5%	9.8%
Minus \$1.50 per case per months to storage rage costs		\$34,857	\$44,836
Net rate of return		5.7%	8.4%

Finally, Sokolin also offers a portfolio of 1985 wines to be bought in early 1986 at futures prices, for a total of \$20,100. This provides the opportunity for us to simulate returns based on actual futures prices at the beginning of our sample period. We consider both the average auction price and the highest auction price in the Edgerton data for each during 1996 and calculate the 1996 value of the portfolio and annualized nominal rate of return, as shown in the last two rows of Table 3. Full details for the portfolio are shown in Table 4. This wine portfolio achieved a total value of \$49,200 at average price and \$61,100 at highest price, yielding potential nominal returns of 9.4% and 11.8% — clearly a better return than for wine purchased overall or for those sticking to the true first growths only.

6. Transaction and Holding Cost Factors

We turn finally to considering additional benefits and costs associated with investing in wine rather than in financial assets. The tax treatment of wine could constitute one compensating differential in favor of wine. Although buyers of wine at auctions are forced to pay sales taxes (if required by state law), auction houses generally do not charge consignors sales tax and generally do not report their capital gains to the government. Indeed, the Internal Revenue Service has not really put forth significant enforcement efforts, ostensibly at least in part because wine can be considered a tax-exempt consumable. Accordingly, collectors can realize tax advantages by trading wine rather than financial assets.

These tax advantages not withstanding, however, the transaction costs on both buying and selling wine are substantial.[27] At Christie's, for example, commissions are charged for both buying and selling. Although the consignor's commission varies according to the total value of the consignment, the seller generally pays a 15% commission, plus 1% insurance and any shipping costs.[28] For consignments with a total value of $100,000 or more on a calendar basis, as well as with individual lots that are worth more than $7,500, Christie's generally charges 9%. Additional prorating begins at the $250,000 level, but this is relevant for very few sellers. On the buyer's side, the 15% premium that is charged on top of all hammer price constitutes a considerable charge that requires long holding of wine to amortize it sufficiently for it to have only a negligible effect on returns.[29] Finally, wine also incurs insurance and storage costs, where one must either pay a

[27]It is potentially possible to reduce these costs by disposing of wine through private sale, directly to the buyer, or using a wine dealer as middleman. Sokolin (1987, 94–95) downplays these ideas as viable options, indicating that most retailers are not interested in buying wine from private sellers and that they take a commission to operate as a broker. Another possibility is to donate the wine at its appraised value and take a tax write-off. This can be an attractive option for high-income owners, but because other assets can also be donated, does not improve wine's return relative to other assets. Also note that wine buyers who are "double agents," namely, restaurants, have no transaction costs over and above what they would have had to incur anyway by buying wine through a wine retailer to stock their cellars.

[28]Shipping costs currently run around $15–$20 per case, with a range of $12–$100 per case depending on required shipping conditions and distance. Sellers occasionally incur catalog-related charges (e.g., photography). Another transaction cost that would deter the small-lot seller is that consignors must frequently forgo several "tasting bottles." As of late 1999, Christie's imposed a consignment minimum for wine of $15,000, down from the 1997 minimum of $25,000, and would usually only auction full cases of wine.

[29]As recently a the early 19, buyer's premiums at the larger, more established auction houses were only 10% but Christie's and Sotheby's both raised the rate to 15% to generate more revenue from this source. Prorating again occurs here, with Christie's dropping the rate to 10% for purchases over $50,000. Smaller auction houses will sometimes waive either buyer or seller premiums to attract business.

wine distributor to store one's investment, or incur the costs of setting up a climate-controlled area in one's house.[30] After taking all these additional differences into account, even though it appears in Figure 2 that a portfolio of wine consisting of only the 1982 vintage would have "beaten" the Dow, it is inconceivable that the actual net return for the average investor would have been this high.

For example, if one considers the effects of sales commission, insurance, and storage costs on Sokolin's futures portfolio, the relative attractiveness of his suggested wine portfolio as an investment instrument diminishes. As shown in Table 4, the effect of a sale commission of 15% and of a 1% insurance charge reduces the net nominal return substantially — to 7.5% or 9.8% under our two alternative scenarios. Moreover, assuming storage costs of \$1.50 per month per case for 120 months (assuming immediate delivery of the wine after the future is purchased), the net nominal return drops to 5.7% or 8.4%. This still leaves out shipping costs and other incidentals that are harder to quantify.[31]

7. Conclusions

Based on the evidence presented in this chapter it appears that wine — like most other noncapital good tangible assets — is only questionably a profitable investment instrument. The recent average annual rate of return on wine, together with the risk inherent in such an investment does not justify retaining it as an alternative to equity, and its volatility likely makes it less desirable than debt for the majority of investors. This conclusion is strengthened if one consider the institutional details and transaction costs outlined above. Such factors as the commission rates associated with buying and selling wine, the cost of storing wine, and the overall thinness of the market all further diminish the attractiveness of wine as a viable alternative to financial asset.

It does appear that if wine investors had engaged in market timing or active, informed investing, they could have gained money relative to blue

[30]Monthly professional storage costs range from \$1.50–1.80 per case for customers storing up to 50 cases, with discounts for larger customers. For recent prices on home wine storage units, see Daspin (1998). Storage conditions are noted in the auction catalogs, see Zachys/Christie's (1998, 62), which describes one set of lots as "Removed from a Substantial Climate-Controlled Underground Home Wine Cellar Maintaining 54°F and 74% Humidity."

[31]These results are roughly comparable to those Weil (1993) obtains in studying an actual wine investor's portfolio, wherein he also omits costs for these incidentals.

chip equity. There are a few examples of individual years when an aggregate portfolio of wine outperformed financial assets (e.g., 1993.2), and it is possible to have constructed a portfolio of a single vintage (i.e., 1982 or 1961), particularly of first growth of that vintage, whose gross return would have outperformed equity over then entire period. However, while it will likely still be possible to identify portfolios ex post that have outperformed either the corresponding market's average or the financial performance of other assets, this is of little use to an investor seeking profitable alternatives to financial assets. As the price index calculated in this chapter indicates, an aggregate portfolio of investments in wine would only have yielded an unimpressive nominal annual return in the 8% range between 1986 and 1996. This result bespeaks that wine should not be saved, but savored.

Acknowledgments

We thank William Edgerton for providing data, the Economics Department of Wesleyan University for financial support, Rachel Mandal for research assistance, and two anonymous referees, Orley Ashenfelter, William Edgerton, Richard Grossman, Peter Kilby, Stan Lebergott, Laurence Levin, Richard Miller, and David Selover for helpful comments.

References

Ashenfelter, O. (1989). How auction work for wine and art. *Journal of Economic Perspectives*, 3, 21–36.

Ashenfelter, O., Ashmore, D., and Lalonde, R. (February 1993). Wine vintage quality and the weather: Bordeaux. *Paper presented at the 2nd International Conference of the Vineyard Qualification Society*, Verona. Italy.

Bailey, M., Muth, R., and Nourse, H. (1963). A regression method for real estate price index construction. *Journal of the American Statistical Association*, 58, 933–942.

Baumol, W. (1986). Unnatural value: Or art investment as floating crap game. *American Economic Review*, 76, 10–14.

Blättel, H., and Stainless, F.E. (1997). *Wine & Price: International Auction Results — Wine and Spirits.* Munich: Arts and Antiques.

Burton, B.J., and Jacobsen, J.P. (1999). Measuring returns on investments in collectibles. *Journal of Economic Perspectives*, 3, 193–212.

Byron, R.P., and Ashenfelter, O. (1995). Predicting the quality of an unborn grange. *Economic Record*, 71, 40–53.

Combris, P., Lecocq, S., and Visser, M. (1997). Estimation for a hedonic price equation for bordeaux wine: Does quality matter? *Economic Journal*, 107, 390–402.

Daspin, E. (July 1998). Wine storage 101. *Wall Street Journal*, 10, 12.

Dickie, M., Delorme, C., and Humphreys, J. (1994). Price determination for a collectible good: The case of rare U.S. coins. *Southern Economic Journal*, 61, 40–51.

Edgerton, W.H. (1997). *Wine Price File*. Darien. CT: Wine Price File.

Ensrud, B. (17 November 1997). A salute to Italian reds. *Wall Street Journal*, 24.

Frey, B.S., and Pommerehne, W. (1989). Art investment: An empirical inquiry. *Southern Economic Journal*, 56, 396–409.

Ginsburgh, V. (1998). Absentee bidders and the declining price anomaly in wine auctions. *Journal of Political Economy*, 106, 1302–1319.

Goetzmann, W.N. (1993). Accounting for taste: Art and the financial markets over three centuries. *American Economic Review*, 83, 1370–1376.

Goetzmann, W.N., and Spiegel, M. (1995). Non-temporal components of residential real estate appreciation. *Review of Economics and Statistics*, 77, 199–206.

Graeser, P. (1993). Rate of return to investment in american antique furniture. *Southern Economic Journal*, 59, 817–821.

Grimond, M. (12 January 1998). A vintage year to bottle up fine profits in your cellar. *Business Day.*

Jaeger, E. (1981). To save or savor: The rate of return to storing wine. *Journal of Political Economy*, 89, 584–592.

Johnson, H. (1971). *The World Atlas of Wine.* New York: Simon & Schuster.

Krasker, W. (1979). The rate of return to storing wines. *Journal of Political Economy*, 87, 1363–1367.

Meltzer, P. (31 December 1997). Third quarter gain nearly double previous result. *Wine Spectator*, 16–17.

Palmer, J. (3 August 1998a). The coming glut. *Barron's*, 25–28.

Palmer, J. (3 August 1998b). A fool's game. *Barron's*, 28.

Parker, R. Jr. (1995). *Bordeaux: The Definitive Guide for the Wines Produced since 1961.* New York: Simon & Schuster.

Peers, A. (2 May 1997). Hot cellars: Wine prices are soaring. *Wall Street Journal*, 8.

Pesando, J.E. (1993). Art as an investment: The market for modern prints. *American Economic Review*, 83, 1075–1089.

Pompe, J. (1996). An investment flash: The rate of return for photographs. *Southern Economic Journal*, 63, 488–495.

Prial, F.J. (17 September 1997). Bordeaux again leads a high-price parade. *New York Times*, 10.

Prial, F.J. (1998). California cabernets join the gold rush. *New York Times*, 7.

Reitlinger, G. (1961). *The Economics of Taste: The Rise and Fall of the Picture Market*, 1760–1960. New York: Holt, Reinhart, and Winston.

Sokolin, W. (1987). *Liquid Assets.* New York: Macrnillan.

Spurrier, S. (December 1997). Auction fever: Can prices rise forever? *Decanter*, 17.

Steele, M., and Goy, R. (1997). Short holds, the distributions of first and second sales, and bias in the repeat-sales price index. *Journal of Real Estate Finance and Economics*, 14, 133–154.

Tanzer, S. (November 1997). Market monitor. *International Wine Cellar: The Consumer's Passport to Fine Wine*, 75.

Thomas, M. (19 January 1998). Alternative investing: Wine collectors drive up prices. *Business News New Jersey (North).*

Weil, R.L. (February 1993). Do not invest in wine, at least in the U.S., unless you plan to drink it, and maybe not even then; or: As an investment, wine is no corker. *Paper Presented at the Second International Conference of the Vineyard Quantification Society*, Verona, Italy.

Zachys Wine and Liquor (9 September 1997). Zachys Gazette. *New York Times.*

Zachys/Christie's. *Finest and Rarest Wines Auction Catalogue.* London: Vauxhall Prepress, for auction of 2 and 3 April 1998.

Chapter 12

Raise Your Glass: Wine Investment and the Financial Crisis*

Philippe Masset† and Jean-Philippe Weisskopf‡

Ecole hôtelière de Lausanne,
HES-SO University of Applied Sciences,
Western Switzerland
†philippe.masset@ehl.ch
‡jean-philippe.weiskopf@ehl.ch

This chapter uses auction hammer prices over the period 1996–2009, with a special emphasis on periods of economic downturns, to examine risk, return and diversification benefits of fine wine. Our research shows evidence that the wine market is heterogeneous with wine regions and price categories evolving differently in terms of volume and turnover. We find that fine wine yields higher returns and has a lower volatility compared to stocks especially in times of economic crises. Forming portfolios for typical investors and taking risk aversion, different financial assets and various wine indices into consideration we confirm that the addition of wine to a portfolio as a separate asset-class is beneficial for private investors. Not only are returns favorably impacted and risk being minimized but skewness and kurtosis are also positively affected. Particularly, during the recent financial crisis these effects are most pronounced and improve portfolio diversification when it is most needed. Most importantly, balancing a portfolio with fine wine has resulted in added return while reducing volatility with the most prestigious and expensive vintages and estates outperforming the General Wine Index (GWI) during the entire research period. Results from the CAPM show that alpha is significantly positive over the period 1996–2009 while showing a low beta coefficient. The use of a conditional CAPM model allows us to clarify the time-variance of alphas and betas depending on the economic environment that is not generally captured by the traditional CAPM. The time-varying dynamics of alphas and betas are in particular explained by the spread between BAA- and AAA-rated bonds and the USD/EUR foreign exchange rate. Our findings confirm that wine returns are primarily related to economic conditions and not to market risk.

*This article originally appeared in *American Association of Wine Economics* (2010), AAWE Working Paper No. 57.

1. Introduction

In 2003, a bottle of 1982 Lafite-Rothschild sold for an average amount of 490 USD at auctions. Six years later the same bottle went for 2,586 USD yielding the seller an annual return of around 70%. As a matter of fact, even investing in fine wines other than from the premier wine estates of the Bordeaux region has been a lucrative affair. The auction price of a 1982 Barbaresco Riserva Santo Stefano, for example, has risen from an average 135 USD in 2002 to 613 USD in 2009. Examples of such hefty price increases for fine wines are frequently cited in newspapers and suggest that the demand and prices for wines have surged in recent years. An ever growing number of positive press commentaries on the favorable risk-return profile of this asset class has helped to convince investors of the advantages of adding wine to their financial portfolio. As a consequence, wine is increasingly viewed not only as a pure consumption good but also as an interesting investment opportunity by many an investor.

As a result, a small but steadily growing investment market for fine wines has established itself. Auction houses have expanded their presence to new geographical regions outside Europe and the United States to reach new customers, especially in Asia, and have simultaneously increased the number of wine auctions throughout the world. The increase in worldwide turnover from some 90 million USD in 2003 to more than 276 million USD in 2008 at major auction houses as noted by Winespectator provides a proof for the growing popularity of this market. At the same time wine-funds and -indices (e.g., Liv-ex in the U.K. or Idealwine in France) have emerged to cater to this new demand from investors. The resulting improvement in transparency and liquidity has rendered this market even more attractive for investors.

In response to the growing interest in wine as an asset class from investors academic research has been conducted on financial characteristics of the wine market. As early as 1979, Krasker (1979) analyzes returns on wine investments but does not find evidence that wine can outperform a riskless asset. In a response to this article, Jaeger (1981) argues that Krasker's use of a low number of observations and a short period (coinciding with the oil crisis in the 1970s) may bias his results. Indeed in using Krasker's methodology and extending the period into the 1960s Jaeger comes up with much more favorable research results. Later studies expand the research framework to incorporate risk and conclude that wines, like other collectibles, have a higher volatility (Burton and Jacobsen, 1999) and are cyclical (Di Vittorio and

Ginsburgh, 1996; Bentzen *et al.*, 2002; Fogarty, 2006). Burton and Jacobsen (2001) using a repeat-sales-regression show evidence that the heterogeneity of the wine market must be taken into account. Even inside the examined Bordeaux region, vintage can widely influence returns on wine investments. Although wine generates positive investment returns throughout the analyzed period, only the 1982 vintage outperforms the Dow Jones Industrial Average. More recently, Fogarty (2006) in a study of premium Australian wines in the 1990s finds similar returns but a lower volatility of wines as compared to Australian equities. However, contrary to Burton and Jacobsen (2001) who find a worse performance for first growth Bordeaux wines than for their aggregate index more expensive wines seem to achieve larger returns and have a lower volatility in Australia.

If fine wines are to be considered as an asset class on its own the risk-return-framework used in the above studies needs to be extended. Potential diversification benefits from a collection of wines in an investor's portfolio and the possibility of a portfolio risk reduction through low correlations between wine and financial assets must be taken into account. Fogarty (2007) shows that the addition of wine to a portfolio consisting of stocks and bonds shifts the efficient frontier to the left which means a better risk-return trade-off for an investor once wine is included in the portfolio. Sanning *et al.* (2008) use the Capital Asset Pricing Model and the Fama-French three factors model to assess the benefits of wine with regard to portfolio diversification. They find evidence of excess returns for wines and suggest a low correlation of wine with financial markets and the Fama-French risk factors. Masset and Henderson (2009) confirm previous findings of a high return and low variance of wine assets and expand the focus by taking portfolio skewness and kurtosis into account. They find a low correlation between wine and other assets and suggest that best-rated wines offer the best portfolio return, volatility, skewness, kurtosis trade-off in the long-run for most investors.

Both common belief and academic research indicate that investing in wine has desirable attributes for portfolio diversification. In times of economic uncertainty investors are increasingly looking for alternatives to diversify their portfolio and often turn to less conventional assets. Fine wines, in line with other collectibles such as art works, coins or stamps, are widely promoted as being interesting choices due to their interesting risk-return profile and low correlation with other asset classes. However, correlation among assets tends to rise during economic downturns. Unfortunately, diversification tends to be less effective when it is most needed. Journalists in the mass media frequently claim that wines have remained unaffected by this correlation breakdown phenomenon and can still be considered as investment grade. There is, however, not yet any solid empirical evidence to reach a consensus on this claim.

The main contribution of this chapter is to analyze risk-, return-, and diversification-benefits of wine in a portfolio in times of economic downturns using a unique dataset covering the period 1996–2009 and several wine regions across the world. We want to assess the impact of the financial crisis on the trading activity and performance of various wine categories. A possible robustness of wine to financial contagion delivers important insights into the stability of portfolio diversification across economic cycles. We construct different wine indices using repeat sales regressions and compare these to different financial assets by forming portfolios for bull and bear markets and different investor types. We also investigate the possibility that wine returns may be cyclical in their nature and unrelated to market risks and therefore affected by prevailing economic conditions by extending our initial analysis to a conditional CAPM model in order to obtain input from additional criteria and parameters. The main advantage of our approach is to keep a standard financial framework that is easy to interpret while controlling for economic variables that might affect the wine market and are not captured by the traditional CAPM. These enhanced modeling efforts as compared to previous studies may allow us to improve our understanding of the dynamics of the wine market, its returns and its future development.

In a nutshell, our findings show that the inclusion of wine in a portfolio and, especially more prestigious wines, increases the portfolio's returns while reducing its risk, particularly during the financial crisis. This is true for all model-portfolios both during bull and bear periods; during crisis-periods the defensive impact of wine is more pronounced in aggressive style portfolios than in conservative ones. The defensive nature of wine is confirmed by a less negative skewness and a kurtosis approaching three. Using the classic CAPM we observe high alphas except during the crisis and low betas. The use of a conditional CAPM model allows us to clarify the time-variance of alphas and betas depending on the economic environment that does not seem to be captured by the traditional CAPM. Especially, the BAA-AAA spread and the USD/EUR exchange rate explain the time-varying dynamics of alphas and betas. Our findings confirm the cyclical nature of wine with returns primarily related to economic conditions and not to market risks.

The remainder of this chapter is structured as follows: Section 2 describes the data and methodology employed in the present analysis. Section 3 shows main results on portfolio diversification and conditional portfolio evaluation while Section 4 gives an outlook on future benefits of the wine market and wine investing. The chapter ends with our conclusions in Section 5.

2. Data and Methodology

2.1. *Data description*

The data for the study is taken from The Chicago Wine Company (TCWC) and covers all auction hammer prices between January 1996 and January 2009. We start our analysis by discarding wines that are not traded on a regular basis and which therefore do not provide comparable results. The remaining data is sorted according to certain characteristics such as region, vintage, producer, and scanned for any apparent errors. Whenever possible, errors in the dataset are corrected or otherwise removed, where the correct value could not be inferred with certainty. All in all, the sample consists of more than 400,000 transactions from 144 auctions and a turnover exceeding 237 million USD. The size of the dataset covering 13 years and therefore larger than earlier studies allows us to cover two significant economic boom phases (1996–2001 and 2003–2007) as well as two major economic and financial crises (2001–2003 and 2007–2009) and is therefore an ideal setting for our research.

After having cleaned up the dataset, we look which wines are traded the most. If wine is to be taken seriously in an investment strategy it must have a minimum sales volume, be liquid and traded on a frequent basis. We, therefore, concentrate on wines that meet these conditions by compiling data as follows:

Step 1: We only use vintages from 1981 to 2005. This enables us to discard wines that are viewed as antiques. Moreover, it eliminates wines that are mostly illiquid and are traded infrequently. A positive side-effect of limiting the sample is the reduction of time-varying characteristics of wine which results in a better price index. Vintages after 2005 are not yet interesting as they appeared on the market in 2008 at the earliest and thus are not reliably priced.

Step 2: We only consider wines from major regions. Wines originating from France (Bordeaux, Burgundy and Rhône Valley), Italy and the United States represent 90% of all trades in the sample and are therefore analyzed. Other regions from the initial sample included Australia, Germany, Spain, Austria but these regions only make up a very small part at auctions and are traded infrequently.

Step 3: Unconventional bottle sizes are equally removed as they represent a very small proportion of our sample and can lead to erroneous price patterns. The analysis only focuses on bottles with 0.375, 0.75, 1.5, 3, 4.5, and 6 liters contents.

Step 4: We only take those wines into account that have traded at least once every 12 months. This ensures that long periods without trades in a wine are eliminated since they lead to erroneous price jumps that are difficult to interpret.

Step 5: We calculate monthly wine prices by taking the median price of every transaction of a specific wine pair for a given month. Observations with price increases of more than 40% in a given month and drops again by 40% or more the following months and vice versa, are removed. Such erratic price movements would seem odd and difficult to explain and are most probably due to erroneous data.

The size of the dataset employed stands in contrast to earlier studies, which focus either on shorter time periods or on Bordeaux wines only. This allows us to draw a comprehensive and reliable picture of the prices and returns investors can hope for in the wine market.

Table 1 shows the number of trades, the USD turnover and the number of 75cl equivalents traded at TCWC during the period 1996–2009. Panel A looks at data per year and region. Obviously, the various wine regions have developed quite differently over time. All regions have, however, experienced substantial volume growth until the peak of the Internet bubble. Wines of U.S. origin have steadily gained in popularity amongst investors even thereafter and growth has not slowed down since. Burgundy wines have been out of favor since 1998/1999. Wines from the Rhône Valley and Italy have seen an increase until 2001/2002 but have then lost their attractiveness even during boom times. During the financial crisis of 2007–2009 Rhône Valley, Italian and especially Bordeaux wines have fared worst while wines form Burgundy and especially the USA have experienced volume gains and yielded higher USD turnovers. All in all, Bordeaux wines have been by far hardest hit by the crisis and volume is now below 1996 levels. It must also be noted that this wine region has been the clear volume leader over many years but its lead has now substantially been reduced over other regions.

Table 1. Trades, USD Turnover and Number of 75cl Equivalent Bottles Traded Per Year and Region (in Absolute Numbers) and Per Year and Price Category (in Relative Terms)

		1996	1997	1998	1999	2000	2001	2002	2003	2004	2005	2006	2007	2008
Panel A: Number of trades, USD turnover and 75cl equivalent bottles sold per year and region														
# trades	Bordeaux	0.5772	0.4861	0.4664	0.4541	0.3947	0.4009	0.4065	0.4307	0.4197	0.4638	0.5162	0.4776	0.3207
	Bourgogne	0.1936	0.2679	0.2988	0.2792	0.2506	0.1600	0.1084	0.0788	0.0613	0.0398	0.0239	0.0120	0.0469
	Rhone	0.0844	0.0972	0.1055	0.1069	0.1536	0.2058	0.2024	0.1795	0.1791	0.1579	0.1621	0.1680	0.1059
	Italie	0.0849	0.0880	0.0656	0.0708	0.1130	0.1467	0.1946	0.1986	0.1932	0.1667	0.1289	0.1095	0.0881
	USA	0.0600	0.0609	0.0636	0.0891	0.0881	0.0866	0.0881	0.1125	0.1468	0.1719	0.1689	0.2329	0.4384
USD turnover	Bordeaux	0.6277	0.6109	0.6154	0.6232	0.5669	0.5511	0.5427	0.5647	0.5639	0.5853	0.6308	0.5948	0.5287
	Bourgogne	0.1960	0.2301	0.2368	0.2121	0.1848	0.1098	0.0801	0.0573	0.0485	0.0403	0.0233	0.0096	0.0794
	Rhone	0.0637	0.0655	0.0646	0.0771	0.1272	0.1786	0.1743	0.1590	0.1559	0.1475	0.1524	0.1615	0.0863
	Italie	0.0752	0.0646	0.0461	0.0405	0.0747	0.1121	0.1573	0.1662	0.1565	0.1381	0.1062	0.0937	0.0524
	USA	0.0374	0.0290	0.0371	0.0472	0.0465	0.0484	0.0456	0.0527	0.0752	0.0887	0.0873	0.1404	0.2532
# 75cl equiv	Bordeaux	0.6383	0.5127	0.4673	0.4683	0.3874	0.4238	0.4404	0.4628	0.4683	0.5157	0.5819	0.5709	0.3827
	Bourgogne	0.1521	0.2464	0.2959	0.2762	0.2557	0.1451	0.0834	0.0572	0.0490	0.0342	0.0172	0.0053	0.0384
	Rhone	0.0770	0.0995	0.1153	0.1162	0.1605	0.1959	0.1935	0.1744	0.1688	0.1520	0.1568	0.1597	0.1050
	Italie	0.0741	0.0869	0.0618	0.0661	0.1286	0.1690	0.2205	0.2261	0.2107	0.1746	0.1422	0.1150	0.0673
	USA	0.0585	0.0545	0.0596	0.0733	0.0678	0.0663	0.0622	0.0795	0.1031	0.1235	0.1020	0.1491	0.4066

(Continued)

Table 1. (*Continued*)

		1996	1997	1998	1999	2000	2001	2002	2003	2004	2005	2006	2007	2008
Panel B: Number of trades, USD turnover and 75cl equivalent bottles sold per year and price category														
# trades	<$99	0.4576	0.3702	0.3459	0.3397	0.3140	0.3306	0.3263	0.3421	0.3851	0.4394	0.4660	0.4453	0.3305
	$100–$199	0.3167	0.3330	0.3497	0.3495	0.3595	0.3224	0.3465	0.3704	0.3558	0.3490	0.3150	0.3127	0.3505
	$200–$399	0.1757	0.1984	0.2091	0.2131	0.2086	0.2297	0.2188	0.1935	0.1855	0.1560	0.1544	0.1677	0.1675
	>$400	0.0501	0.0984	0.0953	0.0976	0.1179	0.1174	0.1084	0.0941	0.0736	0.0557	0.0647	0.0744	0.1515
USD turnover	<$99	0.2752	0.1789	0.1628	0.1554	0.1399	0.1486	0.1544	0.1711	0.2056	0.2439	0.2738	0.2623	0.1332
	$100–$199	0.3184	0.2792	0.2835	0.2715	0.2661	0.2423	0.2785	0.3172	0.3123	0.3356	0.2999	0.2819	0.2293
	$200–$399	0.2722	0.2521	0.2816	0.2897	0.2837	0.3150	0.2878	0.2793	0.2794	0.2332	0.2466	0.2365	0.1858
	>$400	0.1342	0.2898	0.2721	0.2835	0.3103	0.2941	0.2793	0.2324	0.2027	0.1873	0.1798	0.2193	0.4516
# 75cl equiv	<$99	0.5434	0.4545	0.4212	0.4066	0.3840	0.4071	0.4092	0.4180	0.4507	0.4917	0.5449	0.5541	0.4046
	$100–$199	0.3065	0.3302	0.3476	0.3445	0.3540	0.3159	0.3396	0.3609	0.3464	0.3466	0.2980	0.2859	0.3525
	$200–$399	0.1241	0.1505	0.1662	0.1770	0.1781	0.1955	0.1764	0.1584	0.1529	0.1234	0.1197	0.1203	0.1394
	>$400	0.0260	0.0648	0.0650	0.0718	0.0839	0.0816	0.0748	0.0627	0.0499	0.0383	0.0374	0.0396	0.1035

Notes: Panel A illustrates the relative importance of different wine regions for each year in the period 1996–2008 in terms of number of trades, USD turnover and number of 75cl equivalent bottles. Panel B shows the same for different price categories.

Panel B shows the development of different price categories over the same period of time. By far the largest volume has been traded in wines under 200 USD which have also experienced the steepest trade growth and sharpest decline thereafter (for wines under 100 USD). Wines selling for more than 200 USD are showing a steady increase in market share until 2002 but have declined since. The very expensive wines (>400 USD) have, however, experienced upside growth during the recent crisis although coming from a modest level. Volumes in expensive wines have proven to be a lot less volatile than for cheap wines, probably because they are considered collectibles and thus safer investments. The arrival of the outstanding vintage of 2005 has given the market for prestigious and high price wines a noticeable boost that helps explain the doubling of market share for the >400 USD category in 2008 when this vintage dominated this market segment. This illustrates the importance of vintage as a specific valuation criterion and parameter independent of the economic environment and other market factors.

2.2. *Index construction*

We compute a variety of indices using the repeat-sales regression (RSR) method. This technique uses the purchase and sales price of a specific asset with identical properties (in our case a specific wine-vintage pair) to estimate price appreciations. This approach has been extensively used to estimate the price evolution on the real-estate market (e.g., Bailey *et al.*, 1963; Case and Shiller, 1987; Goetzmann, 1992) and has more recently been applied to the arts market (e.g., Goetzmann, 1993; Pesando, 1993).

We start by deflating all prices to obtain constant USD amounts across time and winsorize price data at the 99.9% level to discard very extreme outliers.[1] For each purchase ($P_{i,p}$) and sales ($P_{i,s}$) price of a specific wine in the index, we calculate the log-return $r_{ips} = \ln(P_{i,s}) - \ln(P_{i,p})$ for the period between the purchase (p) and sale (s). Each return is subsequently regressed and is described as $r_{ips} = \sum_{t=1}^{T} b_t x_{it} + w\varepsilon_{ips}$ where b_j is the value of the index at time t; x_{it} is a dummy variable taking the value 1 at the time of sale, -1 at the time of purchase and 0 otherwise; w denotes a weight based on the winsorized average trading volume that can be assimilated to the freefloat market capitalization in stock indices and ε_{ips} is an error term. In aggregate we get $r = bX + w\varepsilon$, with r and ε being a N-dimensional vector

[1] We also (i) omitted the winsorizing process and (ii) winsorized data at the 99% level which both do not alter results significantly.

for N repeated sales pairs and b a T-dimensional vector of the index values to be estimated.

The use of the RSR method offers several interesting properties that make it ideal for the calculation of wine indices. The use of identical goods to calculate price fluctuations constitutes the main advantage of this technique. Compared to a hedonic pricing model in which individual specifications of a good must be collected and modeled appropriately the RSR allows for a simple way to calculate quality-adjusted indices. Over a simple compounding formula using two endpoints and extrapolating annual returns the RSR method has the advantage of generating estimates for each period. It therefore maximizes the information use of intermediate sales. The main drawback of the RSR model is the sample reduction due to the fact that a good must at least be traded twice to be usable. However, examining a market like wine circumvents this problem. Unlike the arts market in which each painting is unique (the printing market marks an exception) any given wine is normally produced in multiples. This dramatically increases the probability that a given wine is sold more than once. However, the problem is not completely resolved as some wines might still be traded infrequently or the number sold at any one auction might be very small and as a result bias the results.

2.3. *Descriptive statistics*

Figure 1 shows the evolution of the general wine index and its split into different wine regions.

The wine index and the Russell 3000 have both gone up between 1996 and 1998. While the Russell 3000 declined heavily between 2001 and 2003 before it recovered again the wine index grew steadily over the period 1998–2005. Neither the terrorist attacks in New York (9.11), nor the burst of the internet bubble or the boycott of French goods after the Iraq invasion (Ashenfelter *et al.*, 2007) have had much effect on wine prices. The period 2005 to 2008 may be called the golden age for wine in which the index doubled. Since mid-2008 the wine index, however, has decreased by 17% as a result of the economic and financial crisis in line with other financial assets but far more moderately than the Russell 3000 which lost 47% over the same period. Interestingly, the general wine index clearly outperformed the Russell 3000 during the crises in this study, be it in 2002/03 or 2007/08. In comparing, first growth wines of top vintages only the general growth trend is similar to the general wine index. However, the amplitude is substantially bigger.

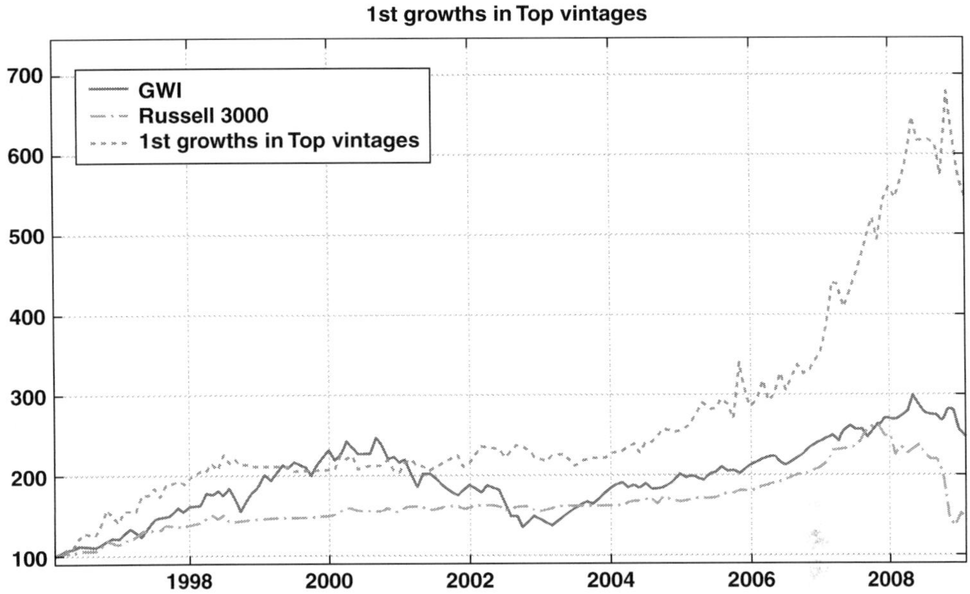

Figure 1. Evolution of the Russell 3000, the General Wine Index and First Growths for Top Vintages for the Period 1996–2008

Especially from 2005 onwards this category hugely outperforms both the general wine index and the Russell 3000.

Figure 2 shows that all the different wine regions follow the upward trend of the general wine index but the amplitude is diverging. Regions outside France show positive returns for the period 1996–2009 but only at a cumulated scale of 66% for the USA or 125% for Italy. Prices for the various French wine regions have developed much more favorably and yielded returns of some 200% in Bordeaux (with very similar returns for the left and right bank) and Burgundy and 300% for the Rhône Valley. Prices have decreased in all regions since March 2008 as a result of the crisis. The effect has however been more moderate (minus about 15% for Bordeaux, the Rhône Valley and Italy and only 6% for U.S. wines) than for major equity markets with the exception of the Burgundy region which suffered a setback of 39% (although from a record high). Over the period subject to our research the wine index has clearly beaten the Russell 3000 and experienced much less volatility.

Looking at different price categories of wines sold at auctions as exhibited in Figure 3 some interesting patterns appear. Wine selling below 200 USD a bottle has seen a steady increase over the period 1996–2009 yielding a return of 120% (wines for 100–199 USD) and 170% (wines below 100 USD). On the

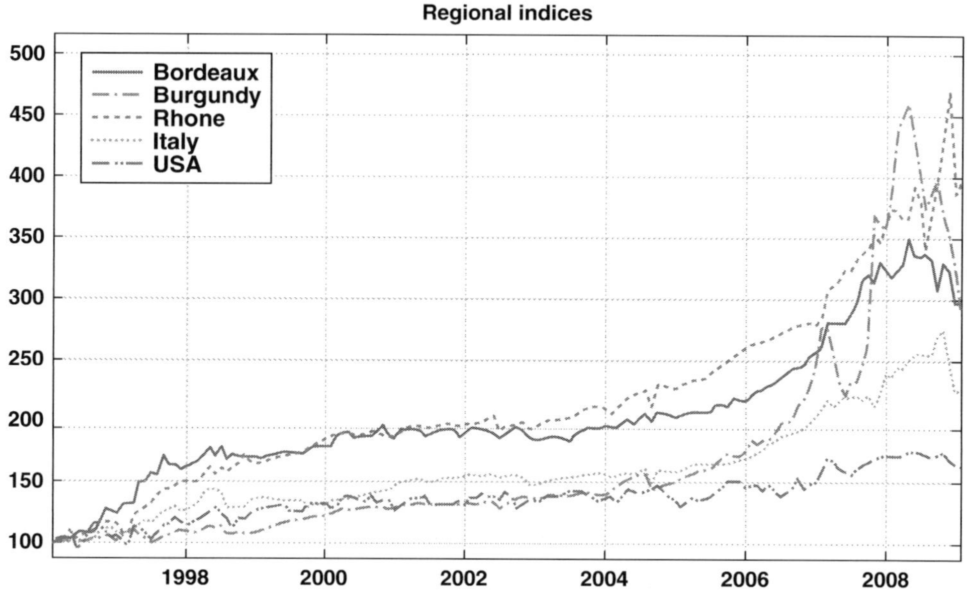

Figure 2. Evolution of Sub-indices for Different Wine Regions for the Period 1996–2008

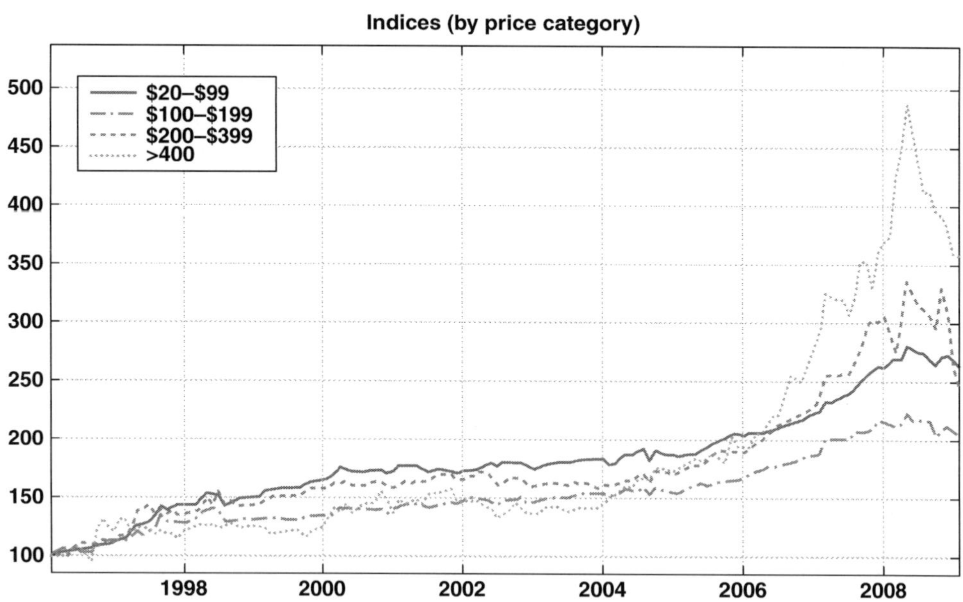

Figure 3. Evolution of Sub-indices for Different Price Categories for the Period 1996–2008

other hand, wines selling for more than 200 USD a bottle and especially those above 400 USD that can be categorized as collectibles have seen a 3–4 fold price increase and have accordingly fallen most during the financial crisis. Since their high in March 2008 wines under 200 USD have only lost 5–10% of their value while those above have lost approximately 25%.

Table 2 illustrates returns and volatilities for different wine indices and the Russell 3000. All wine indices have substantially outperformed the stock index while having a much lower volatility (except for the first growth index that had a similar risk) during the period 1996–2009. Looking at the subperiods it becomes apparent that the outperformance is essentially due to favorable returns in downturns. During economic growth-periods wine underperforms the Russell 3000 but in crises times it substantially outperforms equities and mostly yields positive returns. Volatility is lower for all wine indices (with the exception of best wines) in almost all subperiods. Interesting enough, the 2001–2003 downturn did not result in an increase in wine volatility compared to pre and post boom cycles. The different wine indices are especially solid in down markets and therefore seem to be ideally suited to provide balancing and diversification benefits to an investor's equity portfolio.

3. Empirical Results

3.1. *Portfolio diversification*

We start by building different portfolios that represent the risk attitude of typical investors. This allows us to gauge to what extent investing in wine may be of interest in general and more specifically if risk aversion has an impact on investors' choice when adding wine to their portfolio. Following common bank practice and described in Canner *et al.* (1997) we denote the portfolios as conservative, moderately conservative, balanced, moderately aggressive and aggressive. Table 3 illustrates the asset allocation for each portfolio type.

As can be expected risk averse investors, focus on low risk assets such as Fixed Income products, bonds or Blue Chips. Allocation will gradually move towards more volatile assets once risk aversion declines. We select four different cases for each of the five types of investors described above. The initial case stands for investors that hold a portfolio with the abovementioned assets and do not consider investing in wine. The other three cases include an investment in (i) the general wine index, (ii) first growth wines only, or (iii) first growth wines from top vintages. For these portfolios

Table 2. Return and Risk for Different Indices

	GWI	Bordeaux	Burgundy	Rhône	Italy	USA	< 99 USD	100–199 USD	200–399 USD	> 400 USD	First growth	Russell 3000
Total Return	148.86%	198.15%	190.98%	296.21%	125.75%	63.29%	170.62%	119.30%	146.96%	284.10%	447.91%	42.24%
Period 1	58.30%	88.44%	27.06%	90.11%	35.73%	36.39%	62.54%	57.05%	58.71%	57.04%	119.89%	142.16%
Period 2	0.10%	−2.05%	10.07%	5.55%	10.84%	0.25%	9.84%	0.94%	−3.22%	7.76%	−0.26%	−41.27%
Period 3	51.42%	59.11%	67.02%	65.63%	44.27%	16.46%	37.02%	34.09%	66.29%	105.92%	108.04%	72.11%
Period 4	−3.00%	−5.48%	18.89%	17.26%	3.76%	−0.55%	6.51%	2.51%	−11.00%	2.35%	11.32%	−42.67%
Volatility	8.23%	10.33%	14.71%	11.88%	9.09%	12.73%	6.84%	6.73%	11.20%	13.61%	18.72%	17.89%
Period 1	8.34%	12.77%	7.41%	11.39%	9.78%	17.57%	7.79%	8.44%	13.02%	14.51%	17.93%	15.56%
Period 2	5.28%	6.77%	4.69%	5.29%	4.41%	10.52%	3.86%	4.58%	5.55%	9.69%	11.49%	16.97%
Period 3	6.42%	6.68%	12.70%	7.47%	6.66%	10.76%	5.64%	5.70%	6.85%	11.69%	21.00%	8.63%
Period 4	14.26%	15.14%	34.16%	24.85%	16.68%	5.29%	10.50%	7.23%	19.81%	20.70%	24.34%	31.15%

Notes: Indices include the general wine index (GWI), four sub-indices depending on price categories, an index for first growth from top vintages and the Russell 3000. Periods are divided into two boom and two bear periods. Period one covers the period 1996–2001, period two 2001–2003, period three 2003-mid-2007 and period four mid-2007–2009.

Table 3. Asset Allocation for Different Investor Types

	Conservative	Moderately conservative	Balanced	Moderately aggressive	Aggressive
Fixed income	40%	25%	0%	0%	0%
Bonds	40%	35%	40%	20%	0%
Blue chips	20%	20%	30%	40%	40%
Mid caps	0%	10%	10%	15%	20%
Small caps	0%	10%	10%	15%	20%
International	0%	0%	10%	10%	20%

Notes: Allocation of different asset classes depending on the risk aversion of a typical investor. Fixed Income denotes savings that are invested at the 3-months LIBOR rate, bonds are represented by the CGBI USBIG overall AAA index, blue chips by the S&P500, mid caps by the S&P400, small caps by the S&P600 and international stocks by the MSCI World ex-USA.

a share of 20% is allocated for and the weight of the other assets is reduced proportionally. An investor holding a portfolio with a value between 500,000 and 1 million USD would typically be able to diversify his portfolio in such a way.

Figure 4 shows that the degree of risk has an impact on portfolio returns.[2] In boom-periods risky portfolios clearly outperform all other investor types. Performance trends are, however, reversed in crises periods. Figure 4 illustrates that the performance of all investor types actually finds a common return level in crises periods (2001–2003 and 2007–2009) since all the riskier types are losing the head start they have gained over conservative types during growth periods. The addition of wine, however, produces higher returns for all portfolios (different scale in right figure) including conservative portfolios. Again all portfolio types meet the same performance level during crises periods but at a much higher return level.

As can be seen in Panel A of Table 4 the different initial portfolios appropriately model the risk-aversion of investors (i.e., volatility of a portfolio increases in line with its aggressiveness). However, more risk does not necessarily imply higher returns. During the financial crisis, the aggressive (higher risk) portfolios performed worse than the balanced or conservative ones. The inclusion of wine as an additional asset-class into a portfolio is favorable. Compared to the initial portfolio, portfolio returns rise and

[2]Results for the General Wine Index and different price categories are similar to those shown in Figure 4.

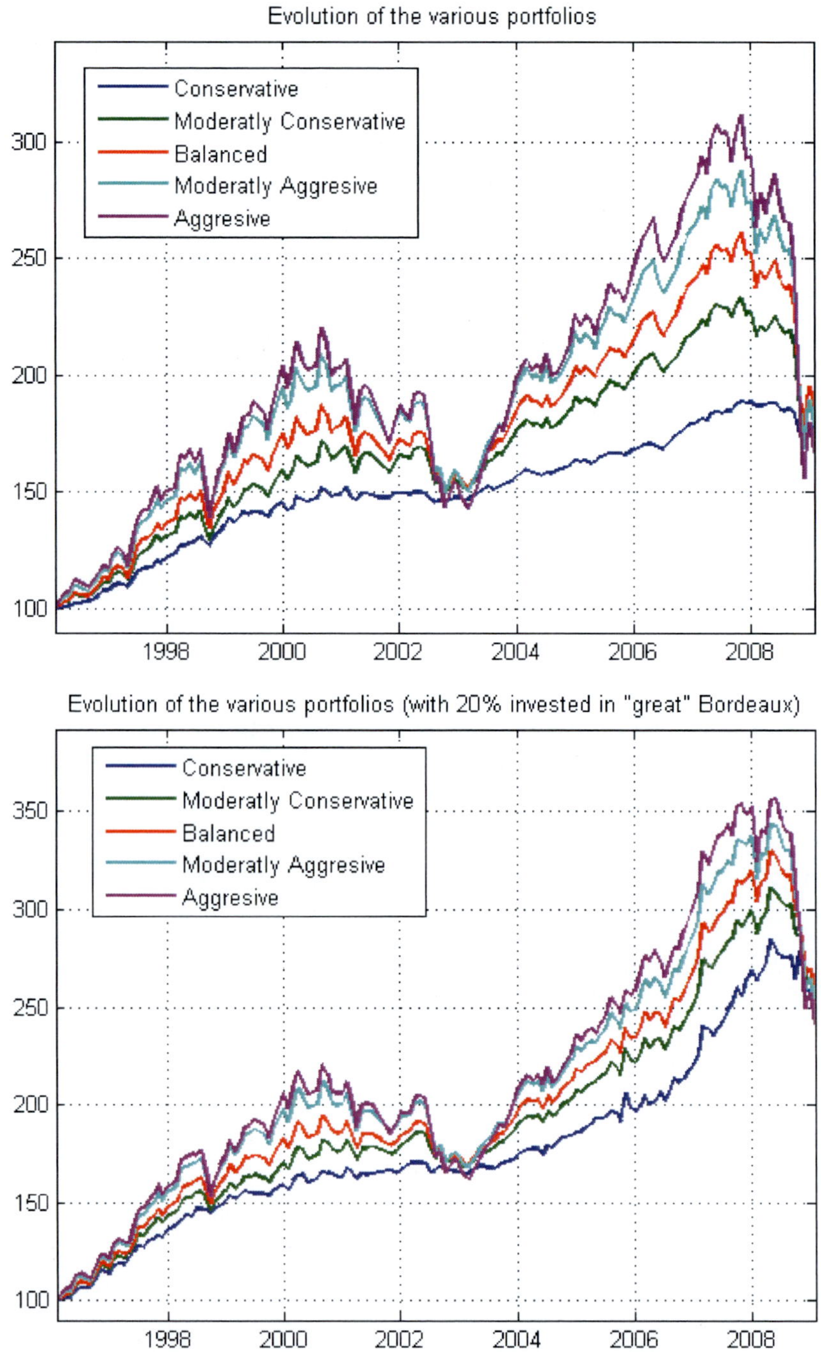

Figure 4. Evolution of Different Portfolios Without and With 20% Invested in 1st Growths from Top Vintage Wines

Table 4. Return, Volatility, Skewness and Kurtosis for Different Portfolios

		Conservative	Moderately conservative	Balanced	Moderately aggressive	Aggressive
		Panel A: Period 1996–2008				
Initial Portfolio	Total returns	77.1237	81.437	87.3863	79.2411	67.3985
	Volatility	0.041	0.0848	0.108	0.1426	0.1761
	Skewness	−0.3347	−1.6096	−1.5141	−1.7208	−1.9434
	Kurtosis	5.4556	10.7716	10.4198	11.3909	12.817
Portfolio with the General Wine Index	Total returns	101.3297	104.7804	109.5399	103.0237	93.5496
	Volatility	0.0368	0.0641	0.0813	0.1074	0.1321
	Skewness	0.0173	−1.0583	−1.1524	−1.39	−1.6252
	Kurtosis	3.287	5.7762	6.3917	7.6735	9.0966
Portfolio with 1st growth wines	Total returns	137.3675	140.8182	145.5777	139.0615	129.5874
	Volatility	0.0483	0.0643	0.0781	0.1005	0.1219
	Skewness	0.226	−0.3646	−0.4889	−0.7282	−0.9537
	Kurtosis	3.0868	3.2889	3.208	3.7384	4.5558
Portfolio with 1st growth from top vintages	Total returns	151.2819	154.7325	159.492	152.9758	143.5017
	Volatility	0.0619	0.072	0.0827	0.1021	0.1214
	Skewness	0.3077	−0.3729	−0.4978	−0.686	−0.8616
	Kurtosis	4.4406	4.1372	3.5315	3.5559	3.9366
		Panel B: Financial Crisis Period (since mid-2007)				
Initial portfolio	Total returns	−4.2401	−20.6806	−26.2372	−36.1765	−44.9145
	Volatility	0.0617	0.1561	0.1984	0.2669	0.3412
	Skewness	−0.3348	−1.1962	−1.105	−1.225	−1.2634
	Kurtosis	5.8931	5.8785	5.8379	5.8293	5.7703
Portfolio with the General Wine Index	Total returns	−3.0023	−15.583	−20.2723	−28.5779	−36.0587
	Volatility	0.0461	0.0998	0.1306	0.1793	0.2315
	Skewness	−0.1748	−1.0759	−1.0835	−1.2398	−1.298
	Kurtosis	2.8868	3.8564	4.3089	4.797	5.0137
Portfolio with 1st growth wines	Total returns	3.5804	−8.8442	−13.657	−21.8397	−29.2053
	Volatility	0.0715	0.0852	0.1054	0.1427	0.1851
	Skewness	0.1282	−0.3417	−0.3035	−0.5575	−0.7333
	Kurtosis	1.9148	2.236	2.0085	2.4715	2.9637
Portfolio with 1st growth from top vintages	Total returns	3.7613	−8.103	−12.7556	−20.6651	−27.8108
	Volatility	0.0977	0.1012	0.1134	0.1429	0.1789
	Skewness	−0.0056	−0.7098	−0.5305	−0.5685	−0.6351
	Kurtosis	2.3208	3.4196	2.8416	2.5156	2.5003

Notes: Panel A shows total returns, volatility, skewness and kurtosis for the period 1996–2008. Investors are categorized according to their risk aversion and hold portfolios that are either conservative, moderately conservative, balanced, moderately aggressive or aggressive. Each investor type can further choose to invest in the initial portfolio consisting of different financial assets but no wine, a portfolio consisting of financial assets and the General Wine Index, of financial assets and first growth wines from the Bordeaux region or of financial assets and first growth wines from the Bordeaux region for top vintages only. Panel B shows the same for the period of the financial crisis (from mid-2007 onwards).

volatility decreases across investor type and wine index. The defensive features of wine are further underlined by a slightly less negative skewness and a kurtosis approaching three. Panel B focuses on the period of the financial crisis (i.e., from mid-2007 onwards). Due to the worldwide crash of stock markets, returns obviously turn negative and volatility increases as compared to the period 1996–2009. It is not a surprise that more aggressive portfolios are the worst performers and have the highest volatility. As for the period 1996–2009 investors with wine in their portfolios perform better than without. In general, returns are higher and volatility is lower. Even more interestingly, a conservative portfolio with 20% first growth wines or first growth wines from top vintages yields a favorable return of some 3.5% during the crisis with a low volatility of 7–9%.[3]

As a further step we run CAPM regressions for the different portfolios. As can be observed in Table 5 the above mentioned results are being confirmed. Portfolios that invest in wine have a significantly higher alpha, which increases the more prestigious the wines are. For first growth wines from top vintages alpha at least doubles. This rise in alpha is accompanied by a significant decrease in beta for all portfolios. We broaden our research to include extended regressions in which a dummy for the crisis is added to obtain the following model:

$$R_P - R_f = \alpha_p + \beta_{pM}(R_M - R_f) + D_{FC}(\alpha_P^{FC} + \beta_{pM}^{FC}(R_M - R_f)) + \varepsilon \quad (1)$$

where the first term represents the initial model and the second term the term for the crisis period with D_{FC} being a dummy taking the value 1 for the crisis period. It can be concluded that results for alphas follow those in the initial model. Alphas do not change for any portfolio type during the crisis and thus similar to the initial model increase in line with the portfolio aggressiveness and wine investment. On the other hand, betas vary significantly during the crisis. For the initial portfolio betas are either significantly positive or insignificant, but for all wine portfolios the beta-dummy for the crisis is significantly negative. It is further proof that the addition of fine wine in portfolios is generating high alphas while reducing the exposition to systematic risk.

[3]We also consider portfolios for economic boom periods only. Results are in line with those presented above. The addition of wine in a portfolio does yield positive results independent of the economic cycle.

Table 5. Market Model Regressions for Different Portfolios

		Conservative	Moderately conservative	Balanced	Moderately aggressive	Aggressive
		Panel A: Market model regressions				
Initial Portfolio	Alpha	0.0008*	0.0015***	0.0019***	0.0020***	0.0018**
		(1.74)	(3.05)	(3.38)	(3.02)	(2.02)
	Beta	0.2124***	0.4787***	0.6135***	0.8138***	1.0006***
		(24.41)	(52.03)	(57.53)	(65.06)	(56.97)
Portfolio with the General Wine Index	Alpha	0.0014**	0.0019***	0.0022***	0.0023***	0.0022***
		(2.02)	(2.85)	(3.23)	(3.15)	(2.59)
	Beta	0.1337***	0.3355***	0.4426***	0.5986***	0.7395***
		(9.91)	(25.98)	(33.35)	(42.28)	(44.29)
Portfolio with the 1st growth wines	Alpha	0.0025**	0.0030***	0.0032***	0.0033***	0.0033***
		(2.21)	(2.79)	(3.07)	(3.10)	(2.88)
	Beta	0.0902***	0.2786***	0.3804***	0.5260***	0.6554***
		(4.11)	(13.59)	(18.69)	(25.35)	(29.75)
Portfolio with the 1st growth wines from top vintages	Alpha	0.0028*	0.0033**	0.0035**	0.0036***	0.0036**
		(1.87)	(2.30)	(2.54)	(2.59)	(2.48)
	Beta	0.0766***	0.2571***	0.3556***	0.4958***	0.6197***
		(2.62)	(9.39)	(13.29)	(18.39)	(22.20)
		Panel B: Market model regressions with financial crisis dummies				
Initial Portfolio	Alpha	0.0004	0.0014***	0.0017***	0.0020***	0.0021**
		(0.90)	(2.74)	(2.92)	(2.87)	(2.29)
	Beta	0.2395***	0.4717***	0.6095***	0.7962***	0.9467***
		(21.28)	(37.96)	(42.28)	(47.39)	(41.52)
	Alpha-Crisis	0.0014	0.0010	0.0015	0.0010	0.0011
		(1.01)	(0.65)	(0.85)	(0.49)	(0.39)
	Beta-Crisis	−0.0557***	0.0194	0.0144	0.0434*	0.1254***
		(−3.17)	(1.00)	(0.64)	(1.66)	(3.52)
Portfolio with the General Wine Index	Alpha	0.0014**	0.0021***	0.0023***	0.0025***	0.0027***
		(1.99)	(3.00)	(3.25)	(3.27)	(2.87)
	Beta	0.1736***	0.3565***	0.4681***	0.6219***	0.7429***
		(9.96)	(20.80)	(26.64)	(33.09)	(33.07)
	Alpha-Crisis	−0.0031	−0.0034	−0.0031	−0.0037	−0.0041
		(−1.42)	(−1.61)	(−1.40)	(−1.59)	(−1.46)
	Beta-Crisis	−0.1010***	−0.0598**	−0.0686**	−0.0660**	−0.0227
		(−3.71)	(−2.24)	(−2.50)	(−2.25)	(−0.65)
Portfolio with the 1st growth wines	Alpha	0.0023**	0.0028***	0.0030***	0.0032***	0.0033***
		(1.96)	(2.63)	(2.87)	(2.97)	(2.82)
	Beta	0.1666***	0.3458***	0.4556***	0.6065***	0.7249***
		(5.94)	(13.14)	(17.69)	(23.31)	(25.60)
	Alpha-Crisis	−0.0032	−0.0039	−0.0037	−0.0045	−0.0050
		(−0.93)	(−1.18)	(−1.15)	(−1.38)	(−1.42)
	Beta-Crisis	−0.1837***	−0.1654***	−0.1827***	−0.1974***	−0.1746***
		(−4.19)	(−4.03)	(−4.54)	(−4.86)	(−3.95)

(*Continued*)

Table 5. (*Continued*)

		Conservative	Moderately conservative	Balanced	Moderately aggressive	Aggressive
		Panel B: Market model regressions with financial crisis dummies				
Portfolio with the 1st growth wines from top vintages	Alpha	0.0027*	0.0032**	0.0034**	0.0035**	0.0036**
		(1.72)	(2.20)	(2.40)	(2.50)	(2.45)
	Beta	0.1528***	0.3296***	0.4381***	0.5872***	0.7042***
		(3.98)	(9.21)	(12.68)	(17.07)	(19.56)
	Alpha-Crisis	−0.0043	−0.0051	−0.0050	−0.0059	−0.0065
		(−0.91)	(−1.14)	(−1.16)	(−1.37)	(−1.46)
	Beta-Crisis	−0.1872***	−0.1817***	−0.2037***	−0.2272***	−0.2140***
		(−3.13)	(−3.25)	(−3.78)	(−4.23)	(−3.81)

Notes: Panel A shows alphas and betas of market model regressions for the period 1996–2008 for different investor types and portfolios with and without wine. Panel B shows the same market model regressions with dummies for the financial crisis. The asterisks show significance levels of 1% (***), 5% (**) and 10% (*).

3.2. *Conditional CAPM*

Literature on wine investments has shown that fine wine has a low correlation with other assets (Masset and Henderson, 2009) and that standard asset pricing models cannot explain wine returns on their own (Sanning *et al.*, 2008). Our results support these findings. Alphas of portfolios including wine seem to turn negative in periods of economic downturns and wines seem, at least graphically, to follow a similar trend as stocks. This indicates that while wines may not directly be correlated with stock returns they might be affected by similar economic factors.

The traditional, unconditional CAPM that is used to evaluate portfolio performance has the major drawback of not taking the changing nature of the economy into account. As a consequence alphas and betas might be miscalculated and misinterpreted. The use of a conditional CAPM model in which alphas and betas can be time-varying is therefore proposed. This approach allows us to identify economic and financial variables that might help explain wine returns more accurately. It, in particular, permits to deepen the understanding of how the wine market works and helps to forecast the evolution of future wine returns while keeping the intuitive interpretation of the CAPM.

The analysis fits the conditional performance of the General Wine Index, 4 sub-indices depending on price category and the first growth from top vintage index, using the Russell 3000 as a benchmark. The model takes the form:

$$\mathrm{r_{p,t}} = \alpha_{0\mathrm{p}} + \alpha'_{\mathrm{p}}\mathrm{z_{t-1}} + \beta_{0\mathrm{p}}\mathrm{r_{m,t}} + \beta'_{\mathrm{p}}(\mathrm{z_{t-1}r_{m,t}}) + \varepsilon_{\mathrm{p,t}} \tag{2}$$

where $\alpha_{0\mathrm{p}}$ and $\beta_{0\mathrm{p}}$ are the average alpha and beta, A'_{p} and $\beta' p$ the response of the conditional alpha and beta to the information variables $\mathrm{z}_{\mathrm{t}-1}$.

The market condition variables z_{t-1} that might influence the evolution of wine prices include: the spread between BAA- and AAA-rated bonds which is suggested by Jagannathan and Wang (1996) as an excellent indicator for the market risk premium; the USD/EUR foreign exchange rate to account for the fact that most wines in the sample come from Europe and are sold in the U.S. Returns should therefore be especially influenced by this exchange rate. Finally, we also use the lagged wine index returns.[4]

We find evidence that neither alpha nor beta is constant over time. As can be seen in Figure 5[5] beta oscillates around zero but does not seem to be too varying and can therefore not be the main driver of the wine market. Alpha, however, is clearly time-varying. It appears that it is strongly influenced by general economic conditions as alpha decreases below the risk-free rate in times of crises (2002/03 and 2007/08) but rises in boom periods.

Following equation 2, we present results of the conditional CAPM model in Table 6. The USD/EUR foreign exchange rate and lagged returns of the wine index are not significant for the beta coefficient but the spread between BAA- and AAA-rated bonds seems to explain some of the variation in market risk. However, it cannot fully explain the beta variation in wines under 200 USD. These wines are predominantly from Italy and the USA and are highly priced *per se*. Therefore they stay expensive but are far less affected by economic conditions and less speculative and volatile than French wines. The sensitivity of the alpha coefficient to the spread and foreign exchange rate is significantly negative for all but one index and thus seems to explain most of the variance. The autocorrelation of the index is also significantly negative apart for wines that cost less than 100 or more than 400 USD.

The explanatory power (R2) can be used to compare the relative performance of the various specifications. The unconditional CAPM has a very low R2 for all portfolios (between 0 and 0.12) which indicates that it is not able to explain the wine market. For the conditional framework it increases (0.07–0.27) which indicates that parameters are time-varying and the estimation with a conditional model more precise. The low R2 of 0.07 and 0.09

[4]We also added the volatility index VIX as an investor fear measure (Whaley, 2000) in our conditional CAPM model. Although the use of the VIX is interesting conceptually and R2 increases slightly it is not significant and causes major multicollinearity problems with the spread variable.

[5]The figure refers to the General Wine Index and the index for first growth wines from top vintages. The same was done for the sub-indices with similar results.

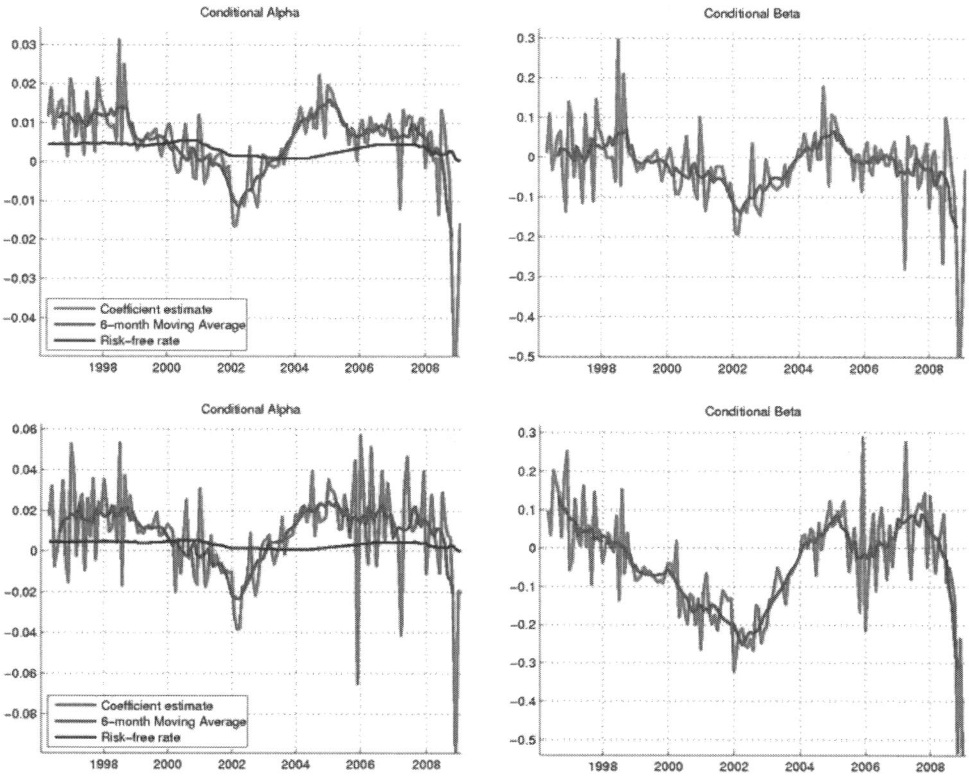

Figure 5. Conditional Alpha and Beta for the General Wine Index (top) and for 1st Growths from Top Vintages Wines (bottom) for the Period 1996–2009

for wines costing between 100 and 200 and more than 400 USD respectively can be explained by the characteristics of the wine market. The lower priced wines, come from less speculative wine regions while the wines costing more than 400 USD can primarily be rated as collectibles and thus are also less speculative and crisis resistant. Consequently, the market conditions do not have as high an impact on these wines as on others.

4. Summary and Conclusions

In times of economic downturns correlation among financial assets tends to rise and diversification becomes less effective when it is most needed. As a result, investors are increasingly looking for alternatives to diversify their portfolio and often turn to less conventional assets. Fine wines are widely recommended as a possible choice due to their interesting risk-return profile and low correlation with other asset classes. In this chapter, we have

Table 6. Conditional CAPM Regressions for Different Portfolios

	GWI	Price <99 USD	Price 100–199 USD	Price 200–399 USD	Price >400 USD	1st growths top vintage
Alpha	0.0606***	0.0338***	0.0303**	0.0757***	0.0721***	0.1183***
	(4.21)	(2.74)	(2.45)	(3.79)	(2.87)	(3.65)
Alpha (Spread)	−0.3861***	−0.4231***	−0.1353	−0.4835***	−0.3010***	−0.2840***
	(−4.90)	(−3.07)	(−0.97)	(−5.00)	(−2.60)	(−2.93)
Alpha (USD/EUR)	−0.6023**	−0.4586	−0.7690*	−0.5271**	−0.6852**	−0.7109***
	(−2.56)	(−1.30)	(−1.88)	(−2.05)	(−1.98)	(−2.62)
Alpha (ACWI)	−3.7046***	−2.5296	−6.2574**	−4.6050***	0.0055	−2.6593***
	(−2.61)	(−0.95)	(−2.13)	(−4.14)	(0.00)	(−3.93)
Beta*Rm	6.5660	−8.3550	10.0759	3.8151	11.5409	5.0034
	(1.22)	(−1.03)	(1.08)	(0.64)	(1.47)	(0.81)
Beta*Rm (Spread)	−2.9290***	−1.5592	−1.4323	−2.6539***	−2.5007**	−1.8090*
	(−3.73)	(−1.31)	(−0.98)	(−2.96)	(−1.96)	(−1.93)
Beta*Rm (USD/EUR)	−4.3828	8.0148	−9.4257	−2.6539	−8.9293	−4.2849
	(−0.84)	(1.02)	(−1.03)	(−0.46)	(−1.16)	(−0.71)
Beta*Rm (ACWI)	−50.5660**	40.3136	−53.6898	−8.2761	−15.1290	11.5959
	(−2.14)	(0.91)	(−1.27)	(−0.50)	(−0.56)	(0.96)
R2	0.2295	0.1928	0.0665	0.2759	0.084	0.2077

Notes: This table presents the average conditional alpha(s), the coefficient estimates for the conditional alpha function and the average conditional beta(s) for the general wine index, price category sub-indices and first growths from top vintages wines using a conditional CAPM model. The information variables are the Spread of BAA- and AAA-rated bonds, the USD/EUR foreign exchange rate and the autocorrelation of the respective wine index (ACWI). R2 is the coefficient of determination, expressed in percentage. The asterisks show significance levels of 1% (***), 5% (**), and 10% (*).

looked into investments in fine wine for the period 1996–2009 with a special emphasis on how they performed in economic crises.

In this chapter we have analyzed risk, return and diversification benefits in the wine market in general and in several submarkets. The use of a unique dataset from TCWC covering over 400,000 auction hammer prices allows us to build repeat-sales regression indices and to look at different wine regions, price categories and vintages. Our results show that since 1996, the General Wine Index and particularly first growth wines from top vintages have performed better than equities while showing a lower volatility.

A further and more detailed research into different investor types and wine indices fully supports this evidence and confirms that wine in a portfolio has produced higher returns and lower risk than the Russell 3000 equity index during this period of time. Especially in times of economic downturns such as in the periods 2001–2003 or 2007–2009 the defensive characteristics of wine are most pronounced. Wine's performance has declined less than for other assets. It had an even lower volatility (with one exception) and also showed improved skewness and kurtosis measures. Fine wines may therefore be regarded as an interesting addition to an investor's portfolio.

Results when using the CAPM indicate higher alphas and lower betas for portfolios containing wine. By focusing on the financial crisis we find that although alpha is not significantly different in periods of economic downturns it also does not seem to be constant over time. We, therefore, extend the analysis to a conditional CAPM framework. This more detailed approach allows us to explain the low explanatory power of the unconditional CAPM and to find which economic variables are best able to describe wine returns while keeping the intuitive interpretation of a CAPM model. Our results suggest that alpha and beta both are time-varying. Wine returns are essentially unrelated to market risk but behave cyclically being affected by the state of the economy.

References

Ashenfelter, O., Ciccarella, S., and Shatz, H. (2007). French wine and the US Boycott of 2003: Does politics really affect commerce? *Journal of Wine Economics*, 2, 55–74.

Bailey, M., Muth, R., and Nourse, H. (1963). A regression method for real estate price index construction. *Journal of the American Statistical Association*, 58, 933–942.

Bentzen, J., Leth-Sørensen, S., and Smith, V. (2002). *Prices of French Icon Wines and the Business Cycle: Empirical Evidence from Danish Wine Auctions*. CIES Discussion Paper 0224.

Burton, B.J., and Jacobsen, J.P. (1999). Measuring returns on investments in collectibles. *Journal of Economic Perspectives*, 13, 193–212.

Burton, B.J., and Jacobsen, J.P. (2001). The rate of return on investment in wine. *Economic Inquiry*, 39, 337–350.

Canner, N., Mankiw, N., and Weil, D. (1997). An asset allocation puzzle. *American Economic Review*, 87, 181–191.

Case, K., and Shiller, R. (1987). Prices of Single-Family Homes since 1970: New Indexes for Four Cities. *New England Economic Review*, September/October, 45–56.

Di Vittorio, A., and Ginsburgh, V. (1996). Pricing red wines of Medoc vintages from 1949 to 1989 at Christie's auctions. *Journal de la Société Statistique de Paris*, 137, 19–49.

Fogarty, J. (2007). Rethinking Wine Investment in the UK and Australia, Working Paper, American Association of Wine Economists.

Fogarty, J.J. (2006). The return to Australian fine wine. *European Review of Agricultural Economics*, 33, 542–561.

Goetzmann, W. (1992). The accuracy of real estate indices: Repeat sale estimators. *The Journal of Real Estate Finance and Economics*, 5, 5–53.

Goetzmann, W. (1993). Accounting for taste: Art and the financial markets over three centuries. *The American Economic Review*, 83, 1370–1376.

Jaeger, E. (1981). To save or savor: The rate of return to storing wine. *Journal of Political Economy*, 89, 584–592.

Jagannathan, R., and Wang, Z. (1996). The conditional CAPM and the cross-section of expected returns. *Journal of Finance*, 51, 3–53.

Krasker, W.S. (1979). The rate of return to storing wines. *Journal of Political Economy*, 87, 1363–1367.

Masset, P., and Henderson, C. (2009). Wine as an alternative asset class, Working Paper.

Pesando, J. (1993). Art as an investment: The market for modern prints. *The American Economic Review*, 83, 1075–1089.

Sanning, L., Shaffer, S., and Sharratt, J.M. (2008). Bordeaux wine as a financial investment. *Journal of Wine Economics*, 3, 61–81.

Whaley, R. (2000). The investor fear gauge. *Journal of Portfolio Management*, 26, 12–17.

Chapter 13

Wine as an Alternative Asset Class*

Philippe Masset[†] **and Caroline Henderson**[‡]

Ecole hôtelière de Lausanne, HES-SO
University of Applied Sciences, Western Switzerland
Route de Cojonnex 18, 1000 Lausanne 25, Switzerland
[†]*philippe.masset@ehl.ch*
[‡]*caroline.henderson@fr.educanet2.ch*

Using a dataset that spans the period 1996 to 2007 and contains transaction prices for all reported auctions at the Chicago Wine Company, we analyze how the prices of high-end wines have evolved during this time period. The best wines according to characteristics like vintage, rating and ranking earn higher returns and tend to have a lower variance than poorer wines. Nevertheless, the different categories of wines seem to follow a rather similar trend over the long run. Wine returns are only slightly correlated with other assets and can consequently be used to reduce the risk of an equity portfolio. Wine looks even more attractive when the investor also has concerns about the skewness of his portfolio. However, the part to be invested in wine is reduced once the kurtosis is included into the analysis. Finally, it seems advisable to diversify across different wine categories as their short-run movements are partially independent of each other. First growths and wines rated as extraordinary by Robert Parker deliver the best tradeoff in terms of portfolio expected returns, variance, skewness and kurtosis for most investor preference settings under consideration.

1. Introduction

During the last few years, wine has been increasingly considered as an alternative investment vehicle. Wine prices have experienced strong inflation (at least until summer 2008). This is particularly true for those wines produced by the most prestigious estates in famous areas like Bordeaux or Burgundy. The demand for these wines has increased because of the massive arrival of new customers from Russia and Asia and also because of bullish

*This article originally appeared in *Journal of Wine Economics* (2010), 5(1), 87–118.

financial markets, which have had an emulation effect on other markets (e.g., collectibles). Moreover, the rarefaction of attractive investment opportunities on financial markets has probably led some investors to reinvest part of their gains on the wine market (see Burton and Jacobsen, 1999). This interest for investing in wines is not restricted to professional investors. A number of articles have been published in popular newspapers and magazines. There are also several investment funds aiming at tracking the performance of the wine market.[1] Euronext launched a wine futures market, the WineFex in 2001; however, it failed to attract sufficient attention from investors and thus disappeared by the end of 2002.

Despite this growing interest in wine as an asset class, finance academics have devoted only limited attention to this realm of research since the pioneering works of Krasker (1979) and Jaeger (1981).[2] Since the late 60's, wine has indeed been presented as a possibly attractive alternative investment (see, e.g., the references in Krasker, 1979). The first attempts to assess formally the validity of this popular belief lead however to mixed results. Krasker (1979) arrives at the conclusion that wine returns are close to the returns on riskless assets. Jaeger (1981) argues that the poor returns reported in Krasker's study could be due to the specific time period considered (1973–1977, 137 observations), which essentially coincides with the oil crisis. Using a sample covering years 1969 to 1977 (199 observations), Jaeger demonstrates that investing in wines can be lucrative.

According to Burton and Jacobsen (1999), collectibles (including wines) are characterized by a higher variance than equities and their price evolution has a typical boom-burst aspect.[3] The latter is confirmed by Fogarty (2006b) who notes that the returns on wine are cyclical. Furthermore, the correlation among various collectible categories seems to increase in falling markets (Burton and Jacobsen, 1999). Burton and Jacobsen (2001) argue that the returns on wine should be higher than for other collectibles (as its

---

[1]Some funds invest in wine companies (see, e.g., The Orange Wine Fund), while others invest directly in wines (see, e.g., The Vintage Wine Fund or The Wine Investment Fund).
[2]Many chapters have addressed the question of how wine is priced; most of them are based on hedonic models; see Ashenfelter *et al.* (1995), Di Vittorio and Ginsburgh (1996), Combris, Lecocq and Visser (1997), Combris, Lecocq and Visser (2000), Jones and Storchmann (2001), Oczkowski (2001), Cardebat and Figuet (2004), Fogarty (2006a) and Lecocq and Visser (2006), Benfratello, Piacenza and Sacchetto (2009) and Ashenfelter (2010). In particular Fogarty (2006a) focuses on Australian wines and provides a thorough literature review.
[3]For instance, Di Vittorio and Ginsburgh (1996) report that prices have increased by 75% between 1981 and 1990 and have then decreased by 15% (up to 1992).

consumption implies destruction) but lower than for stocks (as it provides an intrinsic utility to its beneficiary). These theoretical insights are indeed confirmed by their empirical analysis: wines typically achieve lower Sharpe ratio than stocks. Nevertheless, Burton and Jacobsen (2001) also show that the performance of some specific wine portfolios might be more attractive; in particular, the returns of a portfolio consisting only of wines from the 1982 vintage compare favorably with that of the Dow Jones. More recently, Fogarty (2006b) shows that the returns on premium Australian wines have been almost as large as the returns on Australian equities over the period 1989–2000, while their volatility has been significantly lower than that of Australian equities. Fogarty (2006b) also demonstrates that more expensive wines achieve larger returns and have a lower volatility than less expensive wines.

All the previously mentioned studies have focused on returns and risk solely and have basically compared wines and equities on the basis of these features alone. A problem with such an approach is that it completely disregards the potential benefits of wine in terms of diversification. For a well-diversified investor, it is not sufficient to look at the return and the risk of an investment to assess its profitability. What is relevant is the ability of such an investment to deliver a return in excess of some benchmark rate of return. To the best of our knowledge, only two chapters have tried to assess this issue. Fogarty (2007) derives the optimal frontier for two cases. In the first case, only stocks and bonds are considered, while in the second case the investment universe also includes wines. The results show that the efficient frontier is shifted to the left in case two. Thus it is possible to construct a portfolio with a better risk-return tradeoff when wines are also taken into account. Sanning, Shaffer and Sharratt (2008) use both the Capital Asset Pricing Model and the Fama-French three factors model to assess the risk-return profile of wines as compared to equities. Their results indicate that wines have a low covariance with both the market and the Fama-French risk factors and hence they might be used to improve the diversification of an equity portfolio. They further point out that an investment in wines is rewarded by an excess return that cannot be explained by the model (i.e., the alpha is positive and significant).

The goals of this chapter are the following: (1) we characterize the evolution of high-end wine prices during the last decade, (2) we study long-run, short-run and causality relationships between various wine categories (from first growths to fifth growths) in order to gain a better understanding of the dynamics affecting the wine market, and (3) we address the question of diversification and portfolio allocation in a realistic setting, which includes equities, wines and art works. To achieve this aim, we make use of a large dataset that spans the period 1996 to 2007 and contains the transaction prices of all reported auctions at the Chicago Wine Company. We focus on Bordeaux wines as they represent more than 90% of the worldwide market for high-end wines. We devote much attention to the preparation of the data and carefully control for errors in the dataset. We end up with 77,014 transactions for 92 Bordeaux estates and 29 vintages.

While some authors have already studied the dynamics of wine prices and their interactions with other financial assets, our chapter differs in several respects from earlier works. First of all, the length of our dataset and the frequency of observations permit to complement prior evidence on the features of wine investing. The recent studies of both Fogarty (2007) and Sanning, Shaffer and Sharratt (2008) use samples that end respectively in 2000 and 2003. Our dataset also covers the period from 2004 to 2007, which is often considered as the golden age for wine investing. But stock markets have boomed at the same time and thus it is unclear whether investing in the wine market has been sufficiently rewarding as compared to an investment in equities. In fact, our results indicate that not only the individual performance of wine has been interesting in terms of risk-return trade-off but also that its correlation with equities has remained sufficiently low to maintain its attractive feature as a diversification asset. Because we use monthly data (only Sanning, Shaffer and Sharratt (2008) use a similar frequency) we are also able to analyze precisely the statistical features of wine returns. In particular, the skewness is consistently positive, which is contrary to what is observed on stock markets. The kurtosis always exceeds the threshold value of three and is in general larger than for stocks. These two observations could have important implications for investors as they typically want to maximize the skewness of their portfolio while minimizing its kurtosis.

Our first contribution is that we characterize precisely the returns for different wine categories and verify if it is more profitable to invest in particular wines rather than in a diversified wine portfolio. Several studies have demonstrated that characteristics like vintage, rating and ranking have an impact on pricing. We go beyond this static perspective and show that those characteristics are also important determinants of the returns over time of such wines. Burton and Jacobsen (1999) discuss the fact that returns on specific sub-market portfolios (e.g., portfolios based on outstanding vintages or highly reputable estates) tend to outperform the returns on the overall wine market. Nevertheless, the evidence on this point is mixed. The results in Jaeger (1981) indicate that returns on lesser estates might be larger but also more volatile than those of the best estates. Burton and Jacobsen (2001) find that a general index indeed achieves larger returns than the best estates. We find that wines that are good at one or several of these characteristics earn larger returns and tend to have either a lower or a similar variance than less good wines. A positive premium seems to be attached to these attributes even if an exposition to them does not imply more risk; this looks somewhat counterintuitive and may indeed suggest the presence of inefficiencies on the wine market.

Our second contribution is to study in details long-run, short-run and causal relationships among three categories of Bordeaux wines: first growths, second growths and third to fifth growths. A potential explanation for the aforementioned observation that first and second growths earn larger returns than wines from lesser estates might be that the market is segmented. If, for instance, investors perceive the most prestigious wines as investment grade and merely consider their followers as consumption goods, then investors will most probably not invest in lower ranking wines. As a consequence, those wines will not enter investors' portfolios and, thus, their Sharpe ratio becomes irrelevant. We test this argument and show that it is actually not valid: the three wine categories seem to follow a common long term trend as the hypothesis that a single cointegration relationship links their evolution cannot be rejected. We also document strong correlations between the returns on the three wine categories. In particular, the correlation between first and second growth is large (about 50%) and remains very stable all over the sample period. The correlations between third to fifth growths and first or second growths is less stable but nevertheless important (between 20% and 70%). Finally, we do not find evidence in favor of a causal relationship running from one category to another. This indicates that price evolution is almost synchronous among all categories of wines.

Our third, and probably main, contribution is that we address the question of diversification and portfolio allocation in a realistic setting that accounts for covariance between equities and wines and also for coskewness and cokurtosis. As written above, the evidence concerning the profitability of an investment in wine as compared to an investment in equity is mixed. Yet even if wine does not deliver an attractive risk-return profile per se, it might still improve an equity portfolio through diversification. Several authors argue that focusing on the first two moments of the joint distribution (as in the mean-variance framework of Markowitz (1952) disregards important aspects of the investor preferences and utility function (see Jondeau and

Rockinger, 2006). Furthermore, wines and equities seem to have different marginal distributions and their joint distribution might also diverge from the normal. We therefore employ a polynomial goal programming (PGP) model (e.g., Lay *et al.*, 2006; Davies *et al.*, 2009) to investigate how investor preferences over the first *four* moments of the returns distribution affect the portfolio allocation and the distribution of its returns. In line with Fogarty (2007), we show that wines are only slightly correlated with other assets and as such they can be used to reduce the risk of an equity portfolio. The allocation in the optimal portfolio contains a large part of the most reputable wines because of their high expected returns. This result is robust to various specifications (e.g., including other assets like art works into the analysis) and still holds after having taken into account the various costs inherent to the trading of wines. Wines look even more attractive when the investor also has concerns about the skewness of his portfolio. However, extending the framework to include the kurtosis reduces the part to be invested in wines. Finally, it seems advisable to diversify across the range of rating categories as their moves in the short-run are somewhat independent of each other. First growths and wines rated 100 by Robert Parker deliver the best tradeoff in terms of portfolio expected returns, variance, skewness and kurtosis for most investor preference settings.

This chapter is structured as follows. Section 2 is devoted to the preparation of the data and the calculation of the wine indices. Section 3 presents and discusses the evolution of each index. In section 4, we analyze both the long- and short-run relationships between various categories of wines. In section 5, we study the optimal allocation between equities and wines, first in a standard mean-variance setting and then in a framework including skewness and kurtosis. Section 6 discusses the impact of the financial crisis on wine prices. Section 7 concludes.

2. Data and Index Construction

2.1. *Data*

Our data come from the Chicago Wine Company and cover all auctions that took place between January, 1996 and February, 2007. There is typically one auction per calendar month. However, there are also few months in which no auction took place. In total, our sample consists of 126 months with auctions. We concentrate on the prices of red Bordeaux because they are the most speculative and actively traded wines all over the world. For instance, they account for more than 93% of the Liv-ex 100–Fine Wine Index (as of January

2008).[4] Only transactions involving 0.75L bottles are taken into account. Other formats are traded less frequently and their prices can be subject to erratic changes. There were some mistakes in the original database (e.g., typos or inaccurate entries). These errors were identified and the original entry either corrected or removed depending on whether we could infer the true information from the original dataset or not.

Only few Châteaux can be considered as investment-grade. Indeed many Châteaux remain in the shadow of the biggest names, on which most of the trading activity concentrates. The notoriety of those Châteaux is the result of both their historical situation[5] and the current quality level of the wines they produce.[6,7] We therefore focus on a subset of 92 estates that are actively traded. We classify them into five ranking categories, which are the following: first growths (11 estates), second growths[8] (12), third growths (13), fourth growths (13) and fifth growths (27). We also consider two additional categories: second wines (6) and garage wines (10). Wines from the last two categories are, however, much less frequently traded than the others. Châteaux names are listed in the appendix (their official ranking and the appellation to which they belong are also reported). Our five-tier classification does not match the official one for two reasons. First, in some appellations like Pomerol, no official classification exists. Second, some Châteaux do not deserve their original classification anymore and have not been included; similarly others perform much better than their original classification would indicate. Our classification is mainly based on the trading volume, the *en primeur*[9] pricing and the reputation of each Château over the 11 year sample.

[4]Source: Liv-ex 100 Component List (www.liv-ex.com).

[5]For instance, the 1855 classification is still in use. With the exception of Château Mouton Rothschild, which was upgraded in 1974, the short list of first growths has not changed since 1855!

[6]The latter can be assessed through the ratings they got from, for example, the Wine Advocate (Robert Parker), Wine Spectator, Jancis Robinson and Quarin.

[7]The Saint-Emilion classification is different from the 1855 classification as it is updated every 10 years. It is based on the current level of quality achieved by each estate and the prices at which their recent vintages trade.

[8]Amateurs usually refer to these wines as the super seconds. This denomination comes from the fact that many estates that have not been originally classified as first growth (or even as second growth) are now considered by wine critics as achieving a quality level very close to that of first growths.

[9]Bordeaux estates market most of their wines as *en primeur* in the spring following the harvest. At that moment, the wines are still in cask. Thus, customers do not directly get the wines but have to wait until they are bottled. Buying wines *en primeur* can be considered as a way to secure wines that might be in short supply; this is also a hedge

The wine production in the region of Bordeaux does not achieve the same quality each year. This is due to the typical oceanic climate which is affected by the North Atlantic current. The weather can be rather erratic and each year displays its own features. Hence, every vintage is unique. In recent years, 1982, 1990, 2000, and 2005 turned out to be exceptional. On the other hand, 1984, 1987, 1991–1993 were (almost) of no interest. Amateurs focus on above average vintages and so is the trading activity. We consider all post-1977 vintages (excluding 1980, 1984, 1987, and 1991–1993) up to 2003, and some famous vintages like 1945, 1947, 1955, 1959, 1961, 1966, 1970, and 1975.

We eventually end up with a dataset containing 77,014 transactions for 92 Châteaux and 29 vintages. If a wine has been traded more than once at a particular auction, we set its monthly closing price equal to the average price achieved at this auction. If no trade has been recorded in a given month for a given wine, we set its price to the previous month closing price.

2.2. *Index construction*

We compute a variety of indices using a method, which is very similar to the one employed for stock market indices. That is, the estimation of "our" wine indices is based on weighted average of the observed wine prices.[10] Two alternative routes can be followed to construct a wine index: the first is based on a hedonic pricing regression, while the second uses a repeat sales regression. Hereafter we briefly present each of these three methods and justify our choice in favor of the weighted average approach.

Brief presentation of the hedonic, repeat sales regression and weighted average methods

The literature on price indices (for consumption goods, including wines) relies extensively on the hedonic pricing method.[11] The idea is to split the price into two components; one corresponds to the value attached to some intrinsic features of the good (its quality, rarity, etc.), while the

against rising prices. From a financial point of view, this type of transaction very much resembles a future contract.

[10]See also the discussion and comparison of these methods in Burton and Jacobsen (1999).

[11]See, for example, Jones and Storchmann (2001), Lecocq and Visser (2006), Combris, Lecocq and Visser (1997), Combris, Lecocq, and Visser (2000), Cardebat and Figuet (2004), Oczkowski (2001), Benfratello, Piacenza, and Sacchetto (2009), and Di Vittorio and Ginsburgh (1996). Fogarty (2006a) provides an exhaustive and up-to-date literature review on hedonic pricing.

other part measures the price appreciation over time. It is thus possible to account explicitly for the heterogeneity among the different wines. Hedonic regressions typically involve huge matrices of regressors (with many dummy variables), which leads to multicollinearity problems[12] and renders the index coefficients imprecise and erratic. This is the major drawback of this approach and this why we avoid using it.

The repeat sales regression (RSR) approach is extensively used for estimating housing in dices.[13] The underlying idea is to consider only those (similar) goods that have been traded at least twice during the period under consideration. One can compute the return between two transaction prices and then attribute this *total* return to the different subperiods. It has the advantage over the hedonic method that it compares the price evolution of *similar* goods. It is, thus, not necessary to calibrate a model to account for the differing features of the good under consideration (i.e., no dummy variable is involved). Nevertheless, it also has some drawbacks. First, the index is likely to be updated ex-post. This is because the index level for a given month is definitely fixed only when all goods that have been traded up to this month have been traded again. As a consequence, the true level of the index at time t will not be known before $t + k(k \geq 0)$. Another problem with this method is the potential impact of outliers on the estimated index values. The point is that (i) the number of wines sold at each auction can vary considerably, (ii) a few wines attract most of the interest from investors, while other are seldom traded. So, if the number of wines sold at a particular auction date is small (as compared to other auction dates) and if the prices of these wines diverge significantly from their fair value (i.e., if they are very different from the prices recorded during surrounding auctions), the evolution of the index will reflect this change even if it is only temporary.

As already written, the method we use is a weighted average of the index components (wines) prices. This approach is not only simple to implement but also very flexible and it does not suffer from the drawbacks of the RSR and hedonic methods. Furthermore, the Liv-ex index (www.liv-ex.com), which has became a reference for wine investors, is constructed almost the same way. Another strength of this approach is that the index

[12]For instance, Di Vittorio and Ginsburgh (1996) make use of the hedonic approach and find that a vintage like 1954, which is considered a "worse than average" vintage, outperforms every other vintage (including the great 1961). They also have to exclude vintage 1982 from the analysis because of multicollinearity problems.

[13]In the wine economics literature, it has recently been used by Burton and Jacobsen (2001).

returns effectively correspond to the ones that would have been achieved by an investor with a well-balanced wine portfolio.

Implementation

Wines coming from the same estate but from different vintages do not correspond to a unique homogeneous good. This means that we have to consider each Château-vintage's pair separately. This has an important impact because many of these pairs are traded only on rare occasions. Even the greatest wines are not necessarily traded each month. It is therefore crucial to choose appropriate pricing and weighting schemes when it comes to calculating the index levels.

We refer to each wine using the notation $W_{i,j}$, where i corresponds to the Château ($i \in I = \{1, 2, \ldots, 92\}$) and j to the vintage ($j \in J = \{1, 2, \ldots, 29\}$).[14] We further define $P_{W_{i,j,t}}$ and $V_{W_{i,j,t}}$, which are the price and the trading volume achieved by wine $W_{i,j}$ in month t.

The general wine index and the various subindices (see section 3) are defined on the basis of the set of wines $\Theta_{k,I} = \{I_k, J_I\}$ that enter into their calculation ($I_k \subset I$ and $J_l \subset J$). The index level at time t is denoted by $S_t(\Theta_{k,l})$ and is computed as follows:

$$S_t(\Theta_{k,l}) = \sum_{i}^{I_k} \sum_{j}^{J_l} X_{W_{i,j,t}}(\Theta_{k,l}) \cdot C_{W_{i,j}}(\Theta_{k,l}) \cdot P_{W_{i,j,t}}, \tag{1}$$

where $X_{W_{i,j,t}}(\Theta_{k,l})$ is the weight that wine $W_{i,j}$ has in the index $\Theta_{k,l}$ in month t.

The value of each index in the first period of the sample ($t = 1$) is set to 100. $C_{W_{i,j}}(\Theta_{k,l})$ is a correction factor which is computed as follows:

$$C_{W_{i,j}}(\Theta_{k,l}) = \frac{S_{t_0}(\Theta_{k,l})}{P_{W_{i,j,t_0}}}, \tag{2}$$

where t_0 is the month in which a wine $W_{i,j}$ was traded for the first time. This correction ensures that the standardized price of a wine the first time it was traded is equal to the index level in the same month. If a wine has not been traded in a given month, we set its price equal to the last valid observation we have for this wine.

In the case of an equity index, weights are computed on the basis of the free-float but, in the case of wine, the issue is that we do not know how many

[14]For instance, $W_{1,1}$ corresponds to château Calon Ségur 1945.

full bottles remain available on the market.[15] Moreover, the fact that there is no centralized market place makes it difficult to get a precise picture of the number of trades.[16] We therefore estimate the weights $X_{W_{i,j,t}}(\Theta_{k,l})$ from the average trading volume involved by each wine over the last 12 months. That is, the weight $X_{W_{i,j,t}}(\Theta_{k,l})$ of wine $W_{i,j}$ in the index $\Theta_{k,l}$ at period t is the ratio of the average trading volume of $W_{i,j}$ over the past 12 months divided by the cumulated average trading volume of all wines that enter into the index:

$$X_{W_{i,j,t}}(\Theta_{k,l}) = \frac{\frac{1}{12}\sum_{\tau=0}^{11} V_{W_{i,j,(t-\tau,t)}}}{\sum_{m}^{I_K}\sum_{n}^{J_l}\left[\frac{1}{12}\sum_{\tau=0}^{11} V_{W_{m,n,(t-\tau,t)}}\right]}. \tag{3}$$

3. Evolution of the Wine Market from 1996–2007

3.1. *General wine market index and the Dow Jones*

Figure 1 shows the evolution of the general wine market index and the Dow Jones over the period 1996–2007. The general wine market index is constructed using the prices of wines from all estates and all vintages.

The wine index and the Dow Jones have undergone a strong rise between 1996 and 1998. During the period 1998–2000, both wines and stocks have kept up rising and have achieved almost similar cumulated returns. The burst of the tech bubble and the terrorist attacks in New-York have led the Dow Jones to lose about 7% in 2001.[17] Since spring 2002 the wine market has also started to decline but not as sharply as the Dow Jones. In March 2003 after the invasion of Irak, the Dow Jones began to recover from its previous losses. During the period 2003–2005, wine prices remained rather stable. The last two years of the sample have been bullish for both the wine and the stock markets.

[15]This number decreases through time and we do not know who is holding a given bottle of wine and is willing to sell it.

[16]There are many ways to sell or to purchase wine: auctions, specialized shops, classified advertisements, etc. Moreover, prices are not necessarily arbitrage-free as the same wine can well trade at a different price from one place to another.

[17]Over the period January 1 2001 to September 21 2001, the Dow Jones and the Nasdaq 100 respectively lost 23% and 52%. From March 2000 to the end of 2000, the Nasdaq had already lost more than 50%; though, over the same period, the Dow Jones was down by less than 3%.

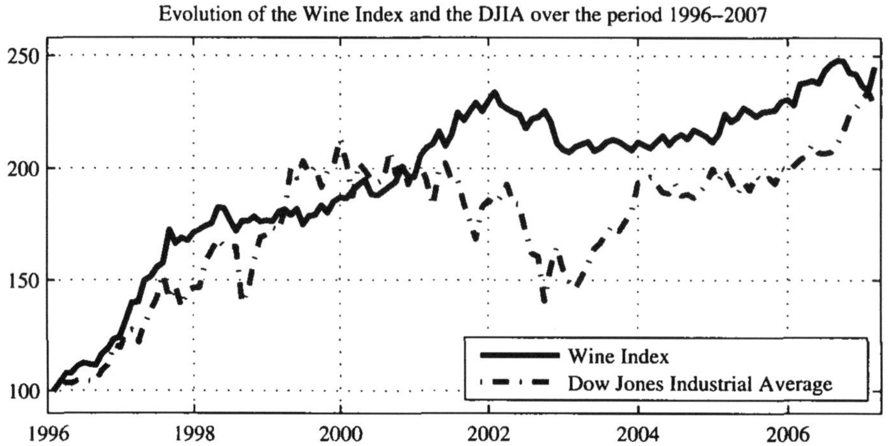

Figure 1. Comparative Evolution of the Wine Market and the Dow Jones from 1996–2007

The total cumulated return of the wine market index is 145%. In comparison, the Dow Jones has achieved a cumulated return of 127% over the same period. Risk features also seem to be more favorable for the wine index than for the Dow Jones: the volatility of the wine index averages 8.1%, while the Dow Jones volatility averages more than 15%. Wine returns are right skewed (skewness of 0.50); this is in sharp contrast with the returns on the Dow Jones, which have a skewness of −0.62. Wine returns also exhibit a very slightly larger excess kurtosis than equity returns (4.38 versus 4.25). These results seem more favorable to an investment in wine than those of Fogarty (2006b), who concludes that "the risk-return profile of [Australian] wines is broadly comparable to the risk-return profile of Australian equities."

A risk-return analysis is, however, not a sufficient tool for assessing the appeal of wine investment. The costs and benefits of holding wine are of various natures. It has the advantage over other investments that it provides a particular utility to its "owner" as it can be both admired and obviously drunk. However, its consumption implies its destruction. For these reasons, one might expect wine to have a lower return than equity (because of its intrinsic utility) but a higher return than other collectibles (as their consumption does not imply their destruction). Explicit costs are storage costs (between I and 2USD per bottle-year) and insurance costs. Obviously wine trading also implies a variety of costs (broker commission, insurance and shipping), which are inherent to the proceeding of wine auctions. They amount to about 10% of the value of the wine for the buyer and 15% to 20% for the seller; though they may vary between various auction houses.

Furthermore, with the development of online auctions, they tend to be much lower now (for instance, ebay charges only 3% to 4%). Illiquidity is an implicit but important cost as the liquidation of a cellar might take months.[18]

3.2. *Vintage, ranking and rating defined indices*

We analyze the price evolution of various subindices defined on the basis of (i) vintages, (ii) ranking, and (iii) Parker's rating. We eventually devote some attention to the price appreciation of second wines and so-called garage wines.

Vintage defined indices

Table 1 shows the evolution of eight wine indices constructed on the basis of vintage's quality. We differentiate between wines from the left and the right bank of the Dordogne.[19] This is because some vintages are better on the right bank than on the left, and *vice versa.*[20]

It is often argued that only very good to great vintages can be considered as investment grade and, indeed, all vintages considered as outstanding have experienced very strong price increases. The best performers are 1961 (total return of 263%), 1982 (216%), 1986 (212%), 1989 (301%) and 1990 (246%). On the other hand, a number of recent vintages have experienced price drops (1995 to 1999 and 2001 to 2002). The reason is probably that these wines were already very expensive when they were released as *en primeur.*[21] The evidence also suggests that the most successful vintages for the left bank

[18]See also Burton and Jacobsen (2001) for an exhaustive discussion of the costs/benefits associated to the holding and trading of wine.

[19]Wines from the appellations of Saint-Estèphe, Pauillac, Saint-Julien, Pessac and Haut-Médoe belong to the left bank. Wines from the Pomerol and Saint-Emilion appellations belong to the right bank. Cabernet Sauvignon dominates the blend in red wines produced on the left bank, while Merlot tends to predominate on the right bank.

[20]The vintages and their corresponding rating are: 1945 (left bank: 5 and right bank: 5), 1947 (5 and 5), 1955 (4 and 4), 1959 (5 and 5), 1961 (5 and 5), 1966 (4 and 4), 1970 (3 and 3), 1975 (3 and 4), 1978 (3 and 2), 1979 (3 and 2), 1981 (3 and 3), 1982 (5 and 5), 1983 (4 and 4), 1985 (4 and 3), 1986 (5 and 3), 1988 (3 and 4), 1989 (4 and 4), 1990 (5 and 5), 1993 (I and 2), 1994 (2 and 3), 1995 (4 and 4), 1996 (5 and 3), 1997 (2 and 2), 1998 (3 and 5), 1999 (3 and 3), 2000 (5 and 5), 2001 (3 and 4), 2002 (3 and 2), 2003 (5 and 3). (1 = below average, 2 = average, 3 = good, 4 = very good, 5 = outstanding).

[21]For a discussion of Bordeaux *en primeur* pricing, see Mahenc and Meunier (2006), who study this issue from a theoretical perspective, and Christensen and Meunier (2006), who analyze empirically this issue and find no evidence suggesting an overpricing.

Table 1. Summary Statistics for Each Vintage Defined Index

	Left Bank					Right Bank				
Vintage's quality	# obs.	Total return[a]	Std. dev.[a]	Skewness[b]	Kurtosis[b]	#obs.	Total return[a]	Std. dev.[a]	Skewness[b]	Kurtosis[b]
Mediocre	1,356	57.52	13.97	0.52	7.42	1,255	31.00	13.04	0.66	9.56
Good	10,722	94.80	11.07	0.50	4.92	7,239	83.25	12.15	5.10	44.04
Very good	13,354	211.20	12.56	1.19	8.19	6,582	74.65	10.71	0.43	4.23
Outstanding	24,679	220.52	10.77	−0.05	3.53	11,827	104.12	12.60	0.31	5.01

Notes: All statistics are calculated for the period from 1996 to 2007. [a]Returns and annualized standard deviations are in%. [b]Skewness and kurtosis are computed from index log-returns.

have experienced higher returns than the best vintages for the right bank.[22] Volatility is higher for these vintage defined indices than for the general index. This is due to the limited amount of data we have for each specific vintage. The skewness is in general positive and the kurtosis is always above three.[23] This indicates that the returns on the different indices are not normally distributed.

Ranking defined indices

In Table 2, we report summary statistics for the five ranking defined indices. Again, the best investment vehicles ought to be the first growths because their "brand" is known all over the world and because they are supposed to have the best ageing potential. Trading activity is heavily concentrated on the first and second growths. Estates from these two ranking categories have almost achieved the same cumulated return over the period under consideration. They have clearly outperformed the third, fourth and fifth growth estates (by about 65% to 110%). Among the first growth, the best performer is Haut-Brion and the worst is Ausone. For the other ranking categories the best performers are Pichon-Longueville Baron, Troplong Mondot, La Fleur-Pétrus and Lascombes and the worst performers are respectively L'Evangile, Le Tertre Roteboeuf, Monbousquet and Quinault L'Enclos. The first and fourth growths are characterized by a lower volatility than the other ranking categories. At the exception of the fifth growths (which are characterized by a much larger volatility than any other ranking category), all indices have a volatility below 12%.[24] The risk-return profile of the best estates looks very attractive in comparison to the Dow Jones.

The fact that less known estates (i.e., third to fifth growths) earn lower returns on average might be justified either by a diversification argument or by the fact that investors in the wine market might be somewhat myopic. That is, if the wine market is segmented such that these wines have a very low correlation with the other wines (and with other financial assets as well), then

[22]We have also studied the price appreciation of the different appellations. Pauillac and Saint-Emilion are respectively the best and the worst performers. Detailed results are available from the authors upon request.

[23]The very high levels of skewness (5.10) and kurtosis (44.04) for the good vintages of the right bank is due to the strong price inflation that these wines have experienced during the first two years of the sample. If we exclude the first two years of observations, the skewness and the kurtosis decrease respectively to 0.5 and 9.6.

[24]A level of 12% can be considered as a lower boundary for the average volatility of the Dow Jones over the long run.

Table 2. Summary Statistics for the Ranking Defined Indices

Classification	#Ch.	#obs.	Total return[a]	Max return[a]	Min return[b]	Std. dev.[b]	Skewness[b]	Kurtosis[b]
1st Growths	11	28,638	188.13	292.97	62.01	9.73	0.08	3.25
2nd Growths	12	20,805	191.84	202.24	14.19	10.75	0.40	5.15
3rd Growths	13	11,092	81.49	233.95	−14.20	8.33	0.95	5.64
4th Growths	13	5,589	123.36	161.52	−18.55	9.15	1.62	9.82
5th Growths	27	5,847	91.07	263.48	−19.34	14.11	1.14	8.56

Notes: All statistics are calculated for the period from 1996 to 2007. [a]Returns and annualized standard deviations are in %. [b]Skewness and kurtosis are computed from index log-returns; max and min returns refer to the best and the worst estate that enters the index.

Table 3. Summary Statistics for the Rating Defined Indices

Parker's points	# wines in index	# obs in index	Total return[a]	Std. dev.[a]	Skewness[b]	Kurtosis[b]
100	40	8,892	249.33	14.66	0.97	5.81
96–99	105	14,944	194.49	10.29	0.46	3.88
93–95	216	19,239	73.41	9.53	0.79	5.54
90–92	313	19,294	47.70	8.23	2.88	24.00
80–89	477	12,563	113.22	8.53	0.18	4.23

Notes: All statistics are calculated for the period from 1996 to 2007. [a]Returns and annualized standard deviations are in %. [b]Skewness and kurtosis are computed from index log-returns.

they should have lower expected returns.[25] On the other hand, it could also be that investors fail to reward these wines for the exposition to systematic risk factors; this explanation implies that these wines are overpriced.

Parker's rating defined indices

Table 3 shows summary statistics for five indices based on Parker's rating. We do not consider wines that have received a rating below 80 as such wines do not attract much attention from wine amateurs and are consequently less frequently traded. Ashenfelter (1989) discusses the so-called "winner's curse," which implies that everyone wants to buy the wines with the highest number of Parker's points. We therefore expect to find a positive relationship between rating and price appreciation.[26]

The index containing the wines that have been rated 100 by Robert Parker achieves a spectacular cumulated return of 249%.[27] This amounts 12% on an annual basis. This index outperforms the general wine index and the Dow Jones. Its annualized standard deviation (14.66%) is higher than for the general index but very comparable to the volatility of the Dow Jones. When looking at the other rating categories, one may also notice that the

[25]For instance, this segmentation might be such that less known estates attract a certain category of customers (wine drinkers), while high-end estates attract other types of customers (like speculators or garish people).

[26]Jones and Storchmann (2001), Ashenfelter (1989) and Lecocq and Visser (2006) use ratings from a jury but do not find any significant relationship between prices and ratings.

[27]50 wines from Bordeaux have been rated 100 by Parker. These wines come from 18 different estates. Though we have enough data only for 40 wines (some estates and some vintages do not attract enough trading volume to get reliable return estimates). From our dataset, six vintages from La Mission Haut Brion got this score; Lafite-Rothschild, Lafleur and Pétrus follow with five "perfect" wines.

best wines are traded much more frequently than the others and achieve higher returns. Skewness and kurtosis are not consistent with a normal distribution. The volatility of returns seems to be larger for the wines that have received the best grades from Parker. This might be due to the fact that we have less observations for this index. Interestingly, the index containing wines rated between 80 and 89 has achieved a spectacular cumulated return. In order to understand more precisely the origins of this performance, we split this category into two subcategories, which contain wines rated between 80 and 85 and between 86 and 89. The cumulated return on the first subcategory is about 24%, while that on the second category exceeds 130%. Overall the best performer is La Mission Haut Brion 1989 (with a cumulated return of 529%); this estate is classified as first growth.

Second wines and "garage" wines

During the last few years, second wines have attracted much interest. This is primarily due to the fact that first growths have become extremely expensive; as a consequence many amateurs have decided to switch to the second wines of these estates. Another trend is the birth of so-called "garage wines." This name comes from the fact that many of these estates are recent and have a very restraint production; some of these wineries look like garages. There is an increasing number of such new wineries in particular in Saint-Emilion. The underlying idea is "small quantities but high quality." The many detractors of these wines would reformulate this marketing formula to an even simpler credo: "highly priced and speculative wines."

We have only few observations for these categories (1,202 for the second wines and 3,841 for the garage wines) and most trades have taken place after year 2000, which makes a performance analysis difficult. We therefore concentrate on the period 2000–2007. Interestingly, both categories of wines have achieved negative returns over this period: 32.05% for the second wines and −13.18% for the garage wines. A possible explanation for this observation is that garage wines might be too expensive when they are released *en primeur*, leading their prices to decline progressively once they arrive on the market.

4. Relationship Among Wines from Different Ranking Categories

In this section, we study the cross-relationships among the ranking indices. In a first step, we analyze whether they follow a single long-run trend or not. Then, we check if some causality relationships (in the sense of Granger) might also exist among these indices. Finally, we compare the evolution of the various indices in the short-run using a correlation analysis. As we have less observations for the third, fourth and fifth growths, we decided to merge them into a unique category.[28] This is in order to avoid spurious results because of low liquidity. This is also a reasonable classification from the point of view of wine amateurs, who usually refer either to the first growths or the so-called super seconds (the second growths in our classification) and consider all other classified Bordeaux as followers.

4.1. *Long-run cross-relationship*

We first run an augmented Dickey-Fuller (ADF) test to analyze whether the series are stationary or not. The specification is as follows:

$$S_{g,t} = \alpha + \beta t + \gamma S_{g,t-1} + \sum_{i=1}^{p} \gamma_i \Delta S_{g,t-i} + u_t,$$

where $S_{g,t}$ is the log of the index level at time t and g designates the growth category; α is a constant, β_t is the time-trend and $\sum_{i=1}^{p} \gamma_i \Delta S_{g,t-i}$ is used to account for possible autocorrelation in the residuals u_t. As we do not find much trace of autocorrelation in u_t, we set p to 1. The ADF test is run on γ. The H_0 hypothesis is that $\gamma \geq 1$; this corresponds to the case in which there is a unit root in the time-series. The critical values are obtained by simulation (see Hamilton, 1994 for details). The evidence demonstrates that we cannot reject the null hypothesis of a unit root in all three wine index series.[29] This is not a surprise as it is well known that most economic and financial indices are non-stationary.

The next step is to test if the series are cointegrated. The purpose of this test is to analyze whether there exists a long-run equilibrium relationship between the different wine indices or not. If all categories of wines share the same clientele, we are likely to find a unique cointegration relation between the indices. Nevertheless, it might be that the highly reputed first growth estates follow a different trend than lesser known estates. We model the three

---

[28]This strategy also mitigates possible multicollinearity problems that might appear when studying the series in a multivariate framework.

[29]The test statistics are between −0.30 and −0.45 for all indices. The critical values according to the length of our sample are respectively −3.16, −3.45, and −4.00 at the 10%, 5%, and 1% percentile.

Table 4. Results of the Johansen Test of Cointegration

# Cointegration relationships	Eigenvalue	Max-eigenvalue statistic	Trace statistic
≤ 0	0.1907	26.23**	40.83**
≤ 1	0.1096	14.40	14.60
≤ 2	0.0016	0.20	0.20

Note: **denotes significativity at the 95% confidence level.

series in a vector error correction model (VECM):

$$\Delta S_t = \mu + \sum_{i=1}^{p-1} \Phi_i \Delta S_{t-i} + \Pi S_{t-1} + \varepsilon_t, \tag{4}$$

where $S_t = [S_{1,t}\ S_{2,t}\ S_{3,t}]$. The order p of the vector autoregression has been chosen on the basis of the Akaike and Schwartz information criteria. Both criteria indicate that $p = 1$ is appropriate. The next step is to identify the rank r of matrix Π. Three cases can be identified. If the matrix is of full rank ($r = 3$), this indicates that all series are stationary. We can discard this case as all series have already been found to be I(1). The opposite case, in which the matrix is of rank zero ($r = 0$), corresponds to a situation in which all series are I(1) but there is no cointegration relation. The last case is when the matrix is singular but $r \geq 0$, this is the cointegration case and r indicates the number of cointegration relations.

The results for the trace and the eigenvalue test statistics are reported in Table 4. Both statistics indicate that there is indeed a single cointegration relationship that links the different indices together.[30] This result supports the assumption that the three wine indices have a common trend. Nevertheless, given the limited time span of our dataset, it is difficult to conclude whether the wine indices are linked together in the long term or just in the mid term.

4.2. *Lead-lag relationships*

We make use of the VECM framework to study the causality relations (in the sense of Granger), which might exist across the different wine indices. This implies imposing and testing some restrictions on the elements of the Φ_i matrices. As the number of lags to be used in the vector autoregression

[30] In this case, ΠS_{t-1} can be rewritten as βZ_{t-1}, where z_{t-1} is the unique (given that $r = 1$) linear combination of the three wine indices ($\alpha' S_{t-1}$) that results in a stationary series.

has been set to 1 (see Section 4.1), we only have to consider the Φ_i matrix, which might be developed as follows:

$$\Phi_1 = \begin{bmatrix} \phi_{11}^{(1)} & \phi_{12}^{(1)} & \phi_{13}^{(1)} \\ \phi_{21}^{(1)} & \phi_{22}^{(1)} & \phi_{23}^{(1)} \\ \phi_{31}^{(1)} & \phi_{32}^{(1)} & \phi_{33}^{(1)} \end{bmatrix}$$

We compare the explanatory power of a model specification in which all the elements of the Φ_i matrix are estimated with a restricted model in which we impose one of the elements of the matrix to be zero (i.e., $\phi_{lk}^{(1)} = 0$). If the mean squared errors (MSE) of both models are not significantly different, we will conclude that variable k fails to Granger-cause variable l (see, e.g., Hamilton, 1994).

Since first growths attract much of the attention of wine lovers and wine investors, we suspect á priori that the causality relation, if any, should run from this category to the other ranking categories. Furthermore, wines from less known estates are traded only rarely and are thus likely to be less reactive to changes in the global wine market. Studying causality in the context of financial asset prices necessarily implies the questions of predictability and arbitrage. The causality relation, if any, should not be too strong, otherwise it would become possible to make money without taking much risk (a "free lunch" in the financial jargon) and one would have to conclude that the wine market is inefficient.

The results indeed indicate that some of the elements of the Γ_1 matrix are significantly different from zero at standard levels: $\phi_{11}^{(1)} = -0.3144$ (p-value: <0.01), $\phi_{13}^{(1)} = -0.1611$ (0.04) and $\phi_{33}^{(1)} = 0.2155$ (0.04).[31] The fact that $\phi_{11}^{(1)}$ is negative suggests first growths tend to overreact in the short-run and then correct back. The returns on third to fifth growths are also influenced by their own lagged realizations but the sign of the correlation is positive, suggesting that there is some delay in the adjustment of the prices of these wines. Furthermore, one may notice that past returns on the first growths have a negative impact on subsequent returns on third to fifth growths. This causality direction is inline with the previous discussion but the sign of the coefficient is a bit more surprising (one would have expected a positive coefficient).

[31] In order to spare space, detailed results are not reported here but they are available from the authors upon request.

The standard VECM-Granger-causality approach is only able to identify linear effects. Given the non-trivial distribution of the returns on the different wine indices, some, more complicated, non-linear lead-lag effects may also link the different indices together. In order to check whether such relations exist, we make use of a non-parametric Granger causality test. We use the test specification of Diks and Panchenko (2006) (see also Baek and Brock, 1992; Hiemstra and Jones, 1994). The test is applied to the residuals ε_t from the previous VECM, see Equation (4). As suggested by Diks and Panchenko (2006), we first uniformize the data. The test is then applied on a bivariate basis; that is, we analyze the causality among each possible pair of series. The bandwidth is set to two standard deviations and the number of lags to one. As a cross-check, we also consider a bandwidth of 1.5 and 2.5 standard deviations and up to two lags.

A significant non-linear autocorrelation can be found in the three indices. This result holds for all test specifications (i.e., for 1 and 2 lags and for bandwidths of 1.5, 2, and 2.5 standard deviations). We also find a nonlinear causality running from first to third to fifth growths and from second to first growths. These results hold for most (not all) test specifications are less significant. It also seems that lesser estates (third to fifth growths) might lead the more renowned Châteaux but this result holds only when we consider at least two lags.[32]

4.3. *Short-run cross-relationship*

We eventually estimate the short-run cross-dependencies between the various index returns series. Once again, we consider the residuals ε_t from the previous VECM regression (4). Because they are not normally distributed, we use the non-parametric Spearman's rank correlation coefficient.[33] These correlation coefficients are informative about the diversification possibilities that the different indices offer. Low or even negative correlations among the different subindices may allow the construction of a more efficient wine portfolio (i.e., a portfolio with a lower volatility). The highest correlation (0.54) is found for the relation between second and third to fifth growths. The correlation between first and second growths amounts to 0.43, while the correlation between first and third to fifth growths is lower (0.28). These

[32]Detailed results can be obtained from the authors upon request.

[33]As a matter of comparison, we also estimated standard Pearson correlation coefficients. The results were very similar.

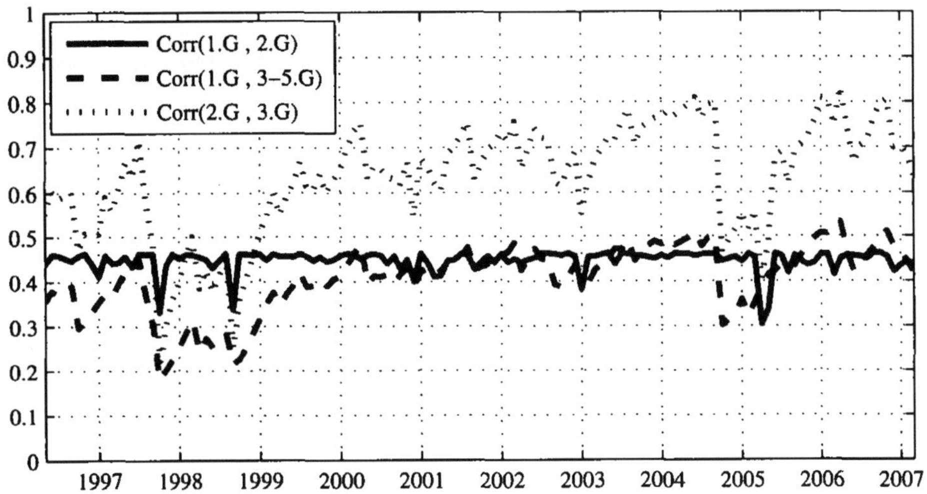

Figure 2. Dynamic (Time-Varying) Correlations between Different Wine Rankings

results, while leaving some space for diversification, clearly show that shocks in the wine market have a direct impact on all wine categories.

We also estimate time-varying correlations among the different wine indices. This should give some insights on the stability of the relations that link the indices together in the short run. A multivariate GARCH model is fitted to the residuals of the VECM regression (4). We opt for the dynamic conditional correlation (DCC) model of Engle (2002) because it explicitly models the time-varying correlations.[34] It is also tractable and relatively parsimonious in comparison with other multivariate GARCH models. The time-varying correlations are reported in Figure 2. One may observe that the correlation between the first and the second growths has remained remarkably stable over the period under consideration. The other two time-series of dynamic correlations are more erratic. Nevertheless, the correlation between first and third to fifth growths has always been lower than the correlation between first and second growths. All in one, the correlation among first and third to fifth growths displays a very similar pattern to the correlation between second and third to fifth growths, although the latter has become more significant in the last two years of the sample.

[34]We skip the technicalities. See, for example, Tsay (2002) and Jondeau, Poon and Rockinger (2007) for an introduction and an up-to-date discussion about the modeling of multivariate financial time-series.

5. Improving Diversification Through Investing in Wines

5.1. *Mean-variance analysis*

We analyze in a standard mean-variance framework if investing in wines might be a way of improving the diversification of an equity portfolio. In order to mitigate the impact of non-synchronous trading, returns are sampled every quarter and expected returns and variance are computed accordingly. We derive the efficient frontier for four different cases. We first consider only equities and we then progressively extend the universe of assets by including first art works[35] and then various wine categories. This permits to observe the additional effect that these assets have on the efficient frontier. The results are reported in Figure 3.[36] The risk-free rate corresponds to the yield of a treasury bond with a constant maturity of 1 year.

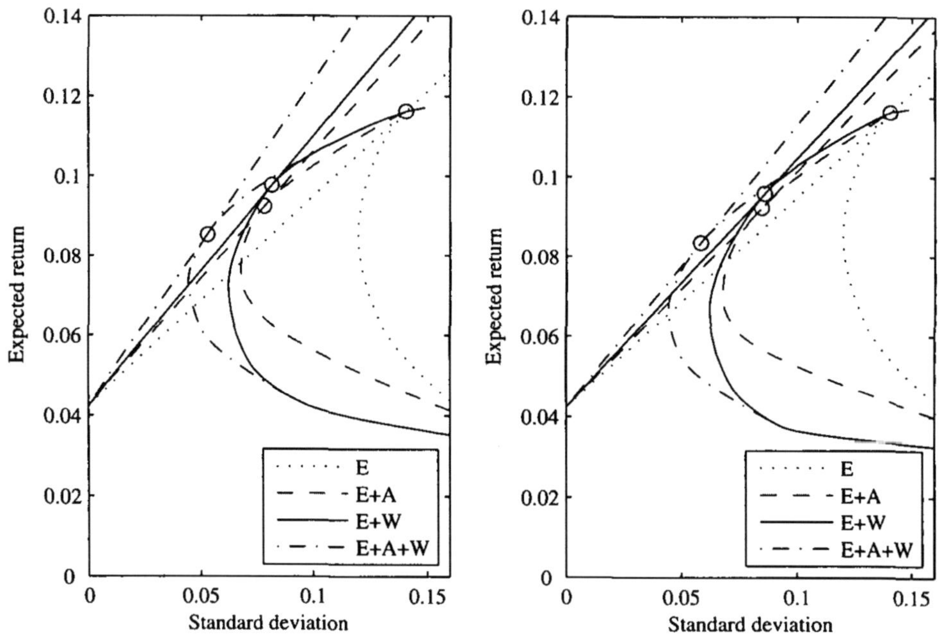

Figure 3. Efficient Frontier for Different Asset Classes: Equities ("E"), Art Works ("A") and Wine ("W")

Note: The left panel is based on raw returns, while the right panel reports the efficient frontier for cost-adjusted returns.

[35] We gather these data from the website www.artprice.com.

[36] We show only the efficient frontiers for the ranking-defined wine indices. Results for the rating-defined indices are very similar and are available from the authors upon request.

In the first case (denoted by "E" in the Figure 3), we derive the efficient line using the following assets: ten US sectorial indices,[37] the MSCI luxury index and the MSCI world index (excluding the USA).[38] This reflects the efficient portfolios for an investor, who focuses on equities only and diversifies across sectors and countries. In the second case ("E + A"), an art index is added to the spectrum of asset classes. For the third case ("E + W"), we study the impact of adding wines to an equity portfolio. The last case ("E + A + W") reports the optimal portfolios for an investor, who diversifies across equities, art works and wines. As wine trading is associated with both transaction costs and periodic costs (insurance and storage), we also calculate the efficient portfolio after having applied a discount of 20% on the final price reached by each wine[39] and a discount of 1% per year on their average returns. These numbers seem to be rather conservative to us. To be fully consistent, we apply the same discount on the returns on art works.[40] Corresponding efficient lines are reported in the left panel of Figure 3.

It is apparent from the figure that adding collectibles like wines and arts to an equity portfolio permits to achieve a better diversification. Notably, the standard deviation of the optimal portfolio becomes much lower, thanks to the low correlations of wines and arts with other assets. The fact that the expected returns are also broadly comparable across the asset classes obviously helps achieving such a result. Furthermore, the impact of taking into account the costs involved by holding and selling wines and art works seems to be quite limited: the expected return of the optimal portfolio is a bit lower and its variance increases slightly. These results are perfectly in line with those of Fogarty (2007) who shows that, even after taking into account transaction costs, investing in wines allows significant risk-reduction benefits. Sanning, Shaffer and Sharratt (2008) arrive at an essentially similar conclusion using another approach (CAPM and Fama-French three factors model). Their results indicate that wine returns covary only minimally with the returns on various factors of systematic risk. Consequently, an investment in wine is rewarded by positive risk-adjusted returns.

[37]These sectors are: oil and gas, basic resource, industrial goods and services, consumer goods, health care, consumer services, telecom, utilities, financials and technology.
[38]Data have been obtained from *Datastream*.
[39]That is, we make the implicit assumption that wine investors have sold their wines in the last period of the sample.
[40]Insurance costs might indeed be very large for art works and transaction costs are also close to or even larger than 20%.

Table 5. Optimal Portfolios for Different Asset Classes

		Ranking defined indices				Rating defined indices			
	PF0	PF1a	PF1b	PF2a	PF2b	PF1a	PF1b	PF2a	PF2b
Exp. ER	7.40	5.54	5.36	4.30	4.12	6.04	5.93	4.51	4.57
Std. dev.	14.06	8.19	8.61	5.28	5.84	8.97	9.43	5.62	6.47
Sharpe	0.53	0.68	0.62	0.82	0.71	0.67	0.63	0.80	0.71
Wines 1	—	41.45	34.24	21.66	21.14	25.64	24.45	13.44	14.76
Wines 2	—	26.46	25.04	17.26	19.20	34.38	31.69	22.04	23.71
Wines 3	—	0.00	0.00	0.00	0.00	0.00	0.00	0.00	0.00
Wines 4	—	0.16	0.00	6.97	1.71	0.00	0.00	0.00	0.00
Wines 5	—	0.00	0.00	0.00	0.00	3.22	0.00	9.23	0.00
Equities	100.00	31.92	40.72	13.73	20.60	36.77	43.86	13.95	23.47
Arts	—	—	—	40.38	37.35	—	—	41.35	38.06

Notes: For each optimal portfolio, the expected excess return (in %), standard deviation (in %), Sharpe ratio and the weights (in %) to be invested in the different asset categories are reported. Wines categories 1–5 refer to the first to the firth growths in the left panel and to the wines with the best (100) Parker's rating to the wines with the worst (80–89) Parker's roting in the right panel. PF1a (PF2a) and PF1b (PF2b) are built on the basis of, respectively, raw and cost-adjusted returns on wines.

Table 5 shows the weighting scheme across the different asset categories for the various optimal portfolios. PF0 is for the case in which the portfolio is fully invested in equities. The left panel (PF1a to PF2b) is for the five ranking defined wine indices and the right panel (PF3a to PF4b) is for the rating defined indices. PFla is invested in both equities and wines; PFlb is constructed in a similar fashion but it also takes into account the impact due to the costs incurred by an investment in wines. PF2a also incorporates art works in the portfolio; PF2b accounts for the costs incurred by an investment either in wines or in art works. We observe that both wines and arts have interesting properties in terms of diversification as they are highly weighted in the optimal portfolio. When wine indices based on ranking are considered, about 42% of the optimal portfolio has to be invested in first, second and fourth growths. Similarly, 38% of the optimal portfolio has to be invested in wines when we employ rating defined wine indices. The most heavily weighted wines in this portfolio are the wines rated 96 or above by Parker. If we do not take into account the costs incurred by an investment in wine (PF2a), wines rated in the range 80 to 89 may also provide a good diversification because of their low correlations with other wine categories and with other asset classes, in particular with art works. A significant part of the optimal portfolios has to be invested in art work, about 37% to 41%

depending on the portfolio considered. As already observed from Figure 3, the discount that we have applied on wine (and art) returns has a minor impact on the optimal portfolio. Furthermore, the weights remain mostly unaltered.

5.2. *Mean-variance-skewness-kurtosis analysis*

In this section, we derive the optimal allocation between wines and equities[41] in a mean-variance-skewness-kurtosis framework. There are at least two major justifications for incorporating higher moments into the analysis:

(1) Wine and equity returns have a non-trivial joint distribution. Their marginal distributions are clearly non-normal and their higher moments are dissimilar. Notably, wines seem to have a positive skewness and a slightly larger kurtosis than equities. Furthermore, wines have rather low correlations with equities. As such it might also prove useful to study how their higher co-moments are related.
(2) The assumptions implied by the mean-variance paradigm are very restrictive. There are many claims suggesting that investors are also affected in their utility by the higher moments of the returns distribution (see Jondeau, Poon and Rockinger, 2007). Investors typically like portfolios with positive skewness and dislike portfolios that have a large kurtosis. Hence, a more realistic approach to optimal allocation would include beneath the usual set of objectives (i.e., maximization of the excepted return and minimization of the variance) the maximization of the skewness and the minimization of the kurtosis.

In order to deal with the difficult task to jointly maximize expected returns and skewness and minimize variance and kurtosis, we use a polynomial goal programming (PGP) model (see Lay, Yu and Wang (2006) and Davies, Kat and Lu (2009) for a full description). That is, we maximize the following expression:

$$Z = \left|1 + \frac{E^* - E_W}{E^*}\right|^{\lambda_1} + \left|1 + \frac{V_W - V^*}{V^*}\right|^{\lambda_2} + \left|1 + \frac{S^* - S_W}{S^*}\right|^{\lambda_3} + \left|1 + \frac{K_W - K^*}{K^*}\right|^{\lambda_4}, \tag{5}$$

[41]Returns on art works are only available on a quarterly basis. This makes it difficult to get reliable estimates of their higher co-moments with wines and equities. We therefore do not include them in the analysis.

where E, V, S, and K stand for the expected return, variance, skewness and kurtosis of the portfolio. We employ returns in excess to the risk-free interest rate (as in Lay, Yu, and Wang, 2006). The symbol * denotes the optimal value for each moment independently of the others (i.e., by optimizing only this moment leaving the others free) and the symbol w denotes the value of each moment when the weighting matrix is $W = w$. The parameters $\lambda_1, \lambda_2, \lambda_3$, and λ_4 allow to give more or less importance to the deviation of each moment from its optimal value. They can be considered as a measure of the investor preferences for each moment. If λ_3 and λ_4 are set to zero, the problem reduces to the standard mean-variance paradigm. Finally, we also impose two conditions on $w : w\,I = 1$ and $w \geq 0$ (short-selling is prohibited).

Tables 6 and 7 show how each asset is weighted in the optimal portfolios for various sets of investor preferences. Table 6 is for wine indices defined on the basis of wine ranking, while Table 7 is for rating defined wine indices. PFl is built on the basis of expected return and variance only; it serves as a benchmark. PF2 to PF4 show the results when we include the skewness (PF2), the kurtosis (PF3) and both the skewness and the kurtosis (PF4) into the analysis.

Table 6. Portfolio Allocation and Summary Statistics for Various Investor Preferences Over the Moments of the Portfolio Return Distribution

	Wine indices based on ranking							
Ranking	PF1	PF2	PF3	PF4	PF5	PF6	PF7	PF8
λ_1	1	1	1	1	12	1	1	1
λ_2	0.25	0.25	0.25	0.25	0.25	0.5	0.25	0.25
λ_3	10	1	0	1	1	1	2	1
λ_4	0	0	0.25	0.25	0.25	0.25	0.25	0.5
E_W	4.41	2.88	4.25	3.96	7.42	3.71	2.55	3.91
V_W	4.82	6.33	4.84	4.77	12.81	4.37	6.93	4.86
S_W	−0.11	3.01	−0.09	0.73	−0.38	0.52	3.30	0.12
K_W	2.90	15.94	2.14	3.24	2.64	2.98	17.75	1.97
1st Growths	22.56	14.39	23.88	25.92	0.00	21.95	12.52	35.52
2nd Growths	14.97	6.40	4.57	22.95	13.27	16.28	3.93	7.08
3rd Growths	0.00	4.25	0.00	0.00	0.00	0.00	10.35	0.00
4th Growths	11.67	44.48	17.51	15.21	0.00	19.34	45.98	11.22
5th Growths	0.00	12.10	0.00	0.00	0.00	0.00	14.15	0.00
Equities	11.26	6.92	15.51	5.92	86.73	6.20	5.85	11.62
Arts	39.53	11.46	38.54	29.99	0.00	36.23	7.22	34.56

Notes: PF1 to PF8 have been estimated for a variety of investor preferences, which are represented by the values attributed to $\lambda_1, \lambda_2, \lambda_3$, and λ_4. For each portfolio, the expected return (E_W, in %), volatility (V_W, in %), skewness (S_W, kurtosis (K_W and the weights (in %) to be invested in the various asset categories are reported.

Table 7. Portfolio Allocation and Summary Statistics for Various Investor Preferences Over the Moments of the Portfolio Return Distribution

	Wine indices based on rating							
Rating	PF1	PF2	PF3	PF4	PF5	PF6	PF7	PF8
λ_1	1	1	1	1	2	1	1	1
λ_2	0.25	0.25	0.25	0.25	0.25	0.5	0.25	0.25
λ_3	0	1	0	1	1	1	2	1
λ_4	0	0	0.25	0.25	0.25	0.25	0.25	0.5
E_w	4.54	4.29	3.89	3.73	6.79	3.46	5.55	3.64
V_w	5.07	5.30	4.56	4.44	10.48	4.22	10.39	4.54
S_w	0.05	0.78	0.14	0.37	0.45	0.36	1.38	0.24
K_w	2.69	3.41	1.81	2.01	3.43	2.02	4.80	1.71
100 points	16.75	16.35	30.51	31.87	0.00	34.95	0.00	33.91
96–99 points	0.00	0.00	0.00	0.00	0.00	0.00	0.00	0.00
93–95 points	0.00	0.00	0.00	0.00	0.00	0.00	0.00	0.00
90–92 points	19.46	39.06	14.68	20.61	0.00	18.32	10.50	16.55
80–89 points	13.73	11.03	8.96	7.06	60.79	6.97	74.17	7.97
Equities	11.03	5.05	9.14	7.04	39.21	5.58	9.05	7.76
Arts	39.02	28.51	36.71	33.42	0.00	34.18	6.28	33.81

Notes: PF1 to PF8 have been estimated for n variety of investor preferences, which arc represented by the values attributed to λ_1, λ_2, λ_3, and λ_4. For each portfolio, the expected return (E_w, in %), volatility (V_w, in %), skewness (S_w), kurtosis (K_w) and the weights (in %) to be invested in the various asset categories are reported.

When investors care about skewness, the expected return of the portfolio is reduced, while both its variance and its kurtosis are increased (comparison of PF2 with PFl). The part of the portfolio that has to be invested in wines (arts) becomes much larger (smaller). Moreover, first and second growths (or wines rated 100, in Table 7) are less heavily weighted relatively to fourth and fifth growths (wines rated between 90 and 92). The impact of taking the kurtosis into account (but without accounting for the skewness, see PF3) depends on whether we consider ranking or rating defined indices. In the first case, the kurtosis is reduced but the other three moments of the return distribution do not change much; the allocation also remains essentially similar except the fact that second growths are less heavily weighted than in PFI. In the second case (i.e., when considering rating defined indices), the expected return and the variance of the portfolio go down and the part of the portfolio invested in the best wines strongly increases. When both the skewness and the kurtosis are considered (PF4), λ_3 and λ_4 tend to cancel each other out as the resulting portfolio has only slightly lower expected return and variance than PFI. The proportion of arts and equities in the optimal portfolio is reduced in favor of first, second and fourth growths (Table 6) and wines rated 100 (Table 7).

PF5 to PF8 focus on the optimal allocation for investors who have a strong preference for expected return (PF5), variance (PF6), skewness (PF7) or kurtosis (PF8). PF5 is characterized by higher expected return than in the base case (PF4) but this is at the cost of a much larger volatility. This portfolio has to be fully invested in second growths (respectively, wines rated between 80 and 89) and equities. On the other hand, the impact of taking a larger value for λ_2 is less pronounced (PF6): the expected return and the variance are only moderately reduced. The allocation among the different asset classes remains mostly unaffected. PF7 displays much larger variance, skewness and kurtosis than PF4. When we consider rating based wine indices, PF7 also has a much larger expected return than PF4. Furthermore, the part of the portfolio invested in first and second growths (respectively wines rated at or above 90) is dramatically reduced, while third to fifth growths (wines rated below 90 in Table 7) goes up to about 75% (respectively 70%, Table 7). Giving more importance to the kurtosis by increasing λ_4 (PF8) leads to a portfolio with rather similar features as PF4 for rating defined indices. Nevertheless, the differences between PF4 and PF8 are more important when we look at Table 6 (ranking defined indices) as the part to be invested in first growths, equities and art works increase, while the proportion of second and fourth growths decrease. This results in lower skewness and kurtosis.

Results from Tables 6 and 7 indicate that the allocation among the different assets almost always gives priority to wines. On average about 20% of the portfolio has to be invested in the best wines (i.e., first growths in Table 6 and wines rated 100 in Table 7). Depending on the preferences of the investors, their weight varies between 0% and 30% (rating defined indices) to 35% (ranking defined indices). When the primary focus of the investors is the expected return (see PF5 in the Tables) of their portfolio (and, to a lesser extent, its skewness — see PF7), the proportion invested in these wines dramatically decrease. The situation is reversed when the investors want to reduce the volatility and the kurtosis of their portfolio; in this case, a substantial part of the portfolio has to be invested in the best wines. Second growths are especially attractive in the perspective of either increasing the expected return of the portfolio or reducing its volatility. On the other hand, investing in lesser wines (i.e., third to fifth growths in Table 6 and wines rated at or below 92 in Table 7) permit to increase both the skewness and, to a lesser extent, the expected return of the portfolio. Thus, even if these categories do not offer the most attractive risk-return profile, they still help improving the portfolio diversification by increasing its skewness. All in one, an investor who wants to increase the expected return of his portfolio, irrespective of its variance, has to invest a larger amount into equities. On the other hand, if he chooses to invest more aggressively in wines, he will see the skewness of his portfolio increases.

Our results indicate that there are several tradeoffs among the different moments of the portfolio returns distribution. In general, the better the expected return, the less attractive are the variance, the skewness and the kurtosis. Similarly, if one wants to increase the skewness of his portfolio, this will come at the cost of higher variance and kurtosis. Hopefully, it seems however possible to reduce the variance, while keeping the kurtosis relatively low.

6. The Financial Crisis and its Impact on Wine Prices

In this section, we study the impact of the financial crisis on the wine market. In order to compensate for the absence of observations for the period 2007–2009,[42] we employ the Liv-ex 100 and Liv-ex 500 indices in addition to our general and first growths indices.[43] The Liv-ex 500 assesses the price evolution of the 500 wines that are the most actively traded on London market place, while the Liv-ex 100 only takes into account the 100 most often traded wines. As such, the Liv-ex 500 is more representative of the dynamic of the complete wine market, while the Liv-ex 100 focuses primarily on the most speculative wines.

Figure 4 shows the evolution of the various wine indices and the S&P 500 between 1996 and 2007.[44] All indices have been standardized in order to have base value 100 in July 2001. The S&P 500 serves us as a benchmark of the evolution of US stock prices. Wine prices have skyrocketed during the period 2006–2008 and have then come back to more reasonable levels. The drop in the Liv-ex 100 in autumn 2008 is particularly spectacular and seems to be related to the financial crisis.

In order to complement graphical observations with a quantitative assessment, we calculate the correlations between the returns on the various wine and stock market indices. To avoid possible non-synchronous trading problems, we focus exclusively on quarterly returns. Furthermore, as wine

[42]Our sample period ends in February 2007.

[43]See www.liv-ex.com.

[44]Historical data for the Liv-ex I00 are only available since July 2001.

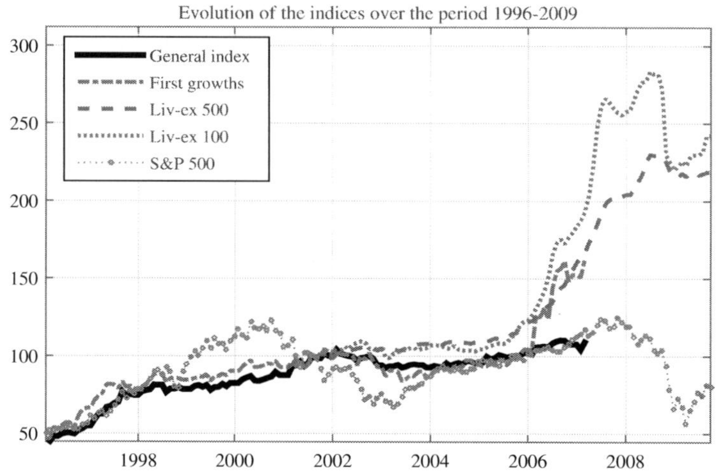

Figure 4. Evolution of the S&P 500, Our General and First Growths Wine Indices (until 2007) and the Liv-ex 100 and Liv-ex 500 (since 2001)

Table 8. Correlation between Wine and Stock Market Indices from 1996 to 2009

	1996–2001		2001–2007				2007–2009	
	GWI	FG	GWI	FG	L500	L100	L500	L100
S&P 500	0.31 ∗ ∗	0.29 ∗ ∗	−0.20	−0.22∗	0.15	0.13	0.41 ∗ ∗	0.50∗∗∗
GWI	1.00	0.94 ∗ ∗∗	1.00	0.81 ∗ ∗∗	0.14	0.23∗	—	—
FG	0.94 ∗ ∗∗	1.00	0.81 ∗ ∗∗	1.00	0.30 ∗ ∗	0.24∗	—	—
L500	—	—	0.14	0.30 ∗ ∗	1.00	0.79∗∗∗	1.00	0.80∗∗∗
L100	—	—	0.23∗	0.14∗	0.79∗∗∗	1.00	0.80∗∗∗	1.00

Notes: GWI, FG, L500, and L100 are abbreviations for the general wine index, the first growths index, the Liv-ex 500 and Liv-ex 100. ***, ** and * denote significativity at the 99%, 95%, and 90% confidence level.

returns are not normally distributed, we use the Spearman's rank correlation coefficient.

Table 8 shows the correlation between the various indices for three different periods: 1996–2001, 2001–2007, and 2007–2009. The correlation between the various wine indices has been consistently positive and significant (at the exception of the correlation between the general wine index and the Liv-ex 500, which is not significant at standard levels). Before 2001, our wine indices have been positively related with the S&P 500, but interestingly the relationship has reverted during the period 2001–2007. On the other hand, the correlation between returns on Liv-ex indices and S&P 500 has been positive (but not significant) during the same period. This suggests that Liv-ex indices are more closely related to the evolution of stock markets. This is presumably due to the fact that the Liv-ex indices trace the evolution of the most speculative wines, while our indices account for the evolution of many more wines, some of them much less speculative. From 2007 onwards, the Liv-ex indices and the S&P 500 have demonstrated a strong correlation.

In order to gain more insight about the impact of the financial crisis on our results from the previous section (i.e., on the diversification benefits from investing in wine), we calculate time-varying correlation coefficients between the different wine and stock market indices. We calculate the correlations using rolling time windows of 24 months. We employ overlapping quarterly returns because of the small number of observations and also in order to smooth the dynamics of correlations. To account for the non-trivial returns distribution, we estimate 90%-confidence bounds using the bootstrap approach. We resample 100,000 times the original data.

Figure 5 shows the evolution of correlations between (1) the general wine index and the S&P 500 (until 2007) and (2) the Liv-ex 500 and the S&P 500 (from 2001 onwards). One may notice that the correlation between wine prices and the S&P 500 has followed a declining trend until 2005 when it reached a low. The correlation between the Liv-ex 500 and the S&P 500 has been larger than the correlation between the general wine index and the S&P 500. Again, we believe that this is because the Liv-ex 500 index gives more weight to speculative wines. Wine has played a defensive role during both the 1998 financial crisis and the burst of the dotcom bubble. On the other hand, wine prices have taken more time to rebound at the end of the 2001–2003 bear market. During the first part of the current crisis, that is, before September 2008, the correlation has started to increase but, in August 2008, wine prices were still close to their all-time highs. At the same moment, the S&P 500 was already 20% down from its 2007 peak.

When entering the eye of the financial tornado in October 2008, the correlation has increased tremendously (see Figure 5) and wine prices have fallen sharply. The most speculative wines (Liv-ex 100) have been the most violently hit. Between September and December, they have lost 25% versus 6% for the Liv-ex 500. It is however worth to point out that the S&P 500 has plunged by over 40% over these three months! This increasing correlation between asset classes can be explained by a well-known flight to liquidity phenomenon that has lead to a "correlation breakdown," which corresponds to a situation in which all asset classes move together thus making diversification

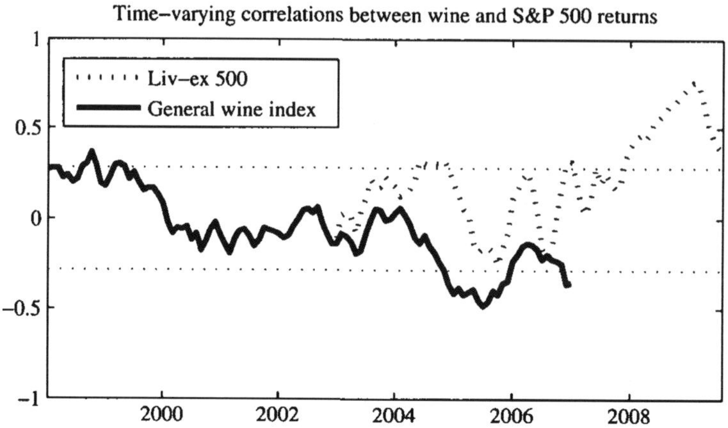

Figure 5. Time-Varying Correlations between the S&P 500 Returns and the Returns on the Liv-ex 500 and Our General Wine Index

Note: Based on rolling time windows of 2 years to calculate the correlations.

strategies inoperative. The impact of such an event is usually limited in time and, therefore, it remains to see if the correlation will rapidly come back to its pre-crisis levels. This could well be the case as wine prices have stabilized since the end of 2008 (i.e., three months before the stock markets started to rebound). Figure 5 also suggests that the correlation has already started to decrease.

7. Conclusions

This chapter studies the evolution of wine prices during the last decade (1996–2007) and analyzes their properties from an investor's viewpoint. Preliminary results show that investing in the wine market might permit to achieve an attractive performance in terms of both average returns and volatility. However, one has to note that this market is far from being homogeneous: the potential for price appreciation of a wine strongly depends on its vintage, its notoriety and ranking as well as its rating. Limited liquidity and market fragmentation make it difficult to establish a precise market price for any bottle of wine. Therefore someone wanting to invest in wines has to be armed with an excellent knowledge of the current conditions prevailing on the market.

We investigate if the wine market can be segmented in homogeneous subcategories. To this aim, we consider a set of wine indices defined on the basis of their ranking. The evidence suggests that these indices follow a unique trend; technically speaking, they are cointegrated. An interesting feature of these subsets of wines is that their short-term codependence is somewhat limited. Furthermore, the correlation of wines with equities is not very significant. This suggests that wines might be a useful diversification device. Indeed, an extensive portfolio allocation analysis shows that wines have to be overweighted relatively to equities in the optimal Sharpe-ratio portfolio. Including higher moments of the distribution does not alter this result: wines allow significantly increasing the skewness of an equity portfolio but equities are more appealing in terms of kurtosis. Even if we consider the costs associated with the holding and trading of wines, the latters still improve the risk-return profile of an equity portfolio. According to a study of the evolution of wine prices during the last two years (in UK), we do not believe that the financial crisis and its impact on the wine market modify our conclusions. All asset classes have been hit sharply by Lehman's failure and, consequently, the correlation between wine and stock returns has increased very significantly. But the empirical evidence suggests that the correlation has already come back relatively close to its pre-crisis levels. Hence, at least from a diversification viewpoint, it looks still attractive to invest in wine.

In summary, the evidence provided in this chapter demonstrates that wine might be an appealing alternative investment vehicle. Nevertheless, our opinion is that such an investment should follow some practical rules. First, one should only invest in wines if one has a real "epicurean" interest in wines. This is because such an investment requires having a very good knowledge of this complex market, which does not function the same way other financial markets do. Second, a long term perspective is necessary (as for equities); wines as other collectibles are also affected by business cycles. The recent financial crisis and its impact on the wine market provides a striking example: prices have dropped by up to 25% for the most speculative wines. Third, we advise against entering the wine market through investment funds. Such funds have large positions in highly illiquid assets. As such, if they had to get out of the market and to sell their positions quickly, they might incur large losses. Fourth, one has to focus on investment grade wines only and to diversify one's positions.

Wine economics remains an understudied realm of research, at least from a financial viewpoint. Now that data have become more easily available and are of better quality, we see several avenues for future research. First, it might be of interest to analyze whether this market is arbitrage-free or not; we suspect that this is not the case. For instance, one may employ a dynamic hedonic pricing model to identify under- and overevaluated wines and then design a trading strategy to take advantage of possible arbitrage opportunities. Second, the variables that lead the evolution of the wine market as a whole remain largely unknown. It might thus prove useful for forecasting purposes to get a better understanding of how such driving variables come into action. Third, it would also be interesting to extend the analysis to an international perspective, including important wine markets like England, France or Germany. Up to now, wine prices have always been investigated in a single-country framework; it is therefore unclear whether there is a unique international trend driving the market. And, of course, it would be definitely useful to study in details the impact of the financial crisis on the wine market. At the time being, it is still very difficult to figure out what would be the long-term impact of this event on wine prices.

Acknowledgments

We are grateful to an anonymous referee and the editor, Karl Storchmann, for their valuable comments and suggestions on earlier versions of this chapter.

References

Ashenfelter, O. (1989). How auctions work for wine and art. *The Journal of Economic Perspectives*, 3, 23–36.

Ashenfelter, O., Ashmore, D., and Lalonde, R. (1995). Bordeaux wine vintage quality and the weather. *Chance*, 8, 7–14.

Ashenfelter, O. (2010). Predicting the quality and prices of Bordeaux wine. *Journal of Wine Economics*, 5(1), 40–52.

Baek, E.G., and Brock, W.A. (1992). A general test for nonlinear Granger causality: Bivariate model. Working Paper, Iowa State University and University of Wisconsin, Madison.

Benfratello, L., Piacenza, M., and Sacchetto, S. (2009). What drives market prices in the wine Industry? Estimation of a hedonic model for Italian premium wines. *Applied Economics*, 41(17), 2197–2209.

Burton, B.J., and Jacobsen, J.P. (1999). Measuring returns on investments in collectibles. *Journal of Economic Perspectives*, 13(4), 193–212.

Burton, B.J., and Jacobsen, J.P. (2001). The rate or return on investment in wine. *Economic Inquiry*, 39, 337–350.

Cardebat, J.M., and Figuet, J.M. (2004). What explains Bordeaux wine prices? *Applied Economics Letters*, 11, 293–296.

Christensen, B.J., and Meunier, V. (2006). Forward and spot prices: Testing the expectations hypothesis in the Bordeaux "en primeur" wine market. Working Paper, University of Aarhus.

Combris, P., Lecocq, S., and Visser, M. (1997). Estimation of a hedonic price equation for Bordeaux wine: Does quality matter? *The Economic Journal*, 107, 390–402.

Combris, P., Lecocq, S., and Visser, M. (2000). Estimation of a hedonic price equation for Burgundy wine. *Applied Economics*, 32, 961–967.

Davies, R.J., Kat, H.M., and Lu, S. (2009). Fund of hedge funds portfolio selection: A multiple-objective approach. *Journal of Derivatives and Hedge Funds*, 15(2), 91–115.

Di Vittorio, A., and Ginsburgh, V. (1996). Pricing red wines of Medoc vintages from 1949 to 1989 at Christies auctions. *Journal de la Société Statistique de Paris*, 137, 19–49.

Diks, C., and Panchenko, V. (2006). A new statistic and practical guidelines for nonparametric Granger causality testing. *Journal of Economic Dynamics and Control*, 30, 1647–1669.

Engle, R. (2002). Dynamic conditional correlation: A simple class of multivariate generalized autoregressive conditional heteroskedasticity models. *Journal of Business and Economic Statistics*, 20(3), 339–350.

Fogarty, J.J. (2006a). Wine investment, pricing and substitutes. Thesis, University of Western Australia. School of Economics and Commerce.

Fogarty, J.J. (2006b). The return to Australian fine wine. *European Review of Agricultural Economics*, 33, 542–561.

Fogarty, J.J. (2007). Rethinking wine investment in the UK and Australia. American Association of Wine Economists, Working Paper No. 6.

Hamilton, J.D. (1994). *Ttme Series Analysis.* Princeton: Princeton University Press.

Hiemstra, C., and Jones, J.D. (1994). Testing for linear and nonlinear Granger causality in the stock price-volume relation. *Journal of Finance*, 49(5), 1639–1664.

Jaeger, E. (1981). To save or savor: The rate of return to storing wine. *The Journal of Political Economy*, 89, 584–592.

Jondeau, E., Poon, S.-H., and Rockinger, M. (2007). *Financial Modeling Under Non-Gaussian Distributions.* London: Springer Finance.

Jondeau, E., and Rockinger, M. (2006). Optimal portfolio allocation under higher moments. *European Financial Management*, 12(1), 29–55.

Jones, G.V., and Storchmann, K.H. (2001). Wine market prices and investment under uncertainty: An econometric model for Bordeaux crus classés. *Agricultural Economics*, 26, 115–133.

Krasker, W.S. (1979). The rate of return to storing wines. *The Journal of Political Economy*, 87(6), 1363–1367.

Lay, K.K., Yu, L., and Wang, S. (2006). Mean-variance-skewness-kurtosis-based portfolio optimization. *Proceedings of the First International Multi-Symposiums on Computer and Computational Sciences*, 2, 292–297.

Lecocq, S., and Visser, M. (2006). What determines wine prices: Objective vs. sensory characteristics. *Journal of Wine Economics*, 1, 42–56.

Mahenc, P., and Meunier, V. (2006). Early sales of Bordeaux grands crus. *Journal of Wine Economics*, 1(1), 57–74.

Markowitz, H.M. (1952). Portfolio selection. *Journal of Finance*, 7, 77–91.

Oczkowski, E. (2001). Hedonic wine price functions and measurement error. *The Economic Record*, 77, 374–382.

Sanning, L.W., Shaffer, S., and Sharratt, J.M. (2008). Bordeaux wine as a financial investment. *Journal of Wine Economics*, 3, 51–71.

Tsay, R.S. (2002). *Analysis of Financial Time Series.* Hoboken, New Jersey: John Wiley and Sons.

Appendix: List of Estates

First Growths (according to our ranking): Lafite Rothschild (official classification: 1st Growth, Pauillac), Latour (1st Growth, Pauillac), Mouton Rothschild (1st Growth, Pauillac), Château Margaux (1st Growth,

Margaux), Haut Brion (1st Growth, Pessac-Léognan), La Mission Haut Brion (Cru Classé, Pessac-Léognan), Lafleur (Pomerol), Pétrus (Pomerol), Le Pin (Pomerol), Ausone (1st Growth "A," Saint-Emilion), Cheval Blanc (1st Growth "A," Saint-Emilion).

Second Growths: Cos d'Estoumel (2nd Growth, Saint-Estèphe), Montrose (2nd Growth, Saint-Estèphe), Lynch Bages (5th Growth, Pauillac), Pichon Longueville Baron (2nd Growth, Pauillac), Pichon Longueville Comtesse (2nd Growth, Pauillac), Ducru Beaucaillou (2nd Growth, Saint-Julien), Léoville Las Cases (2nd Growth, Saint-Julien), Palmer (3rd Growth, Margaux), L'Evangile (Pomerol), Trotanoy (Pomerol), Angélus (1st Growth "B," Saint-Emilion), Pavie (1st Growth "B," Saint-Emilion).

Third Growths: Calon Ségur (3rd Growth, Saint-Estèphe), Grand Puy Lacoste (5th Growth, Pauillac), Gruaud Larose (2nd Growth, Saint-Julien), Léoville Barton (2nd Growth, Saint-Julien), Léoville Poyferré (2nd Growth, Saint-Julien), Talbot (4th Growth, Saint-Julien), Certan de May (Pomerol), Clinet (Pomerol), La Conseillante (Pomerol), L'Eglise Clinet (Pomerol), Vieux Château Certan (Pomerol), Tertre Roteboeuf (Saint- Emilion), Troplong Mondot (1st Growth "B," Saint-Emilion).

Fourth Growths: Pontet Canet (5th Growth, Pauillac), Beychevelle (4th Growth, Saint-Julien), Rauzan Ségla (2nd Growth, Margaux), Sociando Mallet (Haut-Médoc), Pape Clément (Cru Classé, Pessac-Léognan), Bon Pasteur (Pomerol), Fleur de Gay (Pomerol), La Fleur Pétrus (Pomerol), Latour à Pomerol (Pomerol), Figeac (1st Growth "B," Saint-Emilion), Monbousquet (Grand Cru Classé, Saint-Emilion), Pavie Decesse (Grand Cru Classé, Saint-Emilion), Pavie Macquin (1st Growth "B," Saint-Emilion).

Fifth Growths: Lafon Rochet (4th Growth, Saint-Estèphe), Meyney (Cru Bourgeois superiéur, Saint-Estèphe), Les Onnes de Pez (Cru Bourgeois exceptionnel, Saint-Estèphe), Annailhac (5th Growth, Pauillac), Clerc Milon (5th Growth, Pauillac), Branaire Ducru (4th Growth, Saint-Julien), Gloria (Saint-Julien), Smith Haut Lafitte (Cru Classé, Pessac-Léognan), Clos l'Eglise (Pomerol), Nénin (Pomerol), L'Arrosée (Grand Cru Classé, Saint-Emilion), Beau Séjour Bécot (1st Growth "B," Saint-Emilion), Beau Séjour Duffau (1st Growth "B," Saint-Emilion), Canon (1st Growth "B," Saint-Emilion), Lagrange (3rd Growth, Saint-Julien), Brane Cantenac (2nd Growth, Margaux), Giscours (3rd Growth, Margaux), Lascombes (2nd Growth, Margaux), Cantmerle (5th Growth, Médoc), La Lagune (3rd Growth, Médoc), de Chevalier (Cru Classé, Pessac-Léognan), Canon Gaffelière (Grand Cru Classé, Saint-Emilion), Clos de l'Oratoire (Grand Cru

Classé, Saint-Emilion), La Dominique (Grand Cru Classé, Saint-Emilion), La Gaffeliére (1st Growth "B," Saint-Emilion), Magdelaine (1st Growth "B," Saint-Emilion), Quinault l'Enclos (Saint-Emilion).

Garage Wines: Bellevue Mondotte (Saint-Emilion), Clos de Sarpe (Saint-Emilion), La Gomerie (Saint-Emilion), Gracia (Saint-Emilion), Hermitage (Saint-Emilion), Lynsolence (Saint-Emilion), Magrez Fombrauge (Saint-Emilion), La Mondotte (Saint-Emilion), Roi Valentin (Saint-Emilion), Valandraud (Saint-Emilion).

Second Wines: Carruades de Lafite (Second wine of Lafite Rothschild, Pauillac), Forts de Latour (Second wine of Latour, Pauillac), Clos du Marquis (Second wine of Léoville Las Cases, Saint-Julien), Pavillon Rouge de Ch. Margaux (Second wine of Château Margaux, Margaux), Bahans de Haut Brion (Second wine of Haut-Brion, Pessac-Léognan), Pensées de Lafleur (Second wine of Lafleur, Pomerol).

Chapter 14

Wine Investment and Portfolio Diversification Gains*

James J. Fogarty

School of Agricultural and Resource Economics,
University of Western Australia,
35 Stirling Hwy, Crawley 6009, Australia
James.Fogarty@uwa.edu.au

The existing literature on the return to wine is mixed. Some studies have found wine to be an unattractive investment option and others have found wine to be an investment class that provides excess risk adjusted returns. However, provided the return to wine does not have a strong positive correlation with standard financial assets, even if the return to wine is low, it is possible that including wine in an investment portfolio will provide a diversification benefit. Here the repeat sales regression methodology is used to estimate the return to Australian wine, and the return is shown to be lower than for standard financial assets. Several measures are then used to show that despite the return to Australian wine being lower than the return to standard financial assets, wine does provide a modest diversification benefit.

1. Introduction

Although there is now a reasonably established literature that investigates the return to storing fine wine, the potential for wine to provide a diversification gain to an already well diversified investment portfolio is an issue that has not yet been fully investigated. The potential for wine to provide a diversification gain is explored in the remainder of this chapter, and the structure of the discussion is as follows. Section 2 presents a brief overview of the return to wine literature. Section 3 describes the data, explains the method used to estimate the return to wine, and presents estimates of the

*This article originally appeared in *Journal of Wine Economics* (2010), 5(1), 119–131.

return to storing Australian fine wine. Section 4 demonstrates that there is a diversification gain from holding fine wine, and concluding comments are presented in Section 5.

2. Literature Review

The first published study of the return to wine was Krasker (1979). To test whether the return to wine was greater than the return to Treasury bills Krasker considered post 1950 vintages of California Cabernet Sauvignon and Red Bordeaux sold at auction over the period 1973 to 1977. There were 137 observations for the study, although, as the regression approach used requires there to be observations for wine i in adjacent periods, many sales observations would have been excluded from the sample. The estimate of the premium to wine over Treasury bills was not statistically different from zero, and the conclusion drawn was that wine is not an especially good investment. Krasker did however note that the effect of taxes on investment income makes storing wine a viable proposition for those consumers faced with a high marginal tax rate and purchasing only wine they intend to drink.

Jaeger (1981) takes as her starting point the Krasker (1979) data set and approach, and then extends the time series back to 1969 so that there are 199 observations. Using an approach similar to Krasker where storage costs are estimated from the data, the estimated risk premium to wine over Treasury bills for the period 1969 to 1977 was 8.5%, and was statistically significant. However, Jaeger argues the estimate for storage costs generated by the approach ($16.60 per case) is implausibly high, and that the model specification is inappropriate. As an alternative, Jaeger hypothesizes that the return to wine can be decomposed into two parts; a return that accrues to all wine regardless of price, and a return that is a function of price. Reformulating the model to allow for returns to vary with price, Jaeger finds that the risk premium over Treasury bills for an average bottle of wine in the sample (price $410) was 12.4%. Jaeger concludes by using price to separate the sample into thirds and shows that the return to wine in the bottom third of the sample is greater than the return to wine in the top third of the sample. As the risk measure for expensive wine is lower, and statistically different to the risk measure for less expensive wine, the idea that the higher returns to cheaper wine represent compensation for higher risk appears reasonable. Whether the return to wine was greater than the return to other risky financial assets was not considered as part of the study.

Rather than estimating a period by period return to wine calculated from aggregate sales data, Weil (1993) considers the case of an actual wine investor. The 68 transactions evaluated cover a 16 year period, where the earliest wine purchases were in 1976 and the most recent wine sales were in 1992. Wines were held for varying lengths of time, and the size of each investment varied. As such, the actual return the investor achieved was determined via an internal rate of return calculation. For comparison purposes the return to an equity portfolio was also calculated. So that the return to equities would be directly comparable with the return to wine, it was assumed that whenever a wine buy or sell action was initiated by the investor a matching investment or disinvestment in equities was made. For wine, the actual pre-transaction and storage cost annual return achieved was 10%. As the return to the matching equities portfolio was 15%, the conclusion drawn was that the investor would have been better off holding equities.

The regression approach used by Krasker (1979) and Jaeger (1981) is generalized in Burton and Jacobsen (2001) where the semi-annual return to wine for the period 1986 to 1996 is calculated using the repeat sales regression price index methodology due to Bailey *et al.* (1963). The advantage of the Bailey *et al.* method over the approach of Krasker and Jaeger is that it is not necessary to have adjacent period repeat sales. As long as there is a repeat sale, regardless of the amount of time that has passed between the first sale and the second sale, the information can be used in the analysis. The approach therefore permits a substantial increase in the proportion of total wine sales information that can be used to estimate returns. The data used by Burton and Jacobsen to estimate the semi-annual return to wine was restricted to post 1960 vintages of leading Red Bordeaux wines and included 10,558 observations. In the study the return to wine and the return to wine sub-market portfolios of the best wines (first growths), and select high quality vintages (1961 and 1982), were compared to the return of equities and one year Treasury bills. The results showed that the risk-return profile of wine is such that it is dominated by equities in terms of risky investments, and an unattractive alternative to low risk debt.

The adjacent period hedonic price regression approach was used by Fogarty (2006) to estimate the return to post 1965 vintages of Australian premium wine for the period 1989–2000. The hedonic literature is substantial, but modern applications generally attribute the approach to Rosen (1974). The quarterly return to premium Australian wine was estimated from 14,102 observations and compared to the return of Australian equities and three month Treasury bills. The return to wine was found to be lower than equities, but wine was also found to be slightly less risky than equities. Given previous findings that wine returns vary with price, the sample was then split into approximately half and the return to more expensive wine compared to the return to less expensive wine. Unlike the findings of Jaeger (1981), the quarterly return to the most expensive Australian wine (3.17%) was higher than the return to less expensive wine (1.92%), and somewhat surprisingly, the risk to the most expensive wine (S.D. 4.74%) was lower than the risk to the less expensive wine (S.D. 5.35%).

Using data for the period 1996–2003 Sanning *et al.* (2008) use the repeat sales methodology to estimate the return to holding red Bordeaux. Rather than pooling the data to estimate a market return, Sanning *et al.* (2008) estimate monthly returns for individual vintage-producer combinations, and individual vintage-classification combinations, where classification refers to the five classifications recognized in the classic Bordeaux wine ranking, plus all unclassified wines as a sixth group. There are 276 unique vintage-producer combinations and so 276 vintage-producer repeat sales regressions. Averaging across all months and all 276 regressions, the monthly return to wine was found to be 0.51%, with standard deviation 6.05%. Restricting the sample to just the producers recognized in the classic Bordeaux classification the average monthly return was found to be 0.78%, with standard deviation 7.20%. There are 83 unique vintage-classification combinations and the average monthly return across all months and all 83 vintage-classification repeat sales regressions was 0.88%, with standard deviation 7.08%. Restricting the sample to just the producers recognized in the classic Bordeaux classification the average monthly return was found to be 1.03%, with standard deviation 7.29%.

The Capital Asset Pricing Model (CAPM) and the Fama-French Three Factor Model (TFM), which are both standard tools used to study equity returns, are then used to further investigate the return to wine. For the vintage-producer analysis, although average excess returns are found to be positive, most estimates are not statistically significant. The result is somewhat stronger for the vintage-classification regressions. Average excess returns are shown to be positive, with approximately one quarter of the excess return estimates being statistically significant, and of the statistically significant excess returns most are positive. The finding of excess risk adjusted returns is important; however, arguable the most important finding presented in Sanning *et al.* (2008) is that models that do a good job of explaining the return to equities, such as the CAPM and TFM, do an extremely poor job of explaining the return to wine. The finding is important because if wine returns are not explained by equity market risk factors, wine may be able to play a risk diversification role in a balanced investment portfolio.

Masset and Henderson (2010) use an approach that is conceptually similar to the approach used to construct a stock market index to show that for the period 1996–2007 the cumulative return to red Bordeaux wine (145%) was greater than the cumulative return to the Dow Jones (127%). The risk to holding wine, measured as the annualized standard deviation of returns, was also shown to be lower (8%) than the risk associated with holding equities (15%). The data set used included 77,014 wine sale observations, and so the authors were also able to estimate a variety of sub indices based on vintage and wine classification. The results show that in general vintages of higher quality, along with first growth and second growth wines, provide the highest returns, and also have a risk profile at least as favorable as wines from lesser vintages and lower classifications. The mean-variance framework is then used to show that including art and wine in an equity portfolio reduces portfolio risk, and a polynomial goal programming model is used to show that the optimal allocation to wine and art varies if investors care about the skewness and kurtosis of their investment portfolio as well as risk.

The ability of wine to provide a diversification gain to an investment portfolio during a downturn is considered in Masset and Weisskopf (2010). The authors use data covering the period 1996 to January 2009 and the repeat sales methodology to estimate a fine wine price index, as well as individual price indices for wines from Bordeaux, Burgundy, Rhône Valley, Italy, and the U.S. Wine is shown to outperform equities during a downturn, and including wine in a diverse mix of investment portfolios, from conservative to aggressive, is shown to reduce portfolio risk. The CAPM and the conditional CAPM are then used to show that although wine returns are not related to systematic market risk, returns are impacted by general economic conditions.

3. Data and Wine Return Estimates

To investigate the potential for there to be a diversification gain from holding wine requires risk and return information for several asset classes. For standard financial assets it is possible to download data from a commercial service provider such as datastream. For wine it is necessary to obtain raw auction data and then estimate returns. For the current study wine sales data were obtained from the Langton's auction house for sales in Melbourne and

Sydney, and the data allow returns to be estimated for the period 1990Q1 to 2000Q4. For each sale Langton's recorded only the highest and lowest sale price for each item, and information on the quantity associated with each lot sold was unavailable. If several lots of an identical wine were presented for sale at a particular auction, the mean of the highest and lowest hammer price has been used as the sale price. The sample of wines considered was restricted to the post 1965 vintages of the wine brands listed in the Caillard and Langton (2001) classification of Australian investment quality wines and included 12,180 observations.

Observations were recorded for 84 individual wine brands, and while most of the observations were for either Shiraz based or Cabernet based wines, this was not exclusively the case. The specific distribution of observations by dominant grape variety was: Cabernet 43%, Shiraz 37%, Chardonnay 10%, Pinot Noir 4%, Riesling 2%, and Semillon, Merlot, and Botrytis affected wines approximately 1% each. Not all wine brands appeared in the sample with equal frequency, and the most traded wine, Penfold's Grange Shiraz, accounted for almost 9% of the sample. Details on the top eight wine brands by sales volume — along with the price range recorded for sales across all vintages at any point in 2000 — are shown in Table 1, and as can be seen, the top eight wine brands account for more than 36% of the total number of observations. Reflecting the development of the Australian wine investment market, sales observations increase in frequency steadily through time. Specifically, there were 624 sales observations in 1990, followed by 639 sales observations in 1991, then 689 sales observations in 1992, ..., and 2,483 sales observations in 2000.

When considering wines from a specific region it has been shown that it is possible to forecast the vintages that outperform the average by modeling the weather during the growing season (Ashenfelter *et al.*, 1995; Byron and Ashenfelter, 1995; Wood and Anderson, 2006; Lecocq and Visser, 2006; Ashenfelter, 2008). However, in the Australian context, where investment grade wines are drawn from across the country rather than from a single region, such an approach is difficult to implement. As such, for the Australian context it could be argued that an index based on the return achieved from holding wines from all vintages is the most appropriate index to consider. It is however also true that climatic variation in most Australian premium wine growing regions is less pronounced than in Bordeaux, and so the variation in price across wines from different vintages is also less pronounced.

Table 1. Summary Details for the Top Eight Wine Brands by Volume of Sales

Wine brand (1)	Observations 1990–2000 (no.) (2)	Vintage range sold in 2000 (years) (3)	Distinct vintages sold in 2000 (no.) (4)	Max price all vintages in 2000 ($) (4)	Min price all vintages in 2000 ($) (5)
Penfold's Bin 95 Grange Shiraz	1,071	1965–1995	31	426	159
Penfold's St Henri Shiraz-Cabernet	652	1965–1996	31	100	29
Penfold's Bin 707 Cabernet Sauvignon	481	1965–1997	23	151	72
Wynn's Cabernet Sauvignon	467	1965–1997	31	86	19
Penfold's Bin 389 Shiraz	461	1965–1995	31	85	20
Henschke Hill of Grace Shiraz	453	1966–1995	23	281	100
Mount Mary Quintet Cabernet Blend	421	1976–1995	18	226	95
Lake's Folly White Label Cabernets	386	1967–1998	27	60	20

The most commonly used approach to estimating the return to wine has been the repeat sales regression approach, and that is the approach used here. The original application of the repeat sales price index methodology was in the area of house price index construction, and there is now a vast literature that has used the approach to estimate the return to real estate. The approach is however well suited to estimating returns in any market characterized by infrequently traded heterogeneous assets. For example, the approach has also been used extensively to estimate the return to art, and in their review of the art auction process, Ashenfelter and Graddy (2003, p. 769) list nine studies that have used the repeat sales regression approach to estimate the return to art.

The exposition of the repeat sales regressions approach presented in Bailey *et al.* (1963) is timeless, and as such the following outline of the approach draws heavily on the original presentation. Let $w \in W = \{1, \ldots, W\}$ be the set of all observed wine sales, and let $t \in T = \{0, 1, \ldots, T\}$ be the set of time periods under consideration. Now, separate the set W into the subset of wines that sell only once during the sample period,

$i \in I = \{1, \ldots, I\} \subset W$ and the subset of wines that transact more than once over the sample period, $j \in J = \{1, \ldots, J\} \subset W$. The repeat sales approach considers only the observations in the set J. In some applications the proportion of the data discarded can be significant, and this is a criticism of the approach. For Australian wine, individual wine brand-vintage combinations generally trade more than once in a relatively short period of time and so the requirement for there to be a repeat sale is not especially onerous. Now, let the second sale for wine j occur in time period t and let the first sale occur in time period s, where $t > s$. Let the sale observations be denoted P_j^t and P_j^s, respectively, with the price relative (P_j^t/P_j^s) denoted R_j^{st}. Following Bailey *et al.* (1963, p. 934) and using B^t and B^s to denote the true but unknown price index numbers for periods t and s, the repeat sales model can be written as $R_j^{st} = (B^t/B^s) \times U_j^{st}$, or if lower case letters are used to denote logs, as $r_j^{st} = b^t - b^s + u_j^{st}$, where in log form the errors have zero mean and constant variance. If x^τ takes the value minus one when $\tau = s$, the value one when $\tau = t$, and the value zero otherwise, the regression model can then be expressed as $r_j^{st} = \sum_{\tau=1}^{T} \beta^\tau x_j^\tau + u_j^{st}$, where the return to wine is found by taking first differences of the least squares estimates of the β coefficients.

The actual regression point estimates, with robust standard errors, associated quarterly percentage returns, and regression R^2 value are reported in Table 2. Although the R^2 value for the regression is low, it is consistent with that reported in Burton and Jabcosen (2001, p. 343) of 0.17 for all wine, and not that far below the values reported in Jaeger (1981, p. 589) of between 0.29 and 0.41 for a vastly smaller data set. The maximum quarterly return over the period was 12.62%, and the minimum quarterly return was −4.40%. The average quarterly return was 2.05%, and the standard deviation of returns was 3.93%.

4. Diversification Gains

To place the return information in context, Table 3 provides summary details on the return to Australian wine, Australian shares, Australian bonds, and unhedged Australian dollar returns to U.S. shares and U.S. bonds from the first quarter of 1990 to the fourth quarter of 2000. The second column of Table 3 provides total return information, and as can be seen, the return to Australian wine is lower than the return to each of the other four asset classes. There are several measures of risk, and many financial applications focus on systematic risk. Here, details are reported for total risk, measured as the standard deviation of total returns to each asset class, and as can be seen

Table 2. Return to Wine Estimates

	All wine vintages		
Period (1)	Estimate (2)	S.E. (3)	Return (4)
1990Q1	−0.045*	(0.025)	−4.397
1990Q2	−0.031	(0.031)	1.449
1990Q3	−0.024	(0.032)	0.660
1990Q4	−0.034	(0.031)	−1.009
1991Q1	−0.042	(0.035)	−0.749
1991Q2	−0.057	(0.035)	−1.499
1991Q3	−0.026	(0.037)	3.102
1991Q4	0.008	(0.035)	3.503
1992Q1	0.000	(0.036)	−0.783
1992Q2	0.011	(0.038)	1.069
1992Q3	−0.011	(0.039)	−2.179
1992Q4	0.043	(0.041)	5.537
1993Q1	0.036	(0.038)	−0.723
1993Q2	0.096**	(0.038)	6.221
1993Q3	0.111**	(0.039)	1.515
1993Q4	0.106**	(0.040)	−0.540
1994Q1	0.201**	(0.039)	9.990
1994Q2	0.220**	(0.039)	1.946
1994Q3	0.196**	(0.039)	−2.394
1994Q4	0.177**	(0.040)	−1.899
1995Q1	0.229**	(0.042)	5.409
1995Q2	0.322**	(0.043)	9.664
1995Q3	0.355**	(0.041)	3.365
1995Q4	0.372**	(0.042)	1.747
1996Q1	0.491**	(0.042)	12.620
1996Q2	0.541**	(0.043)	5.163
1996Q3	0.512**	(0.042)	−2.897
1996Q4	0.540**	(0.043)	2.907
1997Q1	0.615**	(0.043)	7.778
1997Q2	0.699**	(0.044)	8.757
1997Q3	0.704**	(0.044)	0.449
1997Q4	0.752**	(0.044)	4.947
1998Q1	0.814**	(0.045)	6.419
1998Q2	0.834**	(0.045)	1.956
1998Q3	0.859**	(0.045)	2.528
1998Q4	0.823**	(0.045)	−3.528
1999Q1	0.862**	(0.046)	4.015
1999Q2	0.836**	(0.046)	−2.527
1999Q3	0.874**	(0.046)	3.859
1999Q4	0.885**	(0.046)	1.109
2000Q1	0.891**	(0.047)	0.612

(*Continued*)

Table 2. (*Continued*)

	All wine vintages		
Period (1)	Estimate (2)	S.E. (3)	Return (4)
2000Q2	0.886**	(0.047)	−0.524
2000Q3	0.873**	(0.047)	−1.341
2000Q4	0.861**	(0.048)	−1.206
Observations		12,180	
R^2		0.192	

Notes: *Significant at the 10% level. **Significant at the 5% level or greater.

Table 3. Individual Asset Summary Return Information: 1990Q1–2000Q4

Asset class (1)	Quarterly return (%) (2)	Standard deviation (%) (3)	Sharpe ratio (3)	Correlation coefficient (4)	S. ratio × Corr. coef. (5)	Diversification gain (6)
Australian Wine	2.05	3.93	0.061	1.00	0.061	—
Australian Shares	2.67	5.80	0.150	0.136	0.020	Yes
Australian Bonds	2.84	3.15	0.327	−0.106	−0.034	Yes
U.S. Shares	4.79	8.14	0.366	0.131	0.048	Yes
U.S. Bonds	2.91	6.07	0.181	0.003	0.001	Yes

by considering the information in column three of Table 3, higher returns are generally associated with higher risk. When using total risk rather than systematic risk, a standard measure that can be used to compare the risk adjusted performance of each asset class is the Sharpe ratio. The Sharpe ratio is a measure of excess return per unit of risk and is calculated as the asset return minus the risk free return divided by the asset standard deviation.[1] Here the 90-day Treasury bill return has been used as the risk free return, and by considering the detail in column four of Table 3 it can be seen that of the five asset classes wine has the lowest Sharpe ratio.

In an investment portfolio context both asset returns and asset correlations are important, and as can be seen by considering the correlation coefficient information in the fifth column of Table 3, the return to Australian wine is not strongly correlated with the return to other assets. So, despite the relatively poor performance of wine in both risk adjusted terms and

[1]If using systematic risk rather than total risk the comparable metric is the Treynor measure.

raw return terms, wine could still be a valuable addition to an investment portfolio. The potential for there to be a diversification gain from holding wine can be tested using several different approaches. The first approach considered is based on the ideas outlined in slightly different ways in both Blume (1984) and Elton *et al.* (1987) that there would be an incremental diversification benefit from adding wine to an existing asset if the Sharpe ratio for wine is greater than the Sharpe ratio of the existing asset multiplied by the correlation coefficient between wine and the existing asset. As can be seen by considering the final column of Table 3, based on the Blume/Elton *et al.* measure, there is a diversification gain from adding wine to each of the four broad asset classes considered.

One way to visualize the diversification gain from adding wine to an existing asset is to follow Polwitoon and Tawatnuntachai (2008) and form a sequence of portfolios consisting of the benchmark asset and the asset wine, where the allocation to wine starts at zero and increases in small steps; and then plot the change in the Sharpe ratio. As for the sample period the return to Australian bonds was higher than the return to Australian wine and the risk lower, portfolio combinations comprising these two assets provide a good example to focus on when studying diversification gains in a two asset portfolio setting.

Figure 1 plots excess portfolio return, portfolio risk, and the net gain in the Sharpe ratio compared to a pure Australian bond portfolio, where a sequence of Australian wine and Australian bond portfolios are constructed with the weight to wine gradually increasing from 0% to 100%. In the figure

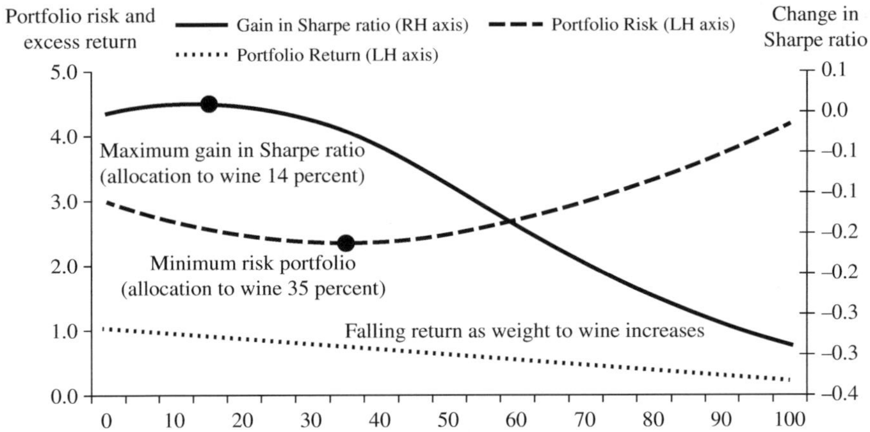

Figure 1. Australian Wine and Bond Portfolio Combinations

risk and excess return information is read off the left axis, and as can be seen, excess portfolio return falls from 1.03% with zero allocation to wine, down to 0.24% with 100% allocation to wine. It can also be seen from Figure 1 that portfolio risk traces a quadratic. The rate of decrease in portfolio risk is equal to the rate of decrease in portfolio return when the allocation to wine is 14%, and it is this point that defines the maximum net gain in the Sharpe ratio from adding Australian wine to an Australian bond portfolio. The plots for pair-wise asset portfolios formed using wine and the other asset classes shown in Table 3 look broadly similar to the result shown in Figure 1.

It is however true that an investor is likely to hold a diversified portfolio of assets rather than a single asset class. As such, it is necessary to consider a more general test of the potential for there to be a diversification gain from holding wine. Mean-variance spanning tests can be used to answer the question of whether or not an investor that currently holds K assets in their portfolio would benefit by adding another asset, or set of assets, to their existing investment portfolio. The Huberman and Kandel (1987) regression based spanning test is a joint test that the intercept equals zero, and that the sum of the β coefficients equal one, in the linear regression $r_t = \alpha + \sum_{i=1}^{k} \beta_i r_{it} + u_t$, where r_t denotes the return to the test asset at time t, r_{it} denotes the return to the benchmark assets at time t, and u_t is a constant variance zero mean error term. If the Huberman and Kandel spanning test restrictions hold, it means the return to the test asset can be written as a linear combination of the existing benchmark assets, plus a zero mean error term. In the current application this would imply that adding wine to the portfolio of existing assets could not raise expected portfolio return, but could only add to portfolio risk. As such, if the restrictions $\alpha = 0$ and $\sum_{i=1}^{K} \beta = 1$ hold, the investor would not add wine to their investment portfolio, and it can be said that wine is dominated, or spanned, by the test assets.

The Huberman and Kandel mean-variance spanning regression was estimated using quarterly return information for the period 1990–2000 where Australian wine was the test asset and the benchmark assets were Australian shares, Australian bonds, US shares, and US bonds. The Wald test statistic for the joint restriction that $\alpha = 0$ and $\sum_{i=1}^{4} \beta = 1$ was 14.3, and strongly significant. The null hypothesis of spanning is therefore rejected. Although the above result suggests wine provides a diversification benefit, before reaching a definitive conclusion there is one further aspect to consider. Unlike standard financial assets, the return to wine has to be estimated, and there is uncertainty surrounding these estimates. The situation is illustrated

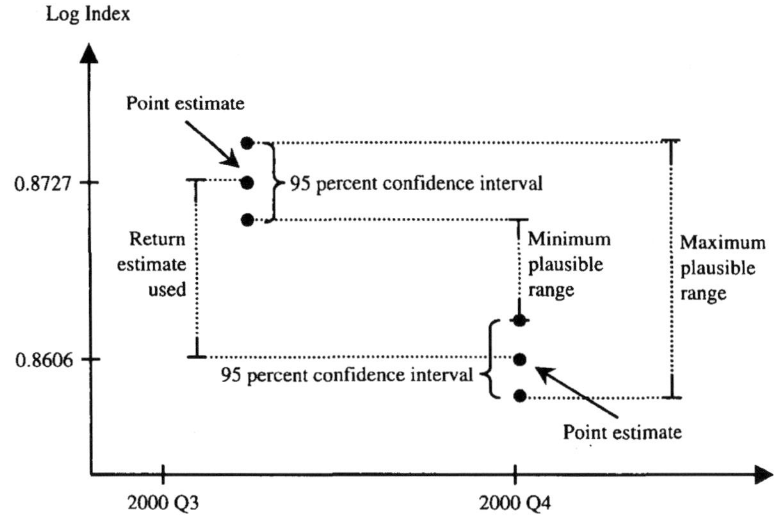

Figure 2. Uncertainty Surrounding Wine Return Estimates

in Figure 2 where the actual estimated index values for 2000Q3 and 2000Q4 are shown, along with estimates of the maximum and minimum plausible range for the change in the index value.

Although using estimated returns is unlikely to have a significant impact on the estimated average return, it does mean that the volatility of the return to wine is likely to be understated. Given this issue, as a final test of the robustness of the result that wine provides a diversification benefit, new wine return estimates were generated as $\hat{\hat{I}}_t = \hat{I}_t + (SE(\hat{I}_t) \times \varphi \times (-1)^t)$ where $\hat{I}_t$ denotes the least squares estimate of the wine price index at time t, $SE(\hat{I}_t)$ denotes the associated standard error, and φ is set at the maximum value consistent with rejecting the hypothesis of mean-variance spanning. The null hypothesis of spanning can be rejected at the 95% confidence level for $\varphi = 0.45$, and with $\varphi = 0.45$ the return to wine is approximately the same as shown in Table 3, but the implied level of risk is 35% higher (5.29%) than reported in Table 3. On balance, it therefore appears reasonable to conclude that in an Australian context, adding wine to an already well diversified investment portfolio provides a further diversification benefit. This finding is consistent with that reported in Masset and Weisskopf (2010) for the U.S. market.

To make tractable the diversification gain attributable to wine where the benchmark portfolio contains several assets, it is helpful to consider only portfolios on the mean-variance efficient frontier. Approaches to finding the

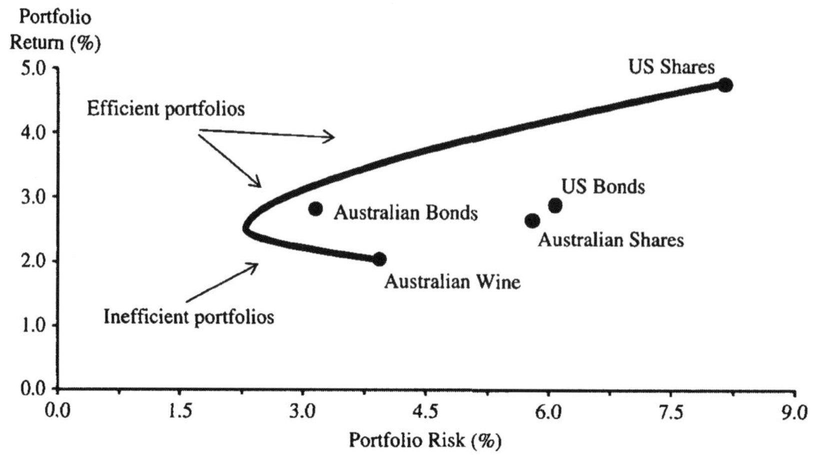

Figure 3. Mean-Variance Efficient Frontier with Wine as an Investment Option

mean-variance efficient frontier have evolved substantially since the concept was proposed by Markowitz (1952), but here the classic approach that uses the covariance matrix and mean return vector with asset weights restricted to non-negative values has been used.[2] The efficient frontier and individual asset risk-return details are shown in Figure 3. The reference portfolio used to calculate the potential diversification gain available from holding wine is the portfolio that generated the highest level of return per unit of risk when wine was not allowed as an investment option. This measure was selected as it is a utility free measure of an optimal portfolio. When wine was excluded from the set of investment options the portfolio that provided the highest return per unit of risk had a quarterly return of 3.10% and risk of 3.15%. The inclusion of wine in the portfolio allowed this same level of return to be achieved with a risk of only 2.94%. So, despite having a relatively low return, including wine as an investment option shifts the efficient frontier to the left.[3]

[2] Alternative approaches include replacing the estimated return vector or covariance matrix with a weighted average of two estimates, where the weights are determined by the data. See Jorion (1985) for an example of the approach applied to expected returns, and Ledoit and Wolf (2003) for a general approach to finding a shrinkage covariance matrix.

[3] Transaction and storage costs when trading wine are much higher than when trading standard financial assets. However, in Australia the profits on the sale of wine are generally tax free. These two effects largely cancel each other out so that when considering after tax and transaction cost return information for the above assets the diversification gain from holding wine is of approximately the same order of magnitude.

5. Conclusions

Over the sample period both the return to Australian wine and the risk adjusted excess return to Australian wine were lower than for standard financial assets. It had previously been proposed that for the investor that wished to drink the wine they store, even when the return to wine is lower than the return to standard financial assets, tax impacts may be such that wine investment remains an attractive option. Given the return information shown in Table 3, and provided the investor has other income such that they face a positive marginal tax rate, this proposition is also true in Australia. Additionally, for the investor that does not intend to drink the wine they hold, the mean-variance spanning test results show that wine investment can provide a diversification benefit that means a positive allocation to wine is worthwhile even if they already have a well diversified investment portfolio. Using the return from the portfolio that provided the highest return per unit of total risk when wine was not allowed as an investment possibility as the reference level of return, a positive allocation to wine was shown to reduce portfolio risk by approximately 6.7%.

Acknowledgments

The author would like to thank Giri Parameswaran and an anonymous referee for several suggestions that helped improve the chapter.

References

Ashenfelter, O., and Graddy, K. (2003). Auctions and the price of art. *Journal of Economic Literature*, 151, 763–786.

Ashenfelter, O., Ashmore, D., and Lalonde, R. (1995). Bordeaux wine vintage quality and the weather. *Chance*, 8, 7–14.

Ashenfelter, O. (2008). Predicting the quality and prices of Bordeaux wine. *The Economic Journal*, 118(529), F174–F184, reprinted in this issue.

Bailey, M.J., Muth, R.F., and Nourse, H.O. (l963). A regression method for real estate price index construction. *Journal of the American Statistical Association*, 58, 933–942.

Blume, M. (1984). The use of "alphas" to improve performance. *Journal of Portfolio Management*, 11, 86–92.

Burton, J., and Jacobsen, J.P. (2001). The rate of return on wine investment. *Economic Inquiry*, 39, 337–350.

Byron, R.P., and Ashenfelter, O. (1995). Predicting the quality of an unborn grange. *Economic Record*, 71, 40–53.

Caillard, A., and Langton, S. (2001). *Langton's Australian Fine Wine Buying and Investment Guide.* Sydney: Media21.

Elton, E.J., Gruber, M.J., and Rentzler, J.C. (1987). Professionally managed, publicly traded commodity funds. *Journal of Business*, 60, 177–199.

Fogarty, J.J. (2006). The return to Australian fine wine. *European Review of Agricultural Economics*, 33, 542–561.

Huberman, G., and Kandel, S. (1987). Mean-variance spanning. *Journal of Finance*, 42, 873–888.

Jaeger, E. (1981). To save or savor: The rate of return to storing wine: Comment. *Journal of Political Economy*, 89, 584–592.

Jorion, P. (1985). International portfolio diversification with estimation risk. *Journal of Business*, 58, 259–278.

Krasker, W.S. (1979). The rate of return to storing wine. *Journal of Political Economy*, 87, 1363–1367.

Lecocq, S., and Visser, M. (2006). Spatial variations in weather conditions and wine prices in Bordeaux. *Journal of Wine Economics*, 1(2), 114–124.

Ledoit, O., and Wolf, M. (2003). Improved estimation of the covariance matrix of stock returns with an application to portfolio selection. *Journal of Empirical Finance*, 10, 603–621.

Markowitz, H. (1952). Portfolio selection. *Journal of Finance*, 7, 77–91.

Masset, P., and Henderson, C. (2010). Wine as an alternative asset class. *Journal of Wine Economics*, 5(1), 87–118.

Masset, P., and Weisskopf, J. (2010). Raise your glass: Wine investment and the financial crisis. *American Association of Wine Economists*, Working Paper No. 57.

Polwitoon, S., and Tawatnuntachai, O. (2008). Emerging market bond funds: A comprehensive analysis. *The Financial Review*, 43, 51–84.

Rosen, S. (1974). Hedonic prices and implicit markets: Product differentiation in pure competition. *Journal of Political Economy*, 82, 34–55.

Sanning, L.W., Shaffer, S., and Sharratt, J.M. (2008). Bordeaux wine as a financial investment. *Journal of Wine Economics*, 3, 51–71.

Weil, R.L. (1993). Do not invest in wine, at least in the U.S., unless you plan to drink it, and maybe not even then. *Paper presented at the 2nd International Conference of the Vineyard Data Quantification Society*, Verona.

Wood, D., and Anderson, K. (2006). What determines the future value of an icon wine? *Journal of Wine Economics*, 1(2), 141–161.

Part V

Wine Tastings and Competitions

Chapter 15

Analyzing a Wine Tasting Statistically*

Orley Ashenfelter† and Richard E. Quandt‡

†*Department of Economics, Princeton University, Princeton, NJ 08540, USA*
C6789@princeton.edu

‡*Department of Economics, Princeton University, Emeritus Princeton, NJ 08544, USA*
Metrics@quandt.com

This chapter discusses the design of wine tasting so as to ensure sensible inferences about wine quality may be inferred from the tasters ratings or rankings. It also proposes some simple statistical techniques for analyzing wine tasting results and implements them on the famous wine tasting comparing California and French wines that is now commonly known as the "Judgment of Paris."

1. Introduction

Wine evaluation has been shrouded in snobbishness for so long that it has become a major source of comedy. As Fran Lebowitz wrote, "Intellectuals talk about ideas: ordinary people talk about things: but boring people talk about wine!" In fact, reports about the evaluation of wine appear in most major newspapers, and there are important publications, like the Wine Spectator, that are devoted to nothing much else. Surprisingly, the reported evaluations of wine, which are subjective in the extreme, are rarely subjected to any serious appraisal. The results of any wine tasting will be solemnly reported, with a winner and a loser being declared, without any concern for whether the results would be replicated the next day (they usually aren't) or for whether there is enough agreement among the evaluators so that any meaningful conclusion may be drawn. After all, if the same wine were served blind in five glasses and the judges did not know this, there would no doubt

*This article originally appeared in *CHANCE* (1999), 12(3), 16–20.

be a first place winner, a last place winner, and everything in between — but the correct conclusion would only be that the judges are variable, not that the wines are different!

The evaluation of wine by a set of appraisers raises many questions about how best to aggregate reported preferences. In fact, many of these issues can and should be raised in other, and to some extent more important, contexts. For example, grant proposals are appraised in subjective peer reviews, diving competitions are subjectively evaluated by judges, and guilt is determined subjectively by juries. Wine appraisal provides a natural, easily replicated, and amusing way to raise and study some important issues.

We relay some of our own experience with wine-tasting evaluations in what follows, and we use this experience to analyze what is arguably the most famous wine tasting ever staged — Stephen Spurrier's famous competition of French versus California wines, conducted on French soil using mostly French judges. Time magazine reported that a California wine had beaten some of France's most famous wines at this wine tasting, and the California wine industry has never been the same. But does a careful analysis verify this result?

2. Do Your Own Wine Tasting (and Circulate the Results!)

After a decade of experience, we think there are three key characteristics that a wine-tasting event should observe to be informative.

1. *Taste the wines blind.* As any experienced taster will admit, identifying wines blind is an incredibly difficult thing to do. As a result, there is no doubt that tasting wines blind is a humbling experience. Perhaps this is why it is resisted. But the failure to taste wines blind leads to terrible biases. Indeed, one of the primary purposes of an independent wine tasting is to test whether common perceptions are really correct. Doing this requires that extraneous information *that reflects the opinions of others* be kept from biasing the tasters. Otherwise, what is the point of creating the wine-tasting event? You might just as well read the score a wine has received in a wine publication and parrot it to everyone who will listen (something which, in our experience, happens all too often!)

2. *Try to keep the tasters' opinions independent.* Wine tasting is a very subjective experience. As a result, even when wines are served blind, the opinions of others often serve as focal points for agreements. For example, a very noticeable feature in many large wine-tasting events is the presence of

"table effects." What seems to happen is that one or two individuals have strong opinions at a table, and this crystallizes the opinions of others. Move some of the same people to a different table and they may have a completely different opinion!

To combat the problem of dependence of tasters, some very professional groups do not permit anyone to speak about the wines until after they have written down their ranking of them. In other groups, including one that we participate with regularly, independence does not seem to require such extreme measures — probably because the tasters in our group revel in disagreement — but even we exercise some discretion in what we say: that is, somebody might say "I think one of the wines is slightly oxidized" rather than "wine C is slightly oxidized."

3. *Analyze the results of the wine tasting systematically.* In their pioneering book, *Wines: Their Sensory Evaluation*, Amerine and Roessler (1983) set out the details of how one should summarize the results of a wine tasting and draw conclusions from it. The basic scientific presumption from which they started is that *human behavior is not perfectly predictable.* Among those with considerable experience with wine tasting, this is hardly a controversial assumption. As Steven Spurrier stated, in reference to the famous tasting of French versus California wines that he hosted in 1976. "The results of a blind tasting cannot be predicted and will not even be reproduced the next day by the same panel tasting the same wines."

Although there has often been broad agreement with the goals of

...a winner and a loser being declared, without any concern for whether the results would be replicated the next day...

Amerine and Roessler, the technical expertise required to implement their approach is far too formidable for most wine lovers, especially when it has to be implemented during a wine-tasting event. (There is alcohol in wine!) So here is what we have done: We have created a software package that will compile the preferences expressed at a wine tasting, analyze the results, and then create a written and comprehensible permanent report of the event. (To see how this software performs, consult our Web site *www.liquidasset.com.*) We have been using this software at wine-tasting events over the past few years, and it has become an invaluable tool and recordkeeping device. To show how it works, we have reanalyzed the most famous wine-tasting event of all time — and with some surprising results.

3. Analyzing the Results of the Paris Tasteoff of 1976 (Did the California Cabernet Really Win?)

The often-discussed French versus California wine challenge took place in Paris in May of 1976. As luck would have it, a *Time* magazine reporter was present to broadcast the results to an eager U.S. audience celebrating the 200th anniversary of the founding of their nation. And the results were shocking: In the presence of distinguished competition, on French soil, and in a blind tasting, the French judges had voted that a California cabernet had defeated its Bordeaux challengers. And a California chardonnay had defeated its Burgundy challengers too.

The Tasting. The complete details of the cabernet tasting, including the scores awarded by each judge to each wine, are contained in Table 1, which is, in turn, cut out of the report written by our *LIQUID ASSETS Winetaster* software. (We transcribed the original data from the *Connoisseurs Guide To California Wine*, July 1976.) As we shall see, not everything reported by the press about this event has been accurate.

The wines were marked against a maximum score of 20. The judges were a distinguished group. Apart from Steven Spurrier and Patricia Gallagher, whose l'Academic du Vin sponsored the event, it included the late Odette Kahn, editor of the *Revue du Vin de France*, the distinguished Jean-Claude

Table 1. The Famous 1976 Tasting: California Cabernet Sauvignon vs. Bordeaux

Number of judges = 11
Number of wines = 10

Identification of the wine	The judges' average grade (out of 20)
Wine A is Stag's Leap Clr. '73 (CA)	14.14
Wine B is Mouton '70 (FR)	14.09
Wine C is Montrose '70 (FR)	13.64
Wine D is Haut Brion '70 (FR)	13.23
Wine E is Ridge Mt.Bello '71 (CA)	12.14
Wine F is Leoville-Las-Cases '71 (FR)	11.18
Wine G is Heitz Martha's '70 (CA)	10.36
Wine H is Clos du Val '72 (CA)	10.14
Wine I is Mayacamas '71 (CA)	9.77
Wine J is Freemark Abbey '69 (CA)	9.64

The judges' grades	Wine									
Judge	A	B	C	D	E	F	G	H	I	J
P. Brejoux	14.0	16.0	12.0	17.0	13.0	10.0	12.0	14.0	5.0	7.0
A. de Villaine	15.0	14.0	16.0	15.0	9.0	10.0	7.0	5.0	12.0	7.0
Michel Dovaz	10.0	15.0	11.0	12.0	12.0	10.0	11.0	11.0	8.0	15.0
Pat. Gallagher	14.0	15.0	14.0	12.0	16.0	14.0	17.0	13.0	9.0	15.0
Odette Kahn	15.0	12.0	12.0	12.0	7.0	12.0	2.0	2.0	13.0	5.0
Ch. Millau	16.0	16.0	17.0	13.5	7.0	11.0	8.0	9.0	9.5	9.0
Ray. Oliver	14.0	12.0	14.0	10.0	12.0	12.0	10.0	10.0	14.0	8.0
Steven Spurrier	14.0	14.0	14.0	8.0	14.0	12.0	13.0	11.0	9.0	13.0
Pierre Tari	13.0	11.0	14.0	14.0	17.0	12.0	15.0	13.0	12.0	14.0
Ch. Vanneque	16.5	16.0	11.0	17.0	15.5	8.0	10.0	16.5	3.0	6.0
J.-C. Vrinat	14.0	14.0	15.0	15.0	11.0	12.0	9.0	7.0	13.0	7.0
Average Grade	14.1	14.1	13.6	13.2	12.1	11.2	10.4	10.1	9.8	9.6

The judges' rankings	Wine										Corr. with group
Judge	A	B	C	D	E	F	G	H	I	J	
P. Brejoux	3.5	2.0	6.5	1.0	5.0	8.0	6.5	3.5	10.0	9.0	0.46
A. de Villaine	2.5	4.0	1.0	2.5	7.0	6.0	8.5	10.0	5.0	8.5	0.70
Michel Dovaz	8.5	1.5	6.5	3.5	3.5	8.5	5.0	6.5	10.0	1.5	−0.07
Pat. Gallagher	6.0	3.5	6.0	9.0	2.0	6.0	1.0	8.0	10.0	3.5	−0.09

(*Continued*)

Table 1. (*Continued*)

The judges' rankings					Wine						Corr. with group
Judge	A	B	C	D	E	F	G	H	I	J	
Odette Kahn	1.0	4.5	4.5	4.5	7.0	4.5	9.5	9.5	2.0	8.0	0.29
Ch. Millau	2.5	2.5	1.0	4.0	10.0	5.0	9.0	7.5	6.0	7.5	0.61
Ray. Oliver	2.0	5.0	2.0	8.0	5.0	5.0	8.0	8.0	2.0	10.0	0.25
Steven Spurrier	2.5	2.5	2.5	10.0	2.5	7.0	5.5	8.0	9.0	5.5	0.47
Pierre Tari	6.5	10.0	4.0	4.0	1.0	8.5	2.0	6.5	8.5	4.0	−0.15
Ch. Vanneque	2.5	4.0	6.0	1.0	5.0	8.0	7.0	2.5	10.0	9.0	0.42
J.-C. Vrinat	3.5	3.5	1.5	1.5	7.0	6.0	8.0	9.5	5.0	9.5	0.65
Group ranking	1	3	2	4	5	7	6	10	9	8	
Votes against	41.0	43.0	41.5	49.0	55.0	72.5	70.0	79.5	77.5	76.0	

(11 is the best possible votes against total, 110 is the worst)

Based on the ranks the wines were preferred by the judges in the following order:

1. 1st place Wine A, Stag's Leap Wine Cellars '73 (CA)
2. 2nd place Wine C, Montrose '70 (FR)
3. 3rd place Wine B, Mouton 70 (FR)
4. 4th place Wine D, Haul Brion '70 (FR)
5. 5th place Wine E, Ridge Monte Bello '71 (CA)
6. 6th place Wine G, Heitz Martha's '70 (CA)
7. 7th place Wine F, Leoville-Las-Cases '71 (FR)
8. 8th place Wine J, Freemark Abbey '69 (CA)
9. 9th place Wine I, Mayacamas '71 (CA)
10. 10th place Wine H, Clos du Val '72 (CA)

Vrinat of the Restaurant Taillevent, the late Raymond Oliver of the restaurant Le Grand Vefour, the sommelier Christian Vanneque of Tour D'Argent, Aubert de Villaine of the Domaine de la Romanee-Conti, Pierre Tari of Chateau Giscours, Pierre Brejoux of the Institute of Appellations of Origin, Michel Dovaz of the Wine Institute of France, and Christian Millau of the eponymous restaurant guide.

The Results. The first thing to notice about this event is that, despite what is usually reported, not all of the judges were French! The scores of Englishman Steven Spurrier and his partner Patricia Gallagher were, in fact, counted in arriving at the results.

The second thing to notice is that the scoring is based on a simple averaging of the numerical grades. As Steven Spurrier acknowledged in Decanter magazine in August 1996, he tallied the winners by "adding the judges marks and dividing this by eleven (which I was told later was statistically meaningless)." The problem with this approach is, of course, that it may give greater weight to judges who put a great deal of scatter into their numerical scores and thus express strong preferences by numerical differences. It is for precisely this reason that, in a typical athletic competition with multiple judges, the judges' numerical scores are converted to ranks before the winners are tallied. Converting the grades to ranks guarantees that each judge has the same influence on the outcome. Absent this, the judge who grades wines from, say, 1 to 20 will have a far greater influence on the outcome than a judge who grades the wines on the same scale but uses only the scores 19 and 20.

To see the problem, suppose there were two wines, A and B, to be scored by two tasters. Suppose the first judge scored wine A with a 1 and scored wine B with a 20, but that the second taster scored the same wines 20 and 19. The average score of the first wine would be 10.5 and the average

score of the second wine would be 19.5. In fact, however, the first wine was preferred by the second taster, while the second wine was preferred by the first taster, so there is no clear group preference. However, we are aware of the fact that ranks can be problematic, because they ignore big and small differences. Grades become a more effective answer to this problem if each judge's grades are divided by the sum of that judge's grades.

In the table, we have also shown the conversion of the judges' scores to ranks, and we also provide the group ranking. The method recommended by Amerine and Roessler for computing the group ranking is to count the "points against." This is done by simply adding the sum of the rankings for each wine. Since there were 11 judges, the best score obtainable would then be 11 first place votes, or 11 "points against." Since there were 10 wines in total, the worst score obtainable would be 11 tenth place votes, or 110 "points against." As the table indicates, the best score achieved was actually 41 (for the 1973 Stag's Leap Wine Cellars California cabernet). So, it was no mistake for Steven Spurrier to declare the California cabernet the winner. (Whew!) The worst score (of 79.5 points against), however, was for the 1972 Clos du Val California cabernet, and this is not the wine that was placed last using the average of the judges' numerical grades. As the table indicates, there is a loose agreement between the ranking of the wines using the average grade and the average rank awarded by the judge, but it is far from perfect.

It is painfully obvious from the table that there was considerable disagreement on the ranking of the wines by the individual judges. This is common in virtually all carefully conducted wine tastings. In fact, to most experienced wine tasters complete agreement is a suspicious sign of collusion!

Despite the disagreement among the judges, there is also considerable evidence of concordance. The value for Kendall's coefficient of concordance is 0.2417, which is statistically significant at the 006 test level. This establishes that there is enough concordance among the tasters that it makes sense to believe that the resulting ranking is not just a product of random chance. A loose grouping of the wines based on an inspection of the "votes against" suggests that the wines may be grouped into three categories. At the top are the 1973 Stag's Leap cabernet, the 1970 Montrose, and the 1970 Mouton. The second group contains the 1970 Haut Brion and the 1971 Ridge Montebello, while the third group contains the remaining wines.

Providing measures of the reliability of the individual rankings of the wines, based on statistical criteria, is considerably more complicated. If we decided *in advance* that we wished to test whether a particular wine was

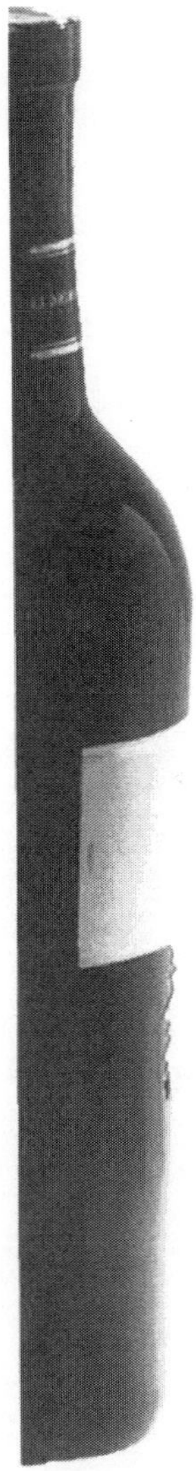

better (or worse) that the others, a straightforward test would be based on the sum of the points against. A Kramer, in the journal *Food Technology* (1956), tabulated the 2% and 10% critical values for testing the null hypothesis that the *pre-selected* wine is significantly better (or worse) that the others. This test would be appropriate if, for example, a winemaker wished to test whether his wine would be judged differently from a reference set. Applying the data on the Paris Tasting and using the 10% level, both the 1973 Stag's Leap cabernet and the 1970 Montrose would have been judged better than the others, but the 1972 Clos du Val cabernet would have been judged worse.

This test is not appropriate, however, when the wine for testing has not been preselected. This was noted by Kramer and R.A. Bradly in 1957, also in *Food Technology.* Because of the *a posteriori* character of the comparisons being made, wider critical values are required. Such values were provided by Kramer in a 1960 *Food Technology* article (with minor corrections in 1963, again in *Food Technology*). For the data on the Paris Tasting, neither the best (nor the worst) wine would be judged significantly better (or worse) than the others, according to Kramer's criterion.

It can be argued that Kramer's *a posteriori* criterion is too conservative because it considers either the smallest or largest rank sum *separately,* rather than considering both the smallest and largest rank sums *simultaneously.* A more detailed analysis would, for example, evaluate the probability that, by chance alone, the smallest rank sum would be 41 or less AND the largest rank sum would be 79.5 or more. Such an analysis has, to the best of our knowledge, never been done. We hope that some interested reader may be concouraged to undertake it!

Converting the grades to ranks guarantees that each judge has the same influence on the outcome.

Judging the Judges. It is also useful to consider how successful the judges were in appraising the wines. One measure of the success of a judge is the extent to which an individual judge's ranking is a good predictor of the group's ranking (where the group's ranking excludes the particular judge in question). To calculate these correlations, we took the judges one at a time, calculated the average rank assigned to the wines by the remaining judges, converted these average to proper ranks, and then calculated Spearman's ρ between the ranking of the particular judge in question and the "average ranking" of the others. By this measure the judges would be ordered as follows (from best predictor to worst): A. de Villaine (0.70 correlation), J.-C. Vrinat (0.65), Ch. Millau (0.61), Steven Spurrier (0.47), Pierre Brejoux (0.46), Ch. Vanneque (0.42), Odette Kahn (0.29), and Raymond Oliver (0.25). Ironically, the preferences of the remaining judges (Dovaz, Gallagher, and Tari), two of whom were French, are unrelated to the group preference.

4. Further Reading

If you taste wines systematically in a group, we hope you will consider circulating the results to others. For the last year we have been posting the results of wine tasting evaluations at our Web site, www.liquidasset.com. Our *LIQUID ASSETS Winetaster* software tabulates the results of a tasting and writes a report in html that can be readily uploaded. (WARNING) Although our software is "plural," our Web site is "singular," not to be confused with the completely unrelated www.liquidassets.com.

If you would like to see a newsletter that uses good analytical practice in reporting the results of its wine tastings, we suggest you take at look at the *California Grapevine* (P.O. Box 22152, San Diego, CA 92192-9973, tel. (619)457-4818; $32 per year, or ask for a sample copy). Edited by engineer N. Ponomareff, this newsletter is primarily a carefully annotated list of California wine-tasting results analyzed by the methods available in the *LIQUID ASSETS Winetaster* software. There should be more publications just like it.

An indispensable analytical book for anyone seriously interested in the sensory evaluation of wine is Maynard Amerine and Edward Roessler, *Wines: Their Sensory Evaluation*, W.H. Freeman, 1983. This book is an extremely rewarding discussion of many of the most important issues raised in wine-tasting evaluations. Other fascinating works include a full Bayesian analysis of wine tasting applied to the 1976 French tasting data in Dennis Lindley's (unpublished) "The Analysis of a Wine-Tasting" and frequentist Richard Quandt's "Measurement and Inference in Wine Tasting" prepared for presentation at the Meetings of the Vineyard Data Quantification Society in Ajaccio, Corsica, on October 2–3, 1998. Both papers and details on the Winetaster software are available at the web site: www.liquidasset.com.

Finally, the Vineyard Data Quantification Society (which has the felicitous acronym VDQS) is a loose group of economists, statisticians, and other professionals who meet annually for the presentation of papers that quantitatively analyze all aspects of the production and distribution of wine. To inquire about membership, or to obtain copies of the papers presented at earlier meetings, contact Marie-Claude Pichery at the University of Bourgogne (email marie-claude.pichery) (au-bourgognr.fr). We have attended VDQS meetings in Verona. Thessaloniki, and Corsica, and they can be great fun — and yes, they even serve wine at lunch during these meetings!

Chapter 16

On Designing Experiments and Analyzing Data to Assess the Reliability and Accuracy of Blind Wine Tastings*

Domenic V. Cicchetti

Yale Home Office, 94 Linsley Lake Road,
North Branford, CT 06471, USA
dom.cicchetti@yale.edu

The author discusses reliability research designs and data analytic strategies that are required in future wine competitions. The sources of variations that are identified and need to be controlled in order to increase both the reliability and, to the extent possible, accuracy of wine tasting evaluations derive from two literature sources, wine research and biostatistical research. These sources of variation include: the manner in which the sample of wine tasters is selected; the type of *a priori* screen required to eliminate inconsistent wine tasters before the competition begins; a careful selection of the specific wine characteristics that the tasters are required to utilize, with specific criteria provided to the tasters; the selection of well defined wine measurement scales; the selection of appropriate wine glasses for the tastings; and the application of appropriate state-of-the-art statistics to analyze the data deriving from the wine competitions.

1. Introduction

In a previous article (Cicchetti, 2004), there was mention of some of the necessary ingredients that one might expect to comprise the design and data analytic strategies of future blind wine tasting competitions. The purpose of this companion piece is to elaborate upon such ideas. Here we shall focus upon both the reliability, and to the extent possible, the validity or accuracy of blind wine tasting. In a more specific sense, the goal is to reduce, as much as is possible, the extent of inter-judge variability in the evaluation of any

*This article originally appeared in *Journal of Wine Research* (2004), 15(3), 221–226.

given wine, on any given characteristic (e.g., color, intensity, aroma, and acidity).

The following sections of the report derive from two areas: first, relevant articles published in wine research; and second, pertinent articles deriving from psychometric research, specifically that body of extant literature that focuses upon data analytic strategies for assessing reliability and accuracy of human judgment. The objective here is to apply what can be learned from both these sources of information to inform the research design and data analytic approach of future wine studies.

2. Identifying Major Sources of Inter-judge (Wine Taster) Variability

Based upon the wine literature, the following sources of variability can and do impinge upon how well one can expect independent judges to agree in their evaluations of the characteristics of red and white wines, broadly defined. The wine literature reveals the following sources of inter-taster variation: the definition of what constitutes an appropriate sample of wine tasters; the specific characteristics upon which the wines are to be evaluated; the scales of measurement that will be used to evaluate the selected wines in a given flight; the specific criteria that are to be used by the wine tasters to assess each wine characteristic; and the type of wine glasses to be used by the tasters and their effects upon the perception of specific wine characteristics. Based upon the relevant biostatistical literature, one can derive the following additional sources of inter-taster variability in the evaluations of given flights of wine: using appropriate state-of-the-art data analytic strategies: to screen out unreliable tasters *a priori*; to assess overall inter-taster reliability (and, to the extent possible), accuracy; to distinguish the most from the least reliable subsets of wine tasters; measuring the extent to which the more reliable tasters remain so in future wine competitions; and finally, reducing the inter-taster variability still further by utilizing the wine expertise of the more reliable wine tasters to train other oenophiles to reach the same or similar levels of reliability.

Each of these issues will now be discussed in more detail.

2.1. *Carefully define or delineate the sample of wine tasters*

Many factors figure in the selection of an appropriate sample of wine judges for a given tasting event or wine competition. As noted by Cliff and King

(1996), judge selection is particularly important since the credibility of the competition is dependent upon the professionalism of the judges. Judge selection committees, however, consider other factors besides technical expertise and wine knowledge (Rankine, 1974; Amerine and Roessler, 1983) when recruiting judges. For example, there is often a requirement for judges to have an international reputation and/or a connection with wine journalism in order to enhance the credibility of the competition and to gain additional publicity.

It also seems to follow that given the known wide variability in judges' rating of any given quality of any given wine, one would indeed be wise to begin with experienced wine tasters. The logic here is that the extent of agreement among experienced tasters should be somewhat higher than that among less experienced tasters.

2.2. *Reduce the inter-judge variability* a priori *by a simple screening test*

One can further reduce the variability, even among experienced wine tasters, by designing an experiment in which each taster is required to evaluate, on two separate occasions, the same flight of wines, presented both times in random order. This reliability design was introduced three decades ago by Detre *et al.* (1975) as a screen for selecting among cardiologists to interpret coronary angiograms. The logic here was that if a given cardiologist could not agree satisfactorily with his/her own previous assessments, then she/he could hardly be expected to agree with the independent assessments of the same angiograms by other cardiologists. The same should apply to independent blind tastings of wine.

2.3. *Carefully specify or control the characteristics upon which the wines are to be evaluated*

As one specific example of how this source of variability is reduced, judges are forced to focus upon specific wine characteristics, rather than rating in an uncontrolled global manner. In the design of one recent tasting, Cain (2004, p. 14) reported that three judges were asked, independently, to score each of a number of flights of wines on the following characteristics: "color and clarity, aroma and bouquet, body and flavor." As is quite common, judges used a 20-point scale in which higher scores denoted higher perceived quality of any of these three characteristics.

2.4. *Select well delineated scales of measurement*

In the heralded 1976 blind wine tasting of French Bordeaux and California Cabernets (see Cicchetti, 2004), a global wine rating scale, consisting of 20 points, was used by wine tasters to evaluate the overall perceived quality of each of 10 red wines.

Subsequently, several modifications of this global 20-point scale have been published (Amerine and Roessler (1980, 1983) and the British Columbia Vintners Quality Alliance, as described by Cliff and King (1996)). These more detailed instruments allow not only for an overall global assessment of a given wine, but also for more specific evaluations that include such attributes as a wine's appearance and color (scored 0–2), aroma and bouquet (0–6), total acidity (0–1), balance (0–2), body (0–1), flavor (0–3), and finish (0–2). This methodological improvement was designed to begin to separate the overall variability in a wine's quality from its variability on more specific and meaningful characteristics.

2.5. *Developing specific criteria for tasting judgments*

In the broader field of biobehavioral research, it is essentially axiomatic that any clinical instrument be designed to provide very specific criteria to distinguish various stages of a person's development or a person's stage of illness. Such specific criteria enhance the probability that independently derived evaluations by different clinical examiners will concur and thereby provide evidence for acceptable levels of the reliability of a given assessment or diagnostic instrument.

Cliff and King (1996) utilized this very principle by providing written descriptions of each attribute a given wine judge scored in the application of a modified Amerine and Roessler scale. As one example, each judge was given the following specific criteria for evaluating *aroma* and *bouquet*.

- 6 = extraordinary. Unmistakable characteristic aroma of grape variety or wine type. Outstanding and complex bouquet. Exceptional balance or aroma bouquet.
- 5 = very good. Characteristic aroma. Complex bouquet. Well balanced.
- 4 = good. Characteristic aroma. Distinguishable bouquet.
- 3 = pleasant. Slight aroma and bouquet, but pleasant.
- 2 = acceptable. No perceptible aroma or bouquet.

- 1 = poor. With slight off odors.
- 0 = objectionable. Objectionable with off odors.

2.6. *Choosing appropriate wine glasses for tasting red and white wines*

Up until rather recently, the use of a given glass for a given wine varietal was based upon tradition, anecdotal evidence and subjectivity, the latter caused by "testing" its usefulness in an open rather than a blind context (Cliff *et al.*, 2000). In her classic research design (Canadian oenology students blinded to the types of wine and glasses), Cliff *et al.* (2000) was able to demonstrate strong linear relationships between such wine characteristics as total intensity and color, and the physical dimensions of the glasses: opening diameter, maximum diameter (cuppa), height and volume. As Cliff (2001) correctly concludes, her research supports the use of a specific type of glass to evaluate a specific varietal of wine.

2.7. *Utilizing appropriate data analytic strategies to assess the reliability and accuracy of all judges' evaluations of wines*

A more subtle and not always realized source of variability that needs to be controlled in the design of future wine competitions is the application of appropriate state-of-the-art data analytic strategies. In Cicchetti (2004) it was shown that the application of non-parametric statistics to assess the results of the 1976 U.S. and French red wine competition resulted in inaccurate conclusions as to who "won" the competition. Because of this serious problem, the recommendation is made again that parametric statistics are to be preferred to their non-parametric counterparts whenever possible or that if non-parametric statistics are to be applied, they should be undertaken with parametric analyses as well.

It was argued (again, Cicchetti, 2004) that the statistic of choice to assess the reliability of judges' blind tasting of wines was the intraclass correlation coefficient (R_i), devised by Bartko (1966, 1974). While there are a number of different models of R_i, depending upon the specifics of the reliability research design, two of them would be statistics of choice for assessing the inter-judge (inter-taster) reliability of wine ratings. The first of these would apply when the same set of judges rates each of the wines in a given competition (here designated as $R_{i(\text{same})}$); the second would apply if the same number of tasters evaluated each wine in a competition, but a given set did not always consist of the same group of tasters (here designated as $R_{i(\text{different})}$). Their formulae, deriving from one-way and two-way analysis of variance designs, respectively, are as follows:

$$R_{i(\text{same})} = \frac{\text{MSS} - \text{MSE}}{[k(\text{MSJ} - \text{MSE})]/[\text{MSS} + (\text{MSE})(k-1) + \mathcal{N}]} \tag{1}$$

where MSS = mean square between subjects (wines), MSE = mean square error (or residual), MSJ = mean square between judges (tasters), k = number of judges (tasters) and $\mathcal{N}$ = number of subjects (wines).

A simplified formula for $R_{i(\text{different})}$ is:

$$R_{i(\text{different})} = \frac{\text{SSS} - \text{SSE}}{\text{SSS} + \text{SSE}} \tag{2}$$

where SSS = sums of squares between subjects (wines) and SSE = sums of squares within subjects (wines).

Schuck (2004) has recently demonstrated that except in the most extreme and unlikely of circumstances, these two models will produce very similar results. My own rater reliability research, over a period of nearly three decades, strongly supports this conclusion. Thus, in my reanalysis of the reliability of the 1976 French and U.S. blind tasting of red Bordeaux and California Cabernets, the reliability coefficient produced by $R_{i(\text{same})}$, or 0.22, was indistinguishable from that of 0.21 produced by the application of $R_{i(\text{different})}$.

Given an overall level of reliability among wine tasters that is less than optimal (<0.40 by agreed upon biostatistical and clinical criteria, e.g., Cicchetti, 2001; Fleiss *et al.*, 2003), the research question becomes: "How representative of the overall reliability level is the reliability level of each of the designated group of wine tasters *vis-à-vis* each other?"

2.8. *Utilizing appropriate data analytic strategies to distinguish the most from the least reliable subsets of judges (wine tasters)*

Is a reliability level as low as 0.22 reflective of a specific tendency for each of the tasters to be inconsistent in her/his wine evaluations? Or, rather, is there a masking effect that blurs what is really happening at a more molecular level? One posits here, as an alternative hypothesis, that there are two distinct or well differentiated subsets of wine tasters: one highly consistent or highly reliable; the other highly inconsistent, therefore highly unreliable. In such a situation, the averaging of these two reliability phenomena, in the form of their respective subset reliability levels, would result in a masking effect that was the etiological agent in producing the overall low and unacceptable level of inter-taster reliability.

Since one can expect to find considerable variability in the overall reliability of the most sophisticated of wine connoisseurs in a given wine tasting (see Cicchetti, 2004), it becomes important to develop and utilize a data analytic strategy that can separate out two subsets of wine tasters from among the total number of tasters, such that one subset will show higher reliability levels relative to the second subset — whenever this indeed is the case.

The technique that was alluded to briefly (Cicchetti, 2004) will now be described in sufficient detail so that it can be utilized in future wine competitions.

The method was previously developed by the author for use in some research involving an assessment of the inter-examiner reliability of the global assessment functioning of patients classified as mentally retarded (Oliver *et al.*, 2003). The steps in the process are as follows.

(1) Using an appropriate computer program (i.e., Cicchetti and Showalter, 1988), obtain the overall as well as separate R_i levels for each possible pairing of wine tasters. The number of such paired comparisons, with WT referring to wine tasters, is determined by the formula WT(WT−1)/2, so that if there were 11 wine tasters, as in Cicchetti (2004), there would be 55 R_i pairings.
(2) Rank-order each of the R_i pairs from lowest to highest.
(3) Obtain the median R_i or the 28th pairing.
(4) The more reliable subset of wine tasters will have R_i values above the median, while the less reliable raters/tasters will fall below the median. Consistent with this information, the more reliable raters will have a higher frequency of R_i values that are acceptable (0.40–1.00) than will the less reliable tasters, who will show more values in the <0.40 range.
(5) After the two sets of wine tasters have been identified, one performs an R_i for each of the two subsets. In our case (see again, Cicchetti, 2004), the respective subset R_i coefficients were 0.69 (good agreement) for the more highly reliable wine tasters and 0.31 (poor agreement) for the less reliable subset of wine tasters.

But even after the serious wine researcher has carefully examined and sought in earnest to control each of the sources of variation just identified, there still remains another major potential source of variability that needs to be examined.

2.9. *Testing whether the more reliable tasters remain so in future competitions*

Would they indeed prove to be the most consistent wine tasters in the next follow-up wine competition? To the extent that they are not, the wine research scientist would be forced to examine why this proved to be the case. To the extent that the most consistent wine tasters remain so over future wine tastings and/or competitions, we can seriously entertain the prospect of utilizing their wine tasting expertise to train others in the field to obtain similar levels of reliability in future blind wine tastings.

Acknowledgment

A preliminary version of this research was presented at the Second Hawaiian International Statistical Conference in Honolulu, HI, 6 June 2003.

References

Amerine, M.A., and Roessler, E.B. (1980). *Wines: Their Sensory Evaluation.* New York: F.H. Freeman.

Amerine, M.A., and Roessler, E.B. (1983). *Wines: Their Sensory Evaluation.* 2nd edn. New York: W.H. Freeman.

Bartko, J.J. (1966). The intraclass correlation coefficient as a measure of reliability. *Psychological Reports*, 19, 3–11.

Bartko, J.J. (1974). Corrective note: "The intraclass correlation coefficient as a measure of reliability." *Psychological Reports*, 34, 418.

Cain, A.B. (2004). Anatomy of a wine judging. *Tasters' Guild*, Summer, 14 and 30.

Cicchetti, D.V. (2001). The precision of reliability and validity estimates re-visited: Distinguishing between clinical and statistical significance of sample size requirements. *Journal of Clinical and Experimental Neuropsychology*, 23, 695–700.

Cicchetti, D.V. (2004). Who won the 1976 blind wine tasting of French Bordeaux and US Cabernets? Parametrics to the rescue. *Journal of Wine Research*, 15, 211–220.

Cicchetti, D.V., and Showalter, D. (1988). A computer program for determining the reliability of dimensionally scaled data when the numbers and specific sets of examiners may vary at each assessment. *Educational and Psychological Measurement*, 48, 717–720.

Cliff, M.A., and King, M.A. (1996). A proposed approach for evaluating expert judge performance using descriptive statistics. *Journal of Wine Research*, 7, 83–90.

Cliff, M.A., O'mahony, M., Fukomoto, L., and King, M.C. (2000). Development of a "bipolar" R-index. *Journal of Sensory Studies*, 15, 219–229.

Detre, K.M., Wright, E., Murphy, M.L., and Takaro, T. (1975). Observer agreement in evaluating coronary angiograms. *Circulation*, 52, 979–986.

Fleiss, J.L., Levin, B., and Paik, M.C. (2003). *Statistical Methods for Rates and Proportions.* 3rd edn. New York: Wiley.

Oliver, P., Cooray, S., Tyrer, P., and Cicchetti, D.V. (2003). Use of the global assessment of function scale in learning disability. *British Journal of Psychiatry,* 182 (Supplement 44), s32–s35.

Rankine, B.C. (1974). Wine tasting and judging. *Food Technology in Australia,* 26, 443–453.

Schuck, P. (2004). Assessing reproducibility for interval data in health-related quality of life questionnaires: Which coefficient should be used? *Quality of Life Research,* 13, 571–586.

Chapter 17

Measurement and Inference in Wine Tasting*

Richard E. Quandt

Department of Economics,
Princeton University, Emeritus Princeton, NJ 08544, USA
metrics@quandt.com

This chapter has three basic objectives: (1) to discuss and analyze the subtleties of ranking wines in blind tastings, (2) to analyze the degree of agreement or disagreement among the tasters (judges), and (3) to shed some light on the problem of identifying the wines and to determine when the identifications of the judges might be called statistically significant. The first issue utilizes the rank sums or the related measure, "votes against," and discusses the appropriateness of a statistical test introduced by Kramer. The second introduces Kendall's W coefficient of concordance and discusses some other, related measures. The third derives the finite sample distribution of the number of correct identifications under the null hypothesis of random identifications, from which critical values can be obtained, both for the case in which each wine has to be identified exactly and the case in which there is a small number of different types of wine that have to be identified.

1. Introduction

Numerous situations exist in which several judges rate a set of objects. Common professional situations in which this occurs are certain types of athletic competitions (figure skating, diving) in which performance is measured not by the clock but by "form" and "artistry," and consumer product evaluations, such as those conducted by *Consumer Reports*, in which a large number of different brands of certain items are compared for performance. Some of these may be items where certain objective measures of performance do exist (such as gas barbecue grills, air conditioners, etc.), (Consumer Union

*This article originally appeared in *Journal of Wine Economics* (2006), 1(1), 7–30.

of United States, 1998). But others may be evaluated purely on the basis of subjective taste sensations, such as orange juice, spaghetti sauce, and the like. These situations are characterized by the fact that a truly "objective" measure of quality is missing, and thus quality can be assayed only on the basis of the (subjective) impressions of judges.

The tasting of wine is, of course, an entirely analogous situation. While there are objective predictors of the quality of wine, which utilize variables such as sunshine and rainfall during the growing season (see e.g., Ashenfelter *et al.*, 1995), they would be difficult to apply to a sample of wines representing many small vineyards exposed to identical weather conditions, such as might be the case in Burgundy, and would not in any event be able to predict the impact on wine quality of a faulty cork. Hence, wine tasting is an important example in which judges rate a set of objects.

In principle, ratings can be either "blind" or "not blind," although it may be difficult to imagine how a skating competition could be judged without the judges knowing the identities of the contestants. But whenever possible, blind ratings are preferable, because they remove one important aspect of inter-judge variation that most people would claim is irrelevant, and in fact harmful to the results, namely "brand loyalty." Thus, wine bottles are typically covered in blind tastings or wines are decanted, and identified only with code names such as **A, B,** etc.[1] But even blind tastings do not remove all sources of unwanted variation. When we ask judges to take a position as to which wine is best, second best and so on, we cannot control for the fact that some people like tannin or are offended by traces of oxidation more than others. Another source of variation is that some judge might rate a wine on the basis of how it tastes *now*, while another judge rates the wine on how he or she thinks the wine might taste *at its peak*.[2]

Wine tastings can generate data from which we can learn about the characteristics of both the wines and the judges. In Section 2, we concentrate on what the ratings of wines can tell us about the wines themselves, while in

[1]In informal wine tastings, it may be difficult to remove all traces of this effect if, for example, the organizer of the wine tasting. who is responsible for decanting bottles and assigning code letters to them, participates in the tasting. Even if he makes no effort to remember which code letter corresponds to which wine, it may well be the case that some residual memory affects his ratings.

[2]In order to eliminate this source of variation, the iron-clad rule in one wine-tasting group is that wines must be judged by how they taste *at the time of the tasting, with no regard to how they might taste in the future.* But it is obvious that this rule is difficult to enforce. Another difficulty is that the wines may often have different tastes at different time intervals after the bottles have been opened.

Section 3 we deal with what the ratings can tell us about the judges. Both sets of questions are interesting and can utilize straightforward statistical procedures. Finally, in Section 4 we consider the problem of correctly identifying wines in a blind tasting and devise some procedures for testing the statistical significance of such identifications.

2. The Rating of Wines

First of all, we note that there is no cardinal measure by which we can rate wines. Two scales for rating are in common use: (1) the well-known ordinal rank-scale, by which wines are assigned ranks $1, 2, \ldots, n$, and (2) a "grade"-scale, such as the well-publicized ratings by Robert Parker based on 100 points.[3] The grade scale has some of the aspects of a cardinal scale, in that intervals are interpreted to have meaning, but is not a cardinal scale in the sense in which a measure of weights is one.

Ranking Wines. We shall assume that there are m judges and n wines; hence a table of ranks is an $m \times n$ table and for $m = 4$ and $n = 3$ might appear as in Table 1.

Notice that no tied ranks appear in the table. The organizer of a wine tasting clearly has a choice of whether tied ranks are or are not permitted. My colleagues' and my preference is not to permit tied ranks, since tied ranks encourage "lazy" tasting; when the sampled wines are relatively similar, the option of using tied ranks enables tasters to avoid hard choices. Hence, in what follows, no tied ranks will appear (except when wines are graded, rather

Table 1. Rank Tables for Judges

	Wine		
Judge	A	B	C
Orley	1	2	3
Burt	2	1	3
Frank	1	3	2
Richard	2	1	3
Rank Sums	6	7	11

[3]This is by no means unique. The restaurant *La Villa des Fleurs* in Talloires employs a 7-point scale (* = Exceptional, 5 = Très grande année, 4 = Grande année, 3 = Bonne année, 2 = Année passable, 1 = Petit année, – = Année mediocre), *Taillevent* a 10-point scale, *The New York Times* alternately a 10-point scale (May 22, 1991), or a 20-point scale (December 16, 1981), or in recent years a 6-point scale.

than ranked). What does the table tell us about the group's preferences? The best summary measure has to be the rank sums for the individual wines, which in present case turn out to be 6, 7, and 11 respectively. Clearly, wine A appears to be valued most highly and wine C the least.

A slightly different interpretation of the rank sums is in terms of "votes against." We might regard each rank assigned to a wine as a vote against it. A rank of "2" is a slightly weightier vote against a wine than a rank of "1," whereas a rank of "3" is a still weightier vote against it. The rank sums can also be expressed as total votes against: thus, for wine A the total votes against is $2 \times 1 + 2 \times 2 = 6$, because it received 2 votes of "1," and two votes of "2." It is noteworthy that if there are m judges and n wines the smallest votes that a wine can theoretically obtain is $m \times 1 = m$ and the largest is $m \times n = mn$.

The real question is whether one can say that a rank sum is significantly low or significantly high, since even if judges assign rank sums completely at random, we would sometimes find that a wine has a very low (high) rank sum.

Kramer computes upper and lower critical values for the rank sums and asserts that we can test the hypothesis that a wine has a significantly high (low) rank sum by comparing the actual rank sum with the critical values; if the rank sum is greater (lower) than the upper (lower) critical value, the rank sum would be declared significantly high (low) (Kramer, 1956). If in assigning a rank to a particular wine, each of m judges chooses exactly one number out of a set $\{1, 2, \dots, n\}$, the total number of rank patterns is n^m and it is easy to determine how many of the possible rank sums are equal to m (the lowest possible rank sum), ..., and nm (the highest possible rank sum). From this it is easy to determine critical low and high values such that 5% of the rank sums are lower than the low and 5% are higher than the high critical value.[4] This test is entirely appropriate if one wishes to test *a single rank sum* for significance.

The problem with the test is that typically one would want to make a statement about each and every wine in a tasting; hence one would want to compare the rank sums of all n wines to the critical values; some of the rank sums might fall below the smaller of the critical values, some might exceed

[4]Kramer gives critical values for the 0.05 and 0.01 levels of significance. His values are correct if one notes that, contrary to his assenion, the observed value needs to be not greater or smaller than the relevant critical value, but greater than or equal or smaller than or equal to the critical value in question.

the larger of the critical values, and others might be in-between. Applying the test to each wine, we could pronounce some of the wines *statistically significantly good* in the tasters' opinion, some significantly bad, and some not significantly good or bad. Unfortunately, this is not a valid use of the test. Consider the experiment of judges assigning ranks to wines one at a time, beginning with wine A. Once a judge has assigned a particular rank to that wine, say "1," that rank is no longer available to be assigned by that judge to another wine. Hence, the remaining rank sums can no longer be thought to have generated from the universe of all possible rank sums, and in fact, the rank sums for the various wines are not independent.

To examine the consequences of applying the Kramer rank sum to test each wine in a tasting, we resorted to Monte Carlo experiments in which we generated 10,000 random rankings of n wines and m judges; for each of the 10,000 replications we counted the fractions of rank sums that were significantly high and significantly low by the Kramer criterion, and then classified the replications in a two-way table in which the $(i, j)^{\text{th}}$ entry, ($i = 0, \ldots, n$, $j = 0, \ldots, n$) indicates the number of replications in which i rank sums were significantly low and j rank sums were significantly high. This experiment was carried out for ($m = 4, n = 4$), ($m = 8, n = 8$) and ($m = 8$, $n = 12$). The results are shown in Tables 2–4.

Thus, for example, in Table 4, 1,915 out of 10,000 replications had a sole rank sum that was significantly low by the Kramer criterion, 1,627 replications had one rank sum that was significantly low *and* one rank sum that was significantly high, 357 replications had one significantly low and two significantly high rank sums, and so on. It is clear that the Kramer test classifies way too many rank sums as significant. At the same time, if we apply the Kramer test to a single (randomly chosen) column of the rank table, the 10,000 replications give significantly high and low outcomes as shown in Table 5.

Table 2. Fraction of Significant Rank Sums According to Kramer for $m = 4, n = 4$

	$j =$		
i	0	1	2
0	0.6414	0.1221	0
1	0.1261	0.1070	0.0016
2	0	0.0012	0.0006

Table 3. Fraction of Significant Rank Sums According to Kramer for $m = 8, n = 8$

	$j =$			
i	0	1	2	3
0	0.4269	0.1761	0.0093	0
1	0.1774	0.1532	0.0211	0.0003
2	0.0097	0.0192	0.0060	0
3	0.0002	0.0003	0.0002	0.0001

Table 4. Fraction of Significant Rank Sums According to Kramer for $m = 8, n = 12$

	$j =$				
i	0	1	2	3	4
0	0.3206	0.1874	0.0252	0.0004	0
1	0.1915	0.1627	0.0357	0.0021	0.0001
2	0.0245	0.0330	0.0121	0.0011	0
3	0.0006	0.0013	0.0012	0.0003	0

Table 5. Application of Kramer Test to a Single Rank Sum in Each Replication

	Significantly	
(m, n)	High	Low
(4, 4)	0.0552	0.0584
(8, 8)	0.0507	0.0517
(8, 12)	0.0478	0.0467

While the observed rejection frequencies of the null hypothesis of "no significant rank sum" are statistically significantly different from the expected value of 500, using the normal approximation to the binomial distribution, the numbers are, at least, "in the ball-park," while in the case of applying the test to every rank sum in each replication they are not even near.

This suggests that a somewhat different approach is needed to testing the rank sums in a given tasting. Each judge's ranks add up to $n(n + 1)/2$ and hence the sum of the rank sums over all judges is $mn(n + 1)/2$. Hence, denoting the rank sum for the jth wine by $s_j = 1, \ldots, n$, we have

$$\sum_{j=1}^{n} s_j = \frac{mn(n+1)}{2} \tag{1}$$

which, in effect, means that the rank sums for the various wines are located on an $(n-1)$-dimensional simplex. The center point of this simplex has coordinates $m(n+1)/2$ in every direction, and if every wine had this rank sum, there would be no difference at all among the wines. It is plausible that the farther a set of rank sums $(s_1, \ldots, s_n)$ is located from this center, the more pronounced is the departure of the rankings from the average. However, judging the potential significance of the departure of a single rank sum from the center point has the same problem as the Kramer measure. Therefore, we propose to measure the departure of the whole wine tasting from the average point by the (squared) sum of distances of each rank sum from the center points, that is, by

$$s_d = \sum_{j=1}^{n} \left(s_1 - \frac{m(n+1)}{2} \right)^2 \tag{2}$$

In order to determine critical values for S_d, we resorted to Monte Carlo experiments. Random rank tables were generated for m judges and n wines ($m = 4, 5, \ldots, 12$; $n = 4, 5, \ldots, 12$), and the S_d-statistic was computed for each of 10,000 replications; the critical value of S_d at the 0.05 level was obtained from the sample cumulative distributions. These are displayed in Table 6.

Table 6. Critical Values for S_d at the 0.05 Level

	$n =$								
m	4	5	6	7	8	9	10	11	12
4	50	88	140	216	312	430	570	746	954
5	60	110	180	278	390	550	716	946	1,204
6	74	134	218	336	480	664	876	1,150	1,468
7	88	158	256	394	564	780	1,036	1,344	1,712
8	102	182	300	452	644	894	1,174	1,534	1,984
9	112	206	338	512	732	1,014	1,342	1,742	2,236
10	122	230	376	580	820	1,128	1,500	1,954	2,508
11	136	252	420	636	902	1,236	1,642	2,140	2,740
12	150	276	458	688	992	1,360	1,836	2,358	2,998

Table 7. Rank Table

	Wine			
Judge	A	B	C	D
Orley	1	2	3	4
Burt	2	1	4	3
Frank	3	1	2	4
Richard	2	1	4	3
Rank Sums	8	5	13	14

It is important to keep in mind the correct interpretation of a significant S-value. Such a value no longer singles out a wine as significantly "good" or "bad," but singles out an entire set of wines as representing a significant rank order. In Table 7, the rank sums for the four wines are 8, 5, 13, 14, and the Kramer test would say only that wine D is significantly bad. In the present example, $S_d = 54$, and the entire rank order is significant at the 0.05 level (i.e., B is significantly better than A, which is significantly better than C, which is significantly better than D).

A final approach to determining the significance of rank sums is to perform the Friedman two-way analysis of variance test (Siegel and Castellan, 1988, p. 180). It tests the hypothesis that the ranks assigned to the various wines come from the same population. The test statistic is

$$F = \left[\frac{2}{mn(n+1)} \sum_{j=1}^{n} s_j^2\right] - 3m(n+1) \tag{3}$$

if there are no ties, and is

$$F = \frac{12\sum_{j=1}^{n} s_j^2 - 3m^2n(n+1)^2}{mn(n+1) + \dfrac{mn + \sum_{i=1}^{m}\sum_{j=1}^{\tau_i} t_{ij}^2}{n-1}} \tag{4}$$

if there are ties, where τ_i is the number of sets of tied ranks for judge i (if there are no ties for judge i, then $\tau_i = n$) and t_{ij} is the number of items that are tied for judge i in his/her j^{th} group of tied observations (if there are no ties, $t_{ij} = 1$). It is easy to verify that the second formula reduces to the first if there are no ties. Critical values for small m and n are given in Siegel and Castellan; for large values F is distributed under the null hypothesis of no differences among the rank sums approximately as $\chi^2(n-1)$. It is clear that the Friedman test and the D-test have very similar underlying objectives.

Grading Wines. Grading wines consists of assigning "grades" to each wine, with no restrictions on whether ties are permitted to occur. While the resulting scale is not a cardinal scale, some meaning does attach to the level of the numbers assigned to each wine. Thus, if on a 20-point scale, one judge assigns to three wines the grades 3, 4, 5, while another judge assigns the grades 18, 19, 20, and a third judge assigns 3, 12, 20, they are seen to be in complete harmony concerning the *ranking* of wines, but have serious differences of opinion with respect to the absolute quality. I am somewhat skeptical about the value of the information contained in such differences. But we always have the option of translating grades into ranks and then analyzing the ranks with the techniques illustrated above. For this purpose, we reproduce the grades assigned by 11 judges to 10 wines in a famous 1976 tasting of American and French Bordeaux wines (see Table 8).[5]

Table 9 contains the judges' grades and Table 10 the conversion of those grades into ranks. It should be noted that grades can be converted into ranks in several ways. The method we are adopting here is to convert each judge's grades into ranks. But if one were to be interested only in the aggregate rank assigned to the wines, one could also add the grades and then rank the grade totals. That method has the disadvantage of being excessively dependent on outlier grades, which is attenuated by ranking the individual judges' grades.[6] Since grading permits ties, the rank into which the grades

Table 8. The Wines in the 1976 Tasting

Wine	Name	Final rank
A	Stag's Leap 1973	1st
B	Ch. Mouton Rothschild 1970	3rd
C	Ch. Montrose 1970	2nd
D	Ch. Haut Brion 1970	4th
E	Ridge Monte Bello 1971	5th
F	Léoville-Las-Cases 1971	7th
G	Heitz Martha's Vineyard 1970	6th
H	Clos du Val 1972	10th
I	Mayacamas 1971	9th
J	Freemark Abbey 1969	8th

[5]For a Bayesian analysis of this tasting, see Lindley (2006) in this issue.

[6]However, analyzing preferences among wines on the basis of rank totals has its own disadvantages; to wit, that method violates the axiom of the Independence of Irrelevant Alternatives.

Table 9. The Judges' Grades

Judge	A	B	C	D	E	F	G	H	I	J
Pierre Brejoux	14.0	16.0	12.0	17.0	13.0	10.0	12.0	14.0	5.0	7.0
Aubert de Villaine	15.0	14.0	16.0	15.0	9.0	10.0	7.0	5.0	12.0	7.0
Michel Dovaz	10.0	15.0	11.0	12.0	12.0	10.0	11.5	11.0	8.0	15.0
Patricia Gallagher	14.0	15.0	14.0	12.0	16.0	14.0	17.0	13.0	9.0	15.0
Odette Kahn	15.0	12.0	12.0	12.0	7.0	12.0	2.0	2.0	13.0	5.0
Christian Millau	16.0	16.0	17.0	13.5	7.0	11.0	8.0	9.0	9.5	9.0
Raymond Oliver	14.0	12.0	14.0	10.0	12.0	12.0	10.0	10.0	14.0	8.0
Steven Spurrier	14.0	14.0	14.0	8.0	14.0	12.0	13.0	11.0	9.0	13.0
Pierre Tari	13.0	11.0	14.0	14.0	17.0	12.0	15.0	13.0	12.0	14.0
Chr. Vanneque	16.5	16.0	11.0	17.0	15.5	8.0	10.0	16.5	3.0	6.0
Jean-ClaudeVrinat	14.0	14.0	15.0	15.0	11.0	12.0	9.0	7.0	13.0	7.0

Table 10. Conversion of Grades into Ranks

Judge	A	B	C	D	E	F	G	H	I	J
Pierre Brejoux	3.5	2.0	6.5	1.0	5.0	8.0	6.5	3.5	10.0	9.0
Aubert de Villaine	2.5	4.0	1.0	2.5	7.0	6.0	8.5	10.0	5.0	8.5
Michel Dovaz	8.5	1.5	6.5	3.5	3.5	8.5	5.0	6.5	10.0	1.5
Patricia Gallagher	6.0	3.5	6.0	9.0	2.0	6.0	1.0	8.0	10.0	3.5
Odette Kahn	1.0	4.5	4.5	4.5	7.0	4.5	9.5	9.5	2.0	8.0
Christian Millau	2.5	2.5	1.0	4.0	10.0	5.0	9.0	7.5	6.0	7.5
Raymond Oliver	2.0	5.0	2.0	8.0	5.0	5.0	8.0	8.0	2.0	10.0
Steven Spurrier	2.5	2.5	2.5	10.0	2.5	7.0	5.5	8.0	9.0	5.5
Pierre Tari	6.5	10.0	4.0	4.0	1.0	8.5	2.0	6.5	8.5	4.0
Chr. Vanneque	2.5	4.0	6.0	1.0	5.0	8.0	7.0	2.5	10.0	9.0
Jean-ClaudeVrinat	3.5	3.5	1.5	1.5	7.0	6.0	8.0	9.5	5.0	9.5
Rank Totals	41.0	43.0	41.5	49.0	55.0	72.5	70.0	79.5	77.5	76.0
Group Ranking	1	3	2	4	5	7	6	10	9	8

are converted by the method selected in this chapter also have to reflect ties; thus, for example, if the top two wines were to be tied in a judge's estimation, they would both be assigned a rank of 1.5. Also note that grades and ranks are inversely related: the higher a grade, the better the wine, and hence the lower its rank position.

If we apply the critical values as recommended by Kramer, we would find that wines A, B, and C are significantly good (in the opinion of the judges) and wine H is significantly bad. The value of the S_d-statistic may be considered significant. Computing the Friedman two-way analysis of variance test yields a χ^2 value of 29.93, which is significant at the 1% level. Hence, the two tests are entirely compatible and the Friedman test rejects the hypothesis that the medians of the distributions of the rank sums are the same for the different wines.

In this section we compared several ways of evaluating the significance of rank sums. In particular, we argued that the S_d-statistic and the Friedman two-way analysis of variance tests are more appropriate than the Kramer statistic.

3. Agreement of Disagreement Among the Judges

There are at least two questions we may ask about the similarity or dissimilarity of the judge's rankings (or grades). The first one concerns the extent to which the group of judges as a whole ranks (or grades) the wines similarly. The second one concerns the extent of the correlation between a particular pair of judges.

The Overall Agreement among the Judges. The natural test for the overall concordance among the judges' rating is the Kendall W coefficient of concordance (Siegel and Castellan, 1988, p. 262–272). It is computed as

$$W = \frac{\sum_{i=1}^{n}(\bar{r}_i - \bar{r})^2}{n(n^2-1)/12} \tag{5}$$

where $\bar{r}$, is the average rank assigned to the ith wine and $\bar{r}$ is the average of the averages. Siegel and Castellan again provide tables for testing the null hypothesis of no concordance for small values of m and n; for large values, $m(n-1)W$ is approximately distributed as $\chi^2(n-1)$. In the case of the wine tasting depicted in Tables 9 and 10, $W = 0.2417$ and the probability of obtaining a value this high or higher under a random assignment of ranks is 0.0059, a highly significant result showing strong agreement among the judges.

It may be interesting to examine the behavior of Kendall's W in a large number of tastings carried out by a highly stable group of wine tasters. Such group is the *Liquid Assets Wine Group*, which consists of eight individuals, who meet about eight or nine times a year. If a member cannot attend a tasting, he may or may not be replaced by an ad hoc invitee; on very rare occasions, the number of tasters is enlarged beyond the core group. We have been analyzing the tastings systematically since March 9, 1998; a total of 92 tastings have taken place in which Kendall's W was computed.

The first question to be answered is whether there is any trend over this period in the W coefficient. However, looking at the W coefficient itself would

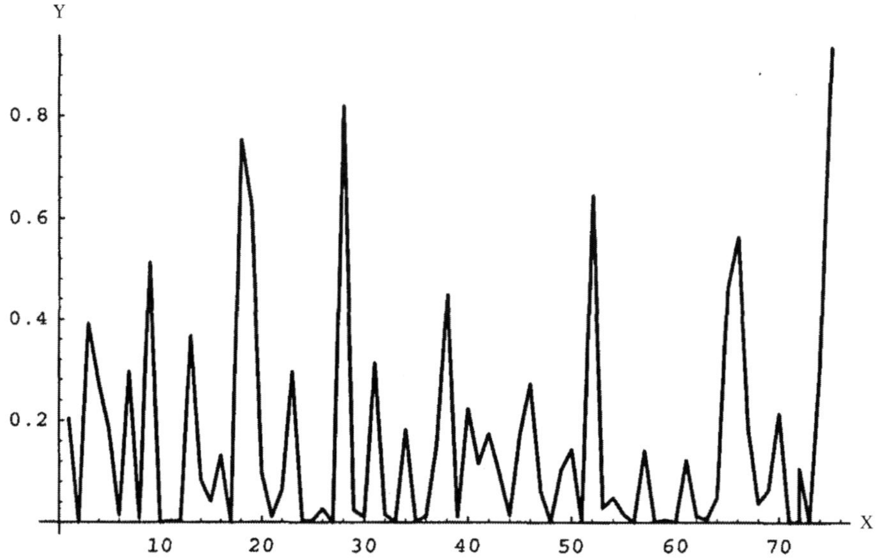

Figure 1. Time Series of p-values for Kendall's W

not be revealing, because the significance of a particular W depends both on the number of tasters and the number of wines, both of which vary from time to time. Thus, for example, $W = 0.4$ is not significant (at the 0.05 level) if the number of judges is 6 and the number of wines 4, but the same value of W is significant if the judges number 6 and the wines 5. It is therefore more appropriate to examine the p-value corresponding to the value of W, the probability that a value of W as high or higher than the observed one would have been obtained if the judges assigned ranks at random. The first question therefore is what the behavior of these p-values is over time. They are displayed in Figure 1, in which the vertical axis denotes p-values and the horizontal axis denotes which tasting they correspond to. If it is fairly clear by inspection, without any sophisticated tests, that the p-values fluctuate randomly, getting neither smaller nor larger as time passes. Hence there is no reason to believe that the agreement among the judges has gotten any better as time has passed.

But an examination of the p-values reveals that 49% are smaller than 0.05 and 57% are smaller than 0.10, indicating that substantial agreement existed among judges more than half the time. A formal test of this hypothesis may be conducted as follows. We may regard the sample realizations of p-values as drawings from some distribution over the unit interval. If the judges judged wines randomly, these drawings would be from a uniform

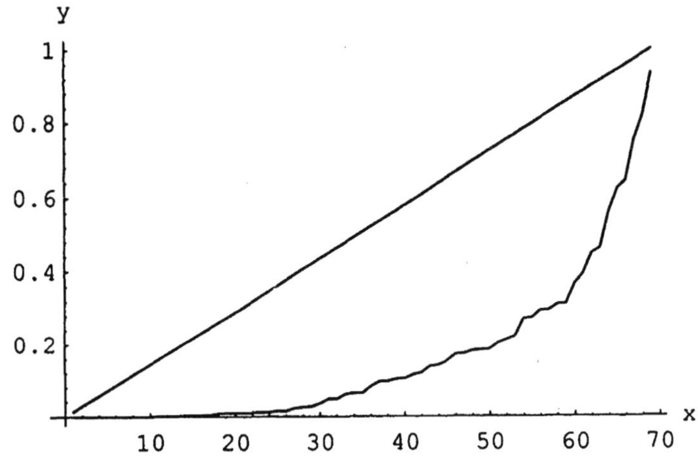

Figure 2. Cumulative Sample Distribution of p-values and the Cumulative $U(0,1)$

distribution.[7] Hence it is relevant to compare the cumulative sample distribution of p-values with the cumulative distribution of $U(0,1)$. The two distributions are displayed in Figure 2, in which the straight line corresponds to the cumulative distribution of $U(0,1)$.

It is obvious by inspection that the two cumulatives are vastly different. For a formal test, it is appropriate to use the Kolmogorov–Smirnov one-sample test to test the hypothesis that the realizations come from the $U(0,1)$ distribution. In fact, the maximal vertical difference between the sample cumulative distribution and the distribution function of the uniform is 0.5530; the Kolmogorov–Smirnov statistic is 4.8211, with a critical value at the 0.05 level of 1.3588, indicating a highly significant departure form the uniform distribution. But exploration of what might explain the differences among the p-values has not been able to shed further light on this. Regressing the p-values on a trend and on six dummy variables with values of 0 or 1 if the tasting was, respectively, one of Bordeaux, Burgundy, Rhone, German, Italian or Spanish, or American wines has yielded no significant coefficients, suggesting that the degree of agreement does not depend on either the trend variable or on what is being tasted.

Pairwise correlations. The pairwise correlations between the judges can be assessed by using either Spearman's ρ and Kendall's τ (Siegel

[7]Let X be a random variable, x a particular value, and let $y = G(x)$, where $G()$ is the cumulative distribution function of X. Then $Pr\{Y < y\} = Pr\{G(X) < G(x)\} = G(x) = y$, which proves that Y is uniform on (0, 1).

and Castellan, 1988, 235–254). Spearman's ρ is simply the ordinary product-moment correlation based on variables expressed as ranks, and thus has the standard interpretation of a correlation coefficient. The philosophy underlying the computation of τ is quite different. Assume that we have two rankings given by r_1 and r_2, where these are n-vectors of rankings by two individuals. To compute τ, we first sort r_1 into natural order and parallel-sort r_2 (i.e., ensure that the ith elements of r_1 and r_2 both migrate to the same position in their respective vectors). We then count up the number of instances in which in r_2 a higher rank follows a lower rank (i.e., are in natural order) and the number of instances in r_2 in which a higher rank precedes a lower rank (reverse order). τ is then

$$\tau = \frac{\text{Number of natural order pairs} - \text{Number of reverse order pairs}}{\binom{n}{2}} \tag{6}$$

Clearly, ρ and τ can be quite different and it does not make sense to compare them. In fact, for $n = 6$, the maximal absolute difference $\rho - \tau$ can be as large as 0.3882 and the cumulative distributions of ρ and τ obtained by calculating their values for all possible permutations of ranks are as shown in Figure 3, where the step-function-like cumulative is that of τ. Since the interpretation of τ is a little less natural, I prefer to use ρ, but from the point of view of significance testing it does not make a difference which is used; in fact, Siegel and Castellan point out that the relation between ρ and τ is governed by the inequalities

$$-1 < 3\tau - 2\rho < 1$$

A final calculation that may be amusing, even though its statistical assessment is not entirely clear, is to calculate the correlation between the rankings of a given judge with the *average ranking* of the remaining judges.[8] To accomplish this, we must first average the rankings of the remaining judges and then find the correlation between this average ranking and the ranking of the given judge. Obviously, repeating this calculation for each of the n judges gives us $n\rho$s that are not independent of another, and hence the significance testing of these n correlations are unclear. But it is an amusing addendum to a wine tasting, since it gives us some insight as to who agrees

[8]Another interesting correlation is between the rankings and the prices of the wines. We calculate this only occasionally, since often the relevant price information is missing.

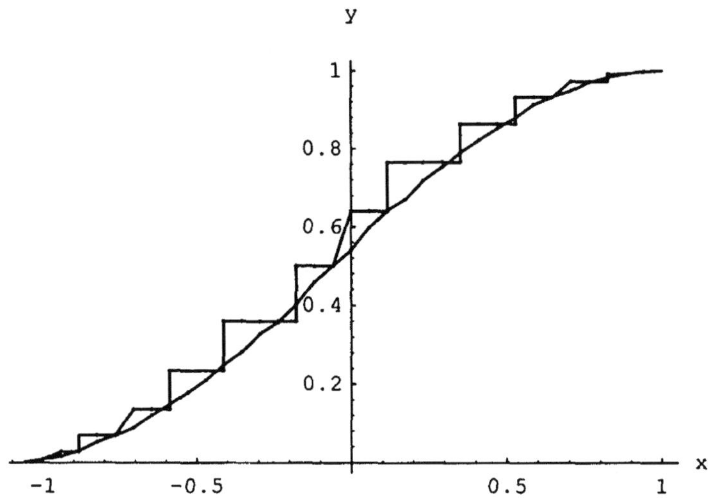

Figure 3. Cumulative Distributions for ρ and τ

Table 11. Correlation of Each Judge with Rest of Group

Judge	Spearman's ρ
Pierre Brejoux	0.4634
Aubert de Villaine	0.6951
Michel Dovaz	−0.0675
Patricia Gallagher	−0.0862
Odette Kahn	0.2926
Christian Millau	0.6104
Raymond Oliver	0.2455
Steven Spurrier	0.4688
Pierre Tari	−0.1543
Christian Vanneque	0.4195
Jean-ClaudeVrinat	0.6534

most with "the rest of the herd" (or, conversely, who is the dominant person with whom the "herd" agrees) and who is the real contrarian. In the case of the 1976 wine tasting, the table of correlations is as in Table 11.

4. The Identification of Wines

We now change the focus of our investigation from how well the judges like the wines and what that can tell us to how good they are in identifying them. This is an aspect that can be both satisfying and challenging. By identification we do not, of course, mean that the judges would have to identify the wines out of the entire universe of all possible wines. It is clear that the judges have to be given some clue concerning the general category of the wines they are drinking, otherwise it is quite likely that no useful results will be obtained from the identification exercise, unless the judges are truly great experts.

There are at least two possibilities. The first one is that the judges have to associate with each actual wine name the appropriate code letter (**A**, **B**, **C**, etc.), that appears on a bottle. In this case, we continue to adopt the convention that at the beginning of the tasting the judges are presented with a list of the wines to be tasted (presumably in alphabetical order, lest the order of the wines in the list create a presumption that the first wine is wine **A**, the second wine **B**, etc.). Thus, if eight wines are to be tasted, the task of the judges is to match the actual wine names with the letters **A**, **B**, **C**, etc. The question we shall investigate is how we can test the hypothesis that the identification pattern selected by a judge is no better than what would be obtained by a chance assignment.

The second possibility is that the judges are not given the names of the wines but are given their "type." Thus, for example, one could have a tasting of cabernet sauvignons from Bordeaux together with cabernet sauvignons from California (as in the 1976 tasting discussed in the previous section), or one could have a tasting of Burgundy pinot noirs, together with Oregon pinot noirs and South African pinot noirs from the Franschhoek or Stellenbosch area. The judges would merely be told the number of wines of each type in the tasting, and their task would be to identify which of the wines **A**, **B**, **C**, etc., is Bordeaux wine and which a California wine.

Guessing the Name of Each Wine. Consider the case in which n wines are being tested and let P be an $n \times n$ matrix, the rows of which correspond to the "artificial" names of the wines (**A**, **B**,...) and the columns of which correspond to the actual names of the wines. We will say that the label in row i is assigned to (matched with) the label in column j if the element $a_{ij} = 1$ and is not assigned to the label in column j if $a_{ij} = 0$. It is obvious that the matrix P is a valid *identification matrix* if and only if (1) each row has exactly one 1 in it and $n - 1$ 0s, and (2) each column has exactly one 1 in it and $n - 1$ 0s. Under these circumstances, an identification matrix is a permutation matrix (i.e., it is a matrix that can be obtained from an identity matrix by permuting its rows). Obviously, the "truth" can also be represented by a permutation matrix; its ij^{th} element is 1 if and only if artificial label i actually corresponds to real label j. This permutation matrix will be denoted by T.

To measure the extent to which a person's wine identification (as given by his or her P matrix) corresponds to the truth (the T matrix), we propose the following measure C:

$$C = \mathrm{tr}(PT)/n \tag{7}$$

where n is the number of wines, which gives just the percentage of wines correctly identified. The justification for this measure emerges from the following considerations.

First note that every permutation matrix is its own inverse; that is,

$$P = P^{-1} \tag{8}$$

The reason is that if we interchange the ith and j^{th} rows of an identity matrix and then premultiply a given matrix by it, that will have the effect of interchanging in the given matrix the same pair of rows. Hence, premultiplying the matrix P by itself, interchanges those rows in P, yielding an identity matrix for the product. Thus, if a person's P matrix is identical to T, PT is an identity matrix, the trace of which is equal to n; hence $C = 1.0$ in the case in which a person identifies each wine correctly. Moreover, C is monotone in the number of wines correctly identified and if no wines are correctly identified, $C = 0$. Therefore, in order to judge whether the observed value of C is significant (under the null hypothesis of random identification by the judge), we require the sampling distribution of C.

There are $n!$ permutations matrices, and any one of these matrices P can be paired with any one of $n!$ possible matrices T, which suggests a formidable number of possible outcomes. However, the possible outcomes are identical for each of the possible T matrices; hence without any loss of generality, we may fix T as the identity matrix. Then $PT = P$ and to compute C it is sufficient to count up how many of the possible $n!$ P matrices have trace equal to $0, 1, \ldots$.

To find the sampling distribution of the trace is formally identical with the following problem. Let there be n urns, labeled **A**, **B**, **C**, etc., and let there be n balls, labeled similarly. We shall randomly place one ball in each urn; we then ask what the probability is that exactly k of the urns contain a ball that has the same label as the urn.

It is obvious that the total possible ways in which balls can be placed in urns is $n!$ It is also obvious that there is exactly one way (out of $n!$ ways) that every ball is in the urn with the same label, and it is also obvious that it is impossible for exactly $n-1$ balls to be like-labeled urn (since if $n-1$ balls are, then the last one must also be in a like-labeled urn).[9]

Denote by $M(i,j)$ the number of ways in which you can place j balls in j urns so that exactly i balls are in like-labeled urns. As long as $i \neq j-1$, having exactly i balls in the like-labeled urns can be done in $\binom{j}{i}$ ways. The remaining urns and balls should produce no match if we want exactly i matches; the number of ways that that can occur is, by definition, $M(0,j-i)$. The total number of ways then is

$$M(i,j) = \binom{j}{i} M(0,j-i) \tag{9}$$

For a value of n, the totality of outcomes is given by

$$\begin{aligned} M(n,n) &= 1 \\ M(n-1,n) &= 0 \\ M(n-2,n) &= \binom{n}{n-2} M(0,2) \\ M(n-3,n) &= \binom{n}{n-3} M(0,3) \\ &\cdots \\ M(i,n) &= nM(0,n-1) \\ M(0,n) &= n! - \textstyle\sum_{j=1}^{n} M(j,n) \end{aligned} \tag{10}$$

with initial conditions being given by $M(2,2) = 1, M(1,2) = 0$ and $M(0,2) = 1$. The $M(i,n)$ are easily computed because the above equations provide a simple recursive scheme for the calculations. We obtain the probability of i matches, $i = 0,\ldots,n$ with n urns by dividing each $M(i,n)$ by $n!$. These probabilities are shown in Table 12.

It is clear that irrespective of the number of n of wines, a trace of 4 or more is a highly significant result and a trace in excess of 2 is still significant

[9]This immediately clarifies why the identification problem is *not* a simple binomial problem. One could have (mistakenly) thought that for each judge there is a probability p that he or she will identify a single wine correctly, and thus the probability of identifying x out of n wines would just be $\binom{n}{x} p^x(1-p)^{n-x}$. This is clearly incorrect for the case we are considering.

Table 12. Sampling Distribution of Trace

	trace =								
n	0	1	2	3	4	5	6	7	8
2	0.500	0.000	0.500						
3	0.333	0.500	0.000	0.167					
4	0.375	0.333	0.250	0.000	0.042				
5	0.367	0.375	0.167	0.083	0.000	0.008			
6	0.368	0.367	0.188	0.056	0.021	0.000	0.001		
7	0.368	0.368	0.183	0.062	0.014	0.004	0.000	0.000	
8	0.368	0.368	0.184	0.061	0.016	0.003	0.000	0.000	0.000
9	0.368	0.368	0.184	0.061	0.015	0.003	0.000	0.000	0.000
10	0.368	0.368	0.184	0.061	0.015	0.003	0.000	0.000	0.000
11	0.368	0.368	0.184	0.061	0.015	0.003	0.000	0.000	0.000
12	0.368	0.368	0.184	0.061	0.015	0.003	0.000	0.000	0.000

at the 0.1 level of significance for $n > 3$. It is also remarkable that the distribution converges very rapidly in n to a limiting form.

The other question that is of interest is whether the judges, as a whole, tend to agree or tend not to agree with one another with respect to wine identification. Here we propose the following measure of the degree of agreement among judges.

Let m be the number of judges and denote their identification matrices by $P_i, i = 1, \ldots, n$. Let $Q = \sum_{i=1}^{n} p_i$ and let q_{ij} be the typical element of Q. Since the sum of the elements of each Pi is exactly n, if there are m judges, the mean value of each element of Q is $mn/n^2 = m/n$. We propose as the measure of concordance the variance of the elements of Q, that is,

$$V = \frac{1}{n^2} \sum_{j=1}^{n} \sum_{i=1}^{n} \left(q_{ij} - \frac{m}{n} \right)^2 \tag{11}$$

If all judges pick the same permutation matrix, n of the elements of Q will be equal to m and the remaining ones will be zero. In that case the variance over the elements of Q is

$$V = \frac{1}{n^2} \left[n \left(m - \frac{m}{n} \right)^2 + n(n-1) \left(\frac{m}{n} \right)^2 \right] = \frac{m^2(n-1)}{n^2} \tag{12}$$

If the judges predominantly pick P matrices that are very different, the elements of Q will be relatively more similar and the variance will be small. In order to determine what level of variance is significant, we have to determine

Table 13. 10 Percent Significance Level for V

	$m =$											
n	4	5	6	7	8	9	10	11	12	13	14	15
4	1.12	1.44	1.75	2.06	2.38	2.69	3.00	3.31	3.62	3.94	4.25	4.56
5	1.88	1.12	1.36	1.60	1.84	2.08	2.32	2.56	2.80	3.04	3.28	3.52
6	0.72	0.92	1.11	1.31	1.50	1.69	1.89	2.08	2.28	2.44	2.67	2.81
7	0.61	0.78	0.94	1.10	1.26	1.43	1.59	1.76	1.92	2.08	2.24	2.41
8	0.53	0.67	0.81	0.95	1.09	1.23	1.38	1.52	1.62	1.80	1.91	2.08
9	0.46	0.59	0.72	0.84	0.96	1.09	1.21	1.33	1.46	1.58	1.68	1.80
10	0.42	0.53	0.64	0.75	0.86	0.97	1.08	1.17	1.30	1.41	1.52	1.63
11	0.38	0.48	0.58	0.68	0.78	0.88	0.98	1.07	1.17	1.26	1.37	1.46
12	0.34	0.44	0.53	0.62	0.71	0.80	0.89	0.98	1.07	1.15	1.25	1.34

Table 14. 5 Percent Significance Level for V

	$m =$											
n	4	5	6	7	8	9	10	11	12	13	14	15
4	1.25	1.69	2.00	2.31	2.75	3.06	3.38	3.81	4.12	4.56	4.75	5.19
5	0.96	1.28	1.52	1.76	2.08	2.32	2.56	2.80	3.12	3.36	3.68	3.92
6	0.78	1.03	1.22	1.41	1.67	1.81	2.06	2.26	2.50	2.64	2.89	3.08
7	0.65	0.82	1.02	1.18	1.39	1.55	1.71	1.88	2.04	2.24	2.41	2.57
8	0.56	0.67	0.81	1.02	1.16	1.33	1.47	1.61	1.75	1.92	2.06	2.20
9	0.49	0.64	0.76	0.89	1.02	1.16	1.28	1.40	1.53	1.68	1.80	1.93
10	0.44	0.57	0.68	0.79	0.90	1.01	1.14	1.25	1.36	1.49	1.60	1.71
11	0.40	0.51	0.61	0.71	0.81	0.93	1.02	1.12	1.22	1.32	1.44	1.54
12	0.35	0.47	0.56	0.64	0.74	0.83	0.93	1.02	1.11	1.20	1.31	1.40

the sampling distribution of the variance under the null hypothesis that the judges pick P matrices at random.

The sampling distributions were determined for the number of wines i, $i = 4, \ldots, 12$ and the number of judges j, $j = 4, \ldots, 15$ by Monte Carlo experiments. An experiment for given i and j consisted of fixing the value of j and picking one out of the $i!$ permutation matrices and then computing V as shown above. Each experiment was replicated 10,000 times. Table 13 contains the 10% and Table 14 the 5% significance levels for V.

Tables 13 and 14 are heuristic, but we may proceed also in a more formal manner by asking what the probabilities are that in a group of m judges with n wines the sum of the traces of the P_i matrices is, respectively

0, 1, 2, etc. Assuming that the judges make their identifications independently of one another (which clearly suggest that *viva voce* identifications are to be eschewed), the sum of correct identifications by m judges has a distribution that is the appropriate discrete convolution of the distributions in Table 12. For example, with eight wines, under the null hypothesis of random identifications, the 10% critical value is 5 for $m = 2$, 6 for $m = 3$ and 7 for $m = 4$. In other words, if four judges jointly succeed making 7 or more correct identifications, we may reject the hypothesis that, as a whole, the group was behaving randomly.

Identifying Types of Wines. We assume, in conformity with previous assumptions, that judges are informed of how many wines of Type I and how many of Type II are present in the sample to be tasted.[10] Before we present tables of the distributions of the number correctly identified under the null of random assignments, consider the following example. Let us assume that there are nine wines in all, four of which are of type X and five of which are of type Y and let us depict the "true" pattern in the sample as

$$X \quad X \quad X \quad X \quad Y \quad Y \quad Y \quad Y \quad Y$$

Now imagine that a particular judge guesses the pattern to be

$$X \quad X \quad X \quad Y \quad X \quad Y \quad Y \quad Y \quad Y$$

In that case, he/she will have identified seven wines correctly by type. In how many ways can this occur? Making two mistakes implies that one X-type wine is identified as a Y and one Y-type wine is identified as an X. In the present case you can choose the X which will be misidentified $\binom{4}{1}$ ways and the Y which will be misidentified as an X in $\binom{5}{1}$ ways, for a total $\binom{4}{1}\binom{5}{1} = 20$ ways. Now, how can you have exactly six or eight wines identified correctly? The answer is that there are no ways in which you can have six or eight correct identifications: for example, to reduce the number of correct identifications, an additional X must be identified as a Y; but that means that an additional Y will also be identified as an X, hence if seven correct identifications is possible, then neither six nor eight will ever be possible. In fact, since if there are n wines, with n_1 of type X and n_2 of type Y, n correct identifications is always a possible outcome, and the number of possible correct identifications is $n, n-2, n-4$, with the last

[10]If, on the contrary, judges were only told that every wine tasted is either a Bordeaux cabernet sauvignon or a California cabernet, with no indication of how many wines of each type are present in the sample, then the problem could, indeed, be formulated as a straightforward binomial problem.

Table 15. Probabilities for the Number of Correctly Identified Wines

	Probability					
Number	$n_1 = 4$ $n_2 = 4$	$n_1 = 4$ $n_2 = 5$	$n_1 = 4$ $n_2 = 6$	$n_1 = 5$ $n_2 = 5$	$n_1 = 5$ $n_2 = 6$	$n_1 = 6$ $n_2 = 6$
0	0.014	0.000	0.000	0.004	0.000	0.001
1	0.000	0.040	0.000	0.000	0.013	0.000
2	0.229	0.000	0.071	0.099	0.000	0.039
3	0.000	0.317	0.000	0.000	0.162	0.000
4	0.514	0.000	0.381	0.397	0.000	0.244
5	0.000	0.476	0.000	0.000	0.433	0.000
6	0.229	0.000	0.429	0.397	0.000	0.433
7	0.000	0.159	0.000	0.000	0.325	0.000
8	0.014	0.000	0.114	0.099	0.000	0.244
9	0.000	0.008	0.000	0.000	0.065	0.000
10	0.000	0.000	0.005	0.004	0.000	0.039
11	0.000	0.000	0.000	0.000	0.002	0.000
12	0.000	0.000	0.000	0.000	0.000	0.001

term in the series for the possible correct number of identifications being $n - 2min(n_1, n_2)$.

We display the distributions for the number of wines correctly identified for selected values of n_1 and n_2 in Table 15.

It is easily seen that there generally does not exist a clear-cut critical value for the number of correctly identified wines at the 5% or 10% level, because of the discreteness of the distributions. So, for example, if $n_1 = 4$ and $n_2 = 5, 7$ or more correctly identified wines mean that the randomness is rejected at the 0.167 (= 0.159+0.008) level. Eight or more correctly identified wines reject the randomness hypothesis at roughly the 0.1 level for the next two columns, nine (respectively ten) reject randomness at roughly the 0.05 level for the last two columns.

The last case we consider is the one in which there are several types of wines. In the first instance, we consider the case with three different types of wines, which we label with X, Y, and Z. An example would be provided by a case in which we are comparing three different vintages of two châteaux. In such a situation, there are two questions that could be asked: (1) How well do the tasters identify the different vintages, and (2) How well do the tasters identify the different châteaux; that is, to what extent can they pick out the wines that are from the same châteaux? The situation is quite different in this case, although two facts remain true: (1) there is exactly one way in which the number of correct identifications can be equal to the number of wines n, and (2) there is no way in which exactly $n-1$ wines are correctly identified. But it is no longer the case that the number of correct identifications is either always an even number or always an odd number. Consider the "true" pattern

$$X \quad X \quad Y \quad Y \quad Y \quad Z \quad Z \quad Z$$

The judges' following potential identification patterns produce, respectively, 0, 1, 2, 3, 4, 5, 6, and 8 correct identifications:

$$\begin{array}{cccccccc} Y & Y & Z & Z & Z & X & X & Y \\ Y & Z & Z & Z & Y & X & X & Y \\ X & X & Z & Z & Z & Y & Y & Y \\ X & Y & Z & Z & Y & Y & Z & X \\ X & X & Y & Z & Z & Z & Y & Y \\ X & Y & Y & Y & Z & X & Z & Z \\ X & Y & Y & Y & X & Z & Z & Z \\ X & X & Y & Y & Y & Z & Z & Z \end{array}$$

For a few selected values of n_1, n_2, n_3 we display the probability distributions in Table 16.

Table 16. Probabilities for the Number of Correctly Identified Wines

	Probability					
Number	$n_1 = 2$ $n_2 = 3$ $n_3 = 3$	$n_1 = 3$ $n_2 = 3$ $n_3 = 3$	$n_1 = 3$ $n_2 = 3$ $n_3 = 4$	$n_1 = 3$ $n_2 = 3$ $n_3 = 5$	$n_1 = 4$ $n_2 = 4$ $n_3 = 4$	$n_1 = 3$ $n_2 = 4$ $n_3 = 5$
0	0.043	0.033	0.019	0.006	0.010	0.006
1	0.150	0.129	0.088	0.049	0.053	0.040
2	0.259	0.225	0.190	0.139	0.131	0.115
3	0.257	0.259	0.246	0.224	0.206	0.198
4	0.188	0.193	0.225	0.237	0.229	0.223
5	0.064	0.112	0.137	0.187	0.183	0.195
6	0.000	0.032	0.071	0.097	0.114	0.126
7	0.002	0.000	0.017	0.046	0.050	0.056
8	0.000	0.001	0.008	0.010	0.020	0.023
9	0.000	0.000	0.000	0.004	0.004	0.004
10	0.000	0.000	0.000	0.000	0.001	0.002
11	0.000	0.000	0.000	0.000	0.000	0.000
12	0.000	0.000	0.000	0.000	0.000	0.000

Thus, with three wines of type X, three of type Y and five of type Z, one needs at least seven correct identifications in order to assert at approximately the 0.05 level that the result is significantly better than random.

A final question is how the critical value depends on how many types of wines there are in a tasting. There is obviously no straightforward answer, because there are two many things that can vary: the total number of wines, the number of types of wines, and the number of wines within each type. But consider a simplified experiment in which we fix the total number of wines at some power of 2; say $2^7 = 128$. We could then consider, alternately, 2 types of wines with 64 wines of each type, or 4 types with 32 wines of each type, or 8 types with 16 wines each, 16 types with 8 wines each, 32 types of 4 wines each, and finally 64 types of 2 wines each. It is intuitively obvious that if we guess randomly, we will tend to score the highest degree of correct identification in the first case and the lowest in the last. For imagine that in the first case we arbitrarily identify the first 64 wines as type X and the last 64 as type Y. If the order in which the wines have been arranged is random, we shall correctly identify on the average 64 of the 128 wines . In the last case, when there are 64 types of 2 wines each, the average number of identifications will be much smaller. To look at this in another way, in the first case there is only a single outcome in which no wine is correctly identified (i.e., the outcome in which the judge guesses the first 64 wines to be of type X, whereas they are all of type Y), but in the last case there is a huge number of possible outcomes in which no wine is correctly identified. We would therefore expect that as the number of types of wine in the tasting declines (with the number of wines in each type increasing), the critical value above which we reject the null hypothesis of randomness in the identification has to increase.

To further illustrate this, take an extreme case in which there are two types of wines, and ten bottles are arrayed left to right as follows

$$X \quad Y \quad Y \quad Y \quad Y \quad Y \quad Y \quad Y \quad Y \quad Y$$

In how many ways can all 10 wines be identified correctly? Our lone X-guess must be assigned to the first spot, and if we make the assignments at random, the probability of this occurring is 0.1. If we do not assign X to the first spot, exactly eight wines will be identified correctly, and hence the probability of that occurrence is 0.9. No other outcome is possible.

We finally display the critical values at the 0.05 and 0.10 levels for a large number of different cases in Table 17. In this table an entry such as

Table 17. Critical Values

	Critical values			Critical values	
Case	0.05 level	0.10 level	Case	0.05 level	0.10 level
6;3,3	6	6	10;2,4,4	7	7
6;4,2	—	2	10;2,2,6	8	7
6;2,2,2	6	6	10;2,2,2,2,2	5	5
7;3,4	7	7	11;5,6	11	9
7;5,2	7	7	11;4,7	11	9
7;2,3,3	7	5	11;3,8	11	11
7;1,2,4	7	7	11;3,4,4	8	7
8;4,4	8	8	11;3,3,5	8	7
8;3,5	8	8	11;2,3,6	8	7
8;2,6	8	8	11;2,2,7	8	8
8;2,3,3	6	6	11;2,3,3,3	6	6
8;2,2,4	6	6	11;2,2,3,4	7	6
8;2,2,2,2	6	5	12;6,6	10	10
9;4,5	9	9	12;5,7	10	10
9;3,6	9	9	12;4,4,4	8	7
9;3,3,3	6	6	12;3,4,5	8	7
9;2,3,4	7	6	12;3,3,6	8	8
9;2,2,5	7	6	12;2,3,7	9	8
10;5,5	10	10	12;2,4,6	8	7
10;4,6	10	10	12;3,3,3,3	7	6
10,3.7	10	10	12;2,3,3,4	7	6
10;3,3,4	7	6	12;2,2,2,2,2,2	5	4
10;2,3,5	7	7			

Note: There is no entry for the second element in the second column because there exists no number of correct identification that has a probability less than or equal to 0.05. In fact, the probability of 6 correct identifications is 0.0667.

n; i, j, k denotes the case in which there are n wines with three subgroups containing i and j and k items respectively.

5. Concluding Comments

In this chapter, we considered three types of questions: (1) How do we use the rankings of wines by a set of judges to determine whether some wines are perceived to be significantly good or bad, (2) How do we judge the strength of the (various possible) correlations among the judges' rankings, and (3) How do we determine whether the judges are able to identify the wines or the types of wines significantly better then would occur by chance alone. We are able to find appropriate techniques for each of these questions, and their application is likely to yield considerable insights into what happens in a blind tasting of wines.

Acknowledgments

I am greatly indebted for useful comments to Burton G. Malkiel, Orley Ashenfelter and Victor Ginsburgh. The responsibility for errors is, of course, mine.

References

Ashenfelter, O., Ashmore, D., and Lalonde, R. (1995). Bordeaux wine vintage quality and the weather. *Chance*, 8, 7–14.

Consumers Union of United States (1998). *Consumer Reports* 63(8). New York: Consumers Union.

Kramer, A. (1956). A quick, rank test for significance of difference in multiple comparisons. *Food Technology*, 10, 391–392.

Lindley, D. (2006). The analysis of a wine tasting. *Journal of Wine Economics*, 1, 33–42.

Siegel, S., and Castellan, N.J. Jr. (1988). *Nonparametric Statistics for the Behavioral Sciences*, New York: McGraw Hill.

Chapter 18

An Examination of Judge Reliability at a Major U.S. Wine Competition*

Robert T. Hodgson

Professor Emeritus, Department of Oceanography,
Humboldt State University, Arcata, CA 95521, USA
bob@fieldbrookwinery.com

Wine judge performance at a major wine competition has been analyzed from 2005 to 2008 using replicate samples. Each panel of four expert judges received a flight of 30 wines imbedded with triplicate samples poured from the same bottle. Between 65 and 70 judges were tested each year. About 10% of the judges were able to replicate their score within a single medal group. Another 10%, on occasion, scored the same wine Bronze to Gold. Judges tend to be more consistent in what they don't like than what they do. An analysis of variance covering every panel over the study period indicates only about half of the panels presented awards based solely on wine quality.

1. Introduction

In the spring of 2003, the author contacted the chief judge of the California State Fair wine competition in Sacramento, proposing an independent analysis of the reliability of its judges. The following questions were asked. Why is it that a particular wine wins a Gold medal at one competition and fails to win any award at another? Is this caused by bottle-to-bottle variability of the wine? To what extent is the variability caused by differing opinions within a panel of judges? Finally, could the variability be caused by inability of individual judges to reproduce their scores? As pointed out by Margaret Cliff and Marjorie King (1997) "Wine judges are rarely, if ever, subjected to rigorous testing. Neither are competitions based on rigorous experimental design with replication to examine judge reproducibility."

*This article originally appeared in *Journal of Wine Economics* (2008), 3(2), 105–113.

The California State Fair hosts the oldest commercial wine competition in North America. Entries are limited to wines produced in California and its judges are selected from a broad range of wine professionals: winemakers, wine buyers, wine critics, and professors of enology and viticulture. Lima (2006) calculates a positive relationship between price and medal status at the State Fair wine competition so awards at the State Fair can be important to a winery's economic health.

The lack of concordance[1] between judges is well known (Ashenfelter, 2006), but an investigation of individual judge consistency has not been published. Ashenfelter and Quandt (1999) and Cicchetti (2004a) appear to disagree on the benefits of rank order statistics (a non-parametric vs. parametric basis) to evaluate wine tastings. However, both approach the reliability of judges based on the principle of concordance, that is, good judges agree with each other, whether by score or by rank. Basing reliability on concordance rather than consistency may be attributed to psychological research, where in order to obtain independent observations, ratings of identical subjects are not possible. Thus, the seminal papers by Bartko (1966) and Shrout and Fleiss (1979) on Intraclass Correlations, which is the approach taken by Cicchetti (2004a, 2006) on evaluating the famous 1976 Paris tasting, base reliability on concordance. This chapter advances the thesis that consistency is more fundamental than concordance in evaluating judge reliability because it is a better basis of measuring experimental error.

2. Methods

The results that follow are based on four triplicate samples served to 16 panels of judges. A typical flight consists of 30 wines. When possible, triplicate samples of all four wines were served in the second flight of the day randomly interspersed among the 30 wines. A typical day's work involves four to six flights, about 150 wines. Each triplicate was poured from the same bottle and served on the same flight. The overriding principle was to design the experiment to maximize the probability in favor of the judges' ability to replicate their scores.

The judges first mark the wine's score independently, and their scores are recorded by the panel's secretary. Afterward the judges discuss the wine.

[1] In this study, *concordance* is used to describe agreement between judges; *consistency* will be used to describe the ability of individual judges to repeat their scores on identical wines. *Reliability* is loosely defined to be a combination of both but is often equated with concordance in the cited literature.

Based on the discussion, some judges modify their initial score; others do not. For this study, only the first, independent score is used to analyze an individual judge's consistency in scoring wines.

3. Data

Approximately 3,000 wines per year were entered during the evaluation period. A typical data set for one panel (2006) is produced below as Table 1. J1 to J4 represent the four judges. The three values associated with R1 represent the scores given the first group of replicate wines, the three for R2, the second, etc. Judges are only asked to provide letter scores, Bronze+, Silver−, etc. Letter scores are later converted to numerical scores ranging from 80 points (No Award) to 100 points.

Table 1. Example of Recorded Data for Panel Q (2006)

	Original score			
Judge code	J1	J2	J3	J4
R1	84	90	80	80
R1	84	88	94	82
R1	80	80	82	86
R2	80	80	84	84
R2	90	90	80	82
R2	96	80	80	82
R3	80	80	80	80
R3	80	80	80	80
R3	80	80	80	80
R4	88	96	80	80
R4	90	96	82	88
R4	96	90	80	84

Notes: Individual statistics are calculated for each judge including four values of range and standard deviation. Also calculated for each judge are their maximum range (maximum error in consistency) and a pooled standard deviation (a typical error in consistency). A two-way Analysis of Variance (ANOVA) was performed for each panel to determine the relative importance of a wine's score between a "wine factor" and the "judge factor." The calculations are performed using Microsoft Excel.

4. Results

The results are divided into two categories, individual judge performance and group (panel) performance.

4.1. *Individual judge performance*

4.1.1. *Range and maximum range*

Figure 1 shows cumulative frequency distributions for range and maximum range for the period 2005–2008. The median range is about 4 points (e.g., Silver− to Silver+). More interesting is the maximum range where only 10% of the judges were *consistently consistent* to a single medal range (a maximum 4-point spread). On the other extreme, another 10% awarded scores ranging from Bronze to Gold (a 12-point spread) or worse (No Award to Gold). Although the median maximum range varies from year to year, it is typically about 8 points corresponding to (e.g., Bronze+ to Gold−).

Examining Figure 1, judges were perfectly consistent (0-point spread) about 18% of the time. However, this usually occurred for wines that were rejected. That is, when the judges were very consistent, it was often for wines that they did not like.

4.1.2. *Pooled standard deviation*

A pooled standard deviation is calculated for each judge based on the four triplicate samples. Since there are two degrees of freedom associated with

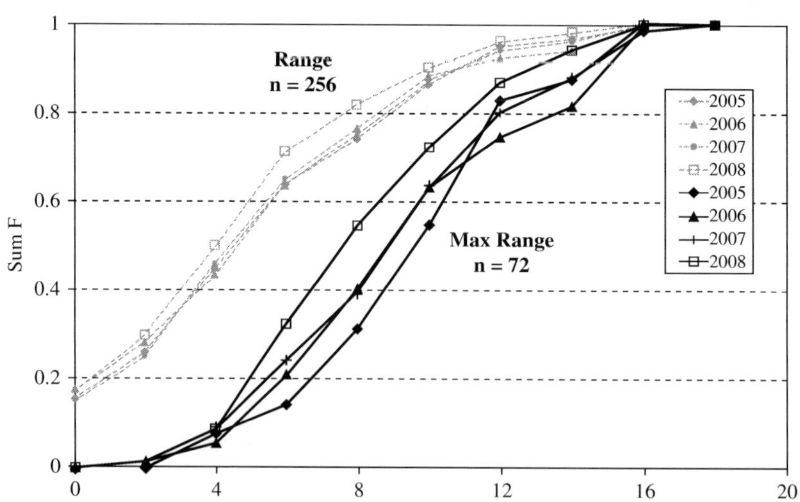

Figure 1. Cumulative Frequency Distribution for Range and Maximum Range 2005–2008

each of the four replicates the pooled standard deviation is

$$s_p = [\{s^2(R_t) + s^2(R_2) + s^2(R_3) + s^2(R_4)\}/4]^{1/2}$$

The median and mean pooled standard deviation for all judges from 2005 to 2008 is 3.6 points. The corresponding 95% confidence interval is 14 points, which includes almost the entire range of medals possible (e.g., No Award to Gold−, or Bronze to Gold+).

4.1.3. *Year-to-year correlation*

Do the most consistent judges repeat their performance year to year? Cicchetti (2004a) asks, "(W)ould the most reliable tasters established in a given competition continue as such, or are these initial findings just another chance phenomenon?" He also asks whether the "'best' judges will continue to remain so in future tastings. To the extent that this is true, it opens up the real possibility of using the more consistent judges to train the less consistent ones to become more highly reliable in their evaluations."

To answer these questions, there is sufficient data to perform a correlation analysis for those judges who participated in at least two competitions. For the 2005–2006 competitions, there were 26 common judges. A scatter diagram, shown in Figure 2, would indicate that a judge's superior performance (in consistency) one year does not correlate with superior performance the next.

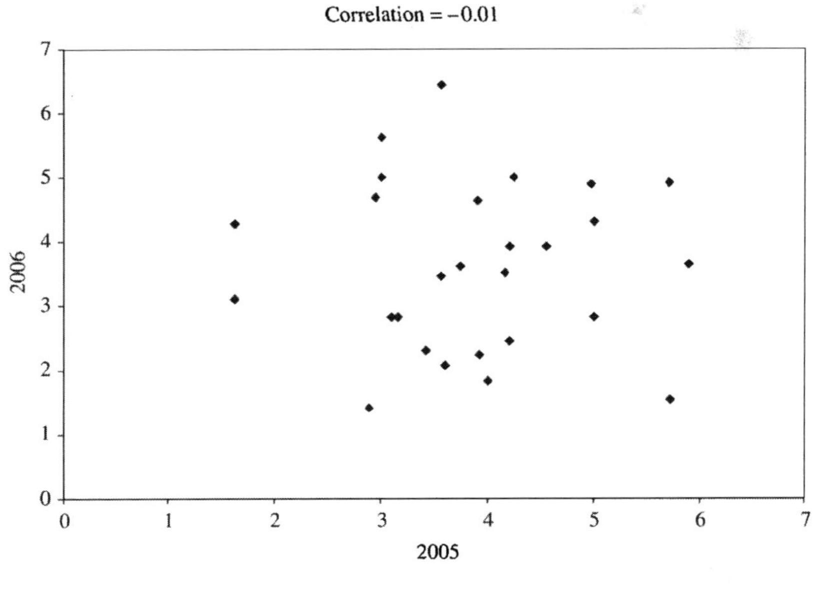

Figure 2. Scatter Diagram of Pooled Standard Deviation for the 26 Judges Who Participated in 2005 and 2006

4.2. *Panel variance*

For each panel, an ANOVA was performed to examine the variation of judge's scores. We presume there are two factors that determine the score given a wine: (1) the quality of the wine and (2) the bias of the judge. Does a wine's score depend on the wine, the judge evaluating the wine, both or neither? In addition to judge bias, judge inconsistency will reduce the significance of the wine factor by increasing experimental error.

Table 2 represents the data from one panel in 2008. Table 3 shows the accompanying ANOVA. Since the P-value for the wine is small (less than 0.05) we assume wine quality is a significant factor in the score it received. As the P-value for the judges is greater than 0.05, it means judge bias is not a significant factor in the wine's final score (case 2 above).

Table 2. Raw Data from Panel xyz, 2008

	J1	J2	J3	J4
R1	84	80	90	96
R1	86	96	96	94
R1	90	84	90	96
R2	80	80	86	84
R2	88	96	92	80
R2	84	80	84	80
R3	84	96	84	80
R3	86	84	84	84
R3	86	84	84	84
R4	86	90	90	88
R4	88	84	94	86
R4	84	84	90	84

Table 3. Analysis of Variance for Data in Table 2

ANOVA Source of variation	SS	df	MS	F	P-value	F crit
Wines	241.7	3.0	80.6	4.4	0.011	2.9
Judges	65.7	3.0	21.9	1.2	0.332	2.9
Interaction	265.7	9.0	29.5	1.6	0.159	2.2
Within	592	32	18.5			
Total	1,165	47				

Table 4. Summary of ANOVA Results for all Panels, 2008

Panel	Wine	Judges	Unknown	Exp error
1	0.461	0.121	0.000	3.2
2	0.005	0.001	0.046	3.5
3	0.108	0.125	0.210	3.7
4	0.000	0.060	0.208	3.3
5	0.030	0.000	0.288	3.3
6	0.000	0.608	0.055	3.0
7	0.037	0.026	0.041	3.6
8	0.164	0.012	0.017	3.5
9	0.006	0.024	0.000	2.6
10	0.011	0.332	0.159	4.3
11	0.000	0.094	0.060	2.2
12	0.296	0.409	0.012	3.8
13	0.000	0.398	0.020	3.3
14	0.199	0.121	0.204	4.1
15	0.007	0.755	0.149	3.9
16	0.286	0.585	0.281	5.8
17	0.526	0.001	0.477	3.5

To recognize a good panel, it is desirable to see a small P-value for the wine and a large P-value for the judges (i.e., the wine is important and the judge bias is not). In addition, judge inconsistency increases experimental error, thus reducing the ability of the wine factor to dominate (i.e., it will increase the P-value for the wine). Table 4 lists the P-values for the wines and judges for all panels in the 2008 competition.

Based on the above guidelines, Panels 4, 6, 10, 11, 13, and 15 meet the requirement that it was the wine, not the judge bias, that contributed to the rankings. In Panels 2, 5, 7, and 9, wine quality evidently was a factor although other factors were also important. In panels 1, 3, 8, 12, 14, 16, and 17, the ranking of the wine did not depend so much on the wine as other factors.

Considering all 65 panels tested during 2005 to 2008, Table 5 summarizes their performance into four groups. The top right panel corresponds to cases where the wine factor and not the judge factor was the primary element responsible for the wine's score. The top left panel shows cases where both the wine factor and the judge factor were significant in determining the wine's score. The bottom left panel shows cases where the judge factor was the primary element in determining the wine's score, and the bottom right panel indicates those cases where the wine's score was determined neither by the wine's quality nor judge bias.

Table 5. Summary of ANOVA Analyses 2005–2008

		Judge factor	Judge factor
		P < 0.05	P ≥ 0.05
Wine factor	P < 0.05	15	30
Wine factor	P ≥ 0.05	9	11

In 30 cases, about 50%, the wine and only the wine was the significant factor in determining the judges' score. For the remaining 50% of the panels, other factors played a significant role in the award received.

5. Discussion

The author's interest over the past four years has been to explain the variability in the results of wine competitions. While this data is from a single competition, there is, in the author's mind, no reason to suspect the results are not general. This is because the format of many competitions is similar and because many of these judges participate in other competitions as well. By serving replicate samples on the same flight and poured from the same bottle, the experiment favored optimum performance by the judges. Had the wines been served on different flights, it is reasonable to assume consistency would be less. While this does not directly explain why wines win Golds in some competitions and fail to place in others, it is reasonable to predict that any wine earning *any* medal could in another competition earn *any other* medal, or none at all. Indeed, in 2003 as reported by The Grapevine,[2] which tracked over 4,000 wines entering 14 major U.S. wine competitions, more than 1,000 wines receiving a Gold medal in one or more competitions failed to place in others.

To lift their brand above the competition, wineries spent more than $1 million in entry fees at just four California competitions alone this year. The benefit of this expense is the belief by wineries that entry fees offer a valid return on investment: gold medals sell wine. However, a recent article in Wine Business Monthly (Thach, 2008) conducted as a joint effort by 10 global universities with specialties in wine business and marketing found that consumers are not particularly motivated by medals when purchasing wine in retail stores. If consumer confidence is to be improved, managers of

[2]California Grapevine, P.O. Box 22152, San Diego CA 92192 www.calgrapevine.com.

wine competitions would be well advised to validate their recommendations with quantitative standards.

Ideally, an examination of the 65 judging panels over four years in Table 5 would show all 65 in the upper right quadrant where wine and only wine is the determinant factor. How can one explain that just 30 panels, less than half, achieved those results? The answers are judge inconsistency, lack of concordance — or both.

6. Conclusions

The purpose of this investigation was to provide a measure of a wine judge's ability to consistently evaluate replicate samples of an identical wine. With such a measure in hand, it should be possible to evaluate the quality of future wine competitions using consistency as well as concordance with the goal to continually improve reliability and to track improvements associated with procedural changes.

Acknowledgments

I would like to thank the administration and advisory board of the California State Fair Wine Competition for supporting this research and agreeing to release the results. Taking such a leadership role benefits the entire wine industry. I would especially like to thank G.M. "Pooch" Pucilowski, chief judge, and Kem Pence, wine department chairperson of the California State Fair Commercial Wine Competition, for their continued support of this study. In addition, Matt Sainson, www.ijudgewine.com, was the programmer responsible for data management for the entire competition. I am also indebted to an anonymous referee.

References

Ashenfelter, O., and Quandt, R.E. (1999). Analyzing wine tasting statistically. *Chance*, 12, 16–20.

Ashenfelter, O. (2006). Tales from the crypt: Bruce Kaiser tells us about the trials and tribulations of a wine judge. *Journal of Wine Economics*, 1(2), 173–175.

Bartko, J.J. (1966). The intraclass correlation coefficient as a measure of reliability. *Psychological Reports*, 19, 3–11.

Cicchetti, D.V. (2004a). Who won the 1976 wine tasting of French Bordeaux and U.S. cabemets? Parametrics to the rescue. *Journal of Wine Research*, 15, 211–220.

Cicchetti, D.V. (2004b). On designing experiments and analyzing data to assess the reliability and accuracy of blind wine tastings. *Journal of Wine Research*, 15, 221–226.

Cicchetti, D.V. (2006). The Paris 1976 tastings revisited once more: Comparing ratings of consistent and inconsistent tasters. *Journal of Wine Economics*, 1(2), 125–140.

Cliff, M.A., and King, M.C. (1996). A proposed approach for evaluating expert judge performance using descriptive statistics. *Journal of Wine Research*, 7, 83–90.

Cliff, M.A., and King, M.C. (1997). The evaluation of judges at wine competitions: The application of eggshell plots. *Journal of Wine Research*, 8(2), 75–80.

Lima, T. (2006). Price and quality in the California wine industry: An empirical investigation. *Journal of Wine Economics*, 1(2), 176–190.

Shrout, P.E., and Fleiss, J.L. (1979). Intraclass correlations: Uses in assessing rater reliability. *Psychological Bulletin*, 86(2), 420–428.

Thach, L. (2008). How American consumers select wine. *Wine Business Monthly* (June 2008), 66–71.

Chapter 19

Reliability and Consensus of Experienced Wine Judges: Expertise Within and Between*

Robert H. Ashton

L. Palmer Fox Professor,
Fuqua School of Business, Duke University, USA
robert.ashton@duke.edu

This chapter considers the levels of reliability and consensus of wine quality judgments found in studies of experienced wine judges. Both reliability, which concerns the similarity of repeat judgments of a particular wine by the *same* judge, and consensus, which concerns the similarity of judgments of a particular wine *across* judges, are necessary requirements for expertise in wine judging. Reliability and consensus levels found in wine judging are compared to those documented by a large body of research in six other fields: medicine, clinical psychology, business, auditing, personnel management, and meteorology. In all fields, including wine judging, reliability is greater than consensus. Both reliability and consensus are, on average, substantially lower in wine judging than in other fields, although tremendous variability exists across judges in every field. Overall, little support is found for the idea that experienced wine judges should be regarded as experts.

1. Introduction

Recent research on wine judging raises questions about both the reliability and consensus of wine quality judgments made by experienced judges in blind tastings (e.g., Gawel and Godden, 2008; Hodgson, 2008, 2009a, 2009b). *Reliability*, an intraindividual notion, concerns the similarity of repeat judgments of the same wine by an individual judge, while *consensus*, an interindividual notion, concerns the similarity of the judgments of

*This article originally appeared in *Journal of Wine Economics* (2012), 7(1), 70–87.

a particular wine between/among two or more independent judges.[1] Both reliability and consensus are necessary requirements for expertise in wine judging. Stated simply, the basic issues are the extent to which individual wine judges repeat their own judgments (which I label "expertise within") and the extent to which different wine judges agree in their judgments (which I label "expertise between").

Although the body of research on the reliability and consensus of experienced wine judges is small (and mostly recent), both the "within" and "between" aspects of judgment variability have been the subject of extensive research across many professional fields over many decades. In this chapter, I review the few wine studies that exist and compare their results with those of a much larger sample of carefully controlled experimental studies that examine reliability and consensus in the fields of medicine, clinical psychology, business, auditing, personnel management, and meteorology. All the studies that I review quantify reliability and consensus using correlational measures. Reliability for each individual judge is measured as the correlation between repeat judgments of identical stimuli on two different occasions. Consensus is measured as the correlation between the judgments of identical stimuli by each *pair* of judges. Correlational measures are by far the most common way of quantifying reliability and consensus, and they offer the advantage of greater comparability of the levels of reliability and consensus across individuals, judgment tasks, and, ultimately, professional fields. I exploit this advantage by contrasting the level of reliability and consensus found in wine judging with that found in other fields.

Of course, professional judges — in any field — cannot be expected to achieve perfect reliability or perfect consensus, especially the latter, for many reasons. These include varying levels of attention to the task and motivation to perform well, differential ability and experience, focusing on different aspects of the phenomenon of interest, the absence of objectively "correct" or "best" answers in many settings, and the evolving and dynamic nature of the phenomenon being judged (Shanteau, 2001). As a result, it is difficult to make statements about the level of reliability and consensus that one should expect to find in a particular field. In controlled experimental

[1] Terminology varies, especially in the wine literature. For example, "consistency" is often used to refer to intrajudge variability (Hodgson, 2008), and both "reliability" and "concordance" are often used to refer to interjudge variability (Cicchetti, 2004b; Hodgson, 2008). In the broader social science literature, in which the judgments of professionals in many fields have been investigated extensively, "reliability" refers to intrajudge variability, while "consensus" refers to interjudge variability. I use the latter terminology in this chapter.

settings, however, many factors that might naturally degrade reliability and consensus will likely operate to a lesser extent, so we might be seeing the various types of judges "at their best" in the research results. In any event, we can get a clear sense of the *relative* extent of reliability and consensus across fields, and that sense can help to inform our understanding of these critical aspects of wine judging.

Section 2 of the chapter considers the roles that reliability and consensus play in the evaluation of professional judgment. It also describes the positive relationship that exists between reliability and accuracy and between consensus and accuracy, in settings where "correct answers" are available and thus accuracy can be measured. Section 3 consists of two parts. The first part summarizes the results of wine studies that examine intrajudge reliability and compares the results to those of 41 studies conducted in these other six fields. The second part summarizes the results of wine studies that examine interjudge consensus and compares the results to those of 46 studies conducted in these same fields. In addition, results from several studies that examine both reliability and consensus in the same study and with the same judges are briefly presented. Section 4 presents a discussion and conclusion.

2. Accuracy, Reliability, and Consensus

The type of setting addressed here is that in which one or more individuals in a professional field, who might be "experts" in varying degrees, make professional judgments concerning specialized aspects of their field, and then communicate recommendations based on those judgments to people who use them as critical inputs in their decision making. Examples abound in such fields as medicine, business, and consumer decision making. Judgments and recommendations made in these settings can be highly consequential to both those who provide them (because of their effect on reputation-building) and those who receive them (because of their effect on decisions).

Those on the receiving end seek confidence in the recommendations they receive and, therefore, are interested in the quality of the professional judgments on which those recommendations are based. Ideally, the quality of professional judgments would be revealed by their *accuracy*, that is, their correspondence with an objectively measured external criterion that is independent of the professional and the judgments he or she makes. In many settings, however, an independent external criterion does not exist (or will not be known for a long time), and therefore judgment accuracy cannot be evaluated. In those settings, attention naturally turns to surrogate evaluation criteria such as intrajudge reliability and interjudge consensus, criteria that are necessary but not sufficient for establishing expertise (or at least for establishing that such judgments are "good enough" for practical purposes). Instead of being three separate features of professional judgment, however, accuracy, reliability, and consensus are closely related both theoretically and empirically, as explained below.

Researchers across many fields consider reliability a more fundamental requirement for expertise than consensus. Cicchetti (2004b) and Hodgson (2008, 2009b), for example, adopt this view in the field of wine judging: "What do we expect from expert wine judges? Above all, we expect [reliability], for if a judge cannot closely replicate a decision for an identical wine served under identical circumstances, of what value is his/her recommendation?" (Hodgson, 2009b, 241). A similar view prevails in medicine. In a setting involving judgments of disease severity, Einhorn (1974, 563) states, "With regard to intrajudge reliability, it should be obvious that unless the expert can reproduce his [judgments], there is little more that can be said in defense of his expertise." Similarly, in a setting involving the evaluation of coronary angiograms, Detre, Wright, Murphy and Takaro (1975, 985) state, "Although high intra- and interobserver agreement does not assure that the observer is right in his judgment, it is certain that he could hardly be right if he disagrees often with himself." Thus, intrajudge reliability is typically regarded as the most important requirement for expertise when the absence of objectively correct answers prevents a definitive determination of judgment accuracy.

It must be recognized, however, that reliability remains an important requirement for expertise even when objectively correct answers are available, and therefore judgment accuracy can be assessed, because of the positive relationship between reliability and accuracy. Theoretical work establishes that intrajudge reliability places an upper limit on the level of accuracy that can be achieved (e.g., Ghiselli, 1964; Lord and Novick, 1968). This fact is captured by Goldberg's (1970, 423) description of intrajudge reliability issues in the field of clinical psychology: "He 'has his days': Boredom, fatigue, illness, situational and interpersonal distractions all plague him, with the result that his repeated judgments of the exact same stimulus configuration are not identical. He is subject to all those human frailties which lower the reliability of his judgments below unity. And, if the judge's reliability is less than unity, there must be error in his judgments — error which can serve no other purpose than to attenuate his accuracy." Thus, intrajudge reliability is a necessary requirement for expertise both when the accuracy of professional judgment cannot be assessed and when it can.

It is worth noting that test-retest reliability is not the only type of intrajudge reliability that has been studied by judgment researchers. The other principal type, often called "linear consistency," concerns the extent to which a linear regression model estimated from the relationship between an individual's judgments and a set of underlying information items can reproduce the individual's judgments. This type of intrajudge reliability is one determinant of the ability of a linear regression model of the individual to produce accurate predictions of an external criterion. Linear-consistency and test-retest reliability are related (see Cooksey, 1996, 205–208) in that linear-consistency reliability is a function of test-retest reliability and the extent to which the individual's linear regression model captures the underlying judgment process, that is, the extent to which the individual's judgment process reflects the linearity and additivity assumptions that underlie regression (Lee and Yates, 1992). Because linear-consistency reliability confounds the effects of test-retest reliability with the effects of systematic departures from linearity and additivity, test-retest reliability is the more fundamental of the two.[2]

Although reliability is widely considered a more fundamental requirement of professional judgment than is consensus, as observed earlier, consensus is nevertheless extremely important. This is especially true in settings where correct answers do not exist (or will not be known within a reasonable period). Decisions must be made and actions must be taken even though the "correctness" of those decisions might never be known. Because agreement among the independent judgments of competent professionals is often an indispensible input to decisions and actions, consensus has emerged as an important criterion for evaluating judgment. As Hodgson (2008, 106) puts it in the wine context, "good judges agree with each other."

To the extent that interjudge agreement is considered a desirable feature of wine judging, it follows that ways of increasing such agreement are likely to be of interest. Indeed, Cicchetti (2004b, 221), in his discussion of research designs and data-analytic strategies for improving blind wine

[2]A full treatment of linear-consistency reliability is beyond the scope of this chapter. Although linear-consistency reliability has not been evaluated in the context of wine judging, scores of studies in other fields find a strong positive relation between this type of intrajudge reliability and accuracy — see, for example, the meta-analyses of Karelaia and Hogarth (2008) and Kaufmann and Athanasou (2009).

tastings, says "the goal is to reduce, as much as is possible, the extent of interjudge variability in the evaluation of any given wine." Cicchetti goes further, however, making a bold suggestion that reducing interjudge variability should "[increase] the validity or accuracy of blind wine tasting" (221).

The idea that reducing interjudge variability (i.e., increasing consensus) will result in increased accuracy has been tested empirically by Ashton (1985) in two important business settings where correct answers exist. One setting involves sales predictions (a continuous executives make quarterly predictions, over 14 years, of the annual number of advertising pages that will be sold by *Time magazine*. The second setting involves predictions by independent auditors (CPAs) of whether a sample of business firms will or will not continue as "going concerns" (a dichotomous judgment variable) for the coming year. In both settings, a strong positive relationship is found between consensus and accuracy.[3] Ashton (1985, 185) concludes: "If an individual's predictions agree strongly with those of others in a group, then that individual will tend to be among the most accurate in the group. This conclusion also holds for *pairs* of individuals; that is, pairs who agree better also tend to be more accurate than other pairs. Similarly, individuals and pairs that exhibit low consensus tend to be less accurate than those exhibiting high consensus."

Ashton's (1985) finding of a strong positive relation between consensus and accuracy is bolstered by the results of Detre *et al.* (1975), who find a strong positive relationship between consensus and reliability. In a medical setting involving evaluations of coronary angiograms, these researchers document considerable variability in both reliability and consensus and, more important for present purposes, a clear relationship between the reliability of individual judges and how often they agree with other judges.

Despite results such as those of Ashton (1985) and Detre *et al.* (1975), consensus is sometimes viewed as a problematic criterion for evaluating judgment. Although it is difficult to dispute the notion that a professional judge should not "disagree with himself," it is often pointed out that even complete agreement among judges does not guarantee accuracy and that the lone dissenter among many judges could, in fact, be correct. As Einhorn (1974, 570) states, "the history of science is replete with oddballs who did not agree

[3]This result held when consensus was measured in noncorrelational terms (e.g., as the mean absolute difference between the judgments of two individuals). The relationship between consensus and accuracy in the field of auditing is further explored by Davis, Kennedy and Maines (2000), Keasey and Watson (1989), and Pincus (1990). Kenny (1991) develops a more general theoretical model of consensus and accuracy in a broader context.

with anyone, yet, were proved to be correct by subsequent events." Einhorn also observes, however, that the later discovery that the oddball was correct requires that a criterion other than consensus eventually become available, which will not be the case in many important judgment settings.

Perhaps a more troublesome aspect of consensus as a criterion for evaluating judgment is its potential dampening effect on learning: "Disagreements are often the route by which experts increase understanding of their field. By seeking out areas of disagreement between one another, experts explore the limits of their own knowledge and stretch their range of competency" (Weiss and Shanteau, 2004, 231). Thus, to the extent that agreement becomes the standard, the benefits of disagreement, alternative viewpoints, devils' advocates, and so on may be lost and learning may suffer. These potential drawbacks notwithstanding, the practical necessity for timely decisions and actions, as well as the positive relationship among consensus, reliability, and accuracy revealed by research, firmly establish consensus as an important criterion for evaluating judgment.

3. Results

3.1. *Judgment reliability: Expertise within?*

Correlational studies of the intrajudge reliability of experienced wine judges have been reported by Brien, May, and Mayo (1987), Gawel and Godden (2008), Gawel, Royal, and Leske (2002) and Lawless, Liu, and Goldwyn (1997). Each study involves several judges who, in blind tastings, independently rate a number of wines and later re-rate those same wines. The researchers determine, separately for each judge, the correlation between the judge's first and second ratings. The results are summarized in Table 1, Panel A.

Brien *et al.* (1987) describe the results of four studies in which either 24 or 48 different wines were tasted — and re-tasted the same day or the following day — by either six or eight experienced judges. Intrajudge reliability varies greatly, ranging from 0.16 to 1.00. On average, reliability is fairly high, with mean reliability across the four studies ranging from 0.45 to 0.74. Note that the mean reliabilities in Studies 2 and 5, in which the repeat tastings occurred the same day (0.73 and 0.74), are considerably greater than those in Studies 3 and 4, in which the repeat tastings occurred one day later (0.45 and 0.54).

Lawless *et al.* (1997) report a study in which four panels of judges tasted — and re-tasted less than an hour later — 14 different wines. Three of the panels were experienced wine tasters (Panels CB, G, and PB), while

Table 1. Summary of Studies Investigating Judgment Reliability

Study	Reliability		
	Mean	Lowest	Highest
Panel A. Wine Studies			
Brien, May, and Mayo (1987)			
Study 2	0.73	0.39	0.91
Study 3	0.45	0.35	0.59
Study 4	0.54	0.16	0.76
Study 5	0.74	0.56	1.00
Lawless, Liu, and Goldwyn (1997)			
Panel CB	0.53	0.10	0.76
Panel G	0.61	0.32	0.85
Panel PB	0.42	0.10	0.80
Panel C	0.31	−0.03	0.69
Gawel, Royal, and Leske (2002)			
Published data	0.46	−0.49	0.98
Unpublished data	0.40	—	—
Gawel and Godden (2008)			
Reds	0.45	−0.39	0.97
Whites	0.35	−0.42	0.97
Mean reliability across studies	0.50		

Field	Number of studies	Mean reliability
Panel B. Studies in Other Fields		
Meteorology	3	0.91
Business	3	0.83
Auditing	10	0.82
Personnel management	13	0.76
Medicine	6	0.76
Clinical psychology	6	0.70

the fourth panel was described as wine consumers (Panel C). The range of intrajudge reliability across the individual judges is −0.03 to 0.85, while the range of mean reliability across the individuals in the four panels is 0.31 to 0.61.[4] The consumer panel produces lower reliabilities than the three

[4]The numbers reported here and in Table 1 are estimated from figure 1 in Lawless *et al.* (1997).

experienced panels (a mean of 0.31 for the former and means of 0.53, 0.61, and 0.42 for the latter).

A particularly interesting aspect of the Lawless *et al.* (1997) results is that the reliability of the *mean ratings* of the individuals in each panel is much higher than the mean reliability of the panel's individual members. To illustrate, consider Panel CB, which has six members. The mean reliability reported for Panel CB in Table 1 (0.53) is the mean of the six judges' individual reliability values, consistent with the notion that reliability is an intraindividual phenomenon. In addition to quantifying these six individual *reliability values*, Lawless *et al.* also calculate the mean of the six judges' *ratings* of each wine, on both the initial and repeat tastings, and then determine the correlation between these mean ratings. The resulting correlation (0.90) is much higher than the mean of the six judges' individual reliability values (0.53).[5] The superiority of mean, or composite, judgments vis-à-vis those of the average individual in the composite has been demonstrated in many settings, including wine judging (Ashton, 2011).

Gawel *et al.* (2002) report a study in which 42 experienced judges tasted a wine that had been aged in four different types of oak. Instead of rating overall quality, however, the judges rated the intensity of eight different characteristics of the wine (e.g., spice, butter, and texture). Only average reliabilities across the eight characteristics are reported. Again, there is tremendous variability across judges, with a mean reliability of 0.46. Gawel *et al.* (2002) also refer to unpublished data from 225 experienced tasters that reveal a mean intrajudge reliability of 0.40, although they provide no further information.

Gawel and Godden (2008) report results from tastings involving 571 experienced judges who tasted an average of 23 reds and 23 whites, with duplicates tasted two or three days later. Again, great variability across judges is evident, with mean intrajudge reliability of 0.45 for the reds and 0.35 for the whites. When the reliability of three-judge panels was evaluated, it was found to be substantially greater than the mean reliability of the individual judges — consistent with the earlier results of Lawless *et al.* (1997).

Finally, Hodgson (2008) reports some fascinating results from the California State Fair Wine Competitions of 2005 to 2008. Hodgson's results

[5]The same result obtains for the other three panels of judges: the correlations between the mean *ratings* of the panel (0.89, 0.82, and 0.52 for Panels G, PB, and C, respectively) are much higher than the mean correlations produced by the individuals who are included in the panel (0.61, 0.42, and 0.31).

concern four triplicate samples that were judged by 16 panels of four judges each. Both of the repeat samples were tasted in the same tasting flight and were poured from the same bottle as the original sample. As Hodgson (2008, 106) explains: "The overriding principle was to design the experiment to maximize the probability in favor of the judges' ability to replicate their scores." Unlike in earlier studies, a correlational measure was not used in this study to quantify judge reliability; instead, the judges awarded medals to each wine (Gold, Silver, Bronze, or No Award), and the reported results concern the judges' ability to replicate their own awards. The key finding is that the judges awarded the same medal only about 18% of the time — and this usually occurred for wines that received No Award. Moreover, in many instances a judge awarded Gold to one of the triplicates and Bronze (or No Award) to another.

Mean reliability across all the wine studies in Table 1 is 0.50. How does this compare to judgment reliability in other fields? In an earlier study, I analyzed published research on the reliability of professional judgment in the fields of meteorology, medicine, clinical psychology, personnel management, business, and auditing (Ashton, 2000). Fifty studies across these six fields were identified, 41 of which measured reliability as the correlation between repeat judgments of identical stimuli by each judge. All 41 correlational studies focus on professional judges who make a series of judgments in the domain of their everyday experience (as opposed to, say, college students responding to abstract and unfamiliar tasks to fulfill a course requirement).

The meteorological studies concerned forecasts of atmospheric events such as microbursts and hail. The medical studies involved professionals such as pathologists and radiologists evaluating the severity of conditions such as gastric ulcers and Hodgkin's disease. The clinical psychology studies concerned the evaluation of traits such as intelligence and sociability. The personnel management studies concerned the evaluation of various dimensions of work-related behaviors, typically for selection or promotion purposes. The business studies concerned financial analysis and taxation. Several studies involved the professional field of auditing. Because the nature of professional judgment in auditing may be unfamiliar to readers of this journal, the Appendix provides a brief explanation of the critical importance of judgment in auditing.

Judgment reliability varied substantially across individual judges in these studies. The mean reliability that emerged in each of the six fields is reported in Table 1, Panel B. Mean reliability ranges from 0.91 in meteorology to 0.70 in clinical psychology — vis-à-vis a mean of 0.50 for the wine studies.

(I defer until Section 4 a consideration of why reliability in wine judging might reasonably be expected to be lower than in other fields.)

My earlier analysis (Ashton, 2000) identified three features of the overall body of results that may provide useful perspective in the wine context. First, reliability decreased with greater time between the original judgment and the repeat judgment, which is also seen in the Brien *et al.* (1987) study of wine judging. Second, group discussion among two or more individual judges had the effect of increasing reliability; a similar effect is seen in the superior reliability of the judge *panels* in Gawel and Godden (2008) and Lawless *et al.* (1997). Finally, reliability was inversely related to the difficulty of the judgment task; this, too, has its counterpart in studies of wine judging — for example, the clear tendency for reliability to be greater for wines at each end of the quality scale than for those in the middle (e.g., Hodgson, 2008).

3.2. *Judgment consensus: Expertise between?*

Correlational studies of the interjudge consensus of experienced wine judges have been reported by Ashton (2011), Baker and Amerine (1953), Brien *et al.* (1987), Cicchetti (2006a, 2006b), and Hodgson (2009a). Each study involves several judges who, in blind tastings, independently rate a number of wines. The researchers determine, for each pair of judges, the correlation between their ratings. The results are summarized in Table 2, Panel A.

Baker and Amerine (1953; cited in Brien *et al.*, 1987) report results from five experienced judges who evaluated 13 reds and 17 whites over multiple sessions, with four or five wines per session. The results reveal greater mean consensus for the whites (0.58) than for the reds (0.39). Substantial variability in consensus exists across pairs of judges, ranging from 0.44 to 0.75 for the whites and from 0.07 to 0.90 for the reds.

One of Brien *et al.*'s (1987) four reliability studies (described above) also examined consensus. Interjudge correlations are reported for both the first occasion on which the wines were tasted and the second occasion (later the same day). Mean consensus is lower in the repeat tasting than in the first (0.37 vs. 45), and the range of consensus across judges is wider (−0.40 to 0.84 vs. −0.09 to 0.79).

Other evidence on the consensus of wine judgments comes from two analyses of the famous 1976 Paris tasting of California and French wines that revolutionized the wine world.[6] Eleven experts (nine of them French)

[6]Taber (2006) provides a fascinating and informative account of the 1976 event.

Table 2. Summary of Studies Investigating Judgment Consensus

Study	Consensus		
	Mean	Lowest	Highest
Panel A. Wine Studies			
Baker and Amerine (1953)			
Reds	0.39	0.07	0.90
Whites	0.58	0.44	0.75
Brien, May, and Mayo (1987)			
Study 2 — Occasion 1	0.45	−0.09	0.79
Study 2 — Occasion 2	0.37	−0.40	0.84
Cicchetti (2004a, 2006b)			
Reds	0.22	0.05	0.93
Whites	0.36	0.09	0.99
Ashton (2011)			
Reds	0.16	−0.62	0.97
Whites	0.44	−0.07	0.94
Hodgson (2009a)	0.11	−0.02	0.33
Mean consensus across studies	0.34		

Field	Number of studies	Mean consensus
Panel B. Studies in Other Fields		
Meteorology	4	0.75
Personnel management	6	0.65
Auditing	23	0.61
Medicine	3	0.56
Business	8	0.49
Clinical psychology	2	0.37

tasted 10 reds (six California and four French) and 10 whites (again, six California and four French). Although much has been written about who "won" the tasting (e.g., Ashenfelter and Quandt, 1999; Cicchetti, 2004a; Hulkower, 2009; Lindley, 2006; Quandt, 2006, 2007), my concern here is the extent to which the 11 judges agreed in their judgments of the wines. Cicchetti (2004a, 2006b), using the intraclass correlation coefficient as the measure of judge consensus, finds an overall consensus level of 0.22 for the reds and 0.36 for the whites. Ashton (2011), using the Pearson correlation as the measure of consensus, reports similar results: mean consensus of 0.16 for the reds and 0.44 for the whites. Both analyses report substantial variability in consensus across pairs of judges.

Hodgson (2009a) analyzed 4,167 wines that were entered in 13 major U.S. wine competitions in 2003. Several of his results speak to the degree of consensus in wine quality judgments across the competitions. First, 106 of the 375 wines that were entered in five competitions received Gold medals in one competition, but only 20 of these 106 received a second Gold medal and only six of these 20 received a third. None of the 375 received Gold medals in more than three competitions. Second, only 132 of the 3,347 wines that were entered in two or more competitions received the *same* medal in all competitions entered (and this almost always occurred in just two competitions). Finally, of the 2,440 wines that were entered in more than three competitions, 1,142 received at least one Gold; however, 957 of these 1,142 failed to receive any medal in at least one competition.

Hodgson (2009a) developed a correlational measure of consensus by first assigning numerical scores to the various medals and then computing correlations between the scores received by wines in each pair of competitions. With 13 competitions, there are 78 such pairwise measures. The mean correlation is 0.11, with a range of -0.02 to 0.33. This clearly reflects poor consensus across the competitions, and most of the consensus that existed concerned wines awarded Bronze medals or No Awards. Hodgson (2009a, 5) concluded that "wine judges concur in what they do not like but are uncertain about what they do," consistent with his earlier findings (Hodgson, 2008) concerning intrajudge reliability.[7]

Lawless *et al.* (1997), whose intrajudge reliability results are reported in Table 1, also examined consensus. They did so, however, by focusing on the mean judgments of each of the four panels, not on the judgments of the individual members. As noted earlier, mean judgments result in inflated reliability values — and the same is true for consensus values. Lawless *et al.* found that the three experienced panels agreed much more with one another (correlations of 0.66, 0.75, and 0.77) than with the consumer panel (correlations of 0.33, 0.44, and 0.46).

Finally, Quandt (2006) summarizes some consensus results from 92 tastings conducted by the eight members of the Liquid Assets Wine Group. Instead of pairwise correlations among tasters, however, Quandt reports

[7]Cliff and King (1997), using a different methodology, report similar results: Judges agree much more on wines perceived to be at both the low and high end of the quality scale than on wines perceived to be of moderate quality.

Kendall's coefficient of concordance (W), a measure of the overall concordance among the judges' ratings. Kendall's W is statistically significant at the 0.05 (0.10) level for 49% (57%) of the tastings, indicating that "substantial agreement existed among judges more than half the time" (Quandt, 2006, 16).

Mean consensus across all the wine studies in Table 2 is 0.34, substantially below mean reliability across wine studies of 0.50. As is the case with reliability, it is of interest to compare the level of consensus found in wine judging to that found in other fields. To my knowledge, there is no comprehensive review of consensus studies comparable to Ashton's (2000) review of reliability studies. However, my recent search of the literature identified 46 studies across the same six professional fields included in Ashton (2000) that report consensus results using a correlational measure.[8] The types of judgments examined in each field are the same as those described above for the reliability studies, with the exception of studies in business; the eight consensus studies in business settings examine a wider range of issues than do the three reliability studies (including sales predictions, actuarial judgments, and predictions of stock prices). As in the reliability studies in Ashton (2000), all the consensus studies focus on professional judges who make a series of judgments in the domain of their everyday experience.

Table 2, Panel B, reports the mean consensus that emerged in each of the six fields. Mean consensus ranges from 0.75 in meteorology to 0.37 in clinical psychology — vis-à-vis a mean of 0.34 for the wine studies. (I defer until Section 4 a consideration of why consensus in wine judging might reasonably be *expected* to be lower than in other fields.) Comparing mean reliability (Table 1) and mean consensus (Table 2) within fields reveals that consensus is lower than reliability in all fields, often substantially so, indicating that judges in all fields agree more with themselves than with others.

It should be recognized, however, that the mean within-field reliability and consensus results reported in Tables 1 and 2 are not completely comparable because the set of reliability studies in Table 1 differs somewhat from the set of consensus studies in Table 2 (i.e., some studies examine only reliability, some examine only consensus, and some examine both). Fortunately, many of these studies evaluate both reliability and consensus in the same study and with the same judges, allowing a direct comparison of reliability

[8]Various subsets of these studies are described by Bédard and Chi (1993), Bouwman and Bradley (1997), Broomell and Budescu (2009), Shanteau (2001), and Wright (1988).

Table 3. Summary of Studies Investigating Both Reliability and Consensus in the Same Study

Field	Number of studies	Mean reliability	Mean consensus
Meteorology	3	0.89	0.77
Personnel management	6	0.83	0.65
Auditing	9	0.81	0.67
Business	3	0.78	0.58
Wine	1	0.73	0.41
Clinical psychology	2	0.73	0.37
Medicine	2	0.70	0.45

and consensus. The results, shown in Table 3, confirm that mean reliability is substantially greater than mean consensus in all fields. The *difference* between mean reliability and mean consensus ranges from 0.12 (0.89 vs. 0.77) in meteorology to 0.36 (0.73 vs. 0.37) in clinical psychology. (This compares to a difference of 0.32 (0.73 vs. 0.41) in the single wine study that examines both reliability and consensus.) Finally, examination of the mean within-study levels of reliability and consensus in the 25 non-wine studies reveals no case in which mean consensus exceeds mean reliability.

4. Discussion and Conclusions

Both intrajudge reliability and interjudge consensus of experienced wine judges are found to be substantially below reliability and consensus in other fields. Quantified in correlational terms, mean reliability across published wine studies is 0.50 while mean consensus is 0.34. Moreover, reliability and consensus vary widely across studies (and across individual judges in a single study), with some judges performing well and others performing poorly. Two questions immediately arise: (1) Why are the *mean* levels of reliability and consensus so much lower among experienced wine judges than among judges in other fields? (2) What accounts for the great *variability* in reliability and consensus across wine judges?

On the first question, it is easy to imagine valid reasons that reliability and consensus in wine judging would be lower than in many other fields. At the risk of stating the obvious, foremost among them is that wine judging is inherently more subjective. Whereas professional judgment in meteorology, medicine, or business, for example, is based largely on relatively objective inputs (such as barometric pressure, x-ray results, and economic data), wine judging involves the senses of sight, smell, and taste. Thus, wine judging is not simply a matter of passively receiving some objective facts about bouquet, clarity, finish, and so forth and then weighting and combining these facts into an overall judgment of quality (which itself possesses a sizable subjective component).

The second question — concerning variability in reliability and consensus across wine judges — is more difficult. In general, however, a useful way of understanding the sources of differential performance across judges — in any field — is to focus on features of the judge, features of the judgment task, and the "interaction" between features of the judge and features of the task (Fischhoff, 1982). By interaction, I mean the extent to which there is a "match" (or a "mismatch") between judge and task.

Considering features of the judge (and assuming that the judge is *motivated* to perform well), voluminous research establishes that differences in ability, experience, and knowledge result in differential judgment performance (e.g., Ashton, 1999; Einhorn and Hogarth, 1981; Schmidt and Hunter, 1992). In the wine context, differences in *preferences* (which may result in part from differences in experience and knowledge and in part from past emotional associations involving particular wines) must also be considered, as must *biological* characteristics, such as differential sensitivity to smells and tastes (e.g., Bartoshuk, 1993; Goode, 2008). Considering features of the judgment task, a multitude of factors are involved in the task of blind wine tasting that might influence the overall results, including those with respect to intrajudge reliability and interjudge consensus (e.g., Amerine and Roessler, 1983; Goldwyn and Lawless, 1991). Examples include the types of wines tasted (and the range of types, if more than one), the number of wines of each type, the order in which they are tasted, the number of tasting flights, and the time between flights.

Such features of the judge and the judgment task surely account for much of the variability in reliability and consensus found across experienced wine judges. However, acquiring a deep understanding of differential performance across wine judges is likely to be more complex than identifying isolated features of judges and judgment tasks that are relevant. The extent to which relevant features of the judge are consonant with relevant features of the task (i.e., the extent to which there is a "match" between judge and task) is likely to be important as well.

To illustrate, imagine a blind tasting of red Bordeaux and red Burgundy involving four judges. Judges 1 and 2 have an affinity for Bordeaux, but not for Burgundy. Such affinity could be the result of greater experience or knowledge, stronger emotional associations, or heightened sensitivity and discriminability with respect to the smells and tastes of Bordeaux. In contrast, Judges 3 and 4 have the opposite affinity — for Burgundy, but not for Bordeaux. I conjecture that Judges 1 and 2 will exhibit greater intrajudge reliability when they taste Bordeaux (a match between judge and task) than when they taste Burgundy (a mismatch between judge and task) and that Judges 3 and 4 will exhibit the opposite pattern of results. Similarly, I conjecture that the Judge 1/Judge 2 pair and the Judge 3/Judge 4 pair will exhibit greater interjudge consensus than will the remaining four pairwise combinations of judges. They key point in this stylized example is that differential levels of reliability and consensus will not be determined solely by features of either the judge or the task in isolation but also by the extent to which those features match one another.

The empirical validity (and practical usefulness) of the various judge and task features mentioned above, as well as the notion that the "match" between judge and task is important in understanding the performance of experienced wine judges, can only be settled by research. Existing studies on the reliability and consensus of experienced wine judges were not designed or conducted in a way that allows the sources of differential performance to be understood. I hope the results reviewed in this chapter will provide a benchmark for future studies that take a systematic approach to understanding why reliability and consensus in wine judging are lower than in other fields and the sources of differential performance across experienced judges.

References

Amerine, M.A., and Roessler, E.B. (1983). *Wines: Their Sensory Evaluation.* New York: W.H. Freeman.

Arens, A.A., Elder, R.J., and Beasley, M.S. (2005). *Auditing and Assurance Services.* Upper Saddle River, NJ: Prentice Hall.

Ashenfelter, O., and Quandt, R. (1999). Analyzing a wine tasting statistically. *Chance*, 12, 16–20.

Ashton, A.H. (1985). Does consensus imply accuracy in accounting studies of decision making? *Accounting Review*, 60, 173–185.

Ashton, R.H. (1999). Enriching the "expertise paradigm" of accounting research: Conscientiousness, general cognitive ability, and goal orientation. *Advances in Accounting Behavioral Research*, 2, 3–14.

Ashton, R.H. (2000). A review and analysis of research on the test-retest reliability of professional judgment. *Journal of Behavioral Decision Making*, 13, 277–294.

Ashton, R.H. (2011). Improving experts' wine quality judgments: Two heads are better than one. *Journal of Wine Economics*, 6, 160–178.

Ashton, R.H., and Ashton, A.H. (1995). Perspectives on judgment and decision-making research in accounting and auditing. In R.H. Ashton and A.H. Ashton (Eds.),

Judgment and Decision-Making Research in Accounting and Auditing. New York: Cambridge University Press. Pages 3–5.

Baker, G.A., and Amerine, M.A. (1953). Organoleptic ratings of wines estimated from analytical data. *Food Research*, 18, 381–389.

Bartoshuk, L.M. (1993). The biological basis of food perception and acceptance. *Food Quality and Preference*, 4, 21–32.

Bédard, J., and Chi, M.T.H. (1993). Expertise in auditing. *Auditing: A Journal of Practice & Theory*, 12(Supplement), 21–45.

Bouwman, M.J., and Bradley, W.E. (1997). Judgment and decision making, part II: Expertise, consensus and accuracy. In V. Arnold and S.G. Sutton (Eds.), *Behavioral Accounting Research: Foundations and Frontiers*. Sarasota, FL: American Accounting Association. Pages 89–133.

Brien, C.J., May, P., and Mayo, O. (1987). Analysis of judge performance in wine-quality evaluations. *Journal of Food Science*, 52, 1273–1279.

Broomell, S.B., and Budescu, D.V. (2009). Why are experts correlated? Decomposing correlations between judges. *Psychometrika*, 74, 531–553.

Cicchetti, D.V. (2004a). Who won the 1976 blind tasting of French Bordeaux and U.S. cabernets? Parametrics to the rescue. *Journal of Wine Research*, 15, 211–220.

Cicchetti, D.V. (2004b). On designing experiments and analysing data to assess the reliability and accuracy of blind wine tastings. *Journal of Wine Research*, 15, 221–226.

Cicchetti, D.V. (2006a). The Paris 1976 wine tastings revisited once more: Comparing ratings of consistent and inconsistent tasters. *Journal of Wine Economics*, 1, 125–140.

Cicchetti, D.V. (2006b). The 1976 blind wine tastings: On the consistency of tasters from chardonnays to cabernets. Vineyard Data Quantification Society (www.vdqs.net).

Cliff, M.A., and King, M.C. (1997). The evaluation of judges at wine competitions: The application of eggshell plots. *Journal of Wine Research*, 8, 75–80.

Cooksey, R.W. (1996). *Judgment Analysis*. San Diego: Academic Press.

Davis, E.B., Kennedy, S.J., and Maines, L.A. (2000). The relation between consensus and accuracy in low-to-moderate accuracy tasks: An auditing example. *Auditing: A Journal of Practice & Theory*, 19, 101–121.

Detre, K.M., Wright, E., Murphy, M.L., and Takaro, T. (1975). Observer agreement in evaluating coronary angiograms. *Circulation*, 52, 979–986.

Einhorn, H.J. (1974). Expert judgment: Some necessary conditions and an example. *Journal of Applied Psychology*, 59, 562–571.

Einhorn, H.J., and Hogarth, R.M. (1981). Rationality and the sanctity of competence. *Behavioral and Brain Sciences*, 4, 334–335.

Fischhoff, B. (1982). Debiasing. In D. Kahneman, P. Slovic, and A. Tversky (Eds.), *Judgment Under Uncertainty: Heuristics and Biases*. New York: Cambridge University Press. Pages 422–444.

Gawel, R., and Godden, P.W. (2008). Evaluation of the consistency of wine quality assessments from expert wine tasters. *Australian Journal of Grape and Wine Research*, 14, 1–8.

Gawel, R., Royal, A., and Leske, P. (2002). The effect of different oak types on the sensory properties of Chardonnay. *Australian and New Zealand Wine Industry Journal*, 17, 14–20.

Ghiselli, E.E. (1964). *Theory of Psychological Measurement*. New York: McGraw-Hill.

Goldberg, L.R. (1970). Man versus model of man: A rationale, plus some evidence, for a method of improving on clinical inferences. *Psychological Bulletin*, 73, 422–432.

Goldwyn, C., and Lawless, H. (1991). How to taste wine (for fun and profit). *ASTM Standardization News*, 19, 32–37.

Goode, J. (2008). Experiencing wine: Why critics mess up (some of the time). In F. Allhoff (Ed.), *Wine & Philosophy: A Symposium on Thinking and Drinking*. Malden, MA: Blackwell. Pages 137–153.

Hodgson, R.T. (2008). An examination of judge reliability at a major U.S. wine competition. *Journal of Wine Economics*, 3, 105–113.

Hodgson, R.T. (2009a). An analysis of the concordance among 13 U.S. wine competitions. *Journal of Wine Economics*, 4, 1–9.

Hodgson, R.T. (2009b). How expert are "expert" wine judges? *Journal of Wine Economics*, 4, 233–241.

Hulkower, N. (2009). The judgment of Paris according to Borda. *Journal of Wine Research*, 20, 171–182.

Karelaia, N., and Hogarth, R.M. (2008). Determinants of linear judgment: A meta-analysis of lens model studies. *Psychological Bulletin*, 134, 404–426.

Kaufmann, E., and Athanasou, J.A. (2009). A meta-analysis of judgment achievement as defined by the lens model equation. *Swiss Journal of Psychology*, 68, 99–112.

Keasey, K., and Watson, R. (1989). Consensus and accuracy in accounting studies of decision making: A note on a new measure of consensus. *Accounting, Organizations and Society*, 14, 337–345.

Kenny, D.A. (1991). A general model of consensus and accuracy in interpersonal perception. *Psychological Review*, 98, 155–163.

Lawless, H., Liu, Y., and Goldwyn, C. (1997). Evaluation of wine quality using a small-panel hedonic scaling method. *Journal of Sensory Studies*, 12, 317–332.

Lee, J.W., and Yates, J.F. (1992). How quantity judgment changes as the number of cues increases: An analytical framework and review. *Psychological Bulletin*, 12, 363–377.

Lindley, D.V. (2006). Analysis of a wine tasting. *Journal of Wine Economics*, 1, 33–41.

Lord, F., and Novick, M. (1968). *Statistical Theories of Mental Test Scores*. Reading, MA: Addison-Wesley.

Pincus, K.V. (1990). Audit judgment consensus: A model for dichotomous decisions. *Auditing: A Journal of Practice & Theory*, 9, 1–20.

Quandt, R.E. (2006). Measurement and inference in wine tasting. *Journal of Wine Economics*, 1, 7–30.

Quandt, R.E. (2007). A note on a test for the sum of ranksums. *Journal of Wine Economics*, 2, 98–102.

Schmidt, F.L., and Hunter, J.E. (1992). Development of a causal model of processes determining job performance. *Current Directions in Psychological Science*, 1, 89–92.

Shanteau, J. (2001). What does it mean when experts disagree? In E. Salas and G. Klein (Eds.), *Linking Expertise and Naturalistic Decision Making*. Hillsdale, NJ: Erlbaum. Pages 229–244.

Taber, G.M. (2006). *Judgment of Paris: California vs. France and the Historic 1976 Paris Tasting that Revolutionized Wine*. New York: Scribner.

Weiss, D.J., and Shanteau, J. (2004). The vice of consensus and the virtue of consistency. In K. Smith, J. Shanteau, and P. Johnson (Eds.), *Psychological Investigations of Competence in Decision Making*. Cambridge: Cambridge University Press. Pages 226–240.

Wright, W.F. (1988). Audit judgment consensus and experience. In K.R. Ferris (Ed.), *Behavioral Accounting Research: A Critical Analysis*. Columbus, OH: Century VII. Pages 305–328.

Appendix

Several of the reliability and consensus studies in Tables 1–3 concern judgments made in the field of auditing, a field that might be unfamiliar to readers of this journal. This Appendix provides some perspective on the critical role that professional judgment plays in auditing.

Briefly stated, auditing provides independent assurance concerning important disclosures provided by business organizations whose ownership shares are publicly held. Such organizations are required to disclose to current and potential investors and creditors substantial information about their past financial performance and current financial condition. Because this information is generated and disclosed by managers of the organization itself, who have strong incentives to portray the results favorably, and because external parties have limited access to such information via other channels, regulatory bodies in both the public and private sectors require the information to be examined by a firm of auditors, or certified public accountants (CPAs), who are independent of the reporting organization.

Auditors examine the reporting organization's financial disclosures and underlying systems and records to judge whether the disclosures are fairly presented in accordance with measurement and disclosure standards adopted by government agencies (e.g., the U.S. Securities and Exchange Commission) and the financial community more generally. Auditors collect and evaluate information that bears on this issue, and they use it as input to several component judgments that, when aggregated, suggest whether the organization's claim of fair presentation is likely to be tenable.

Audit judgments fall into two broad categories — investigation and reporting. *Investigation* judgments concern (1) the likelihood that errors or irregularities have occurred in the organization's processing of financial information and that the organization's own controls would have prevented or detected them, (2) the extent to which errors or irregularities that may have occurred and not been detected are important enough to require close scrutiny by the auditor, and (3) the extent to which evidence collection should be expanded in response to ongoing findings from the audit. *Reporting* judgments concern how best to fulfill the auditors' obligation to report (to the public) the results of their investigation. Auditors' most important reporting options are the standard and modified reports. A standard report provides assurance that the organization's financial disclosures are indeed fairly presented in accordance with accepted measurement and disclosure standards. A modified report, in contrast, signals that the organization's claim of fair presentation is unlikely to be tenable, and it provides an explanation of the circumstances or events that call fair presentation into question.

Auditors' investigation and reporting judgments are made in a setting that imposes significant costs on the various parties from legal, economic, and regulatory sources. Investors, creditors, suppliers, employees, and others can be harmed if auditors fail to detect errors or irregularities or fail to provide adequate disclosure of an organization's financial problems. The organization itself can be harmed if auditors mistakenly believe that they have found errors or irregularities or report that the organization has not provided adequate disclosure when, in fact, it has. Thus, the field of auditing is ripe for the study of professional expertise.[9]

[9]Arens, Elder and Beasley (2005), Ashton and Ashton (1995), and Bédard and Chi (1993) provide detailed accounts of the professional judgment issues faced by auditors.

Part VI

Wine and Expert Opinion

Chapter 20

The Impact of Gurus: Parker Grades and *En Primeur* Wine Prices*

Héla Hadj Ali[†], Sébastien Lecocq[‡], and Michael Visser[§]

[†]*Research Fellow at INRA (National Institute for Research in Agriculture), Toulouse, France*

[‡]*INRA, UR1303 ALISS, Alimentation et Sciences Sociales, F-94205 Ivry-sur-Seine, France*
Sebastien.Lecocq@inra.fr

[§]*CREST, CNRS, ENSAE, University of Paris-Saclay and CRED, University of Paris 2, France*
Michael.Visser@ensae.fr

This chapter looks at the impact of Robert Parker's oenological grades on the so-called *en primeur* prices of young Bordeaux wines. The Parker grades are usually published in the spring of each year, before the wine prices are established. However, the wine grades for 2003 were published much later, in the autumn, *after* the determination of prices. This unusual reversal is exploited to estimate a Parker effect which we find to be, on average, worth 2.80 euros per bottle of wine. We also use grade-specific effects to predict what prices would have been had Parker attended the 2003 spring tasting.

1. Introduction

The judgment of experts and gurus matters in many types of markets. For instance, in art markets for books, music, and movies, opinion leaders have an important effect on consumer decisions via their rankings in all sorts of guides and competitions (Ginsburgh, 2003). Similarly, in auctions of paintings, art experts influence sale prices via the publication of their pre-sale

*This article originally appeared in *The Economic Journal* (2008), 118, F158–F173.

estimates in auction catalogs (Bauwens and Ginsburgh, 2000). Other markets where expert opinion leaders are very active and influential are sports betting markets (Avery and Chevalier, 1999), financial stock markets (Shleifer, 1986) and the market for restaurants (Chossat and Gergaud, 2003).

Given the importance of experts and gurus, it seems of interest to be able to measure their impact on market outcomes precisely. In this chapter we consider a particularly well-known expert, the American wine critic Robert Parker, and study the effect of his opinion on Bordeaux wine prices. More specifically, we analyze the effect of Parker's opinion on the so-called *en primeur* wine prices. These are prices set by Bordeaux châteaux owners just 6 or 7 months after the grape harvest (i.e., when the wines are still very young and not yet bottled).[1]

Robert Parker is widely regarded as the most influential wine expert in the world.[2] It is often claimed by those working in the wine industry that his wine reports and oenological grades, published in the bimonthly journal *The Wine Advocate* and in his wine books, exercise much power over wine prices: good grades may cause prices to rocket sky-high, while, inversely, very bad grades may leave wines practically unsaleable unless their prices are adjusted downwards. His power over prices is thought to be particularly important for *en primeur* wines.[3] A possible explanation for this is that consumers do not have easy access to the *en primeur* market (recall that *en primeur* wines are not yet bottled). As a consequence they cannot judge the products themselves and thus require the judgment of wine connoisseurs.

To assess the effect of Parker's opinion on *en primeur* prices, we exploit the following natural experiment. Each spring (since 1994) Robert Parker comes to Bordeaux to taste and evaluate a number of *en primeur* wines of the latest vintage. He publishes his findings in *The Wine Advocate*, usually in the April issue. The *en primeur* prices are fixed by the châteaux

---

[1]Bordeaux *en primeur* wines should not be confounded with Beaujolais *primeur* wines. The latter are specially produced and bottled for immediate consumption (starting in November, just 2 or 3 months after the harvest), while the former first go through the usual vinification process (a period lasting between one and two years), in the cellars of the châteaux, before being bottled and put on the market.

[2]One can find many quotes about Robert Parker. Here are some found on the web site http://www.erobertparker.com: "Parker is the most influential wine writer in the world today." (*The Los Angeles Times*); "Parker is the world's most experienced and trustworthy taster." (Jancis Robinson, another well-known wine taster and critic); 'The man with the paragon palate... For countless wine lovers Robert Parker's tastes are infallible.' (*Time Magazine*).

[3]See the wine survey "The Globe in a Glass" published in *The Economist*, 18 December 1999, p. 102.

owners in the weeks and months thereafter (the *en primeur* market usually opens at the end of April, and lasts until June), giving them the possibility of incorporating the information contained in the Parker grades. In 2003 things went differently because the wine expert did not come in the spring to taste the 2002 vintage. According to Parker himself, the trip was canceled at the request of his family.[4] The French press however argued that his absence could be explained by the judicial affairs in which one of his collaborators was involved at the time (see, for example, *Libération*, July 1, 2003). Whatever the reasons, it meant that châteaux owners had to determine their prices *without* knowing the grades that Parker would have attributed. So, as Jancis Robinson put it, "the Bordelais are having to re-learn the art of selling a whole vintage, 2002, without his help."[5]

We use this unusual reversal to estimate a Parker effect on *en primeur* prices. Adopting the counterfactual framework introduced by Rubin (1974), this effect is defined as the average treatment effect on the treated. It measures the mean effect of the attribution of Parker grades for those wines that were actually graded. This commonly-used evaluation parameter is identified under a "parallel trend" assumption. Roughly speaking, this assumption states that, had Parker not graded any wine in two subsequent years (which is of course a hypothetical situation), the price evolution over the two years would have been the same for all wines. Under the parallel trend assumption, the treatment effect can be estimated by a difference-in-differences type estimator. Using data on *en primeur* prices established in 2002 (2001 vintage) and 2003 (2002 vintage), we find an estimate of the Parker effect equal to 2.80 euros per bottle of wine. Estimates by appellation show that the treatment effect is the largest for wines from Pomerol, which is quite interesting since these are precisely the wines that Robert Parker appreciates the most. Using data on the grades assigned in 2002, we also estimate grade-specific treatment effects, and show that they steeply increase with the level of grading. Finally we exploit the fact that the grades eventually attributed by Parker to the 2002 vintage (he came to Bordeaux in September 2003) are also observed in our data. Under the hypothesis that these marks have the same interpretation as the ones assigned in the spring (we will explain that this is a plausible hypothesis), we use the autumn grades to predict what the prices would have been had Parker attended the spring tasting in 2003.

---

[4]Early in 2003, his wife and daughter preferred the trip to be postponed in view of the threat of a war in Iraq.
[5]See http://www.jancisrobinson.com/jr7046.htm.

Section 2 summarizes the empirical findings of some other recent chapters on the Robert Parker factor. Section 3 describes our data set, Section 4 gives the definition of the Parker effect, explains how it can be estimated, and presents our empirical results. Section 5 concludes.

2. Review of Literature

Several papers have looked at the influence of Parker marks on wine prices. They are almost all based on the estimation of so-called hedonic price functions, where prices are regressed on a set of characteristics in order to determine which characteristics have a significant effect. Some of these papers compare the impact on prices of official classifications (such as the 1855 classification in the case of Bordeaux wines) with the impact of Parker's own classification but most analyze the marginal effect of Parker grades (i.e., the β-coefficient in the regression of prices on grades).

In what is probably the earliest article on the subject, Ginsburgh *et al.* (1994) apply the hedonic price method to a sample of 102 Médoc wines. Their data set allows them to disentangle the price effects of weather, reputation (as measured by the 1855 classification), natural endowments (soil, exposure of the vineyards or grapes) and all sorts of production factors. They show that technology and weather conditions explain two thirds of the price variation, and once the reputation variable is added the proportion of explained variance increases to almost 85%. They also show that more recent classifications (such as Parker's classification) do not lead to a better fit of the hedonic price equation than the 1855 classification.

Di Vittorio and Ginsburgh (1996) regress auction prices, gathered during public sales held at Christie's London, of 58 top-classified growths from the Haut-Médoc region on the year of vintage and the name of the château. The estimated hedonic function allows them to calculate, for each château and year of vintage, a price index, and these price indexes are compared with several classifications (those of Parker, the wine critics Tastet and Lawton, and the wine magazine *Wine Spectator*). They find that the 1855 classification does better in explaining their price indexes than any other classification.

Jones and Storchmann (2001) use wine auction prices for 21 prestigious Bordeaux wines to assess the respective effects of the year of vintage, the grape composition (acid and sugar levels), and quality (as measured by Parker points). The authors show that the influence of Parker grades on prices is large and varies between châteaux: the price increase induced by a one-point increase in the Parker rating is 7% on average, ranging from less than 4% to more than 10%. The price sensitivity to Parker grades is found stronger for Cabernet Sauvignon-dominated wines than for Merlot-dominated wines, for wines that have achieved high ratings in the past and for small properties.

Février *et al.* (2005) study the role of the buyer's option in multi-unit ascending (or English) auctions using data collected during an important sale of fine wines held in 2000 at Drouot, the largest auction house in Paris. The estimation of an auction model allows them to determine which characteristics influence the willingness to pay for a wine (the production region, the vintage, whether the label is damaged or not, the level of wine in the bottle, the Parker-rating etc.). Parker grades are taken from a Parker guide published in 1995, wherein each wine is ranked between one star (lowest possible rank) and five stars (highest rank).[6] Because the grading system from this particular Parker guide reflects the overall and long-term quality of each wine and does not depend on the vintage, the authors also add a grade, taken from a French wine website, reflecting the quality of the vintage. Their results show that the value bidders attribute to a wine significantly increases with Parker's classification.

Hadj Ali and Nauges (2007) exploit a panel data set covering 132 Bordeaux châteaux over 15 vintages (1983, 1985–1998) to estimate the influence of current quality (as measured by Parker grades and by an overall vintage score given by *Wine Spectator*) and reputation (as measured by the ranking of the wine and by the average of the scores Parker gave to previous vintages) on the pricing of *en primeur* wines. They find that prices mainly depend on the reputation of the châteaux through their ranking. They also find that the marginal impact of Parker grades on *en primeur* prices is significant but small: a one-point increase in the grade leads to a price increase of 1.01%.

Dubois and Nauges (2010) use a subsample of the Hadj Ali and Nauges (2007) data set (108 châteaux over the 1994–1998 vintages). They argue that true quality, which is known by the producer but unobserved by the consumer and the econometrician, will not only influence the pricing of *en primeur* wines but also the Parker-rating, implying an endogeneity issue which may produce biased estimates. Controlling for unobserved quality allows them to disentangle the effect of quality from the effect of Parker grades on prices. They find evidence that Parker grades significantly affect the price of *en primeur* wines: a one-point increase in the grade increases the price by 1.38%. They also show that the impact of Parker's judgment

[6]This contrasts with the other mentioned studies, where wines are graded using a 50–100 point scale.

is clearly over-estimated when unobserved quality is not accounted for since in this case it equals 3.95%, which is much larger than the effect found by Hadj Ali and Nauges (2007) using the whole data set.

There are many differences between the previous papers and the present one, but we will only mention the two most important ones. The first is that most of the previous papers study the marginal impact of Parker grades on prices. We instead focus on the more extreme evaluation parameter "price when wine is graded minus price in the absence of grading." The second difference is that in the previous studies the time lag between the moment the grades are attributed and the moment the wine prices are established is relatively important. For instance in Jones and Storchmann (2001), the wine prices are the prices fetched at auctions in 1996/97, whereas the quality index is the Parker-rating of these wines published in 1994/95. Conversely, in Hadj Ali and Nauges (2007), prices are *en primeur* wine prices but grades are those Parker gave once the wines were bottled, a long time after the end of *en primeur* sales. The grades used in this chapter are the ones assigned by Parker just a few weeks before the start of *en primeur* sales (2001 vintage) or just a few months after these sales (2002 vintage).

3. Data

Our data set combines two sources of information: the 2002 and 2003 *en primeur* prices for approximately 250 châteaux obtained from a Bordeaux wine broker, and Parker grades extracted from *The Wine Advocate*. Section 3.1 gives a short description of the Bordeaux *en primeur* market and explains how wine prices are defined, Section 3.2 outlines how Robert Parker evaluates and grades *en primeur* wines, and Section 3.3 contains a descriptive analysis of the matched data.

3.1. En primeur *wine prices*

The Bordeaux *en primeur* wine market is a forward market where wines are sold as futures. Traditionally the market opens at the end of April and lasts for just 2 or 3 months. The wines that are traded are those from the latest vintage. Thus the wines traded in the spring of 2002 for instance were from the 2001 harvest. Trading therefore takes place when the wines are still very young, unblended and unbottled. The payments on this market are made when the sale contracts are signed and delivery occurs once the wines are bottled, one to two years after the grape harvest. The sales are organized by brokers who act as intermediaries between the châteaux owners and the *négociants* (who in turn sell the wine on to importers, retailers and private consumers). The *en primeur* prices are determined by the châteaux owners themselves and, given these prices, the brokers negotiate with potential buyers about quantities and delivery dates. The Bordeaux *en primeur* market has existed since the eighteenth century and has become increasingly important in recent years. Nowadays it generates a turnover of between 300 and 600 million euros per year and some châteaux sell up to 80% of their production *en primeur* (Hadj Ali, 2002).

The *en primeur* prices in our data correspond to first tranche prices (also called opening prices)[7] and they come from the archives of one of the largest brokers in Bordeaux. The full sample contains the prices of all the 375 Bordeaux châteaux traded by this broker during the period 1994–2003. This chapter only uses the prices established in 2002 and 2003. Furthermore, we restrict ourselves to the 233 châteaux that were traded in both 2002 and 2003.[8] For each of the 233 châteaux in our sample we thus observe the 2002 (2001 vintage) and 2003 (2002 vintage) *en primeur* prices. Prices are in euros per bottle of 75cl. We also observe each château's appellation group and ranking.

Since the broker who gave us the price data is a large and important firm in Bordeaux, there is good reason to believe that our sample is representative of the population of châteaux active in the *en primeur* market. Evidence for this comes from the fact that the sample covers a large spectrum of châteaux, ranging from the best-known wines such as Ausone, Lafite Rothschild, Latour, Margaux and Mouton-Rothschild, to less prestigious ones such as Beaulieu, Chantegrive, Fonréaud, and Pierdon.

3.2. *Parker grades*

Each spring, usually late March or early April, Robert Parker comes to the Bordeaux region to taste *en primeur* wines from the latest vintage. Since the wines are not yet bottled, the infant clarets are extracted from the barrels. The tastings are generally done in peer-group, single-blind conditions. Peer-group tasting means that wines belonging to the same region or appellation

[7]Châteaux owners sell their wine on the *en primeur* market in one, two or three tranches. The tranches are sold successively, which allows the producers eventually to adapt prices to market demand. The first tranche prices are by far the most strategic, awaited and scrutinized prices in the *en primeur* market.

[8]A given château is not necessarily traded by the broker in each year. If it is not traded in some year then its *en primeur* price is obviously not observed in that year.

are evaluated relatively to each other. Single-blind tasting means that the products are judged without the producer's name being known, which has the advantage that neither the price nor the reputation of the châteaux can affect the grading. The Parker grading system uses a 50–100 point quality scale. Unlike the more mature wines, to which Parker assigns single scores (e.g., 82),[9] he generally gives grade intervals to *en primeur* wines (e.g., [88, 90]). This probably reflects the fact that for him there is an extra element of uncertainty in judging the quality of such young wines. The quantitative rating of each wine is complemented by a verbal tasting note containing an overall description of the wine. The grade intervals and tasting notes of all the wines that are tasted in the spring are published in *The Wine Advocate*, usually in the April issue. These pieces of information can also be found on Parker's web site http://www.erobertparker.com. Using this site, we could determine which of the 233 châteaux in our sample were evaluated by Parker in the spring of 2002, and for those indeed evaluated we recorded the 2001 vintage grade intervals.

As explained in the introduction, things were different in 2003. Robert Parker did not come to Bordeaux in the springtime to taste the latest vintage but only during the end of the summer (between August 30th and September 8th),[10] so the 2002 vintage was tasted about 11 months after the harvest, unlike the earlier vintages which were evaluated roughly 6 months after the harvest. According to Robert Parker (see issue 149 of the *The Wine Advocate*), there was not much oenological difference in tasting the 2002s in August/September, as opposed to tasting the other vintages in March/April. This suggests that, *ceteris paribus*, we can attach the same meaning to the grade intervals attributed to the 2002 vintage as the ones assigned to the earlier vintages. The grade intervals for the 2002 vintage were published in the October issue of *The Wine Advocate* (issue 149), and can also be found on Parker's web site. We again consulted the web site, this time to check which of the 233 châteaux were evaluated in the late summer of 2003, and copied the relevant 2002 vintage grade intervals.

3.3. *Descriptive statistics*

Table 1 shows how the 233 châteaux in our data are ranked and from which appellation they originate. Note that about half of the Bordeaux appellations are represented in our sample (there are 25 different appellations in the

[9]See the wine reports in *The Wine Advocate* or his wine books.

[10]Note that in the spring châteaux owners did not know that Parker would come later in the year.

Table 1. Percentage of Châteaux by Ranking and Appellation

Ranking		Haut-Médoc	6.87
1er Cru Classé	5.15	Lalande-de-Pomerol	2.58
2ème Cru Classé	8.58	Listrac	1.29
3ème Cru Classé	4.29	Margaux	10.30
4ème Cru Classé	3.86	Médoc	0.43
5ème Cru Classé	6.44	Montagne-St-Emilion	1.72
Cru Bourgeois	14.16	Moulis	1.72
1er Grand Cru Classé A	0.43	Pauillac	8.15
1er Grand Cru Classé B	2.15	Pessac-Léognan	11.16
Grand Cru Classé	9.44	Pomerol	6.44
Cru Classé	6.01	1ères Côtes de Blaye	0.86
Cru Non Classé	39.48	1ères Côtes de Bordeaux	0.43
Total	100.00	Puisseguin-St-Emilion	0.86
Appellation		St-Emilion Grand Cru	21.89
Barsac	1.29	St-Estèphe	3.86
Bordeaux Blanc	2.15	St-Georges St-Emilion	0.43
Bordeaux Supérieur	0.43	St-Julien	5.58
Côtes de Castillon	2.58	Sauternes	5.58
Fronsac	1.29	Total	100.00
Graves Blanc	1.29		
Graves Rouge	0.86		

Note: The descriptive statistics are based on the sample of 233 châteaux.

sample, while there are roughly 50 of them in the Bordeaux wine region); see Combris *et al.* (1997). Note also that there is much diversity in the ranking of the châteaux: about 28% of the châteaux are ranked according to the famous 1855 classification (1er Cru Classé, 2ème Cru Classé, ..., 5ème Cru Classé), 14% are classified as Cru Bourgeois, and 40% are not classified at all.

Table 2 gives some simple descriptive statistics for the *en primeur* prices and the Parker appreciations. To make the 2002 and 2003 prices comparable, we have divided the latter by 1.019, where 1.9% is the evolution of the consumer price index over that period (source INSEE: http://www.insee.fr). Also, all grade intervals have been replaced by their midpoints (e.g., the interval [94, 98] is replaced by the midpoint 96).[11]

The price statistics are based on all 233 châteaux in our sample. The grade statistics for the 2001 vintage are based on the 158 wines (in our sample) that were evaluated by Robert Parker in the spring of 2002, while those for the 2002 vintage are based on the 121 wines tasted in the late summer of 2003. As the Table shows, the wines from the 2002 vintage received grades that are on

[11]There is not much variation in the observed intervals. In 91% of the cases the interval is either 1 or 2 points, in 8% it equals 3 points, and in 1% it is either 4 (1 case) or 11 points (1 case).

Table 2. *En Primeur* Prices and Parker Grades

	No. of obs.	Mean	Std. dev.	Min.	Max.
2001 vintage					
Grade	158	88.52	2.42	82.5	97
Price	233	19.01	17.86	4	125
2002 vintage					
Grade	121	89.40	2.19	86	96.5
Price	233	15.65	13.23	3.93	98.14

Notes: The grades correspond to the midpoints of the grade intervals. The prices are per bottle of 75cl, in 2002-euros.

average only slightly higher than those received by the wines from the 2001 vintage. Apparently, both vintages were deemed of similar quality. The two vintages differ however markedly in their prices. On average, the 2001 vintage is priced more than 3 euros higher than the 2002 vintage. The variance of the price for the 2001 vintage is also much higher than the one for the 2002 vintage. Recalling that the 2001 vintage prices were released after publication of Parker's grades and that the 2002 vintages prices were released without this knowledge, this last finding suggests that more information leads to more price variation. We also find that the correlation between grades and prices is stronger for the 2001 vintage than for the 2002 vintage: Spearman's correlation coefficient equals 0.74 for the former and 0.64 for the latter.[12]

4. Estimating the Parker Effect

In this section, we give the precise definition of the Parker effect, explain under which condition the effect is identified and how it can be estimated, and present the empirical estimates. The Parker effect will be defined by adopting the counterfactual framework pioneered by Rubin (1974). Let $D_i(t)$ be the treatment status indicator for observation i, for $i = 1, \ldots, 233$, in year t, for $t = 2002, 2003$. Thus $D_i(t) = 1$ if wine i is graded in the spring of year t, and $D_i(t) = 0$ otherwise. Note that since Robert Parker did not grade the 2002 vintage in the spring of 2003, we have $D_i(2003) = 0$ for all i. Let $P_{i0}(t)$ represent the *en primeur* price for wine i not graded in the spring of year t (wine i in the control group at t), and let $P_{i1}(t)$ be the price for wine that is graded (wine i in the treatment group at t). Finally, let $P_i(t)$ be the realized

[12]Pearson's correlation coefficient equals 0.64 for the 2001 vintage and 0.62 for the 2002 vintage.

price, that is, $P_i(t) = D_i(t)P_{i1}(t) + [1 - D_i(t)]P_{i0}(t)$. Note that $P_i(2003) = P_{i0}(2003)$ for all i. We assume that in each time period the treatment status of observation i affects the outcome of observation i in that period only (and not the outcomes of other observations). In the treatment literature this assumption is known as the Stable Unit Treatment Value Assumption (Rubin, 1980). SUTVA is practically always made in empirical evaluation studies (one exception that we are aware of is Heckman *et al.*, 1998). We shall do likewise but acknowledge that the assumption may be quite strong in our particular context. Indeed, SUTVA rules out any interference or relationship between observations. SUTVA thus excludes, for instance, that the grading of a particular château influences the wine prices set by other châteaux owners (through general-equilibrium or imitation effects).

A natural definition of the Parker effect for wine i would be the difference $P_{i1}(2002) - P_{i0}(2002)$. Since the two potential outcomes, $P_{i0}(2002)$ and $P_{i1}(2002)$, cannot both be observed (in 2002, wine i is either in the control group or in the treatment group), it is impossible to calculate wine-specific Parker effects. This is a fundamental problem in the evaluation of treatments in general. Since it is not possible to determine individual treatment effects, the literature has focused on estimating average treatment effects, such as the average treatment effect on the treated (Heckman, 1990; Wooldridge, 2002, ch. 18; Abadie, 2005). In our context this parameter is

$$ATET \equiv \mathrm{E}[P_{i1}(2002) - P_{i0}(2002)|D_i(2002) = 1], \tag{1}$$

which is the expected Parker effect for those wines that were graded in 2002.

For what follows, it is useful to give the mean prices and standard errors, for both vintages, according to whether the wines are in the control or treatment group in 2002. This is done in Table 3.

The effect (1) is not identified from the data in the sense that it is not possible to construct a sample counterpart for the counterfactual expectation $\mathrm{E}[P_{i0}(2002)|D_i(2002) = 1]$. A possible identifying restriction is: $\mathrm{E}[P_{i0}(2002)|D_i(2002) = 1] = \mathrm{E}[P_{i0}(2002)|D_i(2002) = 0]$. Under this assumption the counterfactual expectation is identified since $\mathrm{E}[P_{i0}(2002)|D_i(2002) = 0] = \mathrm{E}[P_i(2002)|D_i(2002) = 0]$. The last expectation can be estimated

Table 3. Mean Prices (Standard Errors) in Control and Treatment Groups

	Control group ($D(2002) = 0$)	Treatment group ($D(2002) = 1$)
$t = 2002$	12.27 (7.32)	22.22 (20.35)
$t = 2003$	10.80 (5.94)	17.95 (15.01)

consistently from the data (as Table 3 shows, the estimate is 12.27). The restriction is, however, very strong in our context as Parker is more likely to grade the prestigious high-quality wines than the low-quality wines. In the absence of treatment, the expected wine price is therefore probably higher in the treatment group than in the control group. Indirect evidence for this selectivity bias comes from Table 3, where the estimate of $\mathrm{E}[P_{i0}(2003)|D_i(2002) = 1] = \mathrm{E}[P_i(2003)|D_i(2002) = 1]$ is shown to be much higher than the estimate of $\mathrm{E}[P_{i0}(2003)|D_i(2002) = 0] = \mathrm{E}[P_i(2003)| D_i(2002) = 0]$ (17.95 vs. 10.80).

Fortunately the $ATET$ is also identified under the following, much weaker, "parallel trend" restriction

$$\begin{aligned} &\mathrm{E}[P_{i0}(2002) - P_{i0}(2003)|D_i(2002) = 0] \\ &\quad = \mathrm{E}[P_{i0}(2002) - P_{i0}(2003)|D_i(2002) = 1]. \end{aligned} \tag{2}$$

This restriction states that, in the absence of treatment, the expected price-evolution would have been the same for the wines in the control group and the wines in the treatment group. Put in other words, it requires that the temporal variation in prices that is not due to the publication of Parker grades (but due to changes in weather conditions, global competition, exchange rates, or other relevant factors) is the same in both groups.

Restriction (2) is essentially the same as the identification restriction considered by Heckman *et al.* (1997) and Abadie (2005).[13] Under restriction (2) and using that $P_i(2003) = P_{i0}(2003)$, the $ATET$ can be rewritten as (Heckman *et al.*, 1997; Abadie, 2005)

$$\begin{aligned} ATET &= \mathrm{E}[P_{i1}(2002) - P_{i0}(2003)|D_i(2002) = 1] \\ &\quad - \mathrm{E}[P_{i0}(2002) - P_{i0}(2003)|D_i(2002) = 0] \\ &= \mathrm{E}[P_i(2002) - P_i(2003)|D_i(2002) = 1] \\ &\quad - \mathrm{E}[P_i(2002) - P_i(2003)|D_i(2002) = 0]. \end{aligned} \tag{3}$$

The Parker effect is thus simply defined as the mean price-evolution (between 2002 and 2003) of the subsample of graded wines minus the mean price-evolution of ungraded wines. This new expression for the $ATET$ is quite intuitive: the difference between mean price-evolutions eliminates, by virtue of the parallel trend assumption, all other factors that could have influenced

[13] Although they also consider a framework with two time periods, say $t = 0$ and $t = 1$, the treatment in their model is only administered in period 1 and never in the initial period 0. Thus in their setting $D_i(0) = 0$ for all i, $D_i(1) = 1$ for the treated and $D_i(1) = 0$ for the untreated.

Table 4. Estimates of ATET by Appellation

Appellation	No. of obs.	Est. (std. error)
Haut-Médoc	16	0.42 (0.29)
Margaux	24	3.53 (1.72)*
Pauillac	19	6.19 (2.45)*
Pessac-Léognan	26	−0.04 (0.95)
Pomerol	15	8.97 (2.89)*
St-Emilion Grand Cru	51	3.85 (1.27)*
St-Estèphe	9	1.32 (0.75)
St-Julien	13	1.36 (0.75)
Sauternes	13	2.78 (0.87)*

Note: *Significant at the 5% level.

the price changes between 2002 and 2003, and thereby isolates the pure Parker effect.

An estimate of the $ATET$ can be obtained by replacing the expectations in (3) by the corresponding sample averages given in Table 3.[14] This leads to the estimate $\widehat{ATET} = (22.22 - 17.95) - (12.27 - 10.80) = 2.80$ euros. The standard error of the estimate equals 0.52, so the effect we find is strongly significant. Estimating the $ATET$ by the rank of the wine shows that the Parker effect increases with ranking. For instance, we find a Parker effect of 3.73 (1.08) for the top classified wines[15] versus only 2.18 (0.59) for the remaining less prestigious wines. Table 4 reports the estimates of the $ATET$ by appellation. We only give the results for the cases with a sufficient number of observations. The estimates are always positive except for Pessac-Léognan, but for this appellation the effect is not significant. Note that the largest

[14]This estimator is sometimes called the "difference-in-differences estimator." This can be seen by considering the regression model $P_i(t) = \delta(t) + \alpha D_i(t) + \eta_i + v_i(t)$, where $\delta(t)$ is a time-specific component, η_i a wine-specific component, and $v_i(t)$ a transitory shock with mean zero at each period. Specifically, η_i may represent factors that are constant over the two years such as technology, natural endowments, and ranking, and $\delta(t)$ gathers all factors that are common to all wines in year t such as weather conditions (although weather conditions may differ substantially from one place to another within the Bordeaux vineyard, thus varying with i, Lecocq and Visser (2006) show that these differences have very little impact on prices). Differencing, and using that $D_i(2003) = 0$ for all i, we get $P_i(2002) - P_i(2003) = \delta + \alpha D_i(2002) + (v_i(2002) - v_i(2003))$, where $\delta = \delta(2002) - \delta(2003)$. Under the assumption that $v_i(2002) - v_i(2003)$ is mean independent of $D_i(2002)$, the OLS estimator of α converges to the $ATET$.

[15]The group of wines with the following ranking: 1er Cru Classé, 2ème Cru Classé, 3ème Cru Classé, 4ème Cru Classé, 5ème Cru Classé, 1er Grand Cru Classé A, and 1er Grand Cru Classé B.

$ATET$ is obtained for Pomerol, which is actually one of the appellations that Robert Parker likes the most.

One may wonder whether the above results are sensitive to the scaling of the outcome variable. It may be that the signs of the estimates of the $ATET$ change when prices are no longer defined in levels. To check this we performed the same kind of calculations as above but now by defining all outcome variables as the natural logarithm of prices. The conclusions obtained with the $ATET$ model in logs are basically the same as those obtained above: the estimate of the $ATET$ is now 0.057 (0.013); the estimate of the $ATET$ for the top classified becomes 0.088 (0.020) and for the less prestigious ones 0.043 (0.016); four out of the five appellations that are significant (and with positive signs) in Table 4 remain so when prices are in logs (St-Emilion Grand Cru is no longer significant however, all appellations with insignificant estimates in Table 4 remain so in the new version of the model), and Pomerol still tops the list with an estimate equal to 0.182 (0.041). Although this is clearly not an exhaustive robustness analysis of the $ATET$ model in levels, it is reassuring to see that our empirical conclusions are not fundamentally modified when the outcome variable is specified in logs. From now on we exclusively focus on the analysis with prices defined in levels.

The $ATET$ is an aggregate and overall measure of the Parker effect as it is the average of grade-specific Parker effects. It is also of interest to study these grade-specific Parker effects. To define these parameters, let $P_{ig}(t)$ now denote the price in the spring of year t had wine i been attributed the grade g, and $P_{i0}(t)$ (as before) the price when the wine is not graded. Let $D_i(t) = g$ if wine i has received the grade g, and $D_i(t) = 0$ (as before) in the absence of treatment. As before $P_i(t)$ denotes the realized price in the spring of year t, and of course we still have $P_i(2003) = P_{i0}(2003)$ for all i. The grade-specific Parker effect is defined as the average treatment effect on the treated at level g

$$ATET(g) \equiv \mathrm{E}[P_{ig}(2002) - P_{i0}(2002)|D_i(2002) = g]. \tag{4}$$

Under an identifying assumption analogous to (2),[16] the $ATET(g)$ can be rewritten as

$$\begin{aligned} ATET(g) = \mathrm{E}[P_i(2002) - P_i(2003)|D_i(2002) = g] - \mathrm{E}[P_i(2002) \\ - P_i(2003)|D_i(2002) = 0]. \end{aligned} \tag{5}$$

Similarly to (3), the Parker effect for wines that received a grade equal to g in 2002 is defined as the mean price-evolution of these wines minus the mean

[16]The restriction that identifies $ATET(g)$ is $\mathrm{E}[P_{i0}(2002) - P_{i0}(2003)|D_i(2002) = 0] = \mathrm{E}[P_{i0}(2002) - P_{i0}(2003)|D_i(2002) = g]$.

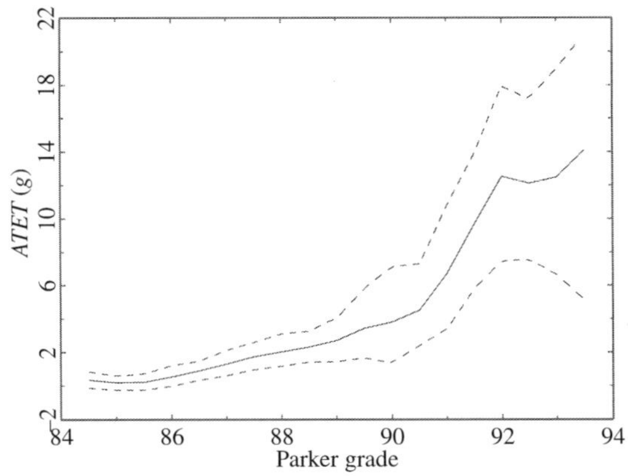

Figure 1. The Estimation of $ATET(g)$ and 95% Point-wise Confidence Band (*full sample*; $h = 0.734$)

price-evolution of ungraded wines. The second expectation in (5) can still be estimated by taking the difference of appropriate sample means, and the first expectation can be estimated using kernel estimation methods. Basically, the kernel estimator can be thought of as a smoothed histogram estimator which may be too erratic when there are small number of observations for particular values of g (see the Appendix for the definition of the kernel estimate $\widehat{ATET}(g)$).

Figure 1 shows the graph of $\widehat{ATET}(g)$ together with the 95% point-wise confidence band.[17] The estimates of $ATET(g)$ tend to increase with the grade, starting around zero for $g = 84.5$ and the maximum is around 14 euros for $g = 93.5$. Note that the null hypothesis "$ATET(g) = 0$" is accepted for grades below 86 but is rejected for grades above that value. The fact that the more highly graded wines benefit relatively more from being evaluated by Parker seems quite intuitive. The fact that $ATET(g)$ does not turn negative for low values of g may come, however, as a surprise. One might expect that very poorly graded châteaux would have been better off had they not received any Parker grade at all. A possible explanation may be that the wines evaluated by Parker in 2002 are simply of too high quality. Indeed, the lowest grade assigned in 2002 was 82.5 (see Table 2), and this is still in the range of wines judged by Parker as "barely above average to very good" (wines with scores between 80 and 89 fall in this category, see *The Wine Advocate*). In other words, had Parker also evaluated châteaux

[17]The confidence band is constructed using the bootstrap method described in Härdle (1990, pp. 103–6). Details can be obtained from the authors.

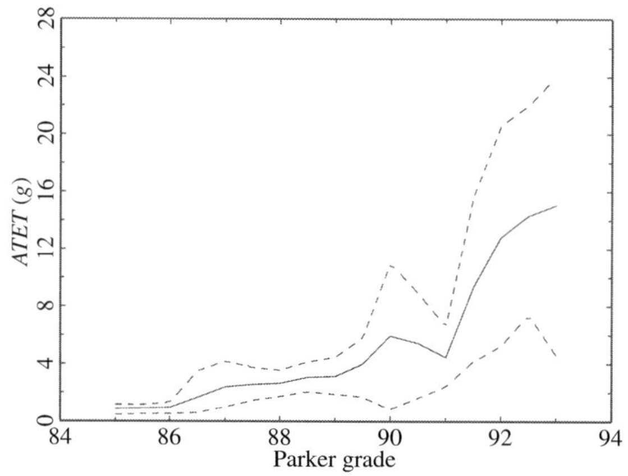

Figure 2. The Estimation of $ATET(g)$ and 95% Point-wise Confidence Band (*top classified wines*; $h = 0.772$)

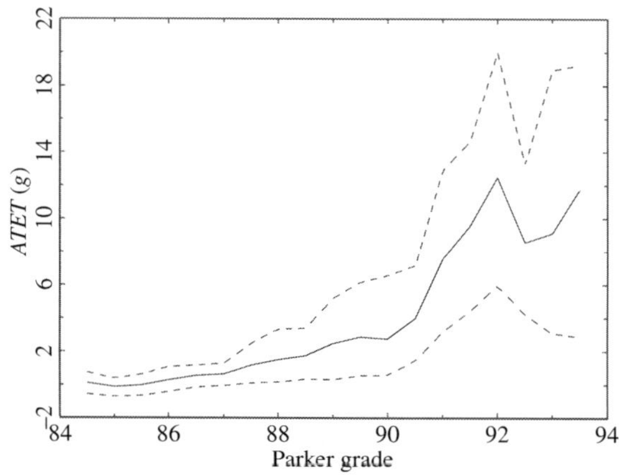

Figure 3. The Estimation of $ATET(g)$ and 95% Point-wise Confidence Band (*less prestigious wines*; $h = 0.813$)

with quality levels well below this range, we might have found $ATET(g)$ to be negative for scores in the 50s ("unacceptable" wines), the 60s ("below average" wines), or may be even the 70s ("average" wines).

Figure 2 displays the estimate of $ATET(g)$ for the top classified châteaux in our sample, and Figure 3 gives the graph for the less prestigious ones.[18] In both figures the estimates start at or slightly above zero, and increase with

[18]The number of observations used to calculate the kernel estimate appearing in the Appendix is 59 for Figure 2 and 96 for Figure 3, and the optimal bandwidths are 0.772 and 0.813, respectively.

the grade g. For the top wines the null "$ATET(g) = 0$" is always rejected, while for the less prestigious wines it is accepted until g around 89. Note that the curve for the top wines is always above the curve for the less prestigious ones, except for grades between 90.5 and 92.

Our estimates $\widehat{ATET}(g)$ are useful to determine what the wine prices would have been had Parker graded the 2002 vintage in the spring of 2003. For this exercise we use the grades assigned in August/September 2003 (see Table 2), and assume that these grades coincide with the ones Parker would have given in the spring. We argued in Section 3.2 that this is a reasonable assumption. Let g_i denote the grade attributed in the late summer of 2003 to wine i. The predicted *en primeur* prices in 2003, $\hat{P}_{i1}(2003)$, can be written as

$$\hat{P}_{i1}(2003) = P_{i0}(2003) + \widehat{ATET}(g_i).$$

Figure 4 shows the actual prices $P_{i0}(2003)$ and the predicted prices $\hat{P}_{i1}(2003)$ for the 117 wines that were graded in August/September 2003 and with grades g_i in the interval [84.5, 93.5].[19] The horizontal axis lists these wines ranked according to their actual prices in 2003. Since $\widehat{ATET}(g)$ is either zero or strictly positive, the predicted prices are always equal or above the actual prices in 2003. The difference between the two series of prices is sometimes substantial (up to around 10 euros) and is more accentuated for the most expensive wines. As the graph shows, there are however

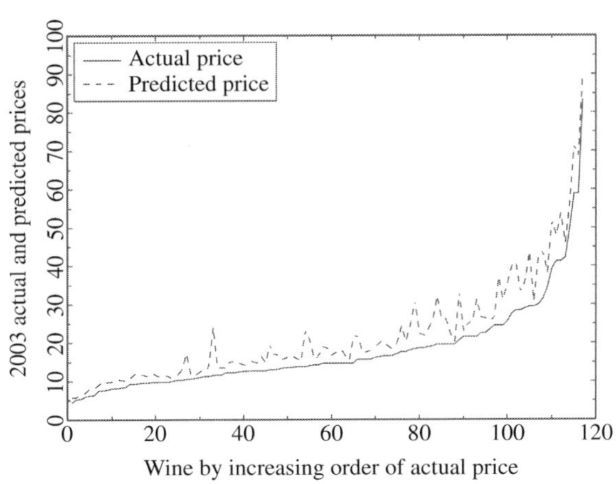

Figure 4. Actual and Predicted Prices in 2003

[19]As Table 2 indicates, 121 wines were evaluated in the late summer of 2003 but 4 of them received grades g_i outside the interval. For such observations $\widehat{ATET}(g_i)$ does not exist.

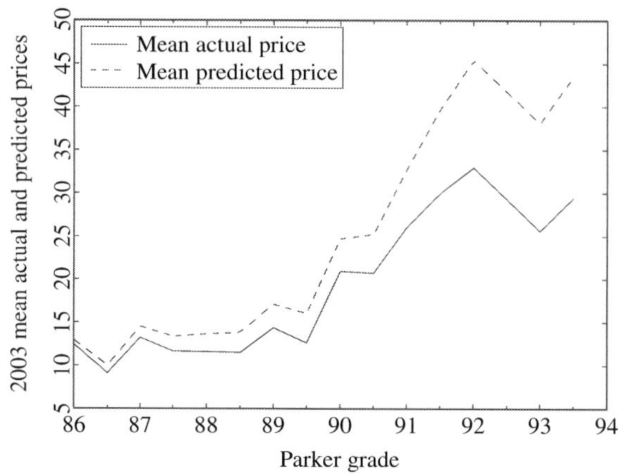

Figure 5. Mean Actual and Mean Predicted Prices in 2003

some sharp peaks for the less expensive wines as well, suggesting that at least some of the high 2003 grades were assigned to wines that fetched low prices in the *en primeur* market.

Figure 5 shows again the actual and predicted prices but here the horizontal axis lists the wines by increasing order of the grade they obtained in 2003. Since we generally observe more than one wine per grade level, mean actual and mean predicted prices are calculated for each observed value of the grade. Figure 5 shows a positive relationship between Parker grades and prices. The slope of the grade/price curve is steeper for predicted prices than for actual prices, and the gap between the two curves increases from 1 euro for $g = 86$ to 14 euros for $g = 93.5$.

5. Conclusions

This chapter measures the effect of Robert Parker's oenological grades on *en primeur* wine prices. We exploit the fact that in 2003 prices were determined before publication of these grades, whereas in all previous years the revelation of grades preceded price determination. This unusual reversal allows us to estimate a treatment effect under relatively weak assumptions. Unlike what is stated by Robert Parker ("I doubt that if I had reviewed the wines six months earlier there would have been any change in their pricing, which, by comparison to recent Bordeaux vintages (1995–2000), is extremely low." *The Wine Advocate*, October 2003), we find an overall effect equal to almost 3 euros per bottle. Our estimates of the grade-specific effects show that the impact of the famous wine expert is very important for highly graded wines.

The impact vanishes for lowly graded wines but without actually turning negative.

Acknowledgments

We are grateful to Patrice Borda, Alan Duncan, Fabrice Etilé, Victor Ginsburgh, Sylvie Lambert, two anonymous referees and participants at the VDQS conference (Dijon, 2004), the RES conference (Nottingham, 2005), the JMA meeting (Hammamet, 2005) and the EEA congress (Amsterdam, 2005), for their helpful comments and suggestions.

References

Abadie, A. (2005). Semiparametric difference-in-difference estimators. *Review of Economic Studies*, 72, 1–19.

Avery, C., and Chevalier, J. (1999). Identifying investor sentiment from price paths: The case of football betting. *Journal of Business*, 72, 493–521.

Bauwens, L., and Ginsburgh, V. (2000). Art experts and auctions. Are pre-sale estimates unbiased and fully informative? *Louvain Economic Review*, 66, 131–144.

Chossat, V., and Gergaud, O. (2003). Expert opinion and gastronomy: The recipe for success. *Journal of Cultural Economics*, 27, 127–141.

Combris, P., Lecocq, S., and Visser, M. (1997). Estimation of a hedonic price equation for Bordeaux wine: Does quality matter? *Economic Journal*, 107, 390–402.

Di Vittorio, A., and Ginsburgh, V. (1996). Des enchères comme révélateurs du classement des vins. *Journal de la Société Statistique de Paris*, 137, 19–49.

Dubois, P., and Nauges, C. (2010). Identifying the effect of unobserved quality and experts' reviews in the pricing of experience goods: Empirical application on Bordeaux wine. *International Journal of Industrial Economics*, 28, 205–212.

Février, P., Roos, W., and Visser, M. (2005). The buyer's option in multi-unit ascending auctions: The case of wine auctions at Drouot. *Journal of Economics & Management Strategy*, 14, 813–847.

Ginsburgh, V. (2003). Awards, success and aesthetic quality in the arts. *Journal of Economic Perspectives*, 17, 99–111.

Ginsburgh, V., Monzak, M., and Monzak, A. (1994). Red wines of Medoc: What is wine tasting worth? Paper, Vineyard Data Quantification Society, Verona.

Hadj Ali, H. (2002). La commercialisation des vins *en primeur*, PhD Thesis, University of Toulouse.

Hadj Ali, H., and Nauges, C. (2007). Reputation and quality effects in the pricing of experience goods: The case of en primeur wine. *American Journal of Agricultural Economics*, 89, 91–103.

Härdle, W. (1990). *Applied Nonparametric Regression*, Cambridge, MA: Cambridge University Press.

Heckman, J.J. (1990). Varieties of selection bias. *American Economic Review*, Papers and Proceedings, 80, 313–318.

Heckman, J.J., Ichimura, H., and Todd, P.E. (1997). Matching as an econometric evaluation estimator: Evidence from evaluating a job training programme. *Review of Economic Studies*, 64, 605–654.

Heckman, J.J., Lochner, L., and Taber, C. (1998). General-equilibrium treatment effects: A study of tuition policy. *American Economic Review*, Papers and Proceedings, 88, 381–386.

Jones, G.V., and Storchmann, K.-H. (2001). Wine market prices and investment under uncertainty: An econometric model for Bordeaux crus classés. *Agricultural Economics*, 26, 115–133.

Lecocq, S., and Visser, M. (2006). Spatial variations in weather conditions and wine prices in Bordeaux. *Journal of Wine Economics*, 1, 114–124.

Rubin, D.B. (1974). Estimating causal effects of treatments in randomised and nonrandomised studies. *Journal of Educational Psychology*, 66, 688–701.

Rubin, D.B. (1980). Discussion of paper by D. Basu. *Journal of the American Statistical Association*, 75, 591–593.

Shleifer, A. (1986). Do demand curves for stocks slope down? *Journal of Finance*, 41, 579–590.

Silverman, B.W. (1986). *Density Estimation for Statistics and Data Analysis.* London: Chapman and Hall.

Wooldridge, J.M. (2002). *Econometric Analysis of Cross Section and Panel Data.* Cambridge, MA: The MIT Press.

Appendix

The estimate of $ATET(g)$ defined in (5) is given by

$$\widehat{ATET}(g) = \frac{\sum_{i=1}^{N_1(2002)}[P_i(2002) - P_i(2003)]K\left[\frac{D_i(2002)-g}{h}\right]}{\sum_{i=1}^{N_1(2002)} K\left[\frac{D_i(2002)-g}{h}\right]} - (12.27 - 10.80),$$

where $K(u) = 0.75(1 - u^2)\mathbf{1}_{\{|u|\leq 1\}}$ is the Epanechnikov kernel function, $\mathbf{1}_{\{\cdot\}}$ the indicator function equal to one if the statement between brackets is true and zero otherwise, h the bandwidth parameter, and $N_1(2002)$ the number of observations in the subsample of wines graded in the spring of 2002 (i.e., $N_1(2002) = 158$). The grades $D_i(2002)$, $i = 1, \ldots, N_1(2002)$, are defined as the midpoints of the grade intervals published in *The Wine Advocate*.[20] The value of the bandwidth parameter is chosen according to Silverman's rule of thumb (Silverman, 1986): $h = 0.9 \min(\sigma, (q_{75} - q_{25})/1.349)\ N_1(2002)^{-\frac{1}{5}}$, where σ is the standard deviation of the grades, and q_{25} and q_{75} are the 25th and 75th percentiles.

[20] We have also calculated estimates of $ATET(g)$ by drawing each grade randomly in its corresponding grade interval, but the resulting graphs were very similar to the ones reported here.

When based on all $N_1(2002) = 158$ observations, the estimate of $ATET(g)$ declines sharply for g beyond 94. This is due to the fact that there are very few observations in this range of the sample. The problem could not be resolved by using a variable bandwidth. We therefore dropped 3 extreme observations from the sample, and our estimate is thus based on $N_1(2002) = 155$, and using this sample we find $h = 0.734$.

Chapter 21

Identifying the Effect of Unobserved Quality and Expert Reviews in the Pricing of Experience Goods: Empirical Application on Bordeaux Wine*

Pierre Dubois[†] **and Céline Nauges**[‡]

[†]*Toulouse School of Economics,*
Université de Toulouse 1 Capitole,
Toulouse 21 Allée de Brienne
31000 Toulouse, France
pierre.dubois@tse-fr.eu

[‡]*Toulouse School of Economics, INRA,*
Université de Toulouse 1 Capitole, Toulouse
21 Allée de Brienne, 31000 Toulouse, France
celine.nauges@inra.fr

We propose a structural empirical approach *à la* Olley and Pakes (1996) to disentangle the effect of experts' grades from the effect of unobserved quality on the pricing of experience goods. Using a panel data set of 108 *châteaux* selling wine on the "en primeur" market of Bordeaux, we confirm that experts' grades affect producers' choice of "en primeur" price above the effect of unobserved wine quality. Our empirical results also show that failing to control for endogeneity caused by the omission of unobserved quality leads to over-estimate the influence of experts' grades on the "primeur" price.

1. Introduction

Since the work by Nelson (1970, 1974), experience goods (i.e., goods for which quality cannot be ascertained before effective consumption) have been

*This article originally appeared in *International Journal of Industrial Organization* (2010), 28, 205–212.

the focus of extensive theoretical and empirical research. The theoretical literature (Shaked and Sutton, 1982; Shapiro, 1983; Tirole, 1996; Mahenc and Meunier, 2003; among others) mainly considers firm's activity of quality signaling (through advertising, product labeling, reputation, experts' ratings, etc.), while most empirical studies (Ackerberg, 2003; Caves and Greene, 1996; Jin and Leslie, 2003; etc.), measure the influence of these various sources of information on consumer demand.

Wine, and "en primeur" wine in particular, has been at the core of several recent articles, both theoretical and empirical. Wine sold "en primeur" is a typical experience good in the sense of Nelson, since the wine is sold 6 to 8 months after the grape harvest, when the wine is not yet mature (the wine is kept in barrels for several more months after the "primeur" sales, before being bottled). Mahenc and Meunier (2003) and Mahenc (2004) provide theoretical evidence for "en primeur" pricing (which can be seen as forward trading) contributing to signal wine quality. Hadj Ali and Nauges (2007) and Hadj Ali *et al.* (2008) estimate the impact of experts on the price set by wine producers at the time of "primeur" sales, using data from the Bordeaux region (France).[1] These authors, who estimate "en primeur" price models using panel data techniques and difference-in-differences methods respectively, find some evidence of a significant but moderate impact of wine experts' ratings on the price set by the producers. In these two articles, it is assumed that consumers rely on experts who are supposed to make correct assessment about "true" wine quality.[2] We argue that experts may be wrong in assessing wine quality at the time of primeur sales though, because the wine is not yet mature. Hence, it is very likely that only the producer, who has been following each step of the wine-making process, knows the wine quality. This assumption, combined with the theoretical assertion that the "primeur" price is used by producers to signal wine quality, calls for the introduction of wine quality as a determinant of the price set by the producers. Because wine quality is unobservable to both the consumers and the econometrician, the main issue when estimating the equation describing the price set by the producers, is that quality may not only influence the pricing of "primeur" wine, but it is also likely to be correlated with experts' grades.

[1]The role of experts' opinion in purchasing behavior has been the focus of several articles in various fields such as art markets (Ginsburgh, 2003), movies markets (Reinstein and Snyder, 2005), or bottled wine markets (Landon and Smith, 1997, 1998).

[2]From now on, "true wine quality" and "wine quality" will stand for the quality the wine will reach at maturity, assuming optimal storage conditions.

We thus face a typical problem of omitted variable which may produce biased estimates if not controlled for.

This endogeneity problem is unlikely to be solved through natural instrumental variables techniques because it would require the availability of variables correlated with experts' grades but not with wine quality. Reinstein and Snyder (2005) face the same endogeneity problem when measuring the influence of movie critics on consumer demand: "products receiving positive reviews tend to be of high quality, and it is difficult to determine whether the review or the quality is responsible for high demand." To circumvent the problem, these authors take advantage of the timing of the reviews relative to a movie's release. Indeed, some reviews came during the opening weekend while other reviews came only after. A difference-in-differences estimator was thus applied using observations from this quasi-natural experiment. As mentioned by the authors, the validity of this approach relies on the assumption that the selection of movies to be reviewed during and after opening weekends is not correlated with quality reviews (see also Hadj Ali *et al.*, 2008, for use of a similar estimation technique).

In this chapter, we use a methodology that builds on the recent literature on production function identification (see Olley and Pakes, 1996; Levinsohn and Petrin, 2003; Ackerberg *et al.*, 2006). This approach not only allows to control for endogeneity bias due to variable omission, but also to disentangle the effect of experts' opinion from the effect of wine quality signaling and to identify unobserved quality of each wine in the sample. Three different models are estimated in order to test for robustness of various identification assumptions.

Using an unbalanced panel data set of 108 Bordeaux *châteaux* over five vintages (1994–1998), we confirm that experts' grades affect producers' choice of "primeur" price above the effect of unobserved wine quality (for previous evidence, see Hadj Ali and Nauges, 2007, and Hadj Ali *et al.*, 2008). Our empirical results also show that failing to control for endogeneity caused by the omission of unobserved quality leads to over-estimate the influence of experts' grades on the "primeur" price.

2. Theoretical Model, Identification and Estimation Procedures

True wine quality, q^*, has to be considered as a potential determinant of the "primeur" price set by the producers as there exists theoretical evidence that primeur prices play an informational role as a signal on wine quality

(Mahenc, 2004; Mahenc and Meunier, 2003, 2006). Mahenc (2004) has shown that a sufficiently high fraction of informed buyers acting in the market eliminates the lemons problem as discussed by Akerlof (1970).[3] We assume this assumption to be satisfied in the Bordeaux primeur market where buyers, for the most part, are wholesale merchants from the same region. The producer, who followed each step of the wine-making process, is assumed to be the only one to know the true quality (or quality at maturity) of his wine, q^*. Indeed, assessing true wine quality is much more difficult for potential buyers since the wine is not yet mature at the time of "en primeur" release and hence does not present the same sensory characteristics as the wine delivered 2 years later (Mahenc and Meunier, 2006).[4]

Producers' pricing strategy is also likely to depend on consumers' expected willingness to pay for the wine. Consumers, who are not perfectly informed about quality, will likely take into account the quality of the wine which was produced in the past (or reputation) and refer to experts' judgment when making their purchase decision. We assume that quality-ranking and appellation, which are clearly labeled on the bottle, convey all information about reputation. We believe this is a reasonable assumption for the Bordeaux region where most of the châteaux have a long-time established reputation and where a system of wine quality-ranking (which is defined inside small geographical regions called "appellations") exists since the nineteenth century (Markham, 1997). However, wine quality is likely to vary from one vintage to another due in particular to the weather conditions that prevailed during the grapes-growing season.[5] There is thus some uncertainty remaining about wine quality when the "primeur" market opens. In that respect, we assume that consumers rely on experts' ratings to assess expected wine quality for the current vintage. Experts' opinion is measured by the grade attributed to the wine during blind tasting sessions that occur before the opening of the "primeur" market. If the producer believes that consumer's willingness to pay for the product is influenced by experts' judgment, then he might price the good accordingly. The choice of the "primeur" price by the producer may thus be influenced by the grade, denoted q_0, which is attributed to his wine. We test this assumption by introducing experts'

[3]Akerlof's lemons problem would occur if producers of a low-quality wine would sell at the same price as producers of high-quality wine.

[4]Mahenc and Meunier (2006) mention that "the samples may be drawn from a particular barrel that has been blended and set aside on purpose."

[5]Contrary to most New World wine regions or countries (California, South Africa, New Zealand, Chile, etc.), weather conditions in the Bordeaux area can vary significantly from 1 year to another.

grades into the "primeur" price function (see also Hadj Ali and Nauges, 2007; Hadj Ali *et al.*, 2008).

The "primeur" price function is written as follows:

$$\ln p = \pi(q^*, q^o, X) + \varepsilon \tag{1}$$

where p represents "primeur" price, q^o is experts' grade given to "primeur" wine, q^* is true wine quality known by the producer only, and the X-vector gathers wine characteristics, namely: categorical variables for vintage, quality-ranking and region of origin (also known as "appellation"). The error term ε is assumed uncorrelated with observed and unobserved covariates, at all time:

$$E(\varepsilon|q^*, q^o, X) = 0.$$

The term ε can be interpreted as idiosyncratic random shocks on price that are unanticipated by experts, or as independent measurement errors, or as independent idiosyncratic deviations when wine producers set the "primeur" price.

2.1. *Structural model*

Under the assumption that the primeur price function $\pi(.,.,.)$ is additively separable between q^*, q^o, and X, we have:

$$\ln p_{it} = E(\ln p_{it}|q^*_{it}, q^o_{it}, X_{it}) + \varepsilon_{it} = X'_{it}\beta + \gamma q^o_{it} + q^*_{it} + \varepsilon_{it}, \tag{2}$$

where i and t are indices for *châteaux* and year or vintage, respectively. The β's and γ are unknown parameters, and the coefficient of q^*_{it} (which is unobserved) has been normalized. Wine quality, q^*_{it}, being unobserved, we cannot identify the coefficient of experts' rating, γ, because

$$E(\ln p_{it}|q^o_{it}, X_{it}) = X'_{it}\beta + \gamma q^o_{it} + E(q^*_{it}|q^o_{it}, X_{it})$$

and, since wine tasting is indeed performed in order to give information on true wine quality, we will have

$$E(q^*_{it}|q^o_{it}, X_{it}) \neq 0.$$

We face an endogeneity problem in (2) because experts' opinion about wine produced by *château* i and vintage t, q^o_{it}, is supposed to signal the true wine quality, q^*_{it}. Thus, unless experts' grades are given completely at random with respect to wine quality, these grades will be endogenous in the price equation.

A first simple solution would be to use instrumental variables. Valid instrumental variables should be correlated with experts' grade, q^o_{it}, and uncorrelated with unobserved wine quality, q^*_{it}. In this particular example of wine as an experience good, no natural instrumental variable appears to be available. Finally, note that a fixed-effects specification, which is the common approach to deal with unobserved heterogeneity in panel data, is not applicable in this particular case as wine quality is not constant over vintages.

To control for endogeneity and disentangle the influence of experts' ratings from the impact of true wine quality on price setting, we use a structural approach based on the methodology started in Olley and Pakes (1996) and further developed by Levinsohn and Petrin (2003) and Ackerberg *et al.* (2006).[6] The approach that we adopt relies on two main assumptions.

A1. Unobserved true quality q^*_{it} is supposed to follow a first order Markov process, that is,

$$E[q^*_{it}|I_{it-1}] = E[q^*_{it}|q^*_{it-1}],$$

where I_{it-1} corresponds to the information set of producers at the end of period $t-1$. Assumption A1 means that average true quality conditionally on previous year information set I_{it-1} only depends on past true quality q^*_{it-1}.

A2. We assume the following relationship between experts' ratings and unobserved true quality:

$$q^o_{it} = h(q^*_{it}, q^o_{it-1})$$

where h is strictly increasing in q^*_{it} and can depend on the past grade q^o_{it-1}.

This monotonicity assumption means that experts' grades are increasing with unobserved quality, given the previous vintage grade. In other words, given lagged ratings q^o_{it-1}, ranking of wine of vintage t according to experts' grades matches the ranking according to the unobserved true quality.[7] Assumption A2 is a "structural" assumption that is crucial for identification.

[6]Olley and Pakes (1996) introduce a technique to deal with unobserved productivity shocks in production functions. See also Levinsohn and Petrin (2003) and Ackerberg *et al.* (2006) for discussions and alternative methods.

[7]Quality, q^*_{it}, may be perceived by experts with some error. This extension is dealt with in the Appendix.

Our main model of interest thus corresponds to the structural Eq. (2) with assumptions A1 and A2. To test for the validity of A2, we estimate alternative models that do not rely on the monotonicity assumption. This however comes at the cost of additional restrictions on the pricing model which consist either in restricting A1 to A1b or in putting a restriction directly on (2) as it is described in turn.

2.1.1. *Alternative A*

Assumption A1 is maintained but we assume that q_{it}^* is the only unobservable in the model (there is no additional error term). The model becomes

$$\ln p_{it} = X_{it}'\beta + \gamma q_{it}^o + q_{it}^*.$$

2.1.2. *Alternative B*

The structure (2) is maintained but we make a more restrictive assumption A1b regarding unobserved true quality.

A1b. Unobserved true quality follows an AR(1) process:

$$E[q_{it}^*|I_{it-1}] = \lambda q_{it-1}^*.$$

Let us now describe the additional assumptions that are needed in order to solve the endogeneity problem under the three alternatives:

A3. The variables in X_{it-1} (categorical variables for vintage, quality-ranking and region of origin) are part of the information set I_{it-1}.

A4. There is state dependence in ratings, that is, experts' ratings are correlated across time for reasons other than correlation in true quality over time. This assumption holds because ratings are provided by a unique expert (namely, Robert Parker) for all years covered by our sample. Any wine expert is likely to exhibit preferences for some wine characteristics related to the grapes or the wine-making process, that are going to be independent of weather conditions and persistent over time.[8]

A5. Lagged experts' rating, q_{it-1}^o, does not enter the pricing equation at time t.

We assume that wine producers do not price wine taking into account experts' rating of the previous vintage and that consumers do not assess

[8]It was acknowledged that some wine makers from the Bordeaux region made their wine according to Robert Parker's own tastes.

quality of a wine produced in t from experts' opinion on the wine produced in $t-1$. The main reason is that wine quality in the Bordeaux region can vary significantly from 1 year to another due to changing weather conditions, which is not the case in most New World wine countries.[9] Hence, experts' rating for a wine produced by *château* i in $t-1$ is likely not to be very informative in itself in terms of the quality of the wine produced in t. Assumption A5 can be interpreted either as a specification restriction or as a bounded rationality constraint. It could be so even if demand is rational and based on q_{it}^o and q_{it-1}^o, the supply side rationally chooses price such that q_{it-1}^o does not enter the price equation $\ln p_{it} = X_{it}'\beta + \gamma q_{it}^o + q_{it}^*$ because there is a one to one relationship between q_{it}^* and q_{it-1}^o given q_{it}^o and thus q_{it-1}^o does not bring information given q_{it}^* and q_{it}^o. However, consumers do not observe true quality and this specification is thus quite restrictive. It can then be interpreted as a bounded rationality assumption on producers or consumers such that producers set prices according to true quality and current grade but not past vintage grade.

2.2. *Estimation procedure*

The estimation procedure and identification strategy for the three alternatives are now described. The first main method is related to Olley and Pakes (1996). Due to the monotonicity assumption, the relationship in A2 can be inverted to obtain:

$$q_{it}^* = g(q_{it}^o, q_{it-1}^o)$$

and substituted into the pricing Eq. (2) to get:

$$\ln p_{it} = X_{it}'\beta + \gamma q_{it}^o + g(q_{it}^o, q_{it-1}^o) + \varepsilon_{it}.$$

Estimation now proceeds as follows: the pricing equation, which is linear in X_{it} and non-parametric in $g(q_{it}^o, q_{it-1}^o)$, is estimated by OLS. A K-order

[9] "In California, for example, it never rains in the summer, and it is always warm in the summer. There is a simple reason for this. In California a high-pressure weather system settles each summer over the California coast and produces a warm, dry growing season for the grapes planted there. In Bordeaux this sometimes happens but sometimes it does not. Summers in Bordeaux can be hot and dry, hot and wet, cool and dry, and, most unpleasant of all, cool and wet. In general, high quality vintages for Bordeaux wines correspond to the years in which August and September are dry, the growing season is warm, and the previous winter has been wet." (Ashenfelter, 2007).

polynomial expansion in q^o_{it} and q^o_{it-1} is used to approximate the non-parametric function $g(.,.)$.[10] OLS estimation produces consistent estimates of the β's. From the set of β estimates denoted $\hat{\beta}$, we compute the implied true quality as:

$$q^*_{it}(\lambda) = \ln p_{it} - X'_{it}\hat{\beta} - \gamma q^o_{it}.$$

Given A1,

$$q_{it} = E[q_{it}|q_{it-1}] + \xi_{it}$$

where ξ_{it} is uncorrelated with the information set at $t-1$: $E[\xi_{it}|I_{it-1}] = 0$. The ξ_{it}, also known as the "innovation" in the production function literature, represents unobserved and unexpected idiosyncratic shocks that may have affected wine quality q^*_{it} during the grapes-growing season and/or during the wine-making process. Such shocks could be local weather events such as frost episodes or pest attacks. The residuals $\xi_{it}(\gamma)$ are obtained from the non-parametric regression of $q^*_{it}(\gamma)$ on $q^*_{it-1}(\gamma)$ such that:

$$\xi_{it}(\gamma) = q^*_{it}(\gamma) - \sum_{k=1}^{K} \hat{b}_k q^{*k}_{it-1}(\gamma)$$

The $\xi_{it}(\gamma)$ are finally used to form a sample analogue of the moment condition:

$$E[\xi_{it} q^o_{it-1}] = 0$$

where experts' rating at time $t-1$ belongs to the information set at time $t-1$ and should not be correlated with the innovation in quality at time t. Under assumptions A4 and A5, experts' rating at time $t-1$ is a suitable instrument for experts' rating at time t: first, under assumption A4, experts' rating at time $t-1$ is going to be informative for experts' rating at time t and second, under assumption A5, experts' rating in $t-1$ do not directly affect price setting in t. So, experts' rating in $t-1$ belongs to the information set I_{t-1}, which implies that ξ_{it} and q^o_{it-1} are uncorrelated. The estimate $\hat{\gamma}$ of γ is then defined as the solution to the following minimization:

$$\min_{\gamma} \sum_{i,t} (\xi_{it}(\gamma) q^o_{it-1})^2.$$

[10]In the forthcoming empirical application, we specify a polynomial of order $K = 3$.

This method allows to obtain consistent estimates (Olley and Pakes, 1996) under model (2) and assumptions A1, A2, A3, A4, and A5.

We now describe the estimation procedure for the two alternative models:

2.2.1. *Alternative A*

In this case, a Generalized Method of Moments (GMM) estimation method can be used. Based on some guess of the parameters (β, γ), we compute the implied true quality:

$$q_{it}^*(\beta, \gamma) = \ln p_{it} - X_{it}^o \beta - \gamma q_{it}^o.$$

Then we do as in the second step of the Olley and Pakes (1996) method. We compute the residuals $\xi_{it}(\beta, \gamma)$ from the non-parametric regression of $q_{it}^*(\beta, \gamma)$ on $q_{it-1}^*(\beta, \gamma)$, and then solve the sample analogue of the moment condition

$$E[\xi_{it}(\beta, \gamma) q_{it-1}^o] = 0$$

as previously explained, where q_{it-1}^o is an element of the information set I_{t-1} that should be orthogonal to $\xi_{it}(\beta, \gamma)$. Other instruments belonging to the information set (e.g., lagged weather variables) could also be used to estimate the model parameters by GMM.

2.2.2. *Alternative B*

In this case, the assumption A1b imposes an AR(1) process for unobserved quality implying that $q_{it}^* = \lambda q_{it-1}^* + \xi_{it}$. We also apply a GMM procedure, using

$$\eta_{it}(\beta, \gamma, \lambda) = \xi_{it} + \varepsilon_{it} - \lambda \varepsilon_{it-1} = (q_{it}^* + \varepsilon_{it})(\beta, \gamma) - \lambda(q_{it-1}^* + \varepsilon_{it-1})(\beta, \gamma)$$

where $(q_{it}^* + \varepsilon_{it})(\beta, \gamma) = \ln p_{it} - X_{it}' \beta - \gamma q_{it}^o$.

Then, under the assumption that ε_{it} is not serially correlated and also uncorrelated with observed and unobserved covariates at all time, the moment condition that $\eta_{it}(\beta, \gamma, \lambda)$ is orthogonal to the information set I_{t-1} is valid. We can then solve the sample analogue of the moment condition

$$E[\eta_{it}(\beta, \gamma) q_{it-1}^o] = 0$$

as previously, where q_{it-1}^o is an element of the information set I_{t-1} that should be orthogonal to $(\xi_{it}, \varepsilon_{it})$, and that we suppose uncorrelated with ε_{it-1}.

In the following empirical application, we compare the "Olley–Pakes" methodology with the alternatives A and B that do not rely on the "inversion" technique of Olley and Pakes (1996), at the cost of more restrictive assumptions. The comparison of the three sets of results will be informative on the reliability of the monotonicity assumption in the first main method if the restrictions used for methods A and B are valid. Note also that when the estimation procedure involves two steps, standard errors are computed using the bootstrap technique along the lines of Levinsohn and Petrin (2003).

3. Empirical Analysis

3.1. *The data and specification issues*

The data, that were provided by one of the most famous broker house in Bordeaux, cover "primeur" wine sales of 108 Bordeaux *châteaux*, over five vintages (from 1994 to 1998).[11] Primeur price is the price of a 75cl bottle in constant euro (1990 base). For each wine, we have data on grades given by Robert Parker (one of the most famous wine experts) to each wine at the time of "primeur" sales, as well as a set of wine characteristics gathering vintage, "appellation" (the French equivalent of Protected Designation of Origin), and ranking.[12] We combine these data with weather data obtained from the company Météo France. Weather data consist in daily observation at Mérignac in the Bordeaux Region, of minimum and maximum temperature, hours of sunshine and rainfall for all years from 1993 to 1998.

The database gathers *châteaux* belonging to ten different "appellations": Haut Médoc (HM), Margaux (MA), Moulis (MO), Pauillac (PA), Pessac Léognan (PL), Pomerol (POM), Saint Emilion Grand Cru (SEGC), Saint Estèphe (SES), Saint Julien (SJ). Some of these *châteaux* are ranked, either inside a region (i.e., a group of appellations) or inside a unique appellation. There are three ranking systems currently in use in the Bordeaux area:

1. The first ranking was created for wines from the Médoc region (appellations HM, MA, MO, PA, SES, SJ). This ranking dates back to 1855 and has been largely unchanged to this day.[13] Wines have been classified following a five-tier classification system ranging from top-quality *Premiers Crus* or First Growth (ME-1 from now on) to *Cinquièmes Crus* or Fifth

[11] Only the price is observed. The data base does not contain any information on quantities sold by each *château* at the time of "primeur" sales.
[12] Tasting usually takes place in spring of each year, before the opening of the "primeur" market. The tasting is generally made in single-blind conditions (i.e., experts do not know the name of the *château* when judging the wine). Wines are graded on a 50–100 scale.
[13] See Markham (1997) for a history of the classification system.

Growth (ME-5). Later on, in 1920, some of the non-ranked *châteaux* have been classified in a sixth-group called *Crus Bourgeois* (ME-6).
2. Saint Emilion wines belonging to the SEGC appellation, formally classified in 1955 (subsequently revised every 10 years), follow a three-tier ranking system: *Premiers Grands Crus Classés A* (SE-1), *Premiers Grands Crus Classés B* (SE-2), and *Grands Crus Classés* (SE-3).
3. Wine from the region of Graves (appellation Pessac Léognan) started to be officially classified in 1953.

Some of the *châteaux* belonging to the three-above cited regions (Médoc, Saint Emilion, Graves) are not ranked. In the empirical analysis these *châteaux* will be gathered into the "non-classified" group. This group will also include all the *châteaux* belonging to the Pomerol appellation that has always refused to rank its own wines.

Tables 1–4 show descriptive statistics on "primeur" price and grade by appellation and by rank.

Robert Parker's grade varied from 73 to 98 over the period, with an average of 87.47. Wines belonging to the Haut Médoc and Margaux appellations got, on average over the 1994–1998 vintages, a lower grade than the other appellations in the database (Table 1). Table 2 shows the average "primeur" price across vintages for each appellation. Primeur price varied significantly from 3.61 to 86.02 euros/bottle, with an average of 15.59. On average over the period, wines belonging to the Pomerol appellation were sold at the highest

Table 1. "Primeur" Grade by Appellation (Average Across Vintages)

	Number of châteaux	Mean	Std. dev.	Min.	Max.
Médoc					
Haut Médoc (HM)	10	85.05	2.85	77	90
Margaux (MA)	16	85.65	4.20	75	98
Moulis (MO)	3	86.39	1.95	83.5	90
Pauillac (PA)	18	88.32	3.89	73.5	96
Saint Estèphe (SES)	8	87.14	3.95	75	93
Saint Julien (SJ)	10	88.49	2.48	83.5	95
Saint Emilion					
Saint Emilion Grand Cru (SEGC)	19	88.13	3.43	77	94.5
Graves					
Pessac Léognan (PL)	16	88.00	2.65	79.5	92
Pomerol (POM)	8	87.96	4.56	73	95.5
Overall	108	87.47	3.72	73	98

Table 2. "Primeur" Price by Appellation, in Euro/bottle (Average Across Vintages)

	Number of châteaux	Mean	Std. dev.	Min.	Max.
Médoc					
Haut Médoc (HM)	10	7.05	2.70	3.61	15.22
Margaux (MA)	16	13.32	11.20	5.00	66.17
Moulis (MO)	3	8.40	1.57	6.28	10.32
Pauillac (PA)	18	18.41	15.37	5.70	66.17
Saint Estèphe (SES)	8	13.62	8.24	5.87	37.05
Saint Julien (SJ)	10	14.68	6.34	7.09	33.08
Saint Emilion					
Saint Emilion Grand Cru (SEGC)	19	19.26	15.77	6.25	86.02
Graves					
Pessac Léognan (PL)	16	13.38	4.34	7.23	27.32
Pomerol (POM)	8	20.90	14.44	6.67	55.93
Overall	108	15.59	12.26	3.61	86.02

Table 3. Primeur Grade by Rank (Average Across Vintages)

	Number of châteaux	Mean	Std. dev.	Min.	Max.
Médoc					
ME-1	4	92.48	2.28	88	98
ME-2	12	88.81	3.95	75	95.5
ME-3	8	85.92	3.11	75	91.5
ME-4	9	86.91	2.04	80	91.5
ME-5	13	86.75	3.52	73.5	95
ME-6	16	84.78	3.39	75	90
Saint Emilion					
SE-1	1	91.70	1.15	90.5	93
SE-2	5	88.13	3.44	79	94.5
SE-3	11	87.90	3.50	77	93.5
Graves	11	87.58	2.59	79.5	91.5
Non-classified	18	88.05	3.96	73	95.5
Overall	108	87.47	3.72	73	98

price, followed by wines from Saint Emilion and wines from Pauillac. The highest ranks (ME-1 and SE-1) got the best grade on average and were priced significantly above the average for all *châteaux* (Tables 3 and 4). The second-highest in the Médoc and in the Saint Emilion region (ME-2 and SE-2 respectively) are priced significantly above the lower ranks from the same region. Note finally that the high "primeur" price for non-classified wines

Table 4. Primeur Price by Rank (Average Across Vintages)

	Number of châteaux	Mean	Std. dev.	Min.	Max.
Médoc					
ME-1	4	43.74	15.67	25.01	66.17
ME-2	12	18.45	8.46	7.09	37.05
ME-3	8	10.15	2.10	6.81	15.88
ME-4	9	10.72	2.99	5.74	15.88
ME-5	13	10.55	4.11	5.70	26.47
ME-6	13	7.87	2.79	3.61	15.22
Saint Emilion					
SE-1	1	62.68	23.48	31.96	86.02
SE-2	5	20.84	9.47	9.45	43.67
SE-3	11	13.36	5.70	6.95	24.48
Graves	11	12.87	3.89	7.23	20.85
Non-classified	18	18.45	12.79	6.25	55.93
Overall	108	15.59	12.26	3.61	86.02

is mainly driven by the wines from the Pomerol region, and especially the famous *Château Petrus.*

The "primeur" price model (1) assumes that the price depends on true quality, q^*, experts' grade, q^o, and a vector X of price determinants. We include in X a dummy variable for each "appellation," a dummy variable for each official ranking class, and a dummy variable for each vintage. Note that, unfortunately, we cannot consider weather variables in the price model since they are the same for all *châteaux* and only vary across years. These three observable elements are labeled on each bottle of wine (ranking is indicated as long as the wine is ranked). The ranking classification may also be considered as an indirect measure for reputation of the *châteaux* (Hadj Ali and Nauges, 2007).

3.2. *Estimation results and tests on vintage quality and the weather*

3.2.1. *Main estimates of the model*

We report in Table 5 estimation results obtained under the three alternatives (standard errors are computed using 500 bootstrap replications).

The estimated effect of Parker's rating is found positive and significant in the three models, ranging from 1.64 in the Olley–Pakes' model to 2.84 in Alternative B. Remember that Alternatives A and B do not rely on the monotonicity of Assumption A2 but on stronger hypotheses on the Markov

Table 5. Estimation of the Price Equation — 392 Observations (108 Châteaux)

	Alternative A		Alternative B		Olley–Pakes	
	Coef.	Std. err.	Coef.	Std. err.	Coef.	Std. err.
Parker's grade ($\log q^o_{it}$)($\hat{\gamma}$)	2.322**	0.987	2.836***	0.798	1.643***	0.632
Médoc (appellation groups)						
Haut Médoc	−0.613**	0.291	−0.613**	0.291	−0.68*	0.404
Margaux	−0.444	0.285	−0.444	0.285	−0.487	0.381
Moulis	−0.441	0.312	−0.441	0.312	−0.553	0.360
Pauillac	−0.325	0.280	−0.325	0.280	−0.415	0.372
Saint Estèphe	−0.311	0.289	−0.311	0.289	−0.440	0.387
Saint Julien	−0.313	0.295	−0.313	0.295	−0.430	0.382
Saint Emilion (appellation groups)						
SEGC	−0.641	0.427	−0.641	0.427	0.029	0.714
Graves (appellation groups)						
Pessac Léognan	−0.286	0.273	−0.286	0.273	−1.183**	0.507
Pomerol (reference group)	—	—	—	—	—	—
Vintages						
1997 vintage	0.464***	0.026	0.464***	0.026	0.319***	0.028
1998 vintage	0.380***	0.031	0.380***	0.031	0.304***	0.036
Médoc (ranking system)						
ME-1	−0.674	0.689	−0.674	0.689	—	—
ME-2	−1.422**	0.694	−1.422**	0.694	−0.587	0.531
ME-3	−1.729**	0.703	−1.729**	0.703	−0.884*	0.537
ME-4	−1.812***	0.698	−1.812***	0.698	−0.911*	0.547
ME-5	−1.850***	0.698	−1.850***	0.698	−1.002*	0.535
ME-6	−1.908***	0.700	−1.908***	0.700	−1.009*	0.544
Saint Emilion (ranking system)						
SE-1 (reference group)	—	—	—	—	—	—
SE-2	−0.958	0.631	−0.958	0.631	−0.837	0.533
SE-3	−1.375**	0.623	−1.375**	0.623	−1.273**	0.534
Graves (ranking system)						
GR	−1.701**	0.704	−1.701**	0.704	—	—
Non-classified	−1.681**	0.684	−1.681**	0.684	−0.870	0.532

Notes: ***, **, * indicates significance at the 1, 5, and 10% level respectively.

process of unobserved quality. Therefore, if unobserved quality satisfies these stricter conditions, the comparison of the results obtained under Alternatives A and B with results obtained with the "Olley–Pakes" methodology, provides a good assessment of the validity of the monotonicity assumption. It shows that results obtained under the monotonicity assumption, and in particular the impact of Parker's grade on the price set by the producer, are quite robust.

We thus find evidence that experts' opinion has some influence on producers' pricing decision. In other words, once the "primeur" price has been chosen on the basis of objective wine characteristics and wine quality, an additional premium is added which depends on experts' judgment. This premium is such that a one percentage-point increase on the average grade induces an increase of the "primeur" price by 1.6% to 2.8%. These results would tend to confirm the idea that Robert Parker is influential in the Bordeaux area (see Hadj Ali *et al.*, 2008, for a discussion of Robert Parker's role in the Bordeaux region). However, our results are not directly comparable to the ones reported in Hadj Ali *et al.* (2008) as these authors consider "primeur" sales in a different period (2002–2003) and measure the impact on the "primeur" price of being graded by Robert Parker.[14]

Ranking is also found to have a significant influence on the pricing of "primeur" wine, in the three models. Wines belonging to all ranks, except top-growths from the Médoc region (ME-1) and second-growths from the Saint Emilion region (SE-2), are priced significantly below the top-growths of Saint Emilion (SE-1) which were taken as the reference group. The rank effect provides an indirect measure of a reputation premium and may also reflect the market power of *châteaux* belonging to top-growths ranking (Hadj Ali and Nauges, 2007). Appellation groups do not come out significantly in the estimated models. Estimates of the β's in Olley–Pakes' model are quite close to estimates of the β's in Alternatives A and B, but, in most cases, the significance is higher in the two latter models. Using the estimation results obtained with the Olley–Pakes' method, we find evidence that the appellation, ranking and vintage variables explain 45% of the total variance of prices, while Parker's grade explains around 10%. The remaining total variance of prices is thus explained by unobserved quality and random shocks.

[14]For the first time, in 2003, Robert Parker wine grades have been published in autumn, after the prices were determined by the producers. Combining these data with observations on prices and grades from 2002, the authors estimate the effect of being graded by Parker using a difference-in-differences procedure. They find an overall effect equal to almost 3 euros per bottle. As stated in their article, the validity of this approach relies on the so-called "parallel trend assumption" which states that, "had Parker not graded any wine in two subsequent years, the price evolution would have been the same for all wines." In our case, we do not rely on such assumption.

Table 6. Correlation Coefficients between Predicted Quality and Other Variables

	Alternative A	Alternative B	Olley–Pakes
Experts' grade	0.2578(0.0000)	0.1921(0.0001)	0.3719(0.0000)
Cumulative hours of sunshine	0.2482(0.0000)	0.2517(0.0000)	0.2481(0.0000)
Cumulative hours of rainfall	−0.1164(0.0212)	−0.1190(0.0185)	−0.1568(0.0018)

Notes: p-value corresponding to the significance level of each correlation coefficient in parentheses.

In order to get an idea of the magnitude of endogeneity bias, we estimate the pricing model (1) using a simple OLS regression. OLS regression would produce consistent estimates of the γ parameter if the expert's grade was not correlated with unobserved true quality or if unobserved true quality did not enter the pricing model. When estimating the model by OLS, the coefficient for the expert's grade is estimated at 3.95 (significant at the 1% level), which indicates that failing to control for endogeneity of unobserved quality in the pricing model leads to over-estimate the impact of Parker's review on the "primeur" price.

3.2.2. *Analysis of predicted wine quality*

A nice feature of our approach is that it allows to recover estimates of the unobserved quality, q^*_{it}, for each *château* i and vintage t. In this section, we propose to test the validity of our quality estimates by analyzing their relationship with other factors such as experts' grade, weather conditions and official rankings.[15] A first test is made by computing simple correlation coefficients between, on the one hand, expected wine quality as predicted by our model, $\hat{q}^*_{it}$, and experts' grade and weather variables on the other hand. As for the latter we consider cumulative rainfall and cumulative hours of sunshine from January to September. Correlation coefficients along with probability values corresponding to the significance level of each correlation coefficient, are shown in Table 6.

Correlation coefficients have the expected signs and are all significant at the 5% level. Correlation coefficient between experts' grade and predicted wine quality is 0.26, 0.19, and 0.37 in Alternatives A and B, and Olley–Pakes'

[15] We assume that local weather conditions on vineyards do not enter the price equation. Including the weather conditions in the X_{it} could be done but it would mean, in this case, that we assume that these weather variables are publicly observed. This is likely to be a too strong assumption though, considering variables like the daily maximum and minimum temperature or the number of hours of sunshine.

model respectively.[16] Predicted wine quality is found positively correlated with cumulative hours of sunshine over the January–September period (correlation coefficient is 0.25 in the three models), and negatively correlated with cumulative rainfall over the same period (correlation coefficient is -0.12 in Alternatives A and B, and -0.16 in Olley–Pakes' model).[17]

Evidence about the effect of weather on wine quality is consistent with Ashenfelter's findings (see Ashenfelter *et al.*, 1995; Ashenfelter, 2007, for a discussion of the relationship between weather conditions and vintage quality), even after disentangling unobserved wine quality from the pure signaling effect of experts' grading on price. Ashenfelter *et al.* (1995) and Ashenfelter (2007) show that the quality for red Bordeaux wines, based on the price of mature wines, can be predicted by weather conditions observed during the grapes-growing season. Here, we find evidence that wine quality known by the producer and taken into account for the pricing of "en primeur" wine, can actually be explained by the weather conditions during the grapes-growing season. It is remarkable that such consistent evidence can be found also on the quality as identified by our structural model after disentangling quality effects from experts' opinion effects.

We then check if wine quality as predicted by our model corresponds to the existing ranking in the Médoc and Saint Emilion appellation groups (see Table 7). As for the wines from Saint Emilion, the ranking based on our predicted quality perfectly matches the "official ranking" inside the appellation group: predicted quality for top-growths wines (SE-1) is found to be higher, on average, than predicted quality for second-growths wines (SE-2), itself being higher than predicted quality of third-growths wines (SE-3). As for the wines produced in the Médoc region, the ordering based on predicted quality matches the official ordering at the top (i.e., top-growths wine (ME-1) and second-growths wine (ME-2) are respectively ranked 1 and 2). This is no longer true for the other groups: ME-3 to ME-6. These findings should not come as a surprise though, knowing that official ranking of wine from the Saint Emilion appellation group is subsequently revised every 10 years while the ranking in the Médoc region has remained almost the same since it was created in the nineteenth century. Our findings would thus support

[16]Graphical tests show that the relationship between experts' grade and wine quality is monotonic. The graph is not shown here but is available from the authors upon request.
[17]Note that correlation coefficients between experts' grade and weather variables are never found significantly different from 0.

Table 7. Ranking Based on Predicted Quality, for Médoc and Saint Emilion Appellation Groups

	Alternative A	Alternative B	Olley–Pakes
Médoc (ranking system)			
ME-1	1	1	1
ME-2	2	2	2
ME-3	5	6	5
ME-4	4	4	4
ME-5	3	3	3
ME-6	6	5	6
Saint Emilion (ranking system)			
SE-1	1	1	1
SE-2	2	2	2
SE-3	3	3	3

the view of some Bordeaux producers who claim that the official ranking in the Médoc region should be revised.

4. Conclusions

In this chapter, we propose an empirical analysis of wine producers' pricing strategy at the time of "primeur" sales in the Bordeaux region. "En primeur" wine is a typical experience good in the sense of Nelson since the wine is not yet mature at the time of "primeur" sales. We use a structural empirical approach, which is based on Olley and Pakes (1996), to disentangle the effect of experts' grades from the effect of true quality on the pricing of experience goods. This technique is particularly useful when one does not have any valid instrumental variables at hand or when panel data techniques allowing for individual specific effects are not well suited. We estimate two alternative models to test the robustness of our main estimation results.

Using a panel data set of 108 *châteaux* selling wine on the Bordeaux "en primeur" market, we confirm that experts' grades affect producers' choice of "en primeur" price above the effect of unobserved wine quality (Hadj Ali and Nauges, 2007; Hadj Ali *et al.*, 2008). Our empirical results also show that failing to control for endogeneity caused by the omission of unobserved quality leads to over-estimate the influence of experts' grades on the "primeur" price.

Finally, an interesting feature of this approach is that it allows to recover unobserved quality of each wine in the sample. The identified wine quality is shown to be correlated with weather conditions at the growing season, an evidence which is consistent with findings by Ashenfelter *et al.* (1995) on the effect of weather on prices of mature wines.

Acknowledgments

We would like to thank Daniel Ackerberg and two anonymous referees for their comments that improved this chapter. All remaining errors are ours.

References

Ackerberg, D.A. (2003). Advertising, learning, and consumer choice in experience good markets: A structural empirical examination. *International Economic Review*, 44, 1007–1040.

Ackerberg, D.A., Caves, K., and Frazer, G. (2006). *Structural Estimation of Production Functions: An Application to the Timing of Input Choices.* Mimeo University of California, Los Angeles.

Akerlof, G. (1970). The market for "lemons": Quality uncertainty and the market mechanism. *The Quarterly Journal of Economics*, 84, 488–500.

Ashenfelter, O. (2007). *Predicting the Quality of Bordeaux Wine.* AAWE Working Paper, Vol. 4.

Ashenfelter, O., Ashmore, D., and Lalonde, R. (1995). Bordeaux wine vintage quality and the weather. *Chance*, 8, 7–14.

Caves, R.E., and Greene, D.P. (1996). Brands quality levels, prices, and advertising outlays: Empirical evidence on signals and information costs. *International Journal of Industrial Organization*, 14, 29–52.

Darolles, S., Florens, J.P., and Renault, E. (2003). *Non-parametric Instrumental Regression.* IDEI Working Paper, Vol. 228.

Ginsburgh, V. (2003). Awards, success and aesthetic quality in the arts. *Journal of Economic Perspectives*, 17, 99–111.

Hadj Ali, H., Lecocq, S., and Visser, M. (2008). The impact of gurus: Parker grades and en primeur wine prices. *Economic Journal*, 118(29), F158–F173.

Hadj Ali, H., and Nauges, C. (2007). The pricing of experience goods: The case of en primeur wine. *American Journal of Agricultural Economics*, 89(1), 91–103.

Jin, G.Z., and Leslie, P. (2003). The effects of information on product quality: Evidence from restaurant hygiene cards. *Quarterly Journal of Economics*, 118, 409–451.

Landon, S., and Smith, C.E. (1997). The use of quality and reputation indicators by consumers: The case of Bordeaux wine. *Journal of Consumer Policy*, 20, 289–323.

Landon, S., and Smith, C.E. (1998). Quality expectations, reputation and price. *Southern Economic Journal*, 64, 628–647.

Levinsohn, J., and Petrin, A. (2003). Estimating production functions using inputs to control for unobservables. *Review of Economic Studies*, 70(2), 317–342.

Mahenc, P. (2004). The influence of informed buyers in markets susceptible to the lemons problem. *American Journal of Agricultural Economics*, 86(3), 649–659.

Mahenc, P., and Meunier, V. (2003). Forward markets and signals of quality. *Rand Journal of Economics*, 34, 478–494.

Mahenc, P., and Meunier, V. (2006). Early sales of Bordeaux grands crus. *Journal of Wine Economics*, 1(1), 57–74.

Markham, D. (1997). *1855: A History of the Bordeaux Classification.* Wiley, New York: NY, USA.
Nelson, P. (1970). Information and consumer behavior. *Journal of Political Economy*, 78, 311–329.
Nelson, P. (1974). Advertising as information. *Journal of Political Economy*, 81, 729–754.
Newey, W., and Powell, J. (2003). Instrumental variables estimation of nonparametric models. *Econometrica*, 71(5), 1565–1578.
Olley, S., and Pakes, A. (1996). The dynamics of productivity in the telecommunications equipment industry. *Econometrica*, 64, 1263–1295.
Reinstein, D.A., and Snyder, C.M. (2005). The influence of expert reviews on consumer demand for experience goods: A case study of movie critics. *The Journal of Industrial Economics*, 53(1), 27–51.
Shaked, A., and Sutton, J. (1982). Relaxing price competition through product differentiation. *The Review of Economic Studies*, 49, 3–13.
Shapiro, C. (1983). Premiums for high quality products as rents to reputation. *Quarterly Journal of Economics*, 98, 659–680.
Tirole, J. (1996). A theory of collective reputations (with applications to the persistence of corruption and to firm quality). *Review of Economic Studies*, 63, 1–22.

Appendix A. The Case of a Perception Error

In the case of the main method of identification that follows Olley and Pakes (1996), we show here how to add a perception error and still obtain identification. We assume that the relationship between q_{it}^* and q_{it}^o is no longer deterministic and is affected by unobserved shocks, ζ_{it}, whatever the signal s_{it} that can be q_{it-1}^o or some other variable in this structural model:

$$q_{it}^o = q_t(q_{it}^* - \zeta_{it}, s_{it}). \tag{A.1}$$

The interpretation of the error ζ_{it} as a perception or reporting error depends on whether one assumes that experts do observe or not wine quality q_{it}^* at period t. If one can assume that wine quality is observed by experts, then ζ_{it} is more a "reporting error." If one assumes that experts do not yet observe perfectly wine quality q_{it}^* then ζ_{it} should be seen as a "perception error."

We first need to assume that the perception error is uncorrelated with signals s_{it}:

$$E(\zeta_{it} s_{it}) = 0.$$

We develop our estimation procedure similarly. The "primeur" price model is assumed linear in the parameters, that is:

$$\ln p_{it} = X_{it}'\beta + \gamma q_{it}^o + q_{it}^* + \varepsilon_{it}, \tag{A.2}$$

where γq_{it}^o is the effect of wine grade and q_{it}^* is true wine quality.

It can be written

$$\ln p_{it} = X'_{it}\beta + \phi_{it}(q^o_{it}, s_{it}) + \zeta_{it} + \varepsilon_{it} \tag{A.3}$$

where $\phi_{it}(q^o_{it}, s_{it})$ is defined as

$$\phi_{it}(q^o_{it}, s_{it}) = \gamma q^o_{it} + q^{*^{-1}}_t (q^o_{it}, s_{it}).$$

In this framework, experts' grade q^o_{it} is endogenous because correlated with ζ_{it}. We thus need to use some instrumental variables for q^o_{it} that are uncorrelated with the perception error ζ_{it}. Remark that while it is difficult to find any instrumental variable that would be correlated with q^o_{it} but not with unobserved quality q^*_{it}, it is easier to think about an instrumental variable correlated with q^o_{it} (and q^*_{it}) but not with the perception error ζ_{it} (a valid instrument would for example be equal to the unobserved quality plus a white noise, and would actually be excluded from the structural equation of q^o_{it}).

If one wants to estimate $\phi_{it}(q^o_{it}, s_{it})$ non-parametrically, then one has to use non-parametric instrumental variables techniques (Darolles *et al.*, 2003; Newey and Powell, 2003). Then, in the first-stage, the price model (A.3) which is linear in X and non-parametric in $\phi_{it}(q^o_{it}, s_{it})$, is estimated consistently, which provides $\hat{\phi}_{it}$. A second step is necessary to identify the experts' grade coefficient γ.

The second stage starts by computing, up to a scalar constant, a prediction for the perceived true quality $q^*_{it} - \zeta_{it}$ that we denote $\hat{q}^*_{\zeta it}$. For any candidate value γ^*, let

$$\hat{q}^*_{\zeta it} = \hat{\phi}_{it} - \gamma^* q^o_{it}. \tag{A.4}$$

Using these values, a consistent (non-parametric) approximation to $E[\hat{q}^*_{\zeta it}|\hat{q}^*_{\zeta it-1}, I_{it}]$ is given by the predicted values $E[q^*_{\zeta it}|\widehat{q^*_{\zeta it-1}}, I_{it}]$ from the regression

$$\hat{q}^*_{\zeta it} = b_0 + b_1\hat{q}^*_{\zeta it-1} + b_2\hat{q}^{*2}_{\zeta it-1} + b_3\hat{q}^{*3}_{\zeta it-1} + b_4 I_{it} + w_{it}. \tag{A.5}$$

Then, using the fact that $q^*_{\zeta it-1} = q^*_{it} - \zeta_{it}$ and denoting $\kappa_{it} = E[q^*_{it}|q^*_{it-1}, I_{it}] - E[q^*_{it}|q^*_{\zeta it-1}, I_{it}]$ the error in the equation defining unobserved shocks on wine quality due to the conditioning on $q^*_{\zeta it-1}$ instead of q^*_{it-1}, we have

$$q_{it}^* - E[q_{it}^* | q_{\zeta it-1}^*, I_{it}] = \xi_{it} + \kappa_{it}.$$

Using $E[\zeta_{it}^* | q_{\zeta it-1}^*, I_{it}] = 0$, we can write

$$q_{\zeta it}^* - E[q_{\zeta it}^* | q_{\zeta it-1}^*, I_{it}] = q_{it}^* - E[q_{\zeta it}^* | q_{\zeta it-1}^*, I_{it}] + \zeta_{it} = \xi_{it} + \kappa_{it} + \zeta_{it}.$$

Given $\hat{\beta}, \gamma^*$, and $E[q_{it}^* | \widehat{q_{it-1}^*}, I_{it}]$, we get

$$\varepsilon_{it} + \widehat{\zeta_{it} + \kappa_{it}} + \xi_{it} = \ln p_{it} - X_{it}'\hat{\beta} - \gamma^* q_{it}^o - E[q_{\zeta it}^* | \widehat{q_{\zeta it-1}^*}, I_{it}].$$

Then, the estimate $\hat{\gamma}$ of γ is defined as the solution to the following

$$\min_{\gamma^*} \sum_{i,t} ((\ln p_{it} - X_{it}'\hat{\beta} - \gamma^* q_{it}^o - E[q_{it}^* | \widehat{q_{\zeta it-1}^*}, I_{it}]) z_{it-1})^2,$$

where z_{it-1} is a valid instrumental variable. Moreover, these errors being independent and identically distributed, we have $E(q_{\zeta it}^* | q_{it}^*)$ so that the average of $q_{\zeta it}^*$ for a given *château*, over vintages, is a consistent estimator of the average of q_{it}^* over vintages. Also the average of $q_{\zeta it}^*$ over a set of *châteaux* is a consistent estimator of the average of q_{it}^* over a set of *châteaux* for a given vintage t.

Chapter 22

Critical Exposure and Price-Quality Relationships for New World Wines in the U.S. Market*

Peter W. Roberts[†] and Ray Reagans[‡]

[†]*Goizueta Business School, Emory University, Atlanta, GA 30306, USA*
peter_roberts@bus.emory.edu

[‡]*MIT Sloan School of Management, Cambridge, MA 02142, USA*
rreagans@mit.edu

Notwithstanding the observed positive correlations between critics' quality ratings and wine prices, the range of these correlations is quite high. In light of this, researchers must consider the factors that either strengthen or weaken the association between quality ratings and prices. In this chapter, we propose that the slope of the relationship between quality ratings and wine prices is moderated by the amount of attention that producers receive. Because attention increases with a producer's critical exposure (i.e., its history of critical coverage), price-quality relationships will be steeper for producers with more critical exposure. This prediction is confirmed in an analysis of New World wines selling into the U.S. market over the 1987 to 2001 period. While a wine's price is a positive function of its own quality rating, the strength of the price-quality relationship increases with a producer's critical exposure.

"A signal hitherto unheard is useless by itself." (Arrow, 1974: 40)

1. Introduction

In the wine industry, quality ratings are provided by (among others) the *Wine Spectator*, the *Wine Advocate* and the *Wine Enthusiast*. Because quality matters to consumers and because the opinions of these experts are

*This article originally appeared in *Journal of Wine Economics* (2007), 2(1), 84–97.

deemed credible, a wine's price should be a positive function of how well it is rated by the critics. In their study of price-quality relationships in a sample of Bordeaux wines, Landon and Smith (1997) find a positive relationship between the quality ratings reported in the *Wine Spectator* and wine prices. A similar result is obtained by Benjamin and Podolny (1999) in their study of California wines (using quality ratings from the *Connoisseur's Guide*) and by Schamel and Anderson (2003) in their study of wines from Australia and New Zealand (using quality ratings from James Halliday and *Winestate*).

These analyses all suggest a strong and unwavering relationship between published quality ratings and product prices. However, using data from *Consumer Reports* covering 1,271 different product markets, Tellis and Wernerfelt (1987) show that despite the positive correlation between quality ratings and prices, the range of these correlations is very high. A similar observation has been made in the wine industry where Jones and Storchmann (2001) conclude that "it is clear that there are great differences between particular châteaux in respect to Parker-point elasticities of the prices." In light of this, it is troubling that existing research has not considered factors that either strengthen or weaken the observed association between quality ratings and wine prices.

One such factor is attention. As Arrow (1974) noted, "each individual economic agent is assumed to start with the ability to receive some signals from the natural and social environment. This capacity is not, however, unlimited, and the scarcity of information-handling ability is an essential feature for understanding ... behavior." We follow Arrow and propose that the strength of the association between a wine's price and its quality rating will depend on the extent to which individuals are paying attention to the product and its rating. A quality rating is a very precise and highly relevant quality indicator because the information that it contains is maximally relevant to the focal product. However, it also lacks salience at low levels of attention; individuals who are not paying close attention will likely miss it.

Consider three variables that are in play when a producer sets the list price for its wine: its underlying quality, the expected likelihood that critics will notice and evaluate the product (P_1), and the expected likelihood that consumers will internalize that quality rating once it is published (P_2). We propose that list prices will be set as a function of product quality weighted by P_1 and P_2.[1] When P_1 and P_2 are thought to be very small,

[1]Note that our theorizing relies on the assumption that producers have a good idea about product quality when they set their list prices, and that there is a correspondence between

a producer is forced to price its products toward the center of the quality distribution; for example, toward "typical" producer quality. Even though the producer knows the product's specific quality, it is not confident that this information will effectively reach the market. As P_1 and P_2 increase, the producer increasingly prices its product in a way that is sensitive to its underlying quality in the belief that critics will publish a quality rating which will then be noticed and internalized by consumers. As consumers gain access to the product-specific quality information, they come to weigh it more heavily (see Figure 1).

Assuming they value product quality, information about higher quality increases demand and translates into a higher price. For lower quality products, greater accessibility reveals negative information, which reduces demand and lowers price.

This leaves the question of what influences the two probabilities, P_1 and P_2. Random events may direct attention toward a given producer or group of

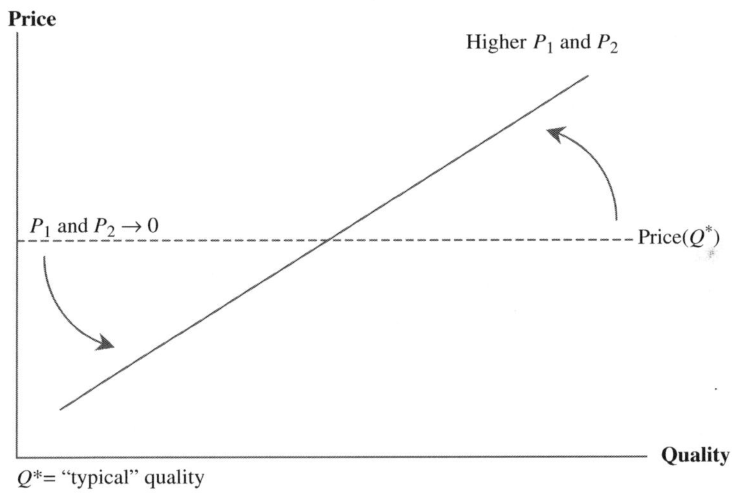

Figure 1. Price-Quality Relationship as Attention Increases

their own and the critics' assessments of quality. In respect of these assumptions, we interviewed several of the major distributors responsible for importing New World wines into the U.S. market. Each confirmed that expert tasting and evaluation are part of the portfolio of activities offered, and that they have a very good idea of a wine's quality before they assist a producer in setting its list price. To confirm that experienced wine tasters tend to reach similar conclusions about quality, we examined the quality ratings of a random sample of 100 wines evaluated by both the *Wine Spectator* and the *Wine Advocate* in 2001 (both publications rate wines on a 100-point scale). For 83% of the wines, the critics publish ratings that are within three points of one another.

producers. For example, the *Judgment of Paris*, which was staged in France in 1976, directed the attention of the world's wine consumers toward U.S. producers and their wines (Taber, 2005). Or, endorsements by, or affiliations with prominent others may attract the attention of potential consumers (Podolny, 1993). A producer's own promotion or advertising initiatives may also attract attention to its products (Hoch and Ha, 1986; Vakratsas and Ambler, 1999). Although accidents, affiliations and strategic actions may influence market attention, we focus on the process whereby attention accumulates as a function of a producer's history of critical coverage.

In addition to providing information about quality, the appearance of a critical review directs the attention of market participants toward certain producers and their products. Zuckerman (1999; 2003) shows that the distribution of legitimacy across firms is influenced by the coverage decisions made by investment analysts. Firms that attract the right kind of coverage are more likely to make it into investors' consideration sets. In his analysis of theater critics at the Edinburgh Festival Fringe, Shrum (1991; 1996) shows that irrespective of the quality of the reviews, simply being reviewed increased the probability that an act will be noticed by potential audience members. Similarly, Ravid (1999) finds that the number of critical reviews is a stronger predictor of film revenues than the actual content of those reviews. We extend these analyses and argue that critics channel attention within wine markets by providing certain producers with more critical coverage over longer periods of time. Two different aspects of this history of critical coverage may influence attention patterns. Attention may accumulate with the number of prior reviews. At the same time, the longer a producer has received critical coverage, the more time consumers have to become familiar with it and its products. In either case, a producer's history of critical coverage enhances the extent to which critics and consumers attend to its products. It increases the likelihood that critics will publish quality ratings for its current product (P_1), and it increases probability that consumers will observe and internalize that ratings once published (P_2). Each of these effects will make a product's list price more sensitive to its underlying quality (see Figure 1). Thus, we predict that *the positive impact of a product's quality rating on its price increases with its producer's critical exposure (i.e., its history of critical coverage)*.

The above studies of price-quality relationships in the wine industry look beyond the quality rating of a focal wine to consider its producer's past quality demonstrations. In the spirit of Shapiro's (1983) model of reputation formation, these demonstrations should translate into a reputation for product quality that is reflected in current prices. Landon and Smith (1997) and Benjamin and Podolny (1999) both find that a producer's previous quality ratings have this predicted impact on the prices of its current product offerings. We continue our examination of the moderating role of attention by asking whether accumulating critical coverage influences the relationship between wine prices and this more indirect indicator of product quality.

A simple extension of our attention story might suggest that as a producer's critical coverage accumulates, consumers place more weight on all of its quality indicators. This would yield a positive moderating effect of critical coverage on the price-reputation relationship. However, we must consider the reputation effect in the context of the specific characteristics of the reputation indicator and of the implications of our first prediction. Because a producer's reputation for quality is an amalgamation of its past quality demonstrations, it offers indirect information about the focal product. At the same time, because it is derived from a larger number of quality demonstrations, it is more accessible when less attentive consumers are unwilling to gather more relevant information. In their analysis of producer reputations and wine prices, Landon and Smith (1997) propose that consumers will make greater use of reputation information when they have difficulty gathering more specific information about product quality. Applying this idea to our theorizing about attention, we expect producer reputation to have its strongest effect when critical exposure is lowest because consumers are not paying attention to and therefore gathering the more relevant product quality ratings. As producers attract more critical coverage, consumers tend to access and make use of the quality ratings. While this increases the impact of these ratings on price, it simultaneously reduces the need for the indirect information housed in the reputation indicator. As one gains access to information about the quality of a particular product, the more indirect information housed in the producer's reputation becomes less relevant. We therefore predict that as critical coverage accumulates *the positive impact of a producer's reputation for quality on the price of its wines decreases with its producer's critical exposure.*

Note how this reputation effect is consistent with existing literature on signaling. In their model, Bagwell and Riordan (1991) conclude that if consumers lack information about quality, then a high quality product may signal its true type by initially pricing above the equilibrium level. As consumers become more informed about quality, prices tend to fall toward expected long run levels. Our framework suggests that a similar dynamic operates at the producer level. If consumers are not paying sufficient attention to evaluate quality differences across products, then charging a premium for its reputation for quality may signal the true "type" of a high quality producer. As attention increases, consumers become better informed about specific products, and give less weight to producer level indicators. Therefore, the price premium attributable to a producer's reputation for quality should fall.

2. Data and Analysis

The data that we analyze come from the *Wine Spectator* and cover quality ratings of New World wines published during the 1987 to 2001 period.[2] "New World" is a shorthand expression for a cohort of seven wine-producing countries that are not among the traditional European producers: these being Australia, New Zealand, Argentina, Chile, South Africa, Canada, and Israel (Allen *et al.*, 1998; Arkell, 1999). In 1987, the volume of wine exported from these New World countries amounted to less than 1.5% of that exported from the four largest Old Word wine countries (France, Germany, Italy, and Spain). By 2001, the situation had changed dramatically — exports from New World wine countries were almost 25% of Old World country export levels.[3] This dramatic ascendance offers an opportunity to examine the relationship between product quality and price in a context wherein a key class of producers were emerging on the world scene.

Because wine is an experience good (Nelson, 1970), the quality of a bottle of wine is not directly observable in advance of purchase. Here, a bottle of wine refers to a specific producer-wine-year combination; for example, Rosemount Estates (producer) Mudgee Hill of Gold Shiraz (wine), 1999 vintage (year). Moreover, despite the best efforts of producers, fluctuations in many different factors lead to irreducible variability in quality across bottles of wine — both within a given year and over time. Consider that Rosemount Estates received *Wine Spectator* reviews for 23 of the wines that it released in 2001. These quality ratings ranged from 79 out of 100 (roughly 1.25 standard deviations below the average quality rating in our sample) to 92 (roughly

[2]Although other publications provide assessments of New World wines, their coverage of non-U.S. wines is more limited. In 2001, the *Wine Spectator* published roughly 1,500 quality ratings from our seven New World countries, while the *Wine Advocate* and the *Wine Enthusiast* published fewer than 600 each. Moreover, "the Spectator ... reaches an audience over six times larger than the Advocate's (Anonymous, 1999)."

[3]Export data are from the FAO Statistical Database, UN Food & Agricultural Organization, Rome, 2001.

1.75 standard deviation above that average). This variability in quality in 2001 persists despite the fact that Rosemount Estates received 206 reviews between 1987 and 2000 — the maximum received by any of our sampled producers.

In this context, the opinions of wine critics clearly matter and posted prices tend to reflect their quality ratings. At the same time, the very large number of products and producers means that securing a visible place in the market is problematic (Lecocq and Visser, 2006). The *Wine Spectator* conducted roughly 9,000 evaluations of New World wines between 1987 and 2001. This number is itself very high, but it pales in comparison to the almost 57,000 evaluations of wines originating in France, Italy, Germany and Spain, and the more than 33,000 evaluations of U.S. wines. This suggests that New World wine producers struggled to get their products noticed.

We obtain our price variable by dividing the list price reported in the *Wine Spectator* by the U.S. consumer price index (normalized to unity in 1987). Because the distribution of real wine prices is highly skewed, we employ the log of real price as the dependent variable. The quality ratings are those reported (on a 100 point scale) in the *Wine Spectator*. These ratings come from blind tastings by wine experts, and the process ensures that tasters do not know who made the wine or its list price when they assign their quality ratings. We are therefore confident that they are not spuriously influenced by the producers' reputations or by the wines' suggested list prices. A producer's reputation for quality is the average quality rating of all other wines made by the same producer in the focal year or in one of the two preceding years (Benjamin and Podolny, 1999).[4]

Because of the relatively recent and dramatic rise of New World wine producers on global markets, there is considerable variability in critical exposure levels during our sample period. Only a handful of New World producers (e.g., Penfolds from Australia) were attracting critical attention in the early 1980s (Allen *et al.*, 1998). As New World producers began to attract more attention throughout the 1980s and 1990s, they did so at different times and at different rates. Figure 2 demonstrates the variability across New World producers in the years in which they first received *Wine Spectator* reviews in the U.S. market. Overall, the products in our sample include those from

[4]There are 430 "isolates" in our sample. Because producer reputation cannot be determined, we assign the average value of the reputation variable to these observations. In addition, all models include an indicator variable set to one for these observations in order to give us unbiased estimates of the producer reputation effect.

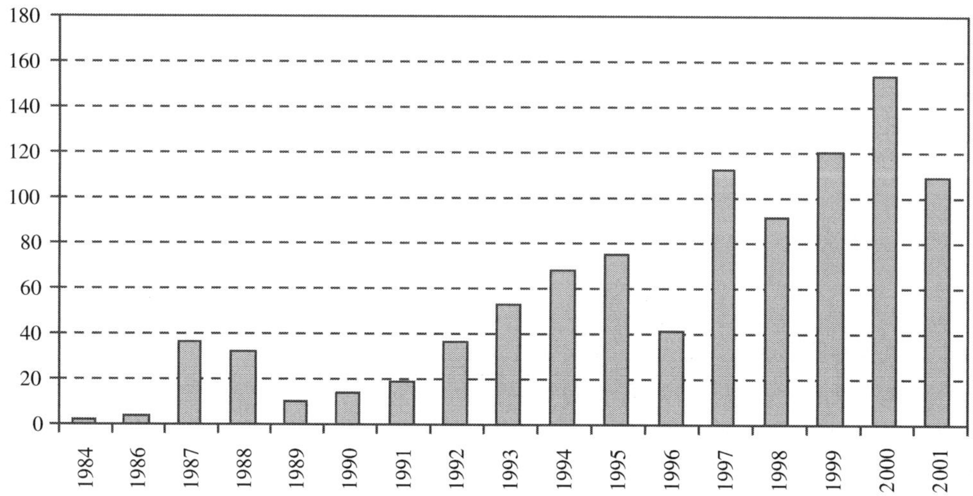

Figure 2. Counts of Producers with First-Time Critical Evaluations, by Year

producers who never before received a single review through those whose producers had garnered more than 200 prior critical reviews. This variance allows us to test whether the producers' different histories of critical exposure influenced the extent to which their product quality ratings and their reputations are reflected in the prices they charge.

Our critical exposure variable is the count of prior reviews received by the focal producer up to year $t-1$, divided by 10. Although we employ this count-based measure in the models that we report, we ran additional models using a variable that reflects a producer's duration of critical coverage. This clock variable dates from the first year in which a producer receives a review. The two exposure variables are highly correlated ($p = 0.70$) and yield virtually identical results. Finally, the tests of our hypotheses require a set of interactions between the quality rating and producer reputation variables and the critical exposure variable. Given concerns about multicollinearity, we mean-centered each variable before creating each interaction term.

The models also include a set of indicator variables for each country, for each grape varietal, and for each year within the sample period. Because the wines in our sample are produced in different countries, exchange rate fluctuations may affect the prices charged in the U.S. In particular, local currency appreciations relative to the U.S. dollar should be associated with higher local production costs (measured in U.S. dollars) and therefore higher U.S. prices. We control for this possibility with a variable that accounts for the percentage change (relative to 1987) of the value of each country's currency relative to the U.S. dollar. Three additional variables account for the extent of competition within each varietal category. One variable counts the number of U.S.-produced wines (divided by 1,000) rated by the *Wine Spectator* in each varietal category in each year. Consistent with ecological models of competition (Hannan and Carroll, 1992), we include the square of this variable to account for possible non-monotonic effects. Because competition may also be quality-based, we include a third variable that measures the average quality rating received by the U.S.-produced wines in the different varietal categories in each year.

Our theorizing relies on the fact that producers and distributors have a reasonably good idea about product quality (see the discussion surrounding Figure 1), which produces a strong correspondence between their own and the critics' assessments of product quality. This begs the question of whether producers tend to become better over time in predicting the reactions of critics to their wines. This is an important issue because if improvements in the ability to accurately assess product quality correlates with accumulating critical exposure, then the interpretation of our results would be suspect. We deal with this issue by controlling for total producer experience. Here, we consulted numerous sources to compile information on the founding dates of 503 wine producers in our sample who are responsible for roughly 84% of the observations.[5] To determine the extent to which producer learning has an impact on the sensitivity of price to quality, we include the producer age variable and its interaction with the quality variables in all of the models that we report.

We also control for the age of each wine at release, because wines that have been aged longer tend to command higher prices. In addition, because wines are produced in different quantities, price-quantity trade-offs may affect our results (Haeger and Storchmann, 2006). The *Wine Spectator* reports quantity data (i.e., the total number of cases produced) for 47% of the observations in our sample. We use the log of the number of cases produced (divided by 1,000) as a proxy for the quantity available for sale in the U.S. Finally, each model also includes an interaction between the product quality and producer reputation variables because prior research documents that returns to quality demonstrations are higher for producers with reputations

[5]As with the reputation variable, observations with missing producer age, wine age and product quantity information are assigned the mean of the respective variables. Each model includes indicator variables set to one for the observations with missing data in order to give an unbiased estimate of each effect.

for producing high quality products (Benjamin and Podolny, 1999; Jones and Storchmann, 2001).

The *Wine Spectator* evaluated 9,217 New World wines during the 1987 to 2001 period. However, we exclude several observations due to missing price data, leaving 8,892 observations. Descriptive statistics and pair-wise correlations for all variables are reported in Table 1 (see Appendix for definitions of each variable). The average of the log of the real price variable corresponds to a real price of $9.47. The averages of the quality rating and producer reputation variables are 84.302 and 84.209. Finally, the number of prior critical evaluations for the average producer is roughly 16.

The observations in our sample are not independent — there can be multiple observations for each producer in each year. We therefore estimate regression models with robust standard errors clustered around producers. Robust standard error estimators provide asymptotically consistent estimates of the variance without making assumptions about the distribution of the errors in our equations.

3. Results

Our results are reported in Table 2. Model 1 includes the control variables and the quality and reputation variables. The count-based competition variables are both significant and in the expected directions. As the number of U.S. wines of the same varietal type increases, price increases and then decreases. The inflection point for this relationship occurs when the count of U.S. wines on offer is roughly 932, which is roughly two standard deviations above the average for this variable. Somewhat surprisingly, the effect of producer age on price is negative and significant. This may reflect the fact we are studying New World producers. Because the New World wine boom is a relatively recent phenomenon, the U.S. market may favor producers founded during the 1980s and 1990s. As expected, a wine's price increases significantly with its own age while the quantity of a wine that is produced has a negative effect on price. The significant coefficient also confirms that wines with higher quality ratings do command higher prices. The producer reputation effect is also positive and significant while the relationship between price and quality increases with producer reputation. Consumers do tend to pay more for quality demonstrations from producers with reputations for high product quality. Finally, note that the null coefficient on the interaction between the quality and producer age variables suggests that producers do not become better at predicting or pricing to product quality as they gain experience.

Table 1. Descriptive Statistics and Pair-wise Correlations ($N = 8{,}892$)

Variable	Mean	Std. Dev.	1	2	3	4	5	6	7	8	9	10	11	12	13	14
1. Log (Real Price)	2.25	0.55														
2. Exchange Rate Appreciation	0.83	0.43	0.02													
3. Varietal Count[a]	0.38	0.24	−0.06	−0.05												
4. Varietal Count Squared	0.21	0.19	−0.04	−0.05	0.97											
5. Varietal Quality	85.65	4.10	0.08	−0.05	0.24	0.23										
6. Producer Age	59.78	59.88	−0.18	−0.05	0.01	0.01	−0.01									
7. Wine Age	2.36	1.53	0.27	0.091	0.01	0.01	0.00	0.11								
8. Log (Quantity)	8.87	1.29	−0.39	−0.02	0.02	0.02	−0.06	0.14	−0.05							
9. Quality Rating	84.30	4.32	0.51	0.00	−0.06	−0.03	0.07	−0.12	−0.02	−0.22						
10. Reputation	84.21	3.11	0.47	−0.01	−0.09	−0.07	0.06	−0.16	−0.11	−0.22	0.52					
11. Quality*Reputation	7.02	16.09	0.05	0.09	−0.03	−0.03	0.01	−0.04	0.089	−0.02	−0.19	−0.18				
12. Quality*Producer Age	−31.25	244.08	−0.03	0.01	0.02	0.02	−0.01	−0.05	−0.01	0.03	0.00	−0.05	−0.06			
13. Critical Exposure	1.62	2.76	0.04	−0.02	0.02	0.04	0.08	0.18	0.06	0.16	0.15	0.10	−0.06	0.01		
14. Quality*Exposure	1.73	12.43	0.09	0.01	−0.01	0.00	0.02	0.01	0.18	0.06	−0.02	−0.07	0.14	0.10	0.47	
15. Reputation*Exposure	0.88	7.97	−0.07	0.01	−0.02	−0.01	−0.00	0.05	0.07	0.11	−0.07	−0.18	0.19	0.04	0.30	0.41

Note: [a]divided by 1,000.

Table 2. New World Wine Results (1987–2001)

	Model 1 Baseline	Model 2 Reputation Interaction	Model 2a Robert Parker
Exchange Rate Appreciation	0.047	0.054	0.067*
	(0.027)	(0.029)	(0.028)
Varietal Count	1.160***	1.171***	1.066***
	(0.171)	(0.174)	(0.167)
Varietal Count Squared	−0.622***	−0.617***	−0.565***
	(0.156)	(0.161)	(0.154)
Varietal Quality	0.002	0.002	0.002
	(0.001)	(0.001)	(0.001)
Producer Age[a]	−0.001***	−0.001***	−0.001***
	(0.000)	(0.000)	(0.000)
Wine Age[a]	0.093***	0.090***	0.091***
	(0.011)	(0.010)	(0.011)
Log (Quantity)[a]	−0.115***	−0.111***	−0.118***
	(0.006)	(0.006)	(0.006)
Quality Rating	0.038***	0.039***	0.038***
	(0.003)	(0.002)	(0.002)
Producer Reputation[a]	0.034***	0.034***	0.032***
	(0.003)	(0.003)	(0.003)
Quality*Reputation	0.005***	0.004***	0.004***
	(0.001)	(0.001)	(0.001)
Quality*Producer Age	0.000	−0.000	0.000
	(0.000)	(0.000)	(0.000)
Critical Exposure	—	0.013***	—
		(0.003)	
Quality*Exposure	—	0.005***	—
		(0.001)	
Reputation*Exposure	—	−0.002**	—
		(0.001)	
Parker Reviewed	—	—	0.085***
			(0.019)
Quality*Parker	—	—	0.013***
			(0.004)
Reputation*Parker	—	—	−0.001
			(0.006)
N	8,892	8,892	8,892
R^2	0.577	0.584	0.584

Notes: $^{***}p < 0.001$; $^{**}p < 0.01$; $^{*}p < 0.05$ (robust standard errors in parentheses). All models include fixed effects for varietal category, country and year.
[a]Models include indicator variables set to one for observations with missing data.

When we add the critical exposure variable in Model 2, its effect is negative and significant. By itself, increased critical exposure imposes a penalty, perhaps in the form of reduced exclusivity. Producers that have produced many different wines in the past may lack the cachet of the boutique wine producer. This said, the interaction between a wine's quality rating and its producer's critical exposure level is positive and significant coefficient, supporting our first prediction. A calculation using the coefficients from Model 2 reveals that the change in the log of real price associated with a unit change in quality increases from 0.031 when critical exposure equals zero, to 0.133 when a producer reaches the maximum critical exposure level. This suggests that at the mean of the price variable a unit increase in quality raises the price of a bottle of wine from a zero exposure producer from \$9.49 to \$9.78. The same increase in quality for the highest exposure producer increases price from \$9.49 to \$10.84. This latter increase is between four and five times as large. Finally, Model 2 also analyzes the effect of increasing critical exposure on the relationship between producer reputation and price. The significant negative interaction effect supports our second prediction. Increasing critical exposure dampens the impact of the more indirect producer reputation variable while stimulating the effect of the product's quality rating.

Taken together, these results suggest that wine prices do reflect the information housed in the different quality indicators. It is a question of which indicators tend to have more impact at different levels of critical exposure. Less attentive consumers do not devote as much effort accessing and processing product quality ratings and therefore rely more heavily on a producer's reputation. Viewing the negative interaction between critical exposure and producer reputation in the context of the positive interaction with the product quality rating, we see that this rating comes to substitute for the more indirect reputation indicator as exposure accumulates. However, note that the negative coefficient on the producer reputation interaction (−0.002) offsets but does not exceed the positive coefficient on the quality rating interaction (0.005). Although consumers are placing less weight on producer reputation, there is evidence of increased overall attention to a producer's quality indicators as critical exposure increases.

A potential concern with this analysis relates to its exclusive reliance on the *Wine Spectator* for the quality ratings and for the information used to generate the critical exposure variable. In our theorizing, we assume that critical exposure in general influences the amount of attention paid to the different New World wine producers within the U.S. market. To check this assumption, we searched back issues of the *Wine Advocate* and recorded the first year in which each producer received a published rating from Robert Parker — another highly influential wine critic. We then created an indicator variable set to one in those years after the producer was "discovered" by Robert Parker, and an interaction between this indicator variable and the product's *Wine Spectator* rating and reputation. As indicated in Model 2a, there is a positive main effect associated with the post-Robert Parker variable, as well as a positive and significant interaction between it and the published quality rating. This latter result suggests that the critical attention offered by Robert Parker intensifies the relationship between a wine's list price and the quality rating it receives from a different set of wine critics. The reputation interaction is again negative (although this time not statistically significant).

4. Conclusions

For a quality rating to influence a wine's price, it must be noticed (Olshavsky, 1994). Therefore, the relationship between quality ratings and wine prices should be moderated by the amount of attention a producer receives. We have argued that the amount of attention paid to a producer increases with its critical exposure or its history of critical coverage. As this accumulates, the information that is housed in the wine quality ratings is given more weight. This reduces the need for the more indirect information housed in the more indirect reputation indicator, which is thereby given less weight. Our analysis of price-quality relationships in the wine industry supports the predictions that follow from our attention-based theory. A wine's price is a positive function of its own quality rating and of its producer's reputation for product quality. However, the strength of the price-quality relationship increases with a producer's critical exposure while the impact of producer reputation on price declines.

These results attest to the dual influence of wine critics. On the one hand, the quality information that they generate can be an important determinant of price. On the other hand, their actions over time channel the attention of the market toward some producers over others. In terms of research into quality signals and prices, this insight highlights a fundamental difference between the information content of a quality indicator and the mechanisms through which it has its impact. In this light, it is tempting to view the critical exposure variable as a quality indicator in and of itself. Risk-averse consumers should prefer products made by producers with legitimate track records. However, our results suggest that the more important impact of critical exposure is to make a product's own quality ratings more impactful. In other words, the information that wine consumers seek resides in the quality indicators, while the associations with prior reviews serve to develop access channels to those indicators.

Finally, we stress that this research should be complemented by additional work that considers other drivers of attention. A producer's critical exposure is but one of the factors that influence the amount of attention paid to it and its wines. Others include random events, advertising and promotional expenditures, and inter-organizational affiliations. While our results provide support for meaningful differences in the amount of attention paid to newer versus more established producers, much additional work is needed to fully articulate the process whereby differential attention levels accumulate within and therefore influence markets.

Acknowledgments

The Authors thank Joel Baum, Marc Busch, Heather Haveman, Greta Hsu, Paul Ingram, Ujwal Kayande, Atul Nerkar, Toby Stuart, Harrison White, Mark Zbaracki, Ezra Zuckerman and an anonymous referee for valuable comments that led to improvements in this chapter.

References

Allen, M. *et al.* (1998). *New World of Wine.* London: Reed Consumer Books: Mitchell Beazley.

Anonymous (1999). Playing the rating game. *The Economist*, September 18, 94–96.

Arkell, J. (1999). *New World Wines.* London: Ward Lock Publishing.

Arrow, K.J. (1974). *The Limits of Organization.* New York: Norton.

Bagwell, K., and Riordan, M.H. (1991). High and declining prices signal product quality. *American Economic Review*, 81, 224–239.

Benjamin, B.A., and Podolny, J.M. (1999). Status, quality, and social order in the California wine industry. *Administrative Science Quarterly*, 44, 563–589.

Haeger, J.W., and Storchmann, K. (2006). Prices of American pinot noir wines: Climate, craftsman-ship, critics. *Agricultural Economics*, 35, 67–78.

Hannan, M.T., and Carroll, G.R. (1992). *Dynamics of Organizational Populations: Density, Legitimation, and Competition.* New York: Oxford University Press.

Hoch, S.J., and Ha, Y.-W. (1986). Consumer learning: Advertising and the ambiguity of product experience. *Journal of Consumer Research*, 13, 221–233.

Jones, G.V., and Storchmann, K.-H. (2001). Wine market prices and investment under uncertainty: An econometric model for Bordeaux crus classés. *Agricultural Economics*, 26, 115–133.

Landon, S., and Smith, C.E. (1997). The use of quality and reputation indicators by consumers: The case of Bordeaux wine. *Journal of Consumer Policy*, 20, 289–323.

Lecocq, S., and Visser, M. (2006). What determines wine prices: Objective vs. sensory characteristics. *Journal of Wine Economics*, 1, 42–56.

Nelson, P. (1970). Information and consumer behavior. *Journal of Political Economy*, 78, 311–329.

Olshavsky, R.W. (1994). Attention as an epiphenomenon: Some implications for advertising. In Clark, E.M., Brock, T.C., and Stewart, D.W. (eds.), *Attention, Attitude and Affect in Response to Advertising*, 97–106. Hillsdale, NJ: Lawrence Erlbaum Associates.

Podolny, J.M. (1993). A status-based model of market competition. *American Journal of Sociology*, 98, 829–872.

Ravid, S.A. (1999). Information, blockbusters, and stars: A study of the film industry. *The Journal of Business*, 72, 463–492.

Schamel, G., and Anderson, K. (2003). Wine quality and varietal, regional and winery reputations: Hedonic prices for Australia and New Zealand. *The Economic Record*, 79, 357–369.

Shapiro, C. (1983). Premiums for high quality products as returns to reputations. *Quarterly Journal of Economics*, 98, 659–679.

Shrum, W.M. (1991). Critics and publics: Cultural mediation in highbrow and popular performing arts. *American Journal of Sociology*, 97, 347–375.

Shrum, W.M. (1996). *Fringe and Fortune: The Role of Critics in High and Popular Art.* Princeton: Princeton University Press.

Taber, G.M. (2005). *Judgment of Paris: California vs. France and the Historic 1976 Paris Tasting That Revolutionized Wine.* New York: Scribner.

Tellis, G.J., and Wernerfelt, B. (1987). Competitive price and quality under asymmetric information. *Marketing Science*, 6, 240–253.

Vakratsas, D., and Ambler, T. (1999). How advertising really works. *Journal of Marketing*, 63, 26–43.

Zuckerman, E.W. (1999). The categorical imperative: Securities analysts and the illegitimacy discount. *American Journal of Sociology*, 104, 1398–1438.

Zuckerman, E.W., Kim, T.-Y., Ukanwa, K., and von Rittmann, J. (2003). Robust identities or non-entities? Typecasting in the feature-film labor market. *American Journal of Sociology*, 108, 1018–1074.

Appendix: Variable Definitions

Log (Real Price)	Natural log of list price reported in the Wine Spectator divided by the U.S. consumer price index (normalized to unity in 1987)
Exchange Rate Appreciation	Percentage change (relative to 1987) of the value of the focal country's currency relative to the U.S. dollar.
Varietal Count	Count of the number of U.S.-produced wines (divided by 1,000) rated by the *Wine Spectator* in the focal varietal category in the focal year.
Varietal Count Squared	Square of the Varietal Count variable.
Varietal Quality	Average quality rating received by the U.S.-produced wines in the focal varietal category in the focal year.
Producer Age	The current year minus the focal producer's founding year.
Wine Age	The current year minus the focal wine's vintage year.
Log (Quantity)	Natural log of the total number of cases produced.
Quality Rating	Quality scores reported (on a 100 point scale) in the *Wine Spectator*.
Reputation	Average quality scores of all other wines made by the focal producer in the focal year or in one of the two preceding years.
Critical Exposure	Count of prior *Wine Spectator* reviews received by the focal producer up to year $t-1$ (divided by 10).

Chapter 23

What Determines Wine Prices: Objective vs. Sensory Characteristics*

Sébastien Lecocq[†] **and Michael Visser**[‡]

[†]*INRA, UR1303 ALISS, Alimentation et Sciences Sociales, F-94205 Ivry-sur-Seine, France*
Sebastien.Lecocq@inra.fr

[‡]*CREST, CNRS, ENSAE, University of Paris-Saclay and CRED, University of Paris 2, France*
Michael.Visser@ensae.fr

The hedonic technique is applied to wines. In the price equation we include objective characteristics appearing on the label, as well as sensory characteristics and a grade assigned by expert tasters. We have three almost identically structured data sets (two on Bordeaux wines, and one on Burgundy wines). The results are used to make comparisons between two of the most important wine regions in France, and comparisons over time (the two Bordeaux data sets are sampled at different points in time).

Another puzzle is the lack of correlation between price and pleasure. Perhaps it is not so surprising that a first-rate example of a little known wine can seem much more memorable than something more famous selling at ten times the price; part of the thrill is the excitement of discovery and the feeling of having beaten the system. What is more extraordinary is the wild price variation at the very top end. Demand bubbles up mysteriously, apparently fuelled by fashion and rumour as much as by intrinsic quality. — Jancis Robinson, *Confessions of a Wine Lover*, Penguin Books, 1997.

1. Introduction

There are many types and kinds of wines.[1] Walking through an arbitrary supermarket, one is impressed by the high number of different wines on

*This article originally appeared in *Journal of Wine Economics* (2006), 1(1), 42–56.

[1]In writing this introduction, the wine survey that appeared in The Economist (1999) was very helpful.

the shelves. Whereas the number of different brands of say beer or whiskey that are on sale does usually not exceed ten or fifteen, shoppers typically have the choice between hundreds or sometimes even thousands of different wines. The wines originate not only from the traditional wine countries such as France, Italy, and Spain, but also from new world countries such as Argentina, Australia, Chile, New Zealand, and the USA. These wine countries produce bottles that can cost just $2 (the simple and plain table wines) but also several hundreds of dollars (for the most prestigious wines such as Bordeaux's Haut-Brion, Lafite-Rothschild, Latour, Margaux, and Mouton-Rothschild; Romanée Conti from Burgundy; Grange, Australia's most famous wine; California's Opus One; Vega Sicilia from Spain; Brunello di Montalcino Riserva from Italy, etc.), young wines that are ready to drink as well as wines that improve even after decades of keeping, wines that are made of different combinations and proportions of grape varieties, and wines that originate from various sorts of soils.

Given the huge variability in both the types of wines and their prices, it is of interest to understand how wine prices and wine characteristics are related: What are the precise effects of the features mentioned on the label of the bottle, such as vintage, name, or ranking? What are the consequences of weather conditions during the growing season? In what way do natural endowments (type of soil, exposure of the vineyards) and technology (the manner in which grapes are picked, pressing and racking techniques, type of barrels in which the wine ferments, etc.), influence wine prices?

Also of interest is how the price of a bottle relates to its quality. Perhaps because the notion of quality is in itself somewhat vague and imprecise, the price-quality debate has always been animated and controversial, with opponents firmly defending their points of view. Some claim that price differences reflect quality differences very accurately, arguing that consumers cannot be fooled all the time and that market forces adjust prices to levels in accordance with quality levels. While this is perhaps true for the select group of top wines that are actively traded in auctions throughout the world (in which wine experts intervene, so that indeed prices are likely to adapt more or less continuously to fluctuations in quality), we feel that this argument is less convincing for the majority of wines that are less known: the sheer range and variety of products, the relative absence of information on these wines (unlike for the very top wines, wine tasting sessions are rarely organized for the less known ones), makes it likely that in this case prices are more rigid and less strongly correlated with quality.

At the other extreme, there are those who claim that there is basically hardly any price-quality relationship. While we do not completely adhere to this either, there is anecdotal evidence that suggests that there is indeed something of a price puzzle. For instance, Ernest Gallo, the patriarch of the family-owned E&J Gallo Winery in California (the largest winemaker in the world), recalls how, in the early stages of his career, he once sold wine in New York. He offered a buyer two glasses of the same red wine, the buyer drank the two glasses and asked for the prices of the "two" wines. Upon hearing that the first wine cost 5 cents per bottle, and the second 10 cents, the buyer declared he wanted the 10 cents bottle. The message behind this anecdote is confirmed by many wine auctioneers who have noticed that in the auction room higher wine prices act as a stimulant rather than as a deterrent, thereby reflecting that for bidders, part of the pleasure is apparently to know that a wine is famous and very expensive.

Other evidence that suggests that the price-quality relationship is far from perfect comes from the results of wine-tasting sessions. One famous wine-tasting session was organized in San Francisco, in 1995. On the initiative of G. Getty, an American billionaire and lover of Bordeaux wine, ten of the most talented wine tasters were reunited to taste blindly a sample of Bordeaux wines. The sample contained all the Médoc wines that were classified in 1855. In 1855, sixty one Médocs were ranked in five categories, and wine experts were asked to establish a new classification (from one to sixty one). Although the reshuffling did not turn out to be dramatic (for instance, the four first-category wines are still in the top fifteen), the 1855 and 1995 rankings were certainly not identical (for instance, one fifth-growth wine can be found among the top ten). Given the prices that these wines fetch at today's auctions are pretty well ordered the same way as the 1855 ordering (Di Vittorio and Ginsburgh, 1996), and interpreting the 1995 ranking as a quality ranking, the San Francisco tasting reflects a disparity between quality and price. This type of result is also found in tasting-sessions in which non-experts evaluate the wines. When non-experts blind-taste cheap and expensive wines they typically tend to prefer the cheaper ones.[2]

Many papers look at the determinants of prices, reporting estimation results of so-called hedonic price functions where wine prices are regressed on a set of characteristics in order to determine which characteristics have

[2]Unlike blind-taste evaluations of whiskies, where usually the more expensive brands are the preferred ones (see The Economist, 1999).

a significant effect. In what is probably the earliest article on the subject, Oczkowski (1994) applies the method to Australian table wine and includes in the set of characteristics attributes that are objective and easily observable for the consumer (vintage, vineyard region, grape variety), and also the grades that are published in a popular Australian wine guide. Grades are measured on a five-point scale, and introducing dummy variables for the five levels, Oczkowski shows that, as expected, wine prices increase with the rating level. Ashenfelter, Ashmore, and Lalonde (1995) (for Bordeaux wines) and Byron and Ashenfelter (1995) (for Australian wines) consider as characteristics vintage and weather conditions that prevailed during the growing season, and show that these variables alone explain more than 80% of the price variation in their samples. Ginsburgh, Monzak, and Monzak (1994) apply the hedonic price method to a sample of Médoc wines. Their fascinating data set allows them to disentangle the price effects of weather, reputation (as measured by the 1855 classification), natural endowments (soil, exposure of the vineyards or grapes), and all sorts of production factors. They show that technology and weather conditions explain two thirds of the price variation, and once the reputation variable is added the proportion of explained variance increases to almost 85%. They also show that more recent classifications (such as Parker's classification) do not lead to a better fit of the hedonic price equation than the 1855 classification. Di Vittorio and Ginsburgh (1996) regress auction prices of Haut-Médoc wines on the vintage and the name of the château. The estimated hedonic function allows them to calculate, for each château and vintage, a price index, and these price indices are compared with several classifications (Parker; Tastet and Lawton; Wine Spectator).

Gergaud (1998) applies the hedonic technique to Champagne wines. He finds that the price of Champagne varies significantly with producer characteristics and the appellation of the wine. His estimations also suggest that neither the sensory variables nor the grade assigned by wine connoisseurs matter in the price determination of Champagne. Lima (1999) examines the prices of Californian wines and uses medals won in nine tasting events in 1995 as indices of quality. Regressing prices on dummy variables for the four possible medals (double gold, gold, silver, and bronze), he finds that the San Francisco Fair is the best predictor for California's wine prices. Schamel and Anderson (2001) estimate hedonic price functions for premium wine from Australia and New Zealand, including as independent variables the ratings compiled in Halliday's wine guide and an Australian wine magazine called Winestate, regional dummies and the grape varieties of the wines. Exploiting the time-series aspect of their data (the observations cover the period from 1992 to 2000), the authors study how the effects of these variables evolve over time. Their results show that the effect of the ratings remains fairly constant over time. The relative implicit prices of grape varieties do vary, and price differences between regions tend to increase in the late nineties.

Jones and Storchmann (2001) use wine auction prices for 21 prestigious Bordeaux wines to assess the respective effects of the vintage, the grape composition (acid and sugar levels), and expert-assessed quality (as measured by Parker-points). The authors distinguish Merlot-dominated and Cabernet Sauvignon-dominated wines. The effect of the Parker-point rating is stronger for the latter ones. In addition, the price of Merlot-dominated wines increases more rapidly with age.

Finally, Oczkowski (2001) estimates a hedonic equation for Australian wines and considers the effects of some objective characteristics (red wine or not, old vintage or not), a quality index (a score assigned to the wine based on the International Show Judging System that allocates 50% of the score for palate, 35% for nose and 15% for color), and a reputation index (a score reflecting the long-term quality over numerous vintages).[3] He argues that the quality and reputation variables are measured with error. Correcting for measurement errors, he finds that reputation has a significant impact but that the effect of quality is insignificant.

The present chapter contributes to this literature. We report estimation results of hedonic price equations based on three data sets. The first one (Bordeaux I) is a sample of Bordeaux wines and formed the basis of the paper by Combris, Lecocq and Visser (1997); the second one (Burgundy) is a sample of Burgundy wines and was exploited in Combris, Lecocq and Visser (2000); the third and most recent data set is another sample of Bordeaux wines (Bordeaux II) and was analyzed in Lecocq and Visser (2001). The three data sets were generated in almost exactly the same way, and all three contain the same set of variables. The results can thus easily be used to make comparisons between two of the most important wine regions in France (Bordeaux and Burgundy), and to make comparisons over time (the Bordeaux I sample is drawn in 1992, and the Bordeaux II sample in 2000).

For each wine in the three samples we observe the price and the following objective characteristics: name, color, ranking, appellation, and vintage. The wines in the three samples were blind-tasted by expert tasters who were

---

[3]See also Landon and Smith (1997, 1998) who estimate similar equations for Bordeaux wines using short-term lagged quality scores as a measure of reputation.

required to record their olfactory (aromatic intensity, finesse of aromas, etc.), and gustatory findings (firmness of attack, suppleness, presence of fine tannins, etc.). These variables will be referred to as sensory characteristics. The experts were also requested to assign a grade between 0 and 20 to each wine, a measure that we will interpret as a measure of quality.

As in the studies described above, our objective is to determine which variables significantly affect the price of Bordeaux and Burgundy wines. At this point it is important to note that our measure of quality differs in several important ways from the quality indices used in the previous literature. First, the wines were evaluated via blind-tasting sessions. Unlike the grades compiled in wine guides or magazines, the wine experts assigned their grades without being influenced by the name of the wine, its price or its ranking. Second, since the wines were purchased before the tasting sessions, the grades were unknown when the wine prices were established.[4] Therefore, it is our feeling that our measure of quality reflects in a better way the pure intrinsic effect of quality on prices, and not an effect that is biased by reputation or publicity factors.

This chapter proceeds as follows. The next section presents the data, Section 3 gives the empirical results, and Section 4 concludes.

2. The Data

This section describes the essential ingredients of our three data sets. For more details we refer to the papers by Combris, Lecocq and Visser (1997, 2000), and Lecocq and Visser (2001).

The data sets come from three very similar experimental studies conducted by the Institut National de la Consommation (INC), and published in 60 Millions de Consommateurs (December 1992 for the Bordeaux I sample, November 1993 for the Burgundy sample, and October/November 2001 for the Bordeaux II sample). The samples were randomly selected. The INC agents bought all the wines anonymously directly from the producers. This circumvents a bias that is present in wine tasting events organized by (even

[4]In the previous literature, there is generally a time lag between the moment the grades are attributed and the moment the wine prices are established. For instance in Jones and Storchmann (2001), the wine prices are the prices fetched at auctions in 1996/97, whereas the quality index is the Parker-rating of these wines published in 1994/95. The reported estimated effect of the Parker-rating therefore reflects not only a direct quality effect (Parker's opinion on the wine), but also an indirect publicity effect, which is not necessarily related to quality but which measures instead how Parker-points modify consumers' purchase behavior and wine producers' price strategy.

famous) guides, where wine producers select specially prepared samples for the contest. Wines were tasted and evaluated by independent wine experts. This avoids the lack of objectivity of some wine guides often sponsored by wine producers where the editor, possibly assisted by a team of colleagues, evaluates the wines.

In the Bordeaux I sample, 519 wines were evaluated; in the Burgundy sample, 613 wines and in the Bordeaux II sample, 255 wines. In each case the wines were evaluated by a jury of 4 or 5 experts. After tasting a wine, each jury member was asked to write down his personal technical comments concerned with olfactory findings (aromatic intensity, finesse and complexity of aromas), gustatory findings (firmness of attack, suppleness, flatness, fat, harmony of components, finish, etc.), as well as some general remarks about alcohol level, need for keeping, etc. A synthesis of these comments is published by 60 Millions de Consommateurs, which leads to the sensory wine characteristics that we use. Each member also assigned a grade between 0 and 20 to the wines he tasted. 60 Millions de Consommateurs only publishes the average of these grades. This average grade will be referred to as the jury grade and constitutes our measure of wine quality. There is also information about the name, color, ranking,[5] vintage, and (in the case of Bordeaux) appellation. These are objective wine characteristics. Finally, the data record the prices at which the bottles were purchased.

The list of variables and some descriptive statistics are given in Appendix 1.

3. Empirical Results

In the hedonic price equations, the dependent variable is the logarithm of the price of a bottle of wine, the explanatory variables are the jury grade (i.e., the average of the individual grades) and the objective and sensory variables defined above. Table 1 presents Ordinary Least Squares (OLS) estimates. To facilitate the comparison of the different variable-effects, the reported estimates are the "β-coefficients."[6] The overall fit of the hedonic

[5]In the case of the two Bordeaux samples the three possible levels are cru and grand cru classé, cru bourgeois, or cru non classé; in the case of the Burgundy sample the four possible levels are AOC grand cru, AOC premier cru, AOC communale, or AOC régionale.

[6]β-coefficients can be interpreted as regression coefficients that would have been obtained had the regressors been standardized (zero mean and unit variance). Their magnitude can thus be used to measure the relative contribution of each regressor (see Goldberger, 1964, pp. 197–198).

Table 1. Hedonic Price Equations

	Bordeaux I		Bordeaux II		Burgundy	
Jury grade	0.081	(0.007)	0.090	(0.018)	0.110	(0.010)
Sensory variables						
Firmness of attack			−0.108	(0.098)		
Well concentrated					0.055	(0.063)
Needs keeping	0.097	(0.041)	0.169	(0.056)	0.070	(0.030)
Objective variables						
Ranking	0.309	(0.030)	0.232	(0.045)	0.650	(0.017)
Vintages						
1989	0.580	(0.074)				
1990	0.413	(0.077)			0.258	(0.043)
1991					0.195	(0.040)
1996			0.646	(0.099)		
1997			0.451	(0.119)		
1998			0.388	(0.118)		
Bordeaux groups						
Bordeaux	−0.326	(0.052)	−0.366	(0.091)		
Côtes	−0.203	(0.050)	−0.280	(0.083)		
St-Emilion Pom. Fr.	0.138	(0.042)				
Blancs doux	0.128	(0.073)				
Constant	1.799	(0.228)	1.694	(0.452)	1.771	(0.167)
$\bar{R}^2$	0.634		0.633		0.606	

Notes: Reported estimates are β-coefficients: standard errors in parentheses; since we are running stepwise regressions, the only coefficients given in the table are those which are significantly different from zero.

price equations is relatively good since the corrected $\bar{R}^2$s range from 0.606 to 0.634. Given the large number of explanatory variables and the absence of theory as to which variable should be kept, we use a stepwise procedure to select the variables that are significant at the 5% level. The final set of selected variables is the same whether we use a backward procedure or a forward procedure.

Nine variables are selected in the two Bordeaux equations and six in the Burgundy equation. It is remarkable that among the nine selected variables in the hedonic price equation for the Bordeaux I (and Bordeaux II, resp.) sample, only one (or two, resp.) belongs to the set of sensory variables. In the Burgundy equation, two out of six are sensory variables, but their effect is considerably smaller than the effect of the objective variables.[7] This

[7]Given that jury grades are highly correlated with sensory characteristics, one might wonder whether the presence of the former prevent the latter to enter the hedonic price equations. To verify this possibility, we performed the same estimations excluding grades

suggests that the price of Bordeaux and Burgundy is essentially determined by objective characteristics (ranking, vintage and appellation) that are easily identifiable by all consumers. A possible explanation for this result could be that sensory characteristics are only available through tasting, learning and the reading of guides. For consumers it may then be less expensive to make purchase decisions primarily on the basis of the information displayed on the label, which causes most of the sensory variables to be insignificant.

The jury grade has a positive and significant impact on prices. Yet this impact is considerably smaller than the impact of any objective variable. As the jury grade seems a priori a reasonable measure of quality, one might have expected this variable to have a more important influence on prices. There are at least two types of explanations for the small correlation between price and average tasting grade.

In the first explanation it is argued that the jury members essentially agree on the quality of the wine but make evaluation errors in determining the precise quality level. The jury grade is then the sum of the intrinsic quality level plus the average of expert-specific evaluation errors. In this setup the jury grade is, therefore, a measure of quality which is contaminated by measurement errors. More formally, let $i = 1, \ldots, N$ be the index of wines, $j = 1, \ldots, J$ the index of expert tasters and g_{ij} the grade assigned to wine i by expert j. The expert-specific grade g_{ij} can be decomposed as $g_{ij} = q_i + \varepsilon_{ij}$, where q_i is a component common to all tasters representing the quality level of wine i and an error term ε_{ij} with zero mean reflecting the judgment error made by jury member j. The true relationship between price p_i and quality q_i is assumed to be

$$p_i = \alpha + X_i\beta + \gamma q_i + \nu_i$$

with ν_i, independent of X_i and q_i. In the data we do not observe q_i but only the average of grades (the jury grade)

$$\bar{g}_i = \frac{1}{J_i}\sum_{j=1}^{J_i} g_{ij} = q_i + \frac{1}{J_i}\sum_{j=1}^{J_i} \varepsilon_{ij}.$$

The estimated hedonic price equation is therefore

$$p_i = \alpha + X_i\beta + \gamma\bar{g}_i + u_i \tag{1}$$

from the set of explanatory variables. The fat variable for the Bordeaux II sample and the excessive acidity and fat variables for the Burgundy sample were the only sensory characteristics to become significant.

Table 2. Impact of Jury Grades on Prices

	Bordeaux I ($J = 4$)	Bordeaux II ($J = 5$)	Burgundy ($J = 5$)
OLS estimate ($\hat{\gamma}$)	0.358	0.316	0.236
True value (γ)	0.442	0.548	0.436

where $u_i = \nu_i - \gamma \frac{1}{J_i} \sum_{j=1}^{J_i} \varepsilon_{ij}$. Since u_i is correlated with $\bar{g}_i$, OLS of equation (1) leads to biased estimates. Using the fact that individual grades are observed in Bordeaux II,[8] we can, however, determine the magnitude of the bias affecting the estimate of γ in our three samples.[9] This is shown in Appendix 2 for the case $\beta = 0$ and $J_i = J$.

Table 2 reports the estimate of γ before correction for measurement errors (OLS of equation 1) and its true value (i.e., the true impact of quality on price). The results show that the bias is important when the average grade is used as a proxy for quality: the true impact of quality is much larger than the estimated one. For example, in the case of the Burgundy sample the OLS estimate of γ is 0.236 whereas the true value of this parameter is 0.436. This is the well known attenuation effect due to measurement errors in an explanatory variable (see for instance Chesher, 1991). Augmenting the number of members in a jury might reduce the variance of the mean of judgment errors, thereby reducing the attenuation effect. In this view the correlation coefficient between price and jury grade might thus increase by adding more persons to the jury.

In the second explanation it is argued that jury members do not make evaluation errors but disagree on the quality of the wine because of taste heterogeneity. As the experts attribute different quality levels to each wine the jury grade will always express a compromise between the different tasters' evaluations. The market, on the other hand, is a reflection of the opposite; a compromise is not needed since the price level can reflect the preferences of subsets of consumers. A high market price can then be compatible with a modest appreciation of the wine (by the public as a whole) if a small group

[8]Unlike the Bordeaux I and Burgundy data sets, in which only the average grades are available, the Bordeaux II data set also records the expert-specific grades. These were directly obtained by us from INC.

[9]The idea is to estimate the variance of ε_{ij} on the Bordeaux II sample and to use it to assess the bias in all three samples, assuming that the dispersion of judgment errors does not differ across samples.

Table 3. Jury Grade Equations

	Bordeaux I		Bordeaux II		Burgundy	
Sensory variables						
Aromatic intensity	0.176	(0.006)	0.109	(0.004)	0.329	(0.007)
Finesse of aromas	0.115	(0.019)	0.105	(0.013)		
Complexity	0.133	(0.018)	0.183	(0.012)	0.094	(0.011)
Firmness of attack	0.073	(0.018)				
Excessive acidity	0.081	(0.021)				
Suppleness	0.096	(0.016)				
Flatness			−0.170	(0.032)	−0.063	(0.034)
Fat	0.126	(0.016)	0.142	(0.012)	0.071	(0.011)
Well concentrated	0.100	(0.021)				
Harmony	0.290	(0.011)	0.319	(0.009)	0.349	(0.007)
Fine tannins	0.065	(0.018)	0.106	(0.018)		
Finish	0.303	(0.015)	0.430	(0.007)	0.138	(0.003)
Traces of staleness					−0.086	(0.015)
Touch of reduction	−0.060	(0.038)				
Needs keeping	0.210	(0.018)	0.207	(0.011)	0.186	(0.009)
Objective variables						
Ranking					0.117	(0.005)
White	−0.107	(0.020)				
Vintages						
1990	0.080	(0.017)				
1991					−0.182	(0.008)
Bordeaux groups						
Côtes			−0.147	(0.016)		
St-Emilion Pom. Fr.	0.144	(0.018)	0.164	(0.010)		
Constant	1.284	(0.099)	2.202	(0.060)	2.301	(0.051)
$\bar{R}^2$	0.597		0.594		0.436	

Notes: Reported estimates are β-coefficients: standard errors in parentheses; since we are running stepwise regressions, the only coefficients given in the table are those which are significantly different from zero.

of individuals intensely likes the product. If indeed there is strong taste heterogeneity among the experts (and if the experts adequately represent the different sub-groups of consumers), it is not surprising that the average tasting grades are not closely connected to price.

We also estimate jury grade equations by regressing the logarithm of jury grades on the attributes of wines. Table 3 presents the OLS estimates for each sample. The $\bar{R}^2$s range from 0.436 to 0.597, again indicating a relatively good overall fit. In the Bordeaux samples, it does not matter whether we use a backward or a forward stepwise procedure, but it does for the Burgundy sample. We only retain variables that are selected in both procedures.

Sixteen variables appear in the Bordeaux I equation, eleven in the Bordeaux II equation, and ten in the Burgundy equation. The only sensory variable that does not have the expected effect is the excessive acidity in the Bordeaux I equation: the jury grade increases if the wine is considered too acidic. In our three samples, the grade increases if the aromatic intensity of the wine is strong, the wine has a complex nose, is considered fat, the harmony between its components is well balanced, its finish is long and if it needs keeping. In contrast to the hedonic price equations, the jury grades are essentially determined by sensory variables: they are thirteen out of sixteen in the Bordeaux I equation, nine out of eleven in the Bordeaux II equation, and eight out of ten in the Burgundy equation.

But the most interesting result is that ranking has a considerable impact on jury grades for Burgundy, whereas it is statistically not significant for Bordeaux wines. This result is not really surprising. In Bordeaux (and particularly in the Médoc region), the classification is old (1855) and the established hierarchy of châteaux does not reflect that the size and shape of vineyards have changed over time. The Burgundy classification, based on the cadastral survey, seems to be less rigid than its Bordeaux counterpart since approval tasting sessions are held each year and serve as the basis for authorizing (or not) a wine to be sold under its appellation class. If a wine loses class membership in a particular year it may be authorized to join a lower appellation class.

4. Conclusions

In this chapter we apply the hedonic technique to wines. In the price equation we include objective characteristics appearing on the label, as well as sensory characteristics and quality, as measured by expert tasters. We use three almost identically structured data sets (two on Bordeaux wines, and one on Burgundy wines), which enable us to make comparisons between two of the most important French wine regions and comparisons over time (the two Bordeaux data sets are sampled at different points in time).

Our results indicate that characteristics that are directly revealed to the consumer upon inspection of the bottle and its label (ranking, vintage and appellation) explain the major part of price differences. Sensory variables do not appear to play an important role. Out of some fifteen sensory characteristics, only two or three have a significant impact in the hedonic price equation.

Wine prices are also hardly affected by the grades assigned by professional wine tasters. Although jury grades have a significant effect, their impact on prices is very small compared to the impact of ranking and vintage. This is surprising given that the jury grade seems a reasonable measure of quality. A possible explanation for this result is that the jury grade is an imperfect measure of quality due to measurement errors in the expert-specific grades. Our most recent data set (Bordeaux II) allows to correct for these measurement errors (see Section 3), and our results suggest that the true effect of quality is much larger than previously thought.

We also find that the jury grade, unlike the price, is primarily determined by sensory characteristics: only one fifth of the variables that have a significant influence on the jury grade equations are objective variables. Furthermore, ranking has no significant effect in the Bordeaux equations, but does significantly affect grades for Burgundy wines, a result that can be explained by the different classification systems used in the two wine-growing regions.

It would be interesting to check whether the findings reported in this chapter are typical for Bordeaux and Burgundy wines, or whether they also hold for other regions and countries. In a comment on the Combris, Lecocq and Visser (1997) paper, Brown (1999) uses a sample of premium California wines to estimate a hedonic price equation and a jury grade equation. Unlike the results of our hedonic price equations, many sensory characteristics of California wines (six out of thirteen) do have a significant impact on prices. The results for his jury grade equation are, however, more in line with ours in that the appreciation of wine experts is essentially determined by sensory variables.

Acknowledgments

This chapter was written while the first author was visiting the Department of Economics at University College London. We would like to thank O. Ashenfelter, F. Etilé, V. Ginsburgh and an anonymous referee for their comments and suggestions.

References

Ashenfelter, O., Ashmore, D., and Lalonde, R. (1995). Bordeaux wine vintage quality and the weather. *Chance*, 8, 7–14.

Brown, D.M. (1999). *Estimation of a hedonic price equation for Bordeaux wine: Does quality matter*? A comment. Mimeo, Georgetown University.

Byron, R.P., and Ashenfelter, O. (1995). Predicting the quality of an unborn grange. *Economic Record*, 71, 40–53.

Chesher, A.O. (1991). The effect of measurement errors. *Biometrika*, 78, 451–462.

Combris, P., Lecocq, S., and Visser, M. (1997). Estimation of a hedonic price equation for Bordeaux wine: Does quality matter? *Economic Journal*, 107, 390–402.

Combris, P., Lecocq, S., and Visser, M. (2000). Estimation of a hedonic price equation for Burgundy wine. *Applied Economics*, 32, 961–967.

Di Vittorio, A., and Ginsburgh, V. (1996). Des enchères comme révélateurs du classement des vins. *Journal de la Société Statistique de Paris*, 137, 19–49.

Gergaud, O. (1998). Estimation d'une fonction de prix hédonistiques pour le vin de Champagne. *Economie et Prévision*, 136, 93–105.

Ginsburgh, V., Monzak, M., and Monzak, A. (1994). Red wines of Medoc: What is wine tasting worth? Verona: Vineyard Data Quantification Society.

Goldberger, A. (1964). *Econometric Theory*. New York: Wiley & Sons.

Jones, G.V., and Storchmann, K.H. (2001). Wine market prices and investment under uncertainty: An econometric model for Bordeaux crus classés. *Agricultural Economics*, 26, 115–133.

Landon, S., and Smith, C.E. (1997). The use of quality and reputation indicators by consumers: The case of Bordeaux wine. *Journal of Consumer Policy*, 20, 289–323.

Landon, S., and Smith, C.E. (1998). Quality expectations, reputation and price. *Southern Economic Journal*, 64, 628–647.

Lecocq, S., and Visser, M. (2001). Is the average of expert tasters' grades a good price predictor? unpublished paper?.

Lima, T. (1999). Price and quality in the California wine industry: An empirical investigation. Mimeo, California State University.

Maddala, G.S. (1977). *Econometrics*. Economics Handbook Series. New York: McGraw-Hill.

Oczkowski, E. (1994). A hedonic price function for Australian premium wine. *Australian Journal of Agricultural Economics*, 38, 93–110.

Oczkowski, E. (2001). Hedonic wine price functions and measurement error. *Economic Record*, 77, 374–382.

Schamel, G., and Anderson, K. (2001). Wine quality and varietal, regional and winery reputations: Hedonic prices for Australia and New Zealand. CIES Discussion Paper 0103, Adelaide University.

The Economist (1999). The globe in a glass, wine survey, December 1999, 97–115.

Appendix 1

Descriptive Statistics

Variables	Modalities	Bordeaux I	Bordeaux II	Burgundy
Price	Continuous	52.78 (31.05)	69.10 (43.75)	55.82 (32.69)
Jury grade	Continuous	11.21 (2.41)	12.93 (1.37)	12.59 (1.44)
Sensory characteristics				
Olfactory examination				
Aromatic intensity	Strong	45.08	43.69	56.68
	Classic	32.64	33.98	32.35

(*Continued*)

(Continued)

Variables	Modalities	Bordeaux I	Bordeaux II	Burgundy
	Discrete	22.28	22.33	13.97
Finesse of aromas	Yes/No	15.61	13.73	15.01
Complexity	Yes/No	23.70	16.08	15.33
Gustatory examination				
Firmness of attack	Yes/No	19.85	5.49	3.43
Excessive acidity	Yes/No	13.87	2.35	6.36
Suppleness	Yes/No	28.90	18.04	9.30
Flatness	Yes/No	8.29	1.96	1.31
Fat	Plump	17.34	10.59	7.50
	Medium	79.19	84.70	87.28
	Lean	3.47	4.71	5.22
Well concentrated	Yes/No	19.08	6.67	4.08
Harmony	Perfect	18.69	0.00	15.17
	Balanced	50.29	49.41	61.99
	Unbalanced	31.02	50.59	22.84
Fine tannins	Yes/No	19.08	6.67	3.59
Finish	Long	34.20	51.46	57.35
	Medium	50.78	13.59	25.00
	Short	15.02	34.95	17.65
General remarks				
Alcohol excess	Yes/No	15.41	13.33	6.69
Traces of staleness	Yes/No	10.60	9.41	7.50
Touch of reduction	Yes/No	3.47	0.00	0.65
Needs keeping	Yes/No	29.87	23.14	28.87
Objective characteristics				
Ranking				
Bordeaux	Cru classé	6.74	5.10	
	Cru bourgeois	9.25	12.55	
	Cru non classé	84.01	82.35	
Burgundy	AOC grand cru			1.80
	AOC premier cru			23.00
	AOC communale			40.29
	AOC régionale			34.91
Red wine	Yes/No	82.08	81.57	60.85
White wine	Yes/No	17.92	18.43	39.15
Vintages				
1989	Yes/No	61.66		
1990	Yes/No	33.33		30.83
1991	Yes/No	5.01		55.95
1992	Yes/No			13.21
1996	Yes/No		59.61	
1997	Yes/No		8.63	
1998	Yes/No		25.88	
1999	Yes/No		5.88	

(Continued)

(*Continued*)

Variables	Modalities	Bordeaux I	Bordeaux II	Burgundy
Bordeaux groups				
Bordeaux	Yes/No	15.99	16.47	
Côtes	Yes/No	15.22	9.02	
Médoc and Graves	Yes/No	20.81	29.02	
St-Emilion Pomerol Fronsac	Yes/No	30.06	27.06	
Blancs secs	Yes/No	12.91	11.37	
Blancs doux	Yes/No	5.01	7.06	
Number of observations		519	255	613

Note: The three last columns contain the mean and standard deviation (in parentheses) for continuous variables, and the share of observations for each modality for discrete variables.

Appendix 2

Let $\sigma_\varepsilon^2 = \text{Var}(\varepsilon_{ij})$ and $\sigma_q^2 = \text{Var}(q_i)$. Since in the Bordeaux II sample we observe all the expert-specific grades g_{ij}, the variance σ_ε^2 can be estimated by

$$\hat{\sigma}_\varepsilon^2 = \frac{1}{N}\sum_{i=1}^{N}\frac{1}{J_i - 1}\sum_{j=1}^{J_i}(g_{ij} - \bar{g}_i)^2, \tag{A.1}$$

where N is the number of observations in Bordeaux II.

Consider the case $\beta = 0$ and suppose that $J_i = J$ for all i. The probability limit of the OLS estimate $\hat{\gamma}$ is (the calculation is similar as in Maddala, 1977, p. 293)

$$\text{plim}\hat{\gamma} = \frac{\gamma}{1 + \frac{1}{J}\frac{\sigma_\varepsilon^2}{\sigma_q^2}}.$$

So the true value γ is approximately equal to

$$\gamma = \left(1 + \frac{1}{J}\frac{\sigma_\varepsilon^2}{\sigma_q^2}\right)\hat{\gamma}. \tag{A.2}$$

Under the assumption that σ_ε^2 is identical in our three samples, the true value of γ can be determined for each of them using (A2), (A1) and the fact that $\sigma_q^2 = \text{Var}(\bar{g}_i) - \frac{1}{J}\sigma_\varepsilon^2$.

Chapter 24

Assessing the Effect of Information on the Reservation Price for Champagne: What are Consumers Actually Paying for?*

Pierre Combris[†], Christine Lange[‡], and Sylvie Issanchou[‡]

[†]*INRA, UR1303, ALISS Alimentation et Sciences Sociales, F-94205 Ivry-sur-Seine, France*
pierre.combris@inra.fr

[‡]*Centre des Sciences du Goût et de l'alimentation, AgroSup Dijon, CNRS, INRA, Université Bourgogne Franche Comté, F-21000 Dijon, France*
christine.lange@inra.fr
sylvie.issanchou@inra.fr

Two series of Vickrey auctions have been performed to assess the effect of packaging information (bottle and label) on the reservation prices of ordinary consumers for five brut non-vintage Champagnes. As in other studies on wine tasting, packaging information is found to explain much more of the variation in willingness to pay than sensory information. Participants are unable, or unwilling, to put different values on the Champagnes after blind tasting, but significant differences in reservation prices appear when labels are disclosed. Detailed analysis of choices reveals a large heterogeneity in individual behaviors and valuations of the Champagnes included in this study.

1. Introduction

Finding out what consumers are actually paying for when they buy a bottle of wine is a recurring question. It is an important issue for producers who have to decide how to allocate their resources to quality improvement and marketing strategies. It is also a matter of concern to consumers who

*This article originally appeared in *Journal of Wine Economics* (2006), 1(1), 75–88.

wonder about the quality they will get for their money. However, the search for quality is costly and, unlike experts or oenophiles, ordinary consumers mainly rely on indicators such as brands or grading systems to make their choices. Thus, it is not surprising that consumers' willingness to pay for a given wine depends, in the first place, on the information carried by the label and the reputation of the wine. If purchases are repeated, consumers' experience will be growing and then the sensory characteristics of the wine should eventually have the decisive impact. Therefore, in equilibrium, market prices should reflect quality, and brands or labels should stand just as signals for quality.

However, hedonic analysis of market prices does not confirm this view. Search characteristics carried by the label are found to have a large and significant impact on prices, but when indicators of sensory quality are available, through experts' tasting for example, the link between quality and price appears to be much less significant (Lecocq and Visser, 2006). This weak relationship between sensory quality and price may result from a lack of convergence in the assessment of quality. The overall sensory quality of a wine summarizes many characteristics that are evaluated along different dimensions. The evaluation of characteristics may be inconsistent because of sensory misperception or true heterogeneity in tastes, both by expert and non-expert consumers.

If the sensory ability of untrained consumers can be rightly questioned, juries of experts are often considered as a reliable method to assess the quality of wines. Usually a jury's grade is viewed as an agreement on a level of quality, but this agreement may be either a consensus or a compromise. To explore the underlying heterogeneity of expert ratings, Lecocq and Visser (2001) have used data from a large test of Bordeaux wines by trained tasters, and have found that when the variance of grades is high, the correlation between the average grade and the price is low. They also found indications of possible sources of heterogeneity: some experts appear, for instance, more sensitive to olfactory characteristics and others to gustatory characteristics. More disturbing are the clues suggesting that wine tasters can easily be misled. Using a white wine artificially colored red with an odorless dye, Morrot *et al.* (2001) showed that undergraduate students from the Faculty of Oenology of the University of Bordeaux described it as a red wine. The interaction between visual and olfactory perceptions is analyzed as a perceptual illusion. The mechanisms of this misperception are an issue open to discussion, but this experiment illustrates that, besides heterogeneity, sensory perception itself may be questioned even for trained tasters.

These different arguments can account for the difficulty to establish a strong link between sensory quality and price and explain the results of hedonic price analyses. Yet, we still have to understand the mechanisms by which the ordinary consumer determines the price he is willing to pay according to the information he has on the product. This chapter presents the results of experiments designed for that purpose. These experiments associate techniques of sensory analysis and experimental economics. We will first briefly describe the different methods that can be used to elicit consumers' preferences in the context of sensory evaluation and experimental analysis, and then turn to the experiments from which the data used here are drawn. After the presentation of the results, we will examine the variability of participants' behaviors.

2. Revealing Consumers' Preferences and Willingness to Pay

Preferences for food products result from a valuation process which uses the information that is available to the consumer: sensory characteristics, packaging, label, specialized guides or books, and general media information. All this information is combined with personal experience to form an overall quality evaluation of a product. Measuring the value of a product, or at least knowing unambiguously the ways a consumer ranks a given set of products, is a difficult issue.

Sensory scientists strive to measure as rigorously as possible appearance, texture and flavor of food products. Sensory analysis relies on trained tasters, who learn to describe their perceptions with standardized attributes and scales (occurrence, intensity, and duration), acting as substitutes to measuring instruments. However, a rigorous and "objective" description of a product is not a measure of the preference for that product.

Preferences are not only based on the sensory characteristics of the product, they also depend on a host of personal and environmental factors. What is sought, here, is not a measure of each factor independently, but an overall assessment of liking at the individual level. To elicit these preferences, sensory scientists use hedonic rating techniques, which amounts to having consumers indicate on a scale how much they like a given product.[1] Hedonic

[1]Hedonic rating tests used by sensory scientists are based on the subjective evaluation of a product by a sample of consumers. Except for the name, they have no link with hedonic

scales are anchored with verbal categories (from "dislike extremely" to "like extremely"). They can be subdivided into intermediate categories, or be just a graphic line where subjects are required to indicate a position which is then converted to a score, from 0 to 10 for example. Sensory scientists think that hedonic tests should be used only with untrained consumers, and that experts and trained subjects should confine themselves to the assessment of the products' conformity to different categories, or at least distinguish very clearly personal hedonic evaluation from sensory descriptive analysis.

Eliciting preferences of the ordinary consumer with hedonic tests raises questions linked to the discriminating power and the predictive ability of these methods. One can wonder whether subjects try really hard to discriminate when they have many products to evaluate, and whether, in an everyday purchase situation, they will actually buy the product they preferred during the test. These two questions are linked through the issue of incentives: evaluating products in the context of a test with nothing at stake may differ greatly from an evaluation that should lead to buying. If the main question is to know what consumers will actually do in real life, then the issue becomes that of the economic value consumers place on products or product characteristics.

Economists use different methods to elicit consumers' values for products. Indirect methods use market price data under the assumption that in a competitive market, prices reflect underlying values for products or for product characteristics. Direct methods consist in asking consumers to state their subjective value for a product, namely to reveal the maximum amount they are willing to pay to purchase it or to obtain a given characteristic. Conjoint analysis or contingent valuation surveys are well-known methods used to elicit reservation prices and estimate willingness to pay for specific characteristics. These methods are limited by the absence of constraints and commitment which leads to very hypothetical choices. Moreover, it is also important to note that consumers have no personal interest in revealing their reservation price, and they usually keep it secret when entering a bargaining situation.

The main contribution of experimental economics to the issue of preference revealing is to devise laboratory settings where participants have an incentive to state their true private values. Experimental auctions have been

---

price techniques used by economists to measure the impact of a product's attributes on its market price.

successfully used for that purpose in different contexts. In an experimental auction, participants submit bids for a product that they commit to purchase at a price determined by the auction rule in case they win the auction. The rule is chosen so that the best individual strategy is to bid one's true reservation price.

Vickrey (1961) has shown that second-price sealed bid auctions have this preference revealing property. Since then, a lot of work has been conducted to test auction theory and to assess the behavioral equivalence of different auction mechanisms (Kagel, 1995). Despite some examples questioning the incentive compatibility of second-price auctions, they have been widely used in experiments to elicit participants' preferences. Since the early nineties, Vickrey auctions have also been used to elicit consumers' willingness to pay for real goods (Menkhaus *et al.*, 1992; Hoffman *et al.*, 1993; Melton *et al.*, 1996) and to assess the value consumers put on food safety (Hayes *et al.*, 1995).

Second-price experimental auctions appear as a very appropriate method for our purpose. First, subjects are placed in front of real choices with constraints and consequences on their well-being. Second, the method allows a good control over the factors influencing choices, and third, it provides a measure of individual reservation prices in each situation. This experimental setting has been used recently by Lecocq *et al.* (1999) to assess the variations of reservation prices for different wines according to the information provided to participants (blind tasting, label characteristics, excerpts from wine guides). They found that sensory characteristics are the least influential information, and that tasting does not modify reservation prices when other characteristics are known.

Our idea was that using both sensory analysis and experimental economics would give us a better control of the tasting conditions and consequently, a better assessment of the weight of sensory factors in the value of wines. The use of auctions was viewed as an incentive for participants both to evaluate more carefully the sensory characteristics of the wines and to reveal their reservation prices.

3. The Experiments

The objectives of the experiments were to assess the respective weights of sensory characteristics and reputation in the evaluation of Champagnes by ordinary consumers and to compare three preference revealing methods. Two series of experiments were performed: in the first one we compared Vickrey to BDM (Becker-DeGroot-Marschak) auctions[2] (Combris *et al.*, 2001), and in the second one a Vickrey auction was compared to a hedonic test (Lange *et al.*, 2002).

In the first series of experiments, 120 subjects were selected and participated in either a Vickrey or a BDM auction (63 and 57 participants respectively). In the second series, 123 new subjects were selected and 57 of these subjects participated in a Vickrey auction and 66 in a hedonic test. Recruitment conditions and Champagnes tested were exactly the same in the two series of experiments in order to allow pooling and comparisons of the data. In this chapter, we concentrate on the factors influencing the value consumers put on Champagnes and use only the results of the two series of Vickrey auctions (63 participants from the first series and 57 from the second one).

In both series participants were asked to perform exactly the same tasks under the same conditions. They had to evaluate and bid for five Champagnes in three different situations. The wines were first evaluated after a blind tasting, then after examination of the bottle with no tasting, and finally after examination of the bottle and tasting.

3.1. *Recruitment of participants*

Our concern was to work with randomly selected individuals who had some familiarity with Champagne consumption and purchases but had never been exposed to experimental methods. To achieve this, participants were sampled from the population of ordinary households, through a stratified design and random selection of phone numbers. The first information was made through a letter explaining that individuals would be contacted by phone to participate in a research conducted by a National Institute. Over the phone, the purpose was first stated in very general terms ("a study of beverage consumption"). Then respondents were asked some questions about all kinds of warm and cold beverages they drink during a regular day and on special occasions. If they mentioned Champagne, they were further asked questions about their Champagne consumption and purchases, and possible previous participation in sensory or consumer studies.

[2]The BDM procedure (named after Becker, DeGroot, and Marschak, 1964) may be described as an individual random second price auction, where *each* participant is committed to buy if his or her bid is higher than a buying price randomly selected from a given price distribution. Winners pay the randomly selected price and all participants can check the price distribution afterwards.

Table 1. Characteristics of the Samples of Participants

	1st experiment (December 2000) (63 participants)				2nd experiment (May 2001) (57 participants)			
Variable	Mean	Std. dev.	Min.	Max.	Mean	Std. dev.	Min.	Max.
Age (in years)	46.17	12.50	25	77	44.56	13.80	23	71
Gender(=1 if woman)	0.40	0.49	0	1	0.37	0.49	0	1
Number of persons in household	2.61	1.18	1	5	2.51	1.43	1	7
Household monthly income (FFr)	20,556	8,353	3,000	40,000	20,518	11,187	4,000	60,000
Monthly income per person (FFr)	9,149	4,565	1,500	20,000	9,150	4,012	1,429	19,000
Usual Price for Champagne (FFr)	87.02	19.00	54	145	91.35	23.65	55	150

Individuals who satisfied all the conditions (drinking Champagne at least four times per year, involved in Champagne purchase decisions, no previous participation in any descriptive sensory test) and agreed to participate received a written notification to attend a given session. They also received a letter describing the experiment as Champagne tasting and were asked whether they would be willing to participate in an auction and buy some of the products they had tasted.

Table 1 presents some summary statistics describing the two groups of participants. The two samples exhibit a large variability in age, household size and income. However, no significant differences appear between the two groups.

3.2. *Sessions*

The experimental sessions were held in Dijon, a medium sized city, situated in Burgundy in the eastern part of France. They took place in the tasting room of the *Institut National de la Recherche Agronomique (INRA)*. A total of 10 sessions were organized (5 for each series). The minimum number of participants per session was 10, and the maximum 15.

Participants were placed in individual booths and had to first read a short note explaining that they were going to taste different Champagnes and will have to state a price (i.e., submit a bid) for each of them. We also stressed that submitting a winning bid implied that the winner had to buy the bottle. If they agreed and signed the consent, they received FFr 200 (EUR30.5) in cash for their participation (each session lasted about two hours, late in the afternoon).

After a training phase with chocolate bars to explain the principle of the auction, participants were invited to ask all the questions they wished before the beginning of the experiment with Champagne. They were then informed that this part of the experiment will consist in submitting bids for different Champagnes under different conditions of evaluation.

Participants were told that the Champagnes will be evaluated sequentially, one at a time, and that they will have to bid after each evaluation. They were informed that *only one out of their fifteen bids* would be randomly selected at the end of the session and become effective. This random selection was designed to avoid endowment effects (lower bids following a winning bid) and strategic behavior (very low bids as long as participants expect that more information will be disclosed). The objective was to make each evaluation situation (i.e., one Champagne in one information condition) as independent as possible of others.

The experimenter also announced that she had a reservation price, which could be disclosed at the end of the session, and that no selling would occur if the highest bid happened to be lower than this price.

The five wines used for the experiments were brut non-vintage Champagnes: three *great brands* (from some of the better-known houses of the former "Syndical des Grandes Marques"), one *middle range* brand, and one *low price* Champagne, that had been selected randomly among the lowest price Champagnes available in Dijon supermarkets. Table 2 exhibits the codes, characteristics and market prices of the five bottles.

Table 2. The Five Champagnes

	Characteristics: Brut Non-Vintage	Market Price (FFr)	Market Price (EUR)
LP	Unbranded, Low Price	69.90	10.66
MR	Middle Range Brand	129.60	19.76
B1	Great Brand	134.95	20.57
B2	Great Brand	144.40	22.01
B3	Great Brand	151.95	23.16

The Champagnes were presented in a different random order to participants, who had first to evaluate each Champagne after tasting (15 mL were served in a glass at a temperature of $9 \pm 2°C$). The only information they had at this stage was that they were served a brut non-vintage Champagne. After tasting, they were asked to state the maximum price they would pay for one bottle of that Champagne, by submitting a written bid that was collected by the experimenter.

After they had evaluated the wines and submitted their bids, they started another round of five evaluations in which they were allowed to handle the bottle and look at the label, but not to taste. They could examine one bottle at a time and had to submit a written bid again. The evaluation order was different from the first round and participants were not told that the Champagnes were the same as in the first round. During this second round, the presentation order of the wines was the same for all participants to prevent them from accidentally, or intentionally, seeing the bottles handed to other participants and being influenced in their evaluations. This presentation order was different across sessions, and in a given session between the second and the third round.

For the last round, participants had access to all the information: the bottle and a glass of the same Champagne (15 mL at the same temperature). The order was again different, but the procedure was otherwise exactly the same as before. Participants were never given any information about the market prices of the five wines.

After participants had submitted their last five bids, they were asked to complete a short questionnaire about their Champagne consumption habits, the brands they knew, the price at which they usually buy Champagne, and the maximum price they happen to pay for very good Champagne. After all the questionnaires had been completed, the experimenter proceeded to the random selection of one evaluation (one Champagne under one information condition) and to the disclosing (on a transparency) of the corresponding bids.[3] The experimenter announced the identification number of the participant who submitted the highest bid and the price he would have to pay (the second highest bid). The winner had to pay the bottle in cash before leaving and no winner was allowed to buy more than one bottle. At the end of the session participants were free to ask questions and remarks were welcome.

[3]The choice was made by one of the participants who was asked to draw at random one of the 15 situations.

4. Results and Discussion

4.1. *Factors influencing the level of reservation prices*

Table 3 exhibits the means of reservation prices according to the product, condition and method. Figure 1 displays the same means with the corresponding 95% confidence intervals. The comparison of means shows that almost no (statistical) differences appear between the Champagnes when participants' information is limited to blind tasting. Information about the bottle and label leads to a significant increase in reservation prices for the

Table 3. Mean Bids According to Product and Condition (in FFr)

	Conditions		
Products*	Blind tasting	Bottle	Bottle and tasting
LP	72.00	59.61	59.93
MR	70.08	85.54	80.78
B1	71.50	105.96	97.93
B2	70.73	111.93	104.11
B3	71.96	111.41	99.25
Mean	71.25	94.89	88.40

Notes: *LP: *low price*; MR: *middle range brand*; B1, B2, B3: *great brands*.

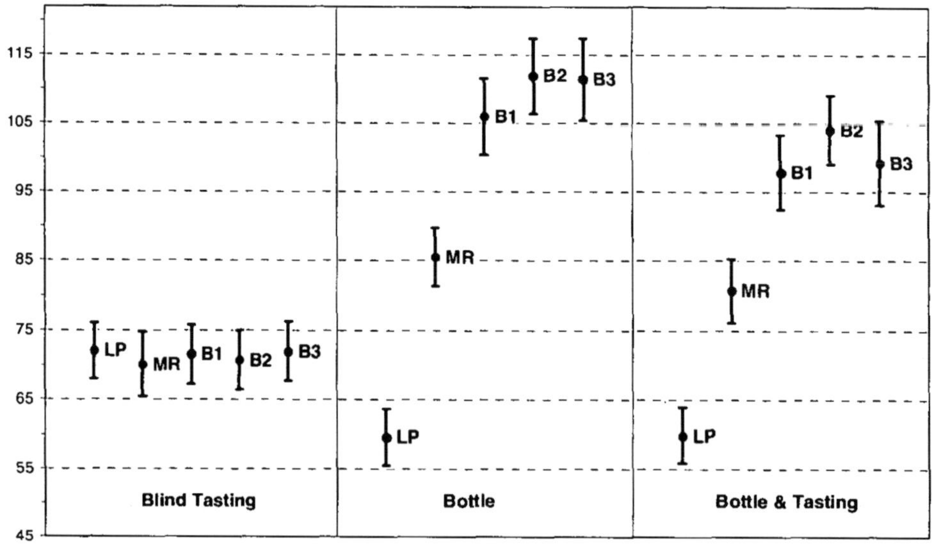

Figure 1. 95% Confidence Intervals of Mean Bids (in FFr)

Table 4. Factors Influencing the Level of Reservation Prices (Bids)

	Factors	Effect on reservation price	Standard errors	P-values
Conditions	Blind tasting	−23.64	1.56	0.000
	Bottle (control)	0.00	—	—
	Bottle and tasting	−6.49	0.89	0.000
Products	Low Price (control)	0.00	—	—
	Middle range	14.92	1.31	0.000
	Great Brand 1	27.89	1.49	0.000
	Great Brand 2	31.71	1.59	0.000
	Great Brand 3	30.33	1.98	0.000
Participants	Maximum price usually paid	0.28	0.07	0.000
	Age	0.53	0.12	0.000
Method	Presentation order	0.83	0.41	0.043
	Session #10	−30.79	4.68	0.000
	Constant	27.52	8.70	0.002

Notes: Linear regression: 1,800 prices observations (120 subject X3 conditions X5 Champagnes).
R-squared = 0.36; OLS with robust standard errors that account for the fact that observations are not independent and that errors may be correlated within each subject.

great brands (B1, B2, and B3) and for the middle range brand (MR), and a decrease for the low price Champagne (LP). Interestingly, full information (tasting and handling the bottle) entails a systematic decrease in prices. This is probably because at that point the differences in taste between the Champagnes appear smaller than expected. This information, however, does not affect the bid for the low price brand and does not lead participants to switch back to their blind evaluation for that brand.

Table 4 shows the results of a linear regression of reservation prices (bids) on the different variables that may influence the participants' valuations. All variables are dummies, with the exception of the maximum price usually paid (in French Francs), the age of the participant (in years) and the presentation order of the 5 wines (coded in deviation from the mean from −2 to 2).

Information conditions and products have the largest and most significant influence. Not surprisingly, compared to the second situation (bottle with no tasting, the omitted dummy), blind tasting leads to lower reservation prices (an average of FFr 23.64 less). The significant decrease in reservation price (FFr 6.49) when participants are fully informed (bottle and tasting) is often observed by sensory scientists. This happens when subjects eventually find out that products taste worse than they expected in the first place. Apart from the unbranded Champagne (LP), that was found better than expected, this is the case here. Participants realize that expected differences in taste between branded Champagnes were much higher than actual differences. This phenomenon is not important enough to eliminate the reputation effect, which appears to have a strong and highly significant influence. Participants are clearly willing to pay more for great brands (B1, B2, and B3) than for the middle range one (MR). The differences with the unbranded Champagne (LP, the control) always remain highly significant.

Among socio-demographic characteristics of the participants (age, gender, income, household size), age is the only one that has a significant impact on reservation prices: an increase of FFr 0.53 per year of age. One important behavioral characteristic of participants is the maximum price they usually pay for Champagne, which increases their mean bids, and also has a positive impact on individual bid variance. Other variables describing usages and habits linked to Champagne (purchase place, storage, purchase frequency, brand loyalty, consumption habits) have no effect on reservation prices.

Some experimental conditions also appear to have influenced bids. As explained previously, the presentation order was varied to control for sequencing effects. The remaining effect of the presentation order is significant at the 4.3% probability level and suggests that bids tend to increase throughout the sessions. A highly significant effect is that of the last session of the second experiment (session #10). At the outset of this session, some participants asked many questions before signing the consent form, and were still very suspicious after they did. This situation led to very conservative behaviors even if there were no more interactions between participants after the beginning of the evaluation. Average reservation prices observed during this session were significantly lower, but exhibit the same pattern as in other sessions (FFr 56 after blind tasting, FFr 67 after examination of the bottle, FFr 60 after examination of the bottle and tasting). Data from this session was not discarded, but a dummy variable was used to control for the shift of mean bids (FFr 30.79).

Besides this unexpected effect, differences between the Champagnes used in the first and second series of experiments might have influenced sensory evaluations. They could be due, in particular, to the fact that two bottles of a given Champagnes may differ slightly through time, because of storing conditions, or because they do not come from the same batch. Some testing (a dummy variable introduced for the second series) showed, however, that there was no significant difference between the two series of experiments.

5. Heterogeneity in Preferences and Reservation Prices

So far, the effect of commercial information appears important. However, mean prices aggregate individual behaviors and hide the heterogeneity of individual preferences. Reservation prices in each evaluation situation vary considerably, but nevertheless individual price rankings reveal preferences and ability to operate some distinctions between the different wines.

Concerning the blind test, it is interesting to check how many participants end up with a ranking of the five Champagnes that corresponds to the hierarchy of market prices. No participant ordering of bids was identical to that of market (LP < MR < B1 < B2 < B3) (See Table 5). Even if we consider that the three great brands are equivalent (LP < MR < B, independent of the order of B1, B2, B3), we find only three participants who have submitted bids corresponding to this ranking (Table 5). This is not more than the outcome of randomness.[4]

If we become even more lenient and just check how many participants ranked the low price Champagne last and one of the three great brands first, we find 25 correct rankings (Table 5). This is still not significant (the expected value under the random choice hypothesis is 18, and the upper limit of the 95% confidence interval is 26). Once again, this outcome rejects

Table 5. Agreement between Rankings and Prices (Number of Agreements)

	Conditions and number of rankings		
Type of ranking	Blind tasting	Bottle	Bottle and tasting
LP < MR < BI < B2 < B3	0	7	5
LP < MR < {BI, B2, B3}	3	68	45
LP < {BI, B2, B3}	25	110	99
Number of distinct rankings	109	50	68

Notes: LP: *low price*; MR: *middle range brand*; B1, B2, B3: *great brands*.

[4]If we assume that the probability of finding this ranking at random is 5% (3!=6 out of 5!=120 possibilities), and that the 120 participants represent 120 "trials," a random choice leads to 6 "successes," with a 95% confidence interval ranging from 2 to 10. Therefore, observing only three participants with rankings corresponding to the market hierarchy (LP < MR < B) gives strong support to the hypothesis that participants did not recognize them.

the hypothesis of a sensory ability of the ordinary Champagne consumer to retrieve the hierarchy of brands from a blind test. These observations do not necessarily mean that participants did not perceive any differences between the five wines; they are also compatible with the possibility that the sensory characteristics to which participants may have been sensible, are not correlated with the hierarchy of market prices.

The analysis of bids shows that participants do make distinctions between the different products during the blind test. If not, a large number of ties would have resulted in the rankings, and this is not the case. Out of the 120 rankings, 48 have no tie at all, and 50 have only two prices that are tied. Moreover, the range of individual bids during the blind test (difference between the maximum and the minimum bid of each participant) is not small. The median range is FFr 30; it is higher than FFr 60 for the 90th percentile, and smaller than FFr 11 for the 10th percentile. This is a reason to believe that participants detected significant differences between the products. However, if we examine all the rankings, we find that there is no unanimity at all. There are 109 different classifications (99 of which appear only once, 9 appear twice, and one three times). This implies that participants made almost all the possible combinations of the five Champagnes.

An indication, that during the blind test some participants perceived sensory differences between the three great brands and the two others, is based on counting the number of times each Champagne has been assigned a given rank. Table 6 shows that under blind tasting conditions, Champagnes LP and MR have been given high or low ranks with equivalent frequencies

Table 6. Ranks of the 5 Champagnes According to Conditions

	Conditions and ranks														
	Blind tasting					Bottle					Bottle and tasting				
Product*	1	2	3	4	5	1	2	3	4	5	1	2	3	4	5
LP	28	31	19	16	26	1	0	7	5	107	1	4	6	21	88
MR	26	18	28	24	24	4	9	32	72	3	6	21	31	53	9
B1	34	24	23	23	16	42	32	26	19	1	39	38	25	14	4
B2	25	27	26	26	16	52	36	26	5	1	50	36	25	8	1
B3	35	20	27	20	18	53	29	30	6	2	45	34	20	17	4
Total	148	120	123	109	100	152	106	121	107	114	141	133	107	113	106

Notes: *LP: low price; MR: middle range brand; B1, B2, B3: great brands. Each cell indicates the number of participants who gave the corresponding rank. Ties have not been broken.

(28 participants put LP in the first position and 26 in the last position; 26 participants ranked MR first and 24 last), but that Champagnes B1, B2, and B3 appear slightly less often in the last position (16, 16 and 18 times respectively). Very few differences appear under the blind tasting condition, which leads us to conclude that sensory differences between the five Champagnes are either small or uncorrelated with prices. This could explain why we observe such a wide range of subjective evaluations.

The disclosing of brands generates more structured evaluations even if some variability persists. Table 6 exhibits clear changes in the frequencies of ranks assigned to each wine, and shows that the low price, the middle range and the great brands are well identified (LP is ranked first only once, B1 and B2 are in the last position once and B3 twice). However, contrary to what could have been expected, this does not lead to a fully homogeneous classification by all participants. After examination of the bottles, the number of participants whose bids clearly discriminate between the three levels of quality is 68 (Table 5). This is highly significant, since the 1% significance level is 12. Bids led to 50 different classifications of the 5 Champagnes, which can still be considered as revealing a large degree of heterogeneity in preferences, which even increases when tasting and examination of the bottles are made jointly. In this case, we end up with 68 different classifications and the number of participants whose bids correspond to the market hierarchy of quality (LP, MR and B) falls to 45. This increase in the number of different choices goes with a slight decrease in the individual and global variance of prices. Sensory information led participants to make some corrections to the ranking they had made using only the information appearing on the bottle, but not to the point of completely toppling the hierarchy of market prices: 99 participants ranked one of the great brands first and the low price Champagne last (Table 5), and, among those who did not, only one subject made a higher bid for the low price Champagne than for any of the three great brands. Commercial information does not unify individual choices, but strengthens the structure within which there is still some room for sensory information and individual heterogeneity.

6. Conclusions

This experiment yields several findings on consumers' valuation of Champagne. Blind tasting shows that ordinary consumers are unable to classify low price, middle range and great brand Champagnes, according to their market prices ranging from FFr 70 to FFr 152. For the five wines included in the test, differences in valuations and rankings that roughly reproduce the hierarchy of market prices appear only when brands are disclosed. Comparative tasting with information leads participants to decrease their reservation prices but does not change their hierarchy of prices. The other important result concerns the very high heterogeneity of valuations of the different Champagnes. Blind tasting leads to almost as many classifications as there are participants. Evaluations using commercial information only reduce strongly the number of different choices, but combining commercial information and tasting leads again to a significant increase in the number of different classifications. This confirms results of previous experiments combining sensory and commercial information: brands and reputation have a decisive impact on reservation prices, preferences are highly heterogeneous, and more information does not necessary lead to a reduced set of "best" choices, but rather to more diversified behaviors.

Acknowledgments

This research is part of a programme of the French Institute of Agronomic Research (INRA) associating economists and sensory scientists. Research support from Mumm Perrier Jouet (Vignobles et Recherches) and the French Ministry of Agriculture (DGAL) is gratefully acknowledged. Claire Chabanet and Christophe Martin provided valuable research assistance.

References

Becker, G., DeGroot, M., and Marschak, J. (1964). Measuring utility by a single-response sequential method. *Behavioural Science*, 9, 226–232.

Combris, P., Lange, C., and Issanchou, S. (2001). Assessing the effect of information on the reservation price for Champagne: Second price compared to BDM auctions with unspecified price bounds. *Oenometrics VIII Conference*, May 21–22, Napa Valley, California, and *6th Conference of Experimental Economics*, May 23–24, 2002, Paris.

Hayes, D., Shogren, J., Shin, S.Y., and Kliebenstein, J. (1995). Valuing food safety in experimental auction markets. *American Journal of Agricultural Economics*, 77, 40–53.

Hoffman, E., Menkhaus, D., Chakravarti, D., Field, R., and Whipple, G. (1993). Using laboratory experimental auctions in marketing research: A case study of new packaging for fresh beef. *Marketing Science*, 12, 318–338.

Kagel, J.H. (1995). Auctions: A survey of experimental research, in Kagel, J.H. and Roth, A.E. (eds.). *The Handbook of Experimental Economics*, Princeton: Princeton University Press, 501–585.

Lange, C., Martin, C., Chabanet, C., Combris, P., and Issanchou, S. (2002). Impact of the information provided to the consumers on their willingness to pay for Champagne: Comparison with hedonic score. *Food Quality and Preference*, 13, 597–608.

Lecocq, S., Magnac, T., Pichery, M.C., and Visser, M. (1999). The Impact of information on wine auction prices: Results of an experiment. *Document de travail CREST*, 9936.

Lecocq, S., and Visser, M. (2006). What determines wine prices: Objectives vs. sensory characteristics? *Journal of Wine Economics*, 1, 42–56.

Lecocq, S., and Visser, M. (2001). Is the average of expert tasters' grades a good price predictor? Mimeo.

Melton, B., Huffman, W., Shogren, J., and Fox J. (1996). Consumer preferences for fresh food items with multiple quality attributes: Evidence from an experimental auction of pork chops. *American Journal of Agricultural Economics*, 78, 916–923.

Menkhaus, D., Borden, G., Whipple, G., Hoffman, E., and Field, R. (1992). An empirical application of laboratory experimental auctions in marketing research. *Journal of Agricultural and Resource Economics*, 17(1), 44–55.

Morrot, G., Brochet, F., and Dubourdieu, D. (2001). The color of odors. *Brain and Language*, 79, 309–320.

Vickrey, W. (1961). Counterspeculation, auctions, and competitive sealed tenders. *Journal of Finance*, 16, 8–37.

Chapter 25

Do More Expensive Wines Taste Better? Evidence from a Large Sample of Blind Tastings*

Robin Goldstein[†,‖], Johan Almenberg[‡], Anna Dreber[§], John W. Emerson[¶], Alexis Herschkowitsch[†], and Jacob Katz[†]

[†]*Fearless Critic Media, 2011 B Bouldin Avenue, Austin, TX 78704, USA*
[‖]*robin@fearlesscritic.com*

[‡]*Department of Economics, Stockholm School of Economics, and the Research Institute of Industrial Economics, Sveriges Riksbank, SE-103 37 Stockholm, Sweden*
johan.almenberg@hhs.se

[§]*Department of Economics, Stockholm School of Economics, and Program for Evolutionary Dynamics, P.O. Box 6501, 113 83 Stockholm, Sweden*
anna.dreber@hhs.se

[¶]*Department of Statistics, Yale University, USA*
john.emerson@yale.edu

Individuals who are unaware of the price do not derive more enjoyment from more expensive wine. In a sample of more than 6,000 blind tastings, we find that the correlation between price and overall rating is small and negative, suggesting that individuals on average enjoy more expensive wines slightly *less*. For individuals with wine training, however, we find indications of a non-negative relationship between price and enjoyment. Our results are robust to the inclusion of individual fixed effects, and are not driven by outliers: when omitting the top and bottom deciles of the price distribution, our qualitative results are strengthened, and the statistical significance is improved further. These findings suggest that non-expert wine consumers should not anticipate greater enjoyment of the intrinsic qualities of a wine simply because it is expensive or is appreciated by experts.

*This article originally appeared in *Journal of Wine Economics* (2008), 3(1), 1–9.

1. Introduction

When symbolic content is an important part of consumption, the enjoyment of a good might become decoupled from its innate qualities. The symbolic content of a price tag has been emphasized in marketing research (e.g., Cialdini, 1998). At the same time, when goods with similar characteristics differ in price, a reasonable prior is that the more expensive good will, on average, be of a higher quality. People have been shown to expect a positive correlation between price and quality (e.g., Rao and Monroe, 1989). Consistent with this expectation, a meta-analysis reports positive correlations between price and quality ratings for most, but not all, of 1,200 product markets, but also finds that the range of these correlations is very large (Tellis and Wernerfelt, 1987).

For some goods, there is much heterogeneity in consumer tastes, making it harder to infer quality from revealed preferences. Nonetheless, a reasonable prior is that consumers on average will derive more enjoyment from the good with the higher price. Wine seems to be a good where consumer tastes are highly heterogeneous (Amerine and Roessler, 1976; Lecocq and Visser, 2006). While individuals may frequently disagree over which wine they prefer, the above hypothesis suggests a positive correlation between the enjoyment of a wine and its price.

A number of studies have reported positive correlations between price and subjective appreciation of a wine for wine experts (e.g., Oczkowski, 1994; Landon and Smith, 1997; Benjamin and Podolny, 1999; Schamel and Anderson, 2003; Lecocq and Visser, 2006). Non-experts, however, may not be particularly sensitive to some of the refinements that are held in high esteem by wine aficionados. Weil (2001, 2005) uses the following experimental setup: two bottles of wine are poured into four containers. Tasters are then given three of the containers and asked to distinguish which one differs from the other two. A random guess has 1/3 chance of being correct. In Weil (2001), the two wines are identical apart from year, but one wine is from a "good" vintage, and the other from a "bad" vintage.[1] The tasters get it right 41% of the time — only marginally better than a random guess.[2] In Weil (2005), the wines are a reserve bottling and a regular bottling, from the same producer and year. The fraction of correct answers is merely 40%. Moreover, Weil

[1] Weil uses pairs for which the famous wine critic Robert Parker has rated one of the bottles "average" to "appalling" and the other bottle "excellent" to "the finest."

[2] All of the significant difference is driven by the testers' ability to distinguish between the good and bad vintages from Bordeaux Pomerol.

finds that even when tasters can distinguish between the vintages, they are about as likely to prefer the good one as the bad one. And among those who can distinguish the reserve bottling from the regular bottling, only half prefer the reserve. In both cases, the wines differ in price by an order of magnitude. These experiments highlight the discrepancy between experts and non-experts and the subjectivity of the wine experience.

Extrinsic factors, such as peer consumption and marketing actions, can also influence how a good is experienced. The price tag may in itself be such a factor. Recent research has shown that individuals appreciate the same wine more when they think that it is more expensive (Brochet, 2001; Plassmann *et al.*, 2008). In other words, the price of a good affects the experienced utility derived from that good. Thus, to test the conjecture that the price of wine and the enjoyment of its intrinsic qualities are positively correlated, we need to examine the enjoyment of wine when individuals are unaware of the price.

In this chapter, we use a large sample of more than 6,000 U.S. blind tastings conducted by food and wine critic Robin Goldstein. We investigate the relationship between price and subjective appreciation of wines when the price is unknown to the taster. Subjective appreciation is measured by overall ratings assigned to wines by individual participants. Blind tastings offer the opportunity to isolate the experience of the wine itself from psychological confounds related to its price, presentation or published expert ratings.

Our main finding is that individuals who are unaware of the price do not, on average, derive more enjoyment from more expensive wine. In fact, unless they are experts, they enjoy more expensive wines slightly *less*. Our results are robust to the inclusion of individual fixed effects, and are not driven by outliers: when we omit the extremes of the price distribution our results are even more pronounced.

This chapter organized as follows. In Section 2, we describe our data. In Section 3, we present our econometric model and report our results. We also perform a robustness check. We conclude in Section 4, where we discuss some implications of our results and suggest directions for future research.

2. Data

The data set contains 6,175 observations from 17 blind tastings organized by Robin Goldstein. The blind tastings took place in the U.S. between April 2007 and February 2008. In total, 506 participants tasted wine flights composed from 523 different wines. The wines were presented in a double-blind manner, so that neither the person serving the wine nor the person tasting the wine knew the identity, price, or any other characteristics of the wine aside from its color. Each taster assigned an overall rating to every wine tasted prior to discussing the wines with the rest of the group, and was not permitted to change his or her answer after discussion. The rating was the response to the question "Overall, how do you find the wine?" and the available answers were "Bad," "Okay," "Good," and "Great." In the data, these alternatives are coded from 1 to 4, with 1 corresponding to "Bad" and 4 corresponding to "Great."[3]

The price per bottle ranged from \$1.65 to \$150. The prices are average retail prices and were obtained from www.wine-searcher.com. The wines represent a broad variety of types (e.g., red, white, rosé, and sparkling), country origins, and grapes.

The participants were unpaid volunteers from 21 to 88 years of age. Selection bias is a concern with any voluntary subject pool, and we have no reason to think that this is an exception. It is quite likely that the sample contains an over-representation of highly educated individuals, and an over-representation of individuals working in the food and wine industries. Nonetheless, the size of the sample and the general diversity of the tasters lead us to hope that inference will not be too restricted. For a more extensive description of the blind tastings, please see Chapters 8 and 9 and Appendix 1 in Goldstein (2008).

3. Results

Throughout the regression analysis, we use both an ordered probit estimator and a linear estimator (OLS). In both cases, we consistently use robust standard errors. The ordered probit estimator is particularly well suited to an ordinal dependent variable, but we find that OLS also performs well, and yields estimates that are easier to interpret. In any case, the two models generate highly consistent results. The dependent variable is the overall rating, measured on a scale from 1 to 4, with 4 being the highest rating. The main independent variable is the price variable, expressed as the natural logarithm of the average retail price per 750 mL of the wine in U.S. dollars.[4]

[3]Tasters ticked one of four boxes. In about 3% of the sample, tasters ticked in between two boxes, suggesting a rating somewhere in between the two responses. For simplicity, we dropped these observations from the regression. Including them makes no difference to our qualitative results, and the changes to the estimates are negligible.

[4]If we didn't do this, we would be expecting a one dollar increase to have the same effect at the \$5 price level as at the \$50 price level. We get similar qualitative results using the

In Model 1, we regress the overall rating assigned to wine i, by individual j, on the price of the wine. About 12% of participants had some wine training, such as a sommelier course. In Model 2, we allow for the possibility that these "experts" rate wines in a different manner. We include a dummy variable for being an expert, as well as an interaction term for price and the expert dummy. In a linear regression, this allows both the intercept and the slope coefficient to differ for experts and non-experts. In terms of the linear specification, we can write these two models as

$$Y_i = \beta_0 + \beta_1 \ln(p_i) + \epsilon_i \quad (1)$$

and

$$y_{ij} = \beta_0 + \beta_2 \ln(p_i) + \beta_2 EXPERT_j + \beta_3 \ln(p_i)^* EXPERT_j + \varepsilon_i \quad (2)$$

where P_i is the price of wine i, and $EXPERT_j$ is a dummy variable indicating if taster j has wine training. If individuals found that more expensive wines tasted better, the correlation between overall rating and price would be positive. In our sample, this is not the case: for both the ordered probit estimates and the OLS estimates, the coefficient on price is negative. In Model 1, the OLS coefficient is about -0.04, implying that a 100% increase in ln(price) is associated with a 0.04 reduction in the overall rating (Table 1, column (c)). The negative effect for more expensive wines is statistically significant.

For non-experts, the relationship between price and overall rating is negative; for experts, however, this is not the case. Our estimates of Model 2 show that the correlation between price and overall rating is positive — or, at any rate, non-negative — for experts (Table 1, columns (b) and (d)). The price coefficient for non-experts is still negative, of about the same size as before, and with greatly improved statistical significance. The coefficient on the ln(price)*expert interaction term is highly statistically significant (ordered probit p-value: 0.017; OLS p-value: 0.015). For experts, the net coefficient on price is the sum of the two (i.e., about 0.11 for the ordered probit and 0.09 for OLS). This net coefficient is significantly different from zero, but only at the 10% level (ordered probit p-value: 0.099; OLS p-value: 0.095), despite the large sample size.

In sum, we find a non-negative relationship between price and overall rating for experts. Due to the poor statistical significance of the price coefficient

---

dollar prices, but the statistical significance of the coefficients is not as good (but still significant).

Table 1. Dependent Variable: Overall Rating

	Ordered probit		OLS	
	(a)	(b)	(c)	(d)
ln(Price)	−0.047	−0.061	−0.038	−0.048
	(0.039)**	(0.013)**	(0.038)**	(0.012)**
ln(Price)*Expert		0.171		0.138
		(0.017)**		(0.015)**
Expert		−0.558		−0.448
		(0.001)***		(0.001)***
Constant			2.297	2.337
			(0.000)***	(0.000)***
N	5986	5972	5986	5972
R^2/pseudo-R^2	0.000	0.002	0.001	0.005

Notes: Robust *p*-values in parentheses. *significant at 10%; **significant at 5%; ***significant at 1%.

for experts, it remains an open question whether this coefficient is in fact positive.

How large are these price effects? The coefficients are of a moderate magnitude, but non-negligible, given that wine prices cover a large range — both in our sample and in the general wine market. Suppose we have two wines, A and B, and Wine A costs ten times more then Wine B in dollar terms. In terms of a 100-point scale (such as that used by *Wine Spectator*), the OLS estimation of Model 2 predicts that non-experts will assign an overall rating that is four points lower for wine A, whereas experts will assign an overall rating chat is seven points higher.[5]

In addition, the coefficient on the expert dummy is negative, quite sizeable, and statistically significant (OLS expert dummy coefficient: −0.448; *p*-value: 0.001). In other words, the OLS estimation of Model 2 consists of two linear relationships, one with a higher intercept (2.337) but a negative slope (−0.048), and one with a lower intercept (1.889) but a positive slope (0.090). The point where the two lines cross each other is the price level at which experts and non-experts are expected to assign the same rating. If we take the model literally, this point occurs at the price of $25.70 (i.e., ln(price) = approx. 3.25). At this price, the model predicts that both groups

[5]If the dollar price increases by a factor of 10, ln(price) increases by about 2.3. Hence the predicted effect on the overall rating of tenfold increase in the dollar price is 2.3 times the ln(price) coefficient for non-experts and experts, respectively, adjusted to a 100 point scale.

Table 2. Individual Fixed Effects

	Ordered probit		OLS	
	(a)	(b)	(c)	(d)
ln(Price)	−0.070 (0.007)***	−0.089 (0.001)***	−0.050 (0.009)***	−0.064 (0.002)***
ln(Price)*Expert		0.209 (0.011)**		0.151 (0.013)**
Individual fixed effects	Yes	Yes	Yes	Yes
Constant			2.487 (0.000)***	2.183 (0.000)***
N	5986	5972	5986	5972
R^2/pseudo-R^2	0.080	0.081	0.181	0.182

Notes: Robust p-values in parentheses. *significant at 10%; **significant at 5%; ***significant at 1%.

will assign a rating of about 2.2. Below this price, the model predicts that experts will assign lower ratings to a wine than non-experts, and vice versa.

We also test a third model, including individual fixed effects. In terms of the linear specification, Model 3 can be written as

$$Y_{ij} = \beta_0 + \delta_j + \beta_1 \ln(P_i) + \beta_2 \ln(P_i) * EXPERT_j + \varepsilon_i \tag{3}$$

where δ_j is a dummy for each individual taster. Including individual fixed effects has very little effect on the qualitative results and the minor differences only serve to reinforce our earlier conclusions, as both the negative effect for non-experts and the positive effect for experts become slightly stronger. These results are presented in Table 2. For each of the four regressions in Table 2, a Wald test rejects that the fixed effects are jointly equal to zero by a wide margin (p-value < 0.001), suggesting that this is a suitable addition to the model.

To make sure that our results are not driven by wines at the extreme ends of the price distribution, we also run our regressions on a reduced sample, omitting the top and bottom deciles of the price distribution. Given the broad range of prices in the sample, this is an appropriate precaution. The remaining wines range in price from \$6 to \$15.

Using the reduced sample, we estimate Model 2 (Table 3, columns (a) and (c)) and Model 3 (Table 3, columns (b) and (d)). This produces consistent and even more pronounced estimates. The coefficient on price is still negative, and in each case larger than when using the full sample. The statistical significance of the coefficients improves further, and the R-squared is higher.

Table 3. Reduced Sample, With and Without Individual Fixed Effects[6]

	Ordered probit		OLS	
	(a)	(b)	(c)	(d)
ln(Price)	−0.225	−0.173	−0.182	−0.122
	(0.001)***	(0.019)**	(0.001)***	(0.025)**
ln(Price)*Expert	0.523	0.515	0.421	0.364
	(0.002)***	(0.006)***	(0.002)***	(0.009)***
Expert	−1.301		−1.044	
	(0.000)***		(0.000)***	
Individual fixed effects	No	Yes	No	Yes
Constant			2.622	1.910
			(0.000)***	(0.000)***
N	4817	4817	4817	4817
R^2/pseudo-R^2	0.003	0.094	0.007	0.206

Notes: Robust p-values in parentheses. *significant 10%; **significant at 15%; ***significant at 1%.

In sum, we use the reduced sample to check the robustness of our results with regard to mid-range price levels. Based on the above, we conclude that our results are not only robust but in fact even more pronounced when omitting observations at the extremes of the price distribution.

4. Conclusions

The pleasure we get from consuming wine depends both on its intrinsic qualities such as taste and smell and external attributes such as price and presentation. One may argue that the former influences our subjective appreciation through a bottom-up process, where the sensory apparatus plays a key role, and that the latter works through a top-down process, where beliefs and expectations about quality are important determinants.[7]

In this chapter we have explored the bottom-up effects by looking at how participants in blind tastings rate wines. We find that, unless they are experts, individuals who are unaware of the price enjoy more expensive wines slightly less.

[6]The reduced sample excludes the top and bottom deciles of the price distribution.

[7]This, inturn, might depend on ulterior motives such as status concerns. Wine as a status signal, and the prospect that expensive wine could function as a positional good, is discussed in Goldstein (2008), Chapter 5.

There is a large relevant literature related to the influence of extrinsic signals on taste experience. Lee *et al.* (2006) look at how knowledge of a beer's ingredients (normal beer with added vinegar) can affect subjective appreciation. They show that the timing of the information plays a substantial role. One group of tasters is told about the vinegar, tastes the beer, and assigns ratings. A second group is told about the vinegar after tasting the beer, but before the ratings are assigned. On average, individuals in the first group assign significantly lower ratings, suggesting that informing participants about the vinegar influences the experience in itself. Using functional magnetic resonance imaging (fMRI), McClure *et al.* (2004) find that having the subject's favorite brand's name on a drink makes it taste better than if it is unlabeled. In another fMRI study, Plassmann *et al.* (2008) test whether marketing actions such as changes in the price can influence the experienced pleasantness of a product such as wine. Testers are given different wines that they are told differ in price. In reality, some of the wines are the same but simply presented with different prices. Prices are found to correlate positively with experienced pleasantness, measured through both subjective reports and tMRI scans.

Marketing provides one channel through which consumers can be influenced to buy certain wines. But it is not the only one: wine critics/experts may also play a role in affecting wine prices and shaping consumer preferences. For example, Hadj Ali *et al.* (2007) find a positive effect of wine critic Robert Parker's ratings on the price of Bordeaux wine.

There is, however, some research expressing skepticism towards wine ratings and their use for the average wine drinker. According to Quandt (2007), many wine ratings do not actually convey any information, nor is there substantial agreement in ratings by experts. Consistent with this view, Weil (2007) investigates whether wine descriptions by experts convey information to wine consumers. This is tested by having testers match wine descriptions to wines. In a similar setup to Weil (2001, 2005), tasters are asked to distinguish the odd one out of three different glasses of wine. Only about 50% of the participants in Weil (2007) can distinguish the odd one out, and of those who manage to do it, only about half can correctly match a wine critic's description of the wine with the wine itself — which is no better than a random guess.

Our results indicate another reason for why the average wine drinker may not benefit from expert wine ratings: He or she simply doesn't like the same types of wines as experts. This is consistent with Weil (2001, 2005), who finds that even among the subset of tasters who can distinguish between good and bad vintages, or reserve or regular bottlings, they are as likely to prefer the "better" one as the "worse" one.

These findings raise an interesting question: is the difference between the ratings of experts and non-experts due to an acquired taste? Or is it due to an innate ability, which is correlated with self-selection into wine training?[8] Investigating this further would be a fruitful avenue for future research.

In sum, in a large sample of blind tastings, we find that the correlation between price and overall rating is small and negative. Unless they are experts, individuals on average enjoy more expensive wines slightly less. Our results suggest that non-expert wine consumers should not anticipate greater enjoyment of the intrinsic qualities of a wine simply because it is expensive or is appreciated by experts.

Acknowledgments

The findings reported here are discussed at length in Robin Goldstein's book *The Wine Trials* (Fearless Critic Media, 2008). We thank Jacopo Anselmi, Zoe Chance, Shane Frederick, Richard Friberg, Barry Goldstein, Erik Grönqvist, Daniel Horwitz, Roy Ip, Magnus Johannesson, Thomas Pfeiffer, Hal Stubbs, Sue Stubbs and an anonymous referee for helpful comments and suggestions. Johan Almenberg thanks the Ragnar and Torsten Söderberg Foundations for financial support, and Johan Almenberg and Anna Dreber thank the Jan Wallander and Tom Hedelius Foundation for financial supp ort. The Program for Evolutionary Dynamics is sponsored by J. Epstein.

References

Amerine, M.A., and Roessler, E.B. (1976). *Wines: Their Sensory Evaluation.* San Francisco: W.H. Freeman and Company.

Benjamin, B.A., and Podolny, J.M. (1999). Status, quality, and social order in the California wine industry. *Administrative Science Quarterly*, 44, 563–589.

Brochet, F. (2001). Chemical object representation in the field of consciousness. Working Paper, General Oenology Laboratory, Talence, France.

Cialdini, R.B. (1998). *Influence: The Psychology of Persuasion.* New York: Collins.

Goldstein, R. (2008). *The Wine Trials.* Austin: Fearless Critic Media.

Hadj Ali, H., Lecocq, S., and Visser, M. (2007). The impact of gurus: Parker grades and *en primeur* wine prices. American Association of Wine Economists, AAWE Working Paper No. 1.

[8]For a further discussion, see Chapter 4 of Goldstein (2008).

Landon, S., and Smith, C.E. (1997). The use of quality and reputation indicators by consumers: The case of Bordeaux wine. *Journal of Consumer Policy*, 20, 289–323.

Lecocq, S., and Visser, M. (2006). What determines wine prices: Objective vs. sensory characteristics. *Journal of Wine Economics*, 1(1), 42–56.

Lee, L., Frederick, S., and Ariely, D. (2006). Try it, you'll like it — the influence of expectation, consumption, and revelation on preferences for beer. *Psychological Science*, 17(12), 1054–1058.

McClure, S.M., Li, J., Tomlin, D., Cypert, K.S., Montague, L.M., and Montague, P.R. (2004). Neural correlates of behavioral preference for culturally familiar drinks. *Neuron*, 44, 379–387.

Oczkowski, E. (1994). A hedonic price function for Australian premium wine. *Australian Journal of Agricultural Economics*, 38, 93–110.

Plassmann, H., O'Doherty, J., Shiv, B., and Rangel, A. (2008). Marketing actions can modulate neural representations of experienced pleasantness. *Proceedings of the National Academy of Sciences*, 105(3), 1050–1054.

Quandt, R.E. (2007). On wine bullshit: Some new software. *Journal of Wine Economics*, 2(2), 129–135.

Rao, A.R., and Monroe, K.B. (1989). The effect of price, brand name, and store name on buyers' perceptions of product quality: An integrative review. *Journal of Marketing Research*, 36, 351–357.

Schamel, G., and Anderson, K. (2003). Wine quality and varietal, regional and winery reputations: Hedonic prices for Australia and New Zealand. *The Economic Record*, 79(246), 357–369.

Tellis, G.J., and Wernerfelt, B. (1987). Competitive price and quality under asymmetric information. *Marketing Science*, 6(3), 240–253.

Weil, R.L. (2001). Parker vs. Prial: The death of the vintage chart. *Chance*, 14(4), 27–31.

Weil, R.L. (2005). Analysis of reserve and regular bottlings: Why pay for a difference only the critics claim to notice? *Chance*, 18(3), 9–15.

Weil, R.L. (2007). Debunking critics' wine words: Can amateurs distinguish the smell of asphalt from the taste of cherries? *Journal of Wine Economics*, 2(2), 136–144.

Chapter 26

Debunking Critics' Wine Words: Can Amateurs Distinguish the Smell of Asphalt from the Taste of Cherries?*

Roman L. Weil

Graduate School of Business, University of Chicago,
5807 S. Woodlawn Avenue, Chicago, IL 60637, USA
roman.weil@gsb.uchicago.edu

I report my tests of the hypothesis that wine consumers cannot match critics' descriptions of wines with the wines themselves. My results suggest that testers' ability to match the descriptions with the wines is no better than random. I report on more than two hundred observations of wine drinkers who engaged in the following experiment. The drinker faces three glasses of wine, two of which contain identical wines and the third contains a different wine. I record whether the drinker can distinguish wines — whether he can tell the singleton from the doubleton and, if the drinker can distinguish, which wine he prefers. I present the testers with descriptions of the two wines written by the same wine critic/reviewer. I find that 51% of the testers who can distinguish the wines correctly match the description of the wine with the wine itself. The percentage matching does not significantly differ from the expected-if-random half. I have recorded the sex of the testers and I can find that men can distinguish the wines better than random, but women cannot. The differences are so small, even though significant, however, that the Exact F test detects no significant difference between the ability of men and women in these experiments. The results span tests of wines from Bordeaux, Burgundy, the Rhône, Spain, Germany, and Australia; the tests use only still wines, all less than 10 years old.

I dedicate this chapter to Adrienne Lehrer, whose 1983 book, *Wine and Conversation*, with a different experimental design, anticipated these results.

*This article originally appeared in *Journal of Wine Economics* (2007), 2(2), 136–144.

1. Introduction

Food and beverage descriptions have been the subject of numerous investigations in linguistic, psychology, and sensory evaluation for more than 30 years; more recently, even economists have become interested in this topic. Although there are several studies on the language of beer (e.g., Cholet and Valentin, 2001) and the language of cheese (Murray and Delahunty, 2000), the wine language is second to none with respect to both its level of publication as well as to its flamboyance (see e.g., Quandt, 2007, in this issue). Robert Parker's data base alone contains descriptions of approximately 100,000 wines. His "glossary of wine terms" comprises descriptors such as *brawny*, *austere*, *backward*, *hedonistic*, *hot*, and *unctuous* (Parker, 2007).

In one of the first studies, the linguist Adrienne Lehrer investigated the wine language in 1975. Lehrer assessed the degree of useful communication of about wine flavors. In one experiment she lets non-experts first describe three distinctly different wines. In the subsequent tastings the subjects were not able to match the descriptions with the wines better than chance. Even when trying to match the wines with presumably better descriptions by individuals with "sensitive palates" the right matches averaged at one of the three.

Lawless (1984) examined the matching performance of non-experts and experts when drawing on descriptions by either group. In his experiments, expert tasters using expert descriptions performed slightly better than chance. In contrast, non-expert tasters fared equally badly using expert or non-expert descriptions. That is, similar to Lehrer's results, non-experts do not perform better than chance regardless of how "accurate" the descriptions are. Solomon (1990) and more recently Sauvageot *et al.* (2006) confirmed these results.

My experiments fall within the Lehrer-Lawless framework, and ask the question of whether wine descriptions facilitate the wine consumer's decision-making by providing useful information about a complex sensory experience.

The research reported here investigates whether the (publicly accessible) words that wine critics (i.e., *experts*) use convey information useful to wine consumer, the subjects in my experiments. Here, I report my tests of wine testers' ability to distinguish wines from critics' descriptions.

My results suggest that:

- In a triangle test, half of my wine tester subjects can distinguish in blind testings the two wines in each of the tests, whereas only one-third could if the process were random, but

- of those who can distinguish, less than half can match the lists of wine words with the wine described by those words, whereas half could if the process were random.

I conclude that (non-expert) wine drinkers cannot match better than chance wines with their descriptions. Wine words used by critics to convey analogy to fruits, vegetables, minerals, and odors have no value.

2. Methods

First, I located pairs of wines with the following characteristics: the testers could afford them (typically, but not always, $40 or less per bottle), the pairs have similar features,[1] and the same writer/critic wrote about these two wines with disjoint word sets. That is, the reviewer used different words in describing the two wines.

To be clear, look at Table 1, testing number 3, for a pair of French Bordeaux. The pair of wines reported here are both from the 2000 vintage — Talbot and Clos du Marquis, both costing around $50 and both reviewed in *The Wine Advocate.* The descriptions of these two wines use disjoint words:

> Talbot–Admirable richness, layered texture, sweet tannin, abundant quantities of smoky cassis, licorice, herb, earth, and leather characteristics. Complex aromatics, blends power with elegance.
>
> Clos du Marquis-Dense, opaque purple-colored, with créme de cassis, vanilla, and cherry notes, medium to full body, an unctuous texture, low acidity.

Second, I split the wine into four containers labeled A, B, C, and D, putting each of the wines into exactly two of the four containers. I gave each tester wines from three of the four containers.[2] I asked each tester to say which of the three wines differed from the other two. Then, which of these did you prefer, the singleton or the doubleton? And, which of two lists of words describes each of the two wines? A typical tester, say one testing from containers A, B, and D, would respond something like, "wine A differs from B/D, I prefer B/D, and list II goes with wines B/D."

---

[1]Common features include grape type, color of wine, sweetness, and age. In some of the tests, the two wines come from different vintages. In all cases the same reviewer wrote the reviews the two wines in a given test.

[2]In the tastings with 20 or more individuals, I had two bottles of each wine/vintage. I did not mix those two bottles and then split them in half, but gave the two bottles separate labels. I wonder if you'd prefer the experimenter to mix identical wines and then split into two containers, which controls somewhat for bottle variation but would not present wines the way individual buyers and drinkers face them.

I tallied how many of the testers correctly distinguished the wines and which they preferred, although we don't care which they say they prefer for these tests. I presented the testers with the two sets of words and asked them to match each set of word lists to the wine. I have recorded data separately for men and women.

After the tally, I matched the wines to the letter labels and counted how many of the testers correctly distinguished between the two wines. I counted whether the tester could correctly match the words to the wines only if that tester correctly distinguished the wines. I announced the result. Refer, for example, to the testing of the Bordeaux wines in testing number 3. I announced, "Eighteen of us tested these two wines; eleven of us got the distinction right and of those eleven, eight correctly matched the word lists to the wines."

I announced the result of each pair-wise testing before going on to the next pair. Most testers tested more than a single pair of wines. Table 1 shows the order in which the subjects tested the wines on each date.

Most of the testers were either MBA students at the Graduate School of Business of the University of Chicago or its alumni and their companions. They are primarily upper middleclass, experienced and enthusiastic wine drinkers, but not experts. All testers paid an entry fee for the testing, which fee covered full costs of the testing, and in the case of some of the alumni, more. (How often do experimenters get their subjects to pay to participate?)

3. Basic Results

Table 1 reports the results. Each individual who tests a vintage pair has a one-third probability of correctly distinguishing the wines by chance: three glasses, one is different; one in three chance of guessing that glass. With n testers and random choices, the expected number of correct distinctions is $n/3$.

Overall Results. Look at the bottom of Table 1, the totals. A total of 166 testers have tested 321 pairs of wines. One-third of 321 is 107, so we'd expect 107 correct distinctions if the process is random where the testers cannot distinguish the wines. The observed number is 162, just over half, 51%. This differs from the expected relative frequency of 33.3% by over 6 standard deviations.

Refer to the last pair of columns in Table 1 which reports the ability of those who correctly distinguished the wines to match the words to the wines. Of the 162 pairs where the tester could distinguish correctly, the tester

Table 1. Testing Results

No.	Date, testers	Wine	Descriptors (source)	Price in $	Sex and number of testers	Getting distinction right		Number getting distinction right who correctly matched lists	
						Total	Share	Total	Share
1	May 2003, GSB Faculty & Students	1998 Fox Creek Shiraz/ Cabernet	Sumptuous nose of black fruits and spicy new oak. . . . Intense black cherry/cassis flavors (Parker, Wine Advocate)	30	W 4	3	75%	0	0%
		2001 Marquis Philips Sarah's Blend	Stunningly sweet bouquet of ground pepper, blackberry liqueur, and toasty oak. (Parker, Wine Advocate)	15	M 9	5	56%	2	40%
2	June 2003, U Chicago Faculty	1999 Ch De Maligny, Carré de Cesar	Sleek and refined pear, green apple, slate, and racy acidity (www.samswine.com)	17	W 2	2	100%	2	100%
		2002 Omaka Springs Marlborough Sauvignon Blanc	Juicy; lively mouthful of lemon, citrus, pepper, and passion fruit flavors (www.samswine.com)	13	M 13	13	100%	6	46%

(*Continued*)

Table 1. (*Continued*)

No.	Date, testers	Wine	Descriptors (source)	Price in $	Sex and number of testers	Getting distinction right		Number getting distinction right who correctly matched lists	
						Total	Share	Total	Share
3	June 2003, U Chicago Faculty	1999 Dujac Morey St. Denis, ler Crus	Nose shows candied cherries, spices. It offers tangy cherries, strawberries, raspberries; sweet, well-balanced. (Rovani, Wine Advocate)	75	W 2	2	100%	1	50%
		1999 Dujac Morey St. Denis	Nose is waxy, sweet cherries. Loads of red fruits (Rovani, Wine Advocate)	50	M 12	3	25%	1	33%
4	June 2003, U Chicago	2000 d'Arenberg "The Footbolt," Australian	Packed with dense blackberry fruit; notes of licorice, smoked meats and bittersweet chocolate. Silky texture. Fine balance and length (Jim Chanteloup)	15	W 2	1	50%	0	0%
	Faculty	Shiraz 2000 Finca Sobreno Crianza, Toro	Wonderful sweet black cherry fruit intermixed with spice box, cedar, toasty oak, and excellent texture, plenty of berry fruit, supple hedonic finish (Anne Pickett and Robert Parker)	10	M 11	8	73%	2	25%

5	Dec 2003, Kansas City GSB Alums	2002 Schloss Lieser Niederberg Helden Spätlese	Delicate and seemingly transparent in texture, framework for the peach, herb and mineral flavors and a creaminess from the midpalate to the fine, lingering, mouthwatering finish ... More defined flavors of rose petal, white and yellow peach, orange peel, sour plums and cherries. Very refined with a driving slate imprint that intensifies the already seething soil/fruit battle creating layer upon layer of flavor (K&L Wines Catalog)	20	W 12	5	42%	1	20%
		2002 Dr. F. Weins-Prüm Erdener Prälat Spätlese	A touch of the tropical in the nose, like spiced pineapple and passion fruit with a dose of rich mineral character. Bright and lively with a silky texture and ripe round acid structure. Very Long (K&L Wines Catalog)	24	M 18	7	39%	4	57%
6	Dec 2003, Kansas City GSB Alums	1999 Bruno Clair Savigny Les Beaune La Dominode	Nose of blackberries and spices. Medium-bodied wine is crammed with dark fruits, hints of licorice, and flavors reminiscent of **freshly laid asphalt**. Powerful, foursquare, austere, long ripe tannin-filled finish (AB, Wine Advocate)	55	W 10	4	40%	3	75%
		1999 Dujac Morey St. Denis	Nose of candied cherries and spices. Light to medium-bodied and well-made; offers tangy cherries as well as strawberries and raspberries in its sweet well-balanced character (Wine Advocate)	50	M 17	12	71%	10	83%

(*Continued*)

Table 1. (*Continued*)

No.	Date, testers	Wine	Descriptors (source)	Price in $	Sex and number of testers	Getting distinction right		Number getting distinction right who correctly matched lists	
						Total	Share	Total	Share
7	Feb 2004, San Francisco GSB Alums	2000 Cabrières Châteuneuf du Pape la Lettre A Louis Arnaud	Deep ruby color includes purpose nuances. Closed aromatically, hints of crème de cassis and black cherries. Cuts broad swath across the palate with considerable depth and concentration. Tannic as well as broodingly backward (Wine Advocate)	50	W 11	6	55%	3	50%
		2000 Cabrières Châteauneuf du Pape Cuvée Prestige Tete de Cru	Deep ruby/purple color; sumptuous perfume of figs, plums, prunes, and jammy black cherry fruit. Large, voluminous mouthfeel, unctuous texture, full body. Low acidity, sweet tannin and gobs of glycerin as well as fruit (Wine Advocate)	30	M 19	12	63%	9	75%

8	Mar 2004, Stanford Faculty	2001 Rasteau Cuvée Prestige Dom. La Soumade	Sweet with lush mouth feel... tremendous Framboise flavors and length on the palate. Tannins are round and very ripe (K&L Wine Catalog).	20	W 5	2	40%	1	50%
		2001 Rasteau Cuvée Confiance Dom. La Soumade	... wealth of red fruits with raspberry scents. It is a dense wine with violet undertones and dark red and black fruits (K&L Wine Catalog)	29	M 9	4	44%	3	75%
9	Apr 2004, U Chicago MBA Students	2001 Rasteau Cuvée Prestige Dom. La Soumade	Sweet with lush mouth feel... tremendous Framboise flavors and length on the palate. Tannins are round and very ripe (K&L Wine Catalog).	20	W 17	5	29%	1	20%
		2001 Rasteau Cuvée Confiance Dom. La Soumade	... wealth of red fruits with raspberry scents. It is a dense wine with violet undertones and dark red and black fruits (K&L Wine Catalog)	29	M 23	10	43%	5	50%
10	Apr 2004, U Chicago MBA Students	1990 Michel-Schlumberger Cabernet Sauvignon Reserve	Rich with layers of berries and spice. [Producer] Deep toasty oak is complimented by blackberries and herbs. Supple and opulent fruit carries through with cigar box and vanilla fragrances (Wine Enthusiast)	120	W 17	8	50%	4	50%

(Continued)

Table 1. (*Continued*)

No.	Date, testers	Wine	Descriptors (source)	Price in $	Sex and number of testers	Getting distinction right		Number getting distinction right who correctly matched lists	
						Total	Share	Total	Share
		1990 Michel-Schlumberger Cabernet Sauvignon	Cherry, cassis, and blackberry; smoky cumin, and cedar. [Producer] Aromas of cherry, currant, chocolate, vanilla, mint, and spice (Underground Wine Journal, K&L Wines)	22	M 24	12	33%	4	33%
Totals				$N = 321$		$M = 62$		80	
Expected Frequency if Process is Random						33.3%		50%	
Observed Relative Frequency						50.5%		49.4%	
Standard Deviation of Relative Frequency if Process is Random						2.63%[a]		3.93%[b]	
Z Score: (Observed — Expected) Divided by Standard Deviation						6.5		−0.2	

Notes: [a]Square Root $(1/3 \times 2/3 \times 1/N)$, [b]Square Root $(1/2 \times 1/2 \times 1/M)$.

matched the word lists to the wines in just under half (49.4% = 80/162) the pairs. The observed 49.4% differs from the expected-if-random 50% by an insignificant 0.2 of one standard deviation. So, even the testers who can distinguish the wines have only an even chance of matching words to wines.

Men outperform women. Men's results differ from random, while women's do not. However, the exact F test suggests that the difference between men and women is not significant.

4. Implications

The results of my testings suggest that you not think that wines will taste or smell to you the way the words the critics use suggest the wines taste or smell to them.

However, I have not tested the following possibility. Consider two tastes, R and C. Imagine that every time a critic says a wine tastes like raspberries, it has taste R and every time the critic says a wine tastes like cassis, it has taste C. To you, taste R resembles apples, and taste C resembles bananas. If the critic is consistent in labeling wines with taste R as raspberries and wines with taste C as cassis, then you can deduce from the review what the wine will taste like to you. I have not assembled testings of wines to ascertain whether others can confirm the consistency of the tastes of the critics.

Some experienced wine drinkers have commented that one requires practice and guidance to identify wine tastes. William Wecker (who devised the taxonomy that distinguishes wine drinkers from wine fondlers) suggests one should drink the wines knowing which list goes with which wine, and use the distinction between the lists to tell you what to expect when tasting. Then, you can learn to align your evaluations with your sensations. He says use the distinction as a teaching guide.

The Wine Aroma Wheel (Noble *et al.*, 1984) provides such a teaching guide, which draws on a three tier system of wine descriptors that are free of hedonic and value-judgment connotations. One can then use these descriptors as a reference standard to train wine tasters to come to consensus about the meaning of wine words.

Maybe so, but don't expect the tastes the wine critics' words bring to your mind to be there when you drink the wine.

Acknowledgments

I prepared this chapter for the 11th Oenometrics Meeting of the Vineyard Data Quantification Society, Dijon, May 21–22, 2004. Natasha Tantsura assisted in the compilation of the data for this research and in the writing of this chapter. Neither she nor I can distinguish better than random. Editor Karl Storchmann contributed even more than one ordinarily expects of the Journal's editor. Thank you.

References

Cholet, S., and Valentin, D. (2001). Impact of training on beer flavor perception and description. Are trained and untrained subjects really different? *Journal of Sensory Studies*, 16(6), 601–618.

Lawless, H. (1984). Flavor description of white wine by "expert" and nonexpert wine consumers. *Journal of Food Science*, 49(1), 120–123.

Lehrer, A. (1975). Talking about wine. *Language*, 51(4), 901–923.

Lehrer, A. (1983). *Wine and Conversation.* Bloomington: Indiana University Press.

Murray, J.M., and Delahunty, C.M. (2000). Selections of standards of reference terms in a cheddar-type cheese flavor language. *Journal of Sensory Studies*, 15(2), 179–199.

Noble, A.C., Arnold, R.A., Masuda, B.M., Pecore, S.D., Schmidt, J.O., and Stern, P.M. (1984). Progress towards a standardized system of wine aroma terminology. *American Journal of Enology and Viticulture*, 35(2), 107–109.

Parker, R. (2007). www.erobertparker.com. Accessed Nov 13, 2007.

Quandt, R. (2007). On wine bullshit: Some new software? *Journal of Wine Economics*, 2(2), 129–135.

Sauvageot, F., Urdapilleta, I., and Peyron, D. (2006). Within and between variations of texts elicited from nine wine experts. *Food Quality and Preference*, 17, 429–444.

Solomon, G.E. (1990). Psychology of novice and expert wine talk. *American Journal of Psychology*, 103(4), 495–517.

Index

G

H

I

J

K

L

M

Y

World Scientific Handbook in Financial Economics Series — Vol.6

WORLD SCIENTIFIC REFERENCE ON

HANDBOOK OF THE ECONOMICS OF WINE

❷ Reputation, Regulation, and Market Organization

World Scientific Handbook in Financial Economics Series

(ISSN: 2010-1732)

The Handbooks in Financial Economics (HIFE) are intended to be a definitive source for comprehensive and accessible information in the field of finance. Each individual volume in the series presents an accurate self-contained survey of a sub-field of finance, suitable for use by finance, economics and financial engineering professors and lecturers, professional researchers, investments, pension fund and insurance portfolio mangers, risk managers, graduate students and as a teaching supplement.

The HIFE series will broadly cover various areas of finance in a multi-handbook series. The HIFE series has its own web page that include detailed information such as the introductory chapter to each volume, an abstract of each chapter and biographies of editors. The series will be promoted by the publisher at major academic meetings and through other sources. There will be links with research articles in major journals.

The goal is to have a broad group of outstanding volumes in various areas of financial economics. The evidence is that acceptance of all the books is strengthened over time and by the presence of other strong volumes. Sales, citations, royalties and recognition tend to grow over time faster than the number of volumes published.

Published

Vol. 6 *Handbook of the Economics of Wine (In 2 Volumes)*
Volume 1: Prices, Finance, and Expert Opinion
Volume 2: Reputation, Regulation, and Market Organization
edited by Orley Ashenfelter, Olivier Gergaud, Karl Storchmann & William T. Ziemba

Vol. 5 *The World Scientific Handbook of Futures Markets*
edited by Anastasios G. Malliaris & William T. Ziemba

Vol. 4 *Handbook of the Fundamentals of Financial Decision Making (In 2 Parts)*
edited by Leonard C. MacLean & William T. Ziemba

Vol. 3 *The Kelly Capital Growth Investment Criterion: Theory and Practice*
edited by Leonard C. MacLean, Edward O. Thorp & William T. Ziemba

Vol. 2 *Efficiency of Racetrack Betting Markets (2008 Edition)*
edited by Donald B. Hausch, Victor S. Y. Lo & William T. Ziemba

Forthcoming

The World Scientific Handbook of Insurance (To be announced)

More information on this series can also be found at http://www.worldscientific.com/series/wshfes

World Scientific Handbook in Financial Economics Series — Vol.6

WORLD SCIENTIFIC REFERENCE ON
HANDBOOK OF THE ECONOMICS OF WINE

❷ Reputation, Regulation, and Market Organization

Orley Ashenfelter, Olivier Gergaud, Karl Storchmann and **William Ziemba**

Editors

World Scientific

NEW JERSEY • LONDON • SINGAPORE • BEIJING • SHANGHAI • HONG KONG • TAIPEI • CHENNAI • TOKYO

Published by

World Scientific Publishing Co. Pte. Ltd.
5 Toh Tuck Link, Singapore 596224
USA office: 27 Warren Street, Suite 401-402, Hackensack, NJ 07601
UK office: 57 Shelton Street, Covent Garden, London WC2H 9HE

Library of Congress Cataloging-in-Publication Data
Names: Ashenfelter, Orley, 1942– editor.
Title: Handbook of the economics of wine / edited by Orley Ashenfelter (Princeton) [and three others].
Description: New Jersey : World Scientific, [2018] | Series: World Scientific handbook in financial economics series ; volume 6 Contents: Volume 1. Prices, finance, and expert opinion -- Volume 2. Reputation, regulation, and market organization.
Identifiers: LCCN 2017044682| ISBN 9789814740579 (hc set : alk. paper) | ISBN 9789814740586 (hc: v.1 : alk. paper) | ISBN 9789814740593 (hc: v.2 : alk. paper)
Subjects: LCSH: Wine industry. | Wine and wine making--Economic aspects.
Classification: LCC HD9370.5 .H36 2018 | DDC 338.4/76632--dc23
LC record available at https://lccn.loc.gov/2017044682

British Library Cataloguing-in-Publication Data
A catalogue record for this book is available from the British Library.

ISBN: 978-981-3270-35-0 (pbk set) For special sales only
ISBN: 978-981-3270-36-7 (pbk: v.1) For special sales only
ISBN: 978-981-3270-37-4 (pbk: v.2) For special sales only

For any available supplementary material, please visit
http://www.worldscientific.com/worldscibooks/10.1142/9834#t=suppl

Desk Editors: Herbert Moses/Lum Pui Yee

Typeset by Stallion Press
Email: enquiries@stallionpress.com

Printed in Singapore

About the Editors

Ashenfelter Orley is Joseph Douglas Green 1895 Professor of Economics and former Director of the Industrial Relations Section at Princeton University. He has been the President of the American Economic Association, the American Law and Economics Association, and the Society of Labor Economics. He is currently the President of the Western Economic Association International and the American Association of Wine Economists. He edited the *American Economic Review* and founded and edited the *American Law and Economics Review.* As Director of the Office of Evaluation of the US Department of Labor in 1972, he began the work that is now widely recognized as the separate field of "quantitative social program evaluation." He is also regarded as the originator of the use of so-called "natural experiments" to infer causality about economic relationships. He has also been the leader in the recent emphasis in quantitative economic analysis on the use of creative methods of data collection.

Gergaud Olivier is Professor of Economics at KEDGE Business School in Bordeaux and Affiliate Researcher at LIEPP in Sciences Po. He holds a Ph.D. from the University of Reims and an accreditation to supervise research from Sciences Po. His research areas are Cultural Economics, Wine Economics, Sports Economics, and Restaurant Economics. He has been a visiting professor at different European (Sciences Po, Université Libre de Bruxelles) and North American universities

(HEC Montréal, NYU, and UCLA). He has published several papers in international journals such as *Economic Journal*, *Economic Inquiry*, *Journal of Economic Behavior and Organization*, *Journal of Wine Economics*, and *Oxford Bulletin of Economics and Statistics*. He currently serves on the Editorial Advisory Board of the *Journal of Wine Economics* and on the Editorial Board of the *Journal of Prediction Markets*.

Storchmann Karl is Clinical Professor of Economics at the New York University, a Co-Founder and the Managing Editor of the *Journal of Wine Economics*, and Vice President of the American Association of Wine Economists (AAWE). He has taught or held permanent or visiting positions in many universities, including Yale University, UCLA, University of Paris II Panthéon-Assas, University of Bordeaux, and Whitman College. His research interests encompass agricultural, energy, and environmental economics. His most recent research focuses on the impact of climate change on the wine industry, particularly on wine prices and vineyard land profitability. He has published in various journals including *American Economic Review*, *Review of Economics and Statistics*, and the *Journal of Wine Economics*.

Ziemba T. William is the Alumni Professor (Emeritus) of Financial Modeling and Stochastic Optimization in the Sauder School of Business, University of British Columbia where he taught from 1968–2006. His Ph.D. is from the University of California, Berkeley. He has been a visiting professor at Cambridge, Oxford, London School of Economics, University of Reading and Warwick in the UK, at Stanford, UCLA, Berkeley, MIT, University of Washington and Chicago in the US, Universities of Bergamo, Venice and Luiss in Italy, the Universities of Zurich, Cyprus, Tsukuba (Japan), Sabanci (Turkey), EDHEC (France), KAIST (Korea), and the National University and the National Technological University of Singapore. His research is in asset-liability management, portfolio theory and practice, security market imperfections, Japanese and Asian financial markets, hedge fund strategies, risk management, sports and lottery investments, and applied stochastic programming. His co-written practitioner paper on the Russell–Yasuda model won second prize in the 1993 Edelman Practice of Management Science Competition. In 2015, he won the futures part of the Battle of the Quants Trading Contest and beat the equity winner as well. He has published widely in journals such as *Operations Research, Management Science, Mathematics of OR, Mathematical Programming, American Economic Review, Journal of Economic Perspectives, Journal of Finance, Journal of Economic Dynamics and Control, JFQA, Quantitative Finance, Journal of Portfolio Management* and *Journal of Banking and Finance* and in many books and special journal issues. He is the series editor for North Holland's Handbooks in Finance, World Scientific Handbooks in Financial Economics and Books in Finance, and previously was the CORS editor of INFOR and the department of finance editor of *Management Science*, 1982–1992. He has continued his columns in *Wilmott* and his 2013 book with Rachel Ziemba have the 2007–2013 columns updated with new material published by World Scientific.

List of Contributors

Anderson Kym
School of Economics, University of Adelaide, Adelaide, South Australia 5005, Australia
Australian National University, Canberra ACT 0200, Australia

Ashenfelter Orley
Professor of Economics, Princeton University, Princeton, New Jersey, USA

Cakal Huseyin
School of Psychology, Keele University, UK

Costanigro Marco
Department of Agricultural and Resource Economics, Colorado State University, Colorado, USA

Deconinck Koen
University of Leuven (KU Leuven), Belgium

Février Philippe
CREST, ENSAE, University of Paris-Saclay, France

Frick Bernd
Paderborn University, Management Department, D-33098 Paderborn, Germany

Galbreath Jeremy
Curtin Graduate School of Business, Curtin University of Technology, Perth, Australia

Ginsburgh Victor
Université Libre de Bruxelles and Centre for Operations Research and Econometrics, Belgium

Goemans Christopher
Department of Agricultural and Resource Economics, Colorado State University, Colorado, USA

Gokcekus Omer
School of Diplomacy and International Relations, Seton Hall University, USA

Heien Dale
Department of Agricultural and Resource Economics, University of California Davis, USA

Hewstone Miles
Department of Experimental Psychology, University of Oxford, UK

Hoffmann Willem
Tshwane University of Technology, Higher Education Institution in Pretoria, South Africa

Jensen G. Hans
Institute of Food and Resource Economics, University of Copenhagen, 1958 Frederiksberg C, Denmark

Kleynhans Theo
Department of Agricultural Economics, University of Stellenbosch. Stellenbosch, South Africa

Landon Stuart
Department of Economics, University of Alberta, Edmonton, Alberta, T6G 2H4, Canada

Mahenc Philippe
University of Montpellier (CEE-M), Avenue Raymond Dugrand, Site de Richter, C. S. 79606, 34960 Montpellier Cedex 2, France

McCluskey J. Jill
School of Economic Sciences, Washington State University, USA

Meloni Giulia
LICOS Centre for Institutions and Economic Performance, KU Leuven, Waaistraat 6, Leuven, Belgium

Podolny M. Joel
Harvard University, William James Hall, Cambridge, MA 02138, USA

Riekhof M. Gina
Associate with Gilmore & Bell, P.C. and a former CORI Graduate Fellow at the University of Missouri, Columbia

Roos William
Student at ENSAE, INSEE 18 Bd Adolphe Pinard, 75014 Paris, France

Schamel Günter
School of Economics, University of Adelaide, Adelaide SA 5005 Australia
Free University of Bozen-Bolzano, School of Economics and Management, Via Sernesi 1, 1-39100, Bozen-Bolzano, Italy

Scott Morton M. Fiona
Yale University and NBER, Box 208200, New Haven, CT 06520, USA

Smith E. Constance
Department of Economics, University of Alberta, Edmonton, Alberta, T6G 2H4, Canada

Swinnen Johan
University of Leuven (KU Leuven), Belgium
LICOS Centre for Institutions and Economic Performance, KU Leuven, Waaistraat 6, Leuven, Belgium

Sykuta E. Michael
Department of Agricultural Economics and Director of the Contracting and Organizations Research Institute (CORI) at the University of Missouri, Columbia

Vink Nick
Department of Agricultural Economics, University of Stellenbosch, Stellenbosch, South Africa

Visser Michael
CREST, CNRS, ENSAE, University of Paris-Saclay and CRED, University of Paris, France

Contents

Part 1

Reputation

Chapter 1

Quality Expectations, Reputation, and Price*

Stuart Landon and Constance E. Smith[†]

Department of Economics, University of Alberta,
Edmonton, Alberta, T6G 2H4, Canada
[†] *constance.smith@ualberta.ca*

Although the theoretical literature on firm reputation is well developed, few empirical studies exist that quantify the importance of reputation effects. This chapter estimates the impact on price of current product quality and reputation using data from the market for Bordeaux wine. A model is proposed in which price is a function of current quality and expected quality, where the latter depends on reputation. Equations determining price and expected quality are estimated jointly. The empirical findings show that the price premium associated with a better reputation far exceeds that associated with improvements in current quality. The impact of reputation on price is disaggregated into individual firm and collective (or group) reputation effects, and the significance and magnitude of these effects are compared. The results indicate that both types of reputation are important, and that in general, the market values collective reputation indicators only to the extent that they are useful predictors of product quality.

1. Introduction

When the true quality of a product is not known before purchase, consumers may rely on a firm's reputation to form expectations of the product's quality. In this case, product prices will depend on firm reputation, as shown by Klein and Leffler (1981), Shapiro (1983), and Allen (1984). Although the theoretical literature on reputation is well developed, there have been few attempts to empirically quantify the magnitude of reputation effects on price or to measure the relative impact on price of reputation and current quality.[1] Jarrell and Peltzman (1985), Borenstein and Zimmerman (1988),

*This article originally appeared in *Southern Economic Journal* (1998), 64(3), 628–647.

[1]A large literature investigates the correlation between quality and price, but it does not incorporate reputation effects. See the surveys by Zeithaml (1988) and Geistfeld (1988).

and Karpoff and Lott (1993) empirically analyze firm reputation, but they examine the impact of reputation on shareholder wealth or product demand rather than on price. Caves and Greene (1996) show how factors that may affect a consumer's ability to evaluate a firm's reputation (such as previous experience with the product) influence the correlation between price and quality. Using U.S. data from the nineteenth-century, Gorton (1996) examines the relationship between a bank's reputation for default and the discount rate on its debt.

This chapter provides empirical estimates of the magnitude of the impact of reputation and current quality on price. By examining the role of reputation in price determination, and comparing this role to that of current quality, it is possible to infer whether firm reputation provides useful information to consumers and whether consumers use this information to guide their consumption decisions. The results can also be used to determine whether a firm that invests in reputation will garner a higher price.

The empirical analysis employs a model in which price depends on both current quality and expected quality, where the latter is a function of reputation. Individual firm data from the market for Bordeaux wine are used to jointly estimate equations determining price and expected quality.[2] The results show that the impact of reputation on price is approximately 20 times greater than the impact of current quality on price. This suggests a major role for reputation in price determination.

The analysis undertaken below distinguishes between the impact on price of two types of reputation. The first of these, *individual firm reputation*, is based on the past quality of a firm's output. This form of reputation is consistent with that used in the theoretical studies of Klein and Leffler (1981), Shapiro (1983), and Allen (1984).

The second type of reputation examined, *collective reputation*, is similar to a concept suggested by Tirole (1996) and is defined as the average quality produced by a group of firms with which an individual firm can be identified. In a market with a large number of firms, such as the market for Bordeaux wine, it may be very costly for consumers to acquire information on the

[2]Recent papers by Nerlove (1995) and Combris, Lecocq, and Visser (1997) also use data from the market for wine but do not examine reputation effects. Landon and Smith (1997) use wine data to analyze reputation effects but do not directly measure the relative importance of reputation and current quality in price determination, nor can their estimates distinguish whether reputation signals affect price directly or only indirectly through expected quality. Di Vittorio and Ginsburgh (1994) and Ginsburgh, Monzak, and Monzak (1992) also use wine data, but do not explicitly model expected quality (reputation).

past quality of the goods produced by all firms. It is typically less costly for consumers to acquire information on collective (or group) quality that can be used as an indicator of the quality of the goods produced by individual firms in the group. For example, a consumer's expectation of the quality of the wine made by an individual Bordeaux winemaker may depend on the average quality of all Bordeaux wines.[3]

Several features of the Bordeaux red wine industry make it especially appropriate for an empirical analysis of the relationship between quality, price, and reputation. Wine is a differentiated product and the large number of producers in the industry makes it costly for consumers to obtain full information on the current quality of all individual wines produced. Furthermore, the industry is relatively stable in the sense that there have not been major changes to the product that might reduce consumers' reliance on reputation as a predictor of current quality. As well, Bordeaux wine is characterized by a number of collective or group reputation indicators. Because these indicators (but not their significance) are often provided on wine labels, information on whether a product belongs to a particular group is frequently available at low cost to consumers.

Although a differentiated product, Bordeaux red wines differ in only a relatively small number of characteristics, in contrast to many consumer products which differ in a large number of dimensions and for which it is much more difficult to obtain a single overall measure of product quality.[4] Bordeaux wine also exhibits wide price variation. In the two years of individual firm data used below, the price per bottle varies from \$8.92 to \$302.56 in 1985 U.S. dollars. Finally, no firm in the Bordeaux wine industry is a large-enough producer to have a significant impact on the market price, a basic assumption of the reputation theories of Klein and Leffler (1981) and Shapiro (1983), for example.

The chapter is organized as follows: The model is outlined in Section 2. In Section 3, the data are described, and in Section 4, the estimation methodology is reviewed. The impact on expected quality and price of the

[3]Jarrell and Peltzman (1985) and Borenstein and Zimmerman (1988) empirically examine issues that are very similar to collective reputation. Jarrell and Peltzman (1985) find that a recall by one U.S. automobile or drug firm has an "externality effect," in that it reduces its U.S. competitors' share value. In contrast, Borenstein and Zimmerman (1988) find that the demand faced by one airline is not affected when another airline has an accident.

[4]Government regulations restrict many of the characteristics of Bordeaux winemaking, including, for example, the region where the grapes are grown, grape varieties used, growing methods, maximum allowable yields, the alcoholic strength of the wine, and the type of bottles used.

individual and collective reputation indicator variables is discussed in Section 5. This section also provides a comparison of the effect on price of expected quality and current quality. Concluding comments are presented in Section 6.

2. The Model

To examine the impact of reputation on price, it is necessary to specify a general model of product price determination. The model used here begins with the standard hedonic approach for differentiated products developed by Rosen (1974). In this model, the equilibrium price of a good reflects the value the market assigns to each of the good's characteristics, where this value is determined by the interaction of consumer bid and firm offer functions. For the case considered here, the equilibrium price is specified to be a function of the following four types of characteristics: the current quality of the good, Q_{it}; the good's expected quality, Q^e_{it}, which depends on reputation; a vector of average group quality or collective reputation indicators, $\mathbf{R}^c_{it}$; and finally, because the product is differentiated, a vector of taste factors, $\mathbf{Z}_i$. Thus, the equation describing the price of good i in period t, P_{it}, takes the form:

$$P_{it}, = P(Q_{it}, Q^e_{it}, \mathbf{R}^c_{it}, \mathbf{Z}_i) + \epsilon_{Pit}, \tag{1}$$

where ϵ_{Pit}, is a mean zero random variable with variance σ^2_P. The partial derivative of this function with respect to each characteristic equals the marginal willingness-to-pay of consumers for that characteristic (Bartik and Smith, 1987).

One of the important attributes of Equation 1 is that it distinguishes between the effects on price of current and expected quality. Expected quality, Q^e_{it}, should have no effect on price if consumers already know actual quality, Q_{it}, because in this case, expected quality does not provide any useful additional information. In contrast, if information on current quality is not available, or is very costly to obtain, Q_{it} will not enter the consumer decision-making process and so cannot affect price. In this case, price will depend only on expected quality and, therefore, on the reputation factors that determine expected quality. Because it includes both Q_{it} and Q^e_{it}, Equation 1 is general enough to allow the data to indicate the extent to which prices are determined by current quality or expected quality and, thereby, does not impose one particular information specification.

The inclusion of the collective reputation indicators ($\mathbf{R}_{it}^{c}$) directly in the price equation allows for the possibility that these indicators may reflect a product characteristic that is valued by consumers independent of its usefulness in predicting quality. This type of effect might occur, for example, if a "snob appeal" is associated with a product from a particular region, of a specific classification, or with a particular type of name. If consumers use collective reputation indicators only to predict firm quality, these indicators will not have a direct impact on price, and the coefficients associated with the elements of $\mathbf{R}_{it}^{c}$ will be insignificant in the estimated price equation.

In order to estimate the price equation, Equation 1, the factors determining expected quality must be specified. Klein and Leffler (1981) and Shapiro (1983) propose that consumers form expectations of the quality of a firm's product based on the firm's reputation for quality when current quality is costly to observe. Reputation, in turn, depends on the quality of the firm's past output. Tirole (1996) suggests that the expected quality of a firm's output may depend on collective reputation, that is, on indicators of the average quality of the goods produced by a group of firms with which the individual firm is identified. Consumers may use collective reputation indicators if information on individual firm reputation is costly to obtain or if the use of these indicators can lead to improved forecasts of current quality even when lagged firm quality information is available. Taking both types of reputation into account, expected quality, Q_{it}^{e}, is defined as the predicted value from the quality forecasting equation:

$$Q_{it} = Q(\mathbf{R}_{it}, \mathbf{R}_{it}^{c}) + \epsilon_{Qit}, \tag{2}$$

where $\mathbf{R}_{it}$ is a vector of variables reflecting an individual firm's reputation for quality, based on the quality of its past output, and ϵ_{Qit}, is a mean zero random variable with variance σ_Q^2. The estimated coefficients associated with $\mathbf{R}_{it}$ and $\mathbf{R}_{it}^{c}$, in Equation 2 will indicate whether information on individual firm reputation or collective reputation (or both) can be used to predict wine quality.

If current quality information is costly to acquire, the reputation indicators, $\mathbf{R}_{it}$ and $\mathbf{R}_{t}^{c}$, working through the expected quality variable in the price equation, could be important determinants of price. The magnitude of the impact of reputation on price will depend on both the ability of reputation to predict quality (the size of the coefficients on the reputation indicators in the quality equation, Equation 2) as well as on the value the market places on this quality prediction (the size of the coefficient on expected quality in the price equation, Equation 1).

3. The Data and Empirical Specification

The relationship between price, quality, and expected quality, where the latter depends on individual firm reputation and collective reputation, can be quantified by jointly estimating the price equation, Equation 1, and the quality equation, Equation 2. Estimation of these two equations requires data on individual product prices (P_{it}), quality (Q_{it}), individual firm reputation ($\mathbf{R}_{it}$), collective reputation ($\mathbf{R}_t^c$), and the other characteristics ($\mathbf{Z}_i$) that may affect the price of the product. The empirical analysis below employs data from the market for Bordeaux red wine because this market has several desirable features that make it particularly appropriate for an analysis of the relationship between price, quality, and reputation. For example, as noted in the introduction, Bordeaux wine has not changed significantly over time and is differentiated in only a small number of dimensions. This facilitates the measurement of the variables that enter the model described in the previous section. As well, the Bordeaux wine market is comprised of many consumers and many firms, none of which is dominant. Furthermore, in contrast to many other products, quality ratings and data on prices and other characteristics are available for a large sample of Bordeaux wines.

Data on the price P and quality Q of individual Bordeaux wines, where P and Q are the empirical counterparts of P_{it} and Q_{it}, are taken from the annual "Bordeaux" issue of the *Wine Spectator*, the world's largest circulation wine magazine, and from the *Wine Spectator*'s buying guide (Shanken 1993).[5] The key advantages of the *Wine Spectator* ranking system (relative to other rankings) are that it includes a large number of different wines, utilizes a finely gradated quality index, provides prices and contemporaneous quality ratings for each wine, and reflects the results of tastings that take place at the same time each year.

The data consist of observations on 151 wines from each of the 1989 and 1990 vintages — 302 observations in all.[6] These two vintages were chosen because they are similar in terms of average price and quality, and as a result, the estimated price and quality equations are less likely to exhibit parameter

[5]Precise definitions of all variables that enter the estimating equations are given in Appendix A. The i and t subscripts have been dropped for convenience where possible. Summary statistics for the data are given in Appendix B.

[6]Every wine listed in the "Bordeaux" issue for which a price is reported and for which two previous annual *Wine Spectator* tastings are available is included in the dataset. The wines of many firms are included for both years, but this is not the case for all the firms in the data set.

instability. The price used is the per-bottle U.S. retail price provided by *Wine Spectator* in its "Bordeaux" issue (converted to constant 1985 dollars).[7]

The quality rating system used by *Wine Spectator* grades wines from 50 (worst) to 100 (best). Quality is assessed in blind tastings, which take into account factors such as a wine's color, aroma, flavor, balance, complexity, and aging potential.[8] Although some wine experts claim that rating wine is an intrinsically subjective process, Robert Parker, the developer of the "100 point" rating system, argues that "wine is no different from any consumer product. There are specific standards of quality that full-time wine professionals recognize" (Robinson 1994, pp. 706–707).[9]

Individual firm reputation, $\mathbf{R}_{it}$, is assumed to be a function of the quality of the firm's past output and depends on both short-term and long-term factors. The short-term reputation of a wine is represented by its quality ratings in the previous two years divided by *Wine Spectator*'s overall quality rating for the corresponding vintage ($Q_{-1}/V_{-1}, Q_{-2}/V_{-2}$). Because the vintage rating is the same for all the wines of a particular vintage year, dividing by vintage quality normalizes for differences across vintages.

As a long-time series of *Wine Spectator* quality ratings is not available, the longer term reputation of each wine is based on a classification of Bordeaux wine producers by Robert Parker (1991). Parker allocates wines to one of five groups based on their quality performance between 1961 and 1990. Membership of individual wines in these groups is represented by five zero-one dummy variables, *R1, R2, R3, R4*, and *R5*, from best to worst, with the base case being those wines that are not of sufficient quality to belong to any of these five groups.

In the Bordeaux wine industry, the most important collective reputation indicators are the government-determined regional designations

[7] *Wine Spectator* calculates prices by surveying a variety of retail price sources. Actual prices could differ from these prices. Note that although their dataset does not include wine, Caves and Greene (1996) obtain very similar results when they use list prices rather than actual transaction prices.

[8] As is the case with many consumer goods, Bordeaux wine is often not consumed at the time of purchase. However, even if consumers intend to let a wine age, they must base their purchase decisions on the quality information currently available.

[9] Quality can be treated as predetermined with respect to price because most of the factors that affect wine quality are exogenous (e.g., weather) or are determined by decisions made by producers years before a wine is released. For example, the producer must decide what types of grapes to grow, the amount of pruning, when to pick the grapes, the type of fermentation tanks to use, the length of time to age the wine in barrels, the quality of the barrels, and when to release the wine.

(appellations)[10] and industry-determined "quality" classifications. Whether a wine is included in a particular designation or classification is generally indicated on the wine's label and so is information easily available to consumers. A zero-one dummy variable is used to represent each of the following ten regional designations: Fronsac and others (*FRONSAC*), Graves (*GRAVES*), Haut-Médoc (*HAUTMEDOC*), Listrac and Moulis (*LISTRAC*), Margaux (*MARGAUX*), Pauillac (*PAUILLAC*) Pomerol (*POMEROL*), St.-Emilion (*STEMILION*), St.-Estèphe (*STESTEPHE*), and St.-Julien (*STJULIEN*), with the remainder of the wines in the dataset being from the rest of the Médoc. Significant coefficients associated with these dummy variables in the quality equation would indicate that they are useful predictors of differences in the quality of the wines from these regions relative to Médoc wines.

Zero-one dummy variables are also used to represent the different gradations in four industry-determined "quality" classifications. The most well known of these is the 1855 classification. Individual wines ranked in this classification belong to one of five groups (from "best" to "worst"): First-Growth (*FIRST*), Second-Growth (*SECOND*), Third-Growth (*THIRD*), Fourth-Growth (*FOURTH*), and Fifth-Growth (*FIFTH*). Dummy variables were also used to represent those St.-Emilion wines that have been classified as either St.-Emilion *Premier Grand Cru Classé* (*SEPGCC*) or St.-Emilion *Grand Cru Classé* (*SEGCQ*)[11] as well as the Graves wines that have been classified as Graves *Cru Classé* (*GRACC*). Finally, three additional dummy variables are used to represent those Bordeaux wines that have been classified as *Cru Grand Bourgeois Exceptionnel* (*CGBE*), *Cru Grand Bourgeois* (*CGB*) or *Cru Bourgeois* (*CB*).[12] Wines that do not belong to any of these classifications form the base case in the estimating equation.

The final two collective reputation indicators that consumers may use to categorize wines are associated with the production of "second" wines.

[10]These regional designations follow the *Appellation d'Origine Controlee* (AOC) system which requires growers to meet certain quality standards, such as the use of certain growing methods and approval of the wine by a tasting panel. Although these regulations are presumably intended to directly maintain wine quality, Molyneux-Berry (1990, p. 11) argues that enforcement of all the AOC regulations is for all practical purposes not possible and "The guarantee of quality today still remains, as it has always done in the past, on the reputations of the grower and the wine merchant involved."

[11]The classification of St.-Emilion wines was first undertaken in 1955. This classification was updated in 1959, 1969, and 1985.

[12]The *Cru Bourgeois* classification was first used in 1932. This classification was updated in 1966 and 1978.

In Bordeaux, firms often produce a "second" wine using grapes that are not good enough for their "first" wine, such as grapes from younger vines. Robinson (1994, p. 861) and Parker (1991, p. 32) argue that this has resulted in a more rigorous selection of grapes and higher quality first wines.[13] The dummy variable *PRODUCESEC* is included in the quality equation to indicate that a wine is the first wine produced by a firm that also produces a second wine. This allows for the possibility that first wines may be superior in quality to otherwise identical wines. The dummy variable *SECWINE* indicates that a wine is a second wine. It is included in the quality equation to determine if, *ceteris paribus*, second wines differ systematically in quality from other wines.

Parker (1991, p. 33) argues that the wine trade has, often misleadingly, promoted second wines as being as good as first wines, but cheaper. If consumers believe this promotion, the prices of second wines should differ, holding everything else constant, from the prices of wines produced by firms with only a single grade of wine. By including the collective reputation variables *SECWINE* and *PRODUCESEC* directly in the price equation, it is possible to determine whether the production of a second wine affects the price of either a firm's first wine or its second wine independent of the impact the production of this second wine may have on expected quality.

The price equation specified in Section 2 above also includes a vector of characteristics ($\mathbf{Z}_i$) which reflect variations in taste across the differentiated product. Because the types of grapes used in a wine have a major impact on its taste and style, grape type may be an important determinant of price. As a result, the estimated price equation includes the percentages used by each producer of four of the five grape varieties that are allowed by Bordeaux production regulations (Cabernet Sauvignon [*CABSAUV*], Cabernet Franc [*CABFRANC*], Malbec [*MALBEC*] and Petit Verdot [*VERDOT*]).[14] As the grape varieties chosen by a grower depend largely on soil type, the inclusion of grape variety data in the price equation also controls for differences in land characteristics that could affect the style and taste of the wine produced.

The dataset includes data from both the 1989 and 1990 vintages, and as a consequence, a dummy variable for 1990 (*D1990*) is included in both the price and quality equations. This variable is intended to capture the influence

[13]It is also possible that, by producing a second wine, firms have not changed their grape selection procedure, but have simply chosen to market wine made from lower quality grapes rather than sell these grapes to producers of generic Bordeaux wine.

[14]The percentage of Merlot used by producers forms the base case and so is not included in the estimating equation.

of factors that differ across the two vintages, such as consumer incomes and the price of substitutes.

4. Empirical Methodology

Equations 1 and 2 specify the types of explanatory variables that should appear in the price and quality equations but do not restrict the functional form of these equations. Five types of linear-in-parameters functional forms were considered for each equation: linear, semi-log, log-linear,[15] reciprocal, and reciprocal square root. The evidence given in Appendix C shows that the linear form provides a reasonable description of the data for the quality equation while the reciprocal square root model is the most appropriate specification for the price equation. The estimates reported below employ these two functional forms.

As noted in Section 2 above, the expected quality variable that enters the price equation, Equation 1, is the predicted value from the quality forecasting equation, Equation 2. To obtain asymptotically efficient estimates of the parameters and correct estimates of the standard errors, the estimation technique used must take account of the presence of this generated regressor in the price equation.[16] This is done by estimating the two equations of the model jointly using the methodology described in Proposition 3.5 of Pagan (1986, p. 528).[17] Iteration of this procedure maximizes the concentrated likelihood function[18]:

$$\log L = \text{constant} - (n/2)\log|\Sigma|,$$

[15]In the log-linear specification, only those explanatory variables that are always strictly positive were transformed.

[16]Some of the difficulties associated with estimating generated regressor models are discussed in Pagan (1984, 1986) and Oxley and McAleer (1993).

[17]This involves the following procedure: The quality equation is estimated and then the price equation is estimated with the predicted value from the quality equation substituted for the expected quality variable in the price equation. Using these parameter estimates, the estimated residuals are calculated for both the quality and price equations. The derivatives of each equation with respect to all the parameters in the model are then calculated for every observation in the data set, and the residuals and derivatives for the two equations are stacked. Finally, a weighted regression of the stacked residuals on the stacked derivatives is undertaken and the estimated parameters from this regression are used to update the initial parameter estimates.

[18]Although iteration is not necessary to obtain asymptotically efficient estimates, it does ensure that the likelihood function is maximized. Convergence took less than 10 iterations in all cases. Convergence was deemed to have occurred if the value of the likelihood function changed by less than 0.00125% between iterations and the largest gradient associated with any of the parameters was equal to zero in its fourth decimal place.

where Σ is the variance-covariance matrix of the two equations, and n is the number of observations.[19] The variance-covariance matrix of the estimated parameters is given by:

$$\frac{2n}{2n-k}\left[\sum_{t=1}^{n}\Omega_t\Sigma^{-1}\Omega_t'\right]^{-1}$$

where k is the total number of parameters in the two equations, Ω_t, is a $k \times 2$ matrix of the partial derivatives of the price and quality equations with respect to each of the k parameters, and both Ω_t and Σ are evaluated at the maximum-likelihood parameter estimates.[20]

5. Estimation Results

5.1. *Estimates of the price and quality equations*

Estimates of the parameters of the price and quality equations are presented in Table 1.[21] For the quality equation, six of the seven individual firm reputation indicators are significant at a 95% confidence level (the seventh is significant at 90%), seven of the 11 "quality" classification variables are significant relative to the base case wine (an unclassified Medoc), as are seven of the ten government-determined regional classification variables. These results suggest that both individual and collective reputation indicator variables are important signals of differences in current product quality across wines.

The estimated coefficients associated with the quality and expected quality variables in the price equation are both significant, and their signs imply that both variables have a positive impact on price. However, the coefficient on expected quality, Q^e, is over 17 times larger than that on current quality, indicating a much greater role for expected quality than actual quality in

[19]In order to identify the parameters associated with Q and Q^e in the price equation, it is necessary to restrict Σ to be diagonal. That there is no contemporaneous correlation across equations is a standard assumption when contemporaneous actual and expected values from a forecasting equation are incorporated in a second equation (see Mishkin 1982; Abel and Mishkin 1983; Hoffman, Low, and Schlagenhauf 1984). Both Abel and Mishkin (1983) and Hoffman, Low, and Schlagenhauf (1984) provide evidence that suggests that imposing this restriction will not affect the results significantly even if the restriction is not true.

[20]This form of the variance-covariance matrix follows Pagan (1986, p. 528) and Davidson and MacKinnon (1993, p. 319).

[21]Because the dependent variable in the reciprocal square root functional form of the price equation is $(P_{it})^{-0.5}$, a negative coefficient associated with an explanatory variable implies a positive effect on price.

Table 1. Quality and Price Equation — Parameter Estimates

	Dependent variable[a]			
Explanatory variable	Quality equation Q		Price equation $P^{-0.5}$	
Q^e			−0.0209	(7.81)***
Q			−0.0012	(3.14)***
Firm Reputation Indicator				
Q_{-1}/V_{-1}	2.488	(1.89)**		
Q_{-2}/V_{-2}	2.293	(1.99)***		
R1	4.429	(7.36)***		
R2	2.919	(6.76)***		
R3	1.959	(6.26)***		
R4	1.558	(4.73)***		
R5	1.081	(5.08)***		
Collective Reputation Indicator				
(a) Quality Classification				
FIRST	2.336	(4.47)***		
SECOND	0.8787	(2.59)***		
THIRD	0.8266	(2.58)***		
FOURTH	0.7355	(1.99)***		
FIFTH	0.8794	(2.77)***		
CGBE	0.5515	(1.60)*		
CGB	0.1198	(0.38)		
CB	0.5455	(1.58)*		
SEPGCC	1.211	(2.51)***		
SEGCC	0.4129	(0.93)		
GRACC	1.500	(3.85)***		
(b) Regional Classification				
FRONSAC	−0.2127	(0.14)	−0.0379	(1.11)
GRAVES	4.248	(3.27)***	0.0528	(1.64)**
LISTRAC	1.520	(1.05)	−0.0066	(0.21)
MARGAUX	2.818	(2.22)***	0.0042	(0.14)
PAUILLAC	4.674	(3.52)***	0.0536	(1.56)*
POMEROL	5.352	(4.05)***	0.0102	(0.29)
STEMILION	3.682	(2.84)***	0.0118	(0.38)
STESTEPHE	4.678	(3.49)***	0.0586	(1.76)**
STJULIEN	4.077	(3.05)***	0.0434	(1.32)
HAUTMEDOC	0.5684	(0.46)	−0.0236	(0.87)
(c) Second Wine Indicator				
SECWINE	0.0913	(0.08)	−0.0087	(0.36)
PRODUCESEC	−0.1911	(0.41)	0.0036	(0.36)
Grape Variety				
CABFRANC			−0.0004	(2.81)***
CABSAUV			−0.0002	(1.44)

(*Continued*)

Table 1. (*Continued*)

Explanatory variable	Dependent variable[a] Quality equation Q	Price equation $P^{-0.5}$
MALBEC		−0.0002 (0.26)
VERDOT		−0.0008 (1.40)
Other Variables		
D1990	0.0659 (0.16)	0.0050 (0.60)
Constant	79.87 (40.0)***	2.193 (9.76)***
R^2	0.464	0.877

Notes: [a]The number in parentheses beside each estimated coefficient is the absolute value of the t-statistic. The estimated coefficient associated with the explanatory variable is significant at ***95%, **90%, and *85%.

price determination. This suggests that consumers rely heavily on reputation when making consumption choices.

Significant coefficients associated with the collective reputation variables in the price equation would imply that these variables have an impact on price that is independent of their ability to predict quality. This would occur if, for example, "snob appeal" caused consumers to have a nonquality-related preference for a good with a particular name, region of origin, or classification. The hypothesis that the 11 industry-determined classification variables do *not* enter the price equation directly cannot be rejected using a 95% confidence interval.[22] This result indicates that the industry-created classifications are valued by consumers only as signals of product quality and, therefore, yield a benefit to wine producers only to the extent that they provide consumers with quality information.

A similar test indicates, in contrast, that the government-designated regional variables have a statistically significant joint impact on price that is independent of their impact on expected quality.[23] Although none of the

[22]The likelihood ratio test statistic, distributed as a χ^2, is 8.44. The 95% critical value with 11 degrees of freedom is 19.68. The hypothesis that the coefficients on the five dummy variables associated with the 1855 classification are zero, while restricting the coefficients on the other classification dummy variables in the price equation to be zero, could also not be rejected. For this case, the test statistic is 5.94 and the 95% critical value is 11.07 with five degrees of freedom.

[23]The hypothesis that the government-designated regional appellation variables do not have a direct effect on price (in addition to their effect through expected quality) is rejected at the 95% confidence level. The likelihood ratio test statistic is 35.78. The 95% critical value for a χ^2 test statistic with 10 degrees of freedom is 18.31. The appellation variables

individual coefficients on the regional variables is significant at the 95% level, the coefficients associated with the Graves, Pauillac, and St. Estéphe variables are significant at either 90 or 85%.[24] The estimated coefficients associated with these three regional dummy variables indicate that wines from these regions obtain a lower price than an otherwise equivalent (from a quality and reputation perspective) Médoc wine.[25]

As noted above, it has been suggested that the production of a "second" wine may have both price and quality implications. The results in the first column of Table 1 indicate that the qualities of both first and second wines are insignificantly different from wines produced by firms that make only one wine (the coefficients on *SECWINE* and *PRODUCESEC* in the quality equation are both insignificant). As well, the insignificant coefficients on both *SECWINE* and *PRODUCESEC* in the price equation indicate that consumers will not pay a premium for a wine just because it is a first or second wine.[26]

5.2. *The quantitative impact of quality, expected quality, and reputation on price*

In order to provide some perspective on the size of the coefficients in Table 1, Table 2 presents the estimated marginal impact on price, in dollar terms, of each variable in the quality and price equations. The first column of figures in Table 2 gives the dollar change in *price* due to a one-unit increase in

should not reflect differences in wine styles across regions because these differences should be captured by the grape variety variables.

[24] A test of the hypothesis that the coefficients on all the regional variables in the price equation are zero, except those associated with these three variables, yields a likelihood ratio test statistic of 14.43. With seven degrees of freedom, the 95% χ^2 critical value is 14.07, and the 99% critical value is 18.48.

[25] A possible explanation for this result is that the names of these three appellations may not be attractive to consumers in the U.S. market. A non-French-speaking consumer could find "Graves" to be an unappealing name (in French "graves" means "gravelly terrain") and "Pauillac" and "St. Estéphe" more difficult to pronounce than the other appellation names. Berger (1994) argues that the price of a Sauvignon Blanc wine is typically lower than a comparable Chardonnay because "Chardonnay is easier to pronounce than Sauvignon Blanc." Kramer (1994) predicts that a wine with "a pronounceable French name" will be more successful in the U.S. market. Thus, rather than acting only as a signal of quality, the appellation names themselves may be viewed as a characteristic which yields positive or negative value to consumers.

[26] One reason why these variables do not have a significant impact on price may be that the average consumer is unaware that a wine is a first or second wine because this information is typically not included on a wine's label.

Table 2. Real Dollar Marginal Effects on Price[a]

Explanatory variable	Quality equation variables	Price equation variables
Q^e		4.91***
Q		0.24***
Firm Reputation Indicator		
Q_{-1}	0.11**	
Q_{-2}	0.12***	
R1	20.40***	
R2	10.24***	
R3	5.93***	
R4	4.45***	
R5	2.89***	
Collective Reputation Indicator		
(a) Quality Classification		
FIRST	13.79***	
SECOND	4.02***	
THIRD	3.75***	
FOURTH	3.29***	
FIFTH	4.02***	
CGBE	2.40*	
CGB	0.49	
CB	2.37*	
SEPGCC	5.85***	
SEGCC	1.76	
GRACC	7.60***	
(b) Regional Classification		
FRONSAC	−0.29	2.96
GRAVES	10.08***	−7.14**
LISTRAC	2.52	0.64
MARGAUX	5.48***	−0.53
PAUILLAC	11.84***	−8.07*
POMEROL	15.15***	−2.45
STEMILION	8.04***	−1.73
STESTEPHE	11.86***	−8.60**
STJULIEN	9.43***	−5.91
HAUTMEDOC	0.85	2.02
(c) Second Wine Indicator		
SECWINE	0.39	1.94
PRODUCESEC	−0.79	−0.67

(*Continued*)

Table 2. (*Continued*)

Explanatory variable	Quality equation variables	Price equation variables
Grape Variety		
CABFRANC		0.08***
CABSAUV		0.04
MALBEC		0.05
VERDOT		0.17
Year Dummy Variable for 1990		
D1990	0.30	−1.07

Notes: [a]The estimated coefficient associated with the explanatory variable is significant at ***95%, **90%, and *85%.

each variable that enters the quality equation (or the impact of each dummy variable relative to the base case). The magnitude of this effect depends both on the ability of the variable in question to forecast quality as well as on the impact of expected quality on price. The second column of dollar values in Table 2 represents the marginal impact on price of the variables that enter the price equation directly.[27]

The results presented in Table 2 make clear the large relative importance of reputation effects in price determination. A one-unit increase in expected quality raises the price per bottle by \$4.91, an amount equal to 17% of the price of the average bottle of wine in the dataset (\$29.51). In contrast, a one-unit increase in actual quality raises the price per bottle by only \$0.24, an increase which is one-twentieth as large. Furthermore, although both short-term and long-term individual firm reputation variables have a significant impact on quality, the impact on price of the long-term reputation variables is far greater in magnitude. For example, a one unit increase in the last period's quality (Q_{-1}) increases the current price by only \$0.11. However, a wine with a quality rating of *R5*, based on its performance from 1961 to 1990 will earn, on average, \$2.89 more than the base case wine. Similarly, wines rated from *R4* to *R1* achieve premiums of from \$4.45 to \$20.40. Because a

[27]The marginal dollar effect on price of variable X_i, is calculated as:

$$\Delta P = \left(\bar{\Pi} + \beta_i\right)^{-2} - \bar{\Pi}^{-2},$$

where β_i is the estimated coefficient associated with variable X_i, Π is the dependent variable ($P^{-1/2}$), P is the price, and $\bar{\Pi}$ is the mean of Π when X_i is a continuous variable and the mean of Π for the observations associated with the relevant base case when X_i is a dummy variable (the observations for which the dummy variable equals zero).

10-point change in quality would be relatively large, the long-term reputation effects are quantitatively much more important than the short-term reputation effects in price determination. These results suggest that consumers are willing to pay considerably more for a wine with a long high-quality track record and that they do not view a recent change in quality to be as valuable an indicator of a product's current quality.

The variables that act as signals of collective reputation are also shown in Table 2 to have a large quantitative impact on price. For example, a wine classified in 1855 as a First-Growth earns, on average, approximately $14 more than the base case wine, whereas a wine classified as Second-Growth to Fifth-Growth earns approximately $4 more than an unclassified wine.[28] Two of the other six classification variables also have large and significant effects on price as do seven of the ten regional variables.

The evidence presented in Table 2 confirms that consumers are willing to pay a significant premium for wines with certain collective reputation signals and that, therefore, they value these variables as predictors of individual wine quality. Given the large number of Bordeaux wine producers, it is not surprising that consumers use signals of product quality other than individual firm reputation to predict current quality and that these collective reputation indicators have an important impact on price.

5.3. *Some indicators of the robustness of the estimates*

A number of tests were carried out to assess the robustness of the estimates. The appropriateness of the functional form used for the estimated price equation could not be rejected at a 95% significance level using a test very similar to that of the standard RESET test.[29] Following Breusch and

[28]Di Vittorio and Ginsburgh (1994) and Ginsburgh, Monzak, and Monzak (1992) also find the 1855 classification to be an important determinant of wine prices. However, their estimates do not reveal whether the 1855 classification is a predictor of wine quality.

Given the estimated standard errors in Table 1, the Second-Growth to Fifth-Growth wines all attain the same quality premium using a 95% confidence level. This finding is inconsistent with a declining quality scale, which the 1855 classification was intended to be. However, except for First-Growth wines, wine labels generally only indicate that a wine was classified in 1855, not its level of classification. As a consequence, wine purchasers do not have easily available information that they can use to differentiate Second-Growth to Fifth-Growth wines.

[29]This test involved using the estimated maximum-likelihood parameters to form the predicted value of the dependent variable in the price equation. This predicted value was squared and this squared value added to the price equation as an additional explanatory variable. The model was estimated exactly as before and iterated until the gradients

Pagan (1979), the price and quality equations were also examined for the presence of heteroscedasticity. The test results indicate that the hypothesis of homoscedasticity cannot be rejected at the 95% level for the quality equation and cannot be rejected at the 99% level for the price equation.[30] Although this test uses a single equation technique, it provides some indication that heteroscedasticity is not a serious problem.

The joint nonlinear estimation of the quality and price equations assumes that the parameters in the quality equation are the same as the parameters that determine expected quality in the price equation. A test of these cross-equation restrictions indicates that the joint restrictions could not be rejected at a 95% confidence level.[31] This suggests that the expectations formation mechanism used is not inconsistent with the data.

Although the insignificance of the coefficient associated with *D1990* suggests that aggregation across time is not inappropriate, the restrictions implied by combining data from the 1989 and 1990 vintages were tested using a likelihood ratio test for the equality of all the parameters across the two years. This test could not reject the parameter constancy restrictions and, thus, suggests that aggregating the data for these two years did not bias the estimates.[32]

During estimation, the predicted values of the price variable were not restricted to be positive (even though only a positive price is reasonable), nor were the predicted values of the quality variable restricted to be between 50 and 100 (the allowable range of values on the "100-point" scale). Although these restrictions were not imposed, the estimated predicted values of both the price and quality variables were within the allowable ranges for every observation in the data set.

---

were zero. The asymptotic t-statistic on the square of the dependent variable in the price equation was 1.32.

[30]The heteroscedasticity test was undertaken by regressing the squared errors from each equation on the explanatory variables that enter each equation (either directly or indirectly) using a simple linear specification. The quality equation regression included 31 regressors in addition to a constant and the price equation included 36. The Lagrange multiplier (LM) test statistics are 33.15 for the quality equation and 52.64 for the price equation. The 95% critical value for a χ^2 statistic with 31 degrees of freedom, as in the quality equation regression, is 44.97. The 95% critical value for a χ^2 statistic with 36 degrees of freedom, as in the price equation regression, is 50.96, and the critical value at 99% is 58.57.

[31]The likelihood ratio test statistic is 17.08. The 95% critical value for the χ^2 distribution with 17 degrees of freedom is 27.59.

[32]The calculated test statistic is 49.40, and the 95% critical value with 50 parameter restrictions is 67.4.

The R^2 statistic in the price equation is 0.877, whereas in the quality equation, it is 0.464. Given that the analysis uses cross-section data, the proportion of the variance in quality explained by the estimated model is of reasonable size whereas the explained proportion of the price variance is quite large.[33]

6. Concluding Comments

The analysis above adds to the small literature that examines the empirical importance of reputation effects. The results indicate that the price of the differentiated product examined, Bordeaux wine, depends significantly on both expected quality (reputation) and current quality. However, the marginal impact of expected quality on price is approximately 20 times greater than that of current quality. This result is consistent with a world in which consumers have incomplete information on product quality, perhaps due to the costs of information gathering. Given this incomplete information on quality, consumers rely heavily on both individual firm reputation — based on the past quality of the firm's output — and collective (or group) reputation indicators — characteristics that allow consumers to segment firms into groups with differing average qualities — to predict current product quality, as in the theoretical models of individual firm reputation proposed by Klein and Leffler (1981), Shapiro (1983), and Allen (1984) and the collective reputation model of Tirole (1996).

The empirical evidence further indicates that consumers consider a long-term reputation for quality to be a better signal of current quality than more recent quality movements. This implies that it may take considerable time for a firm to establish a reputation for high quality that would yield a significant price premium.

The results also show that collective reputation indicators play a significant role in price determination principally through their impact on expected quality. Although some of the government-determined regional designations (appellations) have a weak direct effect on price, this effect is dominated by the role of these collective reputation variables as quality predictors. The industry-determined "quality" classification variables, such as the well-known 1855 classification, are only significant determinants of price to the extent that they are good predictors of quality. Because they do not have an

[33]Given the complexity of the estimation procedure, R^2 is defined here as the ratio of the explained sum of squares to the total sum of squares for each equation.

independent effect on price, they are useful to firms only to the extent that they reflect quality differences.

Akerlof (1970) shows that in a market where consumers lack information on product quality, a firm cannot charge a premium for a high-quality product, and thus in equilibrium, only low-quality products ("lemons") are traded. The existence of quality classifications and other collective reputation indicators that are good predictors of quality, and which consumers use and value, may help higher quality firms differentiate their product from the output of other firms. As a result, collective reputation indicators may be of practical importance to firms and may lead to the production of a wider quality range of goods.

Although the empirical evidence indicates that reputation effects are large in magnitude, current quality also has a significant, although small, impact on price. One explanation for why both current quality and reputation are significant determinants of price may be that there are different types of agents in the market, some of whom are better informed about current quality than others.[34] Alternatively, consumers may view observable quality ratings as noisy indicators of actual quality, so they may rely to a greater extent on the accumulated evidence embodied in reputation.[35] The significance of both current and expected quality in the price equation indicates that it is important to not restrict the model to one particular information specification.

The analysis described above suggests a number of avenues for future research. Estimates derived using alternative price and quality data for wine, as well as for other products, would provide evidence of the robustness of the results. It may also be possible to examine dynamic (learning) effects by using a time series of price data. A further topic for future research is to determine whether there is a systematic difference between the impact of collective reputation signals that are promoted by the industry (such as the quality classifications used above), firm-chosen (such as whether the firm produces a second wine), government-regulated (such as the regional classifications), or exogenous (such as the nationality of a producer).

One of the more puzzling aspects of the results presented above is the finding that the "quality" classification schemes are such useful predictors of quality. The expectation of the periodic reevaluation of *Crus Bourgeois* and St. Emilion wines could provide a possible enforcement mechanism for

[34] Cooper and Ross (1984) present a model with informed and uninformed consumers.
[35] This explanation was suggested by a referee.

the wines that fall into these categories. However, the 1855 classification, empirically a very successful predictor of quality, has never been updated, with the exception of the 1973 elevation of Mouton-Rothschild from Second-Growth to First-Growth status. A classification system with no quality control mechanism would be expected to create an incentive for firms to "free ride" on the quality reputation of the group. However, after 140 years, the premiums accorded wines that were classified in 1855 do not seem to have been dissipated by free riding. The longevity of the value of this classification suggests that firms have found a mechanism to successfully enforce quality standards among the groups' members. More research is needed to expand our understanding of this method of group quality enforcement.

Acknowledgments

The authors thank Robin Lindsey, Douglas S. West, and two anonymous referees for comments on an earlier draft as well as William M. Carter for help in acquiring some of the data. Daisy Ho and Jessica Xu provided efficient research assistance.

References

Abel, A., and Mishkin, F. (1983). An integrated view of tests of rationality, market efficiency and the short-run neutrality of monetary policy. *Journal of Monetary Economics*, 11, 3–24.

Akerlof, G.A. (1970). The market for "lemons": Quality uncertainty and the market mechanism. *Quarterly Journal of Economics*, 84, 488–500.

Allen, F. (1984). Reputation and product quality. *Rand Journal of Economics*, 15, 311–327.

Bartik, T.J., and Smith, V.K. (1987). Urban amenities and public policy. In *Handbook of Regional and Urban Economics*, volume 2, edited by E.S. Mills. Amsterdam: North-Holland, pp. 1207–1254.

Berger, D. (1994). Sauvignon blanc sales a disaster. *Los Angeles Times* reprinted in *The Edmonton Journal*, 12 October, p. D8.

Borenstein, S., and Zimmerman, M.B. (1988). Market incentives for safe commercial airline operation. *American Economic Review*, 78, 913–935.

Breusch, T.S., and Pagan, A.R. (1979). A simple test for heteroscedasticity and random coefficient variation. *Econometrica*, 47, 1287–1294.

Caves, R.E., and Greene, D.P. (1996). Brands' quality levels, prices, and advertising outlays: Empirical evidence on signals and information costs. *International Journal of Industrial Organization*, 14, 29–52.

Combris, P., Lecocq, S., and Visser, M. (1997). Estimation of a hedonic price equation for Bordeaux wine: Does quality matter? *Economic Journal*, 107, 390–402.

Cooper, R., and Ross, T.W. (1984). Prices, product qualities and asymmetric information: The competitive case. *Review of Economic Studies*, 51, 197–207.

Davidson, R., and MacKinnon, J.G. (1993). *Estimation and Inference in Econometrics*. New York: Oxford University Press.

Di Vittorio, A., and Ginsburgh, V. (1994). *Red Wines of Médoc: Vintages from 1949 to 1989 at Christie's Auctions.* Université Libre de Bruxelles. Mimeo.

Geistfeld, L.V. (1988). The price quality relationship: The evidence we have, the evidence we need. In *The Frontier of Research in the Consumer Interest*, edited by E.S. Maynes and the ACCI Research Committee. Columbia, MO: American Council on Consumer Interests, pp. 143–172.

Ginsburgh, V., Monzak, M., and Monzak, A. (1992). *Red Wines of Médoc: What is Wine Tasting Worth?* Université Libre de Bruxelles. Mimeo.

Gorton, G. (1996). Reputation formation in early bank note markets. *Journal of Political Economy*, 104, 46–97.

Hoffman, D.L., Low, S.A., and Schlagenhauf, D.E. (1984). Tests of rationality, neutrality and market efficiency. *Journal of Monetary Economics*, 14, 339–363.

Jarrell, G., and Peltzman, S. (1985). The impact of product recalls on the wealth of sellers. *Journal of Political Economy*, 93, 512–536.

Karpoff, J.M., and Lott, J.R. (1993). The reputational penalty firms bear from committing criminal fraud. *Journal of Law and Economics*, 36, 757–802.

Klein, B., and Leffler, K.B. (1981). The role of market forces in assuring contractual performance. *Journal of Political Economy*, 89, 615–641.

Kramer, M. (1994). Pinot Gris: California's next big white. *Wine Spectator*, 30 September, 19:24.

Landon, S., and Smith, C.E. (1997). The use of quality and reputation indicators by consumers: The case of Bordeaux wine. *Journal of Consumer Policy*, 20, 289–323.

MacKinnon, J.G., White, H., and Davidson, R. (1983). Tests for model specification in the presence of alternative hypotheses: Some further results. *Journal of Econometrics*, 21, 53–70.

Mishkin, F. (1982). Does anticipated monetary policy matter? An economic investigation. *Journal of Political Economy*, 90, 22–51.

Molyneux-Berry, D. (1990). *The Sotheby's Guide to Classic Wines and Their Labels.* New York: Ballantine Books.

Nerlove, M. (1995). Hedonic price functions and the measurement of preferences: The case of Swedish wine consumers. *European Economic Review*, 39, 1697–1716.

Oxley, L., and McAleer, M. (1993). Econometric issues in macroeconomic models with generated regressors. *Journal of Economic Surveys*, 7, 1–40.

Pagan, A. (1984). Econometric issues in the analysis of regressions with generated regressors. *International Economic Review*, 25, 221–247.

Pagan, A. (1986). Two stage and related estimators and their applications. *The Review of Economic Studies*, 53, 517–538.

Parker, R.M. (1991). *Bordeaux.* New York: Simon & Schuster.

Robinson, J. (1994). *The Oxford Companion to Wine.* Oxford: Oxford University Press.

Rosen, S. (1974). Hedonic prices and implicit markets: Product differentiation in pure competition. *Journal of Political Economy*, 82, 34–55.

Shanken, M., editor. (1993). *The Wine Spectator's Ultimate Guide to Buying Wine 1994 Edition.* New York: Wine Spectator Press.

Shapiro, C. (1983). Premiums for high quality products as returns to reputations. *Quarterly Journal of Economics*, 98, 659–679.

Tirole, J. (1996). A theory of collective reputations (with applications to the persistence of corruption and to firm quality). *Review of Economic Studies*, 63, 1–22.

Zeithaml, V.A. (1988). Consumer perceptions of price, quality and value: A means-end model and synthesis of evidence. *Journal of Marketing*, 53, 2–22.

Appendix A: Variable Definitions and Data Sources

CABFRANC A wine producer's average percentage of the Cabernet Franc grape variety. Source: Parker (1991) except for a small number of wines not included in Parker for which data from Molyneux-Berry (1990) were used. Second labels were assumed to have the same grape composition as first labels.

CABSAUV Average percentage of grapes in the wine which are of the Cabernet Sauvignon variety. Source is the same as for *CABFRANC*.

CB A dummy variable which equals one if the wine was classified as a *Cru Bourgeois* in the 1978 Médoc classification and zero otherwise. Source: Parker (1991, pp. 930–931).

CGB A dummy variable which equals one if the wine was classified as a *Cru Grand Bourgeois* in the 1978 Médoc classification and zero otherwise. Source: Parker (1991, pp. 929–930).

CGBE A dummy variable which equals one if the wine was classified as a *Cru Grand Bourgeois Exceptionnel* in the 1978 Médoc classification and zero otherwise. Source: Parker (1991, p. 929).

D1990 A dummy variable which equals one if the wine is from the 1990 vintage and zero otherwise.

FIFTH A dummy variable which equals one if the wine was classified as a Fifth-Growth in the classification of 1855 and zero otherwise. Source: Parker (1991, p. 925).

FIRST A dummy variable which equals one if the wine was classified as a First-Growth in the classification of 1855 and zero otherwise. Source: Parker (1991, p. 924).

FOURTH A dummy variable which equals one if the wine was classified as a Fourth-Growth in the classification of 1855 and zero otherwise. Source: Parker (1991, p. 925).

FRONSAC A dummy variable which equals one if the wine has a Fronsac or "other" appellation and zero otherwise. "Other" includes wine producers from outside the other appellations specified or who combine grapes from more than one appellation and therefore have a Bordeaux designation only. Source is the same as for *Q*.

GRACC A dummy variable which equals one if the wine was classified *Cru Classé* in the 1959 Graves classification and zero otherwise. Chateau Haut-Brion was included in the First-Growth category and not the Graves *Cru Classé* category. It is the only wine that is recognized in two categories. Source: Parker (1991, p. 926).

GRAVES A dummy variable which equals one if the wine has a Graves appellation and zero otherwise. Source is the same as for Q.

HAUTMEDOC A dummy variable which equals one if the wine has an Haut-Medoc appellation and zero otherwise. Source is the same as for Q.

LISTRAC A dummy variable which equals one if the wine has a Listrac or Moulis appellation and zero otherwise. Source is the same as for Q.

MALBEC Average percentage of grapes in the wine of the Malbec variety. Source is the same as for *CABFRANC*.

MARGAUX A dummy variable which equals one if the wine has a Margaux designation and zero otherwise. Source is the same as for Q.

P The price per bottle of wine in 1985 U.S. dollars. The source of the nominal prices is the same as for Q.The deflator is the quarterly average of the U.S. CPI in the first quarter of the year in which the wine is released. This price index is reported in the International Monetary Fund's *International Financial Statistics*, 1994, p. 114.

PAUILLAC A dummy variable which equals one if the wine has a Pauillac designation and zero otherwise. Source is the same as for Q.

POMEROL A dummy variable which equals one if the wine has a Pomerol designation and zero otherwise. Source is the same as for Q.

PRODUCESEC A dummy variable which equals one if the wine is the first wine of a producer that also produces a second wine and zero otherwise. Source: Parker (1991) except for a small number of wines not included in Parker for which data from Molyneux-Berry (1990) were used.

Q Quality measure. Source for 1989: Rating 1989 Bordeaux Reds. In *Wine Spectator*, volume XVI, no. 21, 15 March 1992, pp. 26–32. Source for 1990: Rating Bordeaux's

Generous '90s. In *Wine Spectator*, volume XVII, no. 22, 31 March 1993, pp. 30–39.

Q_1 Lagged quality. Source is the same as for Q; '88 Bordeaux Tasting Notes. In *Wine Spectator*, volume XVI, no. 2, 30 April 1991, pp. 33–43; Shanken (1993).

Q_2 Twice-lagged quality. Source is the same as for Q; Tasting the 87 Bordeaux. In *Wine Spectator,* volume XV, no. 3, 15 May 1990, pp. 46–49; Shanken (1993).

R1 A dummy variable which equals one if a wine producer is included in Parker's list of "First-Growths" and zero otherwise. Source: Parker (1991, p. 932).

R2 A dummy variable which equals one if a wine producer is included in Parker's list of "Second-Growths" and zero otherwise. Source: Parker (1991, p. 933).

R3 A dummy variable which equals one if a wine producer is included in Parker's list of "Third-Growths" and zero otherwise. Source: Parker (1991, p. 933).

R4 A dummy variable which equals one if a wine producer is included in Parker's list of "Fourth-Growths" and zero otherwise. Source: Parker (1991, p. 933).

R5 A dummy variable which equals one if a wine producer is included in Parker's list of "Fifth-Growths" and zero otherwise. Source: Parker (1991, pp. 933–934).

SECOND A dummy variable which equals one if the wine was classified as a Second-Growth in the official classification of 1855 and zero otherwise. Source: Parker (1991, p. 924).

SECWINE A dummy variable which equals one if the wine is a second wine and zero otherwise. Source is the same as for *PRODUCESEC.*

SEGCC A dummy variable which equals one if the wine was classified as a *Grand Cru Classé* in the 1985 St. Emilion classification and zero otherwise. Source: Parker (1991, pp. 928–929).

SEPGCC A dummy variable which equals one if the wine was classified as a *Premier Grand Cru Classé* in the 1985 St. Emilion classification and zero otherwise. Source: Parker (1991, p. 928).

STEMILION A dummy variable which equals one if the wine has a St. Emilion designation and zero otherwise. Source is the same as for Q.

STESTEPHE A dummy variable which equals one if the wine has a St. Estèphe designation and zero otherwise. Source is the same as for Q.

STJULIEN A dummy variable which equals one if the wine has a St. Julien designation and zero otherwise. Source is the same as for Q.

THIRD A dummy variable which equals one if the wine was classified as a Third-Growth in the official classification of 1855 and zero otherwise. Source: Parker (1991, pp. 924–925).

V_{-1}, V_{-2} The average quality of the previous vintage and of the vintage two years before, respectively, in Bordeaux. Source: Rating Bordeaux Vintages 1961–1991. In *Wine Spectator*, volume 18, no. 21, 31 March 1994, p. 35.

VERDOT Average percentage of grapes in the wine which are of the Petit Verdot variety. Source is the same as for *CABFRANC*.

Appendix B: Data Summary Statistics

Variable	Mean[a]	Minimum	Maximum
Q	89.82	75	100
Q_{-1}	88.34	55	100
Q_{-2}	83.05	65	100
R1	0.106 (32)	0	1
R2	0.103 (31)	0	1
R3	0.146 (44)	0	1
R4	0.066 (20)	0	1
R5	0.235 (71)	0	1
Not *Rl-R5*[b]	0.344 (104)		
FIRST	0.033 (10)	0	1
SECOND	0.073 (22)	0	1
THIRD	0.063 (19)	0	1
FOURTH	0.043 (13)	0	1
FIFTH	0.079 (24)	0	1
CGBE	0.066 (20)	0	1
CGB	0.086 (26)	0	
CB	0.043 (13)	0	
SEPGCC	0.066 (20)	0	
SEGCC	0.076 (23)	0	
GRACC	0.073 (22)	0	
Unclassified[b]	0.298 (90)		
FRONSAC	0.033 (10)	0	

(*Continued*)

(*Continued*)

Variable	Mean[a]	Minimum	Maximum
GRAVES	0.116 (35)	0	
LISTRAC	0.043 (13)	0	
MARGAUX	0.126 (38)	0	
PAUILLAC	0.116 (35)	0	
POMEROL	0.109 (33)	0	
STEMILION	0.162 (49)	0	
STESTEPHE	0.073 (22)	0	
STJULIEN	0.086 (26)	0	
HAUTMEDOC	0.106 (32)	0	
MEDOC[b]	0.030 (9)		
CABFRANC	12.42	0	66
CABSAUV	44.19	0	85
MALBEC	0.30	0	10
VERDOT	1.43	0	15
Merlot[b]	41.66	8.0	100
SECWINE	0.036 (11)	0	1
PRODUCESEC	0.589 (178)	0	1
No *SECWINE*	0.374 (113)		
V_{-1}	95	92	98
V_{-2}	82.5	73	92
P	29.51	8.92	302.56

Notes: [a]The numbers in parentheses give the number of observations in the sample for which a dummy variable equals one. The total number of observations is 302.
[b] These variables comprise the base case in the estimating equation.

Appendix C: Choice of Functional Form

When determining the functional form for the price and quality equations, the two equations were analyzed separately. Five functional forms were considered for each equation: linear, log-linear (with the dummy explanatory variables untransformed), semi-log, reciprocal, and reciprocal square root. The models were compared using a RESET test, a heteroscedasticity (Breusch-Pagan) test and a nonnested test — the P_E test of MacKinnon, White, and Davidson (1983).

C.1. *The quality equation*

The RESET and heteroscedasticity test results for different versions of the quality equation are given in Table C1. Neither of the tests could reject

Table C1. Functional form Tests — Quality Equation

Functional form	RESET test[a]	Heteroscedasticity test[b]
Linear	0.44	38.48
Log-linear	0.57	39.25
Semi-log	0.74	39.22
Reciprocal	1.10	40.02
Reciprocal square root	0.91	39.62
Degrees of freedom for test	1,269	31

Linear model compared to other models using P_E nonnested test

	Log-linear[c]	Semi-log	Reciprocal	Reciprocal square root
t-Statistic	−2.58**	−0.68	0.69	0.68

Log-linear model compared to other models using P_E nonnested test

	Linear	Semi-log	Reciprocal	Reciprocal square root
t-Statistic	2.78*	1.90	−1.03	−1.41

Notes: [a]The RESET test statistic is distributed as an F-statistic.
[b]The heteroscedasticity test statistic is distributed as a chi-square statistic.
[c]*Rejects at 5%; **rejects at 5%, but not 1%.

any of the five specifications. As a result, the linear specification was chosen since it is the easiest to interpret. The linear functional form was then compared to alternative specifications using the P_E test. The t-statistics from this test are given in Table C1. The log-linear model rejects the linear model at the 5% level, but not at the 1% level. However, if the log-linear model is the maintained hypothesis, the linear model rejects the log-linear model, even at the 1% level, as shown by the results at the bottom of Table C1. As a result of these tests, the linear specification was chosen as most appropriate.

C.2. *The price equation*

When determining the functional form for the price equation, this equation was specified to include all the variables that would appear in a reduced-form version of the price equation (i.e., with expected quality substituted out, and the cross-equation restrictions not imposed). The results in Table C2 indicate that the reciprocal square root functional form is the only functional form

Table C2. Functional form Tests — Price Equation[a]

Functional form	RESET test[b]	Heteroscedasticity test[c]
Linear	177.18*	70.70*
Log-linear	57.93*	78.10*
Semi-log	57.03*	79.05*
Reciprocal	6.65**	67.19*
Reciprocal square root	2.47	51.77**
Degrees of freedom for test	1,264	36

Reciprocal square root model compared to other models using P_E nonnested test

	Linear	Log-linear	Semi-log	Reciprocal
t-Statistic	2.17**	2.26**	2.17**	1.57

Notes: [a]*Rejects at 5%; **rejects at 5%, but not 1%.
[b]The RESET test statistic is distributed as an *F*-statistic.
[c]The heteroscedasticity test statistic is distributed as a chi-square statistic.

that is not rejected by the RESET test. All the functional forms are rejected by the Breusch-Pagan heteroscedasticity test, but of these, the reciprocal square root form is the only one that is not rejected at the 1% level, and it is just barely rejected at the 5% level. These results indicate that the reciprocal square root functional form for the price equation may be the most appropriate. Taking the reciprocal square root model as the maintained hypothesis, this functional form was then tested against the other four specifications using a P_E test. The test statistics for this test are also given in Table C2. Although three of the four functional forms reject the reciprocal square root functional form at 5%, none reject at 1%. Given the above results, the reciprocal square root functional form was chosen as the most appropriate form for the price equation.

Chapter 2

Wine Quality and Varietal, Regional, and Winery Reputations: Hedonic Prices for Australia and New Zealand*

Günter Schamel† and Kym Anderson‡

School of Economics, University of Adelaide, Adelaide, South Australia 5005, Australia
†*guenter.schamel@unibz.it*
‡*kym.anderson@adelaide.edu.au*

We estimate hedonic price functions for premium wine from Australia and New Zealand, differentiating implicit prices for sensory quality ratings, wine varieties and regional as well as winery brand reputations over the vintages 1992–2000. The results show regional reputations have become increasingly differentiated through time (although less so for New Zealand). In particular, cool-climate regions are becoming increasingly preferred over other regions in Australia. In each country, price premia associated with both James Halliday's and Winestate magazine's sensory quality ratings, and with Halliday's winery ratings and classic wine designations, are highly significant.

1. Introduction

For more than a decade the wine industry has been booming in Australia and New Zealand. Both the area planted to vineyards and the volume of premium wine produced have grown at 7 + per cent per year on average since 1990, while the two countries' exports of wine have been growing at 15 + per cent per year (from a low base). Simultaneously, wine exports from California, South Africa and Chile have been soaring, such that the share of global wine production that is exported has risen from 15% to 30% in just a dozen years. Yet per capita wine consumption has grown little in

*This article originally appeared in *The Economic Record* (2003), 79(246), 357–369.

Australia and New Zealand and has been falling steadily in the traditional wine-consuming countries of Europe and the southern cone of Latin America, more than offsetting demand growth in the U.K., the U.S., and (from a tiny base) East Asia (Anderson and Norman, 2003). In each of these markets, however, there has been a dramatic substitution of quality for quantity: premium (bottled) wine sales are growing steadily while non-premium (cask) sales are declining (Anderson, 2003; Anderson *et al.*, 2003).

With global demand static and export supplies expanding rapidly, the average price of internationally traded wine is bound to come under pressure to decline in the coming years. In this more-competitive and more-globalized environment, the extent to which the price declines (or rises) for a particular group of producers will depend very much on the quality upgrading of its product, absolutely, and relative to that of other producer groups, as perceived by consumers at home and abroad. This raises the question of what determines consumers' perceptions of quality when they buy newly released wine.[1] Many consumers, especially when they are new and inexperienced, are looking for guidance before purchasing wines. Often they are unsure about the quality of a wine they intend to purchase and turn to the published ratings of wine experts for guidance. This begs the question as to how expert ratings, in addition to grape variety and regional reputations, affect the price of wine. What are consumers willing to pay for such things as the reputation of the producing region as distinct from corporate brand reputation, or grape variety reputation, or the published ratings of wine writers/judges/critics; and how has that willingness to pay evolved over time?

This chapter addresses this question as it relates to Australian and New Zealand wines, using a hedonic pricing model. Our analysis extends previous studies in a number of ways. First, we simultaneously examine two very large data samples of quality ratings (Halliday, 2001; Winestate, 2001), each drawn from the same base population of wines and consumers, which enables us to make direct comparisons between them. Second, we are able to expose changes in reputations over the past decade when wine markets

[1]Thanks are due to the editor, referees and numerous colleagues for comments on earlier drafts presented at the AARES Conference in Adelaide in January 2001, the Enometrics VIII Conference in the Napa Valley in May 2001, and the CIES Workshop on Understanding Developments in the World's Wine Markets in Adelaide in October 2001; to Australia's Grape and Wine Research and Development Corporation, Rural Industries Research and Development Corporation, and the Australian Research Council as well as the German Academic Exchange Service (DAAD) for financial support; and to James Halliday and Peter Simic for kindly providing their very extensive tastings databases.

changed dramatically. Finally, we include indicators for sensory quality, producer reputation, variety, and regional origin for not only Australia but also New Zealand, which allows us to directly compare both countries on various grounds (e.g., regional and variety differentials).

This chapter is structured as follows. In Section 2, we briefly review the literature on hedonic pricing models and their application to wine. Section 3 presents the model and the two different data sets used in the analysis. Section 4 details our empirical results for the markets in Australia and New Zealand separately over nine vintages. The final section summarizes what has been learnt and suggests areas for further research.

2. Previous Studies

A number of studies apply hedonic price analysis to estimate implicit prices for wine quality attributes.[2] They are based on the hypothesis that any product represents a bundle of characteristics that define quality. Their theoretical foundation is provided in the seminal paper by Rosen (1974), which posits that goods are valued for their utility-generating attributes. Rosen suggests there are competitive implicit markets that define implicit prices for embodied product attributes, and that consumers evaluate product attributes when making a purchasing decision. The observed market price is the sum of implicit prices paid for each quality attribute.

Since the quality of a particular bottle of wine cannot be known until it is de-corked and consumed, consumers' willingness to pay depends on reputations associated with that wine. In addition to quality ratings, consumers' perceptions of a wine's quality depends on producer reputation, the collective reputation of the wine region of production, and the grape variety (or varieties) used. Shapiro (1983) presents a theoretical framework to examine the effects of individual producer reputation on prices. He develops an equilibrium price-quality schedule for high-quality products, assuming competitive markets and imperfect consumer information, to demonstrate that reputation allows high-quality producers to sell their items at a premium

[2]This is to be distinguished from consumer perceptions over time of the changing quality of ultrapremium wines as they mature in bottle following the initial sale by the winery, as captured by time series of prices in the secondary auction markets. According to Ashenfelter (2000), Ashenfelter *et al.* (1995), Byron and Ashenfelter (1995) and Wood and Anderson (2002), key determinants of the vintage-to-vintage variation in the quality of maturing wines are a few straightforward weather variables in the growing season — information that consumers appear to have ignored in the past.

that may be interpreted as a return from producer investments in building reputation. On the demand side of the market, too, it is costly for consumers to improve their information about product quality. In such an environment of imperfect information, learning about the reputation of a product or of some of its attributes can be an effective way for consumers to become better informed. A favorable producer or winery rating assigned by a wine expert, for example, may serve as a way to reduce consumers' decision-making costs.

Tirole (1996) presents a model of collective reputation as an aggregate of individual reputations where current producer incentives are affected by their own actions as well as collective actions of the past. He shows that new producers may suffer from past mistakes of older producers for a long time after the latter disappear, and derives conditions under which the collective reputation in such cases can be regained. A favorable collective reputation of a particular wine region relative to other regions may provide another effective means of reducing consumers' decision-making costs.

Roberts and Reagans (2001) examine market experience, consumer attention, and price-quality relationships for New World wines in the United States market. They argue that the attention paid to wine quality signals increases with the market experience of its producer and, because of spillover effects, with the experience of associated producers.

Schamel (2000) estimates a hedonic pricing model based on United States data for sensory quality ratings, individual wine quality and regional reputation indicators for two premium wine varieties: a white (Chardonnay) and a red (Cabernet Sauvignon). That paper examines seven regions (Napa and Sonoma Valley, Sonoma County, Oregon, Washington State, Australia, Chile, South Africa) and includes observations from a pool of eight vintages between 1988 and 1995. However, it does not estimate coefficients for individual vintages. The estimated price elasticity of sensory quality is larger for white than red wine, but both regional reputation and individual quality indicators seem to be more important to red wine consumers in the United States. The results also suggest that the marketing of regional origin as a reputation attribute may have a higher payoff for regions primarily growing red wine.

Because wine consumers are uncertain about quality, we assume that, in addition to their own quality perceptions about grape varieties and growing regions, they use expert quality ratings for the wine and/or the winery in their buying decisions. Thus, consumer willingness to pay for a particular wine depends on a critic's quality rating of the wine and/or the producer, as well as their own reputation assessment for grape varieties and growing regions expressed through premia or discounts relative to a base region and variety. The present chapter analyzes such quality and reputation indicators for premium wines from Australia and New Zealand. For each country, we examine Halliday's (1999, 2001) data sets for nine vintages. Moreover, we analyze a second data set with more than 12,500 tasting scores for premium wines for the same two countries and up to eight vintages (Winestate, 2001). This enables us to compare hedonic pricing model results for two different data sets drawn from the same base population of wines and consumers and for the same vintages.

3. The Data and Hedonic Price Model

3.1. *The data*

In Table 1, we provide an overview of the data set from the well-known Australian wine critic James Halliday,[3] which we use to estimate the first set of hedonic price equations for each vintage from 1992 (1993 in the case of New Zealand) to 2000. The set includes 6866 observations from Australia and 1531 from New Zealand. For the Australian sample, the average quality rating is 87.2 points (range 70–97) and the average price is A$23.81 (range A$5–300). For New Zealand, the average quality rating is 88.6 points (range 73–97) and the average price is NZ$23.25 (range NZ$7–90). Halliday's value of sensory wine quality is defined by the variable *vintage rating* (100-point scale). He also provides a *winery rating* (2.5–5 stars) of the producer as a supplier of premium wine, and a *classic wine* classification in recognition of an outstanding wine. To evaluate differences in the willingness to pay for different grape varieties, we distinguish six different red and six white wine varieties or varicty groupings, respectively. In order to assess the value of regional denominations in Halliday's sample, we distinguish wines from 27 different regions in Australia as well as six different regions in New Zealand. Separate equations are estimated for Australia and New Zealand. The endogenous

[3]Halliday data are made publicly available in annual books (see Halliday, 2001 and earlier editions). We were kindly provided with an integrated database for the whole period, however, which minimizes any inconsistencies from one yearbook to the next. There was of course some inflation over the 1990s (though much less than in earlier decades), but that is not a major problem in this study as we assess each vintage separately rather than pool the series.

Table 1. Description of James Halliday's (JH) Data Set

Variable
Dependent Variable: Log(Price), Range A$5–300, NZ$7–90
Vintage Rating: 100-Point Scale, Range 70–97
Winery Rating: 5-Star Rating, Range 2.5–5 (NR = 2)
Classic Wine: 1 = Classic Rating; 2 = Not
Variety Dummies: Red
Cabernet Sauvignon
Cabernet Blends
Shiraz[a] (AUS)
Shiraz Blends (AUS)
Pinot Noir
Merlot (NZ)
Other Red
Variety Dummies: White
Chardonnay[b]
Riesling
Gewurztraminer (NZ)
Sauvignon Blanc
Semillon (AUS)
Sweet White
Other White
Regional Dummies: South Australia
Adelaide Hills
Barossa Valley[a]
Clare Valley
Coonawarra
Eden Valley
McLaren Vale
Other SA
Regional Dummies: ACT and NSW
Canberra
Hunter Valley
Mudgee
Riverina
Other NSW
Regional Dummies: Victoria
Bendigo
Goulburn Valley
Grampians
Macedon Ranges
Mornington Peninsula
Pyrenees
Yarra Valley
Other Vic.

(*Continued*)

Table 1. (*Continued*)

Variable
Regional Dummies: Western Australia
Great Southern
Perth
Margaret River
Other WA
Regional Dummies: Tasmania and Queensland
Northern Tasmania
Southern Tasmania
Queensland
Regional Dummies: New Zealand
Auckland
Canterbury
Hawke's Bay
Marlborough[b]
Wairarapa
Other NZ

Notes: [a](AUS) and [b](NZ) indicate the reference dummies, which we dropped from the regressions.

variable (the tax inclusive recommended retail price) is expressed in local dollars per 750 mL bottle.

Table 2 provides an analogous overview of our second data source from Australia's popular wine magazine *Winestate*.[4] It provides wine ratings for 12,625 combined observations for Australia and New Zealand. In contrast to the 100-point scale for sensory wine quality adopted by Halliday, *Winestate* uses a 5-star rating scheme, assigning between 3 and 5 stars but also using half-stars. (Some wines have no rating at all, which presumably implies less than 3 stars, so we assigned 2.5 stars for all non-rated wines.) For simplicity, we have given two points for every star, to avoid using decimals. From the *Winestate* tastings, a consistent set is available for each vintage from 1992 to 1999 (1994–1999 in the case of New Zealand), amounting to 11,251 observations from Australia and 1374 from New Zealand. For the Australian sample, the average quality rating is 3.25 stars and the average price is A$19.56 (range A$5–385). For New Zealand, the average quality rating is

[4]As pointed out by Oczkowski (1994; footnote 4), *Winestate* uses a panel of judges that changes over time and so it provides a less consistent set of assessments than that provided by Halliday. It also includes a value-for-money consideration in its ratings. Even so, we thought it was worth doing the comparative analysis to see to what extent the *Winestate* data support the findings based on Halliday's data.

Table 2. Description of the Winestate (WS) Data Set

Variable
Dependent Variable: Log(Price), Range A$5–385, NZ$9–90
Star Rating: 3, $3\frac{1}{2}$, 4, $4\frac{1}{2}$, 5 Stars (NR = $2\frac{1}{2}$)
Point Rating: Conversion of star rating to a 10-Point Scale, Range 5–10
Variety Dummies: Red
Cabernet Sauvignon
Cabernet Blends
Shiraz[a]
Shiraz Blends (AUS)
Pinot Noir
Merlot
Other Red
Variety Dummies: White
Chardonnay[b]
Riesling
Sauvignon Blanc
Semillon
Sweet White (AUS)
Other White
Regional Dummies: South Australia
Adelaide Hills
Barossa Valley[a]
Clare Valley
Coonawarra
Eden Valley
McLaren Vale
Other Limestone Coast
Riverland
Langhorne Creek
Other SA
Regional Dummies: ACT and NSW
Canberra
Hunter Valley
Mudgee
Riverina
Other NSW
Regional Dummies: Victoria
Goulburn Valley
Mornington Peninsula
Rutherglen
King Valley
Yarra Valley
Central & West Vic.
Other Vic.

(Continued)

Table 2. (*Continued*)

Variable
Regional Dummies: Western Australia
Great Southern
Perth
Margaret River
Other WA
Regional Dummies: Tasmania and Queensland
Tasmania
Queensland
Regional Dummies: New Zealand
Auckland
Canterbury
Hawke's Bay
Marlborough[b]
Nelson
Other NZ

Notes: [a](AUS) and [b](NZ) indicate the reference dummies, which we dropped from the regressions.

3.44 stars and the average price is NZ$20.59 (range NZ$9–90). In order to assess regional denominations, the *Winestate* sample allows us to distinguish 28 different regions for Australia and six different regions for New Zealand.

3.2. *The model*

Following conventional hedonic models, we propose that a bundle of quality attributes defines any premium wine. Consumer willingness to pay is a function of that bundle of wine quality attributes. In addition to wine experts' sensory quality ratings of a particular wine, of each vintage and of the winery producing it (such ratings books are commonly available for perusal in wine shops), willingness to pay for a wine also reflects consumers' perception of the varietal reputation and the reputation of the producing region. An individual quality indicator such as a classic wine rating assigned by wine critics may also affect buying decisions.

Hedonic price analysis relates the price of a good to its utility-generating characteristics, and generates implicit prices for these characteristics. Thus, any quantitative or qualitative variable that affects consumer utility may be included in a hedonic price function. We formulate a model assuming that consumers, uncertain about the true sensory quality of a particular wine, adjust their willingness to pay using expert ratings of wine quality (vintage ratings) and of the wine producer as well as their own perception of varietal and regional reputations.[5]

The theoretical model described above limits the type of explanatory variables, but it does not restrict the functional form to be estimated. In the empirical literature on hedonic wine pricing, a variety of different functional forms have been explored and reported. For example, Landon and Smith (1997) examine five different functions choosing the reciprocal square root form, Oczkowski (1994) reports a log-linear form, and Nerlove (1995) compares log-linear, log-log and Box–Cox transformations. The log-linear form has been applied in a number of published studies, including Oczkowski (1994, 2001), Nerlove (1995), and Combris *et al.* (1997). In our case, following Oczkowski, the results of applying a RESET-test to the linear, log-linear, and log-log functional forms lead us to prefer the log-linear specification, with log(Price) as the dependent variable (see Table 3). An examination of the correlation matrices for the coefficient estimates suggests that no serious degree of multicollinearity is present in the data. Moreover, we take note of the point stressed by Oczkowski (2001) that serious correlation between a single measure quality regressor and the error term would point to measurement errors and lead to inconsistent OLS (ordinary least squares) estimates. To test for that, we conducted a standard Hausman test using the average of the quality ratings for each producer label as an instrumental variables.[6] As is clear from Table 4, where more than 30 subsets of data are shown, only in five cases were the results significant at the 1% level and another five at the 5% level. We therefore conclude that in this study we do not have a serious problem of dependence between the quality ratings and the error term.

4. What Do the Results Show?

4.1. *Australia*

Tables 5 and 6 present the estimation results for Australia from the Halliday and *Winestate* samples, respectively. Shiraz and Barossa Valley are chosen as

[5]Previous studies have included other variables such as cellaring potential, year of marketing and producer size (see, e.g., Oczkowski, 1994). We did not have such variables available for our full time series, so cannot expect as high an adjusted R^2 value.

[6]There are 765 (923) different producers in the Halliday (*Winestate*) sample for Australia. For New Zealand, there are 203 (205) different producers in the Halliday (Winestate) data set.

Table 3. RESET F-test Statistics

From	Sample	2000	1999	1998	1997	1996	1995	1994	1993	1992
Log-linear	JH AUS	6.14*	6.65*	29	22.9	62.4	52.4	26.3	18.2	6.68*
	JH NZ	0.58**	7.70	6.23*	12.93	6.64*	8.91	1.89**	0.36**	—
	WS AUS	—	0.16**	0.30**	4.73*	19.6	0.04**	6.17*	4.99*	0.09**
	WS NZ	—	1.76**	1.60**	1.42**	2.37**	0.22**	0.04**	—	—
Log-log	JH AUS	7.41	11.0	29.8	22.4	53.2	54.0	29.9	19.6	7.50
	JH NZ	0.55**	13.1	6.33*	14.3	6.73*	11.2	2.18**	0.38**	—
	WS AUS	—	0.08**	0.38**	5.02*	20.4	0.002**	5.46*	5.22*	0.18**
	WS NZ	—	0.35**	2.40**	0.74**	1.55**	2.05**	0.18**	0.09**	—
Linear	JH AUS	26.0	59.1	152.3	82.5	154.9	131.3	97.3	58.6	39.4
	JH NZ	0.09**	23.2	34.1	70.6	52.2	72.7	12.6	1.50**	—
	WS AUS	—	9.47	18.5	19.3	45.5	17.7	185.9	26.7	39.9
	WS NZ	—	2.05**	7.24	11.7	0.05**	1.05**	0.14**	—	—

Notes: **, *indicate significance at least at the 10% and 1% levels, respectively. JH, James Halliday; WS, *Winestate* magazine.

Table 4. Hausman χ^2-test Statistics

From	Sample	2000	1999	1998	1997	1996	1995	1994	1993	1992
Log-linear	JH AUS	7.74	3.58**	15.4	5.81*	2.13***	2.42***	4.41*	0.28***	2.18***
	JH NZ	5.20*	1.35***	3.65**	6.61*	2.69***	0.54***	0.047***	2.60***	—
	WS AUS	—	0.52***	10.12	7.90	6.07*	29.4	16.7	8.72	0.51***
	WS NZ	—	3.18**	0.90**	0.002***	5.80*	0.08***	2.47***	—	—

Notes: ***, **, *indicate significance at least at the 10%, 5%, 1% levels, respectively. JH, James Halliday; WS, *Winestate* magazine.

Table 5. Regression Results for Australia (Halliday Data Set)

Parameter	2000	1999	1998	1997	1996	1995	1994	1993	1992
CONSTANT	0.931*	−0.353	−0.734*	0.093	0.491**	0.503**	0.639**	0.340	−0.337
Vintage Rating	0.023*	0.036*	0.041*	0.032*	0.028*	0.029*	0.025*	0.029*	0.038*
Winery Rating	0.021	0.046*	0.051*	0.055*	0.093*	0.069*	0.093*	0.075**	0.082***
Classic Wine	0.066	0.055	0.159*	0.271*	0.235*	0.259*	0.281*	0.361*	0.275*
Cabernet Sauvignon	−0.243	0.034	−0.045	0.003	−0.059	−0.118**	−0.036−	0.104***	−0.020
Cabernet Blends	−0.444*	0.012	−0.070***−	0.038	−0.065	0.000	0.025	0.013	0.022
Pinot Noir	−0.223**	0.060	0.040	−0.013	−0.086	−0.092	−0.029	0.145	0.245
Shiraz Blends	−0.099	−0.111***	−0.133**	−0.038	−0.110	−0.236*	−0.278*	−0.322*	−0.302**
Other Red	−0.347*	0.073***	−0.009	0.008	−0.110**	−0.110***	−0.136***	−0.119	0.018
Chardonnay	−0.288*	−0.070**	−0.160*	−0.174*	−0.250*	−0.219*	−0.176*	−0.103***	−0.051
Riesling	−0.420*	−0.339*	−0.531*	−0.471*	−0.597*	−0.581*	−0.537*	−0.379*	−0.505*
Sauvignon Blanc	−0.336*	−0.178*	−0.318*	−0.290*	−0.421*	−0.391*	−0.334*	−0.631***	−0.406
Semillon	−0.324*	−0.187*	−0.316*	−0.356*	−0.446*	−0.421*	−0.419*	−0.368*	−0.302
Sweet White	−0.322**	−0.152**	−0.102	−0.337*	−0.375*	−0.200*	−0.205	−0.359*	−0.457**
Other White	−0.316*	−0.183*	−0.382*	−0.353*	−0.423*	−0.513*	−0.447*	−0.466*	−0.186
Great Southern	0.267*	0.094	0.163*	0.192*	0.016	−0.087	−0.004	−0.019	−0.191
Perth	0.086	−0.070	−0.001	0.022	−0.293*	−0.088	−0.243**	−0.151	−0.115
Margaret River	0.276*	0.212	0.278*	0.234*	0.163*	0.055	0.181**	0.173***	0.040
Other WA	0.233**	0.139**	0.297*	0.244**	0.123	0.059	0.040	0.008	−0.030
Adelaide Hills	0.301*	0.183*	0.183*	0.342*	0.136***	0.163***	0.164***	−0.006	−0.023
Clare Valley	0.234*	0.008	0.109**	0.073	−0.099***	−0.154**	−0.105	−0.097	−0.260**
Coonawarra	0.177***	0.032	0.112**	0.066	−0.095***	−0.067	−0.029	−0.065	−0.155
Eden Valley	0.152***	0.080	0.248*	0.288*	0.202**	0.185**	0.205**	0.006	0.287
McLaren Vale	0.056	0.063	0.171*	0.023	−0.099***	−0.150**	0.040	−0.007	−0.193***

(Continued)

Table 5. (*Continued*)

Parameter	2000	1999	1998	1997	1996	1995	1994	1993	1992
Other SA	−0.194**	−0.126**	−0.126**	−0.084	−0.281*	−0.259*	−0.132	−0.119	−0.439**
Canberra	0.253*	0.205**	0.123	0.060	−0.087	−0.098	−0.120	0.055	−0.392**
Hunter Valley	0.163*	0.082***	0.086***	0.055	−0.119**	−0.166**	−0.165**	−0.231**	−0.407**
Mudgee	0.045	0.029	0.131	−0.085	−0.115	−0.346*	−0.323*	−0.483*	−0.523
Riverina	−0.280**	−0.211*	−0.180***	−0.332*	−0.434*	−0.573*	−0.304***	−0.404*	−0.171
Other NSW	0.252*	0.066	−0.008	0.022	−0.239*	−0.245*	−0.170***	−0.200***	−0.382
Bendigo	0.376*	0.073	0.148***	0.117	−0.141	−0.004	0.036	0.023	−0.265
Goulburn Valley	0.009	−0.064	0.074	−0.031	−0.199**	−0.093	0.083	−0.098	−0.074
Grampians	0.218**	0.206***	0.275*	0.188***	−0.020	0.170	0.029	−0.015	0.110
Macedon Ranges	0.322*	0.264*	0.388*	0.211**	0.214***	0.095	0.139	0.055	−0.190
Mornington Peninsula	0.310*	0.233*	0.221*	0.236*	0.158***	0.107	0.126	0.018	−0.541
Pyrenees	0.280**	0.262*	0.146	0.264*	0.056	0.141	0.151	0.168	0.071
Yarra Valley	0.212*	0.173*	0.200*	0.197*	0.056	0.051	0.075	−0.014	−0.075
Other Victoria	0.266*	0.087***	0.044	−0.006	−0.077	−0.033	−0.068	−0.065	−0.151
Northern Tasmania	0.259*	0.083	0.141***	0.120	0.085	−0.005	−0.105	0.142	−0.328
Southern Tasmania	0.386*	0.158*	0.149**	0.122	0.064	0.018	0.067	−0.232	−0.162

Queensland	0.105	0.147	−0.054	−0.073	0.089	−0.130	−0.249	−0.232	−0.015
No. of Observations	429	999	1281	1033	929	767	725	448	255
Adjusted. R^2(%)	29.4	39.4	38.5	44.8	44.4	43.6	42.7	43.7	37.5
Average Retail Price (A$)	18.01	21.57	24.39	24.03	24.45	24.50	24.75	25.24	28.90
Average Vintage Rating (points)	87.0	86.8	87.8	87.5	86.9	86.6	87.1	86.5	87.9
Average Winery Rating (stars)	3.83	3.89	3.96	4.03	4.08	4.08	4.07	4.08	4.15
1-point price effect (A$)	0.41*	0.79*	1.01*	0.77*	0.68*	0.71*	0.62*	0.74*	1.10*
$\frac{1}{2}$-star price effect (A$)	0.19	0.50*	0.62*	0.66*	1.13*	0.84*	1.15*	0.94**	1.19***

Notes: ***, **, * indicate significance at least at the 10%, 5%, 1% levels, respectively.

Table 6. Regression Results for Australia (Winestate Data Set)

Parameter	1999	1998	1997	1996	1995	1994	1993	1992
CONSTANT	2.550*	2.641*	2.767*	2.699*	2.634*	2.419*	2.432*	2.183*
Vintage Rating	0.041*	0.045*	0.044*	0.060*	0.073*	0.092*	0.107*	0.156*
Cabernet Sauvignon	−0.003	−0.019	−0.062**	−0.054***	−0.125*	−0.042	−0.012	−0.238*
Cabernet Blends	−0.149*	−0.094*	−0.141*	−0.161*	−0.199*	−0.112**	−0.103	−0.315**
Shiraz Blend	−0.307*	−0.254*	−0.063	−0.258*	−0.140***	−0.012	−0.322*	−0.240
Pinot Noir	0.105**	0.087**	−0.022	−0.111**	−0.138*	−0.077	−0.011*	−0.357**
Merlot	−0.068	0.067**	−0.016	0.021	−0.097	0.083	0.219	0.039
Other Red	−0.115**	−0.076**	−0.254*	−0.187*	−0.282*	−0.155*	−0.239*	−0.215***
Chardonnay	−0.143*	−0.167*	−0.247*	−0.258*	−0.249*	−0.124*	−0.136*	−0.530*
Riesling	−0.250*	−0.371*	−0.440*	−0.491*	−0.525*	−0.417*	−0.347*	−0.567*
Sauvignon Blanc	−0.121*	−0.253*	−0.396*	−0.418*	−0.401*	−0.250**	−0.088	−0.504*
Semillon	−0.192*	−0.253*	−0.416*	−0.442*	−0.393*	−0.226*	−0.276*	−0.419*
Sweet White	−0.001	−0.116	−0.223**	−0.507*	−0.800*	−0.548*	—	—
Other White	−0.220*	−0.379*	−0.450*	−0.471*	−0.495*	−0.394*	−0.335*	−0.690*
Adelaide Hills	0.248*	0.231*	0.173*	0.121*	0.083***	0.064	−0.110	0.122
Clare Valley	0.103**	0.047	0.010	−0.043	−0.052	−0.082	−0.300*	−0.125
Coonawarra	0.089	0.186*	0.112*	0.105*	0.015	0.078***	−0.053	0.068
Eden Valley	0.147**	0.081	0.316*	0.377*	0.598*	0.905*	−0.414	0.088
McLaren Vale	0.038	0.156*	0.058***	0.007	0.008	−0.152*	−0.318*	−0.159
Other Limestone Coast	0.127*	0.146*	0.067	0.025	0.345**	0.070	−0.667***	—
Riverland	−0.254*	−0.312*	−0.288*	−0.454*	−0.626*	−0.609*	−0.644*	−0.429***
Langhorne Creek	0.059	0.039	0.090	−0.118	0.073	−0.193	−0.129	−0.253
Other SA	0.121	−0.048	−0.057	−0.164*	−0.208*	−0.280*	−0.237*	−0.128
Canberra	0.313***	0.130	0.154	0.030	−0.115	−0.141	−0.306***	−0.294
Hunter Valley	0.179*0.123*	0.058***	0.057	0.019	0.036	−0.085	0.007	
Mudgee	0.009	0.033	0.092***	−0.201*	−0.264*	−0.427*	−0.754*	−0.252

Riverina	−0.407*	−0.321*	−0.328*	−0.222*	−0.351*	−0.239**	−0.230	−0.018
Other NSW	−0.011	−0.003	−0.011	−0.099***	−0.073	−0.015	−0.225	—
Goulburn Valley	0.063	−0.113	−0.021	−0.143**	−0.066	−0.133***	−0.081	−0.303***
Mornington Peninsula	0.300*	0.325*	0.231*	0.211***	0.249*	0.053	−0.259***	0.181
Rutherglen	0.051	−0.019	−0.105***	−0.154**	−0.103	−0.132***	−0.296***	−0.277**
King Valley	0.157	0.063	−0.069	0.003	0.085	0.129	0.424***	0.226
Yarra Valley	0.068	0.253*	0.212*	0.128*	0.161*	0.167**	0.004	0.082
Central & West Vic.	0.187*	0.197*	0.161*	0.090***	0.068	0.060	0.000	0.129
Other Victoria	0.0940.019	−0.069	−0.024	−0.192**	−0.204**	−0.302*	−0.073	
Great Southern	0.219*	0.159*	0.133**	0.112**	−0.031	−0.084	−0.020	0.058
Margaret River	0.287*	0.270*	0.363*	0.347*	0.182*	0.0840.131***	0.069	
Perth	−0.013	0.020	0.017	−0.022	−0.072	−0.170***	—	−0.103
Other WA	0.186*	0.128**	0.035	−0.042	0.071	0.048	−0.280*	−0.357
Tasmania	0.292*	0.269*	0.208*	0.190**	0.199*	0.118	−0.162	0.411
Queensland	0.080	0.013	−0.102	0.047	−0.219	−0.008	−0.280	−0.329
No.of Observations	1345	2154	1993	2001	1551	1186	489	367
Adj. R^2(%)	34.2	30.9	29.7	29.7	30.5	26.3	30.4	40.8
Average Retail Price (A$)	15.87	19.29	20.22	20.31	20.03	20.75	21.33	19.98
Average Vintage Rating (stars)	2.96	3.20	3.29	3.34	3.32	3.35	3.35	3.11
$\frac{1}{2}$-star price effect (A$)	0.65*	0.86*	0.88*	1.21*	1.46*	1.92*	2.28*	3.12*

Notes: ***, **, * indicates significance at least at the 10%, 5%, 1% levels, respectively.

the comparator variety and region (necessary to avoid the dummy variable trap). Thus, all coefficients are relative to what a Shiraz produced in the Barossa Valley would sell for. The columns show the estimation results for each of the eight or nine subsamples of individual vintages. For the Halliday sample, the coefficients for "vintage rating" and "winery rating" measure the percentage price premia for a one-point increase in the 100-point scale, respectively. The dummy variable coefficients for variety and regional origin can be interpreted as a percentage price impact relative to a Barossa Valley Shiraz. The coefficient for "classic wine" reports the percentage price premium for a wine that obtained this special recognition. For the *Winestate* sample, the coefficients for "rating" measure the percentage price premia for a one-point increase (on a 10 point scale), which may in turn be interpreted as the percentage price premium for a 1/2 star rating increase.

Consider first the estimates using the Halliday data (Table 5). The parameters for vintage rating are all significant and fairly constant over time. The price premium is 3.1% on average and varies between 2.3% and 4.1% for a one-point increase in the vintage rating for the 1992–2000 vintages. That amounts to between a 40 and 110 cents increase on an average-priced bottle of wine for each vintage over that period (see second to last row in Table 5). The coefficients for producer reputation ("winery rating") are significant at the 5% level for all vintages except 1992 and 2000 (1992 is significant at 10%). The price premium for an average-priced bottle of wine worth ($23.80) ranges between 50 and 115 cents for another $\frac{1}{2}$ star in Halliday's winery rating and has been declining over the 1990s. Halliday's "classic wine" rating is significant for all vintages in Australia except the three most recent vintages (which were incomplete samples because many premium reds from those vintages were still to be released), and adds a price premium between 16% and 36%, other things equal. The downward trend in this coefficient reflects a premium paid for older vintages.

Turning to the wine variety dummies, the changes over time in the parameter values for varieties reflect relative changes in consumer tastes and preferences for the various varieties. For example, Semillon and sauvignon Blanc parameters become less negative (i.e., the price discount for them relative to Barossa Valley Shiraz decreases), implying that these varieties have become less unpopular over the latter 1990s. For the 2000 vintage, they attract about a one-third discount relative to Barossa Shiraz, other things equal. For Chardonnay, the discount is less whereas for Riesling it averaged almost 50%. In general the reds attracted similar prices relative to Shiraz, and with few exceptions showed no significant difference for most individual vintages. Shiraz blends and other reds were sold at discounts of as much as 20% or more below the Barossa Shiraz price for the early vintages, but this difference has since become insignificant. White wines all sell at a discount relative to Barossa Shiraz and their parameters have become slightly more significant through time.

When examining the regional dummies, note that they clearly become more significant over time. For the 1992 vintage, only four regions are significantly different from the Barossa at the 5% level, while for the 1998 vintage, 10 of the 26 regions are significantly different at the 1% level and another four at the 5% level.[7] This pattern indicates of an intensifying regional quality differentiation in Australia, with coefficients for some regions trending down while others are trending up. For example, the coefficients for wines from Tasmania first become significant in 1998 and then increase further as they became more popular with consumers relative to Barossa Valley wines. Strong upward trends are also evident for the newly developing ultra-premium cool-climate regions of the Adelaide Hills, Mornington Peninsula and Yarra Valley, with average premia up to 31 per cent. By way of contrast, the wines of the warm-climate irrigated region such as Other South Australia and Riverina become heavily discounted by the mid-1990s.

Turning to the estimates for the *Winestate* data (Table 6), the parameters for vintage rating are all significant but less constant over time compared to the Halliday coefficients. The price premium varies between 4 and 16 per cent for a $\frac{1}{2}$-star improvement in the sensory quality rating for the 1993–99 vintages. That is, a $\frac{1}{2}$-star increase in *Winestate's* rating would yield an increase in the price per bottle between 65 and 312 cents on an average-priced bottle of rated wine for the 1992–99 vintages (see last row in Table 6). Unfortunately, the rating schemes are too different to allow a direct comparison of the price premia in the two data sets, since *Winestate* only publishes ratings of three or more stars and the two data providers vary in the extent to which they focus on commercial, super- and ultra-premium wines (as reflected in their different average prices).

For the variety dummies, the *Winestate* data confirm that the Semillon and Sauvignon Blanc parameters become less unpopular relative to Barossa Valley Shiraz over the latter 1990s. On average, the *Winestate* data also

[7]Because the data sets for the 1999 and 2000 vintages exclude many super- and ultra-premium reds that were still awaiting release, less store can be put on the results for those last 2 years.

confirm that they attract about a one-third discount relative to Barossa Shiraz, other things equal, with both coefficients following the declining discount trends observed with the Halliday data. For Chardonnay the discounts are slightly higher in the *Winestate* sample whereas for Riesling they are slightly lower. Among the reds, Merlot attracted similar prices to Shiraz (less than 5% significance), but other red varieties including blends of Cabernet and Shiraz showed significant discounts below the Barossa Shiraz price, other things equal. Compared to the results from Halliday's data set, more of these parameters became significant as the decade proceeded.

When examining the regional dummies, notice again that they become increasingly significant over time, although the trend is more scattered and less clear than in the Halliday sample. In the sample the only region significantly different from the Barossa Valley for the '92 vintage at the 5% level was Rutherglen, while for the 1998 and 1999 vintages about half the regions are significantly different at the 1% level. Again, this pattern is an indication of an intensifying regional quality differentiation in Australia, with coefficients trending up or downward. Moreover, the *Winestate* data confirm the strong upward trends for the newly developing ultra-premium cool-climate regions (e.g., Adelaide Hills, Mornington Peninsula and Tasmania).

4.2. *New Zealand*

The results for New Zealand, shown in Tables 7 and 8, differentiate 10 varieties and five regions in each data set. (Absence of an entry means insufficient or no observations.) The Chardonnay variety and the region of Marlborough are chosen as the New Zealand bases. A number of interesting results, especially when compared with Australia's, are worth highlighting. For example, the parameters for Halliday's "vintage rating" are all significant and fairly constant over time, with somewhat lower price premia for New Zealand as compared with Australia. The coefficients vary between 1.1% and 2.7%, which translate into price premia between 21 and 64 cents calculated at the average NZ price for each vintage. The parameters for "winery rating" also are mostly smaller and less significant for New Zealand than for Australia, while the "classic wine" parameter is equally significant with the premia ranging between 14% and 34%.

Varietal differences are less pronounced in New Zealand too. Note that Riesling is discounted by about one-third and Sauvignon Blanc between one-seventh and one-third relative to the base variety (Chardonnay), whereas the reds enjoy considerable premia, other things equal.

Table 7. Regression Results for New Zealand (Halliday Data Set)

Parameter	2000	1999	1998	1997	1996	1995	1994	1993
CONSTANT	1.914*	1.073*	0.796**	1.031*	0.802**	1.294*	1.248*	0.944
Vintage Rating	0.011**	0.022*	0.023*	0.022*	0.024*	0.018*	0.019*	0.027**
Winery Rating	0.030	0.036**	0.061*	0.049**	0.039	0.042	0.048**	−0.057
Classic Wine	0.279	0.189***	0.343*	0.320*	0.185**	0.315*	0.171**	0.140
Cabernet Sauvignon	—	−0.099	0.131***	0.027	0.240***	0.157	0.170**	0.242
Cabernet Blends	—	0.239*	0.175*	0.311*	0.191**	0.476*	−0.034	—
Merlot	0.096	0.073	0.064	0.158	0.089	0.508*	0.110	−0.168
Pinot Noir	0.278*	0.254*	0.184*	0.112***	0.159**	0.069	0.049	0.133
Other Red	—	0.142	0.296*	—	0.363*	—	−0.155	—
Riesling	−0.118**	−0.321*	−0.385*	−0.304*	−0.365*	−0.359*	−0.505*	−0.462*
Gewurztraminer	—	−0.002	−0.229***	−0.138	−0.187	−0.063	−0.369*	−0.412
Sauvignon Blanc	−0.143*	−0.248*	−0.279*	−0.346*	−0.261*	−0.257*	−0.334*	−0.303***
Sweet White	0.301*	0.043	0.193	0.013	0.000	0.052	−0.021	−0.071
Other White	0.022	−0.100***	−0.184**	−0.187**	−0.193***	−0.253*	−0.363*	−0.271
Auckland	0.053	−0.081	−0.005	−0.042	−0.006	−0.056	−0.017	0.038
Canterbury	−0.005	0.014	0.114**	−0.023	0.096	−0.105	0.148**	0.086
Hawke's Bay	0.020	0.061	0.088**	−0.001	0.008	−0.096	−0.045	−0.144
Wairarapa	0.098	0.165*	0.083	0.100***	0.132***	0.080	0.088***	0.177
Other NZ	−0.053	0.079***	0.103**	0.011	0.101***	0.100	−0.009	0.045
No. of Observations	176	328	289	196	216	117	143	53
Adj. R^2(%)	35.6	56.3	57.8	58.1	47.4	71.7	64.5	36.2
Average Retail Price (NZ$)	19.50	24.68	25.27	21.40	23.39	23.67	22.08	23.45
Average Vintage Rating (points)	89.5	89.0	89.3	88.7	87.3	86.7	89.0	88.2
Average Winery Rating (stars)	4.09	4.08	4.06	3.99	4.104	4.081	4.105	4.151
1-point price effect (NZ$)	0.21**	0.53*	0.59*	0.46*	0.57*	0.43*	0.43*	0.64**
$\frac{1}{2}$-star price effect (NZ$)	0.29	0.45**	0.77*	0.53**	0.46	0.50	0.53**	−0.67

Notes: ***, **, * indicates significance at least at the 10%, 5% and 1% levels, respectively.

Table 8. Regression Results for New Zealand (Winestate Data Set)

Parameter	1999	1998	1997	1996	1995	1994
CONSTANT	2.530*	2.963*	2.782*	2.608*	2.760*	2.804*
Vintage Rating	0.048*	0.014	0.042*	0.065*	0.041**	0.046***
Cabernet Sauvignon	—	0.032	0.031	0.170***	0.000	0.038
Cabernet Blends	—	−0.107	0.269*	0.289*	0.174**	−0.023
Merlot	—	0.032	0.150**	0.047	0.184**	—
Pinot Noir	—	0.352*	0.291*	0.218*	0.090	0.134
Shiraz	—	—	—	0.156	—	—
Othe Red	0.115	−0.179*	0.014	0.145	0.178***	0.042
Riesling	−0.037	−0.212*	−0.256*	−0.220*	−0.282*	−0.343*
Sauvignon Blanc	−0.095***	−0.223*	−0.258*	−0.255*	−0.304*	−0.027
Semillon	—	−0.073	−0.096	−0.135	−0.335**	—
Other White	0.195*	−0.227*	−0.266*	−0.309*	−0.369*	−0.415***
Auckland	−0.061	−0.063	−0.099*	−0.067***	−0.089	−0.052
Canterbury	—	—	−0.157**	−0.041	−0.002	−0.138
Hawke's Bay	−0.111	0.005	0.147*	0.042	0.001	0.137
Nelson	−0.088	−0.118	−0.105***	−0.023	−0.098	—
Other NZ	0.124	−0.054	0.076	0.109**	0.116	0.040
No. of Observations	126	248	344	362	194	90
Adj. R^2(%)	22.4	29.5	45.1	38.1	43.0	14.7
Average Retail Price (NZ$)	17.70	19.62	20.30	21.23	21.14	24.43
Average Vintage Rating (stars)	3.54	3.33	3.38	3.49	3.45	3.66
$\frac{1}{2}$-star price effect (NZ$)	0.85*	0.27	0.84*	1.37*	0.87**	1.12***

Notes: ***, **, * indicates significance at least at the 10%, 5% and 1% levels, respectively.

Most strikingly, however, are the differences in the degree of regional differentiation between the two countries. For New Zealand, only one out of a total of 40 regional dummy coefficients over eight vintages is significantly different from the base region (Marlborough) at the 1% level (plus just four others at the 5% level), and the degree of difference is not large. Nor are any trends in the size or significance of coefficients obvious over time, unlike for Australia.

Very similar findings emerge for New Zealand from the *Winestate* data (Table 8) as those from the Halliday data (Table 7): vintage ratings are nearly all significant with no obvious trend over time, variety and regional differences are not pronounced, and nor are they becoming more significant over time.

Finally on the results, note that in all subsamples the variation in prices explained by the model (adjusted R^2) is higher for New Zealand, despite the much smaller sample sizes. Moreover, note that the estimation results are fairly consistent across the two different data sets for each country, although the Halliday data set has the higher explanatory power. In addition, the size of the price premia that consumers are willing to pay for higher-rated wines is consistently less in New Zealand than in Australia (especially bearing in mind that the NZ$ was worth only 70–85% of the value of the A$ in the 1990s).

5. Implications and Areas for Further Research

At least three clear lessons can be drawn from these results. One is that vintage ratings by independent writers/critics/judges (in this case those of *Winestate* magazine judges and, for James Halliday, as well as his winery ratings and classic wine categorization) appear to have a significant positive impact on the prices that consumers are willing to pay for premium wines, after taking into account their own reputation assessment for grape varieties and growing regions. This is equally true for Australia and New Zealand. It is consistent with the earlier study for Australia for 1991–1992 by Oczkowski (1994) and with Schamel's (2000) findings for the United States (based in that case on ratings published in the U.S. magazine *The Wine Spectator*), and suggests consumers value this information in their quest for greater knowledge about available wines.

Second, the premia consumers are willing to pay for higher-rated wines (both Halliday's and *Winestate's*) appear to have trended downwards slightly over the 1990s. This is true also for Halliday's winery ratings. This is consistent with wine consumers in these two countries becoming more confident in their own ability to discern the quality of different wines, and hence less reliant on critics' ratings.

The third lesson is not unrelated to the second. It is that there is a clear trend towards greater regional and varietal differentiation, at least within Australia. This too suggests a greater proportion of consumers are becoming more discerning, which presumably is being reflected in vineyard land prices in the various regions. Note, however, the weaker regional and varietal differentiation and the absence of any obvious price premia trend in New Zealand. The weaker varietal differentiation may reflect the relatively few varieties grown in New Zealand and (a point emphasized by Roberts and Reagans, 2001) the newness of many of its premium wine-producing regions. The lower price premia New Zealanders seem willing to pay for higher-rated wines and wineries compared with Australians may simply reflect the lower per capita incomes in New Zealand and their weaker preference for wine (their per capita consumption being only 80% that of Australians, and being more heavily focused on non-premium wines).

The difference between the two markets in the degree of regional differentiation also may reflect the fact that Australia has more major premium regions that have been producing continuously for a long time than does New Zealand. The greater extent to which regional differentiation is increasing in Australia is partly a consequence of the rapid growth in the 1990s of new ultra-premium cool-climate regions, which are challenging the supremacy of the long-established regions. But another contributing factor is that, unlike New Zealand, Australia has introduced legislation (in 1993) to allow legal registration of regional names (technically, "geographical indications").[8] That legislation is providing stronger rights over the intellectual property value of regional names, thereby raising the rates of return on investments in regional promotion. Even though they cannot say anything about the profitability of such investments, the above results are not inconsistent with the view that price premia can be generated through such promotion. The European tradition of emphasizing region in addition to nation of origin would appear to be gradually taking hold in Australia. It remains to be seen whether regional reputation indicators become more or less important over time. On the one hand, regions are investing more in generic promotion of their regions; but on the other, globalization is causing individual wineries to agglomerate and put more emphasis on building their corporate brand reputation.

As for the signs and sizes of the premia/discounts attached to variety, they are consistent with common knowledge. But the fact that there are distinct premia for particular varieties, over and above a premium or discount for region of origin, distinguishes the Antipodes from Western Europe where varietal distinctions have until very recently been downplayed.

[8]This was to enable Australia to fulfill its agreement with the European Union on trade in wine, following the Uruguay Round of multilateral trade negotiations. For details see www.awbc.com.au/arms/a_regions.html. An analysis of its possible effects can be found in Kok (1999).

There is much scope for further empirical work of this sort. Two examples of other questions that might be addressed are mentioned by way of conclusion. First, to what extent are subnational regions beginning to enjoy a price premium in markets abroad, or is it still only national recognition ("Brand Australia") and corporate brands that matter in those export markets at this stage? An answer to this question would help to fine-tune the promotional efforts of wine companies and regional wine associations. If national generic promotion can be shown to pay abroad, the bodies responsible for national promotion[9] would find it easier to attract (i) funds for that generic promotion and (ii) support for regulation of wine exports to ensure the national reputation for quality exports is not tarnished.[10] This is especially crucial in light of Tirole's (1996) theoretical result, and the bitter experiences following wine scandals in Austria and Italy in the 1980s, showing that producers can suffer for a very long time from previous mistakes.

Second, how well could hedonic pricing models be applied to better understand the demand for wine grapes by wineries? Various technical features of grapes contribute to the quality of the wines made from them, but in ways that are not very transparent to grape growers. As quantitative measures improve for measuring in the vineyard and/or weighbridge those attributes winemakers are looking for, so will the scope for addressing this issue with hedonic price modeling. This would build on the work begun by Golan and Shalit (1993) with respect to Israeli grapes, and a recent paper by Oczkowski (2002). If indeed weather variables during the grape growing season are crucial, as the empirical results of Ashenfelter (2000) and Wood and Anderson (2002) suggest, those too would need to be included in addition to such variables as grape sugar level, color and acidity.

References

Anderson, K., (ed.). (2003). *The World's Wine Markets: Glabalization at Work.* Edward Elgar, London (forthcoming).

Anderson, K., and Norman, D. (2003). *Global Wine Production, Consumption and Trade, 1961–2001: A Statistical Compendium.* Centre for International Economic Studies: Adelaide.

[9]The Australian Wine and Brandy Corporation and the Wine Institute of New Zealand, respectively.

[10]Care is needed in any such empirical work to separate the influences of quality upgrading national research and development on the supply side and promotional efforts on the demand side (see Zhao *et al.*, 2003), as well as to distinguish corporate, regional and national generic promotion.

Anderson, K., Norman, D., and Wittwer, G. (2003). Globalization and the world's wine markets'. *The World Economy*, 26 (forthcoming).

Ashenfelter, O. (2000). Liquid Assets: The international guide to fine wines. *Optimus: the Magazine for The Private Investor*, 2.

Ashenfelter, O., Ashmore, D., and Lalonde, R. (1995). Bordeaux wine vintage quality and the weather. *Chance*, 8, 7–14.

Byron, R.P., and Ashenfelter, O. (1995). Predicting the quality of the unborn grange. *Economic Record*, 71, 40–53.

Combris, P., Lecocq, S., and Visser, M. (1997). Estimation of a hedonic price equation for bordeaux wine: Does quality, matter? *Economic Journal*, 107, 390–402.

Golan, A., and Shalit, H. (1993). Wine quality differentials in hedonic grape pricing. *Journal of Agricultural Economics*, 44, 311–321.

Halliday, J. (1999). *Australia and New Zealand Classic Wines*, Harper Collins, Sydney.

Halliday, J. (2001). *Australia and New Zealand Wine Companion 2002*, Harper Collins, Sydney.

Kok, S. (1999). The Economics of Geographical Indications: A Case Study of the EU-Australia Wine Agreement. (Unpublished Honours Thesis), School of Economics, University of Adelaide.

Landon, S., and Smith, C.E. (1997). The use of quality and reputation indicators by consumers: The case of Bordeaux wine. *Journal of Consumer Policy*, 20, 289–323.

Nerlove, M. (1995). Hedonic price functions and the measurement of preferences: The case of Swedish wine consumers. *European Economic Review*, 39, 1697–1716.

Oczkowski, E. (1994). A hedonic price function for Australian premium table wine. *Australian Journal of Agricultural Economics*, 38, 93–110.

Oczkowski, E. (2001). Hedonic wine price functions and measurement error. *Economic Record*, 77, 374–382.

Oczkowski, E. (2002). Modelling winegrape prices in disequilibrium. Paper presented at the 31st Annual Australian Conference of Economists. *Adelaide*, 1–3 October.

Roberts, P.W., and Reagans, R. (2001). Market experience, consumer attention and price-quality relationships for New World wines in the US Market, 1987–99, GSIA Working Paper. Graduate School of Industrial Administration, Carnegie, Mellon University, Pittsburgh.

Rosen, S. (1974). Hedonic prices and implicit markets: Product differentiation in pure competition. *Journal of Political Economy*, 82, 34–55.

Schamel, G. (2000). Individual and collective reputation indicators of wine quality, CIES Discussion Paper 0009. Centre for International Economic Studies. University of Adelaide.

Shapiro, C. (1983). Premiums for high quality products as returns to reputations. *Quarterly Journal of Economics*, 98, 659–679.

Tirole, J. (1996). A theory of collective reputations (with applications to the persistence of corruption and to firm quality). *Review of Economic Studies*, 63, 1–22.

Winestate (2001). Tasting Data File 2001, Personal Communication with *Winestate* Magazine, Adelaide.

Wood, D., and Anderson, K. (2002). What determines the future value of an icon wine? Evidence from Australia, CIES Discussion Paper 0233. Centre for International Economic Studies. University of Adelaide.

Zhao, X., Wittwer, G., and Anderson, K. (2003). Who gains from Australian generic wine promotion and R&D? *Australian Journal of Agricultural and Resource Economics*, 4, 181–202.

Chapter 3

Dynamic Analysis of Brand and Regional Reputation: The Case of Wine*

Günter Schamel

Free University of Bozen-Bolzano,
School of Economics and Management,
Via Sernesi 1, 1-39100,
Bozen-Bolzano, Italy
guenter.schamel@unibz.it

Globalization has created an international wine market and global brands. However, consumers continue to regard regional origin as a dominant criterion in their wine buying decisions. Indicators of collective regional reputation as well as individual producer (or brand) reputation guide consumers in their buying decisions. We measure regional and brand reputation indicators for 27 growing regions around the world. Regional reputation is based on a region's overall quality performance through time. Positive and negative brand reputation based on relative regional peer performance is a distinct feature of this empirical application. Noting competing as well as common interest among regional producers, we hypothesize that wines from producers with a high quality reputation rely more on their own strengths and will depend less on their region's reputation and vice versa. We also test whether this assertion is valid over time covering six recent vintages. We apply a hedonic model to measure the significance of these regional and brand reputation indicators in determining wine prices. Our model largely confirms our hypothesis, but it also suggests that for some regions (Germany and New Zealand), high quality brands rely heavily on overall regional reputation. In other regions (including Napa and Sonoma Valley), high reputation brands seem to lose their strength and start to rely on regional reputation. Regions holding on to their strong individual brand reputations include the Rhone Valley, Spain, and Bordeaux. The analysis sheds light on how regional and producer brands are performing as wine markets mature in terms of global branding and consumers becoming more knowledgeable about wine regions, quality, and reputation.

*This article originally appeared in *Journal of Wine Economics* (2009), 4(1), 62–80.

1. Introduction

Demand for specific and identifiable characteristics, including methods of production and geographical origin offers expanded market opportunities for food and beverage products. Outlets for high-value products encourage producers to diversify production and focus on quality. Consumers are able to choose products on the basis of their specific characteristics and to reward them with premium prices in the market. In turn, producers will get the economic benefits from their investment in quality, specificity, regional as well as individual brand recognition.

We often observe price differences for otherwise similar products seemingly based on regional origin. Trade economists have stressed the importance of production cost, product quality, and strategic behavior and associate product origin with a reputation or quality measure (Brooks, 2001). However, this may neglect the impact of subjective preferences based on marketing, brands or product loyalty. For instance, producers from California's Napa Valley known for their high quality wine typically can sell their product at higher prices than those of comparable quality from lesser-known producers in other region. We explain such observations by positing that individual reputation indicators and regional origin affect purchase decisions.

We analyze the demand for different wine varieties evaluating quality aspects based on expert opinion and evaluation. Expert evaluations need to make a sufficiently clear distinction between the qualities available in the market, or consumer will not take them into account in their buying decisions. In our analysis, we use price data that is collected at the time when product quality is evaluated by product experts. When consumers are confronted with a range of qualities, we argue that expert quality evaluations are an important factor directing them to products with the specific quality attributes that they look for.

Our analysis presents a detailed exposition of quality based performance measures. They are isolated as a crucial factor in raising the likelihood that consumers have heard about a product's quality prior to a purchase as well as a crucial factor in attracting consumer awareness for individual producers, associated producer groups and/or wine growing regions. In this respect, expert quality evaluations will direct consumer to specific products or product groups with specific value attributes. Over time, such quality evaluations establish a record of quality performance signaling quality reputation to consumers.

However, there are reasons to believe that such quality evaluations are not fully dispersed across all potential consumers. Arrow (1974) notes limited information-handling ability (bounded rationality) as an essential part of human (i.e., consumer) behavior. While choosing among all possible alternatives, only a few are actually considered (Simon, 1997). In the case of wine, there is an almost infinite amount of quality evaluations available. For example, *Wine Spectator* publishes around 10,000 wine quality assessments each year. Consumers can only take a small part of this information into account and will make their own value assessments also relying on reputation indicators related to producers (brands), regional origin, and varietals. Given that consumers have limited attention levels, not all quality signals will receive equal notice. We assume that the attention level that consumers pay to positive (negative) quality signals is higher for producers that perform significantly above (below) their average peers. Based on this, we argue that unusually high as well as unusually low quality relative peer performance form a lasting impression and define high and low quality producers in the minds of consumers.

Appropriate research into price-quality relationships will not only look at present quality assessments, but also consider indicators of *reputation.* In Shapiro's (1983) model of reputation formation, the sum of all relevant current and previous quality assessments establishes a quality based performance record (reputation) that is reflected in current prices. In this chapter, we assume that consumers have a limited information-handling ability (Arrow, 1974) and calculate brand reputation based on a four vintage peer performance record.

In this chapter, we apply a hedonic model to estimate the potential impact of geographical origin on wine prices controlling for blind-tasted sensory quality, variety, *and* producer reputation to assess their significance in the global wine market. Moreover, we empirically test whether a positive individual brand reputation implies less reliance on the associated collective regional reputation indicator in determining wine prices.

2. Literature Review

Numerous studies have applied pricing hedonic models to estimate implicit prices for wine quality and reputation attributes. They are based on the notion that any product represents a bundle of utility-generating attributes. Rosen (1974) suggests that competitive implicit markets define prices for embodied product attributes, and that consumers evaluate product attributes (e.g., features of a car) when making a purchase. The observed market price is the sum of implicit prices for each quality attribute. Rosen recognizes an identification problem for supply and demand functions derived from hedonic models. Arguea and Hsiao (1993) show that identification is essentially a data issue which can be avoided by pooling cross-section and time-series data specific to a particular side of the market.

In addition to sensory quality and variety, brand and regional reputation will also affect wine prices since a bottle's quality is unknown until it is uncorked. Shapiro (1983) models producer reputation effects on prices in competitive markets but with imperfect information. Improving their knowledge about product quality is costly, to consumers. He demonstrates that reputation allows high-quality producers to sell their items at a premium, which may be interpreted as return on investments in reputation building. In such an imperfect information environment, credible measures of product quality and reputation can be effective in reducing consumer decision-making costs. Expert quality evaluations are an important vehicle enabling consumers to learn about the quality reputation of producers and regions. Tirole (1996) presents a model of collective reputation as an aggregate of individual reputations where current producers are affected by their own actions and past collective actions. Tirole shows that new producers may suffer from past mistakes and derives conditions under which the collective reputation can be regained. Winfree and McCluskey (2005) model collective reputation as a dynamic common resource problem and show that without firm traceability, chosen quality levels may be suboptimal for the group. Klein and Leffler (1981) show that a firm will invest in firm-specific sunk costs only if it can produce a high-quality good to gain a stream of future profits, which are not being realized if the firm "cheats" and produces a low-quality good.

Combris *et al.* (1997) estimate a hedonic price equation and what is referred to as a jury grade equation to explain variations in price and quality for Bordeaux wine. Landon and Smith (1998) focus on a lagged reputation indicator in addition to sensory quality. They use a hedonic model to study the impact of current quality and reputation based on past quality demonstrations. Their main findings are: reputation has a large price impact; an established reputation is much more important than short-term quality improvements; and ignoring reputation indicators will overstate the impact of current quality on consumer behavior.

Oczkowski (2001) argues that single indicators of wine quality and reputation are imperfect measures because tasters' evaluations differ and thus contain measurement errors. Employing factor analysis and 2SLS, he finds significant reputation effects but insignificant quality effects. Brooks (2001) argues that traditional views of international competitiveness emphasize product quality and production cost and neglect the potential impact of marketing and brand development on export demand. Applying hedonic regression analysis, she controls for vintage, blind-tasting quality, variety and also cost differences. Cross-country comparisons that suggest that neither cost nor quality differences, but "country brands" affect a wine bottle's price in excess of 50%, while exchange rate effects are insignificant. Crucial for this conclusion is to interpret the premiums on regional dummies as a marketing premium as opposed to a quality premium.

Schamel (2000) estimates a model with blind-tasting sensory quality, variety, scarcity, and special designations examining seven regions and two varieties. He finds that consumers are willing to pay a higher quality premium for Chardonnay compared to Cabernet Sauvignon. In contrast, red wine consumers put a higher value on regional origin and product scarcity. This suggests that the public-good value is higher for red wine appellations and their producers would benefit more from collective marketing efforts. Schamel and Anderson (2003) evaluate wine quality and regional indicators for wines from Australia and New Zealand. Other empirical studies with specific applications to wine include Jones and Storchmann (2001), Haeger and Storchmann (2003), Anderson and Wood (2006), and Schamel (2006).

Several theoretical models (e.g., Holmstrom, 1982; Diamond, 1989) suggest that performance should have a different impact on expected ability according to how much "reputation" agents have accumulated. Reputation is usually considered to build gradually through learning (i.e., after observing past performance). Modeling positive and negative brand reputation based on relative quality performance is a distinct feature of this empirical application. Consumers have an idea about brand's quality based on its relative regional performance. Consumer willingness to pay depends on expert opinions, wine age, varietal quality perceptions and regional origin effects. To assess the significance of such subjective perceptions on wine trade, we estimate the impact of regional origin *and* brand reputation on wine prices using a hedonic model. Moreover, we empirically test whether a positive (negative) brand reputation rely less (more) on regional reputation indicators. From this, we are able to derive some interesting implications with respect to market development and regional competitiveness. We also draw conclusions with respect to the correlation between prices and regional origin and the interpretation of brand values versus regional quality premiums.

3. Data and Analysis

We propose a hedonic model where the price of a particular wine is a function of important product attributes. The dependent variable is the logarithm of wine prices (P) in US$.[1] Data source for this analysis are expert quality evaluations for wines from the *Wine Spectator* (2005) covering the vintages 1999 through 2004. The *Wine Spectator* publishes U.S. release prices, sensory wine quality ratings based on a 100-point scale (WSP) as well as special expert selections (value designation BB, cellar collectible CC). We also derive an indicator for high (HQ) and low (LQ) quality brands by calculating the deviation of a producer's average quality rating from their respective regional average. We assume that high quality (HQ) and low quality (LQ) brands deviate by at least one standard-deviation from their respective peer average. This procedure classifies about 20% of the wines in the sample as HQ and about 20% as LQ. Following the reasoning in the introductory section, we assume that only such quality demonstrations (either high or low) will be remembered by consumers who are characterized by limited information-handling ability (and thus will command a price premium or discount).

Table 1 provides more information on the data set with 56,661 observations. We differentiate 27 regions in eleven countries and sixteen varieties.[2] Table 2 lists the sample statistics for all regions covered in the model. Over time, regions establish a record of quality performance that signals reputation. Restricting the model to three four vintage periods reflects that consumers have limited attention levels available to affect regional reputation. Table 3 lists average regional quality (AQ) for three periods each spanning four vintages ('99–'02, '00–'03, '01–'04). The final column measures the change in AQ from the '99 to the '04 vintage. Note that the change in average prices from the '99–'02 period to the '01–'04 period is very small (0.9%).

In our analysis, we estimate the full sample for each vintage period. In addition, we also estimate two separate models for positive and negative brand reputations. Producer or brand reputation is defined on the deviation

[1]The reported price is a suggested retail price on *release* and prior to tasting. This price may differ from actual consumer transaction prices due to retail mark-ups and government taxes differ.

[2]New World wines (e.g., California, Australia) are labeled primarily by variety, while Old World wines (e.g., France, Spain) are labeled primarily by their region of origin. The online data set does not classify a "Cabernet Sauvignon" from "Bordeaux." Unless otherwise noted, Bordeaux style wines are grouped as Cabernet blends.

Table 1. Description of the Data

Variable		Short description
Price[1]	*P*	*Suggested* retail price on release published by *Wine Spectator*
Sensory quality[2]	*WSP*	*Wine Spectator* Points (blind tasting: min. 50, max. 100)
Specialty wine	*Spec*	e.g., Amarone, Beerenauslese (BA), Trocken-BA, Eiswein, etc.
High-quality brand	*HQ*	One (1) standard-deviation above regional average (dummy variable)
Low-quality brand	*LQ*	One (1) standard-deviation below regional average (dummy variable)
Value designation[3]	*BB*	Best Buy, Smart Buy, Best Value (dummy variable)
Cellar collectible[4]	*CC*	Cellar Selection, Collectibles (dummy variable)
Age	*Age*	Age of wine when judged (average = 2.34 years, range 0–6 years)
Region[5]	*Reg*	Regional origin (categorical dummy)
Variety	*Var*	Wine Varieties (categorical dummy)

[1]Release prices as published in *Wine Spectator* as well as online.
[2]Scale: 95–100 (classic; a great wine)
90–94 (outstanding; superior character and style)
80–89 (good to very good; with special qualities)
70–79 (average; drinkable, may have minor flaws)
60–69 (below average; drinkable, not recommended)
50–59 (poor; undrinkable, not recommended)
[3]Value for money designation awarded after blind tasting procedure (incl. best buy, smart buy, and best values).
[4]Includes cellar selections (will improve most with aging) and wines regarded as collectibles.
[5]Combined California regions are defined as follows;
South Coast incl. Santa Barbara Co., Paso Robles. Santa Maria, Santa Yncz, and Edna Vlys.
Bay Area/Central Coast incl. Bay Area, Central Coast, and Monterey Co.
Rest of California incl. Mendocino/Lake Co., Sierra Foothills and all other California wines/blends.

of quality for a producer relative to peer producers within their region (WSP average above/below regional average). A positive (negative) brand reputation means that the producer has outperformed (not outperformed) its regional peers in terms of its average quality produced over the last four years. This allows us to test whether or not a positive individual reputation (strong brand) will imply less reliance on the associated collective regional reputation indicator.

A control variable in the model is the age of the wine at time of sensory expert evaluation (*Age*). As we cover only six recent vintages in the model,

Table 2. Regional Statistics (Full Data Set)

		Prices				Scores			
Regions	Count	Avg.	Std. dev.	Min.	Max.	Avg.	Std. dev.	Min.	Max.
Napa	3547	49.29	35.02	8	500	87.09	4.25	55	98
Sonoma	3154	33.72	16.92	7	175	86.56	4.01	55	98
Carneros	656	34.85	15.61	12	125	87.00	3.37	74	95
Bay Area/Cent. Coast	777	32.87	18.70	8	165	85.92	4.19	55	95
South Coast	1640	31.09	13.28	8	115	86.46	3.79	55	97
Rest of California	1953	19.73	13.56	2	120	84.09	3.65	68	94
Oregon	1837	31.68	16.34	7	150	86.99	3.91	55	95
Washington	2050	27.28	16.02	4	200	87.68	3.29	68	98
Rest of N. America	1361	18.26	10.14	6	120	81.44	4.02	59	93
Argentina/Uruguay	1201	19.16	17.81	4	155	84.60	4.67	55	96
Chile	1773	14.92	12.21	4	100	83.41	4.30	60	96
Australia	4069	26.67	24.71	5	400	86.76	3.52	71	99
New Zealand	1431	22.35	11.10	9	100	86.56	3.15	65	93
South Africa	1477	20.19	11.92	6	100	84.94	4.34	55	94
Burgundy	5016	58.99	52.88	7	635	86.58	4.87	55	98
Bordeaux	1719	53.58	104.46	8	1800	87.93	3.75	74	100
Rhone	2574	41.00	49.39	5	496	86.38	5.51	55	99
Languedoc-Rouss.	1266	15.32	9.63	5	75	84.40	4.24	68	94
Rest of France	2629	24.35	17.99	6	166	86.42	4.10	55	96
Tuscany	3819	33.89	27.22	7	340	86.05	3.92	59	100
Piedmont	2500	41.96	43.17	7	570	86.67	4.26	68	100
Northern Italy	1676	24.48	20.20	6	460	85.38	3.76	65	95
Rest of Italy	1300	22.40	17.10	6	220	84.55	4.02	50	95
Germany	2779	44.58	59.70	8	750	88.88	3.96	55	100
Austria	1413	33.08	18.02	8	117	87.23	3.43	68	97
Spain	1982	26.12	35.76	4	450	85.15	3.92	68	96
Rest of World	1002	21.06	16.62	4	125	85.03	4.19	72	97
Overall	56661	33.61	37.98	2	1800	86.19	4.34	50	100

Source: *Wine Spectator* online at www.wincspectalor.com.

the range of the age variable is 0–6 years. Further control variables are categorical dummies for wine variety (*Var*) and regional origin (*Reg*).

We use a mixed log-linear functional form to estimate the model. Similar models have been used in several chapters employing data from *Wine Spectator* including Ramirez (2008), Gokcekus and Fargnoli (2007). Thus, the core model estimated in this chapter is:

$$\log(P) = \alpha + \beta_1, \log(\mathrm{WSP}) + \gamma_1, HQ + \gamma_2 LQ + \gamma_3 BB + \gamma_4 CC + \gamma_5 Spec + \delta Age + \eta_{\mathrm{j}} Var + \theta_{\mathrm{k}} Reg + \varepsilon \quad (1)$$

Table 3. Relative Regional Reputation

	Average quality (*AQ*)		
Regions	'99–'02	'00–'03	'01–'04
Rhone	85.12	85.87	87.01
Burgundy	86.02	86.85	87.56
Languedoc-Roussillon	83.47	84.45	84.97
Rest of World	84.41	85.07	85.63
Germany	88.58	88.88	89.53
Rest North America	81.25	81.57	82.20
Argentina/Uruguay	84.11	84.55	84.91
Australia	86.43	86.66	87.02
Oregon	86.67	86.99	87.19
Rest of France	86.24	86.50	86.73
Chile	83.20	83.39	83.65
Northern Italy	85.24	85.59	85.59
Sonoma	86.30	86.21	86.64
Washington	87.51	87.60	87.76
South Coast	86.26	86.24	86.49
Spain	85.19	85.40	85.33
Bay Area/Central Coast	85.86	85.72	85.98
South Africa	85.04	84.99	85.00
Rest of California	84.00	83.91	83.96
New Zealand	86.59	86.50	86.44
Carneros	87.06	86.80	86.87
Bordeaux	87.88	88.18	87.66
Austria	87.46	87.32	87.10
Tuscany	86.13	85.88	85.73
Rest of Italy	84.92	84.82	84.51
Napa	87.21	86.68	86.77
Piedmont	87.40	86.83	85.66
Overall Average	85.98	86.13	86.38

where $\log(P)$ is the logarithm of the suggested release price in US$. Given the functional form this equation, β_1, measures the price elasticity of the quality rating. The γ coefficients measure the premiums/discounts for high/low-end quality producers, for the two special designations and for specialty wines. The δ coefficient for *Age* indicates the percentage premium paid for older and maturing wines while η and θ measure price premiums/discounts for regional reputation and variety, respectively. *Reg* and *Var* are categorical dummy variable for regional origin and variety. Estimating the equation above yields implicit prices for quality attributes relative to the contribution of the base control. Burgundy was chosen as the base region and Pinot Noir as the base variety.

4. Estimation Results

Tables 4a–4c list the results for the three periods analyzed. The first double column lists the estimation results for the full model while the other two double columns separate the results for positive and negative brand reputation. With respect to sensory expert evaluations in the full model, prices are highly elastic (e.g., about 3.7% or 1.20US$ at average prices for the period '99–'02). Indicators of HQ and LQ producer brands also affect prices significantly. It is interesting that HQ producers receive higher premiums (+28% to +31%) compared to the discount for the LQ producers (−10% to −12%).

Cellar selections and collectibles (CC) receive a 74–80% premium while value designations (BB) carry a discount around 51%. A more detailed look at variety effects suggests that prices for all differentiated varietals are significantly different from the base variety, a Burgundy Pinot Noir. The estimated variety discounts vary from −14% (Cabernet Blends) up to −42% (Sangiovese). All these estimates are relatively stable over the three successive time-periods analyzed in the chapter.

The most interesting results come from the relative effects of regional origin and the mitigating effects of brand reputation on wine prices. The estimated regional price differences are all negative relative to the Burgundy base region. Apart from "Rest of California," all other California regions receive higher prices relative to imports from the New World. New Zealand and Australia are the most successful New World importers. Oregon and Washington are about on par with Australia but exceed Chile, South Africa, and Argentina/Uruguay.

Next, we turn to the mitigating effects of brand reputation on the estimated regional effects. We argue that regional coefficients reflect both, a regional brand and a collective reputation value, because producer reputation signals are significant. Producers within a region may benefit from each other's quality performance due to spillover effects. As consumers pay closer attention to quality differences among producers, the price-quality relationship within a region becomes more competitive and less complementary. A higher level of regional quality would facilitate quality-based competition among producers and in turn may diminish the impact of regional promotion efforts.

The main objective of this chapter was to empirically test whether brands with a positive reputation indicator rely less on their region's reputation and vice-versa. Since positive reputation brands produce wines which perform

Table 4a. Regression Results for Vintages 1999–2002 [dep. variable = log(Price)][a]

	All wines		+ Brand reputation		− Brand reputation	
Parameter	Estimate	(*t*-statistic)	Estimate	(*t*-statistic)	Estimate	(*t*-statistic)
CONSTANT	−13.00**	−36.0	−20.87**	−30.8	−6.238**	−15.9
Log(WSP)	3.655**	45.0	5.436**	35.8	2.124**	23.9
Low-Quality Brand	−0.117**	−17.8			−0.107**	−15.7
High-Quality Brand	0.282**	41.1	0.181**	24.2		
Age	0.222**	70.8	0.196**	41.6	0.235**	56.5
Value Designation	−0.517**	−48.2	−0.569**	−40.8	−0.424**	−26.1
Collectibles/ Cellaring	0.740**	16.7	0.613**	13.4	1.012**	9.8
Specialty Wine	1.024**	27.7	0.968**	21.1	1.066**	18.6
Napa	−0.079**	−5.6	−0.071**	−3.7	−0.068**	−3.4
Sonoma	−0.336**	−26.4	−0.343**	−20.3	−0.320**	−16.9
Cameras	−0.258**	−15.2	−0.259**	−11.2	−0.263**	−10.8
Bay Area/ Central Coast	−0.381**	−19.0	−0.336**	−13.3	−0.423**	−13.5
South Coast	−0.364**	−25.4	−0.360**	−19.6	−0.361**	−16.5
Rest of California	−0.764**	−48.8	−0.659**	−31.4	−0.876**	−36.8
Oregon	−0.510**	−36.0	−0.497**	−28.1	−0.524**	−23.4
Washington	−0.553**	−34.6	−0.454**	−21.7	−0.650**	−28.5
Rest of North America	−0.597**	−35.9	−0.597**	−26.0	−0.558**	−23.5
Argentina/ Uruguay	−0.777**	−38.4	−0.731**	−23.3	−0.828**	−32.8
Chile	−0.885**	−56.5	−0.852**	−38.9	−0.928**	−42.7
Australia	−0.579**	−42.0	−0.536**	−28.9	−0.624**	−30.6
New Zealand	−0.408**	−27.1	−0.467**	−23.3	−0.345**	−15.3
South Africa	−0.685**	−42.3	−0.666**	−30.0	−0.706**	−30.3
Bordeaux	−0.405**	−16.3	−0.246**	−7.3	−0.634**	−19.9
Rhone	−0.180**	−9.0	−0.111**	−4.0	−0.240**	−8.5
Languedoc-Roussillon	−0.994**	−55.3	−0.978**	−38.7	−0.980**	−38.8
Rest of France	−0.509**	−32.4	−0.445**	−19.9	−0.565**	−25.7
Tuscany	−0.179**	−8.9	−0.147**	−5.6	−0.234**	−7.9
Piedmont	−0.142**	−8.3	−0.122**	−5.0	−0.141**	−6.0
Northern Italy	−0.611**	−36.8	−0.549**	−23.8	−0.669**	−28.7
Rest of Italy	−0.584**	−27.6	−0.558**	−20.0	−0.598**	−19.3
Germany	−0.272**	−12.9	−0.285**	−10.6	−0.245**	−7.5

(*Continued*)

Table 4a. (*Continued*)

	All wines		+ Brand reputation		− Brand reputation	
Parameter	Estimate	(*t*-statistic)	Estimate	(*t*-statistic)	Estimate	(*t*-statistic)
Austria	−0.219**	−11.0	−0.200**	−7.5	−0.241**	−8.4
Spain	−0.676**	−35.2	−0.510**	−17.9	−0.805**	−31.5
Rest of World	−0.793**	−33.2	−0.790**	−24.7	−0.776**	−22.0
Cabernet Blends	−0.140**	−9.0	−0.129**	−6.3	−0.155**	−6.4
Cabernet Sauvignon	−0.165**	−13.4	−0.135**	−7.7	−0.205**	−11.9
Merlot	−0.278**	−21.6	−0.235**	−12.3	−0.324**	−18.4
Sangiovese	−0.428**	−21.9	−0.405**	−15.4	−0.419**	−14.8
Shiraz	−0.154**	−13.0	−0.158**	−10.3	−0.177**	−9.7
Zinfandel	−0.256**	−17.5	−0.245**	−12.2	−0.278**	−13.5
Other Red	−0.308**	−24.6	−0.295**	−16.6	−0.317**	−17.7
Red Blend	−0.287**	−20.7	−0.278**	−14.9	−0.309**	−14.6
Chardonnay	−0.269**	−28.0	−0.249**	−19.9	−0.287**	−19.4
Riesling	−0.306**	−18.0	−0.303**	−14.2	−0.352**	−12.8
Sauvignon Blanc	−0.347**	−28.7	−0.351**	−21.3	−0.348**	−19.6
Pinot Gris	−0.249**	−15.3	−0.216**	−9.0	−0.297**	−13.8
Viognier	−0.073**	−3.2	−0.091**	−3.1	−0.049	−1.5
Other White	−0.351**	−25.8	−0.375**	−20.0	−0.339**	−17.3
White Blend	−0.258**	−14.9	−0.215**	−8.3	−0.295**	−13.0
Adj. R^2 [%]	59.53		58.96		55.70	
F-Ratio	1197.3	($n = 39,041$)	627.8	($n = 20,510$)	494.2	($n = 18,531$)

Notes: [a]Least Squares with White Heteroskedasticity-Consistent Standard Errors and Covariance. All estimates are significant at the 1% (**) level.

above their regional average and thus have a stronger brand reputation of their own, we expect that collective regional reputation is less important to consumers. On the other hand, since negative reputation brands perform below their regional average and thus have a weaker reputation of their own, we expect that collective regional reputation is more important to consumers. We estimate separate models for positive and negative reputation brands to test how regional reputation estimates differ *relative* to the full model. Based

Table 4b. Regression Results for Vintages 2000–2003 [dep. variable = log(Price)][a]

	All wines		+ Brand reputation		− Brand reputation	
Parameter	Estimate	(*t*-statistic)	Estimate	(*t*-statistic)	Estimate	(*t*-statistic)
CONSTANT	−13.99**	−35.6	−23.20**	−36.3	−6.429**	−20.4
Log(WSP)	3.880**	44.0	5.961**	41.6	2.165**	30.5
Low-Quality Brand	−0.105**	−15.6			−0.095**	−13.7
High-Quality Brand	0.309**	42.8	0.195**	25.0		
Age	0.227**	67.3	0.201**	39.3	0.238**	54.0
Value Designation	−0.513**	−47.9	−0.560**	−40.7	−0.418**	−17.6
Collectibles/ Cellaring	0.774**	14.0	0.620**	11.5	1.207**	6.3
Specialty Wine	1.034**	26.1	1.012**	21.1	0.960**	22.4
Napa	−0.079**	−5.3	−0.090**	−4.3	−0.064**	−3.4
Sonoma	−0.351**	−26.5	−0.371**	−21.1	−0.325**	−17.5
Carneros	−0.282**	−16.2	−0.310**	−12.5	−0.267**	−9.1
Bay Area/ Central Coast	−0.406**	−19.9	−0.374**	−15.3	−0.415**	−14.9
South Coast	−0.369**	−25.1	−0.377**	−19.7	−0.359**	−16.6
Rest of California	−0.776**	−46.9	−0.666**	−30.1	−0.856**	−39.3
Oregon	−0.516**	−34.6	−0.534**	−28.5	−0.490**	−22.7
Washington	−0.565**	−35.1	−0.529**	−25.1	−0.637**	−28.6
Rest of North America	−0.624**	−34.4	−0.660**	−27.0	−0.558**	−23.0
Argentina/ Uruguay	−0.795**	−40.4	−0.797**	−28.4	−0.809**	−31.1
Chile	−0.898**	−56.3	−0.879**	−39.9	−0.937**	−39.9
Australia	−0.593**	−41.8	−0.556**	−29.0	−0.642**	−35.0
New Zealand	−0.418**	−26.8	−0.473**	−22.2	−0.368**	−15.5
South Africa	−0.708**	−43.5	−0.708**	−32.6	−0.713**	−30.1
Bordeaux	−0.450**	−19.4	−0.331**	−10.2	−0.617**	−23.4
Rhone	−0.282**	−14.6	−0.225**	−8.6	−0.354**	−15.1
Languedoc-Roussillon	−0.982**	−52.7	−0.976**	−36.3	−0.977**	−37.4

(*Continued*)

Table 4b. (*Continued*)

	All wines		+ Brand reputation		– Brand reputation	
Parameter	Estimate	(*t*-statistic)	Estimate	(*t*-statistic)	Estimate	(*t*-statistic)
Rest of France	−0.546**	−33.8	−0.529**	−22.4	−0.567**	−26.5
Tuscany	−0.191**	−9.5	−0.186**	−7.0	−0.217**	−7.8
Piedmont	−0.230**	−13.2	−0.190**	−7.6	−0.251**	−11.1
Northern Italy	−0.639**	−37.0	−0.628**	−26.1	−0.645**	−26.2
Rest of Italy	−0.609**	−30.1	−0.562**	−20.7	−0.657**	−25.8
Germany	−0.250**	−11.8	−0.319**	−11.6	−0.189**	−6.0
Austria	−0.244**	−12.3	−0.244**	−8.7	−0.258**	−9.7
Spain	−0.660**	−34.1	−0.479**	−16.4	−0.804**	−36.2
Rest of World	−0.797**	−33.5	−0.834**	−25.0	−0.765**	−27.8
Cabernet Blends	−0.135**	−8.4	−0.111**	−5.2	−0.154**	−7.2
Cabernet Sauvignon	−0.143**	−10.8	−0.109**	−5.8	−0.181**	−10.2
Merlot	−0.270**	−19.5	−0.207**	−10.1	−0.323**	−16.7
Sangiovese	−0.425**	−21.7	−0.408**	−15.5	−0.415**	−14.6
Shiraz	−0.140**	−11.9	−0.139**	−9.2	−0.172**	−9.8
Zinfandel	−0.228**	−14.4	−0.236**	−10.8	−0.243**	−10.4
Other Red	−0.278**	−21.9	−0.262**	−14.7	−0.290**	−16.1
Red Blend	−0.249**	−17.8	−0.236**	−12.4	−0.261**	−14.0
Chardonnay	−0.253**	−25.7	−0.218**	−16.8	−0.280**	−20.5
Riesling	−0.284**	−16.6	−0.265**	−12.0	−0.329**	−12.2
Sauvignon Blanc	−0.317**	−25.4	−0.328**	−18.6	−0.308**	−16.4
Pinot Gris	−0.219**	−12.8	−0.173**	−6.7	−0.270**	−10.5
Viognier	−0.046*	−2.0	−0.068*	−2.2	−0.042	−1.2
Other White	−0.321**	−23.2	−0.326**	−16.7	−0.313**	−15.7
White Blend	−0.246**	−14.6	−0.213**	−8.5	−0.264**	−11.8
Adj. R^2 [%]	59.00		58.39		53.50	
F-Ratio	1060.8	(n = 38,685)	604.5	(n = 20,216)	452.5	(n = 18,469)

Notes: [a]Least Squares with White Heteroskedasticity-Consistent Standard Errors and Covariance. All estimates are significant at the 1% (**) or 5% (*) level.

Table 4c. Regression Results for Vintages 2001–2004 [dep. variable = log(Price)][a]

	All wines		+ Brand reputation		− Brand reputation	
Parameter	Estimate	(t-statistic)	Estimate	(t-statistic)	Estimate	(t-statistic)
CONSTANT	−14.28**	−33.5	−26.06**	−42.9	−5.641**	−12.5
Log(WSP)	3.944**	41.2	6.608**	48.6	1.981**	19.4
Low-Quality Brand	−0.125**	−18.2			−0.126**	−17.3
High-Quality Brand	0.296**	40.7	0.171**	22.7		
Age	0.234**	60.0	0.202**	35.2	0.241**	48.2
Value Designation	−0.518**	−43.0	−0.575**	−35.0	−0.398**	−22.9
Collectibles/ Cellaring	0.801**	10.8	0.605**	8.1	1.367**	7.6
Specialty Wine	1.138**	27.6	1.050**	21.5	1.183**	16.9
Napa	−0.091**	−5.7	−0.130**	−5.9	−0.059**	−2.7
Sonoma	−0.329**	−24.4	−0.379**	−21.4	−0.292**	−14.5
Carneros	−0.286**	−15.4	−0.323**	−11.7	−0.245**	−9.1
Bay Area/ Central Coast	−0.403**	−18.8	−0.391**	−15.2	−0.407**	−12.2
South Coast	−0.376**	−25.1	−0.419**	−21.8	−0.329**	−14.8
Rest of California	−0.783**	−44.4	−0.680**	−28.8	−0.834**	−33.7
Oregon	−0.469**	−31.0	−0.513**	−28.1	−0.419**	−17.3
Washington	−0.587**	−35.1	−0.525**	−23.2	−0.654**	−28.4
Rest of North America	−0.619**	−31.5	−0.658**	−26.3	−0.514**	−18.9
Argentina/ Uruguay	−0.792**	−39.2	−0.820**	−30.0	−0.785**	−28.7
Chile	−0.889**	−53.0	−0.852**	−36.8	−0.940**	−41.7
Australia	−0.592**	−39.6	−0.543**	−26.5	−0.640**	−30.6
New Zealand	−0.409**	−24.6	−0.524**	−23.6	−0.296**	−12.2
South Africa	−0.701**	−41.3	−0.706**	−31.6	−0.703**	−28.9
Bordeaux	−0.441**	−18.8	−0.351**	−10.7	−0.572**	−18.3
Rhone	−0.331**	−16.5	−0.281**	−10.8	−0.426**	−14.1
Languedoc-Roussillon	−0.961**	−50.0	−0.944**	−35.2	−0.963**	−38.2
Rest of France	−0.538**	−32.3	−0.566**	−24.4	−0.524**	−23.2
Tuscany	−0.223**	−10.5	−0.238**	−8.3	−0.203**	−6.7
Piedmont	−0.333**	−18.6	−0.298**	−11.6	−0.355**	−14.3
Northern Italy	−0.664**	−37.3	−0.639**	−25.5	−0.679**	−28.3
Rest of Italy	−0.642**	−31.7	−0.599**	−22.0	−0.670**	−23.3

(*Continued*)

Table 4c. (*Continued*)

	All wines		+ Brand reputation		− Brand reputation	
Parameter	Estimate	(*t*-statistic)	Estimate	(*t*-statistic)	Estimate	(*t*-statistic)
Germany	−0.274**	−12.7	−0.378**	−13.5	−0.182**	−5.6
Austria	−0.267**	−13.8	−0.283**	−10.4	−0.268**	−10.2
Spain	−0.660**	−33.0	−0.495**	−16.4	−0.799**	−31.9
Rest of World	−0.789**	−31.3	−0.847**	−23.0	−0.732**	−22.7
Cabernet Blends	−0.136**	−8.0	−0.135**	−6.0	−0.111**	−4.4
Cabernet Sauvignon	−0.145**	−10.0	−0.125**	−6.3	−0.152**	−7.5
Merlot	−0.279**	−18.1	−0.243**	−10.5	−0.284**	−13.9
Sangiovese	−0.416**	−19.8	−0.415**	−14.4	−0.394**	−13.4
Shiraz	−0.122**	−10.2	−0.144**	−9.4	−0.114**	−6.0
Zinfandel	−0.199**	−11.9	−0.216**	−8.4	−0.174**	−7.7
Other Red	−0.250**	−18.8	−0.240**	−12.9	−0.238**	−12.9
Red Blend	−0.217**	−15.1	−0.220**	−11.5	−0.191**	−8.8
Chardonnay	−0.227**	−22.4	−0.204**	−15.5	−0.215**	−13.7
Riesling	−0.242**	−13.9	−0.229**	−10.1	−0.255**	−9.4
Sauvignon Blanc	−0.313**	−23.9	−0.333**	−18.1	−0.277**	−15.0
Pinot Gris	−0.182**	−9.7	−0.112**	−3.9	−0.218**	−9.4
Viognier	−0.026	−1.0	−0.073*	−2.1	0.007	0.21
Other White	−0.299**	−21.4	−0.321**	−16.4	−0.260**	−13.2
White Blend	−0.237**	−13.8	−0.215**	−8.6	−0.225**	−9.7
Adj. R^2 [%]	58.24		57.85		51.63	
F-Ratio	1045.4	($n = 35{,}943$)	550.2	($n = 18{,}813$)	388.8	($n = 17{,}130$)

Notes: [a]Least Squares with White Heteroskedasticity-Consistent Standard Errors and Covariance. All estimates are significant at the 1% (**) or 5% (*) level.

on our hypothesis, we expect that positive (negative) reputation brands show a negative (positive) difference *relative* to the full model.

Table 5 reveals that our hypothesis holds true for most of the regions examined during the vintage period 1999–2002. Significant exceptions are New Zealand and Germany (check columns 3 and 5 in Table 5 for large positive and negative numbers, respectively). For these regions, our model suggests that brands performing above the regional quality average still rely more on regional reputation than brands performing below the regional quality average. Thus, producers with a positive brand reputation have some

Table 5. Brand and Regional Reputation 1999–2002

	1	2	3	4	5
	Full discount[a] %	+ Brand discount[a] %	Difference vs. full model %	− Brand discount[a] %	Difference vs. full model %
Napa	−7.9	−7.1	−0.82	−6.8	−1.03
Sonoma	−33.6	−34.3	0.74	−32.0	−1.62
Carneros	−25.8	−25.9	0.10	−26.3	0.50
Bay Area/Central Coast	−38.1	−33.6	−4.50	−42.3	4.25
South Coast	−36.4	−36.0	−0.38	−36.1	−0.30
Rest of California	−76.4	−65.9	−10.49	−87.6	11.21
Oregon	−51.0	−49.7	−1.27	−52.4	1.40
Washington	−55.3	−45.4	−9.84	−65.0	9.76
Rest of North America	−59.7	−59.7	−0.04	−55.8	−3.95
Argentina/Uruguay	−77.7	−73.1	−4.60	−82.8	5.06
Chile	−88.5	−85.2	−3.22	−92.8	4.38
Australia	−57.9	−53.6	−4.31	−62.4	4.49
New Zealand	−40.8	−46.7	5.87	−34.5	−6.38
South Africa	−68.5	−66.6	−1.96	−70.6	2.04
Bordeaux	−40.5	−24.6	−15.89	−63.4	22.94
Rhone	−18.0	−11.1	−6.91	−24.0	6.01
Languedoc–Roussillon	−99.4	−97.8	−1.61	−98.0	−1.36
Rest of France	−50.9	−44.5	−6.37	−56.5	5.61
Tuscany	−17.9	−14.7	−3.15	−23.4	5.55
Piedmont	−14.2	−12.2	−1.97	−14.1	−0.08
Northern Italy	−61.1	−54.9	−6.23	−66.9	5.77
Rest of Italy	−58.4	−55.8	−2.60	−59.8	1.41
Germany	−27.2	−28.5	1.31	−24.5	−2.71
Austria	−21.9	−20.0	−1.90	−24.1	2.24
Spain	−67.6	−51.0	−16.62	−80.5	12.87
Rest of World	−79.3	−79.0	−0.26	−77.6	−1.72
Wald-test F-statistic		6.85**		9.02**	

Notes: [a]Relative to base region/variety (Burgundy/Pinot Noir). **Significance at 1% level.

catching up to do in terms of building a stronger *individual* reputation while producers with negative brand reputations are free-riding.

In Table 6, we list the deviations versus the full model of strong brands (positive brands) and weak brands (negative brands) for all three vintage periods. In general, large negative numbers for positive brand reputations (and large positive numbers for negative brand reputations) indicate strong individual brands. Again, for Germany and New Zealand, positive reputation brands rely heavily on overall regional reputation. For Napa and Sonoma Valley, positive reputation brands are losing their strength and starting to rely on overall regional reputation. This particular effect is shown in Figure 1 with positive and negative brands moving in opposite directions.

Table 6. Brand and Regional Reputation Over Time

Region	Positive brand reputations[a] %			Negative brand reputations[a] %		
	99–02	00–03	01–04	99–02	00–03	01–04
Rhone	−6.91	−5.67	−5.09	6.01	7.27	9.49
Languedoc–Roussillon	−1.61	−0.62	−1.73	−1.36	−0.54	0.18
Rest of World	−0.26	3.70	5.87	−1.72	−3.18	−5.73
Germany	1.31	6.88	10.47	−2.71	−6.18	−9.20
Rest of North America	−0.04	3.53	3.92	−3.95	−6.66	−10.46
Argentina/Uruguay	−4.60	0.20	2.79	5.06	1.32	−0.72
Australia	−4.31	−3.69	−4.86	4.49	4.90	4.77
Oregon	−1.27	1.75	4.43	1.40	−2.63	−4.95
Rest of France	−6.37	−1.77	2.82	5.61	2.04	−1.40
Chile	−3.22	−1.94	−3.75	4.38	3.88	5.01
Northern Italy	−6.23	−1.13	−2.49	5.77	0.61	1.53
Sonoma	0.74	2.04	5.04	−1.62	−2.60	−3.74
Washington	−9.84	−3.66	−6.24	9.76	7.19	6.71
South Coast	−0.38	0.84	4.33	−0.30	−0.97	−4.67
Spain	−16.62	−18.08	−16.57	12.87	14.43	13.86
Bay Area/Central Coast	−4.50	−3.27	−1.14	4.25	0.82	0.42
South Africa	−1.96	0.04	0.49	2.04	0.52	0.13
Rest of California	−10.49	−11.02	−10.34	11.21	8.00	5.06
New Zealand	5.87	5.48	11.47	−6.38	−5.03	−11.29
Carneros	0.10	2.78	3.73	0.50	−1.55	−4.13
Bordeaux	−15.89	−11.86	−9.05	22.94	16.71	13.08
Austria	−1.90	0.00	1.65	2.24	1.44	0.18
Tuscany	−3.15	−0.55	1.48	5.55	2.58	−2.00
Rest of Italy	−2.60	−4.67	−4.28	1.41	4.89	2.83
Napa	−0.82	1.11	3.89	−1.03	−1.56	−3.22
Piedmont	−1.97	−3.96	−3.55	−0.08	2.12	2.14

Notes: [a]Differences versus full model relative to base region/variety.

Regions where positive brands are holding on to their individual reputations include the Rhone Valley, Spain and Bordeaux. This particular effect is shown in Figure 2 with positive and negative brands moving in the same direction.

Finally we note that brand reputation effects have a similar interpretation when it comes to explaining the age premium. As expected, wine prices for the full samples increase with age (+22.2% to +23.4%). However, it is interesting to note that the age premium is always larger for negative reputation brands even though their wines are about 0.135 years younger on average. Since positive reputation brands perform above their regional average and have a stronger brand reputation of their own, we observe that

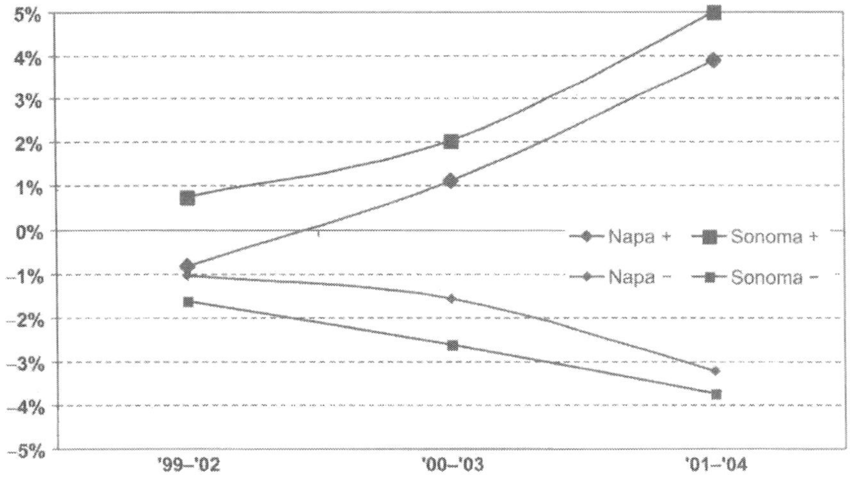

Figure 1. Brand Reputation Premium vs. Full Model for California Regions

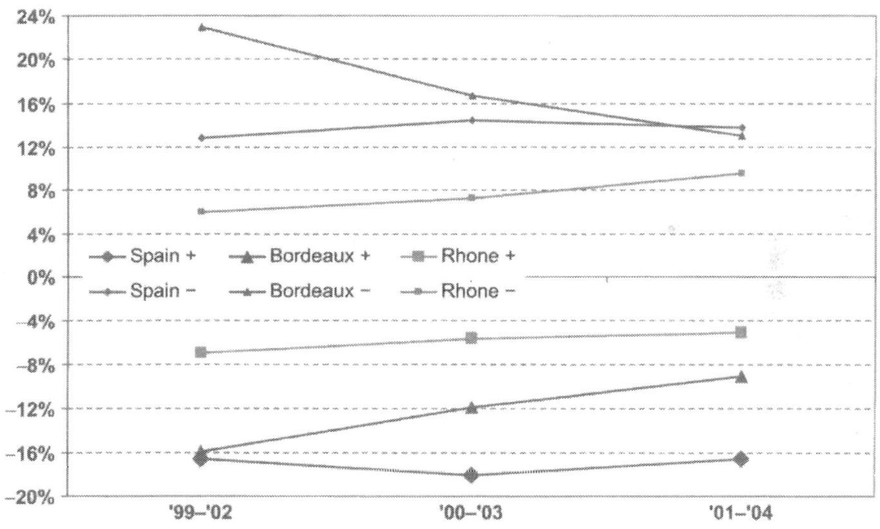

Figure 2. Brand Reputation Premium vs. Full Model for European Regions

the age of their wine is less important to consumers and results in a lower premium. On the other hand, since negative reputation brands perform below their regional average and have a weaker reputation of their own, we observe that the age of their wine is more important to consumers and results in a higher premium.

5. Summary and Conclusions

Producer brands increasingly dominate the international food and beverage markets. In this respect, we argue that one cannot interpret regional reputation as a "regional brand" value (as opposed to a quality premium) without adjusting for brand reputation. Using a hedonic model, we analyze price and product quality indicators for 27 different wine regions. We calculate *regional reputation* indicators based on their relative quality performance through time for three vintage periods in order to examine how different regions have performed over time. We also define positive and negative *brand reputation* based on the quality performance relative to the regional average.

We then investigate the hypothesis that producer brands with a positive quality reputation depend less on their region's reputation and rely more on their own strengths and tested whether this proposition holds over a period covering six recent vintages. Our hedonic model largely confirms this hypotheses, but it also suggests that for some regions (Germany and New Zealand), producers with positive brand reputations rely heavily on their regional reputation while producers with negative brand reputations enjoy a free-ride. In other regions (including Napa and Sonoma Valley), high reputation brands are losing their strength and start to rely on overall regional reputation. Regions holding their individual brand reputations include the Rhone Valley, Spain, and Bordeaux.

Our analysis sheds some light on how regional and producer brands are performing as international wine markets mature in terms of global branding and consumers becoming more knowledgeable about wine regions, wine quality, and producer reputation. As wine consumers become aware of producers (brands) or sub-regional quality and reputation indicators, they will pay more attention to producer and site-specific quality signals and become less reliant on more diffuse signals, such as regional reputation. Then, the producers in regions with strong individual brand reputations are better suited to meet an increasingly discerning consumer demand in maturing market. Producers in regions relying on their overall regional reputation continue to count on less discerning consumers reliant on more diffuse quality signals in a less mature market environment. Targeting the right markets depending on the status of brand development may be a key to success for regional promotion efforts.

Acknowledgments

I would like to thank, without implicating, the two anonymous reviewers for their valuable comments on an earlier version of this chapter. They are not responsible for any errors. This chapter has also benefited from comments of participants at the International Conference on World Wine Markets "Competitive Forces Affecting the Wine and Winegrape Industries" held in Davis, CA August 8–11, 2007. An earlier version of this chapter was presented at the 1st Annual Conference of the American Association of Wine Economists held in Trier, Germany, from May 23–26, 2007. Moreover, I would like to thank the Free University of Bozen–Bolzano for financial support (Project WW5018) to undertake this research.

References

Anderson, K., and Wood, D. (2006). What determines the future value of an icon wine? New evidence from Australia. *Journal of Wine Economics*, 1(2), 141–161.

Arguea, N., and Hsiao, C. (1993). Econometric issues of estimating hedonic price functions. *Journal of Econometrics*, 56, 243–267.

Arrow, K. (1974). *The Limits of Organization.* New York: Norton.

Brooks, E. (2001). Countries as brands: International trade in wine. *Working Paper, Harvard University.* Presented at Oenometrics VDQS XIII in Napa Valley, CA.

Combris, P., Lecocq, S., and Visser, M. (1997). Estimation of a hedonic price equation for Bordeaux wine: Does quality matter? *The Economic Journal*, 107, 390–402.

Diamond, D. (1989). Reputation acquisition in debt markets. *Journal of Political Economy*, 97(4), 828–862.

Gokcekus, O., and Fargnoli, A. (2007). Is globalization good for wine drinkers in the United States? *Journal of Wine Economics*, 2(2), 187–195.

Haeger, J., and Storchmann, K. (2006). Prices of American pinot noir wines: Climate, craftsmanship, critics. *Agricultural Economics*, 35, 67–78.

Holmström, B. (1982). Managerial incentive problems: A dynamic perspective. Republished in *Review of Economic Studies*, 66(1999), 169–182.

Jones, G., and Storchmann, K. (2001). Wine market prices and investment under uncertainty: An econometric model for Bordeaux crus classés. *Agricultural Economics*, 26, 115–133.

Klein, B., and Leffler, K. (1981). The role of market forces in assuring contractual performance. *Journal of Political Economy*, 89(4), 615–641.

Landon, S., and Smith, C.E. (1998). Quality expectations, reputation and price. *Southern Economic Journal*, 64(3), 628–647.

Oczkowski, E. (2001). Hedonic wine price functions and measurement error. *The Economic Record*, 77(239), 374–382.

Ramirez, C. (2008). Wine quality, wine prices, and the weather: Is Napa "different"? *Journal of Wine Economics*, 3(2), 114–131.

Rosen, S. (1974). Hedonic prices and implicit markets: Product differentiation in pure competition. *Journal of Political Economy*, 82, 34–55.

Schamel, G. (2000). Individual and collective reputation indicators of wine quality. *CIES Discussion Paper* 0009. Centre for International Economic Studies, Adelaide University.

Schamel, G. (2006). Geography versus brands in a global wine market. *Agribusiness: An International Journal*, 22(3), 363–374.

Schamel, G., and Anderson, K. (2003). Wine quality and varietal, regional and winery reputations: Hedonic prices for Australia and New Zealand. *The Economic Record*, 79(246), 357–369.

Shapiro, C. (1983). Premiums for high quality products as returns to reputations. *Quarterly Journal of Economics*, 98, 659–679.

Simon, H.A. (1997). *Administrative Behavior: A Study of Decision-Making Processes in Administrative Organizations.* 4th ed. New York: Free Press.

Tirole, J. (1996). A theory of collective reputations (with applications to the persistence of corruption and to firm quality). *Review of Economic Studies*, 63, 1–22.

Wine Spectator (2005). New York: Wine Spectator Press, (http://www.winespectator.com). Last Accessed: August 7th, 2007.

Winfree, J., and McCluskey, J. (2005). Collective reputation and quality. *American Journal of Agricultural Economics*, 87(1), 206–213.

Chapter 4

The Economics of Nested Names: Name Specificity, Reputations, and Price Premia*

Marco Costanigro†, Jill J. McCluskey‡, and Christopher Goemans§

†*Department of Agricultural and Resource Economics, Colorado State University, Colorado, USA*
marco.costanigro@colostate.edu

‡*School of Economic Sciences, Washington State University, USA*
mccluskey@wsu.edu

§*Department of Agricultural and Resource Economics, Colorado State University, Colorado, USA*
chris.goemans@colostate.edu

A good can be identified by its region or country of origin, the firm that produces it, and its product name. In other words, names can nest within each other to categorize goods with increasing specificity. This chapter develops a conceptual framework for jointly analyzing the effect of product, firm, and collective reputations on market price. The model is estimated via quantile regression with California wine market data. The results portray how the structure and relative importance of reputations change as product prices vary. Specifically, reputation premia migrate from collective to specific names as prices increase.

1. Introduction

"What's in a name?" Asking this question, Tadelis (1999) modeled a hypothetical market in which a firm's name is its only asset. We ask a new

*This article originally appeared in *American Journal of Agricultural Economics* (2010), 92(5), 1339–1350.

question: What's in a series of nested names? Like Chinese boxes or Matryoshka Russian dolls, names (or any other term used to identify one or more goods) can nest within each other to categorize goods with increasing specificity. In addition to a product name, a good can be identified by the firm that produces it *and* its region or country of origin, such as designer shoes "made in Italy" or "Irish whiskey." A car may be categorized by the country or continent in which it was manufactured, the make, the model, and the style. As reputations are essentially consumers' *a priori* (preconsumption) association of a name to a quality expectation, multiple reputations may relate to a single experience good, adopting Nelson's (1970) definition.

The primary objective of this chapter is to study the economic rationale underlying the genesis of nested names and reputations. To accomplish this, we develop a conceptual framework for jointly analyzing the effect of product, firm, and collective reputations on market price. A(reduced form) hedonic model of prices as a function of product attributes and the reputations associated with this taxonomy of nested names is then estimated. For firm and collective names, we empirically disaggregate the reputation price premia into the components which can be attributed to a set of different indicators of quality performance (average past quality, consistency of quality, and name longevity). Multiple estimations of the model via quantile regression (Koenker and Bassett, 1978) produce a series of "snapshots" portraying how the structure and relative importance of reputations change as product prices increase. Jointly, our results provide some insight into how firms and groups of firms may manage reputations and obtain price premia.

Historically, economists have studied private and collective reputations independently, perhaps because of the radically different incentive structures inherent to private and collective names. The existing literature has developed in two seemingly parallel streams: one focused on firm reputations, starting with Klein and Leffler (1981) and Shapiro (1982), and another centered on collective reputations (Tirole, 1996).

The main finding of Klein and Leffler (1981) is that reputation-based price premia are necessary to induce producer investment in quality, while Shapiro (1982) shows that for the case of a monopolist, the optimal quality output decreases when consumers cannot immediately verify it. After these seminal chapters, many other contributions on the economics of firm reputation ensued, with a preponderance of theoretical work. Examples include the use of game theory to study the role of reputations in establishing market power (Kreps and Wilson, 1982; Milgrom and Roberts, 1982), the conditions under which high quality and reputation are followed by low quality in a cyclical pattern (Gale and Rosenthal, 1994), and the role of adverse selection (Tadelis 1999 and 2003).

Many empirical studies on firm reputations have examined how the sudden release of information on (generally poor) quality performance affects the value of a firm, as measured by the stock market. For example, Jarrell and Peltzman (1985) and Barber and Darrough (1996) consider product recalls, Karpoff and Lott (1993) consumer fraud, and Mitchell and Maloney (1989) airplane crashes. Similarly, in the agricultural economics literature, researchers have studied the effects of food contamination and recall on markets (Smith *et al.*, 1988; Richards and Patterson, 1999; Piggott and Marsh, 2004; Thomsen and McKenzie, 2001). These studies consistently find that these negative events diminish demand and a firm market value.

Tirole (1996) introduced the term "collective reputation" into the economics literature and used it to study the persistence of corruption in groups of agents sharing a common name. The term is also used in the context of multiple firms sharing a common name (see Blair and Kaserman, 1994 on franchising) or instances in which products are traced to groups of firms. Agricultural products, which are often pooled from multiple producers for the purpose of distribution or processing, offer an illustration of the latter, where quality is associated with the region of production.[1] Theoretical work in this area has focused on the public good nature of collective reputations and how free-rider problems may be addressed (e.g., Winfree and McCluskey, 2005). For many agricultural products, empirical research has quantified, *ceteris paribus*, the existence of price premia specific to certain production regions (e.g., Combris *et al.*, 1997 for French wines; Loureiro and McCluskey, 2000 for Galician veal; Fotopoulos and Krystallis, 2003 for Zagora Greek apples), demonstrating that consumers are indeed willing to pay premium prices for good reputations.

A common trait of all of the cited studies is that the existence of a particular reputation structure is taken as an exogenous product or application-specific matter. It is not clear *why* economic agents form quality expectations on specific names for certain products but use aggregate ones for others. Considering the cases in which multiple reputations coexist provides an opportunity to investigate this research question.

[1]Collective names have been used to "brand" agricultural products since ancient times. Bertozzi (1995) writes, "Already in the fourth century B.C. in ancient Greece, there existed wines from Corinth, almonds from Naxos, honey from Sicily, and marble from Paros, while in the Roman Empire under the reign of Augustus, there were well-known dates from Egypt, cured ham from Gaul, oysters from Brindisi and marble from Carrara" (p. 143).

The automobile industry offers a good example. Since each manufacturer usually has access to different technological resources and managerial skills, forming quality expectations on firm names is a sensible discerning criterion. Barber and Darrough (1996) find that among the six major manufacturers operating in the United States from 1973 to 1992, Toyota produced the most reliable vehicles,[2] while Ford had the greatest number of product recalls. They also show that reputations are embedded in stock prices, and lack of product reliability hinders shareholders' returns. At the same time, since Japanese and U.S. firms operate in different business and cultural environments, we argue that consumers may also form general expectations of the quality of vehicles manufactured in the United States versus those built in Japan. Indeed, Barber and Darrough state, "Japanese automakers have enjoyed a significant advantage over their American counterparts in terms of vehicle reliability" (p. 1097).[3]

Such taxonomical structure of reputations need not be confined to the automobile industry or to firms and country-of-origin names: whenever a number of names share a common, distinctive set of quality-influencing traits (real or perceived), nested reputations may arise. A comprehensive list of examples would be large, spanning from Suisse banks to Bordeaux wines. Indeed, the only chapter (of which we are aware) accounting for the simultaneous existence of firm and collective reputations is a study on French wines by Landon and Smith (1998). Even though the authors do not explicitly study the use of nested names to form quality expectations, they show that firm and collective reputations affect product prices more than current quality performance.[4]

This chapter contributes to the literature on reputation in two principal ways. First, we model the hierarchical structure of names, laying the foundation of how one can think about reputations for nested names. Even though, *ceteris paribus*, name-specific price premia have been generally interpreted as

[2]The series of Toyota recalls in 2010 have likely shattered the manufacturer's reputation in the United States.Toyota's share price fell more than 20% in the month following the recalls of January 21, 2010.

[3]The study does not find evidence of spillover effects relating the quality performance of one firm to the stock market value of its competitors (located in the same or in another country). We suspect that this may be due to the short period of time (three to five days) over which stock market prices are monitored after a product recall.

[4]Two equations are estimated: (1) a prediction of quality as a function of past (lagged) tasting scores (a proxy for firm reputation) and a set of indicator variables for the region of production (a control for collective reputation), and (2) a prediction of prices as a function of current quality, expected quality, and a vector of wine attributes.

direct measures of reputation, we note that such premia capture consumers' willingness to pay for a good's reputation, *net* of the search cost necessary to associate quality expectations and names. This distinction is trivial when firm and collective reputations are studied independently (since search costs are similar across names), but it becomes pivotal for the case of nested names.

Second, we consider several indicators of past quality performance to understand how firms and groups of firms may manage reputations and obtain price premia. The analysis of reputation effects across product prices (i.e., conditional quantiles) reveals how the structure of reputation changes as product prices (and hence consumers' cost of being wrong in their expectations about quality) increase. The empirical application is the California wine industry, for the principal reason that blind quality ratings, exogenous to reputations, are available. Even though wine is the current application, our results are quite general and contribute to several fronts of the reputation literature.

2. The Model

Hedonic price analysis originated with the pioneering work of Waugh (1928) studying the relationship between vegetable prices and qualities (for a review of the methodology and its history, see Nerlove, 1995). The approach is routinely adopted by economists to value bundled product attributes that are not marketed individually and is based on the premise that in a market with perfect information and product differentiation, equilibrium prices will depend on differences in product attributes, *ceteris paribus*. The basic model is in the form $P_i = \Pi(\mathbf{z}_i)$, where P_i is the price of product i, z_i is a row vector of product attributes, and Π is the hedonic function relating product prices and attributes. If we assume that a quality index $\mathbf{q}$ exists and is known to consumers, the model modifies to $P_i = \Pi(qi, \mathbf{zi})$; where the presence of the quality index in the hedonic function may make certain product attributes redundant, whereas other attributes, such as those identifying alternative uses of a product, will maintain nonzero implicit prices.

We posit that for experience goods, consumers approximate the unknown q_i by using the quality expectations they associate with the (nested) names identifying a product. Assuming a three-tiered taxonomy for the case of wine, these will be the reputations associated with the name of the kth region of production, R_k, and the reputation of the jth firm, r_{jk} and of a particular product, b_{ijk} (for wine this includes the specific vintage and variety of a bottle). Introducing reputations and adding the time dimension by using the subscript t, we obtain $P_{ijkt} = \Pi(b_{ijkt}, \mathbf{r}_{jkt}, \mathbf{R}_{kt}, \mathbf{z}_i)$. Although the reputation of a particular product provides more relevant information than that of an aggregate name, some individuals might have formed quality expectations only for the region names and not for products or firms. Thus, it is legitimate to assume that equilibrium prices will depend on the reputation of all names and not only the most specific ones. Adding a vector of parameters, β, and an independently and identically distributed stochastic error term,we can express the equilibrium hedonic price as:

$$P_{ijkt} = \Pi(b_{ijkt}, \mathbf{r}_{jt}, \mathbf{R}_{kt}, \mathbf{z}_i; \beta) + \varepsilon_{ijkt}. \quad (1)$$

Before proceeding further, a clarification is needed. When forming quality expectations, consumers face two important choices. First, they need to decide at what level(s) of name specificity they will collect information and form quality expectations. For example, an uninformed consumer may need to decide whether to focus on collecting information on alternative manufacturing countries, firms, product models, or all of them. This is the process we seek to model. After selecting the level(s) of specificity, sources of information (or an optimal mix of media) need to be chosen. Sources of quality information include direct experiences (personal or reported by others), expert reviews, and advertisement. Each medium provides a different amount of trustworthy information, for a different search cost (in money and time),[5] but we assume that in the long run, consumers will form unbiased expectations.[6] Indeed, if quality is revealed after consumption, in a repeated-purchase scenario, expectations will be based on information regarding present and past quality,[7] independently of the chosen medium.[8]

Our next modeling step consists of specifying how reputations evolve over time, and what affects them. Although it is widely agreed that agents form quality expectations based on indicators of past performance (e.g., Shapiro, 1982; Kreps and Wilson, 1982; Milgrom and Roberts, 1982; Diamond, 1989;

[5]Consumer magazines generally provide reliable information, yet a conscious effort to read them needs to be made, and sometimes subscription fees are required to be paid. On the other hand, the information found in advertisements has almost zero cost, but its informational value may be dubious.

[6]In a general setting, this assumption requires only that consumers can assess quality after consumption.

[7]Note that information on present quality does not eliminate the need to form expectations, as the possibility of purchasing a defective product in the next purchase remains.

[8]We consider advertising as one of the possible sources of information. We do not have the data to test whether advertising influences quality expectations even after quality is revealed by consumption. In any case, we believe that wine advertising in the United States was negligible in the time frame spanned by our data.

Tadelis, 1999; Winfree and McCluskey, 2005); the exact relationship linking quality performance, reputation, and (stock or product) prices remains unknown. In his concluding remarks, Shapiro (p. 33) asked, "How is the choice of product quality related to the information gathering activities of individual consumers or the information flows in the marketplace generally?" After three decades, the issue is not yet resolved. Empirical work, generally constrained by the nature and availability of data, adopted a variety of strategies, relating prices to the release of news on quality performance (Jarrell and Peltzman, 1985; Barber and Darrough, 1996; Karpoff and Lott, 1993; Mitchell and Maloney, 1989), latent reputation constructs (e.g., Quagrainie *et al.*, 2003), or lagged quality ratings from consumer magazines (Landon and Smith 1998).

To summarize, the only consensus arising from the literature is that reputations depend on historical quality performance. Empirical research cited in this chapter generally related prices to location-type measures of quality performance. In dynamic models (Shapiro, 1982; Winfree and McCluskey, 2005), reputations have been represented as state variables whose current value increases or decreases based on the discrepancy between current average quality and past reputation. We adopt this general idea, but in addition to a location measure (the mean), we add two other dimensions to the determinants of reputation: quality consistency and the history of a name. The rationale is that risk-averse consumers should penalize names producing goods of inconsistent quality, and longevity in business may communicate high quality. Moreover, both factors directly relate to the search cost implied by forming quality expectations: inconsistent quality forces consumers to search more (at parity of "true" mean quality and the precision of its estimate), and so does a new name (existing reputations on older names need only be updated). Formally, we assume that the reputation of a name, say the kth region of production, evolves according to the following process:

$$R_{k,t=T} = R[\Psi(\mu(q_{kt})|_{t\leq T}, \sigma(q_{kt})|_{t\leq T}); T - t_{ko}] \tag{2}$$

where $\mu(q_{kt})$ and $\sigma(q_{kt})$ are the mean and standard deviation of the quality of the products marketed under region name k during time period t; Ψ is an unknown weighting function governing how quickly/slowly exceptional performances or past sins are forgotten; and t_{k0} represents the year in which a name enters the market. Firm and product reputations are assumed to evolve analogously.

Jointly, equations (1) and (2) depict a model in which equilibrium prices are a stochastic function of multiple reputations and a vector of product attributes. In turn, reputations evolve through time according to a deterministic process depending on the mean and standard deviation of present and past quality and the longevity of a name.

3. Methods

Quantile regression, a technique pioneered by Koenker and Bassett (1978), provides a straightforward methodological strategy to examine if and how the reputation dynamics change as the cost of being wrong increases. Furthermore, the approach allows controlling for market segmentation and possible structural breaks in implicit prices of the attributes occurring across price ranges (Costanigro *et al.*, 2007). In quantile regression, parameter estimates are obtained by solving the minimization problem: $\min_{\beta \in \Re p} \sum_{i=1}^{N} \rho_{\tau}(y_i - \mathbf{x}_i' \beta)$, where ρ_{τ} represents a function which, by asymmetrically weighting residuals, yields the τth conditional quantile; y is the regressand and $\mathbf{x}$ the regressors; and p specifies the number of parameters to be estimated.

Estimation can be repeated for all the quantiles of interest, thereby obtaining multiple, quantile-specific estimates of the same model parameters. Recasting equation (1) in its conditional quantile-specific form, we obtain:

$$\hat{P}_{ijkt}^{\tau} = \Pi(b_{ijkt}, \mathbf{r}_{jkt}, \mathbf{R}_{kt}, \mathbf{z}_i, \beta^{\tau}); \quad \tau \in (0, 1). \tag{3}$$

4. Data

For several reasons, the wine market provides a unique opportunity to analyze the relationship among prices, reputation, and quality. First, blind quality assessments by experts, *exogenous to prices*, are available from specialized magazines. Second, wine characteristics that can be easily evaluated in-store (i.e., red or white wines, grape variety, and bottle size and label) are relatively homogeneous, yet wine prices span a wide range, suggesting that reputation effects play a prominent role.

Finally, multiple names are used to identify each wine, each with its own reputation. While the winery name relates to the skills of its winemaker, the production region — the American Viticultural Area (AVA), for U.S. wines — identifies groups of wineries with similar weather and "terroir" conditions,[9] which exogenously influence the quality of the grapes and ultimately the wine (Wilson, 1998).

The core of the dataset consists of 9,261 observations obtained from issues of the *Wine Spectator* from 1992 to 2003, spanning ten vintages (1991–2000) of blind tasting quality scores (*SCORE*) for California red wines. We use these quality scores as an unbiased measure of wine quality. Varieties (*VAR*) include cabernet, zinfandel, pinot noir, Syrah and blended reds. For each wine, the producing winery, the AVA,[10] the vintage, the price (Consumer Price Index adjusted to the 2003 base year), and the number of cases produced are also recorded by the *Wine Spectator*. The dataset was compiled with information regarding the year in which the 51 AVAs in the dataset were officially recognized by the U.S. Alcohol and Tobacco Tax and Trade Bureau (TTB), and the year of establishment of the wineries (1,049 in total) from several issues of *Wines and Vines Directory of Wineries/Buyer's Guides*.

Endogeneity problems are common with this type of study, so further discussion of the *PRICE* and *SCORE* variables is worthwhile. First, if price is set after the quality ratings are released, it is possible that observed variations in price simply reflect retailer markups in response to *Wine Spectator* ratings. However, the price data used in this study represent the suggested retail price from the winery for each wine at the time the wine is released. These prices are collected by the *Wine Spectator* prior to tasting, so the above problem is not a concern. This does, however, raise the possibility that high-priced wines are more likely to receive higher ratings. Thus, it is important to note that *Wine Spectator* ratings are the result of a blind tasting process, and no information about price is available to the reviewers at the time of tasting: price is not taken into account when scoring.[11]

[9]Even though *terroir*, terrain, is considered by many wine critics and the popular audience as one of the principal factors in determining wine quality, there is growing empirical evidence that soil characteristics play a limited role compared with the influence of weather (Byron and Ashenfelter, 1995) or technology (Gergaud and Ginsburgh, 2008).

[10]Certain AVAs in California are large, overlapping or entirely containing smaller ones. Generally, wine labels report only the smallest AVA name (and so does the *Wine Spectator*). In the few cases in which two AVA names were found, the name of the oldest AVA was used.

[11]*Wine Spectator* includes the following in its description of the tasting process: "Bottles are coded and bagged, and all capsules and corks are removed. . . . No information about the winery or the price of the wine is available to the tasters while they are tasting." http://www.winespectator.com/display/show/id/tasting-format (accessed June 26, 2010).

Another issue deserving further discussion is the use of expert ratings as an unbiased measurement of quality. In effect, we are making the assumption that consumers' quality assessment are, on average, consistent with that of the *Wine Spectator.* While we have no reason to doubt that wine experts are able to assess the quality of a wine,[12] there is a possibility that the preferences of the wine experts and those of the general public might not coincide. In support of our choice, we found a great deal of evidence that (past or present) expert scores have been found to be positively correlated with wine prices independently of the specific countries, wine magazines, or experts (e.g., Landon and Smith 1997; Angulo *et al.*, 2000; Schamel and Anderson, 2003; Costanigro *et al.*, 2007).

5. Empirical Specification

In order to estimate equation (3), we need to operationalize equation (2). We do so by specifying Ψ as a moving average process and by using blind tasting scores to measure quality.

To be precise, we build *average quality* and *standard deviation constructs*, which, for the kth region of production, take the forms

$$AVAPQ_{jt} = \frac{1}{2}[AVAPQ_{k(t-1)} + \underset{k}{avg}(SCORE_{ijk(t-1)})] \quad \text{and}$$

$$AVASD_{kt} = \frac{1}{2}[AVASD_{k(t-1)} + \underset{k}{sd}(SCORE_{ijk(t-1)})]$$

where t is the issue year of the *Wine Spectator* magazine, and avg_k and sd_k represent the average and standard deviation operators applied to all wines produced in region k, rated in period $t-1$. The longevity component of a region is simply the scalar $AVAY_{kt} = (t - t_{k0})$, the number of years since the kth region of production was officially recognized by the TTB. In summary, $AVAPQ$ and $AVASD$ are computed using information from two adjacent

[12] Alternatively, a sufficient assumption would require the expected error in quality assessment to equal zero and be uncorrelated with the regressors. Reutera (2009) examined the possibility that wineries advertising in the magazine might receive higher ratings and concluded, "*Wine Spectator* appears to largely insulate reviewers from the influence of advertisement."

Table 1. Descriptive Statistics of Dependent and Independent Variables

	PRICE[a]	SCORE	FIRMPQ	FIRMSD	FIRMY	AVAPQ	AVASD	AVAY
N[b]	9261	9261	7717	6115	8183	9074	8949	9199
Mean	\$37.18	86.54	86.65	2.36	25.42	86.25	3.50	14.51
Min	\$6.05	60	62.00	0.00	1	74.67	0.00	1
p25	\$19.76	84	85.00	1.53	9	85.42	3.14	12
p50	\$27.12	87	87.00	2.19	17	86.24	3.49	15
p75	\$39.78	89	88.48	2.98	25	87.68	3.86	18
Max	\$2, 140	99	96.63	14.14	149	91.00	7.78	22

[a]Prices are deflated by the Consumer Price Index with a 2003 base year.
[b]Differences in number of observations across variables are due to non-AVA wines, scarcely populated series of quality ratings, or missing data.

time periods,[13] and recent quality performance affects reputations more than does the quality output of the more distant past. The analogous reputation constructs relative to the jth firm, founded in year t_{j0}, are obtained as

$$FIRMPQ_{jt} = \frac{1}{2}[FIRMPQ_{j(t-1)} + \underset{j}{avg}(SCORE_{ijk(t-1)})],$$

$$FIRMSD_{jt} = \frac{1}{2}[FIRMSD_{j(t-1)} + \underset{j}{sd}(SCORE_{ijk(t-1)})], \quad \text{and}$$

$$FIRMY_{jt} = (t - t_{j0}).$$

We do not have the data to build equivalent constructs at the highest level of specificity (a particular wine),[14] but little is lost by specifying $b_{ijkt} = SCORE_{ijkt}$: for a given winery, we expect the variance in quality across all the bottles of a specific wine to be small; and the relevant name longevity effects are captured by the firm-level name. Table 1 presents descriptive statistics of our dataset and data constructs, and Table 2 reports their pairwise correlations.

[13]The first observation of each series is missing, and the second is calculated using the average quality score of the first year in which a winery appears in the dataset. The process produced 5,764 complete observations.
[14] *Wine Spectator* publishes the rating of a particular bottle of wine only once, and ratings of different vintages of the same wine are rated too sparsely in the dataset.

Table 2. Correlations Among *PRICE*, *SCORE*, and Data Constructs

	PRICE	*SCORE*	*FIRMPQ*	*FIRMSD*	*FIRMY*	*AVAPQ*	*AVASD*	*AVAY*
PRICE	1.00							
SCORE	0.35	1.00						
FIRMPQ	0.34	0.49	1.00					
FIRMSD	−0.06	−0.05	−0.18	1.00				
FIRMY	−0.06	−0.13	−0.18	0.16	1.00			
AVAPQ	0.26	0.32	0.42	−0.05	−0.07	1.00		
AVASD	0.00	0.05	−0.02	0.15	−0.02	−0.13	1.00	
AVAY	0.13	0.08	0.18	−0.10	0.06	0.34	0.02	1.00

Assuming that the price effect of each reputation determinant is additively separable, the model is estimated as:

$$\begin{aligned} P_{ijkt} &= \beta_0^\tau + \beta_1^\tau(SCORE_{ijkt}) + \beta_2^\tau(FIRMPQ_{jt}) + \beta_3^\tau(FIRMSD_{jt}) \\ &\quad + \beta_4^\tau(FIRMY_{jt}) + \beta_5^\tau(AVAPQ_{kt}) + \beta_6^\tau(AVASD_{kt}) + \beta_7^\tau(AVAY_{kt}) \\ &\quad + \sum_{z=9}^{13} \beta_z^\tau(VAR_i) + \varepsilon_{ijkt}. \end{aligned} \tag{4}$$

The following all concur in allowing the identification of the model's parameters: (a) use of current quality scores for b_{ijkt} (while R_k and r_{jk} are based on past scores), (b) the large number of firms residing in each AVA, and (c) the robustness of the AVA-level moving average constructs to changes in the quality and standard deviation of an individual firm.

Although most hedonic studies adopt loglinear specifications, here we allow the implicit prices of each regressor to change with the dependent variable by means of quantile regression, so that the imposition of a specific functional form is not necessary. Therefore, the dependent variable, *PRICE*, is maintained in its linear form, and parameter estimates can be interpreted as quantile-specific marginal effects.

6. Results and Discussion

Table 3 presents quantile regression estimates for the 20th, 40th, 50th, 60th, and 80th quantiles and ordinary least squares (OLS) estimates from a loglinear specification of the model. For the quantile estimates, standard errors

Table 3. 20th, 40th, 50th, 60th, and 80th Conditional Quantile and OLS Estimates[a,b]

	$\tau = 0.2$	$\tau = 0.4$	$\tau = 0.5$	OLS[c]	$\tau = 0.6$	$\tau = 0.8$
SCORE	\$0.84*	\$1.08*	\$1.17*	0.045*/\$1.24	\$1.19*	\$1.49*
	(0.044)	(0.064)	(0.074)	(0.002)	(0.080)	(0.104)
FIRMPQ	\$0.89*	\$1.19*	\$1.34*	0.055*/\$1.49	\$1.65*	\$2.13*
	(0.053)	(0.075)	(0.105)	(0.002)	(0.108)	(0.192)
FIRMSD	−\$0.15	−\$0.30*	−\$0.29	−0.008*/−\$0.24	−\$0.46*	−\$0.61*
	(0.085)	(0.122)	(0.162)	(0.004)	(0.186)	(0.310)
FIRMY	−\$0.04*	−\$0.03*	−\$0.03*	−0.001*/−\$0.03	−\$0.03*	−\$0.02
	(0.004)	(0.005)	(0.006)	(0.000)	(0.007)	(0.010)
AVAPQ	\$1.62*	\$1.78*	\$1.84*	0.073*/\$1.99	\$1.79*	\$1.85*
	(0.095)	(0.125)	(0.128)	(0.004)	(0.180)	(0.252)
AVASD	−\$0.48*	−\$0.72*	−\$0.85*	−0.02*/\$0.54	−\$0.63	\$0.54
	(0.229)	(0.338)	(0.415)	(0.008)	(0.356)	(0.407)
AVAY	\$0.22*	\$0.26*	\$0.29*	0.01*/\$0.28	\$0.34*	\$0.36*
	(0.036)	(0.040)	(0.049)	(0.001)	(0.042)	(0.069)

Note: An asterisk ($*$) indicates significance at the 0.05 level.
[a]Grape varieties and constant are omitted.
[b]Coefficient estimates represent marginal effects. Standard errors are in parentheses.
[c]Coefficients are estimated with log-linear specification, and marginal effects are calculated at median price.

were calculated by bootstrapping.[15] Most parameter estimates are significant at conventional levels, and results are robust to alternative specifications of the data constructs.[16] The coefficients measuring the effect of quality consistency (*FIRMSD* and *AVASD*), are still significant, but have larger standard errors relative to the other coefficient estimates. This is expected, as the mean is estimated more precisely than the variance.[17] All signs, with perhaps the exception of one (i.e., the *FIRMY* parameter estimates) are

[15]Three hundred random draws were taken. The interested reader should see Hahn (1995) and Buchinsky (1998) for discussion about the quantile regression bootstrap estimator of the variance-covariance matrix.
[16]In addition to the model fully presented in the chapter, "fast" and "slow-learning" models were also estimated by varying the weights of the moving average constructs with no appreciable change in the economic significance of the results. To provide an example, a faster-learning process can be imposed by the weights

$$FIRMPQ_{jt} = \left[\frac{1}{3} FIRMPQ_{j(t-1)} + \frac{2}{3} \underset{j}{avg}(SCORE_{ijk(t-1)})\right].$$

Results are summarized in an appendix, which is available upon request from the authors.
[17]It can be shown that at parity of sample size $\text{var}(avg) < \text{var}(s.d.)$

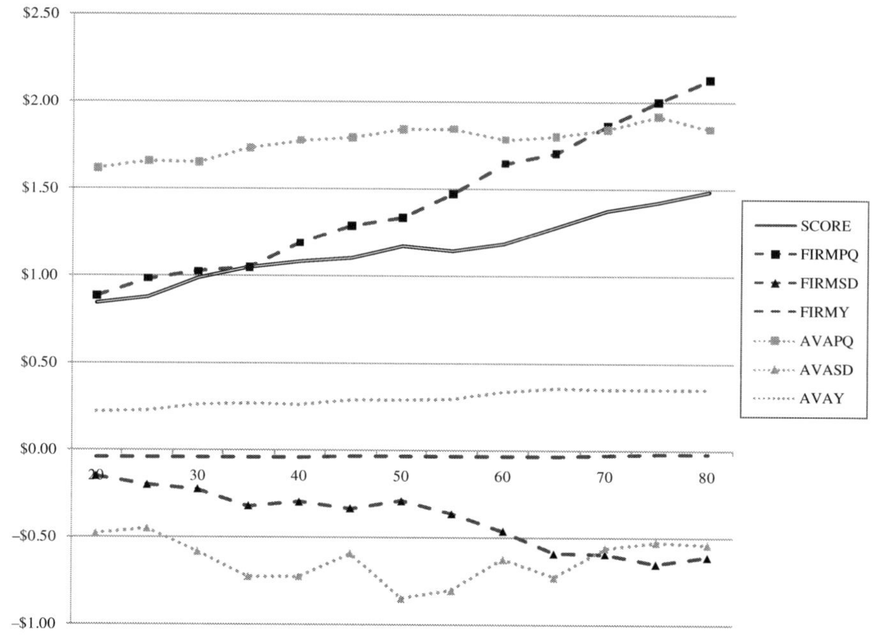

Figure 1. Selected estimates for each 5th conditional quantile $\in [20, 80]$
Note: Grape varieties and constant omitted.

consistent with *a priori* expectations. To ease interpretation, we also estimated the model parameters at each fifth quantile within the 20th and 80th interval and present them graphically in Figure 1. All estimates referring to the same regressors are different when the 20th and 80th quantiles are compared pair-wise (at the nominal size $\alpha = 0.5$), with the exception of the *FIRMSD*, *AVAPQ*, and *AVASD* estimates ($p = 0.11$, 0.32, and 0.88, respectively). Firm-level estimates are statistically different from their AVA-level analogues in the median and lower quantiles, while they are not at the highest quantiles.[18]

There are three main dimensions to our results: first, the estimates relative to the median quantile are discussed to show how firms or groups of firms can obtain and manage reputation premia; then we examine how, at a given conditional quantile, reputation premia distribute across nested names. Finally, estimates are compared across quantiles to understand if and how reputation dynamics are different for low-priced and expensive products.

[18]A Wald test rejected the joint null hypothesis $H_0 : \beta_2^\tau = \beta_5^\tau; \beta_3^\tau = \beta_6^\tau$ at any conventional level of significance for $\tau = 0.2$, 0.4, 0.5 but not for $\tau = 0.6$, 0.8 ($p = 0.74$ and 0.69, respectively).

Jointly, these three dimensions compose a rather general picture, within which we propose some hypotheses regarding the genesis of the use of nested names and its economic rationale.

For the median wine (Table 3), reputation premia are increased by marginal changes in current quality scores (by \$1.17), the firm average quality construct (by \$1.34), and the AVA average quality construct (by \$1.84). Conversely, a marginal increase in the standard deviation construct reduces reputation premia (by −\$0.29 for the firm and by −\$0.85 for the AVA).[19] From a producer's perspective, these results imply that, at parity of cost, policies aimed at increasing average quality *and* consistency should be preferred to the ones focusing on only one of the parameters.[20] More importantly, our results suggest that the mean is not the only parameter of the quality density function relevant in determining reputations, as previous research generally assumed. Consumers' risk aversion and increasing search costs due to inconsistent quality are likely the rationale behind the negative price effects captured by the *FIRMSD* and *AVASD* constructs.

According to our estimates, the AVA premium of the median wine increases each year by an average of \$0.29, implying that older AVAs fetch higher prices at parity of (present and past) quality performance. As argued before, name longevity will affect price premia if consumers consolidate their quality expectations overtime: consumers may be willing to pay a higher price for an older name that has been consistently producing high quality for a long period of time and avoid the hassle of collecting information on other, more recent names.

Counterintuitively, the estimated coefficient for *FIRMY* is negative and significant, implying that older firms earn lower prices at parity of

[19]Note that (Table 3) a set of similar results can be obtained by estimating the model via OLS with a log-linear specification and then calculating marginal effects at the median price.This approach introduces the dependency of the implicit prices on the dependent variable via the transformation imposed on the regressand. The OLS conditional mean estimates are greater than the conditional median ones, since the OLS estimator is sensitive to outliers, while quantile regression is not. More importantly, note that some implicit price functions in Figure 1 cross each other (e.g., *FIRMPQ* crosses *AVAPQ* at the 70th conditional quantile); while others have large effects which remain unchanged across quantiles. Had we estimated only a conditional mean log-linear model, such patterns would have been ruled out.

[20]For example, an AVA seeking to increase its reputation premium might enforce minimum quality standards on its constituents, or incentivize quality by instituting competitions in which wine tasting scores are made public. The first policy will increase mean and reduce variance (by cutting the lower tail of the quality distribution), while the second may have an effect on average quality but not necessarily on variance.

current quality and reputation. Although surprising at first, this finding is consistent with theoretical (Bagwell and Riordan, 1991) and empirical (Benjamin and Podolny, 1999) results in the price signaling literature: if consumers associate high prices with high quality, we should expect a firm to signal the high quality of a new product by raising the price above the full information profit-maximizing level, followed by dampening of the price over time as more and more consumers become aware of the quality of the product. With this insight, our results are consistent with the idea that new, unknown firms tend to price-signal more than older, well-known firms. In further support of this hypothesis, the negative effect of *FIRMY* diminishes in the higher quantiles, where price signaling is no longer necessary.[21]

The second layer of results is found by considering how reputation price premia change as names become more specific. For the median quantiles, the price effect associated with the quality of an individual bottle is smaller than the firm and AVA premia. In turn, AVA-level effects dominate all others in term of absolute magnitude. Indeed, the size and economic significance of collective reputations for California wines is striking, and in some ways paradoxical. If consumers value information, expectations consolidated on specific names should be valued more than the ones relative to more generic names, *ceteris paribus*. This paradox vanishes if we consider that search costs curtail the ability of a name to capture all of consumers' willingness to pay for information on quality. These search costs obviously increase with the level of name specificity: as names become more specific in a nesting sequence, a larger number of quality expectations need to be formed and compared.[22] If these costs are large enough, a consumer will trade the increased accuracy of using specific names for the convenience offered by more aggregated ones. Indeed, the number of wines and winery names can be intimidating for many nonconnoisseurs, and most consumers may prefer a simpler, aggregate reference structure to compare products.

[21] An alternative explanation is that poor quality expectations have crystallized on the names of older Californian wineries because production in the earlier years of industrial winemaking in California was typically bulk and low-quality. Furthermore, older wineries in our dataset also tend to produce large quantities of each wine, suggesting that economies of scale on the cost side might also play a role.

[22] We can think of three main costs associated with forming expectations: one related to accessing source(s) of information, one related to comparing expected quality across names, and finally there is the cost of updating the information through time. All of these costs are proportional to the number of names considered, and hence the level of specificity.

The last layer of interpretation resides in analyzing how estimates change from the lower to the higher quantiles. What can be seen by tracking this dimension in Figure 1 is an increase in the magnitude of the premia associated with the firm quality constructs and individual wine names, while AVA-specific estimates remain stable. From the 70th quantile, the firm-level point estimates become larger than the AVA counterparts. The fact that reputation premia grow larger as wine prices increase is somewhat expected: the greater the monetary investment, the more consumers are willing to pay for information on quality, ensuring against bad experiences. What is perhaps less obvious is that in relative terms, the price impact of reputation premia migrates from aggregate names to specific ones as prices increase. Our interpretation of this result relies once more on the role of search costs. While these are high for specific names and low for aggregated ones, price variations leave the cost of searching relatively unchanged. Thus, most consumers may find it optimal to use aggregated names for inexpensive products but may be willing to search more at high prices, forming quality expectations on more specific names.

Following this reasoning, it is not necessary to invoke exogenous causes to explain why, for many low-priced agricultural products, firm-level information is not available and reputations form only at aggregate levels: given a low cost of being wrong, consumers may just be unwilling to form the reference structure of quality expectations necessary to use firm-specific names. Along the same lines, food contamination (e.g., *Escherichia coli*) and animal disease outbreaks (e.g., bovine spongiform encephalopathy, or "mad cow" disease) represent interesting case studies in which the existing reputation structure is made inadequate and suboptimal by a sudden and unexpected shift in the cost of being wrong.

Returning to the estimates of Figure 1, one may also expect that if a consumer forms quality expectation at the firm level, he or she will not consider at all the less accurate quality cues contained in collective names. Instead, we find that rather than replacing them, firms selling expensive wines "add" their reputation premia to the AVA premia, which remain stable across quantiles. This finding is consistent with a two-stage decision-making process in which, when facing choices related to important consequences, consumers use the reputations of aggregate names as a sorting device to reduce the number of more specific names on which they collect additional information. To provide an analogy, a patient may decide where to have knee surgery based on the reputation of a few alternative hospitals, but he may also collect information on the individual surgeons for more complicated surgical interventions. Such hierarchical structure of decision making would have obvious implications for those high-quality firms which are trapped in collective names with poor reputations.

7. Conclusions and Future Research

In an empirical application to the wine market, this chapter provides evidence that reputation dynamics change across the price spectrum, and reputation premia migrate from collective to specific names as prices increase. These findings suggest that tradeoffs between the (negative) consequences of experiencing poor quality and the variable costs of forming quality expectations determine the level of specificity at which names develop reputations and price premia are captured. This basic intuition, we believe, contains the seed for the formal development of a theory in which firm or collective reputations arise endogenously and, under specific conditions, jointly. Second, we presented empirical evidence that reputation premia are related to a series of factors summarizing the *distribution* of the quality performance of a name, and not only its mean. Here, we considered average quality, quality consistency, and name longevity. The exact process describing how reputations evolve through time and the complete array of factors influencing them remains nevertheless an open question, as the specification of the adopted reputation constructs is a maintained assumption of the chapter rather than a tested one.

Acknowledgments

The authors wish to thank without implicating Stephan Kroll, Ron Mittelhammer, Felix Munoz, Jon Yoder, Jason Winfree, and Orley Ashenfelter for helpful comments on this and related work.

References

Angulo, A.M., Gil, J.M., Gracia, A., and Sanchez, M. (2000). Hedonic prices for Spanish red quality wine. *British Food Journal*, 102(7), 481–493.

Bagwell, K., and Riordan, M.H. (1991). High and declining prices signal product quality. *American Economic Review*, 81(1), 224–239.

Barber, B.M., and Darrough, M.N. (1996). Product reliability and firm value: The experience of American and Japanese automakers, (1973–1992). *Journal of Political Economy*, 104(5), 1084–1099.

Benjamin, B.A., and Podolny, J.M. (1999). Status, quality, and social order in the California wine industry. *Administrative Science Quarterly*, 44(3), 563–589.

Bertozzi, L. (1995). Designation of origin: Quality and specification. *Food Quality and Preference*, 6(3), 143–147.

Blair, R.D., and Kaserman, D.L. (1994). A note on incentive incompatibility under franchising. *Review of Industrial Organization*, 9(3), 323–330.

Buchinsky, M. (1998). Recent advances in quantile regression models: A practical guideline for empirical research. *Journal of Human Resources*, 33(1), 88–126.

Byron, R., and Ashenfelter, O. (1995). Predicting the quality of an unborn grange. *Economic Record*, 71(1), 40–53.

Combris, P., Lecocq, S., and Visser, M. (1997). Estimation of a hedonic price equation for Bordeaux wine: Does quality matter? *Economic Journal*, 107, 390–402.

Costanigro, M., McCluskey, J.J., and Mittelhammer, R.C. (2007). Segmenting the wine market based on price: Hedonic regression when different prices mean different products. *Journal of Agricultural Economics*, 58(3), 454–466.

Diamond, D.W. (1989). Reputation acquisition in debt markets. *Journal of Political Economy*, 97(4), 828–862.

Fotopoulos, C., and Krystallis, A. (2003). Quality labels as a marketing advantage: The case of the "PDO Zagora" apples in the Greek market. *European Journal of Marketing*, 37(10), 1350–1374.

Gale, D., and Rosenthal, R.W. (1994). Price and quality cycles for experience goods. *RAND Journal of Economics*, 25(4), 590–607.

Gergaud, O., and Ginsburgh, V. (2008). Natural endowments, production technologies and the quality of wines in bordeaux. Does terroir matter? *Economic Journal*, 118(529), F142–F157.

Hahn, J. (1995). Bootstrapping quantile regression estimators. *Econometric Theory*, 11(1), 105–121.

Jarrell, G., and Peltzman, S. (1985). The impact of product recalls on the wealth of sellers. *Journal of Political Economy*, 93(3), 512–536.

Karpoff, J.M., and Lott, J.R. (1993). The reputational penalty firms bear from committing criminal fraud. *Journal of Law and Economics*, 36(2), 757–802.

Klein, B., and Leffler, K.B. (1981). The role of market forces in assuring contractual performance. *Journal of Political Economy*, 89(4), 615–641.

Koenker, R., and Bassett, G. (1978). Regression quantiles. *Econometrica*, 46(1), 33–50.

Kreps, D.M., and Wilson, R. (1982). Reputation and imperfect information. *Journal of Economic Theory*, 27(2), 253–279.

Landon, S., and Smith, C.E. (1998). Quality expectations, reputation, and price. *Southern Economic Journal*, 64(3), 628–647.

Loureiro, M.L., and McCluskey, J.J. (2000). Assessing consumer response to protected geographical identification labeling. *Agribusiness*, 16(3), 309–320.

Milgrom, P., and Roberts, J. (1982). Predation, reputation, and entry deterrence. *Journal of Economic Theory*, 27(2), 280–312.

Mitchell, M.L., and Maloney, M.T. (1989). Crisis in the cockpit? The role of market forces in promoting air travel safety. *Journal of Law and Economics*, 32(2), 329–355.

Nelson, P. (1970). Information and consumer behavior. *Journal of Political Economy*, 78(2), 311–329.

Nerlove, M. (1995). Hedonic price functions and the measurement of preferences: The case of Swedish wine consumers. *European Economic Review*, 39, 1697–1716.

Piggott, N.E., and Marsh, T.L. (2004). Does food safety information impact U.S. Meat Demand? *American Journal of Agricultural Economics*, 86(1), 154–174.

Quagrainie, K.K., McCluskey, J.J., and Loureiro, M.L. (2003). A latent structure approach to measuring reputation. *Southern Economic Journal*, 69(4), 966–977.

Reutera, J. (2009). Does advertising bias product reviews? An analysis of wine ratings. *Journal of Wine Economics*, 4(2), 125–151.

Richards, T.J., and Patterson, P.M. (1999). The economic value of public relations expenditures: Food safety and the strawberry case. *Journal of Agricultural and Resource Economics*, 24(2), 440–462.

Schamel, G., and Anderson, K. (2003). Wine quality and varietal, regional and winery reputations: Hedonic prices for Australia and New Zealand. *Economic Record*, 79(246), 357–369.

Shapiro, C. (1982). Consumer information, product quality, and seller reputation. *Bell Journal of Economics*, 13(1), 20–35.

Smith, M.E., van Ravenswaay, E.O., and Thompson, S.R. (1998). Sales loss determination in food contamination incidents: An application to milk bans in Hawaii. *American Journal of Agricultural Economics*, 70, 513–520.

Tadelis, S. (1999). What's in a name? Reputation as a tradeable asset. *American Economic Review*, 89(3), 548–563.

Tadelis, S. (2003). Firm reputation with hidden information. *Economic Theory*, 21(2), 635–651.

Thomsen, M.R., and McKenzie, A.M. (2001). Market incentives for safe foods: An examination of shareholder losses from meat and poultry recalls. *American Journal of Agricultural Economics*, 83, 526–538.

Tirole, J. (1996). A theory of collective reputations (with applications to the persistence of corruption and to firm quality). *Review of Economic Studies*, 63(1), 1–22.

Waugh, F.V. (1928). Quality factors influencing vegetable prices. *Journal of Farm Economics*, 10, 185–196.

Wilson, J. (1998). *Terroir: The Role of Geology, Climate, and Culture in the Making of French Wines.* Berkeley and Los Angeles: Wine Appreciation Guild/University of California Press.

Winfree, J.A., and McCluskey, J.J. (2005). Collective reputation and quality. *American Journal of Agricultural Economics*, 87(1), 206–213.

Part 2

Wine and Regulation

Chapter 5

Politics, Economics, and the Regulation of Direct Interstate Shipping in the Wine Industry*

Gina M. Riekhof[†] and Michael E. Sykuta[‡]

[†]*Associate with Gilmore & Bell, P.C. and a former CORI Graduate Fellow at the University of Missouri, Columbia*
gina_riekhof@yahoo.com

[‡]*Department of Agricultural Economics and Director of the Contracting and Organizations Research Institute (CORI) at the University of Missouri, Columbia*
sykutam@missouri.edu

In 1986, California passed legislation restricting the direct importation of wine from another state by California residents unless the originating state allowed direct shipment from California wineries to residents in that state. The result has been a patchwork of direct shipment regulations across states. We examine how various economic and public interest factors affect the likelihood that a state adopts a change in its direct shipment regulation and the nature of that change. Our results suggest that private and public sector economic considerations lie at the root of direct shipment regulations in the wine industry.

1. Introduction

In 1986, the State of California passed legislation prohibiting the direct shipment of wine from other states to California residents unless the originating state allowed California wineries to direct ship to that state's residents. This "reciprocity" restriction on direct shipment marked a change

*This article originally appeared in *American Journal of Agricultural Economics* (2005), 87(2), 439–452.

from California's previously unfettered direct shipment regime. California consumers, who could previously order wine from anywhere in the country to be delivered to their homes, were now prohibited from such transactions unless the shipping state allowed California wineries reciprocal shipping privileges.

The legislation's intent was to break down other states' barriers to direct shipment of wine by California producers. Prior to 1986, direct shipment of wine to consumers was a misdemeanor crime in forty-seven states. Other than California, only Alaska and Rhode Island permitted direct shipment of wine. In effect, California attempted to leverage its large wine consuming population to open access to the rest of the country for the state's wine industry. A more skeptical interpretation is that the California wine industry — particularly small wine producers — was permitted to hold California wine consumers hostage until other states opened their borders to direct shipment of wine.[1]

The response has been mixed. In the past eighteen years, forty-three states have considered over 160 bills proposing changes to their direct shipment laws. Twenty-five states have adopted some form of direct shipment allowance, ranging from reciprocity regulations to permitting systems to special handling provisions. Four states elected to retain their prohibition, but increased the severity of the penalty by making direct shipment a felony.

The nature of these interstate direct shipment laws has triggered a constitutional debate, drawing the courts into the battle. Proponents of direct shipping have filed suits arguing that state restrictions on direct shipment violate the Commerce Clause (Article I, Section 8) of the U.S. Constitution, which grants the federal government the right to regulate trade "among the several states." However, the states point to the Constitution's 21st Amendment, which gives states the sole authority to regulate the sale and distribution of alcoholic beverages within their borders. As in the legislative arena, the courts' rulings are mixed. Direct shipment cases have been heard in seven of the twelve federal circuits. Thus far, six Circuit Courts of Appeal have ruled on such cases, resulting in a 4-2 split: the 4th, 5th, 6th, and 11th Circuits found direct shipment restrictions unconstitutional, while the 7th and 2nd Circuits have ruled them constitutional.[2]

[1]It should be noted that the interests of California wine producers are not homogeneous on this issue. Large wineries with well-established traditional distribution systems have little to gain from direct shipment allowances and some have even filed opinions opposing direct shipment legislation. However, the industry as a whole, dominated in numbers by small producers, has incentive to open direct shipment channels.

[2]See *Beskind* v. *Easley*, 325 F.3d 506 (4th Cir. 2003); *Dickerson* v. *Bailey*, 336 F.3d 388 (5th Cir. 2003); *Heald* v. *Engler*, 342 F.3d 517 (6th Cir. 2003); *Bainbridge* v. *Turner*, 311

At the heart of the debate in both the legislative and judicial arenas is a question of public interest. In analyzing the enforceability of state laws under both the Commerce Clause and the 21st Amendment, courts consider the public interest concerns addressed by the state regulation. In the case of the Commerce Clause, the regulation must be shown to advance state health, safety, and welfare. In addition to this public interest requirement, courts also require that the social gains exceed the burden on interstate commerce and that no less-restrictive alternative is available to achieve the social objective. Courts' analytical framework under the 21st Amendment involves a lower threshold for permitting states' interventions: regulations are permissible if they (1) promote temperance, (2) raise revenue, or (3) "ensure orderly market conditions"; neither the positive net benefit standard nor the availability of less-restrictive alternatives are typically considered by the courts.[3]

Our purpose in this chapter is to shed light on the motivating factors for regulations on the direct shipment of wine among states. In particular, we use a competing risks hazard model to estimate how various measures of economic and public interests in each of the forty-seven prohibition states affect states' decisions to adopt laws allowing direct shipment of wine and under what terms. We find that economic interests play a significant role in determining a state's adoption of direct shipment, but find no evidence supporting a general public interest motivation.

2. Previous Research

Most economics research on the U.S. wine industry focuses on various dimensions of demand for wine products including price and quality (Krasker, 1979; Jaeger 1981; Blaylock and Blisard, 1993; Buccola and VanderZanden, 1997; Landon and Smith, 1998) and liberalization of North American trade

F.3d 1104 (11th Cir. 2002); *Bridenbaugh* v. *Freeman-Wilson*, 227 F.3d 848 (7th Cir. 2000); and *Swedenburg* v. *Kelly*, Docket No. 02-9511 (2nd Cir. 2004). We considered the possibility that these appellate court rulings may create truncation issues for our empirical estimation by changing the status quo of the incumbent regulatory regimes in the respective appellate jurisdictions. Because the 7th Circuit ruling upheld interstate direct shipment restrictions, it simply affirms states' prerogatives to maintain their restrictions and does not constitute a regime change. The remainder, on the other hand, may constitute a regime change for some states. However, these rulings occur after our sample period.

[3]In July 2003, the Federal Trade Commission released a report finding that restrictions on interstate direct shipment posed a substantial barrier to e-commerce in the wine industry and that, among states adopting direct shipment, direct shipping is not associated with higher incidences of underage drinking. It is not clear how courts will react to the report.

(Heien and Sims, 2000). In his descriptive analysis of recent changes in the global wine industry, Roberto (2003) compares "new world" (particularly United States and Australia) and "old world" industry structures. Wiseman and Ellig (2003) provide the only analysis of direct shipment restrictions of which we are aware, finding that Virginia's prohibition of direct shipment reduces the selection of wines available to Virginia consumers and results in higher wine prices compared to available e-commerce sources of wine.

Similarly, economic research on interstate commerce is focused primarily on transportation industries and the role of the Interstate Commerce Act (ICA) of 1887 (see Childs, 2001) rather than on interstate trade issues stemming from the Commerce Clause of the U.S. Constitution. Elmslie and Milberg (1996) argue the Commerce Clause could be considered a model for regulation of international trade, likening international commerce to commerce between the U.S. states. O'Driscoll, on the other hand, provides an overview of how interstate restrictions on trade in a variety of commodity and service industries effectively circumvent the Commerce Clause. However, O'Driscoll does not specifically offer direct shipment of alcoholic beverages as an example. Inattention among economists notwithstanding, the number and diversity of court cases and opinions described above as well as the plethora of legislation considered in the past eighteen years have spurred debate among legal scholars, (e.g., see Martin, 2000, 2001; Foust, 2000; Douglass, 2000; Kozusko, 2000).

A much larger literature exists concerning the political economy of regulation. This literature can be broadly broken down into two competing camps: the public interest and private interest theories of regulation. Public interest theory argues that government intervention maximizes social welfare by correcting market failures (Joskow and Noll, 1981), particularly in the presence of positive transaction costs (Coase, 1960; Noll, 1989). Heien's (1996) analysis of the appropriate level of alcohol taxes is based on, and a reaction to, applications of a public interest theory approach to alcohol consumption and its social welfare effects as reflected in traditional consumer and producer surplus models.

The private interest or economic theory of regulation argues that regulations result from political competition among private interests attempting to gain or protect economic rents (Stigler, 1971; Posner, 1974; Peltzman, 1976; Becker, 1983). Becker finds that relative, rather than absolute, efficiency of political influence among competing interests will determine which group's interests are reflected in policy. He also finds that competitive interest groups counterbalance and may yield policy outcomes that result in the most (socially) efficient policy. In their analysis of branch banking deregulation, Kroszner and Strahan (1999) argue that private interest theory has been more successful in explaining a wide variety of regulatory interventions, while public interest arguments better explain the removal of such regulations. They go on to conclude that, in the case of bank branching restrictions, private interests appear to drive deregulation.

This chapter is similar to Kroszner and Strahan's (1999) in that we are examining the drivers of deregulation of interstate direct shipment of wine. However, this chapter has broader implications due to the nature of the regulations being considered and the unique constitutional question surrounding such restrictions. Since public interests are the sole redeeming feature of state restrictions on interstate commerce, determining whether public or private interests are the primary drivers of direct shipment laws is of immediate consequence beyond validation of regulatory theories. This chapter also provides a rare glimpse into the economic underpinnings of a rapidly growing and highly regulated sector of the agricultural economy.

3. Structural Change in the Wine Industry and the Direct Shipment Response

The U.S. wine industry has undergone tremendous structural change in the past twenty-five years, resulting in tensions between a growing wine production segment and an increasingly concentrated distribution and retail system. The convergence of these forces has created pressure on the traditional three-tier distribution.

3.1. *Structural change in wine production*

The past twenty-five years have witnessed tremendous growth in the U.S. wine industry. Heien and Martin (2003) report that while U.S. wine consumption was fairly stable through the 1980s, demand increased rapidly through the 1990s, from 106.8 million cases in 1991 to 145.1 million cases in 2001 — most of this growth occurring in the premium priced wine segments. At the same time, the number of U.S. wine producers also grew. The 1974 issue of *Wines & Vines Annual Buyer's Guide* listed 800 wineries operating in thirty-four states. The 2002 issue listed over 3,180 wineries in operation across all fifty states.[4]

[4]The number of wineries listed in *Wines & Vines* may overstate the number of brick-and-mortar wineries or wine companies in operation due to consolidation of brands among

While the total number of wineries increased, Roberto (2003) reports that market concentration in distribution and retail, combined with scale efficiencies in procurement, bottling, and marketing, have led to tremendous consolidation in wine production over the past decade. The February 2004 issue of *Wine Business Monthly* reports the top thirty U.S. wine companies produced over 90% of U.S. production (by case sales) in 2003. Roberto (2003) reports that the top twenty firms accounted for 75% of production in 2001. Heien and Martin (2003) report that the top three firms account for 60% of volume. Thus, the industry is characterized by relatively few large producers, some of which have their own national distribution systems in place, and a large number of small wineries that sell primarily by direct sales to consumers. For smaller wineries to access a larger geographic market, they must develop relations with distributors or larger wineries, or find alternative means for directly accessing distant markets.

3.2. *Structural change in distribution and retail*

While the number of wine producers has increased, the number of licensed wine and spirits distributors in the United States dramatically decreased, from over 1,600 in 1984 to less than 600 in 2002 (*National Beverage Marketing Directory*). This consolidation trend resulted from a 1980 U.S. Supreme Court decision in *California Retail Liquor Dealers Assoc.* v. *Midcal Aluminum* , *Inc.*, (1980) which struck down an alcoholic beverage price posting law in California. This law prohibited distributors from selling alcoholic beverages to retailers at prices below official posted prices, thereby forcing distributors to compete on service rather than price. Similar laws were in place in virtually every state. Everett (2001) argues that when the Supreme Court found such laws in violation of the Sherman Act, distributors were freed to compete on price, thereby driving out less efficient distributors and spurring drastic consolidation.

This consolidation is particularly significant given the traditional three-tier distribution system adopted by most states following the repeal of prohibition. The three-tier system requires alcoholic beverages to be sold to a state licensed distributor that in turn sells the product to a state licensed retailer before consumers purchase the product. In some instances, the state owns and even operates distribution activities in the state; occasionally, the

major wine holding companies such as Constellation Brands and Kendall-Jackson. A search on www.winespectator.com conducted on March 2, 2004, yielded a list totaling 2,440 U.S. wineries.

state also owns or franchises the retail operations. However, most states license private firms to perform these activities within the state. A reduction in the number of distributors means fewer distribution outlets for wineries to get their products into other markets; it also suggests greater opportunity for collusive behavior among distributors.

Moreover, since few distributors have licensed operations in all fifty states, wine producers may have to develop relations with several different distributors to gain access to a broad geographic market. Thus, there are potentially high transaction costs for wineries in identifying and negotiating marketing agreements with distributors across several states. These costs are exacerbated by "franchise laws" in some states that make it difficult, if not impossible, for producers of alcoholic beverages to unilaterally terminate relations with a distributor (Everett, 2001).

From the distributor's perspective, carrying small-volume wine products also creates transaction costs. Alcohol distributors do not simply resell or direct product to established retail outlets. Alcohol distributors are frequently responsible for developing and implementing promotional activities for the products they carry. Distributor-sponsored wine tastings, advertising, and physical displays are just some of the expenses typically incurred. Small-volume products may not justify marketing costs on the part of the distributor.

While distribution has become more concentrated, national retail systems have also become more concentrated. Although the number of retail outlets has grown, in both the off-site (e.g., retail stores and groceries) and the on-site (e.g., hotels and restaurants) sectors, the number of companies controlling those outlets has decreased. Centralized purchasing for these retail systems has created further pressure for higher volume wine products. Moreover, competition for shelf space at the retail level places pressure on both the retailer and the distributor to offer recognized brands with established consumer bases. Although space is typically allocated for smaller specialty runs, shelf space is not proportional to the number of small wine producers, adding to the difficulty small wineries may have in acquiring a distributor relationship.

Anecdotal evidence supports the argument that distribution is difficult and costly to access, even for larger producers. Ernst & Julio Gallo, by far the largest producer in the United States, has developed its own national distribution company. Fosters Brewing of Australia acquired Beringer, another large California winery, in 2001 to leverage Beringer's established distribution system for Foster's expansion in the U.S. market. Constellation Brands grew to be the second largest U.S. producer (by volume) by consolidating a portfolio of medium-sized wineries to take advantage of its distribution capacity, now boasting about sixty-five brands of U.S. wine. Such acquisitions and vertical integration suggest the costs of market transactions to achieve the same market access must be high (Coase, 1937). This is also consistent with Heien and Martin's (2002) prediction that "wineries will get big or small: big enough to offer a portfolio of wines and to be guaranteed shelf space, or small enough to sell their wine to visiting tourists, with the Internet serving as a backup sales channel" (2002, p.33).

3.3. *The direct shipment response*

Given continuing consolidation in the distribution and retail sectors, direct sales are the only economically efficient form of distribution for many small wineries. However, prohibitions on direct shipment to consumers across state lines effectively limit small wineries to on-site visitor sales and intrastate consumer markets. For small wineries seeking to increase their volume, consumer base, and geographic market, direct shipment prohibitions represent a significant obstacle to growth.

California has more wineries than any other state in the United States, accounting for approximately 50% of the national total. Between 1980 and 1986, the number of wineries in California grew by 60%. This growth was primarily in small, often premium, wineries that relied on direct sales. In what might be described as a "tit-for-tat" strategy, California passed legislation in 1986 that effectively shut out direct shipments from wineries in other states unless those states would allow California wineries a like privilege to direct ship into those states. This reciprocity standard created incentives for other states to open their borders to California wines in order to gain access to the largest consuming market in the country for their own wine industries.

As noted earlier, the response has been varied. In the first seven years following California's move, eleven states adopted reciprocity direct shipment legislation, thereby opening their borders to California wines. In the next ten years, fifteen states enacted new legislation regarding direct shipment. Of those, only two adopted simple reciprocity laws. Ten states moved to allow direct shipment, but require some form of permitting on the part of the consumer, the winery, or both prior to shipping. These permitting schemes vary in cost, with some states offering free permits while others require fees that make direct shipment unappealing for most wine purchases. Three states elected to allow consumers to special-order wine through the state's

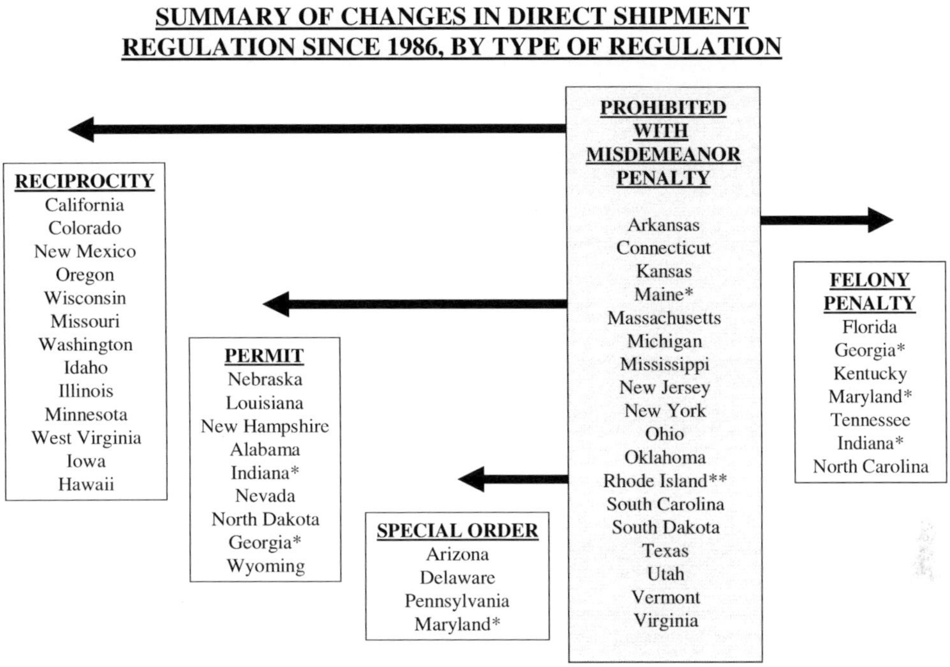

Figure 1. Current State Regulations on Interstate Direct Shipment of Wine

*Denotes states that reacted in multiple ways to direct shipment.

**Rhode Island allowed direct shipment via a permit from 1956 until the regulation was repealed in 2001.

Sources: State statutes, Wine Institute State-by-State Analysis. Note that Alaska is excluded because it allowed imports prior to 1986.

This figure illustrates the current array of state regulations on interstate direct shipment of wine and graphically offers an indication of the direction and relative restrictiveness of the different regulatory regimes. Within permitting, there is an additional degree of restrictiveness related to the cost of permits, who has to purchase the permit, and how easy it is to receive. We make no distinction among these states here.

three-tier system, with delivery either to the distributor or a retailer. Finally, three other states chose not to relax their prohibitions against direct shipment, and increased the penalty for violations from misdemeanor to felony offenses. Figure 1 illustrates the resulting patchwork of state regulations on interstate direct shipment of wine that currently exist.

3.4. *Public versus private in direct shipment regulation?*

As discussed above, the economics literature on regulation assumes two general rationales for regulation: public interests and private interests. If direct shipment prohibitions prior to 1986 were in place solely for public interest reasons, it would be difficult to explain why California's decision to adopt reciprocity would have its intended effect of opening up access to no-shipment states. The reciprocity incentive only affected wine producers in no-shipment states that desired to direct ship their wines to California consumers. Thus, the fact that twenty-three states moved to allow direct shipment under either reciprocity or some form of permitting system suggests the economic interests of wine producers in those states outweighed whatever public interest allegedly supported the original direct shipment prohibition.

Furthermore, differences in timing of adoption of direct shipment and the varied forms in which direct shipment was enacted suggest that the interests driving the move toward direct shipment varied across states. What is not obvious is the degree to which public versus private interests determined those differences. While adopting direct shipment, and thereby gaining access to other reciprocity states, may be good for a state's wine industry, distributors and retailers in the state may object to the possibility of consumers shifting their purchases of higher priced, higher margin wines to direct shipping channels. To the extent the state is a player in the industry, either in terms of ownership of distribution and/or retail operations or in terms of revenues generated by taxes and licenses, the state itself may have economic incentives to support or prohibit direct shipment. Thus, failure to adopt direct shipment, delays in adoption, and the structure of any new regulation might result from either public health and safety interests or competing economic interests in the private or public sectors.

We attempt to assess whether public or private (economic) interests were the driving factors in the adoption of direct shipment legislation, and which private interests were most influential in determining states' decisions. The following section describes the data and methods used to examine whether direct shipment regulation is determined by public interest concerns or private economic interests.

4. Data and Methods

As noted above, at least 160 bills have been introduced across forty-three states to change states' regulation of direct shipment of wine. In the seventeen years since California's opening salvo, twenty-three states have passed legislation allowing direct shipment. These direct shipment rules fall under two categories: straight reciprocity and permitting systems. Thus, the issue involves three questions. First, what factors affect the likelihood that a state will pass direct shipment legislation? Second, are those factors different when states choose reciprocity versus permitting systems?

Finally, why do some states respond quickly with legislation while others take longer?

In order to address these questions, we collected information for all forty-seven original no-shipment states for the period 1986–2001. We collected information on the size and structure of the states' wine production, distribution, and retail sectors, as well as wine consumption. In order to capture the economic interests of the state, we collected information on states' reliance on wine-based tax revenues and their involvement as economic players in the industry. We also collected information concerning public interest issues related to alcohol and general ideology measures. In order to provide a better context for understanding the details of our data collection and variable construction, we begin with a discussion of our modeling technique.

4.1. *The model*

We use a competing risks hazard model to determine the likelihood that a state will choose to deregulate by adopting either reciprocity or a permit system at time t, given that the state has not yet deregulated and given a set of explanatory variables. The competing risks hazard model is an event history, or duration model that seeks to explain both the timing of regulatory adoption and the type of regulation adopted. Such event history models are often used in the political science literature, where "the duration spent in one social state affects the probability that some entity will make a transition to another social state" (Box-Steffensmeier and Jones, 1997). Duration models have also been employed in economics to study the duration of unemployment spells (Kiefer, 1988; Meyer, 1990) and rates of deregulation (Kroszner and Strahan, 1999), and in finance to estimate the effects of bond characteristics on the likelihood of default verses calls (McDonald and Van de Gucht, 1999).[5]

The hazard function, $\lambda(t)$, comprises two parts.[6] The first is a baseline hazard function that varies exclusively as a measure of time, $\lambda_0(t)$. The second part of the hazard function is a function of the explanatory variables, and is commonly noted as $\exp(X'\beta)$, where $\mathbf{X}$ is a vector of the explanatory

[5]Box-Steffensmeier and Jones provide a concise and reader friendly summary of event history models in political science. Keifer explains the relevance of duration models in economics primarily in the context of unemployment, but also discusses several other areas of application.

[6]For a discussion of the statistical properties of hazard functions, see Keifer, (1988); Meyer, (1990); McDonald and Van de Gucht, (1999); or Han and Hausman, (1990).

variables for a given observation and β is a parameter vector. The model allows for either static or time-varying explanatory variables. Therefore, the hazard function can be written as (Kennedy, 1998):

$$\lambda(t) = \lambda_0(t) \exp(\mathbf{X}(t)'\beta). \tag{1}$$

Duration models differ based on the assumed form of the baseline hazard, $\lambda_0(t)$. The baseline hazard may be estimated using a specified form (parameterized) or an unspecified (nonparametric or semiparametric) form. Parametric forms frequently include exponential forms, log-logistic forms, and Weibull distributions. Han and Hausman (1990), and Meyer (1990) show that for competing hazard models, where more than one type of hazard may remove a subject from the risk pool, a semiparametric approach yields the most efficient results when the baseline hazard rate is unknown.

In our study, no-shipment states may exit the pool by adopting either reciprocity or permitting systems. Consequently, we follow Meyer (1990), and McDonald and Van de Gucht (1999), and use a semiparametric specification that includes a vector of time-varying dummies to estimate the effect of time on the baseline hazard. Thus, our estimated hazard model has the form:

$$\lambda(t) = \lambda_0(t) \exp(\mathbf{X}(t)'\beta) \exp(\mathbf{D}(t)'\mathbf{c}). \tag{2}$$

where λ_0, $\mathbf{X}$, and β are as defined above, $\mathbf{D}$ is the vector of time-varying dummies, and $\mathbf{c}$ is a coefficient parameter vector.

4.2. *Dependent variable*

Our sample begins in 1986 with all forty-seven nondirect shipment states and continues through 2001. Because there are some years in which no state adopts direct shipment regulation, we break the sample into eight two-year periods, for example, 1986–1987, 1988–1989, etc., to ensure at least one state experiences a hazard in each period. Our dependent variable takes one of three values. It is set equal to 0, if the state did not pass direct shipment legislation in the observation period. If the state passed reciprocity legislation, the dependent variable assumes a value of 1; if passed a permit system, a value of two. We assume that states can only move from non-direct shipment to direct shipment once.

Thus, if a state's dependent variable takes on a non-zero value in a given year, the state is dropped from the hazard pool and is not observed in the rest of the sample period. States that did not adopt any direct shipment legislation remain in the pool throughout the sample. Such right-censored observations are an additional reason for employing the hazard model framework.

4.3. *Explanatory variables*

As described above, we attempt to capture economic versus public interests as they influence the adoption of direct shipment laws. We collect information on private sector economic interests, public sector economic interests, and proxies for public health and safety interest related to alcohol consumption. For each observation period, we use the average value for each variable in the two years. Table 1 provides summary statistics.

Table 1. Summary Statistics for Explanatory Variables

Variable name	Observations	Mean	Standard deviation	Minimum	Maximum
Wineries per gallon consumed	309	0.0013	0.0013	0	0.0077
Winery HHI	309	4.5404	3.2142	0	10
Winery Gini	309	0.3925	0.2931	0	0.9823
Distributors per gallon consume	309	0.0036	0.0038	0.0001	0.0227
Distributor HHI	309	1.6697	1.3032	0	8.3158
Distributor Gini	309	0.4457	0.1981	0	0.8981
Retail sales of wine as percentage of GSP	309	0.003	0.0178	0.0005	0.314
Excise taxes as percentage of total state revenue	309	0.0117	0.0075	0.0012	0.0465
License fees as percentage of total state revenue	309	0.0008	0.0008	0	0.004
License state (=1)	309	0.5825	0.4939	0	1
Government ideology	282	50.6167	24.4128	0.8333	96.25
Liquor law violations	275	0.0637	0.0481	0	0.2417
DUIs	275	0.1211	0.0586	0	0.3841

Note: The table reports summary statistics for the set of variables used in the empirical estimation. Where the number of observations is less that 610, it reflects a lack of available data for the particular variable in certain years. In the case of government ideology, liquor law violations, and DUIs, data were not available past 1999. HHI and Gini coefficient values were calculated by the authors using the same data that generated the number of operators per gallon of wine consumed in each state. HHI is scaled by a factor of 1/1,000 for the logistic estimation. Both liquor law violations and DUIs are reported as proportions of all arrests in the state.

4.4. *Economic interests in the private sector*

The primary private sector interests we identify relate to the size and structure of the state's wine industry at the production, distribution, retail, and consumer levels. For wine production, we determined the number of wineries in each state by listings in various issues of *Wines & Vines Annual Buyers Guide*. The number of wineries in each state is scaled by the gallons of wine consumed in the state, as reported in *Adam's Wine Handbook*. We also calculate the Herfindahl–Hirschman Index (HHI) and the Gini Coefficient for the state wine industry in each year based on winery storage capacity as reported in *Wines & Vines Annual Buyer's Guide*. Although the two measures are related, they address fundamentally different aspects of market structure. The HHI is primarily a measure of industry concentration. As Waterson (1984, p.170) points out, although the Gini coefficient is sometimes wrongly called a concentration index, it is more properly thought of as a measure of market share inequality among industry participants.

To illustrate the difference, consider one market with equal-sized duopolists and another market with a dominant firm controlling 70% of the market and a competitive fringe of thirty firms each comprising 1% of the market. The HHI measures for these two markets would be 5,000 and 4,930, respectively, on a scale of zero (perfect competition) to 10,000 (monopoly). Conversely, the Gini coefficient for the duopoly would be zero (i.e., perfect equality) while for the other it would be 0.67 on a scale where 1.0 is extreme inequality. We may well expect these markets to behave differently, despite the comparable levels of the HHI. Reliance upon only the HHI or the Gini would not necessarily capture the nature of the market structure. We do check the correlation coefficient to assure no statistical problems, and it is in fact quite low (0.16).

We expect the number of wineries relative to state consumption to be positively associated with adoption of direct shipment regulation. A larger number of wineries suggests not only a larger industry lobby, but a greater need to seek out markets in other states. We also expect the winery HHI to be positively related to direct shipment. Previous research shows more concentrated industries are generally more politically effective, for example, see Kroszner and Strahan (1999). One argument for this result is the reduced opportunity for free-riding by smaller producers. The winery Gini coefficient, on the other hand, we expect to have a negative relationship with the probability of adopting direct shipment. The Gini coefficient value ranges from zero (an evenly distributed market) to one (an extremely unevenly distributed market). The greater the Gini coefficient value, one would infer an industry made up of many disproportionately small producers with a few relatively large firms. We expect this structure to be negatively associated with direct shipment passage; a high Gini coefficient may indicate a dispersion of economic interests (making industry consensus on legislation less likely) or increase the free-rider problem, both of which are likely to make the industry less politically effective.

We use the same measures of sector size and structure for distribution in the state, namely, the number of distributors per gallon of wine consumed, the distributor HHI, and the distributor Gini coefficient in each state in each year. The number of distributors was determined by listings in the "Wines and Spirits Distributors" section of the *National Beverage Marketing Directory*, and was scaled by gallons of wine consumption as with the wineries. The HHI and Gini coefficient measures are calculated based on distributors' sales revenue as reported in the *National Beverage Marketing Directory*. Due to the fact that distributors are an obvious victim of direct shipping, we expect the signs to be opposite those on the winery variables. In particular, we expect the number and concentration of distributors to be negatively related to adoption of direct shipment legislation, while we expect the Gini coefficient (dispersion) measure to be positively related to passage.

For retail, no reliable figures are available for the number and sales of wine retail outlets by state for the entire sample period, so we cannot construct similar measures. Instead, we use the ratio of retail wine sales as a share of gross state product to measure the size of the retail wine industry. This is not a perfect measure, since it could capture either retailers' interests in protecting wine flows through their outlets or consumers' demand for wine, which might suggest greater demand for access to difficult-to-find out-of-state labels. Not surprisingly, retail sales, even as a percentage of gross state product, are highly correlated with per capita wine consumption, so there is no clear way to account for which force might be reflected in this measure. Consequently, we cannot sign this demand measure *ex ante*.

4.5. *Economic interests in the public sector*

The state, and state employees, may not be indifferent with regards to direct shipment of alcoholic beverages. States generate revenue both from excise taxes on alcohol and from licensing fees charged to alcohol distributors and retailers. Moreover, particularly in those states that have state-controlled distribution systems, the state and its employees have similar interests in retaining control as do private distributors and retails.

To account for states' financial interests in the sale of wine, we include variables for both alcohol revenue sources, excise taxes, and licensing fees, as a percentage of total state revenue. The data were collected from the U.S. Department of Commerce's annual *Government Finance Series*. Most state reciprocity laws expressly allow wineries and consumers to avoid the excise tax. States that are more reliant on those funds may be less likely to pass such legislation. In the case of licensing fees, the argument is less clear. Due to the fact that direct shipment is not likely to change the number of licensed distributors or retailers in a state, there may be less concern regarding licensing fees. Moreover, a fee-based permitting system may increase total licensing fee revenues. Consequently, the effect of licensing fee revenue on reciprocity is unclear, and may actually increase the probability of adopting a permit system.

In addition to tax revenues, control system states (those that operate at the distributor, and in some cases retail, level) have business interests similar to private distributors and retailers. In addition to the wholesale margins a state-monopoly distributor may be able to generate, state-run distribution systems also create public sector jobs that have economic interests in preserving the status quo. While license jurisdictions require employees to process and enforce private parties' permits, it is reasonable to presume the public sector employment interests in those states are smaller, if not in line with a permitting system. We employ a dichotomous variable that takes a value of 1 for license jurisdictions and 0 for control states to account for these structural differences, and we expect license states to be more likely to pass direct shipment regulation.[7]

4.6. *Public interests*

As discussed earlier, courts evaluating Commerce Clause cases generally consider whether the state has a compelling public interest, particularly in health and safety, in restricting interstate commerce. In the instance of the Twenty-First Amendment cases, public interest in promoting temperance is typically prime consideration. Since we do not have good direct measures of public interest in the case of direct shipping, we employ a variety of variables to proxy different ways in which such public interests might be reflected or determined.

[7] While we recognize that the control versus license regime may itself be considered endogenous to this process, we argue that such wholesale change of a state's alcohol regulatory structure is less likely given the historical entrenchment of these distribution regimes. What we are examining are in effect changes at the margins of these essentially fixed regimes. Furthermore, no states made a wholesale change in control systems over the period.

We include two variables reflecting negative social impacts of alcohol consumption, namely driving under the influence (DUI) arrests and violations of existing liquor control laws, such as possession by minors, distribution to minors and others. We use data from the U.S. Department of Justice's *Handbook of Criminal Justice Statistics* to calculate the percentage of DUI arrests and the percentage of liquor law violations relative to all arrests each year by state. Unfortunately, the Handbook occasionally omitted data for a given state and was available only through 1999. However, for those observations which were available, we expect higher incidences of alcohol-related arrests, either for DUIs or for liquor law violations more generally, would decrease the likelihood of passing direct shipment legislation.

We also use a measure of government ideology originally created by Berry *et al.* (1998), and now available from the Inter-university Consortium for Political and Social Research (ICPSR). This measure is meant to capture the political conservatism or liberalism of states' governments. The government ideology measure is essentially a weighted index of the political affiliation of elected state officials, adjusted for voting record scores produced by the Americans for Democratic Action and the AFL-CIO Committee on Political Education. A weighted average score is generated for each body of the state legislature and the governor, which are then weighted by 25% for each legislative house and 50% for the governor to arrive at a final score. The score ranges from 0 to 100, with 0 being most conservative (Republican) and 100 being most liberal (Democratic). Although we have no strong a priori argument that one political party would necessarily be more likely to pass direct shipment regulation, Republicans are generally viewed as being more supportive of free trade, suggesting a negative relation between this index and direct shipment. However, Republicans are generally more supportive of states' rights and are more likely influenced by conservative groups that promote temperance.[8] Unfortunately, these data are only available through 1999.

5. Empirical Results

We collected the above data for each state beginning in 1986 and continuing either until the state adopts direct shipment legislation or until 2001. We broke the sample into eight two-year periods, averaging the values of

[8]A more direct measure of temperance interests would be desirable. One such measure would be the percentage of the state's population with a conservation religious affiliation. Unfortunately, we are unable to find state-level religious affiliation data by year for the entire sample period.

the independent variables, resulting in 309 total state-period observations. We estimate the competing risks hazard model described earlier using a maximum likelihood multinomial logistics regression with robust standard errors clustered by state. The multinomial logistic model produces two sets of parameter results; one for the "hazard" of adopting reciprocity legislation and one for adopting a permit system. Both sets of parameters are relative to the default outcome of not passing direct shipment legislation of either sort.

As noted above, a few of our public interest variables are not available past 1999. Consequently, we estimate the model over the first seven time periods (1986–1999), which reduces the possible sample to 282 observations. The results are presented in Table 2 as Model A.

Column 1 of Table 2 shows results for the reciprocity hazard for Model A. As expected, the number of wineries relative to state wine consumption is positive and strongly significant. Winery concentration (HHI) has the expected positive sign but is not significant. Greater winery dispersion (Gini) coefficient significantly reduces the likelihood of adopting reciprocity, as expected. All of the distributor industry variables are significant at the 5% level or better and have the expected signs. More distributors and higher concentration reduce the likelihood reciprocity that direct shipment will be passed, while greater dispersion increases the likelihood of reciprocity. Thus, private sector economic interests appear to affect regulatory outcomes in expected ways.

Of the public sector variables, dependence on excise taxes is significant and negatively related to the likelihood of adopting direct shipment, suggesting states' financial interests play a role in direct shipment. Whether the state operates a control or license distribution system has the expected positive sign, meaning license states are more likely to adopt reciprocity, and is significant at the 1% level. These results are consistent with the argument that economic interests within the public sector also have significant influence on direct shipping regulation.

The public interest results show Democratic state legislatures are less likely to adopt reciprocity, suggesting Republican pro-trade leanings extend to interstate commerce. The one puzzle in the public interest variables is a positive and strongly significant coefficient on the DUI arrests. We have no good rationale for such a result, but we note it is inconsistent with the public interest expectation. Perhaps lawmakers think that allowing direct shipment will reduce the incidence of drunk driving, or that the incidence of drunk driving is reflective of consumer interests in alcohol consumption more generally.

Table 2. Competing Risks Hazard Results, 1986–1999

	Model A		Model B	
Variable name	Reciprocity	Permit	Reciprocity	Permit
Period 1 (1986–87)	−22.772*** (8.65)	−44.257*** (4.82)	−10.421** (94.491)	−40.046*** (2.10)
Period 2 (1988–89)	−18.365*** (5.88)	−44.502*** (4.81)	−10.274** (4.57)	−40.354*** (2.22)
Period 3 (1990–91)	−17.111*** (6.31)	−45.067*** (5.66)	−9.027** (4.37)	−40.844*** (2.13)
Period 4 (1992–93)	−14.528*** (5.67)	−45.570*** (5.66)	−8.134** (4.16)	−41.398*** (2.13)
Period 5 (1994–95)	−56.717*** (5.66)	(5.35) (4.02)	−48.037*** (4.18)	−3.578** (1.84)
Period 6 (1996–97)	−16.588*** (5.71)	(5.30) (4.77)	−9.459** (3.91)	(3.57) (2.25)
Period 7 (1998–99)	−57.653*** (7.19)	(2.34) (3.64)	−46.934*** (3.92)	(0.50) (1.69)
Wineries per gallons consumed	4,024.2*** (1,364.41)	−1,737.5* (1,105.20)	2,360.0*** (876.50)	−1,545.1* (1,050.90)
Wine industry concentration (HHI)	0.29 (0.24)	0.21 (0.19)	(0.04) (0.17)	0.178* (0.13)
Wine industry dispersion (Gini)	−14.481** (6.72)	(2.27) (2.56)	−9.000** (5.10)	(2.76) (2.90)
Distributors per gallon consumed	−1,033.58*** (429.78)	(61.45) (137.27)	(155.81) (190.35)	(36.83) (117.19)
Distribution industry concentration (HHI)	−7.738*** (2.68)	0.11 (0.33)	−2.971*** (1.16)	0.15 (0.32)
Distribution industry dispersion (Gini)	29.433*** (13.94)	8.957* (5.13)	22.726** (9.87)	8.226** (4.12)
Retail wine sales as percentage of GSP	(1,094.80) (1,959.30)	(197.60) (442.74)	(556.02) (1,223.60)	(218.55) (463.62)
Excise taxes as percentage of total revenue	−255.37** (120.12)	−298.53* (201.54)	(44.44) (91.59)	−295.36** (133.48)
License fees as percentage of total revenue	1,453.83** (747.79)	1,267.90 (1,325.40)	(591.01) (1,249.81)	1,046.20 (889.50)
License jurisdiction	9.592*** (3.19)	(0.33) (1.65)	3.837* (2.70)	(0.40) (1.70)
Government conservatism	−0.083*** (0.03)	(0.01) (0.02)	−0.055** (0.03)	(0.02) (0.02)
DUI arrests	56.948** (23.76)	3.63 (14.66)		
Liquor law violations	37.978* (25.31)	8.35 (14.26)		
Number of observations	275.00		282.00	
Log likelihood	(34.02)		(40.49)	
Pseudo R^2	0.89		0.87	

Notes: The table presents results from maximum likelihood multinomial logistic regressions for the likelihood of passing either reciprocity or permit-based direct shipment legislation during the period 1986–1999. The models were estimated with robust standard errors clustered by state (reported in parentheses). Coefficients on the time-varying dummies are not reported for brevity's sake; complete results are available from the authors upon request. ***, **, and * signify statistical significance at the 1%, 5%, and 10% levels, respectively.

Column 2 of Table 2 presents results for the permit system "hazard." In general, few estimates are significant at even the 10% level. Of those that are significant, wine industry concentration, distribution industry dispersion, and excise tax dependence have the expected signs, as in the reciprocity results. Interestingly, the number of wineries is negatively associated with adoption of permit systems. This is counter to our original expectations, but is not necessarily counter-intuitive. Given that new legislation represents a certain degree of "lock-in," wineries may oppose permit-based direct shipment if they believe a reciprocity alternative might otherwise be available. If wineries thought passage of a permit system would preclude the opportunity to pass simple reciprocity, they may opt to retain that legislative option by opposing a permit bill.

The lack of more robust statistical significance in the permit results may also be indicative of political bargaining among competing interest groups. Becker argues that multiple interest groups with competing interests will result in negotiated policies that do not reflect any group's most desired outcome. This is also consistent with the time period dummy variables, which show the probability of passing permit legislation goes up over time while the probability of passing simple reciprocity goes down, *ceteris paribus*. Combined with the results on the economic interest variables, these temporal trends suggest states with relatively stronger wine interests quickly pass legislation most favorable to the wine industry (reciprocity) while states with stronger distributor and state economic interests do not pass any direct shipment allowance; states with relatively balanced interests end up passing compromise legislation (permitting), but only after a more prolonged legislative process.

On the whole, the results from Model A are largely consistent with an economic interest theory of regulation and show little evidence of public interest factors playing a significant role in determining interstate direct shipping regulation. Indeed, the results on alcohol-related arrests indicate a positive, and in the case of reciprocity a significantly positive, effect on allowing direct shipment, counter to a public interest rationale.

Because the above specification has missing observations resulting from flaws in the arrest data, we reestimate the model without the liquor law and DUI arrest variables. The results are reported as Model B in Table 2. Comparing the results to Model A, there are no substantive changes in the direction of relationship, only the level of significance. By and large, the results are consistent across the board. Economic interests in both the private and public sectors appear to significantly affect the likelihood of regulatory change in direct shipment. A log-likelihood ratio test fails to reject the hypothesis that the constrained model performs significantly differently.

Finally, we omit the government ideology and arrest variables and reestimate the model using the full sample across all eight time period (i.e., from 1986 to 2001). The results of this specification are reported in Table 3. Once again, the number of wineries has a strong positive association with passage of reciprocity legislation and dispersion among wineries has a negative, though weakly significant, effect. Increased concentration among distributors reduces the likelihood of passage, though more dispersed

Table 3. Competing Risks Hazard Model, Full Sample

	Model			
	Reciprocity		Permit	
Variable name	Coefficient	RSE	Coefficient	RSE
Period 1 (1986–87)	−10.159***	3.188	−36.561***	1.05
Period 2 (1988–89)	−10.069***	2.987	−36.760***	0.97
Period 3 (1990–91)	−9.302***	2.73	−36.983***	0.96
Period 4 (1992–93)	−9.039***	2.718	−37.178***	0.99
Period 5 (1994–95)	−43.958***	2.486	−3.200***	1.04
Period 6 (199–97)	−9.091***	2.773	−2.909*	1.48
Period 7 (1998–99)	−42.697***	2.568	−0.228	1.06
Period 8 (2000–01)	−8.377***	2.634	−0.402	1.24
Wineries per gallons consumed	1,405.6***	416.7	−916.8*	574
Wine industry concentration (HHI)	−0.041	0.122	0.1632*	0.11
Wine industry dispersion (Gini)	−4.924	2.602	1.275	1.65
Distributors per gallon consumed	56.018	140.8	83.74	77.3
Distribution industry concentration (HHI)	−1.155*	0.699	−0.13	0.25
Distribution industry dispersion (Gini)	13.879***	5.274	1.616	2.81
Retail wine sales as percentage of GSP	−134.09	547.4	−224.4	383
Excise taxes as percentage of total revenue	−55.387	72.46	−166.9*	117
License fees as percentage of total revenue	−841.99	757.5	608.5	784
License jurisdiction	2.098*	1.301	0.482	1.31
Number of observations	309			
Log likelihood	57.8756			
Pseudo R^2	0.8295			

Notes: The table presents results from maximum likelihood multinomial logistic regressions for the likelihood of passing either reciprocity or permit-based direct shipment legislation during the period full sample, omitting some of our public interest variables. The models were estimated with robust standard errors clustered by state. Coefficients on the time-varying dummies are not reported for brevity's sake; complete results are available from the authors upon request. ***, **, and * signify statistical significance at the 1%, 5%, and 10% levels, respectively.

distribution industries increase the likelihood of passage. States with license distribution systems continue to appear more likely to adopt reciprocity. Results on the permit system are likewise consistent with earlier results, both in their lack of overwhelming statistical support for particular economic interests and in their consistency with Becker's argument regarding competing political interests.

6. Conclusions

California's 1986 passage of reciprocity direct shipment regulation represented a tightening of California's borders with respect to wines from other states. The purpose of that legislation was to pry open the borders of the forty-seven states that prohibited interstate direct shipment of wine to their citizens. In the seventeen years that followed, a flurry of legislation has been considered in at least forty-three states, with twenty-three states adopting some form of direct shipment allowance. Our purpose in this chapter has been to identify the factors that drive the adoption of direct shipment. Using data on economic and public interests regarding direct shipping, we estimate a competing risks hazard model and find that private and public sector economic interests appear to play a dominant role in determining the adoption of direct shipment laws.

These results have immediate consequence for the legal battles raging across the country contesting the constitutionality of direct shipment laws. To the extent that public welfare interests are required by courts to justify states' restrictions on interstate commerce, our results cast a shadow of doubt on public interest arguments in the area of direct shipment of wine.

The patchwork of direct shipment regulation also suggests opportunities for further research on the nature and structure of distribution relationships. To the extent small wineries find alternative means for accessing consumer markets through direct shipment, do distribution contracts in those markets change, and do they differ from those in states that continue to prohibit direct shipment? The lessons of direct shipment of wine may also have consequence for other alcoholic beverages, particularly specialty microbrew beers that face similar distribution hurdles to small wineries.

Acknowledgments

The authors thank Jerry Ellig, Eric Helland, Peter Klein, Jennifer Robbennolt, and two anonymous referees for helpful comments.

References

Becker, G.S. (1983). A theory of competition among pressure groups for political influence. *Quarterly Journal of Economics*, 98, 371–400.

Berry, W.D., Ringquist, E.J., Fordig, R.C., and Hanson, R.L. (1998). Measuring citizen and government ideology in the American States, 1960–1993. *American Journal of Political Science*, 42, 327–348.

Blaylock, J.R., and Blisard, W.N. (1993). Wine consumption by U.S. men. *Applied Economics*, 25, 645–651.

Box-Steffensmeier, J.M., and Jones, B.S. (1997). Time is of the essence: Event history models in political science. *American Journal of Political Science*, 41, 1414–1461.

Buccola, S.T., and VanderZanden, L. (1997). Wine demand, price strategy, and tax policy. *Review of Agricultural Economics*, 19, 428–440.

California Retail Liquor Dealers Assoc. v. Midcal Aluminum, Inc., 445 U.S. 97 (1980).

Childs, W.R. (2001). State regulators and pragmatic federalism in the United States, 1889–1945. *Business History Review*, 75, 701–738.

Coase, R.H. (1937). The nature of the firm. *Economica*, 4, 386–405.

Coase, R.H. (1960). The problem of social cost. *Journal of Law and Economics*, 3, 1–44.

Douglass, D.B. (2000). Constitutional crossroads: Reconciling the twenty-first amendment and the commerce clause to evaluate state regulation of interstate commerce in alcoholic beverages. *Duke Law Journal*, 49, 1619.

Elmslie, B., and Milberg, W. (1996). Free trade and social dumping: Lessons from the regulation of U.S. interstate commerce. *Challenge*, 39, 46–52.

Everett, E. (2001). A Changing distribution system, edited by K. Moulton and J. Lapsley *Successful Wine Marketing*. Gaithersburg MD: Aspen, pp. 257–262.

Foust, J. (2000). State power to regulate alcohol under the twenty-first amendment: The constitutional implications of the twenty-first amendment enforcement act. *Boston College Law Review*, 41, 659–697.

Han, A., and Hausman, J.A. (1990). Flexible parametric estimation of duration and competing risk models. *Journal of Applied Econometrics*, 5, 1–28.

Heien, D. (1996). Are higher alcohol taxes justified? *CATO Journal*, 15, 243–257.

Heien, D., and Martin, P.L. (2000). Inside the bottle: The wine business. *Choices*, Fall, 30–33.

Heien, D., and Martin, P.L. (2003). California's wine industry enters new era. *California Agriculture*, 57, 71–75.

Heien, D., and Sims, E.N. (2000). The impact of the Canada-United States free trade agreement on U.S. wine exports. *American Journal of Agricultural Economics*, 82, 173–182.

Jaeger, E. (1981). To save or savor: The rate of return to storing wines: Comment. *Journal of Political Economy*, 89, 584–592.

Joskow, P., and Noll, R. (1981). *Regulation in Theory and Practice: An Overview. Studies in Public Regulation*, edited by G. Fromm. Cambridge MA: MIT Press, pp. 1–65.

Kennedy, P. (1998). *A Guide to Econometrics*. 4th ed. Cambridge MA: MIT Press.

Kiefer, N.M. (1988). Economic duration data and hazard functions. *Journal of Economic Literature*, 26, 646–679.

Kozusko, A.J., III. (2000). The fight to 'Free the Grapes' enters federal court: Constitutional challenges to the validity of state prohibitions on the direct shipment of alcohol. *The Journal of Law and Commerce*, 20, 75–102.

Krasker, W.S. (1979). The rate of return to storing wines. *Journal of Political Economy*, 87, 1363–1367.

Kroszner, R.S., and Strahan, P.E. (1999). What drives deregulation? Economics and politics of the relaxation of bank branching restrictions. *Quarterly Journal of Economics*, 114, 1437–1467.

Landon, S., and Smith, C.E. (1998). Quality expectations, reputations, and price. *Southern Economic Journal*, 64, 628–647.

Martin, S.L. (2000). Wine wars-direct shipment of wine: The twenty-first amendment, the commerce clause, and consumer's rights. *American Business Law Journal*, 38, 1.

Martin, S.L. (2001). Changing the law: Update from the wine war. *Journal of Law and Politics*, 17, 63–98.

McDonald, C.G., and Van de Gucht, L.M. (1999). High-yield bond default and call risks. *Review of Economics and Statistics*, 81, 409–419.

Meyer, B.D. (1990). Unemployment insurance and unemployment spells. *Econometrica*, 58, 757–82.

Noll, R. (1989). *The Politics of Regulation. Handbook of Industiral Organization*, edited by R. Schmalensee and R.D. Willig. vol. II. New York: Elsevier, pp. 1254–1287.

O'Driscoll, G.P., Jr. (1993). *Interstate Obstacles to Commerce. Free Trade within North America: Expanding Trade for Prosperity*, edited by Jr., G.P. ÓDriscoll. Norwell MA: Kluwer Academic Publishers, pp. 151–160.

Peltzman, S. (1976). Toward a more general theory of regulation. *Journal of Law and Economics*, 19, 211–240.

Posner, R.A. (1974). Theories of economic regulation. *The Bell Journal of Economics and Management Science*, 5, 335–358.

Roberto, M.A. (2003). The changing structure of the global wine industry. Paper presented at European Applied Business Research Conference, Venice, Italy.

Stigler, G.J. (1971). The theory of economic regulation. *The Bell Journal of Economics and Management Science*, 2, 3–21.

Waterson, M. (1984). *Economic Theory of the Industry.* Cambridge UK: Cambridge University Press.

Wiseman, A.E., and Ellig, J. (2003). How many bottles make a case against prohibition? Online wine and Virginia's direct shipment ban. Working paper, Federal Trade Commission, Bureau of Economics Working Paper.

Chapter 6

The Economics of Planting Rights in Wine Production*

Koen Deconinck† **and Johan Swinnen**

†*University of Leuven (KU Leuven), Belgium*
koen.deconinck@kuleuven.be

The European Union (EU) is the world's largest wine producer, as well as the world's most regulated wine market. In 2007, the EU decided on a major reform of its wine policy. A crucial element was the abolishment of a system of planting rights to limit the planting of vineyards. However, after intense lobbying by opponents of the liberalization, this decision was reversed in 2013. Despite the importance of planting rights in European (and hence global) wine production, and despite the fierce debates surrounding the reforms, no model exists to study the effects of this policy. We develop the first theoretical model of planting rights, integrating the markets for land, planting rights and wine to analyze efficiency and distributional effects. We use the model to study the effects of differences among EU member states in restrictions on trade in planting rights, the role of government reserves and the impact of imperfect enforcement.

1. Introduction

The European Union (EU) produces and consumes around 60% of the world's wine. 3.6 million hectares of vineyard out of a global total of 7.4 million hectares are in the EU (Anderson and Nelgen, 2011). The EU is also the world's most regulated wine market (Meloni and Swinnen, 2013). The "Common Market Organization" (CMO) for wine was developed in the 1960s. It comprised regulations affecting quality (such as rules on geographical indications (GIs)) and quantity. The wine policy, as many other initial CAP policies, caused major market distortions. A system of minimum prices

---

This article originally appeared in *European Review of Agricultural Economics*, (2015), 42(3), 419–440.

and intervention buying caused oversupply. In 1976, extra regulations were introduced to control supply. The so-called "planting rights" system limits the area under vines in the EU.

In 2007 — in line with policy liberalizations in other agricultural sectors — the EU decided a major reform of the CMO for wine, including the abolishment of the planting rights system by 2018. The European Commission (2007) argued that the liberalization would improve the competitiveness of the sector: "successful wine makers are currently hamstrung by their inability to expand their vineyards — an expansion that would greatly increase their competitiveness by offering economies of scale." However, after the decision in 2007, opponents of the liberalization of planting rights organized themselves and lobbied heavily to have this decision reversed.[1] In June 2013, after trilogue discussions between the Council, the European Parliament and the European Commission, the liberalization decision was reversed. The current system of planting rights would remain in place until 2016, when it would be replaced by a system of "authorizations" for new plantings. This reversal of the decision to liberalize the planting rights presents a unique case in the political economy history of the CAP.

Despite its importance for the sector, its long existence, its distinct features (explained below) and the unique political outcome, the literature on planting rights is surprisingly scant. A few reports on the effects of liberalization (e.g., European Parliament, 2012; Montaigne *et al.*, 2012) provide only qualitative arguments, anecdotal evidence and summary statistics. A more elaborate empirical study by Bogonos *et al.* (2012) focuses on one region (Rheinland-Pfalz). However, none of these studies have a conceptual or theoretical framework to study the effects of planting rights (liberalization). Our chapter is the first to conceptually analyze the effects of planting rights in the wine sector and the effects of liberalization.

Our model and analysis is related to several studies of other agricultural policies. First, there is an extensive theoretical and empirical literature on the effects of production quota in agriculture (e.g., Gardner, 1987; Alston and James, 2002; Lips and Rieder, 2005; Gohin and Bureau, 2006). The analysis of planting rights is different since planting rights impose a constraint on the use of land in viticulture (instead of output) when yields (and thus output) can vary strongly between regions and over time. Planting rights

[1] Opponents claimed that abolishing planting rights would drive small producers out of the market and allow large and powerful producers to delocalize vineyards to higher-yield areas, increasing production and decreasing prices, income and quality (Copa-Cogeca, 2012).

thus not only have an impact on the market for wine, but also on the land market. Hence, one needs to simultaneously consider the markets for output (wine), inputs (land) and quotas (planting rights). Second, in that sense, our analysis is related to that of acreage controls, an instrument used extensively in the USA (Gardner, 1987; Gisser, 1993), and set-aside requirements in the EU (Bourgeon *et al.*, 1995). However, our model of planting rights differs since, unlike acreage controls and set-aside requirements, it allows for trade of rights. Third, our analysis is also related to recent studies on CAP direct payments and their interactions with land and credit market imperfections and trade in entitlements (Ciaian and Swinnen, 2006, 2009; Ciaian *et al.*, 2008; Courleux *et al.*, 2008; Kilian *et al.*, 2012). However, direct payments are not aimed at restricting production.

Moreover, since entitlements give rise to exogenously given monetary benefits, in contrast to planting rights, the market for entitlements functions differently.[2] Fourth, our analysis is also related to the analysis of GIs. However, planting rights are different because (i) the planting rights system applies to all wines, including wines without GI; (ii) whereas GIs are (in principle) designed to protect quality, planting rights restrict production regardless of quality and (iii) there can be trade in planting rights between different regions covered by a GI. Existing studies of GIs ignore planting rights and typically only consider a single region in isolation (e.g., Moschini *et al.*, 2008; Mérel and Sexton, 2012).

The chapter is organized as follows. Section 2 explains the planting rights regulations, discussing both EU-wide principles and variations in implementation between member states (MS). Section 3 develops our basic model integrating the markets for land, planting rights and wine. Section 4 analyzes the effects of differences in implementation between MS (restrictions on trade in planting rights, the "reserve" system, and problems of enforcement). Section 5 discusses conclusions and implications.

2. The System of Planting Rights in the EU

Planting rights were introduced in 1976. Since then, the planting of new vineyards is forbidden unless the grower has a permission ("planting right").

[2]For instance, as our analysis shows, the price of planting rights gradually decreases to zero as the amount of planting rights increases. In contrast, with entitlements the market price may discontinuously drop to zero (and the direct payment gets capitalized in land values) once the number of entitlements exceeds the total eligible area (Ciaian *et al.*, 2008; Courleux *et al.*, 2008).

Planting rights can derive from three sources.[3] *Replanting rights* are granted to a grower who has grubbed up a vineyard. The grower can either use the replanting right for new vineyards or transfer this right to another grower. Second, planting rights can also be obtained from a *reserve*, organized at the national or subnational level.[4] The reserves can grant these planting rights to producers either for free in the case of young producers (under 40) who fulfil certain requirements or against payment for others. Third, *new planting rights* are awarded for experimental purposes or for vineyards which are intended for personal consumption, and therefore of limited practical importance.

Although general rules are laid down by the EU, there are considerable differences in implementation between MS in terms of the relative importance of replanting rights versus reserves, the regulations regarding trade in replanting rights, the organization of reserves and the enforcement of the planting rights regulations.

Replanting rights are by far the most important source of planting rights in the EU (Table 1). In 2010–2011, of all available planting rights in the EU, 76% were replanting rights, 20% were planting rights held in reserves and 4% were planting rights allocated to producers from a reserve but not yet used. Replanting rights dominate in the "old" MS (Austria, France, Germany, Greece, Italy, Luxembourg, Portugal and Spain), where they account for 82% of all planting rights. In contrast, in the new member states (NMS) (Bulgaria, Cyprus, Czech Republic, Hungaria, Malta, Romania, Slovakia and Slovenia) replanting rights only account for 44% of the total. In the NMS, the reserves play a more important role (European Commission, 2012, p. 23).

Replanting rights cannot be transferred between different countries. EU rules also stipulate that MS must ensure that the transfer of planting rights does not lead to an increase in overall production potential (for instance when planting rights are transferred from a non-irrigated to an irrigated area) and replanting rights can only be used for the production of GI wines. In addition, MS are allowed to use national regulations to further restrict trade. Several MS have restrictions on the internal trade in planting rights. In Spain, for instance, planting rights are organized at the level of the regions (the

[3]See Articles 90–97 of Council Regulation (EC) No 479/2008.

[4]Reserves receive replanting rights which were not used by producers in the prescribed time frame. They can also buy replanting rights directly from producers, depending on the specific rules set by the national governments.

Table 1. Sources of Planting Rights

Member state	Replanting rights held by producers but not yet used (%)	Planting rights available in the reserve (%)	Planting rights from the reserve allocated to producers but not yet used (%)
Spain	84	16	0
France	81	19	0
Italy	91	3	6
Portugal	99	1	0
Germany	90	9	1
Greece	34	27	38
Austria	36	64	0
Luxemburg	100	0	0
Eight old MS (EU-8)	*82*	*16*	*2*
Hungary	70	30	0
Slovakia	60	39	1
Czech Republic	50	44	7
Slovenia	11	80	8
Cyprus	81	18	2
Malta	0	100	0
Six new MS (EU-6)	*56*	*42*	*2*
Romania	55	6	39
Bulgaria	17	80	3
Two new MS (EU-2)	*37*	*41*	*21*
EU total	**76**	**20**	**4**

Source: European Commission (2012).

seventeen "autonomous communities" such as Catalonia, Valencia or Basque Country), and the transfer of planting rights between different regions is strictly regulated. A region can only transfer a maximum of planting rights equal to 0.4% of its total area of vineyards each year, and such transfers must be authorized by the national Ministry of Agriculture (Montaigne *et al.*, 2012). Moreover, even transfers of planting rights inside the region must be authorized by the regional government, which also imposes extra limits on how the planting rights can be used (European Parliament, 2012). In Germany, transfers of rights are in principle not allowed between federal regions (Länder) or between wine regions within the same federal region, except if public authorities authorize it. France has even more regulations. Producers also need an "authorization" to use the planting right. Producer organizations set an annual quota of new plantations for wines within a GI.

There is a limit to how much new vineyards a single producer can add in a given year.[5]

For planting rights from a reserve, EU regulations state that the planting right is used such that the location, the varieties and the cultivation techniques are "adapted to market demand," and that the plot of land must have yields which are "typical of the average in the region" (European Commission, 2012, p. 11). MS are allowed to define the price or extra requirements for purchasing planting rights from the reserve, and to decide whether the reserves are organized on the national or subnational level. For instance, France has a national single reserve, while in Spain the reserves are organized at the regional level.[6]

MS also differ in the enforcement of the regulations. In fact, there is considerable uncertainty about the total area under vines in some MS. In 1986, the EU decreed that MS had to set up a vineyard register to manage planting rights by 1992, but Italy and Greece still had not complied by 2004. Different official numbers submitted to the EU put the Greek vineyard area at somewhere between 51,000 and 112,000 ha in the period 1997–2000 (European Commission, 2004). In June 2012, the European Commission fined Greece, Italy and Spain for a total of 250 million euros because of an estimated 120,000 ha of illegally planted vineyards. In contrast, different estimates of the surface under vines in France appear to have an error margin of <1 per cent (European Commission, 2004). Thus, enforcement of planting rights differs between MS.

To model these differences in implementation and national regulations between MS, we first develop a basic model of the markets for planting rights, land and wine. Next, we extend the model to evaluate the impact of MS differences in trade restrictions, reserves and enforcement.

3. The Basic Model

We distinguish four different agents (interest groups): consumers of wine, owners of land, owners of planting rights and producers of wine. For both

[5]For wines with a GI, the limit is set at 3 ha of new vineyards per producer per year and at 1 ha for wines with a protected designation of origin. Requests for authorizations are handled by the Institut National des Appellations d'Origine (INAO) for PDO wines and by FranceAgriMer for all other categories of wines (Montaigne *et al.*, 2012).

[6]In general, a reserve can freely buy and sell planting rights, although MS can again introduce their own rules to govern the reserve. In addition, regional reserves may exchange planting rights with each other or with their national reserve, although this seems to be rare in practice. Spain also has a national reserve in addition to the regional reserves, although the national reserve plays only a minor role.

analytical and policy reasons, it is important to distinguish between these interests. While most current grape producers are also owners of their vineyards (and hence the land and the planting rights), when they want to expand they need to buy new land and new planting rights. The evaluation of a policy should also take into account its effect on future producers; many potential future producers do not own planting rights, and for them planting rights represent a cost, not an asset. We assume that the grape grower produces and sells the wine directly to the consumers, thus collapsing the supply chain of wine.[7] To start, we focus on replanting rights only. We analyze the effect of the reserves later.

Our model assumes for simplicity that land is the only input in wine production. This assumption precludes substitution effects in the production decision. If substitution were possible, restricting the use of land might lead to more intense use of other production factors (Alston and James, 2002). This would clearly reduce the effectiveness of planting rights in restricting wine production. However, in most EU wine regions, there are strict rules on production techniques and the maximum allowable yield. The scope for substitution is therefore limited in most wine regions, which justifies the simplification of considering land as the only input.

Consider a region consisting of producers which can produce wine or an alternative crop with land as the only input in the production process. Each producer has an initial holding of land $\bar{L}_i$. The total area of the region is $\bar{L}$. The producer allocates an amount of land $L_{i,W}$ to wine production and an amount $L_{i,A}$ to an alternative crop. Land can be bought and sold for a price p_L.[8] We assume producer-specific production functions for wine $W_i(L_{i,W})$ and the alternative crop $A_i(L_{i,A})$. For both crops, we assume diminishing returns to the use of land, hence $W_i', A_i' > 0$ and $W_i'', A_i'' < 0$. The price of wine is p_W and the price of alternative crop is normalized to one.[9]

[7]The structure of the wine sector and its supply chain is quite complex and can vary importantly between regions, and even within regions. Some producers produce bulk wine which is sold to commercial enterprises which bottle and market the wine. Others produce wine through a cooperative. Yet other producers produce and bottle their own wines and sell them directly to wine retailers or consumers all over the world.

[8]Throughout, we are working with a one-period model; hence renting or buying are equivalent here.

[9]That is, we assume that producers within one region are producing a homogenous product. In reality, of course, the quality and price of wines can vary a lot between different producers. This could be in corporated in the model by assuming that "high-quality" producers and "low-quality" producers form two separate regions (with or without trade in planting rights between regions, as analyzed later).

The objective function of producer i is

$$Max_{L_{i,W},L_{i,A}} p_W W_i(L_{i,W}) + A_i(L_{i,A}) - p_L(L_{i,W} + L_{i,A} - \bar{L}_i). \quad (1)$$

The first-order conditions defining optimal land use for the individual producer are given by

$$p_W W_i'(L_{i,W}) = p_L, \quad (2)$$

$$A_i'(L_{i,A}) = p_L. \quad (3)$$

Equations (2) and (3) determine producer i's demand for grape-growing land and alternative-crop land. By summing the first-order conditions across producers in the region, we obtain the region-wide value marginal productivity of land in producing wine $p_W W'(L_W)$ or the alternative crop $A'(L_A)$, which represent the region-wide demand curves. Given our assumption of diminishing returns, both are downward-sloping. Since total land use must equal the total area of the region $\bar{L}$, we can depict these demand schedules as in the upper left panel of Figure 1, with land used in wine production measured from left to right, and land used in growing the alternative crop measured from right to left.[10] The equilibrium price of land p_L equals the marginal productivity of both crops.

The equilibrium allocation of land to producing wine L_W and the price of land p_L depends on the price of wine p_W. For instance, with a wine price of p_W^1 the equilibrium allocation of land is L_W^1 and the price of land is p_L^1. A decrease in the wine price p_W corresponds to a downward (counterclockwise) rotation of $p_W W'(L_W)$. Different wine prices p_W thus correspond to different allocations L_W and hence different output levels of wine $W(L_W)$. This allows us to trace out the supply curve of wine in the upper right panel of Figure 1. In the upper left panel, a given price of wine (e.g., p_W^1) determines the allocation of land to the production of wine (e.g., L_W^1). In this panel, we have rescaled the vertical axis such that $W'(0) = 1$.[11] With this convention, the intercept of $p_W W'(L_W)$ equals the output price of wine p_W, which makes it easier to compare the upper left and upper right panel.

[10]For simplicity, we have chosen to draw these demand functions as straight lines; however, no functional form is implied by this choice. Given the assumptions on the producer-level production functions, both demand curves are downward sloping, and total wine production is an increasing but concave function of land use.

[11]This is merely a rescaling of the vertical axis of the drawing, not an assumption on the functional form of the production functions. The rescaling allows us to read the output price of wine p_W on the vertical axis of the upper-left panel.

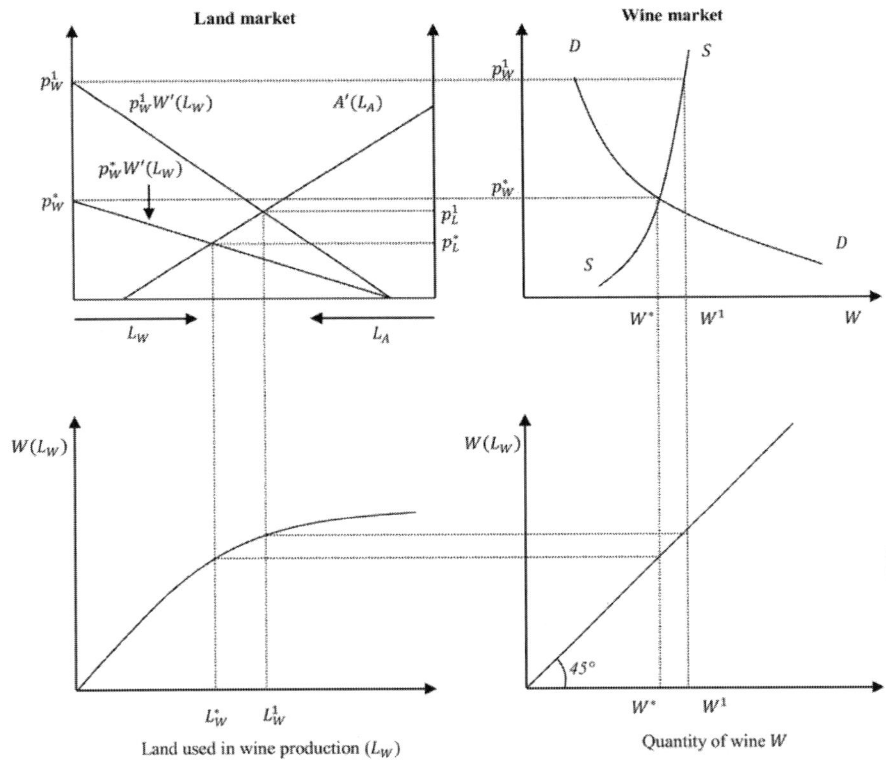

Figure 1. Equilibrium in the Wine and Land Market

The bottom left panel of our graph plots the aggregate (region-wide) production function of wine $W(L_W)$. Given an allocation of land (e.g., L_W^1), this panel gives the resulting output of wine (e.g., $W_1 = W(L_W^1)$). The lower-right panel is merely the 45°-line, projecting the output of wine W on the horizontal axis of the upper right panel, which depicts the market supply of wine as a function of p_W. By varying the wine price p_W, we can trace out the resulting supply of wine in the upper-right diagram and so obtain the supply curve of wine, here denoted by *SS*. By adding the market demand for wine, we are able to find the equilibrium price of wine p_W^*. The corresponding demand curve for land $p_W^* W'(L_W)$ then determines the equilibrium allocation of land L_W^* and the equilibrium land price p_L^*.

3.1. *Welfare effects of planting rights*

Planting rights will affect the equilibrium. We assume that the government fixes a total number of planting rights equivalent to an area $\bar{R}$ which can be used for wine production. We focus on the interesting case, where this area is below the "laissez-faire" optimal area L_W^*. We assume that these planting rights are distributed arbitrarily among the producers, each producer receiving a certain endowment of planting rights R_i. Planting rights can be freely traded at a price p_R, exogenous to the producer. (We later analyze how relaxing the assumption of tradable planting rights affects the results.) The objective function of the producer now becomes

$$\begin{aligned} &Max_{L_{i,W},L_{i,A}} p_W W_i(L_{i,W}) + A_i(L_{i,A}) \\ &\quad - p_L(L_{i,W} + L_{i,A} - \bar{L}_i) - p_R(L_{i,W} - R_i). \end{aligned} \tag{4}$$

And the first-order conditions are now

$$p_W W_i'(L_{i,W}) = p_L + p_R, \tag{5}$$

$$A_i'(L_{i,A}) = p_L. \tag{6}$$

The situation on the land market is depicted in the top panel of Figure 2, where the available quantity of planting rights $\bar{R}$ is denoted by a vertical line. Total land used in wine production cannot exceed $\bar{R}$. Planting rights thus lead to an expansion of the area planted with the alternative crop. In equilibrium, the value marginal productivity of land is higher for wine than for the alternative crop. The latter determines the price of land $p_L^{\#}$, which is lower than the land price without planting rights p_L^*.[12]

At the margin, producers should be indifferent between buying one extra unit of land at price p_L and producing the alternative crop, or buying an extra unit of land and a planting right at a total cost of $p_L + p_R$ and producing wine.

The equilibrium price of planting rights $p_R^{\#}$ is therefore equal to the difference between the marginal productivity of land in wine production and in growing the alternative crop. The supply curve for wine now becomes $SS^{\#}$ in the bottom panel of Figure 2 with maximum wine production of $W^{\#}$.

"Producers" as a group (i.e., land owners, planting rights owners and wine producers) face an efficiency loss b because of the restriction in production. Unless demand is perfectly elastic, the restriction in supply will also lead to a higher wine price $p_W^{\#}$, which decreases consumer surplus by $a + c$, where a denotes an efficiency loss and c is a transfer of surplus from

[12]Throughout, we will denote by* the equilibrium values in a laissez-faire setting, while we use # for the equilibrium outcomes under a planting rights regime.

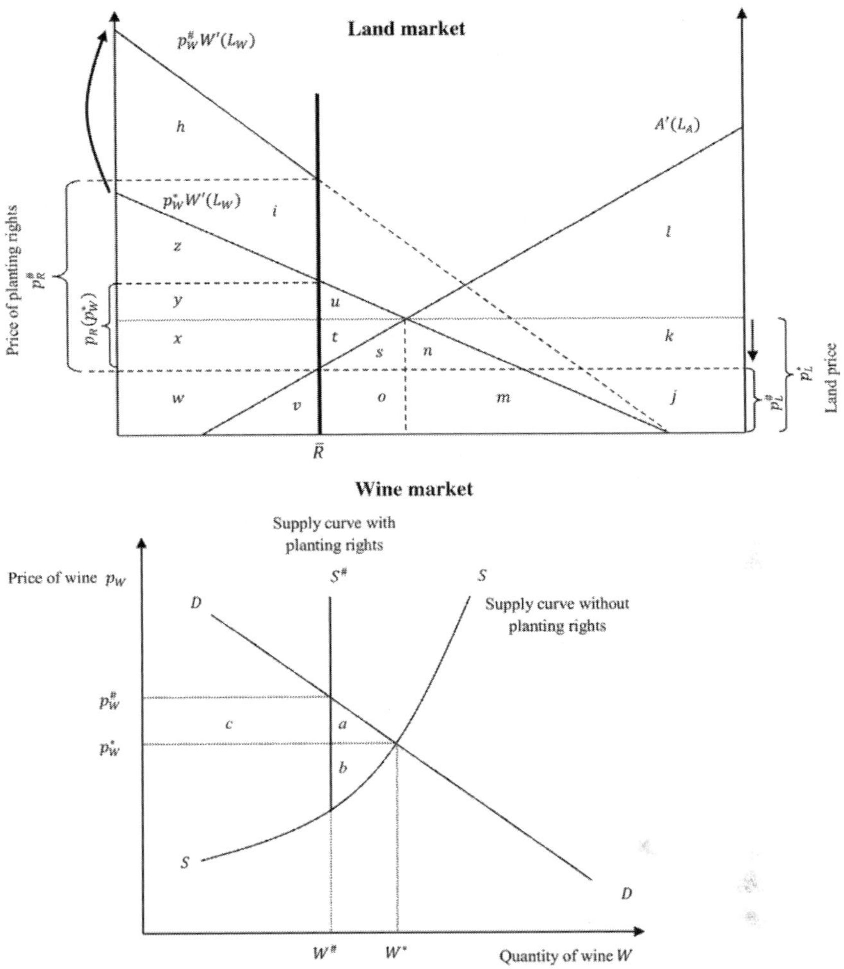

Figure 2. Welfare Effects of Planting Rights

consumers to "producers." Society faces a net loss equal to $a+b$ (see Table 2 for a summary).

The upper panel of Figure 2 allows us to analyze how the transfer c and the efficiency loss b are distributed among land owners, planting rights owners and wine producers. For didactic purposes, we first discuss the welfare effects if the price of wine remains constant, and then discuss the additional impact of an (induced) increase in the price of wine.

Before the introduction of planting rights, wine producers received an area $z + y + u$ as surplus from producing wine while producers of the alternative crop receive area l as surplus. The introduction of planting

Table 2. Welfare Effects of Planting Rights

	Constant wine price	Price effect	Total effect
Wine producers	$-y-u$	$h-z$	$h-z-y-u$
Owners of planting rights	$x+y$	$z+i$	$x+y+z+i$
Landowners	$-x-t-s-n-k$		$-x-t-s-n-k$
Producers of alternative crop	$s+n+k$		$s+n+k$
Net change in total income of producers	$-u-t$	$h+i$	$h+i-u-t$
Efficiency loss on producer side	$-u-t$ $=-b$		$-u-t$ $=-b$
Transfer from consumers to wine sector		$-h-i$ $=-c$	$-h-i$ $=-c$
Efficiency loss on consumer side		$-a$	$-a$
Total change in consumer welfare		$-a-c$	$-a-c$
Total efficiency loss	$-b$	$-a$	$-a-b$

rights (assuming no effect on the price of wine) depresses the land price and landowners lose $(p_L^* - p_L^{\#})\bar{L}$, which is represented by areas $x+t+s+n+k$. Planting rights induce an expansion of the area used in growing the alternative crop. For producers of alternative crops, the expansion of production leads to extra surplus $s+k+n$ (we assume that demand for the alternative crop is perfectly elastic so no price effect occurs). Wine producers who do not own land or planting rights are definitely worse off: their surplus declines by $y+u$ as their production is restricted to $\bar{R}$ and as they have to pay land prices and planting rights which together are more expensive than land prices before the introduction of planting rights.[13] Wine producers' surplus is now equal to an area z, and the area $y+x$ represents total payments on planting rights. Finally, area $u+t$ represents the social deadweight costs (economic inefficiencies) caused by the planting rights system. As the supply curve in the bottom panel of Figure 2 is derived from the land market in the top panel, area $u+t$ is merely a different way of depicting the producers' efficiency loss b.

The initial allocation of planting rights has distributional consequences. If wine producers need to buy the planting rights from the government or from others, the area $y+x$ would be a transfer to the government or other agents; wine producers then lose $y+u$. In contrast, if wine producers initially received these planting rights for free, the value of the planting rights accrues

[13]In Figure 2 we use $p_R(p_W^*)$ to denote the price of planting rights if the wine price remains at p_W^*, and p_R^* to denote the price of planting rights if the wine price increases to p_W^*.

to them. The net effect on their surplus would then be $x - u$, which could be positive or negative. This net effect is the combination of the decrease in land prices due to planting rights, x and the efficiency loss u as a result of reduced output.[14]

Consider now the (additional) effects if the introduction of planting rights increases the price of wine from p_W^* to $p_W^{\#}$. The demand for land for vineyards rotates upward, but does not change the price of land. An increase in the price of wine only increases the price of planting rights: from $p_R(p_W^*)$ to $p_R^{\#}$. Hence, there is no impact on producers of other crops or landowners. Changes in the wine price only affect wine producers and planting rights owners. Benefits for the planting rights owner increase to $x + y + z + i$. The additional benefits for wine producers equal $h - z$, which is always greater than zero.[15] Given a planting rights regime, both planting rights holders and wine producers thus benefit if the wine price increases.

A final question is whether planting rights, compared with a laissez-faire regime, also benefit wine producers. The net effect on their surplus is $h-(z+y+u)$. Whether this is positive or negative depends on the elasticity of wine demand. A more inelastic demand implies a stronger increase in the price of wine following the supply restrictions imposed by planting rights. For strong enough price increases, the triangle h can be larger than the triangle $z + y + u$, so that even producers without planting rights benefit.[16]

4. Effects of Variations in Implementation

As explained in Section 2, MS differ in their implementation of the planting rights regime on three dimensions: the degree to which planting rights are tradable within and between regions; the organization of the reserve system and the degree to which the planting rights system is effectively enforced. In this Section, we use our conceptual model to analyze the effects of these variations in implementation.

[14]Whether $x - u$ is positive depends on the relative steepness of the productivity schedule of wine and the alternative crop. If the marginal productivity of wine production declines only slowly, u will be small. If the marginal productivity of the alternative crop declines strongly, x will be large. In this case, wine producers gain from lower land prices while efficiency losses are limited. In contrast, if efficiency losses are large while the decline in land prices is small, wine producers lose from the introduction of planting rights even if they receive the rights for free.

[15]This can be seen graphically by vertically shifting the triangle z upward.

[16]For a wine production function of the form $W = L^{\alpha}$, for instance, it is sufficient that demand is inelastic, as shown in the Appendix.

4.1. *Trade restrictions*

A well-known result of the literature on output quotas is that when output quotas cannot be traded among producers, extra inefficiencies arise (Alston, 1981; Burrell, 1989). Also with planting rights, trade allows less efficient wine producers to sell their planting rights to more efficient wine producers, until the point where the price of planting rights equals their marginal value for every producer. Hence, trade leads to an efficient allocation of planting rights regardless of the initial allocation.

With trade, the initial allocation of planting rights does not affect the (efficient) allocation outcome, but the resulting distribution will be different. If planting rights are allocated based on historical ownership of vineyards (as in the old MS of the EU), over time there is a transfer from new producers to existing producers (who initially did not have to pay for planting rights). If initially planting rights are auctioned off, the government benefits, as there is a transfer from existing producers to the state budget.

The effect of trade restrictions in planting rights depends on (i) trade in land and vineyards and (ii) differences in land quality. To illustrate this, consider the theoretical case where land is perfectly homogeneous and vineyards and land are perfectly tradable. In this case, restrictions on trade in planting rights will have no effects. While producers with more planting rights than they could profitably use cannot sell these planting rights directly, they could buy land, plant a vineyard and sell the resulting vineyard to producers who wanted to produce more wine. Hence, with homogeneous land and no transaction costs, trade in land and vineyards has the same effect as transfers of planting rights, as it leads to an efficient allocation.

In reality, of course, land is heterogeneous and transaction costs matter. Trade in planting rights will typically have lower transaction costs than trading vineyards and land. Restrictions on trade in planting rights will therefore cause efficiency losses. To analyze this, in Figure 3 we consider the case of trade in planting rights between two regions. Transfers of land from one region to the other are physically impossible, which is equivalent to assuming prohibitively high transaction costs. We assume that the two regions are identical except for their initial endowment of planting rights. The extension to a situation with heterogeneous land quality or productivity is straightforward.[17] Region 1 has a smaller endowment of planting rights than

[17]The wine price p_W^* is assumed constant. Relaxing this assumption would not fundamentally alter the conclusions.

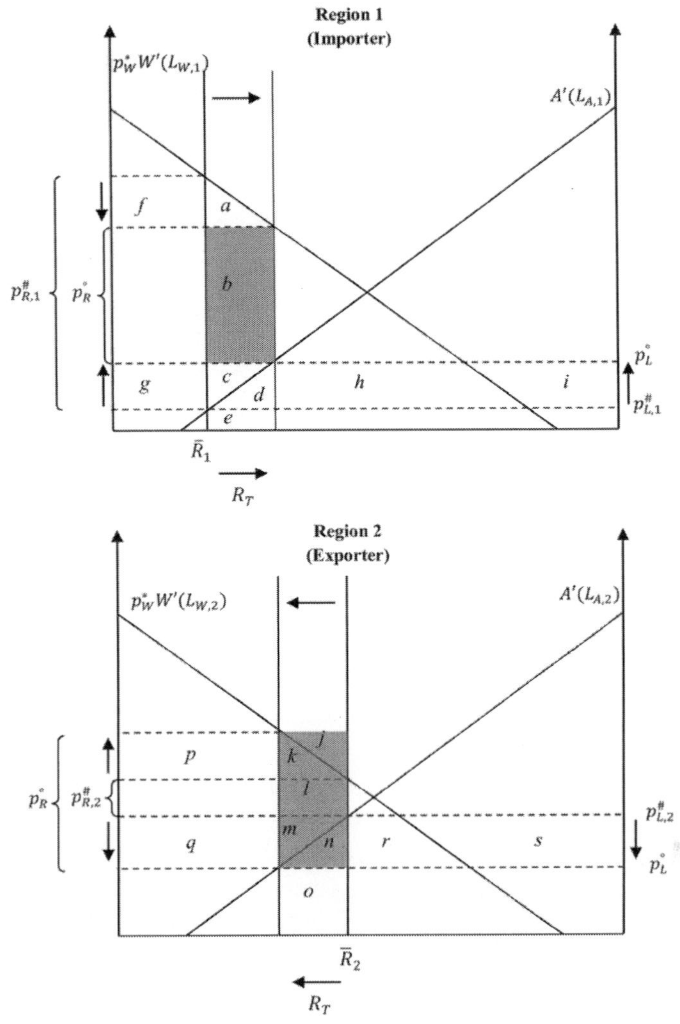

Figure 3. Effects of Transfers of Planting Rights

Region 2 ($\bar{R}_1 < \bar{R}_2$). Without trade, Region 1 has lower wine production, a higher price of planting rights ($p^{\#}_{R,1} > p^{\#}_{R,2}$) and a lower land price ($p^{\#}_{L,1} < p^{\#}_{L,2}$). With trade in planting rights, vineyards in Region 2 will be grubbed up and the planting right will be sold to Region 1. This process continues until the price of planting rights in both regions is equalized. An amount of planting rights R_T is transferred from Region 2 to Region 1.[18]

[18]In Figure 3, we denote by $\circ$ the outcomes for an "open" economy. Thus, $p^{\#}_{L,1}$ is the price of land in Region 1 under a planting rights regime with no trade, while p°_{L} is the price of

Table 3. Welfare Effects of Trade between Regions

	Region 1 (importer)	Region 2 (exporter)
Changes in production		
Change in wine production	$a+b+c+d+e$	$-k-l-m-n-o$
Change in production of alternative crop	$-d-e$	$n+o$
Net production change	$a+b+c$	$-k-l-m$
Transfer to/from other region	$-b$	$j+k+l+m+n$
Net change in total income	$a+c$	$j+n$
Distributional effects		
Wine producers	$f+a$	$-p-k$
Owners of planting rights	$-f-g$	$p+q+j+k+m+n$
Landowners	$g+c+d+h+i$	$-q-m-n-r-s$
Producers of alternative crop	$-d-h-i$	$n+r+s$
Net change in total income	$a+c$	$j+n$

Trade increases welfare in both regions. In Region 1 area R_T is transferred from the production of the alternative crop to wine. The net increase in output value is $a+b+c$. Part of this (area b) will go to Region 2 as payment for traded planting rights. Hence, total welfare in Region 1 increases by $a+c$. In Region 2, the wine area decreases by R_T, leading to an output loss of $k+l+m+n+o$. The value of the alternative crop increases by $n+o$. Total output decreases with $k+l+m$. Since the owners of planting rights in Region 2 receive $j+k+l+m+n$, there is a net welfare gain in Region 2 of $j+n$. In both regions, welfare increases as trade allows producers to reap efficiency gains by transferring planting rights to their most efficient use. The total efficiency gains are $a+c+j+n$ (see Table 3).

However, there are winners and losers in both regions. The distributional consequences depend on whether the region is a "net exporter" or a "net importer" of planting rights. For "importing" regions, wine producers gain from lower planting rights prices, while owners of planting rights lose. Landowners gain because of higher land prices, while producers of the alternative crop lose because of lower output and higher land prices. For "exporting" regions, the opposite effects hold.[19]

land when trade is allowed. (Given our assumption of identical regions, this land price is the same for both regions.)

[19]In Region 1, owners of planting rights lose by area $f+g$; land owners gain $g+c+d+h+i$ and producers of the alternative crop lose because of lower production (area d) and higher land prices ($h+i$). In Region 2, wine producers lose $p+k$. Owners of planting rights gain $p+q+j+k+m+n$. Landowners lose $q+m+n+r+s$. Producers of the alternative crop gain $r+s+n$.

When trade is restricted, the price of planting rights will not be equalized across different regions. One could therefore consider differences in prices of planting rights as an indicator of efficiency losses. In Spain, where trade in planting rights between different regions is highly regulated, prices of planting rights varied between EUR 500/ha and EUR 30,000/ha. They traded at EUR 500/ha in Castilla-La-Mancha, at EUR 2,000/ha in Catalonia, at EUR 4,000/ha in Castilla y León, and at EUR 30,000/ha in La Rioja (Montaigne *et al.*, 2012). These numbers suggest considerable efficiency losses (and strong distributional effects) due to restrictions on trade in planting rights.[20]

However, in France where trade among regions is also highly regulated, price differences in planting rights among regions are much smaller. As we will argue in the next section, this may be because of differences in how the reserve system operates — and how this interacts with the market for planting rights.

4.2. *The reserve system*

To start, consider the case of a reserve in a single region (which could be the entire country). The reserve can acquire planting rights by buying them from producers who grub up their vineyards. We assume the reserve buys and sells at the same price p_R^{reserve} (set by the reserve). Moreover, we make the assumption that the reserve may start off with a stock of planting rights R^{reserve} previously acquired from producers.[21] The total stock of planting rights in the region $\bar{R}$ now includes both the planting rights available on the market and those in the reserve, R^{reserve}. $p_R^{\#}$ is the market price of planting rights which would prevail if the entire stock of planting rights in the region $\bar{R}$ were made available to producers (i.e., the reserve does not "hoard" planting rights). Interestingly, if there is an initial stock of planting rights in the reserve, the price set by the reserve will have "asymmetric" effects depending on whether p_R^{reserve} is above or below $p_R^{\#}$.

If the reserve sets p_R^{reserve} below the equilibrium price $p_R^{\#}$, the total demand for planting rights will exceed the available stock of planting rights $\bar{R}$ in the region. Likewise, the demand for planting rights from the reserve

[20]Inefficiencies arising from limited transferability of quota can be larger than the effect of quota *per se*. For instance, Alston (1986) estimated that limited transferability of hen quota in Victoria dominated the total efficiency effect of the quota system, so that most of the welfare gains of liberalization could be achieved by simply allowing free transferability.

[21]This is a realistic assumption: as shown in Table 1, 20% of all planting rights in the EU are currently held by a reserve.

will exceed the stock of planting rights in the reserve, R^{reserve}. The reserve will sell its entire stock, and competition will push up the price of planting rights in the market to $p_R^{\#}$. Hence, in terms of total efficiency the existence of a regional reserve selling at a low price makes no difference for our analysis. There is, however, a distributional effect. Since at the low price p_R^{reserve} the demand for planting rights from the reserve exceeds the amount available, the reserve will need to ration the allocation of planting rights. This might be done by using criteria for preferential treatment, such as giving priority to younger producers. Those who have been able to buy planting rights paid p_R^{reserve} while the market value is $p_R^{\#}$, which amounts to a transfer to those who have access to the reserve. The magnitude of the transfers depends on the size of the initial stock; if the initial stock were zero, setting the reserve price below the market price would have no effects.

Alternatively, suppose the reserve sets a price p_R^{reserve} above the equilibrium price $p_R^{\#}$. Since we assume that the reserve is willing to both buy and sell at this price, there will be producers who find it profitable to grub up their vineyards and sell the planting rights to the reserve at this price. As a result, the total area under vines in the region will decrease and the market price of planting rights will increase to p_R^{reserve}. The reserve is hoarding planting rights and the stock R^{reserve} will increase. Analytically, this case is similar to what happens in a region which becomes a "net exporter" of planting rights, as in the lower panel of Figure 3. The area under vines decreases by an amount R_T, which is equal to the number of planting rights transferred to the reserve. There is a reduction in the production of wine, an increase in the production of the alternative crop, a decrease in the price of land and an increase in the price of planting rights. In terms of welfare effects for the different stakeholders, the same conclusions apply as for Region 2, the net exporter in our previous analysis. However, in this case the shaded area $j+k+l+m+n$ represents payments from the reserve to producers, instead of payments from producers in a different region. That is, this area now represents costs to the taxpayer. Total income in the region has increased by $j+n$, while taxpayers now pay $j+k+l+m+n$. So, the total efficiency loss to society is given by $k+l+m$. Hence, in contrast to the case where a reserve sets the price of planting rights below the equilibrium price, setting the price above the equilibrium price results in efficiency losses.

The above conclusions are obviously also valid when instead of a single regional reserve we are analyzing a single national reserve. However, the existence of a national reserve has some interesting additional implications. When a national reserve sets one price at which it freely buys and sells planting rights throughout the country, producers in all regions will expand or restrict production to match the marginal productivity of vineyards to the price of land plus the price of planting rights as set by the reserve. That is, even if planting rights cannot be traded across regions, the existence of a national reserve which sets a single price might lead to an efficient allocation of planting rights across regions, as planting rights will be implicitly transferred through the reserve instead of through direct trade. In the absence of trade, an efficient allocation can thus be achieved by a national reserve.

This appears to be the case in France, where the price of planting rights in regional markets has closely followed the price set by the national reserve, even though trade in planting rights is severely restricted by regulations. In contrast, Spain relies mostly on regional reserves; in combination with the restrictions on trade between regions as well as between regional reserves this may explain the enormous disparities in prices of planting rights across different regions.

4.3. *Imperfect enforcement*

The presence of enforcement issues generally changes the welfare analysis of agricultural policies. As shown by Giannakas and Fulton (2000), cheating implies that a given transfer to producers becomes less efficient, since the government now needs to incur enforcement costs. However, most studies (including Giannakas and Fulton (2000)) have focused on efficiency effects, using a representative producer, which ignores the distributional consequences.

So far, we have assumed that the level of planting rights $\bar{R}$ set by the government is also the effective level of planting rights. With imperfect enforcement, this is no longer the case. If replanting rights are issued while vineyards were not grubbed up, or if vineyards are planted without planting rights, this would result in the *de facto* stock of planting rights being greater than the official stock of planting rights. This in turn leads to lower prices of planting rights (as the actual constraint imposed by planting rights is weakened), higher prices of land (as more land can now be used to plant vineyards rather than the less profitable alternative crop), a larger supply of wine and thus in general a lower price of wine than would be the case with perfect enforcement. As a result, the efficiency losses described earlier are smaller when the planting rights system cannot be perfectly enforced.[22]

[22]We are focusing here on the net effects of illegal plantings, abstracting from the social costs of enforcement.

Both the efficiency effects and the distributional consequences of illegal plantings can be analyzed using the top panel of Figure 3, which shows a region that is a "net importer" of planting rights. The creation of false planting rights or illegal plantings is similar to the import of planting rights through trade. The extra production through illegal plantings creates a total value of $a + b + c + d + e$, but displaces production of the alternative crop $(d + e)$; the net gain to society is thus $a + b + c$. Owners of (official) planting rights suffer a decrease in their income of $f + g$, while landowners experience an increase in their revenues due to higher land prices $(g + c + d + h + i)$.

What happens with the surplus $a + b$ depends on the nature of illegal planting rights. If planting rights have been created illegally and sold to unsuspecting producers, the surplus of wine producers increases by $f + a$ because of the lower price of planting rights and the increase in production. The sale of illegal planting rights leads to revenues b for the forgers. Thus, owners of (legal) planting rights lose while other groups gain.

Alternatively, if producers buy land and plant a vineyard without buying planting rights, these producers capture $a + b$, while "honest" producers gain f through lower planting rights prices, but land prices also increase.

In addition, unless demand is perfectly elastic, extra production would depress the output price of wine. While this would again reduce the efficiency loss associated with the planting rights regime, it would create an additional negative effect on producers' income.

5. Discussion and Conclusions

In this chapter, we develop the first conceptual model of the planting rights system, which affects half of the world's vineyards. Our theoretical model integrates the markets for wine, land and planting rights. We identify the efficiency and distributional consequences of planting rights and we show how differences between MS in implementation of planting rights, in particular concerning trade and enforcement of planting rights and the functioning of the reserve system, affect efficiency and welfare.

Our analysis implies that consumers would benefit from a liberalization of the planting rights system because they would benefit from larger supplies of wine at lower prices, and owners of land would benefit from an increase in land prices. A third group of winners are new entrants into the sector, who would be able to plant vineyards without paying for planting rights. The losers are clearly the present owners of planting rights, who would see the value of their rights fall to zero. Whether wine producers benefit depends on how the price of wine changes after liberalization. If there is little or no price change, they gain through a decrease in the costs associated with planting rights. In contrast, if the price of wine falls sharply, wine producers may lose. For a wine producer who currently owns his vineyard (i.e., land and planting rights), the combined effect of liberalization would be negative.

While our theoretical analysis determines the sign of the effects, the magnitude depends how restrictive planting rights are in a given region, as well as on the elasticity of supply and demand. The negative price effect will be large if the area under vines is currently far below the "laissez-faire" equilibrium, if supply can be easily expanded, and if demand is very inelastic so that an increase in supply leads to a strong decline in prices. On the other hand, the price effect would be limited if the current area under vines is close to the post-liberalization equilibrium, if supply cannot be easily expanded (if at all), and if demand for its wines is elastic so that increases in supply have little effect on price.

While no exact information is available on how far the current area under vines is below the "laissez-faire" equilibrium, the price of planting rights in different regions gives some indication of how binding planting rights are. Regions with a higher price of planting rights can be expected to experience larger effects of liberalization, *ceteris paribus*.

The supply response is determined by physical characteristics of the region, by the presence of profitable alternative crops and by remaining other regulations. If most suitable land is already planted with vines, if vines compete against a profitable alternative crop, or if the supply response is limited by GIs which would not be affected by the liberalization (as, e.g., in the Champagne region), the supply response would be limited.

An indicator that is useful in this context is the share of vineyards in the total area under the GI. Data for French wine regions show that the share of the total available land under the GI which is currently planted with vineyards varies widely (Vautrin, 2010). For instancc, only 10% of available land is used in Cognac. In Beaujolais, Bordeaux and Burgundy, the share is around one-half of all available land, while in the Champagne region practically all available land is planted with vineyards. Of course, these aggregates hide considerable heterogeneity. The Bordeaux region contains some 50 sub-appellations; in some of these (e.g., Pomerol), the share of land under vines is as binding as in Champagne. All else equal, when expanding the area under vines is difficult, the expansion of output and the reduction in price would be more modest.

On the other hand, in some regions there may be plenty of suitable land available and it might be possible to easily expand the area under vines. This situation might characterize some northern regions where grape growing is only now becoming feasible due to climate change (Jones *et al.*, 2005); in those regions there may be few existing vineyards and few alternative crops, which makes it easy to expand the area under vines. All else equal, when expanding the area under vines can be done easily and at relatively low costs, the expansion in production and the reduction in price would be larger.

The third factor determining the magnitude of the effects is the elasticity of demand; if demand is highly elastic, expansion will not lead to a negative price effect. Given the heterogeneity of European wine regions and the inefficient allocation of planting rights, one should consider the elasticities for different wine regions separately. This "regional" elasticity depends among other things on whether the price of wine is determined by the local market or is driven more by international markets. In the former case, expansion may have a large negative effect on price; in the latter case, the wine price will be more or less set by the world price and expansion would only have a small effect.

Interestingly, these categories do not neatly coincide with the usual distinction between high-quality and low-quality wines. Regions producing table wine for the local market would face a strong negative price effect if production expanded, while regions producing cheap wines for export may have more opportunities to sell extra output without a strong reduction in price. Regions producing high-quality wines which are mostly sold on the domestic market would face a stronger negative price effect than similar regions which export a sizeable part of their production. For instance, some top wines in Bordeaux which are in high demand in the emerging economies might be able to expand production without any negative effect on the output price. To our knowledge detailed studies on the elasticity of wines from different European wine regions are not available, although the fraction of production exported abroad might be used as a good proxy: regions exporting most of production are probably more dependent on the world price and would therefore undergo smaller price effects from increased output.

Acknowledgments

The authors wish to thank Julian Alston, Paola Corsinovi, Davide Gaeta, and Giulia Meloni for insightful comments on an earlier version of this chapter. This research was financially supported by KU Leuven (Methusalem Funding).

References

Alston, J. (1981). A note on the effects of non-transferable quotas on supply. *Review of Marketing and Agricultural Economics*, 49, 186–196.

Alston, J. (1986). Consequences of deregulation in the Victorian egg industry. *Review of Marketing and Agricultural Economics*, 54(1), 33–43.

Alston, J., and James, J. (2002). *The Incidence of Agricultural Policy*, Handbook of Agricultural Economics, edited by G. Rausser and B. Gradner. vol. 2, ch. 33. Amsterdam: Elsevier Science, pp. 1689–1749.

Anderson, K., and Nelgen, S. (2011). *Global Wine Markets*, 1961–2009: *A Statistical Compendium*, Adelaide, Australia: University of Adelaide Press.

Bogonos, M., Engler, B., Dressler, M., Oberhofer, J., and Dabbert, S. (2012). How the liberalization of planting rights will affect the wine sector of Rheinland-Pfalz, Germany: A partial equilibrium analysis. Working Paper 115, American Association of Wine Economists (AAWE).

Bourgeon, J.M., Jayet, P.A., and Picard, P. (1995). An incentive approach to land set-aside programs. *European Economic Review*, 39(8), 1487–1509.

Burrell, A. (1989). *The Microeconomics of Quota Transfer*, Milk Quotas in the European Community, edited by A. Burrell. wallingford, Oxon, UK: CAB International.

Ciaian, P., Kancs, D., and Swinnen, J. (2008). Static and dynamic distributional effects of decoupled payments: Single farm payments in the European Union. LICOS Discussion Paper 207/2008.

Ciaian, P., and Swinnen, J. (2006). Land market imperfections and agricultural policy impacts in the New EU Member States: A partial equilibrium analysis. *American Journal of Agricultural Economics*, 88, 799–815.

Ciaian, P., and Swinnen, J. (2009). Credit market imperfections and the distribution of policy rents. *American Journal of Agricultural Economics*, 91, 1124–1139.

Copa-Cogeca (2012). The role of planting rights for the future of the European wine sector. http://www.copa-cogeca.be/img/user/file/win_2012/win_E.pdf (accessed July 11, 2014).

Courleux, F., Guyomard, H., Levert, F., and Piet, L. (2008). How the EU single farm payment should be modelled: Lump-sum transfers, area payments or... what else? SMART-LERECO Working Paper No. 08.01.

European Commission (2004). Ex-post evaluation of the Common Market Organization for wine — final report. DG Agriculture.

European Commission (2007). Towards a sustainable European wine sector. http://ec.europa.eu/agriculture/publi/fact/wine/072007_en.pdf. (accessed July 11, 2014).

European Commission (2012). The EU system of planting rights: Main rules and effectiveness. Working document. DG Agriculture.

European Parliament (2012). The liberalization of planting rights in the EU wine sector — study. DG Internal Policies. http://bookshop.europa.eu/en/the-liberalisation-of-plantingrights-in-the-eu-wine-sector-pbBA3112158/ (accessed July 11, 2014).

Gardner, B. (1987). *The Economics of Agricultural Policies*, New York: MacMillan Publishing.

Giannakas, K., and Fulton, M. (2000). Efficient redistribution using quotas and subsidies in the presence of misrepresentation and cheating. *American Journal of Agricultural Economics*, 82, 347–359.

Gisser, M. (1993). Price support, acreage controls, and efficient redistribution. *Journal of Political Economy*, 101(4), 584–611.

Gohin, A., and Bureau, J.C. (2006). Modelling the EU sugar supply to assess sectoral policy reforms. *European Review of Agricultural Economics*, 33(2), 223–247.
Jones, G., White, M., Cooper, O., and Storchmann, K. (2005). Climate change and global wine quality. *Climatic Change*, 73, 319–343.
Kilian, S., Antón, J., Salhofer, K., and Röder, N. (2012). Impacts of 2003 CAP reform on land rental prices and capitalization. *Land Use Policy*, 29, 789–797.
Lips, M., and Rieder, P. (2005). Abolition of raw milk quota in the European Union: A CGE analysis at the member country level. *Journal of Agricultural Economics*, 56(1), 1–16.
Meloni, G., and Swinnen, J. (2013). The political economy of European wine regulations. *Journal of Wine Economics*, 8(3), 244–284.
Mérel, P., and Sexton, R. (2012). Will geographical indications supply excessive quality? *European Review of Agricultural Economics*, 39(4), 567–587.
Montaigne, E., Coelho, A., Delord, B., and Khefifi, L. (2012). Etude sur les Impacts Socio-Economiques et Territoriaux de la Libéralisation des Droits de Plantations Viticoles. AREV & UMR — Moisa Montpellier.
Moschini, G., Menapace, L., and Pick, D. (2008). Geographical indications and the competitive provision of quality in agricultural markets. *American Journal of Agricultural Economics*, 90(3), 794–812.
Vautrin, C. (2010). Les Droits de Plantation: Un outil Eprouvé et Moderne de Gestion Harmonieuse du Potentiel Viticole Européen.

Appendix

When do producers without planting rights benefit?

Whether producers benefit from the introduction of planting rights when they do not receive the planting rights for free depends on whether the triangle h in Figure 2 is larger than $z + y + u$. As we demonstrate in this appendix, this can indeed be the case if demand is sufficiently inelastic.

Algebraically, we can look at small changes in the volume of planting rights R and how these affect the surplus of producers without planting rights. This surplus equals the total value of production $p_W^R W$ minus total payments for land and planting rights, which together equal the total amount of land R multiplied by the marginal productivity of land $p_W^{\#} W'(R)$. Hence, surplus of producers who do not receive planting rights for free is given by

$$\Pi^P = p_W^{\#}(W(R) - W'(R)R). \tag{A.1}$$

A small change in the amount of planting rights changes the wine price as well as production volume and marginal productivity (and hence payments for land and planting rights)

$$\frac{\partial \Pi^P}{\partial R} = \frac{\partial p_W^{\#}}{\partial R}(W(R) - W'(R)R) + p_W^{\#}(W'(R) - W'(R) - W''(R)R). \tag{A.2}$$

Rewriting and expressing the price effect as an elasticity, we get

$$\frac{\partial \Pi^P}{\partial R} = p_W^{\#}\frac{1}{\epsilon^D}\frac{\partial W}{\partial R} - p_W^{\#}\frac{1}{\epsilon^D}\left(\frac{\partial W}{\partial R}\frac{R}{W}\right)\frac{\partial W}{\partial R} - p_W^{\#}W''(R)R. \tag{A.3}$$

Expressing the change in output as an elasticity

$$\frac{\partial \Pi^P}{\partial R} = p_W^{\#}\frac{1}{\epsilon^D}(1 - \epsilon_R^W)W'(R) - p_W^{\#}W''(R)R. \tag{A.4}$$

Because of diminishing returns, $\epsilon_R^W < 1$ and the first term is negative since $\epsilon^D < 0$. Because the production function is concave, $W''(R) < 0$. The first and second term of this expression thus have opposite signs, and the sign of $(\partial \Pi^P / \partial R)$ depends on the relative magnitude of these two effects.

If demand is perfectly elastic, $\epsilon^D \to -\infty$ and the first term becomes zero. In that case, since $W'' < 0$, the effect of an increase in planting rights is to increase producer surplus — or put differently, a reduction in the area under vines (e.g., by the introduction of planting rights where none existed) will reduce the surplus of producers when they do not receive the planting rights for free.

If demand is sufficiently inelastic, however, the first term might dominate the second term, and a reduction in planting rights may increase producer surplus. This will be the case if demand is very inelastic and/or W'' is small in absolute terms — which would imply a relatively horizontal marginal productivity schedule. If the latter is the case, the reduction in planting rights will only lead to a modest increase in the price of planting rights, *ceteris paribus*.

Expressing this differently, producer surplus will increase when planting rights are reduced if

$$\frac{1}{\epsilon^D}W'(R)(1 - \epsilon_R^W) < W''(R)R, \tag{A.5}$$

which can be rewritten as

$$\frac{(1-\epsilon_R^W)W'(R)}{W''(R)R} < \epsilon^D < 0. \tag{A.6}$$

Assume, for instance, that wine production is given by $W = R^\alpha$ with $\alpha < 1$. In this case, $\epsilon_R^W = \alpha, W' = \alpha R^{\alpha-1}, W'' = \alpha(\alpha-1)R^{\alpha-2}$. The term on the left-hand side becomes

$$\frac{(1-\alpha)\alpha R^{\alpha-1}}{\alpha(\alpha-1)R^{\alpha-1}} = -1. \tag{A.7}$$

And a sufficient condition for producers to benefit would be that the demand for wine grapes is inelastic ($-1 < \epsilon^D < 0$).

Chapter 7

The Political Economy of European Wine Regulations*

Giulia Meloni[†] **and Johan Swinnen**

LICOS Centre for Institutions and Economic Performance, KU Leuven, Waaistraat 6, Leuven, Belgium
[†]*giulia.meloni@kuleuven.be*

The wine market in the European Union is heavily regulated. Despite the many distortions in the wine market as a consequence, reforming the regulations has proven difficult. This chapter analyzes the political economy mechanism that created existing wine regulations. We document the historical origins of the regulations and relate these to political pressures that resulted from international integration, technological innovations, and economic developments.

1. Introduction

> They [the Germanic tribes] on no account permit wine to be imported to them, because they consider that men degenerate in their powers of enduring fatigue, and are rendered effeminate by that commodity. (Julius Caesar, 1869; De Bello Gallico, Book IV, Chap. 2)

Almost half the world's vineyards are in the European Union (EU), and the EU produces and consumes around 60% of the world's wine.[1] The EU is not only the largest global wine-producing region and the main importer and exporter of wine but also a highly regulated market.

*This article originally appeared in *Journal of Wine Economics* (2013), 8(3), 244–284.

[1]Worldwide production increased from 213 million hectoliters (hl) in 1961 to 244 million hl in 2011. France, Italy, and Spain together produced 122 million hl of wine in 1961 and about the same in 2011. Wine production in New World wine countries (Argentina, Australia, Chile, China, New Zealand, South Africa, and the United States) increased from 30 million hl in 1961 to 81 million hl in 2011 (FAO, 2012; OIV, 2007, 2012b).

Government intervention has taken many forms in EU wine markets. Regulations determine where certain wines can be produced and where not, the minimum spacing between vines, the type of vines that can be planted in certain regions, yield restrictions, and so on. In addition, EU regulations determine subsidies to EU producers and wine distillation schemes.[2] The EU also subsidizes grubbing up (i.e., uprooting) of existing vineyards and imposes a limit on the planting of new vineyards. The extent of the regulatory interventions — and the associated market interventions — is possibly best illustrated by the observation that in the past three decades every year on average 20 million to 40 million hectoliters (hl) of wine have been destroyed (through distillation), representing 13% to 22% of EU wine production or, in other words, the equivalent of 3 billion to 6 billion bottles (Eurostat, 2013).

Wine regulation in the EU has several noteworthy features. One of the most striking conclusions of economic studies on the EU's wine markets is that the policies have not been effective at solving the problems and may have caused — rather than resolved — some major distortions in the wine sector.[3] This raises some questions related to the introduction of these policies.

The objective of our chapter is to explain why these regulations have been introduced. We analyze the historical origins of these regulations and relate them to various political pressures. Analyzing the historical roots and political motivations of regulations in the EU, how they were introduced, and how they have (not) continued to affect current regulations provides interesting insights on the current EU policy regime. Our chapter also offers some general insights on the political economy of government regulations.[4]

More than two thousand regulations, directives, and decisions on wine have been published in the EU since 1962, and the main wine framework law of 1962 was reformed five times (Council Regulation No. 479/2008;

---

[2]Wine distillation is the process by which wine is transformed either into raw alcohol and spirits, which are sold as potable alcohol, or into industrial alcohol for later use in chemical or carburation processes (European Commission, 2006a).

[3]See various studies on the wine sector by (or commissioned by) the European Commission in 2004, 2006, and 2007. For example, the 2004 Innova *et al.* report asserts: "Distillation of wine measures are neither effective nor efficient in eliminating structural surpluses. Distillation measures involve fairly high EU expenditure. The short-term income support through buying-in of wines for distillation stabilizes surplus production in the long-term .... Additionally, continuous implementation of distillation measures producing industrial alcohol out of wine might be an incentive for higher yields."

[4]There is an extensive literature on the political economy of government regulations and public policy. For a review see Rausser *et al.* (2011); and for applications to EU agricultural policy see Swinnen (2008, 2009).

Petit, 2000). As we argue, some of the regulations were introduced to protect existing economic rents when these were threatened by innovations or surging imports. Other regulations, however, appear to both enhance welfare (efficiency) and redistribute economic rents, which makes analysis of them more complex. Wine regulations offer particular insights because of their long history. The remainder of this chapter is organized as follows: Section 2 develops the conceptual framework for our analysis; Section 3 describes the EU wine policy, the Common Market Organization (CMO) for wine; Section 4 presents a historical perspective on the political economic origins of some of the key regulatory interventions in Europe; Section 5 explains how the process of European integration led to the creation of the EU wine policy; and Section 6 concludes and provides some perspective.

2. Conceptual Framework

> That the vineyard, when properly planted and brought to perfection, was the most valuable part of the farm, seems to have been an undoubted maxim in the ancient agriculture, as it is in the modern through all the wine countries. (Smith, 1776/1904, p. 216)

European policies have tried to regulate quantities, prices, and qualities of wine. As with many government interventions in other food and agricultural markets, the quantity and price regulations can be understood only from a political perspective — that is, by analyzing how political pressures related to regulation-induced rents have influenced government decision-making.[5] Their primary purpose is to redistribute rents between different groups in society, in particular from (potential) new producers of wine and from consumers of wine to the existing producers. These interventions typically reduce overall welfare and efficiency.

In contrast, regulations to guarantee a certain quality of wine, like many products and process standards in general, may increase efficiency and overall welfare. In an environment with asymmetric information between producers and consumers, where consumers have imperfect information and high ex-ante monitoring costs about the quality of a certain product, such as wine, government regulations that guarantee a certain quality or safety level, or that reduce information costs, can enhance overall welfare. Similarly, regulations that forbid the use of unhealthy ingredients may increase consumer

[5]There is an extensive literature on the political economy of agricultural and food policies (see de Gorter and Swinnen (2002), Swinnen (2010) and Anderson *et al.* (2013) for surveys) but there have been no applications to wine policies.

welfare by reducing/eliminating problems of asymmetric information. For example, some of the early regulations target the dilution of wine with water, which hurts consumer interests and producer reputations.[6]

However, quality regulations also affect income distribution. Depending on their implementation, they may create rents for certain groups of producers who face fewer costs in implementing certain quality standards for those who have access to key assets or skills that are required by the regulations.[7] For example, regulations that restrict the production of certain types of (expensive) wines to a certain region will benefit the owners of the fixed factors of production (such as land and vineyard) in that region and will harm the owners of land and vineyards in neighboring regions.

Some of the EU wine quality regulations have strong income distributional effects as they require access to very specific assets, such as plots of land in specific regions. In fact, the official EU regulations explicitly specify that "the concept of quality wines in the Community is based... on the specific characteristics attributable to the wine's geographical origin. Such wines are identified for consumers via protected designations of origin and geographical indications" (Council Regulation (EC) No. 479/2008, Preambles at (27)). Other examples of quality regulations with clear rent distributional effects are those in which regulations do (not) allow certain new techniques, such as the use of hybrid vines, the mixing of different wines (e.g., in rosé wine production), the use of new vine varieties.

In historical perspective, this approach to quality regulation in the EU is not the exception but the rule. In fact, throughout history, quality regulations for wine have been motivated both by efficiency considerations and in order to restrict the production of wines to certain regions (which created rents for land and vineyard-owners in those regions) or certain technologies (again creating rents).[8] Moreover, even when regulations were primarily

[6]More recent regulations specify that the use of certain ingredients must be indicated on the label. Since 2006, sulfites (added to preserve wine) must be disclosed on the labeling since these additives may cause allergic reactions (Article 51 of Council Regulation No. 607/2009).

[7]An emerging literature on the political economy of food standards focuses on the interaction between rent distribution and welfare enhancement (see, e.g., Anderson *et al.*, 2004; Fulton and Giannakas, 2004; Moschini *et al.*, 2008; Swinnen and Vandemoortele, 2008, 2009), but none of these insights have been applied to wine policies.

[8]Throughout history, owners of vineyards and wine producers have been among the rich and powerful. Not surprisingly the profits and power of existing wine producers and vineyard owners attracted others to invest in wine production and induced innovations. These

introduced for efficiency reasons they have invariably created rents and induced lobbying to keep these regulations in place after their efficiency effects had been mitigated (Meloni and Swinnen, 2013).

In summary, to understand the existing set of quantity and quality regulations, it is crucial to look at the interactions of political and economic aspects of the regulations.

3. EU Regulations and the Wine Lake[9]

Since the 1960s, the EU has introduced a vast number of regulations in the wine sector, the Common Market Organization (CMO) for wine.[10] Appendixes 1–3 provide a detailed list of these regulations. Here we summarize some key elements. We focus first on quality regulations and later on quantity and price regulations.

3.1. *Quality regulations in the EU*

> Poured from the bottle, the ruby-colored liquid looks like wine. Swirled around a glass, it smells like wine. Sure enough, it tastes like wine, too. But, at least within the confines of the European Union, the closest it may come to be being called wine is "fruit-based alcoholic beverage." (Castle, 2012)[11]

---

new investments and innovations threatened the rents and power of the established vineyard owners and caused protectionist reactions. There are many examples of such political economy processes which resulted in significant regulations in wine markets during Roman times, the Middle Ages, the Renaissance period and in the past few centuries. Whenever changes threatened to reduce their rents, established producers have sought to constrain or outright remove the threat of new developments through political means. They lobbied governments to constrain threats to their rents through regulatory initiatives. Because of their wealth and power they were often successful (see Meloni and Swinnen, 2013).

[9]For a detailed review of EU wine policies, see Council Regulations of 1962, 1970, 1979, 1987, 1999, and 2008; Europa (2008) and European Commission (2008a). In 2009, the wine regulation of 2008 merged into the Single CMO Regulation (EC) No. 1234/2007, that formally integrates in one document all the CMOs of agricultural products (Council Regulation [EC] No. 491/2009).

[10]"A common market organization is a set of measures that enables the European Union firstly to manage ... markets for agricultural products and secondly to support the incomes of farmers" (European Commission, 2008b). These common rules for agricultural markets include, for instance, public interventions and production standards.

[11]Wine produced in the EU from grapes that are not produced within the EU cannot be named "wine." This principle was already adopted in 1962 where "imported fresh grapes ... shall not be turned into wine" (see Articles 28 of the Council Regulation No. 816/70). In April 2012, English winery Chapel Down could not sell its "wine" made from grapes shipped from Argentina and had to name the beverage a "fruit-based alcoholic beverage" (Castle, 2012).

The EU has introduced regulations with the official intention of affecting the quality and location of wine production. Such "quality regulations" include policy instruments, such as the geographical delimitation of a certain wine area, winegrowing and production rules (as regulations on grape variety, minimum and maximum alcohol content and maximum vineyard yields, the amount of sugar or the additives that can be used — i.e., "oenological practices"), and rules on labeling.

Quality regulations were part of the initial wine policy in 1962[12] and have been strengthened since.[13] They apply to both "low quality" ("wines without a Geographical Indication" (GI), previously called "table wines") and "high-quality" wines ("wines with a Geographical Indication" (GI), previously called "quality wines").[14]

The EU heavily regulates "wines without a GI" and their quality requirements by defining the oenological practices (indicating the recommended/authorized varieties or the maximum enrichment/alcohol per volume allowed), by requiring particular methods of analysis[15] and by restructuring and converting vines.[16] For "wines with a GI," it only sets

[12] "[W]hereas the common organization must aim at stabilizing markets and prices by adjusting supplies to requirements, such adjustment being directed in particular toward quality production" (Council Regulation [EEC] No. 24/1962, Preambles at [3]).

[13] Regulations of 1970, 1979, 1987, 1999, and 2008 included provisions that strengthen the requirements in order to increase quality.

[14] In the pre-2008 system, EU wines were classified into two categories: "quality wines produced in specified regions" (abbreviated to "quality wines") and "table wines" (separated into table wines protected by geographic indications and those not protected by geographic indications). The 2008 regulation transformed the EU wine classification: wines are now divided into "wines with a GI" and "wines without a GI." Within the first category, there are two subcategories: Protected Designation of Origin (PDO) wines and Protected Geographical Indication (PGI) wines, with PDO as the highest quality level. With the 2008 regulation, certain table wines (as French VdP or Italian IGT) were elevated to the rank of wines with a GI (PGI). Even if the new classification harmonized the wine market with other EU food products that already adopted the PDO/PGI system, member states still have the possibility to use their national classifications on the labels. So far only Romania adopted the PDO/PGI system, casting doubts on the "simplicity" of the system (Cagliero and Sardone, 2009).

[15] Grape and must analysis regards three components, sugar, acid and pH. For instance, for wines without GI, the alcoholic strength ranges between 8.5% and 15% by volume and total acidity content of not less than 3.5 grams per liter. In addition, wine analysis involves alcoholic strength, total acidity, pH, density, residual sugar, and mineral elements, such as iron, copper, sodium, and potassium (Council Regulation No. 479/2008; Robinson, 2006).

[16] Support for restructuring and conversion of vineyards includes: varietal conversion, relocation of vineyards and improvements to vineyard management techniques. It involves, for instance, uprooting existing old vines and planting new vines but also, among others,

the minimum legal framework. It is up to each member state to determine its own system of classification and control.[17] For this reason, within the EU, "wines with a GI" can have different meanings among member states (Robinson, 2006, p. 678).

The EU system of geographical indications (GIs) is based on the French concept of *appellation d'origine*. Appellation of origin is "the name of the country, region or the place used in the designation of a product originating from this country, region, place or area as defined to this end, under this name and recognized by the competent authorities of the country concerned" (OIV, 2012a). A place name is thus used to identify the wine and its characteristics, which are thus defined by the delimited geographic area and specific production criteria (*cahier des charges* in France or *disciplinare di produzione* in Italy).[18] These governing rules delimit the geographic area of production, but also determine the type of grape varieties that can be used, the specific wine-making methods, the maximum yield per hectare, and the analytical traits of the respective wines (assessment of organoleptic characteristics — such as appearance, color, bouquet, and flavor — and a chemical analysis that determines the levels of acidity and alcohol). This implies that the wine's denomination can be attributed only if the grapes are grown and pressed in the delimited region and the wine production process fulfills certain criteria. For instance in the case of Chianti Classico wine, specific varieties of grapes have to be grown in one of only nine villages in Italy.[19]

As part of these quality regulations, the EU also specifies the type of labels that can and should be used. Until 2008, labels listed the geographic areas but not the wine's varietal composition. For instance, the indication of "Burgundy" was mentioned but not that of Pinot noir (the name of the

terracing, stone picking, soil disinfection and land leveling, with the aim of improving vineyard's quality (Council Regulation No. 479/2008, Article 11).

[17]For instance, wines with a GI in Italy are regulated by Governmental Legislation 164/92 and by Ministerial Decree 256/97, and three categories are defined: Controlled and Guaranteed Denomination of Origin (DOCG) and Controlled Denomination of Origin (DOC) and Typical Geographical Indication (IGT). The DOCG are subject to stricter requirements than DOC (Federdoc, 2012).

[18]See Appendix 4 for an example of such *cahier des charges* regulation applied to Bordeaux wines.

[19]The area includes the villages of Barberino Val d'Elsa, Castellina in Chianti, Castelnuovo Berardenga, Gaiole in Chianti, Greve in Chianti, Poggibonsi, Radda in Chianti, San Casciano Val di Pesa and Tavarnelle Val di Pesa. In order to produce a Chianti Classico DOCG, the varieties of grapes used in the preparation of the wine are fixed: 80% of Sangiovese, plus 20% of either native varieties like Canaiolo or "foreign" types like Merlot Cabernet and Sauvignon (Consorzio Vino Chianti Classico, 2012).

grape).[20] The 2008 wine reform introduced changes in labeling for wines without a GI. The label now allows mention of the grape variety and harvest year, thus facilitating identification of the product's characteristics.[21] This aligns European producers with wine producers in the New World (e.g., Australia and California) who document on their labels the brand and the grape variety rather than where the wine is produced (Maher, 2001).

3.2. *Quantity and price regulations in the EU*

> The market mechanism measures have often proved mediocre in terms of cost effectiveness to the extent that they have encouraged structural surpluses without requiring structural improvements. Moreover, some of the existing regulatory measures have unduly constrained the activities of competitive producers. (Council Regulation [EC] No. 479/2008, Preamble at [3]).

In addition to the quality regulations, the EU employs policies that influence the amount and price of wine produced in Europe. Since the implementation of the EU Common Wine Policy in 1970, the EU has imposed minimum prices for EU wine, tariffs on the import of wine, and organized public intervention in wine markets to deal with surpluses. Surpluses were either stored or distilled into other products with heavy government financing. In addition to distillation and market intervention, the EU wine policy included measures to restrict production such as restricted planting rights[22] and vineyard grubbing-up programs.[23]

Figure 1 and Table 1 summarize the effect of these regulations. The Organization for Economic Cooperation and Development's (OECD's) estimate of government support to wine producers, the Producer Single Commodity Transfer (PSCT) for wine, fluctuated around 7% in the late 1980s and early 1990s — meaning that government transfers to producers through these regulations were around 7% of the production value of wine. The main instrument of regulation was market interventions (minimum price and tariffs of 10% to 20% — see below). As indicated in Table 1, market price support accounted for 99% of the PSCT from 1985 to 1990. However, the PSCT numbers do

[20]Germany is an exception. The classification system is based on grapes' sugar levels and ripeness of the grapes rather than only on geography (Maher, 2001).
[21]Article 50 of Council Regulation (EC) No. 479/2008.
[22]Planting rights is a system to control European wine grape production, in which the planting of new vineyards require permission ("planting rights"). See Deconinck and Swinnen (2013) for an economic analysis.
[23]The EU provides grubbing-up premiums to winegrowers who permanently (and voluntarily) abandon vineyards.

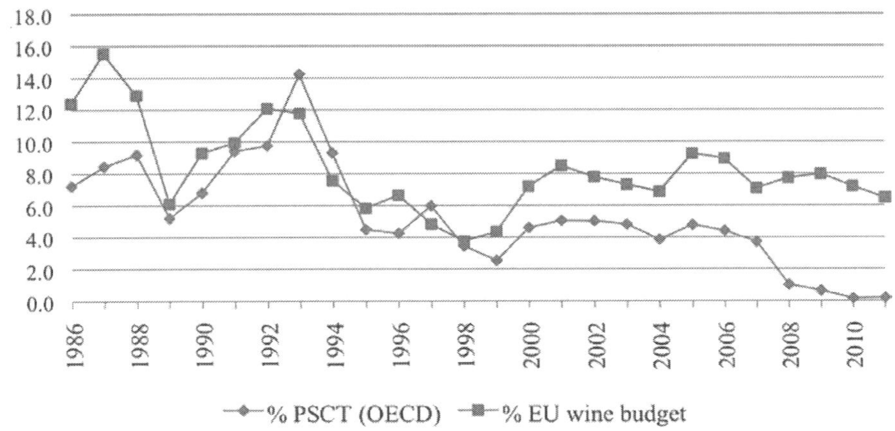

Figure 1. Policy Transfers (PSCT) and EU Budget Expenses on Wine as % of Production Value, 1986–2011

Sources: OECD Producer and Consumer Support Estimates database, 2012 (available at www.oecd.org/tad/agricultural-policies/E27dataPSE2012.xlsx); European Commission budget: Guarantee Section of the EAGGF, various years (see EAGGF financial reports available at http://aei.pitt.edu/view/euannualreports/euann13.html and, from 2007, see EAGF financial reports available at http://ec.europa.eu/agriculture/cap-funding/budget/index_en.htm); authors' calculations.

Table 1. Producer Single Commodity Transfers (PSCT) to Wine (annual average)

	1985–1990		1995–2000		2008–2011	
	Million Euros	% of total PSCT	Million Euros	% of total PSCT	Million Euros	% of total PSCT
Market price support	749.8	98.8	588.9	84.0	55.3	48.0
Payments based on output	0	0	0	0	0.2	0.2
Payments based on input use	0.3	0.1	54.3	7.9	0.9	0.9
Other payments for which production is required	8.5	1.1	54.9	8.1	22.6	50.9
Total transfers	758.6	100	643.1	100	79.0	100
Total transfers/Value of production (%PSCT)	7.4		4.2		0.5	

Source: OECD Producer and Consumer Support Estimates database, 2012 (available at www.oecd.org/tad/agricultural-policies/E27dataPSE2012.xlsx).

Table 2. EU Budget Expenditures on Wine Policy (annual average)

	1985–1990		1995–2000		2008–2011	
	Million Euros	% of total PSCT	Million Euros	% of total PSCT	Million Euros	% of total PSCT
Export refunds	41.1	3.8	37.9	4.8	4.3	0.3
Private storage	75.8	7.1	43.7	5.5	29.4	2.2
Distillation	782.5	73.2	403.3	50.9	270.6	20.4
Aid for the use of must	128.7	12.0	149.7	18.9	106.0	8.0
Grubbing-up premium*	36.7	3.4	156.4	19.8	287.3	21.6
Vineyard restructuring and conversion	—	—	—	—	387.2	29.1
Single Payment Scheme support	—	—	—	—	47.5	3.6
Promotion	—	—	—	—	58.5	4.4
Investments in enterprises	—	—	—	—	41.8	3.1
Other measures	3.9	0.4	0.6	0.1	96.5	7.3
Total budget	1,068.7	100.0	791.7	100.0	1,329.0	100.0
% of total budget in production value	11.2		5.4		7.5	

Note: *The grubbing-up premium was previously called "permanent abandonment premium."
Sources: Guarantee Section of the EAGGF, various years (see EAGGF financial reports available at http://aei.pitt.edu/view/euannualreports/euann13.html and, from 2007, see EAGF financial reports available at http://ec.europa.eu/agriculture/cap-funding/budget/index_en.htm); National support programs, various years (see the financial executions available at http://ec.europa.eu/agriculture/markets/wine/facts/index_en.htm); and authors' calculations.

not include most of the EU budget expenses on wine (see Figure 1 and Appendix 5).[24] These budget expenditures were on average around 1 billion euros per year over the same period — with a peak in 1988 of 1.5 billion euros. This is equivalent to 11% of the production value (see Table 2). In that period, the vast majority (around 70%) of budgetary expenditures comprised subsidies for the distillation of wine. As Table 3 shows, almost one quarter (22%) of total EU wine production was distilled in 1987 to 1993. Moreover, the share was highest for the largest producers: France (22%), Italy (23%), and Spain (28%).

[24]To some extent, this is to avoid "double counting" in the PSCT numbers; another reason is that some of the payments are not considered specific support to wine producers. For example, the OECD calculations consider distillation subsidies support to "consumers" of wine, not producers. Also measures such as grubbing-up premiums are not included in the wine PSCT.

Table 3. Average Annual Distillation by Member States (in million hectoliters)

	Wine production				Volume distilled				% of annual production			
	1987–93	1994–2000	2001–7	2008–11	1987–93	1994–2000	2001–7	2008–11	1987–93	1994–2000	2001–7	2008–11
Greece	4.2	3.7	3.7	3.4	0.4	0.3	0.3	0.0	10	8	8	1
Spain	33.3	28.2	37.9	35.8	10.0	4.0	9.3	5.3	28	13	25	15
France	61.1	54.9	52.8	44.7	14.2	10.7	4.8	1.5	23	19	9	3
Italy	64.7	56.9	49.8	45.3	14.8	5.5	6.1	3.0	22	9	12	7
Portugal	8.6	6.6	7.3	6.2	1.1	0.5	1.0	0.4	11	7	14	7
Total[a]	183.2	161.9	167.7	158.2	40.8	21.1	21.9	14.5	22	13	13	8

Note: [a]Including all EU member states.
Sources: European Commission, 2006a, 2009; Eurostat, 2013.

Despite these regulations, the wine market in the EU has been characterized for decades by what EU Commission documents typically refer to as "structural imbalances," that is, the production of vast surpluses of low-quality wine. Surplus problems were reinforced by two factors. First, overall wine consumption in the EU has decreased since the 1980s. While wine consumption has grown in some North European countries, it has declined strongly in the traditional wine countries. Both French and Italian national consumption decreased from about 60 million hl per year on average in the 1960s to 45 million hl in the 1980s and less than 30 million hl in the 2000s (Eurostat, 2013). Second, since the 1990s, competition and imports have grown from New World wines, that is, those from South America, Australia, and South Africa. Agreements resulting from the 1994 Uruguay Round of the GATT resulted in lower tariffs — which is reflected in the reduction of the PSCT levels from 14% in 1993 to 5% in 1995 (see Figure 1). Even if the EU is still the leading world wine exporter in terms of volume, the share of the five leading EU exporting countries (Italy, Spain, France, Germany, and Portugal) decreased from more than 70% in the late 1990s to 62% in 2012, while the share of South Africa, Australia, New Zealand, Chile, Argentina, and the United States increased from 15% to 28% in 2012 (see Figure 2).

Experts argue that the EU's wine policies, instead of contributing to a solution, have exacerbated the problem. Wyn Grant's (1997) review of

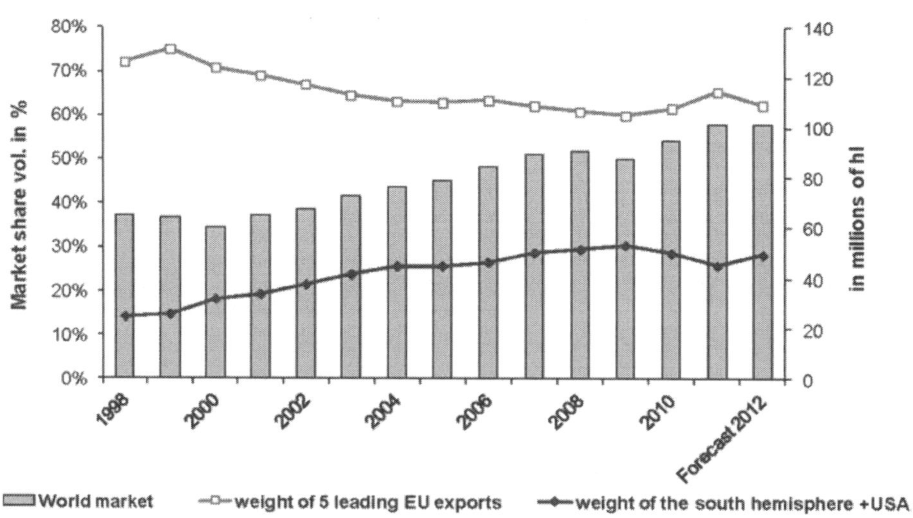

Figure 2. Total World Wine Exports, 1998–2012

Source: OIV, 2013.

the EU's wine policy distortions summarized the problems well under the heading "The Wine Lake":

> The EU tries to cope with the situation by siphoning wine out of the lake for distillation (for example, into vinegar) and by grubbing up vines from the vineyards on the hills around the lake. [However,] the problem is that EU-financed distillation is a positive stimulant of over-production of largely undrinkable wine, since it maintains less efficient growers of poor quality wine which would have given up long since if it were not for the EU support system.... The EU is losing ground in the expanding middle sector of the market [to New World wines].... The EU thus finds itself running a wine support policy that costs around 1.5 billion [euros] a year, involving the annual destruction of an average of 2–3 billion litres of substandard and undrinkable wine. (pp. 137–138)

The situation did not improve much over the next decade: in the mid-2000s, an average of around 24 million hl of wine was being distilled every year (see Table 3).

Over the years, the EU Commission has launched several attempts to reform its wine policy but has faced stiff resistance from wine producers and their governments. Attempts to reform the wine policy — and cut its budget — were supported by other member states, such as the U.K. In 1994, the EU Commission attempted to reform the wine market but failed (Maillard, 2002).[25] In 1999, a new wine CMO was finally adopted, as part of the Agenda 2000 reforms. The reform confirmed the ban on new vineyard plantings until 2010,[26] changed the distillation policy from compulsory to voluntary distillation (i.e., "crisis" distillation in cases of serious and exceptional structural surplus) and introduced restructuring and conversion measures for vineyards (Conforti and Sardone, 2003).

The Eastern enlargement of the EU — which integrated several wine-producing countries (e.g., those in Hungary, Slovakia, and Slovenia in 2004 and Bulgaria and Romania in 2007) into the EU — created another impetus for reforms. In 2006, the EU Commission proposed a set of bold reforms, which included the immediate elimination of traditional market intervention

[25]While all professional winegrowers' organizations are opposed to the reform, in Italy there was strong opposition from southern producers to the proposal to liberalize the concentrated grape must market. The EU Commission proposed allowing wine enrichment through sugar and not only through concentrated grape must. In southern Italy, winegrowers received subsidies for producing concentrated grape must (Maillard, 2002).

[26]The wine-producing countries had different preferences with respect to vineyard plantings. Italy was in favor of liberalizing planting rights (PR) while France wanted to maintain the PR system (Maillard, 2002).

measures (e.g., distillation, aid for private storage,[27] export refunds, and planting rights), the consolidation of previously adopted measures (e.g., restructuring and conversion of vineyards), the parallel introduction of new measures (e.g., subsidies for green harvesting,[28] investment, promotion in third countries, mutual funds, and harvest insurance), and simplified labeling rules with the intention of making EU wines more competitive with New World wines (European Commission, 2006c, 2006d, 2007a, 2007b, 2007c; Cagliero and Sardone, 2009). Surpluses would then be eliminated through ex-ante measures (green harvesting) and not through ex-post measures (aid for private storage or distillation).

Moreover, the available budget would be allocated through national support programs or envelopes (see Appendix 2), according to national priorities, thereby strengthening regional power. Producers could be compensated through decoupled farm payments (under the Single Farm Payment program, which has been implemented in reforms of other commodity market regimes since 2003).[29]

In addition to the pressure caused by the EU enlargement, the political coalitions changed in the 2006 reform debate. While in previous reforms discussions were dominated by winegrowers and their member states' governments, in the 2006 reform debate the EU wine industry and merchant organizations[30] and the Commission united and gained more power in their demand for less market intervention. Winegrowers of different member states were divided in their opposition because of different specific interests (e.g., distillation subsidies for Spain, in particular in Castilla–La Mancha; planting rights in France, in particular in AOC regions; and chaptalization (adding sugar to must) in Germany) (Smith, 2008).

The reform was approved in 2007, albeit after significant modifications. Because of strong opposition, some reform proposals were dropped (e.g., banning enrichment through the addition of sugar) or diluted (e.g., grubbing up was reduced from 400,000 to 175,000 hl)[31] or their implementation was

[27]In years of overproduction, aid for private storage for their wine surplus was given to winegrowers.

[28]Green harvesting is the destruction of the grapes before harvest (Council Regulation No. 479/2008, Article 12).

[29]Member states that have implemented this measure in their national support programs are: Greece, Luxembourg, Malta, Spain, and U.K (European Commission, 2013).

[30]Comité Européen des Entreprises Vins (CEEV) and Federación Española del Vino (FEV).

[31]Because of oversubscription, the Commission's initial proposal proved to be right. The total EU demand for grubbing up was equal to 351.223 ha of vines, a level extremely close

delayed (e.g., crisis and potable alcohol distillation[32] and use of concentrate grape must were phased out in 2012 and not in 2008 as proposed) (Gaeta and Corsinovi, 2009).

The result of the reforms was a further reduction of the PSCT to 1%. However, EU budget expenditures for the wine sector did not fall. The total budgetary expenditures on the wine policy are still more than 1 billion euros per year (around 8% of the production value; see Figure 1). However, the allocation of the wine budget to specific policies has changed significantly. As Table 2 documents, distillation subsidies are much lower (from a share of slightly more than 50% to slightly more than 20%) while grubbing-up premiums (slightly more than 20%) and subsidies to restructure and convert vineyards (about 30%) now comprise the most important budget allocations. Direct payments to wine producers — the Single Payment Scheme — account for about 4% of the budget.

The Commission also proposed that planting rights restrictions be removed by 2013, allowing producers to freely decide where to plant. However, the Council decided to allow a long transition period: the member states wishing to continue the restrictions could do so until 2018. Opposition to the liberalization has grown greatly since then. Opponents of the liberalization have organized to overturn the decision. The first countries to express their wish to do so were Germany and France in 2010. Since then, all EU member states that produce wine have joined in asking for a continuation of planting rights (Deconinck and Swinnen, 2013; EFOW, 2012).[33] This led to a decision

to the initial EU Commission proposal (400,000 ha). Only 50.4% of the areas claimed could be accepted (European Commission, 2012; European Court of Auditors, 2012).

[32]Until the 2008 CMO reform, the alcohol obtained through distillation was sold either as potable alcohol or as industrial alcohol. Four distillation schemes were used, and only the alcohol derived from the "potable alcohol" distillation was sold for the processing of potable alcohol (i.e., spirits and brandy or liqueurs wines). The other three distillation schemes ("by-product" distillation of grape marc and wine lees, "dual-purpose grape" distillation of mainly French Charentes wines and "crisis" distillation in case of "serious market disturbance") produced alcohol for industrial use (i.e., baker's yeast, fuel, or bioethanol) (European Commission, 2006a). Over the past 10 years, on average, the potable alcohol distillation accounted for half the total, while the other half was transformed for industrial use (see Appendix 6). The dual-purpose grape distillation was abolished in 2008, while potable alcohol and crisis distillation was phased out in 2012, leaving by-product distillation as the only remaining option for member states.

[33]In France, there has always been strong opposition to the liberalization of planting rights (Blancaneaux, 2013). The winegrowers' professional organizations (the European Federation of Wines of Origin [EFOW]) and the French Confederation of Wine and Spirits Producers [CNAOC]) were united in opposition. However, in Spain the wine sector was divided (Itçaina *et al.*, 2013). Wine merchants and large producers (Federación Española del Vino

in 2013 to extend the planting rights system until 2030 with a new program of authorizations starting in 2016.

The fact that it is difficult to impose reforms in the face of strong opposition by EU producers is an interesting yet hardly new insight. It is well known that regulations breed their own interest groups, which receive economic rents from the regulations and oppose their removal. Moreover, the particularities of the EU decision-making process tend to contribute to a preservation of the status quo (Pokrivcak *et al.*, 2006).[34]

What is particularly interesting in this case is the historical origins of the EU wine regulations, to see when they were introduced, and why, and how they have persisted or changed since their introduction. A large part of the current EU wine regulations have their roots in French and Italian national regulations prior to their integration in the European Economic Community (EEC) — the predecessor of the EU.

4. The Political Economy of French Wine Regulations in the Nineteenth and Twentieth Centuries[35]

4.1. *The creation of the Appellations d'Origine Contrôlées (AOC)*[36]

By the mid-nineteenth century, viticulture played a major role in France's economic development. It created income, wealth, and employment for many citizens.[37] However, the subsequent appearance of *Phylloxera* had dramatic consequences and destroyed many vineyards. *Phylloxera*, a parasite that lives on the vines' root systems and eventually kills the plant, originated in North America and was introduced to Europe in 1863. Unlike American native

[FEV]) were in favor of liberalization, while small producers, cooperatives, and regional governments (Confederación de Organizaciones de Agricultores y Ganaderos [COAG] and Rioja) were against it. They succeeded in reversing the Spanish government's position from supporting the Commission (in 2007) to opposing it (now).

[34]Swinnen (2008) documents how radical reforms in EU agricultural policy were possible only after several external changes (economic, political, and institutional) occurred simultaneously — a "perfect storm."

[35]Some key French regulations predate the nineteenth century. For example, during the fourteenth century, Philip the Bold laid the first stone for Burgundy's delimitation. The 1395 edict can be seen as a precursor of the modern Appellation d'Origine Contrôlée system. See Meloni and Swinnen (2013) for details.

[36]Many authors analyzed in detail state intervention in the French wine market and the creation of twentieth-century French regional appellations. See, e.g., Lachiver (1988), Loubère (1978, 1990), Simpson (2011), Ulin (1996), and Warner (1960).

[37]Wine employed 1.5 million family winegrowers, contributed about one-sixth of France's revenues, and was the second-largest export after textiles (Paul, 1996, p. 9).

vine species (e.g., *Vitis riparia or Vitis rupestris*), European vine species (*Vitis vinifera*) are not resistant to it.[38] One-third of the total vine area was destroyed,[39] and wine production fell from 85 million hl in 1875 to 23 million hl in 1889 — a 73% decrease (Augé-Laribé, 1950; Lachiver, 1988). While potential cures for *Phylloxera* were tested,[40] France became a wine-importing country. Since the French government wanted to prevent consumers from turning to other alcoholic beverages, table wines were imported from Spain, Italy, and Algeria (which was French territory from 1830 to 1962).[41]

As we document in detail in Meloni and Swinnen (2014), Algerian wine development played a key role in French regulations. The area planted in Algeria increased from 20,000 ha in 1880 to 150,000 ha in 1990, and exports to France grew to 3.5 million hl in 1897. French imports of wine from all sources, not just Algeria, rose from 0.1 million hl in 1870 to 12 million hl in 1888 (Augé-Laribé, 1950; Isnard, 1947).

However, by the beginning of the twentieth century, French vineyards had gradually been reconstructed and production recovered thanks to the planting of hybrid grape varieties and the use of grafting.[42] The first solution — hybrids — was the crossing-breeding of two or more varieties of different vine species. Hybrids were the result of genetic crosses either between American vine species ("American direct production hybrids")[43] or between European and American vine species ("French hybrids"). The second solution — grafting[44] — consisted of inserting European vines on to the roots of the *Phylloxera*-resistant American vine species (Gale, 2011; Paul, 1996).

---

[38]Gale (2003, 2011), Ordish (1987), and Paul (1996) extensively analyzed the causes and cures for *Phylloxera*.

[39]Before *Phylloxera*, about 2.3 million ha were planted with vines. By 1900, vineyard surface dropped to about 1.6 million ha, with replanted vines reaching 1.2 million ha (Lachiver, 1988).

[40]The remedies included flooding vineyards, chemical treatments (using carbon disulfide), or natural brews made, for instance, with tobacco or sea salt (Paul, 1996; Tyman, 1879).

[41]Greece also witnessed a large extension of vineyards, with dried grapes used by French wine producers instead of fresh grapes (Critz *et al.*, 1999).

[42]The initial search focused on chemical treatments. Carbon disulfide managed to halt the vines' destruction temporarily, but it was expensive. Scientists continued to search for cheaper and longer lasting solutions (Loubère, 1978, 1990).

[43]These "American hybrids," such as Clinton, Isabelle, and Noah, were developed in the United States at the beginning of the nineteenth century. They were directly planted in the French soil as a first solution to the vine diseases. However, by 1890–1900, due to their low resistance to *Phylloxera*, they were replaced by either grafting or Euro-American hybrids (Couderc, 2005).

[44]An earlier example of grafting is from sixteenth-century Spanish Mexico, where in 1524 Hernàn Cortés, the Spanish *conquistador*, ordered the grafting of European vines onto American rootstocks in Mexico (Hyams, 1965).

The solutions to *Phylloxera* led to two new problems. First, French domestic production recovered and cheap foreign wines now competed with French wines, thus leading to lower prices. Second, as a reaction to low prices two types of quality problems became common: imitations of brand-name wines to capture higher-value markets and adulteration to compete with cheap wine imports. Examples of imitations were false "Burgundy wines" or "Bordeaux wines," labeled and sold as Burgundy or Bordeaux but produced in other parts of France. Examples of wine adulteration include using wine by-products at the maximum capacity (e.g., by adding water and sugar to grape skins, the *piquettes*), producing wines from dried grapes instead of fresh grapes,[45] mixing Spanish or Algerian wines with French table wines in order to increase the alcoholic content, or adding plaster or coloring additives (e.g., sulfuric or muriatic acids) in order to correct flawed wines (Augé-Laribé, 1950; Stanziani, 2004).

The French government introduced a series of laws aimed at restricting wine supply and regulating quality. An 1889 law first defined wine as a beverage made from the fermented juice of grapes, thereby excluding wines made from dried grapes (Milhau, 1953). A 1905 law aimed at eliminating fraud in wine characteristics and their origins.[46] This and other laws also tried to regulate "quality" by introducing an explicit link between the "wine quality," its production region (the *terroir*), and the traditional way of producing wine. In this way, the regional boundaries of Bordeaux, Cognac, Armagnac, and Champagne wines were established between 1908 and 1912.[47] These regional boundaries were referred to as *appellations*.

A few years later, in 1919, a new law specified that if an *appellation* was used by unauthorized producers, legal proceedings could be initiated against its use. Later, the restrictions grew further: a 1927 law placed restrictions on grape varieties and methods of viticulture used for the *appellation* wine (Loubère, 1990). Not surprisingly, these regulations were heavily supported

[45] In 1887, sugar wines and dried grapes wines accounted for 11% of total wine production (INSEE, 1935, 1966).

[46] A 1907 law forbade *mouillage* (addition of water) and *sucrage* (addition of sugar) of wines (Legifrance, 2011).

[47] These laws were also the result of the winegrower's revolt in southern France and in the Champagne region. Their collective political activities consisted of pressuring politicians through street protests and even violence. For example, in the early twentieth century, during their "revolutionary phase," winegrowers imposed their opinions with so-called *actions directes*, which included mutinies, pillaging, burning down of city halls, with deaths and injuries as a consequence (Bagnol, 2007; Bonal, 1984; Jacquet, 2009; Martin, 1998; Wolikow, 2009).

by representatives of the *appellation* regions who held key positions in parliament.[48]

Finally, in 1935, a law created the Appellations d'Origine Contrôlées (AOC) — which formed the basis for the later EU quality regimes. This law combined several of the earlier regulations: it restricted production not only to specific regions (through areas' delimitation) but also to specific production criteria such as grape variety, minimum alcohol content, and maximum vineyard yields (adding "controlled" to the "appellation of origin" concept). Moreover, the Comité National des Appellations d'Origine (National Committee for Appellations of Origin), a government branch established to administer the AOC process for "high quality" wines, was established (Simpson, 2011; Stanziani, 2004).[49]

Somewhat paradoxically, instead of reducing the number of *appellations*, the 1935 system encouraged the creation of more AOC regions in France. In 1931, the Statut Viticole (see below) tightly regulated French table wines while the AOC wines were exempted from it. This induced many table wines producers to ask for an upgrading to the higher wine category. The share of *appellation* wines production increased from 8% in the 1920s to 16% in the 1930s and to 50% in the 2000s (Capus, 1947; Figure 3).

4.2. *The battle over hybrid vines*

Underlying these increasingly tight "quality" regulations in France was a major battle over the regulation of hybrids, one of the two practices used to cure vines from *Phylloxera*. This battle continued through most of the twentieth century.[50] A strong division of interests existed between the Appellation d'Origine producers in Bordeaux, Champagne, or Burgundy and producers from other regions. Grafting was the preferred solution for the *appellation* regions since it permitted the grapes to retain European *Vitis vinifera* characteristics. At the same time, wine producers from other regions relied on

[48]In 1919, Joseph Capus was elected deputy of the Gironde (the Bordeaux wine area) and he was also the president of the parliamentary committee called *des grands crus* (great growths).

[49]In 1947, the institution was renamed Institut National des Appellations d'Origine, INAO (National Institute for Appellations of Origin), and, in 2007, Institut National de l'Origine et de la Qualité (National Institute for Origin and Quality), keeping the acronym INAO.

[50]Interestingly, the research community also held divergent views. Two schools of agriculture were in opposition: the University of Montpellier in southern France (pro grafting) and the University of Bordeaux (pro hybrids). By the end of the nineteenth century, the government (Ministry of Agriculture and local politicians) allied with the school of Montpellier and promoted grafting (Paul, 1996, p. 100).

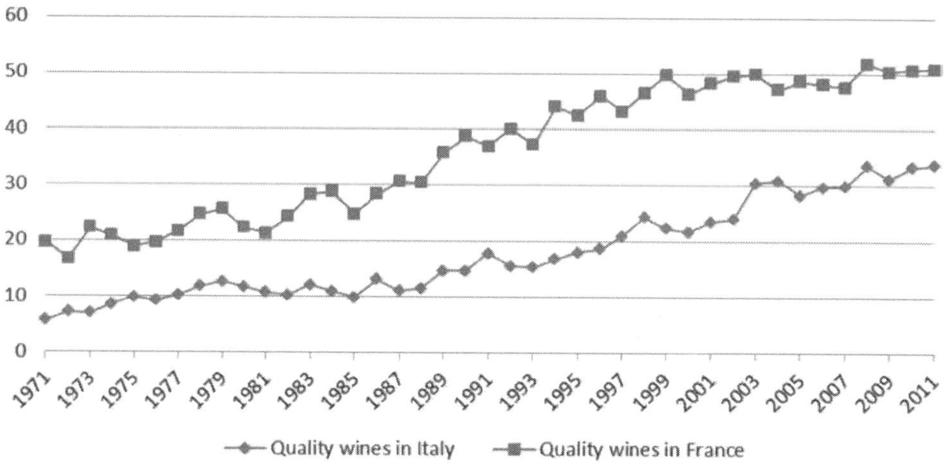

Figure 3. "Quality" Wines Produced in France and Italy as a Share of their National Wine production, 1971–2011

Note: "Quality" wines are defined as "Quality wines produced in specified regions" from 1971 to 2009 and as "Protected Designation of Origin (PDO) wines" from 2010 onward.
Source: Eurostat, 2013 (accessed February 26, 2013).

hybrids since the new vines were more productive, easier to grow, and more resistant to disease in general. They required less winegrowing experience, pesticides, and capital (Paul, 1996).

However, these diverging interests were not equally represented. The *appellation* producers and winegrowers were grouped in associations that were very influential over the government.[51] Wine producers from other regions were not as well organized. For instance, in the Champagne AOC region, three powerful and unified lobbying groups existed: the Fédération des Syndicats de la Champagne that represented winegrowers; the Syndicat du Commerce des Vins de Champagne, which promoted exports of the Maisons de Champagne;[52] and the Association Viticole Champenoise, which lobbied for the interests of both winegrowers, and Maisons de Champagne (Comité Interprofessionnel du Vin de Champagne, 2003; Wolikow, 2009).

[51]The creation of these associations was promoted by a 1884 French law that legalized labor unions (Simpson, 2011).

[52]Champagne houses (the *grandes marques* such as Veuve Clicquot or Moët & Chandon) were producers (*négotiants*) that acquired grapes and established long-term contracts with winegrowers throughout the Champagne region, thereby undertaking the high costs and risks of elaborating *cuvées*. Even now, two-thirds of the sales and 90% of the exports are done by around 100 Champagne houses, which own 4,000 ha, or 12.5% of the land (Union des Maisons de Champagnes, 2012).

The greater political power of the *appellation* wine regions derived from commerce — with brand names, strong reputations, and large economic benefits[53] — and was protected by political organizations.

Under pressure from these politically powerful constituencies, the French government decided to restrict the use of the low-cost technology (hybrid vines). The first "quality law" that limited the use of hybrids was introduced in 1919 and modified in 1927, restricting *appellation* wines to nonhybrid grapes.[54] In addition, three other laws against hybrids were approved in less than ten years. First, the 1929 law forbade chaptalization for hybrids, a technique allowed for European vine varieties (*Vitis vinifera*) to increase wine alcohol content. Second, a 1934 law stated that uprooted *Vitis vinifera* could be replanted only with vines registered (authorized) by local authorities. Third, a 1935 law prohibited six vine varieties derived from hybrids (Clinton, Herbemont, Isabelle, Jacquez, Noah, and Othello). The invoked argument to support the 1935 prohibition was safety, since wines produced with American varieties were said to contain a significant level of methyl alcohol harmful for human consumption.[55]

Yet, despite these regulations, the planting of hybrids spread as many wine producers disobeyed the laws. Since hybrids could survive in a humider and cooler climate, regions that never had a strong wine tradition took advantage of it (Milhau, 1953). By the end of the 1950s, hybrids made up one-third of France's total vine area (see Figure 4) and comprised 42% of table wine production (Paul, 1996).

[53]In 1910, in the Champagne region, in Hérault and Aude, wine was sold at 25–30 francs per hl with production costs of about 12–15 francs per hl (Augé-Laribé, 1950).

[54]The 1927 law regulated the varieties of grape allowed for specific appellation of origin (e.g., Champagne wine producers could only use Pinot Noir, Pinot Meunier, or Chardonnay) and required that wines coming from hybrids could under no circumstance receive an appellation: "Les vins provenant des hybrides producteurs directs n'ont en aucun cas droit à une appellation d'origine" (Capus, 1947).

[55]Methyl alcohol was supposed to drive people mad; this view is obsolete. Moreover, the fact that the first experimental French hybrids produced undrinkable wines certainly influenced the thinking of winegrowers and consumers, thereby giving rise to suspicious reactions to the new technology. Indeed, it took almost 30 years before German researchers, at the Geilweilerhof Institute for Grape Breeding, began to breed the new cultivar *Regent*. This non-*vinifera* variety is part of a new generation of hybrids (called "disease-resistant varieties") that can compete with "high-quality" wines, with the advantage of being more resistant to disease and less polluting because chemical fertilizers are not used. Furthermore, researchers have not found essential differences in characteristics between *vinifera* and non-*vinifera* varieties (European Commission, 2003; Federal Centre for Breeding Research on Cultivated Plants, 2009).

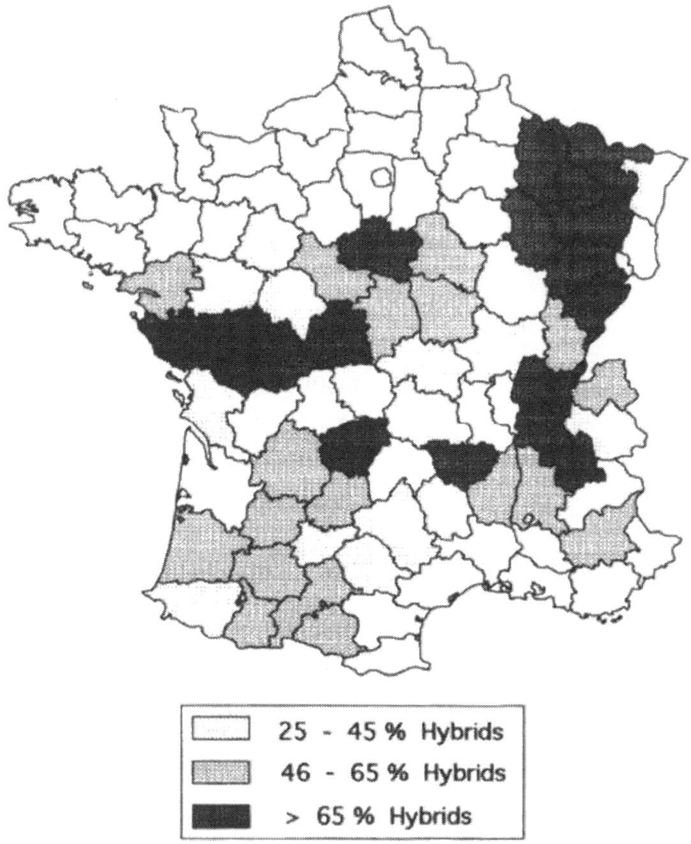

Figure 4. Percentage of Hybrid Vine Varietals in France, 1958
Source: Crowley, 1993.

4.3. *The Statut Viticole*

Other factors also played a role in inducing more regulations. While import restrictions had reduced imports from Spain, Italy, and Greece,[56] vineyards continued to expand in Algeria, exerting pressure on the French market. Algerian wine production doubled from 7 million hl in 1920 to 14 million hl in 1930 (Milhau, 1953). French demand was not able to absorb the extra wine, and the market faced a persistent wine surplus. This resulted in new regulations in the 1930s (Meloni and Swinnen, 2014).

[56]In the late 1880s, France imposed high tariffs on Italy and, in 1892, on Spain and Greece (Critz *et al.*, 1999; Pinilla and Ayuda, 2002; Pinilla and Serrano, 2008).

Between 1931 and 1935, regulations called the Statut Viticole[57] were introduced to reduce the supply of wine (Munholland, 2006; Sagnes, 2009). The Statut Viticole included an obligation to store part of the excess production (*blocage*),[58] obligatory distillation,[59] the establishment of a levy on large crops and yields,[60] a ban on planting new vines, and grubbing up overproductive vines[61] (Gavignaud, 1988; Loubère, 1990). The grubbing-up measure proved inefficient despite its substantial premium (as much as 7,000 francs[62] per hectare (ha)) because mostly old and unproductive vines were uprooted with little effect on total production (Milhau, 1953).

During War World II, French production stagnated due to massive vineyard destruction, and in 1942, in the German-occupied part of France, the Statut Viticole was repealed.

After the war, wine demand grew rapidly and supply fell still lower. This resulted in high prices, which encouraged major vineyard replantings. In the following years, wine production increased strongly, also because young vines were more productive than older ones. The increase in wine production reduced prices again and soon resulted in new pressure for political intervention. In 1953, the Statut Viticole was reintroduced throughout the country under the name Code du Vin. The law reestablished subsidies to uproot vines,[63] as well as surplus storage, compulsory distillation, and penalties for high yields. It also created the viticultural land register (Malassis, 1959; Milhau, 1953; Munsie, 2002). Again, it turned out that the grubbing-up measure was not very effective since it apparently worked only in the French

---

[57]As the *Appellation* producers were represented by Joseph Capus in the French parliament, so the growers of "table wines" had Édouard Barthe, a pharmacist who became a powerful deputy of Hérault in the Languedoc region (from 1910 to 1942). He played an important role in the adoption of the Statut Viticole.

[58]Producers could allocate their product in the market through successive quotas.

[59]Between 1934 and 1935, 24 million hl were distilled (Lachiver, 1988).

[60]The policy was biased toward supporting smaller French winegrowers and hurting larger Algerian winegrowers. For instance, due to the hot climate, the obligation to store part of the excess production was more damaging for Algerian wine producers; the tax on large productions also hurt Algerian producers more than French (Birebent, 2007; Lachiver, 1988; Simpson, 2011).

[61]The unpopularity of the last measure forced the French government in 1934 to introduce a grubbing-up premium (Gavignaud, 1988).

[62]€5340,80 in 2012 (see http://www.insee.fr/fr/themes/calcul-pouvoir-achat.asp).

[63]The French decree 53/977 of 1953 established — on average — a premium of 2,700 francs per ha (Bartoli, 1986). Between 1953 and 1957, 5% (54,000 ha) of the total vine area benefited from this measure.

départements that had already witnessed a decrease in vineyard area planted (Bartoli, 1986).[64]

Finally, the pressure of the AOC producers was ultimately successful in removing the hybrid grapes from France through government regulations. However, this took another few decades and, most importantly, regulatory measures of the EEC (later EU). Through a combination of subsidized grubbing up and specific planting rights, the amount of "hybrid" vines in the country was dramatically reduced. AOC pressure groups continued to lobby the French government, and later the EU Council, to achieve the removal of hybrid grapes. Between the 1960s and the 1980s, the uprooting of "undesirable vines" was subsidized. Authorized hybrids were allowed, but planting rights were reduced by 30%[65] (Council Regulations Nos. 1160/76 and 458/80; Crowley, 1993). Ultimately, these policies were successful in largely removing hybrid wines. By subsiding the replanting of allowed varieties, 100,000 ha of hybrids were removed in the 1960s and 225,000 ha in the 1970s. Thus by the end of the 1980s, less than 3% of French vines were hybrids (Crowley, 1993).

5. European Integration and the Creation of the EU Wine Policy[66]

> The Common Wine Policy today is, to a large extent, the legacy of France's deep rooted interventionism in wine. (Spahni, 1988, p. 9)

Among the initial six members of the EEC, four countries produced wine (France, Italy, Luxembourg, and West Germany). Wine was an important commodity, particularly for France and Italy, which were both major wine exporters. Of the total EEC wine supply, Italy produced 49% and France 47% — together they produced 96%; West Germany produced the remaining 4% (Newsletter on the Common Agricultural Policy, 1969).

The pre-EEC wine policies of France and Italy differed. While France's wine market was highly regulated through government intervention, including prohibitions on new vineyards, wine classification systems, price supports, compulsory distillation, chaptalization, and so on (Kortteinen, 1984;

[64]The grubbing-up measure was temporarily suspended in 1957, following grape losses due to frost (Bartoli, 1986).

[65]For instance, Council Regulation No. 1163/76 (Article 2) granted a conversion premium in the wine sector, including for the conversion of areas planted with varieties "obtained from direct-producer hybrids."

[66]See Table 4 for a chronology of the introduction of key French and EU wine policy measures.

Table 4. Introduction of Wine Regulations in France and in the EU

	Introduced in France	Introduced in the EU
Quality policy (GIs)	1935 (AOC)	1970
Oenological practices	1889	1970
Rules on labeling	1905	1970
Private storage	1931	1970
Distillation	1931	1970 (1999)[a]
Planting rights	1931	1976 (1984)[a]
Grubbing-up premium	1935	1976

Note: [a]The measures were extended to all wines, including "quality wines."

Niederbacher, 1983), Italy had more liberal policies: there were no price interventions or plantation restrictions, but the Italian government did provide tax advantages for distilling wine surpluses and imposed restrictions on imports from non-EEC countries (Newsletter on the Common Agricultural Policy, 1969; Smith *et al.*, 2007, p. 80; Spahni, 1988).[67]

The different wine policies were also reflected in the different tariffs on imported foreign wines imposed by France and Italy. The process of European integration required the abolition of tariffs in intra-EEC trade and the adoption of a Common External Tariff (CET) by 1968. For most products, the CET was calculated as the average of pre-existing tariff rates of the six initial EEC member states. However, for wine, the CET was identical in all but one category to the French tariffs, which were 20–30% higher than the Italian ones (see Table 5).

Economic integration required the further integration of both policy regimes into one EU wine policy (the CMO for wine). An initial EEC regulatory step toward such a common market was taken in 1962.[68] It required that each member state established a viticultural land register;[69] the notification of annual production levels to a central authority (harvest and stock declarations); the annual compilation of future estimates of resources and requirements;[70] and stricter rules on "quality wines" (defined as wines with a GI).

[67]Germany claimed control of new planting and a liberal approach to imports from non-EEC countries (Newsletter on the Common Agricultural Policy, 1970).
[68]Source: Council Regulation No. 24/62.
[69]The viticultural land register contained minimum information, as the total area under vines (Council Regulation No. 24/1962, Article 1).
[70]A forward estimate was calculated at the end of each year to count the Community's resources and forecast its needs, including anticipated imports from and exports to third countries (Council Regulation No. 24/62, Article 3).

Table 5. EEC Wine Tariffs in 1966 (in dollars per hectoliter)

	Common external tariff	France	Italy	West Germany	Benelux
Wines in containers >2 liters					
up to 13%	9	9	6.4	9	5.4
from 13 to 15%	11	11	7.6	11	6.6
from 15 to 18%	14	14	9.4	10.8	8.4
from 18 to 22%	19	19	14.7	15.2	11.4
Wines in containers <2 liters					
up to 13%	12	12	10.5	22.6	13.9
from 13 to 15%	14	14	11.7	23.8	15.1
from 15 to 18%	17	17	13.5	20.8	10.8
from 18 to 22%	19	29.8	14.7	22	14

Source: GATT, 1966.

Initially, the CMO refrained from stronger regulations.[71] However, there was strong pressure from France for a more interventionist approach. In the 1960s, French wine producers had to deal with their internal surpluses and large inflows of Algerian wine on the French market due to a French-Algerian treaty. After Algerian independence was declared in 1962, France committed to purchasing considerable quantities of Algerian wine: 39 million hl in five years (1964–1968) (Isnard, 1966).[72] Since the French wine market was already saturated and had to absorb large inflows of Algerian wine, France was afraid that cheaper Italian wine would swamp the French market and cause a collapse in prices.

The final version of the EEC's Common Wine Policy, agreed upon in 1970,[73] was a compromise between the positions of Italy and France (Arnaud, 1991; Council Regulations 816/70 and 817/70; Spahni, 1988). Minimum price

[71]The EU's policies focused strongly on "table wines" as these represented the vast majority of the wines, and most problems were in that segment of the market. During the 1960s, table wines accounted for 95% of total EU-6 production, while in 2011 they accounted for approximately 54% if we consider "table wines" only as non-PDO wines or 27% of the total EU-6 production if we consider all wines without a GI (non-PDO and non-PGI wines) (Eurostat, 2013; Smith *et al.*, 2007, p. 81).
[72]The agreed import was considerably lower than before independence (e.g., in 1961 Algeria exported 15 million hl to France). However, under pressure from French winegrowers, the French government did not fulfill the agreement in the last two years of the agreement and imported only 6.2 million hl instead of the agreed 14 million hl (Isnard, 1966).
[73]Also in other agricultural commodities, such as grains, dairy, and oilseeds, there was a transition period of approximately ten years after the signing of the Treaty of Rome (in 1957) before a common market organization was fully implemented.

supports were imposed in the wine market in the form of aid for private storage and distillation of table wines.[74] Moreover, new regulations established guidelines for enrichment[75] and alcohol strength, introduced a quality classification of vine varieties,[76] and common rules on labeling and "oenological practices" (European Commission, 2006b; Petit, 2000).

However, due to pressure from the Italians, the EEC wine policy did not restrict planting rights and did not impose grubbing up — although anyone wishing to plant/replant vines had to notify the relevant authority (Council Regulation No. 816/70).[77] This requirement closely followed the pre-EEC policies of France, Luxembourg, and West Germany, where growers had to acquire official permission in order to plant vines (Newsletter on the Common Agricultural Policy, 1970).

Hence, the final version of the EEC Common Wine Policy, agreed upon in 1970, was considerably more interventionist than the Italian wine regime, but still less regulated than the old French wine policies. However, it was only a matter of time before the EEC Wine Policy was adjusted and the French interventionist approach dominated.

As could be foreseen, the 1970 Wine Policy, with its minimum prices and intervention buying of wine, did not solve the problems. In several ways, it exacerbated the problems of oversupply of French wine. Cheaper Italian wine production grew rapidly and increasingly substituted French wine.[78] In addition, because of the price floor, total wine production increased in the EEC and surpassed EEC consumption, causing growing surpluses (see

---

[74]Private storage aid was granted if the average price remained lower than the government-set "threshold price" for two consecutive weeks. Distillation of table wines was enacted if the aid for private storage proved insufficient for stabilizing market. In addition, the new wine policy provided government subsidies to distillers to compensate them for minimum prices paid to wine producers (which were above market prices), and subsidies for the private storage of this alcohol. Trade with third countries was also regulated through government-set minimum import prices and tariffs.

[75]Robinson (2006) defines enrichment as a "wine-making operation whereby the fermentable sugars of grape juice or must are supplemented in order to increase the alcoholic strength of the resultant wine." "Chaptalization" refers to the addition of sugar, whereas enrichment also includes other additives.

[76]Vines were classified as "recommended," "authorized," and "provisionally authorized" varieties — with "recommended" as the highest quality level.

[77]In addition, national assistance for new planting and replanting (which increase wine production) were prohibited and only "recommended" or "authorized" vine varieties could be used for planting or replanting (Council Regulation No. 816/70, Article 15).

[78]French wine prices were on average 25% higher than the Italian ones. In the 1969/70 wine year, Italy exported 4 million hl of table wine to France, which represented 90% of French's wine imports by volume (Arnaud, 1991).

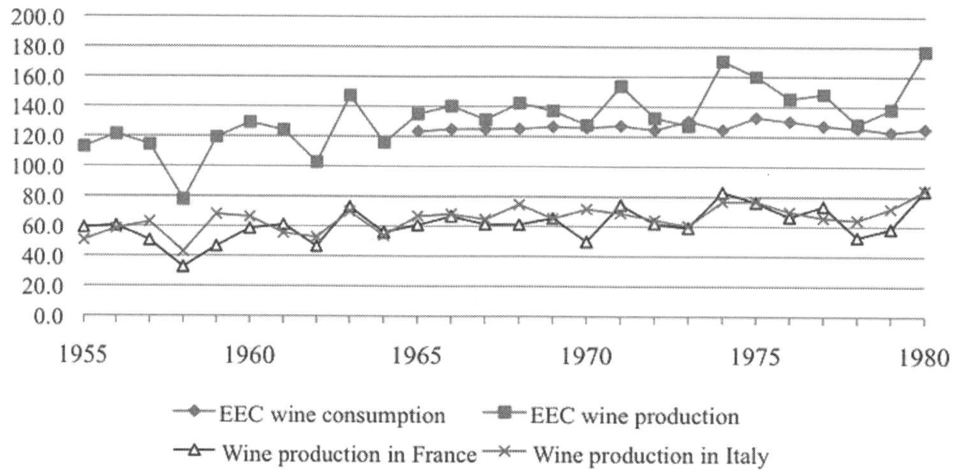

Figure 5. EEC Wine Production and Consumption and Wine Production in France and Italy 1955–1980 (in million hectoliters)

Source: Eurostat, 2013.

Figure 5). Under pressure from French wine producers,[79] the EEC distilled 6.9 million hl of wine between 1971 and 1972 (Niederbacher, 1983). Increasing grape harvests in 1973 and 1974[80] and a devaluation of the Italian lira further lowered prices of exported Italian wines. A full-blown "wine war" exploded in 1974, when French growers physically blocked Italian wine imports at the Sète harbor entrance. In order to settle the crisis, the French government imposed a tax on imported Italian wine and the EEC again intervened in the wine markets by distilling 19.6 million hl of wine in four years (from 1973 to 1976).

Under pressure from French producers and faced with the increasing budgetary costs of its recently imposed wine policy, the EEC Council of Ministers in 1976 decided to reform the Common Wine Policy (Council Regulation Nos. 1162/76 and 1163/76). However, instead of loosening regulation, the Council decided to introduce even more regulations to control the supply of wine. New regulations introduced restrictions on planting rights[81] and

[79]Especially "table wine" growers of the Midi region in southern France.
[80]171 and 161 million hl were produced in the harvests of 1973 and 1974, respectively, compared to a normal 135–140 million hl (Niederbacher, 1983).
[81]At the beginning the limitation on planting was only intended for a limited period (until November 30, 1978) and for a certain type of wines (table wines). However, this regime was repeatedly extended and grew to include wines with a Geographical Indication (GI).

subsidies for grubbing up existing vineyards.[82] In addition, three years later, new regulations now made distillation of table wine surpluses obligatory and provided subsidies for concentrated grape must used for enrichment (Council Regulation No. 337/79; Smith *et al.*, 2007; Spahni, 1988).

In short, by 1979, just a few years after the introduction of a common wine market in the EEC, French wine policy with its extensive regulations and heavy government intervention in markets had become the official wine policy for all EEC members.

The EEC's initial system of quality regulations explicitly referred to (and integrated) the French AOC system, which has existed in France since 1935.[83] In 1963, Italy followed the French model and introduced the Denominazione di Origine Controllata (DOC) and the Denominazione di Origine Controllata e Garantita (DOCG). With the accession of other wine-producing countries into the EU — Greece in 1981, Spain and Portugal in 1986, Austria in 1995, Hungary, Slovakia, and Slovenia in 2004, and Bulgaria and Romania in 2007 — these regulations expanded to cover a vast wine-producing region. All these countries had to adjust their national policies to join the EU. For example, Portugal introduced its Denominação de Origem Controlada (DOC) in 1986 and Spain its Denominación de Origen (DO) in 1996. The spread of Protected Designation of Origin (PDO) wines has led to some odd results (for a definition of PDO wines, see note 14). For example, Belgium, a country with very little wine production or tradition,[84] has seven PDOs, and PDO wine production as a share of total wine production is almost twice as high as in Italy (see Table 6).

Not only did the French regulations heavily influence European wine classification, but they have also influenced the definition of "quality wines." As initially in France, hybrids are now outlawed from the PDO category

[82]EC Regulation 1163/76 introduced a system of subsidies for producers either to abandon vineyards for six years or to grub up vineyards and replace them with other crops.

[83]The French AO system had already influenced other countries policies through earlier international agreements. For instance, the first AO was approved in Spain (Rioja) in 1926 to protect the wines with this origin against imitations or fraud (Pan-Montojo, 1994, p. 288). Moreover, Italy and Spain integrated the notion of AO (applied as a system at national level) respectively in 1930 and 1932. However, the Italian and Spanish regulations were less interventionist than the French, guaranteeing only the origin of the product and not the production practices, as in the French system (Estatuto del Vino, 1932; Federdoc, 2012).

[84]In 2011, wine production in Belgium was only 5,000 hl. In the same year, France and Italy produced 44 and 46 million hl respectively (Eurostat, 2013).

Table 6. Protected Designation of Origin (PDO) and Protected Geographical Indication (PGI) Wines in the European Union, 2011

	Number of PDO	Number of PGI	PDO wine production as a share of total wine production (in %)	PGI wine production as a share of total wine production (in %)
Austria	26	3	84	4
Belgium	7	2	67	—
Bulgaria	52	2	3	31
Cyprus	7	4	1	45
Czech Republic	12	2	53	46
Denmark	0	4	—	—
France	396	158	51	27
Germany	13	26	98	1
Greece	33	123	11	17
Hungary	58	16	62	18
Italy	496	135	34	30
Luxembourg	2	0	95	—
Malta	3	1	38	28
Netherlands	0	12	—	—
Portugal	36	16	47	24
Romania	39	13	10	18
Slovakia	17	3	71	4
Slovenia	14	3	63	28
Spain	97	45	40	10
United Kingdom	2	2	40	60

Sources: Eurostat, 2013 (accessed February 26, 2013); E-Bacchus, 2012 (accessed February 27, 2013).

(the highest quality level) throughout the EU.[85] This has had important implications for some countries. For example, upon its accession to the EU, Romania had to agree to uproot its hybrid varieties, which accounted for half its total area under vines[86] and to replace them with varieties authorized by the EU.[87] Moreover, for both Romania and Bulgaria, around 2,000 ha of

[85]The EU wine regulation states that "'designation of origin' means the name of a region, a specific place . . . that it is obtained from vine varieties belonging to Vitis vinifera" (Council Regulation No. 479/2008, Article 34).

[86]In 2003, out of a total 233,300 ha of vines, 117,500 were planted with hybrids (Manole *et al.*, 2008).

[87]Even if the vineyard area decreased from about 190,000 ha in 2006 to 175,000 ha in 2011, it did not fall dramatically, as Romania obtained replanting rights for 30,000 ha that could be used "exclusively for planting with Vitis vinifera" (Treaty of Accession of Bulgaria and Romania, Annex VII, 2005). However, neither the EU Commission nor Romania (through

new vineyards were granted exclusively for the production of "quality wines" (Treaty of Accession of Bulgaria and Romania, Annexes III and VII, 2005).

6. Conclusions

The EU is the largest global wine-producing region and the main global wine importer and exporter. It is also a highly regulated market. Government intervention has taken many forms. Regulations determine where certain wines can be produced and where not, the minimum spacing between vines, the type of vines that can be planted in certain regions, yield restrictions, and so on. In addition, public regulations determine subsidies to EU producers and wine distillation schemes. The EU also determines public subsidies to finance grubbing up programs to remove existing vineyards, and imposes a limit on the planting of new vineyards.

In this chapter, we document these regulations and analyze the historical origins of these regulations. The introduction of many regulations followed the integration of markets and globalization, technological changes, and resulting political pressures.

Many of the current EU regulations can be traced back to French regulations of the late nineteenth and early twentieth centuries. "Quality" regulations, as the AOC system, were introduced to protect producers of "quality wines," such as wealthy landowners of Bordeaux, from imitations and adulterations. Quantity regulations, such as planting restrictions, were introduced to protect French producers from cheap wine imports.

After the accession of France into the EU, some of the policies were initially liberalized. However, surplus crises in the 1970s caused strong pressure from French producers to reimpose the regulations and extend them to the EU as a whole. For instance, just as, in 1931, wine producers in the Midi (which were threatened by the importation of Algerian wines) pressured the French government into imposing the Statut Viticole, regulating the production of wines, in 1976 French producers (threatened this time by the importation of Italian wines) pressured their government and EU leaders into introducing more wine regulation.

As a consequence, what were initially mainly French and, to a lesser extent, Italian national regulations now apply to approximately 60% of the world's wine production. This demonstrates how inefficient institutions

its national envelope) decided to subsidize the grubbing up of hybrids vines, leaving the cost of replacing the hybrids to the winegrowers (Itçaina *et al.*, 2013).

and regulations can grow because of a combination of economic, political, and institutional integration and the associated political pressure and influence.[88]

Acknowledgments

The chapter benefited from comments from Paola Corsinovi, Koen Deconinck, Alan Olmstead, Vicente Pinilla, and Eline Poelmans and participants in the 2011 AAWE Conference in Bolzano, Italy; the 2011 International Conference on Economics, Management Sciences, and History of Wine in Zaragoza, Spain; the 2011 International Workshop on Economic History of Globalization in Leuven, Belgium; the 2012 ICABR conference in Ravello, Italy; and LICOS. We thank Jill McCluskey and Karl Storchmann for the encouragement throughout this project.

References

Anderson, K., Damania, R., and Jackson, L.A. (2004). Trade, standards, and the political economy of genetically modified food. CEPR Discussion Papers 4526, Center for Economic Policy Research.

Anderson, K., Rausser, G., and Swinnen, J. (2013). Political economy of public policies: Insights from distortions to agricultural and food markets. *Journal of Economic Literature*, 51(2), 423–477.

Arnaud, C. (1991). Le vin et l'organisation commune de marché entre Paris et Bruxelles: Un dialogue quelquefois difficile. *Économie rurale*, 204(204), 3–10.

Augé-Laribé, M. (1950). *La Politique Agricole de la France de 1880 à 1940*. Paris: Presses Universitaires de France.

Bagnol, J.M. (2007). Les députés héraultais et la viticulture dans l'entre-deux-guerres: Organes de décision, relais de pouvoir, législation. *Ruralia*. https://ruralia.revues.org/1857 (accessed on November 3, 2017).

Bartoli, P. (1986). Les primes d'arrachage et la régression du vignoble. Une analyse d'impact de la politique viticole. *Économie rurale*, 175, 3–19.

Birebent, P. (2007). *Hommes, vignes et vins de l'Algérie française: 1830–1962*. Nice: Editions Jacques Gandini.

Blancaneaux, R. (2013). Le Parlement européen post-Lisbonne, une courroie de transmission pour les opposants à la Commission européenne? Le cas de l'opposition à la libéralisation des droits de plantation viticoles. https://www.cairn.info/revue-politique-europeenne-2014-1-page-192.htm (accessed on November 3, 2017).

Bonal, F. (1984). *Livre d'or du Champagne*. (Lausanne: Editions du Grand-Pont, 1984).

[88]There is a large body of literature on the persistence and growth of inefficient institutions (see, e.g., David, 1985). Our argument, however, is not related to scale economies of transaction costs but to political and institutional integration. Meloni and Swinnen (2013) analyze in great detail other pre-EEC regulations, such as the first grubbing-up policies during Roman times, the Middle Ages, and the Renaissance period.

Caesar, C. Julius (1869). *Caesar's Gallic War.* W.A. McDevitte and W.S. Bohn (trans.), 1st ed. New York: Harper & Brothers. Harper's New Classical Library. http://www.perseus.tufts.edu/hopper/text?doc=Perseus:text:1999.02.0001 (accessed on November 3, 2017).

Cagliero, R., and Sardone, R. (2009). *La nuova OCM vino.* L'OCM Vino. La Difficile Transazione Verso Una Strategia di Comparto, edited by E. Pomarici and R. Sardone. Rome: INEA, pp. 25–48.

Capus, J. (1947). *L'évolution de la législation sur les appellations d'origine; genèse des appellations contrôlées.* (Paris: INAOEditions Louis Larmat).

Castle, S. (2012). When is a wine not a wine? When European regulations say it's not. *New York Times*, May 29. Available at http://www.nytimes.com/2012/05/30/world/europe/when-is-a-wine-not-a-wine-when-european-regulations-say-its-not.html (accessed on November 3, 2017).

Comité Interprofessionnel du Vin de Champagne (2003). L'appellation Champagne, les clés des vins de Champagne. Available at http://maisons-champagne.com/IMG/pdf/appellation-2.pdf (accessed on November 3, 2017).

Conforti, P., and Sardone, R. (2003). *Assessing the Effectiveness of the EU Common Market Organization for Wine: A Research Agenda.* Wine in the Old World: New Risks and Opportunities, edited by S. Gatti, E. Giraud-Heraud and S. Mili. Milano: FrancoAngeli.

Consorzio Vino Chianti Classico (2012). Production Code of Chianti Classico denominazione di origine controllata e garantita Wine. Available at http://www.gazzettaufficiale.it/eli/id/1996/09/18/096A5835/sg (accessed on November 3, 2017).

Couderc, F. (2005). *Les vins mythiques de la Cévenne ardéchoise et du Bas-Vivarais.* 2nd ed. Point-Saint-Esprit Cedex: La Mirandole.

Council Regulation (EEC) No. 24/1962 of 20 April 1962 on the progressive establishment of a common organisation of the market in wine. *Official Journal of the European Communities.*

Council Regulation (EEC) No. 816/70 of 28 April 1970 laying down additional provisions for the common organization of the market in wine. *Official Journal of the European Communities.*

Council Regulation (EEC) No. 817/70 of 28 April 1970 laying down special provisions relating to quality wines produced in specific regions. *Official Journal of the European Communities.*

Council Regulation (EEC) No. 1160/76 of 17 May 1976 amending Regulation (EEC) No. 816/70 laying down additional provisions for the common organization of the market in wine. *Official Journal of the European Communities.*

Council Regulation (EEC) No. 1162/76 of 17 May 1976 on measures designed to adjust winegrowing potential to market requirements. *Official Journal of the European Communities.*

Council Regulation (EEC) No. 1163/76 of 17 May 1976 on the granting of a conversion premium in the wine sector. *Official Journal of the European Communities.*

Council Regulation (EEC) No. 337/79 of 5 February 1979 on the common organization of the market in wine. *Official Journal of the European Communities.*

Council Regulation (EEC) No. 458/80 of 18 February 1980 on collective projects for the restructuring of vineyards. *Official Journal of the European Communities.*

Council Regulation (EEC) No. 822/87 of 16 March 1987 on the common organization of the market in wine. *Official Journal of the European Communities.*

Council Regulation (EC) No. 1493/1999 of 17 May 1999 on the common organisation of the market in wine. *Official Journal of the European Union.*

Council Regulation (EC) No. 479/2008 of 29 April 2008 on the common organisation of the market in wine, amending Regulations (EC) Nos. 1493/1999, 1782/2003, 1290/2005, and 3/2008 and repealing Regulations (EEC) Nos. 2392/86 and 1493/1999. *Official Journal of the European Union.* Available at http://eur-lex.europa.eu/LexUriServ/LexUriServ.do?uri=OJ:L:2008:148:0001:0061:EN:PDF/. Accessed on November 3, 2017.

Council Regulation (EC) No. 491/2009 of 25 May 2009 amending Regulation (EC) No. 1234/2007 establishing a common organisation of agricultural markets and on specific provisions for certain agricultural products (Single CMO Regulation). *Official Journal of the European Union.* Available at http://eur-lex.europa.eu/LexUriServ/LexUriServ.do?uri=OJ:L:2009:154:0001:0056:EN:PDF/. Accessed on November 3, 2017.

Council Regulation (EC) No. 607/2009 of 14 July 2009 laying down certain detailed rules for the implementation of Council Regulation (EC) No. 479/2008 as regards protected designations of origin and geographical indications, traditional terms, labelling and presentation of certain wine sector products. *Official Journal of the European Union.* Available at http://eur-lex.europa.eu/LexUriServ/LexUriServ.do?uri=OJ:L:2009:193:0060:0139:EN:PDF (accessed on November 3, 2017).

Critz, J.M., Olmstead, A.L., and Rhode, P.W. (1999). "Horn of Plenty": The globalization of mediterranean horticulture and the economic development of Southern Europe, 1880–1930. *Journal of Economic History*, 59(2), 316–352.

Crowley, W.K. (1993). Changes in the French winescape. *Geographical Review*, 83(3), 252–268.

David, P.A. (1985). Clio and the economics of QWERTY. *American Economic Review*, 75(2), 332–337.

de Gorter, H., and Swinnen, J.F.M. (2002). *Political Economy of Agricultural Policies.* The Handbook of Agricultural Economics, edited by B. Gardner and G. Rausser. Amsterdam: Elsevier Science, North-Holland, pp. 2073–2123.

Deconinck, K., and Swinnen, J. (2013). The economics of planting rights in wine production.

Deconinck K., and Swinnen J. (2015). The economics of planting rights in wine production. *European Review of Agricultural Economics*, 42(3), 419–440.

E-Bacchus (2012). Wine register of designations of origin and geographical indications protected in the EU. European Commission, online database. Available at http://ec.europa.eu/agriculture/markets/wine/e-bacchus/. Accessed on November 3, 2017.

EFOW (2012). Planting rights: Commissioner Ciolos set up a high level group. European Federation of Origin Wines (EFOW), March 22. Available at www.efow.eu/press/planting-rights-commissioner-ciolos-set-up-a-high-level-grou_id_124/.

Estatuto del Vino (1932). Estatuto del vino: regulación de su producción y venta. Decreto del Ministerio de Agricultura, Industria y Comercio de 8 de septiembre de 1932, elevado a ley por la de 26 de mayo de 1933 y disposiciones posteriores. Available at www.magrama.gob. es/es/ministerio/pags/biblioteca/fondo/40869.htm.

Europa (2008). Markets for Agricultural Products — Wine. Brussels. Available at http://europa.eu/scadplus/leg/en/lvb/l60031.htm.

European Commission (2003). *Study on the Use of the Varieties of Interspecific Vines.* Contract No. AGR 30881 of 30 December 2002. Available at http://ec.europa.eu/agriculture/markets/wine/studies/vine_en.pdf.

European Commission (2006a). *WINE — Common Market Organisation.* Available at http://ec.europa.eu/agriculture/markets/wine/studies/rep_cmo2006_en.pdf.

European Commission (2006b). *WINE — Economy of the Sector.* European Commission. Available at http://ec.europa.eu/agriculture/markets/wine/studies/rep_econ2006_en.pdf.

European Commission (2006c). *Communication from the Commission to the Council and the European Parliament — "Towards a Sustainable European Wine Sector."* COM(2006) 319 final. Available at http://ec.europa.eu/agriculture/capreform/wine/com2006_319_en.pdf.

European Commission (2006d). *Impact Assessment — Annex to the Communication from the Commission to the Council and the European Parliament "Towards a Sustainable European Wine Sector."* Available at http://ec.europa.eu/agriculture/capreform/wine/fullimpact_en.pdf.

European Commission (2007a). *Fact Sheet — Towards a Sustainable European Wine Sector.* Available at http://ec.europa.eu/agriculture/publi/fact/wine/072007_en.pdf.

European Commission (2007b). *Proposal for a Council Regulation on the Common Organization of the Market in Wine and Amending Certain Regulations.* COM(2007) 372 final. Available at http://eur-lex.europa.eu/LexUriServ/LexUriServ.do?uri=COM:2007:0372:FIN:EN:PDF/.

European Commission (2007c). *Accompanying Document to the Proposal for a Council Regulation on the Common Organisation of the Market in Wine and Amending Certain Regulations — Impact Assessment.* Available at http://ec.europa.eu/agriculture/capreform/wine/impact072007/full_en.pdf.

European Commission (2007–2012). *Agriculture and Rural Development budget: European Agricultural Guarantee Fund (EAGF) financial reports, 2007–2012.* Office for Official Publications of the European Communities, Luxembourg. Available at http://ec.europa.eu/agriculture/cap-funding/budget/index_en.htm.

European Commission (2008a). *Reform of the EU Wine Market.* Available at http://ec.europa.eu/agriculture/capreform/wine/index_en.htm.

European Commission (2008b). *The Common Agricultural Policy — A Glossary of Terms.* Available at http://ec.europa.eu/agriculture/glossary/glossary_en.pdf.

European Commission (2009). *Market Situation (History).* Available at http://ec.europa.eu/agriculture/markets/wine/facts/winehist_fr.pdf.

European Commission (2009–2012). *Wine CMO: Financial Execution of the National Support Programme.* Directorate-General for Agriculture and Rural Development. Available at http://ec.europa.eu/agriculture/markets/wine/facts/index_en.htm.

European Commission (2012). Grubbing-up scheme 2008–2009–2010. *In Statistics and Data. European Commission — DG AGRI.* Available at http://ec.europa.eu/agriculture/markets/wine/facts/grubbing_2008-2009-2010_en.pdf.

European Commission (2013). Execution 2012. *In Statistics and Data. European Commission — DG AGRI.* Available at http://ec.europa.eu/agriculture/markets/wine/facts/execution- 2012_en.pdf.

European Court of Auditors (2012). The reform of the common organisation of the market in wine: progress to date. Special Report No. 7. Available at http://eca.europa.eu/portal/pls/portal/docs/1/14824739.PDF.

Eurostat (2013). Eurostat Statistics Database. Luxembourg: Eurostat. Available at http://ec.europa.eu/eurostat/data/database (accessed on November 3, 2017).

FAO (2012). Food and Agriculture Organization of the United Nations. FAOSTAT. Available at http://faostat.fao.org.

Federal Centre for Breeding Research on Cultivated Plants (2009). IRZ Institute of Grapevine Breeding Geilweilerhof. Available at www.bafz.de/baz2006V4/index.php?id=319/.

Federdoc (2012). I vini italiani a Denominazione d'Origine 2012. Available at www.federdoc.com.

Fulton, M., and Giannakis, K. (2004). Inserting GM products into the food chain: The market and welfare effects of different labelling and regulatory regimes. *American Journal of Agricultural Economics*, 86(1), 42–60.

Gaeta, D., and Corsinovi, P. (2009). *Evoluzione del processo di riforma tra mutamenti del mercato, gruppi di pressione e alleanze nazionali.* L'OCM Vino. La Difficile Transazione Verso Una Strategia Di Comparto, edited by E. Pomarici and R. Sardone. Rome: INEA, pp. 49–69.

Gale, G. (2003). *Saving the Vine from Phylloxera: A Never-ending Battle.* Wine: A Scientific Exploration, edited by S. Merton and R. Pinder. London and New York: Taylor & Francis, pp. 81–84.

Gale, G.D. (2011). *Dying on the Vine. How Phylloxera Transformed Wine.* Berkeley: University of California Press.

GATT (General Agreement on Tariffs and Trade) (1966). *World Trade Prospects for Ordinary Wine.* Trade Intelligence Paper No. 8, Geneva.

Gavignaud, G. (1988). Etat et propriété: Le vignoble méridional (1880–1980). *Économie rurale*, 184(184–186), 92–99. Available at www.persee.fr.

Grant, W. (1997). *The Common Agricultural Policy.* London: Macmillan.

Hyams, E. (1965). *Dionysus: A social history of the wine vine.* Bristol: Thames & Hudson.

Innova SpA (2004). Ex-post evaluation of the Common Market Organisation for wine. Final report prepared for European Commission, DG Agriculture, Tender AGRI/EVALUATION/2002/6. Available at http://ec.europa.eu/agriculture/eval/reports/wine/fullrep_en.pdf.

INSEE (1935). *Annuaire statistique de la France. Résumé rétrospectif.* Paris: Institut National de la Statistique et des Etudes Economiques.

INSEE (1966). *Annuaire statistique de la France. Résumé rétrospectif.* Paris: Institut National de la Statistique et des Etudes Economiques.

Isnard, H. (1947). Vigne et colonisation en Algérie (1880–1947). *Annales. Économies, Sociétés, Civilisations*, 2(3), 288–300. Available at www.persee.fr.

Isnard, H. (1966). La Viticulture Nord-Africaine. In *Annuaire de l'Afrique du Nord-1865*, vol. 4. Paris: Editions du CNRS.

Itçaina, X., Roger, A., and Smith, A. (2013). Institutionalizations compared: Implementating the EU's 2008 wine reform. *Comparative European Politics*, 11(1), 119–142.

Jacquet, O. (2009). Les appellations d'origine et le débat sur la typicité dans la première moitié du XXème siècle: le rôle du syndicalisme viti-vinicole bourguignon. *Territoires du vin — Pour une redéfinition des terroirs.* Available at https://revuesshs.u-bourgogne.fr/territoiresduvin/document.php?id=125 (accessed on November 3, 2017).

Kortteinen, T. (1984). Wine production in the European Community since 1975. *British Journal of Addiction*, 79(4), 319–325.

Lachiver, M. (1988). *Vins, vignes et vignerons. Histoire du vignoble français.* Paris: Fayard.

Legifrance (2011). Loi du 29 juin 1907 tendant à prévenir le mouillage des vins et les abus de sucrage. Les textes législatifs et réglementaires, Détail d'un texte. Available at www.legifrance.gouv.fr/affichTexte.do?cidTexte=LEGITEXT000006071147&dateTexte=20110803/. Accessed on November 3, 2017.

Loubère, L.A. (1978). *The Red and the White. The History of Wine in France and Italy in the Nineteenth Century.* Albany: State University of New York Press.

Loubère, L.A. (1990). *The Wine Revolution in France: The Twentieth Century.* Princeton, NJ: Princeton University Press.

Maher, M. (2001). On vino veritas? Clarifying the use of geographic references on American wine labels. *California Law Review*, 89(6), 1881–1925.

Maillard, J. de (2002). La commission, le vin et la réforme. *Politique Européenne*, 1(5), 68–84.

Malassis, L. (1959). La politique agricole de 1946 à 1958. La recherche d'une politique agricole. In *Économie rurale. N° 39–40. L'économie agricole française 1938–1958.* Paris: Société Française d'économie rurale, 233–251.

Manole, V., Ion, R.A., and Ladaru, G.R. (2008). Wine chain in Romania — A marketing approach. *Annales Universitatis Apulensis Series Oeconomica*, 2(10), 52.

Martin, J.-P. (1998). Viticulture du Languedoc: Une tradition syndicale en mouvement. *Pôle Sud*, 9(1), 71–87.

Meloni, G., and Swinnen, J.F.M. (2013). The political economy of quality regulations: Geographical origins, production regulations, and labelling. Unpublished mimeo.

Meloni G., and Swinnen J. (2014). The rise and fall of the world's largest wine exporter– and its institutional legacy. *Journal of Wine Economics*, 9(1), 3–33.

Milhau, J. (1953). L'avenir de la viticulture française. *Revue Économique*, 4(5), 700–738.

Moschini, G., Menapace, L., and Pick, D. (2008). Geographical indications and the competitive provision of quality in agricultural markets. *American Journal of Agricultural Economics*, 90, 794–812.

Munholland, K. (2006). "Mon docteur le vin": Wine and health in France, 1900–1950, edited by M.P. Holt. *Alcohol: a Social and Cultural History.* Oxford: Berg, pp. 77–90.

Munsie, J. (2002). *A Brief History of the International Regulation of Wine Production.* Harvard Law School, Cambridge, MA.

Newsletter on the Common Agricultural Policy (1969). *A Common Wine Policy: New Moves by the Commission.* No. 7/69. European Communities — Directorate General Press and Information. Available at http://aei.pitt.edu/6530/. Accessed on November 3, 2017.

Newsletter on the Common Agricultural Policy (1970). The background to the common organization of the market in wine. No. 2/70. *European Communities — Directorate General Press and Information.* Available at http://aei.pitt.edu/5482/. Accessed on November 3, 2017.

Niederbacher, A. (1983). Wine in the European Community. Office for Official Publication of the European Communities, Periodical 2/3–1983, Luxembourg.

OECD (Organisation for Economic Co-operation and Development) (2012). Producer and Consumer Support Estimates database, OECD database 1986–2011, Paris. Available at www.oecd.org/tad/agricultural-policies/E27dataPSE2012.xlsx. Accessed on November 3, 2017.

OIV (International Organization of Vine and Wine) (2007). World Vitivinicultural Statistics 2007 — Structure of the World Vitivinicultural Industry 2007. Paris. Available at www. oiv.int/oiv/info/enstatistiquessecteurvitivinicole#secteur/.

OIV (International Organization of Vine and Wine) (2012a). International Standard for Labelling Wines. Paris. Available at www.oiv.int/oiv/info/enplubicationoiv/.

OIV (International Organization of Vine and Wine) (2012b). Statistical Report on world vitiviniculture. Paris. Available at www.oiv.int/oiv/info/enizmiroivreport/.

OIV (International Organization of Vine andWine) (2013). State of the Vitiviniculture-World Market. Paris. Available at www.oiv.int/oiv/info/enconjoncture/.

Ordish, G. (1987). *The Great Wine Blight.* 2nd ed. London: Sidgwick and Jackson.

Pan-Montojo, J. (1994). *La Bodega del Mundo. La Vid y el Vino en España (1800–1936).* Madrid: Alianza.

Paul, H.W. (1996). *Science, Vine and Wine in Modern France.* Cambridge: Cambridge University Press.

Petit, G. (2000). Pour une histoire de la réglementation vitivinicole des Communautés européennes. *Bulletin de l'OIV*, May–June, 324–339.

Pinilla, V., and Ayuda, M.-I. (2002). The political economy of the wine trade: Spanish exports and the international market, 1890–1935. *European Review of Economic History*, 6, 51–85.

Pinilla, V., and Serrano, R. (2008). The agricultural and food trade in the first globalization: Spanish table wine exports 1871 to 1935 — A case study. *Journal of Wine Economics*, 3(2), 132–148.

Pokrivcak, J., Crombez, C., and Swinnen, J.F.M. (2006). The status quo bias and reform of the common agricultural policy: Impact of voting rules, the European Commission, and external changes. *European Review of Agricultural Economics*, 33(4), 562–590.

Rausser, G., Swinnen, J.F.M., and Zusman, P. (2011). *Political Power and Economic Policy: Theory, Analysis, and Empirical Applications.* New York: Cambridge University Press.

Robinson, J. (2006). *The Oxford Companion to Wine.* 3rd ed. Oxford: Oxford University Press.

Sagnes, J. (2009). Edouard Barthe, Député du vin, 1882–1949. In G. Gavignaud-Fontaine (ed.), *Vin et république, 1907–2007: colloque, Montpellier, October 18–19, 2007.* Paris: Pepper-L'Harmattan, 126–132.

Simpson, J. (2011). *Creating Wine: The Emergence of a World Industry, 1840–1914.* Princeton, NJ: Princeton University Press.

Smith, A. (1776/1904). *An Inquiry into the Nature and Causes of the Wealth of Nations.* Edwin Cannan (ed.), 5th ed. London: Methuen. Available at www.econlib.org/library/Smith/smWN.html. Accessed on November 3, 2017.

Smith, A. (2008). Globalization within the European wine industry: Commercial challenges but producer domination, edited by B. Jullien and A. Smith. *Industries and Globalization: The Political Causality of Difference.* Basingstoke, UK: Palgrave.

Smith, A., Maillard, J. de, and Costa, O. (2007). *Vin et Politique. Bordeaux, la France, la Mondialisation.* Paris: Presses de Sciences Po.

Spahni, P. (1988). *The Common Wine Policy and Price Stabilization.* Aldershot, UK: Avebury.

Stanziani, A. (2004). Wine reputation and quality controls: The origin of the AOCs in 19th century France. *European Journal of Law and Economics*, 18(2), 149–167.

Swinnen, J.F.M. (2008). *The Perfect Storm: The Political Economy of the Fischler Reforms of the Common Agricultural Policy.* Brussels: CEPS.

Swinnen, J.F.M. (2009). The growth of agricultural protection in Europe in the 19th and 20th centuries. *World Economy*, 32(11), 1499–1537.

Swinnen, J.F.M. (2010). The political economy of agricultural and food policies: Recent contributions, new insights, and areas for further research. *Applied Economic Perspectives and Policy*, 32(1), 33–58.

Swinnen, J.F.M., and Vandemoortele, T. (2008). The political economy of nutrition and health standards in food markets. *Review of Agricultural Economics*, 30(3), 460–468.

Swinnen, J.F.M., and Vandemoortele, T. (2009). Are food safety standards different from other food standards? A political economy perspective. *European Review of Agricultural Economics*, 36(4), 507–523.

Treaty of Accession of Bulgaria and Romania: Protocol, Luxembourg, April 25 (2005). *Official Journal of the European Union L157.* Available at http://ec.europa.eu/enlargement/archives/enlargement_process/future_prospects/negotiations/eu10_bulgaria_romania/treaty_2005_en.htm.

Tyman, R. (1879). *Le Phylloxéra.* Gand: Vanderhaegen.

Ulin, R.C. (1996). *Vintages and Traditions: An Ethnohistory of Southwest France Wine Cooperatives.* Washington, DC: Smithsonian Institution Press.

Union des Maisons de Champagnes (2012). "Organisations des vins et spiritueux en France, en Europe et dans le monde." Available at www.maisons-champagne.com/orga_prof/schema_org_prof.htm.

Unwin, T. (1991). *Wine and the Vine: An Historical Geography of Viticulture and the Wine Trade.* London: Routledge.

Warner, C.K. (1960). *The Winegrowers of France and the Government Since 1875.* New York: Columbia University Press.

Wolikow, C. (2009). La Champagne viticole, banc d'essai de la délimitation (1903–1927). *Territoires du vin — Pour une redéfinition des terroirs.* Available at http:// revuesshs.u-bourgogne.fr/territoiresduvin/document.php?id=275 (accessed on November 3, 2017).

Appendix 1: Chronology of European Wine Regulations

1962	— establishment of a viticultural land register — notification of annual production levels (harvest and stock declarations) — annual compilation of future estimates of resources and requirements — stricter rules on "quality wines psr"
1970	— rules on viticulture: vines were classified into "recommended," "authorized," and "provisionally authorized" varieties — definition of different types of wine: "table wine" that had to contain an alcoholic strength of between 8.5° and 15° and "quality wines psr"* that included French AOC and VDQS wines**, Italian DOC wines, German *Qualitätsweine* and *Qualitätsweine mit Prädikat* and Luxembourg *Marque Nationale wines.* — rules on wine production (as the maximum amount for enrichment and alcohol strength) — introduction of common rules on labeling and oenological practices — rules for determining guide prices activating the intervention system — introduction of distillation of excess production in times of crises and obligatory distillation of the by-products of wine-making — aid for short-term and long-term storage — monitoring of trade with non-member countries was established — declaration of *free movement of wine* within the Community
1979	— introduction of subsidies for concentrated grape must used for enrichment — compulsory distillation of wines obtained for table grapes — definition of oenological practices
1987	— for table wines, the measures maintained price supports, prohibition of new planting and temporary storage of surpluses — widening of compulsory distillation (see Annex 3) — introduction of further subsidies for the conversion of vineyards — new rules for the production of quality wines
1999	— prohibition until 2010 on the planting of vines — market mechanisms are maintained: private storage, obligatory by-product distillation, distillation of table wines and voluntary crisis-distillation — introduction of restructuring and conversion measures for vineyards — wine-making processes and practices are laid down — trade with countries outside the EU is brought in line with the Uruguay Round agreement

Notes: *Quality wines psr stands for Quality wines produced in specified regions.
**VDQS wines stands for Delimited Wine of Superior Quality.
Sources: Council Regulations of 1962, 1970, 1979, 1987, 1999; Europa, 2008; Munsie, 2002; Niederbacher, 1983; Unwin, 1991.

Appendix 2: The 2008 Reform of European Wine Policy

Support measures	• National envelopes: each country is entitled with a funding budget adapted to their particular situation. Support programs contain one or more of the following measures: (a) Single Payment Scheme support (Article 9); (b) promotion (Article 10); (c) restructuring and conversion of vineyards (Article 11); (d) green harvesting (Article 12); (e) mutual funds (Article 13); (f) harvest insurance (Article 14); (g) investments (Article 15); (h) by-product distillation (Article 16); (i) potable alcohol distillation (Article 17) (until July 31, 2012); (j) crisis distillation (Article 18) (until July 31, 2012); (k) use of concentrated grape must (Article 19) (until July 31, 2012). • Chaptalization: lower limits for added sugar and must • Introduction of Single Farm Payment • Rural Development and environmental protection
Trade with third countries	The reform took into account WTO policies, that is, the phasing-out of market intervention measures (as distillation and public storage)
Regulatory measures	• Oenological practices: the Commission now approves or changes winemaking practices • New classification: wines are now divided into "wines with a Geographical Indication" and "wines without a Geographical Indication." Within the first category, there are two subcategories: Protected Designation of Origin (PDO) wines and Protected Geographical Indication (PGI) wines, with PDO as the highest quality level • Labeling: national quality-labeling schemes are kept for PDO wines, while wines without an Geographical Indication can now be labeled with grape variety and vintage
Production potential	• The planting rights regime will end at EU level from January 1, 2016 (Member states can decide to extend the limit until 2018) • A voluntary grubbing-up scheme was enacted (175,000 ha were uprooted)

Sources: Council Regulation (EC) No. 479/2008; European Commission, 2008a.

Appendix 3: Distillation Schemes in the EUO

1962	No distillation scheme provided
1970	Distillation of excess production in times of crises Distillation of the by-products of wine-making (compulsory)
1979	Preventive distillation (voluntary) Distillation with special price maintenance for long-term storage contracts Distillation of wines obtained for table grapes (compulsory)
1987	Support distillation Preventive distillation (voluntary) Distillation of table wines (compulsory) Distillation of wines other than table wines (compulsory) Distillation of by-products (compulsory)
1999	Distillation for potable alcohol (voluntary) Crisis distillation (voluntary, all wines)* Distillation of wine from dual-purpose grapes (compulsory) Distillation of by-products (compulsory)
2008	Phasing-out of crisis distillation and potable alcohol distillation (support granted until 31 July 2012) Support for (voluntary or compulsory) distillation of by-products of wine-making maintained

Note: *From 1999 onward, crisis distillation could also be applied to "quality wines."
Sources: Council Regulations (EC) Nos. 817/70, 822/87, 1493/1999, and 479/2008; and European Commission, 2006a.

Appendix 4: An Example of an Appellation d'Origine Contrôlée Regulation (applied to Bordeaux Wines)

The *Cahier des charges de l'Appellation d'Origine Contrôlée "Bordeaux Supérieur"* is a 51-page document pages laying out the governing rules of production, vinification and bottling of the AOC. The document is available at http://agriculture.gouv.fr/IMG/pdf/AOC_DGPAAT_SOMM42–2.pdf

The main rules for local winegrowers refer to:

a) Territory: the specific area is defined in which the harvest/vinification/bottling has to be carried out. A list of approximately 500 *communes* are specified in the Gironde territory;

b) Authorized grape varieties: grapes have to grow within the specified geographical region. For example, for the red Bordeaux wines, only 6 varieties are permitted, namely, Cabernet Sauvignon — Cabernet Franc — Merlot — Cot (or Malbec) — Carmenère — Petit Verdot;

(*Continued*)

Appendix 4: (*Continued*)

c) Growing and winemaking methods, as:
- maximum number of vines per hectare (4,500 plants per hectare);
- distance between rows (not more than 2.20 meters) and between vines (not less than 0.85 meter);
- pruning methods. For instance, for the Merlot variety, the number of fruiting branches per plant cannot exceed 11 shoots per vine;
- the fence height must be at least equal to 0.55 times the spacing between rows.

d) the minimum natural alcoholic strength (in % of volume) must be 11% for red wines;
e) the maximum yield allowed (50 hectoliters per hectare);
The bottling and labeling: wines must age for at least 12 months before they can be sold; and the label must indicate Bordeaux Supérieur together with the Appellation Contrôlée reference.

Appendix 5: Producer Single Commodity Transfers (PSCT), Consumer Support Estimate (CSE) and General Services Support Estimate (GSSE) for Wine in 2011

	Currency/ unit	
I. Level of production	000 tons	16,381.4
II. Value of production (at farm gate)	ECUmn	16,024.9
III.1. Producer Single Commodity Transfers (PSCT): Includes Wine specific programs in A, B, C and D	ECUmn	31.9
A. Support based on commodity outputs	ECUmn	2.1
A1. Market Price Support	ECUmn	2.1
A2. Payments based on output	ECUmn	0.1
B. Payments based on input use	ECUmn	3.2
B1. Variable input use	ECUmn	0.0
B2. Fixed capital formation	ECUmn	0.0
B3. On-farm services	ECUmn	3.2
C. Payments based on current A/An/R/I, production required, single commodity	ECUmn	26.6
D. Payments based on non-current A/An/R/I, production required	ECUmn	0.0
III.2. % Producer Single Commodity Transfers (PSCT)	%	0.2
F. Payments based on non-commodity criteria		
F1. Long-term resource retirement		
Permanent abandonment premiums	ECUmn	0.0
Grubbing-up scheme (wine reform 2007)	ECUmn	20.0

Appendix 5: (*Continued*)

	Currency/ unit	
IV. General Services Support Estimate (GSSE)		
L. Marketing and promotion		
Aid for the use of must	ECUmn	0.0
National support programs for the wine sector	ECUmn	1,086.7
M. Public stockholding		
Buying-in of alcohol from compulsory distillation	ECUmn	0.2
V.1. Consumer Support Estimate (CSE)		
Q. Transfers to consumers from taxpayers		
Q.1. Commodity specific transfers to consumers		
Distillation of wine	ECUmn	0.0
Compulsory distillation of by-products of wine making	ECUmn	0.0

Source: OECD Producer and Consumer Support Estimates database, 2012 (available at www.oecd.org/tad/agricultural-policies/E27dataPSE2012.xlsx).

Appendix 6: Annual Distillation Disposal, 2001–2011*

	By-product distillation		Dual purpose grape distillation		Potable alcohol distillation		Crisis distillation		Total Distillation
	(million hl)	%	(million hl)	%	(million hl)	%	(million hl)	%	(million hl)
2001	5.1	21	1.1	5	12.6	53	5.1	21	23.9
2002	5.5	21	1.2	4	11.8	44	8.1	30	26.7
2003	5.4	34	1.0	6	8.7	54	0.9	6	16.0
2004	5.5	33	0.8	4	10.2	60	0.4	3	16.9
2005	6.6	30	1.4	6	10.9	49	3.1	14	22.0
2006	6.3	24	1.2	4	12.7	49	5.9	23	26.0
2007	5.9	24	0.9	3	12.5	50	5.7	23	25.0
2008	5.1	42	0	0	6.9	57	0	0	12.1
2009	4.5	35	0	0	8.3	65	0	0	12.8
2010	4.9	36	0	0	7.6	55	1.1	8	13.6
2011	5.9	66	0	0	3.0	34	0.1	1	9.0

Note: *The dual purpose grape distillation was abolished in 2008 and potable alcohol and crisis distillation were phased out in 2012, leaving the byproduct distillation as the only remaining option for member states.
Source: Eurostat, 2013.

Chapter 8

How Much Government Assistance Do European Wine Producers Receive?*

Kym Anderson[†,‡] **and Hans G. Jensen**[§]

[†]*School of Economics, University of Adelaide, Adelaide, South Australia 5005, Australia*

[‡]*Australian National University, Canberra ACT 0200, Australia*
kym.anderson@adelaide.edu.au

[§]*Institute of Food and Resource Economics, University of Copenhagen, 1958 Frederiksberg C, Denmark*
hans@ifro.ku.dk

The European Union's (EU) long-standing financial support for its wine industry has been nontrivial but very difficult to estimate. The Organization for Economic Cooperation and Development's (OECD) generic producer support estimate methodology has been able to capture some of the supports, but it excludes such measures as subsidized distillation of low-quality wine, grants to promote wine generically, protection via import tariffs, and grubbing-up premiums. Nor does the OECD disaggregate EU supports to individual member countries. This chapter provides a new set of a complete estimates of support to EU wine producers. It also reveals how unevenly those supports are spread across EU member countries. The new estimates suggest that during 2007–2012, annual assistance amounted to approximately 700 euros per hectare of vines or 0.15 euros per liter of wine produced in the EU as measured at the winery gate. That is equivalent to a nominal rate of direct plus indirect producer assistance of approximately 20%. (JEL Classifications: F14, H25, L66, Q18)

1. Introduction

For decades the European Union (EU) and its predecessors have had a Common Market Organization (CMO) for wine that has heavily regulated or

*This article originally appeared in *Journal of Wine Economics* (2016), 11(2), 289–305.

influenced the quantity, quality, and price of wine grapes and wine produced in the EU (Gaeta and Corsinovi, 2014; Meloni and Swinnen, 2013; Spahni, 1988). Following a review in 2006 (European Commission, 2006), the policy went through a major reform in 2008, which included a 3-year grubbing-up program that paid growers to remove vines. Meanwhile, financial support for generic promotion of EU wines has been expanding considerably and is budgeted for further expansion during 2014–2018.

The Organization for Economic Cooperation and Development (OECD) has tracked support for farm industries in its member countries since 1986. In the case of the EU (but not other member countries) that has included support for the wine industry. However, using the OECD's generic methodology means that various support measures are not included in its producer support estimates (PSEs). It also means support is shown only for the EU as a whole, not for individual EU member countries. The omitted measures include subsidies for distillation of low-quality wine and any domestic price-raising effect of tariffs on imports of non-EU wines. The industry has also benefitted, along with other farm industries, from non-product-specific support to the rural sector of EU member countries. That support is treated as a generic rural benefit rather than supporting winegrowers or producers of any other particular agricultural product.

This chapter is not meant as a criticism of that generic OECD methodology. Rather, its purpose is to provide a set of a complete estimates of government support to EU wine producers because many other countries' wine producers are struggling and would like to compare the types and extent of EU support with that from their own government.

The focus is on the period 2007–2012, after which the OECD changed its generic methodology. We show how much the level and types of support have altered over that period and how unevenly they are spread across EU member countries. The chapter begins by describing the data sources. Results presented in tables and figures are then discussed, and the final section draws out implications and concludes.

2. Data

The OECD's PSE database has altered its methodology several times since it was first released more than two decades ago. The latest version, uploaded in July 2015 (OECD, 2015), not only has updated numbers to 2014 but also has altered past numbers back to 1986. The latest estimates are summarized in Table 1. They suggest EU wine producers benefitted from transfers from

Table 1. OECD Estimates of Direct Transfers[a] to Wine Producers and Their Nominal Rate of Direct Producer Protection,[b] European Union (EU-28), 1986–2014 (Annual Averages)

	1986–1992	1993–1999	2000–2006	2007–2013	2014
Transfers to producers (million euros per year)[a]	858	705	716	417	489
Of which, transfers due to market price support (million euros per year)	848	769	255	51	0
Nominal rate of direct protection (NRP, %)[b]	8.6	6.4	1.7	0.3	0.0

Notes: [a]The Organization for Economic Cooperation and Development's (OECD) single commodity transfers do not include such supports as subsidies to distill unwanted wine and to promote wine generically, grubbing-up premiums, price support from import tariffs, or any proportion of non-product-specific assistance to the agricultural sector and rural areas. [b]Based on OECD's estimate of nominal protection coefficient (NPC), where NRP = 100(NPC − 1). The NRP expresses the estimated direct transfer as a percentage of the gross value of wine production (net of assistance).
Source: OECD (2015).

consumers and taxpayers to the extent of about 800 million euros per year in the latter 1980s and the 1990s, but that this fell to less than 500 million euros per year in the past 10 years. Most of that was market price support prior to the policy reforms that began in the early 1990s, but these estimates suggest that has now disappeared, with producer returns being raised by just 0.3% during 2007–2013 and zero in 2014 (see the nominal rate of protection [NRP] row in Table 1), down from approximately 7% in the latter 1980s and 1990s. This recent estimate, however, is not consistent with the fact that tariffs still apply on the EU's wine imports from all countries without a free-trade or association agreement with the EU-28. Those tariffs would have some positive impact on the domestic price of wine in EU countries, but the OECD chooses not to try to measure that because of the heterogeneous nature of wines.

It is possible to amend the OECD's estimates using the data contained in its database plus data available from Eurostat. In the Appendix (Table A1), we focus on aggregated EU-27 wine production from 2007 to 2012 and domestic support given directly to the industry's producers. That table is built up following the OECD's PSE structure prior to its latest methodology revision, which categorizes payments as either "single commodity transfers" or group commodity transfers. To that we have added a pro rata fraction of "all commodity transfers," based on wine's share of agriculture's gross value of production,[1] and "other transfers to producers" that are specific to grape and wine production. At the top of that table, the value of production (at the farm gate, inclusive of transfers) is taken directly from the PSE tables and originates from the Eurostat Dissemination Database, formerly New Cronos database, the official EU data portal. The single farm payment scheme data for wine are from the European Commission (2013) because the OECD no longer itemizes those payments by commodity.[2]

The Appendix (Table A2) includes additional payments not specifically linked to the wine industry and specified by the OECD as "general services support estimates" (GSSEs), again for the EU-27 as a whole and for the period 2007–2012. These include some general payments from which the wine industry could benefit, so these are calculated as a pro rata fraction based on wine's share of agriculture's gross value of production within the EU-27 each year.

It might be argued that basing shares on gross production value in these two tables exaggerates the shares attributable to the wine industry because wine's share of total agricultural production exceeds considerably its share of total utilized agricultural land (e.g., 4.2% compared with 1.8% in 2012). For that reason, we also calculated how much lower the total support would be had we used the land share instead of the production value share to calculate that nondirect assistance. It turns out to be about one-ninth lower (see Table 2 notes).

Tables A3 and A4 in the Appendix are structured the same as Tables A1 and A2, but they decompose the EU-27 data into the various receiving member countries, but just for 2012 in the interests of space. The GSSE payments in the OECD data-base that are not commodity specific are allocated in Table A4 to each member country using (1) official (but not publicly available) EU data taken from the Clearance Audit Trail System database that includes both EU-funded and national payments by member states and

[1]For example all commodity transfer payments given to the agricultural sectors of EU countries in 2012 amounted to €18.7 billion, of which €11.6 billion was national payments (according to information provided by the OECD) and the remainder was EU-funded payments. We allocated that residual to member countries in proportion to their national payments. The types of support that amounted to more than 5% of that 2012 total are as follows: investments in agricultural holdings (25%), fuel tax rebates/subsidies (22%), less-favored area payments (16%), environmentally friendly production (10%), disaster payments (6%), and extensive management of land (6%).

[2]Note also that the EU's Farm Accountancy Data Network provides subsidy information on a per hectare basis, albeit just for their sample farms, at http://ec.europa.eu/agriculture/rica/database/database_en.cfm.

Table 2. Direct Plus Other Support to Wine Producers and Their Nominal Rate of Assistance,[a] European Union (EU-27), 2007–2012

	2007	2008	2009	2010	2011	2012[b,c]	2007–2012 Average
Total (direct + other) support (million euros)	2,225	2,488	2,495	2,189	2,364	2,285	2,341
Of which, direct support (million euros)	1,415	1,295	1,172	1,053	978	924	1,140
Nominal rate of total producer assistance[a] (NRA, %)	19.3	22.0	23.2	20.3	18.8	18.7	20.4
Total support per hectare of vines (€)	616	702	716	655	734	712	689
Total support per kiloliter of wine produced (€)	140	157	154	141	152	144	148

Notes: [a]NRA is total support as a percentage of gross value of wine production (net of assistance). The NRA is broader than the Organization for Economic Cooperation and Development's nominal rate of direct protection in Table 1, the latter referring just to price-support measures, whereas the NRA also includes the other transfers to producers that may not alter the price they receive for their output but are part of the total support shown in row 1 of this table (see Anderson *et al.*, 2008). [b]An assumption in Tables A2 and A4 (see Appendix) is that wine's share of some general services supports is proportional to the gross value of total agricultural production. If instead it is proportional to the share of vines in the total area of land used for agriculture, the numbers in the 2012 column other than for direct support would be one-tenth lower. [c]The tariffs in EU wine imports had a weighted average in 2011 of 5.8% when expressed in ad valorem terms (estimated from the latest Global Trade Analysis Project Version 8 database; see http://www.gtap.org). Had they raised the domestic producer price in 2012 by a full 5.8% (an upper bound; or by just 1% as a possible lower bound), the market price support in 2012 would have been not zero but 788 million euros (or 136 million euros), thereby raising total producer support by the same amount. The 2012 NRA would then be not 18.7% but 26.4% (or 20.0%), the support per hectare of vines would rise from 712 to 946 (or 754) euros, and support per kiloliter of wine produced would rise from 144 to 191 (or 152) euros.
Source: Authors' calculations based on Tables A1 and A2 (see Appendix).

(2) wine CMO financial execution data on the national support program (European Commission, 2013).

In all tables, support payments are expressed in millions of euros. The vine bearing area and wine production volumes are shown as well, allowing the calculation of support per hectare of vines and per liter of wine produced. Those summary estimates are depicted in Figures 1 and 2 just for 2012, and the key forms of support since 2007 are summarized in Figure 3.

Table 2 aggregates the data at the bottom of Tables A1 and A2 for the years 2007–2012. These can now be compared with the OECD's estimates of

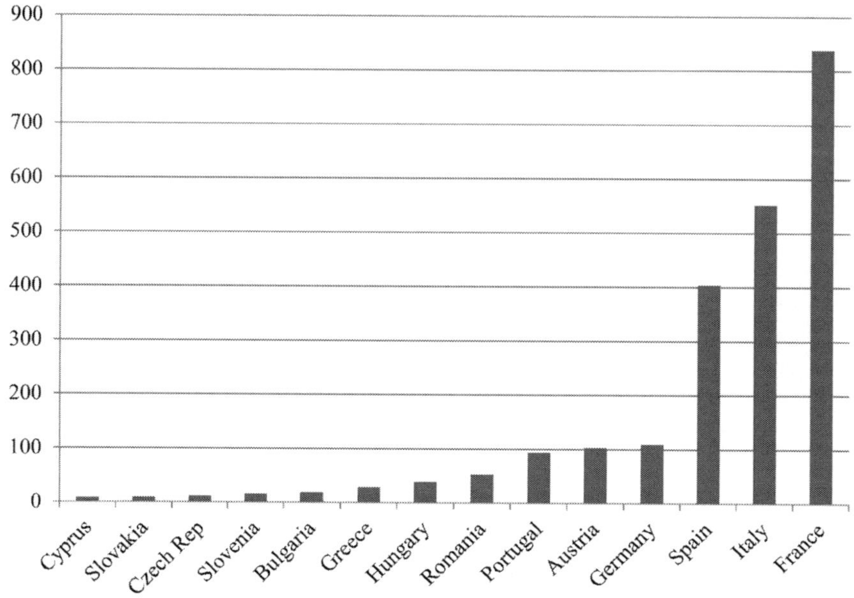

Figure 1. Total Support to Wine Producers, Individual European Union Member Countries in Million Euros, 2012

Source: Authors' calculations by summing final rows of Tables A3 and A4 (see Appendix).

transfers to producers, as summarized in Table 1. In Table 2 we report also what our estimates imply in terms of a nominal rate of assistance (NRA). The NRA is broader than the OECD's NRP in Table 1, the latter referring just to price-support measures, whereas the NRA also includes the other identified transfers to producers that may not alter the price they receive for their output (see Anderson *et al.*, 2008).

3. Results

The comparison of Tables 1 and 2 suggests that the OECD estimates, at least since 2007, understate considerably the full extent of government support to the EU wine industry. In contrast to the OECD's estimate of an average transfer of less than 500 million euros per year during 2007–2012, our Table 2 suggests the number is more than 2,300 million euros per year — and it has not been declining (see also Figure 3a). This implies that gross returns are about one-fifth above what they would be without those supports (an average NRA for the 2007–2012 period of 20.4%). That annual assistance amounts to approximately 700 euros per hectare of vines, or 0.15 euros per liter of wine produced in the EU as measured at the winery gate (Table 2 and Figure 2).

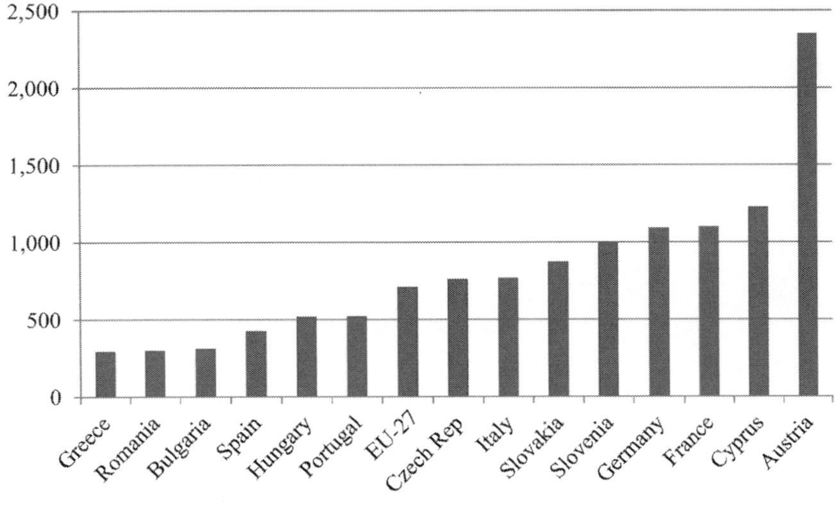

(a) Euros per hectare of vines

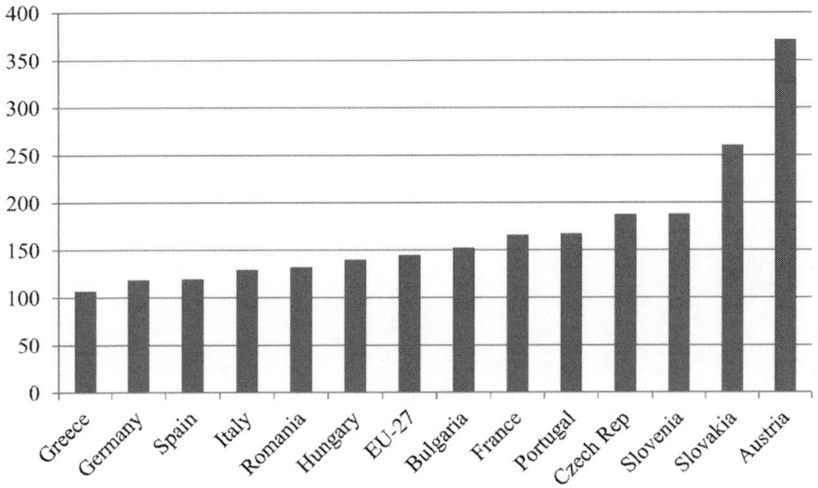

(b) Euros per kiloliter of wine produced

Figure 2. Total Support to Wine Producers Per Hectare and Per Kiloliter of Wine, Individual European Union Member Countries, 2012

Source: Authors' calculations by summing final rows of Tables A3 and A4 (see Appendix).

Even these new estimates probably understate the transfers to producers. One reason the numbers in Table 2 are likely to be understated is because the effect of tariffs on imports of non-EU wine in raising producer prices is not included. An upper bound on the extent to which tariffs raised the domestic producer price in 2012 is 5.8%, which is the import-weighted average tariff

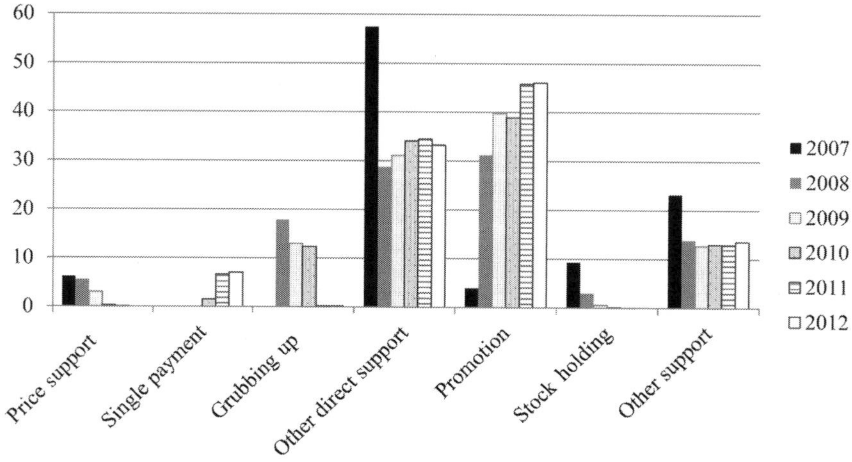

(a) European Union (EU-27) in Total, 2007–2012

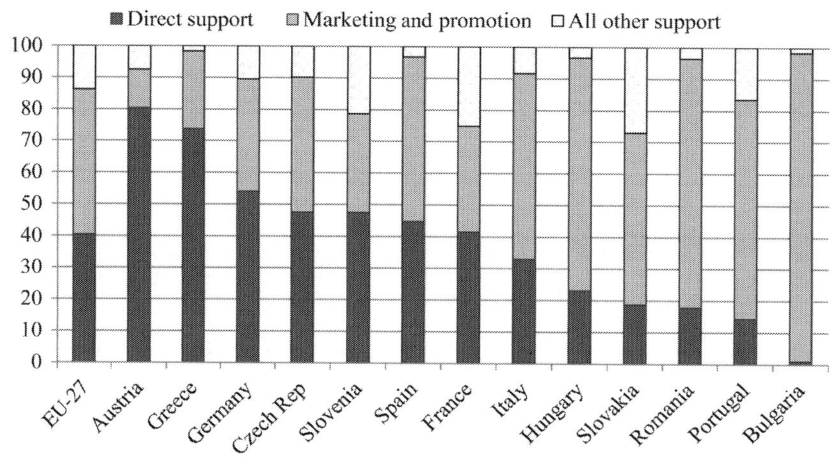

(b) By European Union member country, 2012

Figure 3. Shares of European Union Wine Producer Supports by Measure, 2007–2012 (%)
Source: Authors' calculations from Tables A1–A4 (see Appendix).

that year when converted to ad valorem terms. A lower bound might be one-sixth of that (bearing in mind that the EU accounts for a large share of the global wine market and thus is hardly a price taker). As reported in Table 2 notes, the 2012 NRA would then be not 18.7% but 26.4% (or 20.0%), the estimated support per hectare of vines would rise from 712 to 946 (or 754) euros, and the support per kiloliter of wine produced would rise from 144 to 191 (or 152) euros.

However, the numbers in Table 2 assume wine's shares of general services supports are proportional to the gross value of total agricultural production. Had we assumed they are proportional to the share of vines in the total area of land used for agriculture, the numbers in the 2012 column of that table, apart from direct support, would be one-tenth lower. This may more or less than offset the effect of omitting tariff protection.

It might also be argued that payments for grubbing up vines should be omitted because they are unrelated to current production and are reducing the future EU (and hence global) supply of wine. However, because this chapter is trying to estimate not price distortions but financial support to the industry, their inclusion is appropriate.

In addition to an overview estimate of the size of payments given to the wine sector in the EU-27 as a whole there is also an interest in the allocation of payments between EU member countries. In the Appendix (Tables A3 and A4), estimates of the individual payments by country are given for the year 2012 for all of the EU-27's wine-producing countries. These are summarized in Figures 1 and 2. Of course, France, Italy, and Spain get the lion's share of total payments, being by far the largest wine producers (Figure 1). However, per hectare support ranges from 300 euros in Greece to 2,350 euros in Austria (Figure 2a), and support per liter of wine produced ranges from 0.11 euros in Greece to 0.37 euros in Austria (Figure 2b).

By far the largest — and still growing — category of support is for marketing and generic promotion of EU wines. It accounts for about two-fifths of the estimated total in aggregate (Figure 3a). Direct price supports were most important in 2007, but since then they have been eclipsed by other direct supports and support for marketing and promotion. Although grubbing-up support was nontrivial during the 2008–2010 reform period, those payments are no longer being made. In 2012, direct supports were relatively more important to the Czech Republic, Germany, Slovenia, and Spain, whereas marketing and promotion supports were relatively more important to Bulgaria and Romania (Figure 3b).

4. Implications and Conclusion

According to our new estimates, government support for European wine producers continued unabated between 2007 and 2012, albeit in changing forms. The support per hectare of vineyard in 2011 and 212 exceeded 700 euros in the EU in aggregate and more than 1,000 euros in Austria, Cyprus,

France, and Germany. That almost certainly exceeds the support provided by governments in any other major wine-producing country. It is equivalent to an average of 0.15 euros per liter of wine produced and more than 0.25 euros in Cyprus (at 1.02 euros, not shown in Figure 2b), Austria, and Slovakia.

Generic promotion accounted for a growing share of total EU support, amounting in 2012 to 0.009 euros per liter of wine produced. By contrast, Australia's expenditure per liter on generic promotion that year was half that amount (Anderson and Aryal, 2015). The EU provided a total of 522 million euros for wine promotion during 2008/2009–2012/2013 (Table A2), and, despite the uncovering of many mis-appropriations, that expenditure is to be more than doubled to 1,156 million euros for the period 2013/2014–2017/2018 (European Court of Auditors, 2014). Given that this promotion item (an average annual 231 million euros) is but one-tenth of the total support to the EU industry in 2012, it is little wonder that other wine-producing countries worry about their ability to compete in international markets against supported EU producers. True, vineyard planting restrictions may have reduced the extent to which the previously mentioned financial supports add to EU wine output and exports (Deconinck and Swinnen, 2015), but they are being relaxed. The empirical impact of past area restrictions and their recent relaxation is a topic worthy of further research.

Acknowledgments

The authors are grateful for very helpful comments from two referees and for funding support from the University of Adelaide and the University of Copenhagen. The views expressed are the authors' alone.

References

Anderson, K., and Aryal, N.R. (2015). *Growth and Cycles in Australia's Wine Industry: A Statistical Compendium, 1843 to 2013*. Adelaide, South Australia, Australia: University of Adelaide Press.

Anderson, K., Kurzweil, M., Martin, W., Sandri, D., and Valenzuela, E. (2008). Measuring distortions to agricultural incentives revisited. *World Trade Review*, 7(4), 675–704.

Deconinck, K., and Swinnen, J. (2015). The economics of planting rights in wine production. *European Review of Agricultural Economics*, 42(3), 419–440.

European Commission (2006). *Communication from the Commission to the Council and the European Parliament: Towards a Sustainable European Wine Sector*. COM(2006) 319 and SEC(2006) 770. Brussels, Belgium: Commission of the European Communities.

European Commission (2013). *Wine CMO Financial Execution 2012.* Commission Regulation EC 555/2008. Brussels, Belgium: Commission of the European Communities. http://ec.europa.eu/agriculture/wine/reforms/index_en.htm. (accessed March 15, 2015).

European Court of Auditors (2014). *Is the EU Investment and Promotion Support to the Wine Sector Well Managed and Are Its Results on the Competitiveness of EU Wines Demonstrated?* Special Report No. 9. Luxembourg: Publications Office of the European Union.

Gaeta, D., and Corsinovi, P. (2014). *Economics, Governance, and Politics in the Wine Market: European Union Developments.* London: Palgrave Macmillan.

Meloni, G., and Swinnen, J. (2013). The political economy of European wine regulation. *Journal of Wine Economics*, 8(3), 244–284.

Organization for Economic Cooperation and Development (OECD) (2013). Producer and Consumer Support Estimates database. http://www.oecd.org/tad/agricultural-policies/producerandconsumersupportestimatesdatabase.htm#country. (accessed March 15, 2015).

Organization for Economic Cooperation and Development (OECD) (2015). Producer and Consumer Support Estimates database. http://www.oecd.org/tad/agricultural-policies/producerandconsumersupportestimatesdatabase.htm#country. (accessed July 20, 2015).

Spahni, P. (1988). *The Common Wine Policy and Price Stabilization.* Aldershot, UK: Avebury.

Appendix

Table A1. Direct Supports for Wine Producers, European Union (EU-27), 2007–2012 (Million Euros)

	2007	2008	2009	2010	2011	2012
Value of production (at farm gate, inclusive of price support)	13,769	13,785	13,266	12,954	14,937	14,523
Single commodity transfers (SCTs)						
Market price support	136.9	137.0	74.7	5.5	2.2	0.0
National output payments for wine	1.2	0.4	0.1	0.0	0.0	0.0
Agri-monetary (labor insurance 35%) wine	−0.3	0.0	0.0	0.0	0.0	0.0
Restructuring and conversion of vineyards	447.8	−3.7	−5.2	−10.4	0.0	0.0
Vineyard restructuring national expenditures	17.9	4.7	2.2	3.3	3.1	4.0
Payments for wine in most remote regions	1.7	2.5	2.5	2.5	2.5	2.5
Area payments for wine national expenditures	0.0	0.0	0.8	0.8	0.8	0.7
Payments for integrated production of wine: Rural Development Regulation (RDR) expenditures	5.5	9.6	10.9	11.9	11.0	11.4
Payments for integrated production of wine: national expenditures	8.5	10.7	10.6	10.3	10.6	10.2
Vineyard improvement/restructuring national expenditures	7.0	0.3	0.3	0.3	0.1	0.1
Total SCT	626.1	161.6	96.9	24.3	30.4	29.1
Group commodity transfers (GCTs)						
Total GCT5 Investments in vineyards, national expenditures	6.2	6.9	25.9	14.3	5.5	9.9
All commodity transfers (ACTs)						
Wine's share of total ACT payments (based on gross value of production)	683.2	669.1	727.0	711.7	782.9	718.9

Other transfers to producers (OTPs)						
Single payment scheme	0.0	0.0	0.0	33.4	156.6	159.9
Permanent abandonment premiums in respect of areas under vine	97.7	12.9	0.0	0.1	0.0	0.0
Grubbing-up scheme (following wine reform of 2007/2008)	0.0	444.1	322.7	269.2	4.8	4.9
Other	1.9	0.2	0.0	0.2	−2.7	1.0
Total OTP	99.6	457.1	322.7	302.8	158.8	165.7
Total direct support (SCT + GCT + ACT + OTP)	1,415.2	1,294.8	1,172.4	1,053.0	977.5	923.6
Total EU-27 vineyard area (1,000 ha)	3,609	3,545	3,487	3,342	3,219	3,209
Total EU-27 wine production (billion liters)	15.91	15.81	16.22	15.48	15.57	15.90
Direct support per hectare of vines (€)	392	365	336	315	304	288
Direct support per thousand liters of wine produced (€)	89	82	72	68	63	58

Sources: Authors' calculations building on producer support estimates by Organization for Economic Cooperation and Development (2013) and single farm payments from European Commission (2013).

Table A2. Other Supports for Wine Producers, European Union (EU-27), 2007–2012 (Million Euros)

	2007	2008	2009	2010	2011	2012
General services support estimate						
H. Research and development						
Wine's share of total payments (based on gross value of production)	85.4	85.9	91.3	77.9	84.7	125.2
I. Agricultural schools						
Wine's share of total payments (based on gross value of production)	55.5	49.7	52.5	59.0	63.8	93.8
J. Inspection services						
Wine's share of total payments (based on gross value of production)	26.8	29.0	31.1	27.8	22.5	13.9
K. Infrastructure						
Wine's share of total payments (based on gross value of production)	182.0	154.9	138.2	115.8	130.8	75.7
L. Marketing and promotion						
Aid for the use of must	164.2	21.5	1.7	0.6	0.0	0.0
National support programs for the wine sector (EC 479/2008 EU funded)						
Promotion	0.0	35.2	87.2	111.7	142.5	145.4
Restructuring and conversion	0.0	263.8	368.6	406.4	585.1	594.3
Ongoing plans N 1493/1999	0.0	62.4	31.9	19.5	6.3	4.8
Green harvesting	0.0	0.1	16.8	24.6	7.6	0.8
Harvest insurance	0.0	2.0	38.3	31.2	36.9	42.2
Investments	0.0	18.6	74.3	74.4	141.3	209.6
By-product distillation	0.0	85.5	95.9	85.5	92.0	49.1

Portable alcohol distillation	0.0	145.1	165.5	15.9	11.8	0.0
Crisis distillation	0.0	50.0	19.2	10.6	−0.6	0.0
Concentrated grape must	0.0	84.6	78.8	62.4	46.8	0.3
Marketing aid to producer groups in most-remote regions (processing of Madeira wine)	0.5	0.5	0.4	0.0	0.0	0.0
Marketing aid to producer groups in most-remote regions (marketing of Madeira wine)	0.4	1.4	1.2	0.0	0.0	0.0
Marketing aid to producer groups in most-remote regions (quality wine)	2.2	2.4	2.8	2.9	2.9	0
Wine's share of total payments (based on gross value of production)	84.1	24.7	10.2	5.7	10.0	6.0
M. Public stock holding						
Intervention for products of the wine-growing sector	73.8	34.2	0.2	0.3	0.0	0.0
Buying-in of alcohol from compulsory distillation	128.3	36.6	12.1	1.6	0.1	0.0
Wine's share of total payments (based on gross value of production)	4.6	3.3	3.2	0.6	0.5	0.1
N. Miscellaneous						
Wine's share of total payments (based on gross value of production)	1.9	2.1	1.5	1.8	1.7	0.2
Total other support	809.6	1,193.5	1,322.8	1,136.1	1,386.8	1,361.4
Total EU-27 vineyard area (1,000 ha)	3,609	3,545	3,487	3,342	3,219	3,209
Total EU-27 wine production (billion liters)	15.91	15.81	16.22	15.48	15.57	15.90
Other support per hectare of vines (€)	224	337	379	340	431	424
Other support per thousand liters of wine produced (€)	51	75	82	73	89	86

Sources: Authors' calculations building on producer support estimates by Organization for Economic Cooperation and Development (2013).

Table A3. Direct Supports for Wine Producers, European Union (EU-27), by Country, 2012 (Million Euros)

EU-27 wine year 2012	EU-27	Bulgaria	Czech Republic	Germany	Greece	Spain	France	Italy	Cyprus	Hungary	Austria	Portugal	Romania	Slovenia	Slovakia
Value of production	14,523	38	31	1,189	29	1,699	8,064	2,101	5	106	524	372	202	99	43
Single commodity transfers (SCTs)															
Market price support	0.0	0	0	0	0	0	0	0	0	0	0	0	0	0	0
National output payments for wine	0.0	0	0	0	0	0	0	0	0	0	0	0	0	0	0
Agri-monetary (labor insurance 35%)	0.0	0	0	0	0	0	0	0	0	0	0	0	0	0	0
Restructuring/conversion of vineyards	0.0	0	0	0	0	0	0	0	0	0	0	0	0	0	0
Vineyard restructuring national expenditures	4.0	0.0	0.0	0.0	0.0	0.0	0.0	0.0	0.0	0.0	0.0	0.0	3.9	0.0	0.0
Vineyard restructuring	0.0	0.0	0.0	0.0	0.0	0.0	0.0	0.0	0.0	0.0	0.0	0.0	0.0	0.0	0.0
Payments for wine in remote regions	2.5	0.0	0.0	0.0	2.5	0.0	0.0	0.0	0.0	0.0	0.0	0.0	0.0	0.0	0.0
Area payments for wine national expenditures	0.7	0.0	0.0	0.0	0.0	0.0	0.0	0.0	0.0	0.0	0.0	0.0	0.0	0.0	0.0
Payments for integrated production of wine: RDR expenditures	11.4	0.0	1.5	0.0	0.0	0.0	0.0	0.0	2.0	0.0	7.2	0.0	0.0	0.7	0.0

Payments for integrated production of wine: national expenditures	10.2	0.0	1.4	0.0	0.0	0.0	0.0	0.0	1.8	0.0	6.4	0.0	0.0	0.7	0.0
Vineyard improvement/restructuring national expenditures	0.1	0.0	0.0	0.0	0.1	0.0	0.0	0.0	0.0	0.0	0.0	0.0	0.0	0.0	0.0
Total SCT	29.1	0.0	2.9	0.0	2.6	0.0	0.0	0.0	3.7	0.0	13.6	0.0	3.9	1.4	0.0
Group commodity transfers (GCTs)	0.0	0.0	0.0	0.0	0.0	0.0	0.0	0.0	0.0	0.0	0.0	0.0	0.0	0.0	0.0
GCT5 Investments in vineyards, national expenditures	9.9	0.0	2.0	0.0	0.0	2.1	0.0	0.0	0.0	5.8	0.0	0.0	0.0	0.0	0.0
Total GCT	9.9	0.0	2.0	0.0	0.0	2.1	0.0	0.0	0.0	5.8	0.0	0.0	0.0	0.0	0.0
All commodity transfers (ACTs)	0.0	0.0	0.0	0.0	0.0	0.0	0.0	0.0	0.0	0.0	0.0	0.0	0.0	0.0	0.0
Wines share of total ACT payments	718.9	0.2	0.9	59.0	3.0	32.7	348.2	180.4	0.3	3.2	60.6	13.4	5.5	6.2	1.8
Total ACT	718.9	0.2	0.9	59.0	3.0	32.7	348.2	180.4	0.3	3.2	60.6	13.4	5.5	6.2	1.8
Other transfers to producers (OTPs)															
Single payment scheme	159.9	0.0	0.0	0.0	16.0	142.7	0.0	0.0	0.0	0.0	0.0	0.0	0.0	0.0	0.0

(*Continued*)

Table A3. (*Continued*)

EU-27 wine year 2012	EU-27	Bulgaria	Czech Republic	Germany	Greece	Spain	France	Italy	Cyprus	Hungary	Austria	Portugal	Romania	Slovenia	Slovakia
Permanent abandonment premiums	0.0	0.0	0.0	0.0	0.0	0.0	0.0	0.0	0.0	0.0	0.0	0.0	0.0	0.0	0.0
Grubbing-up scheme	4.9	0.0	0.0	0.0	0.0	3.0	0.1	1.7	0.0	0.0	0.0	0.0	0.0	0.0	0.0
Other	1.0	0.0	0.0	0.0	0.0	0.0	0.1	0.1	0.0	0.0	0.1	0.1	0.0	0.1	0.0
Total OTP	165.7	0.0	0.0	0.0	16.0	145.8	0.2	1.8	0.0	0.0	0.1	0.1	0.0	0.1	0.0
Total direct support (SCT + GCT + ACT + OTP)	923.6	0.2	5.8	59.1	21.7	180.6	348.4	182.1	4.0	9.1	74.3	13.5	9.5	7.6	1.8
Vineyard area (1,000 ha)	3,209	60	16	100	99	943	761	718	7	76	44	180	177	16	11
Total wine production (billion liters)	15.90	0.12	0.07	0.92	0.28	3.37	5.08	4.27	0.01	0.28	0.28	0.56	0.41	0.09	0.04
Direct support per hectare of vines (€)	288	3	367	594	218	192	458	254	600	120	1,704	75	54	466	172
Direct support per thousand liters of wine (€)	59	2	89	64	79	54	69	43	473	32	267	24	23	89	49

Sources: Authors' calculations building on producer support estimates by Organization for Economic Cooperation and Development (2013) and single farm payments from European Commission (2013).

Table A4. Other Supports for Wine Producers, European Union 27 (EU-27), by Country, 2012 (Million Euros)

EU-27 wine year 2012	EU-27	Bulgaria	Czech Republic	Germany	Greece	Spain	France	Italy	Cyprus	Hungary	Austria	Portugal	Romania	Slovenia	Slovakia
H. Research and development															
Wine's share of total payments	125.2	0.0	0.3	1.1	0.1	0.5	103.6	17.9	0.0	0.1	0.3	0.1	0.1	0.9	0.2
I. Agricultural schools															
Wine's share of total payments	93.8	0.0	0.1	0.4	0.0	0.9	83.6	1.8	0.0	0.3	4.5	1.3	0.4	0.2	0.1
J. Inspection services															
Wine's share of total payments	13.9	0.0	0.0	1.5	0.0	0.1	7.9	1.9	0.0	0.4	0.0	0.3	0.0	0.8	1.0
K. Infrastructure															
Wine's share of total payments	75.7	0.2	0.7	8.1	0.4	11.2	13.2	22.1	0.0	0.5	1.4	13.6	1.4	1.4	1.5
L. Marketing and promotion															
National support programs for the wine sector (EC 479/2008 EU funded)															
Promotion	145.4	0.0	0.0	1.2	3.3	38.3	17.1	73.6	0.0	0.0	1.2	9.2	0.7	0.8	0.1
Restructuring and conversion	594.3	17.7	3.2	16.9	3.9	163.7	108.5	154.4	3.7	22.6	2.2	50.9	41.2	4.2	1.3

(Continued)

Table A4. (*Continued*)

EU-27 wine year 2012	EU-27	Bulgaria	Czech Republic	Germany	Greece	Spain	France	Italy	Cyprus	Hungary	Austria	Portugal	Romania	Slovenia	Slovakia
Ongoing plans N 1493/1999	4.8	0.0	0.0	0.0	0.0	0.1	1.7	0.0	0.0	0.0	0.2	0.0	0.0	0.0	2.8
Green harvesting	0.8	0.0	0.0	0.0	0.0	0.0	0.0	0.8	0.0	0.0	0.0	0.0	0.0	0.0	0.0
Harvest insurance	42.2	0.6	0.0	1.5	0.0	0.0	0.0	35.1	0.2	0.0	0.0	4.3	0.2	0.0	0.3
Investments	209.6	0.0	2.0	19.2	0.0	0.0	118.4	55.2	0.8	5.7	7.6	0.0	0.0	0.0	0.7
By-product distillation	49.1	0.0	0.0	0.0	0.0	7.8	34.7	5.2	0.0	0.8	0.0	0.7	0.0	0.0	0.0
Portable alcohol distillation	0.0	0.0	0.0	0.0	0.0	0.0	0.0	0.0	0.0	0.0	0.0	0.0	0.0	0.0	0.0
Crisis distillation	0.0	0.0	0.0	0.0	0.0	0.0	0.0	0.0	0.0	0.0	0.0	0.0	0.0	0.0	0.0
Concentrated grape must	0.3	0.0	0.0	0.0	0.0	0.0	0.0	0.3	0.0	0.0	0.0	0.0	0.0	0.0	0.0
Wine's share of total payments	6.0	0.0	0.0	0.1	0.0	0.6	1.8	2.5	0.0	0.0	0.7	0.2	0.0	0.0	0.0
M. Public stock holding															

Wine's share of total payments	0.1	0.0	0.0	0.0	0.0	0.0	0.0	0.1	0.0	0.0	0.0	0.0	0.0	0.0	0.0
N. Miscellaneous															
Wine's share of total payments	0.2	0.0	0.0	0.2	0.0	0.0	0.0	0.0	0.0	0.0	0.0	0.0	0.0	0.0	0.0
Total other support	1,361.4	18.6	6.4	50.2	7.7	223.1	490.4	370.7	4.6	30.4	29.1	80.5	44	8.4	7.8
Vineyard area (1,000 ha)	3,208	60	16	100	99	943	761	718	7	76	44	180	177	16	11
Total wine production (billion liters)	15.90	0.12	0.07	0.92	0.28	3.37	5.08	4.27	0.01	0.28	0.28	0.56	0.41	0.09	0.04
Other support per hectare of vine (€)	424	310	400	502	78	237	644	516	657	400	661	447	249	525	709
Other support per thousand liters of wine (€)	86	155	91	55	28	66	97	87	460	109	104	144	107	93	195

Sources: Authors' calculations building on producer support estimates by Organization for Economic Cooperation and Development (2013) and European Commission (2013).

Part 3

Wine Auctions

Chapter 9

The Buyer's Option in Multi-Unit Ascending Auctions: The Case of Wine Auctions at Drouot*

Philippe Février[†], William Roos[‡], and Michael Visser[§]

[†] *CREST, ENSAE, University of Paris-Saclay, France*
philippe.fevrier@ensae.fr
[‡] *Student at ENSAE, INSEE 18 Bd Adolphe Pinard, 75014 Paris, France*
william.roos@laposte.net
[§] *CREST, CNRS, ENSAE, University of Paris-Saclay and CRED, University of Paris, France*
michael.visser@ensae.fr

This chapter studies multi-unit ascending (English) auctions with a buyer's option. The buyer's option gives the winner of an auction the right to purchase any number of units at the winning price. We develop a theoretical model and derive the optimal strategies for the bidders. The model predicts various behavioral implications (e.g., the winner never exercises the option, the price declines...) that are tested using a unique dataset on wine auctions held at the Paris-based auction house Drouot. We also analyze why the buyer's option is used. Estimating the model in a structural econometric way, and using counterfactual comparisons, we find that the buyer's option does not affect the seller's revenue (relative to a system where the units are auctioned sequentially without the option). Drouot, however, saves a lot of time with the option and this effect represents a considerable amount of money. The time-saving effect seems thus to be the primary purpose of the buyer's option.

1. Introduction

Whenever several *fully identical* goods have to be sold, many auction houses use the following auction mechanism. The first unit of the good is auctioned. Once this first auction is over, the winner of the auction is given the

*This article originally appeared in *Journal of Economics & Management Strategy*, 14(4), (2005), 813–847.

possibility to exercise a so-called buyer's option. The buyer's option gives him the right to buy any number of units of the good he desires, the price per unit being the price established at the first auction.[1] In case the winner decides to purchase all units, the sale is over. If he decides to buy only part of the total quantity of goods on sale, a second auction is held for the remaining units. And this scheme repeats itself until all units are eventually sold. As an illustration, suppose there are initially 2 units of a particular good on sale, and let the first-auction price be p. The winning bidder then has the choice between buying just one unit (in which case he pays p to the seller) or both units (in which case he pays $2p$). If the winner does not exercise his option, another auction is organized for the second unit. It is important to note that the first-auction winner is allowed to participate and compete in this second auction.

The buyer's option is used in many auctions throughout the world. At the flower auction of Aalsmeer, the Netherlands, huge quantities of flowers and garden plants are auctioned each day. The products are sold via descending (or Dutch) auctions with a buyer's option (see van den Berg *et al.* 2001). Prestigious auction houses such as Christie's and Sotheby's in the UK and the United States (see Ashenfelter, 1989; Ginsburgh, 1998), and Drouot in France, systematically use the buyer's option in their ascending (or English) auctions of wine and champagne. Cassady (1967, pp. 154–156) gives historical examples of auctions where the buyer's option or variants of this mechanism have been practiced (fur auctions in Leningrad and London; fish auctions in English port markets).

The purpose of this chapter is to study, both theoretically and empirically, the buyer's option in ascending (or English) auctions. We consider an Independent Private Value (IPV) model where two identical units are sold to n risk-neutral buyers. It is assumed that the valuations attributed to the two units are either the same (flat demand), or that a buyer's valuation for the second unit is less than his valuation for the first unit (decreasing demand). This is exactly the framework studied by Black and De Meza (1992). Our analysis differs from Black and De Meza since we assume that the units are sold via English auctions (while they considered second-price (or Vickrey) auctions). We derive the optimal bidding strategies, and, comparing our results with those given in Black and De Meza, show that English and

[1]Another and related kind of option exists in the so-called "right to choose" auctions. In these oral ascending sequential auctions of a collection of heterogeneous objects, the winner of a round has the option to choose the object he wants among the objects that are so far unsold (Ashenfelter and Genesove, 1992; Gale and Hausch, 1994; Burguet, 1999).

second-price auctions with a buyer's option are not theoretically isomorphic (except when the number of bidders is $n = 2$). This can be explained by the fact that in an "oral" auction, such as the English auction, more information is released than in a "sealed-bid" auction, such as the second-price auction. We also derive the equilibrium bidding strategies under the assumption that the two units are auctioned sequentially without the buyer's option. The model has various behavioral implications. It predicts, for instance, that successive winning prices should be declining. It also predicts that the winner of the first auction, if the buyer's option is not exercised, cannot win the second auction. Finally, our model predicts that players should bid more aggressively in a one-unit auction than in a two-unit auction.

One of our empirical objectives is to test these predictions. We use data that we were collected during an important sale of fine wine held at Drouot, the largest auction house in Paris, in April 2000. As explained in the data section of the chapter, by being present in the auction room, we were able to register all sorts of information that is crucial for testing the theoretical predictions (such as the numbers of potential bidders in the room at different points in time, the winning bid price for each unit of wine sold at auction, and especially details on the use of the buyer's option). These auction-specific data are matched with information that was available in wine catalogues. The catalogues could be consulted by potential buyers prior to the auction and describe, for each wine on sale, its name, color, vintage, the production region (Bordeaux, Burgundy, Cotes du Rhone, etc.), the condition of the etiquette on the bottle (whether it was readable or not, whether it was numbered or not, etc.), the level of wine in the bottle, etc. We finally complemented this unique dataset by adding to the data, for each wine, the highly influential Parker's grade, and also a grade taken from a wine website. Using these data on wine auctions, we find that all theoretical predictions are verified.

Another empirical objective is to answer the following question: why does Drouot (and the other auction houses mentioned above) sell the goods with the buyer's option arrangement, and not via some other auction mechanism? What explains that the auction mechanism with a buyer's option is apparently preferred over a mechanism where all units are sold sequentially, that is, one after the other, via independent auctions? Or, alternatively, what explains that Drouot does not sell all available units simultaneously, in a single one-shot auction?

Several explanations have been given in the literature for the fact that the buyer's option arrangement is so popular among auctioneers. According to Ashenfelter (1989), auctioneers use the buyer's option as a device to conceal the declining price anomaly. This phenomenon is typically observed when identical objects are auctioned sequentially. Auctioneers are afraid that bidders find something fishy about the fact that identical objects do not fetch identical prices. By introducing a buyer's option, auctioneers render any possible price decline less transparent, and they can thereby limit the extent to which bidders become aware of the declining price anomaly. Cassady (1967) gives another explanation. He argues that an auction mechanism based on the buyer's option is more flexible than a one-shot auction, and that it is faster than a pure sequential auction. Indeed, an auction wherein all units are sold simultaneously is not flexible in the sense that it may not fit the "small" buyers. Small buyers are not much interested in the total quantity of units on sale, and might not want to participate in a one-shot auction. An auction procedure that includes a buyer's option, however, accommodates even the small buyers as they are allowed to purchase any number of units, provided, of course, that they manage to win an auction. On the other hand, a sequential auction can be very time-consuming, especially when the total number of units is large, and according to Cassady a motive for auctioneers to introduce a buyer's option is to accelerate the auction operations. The auctioneers with whom we spoke at Drouot appear to share this point of view. They find that sequential auctions tend to take too much time, and mentioned higher speed as the main reason for making a buyer's option available. A revenue argument is never invoked in this debate, that is, "higher expected earnings" is never explicitly mentioned as a motive for adopting a buyer's option. However, it is *a priori* not unreasonable to think that the buyer's option may have a direct revenue-enhancing effect. The decision to introduce a buyer's option may thus be motivated by revenue considerations.

In answering the above question, we first study whether the buyer's option has a revenue effect. To do this, we estimate our auction model in a structural econometric way. The fundamental parameters to be estimated are the distribution function of the private values for the wines and the parameter that determines the shape of the demand function. We estimate the parameters of the distribution function (conditionally on the wine characteristics) by the maximum likelihood method, and the shape parameter by the method of moments. The estimations allow us to determine which of these characteristics influence the willingness to pay for wine (the effects of wine regions, the condition of the label, the vintage, the Parker rating, the level of wine in the bottle, etc.) and to conclude that the demand function is decreasing. But the estimation results are especially used to evaluate the revenue effect of the buyer's option. We study the effect on the seller's income in switching from a system where units are sold sequentially with a buyer's option to a system whereby they are sold via a pure sequential auction without option. Using a counterfactual comparison based on simulations, we find that the seller's expected revenue in the pure sequential auction is not statistically different from the revenue in a mechanism with buyer's option.

The revenue effect being negligible, we next study to what extent a time-saving argument may explain the popularity of the buyer's option. Our data allow us to determine that Drouot saved 37% of its time thanks to the buyer's option. We show that this gain in time represents a huge amount of money. It thus seems that time saving, as argued by Cassady (1967) and the auctioneers at Drouot with whom we spoke, is the primary motivation for introducing the buyer's option.

The chapter proceeds as follows. The next section presents the theoretical model. Section 3 describes the wine auction data, Section 4 presents the estimation method, Section 5 presents the estimation results and the revenue comparison, and Section 6 concludes.

2. A Model for Two-Unit Ascending Auctions With and Without the Buyer's Option

The two-unit auctions with and without buyer's option are modeled as non-cooperative games. First we consider the model with the buyer's option. Two units of a good are sold to $n \geq 2$ buyers. The first unit is auctioned using an English auction (ascending auction). At the end of the first auction, the winner has the possibility to use a buyer's option, which allows him to purchase the second unit at the price of the first unit. If the winner uses this option, the game ends. If the winner does not use the option, the second unit is auctioned, again via an English auction. The first-auction winner is allowed to participate in this second auction.

Adopting the IPV framework, let vi represent the value that buyer i places on the first unit. The values $v_i, i = 1, \dots, n$, are independently drawn from a distribution $F(\cdot)$ on the support $[0, +\infty]$. The associated density is denoted $f(\cdot)$, and it is assumed that this density is strictly positive on the whole support, and that beyond some large value of the valuation the density $f(\cdot)$ is a decreasing function. As usual in the IPV paradigm, only player i knows the valuation v_i. The opponents of i only know that this valuation is drawn from the commonly known distribution $F(\cdot)$.

It is assumed that the value that i places on the second unit is kv_i, with $0 < k \leq 1$. The value of k is the same for all bidders, and this is common knowledge. Note that $0 < k < 1$ implies that the second unit is valued less than the first unit (decreasing demand), and $k = 1$ implies that both units are valued the same (flat demand).

Let p_1 and p_2 be the winning prices in, respectively, the first and second auction. If the buyer's option is exercised, we automatically have $p_2 = p_1$. The n players are supposed to be risk neutral. Thus, for a player with valuation v, the following outcomes are possible in the game: if he wins the first unit and uses the option, his utility is $(1 + k)v - 2p_1$; if he wins the first unit but does not exercise the option, he has utility $(1 + k)v - p_1 - p_2$ when he wins the second auction, and utility $v - p_1$ otherwise; if he loses the first auction but wins the second, his utility is $v - p_2$ (note that this outcome can only occur if the opponent who won the first auction does not use the buyer's option); finally, his utility equals 0 if he does not win any unit.

The above framework is identical to the one introduced by Black and De Meza (1992). There is one crucial difference, however, with their model and that is that we consider the case where each unit is sold via an English auction, and not, as in Black and De Meza, via a Vickrey auction (sealed-bid second price auction). For this reason, the Nash equilibrium strategy given in Proposition 1 differs from their optimal bidding strategy (Black and De Meza, 1992, Proposition 5, p. 613).

Proposition 1. *The following strategy forms a Bayesian Nash equilibrium of the game.*

1. *In the first auction,*
   - *As long as there are at least three active agents, each bidder i should bid up to his valuation v_i.*
   - *Once the $(n-2)$ "smallest" bidders have dropped out of the game, each of the two remaining players should bid according to the strategy $b^O(\cdot)$. The form of $b^O(v)$ depends on whether v is smaller or larger than $\frac{v_{(n-2)}}{k}$, with $v_{(n-2)}$, being the third largest valuation,*

$$b^O(v) = \begin{cases} c(v) & if\ v_{(n-2)} \leq v \leq \dfrac{v_{(n-2)}}{k}, \\ d(v) & if\ v \geq \dfrac{v_{(n-2)}}{k}. \end{cases}$$

The strategies $c(\cdot)$ *and* $d(\cdot)$ *are the solutions of the following differential equations:*

$$k(c(v) - v_{(n-2)})f(v) = (v - c(v))f(c(v)/k)c'(v) \quad \textit{if } v_{(n-2)} \leq v \leq \frac{v_{(n-2)}}{k},$$

$$k(d(v) - kv)f(v) = (v - d(v))f(d(v)/k)d'(v) \quad \textit{if } v \geq \frac{v_{(n-2)}}{k}.$$

2. *The strategy* $d(\cdot)$ *is the unique solution of the second differential equation defined on* $[\frac{v_{(n-2)}}{k}, +\infty]$, *and* $c(\cdot)$ *is the unique solution of the first differential equation that satisfies the conditions* $c(\frac{v_{(n-2)}}{k}) = d(\frac{v_{(n-2)}}{k})$ *and* $c(v_{(n-2)}) - v_{(n-2)}$.
3. *At equilibrium, the first-auction winner exercises the buyer's option iff* $kv > p_1$, *that is, iff his second valuation is above the first-auction winning price.*
4. *In the second auction, each bidder should bid up to his valuation. The first-auction winner (who has not exercised the buyer's option!) should thus participate until the price has reached the value he attributes to having a second unit, while all other bidders should continue until the price reaches their valuation for the first unit.*

Proof. See the Appendix. □

Next we study the pure sequential auction model. The framework described above remains exactly the same except that the 2 units are now always sold sequentially via two English auctions.

Proposition 2. *The following strategy forms a Bayesian Nash equilibrium of the game.*

1. *In the first auction,*
   - *As long as there are at least three active agents, each bidder* i *should bid up to his valuation* v_i.
   - *Once the* $(n-2)$ *"smallest" bidders have dropped out of the game, each of the two remaining players should bid according to the strategy,*

$$b^{\varnothing}(v) = \begin{cases} v_{(n-2)} & \textit{if } v_{(n-2)} \leq v \leq \dfrac{v_{(n-2)}}{k}, \\ kv & \textit{if } v \geq \dfrac{v_{(n-2)}}{k}. \end{cases}$$

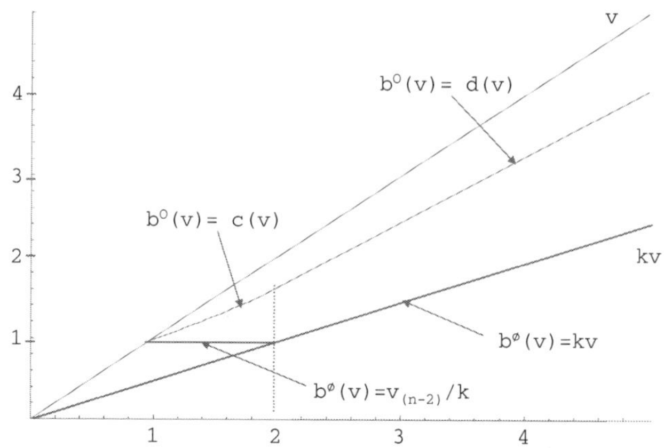

Figure 1. Equilibrium Functions $b^{\varnothing}(\cdot)$ and $b^{O}(\cdot)$.

2. *In the second auction, each bidder should bid up to his valuation. The first-auction winner should thus participate until the price has reached the value he attributes to having a second unit, while all other bidders should continue until the price reaches their valuation for the first unit.*

Proof. The proof is similar to the proof of Proposition 1. □

Figure 1 depicts the equilibrium functions $b^{\varnothing}(\cdot)$ and $b^{O}(\cdot)$ on $[v_{(n-2)}, +\infty]$, for the case where the private value is exponentially distributed with parameter 1, i.e., $F(v) = 1 - e^{-v}$ and $v_{(n-2)} = 1$ and $k = 0.5$.

In both models, players have a dominant strategy to play their valuation in the second auction, as in the standard (single unit) English auction. This result does not however, hold, in the first auction where bidders have an incentive to bid less than their valuation. The intuition for this bid shaving is the following. By bidding less than their valuation, players take the risk of losing the first auction. However, it also reduces the valuation of the highest bidder for the second unit, which decreases from $v(n)$ to $kv_{(n)}$, and this increases their expected gain in the second auction. Consider, for example, an auction without a buyer's option, just two players, and $k = 0$. In the auction for the first unit, players do not want to bid their valuation because by losing the first auction they are sure to win the second one at a price 0. They thus bid 0 in the first auction.

Players thus bid less than their valuation in the first auction and increase their bids in the second auction. As a consequence, the winner of the first auction should exercise his option whenever it is profitable to do so. If he, instead, waits for the second auction, he either loses the second auction or wins at a price above the first-auction price. This also means that the winner of the first auction, if he does not use his option, cannot win the second auction. This result is summarized in the following corollary.

Corollary 1. *In the model with buyer's option, the winner of the first auction, if he does not exercise his option, cannot be the winner of the second auction.*

A consequence of this corollary is that the buyer's option reduces players' incentive to bid less than their valuation. Players do not want the winner to exercise his option. Indeed, they bid less than their valuation in the hope to have a higher gain in the second auction. If there is no second auction because the winner of the first auction uses his option, they have no incentive to do so. At the end, with or without buyer's option, players bid less than their valuations, but bid more aggressively when the buyer's option is available. This is summarized in the next corollary, and is illustrated in Figure 1.

Corollary 2. *For every* $v \in [v_{(n-2)}, +\infty[, b^{\varnothing}(v) < b^{O}(v) < v$.

A comparison of the equilibrium strategies obtained by Black and De Meza (1992) and those given in our Propositions 1 and 2 shows that the English and second-price auctions are not theoretically isomorphic in a sequential auction. This follows from the fact that the English auction mechanism reveals more information about competitors than the second-price auction.[2] Indeed, contrary to the sealed-bid auction, bidders in the oral auction can learn at which prices their competitors drop out. They learn, in particular, at which price the person with the third highest valuation abandons the first auction, and, given the equilibrium strategy, they thereby know the valuation $v_{(n-2)}$ of the third largest bidder. The two strongest competitors use this information in updating their optimal bidding strategy. The only case where the English and second-price auctions are strategically equivalent is when there are just two bidders. That Black and De Meza's strategy and our strategy coincide in this case is quite intuitive because $n = 2$ implies $v_{(n-2)} = 0$.

Black and De Meza study the buyer's option to explain the declining price anomaly observed by Ashenfelter (1989) in sequential wine auctions. They find that in a sequential second price auction, the sequence of winning

[2]This fundamental difference between the two auction mechanisms also explains why in a common value model the optimal bidding strategies are no longer identical (see, for instance, Milgrom and Weber, 1982).

prices increases without a buyer's option, but decreases when the option is available. The same result is obtained for sequential English auctions.

Corollary 3. *Without a buyer's option, prices increase. The winning price in the second auction is greater than the winning price in the first auction.*

With a buyer's option, prices decrease. The winning price in both auctions is the same when the winner uses his option. If he does not, the winning price in the second auction is less than the winning price in the first auction.

In the model without a buyer's option, the winning price p_1 in the first auction is $\max(kv_{(n-1)}, v_{(n-2)})$. The winner is the player with the highest valuation and he pays the bid submitted by the agent with the second highest valuation. Who wins the second auction depends on the comparison between $kv_{(n)}$ and $v_{(n-1)}$. If the winner is the same as in the first auction, he pays a price $p_2 = v_{(n-1)}$, which is greater than p_1 because players bid more aggressively. If the winner is the player with the second highest valuation $v_{(n-1)}$, he pays a price $p_2 = \max(kv_{(n)}, v_{(n-2)})$, which is also greater than p_1.

In the model with buyer's option, the winning price p_i in the first auction is $b^O(v_{(n-1)})$. He uses his option if his valuation for the second unit is sufficiently high ($kv_{(n)} > p_1$). In this case, $p_2 = p_1$. He does not use his option if his valuation is too low ($kv_{(n)} < p_1$). In that case, the competition for the second unit is reduced. The player with valuation $v_{(n-1)}$ is sure to win the second unit at a price $p_2 = \max(kv_{(n)}, v_{(n-2)})$, which is smaller than p_1.

Let us now turn to the effect of the buyer's option on prices and revenue. As explained in Corollary 2, first-auction bidding is more aggressive when a buyer's option is available. The winning price for the first unit is therefore higher in the presence of the option. On the contrary, the winning price for the second unit is lower when a buyer's option is offered to players. If the buyer uses the option ($kv_{(n)} \geq b^O(v_{(n-1)})$), he obtains the second unit at a price $b^O(v_{(n-1)})$. This price is smaller than the price of the second unit without option ($\min(v_{(n-1)}, kv_{(n)})$). If the buyer does not use the option, the winning price is the same in both cases ($\max(kV_{(n)}, v_{(n-2)})$).

Corollary 4. *The buyer's option has a positive impact on the price of the first unit, but a negative impact on the price of the second unit.*

This result proves that the introduction of the buyer's effect has two opposite effects, a positive effect for the sale of the first unit and a negative effect for the sale of the second unit. Given the complicated form of the equilibrium strategies with buyer's option, it is hard to find a general theoretical result that compares the magnitude of both effects, and one should rely on the data to determine which is the best mechanism for the seller in terms of his expected revenue.

3. The Data

The data are based on auctions that were held at the Paris-based auction house Drouot. The wine auctions took place in the afternoon of 20 April (from 14:15 P.M. to 16:45 P.M), and in the morning of 21 April (from 11:15 A.M. to 12:30 A.M.), and were headed by the same auctioneer. The auctioneers of Drouot organize wine auctions on almost every working day of the year. The two sale days were chosen arbitrarily by us, so that *a priori* there is no reason to think that the auction results are in some way specific or nonrepresentative.

Auctions at Drouot are open to the public and anyone who wishes to attend them can do so. Two authors of this paper were present in the auction room of Drouot during the sales of April 20 and 21. They recorded all relevant information released during the auctions (number of bidders, winning prices, identity of the winners, use of the buyer's option, etc.). We added to these auction-specific data the information published in the wine catalogue of the sales. The catalogue could be consulted prior to the sales and record the precise characteristics of each wine on sale. We finally complemented the data set by adding for each wine two indicators for quality. One indicator is the grade assigned by the highly influential wine connoisseur Robert Parker, and the other is taken from a wine website.

The next three subsections describe these three different sorts of information in our dataset. The fourth subsection describes the link between the theoretical model and the real-life auctions as they were held at Drouot.

3.1. *Auction-specific information*

During the two sale days different sorts and kinds of wine were auctioned. The notion of "unit" that we have used so far in this chapter can vary from wine to wine. In our data there is, for instance, a unit of wine consisting of a crate of 12 bottles of *Château Latour 1985*, a unit that is made up of six bottles of *Château Lafite Rothschild 1890*, a unit made up of a single bottle of *La Romanée Conti 1976*, etc. In the sequel, a "lot" of wine designates a group of strictly identical units of wine. In our data the lot of *Château Latour 1985* has 3 units (three identical crates of 12 bottles), the lot of *Château Lafite Rothschild 1890* consists of 4 units (4 units of six bottles), and the lot of *La Romanée Conti 1976* only has 1 unit (of one bottle).

Table 1. Number of Units Per Lot

Number of units	Number of lots
1	152
2	31
3	21
4	8
5	1
6	3
7	2
8	2
9	2
10	1
11	1
12	1

During the two sale days a total of 225 lots of wine were sold. The 225 lots were made up of 413 units, thus the average number of units per lot is 1.8. Table 1 gives the empirical distribution of the number of units per lot.

Thus 152 lots of wine were made up of just 1 unit, 31 lots had 2 units, 21 lots had 3 units, and so forth.

The lots were sold one after the other using ascending oral auctions. After announcing the number of units in a lot,[3] the auctioneer started the auction for the first unit at a low starting price. As in practically all ascending auctions, a bidder in the auction room could indicate that he wished to bid above the current price by raising his hand. The increments by which successive prices jumped were most of the time chosen by the auctioneer himself, but occasionally by a bidder (he could do this by simultaneously raising his hand and shouting out the new price). In any case, the winner was the bidder who was the last to remain active, and the winning price was the price established at the moment he raised his hand for the last time. The auctioneer asked the winner how many units he desired to purchase (the price per unit being the winning price). If he bought all units in the lot, the auctioneer immediately went on with the sale of the next lot; if the winner purchased only part of the lot, a second ascending auction was organized for the remaining units, and this sequence was repeated until all units in the lot were auctioned. For each lot sold in this way we recorded the identity of the

[3]Each time a lot consisted of more than 1 unit, the auctioneer emphasized that the winner could exercise a buyers option (At Drouot, the buyer's option is called *faculté de réunion*).

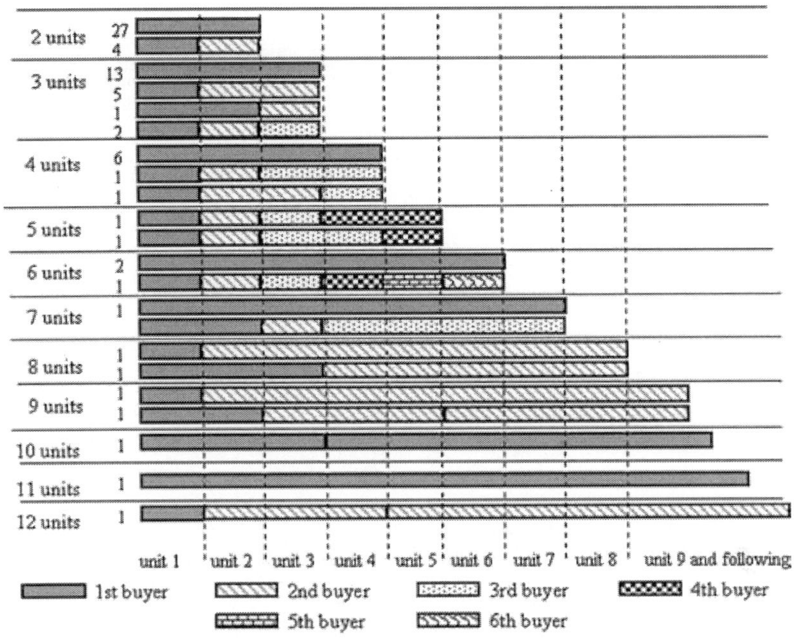

Figure 2. On the Use of the Buyer's Option

winner of each auction and the number of units purchased by the winner. This information is synthesized in Figure 2.

There is a lot of variation in the outcomes of the sales of lots. For instance, 13 lots of 3 units were sold in one shot, whereas two of such lots were each sold to three different buyers. Similarly, 2 lots of 6 units were sold in a single shot, and 1 lot was sold to six different buyers! For the 31 lots that were made up of 2 units, 27 were sold via a single auction (i.e., the first-auction winner exercised his buyer's option in these cases), and 4 were sold via two auctions (the winner did not use the option). Note that a small and thick vertical line in the bars indicates a separation of auctions. For instance, in the lot of 10 units, the first buyer bought 3 units in the first auction, and then bought all the remaining 7 units in the second auction.

The figure also shows that winners often use the buyer's option. More precisely, when the option is available (i.e., if there are at least 2 units on sale), the winner exercises it in 72% of the cases. Furthermore, when the option is exercised, the winner often takes all the remaining units in the lot (90% of the cases).

Figure 2 also allows us to test directly the theoretical prediction stated in Corollary 1. We see that in all of the four cases where two-unit lots are

Table 2. Winning Price Per Lot (in FFr)

Mean	1,322
Std. dev.	2,956
Max	30,833
75% quantile	1,200
50% quantile	500
25% quantile	217
Min	29

sold in two shots, the first- and second-auction winners are different persons. This result is in line with Corollary 1: the first-auction winner who does not exercise his buyer's option never wins the second auction.[4] Note that this result is not necessarily true for the lots made up of more than two units. However, we do not know what the theory predicts in such cases.

For each lot we also recorded the successive winning prices. To make the winning prices in different lots comparable, we normalized each price to the price of a single bottle containing 75 cl. For instance, if a unit of 12 bottles (containing 75 cl each) is sold at price p, the normalized price of that unit is $p/12$. Table 2 gives statistics on the winning prices for all lots. If there is more than one winning price per lot, then we calculate an average of the winning prices for that lot (weighted by the number of units sold at each auction).[5] The statistics are therefore based on 225 observations. As the table indicates, the average winning price is quite high (more than FFr1300), and there is substantial heterogeneity in the winning prices, since they vary from slightly less than FFr30 to more than FFr30,000 per bottle of 75 cl.

Table 3 gives some statistics concerning the price patterns in our data. In this table, p_i represents the price in the ith auction.[6] The results clearly indicate that the sequence of prices is declining, a finding in line with other empirical studies (Ashenfelter, 1989; Ginsburgh, 1998; van den Berg *et al.*, 2001). As predicted by Corollary 3, the winning price of the second auction is always lower than the winning price of the first auction.

[4]Given Corollary 1, one may wonder whether a first-auction winner should even participate at all in the second auction. At the auctions that took place at Drouot, all first-auction winners remained in the room during the second auction.

[5]For instance, if a two-unit lot is sold via two auctions with winning prices p_1 and p_2, the average winning price for that lot is simply $\frac{p_1+p_2}{2}$.

[6]Thus the mean of $p_1 - p_2$ is calculated using all multiple-unit lots where the units are sold in at least two shots; similarly, the mean of $p_2 - p_3$ is calculated using all lots with more than 2 units, that are sold in at least three shots.

Table 3. Evolution of the Winning Prices

	Mean	Min	Max
$p_1 - p_2$	65.9	0	250
$p_2 - p_3$	14.8	−8.3	50
$p_3 - p_4$	20.8	0	41.7

Table 4. Number of Persons in the Auction Room

Time	Lots auctioned	Number of persons
20 April		
14:15–14:30	1–23	65
14:30–14:45	24–45	65
14:45–15:00	46–53	70
15:00–15:15	54–65	80
15:15–15:30	66–75	80
15:30–15:45	75–86	75
15:45–16:00	87–105	60
16:00–16:15	106–118	70
16:15–16:30	119–123	60
16:30–16:45	124–136	50
21 April		
11:15–11:30	137–145	45
11:30–11:45	146–176	50
11:45–12:00	177–185	65
12:00–12:15	186–207	65
12:15-12:30	208–225	55

Another explanation for the declining price phenomenon is risk aversion (McAfee and Vincent, 1993). The bidders may be willing to pay premia to secure purchase in the first auction because there may be none left in the subsequent auctions if the winner exercises his option. In our theoretical model, we assume that bidders are risk-neutral. We will discuss the implication of this restriction when commenting the empirical results (Section 5).

A final source of auction-specific information comes from the fact that we counted, every 15 minutes, the number of persons in the auction room. In counting the number of individuals we did not include the auctioneer, those who assisted him, or ourselves. Table 4 summarizes this information. Thus on April 20 at 14:15 PM., that is when the sale started, 65 persons were present in the auction room; 15 minutes later, when we counted again, there were still 65 persons in the room; at 14:45 PM there were 70 participants, and so on. Note that the number of participants over time follows the same pattern during both auction days: at the start of both sale days the number of participants is relatively low, this number then increases to reach its peak at about halfway the sale day, and then decreases until the end of the sale. Table 4 also indicates which lots were sold during which time interval. Thus, on April 20 between 14:15 PM and 14:30 PM the lots 1 to 23 were sold, between 14:30 PM and 14:45 PM the lots 24 to 45, and so on.

The number of persons in the room may not reflect exactly the number of bidders (as defined in the theoretical model). Given that more than 200 lots were sold during the two auction days, it is likely that not all persons in the room are in contention for each lot. If this is the case, the numbers given in Table 4 constitute an upper bound for the real number of bidders. For this reason, we will report empirical results not only for values of n close to those reported in Table 4, but also for much smaller values (down to 5).

3.2. *Data from the wine catalogue*

The wine catalogue[7] could be consulted by potential buyers before and during the auctions. It records all kinds of information about the wines on sale. For each lot auctioned, the catalogue lists the number of units, the number of bottles of wine per unit (1 bottle, 6 bottles, 12 bottles, etc.), the type of bottle (a standard size bottle of 75 cl., or a magnum bottle of 150 cl.), and a number of other variables that characterize the wine in the lot. Table 5 gives these wine characteristics together with some descriptive statistics.

All variables except "Age of wine" are 0–1 indicator variables. The variable "Authentic wooden crate" equals 1 if the wine is sold in an authentic wooden crate and 0 otherwise; the variable "Label damaged" equals 1 if the label on the bottle is in some way damaged, and 0 otherwise; "Level wine low" is equal to 1 if the level of wine in the bottle is low (this may indicate that the cave where the wine has been kept and stored was too dry and too hot), and 0 otherwise; the variable "Wine reconditioned" is 1 if the wine had at some point in time (while still at the chateau or domain) been uncorked and refilled with the original wine, and 0 otherwise; finally, the four region variables indicate from which wine-producing region the wine originates (Bordeaux, Burgundy, Champagne, or Côtes du Rhone).

[7]Published by Millon & Associés, the auctioneer in charge of the April 20–21 sales. A copy of the catalogue can be obtained from the authors.

Table 5. Wine Characteristics

Variables	Mean	Std. Dev.
Age of wine (in years)	27.09	21.04
Authentic wooden crate	0.19	0.39
Label damaged	0.13	0.34
Level wine low	0.08	0.27
Wine reconditioned	0.13	0.34
Wine region:		
Bordeaux	0.65	0.48
Burgundy	0.05	0.22
Champagne	0.22	0.41
Côtes du Rhône	0.08	0.27

Note: The variable "Age of wine" is missing for one observation; descriptive statistics are therefore based on 224 observations.

3.3. *Two quality indicators*

Because the wine characteristics described in the previous subsection may perhaps not capture all the quality differences between the wines in our sample, we added two additional quality indicators to our dataset. One is taken from Parker's guide (1995). Each wine in the guide is ranked between one star (lowest possible rank) and five stars (highest rank). This grading system reflects the overall and the long-term quality of each wine and does not depend on the vintage. Precisely because the Parker ranking does not take into account the specific vintage effects, we also added a grade reflecting the quality of the vintage. This vintage grade is taken from the French wine website http://www.vindelice.com. This site grades wines according to their vintage, their production region and their color (e.g., it attributes a grade to red Burgundy 1989, or to white Bordeaux 1950, etc.). The site ranks wines as "To avoid," "Average," "Good," "Very good," or "Exceptional." Table 6 lists the frequencies of the values taken by the Parker grade and the vintage grade.

The majority of lots are made up of top-quality wines: 121 lots consist of wines with five Parker stars; for 21 lots of wine the vintage grade is "Excellent" and for 110 lots it is "Very good."

3.4. *The link between theory and practice*

From the description of the sales at Drouot, it is clear that our theoretical framework differs in several ways from practice. This subsection comments on these differences.

Table 6. Parker Grade and Vintage Grade

		Parker Grade			
	Unknown	**	***	****	*****
Number of lots	16	4	52	32	121
		Vintage Grade			
	To avoid	Average	Good	Very good	Excellent
Number of lots	11	11	72	110	21

The first difference is that the model described in Section 2 is a model for lots made up of 2 units. As Table 1 indicates, our data not only contain two-unit lots, but also single-unit lots and lots with more than 2 units. The optimal bidding strategy for the English auction of a single unit being well known, our method of statistical inference will also use the one-unit lots to estimate the parameters of interest of our model. However, we will not use the remaining observations in the sample; that is, the observations corresponding to lots with more than 2 units. The reason is that we do not know the optimal bidding strategies in a model where more than 2 units are auctioned. Discarding these observations from the estimation sample does not, however, bias our estimates if the process that determines the number of units per lot is independent of bidders' valuations. To support this hypothesis, we estimate a probit of a "multiple-unit lot" dummy (equal to 1 if the lot has more than 1 unit, 0 otherwise) on wine characteristics. The results are reported in Table 7.

Except for the authentic wooden crate, no variable is significantly different from 0. The probit estimation seems to support the claim that there are no clear observable differences between multiple-unit lots and single-unit lots.

A second difference is that the model treats the sale of a lot as a completely isolated event. The model does not take into account that sales of other lots take place almost simultaneously and that a given bidder might be interested in buying several of these lots. However, at Drouot such interdependencies might well have existed. Most bidders stayed in the auction room not just for the sale of one particular lot, but for several different lots. It is plausible that some of such bidders were interested in more than one lot at the same time and that their bidding strategies reflected these synergies. It does not appear easy to extend our model to take into account

Table 7. Estimation of a Probit of a "Multiple-unit Lot" Dummy

Variables	Est.	T-stat.
Constant	−0.76	−1.33
Age of wine	−0.004	−0.45
Authentic wooden crate	1.61	4.98++
Label damaged	0.44	1.30
Wine reconditioned	0.13	0.28
Wine region		
Bordeaux	−0.21	−0.56
Burgundy	−0.23	−0.43
Côtes du Rhone	−0.66	−1.08
Parker grade		
Unknown	0.30	0.72
** or ***	−0.43	−1.19
****	−0.31	−0.82
Vintage grade		
Average or good	0.58	1.59
Very good	0.34	1.00

Notes: ++significant at 5%. Reference variables are Champagne, Parker grade = **, ***, and ****, Vintage grade = Excellent.

these possible interactions between auctions of different lots. Furthermore, given our data, it would certainly be impossible to identify and estimate such an extended model. We will therefore ignore the (hopefully small) effects of interdependency. We thus assume that there are no interactions whatsoever between the auctions of the different lots, so that the sales of the different lots constitute independent observations.

A third difference is that in our model it has implicitly been assumed that bidders know at each moment the precise number of active competitors, and the prices at which each opponent drops out of the game. They are in particular assumed to know when and at which price the third strongest bidder quits the first auction. In contrast, the bidders in the auction room of Drouot had less information at their disposal. Basically, all they learned during the course of the auction was the sequence of successive prices proposed by the auctioneer and, for each of these prices, the identity of the bidder who raised his hand (see Section 3.1).

4. The Estimation Method

We now turn to the structural estimation of our theoretical model. The estimation method we propose is a two-step estimation method. In the first step, we use the data on the single-unit lots to estimate the distribution function of private values by maximum likelihood. In the second step, we use the data on the two-unit lots to estimate the shape parameter of the demand function, k, by using the method of moments.

4.1. *The first step: Estimation of the distribution of private values*

We use the data on the one-unit lots to estimate the distribution function of private values. To capture the between-lot heterogeneity of wines, we introduce the vector of variables z characterizing the wine sold in the lot. Thus z contains all variables that appear in Tables 5 and 6. We adopt a parametric framework. Let us denote the parametric density and distribution functions of the valuation v given z by, respectively, $f(v|z;\theta)$ and $F(v|z;\theta)$, with θ an unknown parameter that has to be estimated. Let n be the number of bidders at the moment the lot is auctioned (see Table 4 and its discussion), and let p be the (normalized) price at which the single unit in the lot is sold. Let $f_{(n-1),(n)}(v_{(n-1)}, v_{(n)}|z;\theta)$ be the joint density of the second largest and largest evaluation conditional on z in a sample of size n (see Mood *et al.*, 1982),

$$\begin{aligned}f_{(n-1),(n)}&(v_{(n-1)}, v_{(n)}|z;\theta)\\ &= n(n-1)F^{n-2}(v_{(n-1)}|z;\theta)f(v_{(n-1)}|z;\theta)f(v_{(n)}|z;\theta)1\{v_{(n-1)} \leq v_{(n)}\}.\end{aligned}$$

It is well known (see, e.g., the survey of Klemperer, 1999) that in an English auction for a single good the optimal strategy is for all agents to bid up to their private value. The contribution to the likelihood function of a single-unit lot sold at the price p (when there are n bidders and the characteristics of the wine are z) is therefore the probability of the event that the second largest evaluation equals p and the largest evaluation exceeds p,

$$\begin{aligned}h(p,n,z;\theta) &\equiv \int_p^\infty f_{(n-1),(n)}(p, v_{(n)}|z;\theta)dv_{(n)}\\ &= n(n-1)f(p|z;\theta)F^{n-2}(p|z;\theta)(1-F(p|z;\theta)). \qquad (1)\end{aligned}$$

This corresponds, of course, to the contribution to the likelihood function of a standard IPV single-good-English-auction observation (see, e.g., Paarsch, 1997). Note that in writing the contribution to the likelihood (1), it is implicitly assumed that the n evaluations are independent drawings from the density $f(\cdot|z;\theta)$, and not from some truncated density of v. It is thus assumed that potentially all types of bidders could have been present in the bidding room, and not just the bidders with an evaluation above some truncation point.[8]

The likelihood function consists of the product of all likelihood contributions corresponding to the single-unit lots,

$$\prod_{l=1}^{L_1} h(p_l, n, z_l; \theta), \tag{2}$$

where L_1 is the number of single-unit lots in the sample, and p_l and z_l are the price and wine characteristics in the auction of lot l. The maximum likelihood estimate is obtained by maximizing this likelihood function over θ.

4.2. *The second step: Estimation of k*

Now that we have an estimator for the distribution function parameter θ, we need to propose an estimator for the shape parameter k. The idea is to define the probability of exercising the buyer's option using the equilibrium strategy given in Proposition 1. This probability depends, among other things, on θ and k. Replacing θ by the first-step estimate $\hat{\theta}$, the parameter k can be estimated by the method of moments using the data from the two-unit lots.[9]

Let us now define the moment estimator for k. From Section 2, we know that the winner uses his option if and only if $kv_{(n)} > b^O(v_{(n-1)}, v_{(n-2)})$. Using the definition of $f_{(n-2),(n-1),(n)}(v_{(n-2)}, v_{(n-1)}, v_n|z; 0)$, the joint density of the third largest evaluation, the second largest evaluation, and the largest evaluation, conditional on z, in a sample of size n (see Mood *et al.*, 1982)

$$\begin{aligned} &f_{(n-2),(n-1),(n)}(v_{(n-2)}, v_{(n-1)}, v_{(n)}|z; \theta) \\ &\quad = n(n-1)(n-2)F(v_{(v-2)}|z; \theta)^{(n-3)} f(v_{(n-2)}|z; \theta) \\ &\qquad \times f(v_{(n-1)}|z; \theta) f(v_{(n)}|z; \theta) 1\{v_{(n-2)} \leq v_{(n-1)} \leq v_{(n)}\}, \end{aligned}$$

[8] For instance, had the auctioneer published, *ex ante*, a binding reservation price for a unit of wine, it would have been appropriate to assume that only bidders with an evaluation above the reservation price are in the bidding room, in which case the evaluations are drawings from the truncated distribution of v (truncated at the reservation price).

[9] An alternative way to estimate k is to write the likelihood function of the two-unit lots and maximize this likelihood with respect to k. However, when doing so, we have a "boundary" problem that potentially affects the properties of the maximum likelihood estimator. The reason is that the support of the endogenous observed variables depends on the model parameters (see Donald and Paarsch, 1993). Because this problem is difficult to handle, we opt for the method of moments.

we obtain the probability that the winner exercises his option,

$$\begin{aligned}
&\Pr(\text{option used}|n, z; k, \theta) \\
&= n(n-1)(n-2)\int_0^{+\infty}\int_0^{v_{(n-1)}}\left(1 - F\left(\frac{b^O(v_{(n-1)}, v_{n-2})}{k}\middle| z;\theta\right)\right) \\
&\quad \times F^{n-3}(v_{(n-2)}|z;\theta)f(v_{(n-2)}|z;\theta)f(v_{(n-1)}|z;\theta)dv_{(n-1)}dv_{(n-2)}. \qquad (3)
\end{aligned}$$

Replacing, in the above probability, θ by the first-step estimate $\hat{\theta}$, a method of moments estimator $\hat{k}$ is the value of k that minimizes

$$\left[\frac{1}{L_2}\sum_{l=1}^{L_2}[\Pr(\text{option used}|n, z_l; k, \hat{\theta}) - 1\{\text{option used in lot } l\}]\right]^2, \qquad (4)$$

where L_2 is the number of two-unit lots in the sample. This estimator for k is consistent and is normally distributed asymptotically.[10]

5. Results

We first have to select a parametric form for the distribution function of the valuations. We will estimate various distribution functions and select the one that fits best. In this selection test, we only use the data for the one-unit lots where we know players bid their valuation. Furthermore, we do not consider the observed variations in z. Given a distribution function $F(\cdot|\theta)$ and a particular value for n, and using obvious notation, we maximize the likelihood $\prod_{l=1}^{L_1} h(p_l, n; \theta)$ to obtain an estimation $\hat{\theta}$. Table 8 reports the results of the estimations for $n = 5, 10, 20, 60$, and four different distribution functions: a normal distribution $N(\mu, \sigma^2)$, a lognormal distribution $f(v) = \frac{1}{v\sigma\sqrt{2\pi}}e^{\frac{(ln(v)-\mu)^2}{2\sigma^2}}$, a Weibull distribution function $f(v) = \frac{\alpha}{\beta^\alpha}v^{\alpha-1}e^{-\frac{v^\alpha}{\beta^\alpha}}$, and a gamma distribution function $f(v) = \frac{1}{\beta^\alpha\Gamma(\alpha)}v^{\alpha-1}e^{-\frac{v}{\beta}}$.

One can construct, using the estimated distribution function $F(.|\hat{\theta})$, an estimation for the distribution function of the second highest valuation among n players, $G(.|n;\hat{\theta})$. We now select, using a Kolmogorov test, the distribution that is the closest to the empirical distribution function of the

[10]When estimating the variance of $\hat{k}$ we will neglect the fact that θ was estimated in the first step.

Table 8. Estimation of Different Parametric Specifications

Distribution Function	Parameters	$n = 5$	$n = 10$	$n = 30$	$n = 60$
Normal	μ	−183.12	−1,651.07	−3,951.50	−5,410.17
	σ^2	2,291.97	2,595.28	3,028.33	3,280.07
Lognormal	μ	5.18	3.74	1.26	−0.42
	σ	2.03	2.43	3.04	3.41
Weibull	α	0.45	0.33	0.23	0.19
	β	375.13	81.19	4.28	0.50
Gamma	α	0.26	0.12	0.04	0.02
	β	3,628.00	3,628.00	3,557.21	3,596.57

observed winning bids

$$\hat{G}(p) \equiv \frac{1}{L_1} \sum_{l=1}^{L_1} 1\{p_l < p\}.$$

More precisely, we calculate the statistic $\sqrt{L_1}D \equiv \sup_p |\hat{G}(p) - G(p|n;\hat{\theta})|$. The results are given in Table 9.

Under the null hypothesis that $G(p) = G(p|n;\theta)$, there is a probability of 95% (resp. 99%) for $\sqrt{L_1}D$ to be less than 1.358 (resp. 1.628).[11] The lognormal distribution is the only distribution for which the null hypothesis is accepted, although admittedly only for large values of n. We will thus assume that the private values are drawn from a lognormal distribution function. We assume that the conditional mean is $E(v|z) = (1, z')\beta$ and the conditional variance is $\text{Var}(v|z) = \sigma^2$, where β and σ are unknown parameters. The complete vector of parameters describing the distribution function is thus $\theta = (\beta', \sigma)'$.

We maximize the likelihood (2) with respect to θ for different values of n. Given the estimation of θ, we estimate k in a second step by minimizing (4) over k. The integral and the function $b^O(\cdot,\cdot)$ appearing in the moment condition are approximated numerically.[12] The results are reported

[11] It is also possible to test if the sample comes from a distribution $G(.|n;\theta)$. This requires use of a Kolmogorov test corrected for the fact that the parameters in the parametric distributions are estimated by maximum likelihood (see D' Agostino and Stephens, 1984).

[12] We calculate the integral by simulation. First, for every lot l, we randomly generate 300 values $(v_{(n-1)}, v_{(n-2)})$ using the distribution $(n-1)(n-2)F^{n-3}(v_{(n-2)}|z_l;\hat{\theta})f(v_{(n-2)}|z_l;\hat{\theta})$ $f(v_{(n-1)}|z_l;\hat{\theta})$. We then approximate the integral by $\sum_{s=1}^{300} n(1 - F(\frac{b^O(v^s_{(n-1)}, v^s_{n-2})}{k}|z;\theta))$. In this expression, the function $b^O(v^s_{(n-1)}, v^s_{(n-2)})$ is itself approximated. Using the

Table 9. Kolmogorov Test

Distribution function	$n = 5$	$n = 10$	$n = 30$	$n = 60$
Normal	2.97	2.93	2.86	2.83
Lognormal	1.76	1.70	1.62	1.59
Weibull	1.91	1.87	1.79	1.74
Gamma	2.56	2.17	2.18	2.18

in Table 10. Most parameters are significant and take the expected sign. The results are very robust to changes in the number of bidders. The value bidders attribute to wine increases with its age and if the bottles are sold in an authentic wooden crate. When the label on the bottle is damaged, the willingness to pay for the wine is reduced. Wine experts tend to say, however, that a damaged label is an indicator of good quality. Our result suggests that consumers neglect this and prefer the label to be in good shape. As expected, the value of wine decreases when the level in the bottle is low and increases when the wine has been reconditioned. Burgundy wines are valued the most, followed by Côtes du Rhône, Bordeaux, and Champagne. The Parker and vintage parameters are ranked as expected. The parameter k varies between 0.82 and 0.87 and is always significantly smaller than 1. This suggest that the bidders in our sample had decreasing demand for wine.

To evaluate the effect of the buyer's option on the revenue of the seller we simulated, for each of the 31 two-unit lots in our sample, the revenue under both the pure sequential auction (using the equilibrium strategy in Proposition (2) and the auction with a buyer's option (using the equilibrium strategy in Proposition (1). We simulated 100 times and calculated for each lot the simulated revenues over the 100 observations. The results are described in Table 11.

In conformity with theory (Corollary 3), the revenue appears greater for the second unit than for the first unit in the absence of the buyer's

results and the notations of the appendix, we approximate $b^O(v^s_{(n-1)}, v^s_{(n-2)})$ by $\frac{d^A(v^s_{(n-1)})+d_A(v^s_{(n-1)})}{2}$ over $[v^s_{(n-2)}/k, A]$. $A = 100,000$ is chosen sufficiently large such that $|d^A(v^s_{(n-1)}) - d_A(v^s_{(n-1)})| < 0.001$ for all simulated values $(v^s_{(n-1)}, v^s_{(n-2)})$.$d^A(.)$ and $d^A(.)$ are calculated numerically as the solutions of the first differential equation in Proposition 1 that satisfy, respectively, $d_A(A) = kA$ and $d^A(A) = A$. Finally, $b^O(v^s_{(n-1)}, v^s_{(n-2)})$ is approximated over $[v^s_{(n-2)}, v^s_{(n-2)}/k]$ by $c(.)$ where $c(.)$ is numerically calculated as the solution of the second differential equation in Proposition 1 that satisfies $c(v^s_{(n-2)}/k) = \frac{d^A(v^s_{(n-2)}/k)+d_A(v^s_{(n-2)}/k)}{2}$.

Table 10. Estimation of the Parameters θ and k

	$n = 5$ Est. (T-Stat)	$n = 10$ Est. (T-Stat)	$n = 30$ Est. (T-Stat)	$n = 60$ Est. (T-Stat)
Mean of valuation (β)				
Constant	5.76 (29.5^{++})	5.15 (25.91^{++})	4.10 (18.67^{++})	3.39 (14.00^{++})
Age of wine	0.01 (4.98^{++})	0.01 (4.89^{++})	0.01 (4.78^{++})	0.01 (4.74^{++})
Authentic wooden crate	0.40 (2.20^{++})	0.41 (2.27^{++})	0.42 (2.36^{++})	0.42 (2.40^{++})
Label damaged	−0.24 (−1.67^{+})	−0.21 (−1.50)	−0.19 (−1.31)	−0.18 (−1.24)
Level wine low	−0.24 (−1.62^{+})	−0.22 (−1.52)	−0.20 (−1.37)	−0.19 (−1.31)
Wine reconditioned	0.95 (5.20^{++})	0.98 (5.33^{++})	1.02 (5.48^{++})	1.04 (5.52^{++})
Wine region Bordeaux	0.28 (2.16^{++})	0.27 (2.10^{++})	0.26 (2.03^{++})	0.26 (2.00^{++})
Burgundy	1.01 (5.13^{++})	1.00 (5.13^{++})	0.98 (5.13^{++})	0.98 (5.15^{++})
Côtes du Rhône	0.79 (3.91^{++})	0.81 (4.02^{++})	0.82 (4.15^{++})	0.83 (4.21^{++})
Parker grade				
Unknown	−1.95 (−11.31^{++})	−1.98 (−11.48^{++})	−2.01 (−11.70^{++})	−2.03 (−11.86^{++})
** or ***	−1.15 (−8.87^{++})	−1.12 (−8.80^{++})	−1.09 (−8.71^{++})	−1.08 (−8.68^{++})
****	−0.94 (−6.53^{++})	−0.92 (−6.47^{++})	−0.90 (−6.40^{++})	−0.88 (−6.36^{++})
Vintage grade				
Average or good	−0.40 (−3.46^{++})	−0.38 (−3.28^{++})	−0.35 (−3.07^{++})	−0.34 (−2.98^{++})
Very good	−0.19 (−1.70+)	−0.16 (−1.53)	−0.14 (−1.35)	−0.13 (−1.26)
Variance of valuation (σ)	0.83 (16.42^{++})	1.00 (16.36^{++})	1.25 (16.28^{++})	1.40 (16.23^{++})
k	0.82 (13.67^{++})	0.84 (14.00^{++})	0.87 (14.50^{++})	0.87 (14.50^{++})

Notes: $^{++}$significant at 5%; $^{+}$significant at 10%. Reference variables are Champagne, Parker grade = **, ***, and ****, Vintage grade = Excellent.

option, whereas the opposite holds when the option is available. Also in line with theory (Corollary 4), the revenue obtained from the first (resp. second) unit is lower (resp. higher) in the pure sequential auction than in the auction format with a buyer's option. Note that the total revenues are very similar in the two auction formats. Revenue is slightly higher (except for $n = 30$) with the buyer's option, but the difference is not significant (except for $n = 5$): the two opposite effects of the buyer's option appear to compensate each other, so that the total impact of the option on revenue is negligible.

As mentioned previously, we assume in the theoretical model that bidders are risk-neutral. The question that arises is whether our results strongly depend on this assumption. We have reasons to believe that they are quite robust. Indeed, since the estimation of θ uses only one-unit lots, the estimate of θ would not be different in an extended model with risk aversion (players

Table 11. Revenue Simulations

	$n = 5$ Est. (Std. Err)	$n = 10$ Est. (Std. Err)	$n = 30$ Est. (Std. Err)	$n = 60$ Est. (Std. Err)
Without option				
First unit	15,419 (27)	15,041 (26)	13,814 (22)	14,239 (25)
Second unit	17,672 (27)	16,794 (26)	15,190 (22)	15,650 (25)
Both units	33,091 (56)	31,836 (55)	29,004 (46)	29,889 (52)
With option				
First unit	16,766 (29)	16,047 (28)	14,493 (23)	15,024 (27)
Second unit	16,586 (28)	15,936 (28)	14,457 (23)	14,937 (26)
Both units	33,351 (56)	31,983 (56)	28,950 (46)	29,962 (53)

have a dominant strategy to bid their valuation regardless of whether they are risk-averse or not). Our estimate of k may, however, be biased when the underlying true model is a model with risk aversion. Intuition suggests that in two-unit lots, risk-averse bidders should bid more aggressively than risk-neutral bidders. Because bidders often use the buyer's option in our data, we may therefore have underestimated the true value of k. To check if the revenue comparisons reported in Table 11 are sensitive to the introduction of risk aversion, we have therefore performed the above simulations for values of k (above the estimate $\hat{k}$). As it turns out, our previous conclusions remain unchanged.

The results reported in Table 11 suggest that the buyer's option has no impact on the revenue of the seller. Another reason why Drouot may have opted for the auction format with a buyer's option is to accelerate the sales and thereby save time. Our data allow us to calculate the amount of time Drouot has saved thanks to this mechanism. During the two sale days, Drouot sold 413 units via 263 separate auctions. Had the option not been available, the 413 units would have been sold in 413 separate auctions (see Figure 2). The sales lasted 3 hours and 45 minutes (see Table 4); had the auctions been carried out without buyer's option, the sales would have lasted an estimated 5 hours and 41 minutes. Therefore, through the use of the buyer's option, Drouot appears to have saved almost two hours (37% of time savings). The revenue generated during the two days was 225 lots $\times$ $FFr1,322 = FFr297,450$ (see Table 2). Given the time savings of two hours, the use of the buyer's option amounts to a gain of *FFr*160,000. We do not know how much commission Drouot makes from its wine sales. Assuming a commission of 10% (resp. 20%), the gain in time can be evaluated at *FFr*16,000 (resp. *FFr*32,000). This amount of extra income for Drouot is huge compared to the impact of the buyer's option on the revenue that we estimated previously. These simple calculations lead us to us think that the primary reason the auction house use the buyer's option is to accelerate sales and increase the volumes they trade.

6. Conclusions

This chapter has studied bidding behavior in multi-unit ascending auctions with a buyer's option. We have presented a theoretical model for two-unit English auctions. The two units are sold sequentially. Equilibrium strategies have been derived for the case where the buyer's option is available and also when it is not. The model predicts various behavioral implications that have been tested using a rich dataset on wine auctions. All predictions are empirically verified. The model has also been estimated using structural econometric techniques. The analysis in this chapter suggests that the buyer's option has no impact on the revenue of the seller. However, the buyer's option helps the auction house to save time that can be used to conduct additional auctions. This effect generates significant revenues and can be seen as an *ex post* justification for the fact that so many auction houses use the buyer's option.

Appendix: Proof of Proposition 1

Strategy in the second auction

The fourth claim in the proposition follows immediately from the standard dominated-strategies argument: in the second auction, players have a dominant strategy that consists in bidding until their valuation.

Strategy for the buyer's option

The proof of the third claim is also immediate. Given the equilibrium strategies, players bid more aggressively in the second auction than in the first auction ($c(v) \leq v; d(v) < v$). The winner in the first auction must thus use his option whenever this decision implies a direct gain, that is, if his second valuation is higher than the first-auction equilibrium price.

Strategy in the first auction

Let us now turn to the proof of the first claim.

The "Final" stage

Consider first the "final" stage of the first auction, that is the game once there are only two bidders left. We suppose, for the moment, that the players have not deviated from the optimal strategy *before* the final stage. We thus suppose that the $(n-2)$ smallest bidders have stopped bidding once the price reached their valuation, and that the two remaining bidders have valuations above $v_{(n-2)}$.

Suppose the ascending auction has reached the price p. Let $G(0,p)$ denote the expected total gain (gain in first plus second auction) for a player with valuation v who decides to withdraw at p. His opponent thus wins the first unit at the price p. The form of $G(0,p)$ depends on whether p is smaller or larger than $b^O(v_{(n-2)}/k)$,

$$\begin{aligned}G(0,p) &= \int_{(b^O)^{-1}(p)}^{p/k} (v - \max(v_{(n-2)}, kw))\frac{f(w)dw}{1-F((b^O)^{-1}(p))}\\ &= \int_{(b^O)^{-1}(p)}^{v_{(n-2)}/k} (v - v_{(n-2)})\frac{f(w)dw}{1-F((b^O)^{-1}(p))}\\ &\quad + \int_{v_{(n-2)}/k}^{p/k} (v - kw)\frac{f(w)dw}{1-F((b^O)^{-1}(p))} \quad \text{if } (b^O)^{-1}(p) \le v_{(n-2)}/k\end{aligned}$$

and

$$G(0,p) = \int_{(b^O)^{-1}(p)}^{p/k} (v - kw)\frac{f(w)dw}{1-F((b^O)^{-1}(p))} \quad \text{if } (b^O)^{-1}(p) \ge v_{n-2}/k.$$

The expression for $G(0,p)$ can be explained as follows. Clearly, the first-auction loser (who decided to drop out at p) can only win something in the game if there is a second auction. A second auction takes place only if the first-auction winner does not exercise his option; that is, if his valuation is smaller than p/k (note that the winner's valuation is necessarily above $(b^O)^{-1}(p)$). The first-auction loser then automatically wins the second auction at the price equal to the maximum of $v_{(n-2)}$ and k times the valuation of the winner. Note that the density in the above integrals is the conditional density of the valuation given that the valuation is larger than $(b^O)^{-1}(p)$.

Let us now again assume that the ascending auction has reached p, and let $G(\varepsilon,p)$ now be the expected total gain if the player with valuation v decides that he will stop participating once the auction has reached

$p+\varepsilon$ (whereas $G(0,p)$ denotes the expected gain when he decides to stop *immediately*),

$$\begin{aligned}G(\varepsilon,p) = &\int_{(b^O)^{-1}(p)}^{(b^O)^{-1}(p+\varepsilon)} (v-b^O(w))\frac{f(w)dw}{1-F((b^O)^{-1}(p))}\\ &+\int_{(b^O)^{-1}(p+\varepsilon)}^{v_{(n-2)}/k} (v-v_{(n-2)})\frac{f(w)dw}{1-F((b^O)^{-1}(p))}\\ &+\int_{v_{(n-2)}/k}^{(p+\varepsilon)/k} (v-kw)\frac{f(w)dw}{1-F((b^O)^{-1}(p))}\\ &\qquad \text{if } (b^O)^{-1}(p+\varepsilon)\le v_{(n-2)}/k\end{aligned}$$

and

$$\begin{aligned}G(\varepsilon,p) = &\int_{(b^O)^{-1}(p)}^{(b^O)^{-1}(p+\varepsilon)} (v-b^O(w))\frac{f(w)dw}{1-F((b^O)^{-1}(p))}\\ &+\int_{(b^O)^{-1}(p+\varepsilon)}^{(p+\varepsilon)/k} (v-kw)\frac{f(w)dw}{1-F((b^O)^{-1}(p))}\\ &\qquad \text{if } (b^O)^{-1}(p+\varepsilon)\ge v_{(n-2)}/k.\end{aligned}$$

The first part in the expression of $G(\varepsilon,p)$ corresponds to the total expected gain of the player if he wins the first auction. The player with valuation v wins the first auction if the valuation of his competitor is between $(b^O)^{-1}(p)$ and $(b^O)^{-1}(p+\varepsilon)$. It is easy to verify that, at the equilibrium, he will not exercise the buyer's option and he will not win the second auction. The remaining term(s) in $G(\varepsilon,p)$ correspond to the total expected gain if the valuation of the competitor exceeds $(b^O)^{-1}(p+\varepsilon)$. The agent with valuation v can then only hope to win the second auction and his total expected gain is determined similarly as above (indeed the expression of his gain in this case is very similar to $G(0,p+\varepsilon)$.

Derivation of $G(\varepsilon,p)$ with respect to ε gives,

- if $(b^O)^{-1}(p+\epsilon)\le v_{(n-2)}/k$,

$$\begin{aligned}\frac{\partial G}{\partial\varepsilon}(\varepsilon,p) = &((b^O)^{-1})'(p+\varepsilon)\frac{(v-(p+\varepsilon))f((b^O)^{-1})(p+\varepsilon)}{1-F((b^O)^{-1}(p))}\\ &-((b^O)^{-1})'(p+\varepsilon)\frac{(v-v_{(n-2)})f((b^O)^{-1}(p+\varepsilon))}{1-F((b^O)^{-1}(p))}\end{aligned}$$

$$+\frac{\frac{1}{k}(v-(p+\varepsilon))f((p+\varepsilon)/k)}{1-F((b^O)^{-1}(p))}$$

$$+\frac{((b^O)^{-1})'(p+\varepsilon)[v_{n-2}-(p+\varepsilon)]F((b^O)^{-1}(p+\varepsilon))}{k(1-F((b^O)^{-1}(p))}$$

$$+\frac{[v-(p+\varepsilon)]f((p+\varepsilon)/k)}{k(1-F((b^O)^{-1}(p))}$$

$$=\frac{f((p+\varepsilon)/k)}{k(1-F((b^O)^{-1}(p)))}[v-(b^O)^{-1}(p+\varepsilon)],$$

where the last equality uses the differential equation satisfied by $b^O(.)$ when $(b^O)^{-1}(p+\varepsilon)\leq v_{(n-2)}/k$.

- if $(b^O)^{-1}(p+\epsilon)\geq v_{(n-2)}/k$,

$$\frac{\partial G}{\partial \varepsilon}(\varepsilon,p)=((b^O)^{-1})'(p+\varepsilon)\frac{(v-(p+\varepsilon))f((b^O)^{-1}(p+\varepsilon))}{1-F((b^O)^{-1}(p))}$$

$$-((b^O)^{-1})'(p+\varepsilon)\frac{(v-k(b^O)^{-1}(p+\varepsilon))f((b^O)^{-1}(p+\varepsilon))}{1-F((b^O)^{-1}(p))}$$

$$+\frac{\frac{1}{k}(v-(p+\varepsilon))f((p+\varepsilon)/k)}{1-F((b^O)^{-1}(p))}$$

$$+\frac{f((p+\varepsilon)/k)}{k(1-F((b^O)^{-1}(p))}[v-(b^O)^{-1}(p+\varepsilon)],$$

where the last equality uses the differential equation satisfied by $b^O(.)$ when $(b^O)^{-1}(p+\varepsilon)\geq v_{(n-2)}/k$.

In both cases, the expected total gain for the player increases until $p+\varepsilon=b^O(v)$ and decreases after. Stay active in the auction until the price reaches $b^O(v)$ is thus a best reply for a bidder with valuation v when the other player bids following strategy $b^O(.)$. This proves the second point (the "final" stage) of Proposition 1 first claim.

The "Early" stage

To end the proof of the first claim, we must verify that it is not profitable for the players to deviate from the optimal strategy before the final stage of the first auction. We thus have to show that as long as there are at least three persons actively bidding, each bidder should bid up to his valuation.

To show this, we first consider the deviation that consists in bidding *less* than one's valuation when two other players are still active. This strategy is clearly dominated by the following strategy (that we shall call "strategy s"): stop participating in the auction either when the price has reached the valuation or when one of the two remaining opponents has stopped bidding. Both strategies (the strategy that consists in bidding less than the valuation and "strategy s") lead to the same first-auction winner; similarly, under both strategies the identity of the second- auction winner is identical. However, "strategy s" leads to a higher first-auction equilibrium price, which reduces the probability that the first-auction winner uses the buyer's option, and the expected payoff is thus higher. The "strategy s" is in turn dominated by the strategy given in Proposition 1. We can therefore conclude that it is not profitable to quit the auction before the price reaches one's valuation if there are still at least two other players bidding.

Next we have to consider the deviation that consists in bidding *above* one's valuation when at least two other players are active. Suppose thus that the price reaches the valuation of a player when two other players are still active and that this player decides to continue bidding. The two remaining players are playing the equilibrium strategy and have therefore greater valuations than the deviating agent. As a consequence, he is sure to lose the second unit. At least one of the remaining player will not win the first unit and will bid more than him in the second auction.[13] It is finally possible that the deviating agent win the first auction but the profit he obtains is negative in that case. We can therefore conclude that it is not in the interest of an agent to bid above the valuation when at least two other bidders still participate in the game.

Existence and uniqueness of $c(\cdot)$ and $d(\cdot)$

In this part, we prove Claim 2 of Proposition 1. The equilibrium strategy is defined by a system of differential equation and one must prove that these functions are well defined.

Existence of the Function $d(\cdot)$

Let us first consider the following differential equation:

$$k(d(v) - kv)f(v) = (v - d(v))f(d(v)/k)d'(v).$$

[13]By bidding more than his valuation, the player decreases the probability that the winner in the first auction will use the option. However, this will have no effect on his gain as he is sure to lose the second auction.

We look for a solution defined on $[0, +\infty[$ such that for all $v, d(v) \in [kv, v]$. On this interval, the function should be increasing as $d' > 0$. The problem is, however, not well defined because, at the border condition $d(0) = 0$, the derivative $d'(0)$ is undefined. To overcome this problem, we will proceed in three steps. First, we study the well-defined function d_A, solution of the differential equation that satisfies the condition $d_A(A) = kA, A \in]0, +\infty[$. We then study the well-defined function d^A solution of the differential equation that satisfies the condition $d_A(A) = kA, A \in]0, +\infty[$. We finally prove that there exists a solution of the differential equation $d(.)$ that satisfies our conditions. This function is such that for all $v, d_A(v) \leq d(v) \leq d^A(v)$. Figure A1 represents these functions for $f(x) = e^x$ and $k = 0.5$.

Let us thus introduce the solution d_A of this differential equation that satisfies the condition $d_A(A) = kA, A \in]0, +\infty[$. The Cauchy–Liptchitz conditions are satisfied in A, which insures the existence and the uniqueness of the function d_A. The aim of what follows is to study this function and to prove that $d_A(v)$ belongs to $[kv, v]$ for $v \in [0, A]$ and satisfies the condition $d_A(0) = 0$.

- As $d'_A(A) = 0, d_A$ satisfies $d_A(v) \in [kv, v]$ at least locally for $v \leq A$.
- Suppose that there exists $B, B < A$, such that $d_A(B) = kB$. If there is more than one B satisfying this condition, then we consider the greatest real value. If $B \neq 0$, we have $d'_A(B) = 0$. So locally $d_A(v) < kv$ for $v > B$. As a consequence, B cannot be the greatest real that satisfies the previous condition and we obtain a contradiction. There is no B strictly positive such that $d_A(B) = kB$.

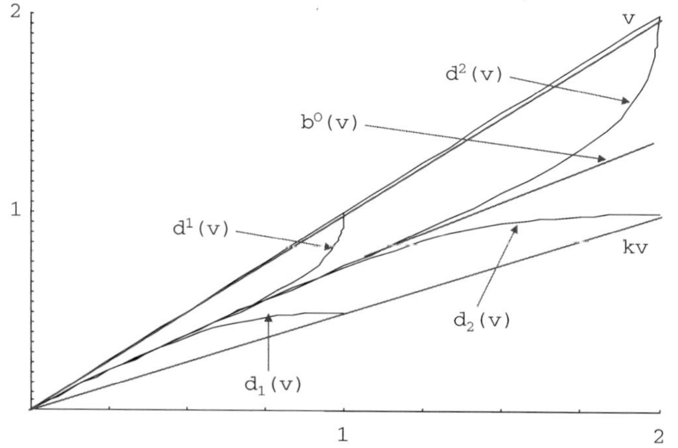

Figure A1. Construction of the Equilibrium Function $B^O(\cdot)$.

- Suppose then that there exists $B \neq 0$ such that $d_A(B) = B$. Suppose again that B is the greatest deal that satisfies this condition. Because $d'_A(B) = +\infty$, locally $d_A(v) > v$ for $v > B$, again a contradiction with the definition of B. There is no B strictly positive such that $d_A(B) = B$.

We just proved that $d_A(.)$ is included between the straight lines kv and v and do not cross them on $]0, A]$. We can thus conclude that the function $d_A(.)$ is defined on $[0, A]$ and satisfies $d_A(0) = 0$.

We prove in the same way that the solution d^A of the differential equation that satisfies the condition $d^A(A) = A, A \in [0, +\infty[$ is defined on $[0, A]$ and satisfies $d^A(0) = 0$.

The aim of what follows is to prove that there exists at least one function d between the functions d_A and d^A that satisfies the differential equation. Such a function will be defined on $[0, +\infty[$ and satisfies $d(0) = 0$. Let $x \neq 0$ be a real fixed number. We introduce $I = \{d_A(x), A \in [x, +\infty[\}$ and $J = (d^A(x), A \in [x, +\infty[\}$.

- We first prove that I is an interval of the form $[kx, \underline{x}[$. As $d_x(x) = kx$, we have $kx \in I$. Moreover, let us verify that if $y \in I$, then $z \in [kx, y[$ also belongs to I. To do so, let $\tilde{d}_z(\cdot)$ denote the solution of the differential equation that verifies $\tilde{d}_z(x) = z$. The Cauchy-Liptchitz properties imply that the solutions $\tilde{d}_z(\cdot)$ and $d_\Upsilon(\cdot)$, which satisfy, respectively, $\tilde{d}_z(x) = z$ and $d_\Upsilon(x) = y$, are functions that do not cross each other (except in 0). We then deduce that $\tilde{d}_z(\cdot) < d_\Upsilon(\cdot)$. As a consequence, $\tilde{d}_z(\cdot)$ crosses the straight line kv before $d_v(\cdot)$ and Z exists such that $\tilde{d}_z(\cdot) = d_Z(\cdot)$. As a consequence, z belongs to I, which proves that I is an interval.

One must finally prove that I is an open interval. Let $\underline{x}$ be the superior bound of the interval. If $\underline{x} \in I$, then there exists $A_{\underline{x}}$ such that $d_{A_{\underline{x}}}(x) = \underline{x}$.A reasoning similar to the previous one will prove the existence of a solution d_A with $A > A_{\underline{x}}$ that satisfies $d_A(x) > d_{A_{\underline{x}}}(x) = \underline{x}$, a contradiction with the definition of $\underline{x}$.

I is therefore of the form $[kx, \underline{x}[$.

- Using similar reasoning, we prove that J is of the form $]\bar{x}, x]$.
- Finally, I and J are two disjointed sets as the solutions that correspond to the interval I cannot cross the line v and the solutions that correspond to the interval J cannot cross the line kv. We then conclude that $\underline{x} \leq \bar{x}$, which proves the existence of a function $d(.)$ that satisfies the required conditions.

Uniqueness of the function d(·)

To prove that there exists a unique solution of the differential equation that is defined on $[0, +\infty[$, one has to show that $\underline{x} = \bar{x}$.

Suppose on the contrary that $\underline{x} = \bar{x}$, and consider the solutions $d_{\underline{x}}(.)$ and $d_{\bar{x}}(.)$ defined on $[0, +\infty[$. If v exists such that $d_{\underline{x}}(v) = d_{\bar{x}}(v)$, the Cauchy–Liptschitz conditions imply $d_{\underline{x}}(.) = d_{\bar{x}}(.)$, and therefore $\underline{x} = \bar{x}$. We can then conclude that $\underline{x} \neq \bar{x}$ implies $d_{\underline{x}}(v) < d_{\bar{x}}(v)$ for every v. Using the differential equation, we obtain

$$d'_{\bar{x}}(v) f\left(\frac{d_{\bar{x}}(v)}{k}\right) - d'_{\underline{x}}(v) f\left(\frac{d_{\underline{x}}(v)}{k}\right) = \frac{k(1-k)v[d_{\bar{x}}(v) - d_{\underline{x}}(v)]f(v)}{(v - d_{\bar{x}}(v))(v - d_{\underline{x}}(v))}.$$

The function $f(v)$ being decreasing for large enough v, we obtain for large enough v,

$$\begin{aligned}\frac{d'_{\bar{x}}(v) - d'_{\underline{x}}(v)}{d_{\bar{x}}(v) - d_{\underline{x}}(v)} &\geq \frac{k(1-k)vf(v)}{(v - d_{\bar{x}}(v))(v - d_{\underline{x}}(v))f(\frac{d_{\underline{x}}(v)}{k})}\\ &\geq \frac{kf(v)}{(1-k)vf(\frac{d_{\underline{x}}(v)}{k})}\\ &\geq \frac{1}{(1-k)v},\end{aligned}$$

where the second inequality follows from the fact that $v - d_{\underline{x}}(v) \leq (1-k)v$, and $v - d_{\bar{x}}(v) \leq (1-k)v$. The first and third inequalities follow from the fact that f is decreasing.

Integrating the previous inequality allows us to obtain

$$d_{\bar{x}}(v) - d_{\underline{x}}(v) \geq Cv^{1/(1-k)}$$

which is a contradiction for large enough v with the fact that $d_{\bar{x}}(v) - d_{\underline{x}}(v) \leq (1-k)v$.

This proves $\underline{x} = \bar{x}$ and there exists a unique solution of the differential equation, $d(\cdot) = d_{\bar{x}}(\cdot) = d_{\underline{x}}(\cdot)$ that is defined on $[0, +\infty[$. This solution is increasing, satisfies $d(0) = 0$, and belongs, for all $v > 0$, to $]kv, v[$.

Existence and uniqueness of the function c(·)

The solution $d(.)$ that we just found interests us only on the interval $[\frac{v_{(n-2)}}{k}, +\infty[$. We must study the second differential equation that defines the equilibrium strategy $c(.)$ on $[v_{n-2}, \frac{v_{(n-2)}}{k}]$,

$$k(c(v) - v_{(n-2)})f(v) = (v - c(v))f(c(v)/k)c'(v).$$

The solution $c(.)$ has to satisfy the two border conditions $c(\frac{v_{(n-2)}}{k}) - d(\frac{v_{(n-2)}}{k})$ and $C(v_{(n-2)}) = v_{(n-2)}$.

The Cauchy–Liptchitz conditions show that there exists a unique solution of this differential equation that satisfies $c(\frac{v_{(n-2)}}{k}) = d(\frac{v_{(n-2)}}{k})$. Using arguments that are similar to those used to study the function $d(.)$, it is easy to prove that this solution also satisfies $c(v_{(n-2)}) = v_{(n-2)}$. The function $c(.)$ is thus well defined and unique.

Acknowledgments

We thank the referees and a coeditor of this journal for their careful reading and insightful suggestions. We also thank Dan Ackerberg, Andrew Chesher, Jeanne Fraysse, Christophe Gegout, and participants at the 5th INRA-IDEI Conference on "Industrial Organization and the Food Processing Industry," the 2002 ESEM in Venice, the VDQS meeting in Budapest, and a seminar at UCL, for their help and comments.

References

Ashenfelter, O. (1989). How auctions work for wine and art. *Journal of Economic Perspectives*, 3, 23–36.

Ashenfelter, O., and Genesove, D. (1992). Testing for price anomalies in real-estate auctions. *American Economic Review*, 82, 501–505.

Black, J., and de Meza, D. (1992). Systematic price differences between successive auctions are no anomaly. *Journal of Economics and Management Strategy*, 1, 607–628.

Burguet, R. (1999). Right to Choose in Oral Auctions, UFAE and IAE Working Paper.

Cassady, R. (1967). *Auctions and Auctioneering*, Berkeley, CA: University of California Press.

D'Agostino, R., and Stephens, M. (1984). *Goodness-of-Fit Techniques*, Statistics: Textbooks and Monographs, Vol. 68, New York: Marcel Dekker.

Donald, S., and Paarsch, H. (1993). Piecewise pseudo-maximum likelihood estimation in empirical models of auctions. *International Economic Review*, 34, 121–148.

Gale, I., and Hausch, D. (1994). Bottom-fishing and declining prices in sequential auctions. *Games and Economic Behavior*, 7, 318–331.

Ginsburgh, V. (1998). Absentee bidders and the declining price anomaly in wine auctions. *Journal of Political Economy*, 106, 1302–1319.

Klemperer, P. (1999). Auction theory: A guide to the literature. *Journal of Economic surveys*, 13, 227–260.

McAfee, R., and Vincent, D. (1993). The declining price anomaly. *Journal of Economic Theory*, 60, 191–212.

Milgrom, P.A., and Weber, R.J. (1982). A theory of auctions and competitive bidding. *Econometrica*, 50, 1089–1122.
Mood, A.M., Graybill, F.A., and Boes, D.C. (1982). *Introduction to the Theory of Statistics*, New York: McGraw-Hill.
Paarsch, H. (1997). Deriving an estimate of the optimal reserve price: An application to british columbian timber sales. *Journal of Econometrics*, 78, 333–357.
Parker, R. (1995). *Guide Parker des Vins de France*, Paris: Editions Solar.
Van den Berg, G., van Ours, J. and Pradhan, M. (2001). The declining price anomaly in Dutch Dutch rose auctions. *American Economic Review*, 91, 1055–1062.

Chapter 10

How Auctions Work for Wine and Art*

Orley Ashenfelter

Professor of Economics,
Princeton University, Princeton, New Jersey, USA
c6789@princeton.edu

At the first wine auction I ever attended, I saw the repeal of the law of one price. This empirical surprise led me to begin collecting data on wine auctions, to interview auctioneers, and even to buy a little wine. In the meantime, I have also had the opportunity (with John Abowd) to observe and collect data on the auction sale of impressionist and contemporary paintings. This paper reports on some of the empirical regularities that I and others have observed in the actual operation of the auction markets for these items. In view of the rich and diverse array of theoretical literature on auctions, it seems high time economists began to spell out precisely what facts it is meant to explain.

1. Introduction

At the first wine auction I ever attended, I saw the repeal of the law of one price. The wine being sold was Chateau Palmer, a red Bordeaux, from the glorious 1961 vintage. The results of the auction I watched are contained in Table 1. Each lot (of 12 bottles) of wine for sale was identical, and three lots were sold in a matter of seconds by Sotheby's according to the usual English auction practice. The first lot fetched 920 pounds, the second lot fetched 800 pounds, and the third lot fetched 700 pounds. The first bidder paid 31% more for his 1961 Chateau Palmer than did the third bidder!

I was, of course, stunned to see such enormous price variability for identical objects sold at the same time and place. Even more amazing, as I looked around the auction room it seemed obvious that no one else in the room thought anything was amiss. The law of one price was repealed and no one even seemed to notice!

*This article originally appeared in *Journal of Economic Perspectives* (1989), 3(3), 23–36.

Table 1. Typical Price Sequences for Identical Wines Sold in a Single Auction (*in £ sterling per dozen bottles*)

	Chateau palmer 1961		Croft (Port) 1927		Chateau margaux 1952		Quinta de norat (Port) 1934	
Wine type	Lot size	Price	Lot size	Price	Lot size	Price	Lot size	Price
Lot 1	12 bts	920	12 bts	800	12 bts	480	10 bts	400
Lot 2	12 bts	800	12 bts	800	12 bts	480	12 bts	500
Lot 3	12 bts	700	12 bts	750	12 bts	480	12 bts	500
Lot 4			12 bts	650	24 bts	480	12 bts	480
Lot 5			12 bts	650	24 bts	480	12 bts	480
Lot 6			12 bts	650	20 bts	480		
Lot 7			12 bts	650				

Source: Author's tabulation of the results of Sotheby's Auction of Finest and Rarest wines, December 11, 1985.

This empirical surprise led me to begin collecting data on wine auctions, to interview auctioneers, and even to buy a little wine.[1] In the meantime I have also had the opportunity (with John Abowd, 1988) to observe and collect data on the auction sale of impressionist and contemporary paintings. This chapter reports on some of the empirical regularities that I and others have observed in the actual operation of the auction markets for these items. In view of the rich and diverse array of theoretical literature on auctions it seems high time economists began to spell out precisely what facts it is meant to explain.[2]

2. How "English Auctions" Really Work

Many people think they understand the rules of an English auction because they are so commonly used.[3] Sotheby's, Christie's, Phillips, and the other English auction houses have invented and refined these rules over two centuries, and they are now common in many other parts of the world. It is well known that in an English auction the bidding begins low and edges upward

[1]Collecting data is an expensive hobby; to support it I began publication of the results of the world's wine auctions in a convenient financial format. See Liquid Assets: The International Guide to Fine Wines, 169 Nassau St., Princeton, NJ 08542.
[2]Recent empirical analyzes of oil leases by Hendricks and Porter (1988) and of highway bidding by Thiel (1988) show how rich is the potential for the study of actual auction outcomes.
[3]What is called an English auction is, in fact, Roman. The word auction comes from the Latin "auction," which means to ascend.

as bidders escalate their bids. When the bidding stops, the item for sale is said to be "knocked down" or "hammered down." The price at which an item is knocked down or hammered down is called the "hammer price."

What is not so well understood is that the items knocked down have not necessarily been sold. Here is the reason. The seller will generally set a "reserve price," and if the bidding does not reach this level the item will go unsold. Auctioneers say that an unsold item has been "bought in." (This terminology is somewhat misleading since unsold items are rarely, if ever, bought by the auction house.) An item that has been bought in may be put up for sale at a later auction, sold elsewhere, or taken off the market. John Abowd and I (1988) found that about one-third of the Impressionist paintings put up for sale in the early 1980s did not find buyers. In wine auctions, on the other hand, the typical "buy in" rate ranges from 5% to 10%. It is my impression that the typical buy in rates for other auction items — European paintings, silver, furniture, and jewelry — fall between these extremes.

Auctioneers are very secretive about whether and at what level a reserve price may have been set, and there is a real auctioneer's art in getting the bidding started on each item without revealing the reserve price. For example, the auctioneer may have to accept and announce fictitious bids "off the wall" or "from the chandelier" to start the "real" bidding. Bids from off the wall are legally being placed on behalf of the seller. At the same time, sellers are forbidden by contract with the auctioneer from bidding in the auction. This is the protection that the auctioneer offers to the prospective buyers to ensure that they are not being artificially "bid up."

If you sit through an auction you will find that every item is hammered down and treated as if it were sold.[4] Only after the auction does the auctioneer reveal whether and at what price an item may have actually been sold. In short, the auctioneers do not reveal the reserve price and they make it as difficult as they can for bidders to infer it.

Although the above description outlines commonly accepted practice in auctions, many economists who write about auctions describe them differently. For example, Milgrom (in this journal) states "the auctioneer begins with the lowest acceptable price — the reserve price — and proceeds to

[4]There are exceptions to this rule. In New York City the auctioneer is legally required to state whether an item has been sold at the conclusion of the bidding. The New York auctioneers did not reveal this information before this rule was promulgated, and they do not reveal this information in other locations except where required by law.

solicit successively higher bids from the customers until no one will increase the bid. Then the item is 'knocked down' (sold) to the highest bidder." As I have noted, real auctioneers do not reveal the reserve price in this way, and many "knocked down" items may be unsold. In another example, Graham and Marshall (1987) state that, "when the bidding stops, the auctioneer will generate a false or phantom higher bid if he feels that the high bidder is 'good for another bump.'" However, inventing fictitious bids above the reserve price is certainly unethical and probably illegal, too. Since the auctioneer's rules are known to an entire array of personnel who often move on to become bidders or their agents, it would soon become common knowledge if an auction house systematically engaged in the generation of fictitious bids above the reserve price. No auction house that values its reputation — and the long run profits its reputation secures — would systematically engage in this practice.[5]

Secret reserve prices and high "buy in" rates have some interesting implications for the theoretical study of auctions. In the optimal auctions model of Riley and Samuelson (1981), for example, the reserve price serves to extract a slightly higher price from the bidder with the highest valuation of the item on offer.[6] The reason is that in an English auction the seller only receives an amount equal to the second highest valuation placed on the object among the bidders. By setting a reserve price the seller takes a chance on extracting part of the valuation gap between the two bidders with the highest valuations in exchange for the risk of losing the sale altogether.

[5]It should be appreciated that an auctioneer faces a real tradeoff in deciding whether to follow the standard ethical auction practices. If the auctioneer gains a reputation for following these practices he receives the benefit that buyers will be willing to reveal their true valuation of an item, and this will, in the long run, lead to higher prices for the items sold. On the other hand, there are always short term gains to be obtained by abandoning the standard practices. I do not mean to suggest that all auctioneers follow the standard practices considered ethical in the auction trade, although I do believe that the large auction houses with substantial reputations follow them. Many sellers try to give the impression that they follow standard auction practices even when they do not, apparently because they believe that it increases their sale prices to uninformed buyers. Some of the most amusing examples of this practice are depicted by the home shopping clubs broadcast on late night cable television. This kind of cheating seems to be endemic to any kind of economic activity where reputations are valuable.

[6]The term "reserve price" is an unfortunate choice of words in this context. In reality virtually every seller has some price below which they would not agree to sell an object; the theory of optimal auctions indicates why, for strategic reasons, a seller should set a reserve price that is strictly higher than the minimum price for which they would sell the object.

However, this optimal auctions model is probably not much help in understanding how reserve prices are set in most auctions. First, since it is a dominant strategy for each bidder in an English auction to bid up to their true valuation of the object, the optimal reserve price is identical no matter whether it is kept secret or not. This model therefore offers no explanation for why the reserve price should be secret. Second, in the optimal auctions model the reserve price is independent of the number of bidders. It follows that the probability that an item will be sold increases with the number of bidders. In fact, however, as I noted above buy in rates are very high for some types of items despite a large number of bidders. Moreover, buy in rates differ systematically across types of items in a manner that is almost certainly not related to the number of bidders in these auctions. It seems very unlikely that actual buy in rates can be explained primarily by the considerations important in the optimal auctions literature.

One likely explanation for the secrecy surrounding reserve prices is that it serves to thwart "rings."[7] There is always random variation in the interest and turnout of bidders; when the turnout is low, some sellers may prefer that their goods be bought in and offered for sale at a later date rather than risk a collusive ring bidding to depress the item's price. The auctioneer may also engage in other practices that weaken rings. For example, the auctioneer typically does not reveal the identity of the purchaser, if there was one, and this creates strong incentives for the ring members to bid privately in opposition to the interests of the ring.

An explanation for the key determinants of the seller's reserve price may be found in models of search (Mortensen, 1970), where the seller may expect to offer the item at auction more than once, or even to sell it privately to a dealer as an alternative. The highest observed price in a particular auction may be thought of as a "job offer" which will be accepted only if it exceeds the reserve price. In these models there is a "natural rate of unemployment" that may well be related to the "normal buy in rate" that characterizes auction markets. Abowd and I (1988) find that time-series movements in the auction market for Impressionist paintings do seem consistent with the dynamics of search models, so perhaps the other characteristics of these markets are consistent with them as well.

[7]Webster defines a "ring" as, "An exclusive combination of persons for a selfish, and often corrupt, purpose, as to control the market."

3. Competition among Auction Houses

It is sometimes said that the auctioneers at Christie's (still owned by Englishmen) are gentlemen who try to act like businessmen, while the auctioneers at Sotheby's (now owned by Americans!) are businessmen who try to act like gentlemen. There is no doubt an element of truth to this characterization of the style of these two auction houses. The competition among auctioneers is more than a matter of style, however. The auction business is an interesting example of an industry where the cost of building a reputation may act as a significant entry barrier to new competitors. Surprisingly little attention has been paid in the literature about auctions to the role of the auctioneer.

In principle the auctioneer acts on behalf of the seller, but the auction house typically receives compensation from both the buyer and the seller for items that are sold. The *buyer's premium* is a percentage of the sale price paid to the auctioneer by the buyer. In most auction houses the buyer's premium is 10% of the sale price, and the amount is generally not negotiable. The *seller's commission* is a percentage of the sale price paid to the auctioneer by the seller. It varies with the type of item being sold, ranging from 15% for wine to as little as 5% for certain kinds of paintings. (Thus, if a single lot of wine is sold at an auction for a hammer price of $100 the buyer will pay $110 to the auctioneer, and the seller will receive $85 from the auctioneer.)

If an item goes unsold, the auctioneer will receive neither a buyer's premium nor a seller's commission. To make sure the seller bears some of the cost of auctioning but not selling an item, auctioneers usually charge the seller a fee on unsold items. This fee is often a percentage of the reserve price set by the seller, which obviously gives the seller an incentive to keep the reserve price low. In addition, some auction houses will not allow a seller to put up an easily recognized item for resale until some time has passed. Sometimes it is claimed that when an advertised item goes unsold its future value will be affected. Such items are said to have been "burned."

Whether an item can be "burned" has some implications for the set of assumptions used in studying auctions. When bidders have independent private valuations of the items on offer, as in Riley and Samuelson (1981), it should not be possible for any item to be burned. The failure of an item to sell should not influence its future salability either at auction or privately. But in models where bidder valuations are correlated, as in Milgrom and Weber (1982), the failure of an item to sell is informative about the value it might achieve in another sale. If an object can be burned, the assumption of correlated valuations becomes more appropriate. However, it is not clear whether paintings really are burned, or whether this is a fiction invented to encourage sellers to be satisfied with lower reserve prices.

Most auction houses now collect a much larger part of their revenues from the buyer's premium than was true in the past. The most commonly given reason is that auction houses have been increasingly forced to bargain down the size of the seller's commission when they deal with large consignors. Since it is far more difficult for a large number of small buyers to bargain effectively, the buyer's premium has provided a new source of revenue. This suggests that real bargaining costs have changed in recent years, but I am unaware of why this might have happened.

The result of an interesting natural experiment in the variation of the buyer's premiums is contained in Table 2. This table contains a comparison of the hammer prices (i.e., not including the buyer's premium) for identical wines sold at six auction houses at four points in time. In the spring of 1986 buyer's premiums were 10% in Sotheby's London, Christie's Chicago, Butterfield's San Francisco, and Christie's and Sotheby's Geneva auctions. The buyer's premium was 16% in Amsterdam at this time, and there was no buyer's premium in Christie's London auctions.

It is reasonable to consider Sotheby's London, Christie's London, and Christie's Amsterdam auctions to be conducted in the same market. The other auctions take place in markets that are divided by both regulatory and transportation cost barriers. Rational buyers will, of course, discount the price of a wine to the extent that it carries a buyer's premium. Thus, the price differences among Christie's London, Sotheby's London, and Christie's

Table 2. Wine/Hammer Price Differences across Auction Houses

	% Difference from Christie's London prices			
Auction house	Spring 1986	Fall 1986	Spring 1987	Fall 1987
Sotheby's London	−12%	0%	+5%	−4%
Christie's Chicago	+14%	+18%	+15%	+4%
Butterfield's San Francisco	+27%	+21%	+10%	0%
Christie's Amsterdam	−16%	−8%	−8%	−8%
Christie's Geneva	+13%	+37%	+25%	+19%
Sotheby's Geneva	+27%	+34%	+27%	+30%

Source: "Liquid Assets," *The International Guide to Fine Wines*, Issue No. 4, Spring 1988.

Amsterdam auctions in Spring 1986 are consistent with the assumption that these auctions are taking place in a single market and that buyers have caused buyer's prices to be equalized. Prices in the United States and Geneva, on the other hand, offered opportunities for arbitrage in early 1986.

In the fall of 1986, Christie's instituted a 10% buyer's premium in their London auctions. The Christie's auctioneer had earlier condemned Sotheby's for instituting a buyer's premium, and had promised not to follow suit, but some aspect of the commercial realities did not allow Christie's to keep this pledge. Most observers believed that having instituted a buyer's premium which would definitely generate some revenue, Sotheby's had then proceeded to negotiate with the larger trade-oriented sellers over the seller's commission and had threatened to take away some of Christie's larger and more lucrative clients. Christie's put a halt to this behavior by implementing their own buyer's premium.

As shown in Table 2, the institution of a buyer's premium by Christie's London immediately resulted in a realignment of hammer prices, so that buyer's prices remained the same among Christie's and Sotheby's London auctions and Christie's Amsterdam auctions. In the meantime, buyer's prices have also converged between London and the United States, albeit much more slowly. Perhaps some arbitrage did take place. Geneva prices, on the other hand, remain remarkably high, suggesting the existence of some permanent barriers to trade between Switzerland and both the U.S. and England.

4. The Price Decline Anomaly

I believe it is common knowledge among auctioneers that, when identical lots of wine are sold in a single auction, prices are more likely to decline than to increase with later lots. This does not mean that price declines always occur, but they are far more common than would be expected by chance alone. Table 1 provides some examples of the pattern of results that you are likely to see in a wine auction.

A more formal analysis is contained in Table 3. I have compared the prices of every pair of identical wines sold in the same lot size in the years 1985 through 1987 in London, Chicago, and San Francisco. Although it is most common for the price to remain constant, prices are at least twice as likely to decline as to increase. This pattern is true for every auction house in London or the United States.

Table 3. The Distribution of Price Patterns for Identical Wines Sold in the Same Auction (August 1985–December 1987)

	Auction house			
	Christie's London	Sotheby's London	Christie's Chicago	Butterfield's San Francisco
Later Price Higher	271	143	90	20
Later Price Lower	628	430	183	41
Later Price Identical	1498	1073	226	39
Mean Ratio (2nd to 1st price)	.9943	.9875	.9884	.9663
Standard Error of the Mean	.00128	.00188	.00335	.0103
Number of Comparisons	2370	1646	499	100

Source: "Liquid Assets," *The International Guide to Fine Wines*, Issue No. 4, Spring 1988.

Table 3 also contains the means (and estimated standard errors) of the ratios of the second to the first prices. If prices followed a random walk these ratios would be unity, but all the ratios are less than unity, and the differences are statistically significant. However, since the cost of buying and then selling these lots of wine will rarely, if ever, be less than 15% of their value, these discrepancies will not support a profitable trading strategy. Still, if you attend a wine auction it is worth remembering that it does not pay to be too aggressive in bidding for early lots of a particular wine!

Most auctioneers are aware that later bidders on similar items are more likely to pay lower prices, but they are uncomfortable about revealing this information to uninformed bidders. Apparently most bidders, like economists, expect to see identical items sold at identical prices! When inexperienced bidders see exceptions to this rule they may think something fishy is going on. As a result, auctions are set up to disguise this regularity. For example, the auctioneer will usually offer smaller lots of the same item before larger lots. Since most bidders see nothing anomalous in quantity discounts, declining per unit prices seem more acceptable. Of course, the statistical analysis I reported above deletes cases where different lot sizes are being offered, and this selection bias has probably led me to underestimate the extent of the decline in prices.

Auctioneers have another device for limiting the extent to which bidders are likely to see price declines for identical items. When a series of lots of identical items is offered, the winning bidder on the first lot has the option of immediately taking all the subsequent lots at the same price.[8] This rule has two effects. On one hand, for a bidder who wants some (but not all) of the items on offer, it increases the risk of waiting for the lower prices that may materialize with later lots. Risk averse buyers are thus forced to pay a real price for any attempt to exploit the typical pattern of price declines: they may lose the opportunity to buy any of the lots they want. Thus, this rule increases the seller's revenue so long as there are risk averse buyers. In addition, since the option to purchase several lots is often exercised, bidders will in this case see a uniform price for all items. (This is also another reason to believe that I have underestimated the extent of the anomalous declines in prices that would otherwise have taken place in Table 3.)

These anomalous price declines appear to be characteristic of many other auction markets. For example, Penny Burns (1985) compared the behavior of student subjects and a group of experienced Australian wool traders in a simulated auction environment identical to that used in the wine auctions described here. After a few "weeks" of simulated trading, the students learned to maximize their profits and market prices followed a random walk throughout trading "days." The wool traders operating in the same environment did not learn to maximize their profits and market prices in their simulated trading declined as in the wine auction results above. Burns asked the wool traders whether they had noticed the pattern of declining prices and reports that, "Despite its consistency over 15 consecutive auction sessions, they had not seen the price fall!" This suggests that in the market trading to which they are accustomed, wool traders do not consider a declining price pattern to be a signal of unexploited profits.

These results suggest that risk aversion or quantity constraints play a significant role in real auction markets. Indeed., assuming bidders are risk averse may simply be a convenient analytical device for dealing with the fact that many bidders at auctions are buying to fill orders and are effectively quantity constrained. In fact, the mechanism used in practice by the auctioneers that gives the first buyer the option to purchase subsequent lots at

[8]Since the buyer must exercise this option immediately, this rule does not establish an option value for risk neutral traders which could be used to explain the price decline anomaly. Here is the reason. Since the option expires as soon as it is purchased, it is only of value if it is exercised. If it is exercised, however, there will be no price decline. Thus, the existence of an option value is not consistent with the price declines. For those who like empirical tests of such theoretical arguments I might also add that Butterfieid's San Francisco auctions have no "buyer's option" — but the price decline anomaly is even more severe there.

an identical price is clearly related to the optimal auction design suggested by Maskin and Riley (1984) when there are risk averse bidders. Theoretical work on auctions will almost certainly have to remove the assumption of risk neutral bidders if it is to explain the full range of interesting empirical results from real auctions.

5. The Information in Auction Results: An Externality

A young woman called me with an unusual request just before Christmas: "Professor Ashenfelter, my husband was killed in a car accident last month, and I am going to have to sell his wine cellar. A relative has offered to take the wine for $3,000, but I am suspicious it may be worth more. Would you tell me what it is worth?"

Oh my, what a sad situation. Knowing that younger wine collectors have young (and not very valuable) wines I wasn't quite sure what to say. So, after offering my own condolences I asked, "What sorts of names are on the bottles?"

"I have a list; there are Chateau Lafite, Chateau Latour, Chateau Mouton..."

These are, of course, the names of the finest red Bordeaux wines. Maybe, I thought, this young woman had a little better luck than I had first guessed. So I asked, "What vintages are on the bottles?"

"There are quite a few. The oldest is 1945, but there is 1961, 1959..."

As it turned out, my estimate was that this young woman's wine cellar would fetch about $18,000 if it were put up at auction, about six times what her relative had offered her!

This story illustrates one way that regular auctions confer information benefits that are typically not captured by the profits of the auctioneer. In essence, the presence of an auction system provides a way for an uninformed seller to obtain approximately the market value for the items they own.

The value of a public auction system as protection for uninformed sellers has long been understood in Europe, but it is not widely appreciated in the United States. In both Sweden and Austria, for example, the auction houses are run as state-owned monopolies. The major auction houses in both the U.S. and England are certainly not state-owned, but they are watched with some care by institutions like the Metropolitan Museum of Art, which disposes of its property only through public auctions.

My advice to the young woman whose wine cellar I appraised was, of course, to sell her wine at auction unless she could find a private buyer who would pay her at least (the certainty equivalent of) what I estimated she would receive for the wine if it were sold at auction. The information on prices I used would not exist without a system of public auctions. In other words, the auction system allows traders to make private transactions outside the auction system, but if everyone traded in this way there would be no auctions in the first place. I believe that the inability of auctioneers to capture a significant part of the benefits of the information they produce leads to less use of the auction system than is optimal for society.

Of course, some people oppose the use of the auction system as a matter of principle. For example, many wine merchants argue that the auctioneers pose "unfair competition" because they do not have to maintain an expensive inventory and therefore the prices realized at auction will be lower than the merchant's. To an economist, such special interest pleading is hard to take seriously, but state legislators are not so immune. The result is that wine auctions are illegal except in Illinois and California.

6. The Information in Auction Results: Taking Advantage of It

In 1987, not long after public wine auctions had begun in California, I asked Dennis Foley of the San Francisco auction house of Butterfield and Butterfield how I could find the "real bargains" in his wine auctions. He said, "Buy the wines Robert Parker doesn't like. Parker's book (1985) has an enormous influence on U.S. auction prices. Wines he doesn't rate or mistakenly rates make fabulous bargains."

To U.S. wine buyers this advice may border on the heretical. Here is the reason. Most of the information available about the quality of wine appears in publications that are run by advertisers. Newspaper writers often accept direct and indirect payoffs for touting wines and many knowledgeable consumers are aware of this practice. (After a detailed expose by media reporter David Shaw in the *Los Angeles Times* in the summer of 1987, the *Times* fired its own wine writer!) The result is that there is a market for independent information. Robert Parker, lawyer turned wine writer, has captured that market and the absolute faith of his readers by refusing to accept handouts and payoffs.

What Parker and many other wine writers attempt to do is to infer the likely quality of a red Bordeaux, Burgundy, or California wine when it is 10 or 15 years old from the taste of the wine when it is a few months old. In other words, wine consumers in search of their liquid asset are much the same as oil drillers in search of their own liquid asset. In the future the true value of the asset will be revealed, but meanwhile the consumer must he satisfied with an estimate of its value. What Dennis Foley seemed to be telling me was that U.S. wine consumers were suffering from an extreme version of the winner's curse. Consumers would bid on a wine in his auctions only up to Parker's valuation of it, as if Parker's appraisals could not possibly contain error. It is precisely this kind of failure to make probability judgments that seems to be the cause of the winner's curse found in experiments by Kagel and Levin (1986).

The question is, of course, how to take advantage of the errors of these bidders. As it turns out, the theoretical literature on the information content of auctions suggests a possible way to do this. In a classic paper Wilson (1977) shows that the auction price is a better estimator of the true value of an item as the number of bidders gets larger. Since the volume of wine sold at auction in London is more than ten times the U.S. equivalent, and the number of potential bidders may be greater still, why not use the prices from London's auctions as benchmarks, buying wine in the U.S. auctions only when its price is systematically lower than in London?

If this form of arbitrage works, it will not make you (or anybody else) any money. Unless the wine is shipped to London, no one in the U.S. is likely to buy it for more than you paid for it. But if you buy the wine to drink, you may have purchased a great bargain.

Over the last year or so I have tested this strategy for wine auction buying several times. So far it has worked very well, although there are signs that enough market participants are learning about it so that it may not last a great deal longer. Here is a recent example that you might still run across: 1970 Chateau Brane-Cantenac, a red Bordeaux, sells for about $330 per dozen bottles in London, while it regularly fetches about 20% less in both San Francisco and Chicago. I and several colleagues recently sampled this wine and found it to be excellent.[9] Why is this wine so much cheaper in the United States? Well, here is what Parker (1985) says about it: "This is a distressingly poor wine, particularly in view of the vintage. The 1970 has quite a foul aroma and dirty barnyard scent. On the palate, the wine is beginning to fall completely apart. Lacking fruit and concentration, this is a vivid example of a very poorly and sloppily made wine." I can assure you

[9]I am indebted to my colleagues Dwight Jaffee and Richard Quandt for their help in this empirical work and to Burton Malkiel who also supplied the wine.

that neither I nor my colleagues detected any barnyard scents in this wine and I do not believe that Parker would either.

7. Auctioneers and Accurate Information

The theoretical literature about auctions emphasizes that there are good reasons for auctioneers to provide truthful information about the items being sold (Milgrom and Weber, 1982). The basic idea is that revealing information tends to remove uncertainty and make low bidders more aggressive; this puts upward pressure on the bidding of others, which is in the interest of the auctioneer. It may seem surprising to some, but auctioneers do appear to act consistently with this prediction.

For example, auction houses typically go to considerable effort to estimate the price that an item offered for sale will fetch. Predicting the price at which a unique item will sell requires considerable expertise, so it is of some interest to see just how good these predictions are. The usual practice is for the auctioneer to provide a high estimate and a low estimate in an auction catalogue.

Taking the auctioneer's point estimate to be the midpoint of the high and low estimates, Table 4 contains the results of an empirical study of how well the auctioneers predicted the prices fetched by Impressionist paintings in London and New York in auctions held by Sotheby's and Christie's. Figure 1 provides a scatter plot of the actual prices against the auctioneer's estimates.

These data reveal some important results. First, the auctioneer's price estimates are very highly correlated with the actual prices fetched and they

Table 4. Comparison of Actual and Estimated (by the Auctioneer Prior to the Auction) Sale Price of Impressionist Paintings 1980–1982

Auction house	Number of paintings put up for auction	Percent not sold	Percent sold at price below the "Low Estimate"	Percent sold at price above the "High Estimate"	Percentage difference between sate price and estimated sale price
Christie's London	211	44%	18%	20%	3.9%
Christie's New York	433	30%	21%	24%	2.1%
Sotheby's London	918	34%	21%	24%	1.5%
Sotheby's New York	617	26%	19%	28%	3.6%

Source: Abowd and Ashenfelter (1988).

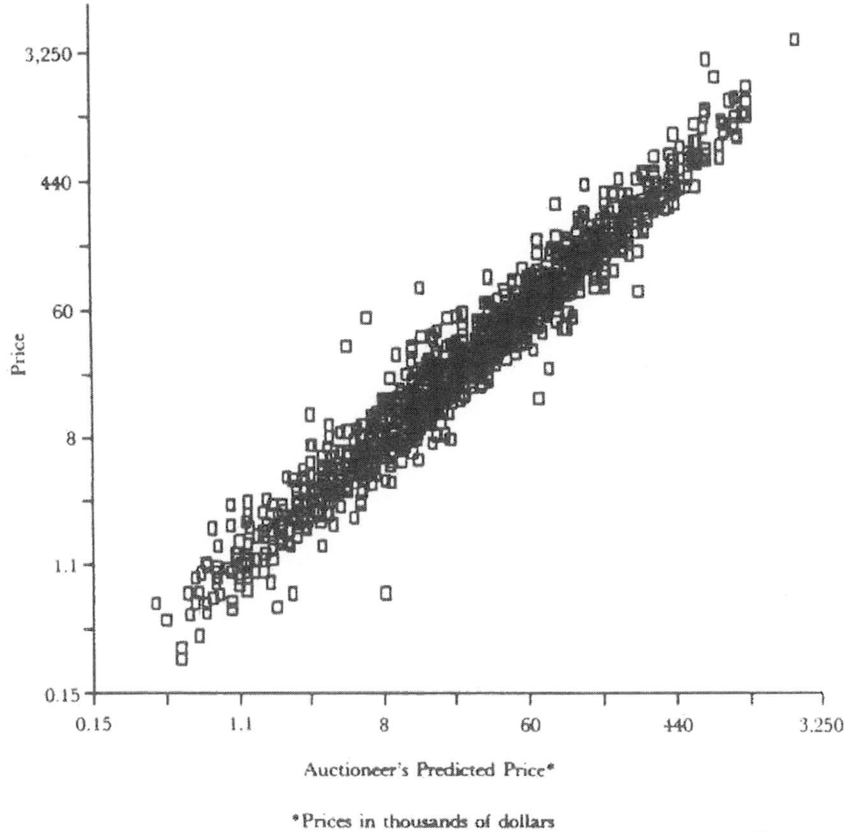

Figure 1. The Relationship between Predicted and Actual Prices for Impressionist Paintings

are very close to unbiased. Since the prices fetched are available only for pictures that are actually sold, unbiased estimates averaged over only those pictures who find a buyer will appear downward biased. Although the extent of this selection bias is very small, this is precisely what the data indicate for both auction houses operating in both London and New York. It is also worth observing that, whatever implicit rules the auction houses use for defining their high and low price estimates, the results of these rules lead to very similar points on the empirical frequency function of forecast errors.

In sum, auctioneers do seem to provide genuine expertise in predicting prices. In fact, Abowd and Ashenfelter (1988) find that the auctioneer's price estimates are far better predictors of the prices fetched than any hedonic price function presently available. Perhaps honesty is an auctioneer's most profitable policy rule.

Acknowledgments

I am deeply indebted to several people in the auction trade who have been very generous in describing the institutions with which they work. Brian Cole, Director of Auctions at Christie's New York, Michael Broadbent, Director of the Wine Department at Christie's, and Bruce Kaiser, Director of the Wine Department at Butterfield and Butterfield, San Francisco have all been exceptionally helpful. I have also received helpful comments on an earlier draft of this chapter from David Card, Robert Marshall, Robert Wilson, and the editors of this journal.

References

Burns, P. (1985). Experience and decision making: A comparison of students and businessmen in a simulated progressive auction. Vol. 3 *of Research in Experimental Economics*. Greenwich, Conn.: JAI Press, Inc.

Eric, M., and Riley, J. (1984). Optimal auction with risk averse buyers. *Econometrica*, 52, 1473–1518.

Graham, D.A., and Robert, C.M. (1987). Collusive bidder behavior at single-object second-price and English auctions. *Journal of Political Economy*, 95, 1217–1239.

John, A., and Ashenfelter, O. (1988). Art Auctions: Price Indexes and Sale Rates for Impressionist Pictures, unpublished manuscript.

Kagel, J.H., and Levin, D. (1986). The winner's curse and public information in common value auctions. *The American Economic Review*, 75, 894–920.

Kenneth, H., and Porter, R.H. (1988). An empirical study of an auction with asymmetric information. *The American Economic Review*, 78, 865–883.

Milgrom, P.R., and Robert, J.W. (1982). A theory of auctions and competitive bidding. *Econometrica*, 50, 1089–1122.

Mortensen, D.T. (1970). Job search, the duration of unemployment, and the phillips curve. *The American Economic Review*, 60, 847–862.

Parker, R.M., Jr. (1985). *Bordeaux: The Definitive Guide for the Wines Produced Since 1961.* New York: Simon and Schuster.

Riley, J.G., and William, F.S. (1981). Optimal auctiorw. *The American Economic Review*, 71, 381–392.

Robert, W. (1977). A bidding model of perfect competition. *Review of Economic Studies*, 44, 511–518.

Thiel, S.E. (1988). Some evidence on the winner's curse. *The American Economic Review*, 78, 884–895.

Chapter 11

Absentee Bidders and the Declining Price Anomaly in Wine Auctions*

Victor Ginsburgh

Université Libre de Bruxelles and
Centre for Operations Research and Econometrics, Belgium
vginsbur@ulb.ac.be

The anomaly is concerned with the observation that in multiple-item auctions of identical objects, prices tend to decline over time. I show that in the case of wine auctions, which have been analyzed frequently, the anomaly is likely to be caused by the fact that most bids are entered by absentees, who use nonoptimal bidding strategies. Therefore, wine auctions can hardly be used to illustrate the standard multiple-object auction model.

1. Introduction

An interesting overview of the behavior of auctioneers and the atmosphere that is pervasive in many salesrooms is provided by Smith (1989), who discusses several anomalies. One of these, the so-called declining price anomaly, was brought to the attention of a wider audience of economists by Ashenfelter (1989). The anomaly is concerned with the observation that in multiple-item auctions of identical objects, prices tend to decline over time.

The anomaly is reported to occur under various forms by Buccola (1982) for livestock auctions; Burns (1985) for wool auctions; Ashenfelter (1989), McAfee and Vincent (1993), and Di Vittorio and Ginsburgh (1994) for wines; Ashenfelter and Genesove (1992) for real estate; Beggs and Graddy (1997) for impressionist and modern paintings; Chanel *et al.* (1996) for jewelry; and Pesando and Shum (1996) for Picasso prints. Burns (1985) and Keser and

*This article originally appeared in *Journal of Political Economy* (1998), 106(6), 1302–1319.

Olson (1996), among many others, have set up experiments and reach the same conclusion.

Several reasons, both theoretical and institutional, have been advocated to explain the anomaly. Ashenfelter (1989) suggests that risk aversion is at the root of the anomaly. McAfee and Vincent (1993) show that the more restrictive, and less likely, assumption of nondecreasing absolute risk aversion is needed for pure strategies to exist and for the result to hold. Beggs and Graddy (1997) show that if the quality of lots in a multiobject auction declines, the ratio "hammer price/presale estimate" should also decline, even if bidders are risk neutral. For wine auctions, rules at Christie's provide that the (winning) buyer of the first lot "will, at the discretion of the auctioneer, have the option to take further lots of a similar bottle size [at the same price]" (Christie's wine catalog). Black and de Meza (1992) and Burguet and Sakovics (1994) show that the uncertainty about future possibilities to buy that is introduced by this rule leads to declining prices.[1]

Burns (1985) argues that, in wool auctions, bidders are often agents who act for others and place higher bids than would be necessary to ensure their obtaining at least one of the items. This is close to the idea of buying to fill orders. Pesando and Shum (1996) observe that in multiple-item auctions of Picasso prints, salesrooms consciously order the items by decreasing quality. If this were systematic,[2] it could provide a ready explanation for the anomaly. To eliminate this possibility, Pesando and Shum look at identical prints sold in different auctions that occur sufficiently close in time (no more than 5 days apart). The number of cases is too small, and the results provide no support for the anomaly.

Both Ashenfelter (1989) and McAfee and Vincent (1993) discuss wine auctions and confirm the existence of the declining price anomaly. The empirical tests conducted by Di Vittorio and Ginsburgh (1994), Chanel *et al.* (1996), and Beggs and Graddy (1997) need some qualification since they measure the price decline in an indirect way. In all three cases, the authors deal with heterogeneous objects, which they homogenize by regressing prices on characteristics and, in some cases, on presale estimates. The declining price anomaly is analyzed by introducing among the exogenous variables an additional one that represents the order in which the item is auctioned. If prices decline (relative to presale estimates in Beggs and Graddy), the

[1]Though Ashenfelter notes that in wine auctions the winning bidder on the first has the option of taking any number of subsequent lots at the same price, this is not assumed in the McAfee-Vincent model.

[2]Several departments at Christie's London confirm that this is the rule used in most cases.

coefficient picked by the "order in sale" variable should be negative. For wines, Di Vittorio and Ginsburgh find that the coefficient is indeed negative, but not significantly so. Beggs and Graddy report that both presale estimates and prices relative to presale estimates decline with order. Chanel *et al.*, who deal with jewels sold at judiciary auctions, find that price behavior for "identical" homogenized lots varies: Prices increase in the case of watches, decrease for objects in gold, and are constant for other collectibles (bracelets, necklaces, and rings). Ashenfelter and Genesove also proceed indirectly for their real estate auctions. They compare prices obtained at auction with those obtained in later face-to-face bargaining for identical condominium units. Prices decline as the auction progresses. This relation is not observed for units sold later on and can therefore be due not to declining quality, but to the auction mechanism itself.

2. An Analysis of Wine Auctions at Christie's London

I now concentrate on wine auctions and show that the declining price anomaly is indeed observed but is essentially due to the institutional functioning of auctions. I collected detailed data on four such sales held at Christie's in London in December 1995 and January and February 1996. All four sales were held at King Street, where the better wines are usually sold.[3] It is important to note that one of the sales is described as "remarkable" (February 22, fine and rare wines), two others as featuring fine wines and vintage ports (December 14, end-of-year fine wines, and February 8, fine wines and vintage port), and the last one can probably be considered as relatively standard (January 25, Claret and white Bordeaux).[4] Though the number of sales I study is probably too small to be considered as representative,[5] the sample converts different situations, and there is no reason to believe that attendance and bidding strategies during these auctions were very different from what they are in general.

There are three types of bidders: those who attend the sale (in person or through an agent, sometimes a Christie's employee), those who bid on the telephone,[6] and absentees who turn in written bids before the sale starts.

[3]The more "standard" sales take place in rooms located in South Kensington.

[4]Some details and the catalog descriptions are given in the Appendix.

[5]Note that this is the same number as in McAfee and Vincent (1993).

[6]Though this is rare for wines since the rule at Christie's is that telephone bids will not be accepted for lots under £2,000. There were no telephone bids during any of the four sales at which I was present.

Table 1. General Characteristics of the Sales

	December 14	January 25	February 8	February 22	All	Percentage
Number of lots offered	1,078	522	577	770	2,947	100.0
Single lots	382	309	183	257	1,131	38.4
Lots in parcels	696	213	394	513	1,816	61.6
Number of lots sold	840	483	493	730	2,546	86.4
Number of parcels[a]	142	54	86	117	399	
Number of lots per parcel	4.9	3.9	4.6	4.4	4.6	

Note: [a]In each of these parcels, at least two lots were sold.

Except in very rare cases, the auctioneer has the absentees' reservation prices registered in the so-called auctioneer's book and bids on their behalf.

Table 1 provides a general overview of the four sales. Almost 3,000 lots came up, and 86.4% were sold.[7] Over 60% of the lots came in parcels, which, on average, contain 4.6 lots of one or several (dozens of) bottles. I shall mainly be concerned with a detailed study of these 399 parcels (1,816 lots).[8]

All this is public information contained in the sales catalogs and price lists released after the auction. However, I also had access to the auctioneer's books, which provide the reservation prices of the vendors as well as the names (in fact, numbers) of the absentees together with their bids. The books also identify the winning bidders and the prices at which they obtained the lots.[9] This makes it possible to determine, lot by lot, whether there were written bids and who, whether present or absent, won the lot.

A summary of this information for parcels only is given in Table 2. It is immediately apparent that in the vast majority of cases, there are bids entered by absentees; in 3.2% of the cases (13), there was no written bid recorded, and in 12.8%, the number of written bids was smaller than the

[7]The number of bottles sold is much larger since a lot may contain as many as five to 10 dozens of bottles.

[8]Note that similar wines may also be sold in different parcels and not sequentially. This will happen if the sellers are different. Such parcels may be considered by customers as being of different "quality" since they were stored in different cellars. I ignore these cases here since they do not occur frequently.

[9]Unfortunately, they do not provide information on the starting bid nor on the sequence of bids. This information is of course public and is released during the auction, but it is very difficult to keep track of it if not recoded. Even so, it would often be hard to see whether the bid is made by someone in the room or by the auctioneer acting for an absentee.

Table 2. Characterizing Bids on Parcels

	December 14	January 25	February 8	February 22	All	Percentage
Total number of cases	142	54	86	117	399	100
No written bid	9	0	1	3	13	3.2
Fewer written bids than lots	20	4	15	12	51	12.8
More written bids than lots	113	50	70	102	335	84.0
Price dynamics	60	15	51	53	179	44.9
Decreasing prices						
Increasing prices	7	4	0	10	21	5.3
Both ways	9	4	13	21	47	11.8
Constant prices	66	31	22	33	152	38.1
Option						
Exercised	57	30	25	38	150	37.6
Not exercised	85	24	61	79	249	62.4
Decreasing prices	60	15	51	53	179	44.9
Due to quality effect	1	0	3	0	4	
Due to quantity effect	14	4	9	17	44	
Other	45	11	39	36	131	
Price decreases[a] (%)						
Average	11.4	8.3	7.6	12.0	10.2	
Largest	55.6	22.7	23.5	45.4	55.6	

Note: [a]Ratio of first (largest) to last (lowest) price in a parcel.

number of lots in a parcel.[10] Therefore, the remaining 84% of the parcels would have been sold even with no one bidding from the room.[11]

Table 2 also illustrates the number of times prices for subsequent lots in a parcel increase, decrease, or remain constant. The results show that the number of decreases is much larger than the number of increases — and that some price decreases are substantial — but also that prices are constant or move both up and down in half of the cases. I now turn to a more detailed analysis of the decreases by discussing four reasons why declining prices are indeed observed but may have little to do with auction theory: The reasons are essentially linked to the organization of wine auctions, though one may argue that wine auctions are organized that way because auctioneers have

[10]This takes into account that one bidder can bid for several lots; in several cases, there are fewer bidders than bids.

[11]In all these cases, bids were higher than the lower bounds of the range of the presale estimate, which, according to the rule set by Christie's, should be at least as large as the reservation price set by the seller.

observed that prices decline.[12] I distinguish the option effect, the decreasing quality effect, the varying (size and) quantity effect, and the absentee bidder effect.

2.1. *The option effect*

The first issue is the option offered to the winning bidder of the first lot (in a parcel) to buy, at the same price, any number of subsequent lots, as long as the size of the bottles in these lots is the same as in the first one. This is so at Christie's. Sotheby's seems even to extend this option to any winning bidder, and not only to the one who won the first lot. According to Ashenfelter (1989), there is no such option at Butterfield's San Francisco, and declining prices are nevertheless observed. As already mentioned, this rule has been the subject of theoretical developments by Black and de Meza (1992) and Burguet and Sakovics (1994), but the intuition for its effect on prices is obvious: The price for the first lot is equal to later ones, plus a risk premium. However, if the option were infrequently used, it would not be threatening. Table 2 shows that the option is exercised in more than 37% of the cases (much more frequently by absentees) and constitutes, therefore, a credible threat: Those who wait may not have the opportunity to buy any lot should the first buyer exercise this option.

Moreover, the fact that the option exists but is not exercised on all the lots signals that the price paid for the first lot is higher than the market-clearing price. Therefore, the market-clearing price will, on average, be higher in the cases in which the option is exercised and lower when it is not.

2.2. *The decreasing quality effect*

Second, prices may decline because lots are ordered by decreasing quality.[13] Though, indeed, ordering by decreasing quality is the rule at Christie's, there are only four such cases. This is negligible and cannot provide an explanation for declining prices in wine auctions.

---

[12] It is impossible to decide on this by just looking at auction results. Experiments such as the ones run by Keser and Olson (1996) convey the feeling that declining prices can be generated under various experimental conditions.

[13] The "fullness" characteristics of a bottle is said to influence quality since the contact of wine with air should be minimal. "Ullage," as the seepage of wine from a bottle is called, results in different levels of fullness (from high fill to below low shoulder). Condition is usually described in the sales catalogs.

2.3. *The bottle size and quantity effects*

Third, for many parcels with lots of identical wine and vintage, the number of bottles and their size vary across lots. Large bottles (magnums, double magnums, jeroboams, and imperials) are often listed before standard 75-cl ones. Wine connoisseurs claim that larger bottles make for better wines;[14] they are also less frequent than standard bottles, and collectors may be willing to pay for rarity.

Moreover, the number of bottles of identical size offered in a lot often increases in later lots, and standard demand theory would predict a decrease in the price per bottle. This is probably compounded by the fact that high transaction costs (see, e.g., Weil, 1993) make it costly to resell any undesirable surpluses acquired if later (and usually larger) lots are bought.

In my calculations, I compute for each lot in a parcel a price per standard 75-cl bottle. Therefore, a declining price effect, if present, could show at breakpoints, that is, when bottle size or number of bottles changes from one lot to the next. The number of such "breaks" is reported in Table 2, in the row labeled "due to quantity effect." It is observed in 44 cases and seems thus to be responsible for 24.5% of the total number of declines.

2.4. *The absentee bidder effect*

This is the fourth and probably most important observation. As can be seen from Table 3, in 60% of the parcels, all the lots were sold to absentees; this does not mean that there were no bidders in the room, but only that none of them could purchase a lot of this particular parcel. For another 30.8%, there was some competition between the room and absentees. Finally, in 9.2% of the cases, only customers in the room entered bids that were high enough to buy all the lots in a parcel. One can also observe that in 81.5% of the cases, the first winning lot goes to an absentee.

Though there may have been bidders present in the room competing, but unsuccessfully, with written bids, there is a strong indication that most wine sales, at least in London, are not attended by many bidders. For reasons

[14]Because of the porous nature of the cork, there is some exchange between the wine and air through the cork. Since there should be as little air-liquid contact as possible while a wine is aging, one way to minimize this contact is to maximize the volume of liquid for a given amount of air-exposed surface area. This can be achieved by using larger bottles. Consequently, one would expect this quality effect to be reflected in the price of larger bottles. Di Vittorio and Ginsburgh (1994) show that this is indeed the case: The price increase (for a standard 75-cl volume) can be as large as 42% for imperials (eight bottles).

Table 3. Detailed Overview of the Bids

	December 14	January 25	February 8	February 22	All	Percentage
Total number of cases	142	54	86	117	399	100
Cases with lots won by						
Absentees only	85	36	52	66	239	60.0
Room only	18	4	4	11	37	9.2
Both	39	14	30	40	123	30.8
First winning bid won by						
Absentee	111	44	74	96	325	81.5
Room	31	10	12	21	74	18.5
Option exercised by	57	30	25	38	150	37.6
Absentee	47	26	20	32	125	31.3
Room	10	4	5	6	25	6.3
Decreasing prices	60	15	51	53	179	44.9
Absentees only	33	9	29	28	99	24.8
Due to quality effect	1	0	3	0	4	
Due to quantity effect	8	3	4	8	23	
Other	24	6	22	20	72	
Room only	0	0	1	0	1	.2
Other	0	0	1	0	1	
Both	27	6	21	25	79	19.8
Due to quantity effect	6	1	5	9	21	
Other	21	5	16	16	58	
Increasing prices	7	4	0	10	21	5.3
Absentees only	3	2	0	8	13	
Room only	1	0	0	1	2	
Both	3	2	0	1	6	
Both ways	9	4	13	21	47	11.8
Absentees only	3	2	6	7	18	
Room only	0	0	0	0	0	
Both	6	2	7	14	29	
Constant prices	66	31	22	33	152	38.1
Absentees only	48	23	18	27	116	
Room only	15	4	2	6	27	
Both	3	4	2	0	9	

that are unclear[15] — the relatively low value of the items is probably one of the explanations — wine auctions often seem to deal with a large number of written bids, and this could obviously have an effect on the way the sale proceeds. In auctions for more expensive items, collectors use agents to bid

[15]One of the reasons given by Christie's wine specialists is that the number of overseas clients is large.

on their behalf or bid themselves on the telephone.[16] This helps bidders to capture the atmosphere of the sale (in particular, the number of bidders) and makes it possible for them to adapt their strategies.

Price decreases are observed 179 times. In 99 cases, they occur when only absentee bidders win; in 79 (52 + 27) additional cases, both absentees and room bidders complete.[17] Finally, there is *only one case* in which the declining price anomaly is observed and in which all the lots are knocked down for bidders attending the auction.

Some details on the organization of an (English and not sealed-bid) auction with written bids are useful at this stage. Written bids come in before the sale starts and are registered in the auctioneer's book. The auctioneer bids on behalf of absentees, who may enter their bids under various alternative strategies: (1) quote a price for only one specific lot in the parcel; (2) quote different prices for several or all of the identical lots and instruct the auctioneer to stop bidding after having won one lot; (2C) same as strategy 2, except that prices quoted are equal; (3) quote different prices for several or all of the identical lots and instruct the auctioneer to stop bidding after having won several (a specified number of) lots; (3C) same as strategy 3, except that prices quoted are equal; and (4) enter more complicated conditional bids or state an upper limit for total expenditure. These forms are much less frequent, and if they become too complicated (for instance, if the conditional bids are spread over various parcels), they are handled by a salesroom employee who bids from the room.

The classical result on equilibrium bidding strategies in the case of multiple lots is due to Weber (1983), who derives bid functions under the assumptions that bidders are symmetric and risk neutral, have identically, independently distributed private values drawn from a uniform distribution with lower support of $\underline{v}$, and desire one unit each. In the case of second-price auctions, these functions are $b_i = \underline{v} + [(v_i - \underline{v})(n - k)/(n - s)]$, where b_i is the equilibrium bid of bidder i; v_i is his private value; and n, k, and s are, respectively, the number of bidders, the number of identical lots in a parcel, and the order in which the lot is auctioned. These functions imply that the equilibrium bid should increase for each subsequent lot. It can then be shown that hammer prices should, on average, be equal. A similar result holds in the case of common values (instead of private values), whereas the

---

[16] I have seen a fairly large number of cases of art sales in which *all* the bids were entered exclusively by Christie's employees acting for telephone bidders.

[17] In 52 cases, the first lot goes to an absentee; in 27 cases, to a bidder present in the room.

affiliated values model predicts even steeper bidding functions. Nondecreasing absolute risk aversion produces declining prices but is unlikely to prevail for wine auctions (values are relatively small) and would lead to increasing bids. Therefore, one should expect absentees to bid for several lots, even if they wish to buy only one lot (strategies 2 and 3 above), and bids should be increasing with lot number. Though there exists no theoretical result for the case in which a bidder wishes to buy several units, intuition suggests that the strategies are likely to be similar. Of course, the theory implies that every bidder, whether in the room or absent, needs to know how many bidders will enter the game for each parcel; moreover, the number of bids should be larger than the number of lots, which is very often the case (see Table 2).

Observed bidding strategies, summarized in Table 4, are strikingly different from this theoretical prediction. In more than 90% of the cases in which there were written bids, these bids are constant; that is, either strategy 2C or strategy 3C is followed in only three cases.

Therefore, if only absentees are interested and each of them sends a unique bid for (any) one or several lots in a parcel, it is obvious that the auctioneer will sell the lots to satisfy bids in decreasing order of value. A typical example is the following. In the sale of February 22, lots 479–81 each consisted of 12 bottles of Echézeaux 1988. Four written bids were registered, with each bidder willing to buy at most one lot. Bids were as follows: bidder 1006, £500; bidder 1010, £400; bidder 1013, £340; and bidder 874, £330. The first lot went to bidder 1006 for £360, the second one to bidder 1010 for £350, and the last one to bidder 1013 for £340.[18]

In the 99 cases mentioned earlier, little or no competition at all from the room would readily explain the declining price anomaly. If both absentees and bidders in the room compete (79 occurrences), this effect may still be driving the result, especially in the 52 cases in which the first winning bid was placed by an absentee, who can have no feeling about what happens in the room during the auction.

[18]When there is no supporting bidding in the room up to the levels set by absentees, they will often get the lot well below their bid. In this case, the fourth bidder at £330 did not win, the third got one lot at his bid value (£340), and the two others who entered bids of £400 and £500, respectively, were charged only £350 and £360. Note that this is far from corresponding to a second-price auction since, in that case, the highest bidder would have paid £400, the next one £340, and the last one £330. According to Christie's auctioneer, this "rule" prevents prices from "declining too much." This implies that hammer prices usually decline less rapidly than if a second-price auction mechanism were used. Note also that the auctioneer could have chosen to auction all these lots at £340, which would not have led to declining prices.

Table 4. Absentees' Bidding Strategies

	December 14	January 25	February 8	February 22	All	Percentage
Total number of cases	142	54	86	117	399	100
No written bid	9	0	1	3	13	3.2
Strategy 2C[a]	31	6	25	30	92	23.1
Strategy 3C[b]	91	44	50	75	260	65.2
Other strategies	11	4	10	9	34	8.5
Increasing bids for identical quantities	0	0	1	2	3	
Decreasing bids for identical quantities	0	3	6	1	10	
Different bids but different quantities	3	0	2	3	8	
Different bids but different sizes	7	1	1	3	12	
Decreasing bids but decreased quality	1	0	0	0	1	

Notes: [a]Quote equal prices for several of the identical lots and instruct the auctioneer to stop bidding after having won one lot.
[b]Quote equal prices for several of the identical lots and instruct the auctioneer to stop bidding after having won several (a specified number of) lots.

A bidder who attends the sale has the possibility of gathering information about the number of bidders for a specific parcel and thus computing his optimal strategy. This is of course impossible for absentees and may turn out to be the reason for their apparently non-optimal bidding behavior. Moreover, there is a large number of cases in which absentees offer to buy several lots, a situation that is not analyzed (and seems very hard to formalize) in auction theory. This also makes it impossible for absentees to infer how many lots remain unsold after each round and thus the number of the lot that is auctioned (s in the optimal bidding formula discussed earlier).

The "law of one price" could indeed be said to be violated if declining prices were observed when all customers bid from the room, but this seems to happen very seldom. As shown in Table 5, all the lots in a parcel went to room bidders in 37 cases, with 34 instances of constant prices (23 in which the first winner exercised his option). This may well indicate that bidders in the room are likely to follow the strategy predicted by theory so that, on average, realized prices are constant.

Table 5. Cases for Which all Lots in a Parcel Are Obtained by Room Bidders

	December 14	January 25	February 8	February 22	All	Percentage
Total number of cases	18	4	4	11	37	100
No written bids	9	0	1	3	13	35.1
Constant prices	9	0	1	3	13	35.1
Decreasing prices	0	0	0	0	0	0
Increasing prices	0	0	0	0	0	0
Written bids, but no winning one	9	4	3	8	24	64.9
Constant prices	8	4	2	7	21	56.8
Decreasing prices	0	0	1	0	1	2.7
Increasing prices	1	0	0	1	2	5.4

If the declining price anomaly were often observed with room bidders, rational behavior would make them all wait for the last lot. An obvious contradiction results.[19]

3. Concluding Comments

In this chapter, I show that declining prices are indeed observed in wine auctions. This "violates" the law of one price, but mainly for institutional reasons. One could wonder why, knowing this, bidders do not show up more frequently at auctions and are satisfied with sending in written bids.

Since identical wines come up for sale quite frequently, it is not very difficult to predict their prices, at least in the short run. Christie's wine department computes price indexes and may be using them to predict the presale estimates published in their catalogs. Therefore, with the exception of items that are collectibles, such as the bottle of Château d'Yquem 1811 sold in the December 14 auction for £14,000 ($21,000),[20] customers know with reasonable accuracy how much a wine is worth and cannot be very much off when submitting written bids. For those cases in which prices do decline, the average decrease is equal to 10%. This represents £2 ($3) for a

[19]Note that bidders and auctioneers are aware of the difficulties and possible inconsistencies that appear when parcels are auctioned. See, for example, a letter entitled "Fair Bidding at Auctions?" to the editor of the renowned wine review *Decanter* (May 1992, p.7) and the answer in the June 1992 issue by Michael Broadbent, Christie's wine specialist and auctioneer.

[20]Note that, even for that case, the presale estimate (£15,000–20,000) was close to the hammer price.

£20 bottle or, for a 12-bottle buyer, approximately the cost of a cab ride to and back from the auction room. At least in the case of wines, prices decline for very obvious (institutional) reasons. These reasons cannot be invoked for auctions of other commodities, such as collectibles or real estate, where multiple-object parcels are rare and bidders are usually present at the auction.

It would be interesting to study why absentees use bidding strategies that do not conform with Weber's (1983) or similar models' theoretical predictions, which all yield increasing bids. One reason may be that they cannot use optimal bidding rules since they are unable to infer the number of bidders. Another reason may be linked to the fact that bidders are often willing to buy more than one lot of a parcel, a situation for which theoretical results seem to be particularly difficult to obtain.

Acknowledgments

I am grateful to the wine department of Christie's London for allowing me to access some of its auctioneer's books and collect the data used in this chapter. The conversations I had with Paul Bowker, Michael Broadbent, and Duncan McEuen from the Christie's London wine department on the functioning of wine auctions were very useful. Gian-Luigi Albano, Orley Ashenfelter, Claude d'Aspremont, Sherwin Rosen, Jonathan Shalev, and Mary Sullivan made very useful comments on previous drafts. I am particularly grateful to a referee who forced me to look more carefully at my data. Support from the centre Interuniversitaire pour les Etudes en Management, Brussels, and from the John M. Olin Foundation, which made possible my visit to the University of Chicago, is gratefully acknowledged.

References

Ashenfelter, O. (1989). How auctions work for wine and art. *Journal of Economic Perspectives*, 3, 23–36.

Ashenfelter, O., and Genesove, D. (1992). Testing for price anomalies in real-estate auctions. *A.E.R. Papers and Proceedings*, 82, 501–505.

Beggs, A., and Graddy, K. (1997). Declining values and the afternoon effect: Evidence from art autions. *RAND Journal of Economics*, 28, 544–565.

Black, J., and de Meza, D. (1992). Systematic price differences between successive auctions are no anomaly. *Journal of Economics and Management Strategy*, 1, 607–628.

Buccola, S. (1982). Price trends at livestock auctions. *American Journal of Agricultural Economics*, 64, 63–69.

Burguet, R., and Sakovics, J. (1994). Sequential auctions with supply and demand uncertainty. Manuscript. Barcelona: Inst. Analisis Economico.

Burns, P. (1985). Experience and decision making: A comparison of students and businessmen in a simulated progressive auction. In *Research in Experimental Economics: A Research Annual*, vol. 3, edited by V.L. Smith. Greenwich, Conn.: JAI.

Chanel, O., Gerard-Varet, L.-A., and Vincent, S. (1996). Auction Theory and Practice: Evidence from the Market for jewellery. In *Economics of the Arts: Selected Essays*, edited by Victor Ginsburgh and Pierre-Michel Menger. Amsterdam: Elsevier.

Di Vittorio, A., and Ginsburgh, V. (1994). Vintages from 1949 to 1989 at Christie's Auctions. Manuscript. Brussels: Univ. Libre de Bruxelles.

Keser, C., and Olson, M. (1996). Experimantal examination of the declining price anomaly. In *Economics of the Arts: Selected Essays*, edited by Victor Ginsburgh and Pierre-Michel Menger. Amsterdam: Elsevier.

McAfee, R.P., and Vincent, D. (1993). The declining price anomaly. *Journal of Economic Theory*, 60, 191–212.

Pesando, J., and Shum, P. (1996). Price anomalies at auction: Evidence from the market for modern prints. In *Economics of the Arts: Selected Essays*, edited by Victor Ginsburgh and Pierre-Michel Menger. Amsterdam: Elsevier.

Smith, C.W. (1989). *Auctions: The Social Construction of Value.* New York: Free Press.

Weber, R.J. (1983). Multiple-object auctions. In *Auctions, Bidding, and Contracting: Uses and Theory*, edited by Richard Engelbrecht-Wiggans, Martin Shubik, and Robbert M. Stark. New York: New York University Press.

Weil, R. (1993). Do not invest in wine, at least in the U.S. unless you plan to drink it, and maybe not even then. Paper presented at the second International Conference of the Vineyard Data Quantification Society, Verona.

Appendix

Characteristics of the four wine auctions used in the chapter

The descriptions are taken from the sales catalogs.

1. December 14, 1995. — 1,078 lots for sale; 840 lots sold.[21]

> End of Year Fine Wines. *In the morning:* Excellent vintage Port, mainly private cellars, vintages 1958 to 1987; fine Claret including an impériale of Latour 1961 and many top Châteaux of the sought-after 1982 and 1990 vintages; excellent Graves and Yquem; top-quality red Burgundy, including Grand Cru of the excellent 1978 vintage; fine white Burgundy; an excellent range of mixed stocks, including top-quality wines from a Swedish cellar, excellent Rhône; Loire; Alsace; rare Apostelwein; fine Hock and Mosel; Tokay; Napa Valley Cabernet and excellent Champagne. *In the afternoon:* Fine red and white Graves from Château Rahoul, including a range of formats; an impressive stock of wines, predominantly Claret and Sauternes, from a Continental cellar; excellent red and white Burgundy including mature wines for current drinking and a wide range of top

[21]The sale included one imperial of Château Latour 1961 (knocked down at £7,200) and one bottle of Château d'Yquem 1811 (£14,000).

wines from Leroy; venerable Cognac and other spirits, including rare Chartreuse.

2. January 25, 1996. — 522 lots for sale; 483 lots sold.[22]
   Claret and White Bordeaux.

3. February 8, 1996. — 577 lots for sale; 493 lots sold.[23]

   Fine Wines and Vintage Port. Excellent stock of vintage Port, incorporating many shippers of the 1963, 1970 and 1977 vintages; fine Claret, vintages 1928 to 1986, including excellent private stock or rare wines: Yquem of highly regarding vintages, substantial stocks of top-quality red and white Burgundy, incorporating many wines from top Domaines; excellent mixed stocks of fine wines, many from private cellars; a wide range of top-quality Rhône; excellent Champagne and venerable Brandy.

4. February 22,1996. — 770 lots for sale; 730 lots sold.[24]

   Fine and Rare Wines from a Scandinavian Cellar. *In the morning:* An impressive range of Vintage Port, 1948 to 1985, also large parcels of Port from Fonseca for everyday drinking; excellent Claret, vintage 1970 to 1990, including many first-growths; a remarkable range of Le Pin; a wide range of Bordeaux from Francois Mitjaville; top-quality red and white Burgundy from excellent producers, including Domaine de la Romanée-Conti, Leroy and Comte Lafon; fine Rhône, including single vineyard Côte-Rôtie from Guigal and excellent champagne from Bollinger, Deutz and Pol Roger. *In the afternoon:* A remarkable range of excellent red and white Burgundy from the highly-regarded firm of Joseph Faiveley including a number of Grand Crus from the excellent 1988, 1989 and 1990 vintages as well as their rare Corton-Charlemagne; an impressive collection of small and mixed lots of fine and rare wines and venerable Brandy.

   This sale is further described as follows in Christie's Wine Department sales Memorandum no. 362:

   Remarkable sale of Fine and Rare Wines... Remarkable not only for the size of the cellar as a single-owner collection, but also for the range and breadth of wines on offer. The wines included in this catalogue have been acquired over a period of time by a Scandinavian institution, and were impeccably stored under quite exceptional conditions in three purpose-built cellars, equipped with elaborate temperature and humidity controls. Two of the three cellars contained the majority of the cased stock, the third was fully racked and included all of these loose, buried wines. All wines featured

[22]The sale included 12 bottles of Château Petrus 1975 (£3,700).

[23]The sale included several one-bottle lots of Château Mouton-Rothschild 1961 (£1,900 each).

[24]The sale included six bottles of Château Latour 1961 (£3,600), 12 bottles of Château Le Pin 1982 (£11,000), 12 bottles of La Tâche 1978 (£4,400), and several one-bottle lots of Romanée-Conti 1978 (£1,500 each).

in this sale were carefully checked and, where appropriate, packed over a period of three days by a team from Christie's Wine Department. The total consignment (in excess of 2,000 cases) was then loaded on two trailers for specialised transport to London, and is now lying under bond at Trapp Cellars.

Part 4

Supply and Its Implications

Chapter 12

Price Formation in the California Winegrape Economy*

Dale Heien

Department of Agricultural and Resource Economics,
University of California Davis, USA
dale@primal.ucdavis.edu

This chapter presents a theory of price determination for winegrapes in California. As the California wine economy developed, winegrape contracts took on a role as one of the centerpieces of this transformation. The theory is presented and it is shown how two important factors, weather and financial uncertainty, served to shape the contracts. Hence, long-term planting contracts for new vineyards, specifying the price, helped ameliorate the uncertainty to growers. Similarly, shorter contracts played a similar role for established vintners. The model deals with two types of growers: those with contracts made well before the year in question and those who will sign a contract in the Spring of the year of harvest. This chapter hopes to illuminate these elements and their interaction. The model is then empirically estimated and tested.

1. Introduction

The manner in which price determination takes place in agriculture markets often differs from the static paradigm of instantaneous adjustment of supply and demand. Transparent and well organized grain and livestock exchanges facilitate the equilibration of supply and demand, while price determination in some areas of agriculture occurs under conditions of asymmetric information, imperfect competition, and uncertainty. Although there is considerable literature on price determination for grains,[1] livestock[2] and, to some

*This article originally appeared in *Journal of Wine Economics* (2006), 1(2), 162–172.

[1]See, for example, Williams and Wright (1991) for models of storable commodity price determination.
[2]See, for example, Brandt and Bessler (1981) and Chavas and Holt (1991).

extent, vegetables,[3] comparatively little research has been done on fruit price formation.

This chapter deals with price formation for winegrapes. In terms of cash receipts, grapes are the largest fruit crop in the U.S. with over three-fourths of these receipts coming from winegrapes. Winegrapes are a high value crop with relatively steep entry costs. Since time is required to recoup large initial investments, price variation and future price levels are major concerns. Both of these concerns are often handled in contracts.

Prices in the California winegrape economy do not adjust instantaneously to supply and demand. This failure to adjust within any given crop year arises out of the interaction of two characteristics of the winegrape economy: (1) the widespread use of long-term contracts between growers and wineries and (2) the impact of weather and disease on the grape crop level. The contracts, to some extent, lock in current and future prices while the weather and disease determine crush levels. Hence, there are considerable latitude for a disconnect between actual crush levels and prices paid since contract prices are often based on expected crush levels and may be locked in for several years.

This independence was demonstrated in 1997 in Napa county. The quantity crushed of Cabernet and Chardonnay increased 43% and 51% respectively, while grower prices increased 11% and 13%. Slightly increased bearing acreage augmented by ideal weather produced a bumper crop. While demand was increasing, it is difficult to imagine a demand shift sufficient to warrant these increases in price, given the increase in quantity crushed. Wineries that were locked into long-term contracts, were not able to take advantage of the large crop by paying lower prices. This occurred because the prices were specified in long-term contracts long before it was realized that the crop would be relatively large.[4]

The purpose of this chapter is: (1) to describe the price formation process for winegrapes and its unique characteristics; (2) to model this process analytically; and (3) to test several hypotheses regarding price determination. To achieve these goals the chapter uses annual data on three winegrape varieties (Cabernet Sauvignon, Chardonnay, and Merlot) from three different areas (North Coast, Central Coast, and Central San Joaquin Valley).

[3]See, for example, Sexton and Zhang (1996) and Hammig and Mittelhammer (1980) and on celery by Shonkwiler and Pagoulatos (1980) and Taylor and Kilmer (1988).

[4]Many of these were planting contracts which typically run 10 years.

2. The Winegrape Market: Institutional Setting

In California there are roughly 12,000 grape growers and 600 wineries. There is no organized winegrape market. Although there are two grape brokerage houses most contracts are formed through personal contact between growers and wineries. A large proportion of these growers are under long-term contracts. A recent survey showed that 51% of growers had contracts of three years or greater while 36% had one-year contracts.[5] As a result, the majority of growers are removed from the year to year price negotiation process due to the multiyear nature of their contracts. Data on prices paid the previous year is published in the *Grape Crush Report* each March. These prices play an important role as the escalator in many long-term contracts. Long-term contract base prices are often "moved" by the percentage change in the previous year's crush district average price.[6] Arrangements such as these tend to make price behavior independent of current year market conditions.

The remaining growers are in reality spot market participants although they will eventually make a contract (oral or written) for the coming harvest. Growers in the spot market generally make contracts in late Spring or early Summer for that Fall's crop. At this point in time information on Spring weather (i.e., frost or excessive heat) and its impact on crop size is more clearly understood. Because of this weather variability long-term contracts do not specify the amount to be crushed in terms of tons. Eighty percent of California grape contracts do not even specify a maximum tonnage (Goodhue *et al.*, 1999). Due to yield variability growers are reluctant to enter maximum tonnage contracts.

Wineries enter into long-term contracts and predict quantity on the basis of the expected yield with the understanding that some years will be short and others long. Wineries are in a better position to deal with this variability because it is easier for them to expand storage, for example, new tanks can be added and aging wines can be marketed sooner or later. Growers desire long-term contracts to obtain bank financing, deal with future price uncertainty, and avoid unfamiliar marketing tools. Wineries, on the other hand, need contracts because they need to be assured of a steady supply of grapes at a known quality, without having to deal with the problems associated with growing grapes.

---

[5]See Goodhue *et al.* (1999). In addition to the 51%, there are those with two-year contracts and others waiting to renew multiyear contracts.

[6]The California winegrape economy is divided into 17 crush districts. Some districts are unique counties while other districts are comprised of several counties.

In most contracts it is either explicitly stated or implicitly assumed that all grapes produced on the stated acreage will be purchased by the winery.[7] Hence, with supply relatively inelastic in the short-run, one way to model price determination is via a price dependent demand curve. Such a model is useful when supply is inelastic and markets adjust rapidly to demand shifts through price changes. For winegrapes such is partially, but not wholly, the case. The important intervening factor is, of course, the presence of multi-year contracts.

Contracts usually make some mention of the acreage covered, but seldom specify an exact tonnage. This omission is due to the difficulty in forecasting the crop size as discussed above. For contracts over one year, the best estimate of tonnage will be based on (known) bearing acreage and some notion of expected yield. This implies that quantity demanded is based on expected harvest, that is, bearing acreage times expected yield.[8] For those growers with long-term contracts the quantity demanded is the expected crop level. For those selling in the spot market the actual quantity is the relevant quantity because at the time they enter into a contract the actual level is more accurately known. Hence, the weighted average crush district price will depend on both spot (one-year contract) and long-term contract prices.

3. Winegrape Price Formation: Model Formulation

This section uses the institutional setting described above to specify a grape price formation relationship. It is only one of several relations needed to construct a complete model of the winegrape sector. However, due to the above mentioned disconnect between supply and demand, excess demand relations provide an interesting vehicle to attempt to model the disequilibrium. The model assumes there are two distinct groups of growers: spot market operators, that is, individuals with one-year contracts, and longer-term contract growers. Winegrape contracts typically run three to five years with planting contracts up to 10 years. Renewal of these contracts is typical, so a hiatus forcing contract growers into the spot market is not typical. Hence, the price

[7] The survey by the Agricultural Issues Center showed that only 22% of winegrape contracts stipulated a maximum tonnage (Goodhue *et al.*, 1999).

[8] Expected yields were estimated by regressing the yield on a time trend. While there are many economic factors affecting yields, these effects are of a long-run nature and are essentially exogenous in the short-run. Weather and disease induced effects on yields are current, but also exogenous to economic variables.

formation relation here will consider both scenarios and incorporate them in a single relation which determines market price.

Begin by considering the price formation relation for a grower who has a long-term contract. Often, there is a reference price, frequently last year's average return for that district (e.g., North Coast) and variety (Cabernet), which "moves" the price the grower receives. Such a relation can be specified as

$$cp_t = \beta_0 + \beta_1 dp_{t-1} + \beta_2(S_{t-1} - S^*_{t-1}), \tag{1}$$

where cp is the contract price, dp is the crush district average price for that variety, S is the actual crush level, and S^* is the expected crush level. The lagged district price reflects the use of last year's district price as an escalator for contract price movement as discussed above. The latter term reflects contact price renegotiation considerations which occur in the year following the current crush year. If actual crush exceeds expected crush growers' revenues will be greater than expected under the contract.[9] This provides a bargaining chip for the winery, especially if the contract comes up for renewal the next year. Conversely, if actual crush falls short of expected crush, the growers will have an argument for higher contract prices.

Spot prices will be determined by the supply and demand for grapes not under contract. The price adjustment process for these spot market grapes is in the tradition of excess demand relationships.[10] When demand is based on expected crush there will be unfulfilled expectations when the actual crop differs from the expected one. In any given crop year, the spot market reduces this imbalance to some extent. Hence, the corrective mechanism must be specified for the spot market as well. Since we assume that crush levels are relatively inelastic and known to some extent at this time, the excess demand relation is given by

$$sp_t = \gamma_0 + \gamma_1(D_t - S_t) + \gamma_2(S_{t-1} - S^*_{t-1}), \tag{2}$$

where sp is the spot price and D is the expected demand for wine. Again, the term $S_{t-1} - S^*_{t-1}$ is used as an indicator of market over/under-supply carried forward from last year. As such, this difference is a relevant part of this year's

[9]Unfulfilled demand expectations do not seem to have the same effect. This may be due to the fact that wine is often marketed longer than one year after crush. Also, marketing problems may be considered more in the domain of the winery, wholesalers and retailers rather than a shared problem between growers and wineries.

[10]See Baumol (1959, pp. 82–135) and Samuelson (1961, pp. 257–284).

demand or supply. Last is the crush district average price equation,

$$dp_t = w \cdot cp_t + (1 - w)sp_t, \tag{3}$$

where it is assumed that the proportion of the crop going to the spot market, w, is fixed over time.[11] Aggregating over both classes of growers gives the crush district average price determination relationship. Substituting (1) and (2) into (3) gives

$$dp_t = \alpha_0 + \alpha_1 dp_{t-1} + \alpha_2(S_{t-1} - S^*_{t-1}) + \alpha_3 \phi Y_t - \alpha_4 S_t, \tag{4}$$

where

$$\begin{aligned} D_t &= \phi Y_t \\ \alpha_1 &= w\beta_1 > 0 \\ \alpha_2 &= w\beta_2 + (1 - w)\gamma_2 < 0 \\ \alpha_3 &= (1 - w)\gamma_1 > 0 \end{aligned}$$

Y is real Personal Consumption Expenditures which represents demand effects and ϕ is a constant which converts dollars to tons.

4. Empirical Estimation and Results

Annual data on winegrape prices and crush tonnage for the three main grape growing regions of California was obtained from the *Grape Crush Report* (California Department of Food and Agriculture, 1981a–2005a). The period covered was 1980–2004. The regions with crush districts in parenthesis are: North Coast (Lake, Mendocino, Napa, and Sonoma counties); Central Coast (Alameda, Contra Costa, Monterey, San Luis Obispo, Santa Barbara, Santa Clara, and Santa Cruz counties); and Central San Joaquin Valley (Merced, Sacramento, San Joaquin, Stanislaus, and Yolo counties). Annual data on bearing acreage was obtained from corresponding issues of *California Grape Acreage* (California Department of Food and Agriculture, 1981b–2005b).

The *Grape Crush Report* contains data on price received, quantity crushed and other information on every load of grapes crushed in California. For each Crush District a quantity weighted average price (i.e., a "unit value" index) is created. These unit value indices, technically called Average Grower Returns, were aggregated into unit value indices for each of the three regions given above. These are the prices given by (4) and are the dependent variable

[11] Data does not exist on w (the proportion of the crush coming from spot market growers).

for the model to be estimated. This price data does not distinguish between contract grapes and those sold in the spot market.

In California all loads of grapes to be crushed are required to be weighed at a state designated weigh station. The weight of the grapes, the price of the grapes, the buyer and seller, and various other data called Brix Factors are collected. These Brix Factors include incentives and penalties, weight loss in late harvest grapes, limits for acceptable grapes, and various other information. This data is not a sample. It covers all grapes crushed in California (e.g., 1,400 loads of Cabernet in Napa county). Each and every "weighed in load" appears in the crush report. Since the law requires that all grapes to be crushed must be weighed by state officials all loads will be counted. Hence, much useful information is available on each crop. However, the information does not link to any grower information such as education, age, acres, etc.

The varieties selected are Cabernet Sauvignon, Chardonnay, and Merlot. Hence, nine regressions are estimated to test the theory of price determination presented above. All of these grapes are prominent wine varietals and do not constitute blending grapes. Also, none of these varieties are suitable for the concentrate market. The expected crop is obtained by multiplying actual bearing acreage by the expected yield. The expected yield is obtained by regressing the actual yield on time. Yields have increased gradually over time due to improved rootstock, better equipment and closer row spacing. The estimated yield from the regression is then taken as the expected yield. Table 1 gives the regression coefficients for these yield functions.[12] The regression residuals will capture the unexpected effects. The yield regressions (Table 1) generally show the time trend to be significant. The coefficient of variation (σ/μ) averaged 0.195, somewhat large for time series data indicating considerable variation in yields.

The statistics in Table 2 which present the price determination relationships are of much greater interest. All coefficients have the correct sign with the exception of α_3 for Central Coast Merlot which has a t-ratio of 0.33. The overall F-statistic is significant in all nine cases. The lagged price coefficients' t-ratios exceed 2.0 in all regressions except one. Table 3 provides a summary of the statistics generated by the model. The top row labeled "All Variables" gives the average t-statistics for all four variables by variety and by region. The next four rows give the average t-statistic first by variety and then by region for each of the four slope coefficients. Since there is a

[12]The yield regressions were estimated in both the linear and log-linear form. Based on the MacKinnon, White, Davidson (1983) test the linear form was chosen.

Table 1. Yield Regression (Dependent Variable: Yield (tons per acre)[a])

	Cabernet Sauvignon			Merlot			Chardonnay		
Region	N Coast	C Coast	C SJ	N Coast	C Coast	C SJ	N Coast	C Coast	C SJ
Time	0.044	0.151	0.387	0.052	0.119	0.513	0.105	0.149	0.375
t-ratio	(1.50)	(4.94)	(6.52)	(1.24)	(2.64)	(5.01)	(3.81)	(4.41)	(6.59)
Adj. R^2	0.072	0.594	0.722	0.033	0.272	0.602	0.457	0.059	0.726
DW	2.23	1.15	1.16	2.13	1.06	1.58	1.75	1.51	2.08
Regression standard deviation	0.60	0.62	1.21	0.84	0.84	2.07	0.56	0.69	1.15
Mean dependent variable	3.66	3.67	7.34	4.32	3.81	7.24	4.21	3.61	7.15
Coef. of variation	0.16	0.17	0.16	0.19	0.22	0.29	0.13	0.19	0.16

Note: [a]Crush divided by bearing acreage.

lagged dependent variable the Durbin-Watson statistic is biased toward 2.0. Hence the "Durbin h" statistic was used to test for autocorrelation.[13] Table 4 gives the short- and long-run elasticities of price with respect to expenditure and crop yield (expected crush).

5. Conclusions

This chapter sets out a model of price determination for winegrapes. Grapes are harvested once a year and the crop level is difficult to forecast before late Spring or early Summer. For reasons discussed above, long-term contracts frequently arise between wineries and growers. These contracts specify forward prices or the mechanism by which they are to be computed. The price model given here incorporates the price determination process for growers with contracts as well as the process for spot market growers. The combined market price determination process gives current price as a function of the last year's price, the current excess demand and the lagged excess supply. Lagged price represents the fact that many contracts call for annual updating of the current price based on last year's district average price. Excess demand is specified as the difference between current demand (represented by real

[13]For cases when the Durbin h requires the square root of a negative number the Breusch-Godfrey LM is the appropriate test. This was the case for Chardonnay in the Central San Joaquin. The LM Chi-squared statistic is 3.55 for this case.

Table 2. Price Determination Relations (Dependent Variables: Price[a])

	Cabernet Sauvignon			Merlot			Chardonnay		
Region	N Coast	C Coast	C SJ	N Coast	C Coast	C SJ	N Coast	C Coast	C SJ
Lagged	0.881	0.715	0.506	0.836	0.597	0.501	0.884	0.671	0.415
endogenous	(5.51)	(4.64)	(2.16)	(4.64)	(2.84)	(2.52)	(3.77)	(2.95)	(1.47)
Real personal	0.125	0.109	0.208	0.093	0.121	0.171	0.078	0.13	0.073
consumption	(2.58)	(2.88)	(2.20)	(1.32)	(1.49)	(3.13)	(1.17)	(1.71)	(1.14)
expenditures									
$(S_{t-1} - S^*_{t-1})$	−0.0082	−0.013	−0.0058	−0.0215	−0.061	−0.0082	−0.0041	−0.0059	−0.0006
	(−3.13)	(−2.51)	(−0.91)	(−2.02)	(−1.35)	(−0.82)	(−1.75)	(−1.36)	(−0.16)
S	−0.0064	−0.0042	−0.0059	−0.0034	0.003	−0.0027	−0.0013	−0.0024	−0.0007
	(−2.54)	(−1.16)	(−1.59)	(−1.20)	(0.33)	(−1.71)	(−0.56)	(−0.96)	(−0.46)
Adj. R^2	0.96	0.95	0.77	0.97	0.94	0.95	0.68	0.74	0.41
Durbin's h	0.90	0.43	1.52	2.13	1.17	2.44	5.59	2.93	3.55

Note: [a]Crush divided by bearing acreage.

Table 3. Average t-Statistics and Adjusted R^2 by Region and Variety

	By variety			By region		
	Cabernet Sauvignon	Merlot	Chardonnay	N Coast	C Coast	C SJ
All variables	2.65	1.95	1.46	2.52	2.01	1.61
Lagged price	4.64	3.33	2.73	4.64	3.47	2.05
Real personal consumption expenditures	2.55	1.98	1.34	1.69	2.03	2.16
$(S_{t-1} - S^*_{t-1})$	−2.18	−1.40	−1.09	−2.30	−1.74	−0.63
S	−1.76	−1.08	−0.66	−1.43	−0.81	−1.25
Adj. R^2	0.89	0.95	0.61	0.87	0.88	0.71

Table 4. Long- and Short-Run Elasticities: All Regressions

	N Coast	C Coast	C SJ
		Cabernet Sauvignon	
Expenditure			
Short-run	0.41	0.57	1.59
Long-run	3.43	2.01	3.22
Crop yield			
Short-run	−0.31	−0.14	−0.38
Long-run	−2.61	−0.49	−0.75
		Merlot	
Expenditure			
Short-run	0.29	0.51	1.15
Long-run	1.71	1.24	2.50
Crop yield			
Short-run	−0.21	−0.48	−0.46
Long-run	−1.98	−1.44	−0.78
		Chardonnay	
Expenditure			
Short-run	0.24	0.48	0.45
Long-run	2.05	1.45	0.78
Crop yield			
Short-run	−0.09	−0.12	−0.05
Long-run	−0.75	−1.03	−0.08

Notes: Elasticity of price (dp) with respect to PC expenditure (Y): SR & LR elasticities. Elasticity of price (dp) with respect to crop yield (S): SR & LR elasticities. dp is crush district price defined by (3); long-run is when all variables in (4) are at current time period t.

personal consumption expenditures) and the current crush. Excess supply, the difference between last year's actual crush and last year's expected crush, is termed a contract renegotiation mechanism.

Table 2 reports the effect of lagged prices. It shows that for any given variety the biggest effect is in the relation for the North Coast with the Central Coast always second and Central San Joaquin smallest. This larger lagged effect for the North Coast reflects the greater use of escalator price contracts by North Coast growers. Evidence from the winegrape contract survey showed that contracts with a reference price were most prevalent in the Coastal regions, further verifying the model results. Reference price contracts use the previous year's crush district average price as a basis for a price adjustment in the current year. The AIC survey (Goodhue *et al.*, 1999, p. 3) showed the following percentages of contracts with reference prices: North Coast — 50%; Central Coast — 41%; and Central Valley — 34%.

This more frequent escalator price usage might also be due to a more competitive environment. Napa county, a North Coast crush district, has over 300 of the states 600 wineries. Also, a strong lagged effect will mean that current demand or supply shocks will play a smaller role than relations with smaller lagged price coefficients. The short-run elasticity of price with respect to real income is inelastic in seven of the nine regressions. However, the long-run elasticities are substantially greater than one in all cases except one.

In terms of significance, the demand effects and price renegotiation effects are generally second to the lagged price effects with the current supply effect generally last. The effect of current supply is due to two factors. First, while it is likely of considerable impact for spot market prices, it is true that there are fewer spot market growers.

Second, the results also confirmed the hypothesis that contracts have more price inertia in areas where there is more competition and hence a greater desire to have good grower-winery relations by smoothing price realizations. This was confirmed by the fact that the coefficient on the lagged dependent variable in the three areas declined monotonically by level of concentration, percentage of contracts with price specification, and by grape price over the three areas considered. As the point estimates declined there was an accompanying decline in the t-ratios.

The results show that specification of price determination relations for the winegrape sector should include knowledge of the impact of contracts and their provisions as opposed to static instantaneous market clearing models. In areas where there is more competition and higher valued grapes, these contractual provisions are more significant. Lastly, inertia in price determination was found to have a greater effect in the areas where there is less buyer concentration. The inertia reflects the fact that prices adjust more slowly in these regions because contracts which state prices in advance of knowledge of crop levels are more prevalent.

An alternative rationale for this model is to envision a market with two price regimes. The first is a competitive market with spot participants whose prices are determined solely by the equilibration of supply and demand. The second is a market with long-term contracts with prices set equal to last year's market average. The final market price will be a weighted average of the two, the weights depending on the relative sizes of each class of growers. Such a model is a (stable) first order difference equation.

A second explanation is risk incidence, which is very similar to the efficiency wage theory. Prices based on expected crop reduce income risk to the grower. This occurs because, presumably, wineries are less risk averse than growers. They are less risk averse because: (a) they are bigger; (b) perishability of crop is less a problem for wineries; (c) wineries are more diversified than growers; (d) wineries have better bank connections and (e) growers face uncertainty due to weather, disease, and labor availability. Also, it is costly to search a heterogeneous market when a product is perishable. Custom crushing has shifted this balance somewhat since growers can have their crop crushed, vinted, and marketed at the facility.

There are several explanations which are consistent with multiperiod profit maximization. Wineries pay a premium in the form of a known price over time to insure future supply from these growers. This is analogous to an employee who values security of employment. Contracts also provide a mechanism for better viticultural practices. Also, consumers, and hence wineries, want this higher quality in the wine they drink and make.

The results indicate that in markets with fewer buyers, supply and demand adjust faster than in markets with many buyers. This seeming contradiction is resolved when one considers the dynamics of the market. Wine is not a homogeneous product. Reputation, product differentiation, and quality are extremely important. Hence, in order to insure an adequate supply of grapes over time, wineries must be far-sighted in their relations with growers. Financial market models are also adaptable since disequilibrium is often a financial phenomenon. Taylor (1980) has presented a model of "Over-lapping Contracts" which for macro models generates cyclical patters similar to those found in GNP. Since winegrapes have cyclical patterns due to planting lags, this model might be useful in understanding agricultural markets also.

Acknowledgments

My thanks to colleagues Rachael Goodhue and Richard Sexton, to the referees and Karl Storchmann, all of whom gave useful insights and comments.

References

Baumol, W.J. (1959). *Economic Dynamics.* 2nd ed. London: Macmillian Co.

Brandt, J.A., and Bessler, D.A. (1981). Composite forecasting: An application with U.S. hog prices. *American Journal of Agricultural Economics*, 63, 135–140.

California Department of Food and Agriculture (1981a–2005a). *Final Grape Crush Report.* Sacramento.

California Department of Food and Agriculture (1981b–2005b). *California Grape Acreage.* Sacramento.

Chavas, J.P., and Holt, M.T. (1991). On nonlinear dynamics: The case of the pork cycle. *American Journal of Agricultural Economics*, 73, 819–828.

Goodhue, R., Heien, D., and Lee, H. (1999). Contract use in the California winegrape economy. *Agricultural Issues Center Issues Brief*, 11, December 1999.

Hammig, M.D., and Mittelhammer, R.C. (1980). An imperfectly competitive market model of the U.S. lettuce industry. *Western Journal of Agricultural Economics*, 5, 1–12.

Heien, D.M. (1977). Price determination processes for agricultural subsector models. *American Journal of Agricultural Economics*, 59, 126–132.

MacKinnon, J., White, H., and Davidson, R. (1983). Tests for model specification in the presence of alternative hypothesis; some further results. *Journal of Econometrics*, 21, 53–70.

Samuelson, P.J. (1961). *Foundations of Economic Analysis.* Cambridge, Mass.: Harvard University Press.

Sexton, R., and Zhang, M. (1996). A model of price determination for fresh produce with application to California iceberg lettuce. *American Journal of Agricultural Economics*, 78, 924–934.

Shonkwiler, J.S., and Pagoulatos, E. (1980). A model of weekly price discovery for Florida celery. *Southern Journal of Agricultural Economics*, 12, 113–118.

Taylor, J.B. (1980). Aggregate dynamics and staggered contracts. *Journal of Political Economy*, 88, 1–23.

Taylor, T.G., and Kilmer, R.L. (1988). An analysis of market structure and pricing in the Florida celery industry. *Southern Journal of Agricultural Economics*, 20, 35–43.

Williams, J., and Wright, B. (1991). *Storage and Commodity Markets.* Cambridge, U.K.: Cambridge University Press.

Chapter 13

Does Ownership Matter? Empirical Evidence from the German Wine Industry*

Bernd Frick

Paderborn University, Management Department,
D-33098 Paderborn, Germany
bfrick@uni-wh.de

There is widespread belief among economists that the separation of ownership and control tends to reduce the performance of companies while competition tends to improve it. Irrespective of their theoretical appeal these assumptions have not been tested very often. Using an unbalanced panel of about 300 German wineries (compiled from four different editions of a highly respected and widely used wine guide), the chapter shows that firms run by "managing directors" produce higher quality and more expensive wines than otherwise identical owner-managed firms. Since firms have identical production functions and due to the intense competition in the sector under consideration it is very likely that differences in human capital explain the observed productivity differences.

1. Introduction

There is widespread belief among economists that the separation of ownership and control tends to reduce the performance of companies while competition tends to improve it. On the one hand, the specific details of the "organizational architecture" of firms, that is their structures, policies, and procedures designed to achieve efficiency in coordinating and motivating its members, are likely to influence their performance. On the other hand, competition not only leads to allocative efficiency by forcing prices to equal marginal costs, but it is also thought to provide incentives for an efficient organization of production and reducing slack. Thus, competition

*This article originally appeared in *KYKLOS* (2004), 57, 357–386.

may sharpen managerial incentives by enabling owners to compare the performance of managers within the same industry. Irrespective of their theoretical appeal, these assumptions have not been tested very often. Due to a lack of longitudinal data on the performance of firms with different organizational forms, the empirical evidence is not very compelling yet.

The chapter is organized as follows: Section 2 discusses the conditions under which different types of organizations (owner-managed firms, firms run by "managing directors," foundation owned firms, firms owned by public authorities and cooperatives) may be efficient responses to the needs of coordination and motivation. Any attempt to empirically assess the efficiency of different organizational forms has to deal with the problem of data availability. Most research is based on data from manufacturing firms that are very often highly heterogeneous with regard to their stocks of physical and human capital, their production functions and a number of other variables that may influence firm performance, but are difficult to measure (see, e.g., Thomsen, 1996; Czarnitzki and Kraft, 2000; Gorriz and Fumas, 1996). Moreover, the fact that most analyzes use cross-sectional data implies that it is not possible to control for firm specific effects (see, e.g., Ford and Kaserman, 2000; Michael, 2000). Therefore, Section 3 first describes the longitudinal data used to assess the influence of ownership structures on firm performance in a sample of about 300 wineries in Germany, covering the years 1996–1999. Apart from the simple fact that the necessary data is available, the wine industry is especially suitable for an empirical analysis like the one performed below because firm heterogeneity is, first, rather limited (all firms employ the same input factors and have the same production function) and, second, because that heterogeneity can be accounted for by estimating, *inter alia*, random effects-models. Third, organizational forms in the German wine industry differ more than in most other sectors. Here we observe not only owner-managed firms and firms run by "employee managers," but also a significant number of firms owned and operated by public authorities or non-profit organizations as well as a quite considerable number of cooperatives. Section 3 presents estimates of the influence of ownership structure on two different dimensions of firm performance, that is, the quality of the products as perceived by distinguished experts and product prices. It appears that ownership has indeed a considerable impact. Section 4 summarizes the main findings and raises some of the questions that should be the subject of future research.

2. Governance, Incentives, Competition, and Performance

2.1. *Theory*

Economic organizations are created entities within and through which people interact to reach individual and collective economic goals.[1] From an economic point of view, an organization is a nexus of contracts among its individual members. Thus, the firm — whatever its specific form — is a legal fiction that enters relatively simple bilateral contracts with its suppliers, workers, investors, and customers. However, defining organizations as distinct legal entities only can be quite misleading, because such a definition conceals important differences in the "organizational architecture" of firms that involves different elements, such as the allocation of responsibilities and decision rights, the authority and control relationships, the pattern of information and resource flows as well as the means used to align the interests of individual members of the organization and the goals of the organization as a whole (Milgrom and Roberts, 1992, pp. 19–20).

Prior to the publication of "The Modern Corporation and Private Property" by Berle and Means in 1932, economic theory did not explicitly distinguish between "owners" and "employee managers."[2] Since then, however, ownership came to be seen as a key organizational variable in determining firm outcomes. Berle and Means not only documented the increasing separation of ownership and control in modern corporations but also depicted the firm as a largely autonomous entity, where "managers" more or less successfully pursue their own objectives rather than maximize the returns to the

[1] Another "natural candidate" to explain the impact of the observed governance arrangements on the performance of different firms within the same industry is the "resource-based view," which has become one of the dominant perspectives in the more business oriented literature (see Conner, 1991; Mahoney and Pandian, 1992; Peteraf, 1993; Wernerfeldt, 1984, 1995). The problems with this approach are twofold and have not been solved yet (see Poppo and Weigelt, 2000, p. 586): First, as long as we cannot empirically examine the performance-cost link, any asset can be said to provide a competitive advantage which, in turn, points to the possibility that the theory is tautological (this argument has been discussed in a recent controversy between Priem and Butler (2001a, 2001b) and Barney (2001)). Second, determining the contribution of a single asset within a joint production function is quite difficult.

[2] Jagannathan and Srinivasan (2000) quote from Adam Smith's "The Wealth of Nations" to prove that the agency theoretic view that managers do not maximize the returns to owners but preserve the firm's value only because it is necessary for their survival in the job dates back to the 18th century already.

owners. Thus, management opportunism may lead to a waste of corporate resources or reduced effort ("shirking"). Owners face a delegation problem: On the one hand, they hire managers because of their knowledge and their ability to perform certain tasks (their "human capital"), while on the other hand, they cannot completely control the actions of these managers.[3] Principal agent-theory shows that, in principle, the moral hazard problem can be solved, or at least improved, through a mix of control and incentives. Due to monitoring costs, owners try to develop incentive compatible contracts that align the interests of the two parties. Although the concept of reward based on effort is rather appealing, it is difficult to enforce contracts based on the manager's physical or intellectual input. This, in turn, is not only due to problems of measurement and monitoring, because the firm's cash flow is the result of the manager's effort and external (random) factors. If both cannot be distinguished or if they are unobservable, owners do not know whether good performance is due to effort or luck. Usually problems arise due to lack of competence on the side of owners to evaluate the adequacy of managerial decisions and actions. Such incomplete information leads to attempts by the owner(s) to mitigate these asymmetries by implementing more or less complex monitoring systems and by devising more or less elaborate systems of performance-related pay. Apart from the fact that most managers are motivated by concerns about their status and reputation in the managerial labor market (Fama, 1980), competition in the product market reduces managerial opportunism and slack as well. Machlup (1967), for example, argues that imperfect competition in the product market is a necessary condition for the existence of agency costs. As Holmstrom (1982) and Nalebuff and Stiglitz (1983) have shown, explicit incentive schemes will generate sharper incentives the greater the number of players involved. This arises because of the greater opportunities for comparison of performance.

In addition to owner-managed firms and firms run by managing directors,[4] further types of organizations exist that — under specific

[3] Scott Morton and Podolny (1998) further distinguish between owners who try to maximize utility and those who maximize their profits and analyze how the differing objectives among these two types affect competition, prices, production, and quality levels.

[4] If owning a winery has recently become a "hobby" for rich "baby boomers" (as is apparent especially in California and — to a lesser extent — in Australia) one might expect to observe a poor performance of firms run by professional managers (the hobby owners are unlikely to run their estates themselves). This, however, is unlikely to occur because especially the richer owners are typically interested in producing high quality wines (which may not always sell out) and gaining prestige (see Scott Morton and Podolny, 1998). A more general point is that the motivation to run a winery may differ considerably between

circumstances — must be efficient, because otherwise competition would have driven them out of the market. In some sectors, such as personnel services (medical doctors and lawyers) partnerships play an important role while in others (such as agriculture and fishing) cooperatives seem to fulfill certain tasks better than other organizational forms (Kräkel, 1999, pp. 331–374). There are several reasons why the latter type of organization may operate more productively than "classical" firms. First, cooperatives are a hybrid form of organization with economically independent members who pool their resources to acquire capital intensive input factors, such as a winepress, while simultaneously using the advantages of decentralization, that is, the incentive effects of "capitalist entrepreneurship." Second, cooperatives may mitigate agency costs associated with a firm's division between ownership and control, because worker ownership eliminates the separation of interests between workers and owners. In the presence of asymmetrical information, cooperatives offer the opportunity of productivity gains from eliminating the division of interests between the two groups. Third, workers may be able to monitor each other's effort more effectively than in firms where the monitor is the owner's agent (Craig and Pencavel, 1995, pp. 124–126). Finally, especially with regard to the specific conditions in agriculture and forestry, some additional reasons to form a cooperative may be important: Due to their specific capital (knowledge and equipment), small estate owners who sell their grapes instead of producing wine themselves can avoid a hold-up situation only through vertical integration, that is, by founding a joint enterprise (a cooperative) that buys and processes the grapes. In the context of this chapter, another argument may be even more important: If products from a specific region that have a high reputation among consumers (i.e., wine from the Mosel valley) are sold throughout the country (or even worldwide), individual estate owners may have an incentive to produce low-quality wines thereby saving production costs while simultaneously damaging the reputation of all other producers. In this case, cooperatives may act as an institution to prevent negative external effects by guaranteeing a high product quality. In order to avoid the free rider-problem cooperatives typically use complex incentive schemes rewarding members not only for the quantity, but also the quality of the products delivered for manufacturing.

---

those who produce wine because of their affection for the product and those who produce wine to make as much money as possible. The empirical part of my paper (see Section 3) implicitly takes this argument into consideration by using two different, though related, performance measures.

A further organizational form to be found among German wine producers is a foundation, that is, a legal entity that has been created by an irrevocable donation. In principle, a foundation is an independent institution that has no owners and no members. It is formally governed by a charter which defines its purpose and organization. The foundation may, for example, be obliged to do business in the spirit of the founder and therefore, engage in a certain type of economic activity. A foundation-owned company seems to violate some of the basic principles of the modern corporation: It is neither monitored by the stock market nor exposed to the market for corporate control. Its owner (the foundation) does not have a personal profit motive and its board is usually dominated by representatives from the local political elite. Therefore, foundations are neither incentive efficient (managers that run them are not fully compensated according to their performance) nor are they risk efficient (risk bearing is mainly confined to the owner). On the other hand, companies owned by foundations may have a comparative advantage in long-term decision making. They may, for example, be even more patient investors in firm specific assets than private owners.

The wine industry in Germany offers a particularly well suited environment to study the relative performance of owner-managed firms, firms run by employee managers, public firms, cooperatives, and foundations. All firms use identical input factors and have an identical production function. Moreover, since the industry is highly competitive, all firms should produce rather efficiently because otherwise they would be driven out of the market. Summarizing the discussion above, the following competing and testable hypotheses can be derived:

- H_1 As monitoring of "managing directors" is costly and difficult to perform owner-managed firms and cooperatives should be — other things equal — more efficient than firms run by "expert" managers (i.e., they should produce better and more expensive wines).
- H_2 If, on the other hand, the (sector-specific) skills and knowledge of expert managers are of primary importance (because monitoring costs are low and benchmarking is easy to perform), then managed firms should be more successful than the other two types of organizations. In the case of specialized managers, however, monitoring intensity is likely to vary between public and private firms, suggesting that the managers of public firms are less successful than those managing private enterprises.
- H_3 Finally, it is also possible that "variety in organizational forms is most likely to be observed where organizational form matters least, so that

small changes in the underlying environment can tip the net benefit calculation from one arrangement to another. Where, on the other hand, organizational form is important, in the sense that one form of organization has large efficiency advantages over the alternatives, the superior alternative will tend to dominate, and little variety will be seen in organizational arrangements" (Masten, 2002, p. 429). This, in turn, suggests that the organizational form should have no impact on firm performance.

2.2. *Previous evidence*

Two different strands of literature deserve to be reviewed in the context of this chapter: On the one hand, a few papers have investigated the determinants of firm survival (an easily accessible measure of long-run firm performance) in the California and the Missouri wine industry (Delacroix *et al.*, 1989; Delacroix and Swaminathan, 1991; Stoeberl *et al.*, 1998). Unfortunately, however, these studies do not take into account the ownership and governance structures of their sample firms, but concentrate on an analysis of the influence of organizational characteristics (such as age and size), calendar time, level and change in wine consumption, organizational change (measured by, *inter alia*, the number of land acquisition and divestment events and the number of brand and product increase/decrease events), and environmental change (number of foundings and disbandings) on the failure rate of individual wineries in the period 1940–1985 (California) and 1973–1990 (Missouri), respectively. Using event-history analysis as an econometric tool, the studies unequivocally conclude that although organizational change is responsive to environmental variation, it does not at all affect the probability of firm survival.

This, in turn, implies that business organizations typically have the ability to avoid elimination by migrating to neighboring niches and by enlarging their initial niche.

On the other hand, a number of papers have analyzed the influence of the ownership and governance structures of mostly publicly traded firms from various parts of the private sector on their economic performance.[5] Apart from three notable exceptions, however, these studies typically use

[5]These papers include, among others, the widely quoted studies by Demsetz and Lehn (1985), Morck *et al.* (1988), Hermalin and Weisbach (1988), Loderer and Martin (1997), Cho (1998), Himmelberg *et al.* (1999), Holderness *et al.* (1999), Demsetz and Villalonga (2001), and Schulze *et al.* (2001).

data from very broadly classified industries, such as manufacturing, and are thus unable to control adequately for the heterogeneity among their sample firms. Unfortunately, however, these three exceptional studies do not distinguish between owner-managed firms and firms run by employee managers, but only between profit oriented and not-for-profit organizations (with all of them being run by professional management) or between publicly and privately financed endeavors.

Using data from a country-wide survey that was conducted in 1986 in 4739 hospitals, Deily *et al.* (2000) first estimate a translog cost function to measure the degree of relative (in-)efficiency. They find that, on average, hospitals in their data set had costs approximately 15% higher than the observed best practice cost. The mean relative inefficiency residual for the for-profit hospitals was 0.185, for non-profit hospitals it was 0.148, and for government hospitals it was 0.154, with the means significantly different from one another at conventional levels. Five years after the survey had been conducted (in 1991) exactly 177 of the hospitals had been closed down. The mean relative inefficiency residual for hospitals that subsequently closed was 0.194, in contrast to 0.153 for hospitals that remained open and the difference between these two means was once again statistically highly significant. Controlling for a large number of possible determinants of hospital exit, the study finds that the relative inefficiency residual has the predicted significantly positive influence on the exit probability. Moreover, it appears that government hospitals have — irrespective of their efficiency — a significantly lower exit probability than observationally similar for-profit and non-profit hospitals. Separate estimates for the three ownership categories revealed that both for-profit and not-for-profit hospitals with higher relative inefficiency results were more likely to exit, while relative inefficiency did not have a statistically significant effect on the probability of exit for government hospitals.

Using longitudinal data on essentially all non-rural elderly Medicare recipients hospitalized for a treatment of a new heart attack over the period 1985–1996, matched with comprehensive data on all non-rural US hospitals over the same period, Kessler and McClellan (2001) find that areas with a presence of for-profit hospitals have approximately 2.4% lower levels of hospital expenditures, but virtually the same patient health outcomes (measured by the one-year mortality rate and the one-year re-admittance rate) — a finding that points to significant spillover benefits of for-profit hospitals for medical productivity.

Finally, Karpoff (2001) compares the relative performance of 35 government and 57 privately funded expeditions that, during the years 1818–1909, sought to find a Northwest Passage, discover the North Pole and make other significant discoveries in arctic regions (such as finding the members of an expedition who got lost in 1845). He finds that most of the major arctic discoveries were made by private expeditions while most tragedies were publicly funded. This is surprising insofar as, on average, public expeditions were better funded than private ones (measured by the number of ships (1.6 vs. 1.2), vessel tonnage employed (596 vs. 277), and crew size (70 vs. 16)). This, in turn, suggests that the former ones lost more ships (0.5 vs. 0.2), had more men die (5.9 vs. 0.9), and experienced poorer crew health (measured by the incidence of scurvy (47% vs. 13%)). According to the estimates, public expeditions' poor performance cannot be attributed to differences in objectives, available technologies, or country of origin. Rather, the results point toward poor leadership structures, slow adaptation to new information, and perverse incentives in publicly funded expeditions.

Summarizing the available evidence, it appears that no study exists that tries to isolate the impact of the various forms of ownership on the economic performance of firms: While most studies concentrate on the impact of ownership concentration ("dispersed ownership" vs. "blockholding") or the identity of the owners (banks, families, other firms, etc.[6]), others just compare profit-oriented and not-for-profit organizations, leaving aside the important distinction between different forms of profit oriented firms. It is the possible differences between owned-managed firms and firms run by employee managers on the one hand, public, collective and private ownership on the other hand that this chapter addresses using data from a setting that is especially suited for an econometric study.

3. Data, Estimation Procedure and Empirical Findings

In 1999, there were about 34,000 individual wine producers in Germany who cultivated about 245,000 acres of land (Gurrath, 2001, p. 37);[7] nearly 90% of these individual producers belong to one of the approximately 300 cooperatives (Sälzer, 1998, pp. 94, 156). Thus, the number of distinct organizational entities is about 3500. Average estate size is about 7.1 acres (compared

[6]For a recent overview of the available evidence for Germany see Frick and Lehmann (2004).
[7]In 1979, some 52,000 wine producers cultivated about 218,000 acres. In 1989, the former figure had fallen to 46,000 while the latter had increased to 240,000. Thus, the number of individual wine producers has decreased by about a third in twenty years (Gurrath, 2001, p. 37). Given the rather small increase in acreage these figures imply a significant increase in average estate size (from 4.2 acres in 1979 to 7.1 acres in 1999).

to more than 250 acres in California, cf. Scott Morton and Podolny, 1998, p. 31); members of cooperatives on average cultivate about 1.3 acres only.[8] The individual producers are located in 13 different regions of varying quantitative as well as qualitative importance. The smallest regions, like Sachsen, Hessische Bergstrasse, Ahr, Saale-Unstrut and Mittelrhein cover at most 1,500 acres, while the largest ones (Rheinhessen, Pfalz, Baden, Mosel-Saar-Ruwer, and Wuerttemberg) cover more than 25,000 acres each.[9]

The data set used in this section to empirically test the hypotheses derived above has been compiled from four different editions of a well-known wine guide called "Der Feinschmecker" (literally translated "The Gourmet"). Originally a hotel and restaurant guide, it was enlarged by its publishers in 1996 to include the "Top 300" wineries in the country. Combining the data for the years 1996–1999 resulted in an unbalanced panel of 305 wineries (about 9% of all wine producing organizations in Germany). Apart from detailed information concerning its size and its products the description of every estate contains information on its ownership structure, that is, whether it is an owner-managed firm, a firm run by an "employee manager" or a cooperative. Moreover, it is possible to distinguish between private firms and those that are owned by public authorities or belong to a foundation. The wineries included in the 1999 sample cultivate some 25,000 acres (about 9% of all land that is used to grow grapes). Thus, the sample estates are much larger than the average winery (82.5 vs. 7.1 acres).

The data underlying Table 1 (as well as the estimations presented below) were collected as follows: In an effort to reproduce the environment in which an ordinary customer buys wine, the cultivators are never informed about the identity of the jury members. The "expert customers" are instructed to buy three "representative" bottles of wine upon visit of the winery and not in a supermarket, at a wine merchant's or somewhere else. Thus, if all wineries provided complete information the data set should consist of 3,660 cases (305 wineries with three wines per year over a period of four years). Since some of

[8]Each cooperative has, on average, about 250 members; the small ones have less than 100 members, the large ones about 1000.

[9]The remaining three regions are Franken, Nahe, and Rheingau with 4,500–9,000 acres each. Average firm size varies between these regions. The largest wineries are located in Rheinhessen (13.8 acres), Saale-Unstrut (12.4 acres), and Pfalz (11.9 acres) while the smallest ones can be found in the Ahr region (3.2 acres), Baden (4.0 acres), and Wuerttemberg (4.2 acres). Not surprisingly, the latter three regions are the ones where cooperatives have a market share of more than 75% (on average, the cooperatives' market share is 30% only; Sälzer, 1998, p. 179).

Table 1. Wine Prices and Wine Quality in the Different Wine Regions

	Average price per bottle (in DM)		Average quality as perceived by Jury Members (Grades 0.5–5.0)	
Region	Mean	Std. Dev.	Mean	Std. Dev.
Ahr	21.97	8.76	2.95	3.21
Baden	17.61	9.56	2.25	2.28
Franken	22.02	29.42	2.39	2.41
Hessische Bergstrasse	21.83	36.64	2.08	2.17
Mittelrhein	32.60	66.57	2.05	2.00
Mosel-Saar-Ruwer	23.62	34.46	2.88	2.90
Nahe	16.60	16.11	2.46	2.52
Pfalz	20.93	29.82	2.60	2.64
Rheingau	26.79	40.20	2.83	2.93
Rheinhessen	14.68	15.39	2.18	2.10
Saale-Unstrut	13.39	3.19	1.21	1.25
Sachsen	18.58	9.04	1.08	1.00
Wuerttemberg	26.88	53.15	2.26	2.25
Average	21.58	31.89	2.50	1.13
F-Value	5.10^{***}		29.86^{***}	

Note: $^{***}p < 0.01$.

the wineries are not permanently included in the "Top 300" and due to some missing values the number of cases available for the estimations is about 10% lower (3,298 and 3,269). When testing and classifying the purchased wines the experts do not know the identity of the winery. The results of this testing, in turn, give a quality measure that ranges from 0.5–5.0 (with values of 1.5, 2.5, 3.5, and 4.5 also possible). For all the wines, objective and easily observable characteristics (price, vintage year, vineyard region, etc.) are available. Finally, some weeks after the visit a questionnaire is sent to each enterprise asking for, *inter alia*, its size, the annual production of wine (in bottles), and grape varieties.

Table 1 shows that wine prices as well as wine quality (as perceived by the members of an independent professional jury) vary significantly between the thirteen wine growing regions of Germany. On the one hand, the most expensive wines are produced in Mittelrhein, Rheingau, and Wuerttemberg while the cheapest ones come from Saale-Unstrut, Rheinhessen, and Nahe (note, however, that in the most expensive regions the standard deviation of bottle prices is rather high). On the other hand, the best quality is produced in the Ahr region, in the valleys of Mosel, Saar, and Ruwer and in the

Rheingau while the by far poorest quality is produced in Saale-Unstrut and Sachsen.[10]

Apart from the variation in wine prices and wine quality[11] the distribution of ownership types is also quite different among the thirteen wine growing regions: In the Ahr region, Mittelrhein, Nahe, and Rheinhessen, owner-managed firms are heavily over-represented among the top wineries (by 12–41 percentage points) while in Pfalz and Rheingau firms run by employee managers have a significantly higher market share (12–22 percentage points) than the one that would be observed if ownership type and region were uncorrelated. Moreover, firms owned by public authorities are over-represented in Hessische Bergstrasse, Saale-Unstrut, and Sachsen (by 19–29 percentage points) while Baden, Hessische Bergstrasse, Saale-Unstrut, and — to a lesser extent. Wuerttemberg have a high percentage of cooperatives among their top wineries (9–28 percentage points above the average). Finally, the valleys of Mosel, Saar, and Ruwer — a predominantly catholic area with strong religious ties of most of its inhabitants — are the only region with top wineries owned and operated by the Catholic Church.

Using the data described above two different regression models can be estimated. The dependent variable in the first estimate is the jury grade as the most readily available measure of product quality. The dependent variable in the second estimate is the natural logarithm of the price per bottle.[12] Assuming that all producers in this highly competitive industry set their prices at levels that allow them to sell out their annual production, price per bottle can be interpreted as a complementary measure of product quality. Thus, the model to be estimated is of the following general

---

[10]The latter two regions are located in the former German Democratic Republic, where professional wine making ceased to exist immediately after WW II. In the early 1990s the first private enterprises started to produce wines (again). Most likely, it will take at least another 10 years before these producers become really competitive.

[11]For means, standard deviations, and the distribution of the dependent variables, see Figures 1 and 2 as well as Tables A1, A2, A3 and A4 in the appendix.

[12]Unfortunately, performance measures such as revenues, profits, or returns on investment are not available. Therefore, I use price per bottle and jury grade as proxies for firm performance. The correlation between the two measures used is $r = +0.265$ ($p < 0.01$). Of course, neither price per bottle nor product quality can be considered a valid proxy for the economic returns of the firm. On the one hand, production costs are not identical for all wineries and second, I have no information on investments. Moreover, production costs vary according to the marketing strategy chosen by the owner or the manager (does he sell his products directly to the consumer or to distributors?).

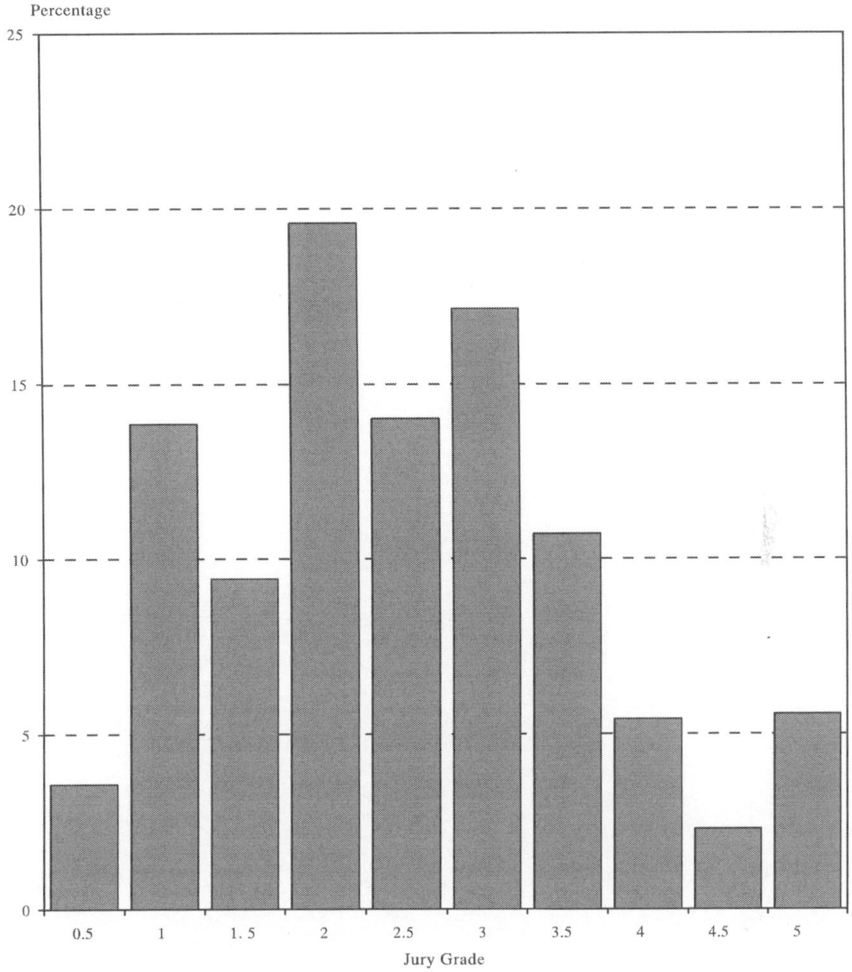

Figure 1. The Distribution of the Jury Grades

form:[13]

$$Y = \alpha_0 + \alpha_1 MANF + \alpha_2 PUBF + \alpha_3 COOP + \alpha_4 SIZE + \alpha_5 BPY + \alpha_6 MEM + \alpha_7 MMS + \alpha_8 BARR + \alpha_9 \sum RED + \alpha_{10} \sum VD + \alpha_{11} \sum RAD + \alpha_{12} \sum YD + \varepsilon \quad (1)$$

where

[13]Another variable one would like to control for in the estimates is the age of the winery. Unfortunately, age is available only for a small number of estates in the sample.

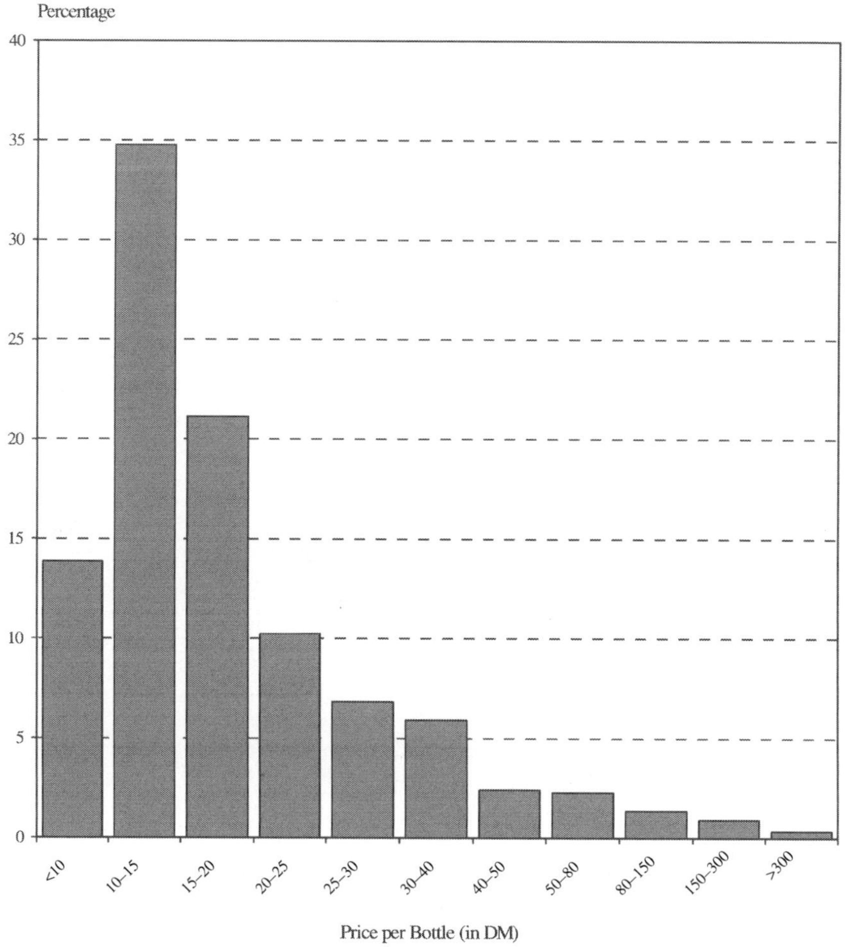

Figure 2. The Distribution of Wine Prices

Y: is either jury grade (JG), that is, the quality of the wine as perceived by independent experts, or the natural logarithm of the price per bottle ($\ln(PB)$)

MANF: managed private firm (dummy variable, no = 0; yes = 1)

PUBF: public or non-profit firm (dummy variable, no = 0; yes = 1)

COOP: cooperative (dummy variable, no = 0; yes = 1)

OWN: owner-managed firm (dummy variable, no = 0; yes = 1; omitted reference category)

SIZE: acreage

BPY: annual production of bottles of wine[14]
MEM: membership in professional associations (dummy variable, no = 0; yes = 1)
MMS: multiple membership in professional associations (dummy variable, no = 0; yes = 1)
BARR: wine fermented in oak barrels (dummy variable, no = 0; yes = 1)
RED: series of region dummies[15]
VD: series of vintage dummies
RAD: series of ranking dummies
YD: series of year dummies

The model outlined above is first estimated by OLS. The coefficients are then compared to the ones from a random effects model and a 2SLS model.[16] Finally, a seemingly unrelated regression is estimated that takes into account the fact that the error terms of the two equations are likely to be correlated. The upper part of Table 2 shows that — compared to owner-managed firms — private estates run by employee managers are perceived as producing higher quality while cooperatives are seen as producing less quality.[17,18]

Albeit not significant in a statistical sense, the latter is also true for wineries owned by public authorities or foundations. Moreover, larger estates (with more acreage) produce — other things equal — higher quality, while a higher

[14]Acreage and annual production (in thousands of bottles) are significantly correlated. However, the correlation coefficient of +0.787 suggests that two different ways of producing wines ("intensive" vs. "extensive") seem to coexist. A table with the correlation matrix of the variables used in the analyzes is available from the author upon request.

[15]Admittedly, region dummies are rather poor proxies for differences in soil quality and surface conditions (such as flat fields vs. steep hills). The latter characteristic is important insofar as the use of machines to maintain the vineyards and to harvest the grapes is restricted to flat fields, suggesting that labor costs (and product prices) tend to be higher in hilly environments. However, since in most of the wine growing regions soil quality and surface conditions vary to a considerable degree, this omission should not lead to a systematic bias in the estimated coefficients.

[16]The coefficients of the region, vintage, ranking, and year dummies are not reported but can be obtained from the author upon request.

[17]Wineries owned by public authorities, foundations, and religious communities are grouped together because neither the quality of their products nor the prices they charge differ between the three types of organization.

[18]The R^2 is considerably higher than in comparable estimates presented by Scott Morton and Podolny (1998) using data from Californian wineries.

Table 2. Determinants of Product Quality

Variable	B	SE B	T	P
		Estimation method: OLS		
MANF	0.213	0.042	5.09	***
PUBF	−0.360	0.087	−4.15	***
COOP	−0.516	0.145	−3.56	***
OWN		reference category		
SIZE	0.005	0.002	3.09	***
BPY#	−0.473	0.161	−2.94	***
BARR	−0.003	0.074	−0.04	+
MEM	0.551	0.039	14.16	***
MMS	0.451	0.058	7.74	***
CONST	1.945	0.091	21.26	***
Region dummies ($n = 13$)		yes		
Vintage dummies ($n = 14$)		yes		
Ranking dummies ($n = 11$)		yes		
Year dummies ($n = 4$)		yes		
N of Cases		3298		
F-value		24.03		
Adj $R^2 \cdot 100$		25.4		
		Estimation method: RE		
MANF	0.193	0.090	2.14	**
PUBF	−0.002	0.152	−0.11	+
COOP	−0.696	0.170	−4.09	***
OWN		reference category		
SIZE	0.006	0.004	1.36	+
BPY#	−0.622	0.453	−1.37	+
BARR	0.003	0.024	0.11	+
MEM	0.064	0.028	2.30	**
MMS	0.037	0.037	0.97	+
CONST	2.181	0.197	11.07	***
Region dummies ($n = 13$)		yes		
Vintage dummies ($n = 14$)		yes		
Ranking dummies ($n = 11$)		yes		
Year dummies ($n = 4$)		yes		
N of Cases		3298		
N of Groups		305		
Adj $R^2 \cdot 100$		15.3		

(*Continued*)

Table 2. (*Continued*)

Variable	B	SE B	T	P
		Estimation method: 2SLS		
MANF	0.997	0.144	6.92	***
PUBF	−1.069	0.232	−4.61	***
COOP	−0.425	0.105	−4.05	***
OWN		reference category		
MEM	0.562	0.042	13.37	***
MMS	0.371	0.061	6.11	***
CONST	1.949	0.048	40.91	***
N of Cases		3298		
F-value		115.01		
Adj $R^2 \cdot 100$		5.4		

Notes: # coefficient multiplied by 100,000 for ease of presentation.
+ n.s.; $^{***}p < 0.01$.

output per acre reduces perceived quality.[19] Finally, the finding that membership in a single professional association as well as multiple membership results in higher quality may be surprising. However, since membership is costly (fees, controls, etc.) it is very likely that owners as well as managers see membership as an investment in reputation, which — in turn — has to be amortized.[20]

Looking at the findings of the random effects estimate in Table 2, it appears that all coefficients retain their sign and that most of them are still significant (the dummy denoting public firms is no longer significantly different from the reference category). However, the LM-Test statistic indicates that the random effects estimate is superior to the OLS-estimate ($\chi^2 = 12{,}993.0$; $p < 0.001$). Comparing the coefficients of the ownership dummies it appears that unobserved heterogeneity is indeed present in the sample, that is, some unobserved characteristics seem to be relevant for the

[19]If, as suggested by an anonymous referee, larger organizations may be simply better equipped to process grapes of different quality, product quality should not differ between large private firms (whether owner-managed or not) and cooperatives. However, the estimates show that this is clearly not the case.

[20]Given the characteristics of one of the dependent variables (the jury grade) an ordered probit and/or a tobit-model may be better suited in the context of this chapter. The respective findings — available upon request — are very similar to the ones presented above.

quality of the wines produced. These characteristics seem to vary systematically across organizations and conduce to the documented quality differentials. Basically, the coefficients of the ownership dummies remain significant, but their magnitude is reduced.

If, as suggested by Demsetz and Lehn (1985), ownership is an endogenous variable, OLS- as well as RE-models may be inappropriate to test the influence of ownership on product quality. In this case, only a 2SLS-model is likely to produce unbiased estimates of the ownership dummies.[21] The coefficients in the lower part of Table 2 reinforce the findings from the OLS-regression: All of the ownership dummies are significantly different from the reference group (the owner-managed firms) with the coefficient of the manager-dummy deviating positively and the cooperative- and the public firm-dummy deviating in the opposite direction.[22] Thus, private firms run by managing directors seem to produce significantly higher quality while public firms and cooperatives show a rather poor performance compared to observationally similar firms that are run by owner managers.

The determinants of bottle prices (see Table 3) are also relatively unaffected by the estimation method: All of the models show that estates run by an employee manager can — other things equal — charge significantly higher prices for their products than other wineries (the coefficient of the foundation/public firm-dummy proved to be significant in only one of the respective estimates while the coefficient of the coop-dummy failed to reach significance in either case). However, in a statistical sense as well as regarding their economic relevance some of the other independent variables seem to be even more important determinants of product prices than company ownership: Wine fermented in oak barrels instead of steel tanks is *c.p.* about 35% more expensive and wine produced at estates that belong to one (or more)

---

[21]In the 2SLS-estimate, the three ownership dummies (managing director, public firm/foundation, cooperative) were instrumented. I used the region and the vintage dummies, acreage and bottles per year as instruments. Type of ownership and, therefore, size and annual production vary across the regions: While in some areas (Baden, Hessische Bergstrasse, Saale-Unstrut, and Wuerttemberg), cooperatives have secured a large market share, in others it is either owner-managed wineries (Ahr, Mittelrhein, and Rheinhessen) that dominate or firms run by employee managers (Mosel-Saar-Ruwer, Pfalz, and Rheingau). In the Nahe region, in Franken and in Sachsen none of the ownership types is over-represented. Of course, acreage and annual production (in thousands of bottles) are correlated with the different ownership types.

[22]This result is robust on changes in the list of variables that are used to instrument the ownership dummies. The detailed findings of various specifications are available from the author on request

Table 3. Determinants of Product Prices

Variable	B	SE B	T	P
		Estimation method: OLS		
MANF	0.131	0.013	9.47	***
PUBF	−0.005	0.028	−0.19	+
COOP	−0.204	0.047	−4.32	***
OWN		reference category		
SIZE	0.001	0.000	2.79	**
BPY #	−0.107	0.053	−2.04	**
BARR	0.381	0.024	15.73	***
MEM	0.123	0.013	9.64	***
MMS	0.044	0.019	2.33	**
CONST	2.089	0.030	69.88	***
Region dummies ($n = 13$)		yes		
Vintage dummies ($n = 14$)		yes		
Ranking dummies ($n = 11$)		yes		
Year dummies ($n = 4$)		yes		
N of Cases		3269		
F-value		186.94		
Adj $R^2 \cdot 100$		72.7		
		Estimation method: RE		
MANF	0.138	0.030	4.56	***
PUBF	−0.026	0.060	−0.43	+
COOP	−0.141	0.091	−1.55	+
OWN		reference category		
SIZE	0.001	0.001	1.14	+
BPY	−0.132	0.120	−1.10	*
BARR	0.378	0.022	17.36	***
MEM	0.068	0.020	3.43	***
MMS	0.042	0.028	1.51	+
CONST	2.143	0.051	41.27	***
Region dummies ($n = 13$)		yes		
Vintage dummies ($n = 14$)		yes		
Ranking dummies ($n = 11$)		yes		
Year dummies ($n = 4$)		yes		
N of Cases		3269		
N of Groups		305		
Adj $R^2 \cdot 100$		72.1		

(*Continued*)

Table 3. (*Continued*)

Variable	B	SE B	T	P
		Estimation method: 2SLS		
MANF	0.324	0.080	4.03	***
PUBF	0.052	0.126	0.41	+
COOP	−0.015	0.058	−0.26	+
OWN		reference category		
MEM	0.154	0.023	6.68	***
MMS	0.059	0.034	1.75	*
CONST	2.609	0.026	99.34	***
N of Cases		3298		
F-value		23.73		
Adj $R^2 \cdot 100$		3.1		

Notes: # coefficient multiplied by 100,000 for ease of presentation; + n.s. $^*p < 0.10$; $^{**}p < 0.05$; $^{***}p < 0.01$.

professional association(s) is about 5–10% more expensive. Moreover, product prices are lower, the higher the output (in bottles) per year and acre.[23]

Since the wines have been purchased before the tasting, the jury grade cannot have any causal impact on the price level. It is, nevertheless, tempting to include the quality index in the vector of explanatory variables, because a major shortcoming of the data used to estimate the price equation is the lack of sensory characteristics (color, smell, taste, etc.) of the wines.[24] In a situation of imperfect information rational consumers gather (additional) information about the product under consideration only as long as the marginal cost of obtaining it is lower than or equal to the marginal utility it generates.[25] Since it is rather expensive to obtain information about the

[23]Again, the R^2 is much higher than in comparable studies by Scott Morton and Podolny (1998) for Californian wines and by Combris *et al.* (1997, 2000) for Bordeaux and Burgundy wines.

[24]It is also possible that the jury grade has an impact on future prices: Following a positive evaluation a winery may increase its prices and following a bad rating, prices may decrease. Given the short period of time for which the data is available so far (1996–1999), it is unfortunately not possible to empirically study the development of future prices.

[25]In such a situation, the rise of "superstar winemakers" may be the result of a random process as described by Adler (1985, p. 212): "... the phenomenon of stardom exists where consumption requires knowledge. The acquisition of knowledge by a consumer involves discussion with other consumers, and a discussion is easier if all participants share common prior knowledge. If there are stars, that is, artists that everybody is familiar with, a consumer would be better off patronizing these stars even if their art is not superior to that of others."

sensory characteristics consumers tend to make their choice primarily on the basis of objective characteristics that are printed on the label of the bottle as well as on the information obtained from one or more wine guide(s). Additional estimates (not reported here) including the quality index as a series of dummy variables (Frick, 2004) reveal that — not surprisingly — higher quality goes hand in hand with higher prices. More important in the present context is yet a second finding: Controlling for product quality in the price equation leaves the significance as well as the magnitude of the ownership dummies virtually unchanged.[26]

Moreover, from an econometrician's point of view it may seem problematic that the price and the quality equations have been estimated separately, although the same set of right hand side variables has been used. Therefore, it is certainly advisable to estimate a seemingly unrelated regression of the two equations and to use the Breusch Pagan-Test to control for possible dependence among the error terms. It appears from Table 4 that wineries that are run by managing directors produce higher quality wines and are thus able to charge higher prices for their products than otherwise identical owner-managed firms. Wineries owned by public authorities or foundations as well as cooperatives are — on the other hand — less efficient than owner-managed firms: In the case of the former, the quality of the wines produced is lower but — surprisingly — their prices are not. Finally, wines produced by cooperatives are perceived to be of a lower quality and, at the same time, sell at a significantly lower price than the ones produced by wineries that belong to the reference group.[27]

Apart from the ones mentioned above, a further econometric issue warrants attention: Since the sample contains about 3,300 different wines but only 305 separate estates and most of the independent variables vary by estates, not by individual wines, we may encounter the "Moulton problem" in calculating the standard errors of the coefficient estimates (Moulton, 1986, 1990): When the observations in the sample are independent across groups (i.e., wineries) but not independent within groups, the estimated standard

[26]In the random effects estimate presented in Table 3, for example, the adjusted R^2 increases from 72.1% to 73.4%. The coefficient of the manager dummy now becomes 0.119 instead of 0.138 (with a t-value of 4.12 instead of 4.56) and the coefficient of the public firm/foundation dummy now is -0.043 (as opposed to -0.026 in the estimation presented above). Finally, the coefficient of the coop-dummy now is -0.132 (both coefficients are statistically not significant, thus confirming the results presented above).

[27]The correlation of the residuals is $r = +0.294$; the Breusch-Pagan test of independence gives a χ^2 of 284.2 ($p < 0.01$).

Table 4. The Simultaneous Determination of Product Quality and Product Prices

Variable	B	SE B	T	p
		Estimation method: SURE		
		Dependent variable: JG		
MANF	0.176	0.042	4.16	***
PUBF	−0.397	0.087	−4.58	***
COOP	−0.575	0.144	−3.98	***
OWN		reference category		
SIZE	0.005	0.002	3.19	***
BPY#	−0.482	0.161	−3.00	***
BARR	0.092	0.072	1.28	+
MEM	0.538	0.039	13.79	***
MMS	0.498	0.058	8.57	***
CONST	2.118	0.084	25.36	***
Region dummies ($n = 13$)		yes		
Vintage dummies ($n = 14$)		yes		
Ranking dummies ($n = 11$)		no		
Year dummies ($n = 4$)		yes		
N of Cases		3269		
$R^2 \cdot 100$		23.4		
χ^2		1000.67		
		Dependent variable: ln(PB)		
MANF	0.130	0.014	9.47	***
PUBF	−0.008	0.028	−0.28	+
COOP	−0.208	0.047	−4.43	***
OWN		reference category		
SIZE	0.001	0.000	2.80	***
BPY	−0.106	0.052	−2.03	**
BARR	0.390	0.024	16.25	***
MEM	0.123	0.013	9.71	***
MMS	0.048	0.019	2.53	**
CONST	2.105	0.029	71.37	***
Region dummies ($n = 13$)		yes		
Vintage dummies ($n = 14$)		yes		
Ranking dummies ($n = 11$)		yes		
Year dummies ($n = 4$)		yes		
N of Cases		3269		
$R^2 \cdot 100$		72.7		
χ^2		9091.57		

Notes: # coefficient multiplied by 100,000 for ease of presentation; + n.s.; $^{**}p < 0.05$; $^{***}p < 0.01$.

errors are likely to be biased downward. However, re-estimating the price- as well as the quality-model using a robust variance estimator produces virtually identical results.[28] Thus, in the present context clustering is apparently not the source of any bias.

Finally, the composition of the sample used to estimate the models presented above may be a matter of serious concern, because the 305 estates are certainly not a random, but a positive selection from the population of German wineries. While in most cases such a selection bias is detrimental to a clear-cut interpretation of the findings, it tends to even strengthen the results obtained here: Since estates that produce mediocre wines are virtually non-existent in the sample and since owner-managed firms have a significantly higher probability of belonging to the mediocre producers (their average quality rating is 2.49 as opposed to 2.83 for the firms run by expert managers), the findings presented above most likely underestimate the "true" differences in product quality and product prices between firms that are owner-managed and those that are run by expert managers hired from outside.

4. Summary and Implications for Future Research

Using an unbalanced panel of some 300 German wineries (compiled from the information provided by a very respected and widely used wine guide), the above analysis shows that ownership does indeed influence the performance of firms, that is, their product quality as well as their product prices: Firms run by "managing directors" produce higher quality and more expensive wines than otherwise identical owner-managed firms. Given the problems that may occur when ownership and control are separated, these findings may seem counterintuitive. They can, however, be reconciled with principal agent-theory: First, there is certainly intense competition among the wineries in the sample used here and competition is likely to deter management opportunism. In an attempt not to lose their reputation and to keep their jobs, employee managers are unlikely to take actions that are not in the interests of owners. Moreover, in homogeneous industries (i.e., those where firms have more or less identical production functions and use the same input factors) competition creates opportunities for benchmarking which, in

[28] I used the Newey-West estimator which produces the same results as the Huber-White sandwich robust variance estimate if the lag is assumed to be zero (a plausible assumption in the present context). For the sake of brevity I do not report the results; they can be obtained upon request.

turn, gives reliable information about the effort levels chosen by employee managers.

Furthermore, the superior performance of employee managers may be due to their level of education, that is, managing directors are, on average, better qualified than owner managers. This human capital advantage, however, guarantees a better performance only in the case of privately owned wineries: Estates that are owned by a public authority or belong to a foundation do not benefit very much from the superior knowledge of their managing directors. Here the costs associated with a separation of ownership and control apparently outweigh the benefits of having an especially qualified management.

Some additional features of the data and the estimates tend to reinforce the interpretation outlined above: First, due to its specific nature, the data used in this study are likely to underestimate the significantly positive impact of employee managers on different dimensions of firm performance: An estate has been classified as run by an employee manager if different names have been given in the wine guide for the owner and the "managing director" in the short description provided for every estate that belongs to the "Top 300" in a given year. If, for example, the son-in-law or a brother of the owner's wife is acting as managing director, wineries are falsely classified as being managed by an "outside director" although in reality they are family owned and managed. Since firms run by employee managers seem to be more efficient, these misclassifications are likely to reduce the coefficient of the associated dummy variable. Second, since the manager-dummy proved to be significantly different from the reference category (owner-managed firms) in all of the eight different specifications although the data used does not contain any information neither on the duration of individual winery-manager matches nor on contract design (such as the existence of incentive clauses), the findings are likely to be very robust.

Apart from the question whether the findings presented in this chapter can be generalized to other sectors, they suggest at least two promising avenues for future research: First, the prices given in most of the wine guides have been criticized as being unrealistically high. Most producers would sell their products at significantly lower prices than the ones indicated. This, however, would be a problem only if the rebates given to (large) customers differed between owner-managed firms and wineries run by employee managers. Although it is not very likely that this is the case, (potential) differences in price setting behavior can be analyzed empirically by using data on prices paid at wine auctions. In principle, such data is available and will be analyzed in the near future. Second, a question that should also be dealt with is whether the situation in the German wine industry can be described as a separating equilibrium where firms of different organizational architecture and/or productivity can survive, because some consumers prefer buying wine from a cooperative (e.g., due to ideological reasons) while others have a preference for small and independent estate owners (both of which produce — according to the estimates presented above — lower-level quality). Unfortunately, due to a lack of customer-related data an empirical test of a separating equilibrium is quite difficult to achieve.[29]

Finally, an additional question remains to be answered by future research: Are the main findings presented above — other things equal, owner managers produce less quality and sell their products at lower prices — specific to the sector under consideration, the German wine industry, or can they be generalized to other sectors with similar characteristics, such as the high degree of product market competition and the low level of monitoring costs? To the extent that product market competition and the opportunities of (nearly) costless monitoring of employee managers are only necessary (but not sufficient) conditions for the emergence of the observed differences in product prices and product quality, additional explanations are required. For example, it may well be that the distribution of talent is different within the two winemaker populations.[30] Assuming that the jury grades reflect talent and ability, it appears that both distributions are highly skewed: While in the case of employee managers the distribution is skewed to the right (indicating a rather low percentage of less talented winemakers), the opposite seems to be true for the owner population here the distribution is clearly skewed to the left (indicating a rather low percentage of "top talent"). Most owner managers have inherited their estates, suggesting that many of them

[29]Using data from various annual drafts in the National Football League, Conlin (1999) and Conlin and Emerson (1999) provide a convincing example of such a test.

[30]Differences in talent should be correlated with differences in the extent of vocational education, because only the more able individuals will have an incentive to invest in the acquisition of specific skills. In the context of this chapter, there are three different levels of formal qualification to be distinguished: First, many owner managers (but none of the employee managers) have never obtained a formal degree, but acquired the necessary skills on-the-job. Second, most of the employee managers and a large minority of the owner managers have completed a regular apprenticeship and later on acquired a craftman's degree. Moreover, a considerable percentage of the employee managers (but only few owner managers) have obtained a degree as an engineer from the only technical college in Germany that is specialized in teaching winemakers (located in Geisenheim, a small city in the Rhine valley).

engage in the production of wine because their second-best alternative is a low-paying job as a poorly qualified blue-collar worker in a rural area (or even unemployment).[31] Or, to put it in other words: The percentage of especially gifted winemakers is likely to be significantly lower among the owner managers than among the employee managers.[32] If this explanation is of wider applicability, we should observe similar differences in the performance of firms run by owner managers and managing directors in other sectors too.

Acknowledgments

I thank David Forrest, Victor Ginsburgh, Hans Pechtl, Jürgen Weigand, Reiner Eichenberger (the editor), and the referees for their detailed and valuable comments that helped to improve the paper. Moreover, I am indebted to Joachim Prinz for his research assistance and to Lucas Bretschger, Helmut Dietl, and Hans Hirth for suggestions and recommendations. All remaining errors are, of course, my own.

References

Adler, M. (1985). Stardom and talent. *American Economic Review*, 75, 208–212.

Barney, J.B. (2001). Is the resource-based 'View' a useful perspective for strategic management research? Yes. *Academy of Management Review*, 26, 41–56.

Berle, A.A., and Means, G.C. (1932). *The Modern Corporation and Private Property*. New York: Macmillan.

Cho, M.-H. (1998). Ownership structure, investment and the corporate value: An empirical analysis. *Journal of Financial Economics*, 47, 103–121.

Combris, P., Lecocq, S., and Visser, M. (1997). Estimation of a Hedonic price equation for Bordeaux wine: Does quality matter? *Economic Journal*, 107, 390–402.

Combris, P., Lecocq, S., and Visser, M. (2000). Estimation of a Hedonic price equation for Burgundy wine. *Applied Economics*, 32, 961–967.

Conlin, M. (1999). Empirical test of a separating equilibrium in National Football League contract negotiations. *Rand Journal of Economics*, 30, 289–304.

[31] Another possibility is that it is not the quality of the management that differs between owner-managed firms and those run by employee managers, but the quality of the other staff — and that may drive the results instead. This, however, is rather unlikely: Apart from one or two foremen, the staff of a winery (be it an owner managed one or one run by an employee manager) typically consists of poorly qualified seasonal blue-collar workers who have been recruited from the local area in which the winery is located. Since most of the jobs pay low wages only (approximately 6–7€ per hour), they are not at all attractive to workers from outside the respective village.

[32] Winery sales are very rare events suggesting that, on the one hand, there is no takeover threat by the capital market. On the other hand, "altruism" toward their children may inhibit some private estate owners to sell their winery although the potential heirs have already proved to be rather poor wine makers (there is some anecdotal evidence to this latter point).

Conlin, M., and Emerson, P. (1999). Double moral hazard and a multi-dimensional separating equilibrium in contract negotiations: A study of the National Football League. Discussion paper, Department of Economics, Cornell University.

Conner, K. (1991). A historical comparison of resource-based theory and five schools of thought within industrial organization economics: Do we have a new theory of the firm? *Journal of Management*, 17, 121–154.

Craig, B., and Pencavel, J. (1995). Participation and productivity: A comparison of worker cooperatives and conventional firms in the plywood industry. *Brookings Papers on Economic Activity: Microeconomics*, 121–160.

Czarnitzki, D., and Kraft, K. (2000). Management control and innovative activity. Discussion paper, Centre for European Economic Research, Mannheim.

Deily, M.E., McKay, N.L., and Dorner, F.H. (2000). Exit and inefficiency: The effects of ownership type. *Journal of Human Resources*, 35, 734–747.

Delacroix, J., and Swaminathan, A. (1991). Cosmetic, speculative, and adaptive organizational change in the wine industry: A longitudinal study. *Administrative Science Quarterly*, 36, 631–661.

Delacroix, J., Swaminathan, A., and Solt, M.E. (1989). Density dependence versus population dynamics: An ecological study of failings in the california wine industry. *American Sociological Review*, 54, 245–262.

Demsetz, H., and Lehn, K. (1985). The structure of corporate ownership: Causes and consequences. *Journal of Political Economy*, 95, 1155–1177.

Demsetz, H., and Villalonga, B. (2001). Ownership structure and corporate performance. *Journal of Corporate Finance*, 7, 209–233.

Fama, E. (1980). Agency problems and the theory of the firm. *Journal of Political Economy*, 88, 288–307.

Ford, J.M., and Kaserman, D.L. (2000). Ownership structure and the quality of medical care: Evidence from the dialysis industry. *Journal of Economic Behavior and Organization*, 43, 279–293.

Frick, B. (2004). The revenue potential of superstardom: Empirical evidence from German restaurants and wineries. Mimeo, Witten/Herdecke University, Department of Business Administration and Economics.

Frick, B., and Lehmann, E. (2004). Corporate governance in Germany: Ownership, codetermination and firm performance in a stakeholder economy, edited by H. Gospel, and A. Pendleton. *Corporate Governance and Labour Management*. Oxford: Oxford University Press (forthcoming).

Gorriz, C.G., and Fumas, V.S. (1996). Ownership structure and firm performance: Some empirical evidence from Spain. *Managerial and Decision Economics*, 17, 575–586.

Gurrath, P. (2001). Weinbau in Deutschland. *Wirtschaft und Statistik*, 1, 30–45.

Hermalin, B., and Weisbach, M. (1988). The determinants of board composition. *Rand Journal of Economics*, 19, 589–606.

Himmelberg, C.P., Hubbard, R.G., and Palia, D. (1999). Understanding the determinants of managerial ownership and the link between ownership and performance. *Journal of Financial Economics*, 53, 353–384.

Holderness, C., Kroszner, R., and Sheehan, D. (1999). Were the good old days really that good? Evolution of managerial stock ownership and corporate governance since the great depression. *Journal of Finance*, 54, 435–469.

Holmstrom, B. (1982). Moral hazard in teams. *Bell Journal of Economics*, 13, 324–340.

Jagannathan, R., and Srinivasan, S.B. (2000). Does product market competition reduce agency costs? Working Paper No. 7480, National Bureau of Economic Research, Cambridge, MA.

Karpoff, J.M. (2001). Public versus private initiative in Arctic exploration: The effects of incentives and organizational structure. *Journal of Political Economy*, 109, 38–78.

Kessler, D., and McClellan, M. (2001). The effects of hospital ownership on medical productivity. Working Paper No. 8537, National Bureau of Economic Research, Cambridge, MA.

Kräkel, M. (1999). *Organisation und Management*. Tübingen: Mohr Siebeck.

Loderer, C., and Martin, K. (1997). Executive stock ownership and performance: Tracking faint traces. *Journal of Financial Economics*, 45, 223–255.

Machlup, F. (1967). Theories of the firm: Marginalist, behavioral, managerial. *American Economic Review*, 57, 1–33.

Mahoney, J., and Pandian, J. (1992). The resource based view within the conversation of strategic management. *Strategic Management Journal*, 13, 363–380.

Masten, S.E. (2002). Modern evidence on the firm. *American Economic Review, Papers and Proceedings*, 92, 428–432.

Michael, S.C. (2000). The effect of organizational form on quality: The case of franchising. *Journal of Economic Behavior and Organization*, 43, 295–318.

Milgrom, P., and Roberts, J. (1992). *Economics, Organization and Management*. Englewood Cliffs, NJ: Prentice Hall.

Morck, R., Shleifer, A., and Vishny, R. (1988). Management ownership and market valuation: An empirical analysis. *Journal of Financial Economics*, 20, 293–315.

Moulton, B.R. (1986). Random group effects and the precision of regression estimates. *Journal of Econometrics*, 32, 385–397.

Moulton, B.R. (1990). An illustration of a pitfall in estimating the effects of aggregate variables on micro units. *Review of Economics and Statistics*, 72, 334–338.

Nalebuff, B., and Stiglitz, J. (1983). Prizes and incentives: Towards a general theory of compensation and competition. *Bell Journal of Economics*, 14, 21–43.

Peteraf, M. (1993). The cornerstones of competitive advantage: A resource-based view. *Strategic Management Journal*, 14, 179–191.

Poppo, L., and Weigelt, K. (2000). A test of the resource-based model using baseball free agents. *Journal of Economics and Management Strategy*, 9, 585–614.

Priem, R.L., and Butler, J.E. (2001a). Is the resource-based view a useful perspective for strategic management research? *Academy of Management Review*, 26, 22–40.

Priem, R.L., and Butler, J.E. (2001b). Tautology in the resource-based view and the implications of externally determined resource value: Further comments. *Academy of Management Review*, 26, 57–66.

Sälzer, G-L. (1998). *Die Effizienz deutscher Winzergenossenschaften: Institutionelle und empirische Analysen*. Doctoral dissertation, Department of Business Administration and Economics, University of Würzburg.

Schulze, W.S., Lubatkin, M.H., Dino, R.N., and Buchholtz, A.K. (2001). Agency relationships in family firms: Theory and evidence. *Organization Science*, 12, 99–116.

Scott Morton, F.M., and Podolny, J.M. (1998). Love or money? The effects of owner motivation in the California wine industry. Discussion paper, Chicago Graduate Business School and Stanford Graduate Business School.

Stoeberl, P.A., Parker, G.E., and Joo, S.-J. (1998). Relationship between organizational change and failure in the wine industry: An event history analysis. *Journal of Management Studies*, 35, 537–555.

Thomsen, S. (1996). Foundation ownership and economic performance. *Corporate Governance*, 4, 212–221.

Wernerfeldt, B. (1984). A resource-based view of the firm. *Strategic Management Journal*, 5, 171–180.

Wernerfeldt, B. (1995). A resource-based view of the firm: Ten years after. *Strategic Management Journal*, 16, 171–174.

Appendix

Table A1. Means and Standard Deviations of Dependent Variables

	Quality model ($n = 3.298$)		Price model ($n = 3.269$)	
	Mean	Std. Dev.	Mean	Std. Dev.
Quality	2.50	1.13	—	—
Price	—	—	21.69	31.98
ln(Price)	—	—	2.80	0.61

Table A2. Means and Standard Deviations of Independent Variables

	Quality model ($n = 3.298$)		Price model ($n = 3.269$)	
Independent variables	Mean	Std. Dev.	Mean	Std. Dev.
OWN (reference category)	0.673	—	0.672	—
MANF	0.174	—	0.177	—
PUBF	0.051	—	0.050	—
COOP	0.102	—	0.101	—
SIZE	33.2	64.4	33.0	64.2
BPY	263.590	605.900	261.740	603.600
BARR	0.066	—	0.065	—
MEM	0.556	—	0.559	—
MMS	0.147	—	0.147	—
	Region dummies			
Ahr	0.024	—	0.025	—
Baden	0.158	—	0.156	—
Franken	0.081	—	0.080	—
Hessische Bergstrasse	0.011	—	0.011	—
Mittelrhein	0.029	—	0.029	—
Mosel-Saar-Ruwer	0.200	—	0.205	—
Nahe (reference category)	0.072	—	0.071	—
Pfalz	0.130	—	0.130	—
Rheingau	0.128	—	0.127	—
Rheinhessen	0.079	—	0.078	—
Saale-Unstrut	0.012	—	0.013	—

(*Continued*)

Table A2. (*Continued*)

	Quality model ($n = 3.298$)		Price model ($n = 3.269$)	
Independent variables	Mean	Std. Dev.	Mean	Std. Dev.
Sachsen	0.012	—	0.012	—
Wuerttemberg	0.064	—	0.063	—
	Vintage dummies			
1983	0.001	—	0.001	—
1985	0.001	—	0.001	—
1986	0.001	—	0.001	—
1987	0.001	—	0.001	—
1988	0.001	—	0.001	—
1989	0.003	—	0.003	—
1990	0.009	—	0.009	—
1991	0.002	—	0.002	—
1992	0.023	—	0.023	—
1993	0.075	—	0.075	—
1994 (reference category)	0.133	—	0.134	—
1995	0.174	—	0.174	—
1996	0.345	—	0.343	—
1997	0.231	—	0.232	—
	Ranking dummies			
Tafelwein	0.014	—	0.014	—
Landwein	0.069	—	0.068	—
Qualitätswein	0.157	—	0.155	—
Kabinett (reference category)	0.251	—	0.253	—
Spätlese	0.344	—	0.343	—
Auslese	0.117	—	0.118	—
Beerenauslese	0.012	—	0.012	—
Trockenbeerauslese	0.007	—	0.008	—
Eiswein	0.010	—	0.010	—
Sekt	0.017	—	0.017	—
Sonstige	0.002	—	0.002	—
	Year dummies			
1996 (reference category)	0.227	—	0.227	—
1997	0.274	—	0.272	—
1998	0.232	—	0.231	—
1999	0.267	—	0.270	—

Table A3. Quality by Year

Year	Mean	Std. Dev.
1996	2.52	1.13
1997	2.38	1.15
1998	2.61	1.11
1999	2.52	1.12
Average	2.50	1.13

Notes: F-Value = 6.33; $p < 0.01$.

Table A4. Prices by Year

Year	Mean	Std. Dev.
1996	22.73	34.55
1997	21.78	37.98
1998	21.08	25.86
1999	20.92	26.92
Average	21.69	31.98

Notes: F-Value = 0.53; n.s.

Chapter 14

Financing Wine Barrels: The Vincorp Model*

Nick Vink[†,‡], Theo Kleynhans[†], and Willem Hoffmann[§]

[†]*Department of Agricultural Economics, University of Stellenbosch, Stellenbosch, South Africa*
[‡]*nv@sun.ac.za*

[§]*Tshwane University of Technology, Higher Education Institution in Pretoria, South Africa*

Wine barrels constitute a considerable share in the cost of making a fine wine, yet there is not much in the literature on how farmers decide to finance wine barrels. This is arguably because there are really only two financial models in use around the world: buy the barrels with own funds, or borrow from a bank using a conventional loan instrument with collateral. However, in South Africa there has been innovation in the marketplace. The purpose of this paper is to describe the origins of this new model, to identify those characteristics of the market in wine barrels that make the model suited to the needs of the market, and to describe the business model that has been put in place to gain access to the market. The paper ends with some information on international trade in wine barrels as an indication of market size.

1. Introduction

The use of oak barrels to improve the quality of wine and to aid in the maturation process has a long history (Garde-Cerdán and Ancín-Azpilicueta, 2006), and has become a core part of the expertise of wine makers globally. Wine barrels are expensive, and constitute a considerable share in the cost of making a fine wine — this is why it is estimated that only 4% of wineries world-wide use them (Anson, 2013). Yet there is not much in the literature

*This article originally appeared in *American Association of Wine Economists* (2014), AAWE Working Paper No. 161.

on the financing models available to wine makers, or on how they decide on the optimal financing strategy, although some authors do address the issue tangentially (e.g., Carter, 2012; Monday and Wood-Harper, 2010; Blake *et al.*, 1998). This is arguably because there are really only two financial models in use around the world: buy the barrels with own funds, or borrow directly or indirectly from a bank using a conventional loan instrument with collateral. This neglect exists despite the more recent emphasis on value chain financing in the literature (e.g., Miller and Jones, 2010).

Elsewhere in the world wine makers have the option of (a) buying barrels with their own funds; (b) of borrowing in the form of a collateralized loan or a lease from the traditional banking sector or from a wine industry-specific bank; or (c) of taking out a lease in the form of barrel-specific lending. The second of these options represents a conventional financial model. The lease option works much like vehicle finance. The owner of the equipment (in this case wine barrels), also called the lessor, gives a client the opportunity to rent the equipment over a fixed time period against an agreed rental payment. The lessee has the option to return the equipment after the expiry of the agreed term, or to take over ownership in the event that there was a buyout option (Kirkham, 2011). The lessor typically gains a tax advantage in writing down the value of the capital asset. The lessee frees their capital for other uses, especially after the harvest when wine making incurs a host of other costs. In a lease the equipment itself is the collateral for the loan, unlike a regular loan, where additional collateral may be required.

The third option, barrel-specific lending, is found in different variations in France and in South Africa. The purpose of this chapter is to describe the origins of the rental model in use in these two countries, and to describe the business model that has been put in place to gain access to the market. The attention then shifts to the identification of those characteristics of the market in wine barrels that make the South African version of the model suited to the needs of the local market. The chapter ends with some information on international trade in wine barrels as an indication of market size and some reflections on how to grow the business.

2. Origins

As will be seen below, the French and South African versions of a barrel-specific leasing model differ from each other in quite significant ways. Nevertheless, they share some degree of common heritage, as one of the two progenitors of the French model and currently the President of the company H&A Financing and Services, Richard Hardillier, is described as French-South

African (Anson, 2013). Another common feature is that both are expanding globally.

2.1. *France*[1]

The French company H&A Location was established in 2004 by Richard Hardillier and Florent Arrouy, after two years of development of the business plan and the piloting of the first leasing contract. The business model was focused on the management of barrel inventory on behalf of the client — H&A Location does not put up its own capital to purchase barrels, but refers the buyer to a bank. Offices were opened in Bordeaux, Beaune in the Burgundy region and Limonest in the Rhône region. In 2006 the company opened a subsidiary, H&A Renting, in Madrid, Spain, in 2010 H&A Finance in San Francisco, USA, and H&A Locazione in 2013 in Milan, Italy. By 2006 the company was servicing its 100th customer and had a turnover of \$10 m and by 2013 the 1,000th customer and a \$130 m turnover, a Figure that has now grown to \$155 m. It is estimated that the company has a 40% share of the French barrel market, and 50% of the Bordeaux market (Anson, 2013), and has 400,000 barrels under management.

2.2. *South Africa*[2]

The South African version of a dedicated business model for barrel financing has a unique provenance. It started in the fruit industry in the early 1990s: a fruit farmer in the Stellenbosch area, JP du Plessis, became concerned about the cost of the bins used to store and transport fresh fruit — a highly seasonal market. At that time GKN Chep South Africa, a company with its origins in Australia, and whose parent company is currently a global leader in pallet and container pooling services across all industries and modes of transport, was renting out these bins. However, he thought he could out-compete them. When he subsequently sold his farm he used the capital to buy bins in order to rent them out to farmers. While the returns were good, he realized that he would not be able to compete with GKN Chep in the long run.

Then, in the mid-1990s, KWV approached Du Plessis. They were planning expansion and wanted to know whether he would consider including the financing of wine barrels as part of his business plan. At that time KWV was still incorporated as a cooperative and had statutory powers over the entire

[1] Most of this information is available on the Company website at http://www.hafinancing.com/en/corporate-missionstatement.php (accessed February 25, 2014).

[2] Most of the information in this section was gained from interviews with the principals of Vincorp. The schedule of interviews are provided at the end of the article.

wine industry. Also, at that time barrel aging was a virtually unknown practice in the industry, used only by the large players such as Distell and KWV. Where individual farmers did use barrels, it was invariably under advice and instruction from KWV. The fact that KWV had statutory powers over the industry, therefore, enabled the institution to adopt a bird's-eye view of what they thought would be the total requirement for barrels in the industry.

This changed in 1996 when the KWV filed court papers to convert from a cooperative to a company, a move that was opposed by the Minister of Agriculture and Land Affairs (Derek Hanekom) pending further investigation (Vink *et al.*, 2004). The Court instructed the parties to come to an agreement before making a ruling. The Minister then appointed three Committees of Inquiry in early 1997, one of which was charged with recommending whether KWV should keep its statutory powers and what should be done if the status quo was to change. This Committee, chaired by Prof WE Kassier, recommended against allowing a private company to exercise such powers, and this recommendation then became part of the settlement which caused the Minister to withdraw his objection to the transformation. This occurred later in 1997, with new industry legislation and a new institutional framework for industry functions such as the funding of research and the provision of information.

Of course, this was also the time when the South African industry was experiencing a boom in exports (Vink *et al.*, 2004), and a revolution in the production of high quality wines (Ponte and Ewert, 2009). The result was a rapid expansion in the market for new barrels, thus the time was ripe for the establishment of Vincorp, currently a division of Anglo African Finance, a Stellenbosch-based financing company.

3. The Business Model

3.1. *France*

H&A Financing and Services, a French (and now global) \$155 m enterprise was established a decade ago in Bordeaux and has expanded into Spain, the USA and Italy, with discussions around expansion into Argentina and Chile. The firm currently has more than 1,000 clients and 45 employees. According to their website (http://www.hafinancing.com), the business model consists of a three-pronged approach: (a) leasing of barrels; (b) inventory management on behalf of the wine maker; and (c) management of the resale of the barrels. As part of this third activity, buyers of second and third fill barrels can be provided with a guarantee in the event that the barrels were used by one of the premier Chateaux as first fill. These barrels come at a price premium that can vary according to the reputation of the Chateaux in question, and the renter guarantees a buy-back to that Chateau — a business that can survive only as long as there is a demand for the second fill barrels.

Importantly, H&A Financing and Services does not commit its own capital to the purchasing of first fill barrels, but connects the wine farmer to a financier, mostly commercial banks that lend on conventional leasing terms — their biggest financier is BNP Paribas (e.g., Kirkham, 2011).

The French enterprise started with the provision of a service to the wine maker, namely managing the logistics of their barrel inventory, which included the provision of financing in the form of a lease that allows the wine maker to move the barrels from the balance sheet to the operating budget. The three main services that are provided are implemented as follows:

- A leasing solution that consists of a customized contract that evolves with the lifecycle of the barrel inventory and that provides the lessee with depreciation and tax benefits, frees up their cash flow, and reduces their administration costs.
- An online barrel inventory management system that is accessible by smartphone. A unique barrel ID is created along with a customized view of inventory, tracking of work orders, and tracing of all historical activity.
- Resale management of barrels in a service that operates globally. One variant of this activity is that the company can guarantee the lessee that particular barrels were used by a particular grower for first fill — the better known the Chateau, the higher the price. As part of this service the company offers advice on the proper maintenance of barrels, traceability, an international sales force with local knowledge, logistical support in sourcing barrels internationally, and recycling at the end of the life of the barrel.

3.2. *South Africa*

It is obvious why a wine producer would normally prefer to rent wine barrels rather than buy them. However, it is not as obvious why a wine producer would prefer to rent through Vincorp rather than through their bank. The reason why Vincorp handles some 60–65% of the market for new barrels in South Africa is because:

(1) Vincorp does not ask for collateral from the borrower. This it can do because of the active market in purchase or rental of second-hand barrels, and its own intimate knowledge of this market.

(2) The focus is on new barrels for first fill; hence loans are typically for a year to 18 months. At the end of the period the barrel is bought by the wine maker for a nominal sum, and then also takes responsibility for the further use or disposal of the barrels.
(3) In return, Vincorp has the benefit of being able to draw back on Value Added Tax (VAT) for the full value of the barrels on purchase (the buyer can also claim back on VAT, but only for the rental amount as this is paid). This also serves to emphasize that the ownership of the barrel remains with Vincorp until the full rental has been paid. At the end of the rental agreement a nominal payment is made by the buyer to secure ownership of the barrels.
(4) Vincorp sees to all the necessary logistical arrangements involved in finding, purchasing, financing, and moving the barrels from source to the client. Few banks know the market well enough to compete with Vincorp in these respects.
(5) Vincorp runs its business with very low overhead costs. The logistics involved in getting the barrels to the client are, for example, outsourced, and delivery is on a just-in-time basis, that is, there are no warehousing costs. The business basically consists of four people.
(6) Vincorp does not interfere in the normal business relationship between the wine producer and the agents of the firms that sell barrels in South Africa. Once the wine producer has decided on what barrels they want, they approach Vincorp for financing and get a quote from Vincorp for the quantities, specifications, and payment terms that the client wants. Obviously, Vincorp will also advise a client on what is available on the market if requested.

Vincorp's market share consists of the barrels that they finance, as well as the barrels where they provide an import service to farmers who provide their own financing, and for agents who basically use Vincorp as a back office. By Vincorps calculation, the market for new barrels in South Africa is some 20–25,000 barrels a year. Their turnover consists of rentals (R70 million per year) and the provision of the logistical service around the import processes (some R50 million per year).

In 2003 the concept was taken to Australia, principally through a partnership with Boar's Rock Winery, described as a purveyor of "premium bulk wine or contract winemaking and storage services in Adelaide, Australia"[3] who at that stage had a crush capacity of some 35,000 tons of grapes. The

[3]http://www.boarsrock.com.au/

Australian enterprise is called Barrel Finance and Logistics, and it currently finances over 17,000 barrels and is considering expansion into cellar equipment. It expanded into New Zealand in 2009.[4] However, given the current problems in Australia, the business there has not grown substantially and needs attention. Vincorp currently has about 20–25% of the Australian market in new barrels.

3.3. *A comparison between the business models*

Table 1 provides a comparison between the French and South African business models. The two models differ in important respects. Vincorp uses its own capital to finance the purchase of the barrels, resulting in a lot less red tape in accessing funds for the wine maker as opposed to the H&A Location model, where clients are recommended to a commercial bank. H&A Location on the other hand includes a buy-back guarantee, and lends for a far longer period together with the provision of an inventory management system. Yet the two models also have some common features: both allow the renter/lessee of the barrels the freedom to choose which barrels they prefer, that is, they do not interfere with their relationship with the coopers or agents as the case may be. Both also provide logistical and administrative support to the renter/lessee. The French enterprise is at least 10 times as big as the South African counterpart by most measures.

Table 1. A Comparison between the French and South African Barrel Leasing Models

	French	South African
Source of finance	Bank	Own capital
Collateral?	Yes — the asset	No
Buy-back clause?	Yes — for a fee	No
Term	Up to 10 years	Typically 12–18 months
Online inventory management	Yes	No
Buyer cooper preferences respected?	Yes	Yes
Logistical support	Yes	Yes
Administrative support	Yes	Yes
Finance second and third fill barrels?	Yes	No
Number of barrels owned (current)	400,000	At most 40,000
Turnover	€155 m	ZAR 120 m
Employees	45	4

[4] http://www.bfl.net.au/company-profile.html

4. Characteristics of the South African Market

The precise nature of the business model is evidently derived from the special characteristics of the environment within which it is implemented. In the South African case, the most important features of the wine industry and its environment are:

(1) The main barriers to entry into the market are the capital required to buy the barrels; the knowledge of the product and the ties with the (French) suppliers; and the ability to provide a service in terms of the processes of getting the barrels to the wine farmer in South Africa.

(2) The market dominance of oak and particularly French oak, as the wood of choice. There is no particular reason why oak, and particularly French oak, is the wood of choice globally for aging wines other than a form of path dependence. All woods enhance the quality of the wine drinking experience, but the world has come to associate oak wood with the taste of the best premium wines, and so oak wood is the most widely used. For the same reason, French oak is preferred because of the French influence on perceptions about wine quality, although oak from Eastern Europe and from the USA is also used worldwide.

(3) The result is that French cooperages dominate the global market for oak for the production of wine barrels. In South Africa, it is estimated that some 90% of the oak that is imported comes from French coopers, with $7\frac{1}{2}\%$ from other parts of Europe and $2\frac{1}{2}\%$ from the USA. To complicate matters, French coopers also sell oak from other origins, so the proportion of American oak used in South Africa could actually be as high as 15%. The dominance of the French coopers also means that even a buyer of large volumes such as Vincorp does not really get a discount on prices, but this is still an old-fashioned trade where Letters of Credit are not normally required from large buyers. This represents a large saving on normal financing costs for the importer that qualifies.

(4) Although global supply of oak wood for barrels is largely confined to France, the USA, and certain Eastern European countries, there is a wide variety of barrels available on the market. A typical price list for September 2013 for one of the better-known coopers has two pages of different sizes (205 and 225 liters plus larger sizes), stave thicknesses (22 mm and 27 mm), length of seasoning (24 or 26 months), shapes (Bordeaux and Burgundy) as well as further options such as barrels for organic and biodynamic producers, toasting of barrel heads, and the placement of the logo of the winery on the barrel. Knowledge of the product provides

the specialist financier with a strong competitive advantage over a more generalized financier such as a bank.

(5) There is an active rental and purchase market for second-hand barrels in South Africa (and elsewhere), although the South African market is less liquid than the market in the USA, for example. Nevertheless, Vincorp is prepared to finance without collateral because they retain ownership of the barrel until it is paid up. Most of Vincorp's new clients (some 85%) ask for financing for the barrels for one year only. The typical client requires 30 to 60 barrels, with a third used for white wine and two thirds for red wine. Barrels for white wine are typically landed in January, and those for red in February, with payment starting from May 1 or June 1, for a period of 12 months, so the payment period is in any case longer than a year. Vincorp is flexible in its repayment terms, and is prepared to lend over three years, but for the producer the issue is that in the second and third year they are paying installments on the new barrels bought in those years, so the savings of an extended term are not very large. Once the barrels have been paid off they become the property of the buyer. Because the market in South Africa is relatively less liquid, buyers will use these barrels for second and third, etc. fills, even for second labels.

(6) Given that buyers have few choices of where to buy, it would be more efficient to transport the wood to the country where the barrels are to be used, and to make the barrels locally. Usually it is cheaper to transport the value-added product, but in this case the barrel is an awkward shape (traditionally to make it easier to handle) and is itself a means of storage. Transporting barrels is akin to putting an empty container into an empty container — it uses up a lot of space, hence transport costs are very high.

(7) The South African industry is geographically concentrated, with most of the barrels delivered within a 3 to 4 hour drive from Vincorp's warehouse in Paarl. This is in sharp contrast with Australia, for example, where there is a continent between the Western Australian wineproducing areas and the rest of the industry, which is in any event widely scattered.

5. Characteristics of the Global Market

Figure 1 shows South African imports under the relevant HS code from 2002–2012. These data need to be treated with caution because the HS category in question (HS 441600) is defined as including "*Casks, barrels, vats, tubs and other coopers products, parts thereof, of wood, incl. staves.*"

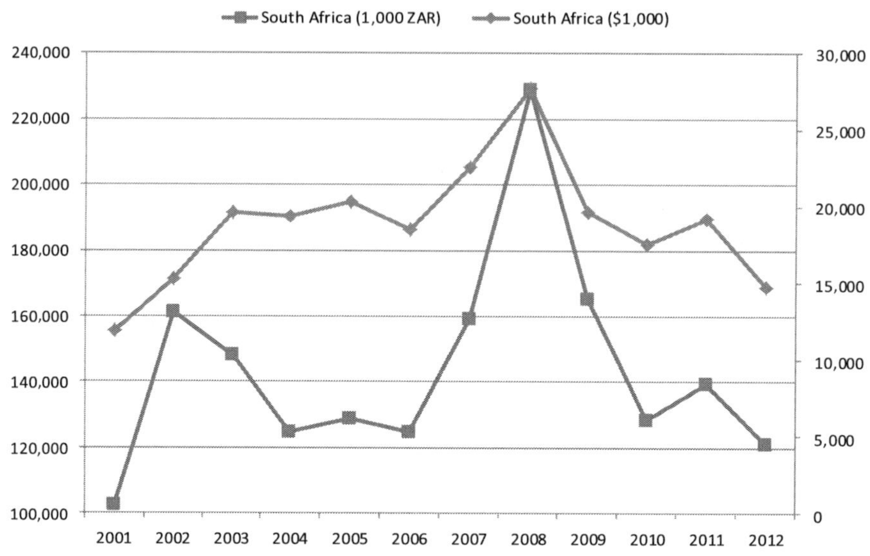

Figure 1. South Africa's Imports of Barrels, 2001–2012
Note: US$ values measured on right axis.
Source: US International Trade Commission (http://usitc.gov/); South African Reserve Bank (www.resbank.co.za).

Table 2. HS Codes for Barrels

44160030	Wooden casks, barrels, and hogsheads
44160060	Wooden staves and hoops; tight barrelheads of softwood
44160090	Wooden vats, tubs and other coopers' products and parts thereof

The relevant databases provide tariff data at an even more disaggregated level, as illustrated in Table 2, but trade data to this level do not seem to be available. From this definition it seems as if the appropriate HS category would be 44160030, but even here it is unclear whether these are new barrels, or whether they are intended for use in the wine industry.

Notwithstanding, it is clear from Figure 1 that South Africa's imports peaked in 2008 in both Rand and Dollar terms and declined thereafter with the strengthening of the Rand and the global recession. Imports are expected to increase with the current weakening of the Rand and an expected increase in packaged wine exports.

It is also interesting to note South Africa's relative position as a buyer of barrels from the EU in the international market. The data are shown in Table 3. The USA is by far the largest buyer of barrels, but its share has

Table 3. South Africa as a Buyer of Barrels (%)

	2001	2002	2003	2004	2005	2006	2007	2008	2009	2010	2011	2012
Argentina	1.90	1.88	2.36	3.29	3.07	3.62	3.37	4.47	4.92	4.90	4.26	3.53
Australia	15.66	13.52	13.95	14.75	13.77	12.47	10.22	11.39	11.65	12.31	10.91	12.67
Chile	5.24	5.79	7.24	7.25	7.26	6.27	6.83	7.80	8.69	8.19	7.48	7.17
New Zealand	4.19	3.81	4.79	4.63	5.77	4.13	4.43	4.35	4.68	5.24	3.84	3.97
South Africa	6.33	7.33	8.53	8.18	7.80	5.97	6.39	6.75	6.42	6.30	5.83	4.40
USA	60.77	61.82	55.11	52.71	54.51	59.15	59.65	57.18	52.84	50.34	54.15	54.42
Rest of World	5.92	5.85	8.03	9.18	7.82	8.40	9.11	8.05	10.80	12.72	13.53	13.84
Total	100	100	100	100	100	100	100	100	100	200	100	100

Source: Global Trade Information Services (Brasher). http://www.gtis.com/english/

declined from over 60% to below 55% since 2001. Argentina and Chile have increased their share of world imports, as has the rest of the world, while the share of Australia, New Zealand, and South Africa has declined.

Table 4 provides the structure of tariffs for the importing of barrels into the main new world wine producing countries. In all cases the MFN tariffs are the same as these applied rates. Argentina and the USA levy a small tariff, while Chile has a standard tariff on all its imports. Australia, New Zealand, and South Africa levy no tariffs, and there is no evidence of tariff escalation to encourage cooperage within these countries rather than importing ready-made barrels.

6. The Potential for Expansion

It is clear that the South African market in new barrels presents a unique business opportunity, but because the market is finite, it also places a ceiling on the expansion potential of the firm. There are, however, a number of potential ways in which this business can expand over time. At the same time, competition, domestic or foreign, could effectively shrink the market. These are all possibilities that warrant further investigation.

(1) The business started with the rental of fruit bins, and this has been continued through Binfin, also part of Anglo African Finance. The renting out of fruit bins differs from wine barrels in two important respects. First, while seasonal, it is also a cyclical business. Second, because of market concentration (there is only one supplier of plastic crates and four of wooden crates in South Africa) bin sizes are more uniform, so

Table 4. Trade Barriers in the Market for Barrels

HS Code	Product description	Argentina	Australia	Chile	New Zealand	South Africa	USA
44160000	Casks, barrels, vats, tubs and other coopers' products parts thereof, of wood, incl. staves	na	0	na	0	0	na
44160010	Barrels vats, tubs and other articles of cooperage and their parts of wood, including staves: of holm oak, Cork oak, and other oaks (quercus spp.)	2%	na	na	na	na	na
44160030	Wooden casks, barrels, and hogsheads	na	na	6%	na	na	0%
44160060	Wooden staves and hoops; tight barrelheads of softwood	na	na	6%	na	na	0%
44160090	Wooden vats, tubs and other coopers' products and parts thereof	10%	na	6%	na	na	3.20%

that industry information is less of a market differentiator and barrier to entry. Thus, expansion prospects exist, but are limited.

(2) As shown above, the business model can be expanded geographically, as has been done in Australia and New Zealand. A former partner has also started to pilot the model in the USA.

(3) While rentals are known in the USA, the available evidence shows that it is largely in the form of traditional bank lending (either directly or "back-to-back" lending), that is, with collateral and a lot of red tape, and largely without the additional element of service provision.

(4) Vincorp already finances cellar equipment such as forklifts and wine making equipment. However, this calls for caution, especially where the assets being financed do not have a ready second hand market (e.g., custom built tanks in the winery). Again, this presents expansion potential, but is limited to products that have the same characteristics

Table 5. The Share of Noble Varieties in the South African Crush, 1990–2012

	1990	1995	2000	2010	2011	2012
			%			
Orange River	0.38	0.97	1.91	4.57	7.00	7.00
Little Karoo	1.33	2.21	6.13	20.69	27.51	26.00
Olifants River	1.56	3.43	15.60	36.14	35.60	34.00
Worcester	1.82	5.23	17.35	41.40	46.46	45.00
Robertson	6.34	9.25	22.96	51.36	54.10	55.00
Malmesbury	10.87	16.22	34.26	67.64	63.00	64.00
Paarl	19.63	25.20	41.63	68.19	61.00	60.00
Stellenbosch	30.06	40.21	59.19	83.43	77.00	79.00
Total	11.68	16.45	29.76	54.58	52.00	52.00

Notes: Noble varieties include Cabernet Sauvignon, Cabernet Franc, Pinotage, Shiraz, Sauvignon Blanc, and Chardonnay.
Source: SAWIT, 2013.

as wine barrels (especially the existence of a second-hand market) or alternatively to an additional service to existing clients, in which case a premium is charged.

(5) The South African market has grown considerably over the past two decades, largely because the average price at which wine is sold has increased, in turn largely because of the improved quality of wine, as evidenced by the increasing proportion of wine that is made from the noble varietals. This is reflected in Table 5, which shows that less than 12% of the grapes grown in South Africa in 1990 were one of the "noble" cultivars, and that this has increased to more than 50%, which still leaves scope for further upgrading. This will increase the demand for oak barrels.

7. Conclusions

Value chain finance in agriculture consists of "The flows of funds to and among the various links within a value chain" (Miller and Jones, 2010). The models of barrel-specific funding described here are a prime example of value chain financing, and illustrate how different financing models can be adapted to different circumstances. In this chapter, two such dedicated financing models have been analyzed, namely that of H&A Financing and Services in France, and Vincorp in South Africa. In the case of the latter, the way in which the model has been adapted to local circumstances has also been described. In this regard, it would also be interesting to investigate further how the clients (wine makers) respond to this opportunity in the market. More specifically, research on the following aspects would be useful:

(1) How do farmers decide what the best financing model is for their purposes?
(2) Are there any patterns (demographic, geographic, etc.) to farmers' decisions in this regard?
(3) What features do wine makers like and dislike about the current model (i.e., how can the model be adapted to suit their needs even better)?
(4) Is it possible to cost the ancillary services provided to wine farmers?
(5) What is the short, medium, and long term expansion potential for the model — within agriculture or even in other sectors of the economy?

References

Anson, J. (2013). The barrel men. Decanter China, 3 October 2013. Available at https://www.decanterchina.com/en/index.html?article=591 (accessed February 25, 2014).

Blake, J., Oriol, A., and Jack, D. (1998). The drive for quality: The impact on accounting in the wine industry. *Journal of Wine Research*, 9(2), 75–85.

Carter, E. (2012). Cooperation, competition, and regulation: Constructing value in French and Italian wine markets. A dissertation submitted in partial satisfaction of the requirements for the degree of Doctor of Philosophy in Political Science in the Graduate Division of the University of California, Berkeley.

Garde-Cerdán, T., and Carmen, A. (2006). Review of quality factors on wine ageing in the oak barrels. *Trends in Food Science & Technology*, 17(8), 438–447.

Kirkham, K. (2011). Barrel leasing and cash flow: How to address your fast-depreciating oak inventory through finance. Wines & Vines, September 2011. Available at http://www.winesandvines.com/template.cfm?section=features&content=91414&ftitle=Barrel%20 Leasing%20and% 20Cash%20Flow (accessed February 25, 2014).

Miller, C., and Linda, J. (2010). Agricultural value chain finance: Tools and lessons. Rome, Food and Agriculture Organization of the United Nations.

Monday, A., and Trevor, W. (2010). Exploring the supply chain of small and medium-sized South Australian wine producers. *Supply Chain Forum*, 11(1), 16–26.

Ponte, S., and Ewert, J. (2009). Which way is "up" in upgrading? Trajectories of change in the value chain for South African wine. *World Development*, 37(10), 1637–50.

SAWIT (2013). South African Wine Industry Statistics No 37. Paarl, South African Wine Industry Information and Systems.

Vink, N., Gavin, W., and Johann, K. (2004). *South Africa. The World's Wine Markets: Globalization at Work*. London: Edward Elgar, pp. 227–251.

Interviews at Vincorp

JP du Plessis, January 16, 2014
Chris Krige, Paul Haumann and Hendrik de Waal, January 31, 2014
Chris Krige, February 24, 2014

Part 5

Organization

Chapter 15

Love or Money? The Effects of Owner Motivation in the California Wine Industry*

Fiona M. Scott Morton[†] **and Joel M. Podolny**[‡]

[†]*Yale University and NBER,*
Box 208200, New Haven, CT 06520, USA
fiona.scottmorton@yale.edu

[‡]*Harvard University, William James Hall,*
Cambridge, MA 02138, USA
jpodolny@hbs.edu

Models that assume only consumer tastes determine the characteristics of supply are restrictive; producers can gain utility from aspects of production and pay for deviating from demand by accepting lower financial returns. We model and measure motivations of California winery owners, and analyze their effects on quality and price. We find utility-maximizers are more likely to produce high quality and set higher quality-adjusted prices. Profit-oriented owners are less likely to produce high-quality wines. These results suggest that the presence of hobbyists who enjoy producing high quality may lower financial returns in the segment and discourage profit-maximizers from locating there.

1. Introduction

In a neoclassical model, firms supply those goods and services demanded by consumers. In many markets, this description of the supply is not complete. Suppliers themselves may have preferences about what to supply; that is, *producers* may get utility from certain characteristics of the product or production process. To the extent these preferences deviate from consumer preferences, the owners will pay for this type of consumption through a lower

*This article originally appeared in *The Journal of Industrial Economics* (2002), 50(4), 431–456.

rate of return. For privately-owned firms, this is often quite feasible. For example, professional sports teams, newspapers, art galleries, and wineries are often privately-owned by people who enjoy some aspect of the product or production process. Integrating owner preferences into a study of the supply-side of an industry enlarges the scope of Industrial Organization.

The typical assumption that the objective of the firm is pure profit-maximization seems justifiable on evolutionary grounds. Because profit-maximization implies tremendous incentives to minimize costs, any firm that does not behave *as if* it is a profit-maximizer may not be able to survive in the long-run. While this evolutionary argument is not always explicitly invoked as justification for the assumption of profit-maximization (see Alchian (1950) for an explicit statement), the essential claim has rich historical roots, dating back to the classic writings of Smith, Marx, and Weber.

Our model allows owners to maximize utility, rather than profits. Any nonprofit-related motives an owner has can raise a firm's costs or create inefficiencies. However, an owner's utility for the processes or features of the firm that generate these costs or inefficiencies can compensate the owner for the lower financial rate of return. For example, if the firm produces a high-quality product, the owner may value the association with the product. Or, if the firm's activities further some social cause, the owner may derive utility from the cause's advancement. If the additional utility derived from the inefficient features of the firm is greater than the disutility from the lower return, then the owner is willing to subsidize the firm and it can survive in the market.

In this chapter we attempt to measure how much utility versus profit-maximization a firm's owner engages in, we discuss the type, extent, and implications of departures from the profit-maximization principle, and then we empirically examine the behavioral consequences of utility-maximization. In the process, we gain insight into the market consequences that result from the co-existence of utility- and profit-maximizing firms.

We begin with data on prices and characteristics of California wines and supplement it with a survey of winery owners' attitudes toward their firm and product. We find that many of the people owning and running wineries in California have goals that depart from standard profit-maximization (PM). For example, 78% of our respondents would be "somewhat" or "very" unlikely to sell their winery if they could get a higher return in the stock market. Our model allows winery owners to care about the quality of their wine (separately from the effect of quality on profits) and to gain utility from lifestyle expenditures that raise production costs.

We find that owners who derive strong non-financial returns from ownership charge more for their product on a quality-adjusted basis. The price premium declines with the length of time the owner's family has owned the winery, which we interpret as evidence of learning-by-doing. Those same owners locate at the higher end of the quality spectrum and are also unlikely to make the lowest quality wine. Owners who primarily care about financial returns from their winery are less likely to produce high-quality wine.

The results of this chapter have implications for the equilibrium of the wine industry. Our first conclusion is that utility-maximizing owners price higher, or more "softly," and consequently one might expect the existence of utility-maximizers to raise profits and attract entry, relative to a situation where utility-maximizers were not in the industry. However, if utility-maximizing owners "oversupply" quality, they can drive down the financial rate of return to producing high-quality wine for any producer. The highest quality grape-growing land is in relatively fixed supply. Utility-maximizers may be willing to bid for scarce high-quality inputs up to the point justified by the sum of the financial and psychic returns.

The wine industry is not the only one in which we expect a significant proportion of owners to have non-financial motivations. The owners of "Mom and Pop" firms, family businesses, and larger private businesses are not constrained by shareholders with a simple financial claim on the firm.[1] Thus, while our focus is on the wine industry, we believe that the findings of this chapter have broader applicability.

The remainder of this chapter will proceed as follows. A review of the existing literature is in Section 2; a discussion of the theoretical implications of this phenomenon is contained in Section 3. Section 4 describes the data on California wines and the survey we designed and administered. It also discusses the general types of owners we find in the industry. Section 5 tests the hypotheses on quality and price generated earlier in this chapter, and Section 6 concludes.

2. Literature Review

Our interest in the market consequences of different objective functions than profit-maximization is related to a number of distinct areas of research.

[1] The Family Business Center at Loyola University estimates that 80% of American businesses are privately owned. (Steinberg, 1996). This estimate is most likely conservative. Eddy (1996) includes estimates that as much as 90% of American business is private and as much as 40% to 60% of the U.S. Gross Domestic Product comes from privately owned enterprises. Prince (1996) reports that as many as 95% of U.S. businesses are family owned.

For instance, there is a considerable literature on the differences between, and competition among, for-profit and not-for-profit institutions such as hospitals and daycare centers (see Rose-Ackerman (1996) for a survey of nonprofit organizations and economic theory). Rose-Ackerman (1986) shows that nonprofit daycare centers produce high-quality service, charge a low price and survive in a competitive market because of donations. Customers queue for the right to purchase the nonprofit product, while unmet demand patronizes the for-profit sector. Schiff and Weisbrod (1991) examine the issue of competition between nonprofit and for-profit organizations in ancillary commercial markets. In their model, nonprofits get disutility from producing the ancillary commercial good, but produce it to earn profits to finance charitable production. They find that the tax-free status of nonprofits causes distortions in the commercial market, and that changes in donations will affect competition in the commercial market by causing nonprofits to compensate for lost donations with commercial output.

Lakdawalla and Philipson (1998) try to explain the share of an industry that chooses nonprofit status. In their setup, there is a limited supply of altruists in the world; altruists value the output of the firm as well as profits, while traditional firms only value profits. As the level of available economic profit drops, the altruists will give up the ability to distribute profits and choose to take nonprofit status because that frees up resources to increase output. They find support for the comparative statics of their model in the US long-term care industry. In Lakdawalla and Philipson (1998), Schiff and Weisbrod (1991), and our model, "altruists" can drive profit-maximizing firms out of the industry if there are enough of them to satisfy demand.

Becker's (1957) theoretical work on discrimination in labor markets is also related to our interest in the market consequences of utility-maximizing firms. In contrast to the already mentioned research which uses legal form of the organization to infer objective function, Becker allows employers (and consumers and employees) to have individual tastes for discrimination. Firms that have tastes for discrimination against a minority group will face higher total costs than firms that are not discriminatory.[2]

A second area of the literature that is closely related to our problem is analysis of worker-run firms. The classic choice of objective function for a firm owned by its workers is income per worker (Ward [1958]). Futagami and Okamura (1996) show that the labor-owned firm will use

[2]Managers have a legal obligation to maximize shareholder value, but may have personal incentives to utility-maximize; in this sense our work is related to the agency literature.

more capital-intensive technology and produce more output than the profit-maximizing firm in a duopoly. Craig and Pencavel (1996, 1992) undertake a similar project to ours by empirically examining worker-cooperative and profit-maximizing sawmills in the Pacific Northwest. They find that when output prices change, cooperatives adjust wages more than for-profit firms do. Traditional for-profit corporations are more likely to adjust working hours or employment with the price of plywood.

While these lines of research document or postulate the existence of organizations with objective functions that contain more than profits, or model competition between types, there is no work we know of that attempts to measure directly owner motivations within one industry and then relate these motivations to variations in market behavior. Our empirical work seeks to accomplish this for the California wine industry.

3. Theory

Potential entrants (owners) into the wine industry have varying levels of ability. This ability parameter, α, determines a winery's initial level of marginal cost of production; higher ability leads to lower marginal costs. Starting a winery also requires paying a fixed entry cost. Some potential owners also enjoy (get utility from) making wine. We will call these utility-maximizing owners, or UMs. We make an important assumption here, which is consistent with our knowledge of the industry, that UM owners only get utility from producing good quality wine. Because UM owners maximize total utility and not simply profits, UM owners are willing to accept a lower financial return on their winery.[3] Profit-maximizing owners (PMs) care solely about financial return from the winery.

One can immediately see that the entry decision will differ for the two types of owners. There will be a cutoff level of ability α^* below which a PM owner would earn negative profit if he entered. PMs with ability levels below α^* will choose to stay out. However, a UM owner with ability just below α^* *will* enter because he requires a lower rate of financial return. This owner's net costs — financial and psychic — are lower than the costs of an identical

[3]Our problem is also analogous to the compensating differential labor literature as in Weisbrod (1983). Suppose the manager of the winery were an employee instead of the owner, but this manager still gained utility from making good quality wine. One possible contract the owners might choose is to allow the manager to run the winery but lower his wage by an amount that makes him indifferent to his outside option. Naturally, this sort of contract is limited by the initial wealth of the manager. However, our interests in either case are policy changes due to the particular preferences of the manager-owner.

profit-maximizing firm. The entry of the UM will drive out a fraction of the marginal PM, who is now making negative profits. Because the UM produces a smaller quantity than the PM, the substitution is not one for one. Thus the entry of UMs increases the total number of firms in the industry. In addition, UMs will only enter where they have an opportunity cost advantage, at the upper end of the quality spectrum. The first important implication of the model is that UM owners will locate disproportionately at the high end of the quality spectrum because they value producing quality separately from, and in addition to, profits.

We assume that competition in the wine industry is differentiated Bertrand. For example, one of two bottles of the same quality level (no vertical differentiation) will generally be preferred by a consumer due to personal taste (horizontal differentiation). Each producer faces a downward-sloping demand curve due to this differentiation. The wine industry is an excellent example of a market in which small price differences can be sustained in equilibrium due to heterogeneous tastes on the part of consumers for the wine, its label, the shape of the bottle, etc. Entry will drive economic profit to zero for the marginal PM and below zero for the marginal UM. We assume the relevant UMs have an existing stock of wealth out of which they can cover the losses of their winery, should there be any.

We can combine our assumption about the ability of UM entrants and our assumption about competition to generate our second prediction: UM owners will price higher, on a quality-adjusted basis, and sell somewhat less than would an identical PM owner in the same market. The reason is that UM owners have, on average, higher marginal costs because they have lower ability. These higher marginal costs cause owners to set higher profit-maximizing prices. *Ceteris paribus*, this also leads to a lower quantity sold.

We assume that both UM and PM owners can reduce their marginal costs with experience producing wine at their winery. Interviews with owners and general knowledge of the industry suggest that learning by doing is likely to be an important part of wine-making. Because many aspects of making wine are not scientific, but must be experienced, every owner is likely to be able to reduce costs over time. If learning by doing is proportional to cost, UM owners (who begin with higher costs) can reduce costs more quickly with experience, and will therefore have a larger reduction in their price premium over time than PM owners.[4]

[4]A second plausible — and related — explanation is selection. UM owners who do not reduce costs and prices over time may exit and no longer be in the sample. However, we

It could also be the case that UM owners are more likely to have x-inefficiency in the management of their winery. There are many tastes an owner could indulge that do not add to the value of the wine. For example, the owner could live the life of a landowner engaging in rural and social pursuits in the company of like-minded friends. Such an owner might tolerate some inefficiencies in running the winery that cater to that lifestyle, such as paying employees more than marginal product, not exerting enough effort to reduce costs, or continually interfering in the production process. This could generate higher marginal costs, perhaps without any effect on quality.[5] This cost structure would also produce higher quality adjusted prices and a lower quantity sold. However, x-inefficiency by itself does not generate the learning by doing implication above, nor does it predict location on the quality spectrum.

The arguments of an owner's utility function are likely to be quite different in other industries; we are not claiming that the specifics of the model above (quality and ability) apply to art galleries or other utility-maximizing settings. For example, the owner of a magazine of opinion probably gets utility from higher circulation figures for the magazine. We assume that quantity produced or sold is *not* an argument of a winery owner's utility function. Our interviews with owners did not ever indicate quantity was a goal. While an owner wants to make enough wine to supply the restaurants, competitions,

---

think selection should operate quite quickly, which is inconsistent with our small estimated interaction term. (See Table 6.)

[5]Consider a model of x-inefficiency: There are two types of inputs the owner may value: quality, s, that consumers also value, and t (a wine-maker who has a French accent and costs more, but is not better than other wine-makers) that consumers do not value. A change in t does not alter the demand curve. $\gamma[g(s) + h(t)]$, represents the value of these benefits. PMs have $\gamma = 0$ while UMs have $\gamma = 1$. ($h'(t) > 0, h''(t) < 0$, $g'(s) > 0$, $g''(s) < 0$). The utility function of the owner is therefore:

$$U(p, s, t) = q(p, s) \cdot p + \gamma[g(s) + h(t)] - C[q(p, s), s, t]$$

PM owners choose $t = 0$ because t has a positive cost and does not increase revenue. However, the UM owner will invest in input t up to the point where marginal benefit equals marginal cost. A UM firm will have higher marginal costs than a PM firm, and will therefore charge a higher price relative to the wine's merits and sell a smaller quantity than a PM owner. When the UM owner gets both a financial *and* private return on quality, he will invest more than is justified by the financial return alone. Thus we predict that UM owners will position their wines higher on the quality spectrum than PM owners. The three choice variables, price, quality expenditures, and lifestyle expenditures, will move together for UM owners if the utility function is supermodular (Milgrom and Shannon, 1994). However, supermodularity is not necessary (although certainly sufficient) for the specific relationships above to be true.

and friends he is anxious to impress; beyond the small-scale production that can supply those parties, additional quantity does not increase private benefits.

In a world where suppliers have preferences, consumers face a different mix of products and product characteristics than their own demand would generate in a neoclassical world. In addition, characteristics "over-supplied," or subsidized, by owners will fall in price relative to a world of pure profit-maximization. We can see that the attractiveness of an industry for PM owners depends in part on the distribution of tastes across both UMs and consumers. If UMs provide daycare facilities in poor neighborhoods, PM demand from wealthy neighborhoods is not affected. In contrast, if UM winemakers get utility from producing high quality, the high-quality segment will be crowded with hobbyist suppliers. If consumers like the attribute too, then that same space would normally be desirable for PMs. However, it may be sufficiently crowded with hobbyists that positive financial returns are not attainable. This may be true despite relatively "soft" price competition from UMs.

4. Data

4.1. *Wine data*

The data on wine characteristics was collected by Beth Benjamin from the Bureau of Alcohol, Tobacco, and Firearms, *Wines and Vines Buyers Guide, Connoisseur's Guide*, and other industry sources. The dataset has complete information on California wines and wineries during the time period 1980–1990 (see Benjamin (1994) for detailed information regarding collection of this data). A bottle of wine is described by its price, the year it appears in *Wines and Vines*, vintage, grape varietal, the appellation on the label, the quality of the bottle and its vintage, whether it is ready to drink, and a variety of characteristics of the winery producing the bottle. The same bottle can appear in the data in more than one year; over time the bottle's price and some other characteristics (e.g., ready to drink) may vary. Prices therefore belong to a bottle-calendar year combination. Though the panel is not balanced, 71% of the observations describe a bottle that only appears once, and 95% of observations describe bottles that appear three or fewer times.[6] Price is taken from the *Connoisseurs' Guide to California Wine*; they

[6]The maximum number of times a bottle is surveyed is 8 out of 11 years; the bottles with over five showings comprise 1% of the dataset.

report the suggested retail price of a bottle sold individually in a particular year in California.[7]

A winery may produce many types of wine: wineries can produce different varietals under the same or different labels (brands) that may reflect a particular quality positioning. The winery can also make multiple products. Examples of popular products include table wine, dessert wine, sparkling wine, and brandy. The average cost of a bottle in the dataset is \$9.50; the minimum price is \$2. The group of wines in the \$2–\$3.50 range includes many varietals: red table wine, Zinfandel, Cabernet Sauvignon, and Chenin Blanc are the most popular. The producers of these inexpensive wines include a range of producers such as Almaden, Beaulieu Vineyards, Fetzer, Gallo, Glen Ellen, and Paul Masson. The most expensive wine in the dataset is Stag's Leap Cabernet Sauvignon which cost \$75; other expensive wines in the dataset are produced by Heitz Cellar, Chateau Woltner, Caymus, and Silver Oak Cellars. See Table A1 on the journal's website, (www.stern.nyu.edu/~jindec/supp.htm) for means and standard deviations of the variables in the wine dataset.

4.2. *Survey data*

To determine the motivations of the owners in our dataset, we mailed a survey in January of 1997 to each winery in the dataset for which we could find an address. A copy of the survey is located on the journal website. Approximately 13% of the wineries in the dataset were un-locatable; we searched in several data sources and if we could not find an address, that winery did not get a survey. We asked the owner or majority partner of the winery to fill out the survey and return it, which resulted in a total of 184 survey replies out of 411 mailed. We received the replies in February–April of 1997. Our response rate is therefore 45%. Summary statistics for surveys are also on the journal website in Table A2. We tried to construct questions that would get owners to quantify their non-monetary benefits and describe what kinds of things the non-monetary benefits are. The replies indicate there is a substantial amount of utility-maximizing behavior going on in the

[7]The *Connoisseur's Guide's* goal is to provide a price that will resemble what the reader encounters at the local wine store. The price they report is the actual price of the bottles they buy. Since the wines have just been released, they are not on sale. Occasionally, the *Connoisseur's Guide* buys a bottle at a "discount" store, in which case they do not use the discounted price, but report the suggested retail price obtained from the winery. This winery suggested retail price is what a reputable wine store would usually charge.

industry. 78% of owners would be "somewhat" or "very" unlikely to sell their winery if they could get a higher return in the stock market. Almost 40% of respondents would lose over $10,000 to improve the quality of their wines. Although almost all respondents aim to cover costs and earn some profit, less than half have a specific target rate of return in mind. The mean respondent does between a quarter and a half of his socializing with "wine people."

We assume the responses reflect actual preferences of the respondents. They were told the survey contents would remain confidential, so unless they felt a need to convince the authors of their preferences, there is no one to whom they could be sending a message.

Table 1 shows how different non-monetary benefits of owning a winery are correlated. Those who socialize with "wine people" and list non-financial reasons for owning their winery are more likely to say that an increase in resources would cause them to improve their winery. Being in business for the love of wine is negatively correlated with the length of time the winery has been owned by the family. Feeling family ownership of the winery is important is correlated with having a non-financial reason for owning the winery, being unlikely to sell the winery for fair market value, and entertaining.

An owner's view of Gallo seems to do a good job of capturing his general type. Gallo is the largest winery in California and is known to be run in a professional manner that takes full advantage of its size and market power, although it is family owned. The vast majority of the wines and spirits they produce are generally regarded as being quite low quality, although the firm now makes some higher quality wines. Respondents who rate Gallo as "a superior winery" have owned their wineries longer, have a particular target rate of return in mind, are not in the wine business for the lifestyle, and earn a significant portion of family income from their winery.

We undertake a formal factor or "principal components" analysis to consolidate the data we gather in the survey.[8] The reason for this is that we have 16 questions that are all trying to get at the same concept in different ways. We suspect that the response to any one question does not fully capture the concept we are interested in: the strength of the non-financial benefits from owning the winery. The intuition behind principal components is to find (fewer) new variables that summarize an owner's responses. The result of the factor analysis will be two new variables that are correlated with the responses to the questions.

[8]See Hotelling (1933) or Harman (1960) for an explanation of this technique.

Table 1. Correlations between Survey Variables and Correlations between Factors and Selected Variables

	1tot	2	3	4	5	6	7	8b	9tot	91v	91f	9ot	10	11	12m
1tot	1														
2	−0.26*	1													
3	−0.13	0.14	1												
4	0.14*	−0.11	−0.14	1											
5	0.14	0.04	−0.09	−0.07	1										
6	−0.12	−0.03	−0.02	0.02	−0.26*	1									
7	−0.08	−0.04	0.09	0.18*	−0.01	−0.03	1								
8b	0.27*	0.02	−0.01	−0.01	0.01	−0.05	0.00	1							
9tot	0.19*	0.04	0.11	0.00	−0.01	0.12	−0.06	0.09	1						
91v	0.23*	0.02	0.11	−0.03	0.01	0.02	−0.15*	0.13	0.73*	1					
91f	0.22*	0.07	−0.05	0.12	0.08	0.10	−0.02	0.09	0.66*	0.36*	1				
9ot	−0.03	0.02	0.19*	0.12	−0.19*	0.07	0.06	0.02	0.42*	0.11	0.00	1			
10	0.16*	−0.07	−0.26*	−0.10	0.11	−0.03	−0.12	−0.02	−0.17*	−0.15*	0.02	−0.22*	1		
11	0.08	−0.01	−0.01	−0.06	0.02	−0.11	−0.21*	−0.00	−0.08	−0.15*	−0.06	−0.03	0.13	1	

(Continued)

Table 1. (*Continued*)

	1tot	2	3	4	5	6	7	8b	9tot	91v	91f	9ot	10	11	12m
12m	−0.21*	−0.10	0.11	−0.05	0.09	0.08	0.16*	−0.24*	−0.10	−0.08	−0.13	0.04	−0.13	−0.12	1
12g	−0.10	−0.05	−0.04	−0.02	0.03	−0.03	0.25*	−0.26*	−0.13	−0.12	−0.18*	0.05	0.07	−0.15*	0.52*

	Love	Money	Price	Quality	Status
Money	−0.055	1			
Price	0.137	−0.080	1		
Quality	0.109	−0.084	0.342	1	
Status	−0.035	−0.107	0.175	0.152	1

Notes: *Significant at 5% level or better, $N = 172$. All correlations significant at 1% or better except (love, status) at 4.5%. $N = 10341$.

Key for Table 1

1tot	Tot Entertain business + entertain nonprofits + entertain wine people
2	Willing to lose money for quality
3	Unlikely to sell winery for fair value
4	Percentage of wines named after family
5	Increases in resources would cause little additional investment in winery
6	Amount of socializing with wine people
7	Length of time owned winery
8b	No specific target rate of return in mind
9tot	Sum of motivations checked or written in. One point for each
91v	Motivated by love of wine
91f	Motivated by lifestyle
9ot	Other non-financial reason for owning winery written in
10	Continuing family ownership of winery unimportant
11	Winery profits small part of family income
12m	Mondavi superior
12g	Gallo superior

Table 2. Factor Loadings

Survey variable	Love	Money
Entertain wine community	0.202	0.404
Willing to lose money for quality	0.116	−0.295
Unlikely to sell winery for fair value	0.040	−0.462
Percentage of wines named after family	0.006	0.107
Increases in resources would cause little additional investment in winery	0.005	0.218
Amount of socializing with wine people	−0.044	−0.093
Length of time have owned winery	−0.242	−0.110
No specific target rate of return in mind	0.489	0.049
Motivated by love of wine	0.403	−0.074
Continuing family ownership of winery unimportant	−0.127	0.461
Winery profits small part of family income	−0.009	−0.001
Gallo superior	−0.499	0.083

We perform a standard factor analysis to obtain six principal components and then rotate the components using a varimax rotation. We use only two factors, those with the highest contribution to variance. The factor loadings are presented in Table 2. The first factor positively loads on entertaining, being willing to lose money to improve quality, short ownership tenure, not having a particular rate of return in mind, being in business for the love of wine, thinking that continuing family ownership of the winery is important, and disliking Gallo. We call this the *love* factor; it is clearly picking up owners who derive substantial non-monetary rewards from owning a winery. The second factor is complementary. It loads on entertaining also (including business and community entertaining), being unwilling to lose money to improve quality, being willing to sell the winery for a fair price, not socializing with "wine people," not feeling it is important for the winery to stay in the family, and undertaking little new investment if cash becomes available.[9] This factor will be called the *money* factor and summarizes a profit-maximizing and businesslike attitude on the part of owners.

Wineries that answered the survey clearly differ from wineries that did not. Principally, the non-respondents are bigger; the mean storage capacity for a respondent is 705 (1,000 gallons) versus 2,337 for the non-respondents. Kendall Jackson and Gallo did not return a survey. In terms of acreage,

[9]This last correlation is likely due to the fact that a PM owner has access to capital markets and has therefore optimally improved his winery, whereas a UM owner might not be able to borrow for a project that will not yield adequate profits.

the respondents are actually somewhat bigger (333 vs. 181). These statistics suggest that the larger wineries producing the lowest quality wines were less likely to answer; these wineries do not own their own land since the grapes they use are a commodity, but their large scale of production requires more storage capacity. This group of wineries likely contains the few public wineries that existed at the time. Additionally, we suspect that as wineries grow in size, the use of professional management reduces the impact of owner preferences on particular operational choices. Hence, the non-respondents may be a group of wineries with less variation in the characteristics we are studying. However, mean price and quality ranking are almost equal across the two samples. Slight differences exist in status, age, and availability; respondents are higher status (0.53 vs. 0.48), older (31 vs. 21), and have slightly less available wine (1.84 vs. 1.93). Distribution capabilities do not differ significantly across the two groups.

5. Empirical Testing

5.1. *Quality choice*

There are few exogenous features of a winery that predict quality, rather than being chosen simultaneously with it. As a consequence, the quality regressions reported in Table 3 will be sparse. Bottle quality is postulated to be a function of varietal (type of grape), vintage (year grape is grown), and appellation (geographic source of grapes). Clearly a winery has no control over the weather, and in the short run, particularly if it grows the majority of its own grapes, has less control over appellation and varietal selection.[10] Winery age is also included as an explanatory variable. We use a random effects regression specification, which allows the errors within a winery to be correlated.

Column one of the table includes answers to survey questions to see if these can predict bottle quality. Two are significant at the 5% level, and the rest at 10%. Specification two includes *love* and *money* rather than the raw survey answers and confirms the hypothesis of the theory section. The love factor significantly increases the likelihood that a particular bottle will be high-quality wine. A one standard deviation increase in *love* increases

[10]Even when a winery purchases its grapes from a grower in another appellation region, the contracts for such purchases are typically of at least a three-year duration. Therefore, even if a winery does not use its own grapes, there are some constraints on the ability to chose an appellation.

Table 3. Random Effects Regression of Bottle and Vintage Quality Rating (Rating Takes on Four Values Only, 0–3)

Dependent variable	Bottle rating	Bottle rating	Bottle rating	Bottle rating	Avg. winery rating	Min. winery rating	Max. winery rating
Love factor	—	0.160*	0.167*	0.109	0.091	0.100*	0.021
		(0.056)	(0.055)	(0.060)	(0.057)	(0.079)	(0.078)
Money factor	—	−0.013	−0.013	−0.025	−0.035	0.037	−0.154*
		(0.053)	(0.052)	(0.060)	(0.056)	(0.046)	(0.076)
Willing to lose money for quality	0.065*	—	—	—	—	—	—
	(0.031)						
Own winery because love wine	0.146*	—	—	—	—	—	—
	(0.072)						
No further investment if more resources	0.056†	—	—	—	—	—	—
	(0.032)						
Think Gallo is superior winery	−0.027†	—	—	—	—	—	—
	(0.014)						
Age	−0.0015†	−0.0013	−0.0013	−0.0013	−0.0020†	−0.0017*	−0.0021
	(0.0009)	(0.0009)	(0.0009)	(0.0010)	(0.0011)	(0.0009)	(0.0015)
Varietal dummies?	yes	yes	no	no	no	no	no
Vintage dummies?	yes	yes	yes	yes	yes	yes	yes
Appellation dummies?	yes	yes	yes	no	no	no	no
Random winery effects?	yes	yes	yes	yes	yes	yes	yes
R-squared	0.153	0.136	0.124	0.052	0.083	0.106	0.077
Observations	2,608	2,608	2,608	2,608	807	807	807

Notes: The sample in columns 1 and 2 is bottle quality of respondents who owned their winery for the relevant observation. Average, minimum, and maximum winery qualities are defined within a vintage. In columns 3–5 each winery-vintage combination that responded to the survey and owned the winery within three years after the vintage has one observation in the sample. *indicates significant at the 5% level or better, †indicates significant at the 10% level.

bottle quality by 3.3%. The money factor has a negative coefficient, but is not statistically significant. Interestingly, the significant coefficients on owner motivations are conditional on varietal choice. Since grape varietal is a choice variable in the medium to long run, this specification is a relatively strong test. The next column shows similar results if the varietal dummy variables are omitted. However, removing appellation dummy variables considerably reduces the significance of *love*.

We also examine the determinants of a winery's average, minimum, and maximum quality. The variables are defined for a particular vintage year belonging to a particular winery. Average quality is not weighted by volume or sales since we do not have that information. Only vintage dummy variables are included since a winery's average, best, or worst bottle in a given vintage could be one of a number of varietals or appellations. In these regressions each winery-vintage has only one observation, so the number of observations drops considerably. Average winery quality is again affected by the love factor, but its p-value is only 0.11. One might think a winery's minimum quality represents something about an owner's taste and his or her willingness to manufacture cheap products. Indeed, a one standard deviation increase in *love* increases the lowest quality a winery will manufacture by 2.1% (while *money* is insignificant). Owners with substantial private benefits from making wine are less willing to make low-quality wines. The outcome is exactly reversed when predicting maximum winery quality. A one standard deviation increase in the money factor lowers a winery's maximum quality by 3.5% (while *love* is insignificant).

The relationship documented in Table 3 can also be seen in the plot of average winery quality against *money* shown in Figure 1. There is hardly any slope to the cluster of points. While the high quality and high *money* quadrant is relatively empty, there are many owners who do not care about profits but do not seem to be able to produce high quality either. *Love* is associated with high quality as can be seen in Figure 2. Here, as in the regression, the correlation between winery quality and owner motivation is stronger.

We also expect to see winery owners who care more about financial returns being more likely to compete in the low-end segment. We focus on the survey questions that most closely pick up an owners attitude toward financial return. The question, "Do you have a specific rate of return in mind?" is the best match for our problem. We also include the other survey questions that particularly refer to financial conditions: "Are you willing to lose money to improve the quality of your wines?" and "winery improvements would not be undertaken with more resources." Because we use many individual questions in this regression, including the love factor would be redundant. Therefore we include questions that are correlated with *love*. Being unwilling to sell the winery, wanting it to continue in the family, and being motivated

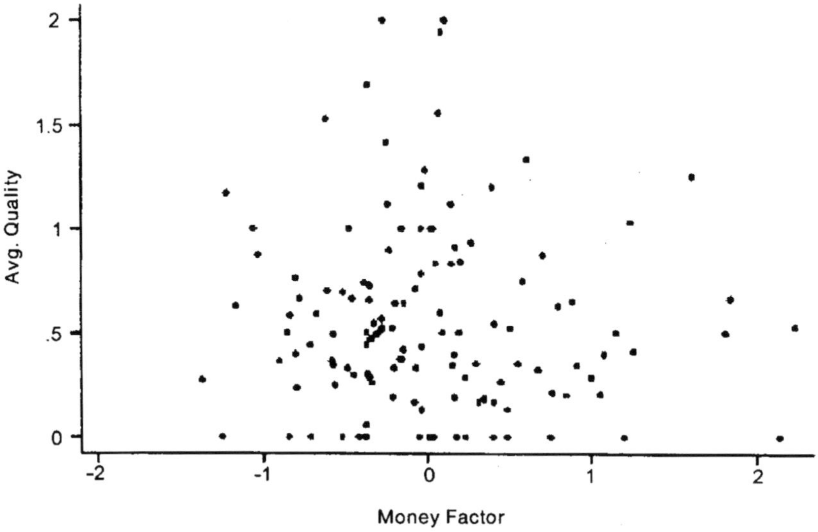

Figure 1. Winery Quality versus Money

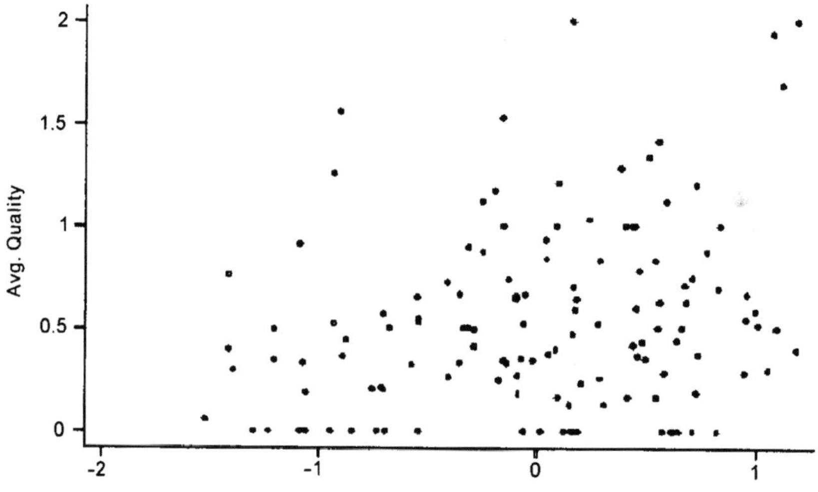

Figure 2. Winery Quality versus Love

by love of wine are in the specification. These variables are used to explain whether or not the winery chooses to make a wine of quality level zero, the minimum level. To test this proposition we use a random effects logit where the dependent variable is a one if the winery chooses to make a wine of quality zero. The results are presented in Table 4. Little attention to financial return decreases the probability of producing the lowest quality wines

Table 4. Financial Concerns Explain Choice to Produce Low Quality

Dependent variable	1 if winery produces 0-level quality
No specific rate of return in mind	−0.567*
	(0.306)
Willing to lose money for quality	0.033
	(0.138)
No further investment if more resources	−0.377*
	(0.136)
Unlikely to sell winery	−0.169
	(0.135)
Important winery remains in family	0.056
	(0.149)
Own winery because love wine	−0.087
	(0.310)
Age	0.021*
	(0.006)
Vintage dummies?	yes
Random winery effects?	yes
Observations	912

Note: Minimum winery quality is defined within a vintage. Each winery-vintage combination that responded to the survey and owned their winery for the relevant observation is in the sample. (Stata xtlogit used as estimation procedure.)
*indicates significant at the 6% level or better.

(*p*-value 0.08). Having undertaken all desired improvements also raises the minimum quality choice of the winery, while older wineries are more likely to produce the lowest quality wine.[11]

The implications of the dependence of quality choice on owner motivation are interesting. There are some competitors who have a preference for the high-quality segment of the market. We provide indirect evidence that UMs are sacrificing financial returns to buy quality as a consumption good. Over-entry into the high-quality end of the spectrum would lower returns to producers of high-quality wines. We also find evidence consistent with this, namely, PMs are less interested in occupying the high-quality segment.[12]

[11]The large positive demand shock for high-quality wines in the late 80's may have counteracted the crowding effect caused by utility-maximizing producers and raised the *ex post* return to producing high-quality wines. However, this shock was unanticipated and, because our sample ends in 1990, would only have affected prices for wines that had already been made.

[12]The PMs most likely to remain in the high-quality segment are those whose high-quality wines create a positive externality for their lower quality wines. We test this idea by including variables measuring if a winery has a bottle on the shelf in the previous year of

5.2. *Predicting price*

How should owner motivations affect price? Our theory predicts that quality-adjusted prices should fall with marginal cost, or the owner's ability parameter, α. This parameter is higher on average for UM owners, whom we are able to identify from our survey. First we develop a specification that predicts price and compare wineries that responded to the survey and those that didn't. Secondly, we capture the broad types of owners from the survey by including in the price regression the *love* and *money* variables constructed from the factor analysis.

We use the natural log of price as the dependent variable. Several categories of fixed effects must be included to pick up wine characteristics that strongly influence price. Varietal fixed effects control for different prices attached to different species of grapes. Grapes differ in their difficulty and cost of cultivation and also in their popularity. Vintage fixed effects are included because quality varies systematically across years, but is more constant within years. Finally, there are of course year fixed effects to control for demand in any particular year. We again use a random effects specification to allow the errors to be correlated within a winery. The results are not surprising, so they are discussed only briefly and reported in Table 5.

We expect price to be driven primarily by the quality of the wine. Quality is measured on different dimensions by numerous variables in the dataset. The first quality variable is a numeric rating of bottle quality from the *Wines and Vines Buyers Guide* that is an integer between zero and three inclusive. Although this particular rating takes on only four values, we use it because of its complete coverage of varietals and the fact that blind tasting determines the ratings.[13] Secondly, the average quality rating of all the bottles produced by a winery over the previous three years is also constructed. Other important quality variables are *status* and *three year average of winery status*, which essentially measure the quality one would expect based on reading the

a higher or lower quality level. We find that higher "sister" products do create a positive externality on the price of the reference bottle, while lower sister products do not. The "sister" premium is substantial (at the mean, approximately 40 cents for each quality level difference) and could be a reason for a winery to continue to produce high-quality wines despite unremunerative direct financial returns. Large wineries will earn the premium on a greater volume of low-quality wines and have distribution clout with supermarkets and other retailers that allows them to get a high-quality sister wine with low volume onto the shelf where it can be seen by and influence consumers.

[13]The tasters taste different wines of the same vintage and variety at the same time, but do not know the identities of individual bottles.

Table 5. Random Effects Regressions of Price on Wine and Winery Characteristics

Dependent variable: ln(price)	Whole sample $N = 8{,}223$		Wineries who returned survey $N = 4{,}043$	
	Coefficient	Std err	Coefficient	Std err
Age	−0.0006*	0.0002	−0.0005	0.0003
Quality level 0 (3 omitted)	−0.214*	0.019	−0.255*	0.027
Quality level 1	−0.149*	0.018	−0.191*	0.026
Quality level 2	−0.060*	0.019	−0.072*	0.027
3yr quality of winery	0.058*	0.009	0.049*	0.014
Rating of vintage	−0.002*	0.0003	−0.0024*	0.0005
Status	0.053*	0.009	0.050*	0.014
3yr status	0.022	0.012	0.028	0.019
Availability	0.048*	0.004	0.052*	0.007
Drinkability	0.064*	0.005	0.069*	0.008
Irregular	−0.101*	0.018	−0.098*	0.026
Ready to drink	−0.052*	0.013	−0.035	0.019
Tannic	0.053*	0.022	0.081*	0.031
Wholesale	−0.015	0.013	0.012	0.021
Shipout	−0.010	0.010	−0.013	0.015
Number of brands	−0.019*	0.007	0.0004	0.020
Brands squared	0.0004	0.0005	−0.0018	0.0029
Acreage	−0.00004*	0.00002	0.00001	0.00004
Acreage squared	5.1E-10	4.5E-09	−8.4E-09	1.7E-08
Storage capacity	−1.1E-06	1.3E-06	−1.5E-05	9.3E-06
Storage capacity squared	6.8E-13	3.4E-12	2.2E-10	2.8E-10
Random winery effects?	yes		yes	

Note: *Varietal dummies*: Cabernet Sauvignon, Chardonnay, Marsanne, Voigner, Merlot, Pinot Noir are significantly positive. Negative coefficients include Gamay, White Zinfandel, Chenin Blanc.
Vintage dummies: One set of vintage dummies for all varietals. Peak coefficients are 1975–1983.
Year dummies: Increasing over time, especially in late 80's.
Adjusted $R^2 = 0.620$ and 0.626, respectively. *Significance at 5% level or better.

label. These were constructed by Benjamin and Podolny (1997) according to the deference ordering among the appellations used on the labels of bottles of wine produced in California. A higher status appellation is one that a winery chooses — over other options allowed by the grapes that compose the wine — to write on a label.[14] Note that status is picking up other aspects

[14]See Benjamin and Podolny (1997) for a detailed discussion of the construction of the status variables and their implications for price and the returns to investments in quality. Benjamin and Podolny investigate a series of involved interactions involving status and lagged status with quality and lagged quality. Because our focus in this chapter is not on

of quality than those measured in the simple rating above; the correlation between status and tasting rating is only 0.15. However, over the longer term the two are more closely related; a winery's average tasting rating over three years and the average status of its bottles over three years have a correlation coefficient of 0.59. The remaining quality variables include *vintage* and *varietal*, a *rating* of the vintage, whether the wine is *drinkable*, whether or not the wine is considered to have a *tannic* character, and whether the wine is *irregular*. *Wines and Vines* also notes if the wine is *early maturing*, whether the wine is *available*, and whether it is *ready to drink*.

We would expect a winery's marginal cost to affect its choice of an optimal price for a bottle of wine when it faces a downward sloping demand curve.[15] The most important determinant of costs observable to the econometrician is the scale of production. There are several variables in the dataset that proxy for winery size, although, unfortunately there is no direct measure of output or cases sold in a particular year. *Vineyard acreage*, and *storage capacity* reflect size, and therefore economies on the manufacturing side.[16] Additional economies of distribution are picked up in several distribution and wholesaling variables (e.g., *wholesale, export*) that indicate the firm has permission from ATF to ship the wine to different places. We also include *number of brands* (e.g., Turning Leaf) because this might be another proxy for size, although we would expect costs to be higher as the number of brands increases.

The effects of the variables on log price are reported in Table 5. Because the tasting rating variable takes on only four values, it is included as three separate quality dummies rather than as a continuous variable. The results

the effects of status and because of the relatively low correlation between status and the love and money factors that are of central interest (see Table 1), we include the main effect for status as a control variable in the subsequent analysis, but do not include the more involved interactions.

[15]Wineries are not tax shelters and never have been. However, before 1986 a vineyard was a tax shelter because it is agriculture. The farming cost of planting new vines could be immediately expensed, generating a loss for the vineyard that year even though the project as a whole might have positive net present value. The tax shelter reason for owning a vineyard has disappeared due to the tax reform act of 1986. As far as we can tell there is not really a reason to think that marginal costs differ across firms for tax reasons, for example.

[16]Note that a winery makes wine and a vineyard grows grapes. A winery can be vertically integrated, leading to the usual results on relationship-specific investment in grape-growing by the vineyard. A winery could instead have a long-term contract(s) with vineyard(s) or purchase grapes of any quality on the spot market. Hence acreage may be correlated with production but is not necessarily an accurate sign of production levels.

are what one would expect. Higher rated wines and higher status wines cost more. All the quality coefficients show that price increases as quality increases except for the vintage rating, which has a negative and significant coefficient. *Ready to drink* has a negative coefficient, which may be the cost to the buyer of not being able to store the wine.[17] The cost variables are largely insignificant, although they have the predicted signs. However, larger wineries, measured by number of brands or acreage, charge less for their wines. The most expensive varietals include the most popular grapes, Cabernet, Chardonnay, Merlot, and some others such as Marsanne, Voigner, and Pinot Noir. Prices increase over the years in the dataset, particularly in the late 80's.[18] The age of the winery has a negative and significant coefficient; increasing age from zero to the mean of 23 years reduces price by 1.3%.

Note that the measures we have of scale are not measures of quantity. Unfortunately, the dataset does not have production quantity information. Thus, the storage capacity and distribution variables actually measure the size of the winery's operation, not its choice of quantity in response to price in a particular year.[19]

5.3. *The effect of preferences on prices*

Table 6 reports the same price regression as Table 5 with the addition of *love* and *money*.[20] Those wineries scoring high on the *love* factor have higher prices, while the *money* factor has an insignificant effect on price. This

[17] *Ready to drink* may also be picking up unobserved quality, since lower quality wines are not intended for storage and are always ready to drink.

[18] An interesting feature of the results is the importance of the age of the vineyard, which is not present in the later years of the dataset. The effect of age on pricing is quite robust and is shaped like a sideways, backwards "s". Prices increase steeply in age from zero up to ten or so, then there is a gentle dip that bottoms out at about 75 years, followed by an increase in price for older firms, catching up to the earlier peak at about age 120. Very new firms have no reputation among consumers and appear to charge an "introductory" price to build demand; wineries 10 years old or less charge less for a bottle conditional on quality and scale of operation. Firms in their prime — those between 10 and 50 years old — have the highest prices.

[19] In addition, simultaneity between price and quantity is not a problem because of the nature of wine production, particularly at the top end. Producers presumably do make quantity choices based on current and expected prices, but by the time the wine is ready to be sold the demand curve has moved in unexpected ways (several years have gone by) and by then price cannot physically affect quantity provided.

[20] We do not report the regression using the raw answers to the survey questions as the factors do a much better job explaining prices.

Table 6. Random Effects Regression of Loo Price on Factors as well as Wine and Winery Characteristics

Dependent variable: ln(bottle price)	1	2	3
Money factor	0.0007	−0.014	0.022
	(0.023)	(0.024)	(0.050)
Love factor*	0.054*	0.051*	0.091*
	(0.024)	(0.024)	(0.036)
Additional outside resources would not result in more winery investment	—	0.029*	—
		(0.015)	
Money*Years owned by family	—	—	−0.0016*
			(0.0019)
Love*Years owned by family	—	—	−0.0025*
			(0.0013)
Years owned by family	—	—	−0.0031*
			(0.0012)
Quality level 0	−0.256*	−0.255*	−0.254*
	(0.032)	(0.033)	(0.033)
Quality level 1	−0.201*	−0.200*	−0.200*
	(0.032)	(0.032)	(0.032)
Quality level 2	−0.073*	−0.072*	−0.072*
	(0.034)	(0.034)	(0.034)
Random winery effects?	yes	yes	yes
Adj. R^2	0.633	0.637	0.645
N	2,567	2,567	2,567
Dollar change in mean bottle price when *love* increases by one standard deviation and years owned is 23 (mean).	+0.36	+0.34	+0.21

Notes: The full sample is respondents who owned their winery for the relevant observation. The sample size drops from Table 3 to this table because of missing observations, (love and money cannot be constructed if a survey is missing responses.) All explanatory variables from Table 2 are included in all regressions, but their coefficients are not reported to conserve space. The *love* and *money* factors in column 3 are constructed without family ownership years; it enters separately and in interactions with *love* and *money*. *indicates significant at the 5% level, two-tail test.

evidence is consistent with our theory that UMs have higher (marginal) costs than PMs. A one standard deviation increase in the love factor increases a wine's price by 3.4%, which is 36 cents for the mean bottle of wine in the sample ($10.60). This result is the second major contribution of this chapter. The coefficients measuring quality do not change significantly from the previous specification. However, including owner preferences makes *age of winery* insignificant.

It is possible that the love variable is picking up unobserved quality, which then drives price. In such a case, the estimated coefficient on *love* will represent unobserved quality correlated with *love* rather than the behavioral effect of those owners who love making wine. Note, however, that quality is well controlled for in the regression; we have the quality rating variable, status of the label, three-year quality of winery, three-year status of winery, vintage dummies, varietal dummies, *tannic*, and *ready to drink*, among other variables that all measure aspects of the quality of the wine. We also include question 5 from the survey ("additional resources would not cause winery improvements") which is not an important component of love but will pick up any unobserved quality. The only change is an increase in magnitude of the *money* coefficient, although it remains statistically insignificant.[21]

We create a test for the presence of unobserved quality in an indirect manner. We examine how *love* and *money* owners' prices vary with the length of time they have owned their wineries. Our assumption is that two owners with the same *love* score should have the same unobserved quality, regardless of the length of time each has owned his winery. However, if there is learning by doing in the wine industry, we might expect marginal costs to decline, and therefore the price premium to decline, with years of experience running the winery. We interact the number of years the owner or his family has owned the winery with *love* and with *money*. To make the experiment as clean as possible, we construct new *love* and *money* factors that are identical to the original ones except they do not include the ownership years variable.[22] Ownership years is included separately in the regression. The third column of Table 6 shows the results of the specification. The coefficient on years of ownership is −0.0031, which means that all wineries reduce quality adjusted prices with experience. The important finding is that *love* owners show more strongly declining prices with the amount of time they have owned the winery. Their coefficient is an additional significant −0.0025. The main *love* coefficient is positive, significant, and almost twice as large as in previous results.

These results imply that an owner who has just purchased his winery will price 5.5% higher than his PM peers (60 cents on the average bottle). An owner with the mean number of years of experience (23) who raises his love

[21]We also experimented with interactions between these variables and financial resources to reflect the situation where the owner has a preference for quality and additionally has sufficient wealth to carry out that preference. Importantly, the coefficients on the *love* and *money* factors are almost entirely unchanged and continue to be significant regardless of the specification.

[22]These factors are correlated 0.98 with the original ones and have nearly identical means and standard deviations.

score by one standard deviation will price 2.0% higher (21 cents). The effect of increasing an owner's love score reaches zero at 36 years of ownership. Only 10% of the wineries in the sample have been owned by the same family for longer than 36 years, so for the vast majority of owners, the net effect of the love variable is positive. The love variable, therefore, does not seem to be measuring only unobserved quality. The main *love* result may be unobserved quality, but the decline over time in *love* firms' prices is most consistent with initially high marginal costs.

Another alternative hypothesis we want to address is that hobbyist owners are selling their image and story, rather than the quality of the wine. Buyers know the attitude of the owner, and they place a higher value on wine produced by someone who shares their values. In our view, such an explanation for the price difference is likely to apply to few consumers and few wineries since the explanation hinges on consumers having a relatively intimate knowledge of the motivations of individual owners. Most consumers are not well-enough informed to be paying for "values," particularly in the face of advertising by PMs intent on convincing consumers that they too have values.

In conclusion, we find evidence that owners with strong non-financial motivations choose higher prices for their wines, controlling for quality. That price premium declines with the length of time the winery has been in the owner's family.

6. Conclusions

In this chapter we argue that non-profit-maximizing organizations should be observed in a market economy — despite higher costs — when production creates some sort of non-financial return for the firm's owner. In this chapter we document several ways in which such owner motivation alters the policy choice of the firm. We conclude that explicitly recognizing heterogeneity of objective functions among firms in an industry is important in understanding outcomes such as quality provision and price. Our results have implications for several areas of the economics literature. Producers who gain utility from some aspect of their product or process supply more of those characteristics to the market than consumers would demand on their own. The equilibrium relative price of those characteristics will be lower than in a world without the UM producers. Consumers who happen to enjoy the same characteristics that producers value will be better off, since their preferred goods will be "over" supplied. The mixture of goods we see in the economy will therefore not just be driven by consumer tastes, but by producer tastes also.

Because we find that different types of owners systematically price differently and the type of owner is correlated with the quality of the wine, ordinary hedonic regressions of wine prices will not be correct. A standard hedonic pricing regression using data from wineries with different objective functions will consistently mis-specify the cost of the features of a high quality bottle of wine. Further, our results are also relevant for the traditional strategy literature; for example, the classic strategy of moving first with a large capacity in order to deter entry by UM competitors will need to be re-evaluated. When competitors are not maximizing profit, they will not respond according to the standard model.

The fact that UMs have a lower threshold for profits has clear and important implications for the evolutionary argument to which we alluded at the outset. Rather than PMs driving UMs from the market or selected market segments, the UMs end up being more "competitive" than their PM counterparts. An obvious extension of this empirical research is to undertake a dynamic analysis of the entry and exit of firms, and see how the motivations and wealth levels of owners explain operational choices of the firm over time. Another interesting area for thought and future research lies in how motives of subsequent generations of owners differ from the original owner and the implications for evolution of an industry.[23] We suspect that this kind of research project could be carried out in industries other than the wine industry. For example, opinion magazines, films, bars, and horse-racing would also seem to be activities where a large proportion of owners derive utility from some feature of the organization other than its level of profitability.

Acknowledgments

We thank Ben Polak, John Roberts, Scott Schaefer, lunch participants at Stanford GSB, and seminar participants at Chicago GSB, Cornell University, and the NBER Summer Institute IO Meetings for helpful comments. An anonymous referee and the editor improved the chapter considerably. We are also grateful to the winery owners who shared their knowledge and insights

[23]If non-financial benefits are not as strong (regression to the mean) for subsequent owners then the objective function of the organization will revert to profit maximization. This sort of pattern seems to describe entry in the software industry, for example, where founders have goals other than profit-maximization, but after selling to shareholders and professional management, the organization changes its behavior and maximizes profits.

with us. Fiona Scott Morton was partially supported by NSF grant SBR-9810178.

References

Alchian, A. (1950). Uncertainty, evolution, and economic theory. *Journal of Political Economy*, 58(3), 211–221.

Becker, G. (1957). *The Economics of Discrimination*. Chicago: University of Chicago Press.

Benjamin, B.A. (1994). Identity construction through collective affiliation. PhD Dissertation, Stanford University.

Benjamin, B.A., and Podolny, J.M. (1999). Social order and status in the California wine industry 1981–1991. *Administrative Science Quarterly*, 44, 563–589.

Cremer, H., and Cremer, J. (1992). Duopoly with employee-controlled and profit-maximizing firms: Bertrand vs Cournot competition. *Journal of Comparative Economics*, 16, 241–258.

Craig, B., and Pencavel, J. (1992). The behavior of worker cooperatives: The plywood companies of the Pacific Northwest. *American Economic Review*, 82(5), 1083–1105.

Eddy, P. (1996). Lessons, legends, and legacies: Serving the family business. *Journal of Financial Planning*, 9, 76–79.

Futagami, K., and Okamura, M. (1996). Strategic investment: The labor-managed firm and the profit-maximizing firm. *Journal of Comparative Economics*, 23, 73–91.

Hotelling, H. (1933). Analysis of a complex of statistical variables into principal components. *Journal of Educational Psychology*, 24, 417–441 and 498–520.

Harman, H. (1960). *Modern Factor Analysis*. Chicago: University of Chicago Press.

Lakdawalla, D., and Philipson, T. (1998). Nonprofit production and competition. University of Chicago, Harris School of Public Policy, manuscript.

Milgrom, P., and Shannon, C. (1994). Monotone comparative statics. *Econometrica*, 62(1), 157–180.

Pencavel, J., and Craig, B. (1994). The empirical performance of orthodox models of the firm: Conventional firms and worker cooperative. *Journal of Political Economy*, 102(4), 718–744.

Prince, A. (1996). Understanding the eight types of business owners. *Trusts and Estates*, 135, 41–43.

Rose-Ackerman, S. (1986). Altruistic nonprofit firms in competitive markets: The case of day-care centers in the united states. *Journal of Consumer Policy*, 9, 291–310.

Rose-Ackerman, S. (1996). Altruism, nonprofits, and economic theory. *Journal of Economic Literature*, 34, 701–728.

Schiff, J., and Weisbrod, B. (1991). Competition between for-profit and nonprofit organizations in commercial markets. *Annals of Public and Cooperative Economics*, 62(4), 619–639.

Steinberg, C. (1996). The next generation. *Success*, 43, 85–88.

Stewart, G. (1991). Strategic entry interactions involving profit-maximizing and labour-managed firms. *Oxford Economic Papers*, 43, 570–583.

Stewart, G. (1992). Management objectives and strategic interactions among capitalist and labour-managed firms. *Journal of Economic Behavior and Organization*, 17, 423–431.

Weisbrod, B. (1983). Nonprofit and proprietary sector behavior: Wage differentials among lawyers. *Journal of Labor Economics*, 1(3), 246–263.

Chapter 16

Influence of Informed Buyers in Markets Susceptible to the Lemons Problem*

Philippe Mahenc

University of Montpellier (CEE-M),
Avenue Raymond Dugrand, Site de Richter,
C. S. 79606, 34960 Montpellier Cedex 2, France
philippe.mahenc@umontpellier.fr

It is shown that the presence of informed buyers is necessary but not always sufficient for producers to use prices as signals of product quality. A sufficiently high fraction of informed buyers eliminates the lemons problem. A small fraction of informed buyers mitigates the lemons problem, provided that buyers' prior belief of high quality is sufficiently pessimistic: price reveals high quality at a signaling cost which increases with market power. However, if buyers prior belief of high quality is optimistic when the market is poorly informed, then the lemons problem is not overcome.

1. Introduction

Whatever the degree of competition, markets in which the producer knows the quality of his good but the buyer does not are susceptible to Akerlof's (1970) lemons problem: a low-quality good sells at the same price as a high-quality good because it is impossible for most of the buyers to tell the difference between a high and a low quality. The lemons problem is important to the food sector and to markets for products that generate less environmental harm such as organically grown agricultural products. The latter are often either experience or credence goods. Both Karl and Orwat (1999) and Cason and Gangadharan (2002) explicitly address the issue that consumers often find it difficult to identify the environmental quality of clean products.

*This article originally appeared in *American Journal of Agricultural Economics* (2004), 86(3), 649–659.

Similarly, the quality of Bordeaux *grands crus* can hardly be observed prior to purchase. When prices alone fail to signal quality, uninformed buyers rely on private expert opinion, public disclosure programs, or the externality exerted by informed buyers to acquire information. The objective of this chapter is to examine to what extent the presence of informed buyers might be used by producers to signal quality through prices.

In order to illustrate, consider the market for Bordeaux *grands crus*. Each year, the Bordeaux "primeur" release deals with 80% of the châteaux total production. While the wine is still in barrels, hence is not yet mature, the owners of the foremost châteaux set a price called the "primeur" price. One special feature of this marketing strategy is that wine becomes an experience good in the sense of Nelson since full information on quality is not available to buyers at the time of purchase. Another feature is that buyers rely on expert opinion to make their purchase decisions. Figures 1 and 2 illustrate that the "primeur" release of *grands crus* is susceptible to Akerlof's (1970) lemons problem. The four curves that are almost superimposed in Figure 1 depict the changes in the "primeur" prices of four *grands crus* classified as First-Growth of the appellation *Médoc*. One can see that these four châteaux have been setting the same price since 1980 for almost all the vintages. Figure 1 might suggest that, for a given vintage, the wine quality is even regardless of the château, *provided that* the "primeur" price is an effective signal of quality. However, Figure 2 shows that the scores assigned in January 2002 to the four wines by Robert Parker, a famous wine expert and editor of

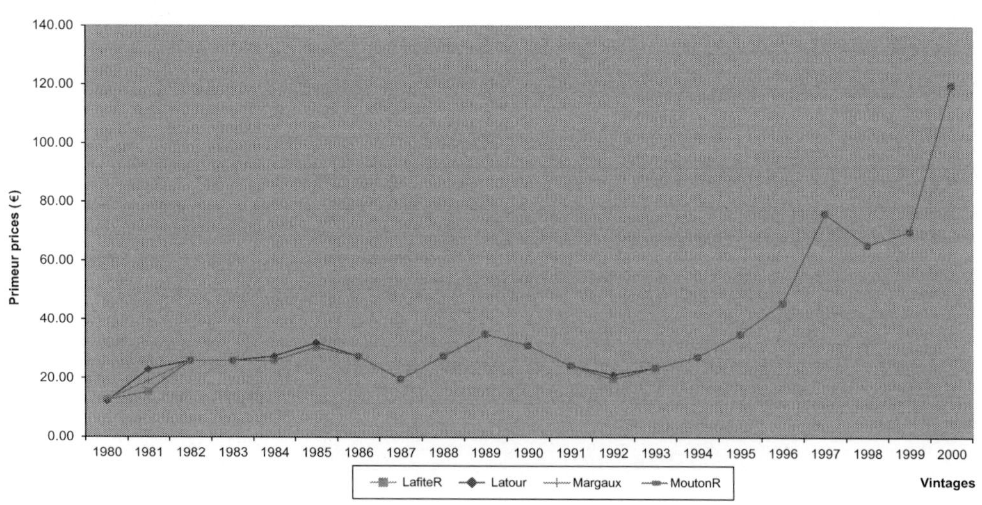

Figure 1. Primeur Prices of 4 Médoc Grands Crus

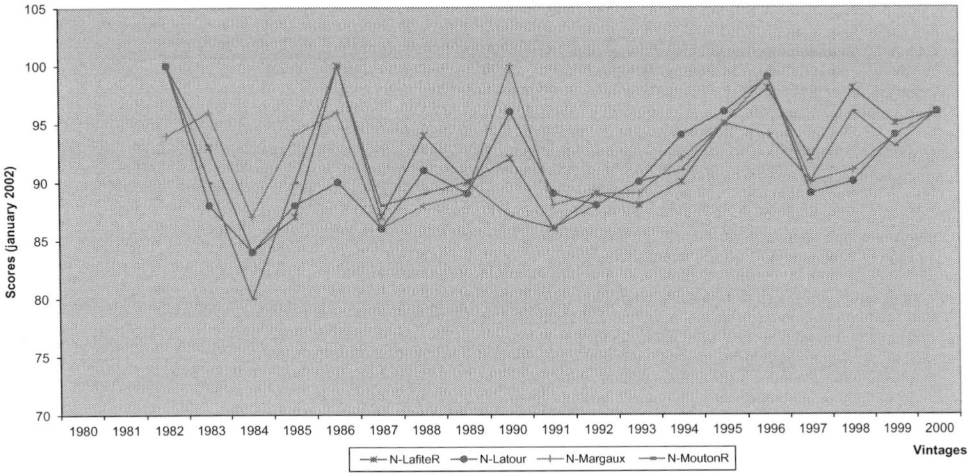

Figure 2. Parker's Scores for 4 Médoc Grands Crus

The *Wine Advocate*, noticeably differ from one château to another. If the expert opinion provides accurate estimates of quality, then "primeur" prices have failed to signal quality at least for the aforementioned châteaux.

This chapter investigates a signaling model of price in the spirit of Milgrom and Roberts, and Bagwell and Riordan (1991), which is inspired by the main features of the Bordeaux *grands crus* industry.

A wine is a bundle of characteristics: taste, quality, color, aroma, balance, aging potential, location, time, and so on. Two differentiated goods which differ in taste and quality are considered. Taste is a horizontal characteristic in the sense that it differs from one buyer to another. On the other hand, quality is a vertical characteristic and so it is assumed that there exists a single ranking of qualities based on the expert opinion, with which all buyers agree.[1] In this framework, one good can be seen as a wine produced by one of the foremost châteaux dominating the Bordeaux wine industry in terms of quality, while the other good is a second wine sold by lesser known wine producers.[2] The superior good is more costly to produce than the other good (hence production techniques determine quality), and it endows the producer with a monopolistic position. Furthermore, the superior good is an experience good: all buyers know that its quality is higher than that of the other good, but some buyers cannot ascertain whether it is much higher or

[1]Robert Parker argues that "there are specific standards of quality that full-time wine professional recognize" (quoted in Landon and Smith, 1997).

[2]Wine producers classified, for instance, as *Crus Bourgeois*.

a little higher. These differences in the quality of the superior good are due to exogenous factors, that is, factors outside the control of the monopolist such as weather (hence nature also determines the quality of the superior good). The lemons problem is formally captured by the benchmark that the monopoly price of the superior product could not signal quality were all buyers uninformed. The other good is sold by a competitive fringe of small producers and its quality is perfectly known.

As a result, whatever the degree of monopoly power, the presence of informed buyers is necessary for the monopoly price to be an effective signal of quality but not always sufficient. A sufficiently high fraction of informed buyers eliminates the lemons problem by exerting a negative externality on the low-quality monopolist. These informed buyers so increase the cost of pricing for the low-quality monopolist that replicating the high-quality product price becomes unprofitable. Thus, the condition emphasized by Spence (1973) for a signal to be effective is met: the high-quality monopolist bears lower costs for signaling through price. A small fraction of informed buyers mitigates the lemons problem, provided that buyers' prior belief of high quality is sufficiently pessimistic. In the case of such a poorly informed market, the monopolist bears a signaling cost to reveal the high quality by distorting his price above the full information level. However, if buyers' prior belief of high quality is optimistic when the market is poorly informed, then signaling the true quality is more costly than accepting mimicry for the high-quality monopolist, and so uninformative prices prevail.

Furthermore, in this chapter the impact of the monopolist's market power on price signaling is evaluated. The main idea is that more market power increases the signaling cost to reveal high quality because the low-quality monopolist finds mimicry more attractive: the more market power, the lower the loss of buyers who refuse to buy at a higher-mimicking price.

While the present model is closely related to the work by Bagwell and Riordan, their conclusions contrast in three respects with the results presented in this chapter. First, they find that informed buyers are not necessary for the signaling of a given quality. Second, uninformative prices occur only when the fraction of informed buyers is intermediate. Third, they do not take into account the monopolist's market power. The main reason for the first result in Bagwell and Riordan is that higher-quality products entail higher costs of production. In the present chapter, higher-quality products do have a higher cost of production, but due to uncontrollable factors such as weather, nature introduces randomness into the quality. This simple fact renders crucial the presence of informed buyers to achieve separation of quality types. The second result mentioned above stems from Bagwell and Riordan's choice of the *intuitive criterion* (Cho and Kreps, 1987) to prune equilibria. The logic of *undefeated equilibria* proposed by Mailath, Okuno-Fujiwara, and Postlewaite (1993) is proved to provide more intuitive insights in the present case. In particular, this criterion eliminates separating equilibria rather than pooling equilibria, hence informative prices rather than uninformative prices, when uninformed buyers are numerous and prone to believe that quality is high. The idea is that, in such circumstances, it is of no avail to make an effort to fully reveal that quality is high. This result is noteworthy, although it would be overturned by the *intuitive criterion.*

2. Basic Model with Uninformative Prices

Following Hotelling, an industry is considered in which two differentiated goods are located at the two endpoints of the segment [0,1]. Buyers do not rank both goods in the same way and their heterogeneous tastes are assumed to be continuously distributed along the segment. The location of a buyer with taste x is interpreted here as his disutility from buying the less-than-ideal good located at the left endpoint of the segment (henceforth the left good). The monetary equivalent losses of the buyer x purchasing the left good and the good located at the right endpoint of the segment (henceforth the right good) are tx^2 and $t(1-x)^2$, respectively. The parameter t measures the degree of differentiation between goods and can also be seen as an index for the degree of competition.

The left good is assumed to be an experience good, that is, quality is not observable to buyers. This good is sufficiently differentiated in taste and/or quality to provide the producer with a monopolistic position, like a First-Growth wine in Bordeaux.[3] In contrast, the right good is produced by a competitive fringe of small producers and its quality is perfectly known to buyers. This fits the presence in Bordeaux of numerous wines, which are close, but imperfect substitutes in taste to a wine classified as First-Growth, and of lower quality too. An immediate consequence of the competition between the producers of the right good is that its price drops to marginal cost of production which is normalized to zero. Hence, the purpose of the present framework is to focus on the monopoly behavior of the producer of the left good (henceforth the monopolist), using t as an index for the degree

[3]Another interpretation could be that a few Bordeaux châteaux among the foremost ones form a dominant cartel or achieve price collusion.

of monopoly power. If $t = 0$, the taste characteristic becomes irrelevant. If t is positive, the producer of the left good attains some degree of monopoly power.

Moreover, the left good is vertically differentiated in the sense that all buyers agree that higher quality is preferable.[4] The left good is more costly to produce than the right good, hence the superior quality of the left good is partly due to production techniques. Nevertheless, some differences in quality are assumed to be gifts of nature and so are exogenous to the monopolist. The quality of the left good takes one of two values, either high (H) or low (L). The marginal production costs for the left good are constant and equal to $c > 0$, regardless of quality. Throughout the chapter it is assumed that $L = c$: this implies that buyers with taste $x < 1/2$, who exhibit a "personal" preference for the left good, are the only ones to purchase this good when its quality is low and its price is set at marginal cost. Thus, the monopolist is able to "steal" buyers from the competitive fringe of producers only when the quality of the left product is high.

A crucial feature of the markets considered in this chapter is that information is asymmetric: the monopolist knows the actual quality measured by a quality index q, while buyers do not.[5]

The expected utility of a buyer with taste x and income R purchasing the left good is given by $R + q - p - tx^2$ if he purchases a good of quality q at price p, and R if he does not buy. On the other hand, if the same buyer (x, R) purchases the right good, he obtains the utility $R - t(1-x)^2$. It is assumed that buyers buy at most one unit of the differentiated good. It is also assumed that R is large enough for all buyers to find a product for which their utility is positive (in equilibrium). The market is split at the marginal buyer with taste $\tilde{x} \in [0, 1]$ satisfying,

$$R + q - p - t\tilde{x}^2 = R - t(1-\tilde{x})^2.$$

This implies a linear demand function $D(p) \equiv \tilde{x} = (q + t - p)/2t$ for the left good, as long as this is nonnegative and does not exceed 1. Note that

[4]For the Bordeaux "primeur" release, this amounts to saying that the expert predictions of quality are supposed to be infallible and everybody is agreed on them. An extension of the present model has been examined to capture the possibility of expert errors. Results are generally the same as in the present chapter except in a particular case, namely when experts are unanimous on quality regardless of whether they are right or wrong.

[5]As far as Bordeaux *grands crus* are concerned, Di Vittorio and Ginsburgh (1996) stress that weather information concerning a whole area is publicly available, while local weather phenomena that mar the grapes, such as hail, remains the château's private information.

the demand price elasticity $|\frac{\partial D(p)}{\partial p}\frac{p}{D(p)}| = \frac{p}{q+t-p}$ decreases with the degree of monopoly power.

As the actual quality of the left good is not observable to buyers, they must rely on their beliefs about quality when deciding to purchase the good. The monopolist, in turn, will have to take into account how his choice of price affects the buyers' beliefs. Observing p, buyers try to infer some information about quality and update their beliefs. Let $\mu(p)$ denote the buyers' posterior belief that quality is H when the price is p. If the buyers assign probability $\mu = \mu(p)$ to the high quality, then $g(\mu) \equiv \mu H + (1-\mu)c$ is the buyers' perception of quality upon seeing p and the monopolist's demand is represented by the demand curve,

$$D(p,\mu) = (q(\mu) + t - p)/2t. \tag{1}$$

Let μ_0 be the prior probability assigned to the quality being H. This belief is common knowledge: it summarizes all the information that is publicly available in popular quality reports.[6] For instance, it includes information on weather and reputation.[7] When buyers perfectly identify quality, the monopolist with quality q has a profit function explicitly defined by $(p-c)(q+t-p)/2t$. Thus, $\frac{(q-c+t)^2}{8t}$ is the maximum profit he can get by charging his full information price $\frac{q+c+t}{2}$. Clearly, when q or t increase, the left good becomes more differentiated from the right good either in quality or in taste, enhancing the market power of the monopolist who, in turn, raises his price. When buyers cannot ascertain quality, the monopolist may choose either to fully reveal information on quality through separating prices, or to conceal information through pooling prices. The following lemma can be stated:

Lemma 1. *When all buyers are uninformed, prices fail to signal quality.*

Suppose that the price p does reveal high quality. Then the monopolist must not be able to duplicate such a price when his product is of low quality. His demand when doing so would be $D(p,1) = (H+t-p)/2t$, hence he would make a mimicking profit of $(p-c)(H+t-p)/2t$, whereas his maximized

[6]In the case of Bordeaux wine, there are numerous guides and reviews such as *La Revue du Vin de France, La Lettre du Club Vinophile*, the annual "Bordeaux" issue of the Wine Spectator which provides a wine quality index that takes into account factors such as color, aroma, flavor, balance, complexity, and aging potential.

[7]Following Landon and Smith, information on the past quality performance of Bordeaux châteaux largely influences the buyers' beliefs on current quality.

profit is $\frac{t}{8}$ when quality is perfectly identified. Therefore, to signal the high quality, the price p must satisfy,

$$(p-c)(H+t-p)/2t \leq \frac{t}{8}. \tag{2}$$

However, $\frac{t}{8}$ is also the opportunity cost that the high-quality monopolist must bear to reveal quality since it is the highest profit that he can make when he is believed to sell a low-quality product. Thus, the high-quality monopolist finds it profitable to charge an informative price p yielding a profit $(p-c)(H+t-p)/2t$, provided that,

$$(p-c)(H+t-p)/2t > \frac{t}{8}. \tag{3}$$

This contradicts inequality (2). As in the lemons problem identified by Akerlof (1970), the equilibrium price cannot be informative.

The reason why there is no separating equilibrium is that pricing entails the same cost regardless of quality, that is, namely the monopolist's profit in the absence of informed buyers, $(p-c)D(p,\mu)$, has the same derivative with respect to p for all q.

In fact, the high- and low-quality monopolists charge the same price in equilibrium. Given that buyers assign a prior probability μ_0 to the high-quality monopolist, such a price p must yield a profit no lower than $\frac{t}{8}$, which is what the monopolist could get at best, were he thought to be low-quality, that is, $(p-c)(q(\mu_0)+t1-p)/2t \geq \frac{t}{8}$. Obviously, this inequality holds for infinitely many equilibrium prices.

Nevertheless, some equilibrium prices are less plausible than others. To discard them, it is useful to apply the logic of *Undefeated Equilibrium* (UE) proposed by Mailath, Okuno-Fujiwara, and Postlewaite. Define π_q^* and $\pi_q^{\#}$ as the equilibrium profits of the monopolist selling quality q at prices p_q^* and $p_q^{\#}$, respectively. Furthermore, let $\mu^*(p)$ be the posterior belief held after observing p, that sustains p_q^* as an equilibrium. Following Mailath, Okuno-Fujiwara, and Postlewaite, the equilibrium price p_q^* survives the UE criterion, provided that there does not exist another equilibrium $p_q^{\#}$ "defeating" p_q^*, that is:

$$\begin{aligned}&\text{If } p_H^{\#} = p_L^{\#}, \quad \text{then } \pi_q^{\#} \geq \pi_q^* \quad \text{for} \\ &\quad q = H, L \text{ with one inequality strict} \\ &\quad \text{and } \mu^*(p_H^{\#}) \neq \mu_0.\end{aligned} \tag{4}$$

$$\text{If } p_H^{\#} \neq p_L^{\#}, \quad \text{then } \pi_H^{\#} > \pi_H^{*},\ \pi_L^{\#} \leq \pi_L^{*} \quad \text{and } \mu^*(p_H^{\#}) \neq 1. \tag{5}$$

The existence of such an equilibrium $p_q^{\#}$ would induce the monopolist to deviate from p_q^*. Some persuasive arguments in favor of the UE criterion can be found in Mailath, Okuno-Fujiwara, and Postlewaite. In the present context, the logic of this refinement is parallel to a Pareto dominance argument in reference to the monopolist only. As the monopolist is potentially of two quality types, both of these types should not be wastefully competitive with themselves. In the case without informed buyers, the UE criterion singles out the equilibrium price $(q(\mu_0)+c+t)/2 = \arg\max_p (p-c)D(p,\mu_0)$ simply because it is the equilibrium that Pareto dominates all the other pooling equilibria from the monopolist's viewpoint. Clearly, there does not exist another pooling equilibrium such that requirement (4) is met, hence the monopolist is not tempted to deviate from $(q(\mu_0)+c+t)/2$, whatever his quality.

Lemma 2. *When all buyers are uninformed, the monopolist charges the uninformative UE price* $(q(\mu_0)+c+t)/2$.

Lemma 2 states the existence of a lemons problem in the market under consideration, in that the monopolist has no way of signaling quality through price. Such a situation prevailing in the absence of informed buyers will serve as a benchmark to shed light on the role of informed buyers. Furthermore, the only reasonable prediction is that the monopolist will choose the uninformative price $(q(\mu_0)+c+t)/2$ which depends on the buyers' prior information about quality. The reason why prices fail to signal quality is that the cost of pricing does not depend on the level of quality.

As the incentive to "tell" buyers about quality through price is not higher for a monopolist with a high-quality product, mimicry can emerge: the low-quality monopolist charges the same price as his high-quality counterpart, hence prevents buyers from learning the true quality and turns their misinformation to profit.

In the remainder of the chapter, it is shown that the presence of informed buyers enables prices to signal quality because it lowers the cost of pricing for the monopolist when quality is higher.

3. The Model with Informed Buyers

Now assume that some buyers can ascertain the quality of the left good. A fraction I of buyers, say the readership of reviews publishing accurate advice on quality, learn the product quality before purchase, while the remaining fraction $1-I$ of buyers believe that quality is high with probability μ. Then the total demand is,

$$\begin{aligned} D(p,q,\mu) &\equiv ID(p) + (1-I)D(p,\mu) \\ &= (\phi_q(\mu) + t - p)/2t \end{aligned} \tag{6}$$

where $\phi_q(\mu) \equiv Iq + (1-I)q(\mu), q = H, L$.

The profit of a monopolist selling a product of true quality q at a price p, that is believed to be of quality H with probability μ, is now given by $\pi_q(p,\mu) = (p-c)\mathrm{D}(p,q,\mu)$. This is a strictly concave function with a single turning point at $\frac{\phi_q(\mu)+c+t}{2}$, which yields a maximized profit of $\frac{(\phi_q(\mu)-c+t)^2}{8t}$.

The presence of informed buyers modifies the framework in a crucial way. From (6), the monopolist's marginal benefit from slightly increasing the price can now be expressed as,

$$\begin{aligned} \frac{\partial \pi_q(p,\mu)}{\partial p} &= Iq/2t + ((1-I)q(\mu) \\ &\quad + t + c - 2p)/2t, \quad q = H, L. \end{aligned} \tag{7}$$

It is instructive to note that the right-hand side expression depends on q only in the first term. The marginal benefit is higher for a higher-quality monopolist provided that $I > 0$. This single-crossing property no longer holds in the absence of informed buyers.

Denoting by p_H^I and p_L^I the separating prices for the high quality and the low quality, respectively, the corresponding equilibrium profits will be π_H^I and π_L^I. Since the monopolist selling a product of one quality has the option to pretend to sell a product of another quality, the separating prices must satisfy the requirements ensuring that revealing the actual quality is profitable. When quality is perfectly identified, the low-quality monopolist earns more by charging his full information price $\frac{2c+t}{2}$ than any other price. Thus, $p_L^I = \frac{2c+t}{2}$ is the only separating price open to the low-quality monopolist. On the other hand, when the low-quality monopolist is thought to be high quality after choosing a price p, he faces a demand $D(p, L, 1)$ and has a mimicking profit $\pi_L(p,1) = (p-c)(\phi_L(1) + t - p)/2t$. To achieve separation, the high-quality monopolist must set a price p_H^I that satisfies the condition,

$$\pi_L(p_H^I, 1) \leq \pi_L^I. \tag{8}$$

Otherwise, the low-quality monopolist would strictly prefer to spurn p_L^I and choose p_H^I. Note that the derivative of the mimicking profit in the left-hand side of (8) with respect to p decreases with I, namely $\frac{\partial^2 \pi_L(p,1)}{\partial p\, \partial I} = (c - H)I < 0$. In other words, the more informed the market, the more difficult it is fooling buyers. Denoting respectively by L, the set of prices defined by requirement (8) and by $\bar{p}_L^I$ the upper root solving the equality version of (8) (see Appendix A for more details), the constraint to choose a price in L to avoid mimicry may distort the price charged by the high-quality monopolist with respect to the full information case, hence creating a signaling cost.

Moreover, if the high-quality monopolist quotes a price p on the basis of which he is believed to sell low quality, then he makes a profit $\pi_H(p,0) = (p-c)(\phi_H(0)+t-p)/2t$. Maximizing this profit by setting the price $\frac{\phi_H(0)+c+t}{2}$, would give him a profit of $\frac{(\phi_H(0)-c+t)^2}{8t}$. This can be interpreted as the opportunity cost to signal high quality, which increases with the number of informed buyers since $\phi_H(0)$ increases with I. Thus, the more informed the market, the weaker the incentive to reveal information through price. The separating price p_H^I must be such that,

$$\pi_H(p_H^I, 1) > \frac{(\phi_H(0) - c + t)^2}{8t}. \tag{9}$$

Otherwise the high-quality monopolist would deviate to $\frac{\phi_H(0)+c+t}{2}$, no matter what inferences buyers might draw from the observation of such a price. Let H denote the interval of prices for which condition (9) is met.

In order to reveal quality, the high-quality monopolist must choose a separating price p_H^I in the set $L \cap H$, which turns out to be nonempty for all $I > 0$ (see the proof in Appendix B). As a result, informed buyers are necessary for the price to be an effective signal of high quality. To state the result in Proposition 1, the following function is denned,

$$I(t) \equiv \frac{2t + H - c}{2(t + H - c)}$$

where $I = I(t)$ solves equation $\bar{p}_L^I - \frac{H+c+t}{2} = 0$, that is, $\bar{p}_L^I$ is equal to the full information price for the high-quality product (see Appendix C for further calculations). In Figure 3, the function $I = I(t)$ represents the borderline between the two regions I and II. Proposition 1 states that the monopolist sells both the low- and high-quality products at the full information price for the parameter values in region I, hence, the lemons problem is fully solved due to the presence of informed buyers. On the other hand, the monopolist charges a price exceeding the full information price to reveal high quality for values of I and t in region II. For these values, the presence of informed buyers mitigates the lemons problem since buyers can infer the

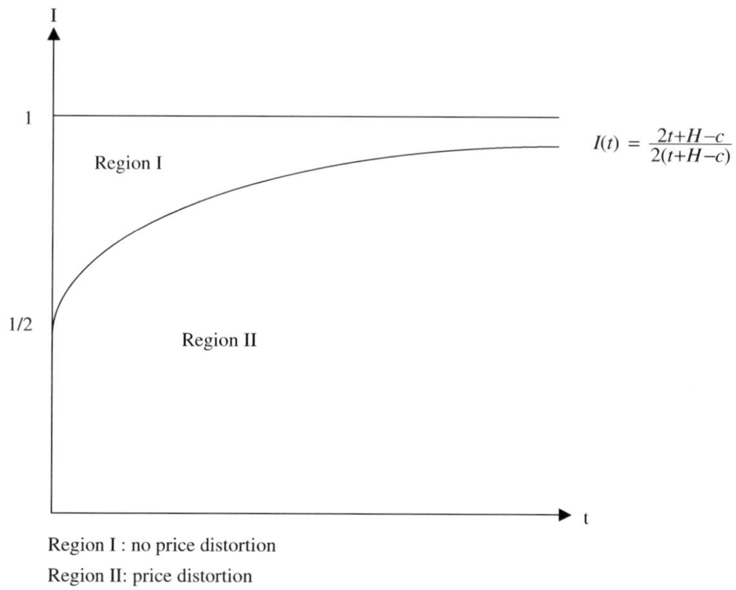

Figure 3. Parameter Values for Price Distortion

true quality from observing the monopoly price. Nevertheless, they pay a signaling cost through the price distortion when purchasing the high-quality product.

Proposition 1. *Separation is achieved provided that $I > 0$. All the revealing prices are defeated by the following pair of least-costly revealing prices:*

- $p_L^I = \frac{2c+t}{2}$ *for the low-quality product*
- *and* $p_H^I = \begin{cases} \frac{H+c+t}{2} & \text{if } I \geq \mathtt{I}(t), \\ \bar{p}_L^I & \text{otherwise}, \end{cases}$ *for the high-quality product.*

The presence of informed buyers enables prices to signal quality because it lowers the cost of pricing when quality is higher. There is a conflict between two effects, due to the presence of informed buyers. First, the mimicking profit, hence the temptation to mimic for the low-quality monopolist, decreases with I. Second, the opportunity cost to reveal high quality increases with I. However, the former effect dominates the latter for prices inside $L \cap H$: for these prices, the low-quality monopolist does not find it profitable to imitate the price set by the high-quality monopolist. There are now buyers who can ascertain the product quality on the market and, hence, are not fooled. It follows that increasing price has become more damaging to the low-quality monopolist. The price can now function as an effective signal of quality.

There exists a range of prices, namely $\mathtt{L} \cap \mathtt{H}$, at which the high-quality monopolist can profitably distinguish himself. However, from requirement (5), the price entailing the least costly signal defeats all the other revealing prices. Some calculations given in Appendix C show that there are two cases to consider, depending on the value of I. First, if the fraction of informed buyers is higher than the threshold $I(t)$, then the full information price for the high-quality product, that is, $\frac{H+c+t}{2}$, is inside $\mathtt{L} \cap \mathtt{H}$, and so will be chosen by the monopolist to signal high quality. When the market is sufficiently well informed, signaling the true quality is possible at no cost. Second, if I is lower than $I(t)$, signaling the true quality is still possible, albeit at a positive cost for the high quality. In this case, the full information price $\frac{H+c+t}{2}$ does not belong to $\mathtt{L} \cap \mathtt{H}$, thus the high-quality monopolist must distort his price above the full information price to prevent the low-quality monopolist from mimicking. By charging $\bar{p}_L^I$, the high-quality monopolist minimizes the loss of buyers resulting from the upward distortion. The signaling cost incurred by the high-quality monopolist is then measured by the difference $\frac{(H-c+t)^2}{8t} - \pi_H(\bar{p}_L^I, 1)$, where $\frac{(H-c+t)^2}{8t}$ is the full information profit when the product is of high quality. One can easily check from Appendix C that $\bar{p}_L^I$ decreases with I. The signaling cost declines as the fraction of informed buyers increases, until this fraction reaches the threshold $I(t)$ above which the signaling cost vanishes and so, too, the lemons problem.

What is the impact of the monopoly power on the signaling activity? From Appendix C, $\bar{p}_L^I - \frac{H+c+t}{2}$ increases with t, meaning that the more market power that the monopolist has, the higher the price distortion to signal high quality. It follows from the single-crossing condition stated in (7) that the low-quality monopolist finds mimicry unattractive whatever his market power. As market power drops, it becomes increasingly costly for the low-quality monopolist to duplicate the high-quality price since demand is more elastic: the more competitive the market, the more damaging the loss of buyers who refuse to buy at a higher price.

The emergence of separating prices due to the presence of informed buyers does not dismiss uninformative prices. Recall that $\mu_0 \in (0, 2)$ is the initial probability assigned by buyers to the high quality. Let p^I denote an uninformative price. Since it is the same price charged by the monopolist, regardless of quality, the buyers' posterior beliefs after observing this price are the same as their prior beliefs. The monopolist earns $\pi_q(p^I, (\mu_0))$ with the uninformative price p^I, if such a price does exist. To exist, it suffices that

p^I satisfies the two following conditions:

$$\pi_q(p^I, \mu_0) \geq \frac{(\phi_q(0) - c + t)^2}{8t}, \qquad q = H, L. \tag{10}$$

Any price yielding a profit in both states of nature, no lower than the right-hand side of (10) — that is, what the monopolist could get at best if he were thought to be of low quality with certainty — is a candidate for concealing information. Note that letting the low-quality monopolist mimic is costly for the high-quality monopolist: the loss in profit with respect to the full information situation is given by $\frac{(H-c+t)^2}{8t} - \pi_H(p^I, \mu_0)$. Moreover, requirement (5) imposes the further restriction on p^I:

$$\pi_H(p_H^I, 1) \leq \pi_H(p^I, \mu_0). \tag{11}$$

If inequality (11) holds, then the high-quality monopolist is better off with the uninformative price p^I than with the separating price p_H^I. Since the low-quality monopolist will also find it more profitable to imitate p^I than to reveal information, requirement (11) guarantees that the uninformative equilibrium defeats the least-costly separating equilibrium in the sense of Mailath, Okuno-Fujiwara, and Postlewaite. In such a case, it is more plausible that quality will not be revealed in equilibrium. Clearly, if the market is sufficiently well informed so that $I > I(t)$, then (11) is not met since $\pi_H(P_H^I, 1) = \frac{(H-c+t)^2}{8t}$, which is the full information profit level. But when $I < I(t)$, the returns from signaling high quality with $p_H^I = \bar{p}_L^I$ are lower than $\frac{(H-c+t)^2}{8t}$. Thus, (11) will hold for sufficiently high values of μ_0. More accurately, let $\bar{\mu}$ define the unique probability μ such that,

$$\pi_H(\bar{p}_L^I, 1) = \frac{(\phi_H(\mu) - c + t)^2}{8t}. \tag{12}$$

The right-hand side of (12) is the maximum profit that the high-quality monopolist can make by holding back information, when buyers believe the product to be of high quality with probability μ. The critical value $\bar{\mu}$ is the level of beliefs such that the high-quality monopolist is indifferent between signaling quality at some cost and concealing information about quality. If μ_0 is strictly lower than $\bar{\mu}$, then inequality (11) is violated regardless of the uninformative price p^I considered. Consequently, it is more plausible that information will be revealed in equilibrium. The result is reversed for values of μ_0 higher than $\bar{\mu}$. Then, the monopolist will prefer to conceal his private information about the quality of the product. In Figure 4, $\bar{\mu}$ is depicted as a

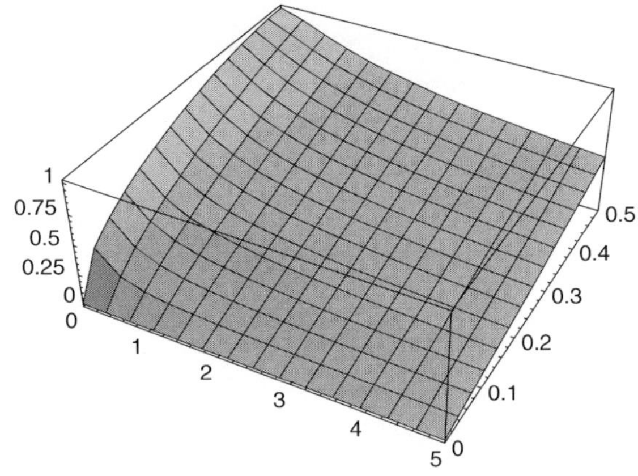

Figure 4. The Critical Value for Buyers' Beliefs

function of t and I, for $t \in [0,5], I \in [0,1/2]$, and $H - c = I$.[8] It shows that, given I, $\bar{\mu}$ declines for higher values of t. Thus, it is more likely that the monopolist conceals his private information as his market power increases.

Proposition 2. *The presence of informed buyers is necessary for price to be an effective signal of quality, but not always sufficient in the following sense:*

1. *If $I \geq I(t)$, then separation is achieved at no signaling cost with the full information prices $p_L^I = \frac{2c+t}{2}$ and $p_H^I = \frac{H+c+t}{2}$.*
2. *If $I < I(t)$, then*
   a. *separation is achieved at a signaling cost with the pair of UE prices $p_L^I = \frac{2c+t}{2}$ and $p_H^I = \bar{p}_L^I$, provided that $\mu_0 \leq \bar{\mu}$;*
   b. *separation fails and a continuum of uninformative UE prices prevails for all $\mu_0 \leq \bar{\mu}$.*

Proposition 2 summarizes all the results in the model with informed buyers. If the market is well informed, the presence of informed buyers eliminates the lemons problem by increasing the cost of pricing for a lower-quality monopolist so much that mimicking becomes unprofitable (case 1). If the market is poorly informed (case 2), the presence of informed buyers mitigates

[8]Equation (12) has a unique positive root which has the following expression for: $H - c = 1$: $\bar{\mu} = [2(I-1)(I+t) + \sqrt{4(I+t)^2(1-I)^2 - 4I(1-I)^2(3I-2) - 2\sqrt{(1-I)(1-I+2t)}}]/2(1-I)^2$.

the lemons problem, provided that buyers' prior beliefs of high quality are sufficiently pessimistic (case 2(a)); due, for instance, to bad weather or a bad reputation. In this case, the monopolist must incur a signaling cost to reveal high quality by distorting his price above the full information price. However, optimistic prior belief of high quality when the market is poorly informed (case 2(b)) causes separation to fail because signaling the true quality is more costly than accepting mimicry for the high-quality monopolist.

4. Conclusions

This chapter investigates to what extent the presence of informed buyers permits price to credibly signal quality in markets that are susceptible to a lemons problem. As a general result, informed buyers are necessary but not always sufficient for a monopolist to use prices as signals of product quality, regardless of the monopoly power. The essential effect of the presence of informed buyers is to reduce the benefit accruing to a low-quality monopolist from mimicking his high-quality counterpart. This in turn increases the incentive for signaling high quality through price.

If the market is poorly informed, then the monopolist's price will signal the actual quality provided that buyers a priori hold pessimistic beliefs about high quality. Such beliefs may be due either to unfavorable weather reports or to bad quality performances in the past that have spoilt the monopolist's reputation. Nevertheless, the price is not restored as a signal of quality without entailing some cost. To signal high quality, the price must be distorted above the full information level: the monopolist sacrifices buyers to prove that quality is high. The signaling cost increases with monopoly power. It becomes a too high burden when numerous buyers are uninformed and a priori hold optimistic beliefs on high quality. In such a case, the high-quality monopolist is better off choosing uninformative prices, hence the lemons problem is not overcome.

These results shed light on the lemons problem identified in Figures 1 and 2. There is evidence that the "primeur" price has never been an effective signal of quality since 1982 for the châteaux under consideration. The most general explanation can be found in Spence (1976): "For a signal to be effective, it must be unprofitable for sellers of low-quality products to imitate it." Obviously, the cost of using the "primeur" price as a signal of quality is the same for the four *Médoc* châteaux endowed with different qualities. The main insight that this chapter adds is that the market is poorly informed and buyers, a priori, hold optimistic beliefs about the quality offered by the four châteaux. The high reputation of the four châteaux may explain why uninformed buyers unrealistically believe quality to be high before purchase. That the market is poorly informed means that either few buyers rely on expert opinion or few buyers develop sufficient skills to estimate the true quality. This is consistent with two empirical studies on the Bordeaux wine industry: Landon and Smith find no evidence that buyers use expert predictions when purchasing Bordeaux wine and Ashenfelter and Jones (1998) argue that expert opinion neglects some information that is useful in making predictions, such as weather data.

The explanation above as to why some châteaux are better off charging uninformative "primeur" prices does not exhaust the subject. Further research is necessary to determine whether the practice of concealing information obeys insurance motives or serves as a coordinating device in a situation of repeated competition. Moreover, it may be instructive to extend the present analysis by considering that the Bordeaux "primeur" release has the features of forward trading. A model along this line can be found in Mahenc and Meunier (2003). This work exhibits forward pooling equilibria which can be here interpreted as follows: low-quality producers earn positive speculative profits by selling forward at "primeur" prices that are both uninformative and upward-distorted, while high-quality producers need uninformative "primeur" prices to reduce the cost of signaling quality on the market of bottled-wine.

References

Akerlof, G.A. (1970). The market for "lemons": Qualitative uncertainty and the market mechanism. *Quarterly Journal of Economics*, 84, 488–500.

Ashenfelter, O., and Jones, G. (1998). The demand for expert opinion: Bordeaux wine. Paper presented at 6th annual meeting of the Vineyard Data Quantification Society.

Bagwell, K., and Riordan, M.H. (1991). High and declining prices signal product quality. *American Economic Review*, 81, 224–239.

Cason, T.N., and Gangadharan, L. (2002). Environmental labelling and incomplete consumer information in laboratory experiments. *Journal of Environmental Economics and Management*, 43, 113–134.

Cho, I.-K., and Kreps, D. (1987). Signaling games and stable equilibria. *Quarterly Journal of Economics*, 102, 179–221.

Di Vittorio, A., and Ginsburgh, V. (1996). Des Enchéres comme révélateurs du classement des vins. *Journal de la Société Statistique de Paris*, 137, 19–49.

Karl, H., and Orwat, C. (1999). *Economic Aspects of Environmental Labelling.* In Yearbook of Environmental and Resource Economics 1999/2000. Cheltenham, UK: Elgar pp. 107–170.

Landon, S., and Smith, C.E. (1997). The use of quality and reputation indicators by consumers: The case of Bordeaux wine. *Journal of Consumer Policy*, 20, 289–323.

Mahenc, P., and Meunier, V. (2003). Forward markets and signals of quality. *RAND Journal of Economics*, 34, 478–494.
Mailath, G., Okuno-Fujiwara, M., and Postle-Waite, A. (1993). Belief-based refinements in signaling games. *Journal of Economic Theory*, 60, 241–276.
Milgrom, P., and Roberts, J. (1986). Price and advertising signals of product quality. *Journal of Political Economy*, 94, 796–821.
Nelson, P. (1974). Advertising as information. *Journal of Political Economy*, 82, 729–754.
Spence, A.M. (1973). Job market signaling. *Quarterly Journal of Economics*, 85, 355–379.
Spence, A.M. (1976). Informational aspects of market structure: An introduction. *Quarterly Journal of Economics*, 90, 591–597.

Appendix A

The Set L

Requirement (8) can be rewritten

$$(p_H^I - c)(\phi_L(1) + t - p_H^I)/2t - t/8 \leq 0$$

which holds only for prices p_H^I in the set

$$L \equiv \left[c, \left(\phi_L(1) + c + t - \sqrt{(\phi_L(1) + c + t)^2 - 4c(\phi_L(1) + t) - t^2}\right)\Big/\, 2\right]$$
$$\cup \left[\left(\phi_L(1) + c + t + \sqrt{(\phi_L(1) + c + t)^2 - 4c(\phi_L(1) + t) - t^2}\right)\Big/\, 2, H + t\right]$$

where

$$\bar{p}_L^I \equiv \left(\phi_L(1) + c + t + \sqrt{(\phi_L(1) + c + t)^2 - 4c(\phi_L(1) + t) - t^2}\right)\Big/\, 2$$
$$= \left(H - I(H - c) + c + t + \sqrt{(H - c)(1 - I)((H - c)(1 - I) + 2t)}\right)\Big/\, 2.$$

Appendix B

The Set H

Condition (9) can be rewritten

$$(p_H^I - c)(H + t - p_H^I)/2t - (\phi_H(0) - c + t)^2/8t > 0.$$

This inequality is met for prices p_H^I in the interval

$$H \equiv \left(\left(H + c + t - \sqrt{(H + c + t)^2 - (\phi_H(0) - c + t)^2 - 4c(H + t)}\right)\Big/\, 2,\right.$$
$$\left.\left(H + c + t + \sqrt{(H + c + t)^2 - (\phi_H(0) - c + t)^2 - 4c(H + t)}\right)\Big/\, 2\right)$$

$$= \left(\left(H + c + t - \sqrt{(H-c)(1-I)((H-c)(1+I)+2t)}\right) / 2,\right.$$
$$\left.\left(H + c + t + \sqrt{(H-c)(1-I)((H-c)(1+I)+2t)}\right) / 2\right).$$

It follows that, for all $I > 0$,

$$\bar{p}_L^I = \left(H - I(H-c) + c + t + \sqrt{(H-c)(1-I)((H-c)(1+I)+2t)}\right) / 2$$
$$< \left(H + c + t + \sqrt{(H-c)(1-I)((H-c)(1+I)+2t)}\right) / 2$$

Thus, for all $I > 0$, the set $L \cap H$ is nonempty.

Appendix C

The Price Distortion for High Quality

The price distortion to reveal high quality can be expressed as follows

$$\bar{p}_L^I - \frac{H+c+t}{2} = \left(-I(H-c) + \sqrt{(H-c)(1-I)((H-c)(1-I)+2t)}\right) / 2$$

It can be seen that this distortion decreases with I and increases with t. Moreover, straightforward calculations give that $\bar{p}_L^I - \frac{H+c+t}{2} \leq 0$ for all $I \geq I(t)$.

Chapter 17

A Study of Women in Top Business Roles: The Case of the Wine Industry*

Jeremy Galbreath

Curtin Graduate School of Business,
Curtin University of Technology,
Perth, Australia
jeremy.galbreath@gsb.curtin.edu.au

Purpose — The purpose of this chapter is to empirically explore the extent to which women are advancing in the wine industry, and whether there are conditions which help facilitate their advancement. There is a perception that women are making great strides in the wine industry. However, this perception is largely anecdotal.

Design/methodology/approach — All wineries in Australia are examined in each year for the years 2007 to 2013. By relying on a leading wine industry database, women in CEO, winemaker, viticulturist and marketing roles are examined.

Findings — With the exception of the marketing role, women are under-represented relative to predicted representation rates. Regarding regional differences, there is no consistent pattern with respect to where women representation in the roles is higher. The findings also suggest that where there is a woman CEO, women are more likely to be represented in winemaker, viticulturist and marketing roles.

Research limitations/implications — The study represents Australian wine regions and should not be taken as a general population sample. The representation rates of women in top roles in other wine firms around the world may vary, which could lead to results different than those found in this study.

Practical implications — For firms and policy makers interested in increasing the representation rates of women in the wine industry, the results of this study offer some insight into where current rates stand, and what might be underlying these representation rates. This is expected to facilitate debate around the means

*This article originally appeared in *International Journal of Wine Research* (2015), 27(2), 143–158.

and mechanisms through which to increase the representation of women in the wine industry.

Originality/value — This is the first known large-scale study to examine the representation rates of women in top roles in the wine industry; therefore, it offers both new insights and avenues for future research.

1. Introduction

Statistics across the world suggest that, in the absence of gender quotas, women appear to struggle to reach top roles in business firms (Catalyst, 2014; HRReview, 2013; Marcus Evans, 2013; WGEA, 2012). However, in some cases, the public is lead to believe that women's representation in top roles in business is significantly increasing. For example, in the wine industry, reports highlight that women now make up a significant part of the industry (Cooper, 2009, as cited in Bryant and Garnham, 2014). Industry prizes and leading roles (e.g., winemaker) in prestigious wineries give women high profiles through media discourse and exposure (Fuller, 2008, as cited in Bryant and Garnham, 2014). Further, evidence suggests that in some universities, enrolment of women in viticulture and oenology programs equals that of men (Ting, 2013). One report goes as far as to say that women in top roles in the wine industry, such as winemaking, now constitute at least a 15% representation rate (Kauffman, 2009), well above rates in top roles in other industries (Catalyst, 2014; HRReview, 2013; Marcus Evans, 2013; WGEA, 2012). This has led some to suggest that the wine industry, given its history of male dominance, has undergone significant cultural and structural change when it comes to gender representation in top roles (Matasar, 2006).

The progression of women to top roles in the wine industry should be seen as a welcome development. Women are known for their creativity, are strong in the areas of idea generation and innovation, are noted for having high moral and ethical standards, are environmentally sensitive and demonstrate transformational leadership styles (Galbreath, 2016), all of which should be a positive for the competitiveness and social responsibility of the wine industry. Yet, there is no empirical support to prove or disprove the rate at which women are advancing to top roles in the wine industry. Further, where a certain level of achievement of women in top roles is perceived, this can create a halo effect of positivity, where a deeper understanding of what helps (or hinders) women's advancement is either ignored or becomes irrelevant. Some scholars, however, are looking closer at the predictors of women in top roles.

In a study of women on boards of directors in 950 of the largest public firms in the USA, Hillman *et al.* (2007) find that firm size, industry type, firm diversification strategy and network effects (i.e., a firm's number of links to other firms with women on their boards) predict women representation on corporate boards. In their study of 85 large, publicly traded French firms, Nekhili and Gatfaoui (2013) find that family ownership, board size, firm size and demographic attributes (e.g., education level, business expertise such as network links) are linked to the appointment of women to boards of directors. These studies are important in that they highlight the fact that the assumption that the representation of women in top roles, such as boards of directors, is determined exogenously, may need to be challenged.

While having improved our understanding of women in top roles, the contributions of prior research are limited in three ways. First, little empirical research has examined the role of women in the wine industry. However, there is evidence to suggest that a false notion of women's advancement to top roles is being created (Bryant and Garnham, 2014), leading to a lack of understanding of the characteristics that impede or support progress. Second, previous research on gender in the wine industry predominately focuses on women as wine drinking consumers (Barber, 2010; Barber *et al.*, 2006; Forbes, 2012), leaving little understanding of the role they play in the industry from a commercial perspective. Third, given the paucity of research, as noted by Hillman *et al.* (2007) and Nekhili and Gatfaoui (2013), there still remains the need to study predictors of women to top roles to advance knowledge.

Given that women in business is seen as a critical imperative (Curtis *et al.*, 2012; Krishnan and Park, 2005; McCabe *et al.*, 2006), to address current research gaps, this chapter makes three contributions to the literature. First, the study seeks to challenge the current estimated rate of the representation of women in top roles in the wine industry, while examining factors that predict women representation rates in these roles. This may help to dispel an overinflated perception that can mask the reality of actual representation rates and the barriers that need to be overcome to achieve more balanced gender equality. Second, by relying on a unique database, this study tracks gender in the wine industry in Australia across CEO, winemaking, viticulture and marketing roles, in each year for the years 2007–2013. This advances the literature by studying the role of women beyond consumers of wine, to what ways they contribute to the business of wine production. Lastly, the study has practical implications. In Australia, the percentage of full-time women employed across all agriculture industries (including wine production) is estimated at around 14% (WGEA, 2012). This chapter provides some insights that could inform future gender diversity policy.

2. Background and Some Current Statistics

2.1. *Women and top roles in business*

Though gender diversity in business organizations has become prominent in both academia and the popular press, the issues of equality and discrimination are driving most discussions about the increase of women in top leadership roles. Such issues frame gender diversity as an ethical imperative (Kelan, 2008; McCabe *et al.*, 2006). On the other hand, women are thought to bring specialist skills and expertise that increase the effectiveness and efficiency of firms (Kallenberg and Keicht, 1991; Torchia *et al.*, 2011). These couch gender diversity as a resource imperative (Burke, 1997; Galbreath, 2011). In both cases, management research examining gender diversity appears to coalesce around one common theme: gender diversity in upper echelon positions.

Although it is increasingly widespread, the study of gender diversity in upper echelon positions is somewhat recent. Such research has gravitated toward studying women on boards of directors of large, publicly traded firms (Adams and Funk, 2012). This is because corporate governance is seen as critical to these firms' decision making, particularly strategic, operational and financial decisions, as well as to the setting of policy objectives (Nekhili and Gatfaoui, 2013). One of the larger debates to surface is the issue of quotas. For example, in 2003, Norway was one of the first countries to impose a gender quota for boards of directors, set at 40%. More recently, in 2011, the French parliament imposed a gender quota for corporate boards, which stipulates that, by 2016, women must represent 40% of a firm's board members (for firms with more than 500 employees and annual turnover exceeding 50 million Euros). Similarly, Sweden and Spain have imposed quotas of 25 and 40% gender representation on boards, respectively. Outside of Europe, government imposed gender quotas are rare, which may be resulting in lower representation rates. For example, the proportion of women on boards in Australia is 15.6%; in China, it is 7.2%; in Hong Kong, it is 8.9%; in Japan, it is (0.4%); and in the USA, it is 16.1%.

Apart from board roles, less research examines gender diversity in other top roles. One exception is the study of women CEOs (Cook and Glass, 2014). In Australia, for example, a recent study on women in leadership identified that, in 2012, women CEOs in the ASX500 accounted for approximately 3% (WGEA, 2012). Similarly, in the UK, women CEOs in the FTSE350 stood at 3% in 2013 (HRReview, 2013). In the USA, the percentage of women CEOs in the Fortune 500 was 4.4% in 2013 (Catalyst, 2014), slightly higher than in Australia and the UK. In Germany, in 2013, firms in the major DAX 30 index did not boast a single woman CEO (Marcus Evans, 2013). Generally, the statistics suggest that while, over time, the percentage of women on boards and in other leadership roles such as CEO has increased in most countries under study, it is clear that women remain largely under-represented, particularly in countries without gender quotas.

2.2. *Women and the wine industry*

Historically, the production of wine has been concentrated in Europe, a trend which continues. Europe still represents around 60% of the global surface area used for wine grape growing and production (OIV, 2014). Notwithstanding this, New World producers, including Argentina, Australia, Chile, South Africa and the USA, have made significant inroads in recent decades in terms of both quantity and quality of wine production. For example, Argentina, Australia, Chile, South Africa, the USA and, recently, China, now all rank as top 10 global wine producers. Surprisingly, despite its age as a product, its cultural significance and its reputational impact, little research has examined women in the wine industry (Ting, 2013). The few studies that do exist reveal some important insights.

In one study, Gilbert (2011) examines 3,200 wineries based in California to determine the gender of winemakers. The study classifies the wineries into eight wine regions: Mendocino/Lake County, Napa Valley, Sonoma/Marin, Sierra Foothills, Central Valley, North Central Coast, South Central Coast and Southern California. The findings suggest that 9.8% of Californian wineries have women winemakers, a higher percentage of these being found in the state's premier wine sub-regions, namely, Sonoma/Marin and Napa, which have 12.4 and 12.2% of women winemakers, respectively. In a follow-up study, Gilbert and Gilbert (2012) compare the quality of wine produced from the earlier sample of Gilbert (2011) by comparing men versus women winemakers listed in *Opus Vino*, a global ratings guide that identifies the highest quality wines. Their study of 450 wineries, using a matched-pair analysis (men versus women winemakers), finds that women winemakers are more likely than men winemakers to be listed in the *Opus Vino* quality wine guide.

In their study, Bryant and Garnham (2014) seek to challenge a perception that women in the traditionally patriarchal wine industry are no longer subject to structural constraints based on gender. Interviewing 16 women working in one of the largest wine producers in Australia, they find that within the corporation, a male-dominated hierarchy exists, particularly in upper-level positions. The interviewees expressed views that within the organization, the ideal worker is conceived of as "masculine." This includes, for example, the need to work long hours, to demonstrate commitment to the organization ahead of social or family responsibilities, to adhere to cultural norms such as golf days and watching football and to have the physical strength required for heavy lifting and using machinery. Ultimately, this led the researchers to conclude that (p. 9):

> [...] the majority of roles [within the corporation] are occupied by men, work roles are shaped by assumptions about gender that position men higher in the organizational hierarchy, masculine benchmarks for skills and experience to achieve promotion into higher levels requires women to "match" their careers to those of men to be competitive, and masculine culture, norms and value practices are embedded in the everyday practices and processes of the organization. Within this organization, the ideal labouring body is therefore constituted "male," where work and worker identity are shaped by masculine norms.

3. Research Questions

3.1. *Overall representation of women in top roles in the wine industry in Australia*

On any given day around 30 million glasses of Australian wine are enjoyed worldwide (Ting, 2013). This reflects an approximately $8 billion contribution to the Australian economy and an industry that has made significant strides as a global competitor over the past 20–30 years, including becoming the world's fifth largest wine exporter (Connell, 2012). The industry also has had a valuable impact on regional and rural employment in Australia (directly and indirectly employing 120,000 people), while contributing positively to the reputation of the country around the world (IBISWorld, 2013; Kansil and Roberts, 2013). However, the Australian wine industry has struggled recently. For example, evidence suggests revenue growth is actually in *decline* relative to its major global competitors (IBISWorld, 2013), with a conservative estimate that as much as 70% of current production is uneconomic (Kansil and Roberts, 2013). Given the human capital that women possess, some have called for their increased participation in the Australian wine industry as a means to improve competitiveness (Galbreath, 2014b). Anecdotal evidence suggests that this may be happening. In Australia:

> [...] according to media representation (Allen, 2000; Cooper, 2009; Fuller, 2008) the [...] wine industry has undergone a *gender sea change* such that the once male-dominated industry 'now *abounds* with successful women' (Cooper, 2009). The names and profiles of women winemakers occupying senior positions at leading and prestigious wineries or their own enterprises and winning industry prizes illustrate stellar heights of career success that suggest 'women and wine are a perfect blend' (Fuller, 2008) (italics added) (Bryant and Garnham, 2014, p. 1).

However, there is reason to question the perception that a sea change has occurred for women in the wine industry in Australia.

Current estimates suggest that women representation rates in top roles in the wine industry are 15% (Heimoff, 2007; Kauffman, 2009), which would put them at a higher rate of representation in such roles than many (if not most) industries. To what extent this represents a "sea change" is unclear, and in fact, perceptions that women are well-represented in a traditionally male-dominated field can serve as a barrier to their increased participation (Morrison *et al.*, 1994; Rossi, 1985; Schmitt *et al.*, 2009). For example, the high visibility of women in the wine industry such as Vanya Cullen and Severine Logan in Western Australia, and Kerri Thompson and Pam Dunsford in South Australia, can create a perception of a high level of presence of women in a field dominated by males. More specifically, high visibility or celebrity status of a few acclaimed women in a field can actually create perceptions that can lower the perceived need to encourage women to enter the field, resulting in lower representation rates (Morrison *et al.*, 1994; Rossi, 1985; Schmitt *et al.*, 2009). That is, as perceptions are formulated that inequality does not exist as a result, for example, of tokenism, women can be less motivated to challenge perceived gender equality, which can result in their unwillingness to take up roles that are, in fact, dominated by men (Schmitt *et al.*, 2002; Wright, 1997). Thus:

RQ1. Are there significantly fewer women in top roles in the wine industry in Australia than is estimated?

3.2. *Location as a predictor of representation of women in top roles in the wine industry in Australia*

Following Unger (2006), as women strive to take on roles that have been historically unavailable to them, they seek to achieve "exceptional" status. There are two key ways that women might seek to achieve such status. First, they could seek to be a part of a group because of the status or recognition it provides. By becoming part of certain groups, members believe that their social status is automatically looked upon as special and peculiar, endowing them with a level of prestige (Unger, 2006). Second, they could seek to achieve exceptional status by aligning themselves with groups that align to their personal goals. Here, because the group's goals are seen as cutting-edge or advanced, gaining entrance into the group could afford them the opportunity to achieve their personal goals of excellence (Unger, 2006). In the case of women in the wine industry in Australia, this group identification phenomenon is potentially tied to location or region as a specific form of social identification.

In Australia, South Australia is arguably the most acclaimed wine-producing region and is recognized around the world for many of its leading brands. South Australia is the largest producer (nearly 50% of total wine production) and arguably has the country's most iconic and reputable sub-regions (e.g., Barossa Valley). South Australia is also Australia's hub for wine research and innovation, and produces some of the most respected — and expensive — wines in the world (Aylward, 2007). Further, the region boasts the country's highest implementation levels of environmental practices (Galbreath, 2014c), creating a reputation for being the Australian wine industry's leading steward of natural resources. In free and open labor markets, as women strive for top roles that can afford the highest visibility and accolades, the expectation is that they would seek to gain employment in a region that could more readily help them achieve their goals or to gain recognition. In this way, they seek to penetrate the regional group that is the most prestigious. This is supported by Gilbert's (2011) findings, where the most famous wine sub-regions in California boast the highest rate of women winemakers. Hence:

RQ2. Are there more women in top roles in the wine industry in South Australia than in other wine-producing regions in Australia?

3.3. *The influence of women in the CEO role on other representation rates*

As women attempt to enter the wine industry, they are likely to seek out positions in firms that have a woman leader, particularly in the top role (i.e., CEO). This is because feelings of anxiety can be reduced (Riek *et al.*, 2006), self-esteem can be increased (Morton *et al.*, 2009) and a sense of belonging and self-enhancement achieved (Hogg, 2006). Alternatively, top-level decision-makers, such as CEOs, can reserve attractive or prestigious positions (e.g., the winemaker position) for members of the same sex (Powell and Butterfield, 2002; Tajfel and Turner, 1979). This may be a due to loyalty shared between individuals of the same sex, as they are seen as more essential to the firm, or because of the comfort level with individuals of the same sex. Cook and Glass (2014) and Elsaid and Ursel (2011), for example, find that when there is greater gender diversity on boards of directors, there is a greater likelihood that a woman will be appointed to the CEO role of the firm. Considering these findings:

RQ3. Where a wine firm has a woman CEO, is there a greater likelihood that there will be women in the winemaker, viticulturist or marketer roles?

4. Data and Methods

4.1. *Sample*

Due to the nature of work and the possibility of employee turnover, this study did not rely on a single snapshot in time. More specifically, data were collected from the annual Winetitles *Australia and New Zealand Wine Industry Directory* database (Winetitles, 2013), in each year for the years 2007–2013. Updated on a yearly basis, the Winetitles directory is the most comprehensive guide to wine producers in Australia, where a wide variety of detailed data is collected annually, including variables of interest such as regional location and names of key personnel (e.g., CEO, winemaker). All data were coded appropriately (see below under Variables section) and entered into SPSS for analysis.

In terms of sample size, in 2007, there were 2,145 total wineries in Australia; in 2008, there were 2,298 total wineries; in 2009, there were 2,319 total wineries; in 2010, there were 2,419 total wineries; in 2011, there were 2,476 total wineries; in 2012, there were 2,532 total wineries; and in 2013, there were 2,574 total wineries. For women in the roles of interest, averages were taken across the seven years for statistical analysis.

4.2. *Variables*

To capture the roles of interest, a series of dichotomous variables were calculated. CEOs are critical because these are the top decision-makers of the firm and have substantial control and authority over strategy and resource allocation. Winemakers can be considered the "rock stars" of the industry in the sense that they produce the product, generally receive the most press coverage and attention from wine critics and can gain global reputations for their vintages. Viticulturists work in the vineyard to ensure that a quality grape is produced, without which a vintage can be sub-par or abandoned altogether, and thus play a vital role in wine production. Marketers are critical because they market and sell wine, generating the revenue stream that sustains the business. Thus, to capture gender diversity, for each CEO, winemaker, viticulturist and marketer, women in these roles were coded 1, 0 otherwise (but only where the women in these roles differed to avoid double counting). Where names occurred that could be those of men or women (e.g., Chris, Jamie and Sam) or where gender was not obvious, images of the person were sought on company Web sites, and/or firms were called for confirmation. As for reliability of the data, a random sample of the names of 100 winemakers from each year was compared to the listed winemaker in the James Halliday *Australian Wine Companion* guidebooks (Halliday, 2013). The *Wine Companion* guidebooks offer quality ratings and prices for thousands of wines. Where matches were found between both sources for the name of the winemaker,[1] inter-rater agreement across all years revealed kappa's <0.93, demonstrating more than satisfactory agreement and reliability of the data.

To make regional comparisons across the roles, each wine-producing region was given its own unique identifier. The regions were New South Wales, Queensland, South Australia, Tasmania, Victoria, and Western Australia. Together, these regions represent 99.8% of total Australian wine production.

Control variables include firm age, firm size and export orientation, as inertia and other factors can impact the level of representation of women in top roles (Bryant and Garnham, 2014; Hillman *et al.*, 2007). For firm age, categorical variables were established as follows: 1 = 10 years old or less, 2 = 11 to 20 years old, 3 = 21 to 30 years old, 4 = 31 to 40 years old, 5 = 41 to 50 years old and 6 = 51 years old or more. For size, number of cases produced was used, where 1 = 1 to 2,499 cases, 2 = 2,500 to 19,999 cases, 3 = 20,000 to 99,999 cases, 4 = 100,000 to 1,499,999 cases and 5 = over 1,500,000 cases. For export orientation, firms where coded on the basis of their percentage of export sales, where 1 = do not export, 2 = 1 to 25%, 3 = 26 to 50%, 4 = 51 to 75% and 5 = 76 to 100%. Data for these variables were collected from company Web sites and the Winetitles databases.

[1]The Halliday guidebook only lists the names of the winemakers and does not cover all wineries listed in the Winetitles database.

5. Results

Means and correlations are presented in Table 1 and descriptive statistics in Figure 1 and Table 2. The descriptive statistics suggest a few interesting patterns. First, although the wine industry in Australia has demonstrated growth in the number of firms (albeit modest growth at 2.86%), women in the leadership roles studied have not kept pace with this growth: women CEOs were the closest at a 2.24% growth rate for the 2007–2013 period.[2] Second, the representation of women in marketing roles, across all regions, is clearly at the highest level. The 2007–2013 average across all firms and all regions for a woman in the marketing role is 53.5% (with a growth rate

Table 1. Means and Correlations

Variable	Mean	SD	1	2	3	4	5	6	7
1. Gender CEO	0.13	0.33	1.00						
2. Gender winemaker	0.09	0.28	0.18**	1.00					
3. Gender viticulturist	0.10	0.30	0.22**	0.12**	1.00				
4. Gender marketer	0.54	0.49	0.11**	0.01	−0.01	1.00			
5. Firm age	2.30	1.26	−0.04**	0.01	−0.06**	−0.02	1.00		
6. Firm size	1.63	0.78	−0.10**	0.00	−0.13**	−0.16**	0.28**	1.00	
7. Export orientation	2.31	1.02	−0.07**	−0.03**	−0.08**	−0.07**	−0.02	0.42**	1.00

Note: $^{**}p < 0.01$.

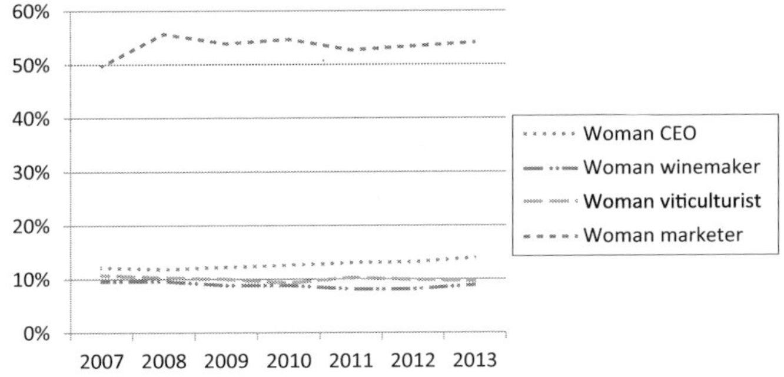

Figure 1. Percentage of Women by Role by Year (Overall Sample)

[2]Growth rates use the straight-line method, where: (present value — past value)/past value ×100. The resulting factor is divided by n (in this case, 7).

Table 2. Descriptive Statistics

	2007	2008	2009	2010	2011	2012	2013	Averages	Growth rates[a] (%)
Percent women by role (Overall sample)									
Women CEOs	12.1	11.8	12.2	12.6	13.1	13.2	14.0	12.7	2.24
Women winemakers	9.6	9.6	8.8	8.8	8.1	8.1	8.9	8.8	−1.04
Women viticulturists	10.7	10.3	10.0	9.3	10.3	9.9	9.6	10.0	−1.47
Women marketers	49.8	55.7	53.9	54.7	52.7	53.4	54.1	53.5	1.23
Number of firms	2,145	2,298	2,319	2,419	2,476	2,532	2,574	2,395	2.86
Percent women by role (New South Wales)									
Women CEOs	13.4	12.9	12.6	13.9	13.2	14.3	16.1	13.8	2.88
Women winemakers	7.9	8.9	8.5	9.3	10.2	9.8	9.5	9.2	2.89
Women viticulturists	12.7	11.2	10.4	9.2	10.4	10.5	10.7	10.7	−2.25
Women marketers	43.4	60.7	53.3	60.4	59.1	61.2	58.3	56.6	4.90
Number of firms	432	452	443	467	474	474	487	461	1.82
Percent women by role (Queensland)									
Women CEOs	16.7	14.0	13.3	15.6	15.6	14.4	12.9	14.6	−3.25
Women winemakers	3.9	4.1	4.1	6.9	4.0	3.1	3.3	4.2	−2.20
Women viticulturists	6.1	6.0	10.8	10.2	12.2	10.4	8.6	9.2	5.85
Women marketers	25.0	53.8	60.0	57.7	53.8	52.2	56.5	51.3	18.00
Number of firms	109	107	106	111	111	106	102	107	−0.92
Percent women by role (South Australia)									
Women CEOs	10.3	10.7	10.9	10.9	12.4	12.3	13.2	11.5	4.02
Women winemakers	9.9	9.5	9.8	10.1	8.8	9.4	11.1	9.8	1.73
Women viticulturists	9.4	9.7	8.8	7.9	9.3	8.8	7.3	8.7	−3.19
Women marketers	48.0	48.7	49.6	49.4	48.2	49.4	50.0	49.0	0.59
Number of firms	564	607	619	648	667	697	705	644	3.57

(Continued)

Table 2. (*Continued*)

	2007	2008	2009	2010	2011	2012	2013	Averages	Growth rates[a] (%)
Percent women by role (Tasmania)									
Women CEOs	17.7	14.6	14.4	15.1	14.4	15.2	15.9	15.3	−1.45
Women winemakers	10.0	10.3	10.0	7.1	5.7	6.7	9.4	8.5	−0.86
Women viticulturists	12.1	10.8	10.7	11.4	7.8	10.3	6.7	10.0	−6.38
Women marketers	44.4	61.9	60.9	60.0	52.0	50.0	58.3	55.4	4.72
Number of firms	81	90	92	98	104	112	115	99	6.00
Percent women by role (Victoria)									
Women CEOs	11.6	11.3	12.6	13.0	13.2	12.6	13.5	12.5	2.34
Women winemakers	8.6	7.0	6.7	6.5	6.1	6.0	7.5	6.9	−1.83
Women viticulturists	12.3	13.0	12.4	12.7	13.7	12.8	12.9	12.8	0.70
Women marketers	55.4	56.5	55.6	53.6	51.0	51.8	54.1	54.0	−0.34
Number of firms	627	686	698	723	738	749	776	714	3.39
Percent women by role (Western Australia)									
Women CEOs	11.0	11.4	12.0	11.4	12.8	13.6	13.5	12.2	3.25
Women winemakers	15.1	17.1	12.9	11.4	10.0	9.8	8.6	12.1	−6.15
Women viticulturists	8.1	6.5	6.5	4.8	5.2	5.2	6.1	6.1	−3.53
Women marketers	60.0	61.7	58.5	58.5	56.5	55.6	55.7	58.1	−1.02
Number of firms	332	356	361	372	382	394	389	369	2.45

Note: [a]Calculated using straight-line growth rates.

of 1.23%). Third, women in the CEO role have the second highest representation at 12.7%. Fourth, in the prestigious winemaker role, only 8.8% are women across the reporting period. This is less than, although close to, the 9.8% of women winemakers in California (Gilbert, 2011). Lastly, overall, the percentages of women in the winemaker role have *declined* since 2007 (−1.04% growth). This is perhaps most evident in Western Australia, where there has been a 6.15% decline in the percentage of women winemakers. Conversely, New South Wales demonstrates the highest growth of women winemakers at 2.89%. These figures need to be considered with respect to

Table 3. Actual versus Predicted Percentage of Women by Role

Actual versus predicted percentage of women by role (2007–2013 average)					
	Actual (%)	Predicted (%)	χ^2	df	Significance
Women CEOs	12.7	15	65.20	1	0.000[a]
Women winemakers	8.8	15	429.92	1	0.000[a]
Women viticulturists	10.0	15	224.51	1	0.000[a]
Women marketers	53.5	15	5,379.98	1	0.000[a]

Note: [a]Statistically significant.

the fact that the rate of women entering Australia's oenology and viticulture programs is much *greater* in the past 10–20 years, suggesting the difficulty of translating a formal education into higher ranking roles in the wine industry.

Regarding the control variables, ANOVA tests reveal differences between firms. There are statistically significant differences with respect to firm age ($F = 3.196, p = 0.000$), with firms in South Australia being the oldest. There are also differences in firm size (as measured by case production), indicating that South Australian firms are the largest ($F = 14.659, p = 0.000$). Lastly, there are statistically significant differences in export orientation as well ($F = 23.857, p = 0.000$), with South Australian firms exporting more product than other states. These differences should be considered in light of the analyzes.

To explore the research questions, chi-square tests were used. As for *RQ1*, with the exception of women in the marketing role, the actual percentage of women in all other roles was significantly less than the 15% predicted rate (Table 3). Thus, there is some question as to the extent to which women representation rates in the Australian wine industry are as high as perceived. With respect to *RQ2*, South Australia is compared to other regions across all of the roles (Table 4). Relative to New South Sales, South Australia has a lower proportion of women CEOs ($\chi^2 = 7.93, p = 0.005$), lower percentages of women viticulturists ($\chi^2 = 5.63, p = 0.018$) and a lower representation of women marketers ($\chi^2 = 17.27, p = 0.000$). Compared to Queensland, South Australia has a lower representation of women CEOs ($\chi^2 = 5.62, p = 0.018$) and higher proportion of women winemakers ($\chi^2 = 22.25, p = 0.000$). With respect to Tasmania, South Australia has lower percentages of women CEOs ($\chi^2 = 7.36, p = 0.007$) and a marginally lower percentage of women marketers ($\chi^2 = 2.78, p = 0.096$). As for Victoria, South Australia has a higher proportion of women winemakers ($\chi^2 = 23.03, p = 0.000$), lower percentages of women viticulturists ($\chi^2 = 27.48, p = 0.000$) and

Table 4. South Australia versus Other Regions

Percentage of women by role (2007–2013 average)					
	South Australia (%)	New South Wales (%)	χ^2	df	Significance
Women CEOs	11.5	13.8	7.93	1	0.005[a]
Women winemakers	9.8	9.2	0.69	1	0.406
Women viticulturists	8.7	10.7	5.63	1	0.018[a]
Women marketers	49.0	58.0	17.27	1	0.000[a]
	South Australia (%)	Queensland (%)	χ^2	df	Significance
Women CEOs	11.5	14.6	5.62	1	0.018[a]
Women winemakers	9.8	4.2	22.25	1	0.000[a]
Women viticulturists	8.7	9.2	0.13	10.716	
Women marketers	49.0	51.3	0.84	1	0.360
	South Australia (%)	Tasmania (%)	χ^2	df	Significance
Women CEOs	11.5	15.3	7.36	1	0.007[a]
Women winemakers	9.8	8.5	1.17	1	0.280
Women viticulturists	8.7	10.0	0.80	1	0.371
Women marketers	49.0	55.4	2.78	1	0.096[a]
	South Australia (%)	Victoria (%)	χ^2	df	Significance
Women CEOs	11.5	12.5	2.03	1	0.154
Women winemakers	9.8	6.9	23.03	1	0.000[a]
Women viticulturists	8.7	12.8	27.48	1	0.000[a]
Women marketers	49.0	54.0	5.29	1	0.021[a]
	South Australia (%)	Western (%)	χ^2	df	Significance
Women CEOs	11.5	12.2	0.70	1	0.404
Women winemakers	9.8	12.1	7.53	1	0.006[a]
Women viticulturists	8.7	6.1	11.54	1	0.001[a]
Women marketers	49.0	58.1	15.31	1	0.000[a]

Note: [a]Statistically significant.

Table 5. Likelihood of Women in Other Roles where CEO is a Woman

Likelihood of firms with women in the CEO role having women in other roles (2007–2013 average)	χ^2	df	Significance
Likelihood of firms with women CEOs (vs men CEOs) having women winemakers	444.47	1	0.000[a]
Likelihood of firms with women CEOs (vs men CEOs) having women viticulturists	538.22	1	0.000[a]
Likelihood of firms with women CEOs (vs men CEOs) having women marketers	48.77	1	0.000[a]

Note: [a]Statistically significant.

lower percentages of women marketers ($\chi^2 = 5.29, p = 0.021$). Finally, regarding Western Australia, South Australia has a lower proportion of women winemakers ($\chi^2 = 7.53, p = 0.006$), higher percentages of women viticulturists ($\chi^2 = 11.54, p = 0.001$) and a lower proportion of women marketers ($\chi^2 = 15.31, p = 0.000$). The results suggest that there is not a strong pattern with respect to higher women representation rates in South Australia; hence, there is not significant evidence suggesting that location is a strong predictor of the representation rates of women in top roles in the Australian wine industry.

As for *RQ3*, in all cases (Table 5), wine firms with women CEOs tend to have women in winemaker ($\chi^2 = 444.47, p = 0.000$), viticulturist ($\chi^2 = 538.22, p = 0.000$) and marketing roles ($\chi^2 = 48.77, p = 0.000$). Therefore, the findings offer some support that when women take up top roles in business, there is likely to be a flow-on effect regarding the appointment of women to other top roles (Cook and Glass, 2014; Elsaid and Ursel, 2011).

6. Conclusions

The place of women in top business roles is subject to much popular press and has become a topic of interest to organization scholars. Although arguments have been put forth that women in the wine industry are breaking through the glass ceiling with "relative" ease (Cooper, 2009; Fuller, 2008, both cited in Bryant and Garnham, 2014), the findings here challenge perceptions of the advancement of women, while enhancing an understanding of the characteristics that might help or hinder their advancement to top roles.

As this study is the first known large-scale research on women in the wine industry, it contributes to the on-going debate on gender diversity in top business roles, particularly in the Australian context. Relative to women CEOs in Australia's largest 500 firms (a 3% representation rate), women in the wine industry are filling this role at a much higher rate overall (nearly a 13% representation rate), and further, these rates increased from 2007 to 2013, just under industry growth rates in the same period (2.24% and 2.86%). Similarly, with the exception of Queensland and Tasmania, the percentages of women in the CEO grew in all other regions under the study period. Given that across all agriculture industries, the current full-time employment rate of women is around 14%, that there is good representation at the CEO level in the wine industry is a positive. However, in winemaking and viticulturist roles, there appears to be much room for improvement.

The study also expands the work of Hillman *et al.* (2007) and Nekhili and Gatfaoui (2013) on the characteristics that predict women in top roles. Notably, as women face far greater barriers than men in reaching top roles in firms (Terjesen *et al.*, 2009), the expectation is that they strive to achieve "exceptional" status (Unger, 2006). One way they can achieve this is by breaking into top positions in highly visible industries or regions. The results of this study state that while demonstrating that the leading wine region of South Australia does boast some higher representation rates of women in the studied roles than other regions, there are clearly inconsistencies. Hence, penetrating top roles in a firm in a prestigious location might, in some cases, actually be more difficult. For example, in Silicon Valley, the world's most prestigious information technology region, gender representation rates at high levels (e.g., CEO, partner-level positions in venture capital firms) are extremely low (Wadhwa, 2014). Alternatively, this study demonstrates that once a woman reaches the CEO role, this appears to have positive flow-on benefits for the representation rates of women in other top roles. The finding confirms previous research (Cook and Glass, 2014; Elsaid and Ursel, 2011), extending the idea that women "look after their own."

Lastly, this study has practical implications. Specifically, the Australian wine industry is considered to be at cross-roads: overall revenue growth is weak relative to its New World (e.g., Chile and South Africa) competitors; exports have declined; profitable production is conservatively said to be at less than 30% of total production; and climate change appears to be an increasing threat. If women in leadership roles are noted for their creativity, innovativeness and sensitivity to environmental concerns (Galbreath, 2016), then there is a real possibility that the government in Australia will need to debate the issue of gender quotas in the wine industry as a potential means of improving competitiveness. For example, given that in Australia's leading oenology programs around half of the students are now women (Ting, 2013), the federal government could consider an innovative policy by mandating gender quotas for internships or apprentices for specific roles such as winemaking and viticulture to facilitate the movement of women into the industry. In another example, wine-producing states could offer financial incentives that encourage women to own or start wineries. Lastly, wineries could be provided tax breaks by the government for employing women, particularly in the roles studied here.

7. Limitations and Future Research Directions

This study is not without limitations. First, only a single industry in a single country was studied; therefore, generalizability is limited. However, there is some evidence to suggest that the findings are similar to those in other countries, such as the USA (at least with respect to the percentage of women in the winemaker role). Future research needs to take into account other countries to gain a better understanding of whether women are reaching top roles in the wine industry and what factors might be advancing — or impeding — progress. Second, given the nature of the industry and the available data, the study relied mainly on smaller, private firms. However, because a good deal of the published research in the management literature examines women at the boardroom level and top executive positions in the largest, publicly traded firms, this study provides much needed insight beyond such a narrowly defined context. Future research could include large samples of small and medium-sized enterprises (SMEs), as such firms create many jobs (e.g., in Australia, SMEs make up 99% of employing businesses), and the opportunity for women to add value (or advance) here might be greater than in large, high profile companies typically found in the literature. This could also be expanded to examine how and why women in top roles might have more success in specific regions or clusters, as the present study suggests that this is an areas requiring further study. Third, due to lack of available data, this study did not compare family-owned firms to other types of ownership structure. This could influence the results, and future study is needed that examines whether differences exist in the representation rates of women in top roles in family firms versus non-family firms in the wine industry. Finally, that some evidence suggests that women winemakers are producing higher quality wine than men is intriguing. That is study did examine this aspect is a limitation, and future research could expand this area of study beyond the present known work in the USA (Gilbert and Gilbert, 2012).

References

Adams, R.B., and Funk, P. (2012). Beyond the glass ceiling: Does gender matter? *Management Science*, 58(2), 219–235.

Aylward, D. (2007). Innovation and inertia: The emerging dislocation of imperatives within the Australia wine industry. *International Journal of Technology and Globalization*, 3(2/3), 246–262.

Barber, N. (2010). 'Green' wine packaging: Targeting environmental consumers. *International Journal of Wine Business Research*, 22(4), 423–444.

Barber, N., Almanza, B.A., and Donovan, J.R. (2006). Motivational factors of gender, income and age on selecting a bottle of wine. *International Journal of Wine Business Research*, 18(3), 218–232.

Bryant, L., and Garnham, B. (2014). The embodiment of women in wine: Gender inequality and gendered inscriptions of the working body in a corporate wine organization. *Gender, Work & Organization*, 21(5), 411–426.

Burke, R.J. (1997). Women on corporate boards of directors: A needed resource. *Journal of Business Ethics*, 16(9), 909–1015.

Catalyst (2014). Women CEOs of the Fortune 500. Available at: www.catalyst.org/knowledge/women-ceos-fortune-1000 (accessed January 6, 2014).

Connell, S. (2012). *Wine Manufacturing in Australia*. IBISWorld, Sydney.

Cook, A., and Glass, C. (2014). Women and top leadership positions: Towards an institutional analysis. *Gender, Work & Organization*, 21(1), 91–103.

Curtis, M., Schmid, C., and Struber, M. (2012). *Gender Diversity and Corporate Performance*. Credit Suisse, Zurich.

Elsaid, E., and Ursel, N.D. (2011). CEO succession, gender and risk taking. *Gender in Management: An International Journal*, 26(7), 499–512.

Forbes, S.L. (2012). The influence of gender on wine purchasing and consumption. *International Journal of Wine Business Research*, 24(2), 146–159.

Galbreath, J. (2011). Are there gender-related influences on corporate sustainability? A study of women on boards of directors. *Journal of Management & Organization*, 17(1), 17–38.

Galbreath, J. 2016. When do board and management resources complement each other? A study of effects on corporate social responsibility. *Journal of Business Ethics*, 136, 281–292.

Galbreath, J. (2014b). My view. *Australian & New Zealand Grapegrower & Winemaker*, June, p. 6.

Galbreath, J. (2014c). An exploratory study of climate change innovations in wine regions in Australia. Working Paper, Curtin Graduate School of Business, Curtin University, Western Australia.

Gilbert, L.A. (2011). California women winemakers, their accomplishments, and their progress in a male-dominated field. Working Paper, Santa Clara University, Santa Clara, CA.

Gilbert, L.A., and Gilbert, J.C. (2012). Evidence of women winemakers' success in a male-dominated field. Working Paper, Santa Clara University, Santa Clara, CA.

Halliday, J. (2013). *The Australian Wine Companion.* Hardy Grant Books, Richmond, VA.

Heimoff, S. (2007). *New Classic Winemakers of California: Conversations with Steve Heimoff.* University of California Press, Berkeley, CA.

Hillman, A.J., Shropshire, C., and Cannella, A.A. Jr. (2007). Organizational predictors of women on corporate boards. *Academy of Management Journal*, 50, 941–952.

Hogg, M.A. (2006). *Social Identity Theory.* Contemporary Social Psychological Theories, edited by P. Burke. Stanford University Press, Stanford, CA, 111–121.

HRReview (2013). Just 3% of FTSE350 companies have female CEO's now. Available at: www.hrreview.co.uk/hr-news/diversity-equality/just-3-of-companies-have-female-ceos-now/49078 (accessed January 6, 2014).

IBISWorld (2013). Industry insight. Available at: www.ibisworld.com.au/newsletter/news.aspx?id=fe63c5dl-925b-43f7-9168-e703e93b45cc&mgsl=9289bOFFUp#aIndustryl (accessed May 30, 2013).

Kallenberg, A.L., and Keicht, K.T. (1991). Gender and organizational performance: Determinants of small business survival and success. *Academy of Management Journal*, 34, 136–161.

Kansil, M., and Roberts, J. (2013). *Wine Industry Report.* Centaurus Partners, Sydney.

Kauffman, E. (2009). Women in wine. Available at: http://ucdavismagazine.ucdavis.edu/issues/su09/women_in_wine.html (accessed January 7, 2014).

Kelan, E.K. (2008). The discursive construction of gender in contemporary management literature. *Journal of Business Ethics*, 81(2), 427–445.

Krishnan, H.A., and Park, D. (2005). A few good women — on top management teams. *Journal of Business Research*, 58(12), 1712–1720.

McCabe, A.C., Ingram, R., and Dato-on, M.C. (2006). The business of ethics and gender. *Journal of Business Ethics*, 64(2), 101–116.

Marcus Evans (2013). 'Abysmal' that no female CEO among Germany's DAX 30 companies. Available at: www.marcusevans.com/reviews/news.aspPnewsID=202 (accessed January 6, 2014).

Matasar, A.B. (2006). *Women of Wine: The Rise of Women in the Global Wine Industry.* University of California Press, Berkeley, CA.

Morrison, A.M., White, R.P., and Velsor, E.V. (1994). *Breaking the Glass Ceiling.* Basic Books, New York, NY.

Morton, T.A., Postmes, T., Haslam, S.A., and Hornsey, M.J. (2009). Theorizing gender in the face of social change: Is there anything essential about essentialism? *Journal of Personality and Social Psychology*, 96(3), 653–664.

Nekhili, M., and Gatfaoui, H. (2013). Are demographic attributes and firm characteristics drivers of gender diversity? Investigating women's positions on French boards of directors. *Journal of Business Ethics*, 118(2), 227–249.

OIV (2014). 271 mhl of wine produced in 2014. Available at: www.oiv.int/oiv/info/en_OIV_Press_Conference_23_October_2014 (accessed January 7, 2015).

Powell, G.N., and Butterfield, D.A. (2002). Exploring the influence of decision makers' race and gender on actual promotions to top management. *Personnel Psychology*, 55(2), 397–428.

Riek, B.M., Mania, E.W., and Gaertner, S.L. (2006). Intergroup threat and out-group attitudes: A meta-analytic review. *Personality and Social Psychology Review*, 10(4), 336–353.

Rossi, A.S. (1985). *Gender and the Life Course*. Aldine, New York, NY.

Schmitt, M.T., Branscombe, N.R., Kobrynowicz, D., and Owen, S. (2002). Perceiving discrimination against one's gender group has different implications for well-being in women and men. *Personality and Social Psychology Bulletin*, 28(2), 197–210.

Schmitt, M.T., Spoor, J.R., Danaher, K., and Branscombe, N.R. (2009). Rose-coloured glasses: How tokenism and comparisons with the past reduce the visibility of gender inequality. *The Glass Ceiling in the 21st Century*, edited by M. Barreto, M. Ryan, and M.T. Schmitt, American Psychological Association, Washington, DC, 49–71.

Tajfel, H., and Turner, J.C. (1979). An integrative theory of intergroup conflict. *The Social Psychology of Intergroup Relations*, edited by W.G. Austin, and S. Worchel. Brooks/Cole, Monterey, CA, 33–47.

Terjesen, S., Sealy, R., and Singh, V. (2009). Women directors on corporate boards: A review and research agenda. *Corporate Governance: An International Review*, 17(3), 320–337.

Ting, I. (2013). Women in wine are pushing open the cellar door. Available at: www.theage.com.au/action/printArticle?id=4186716 (accessed April 18, 2013).

Torchia, M., Calabro, A., and Huse, M. (2011). Women directors on corporate boards: From tokenism to critical mass. *Journal of Business Ethics*, 102(2), 299–317.

Unger, R.K. (Ed.) (2006). *Handbook of the Psychology of Women and Gender*. John Wiley & Sons, New York, NY.

Wadhwa, V. (2014). The glaring gender dilemma Silicon Valley venture capitalists are hiding from. Available at: www.huffingtonpost.com/vivek-wadhwa/the-glaring-gender-dilemm_b_5948588.html (accessed January 7, 2015).

WGEA (2012). *Australian Census of Women in Leadership*. Commonwealth of Australia, Canberra.

Winetitles (2013). *The Australian and New Zealand Wine Industry Directory*, 31st ed. Winetitles, Prospect East.

Wright, S.C. (1997). Ambiguity, social influence and collective action: Generating protest in response to tokenism. *Personality and Social Psychology Bulletin*, 23(12), 1277–1290.

Chapter 18

In Vino Veritas? Social Influence on "Private" Wine Evaluations at a Wine Social Networking Site*

Omer Gokcekus[†], Miles Hewstone[‡], and Huseyin Cakal[§]

[†]*School of Diplomacy and International Relations,*
Seton Hall University, USA
Omer.Gokcekus@shu.edu

[‡]*Department of Experimental Psychology,*
University of Oxford, UK
miles.hewstone@psy.ox.ac.uk

[§]*School of Psychology, Keele University, UK*
h.cakal@keele.ac.uk

An archival analysis of evaluations of wines provides a unique context in which to investigate social influence in a naturalistic setting. We conducted analyzes based on 6,157 notes about 106 wines posted by wine drinkers at a wine social networking site. Our findings suggest that social influence on private wine evaluations occurred by communicating a descriptive norm via written information. We provide empirical evidence that there is social influence on private wine evaluations that is greater than the effect of experts' ratings and prices combined. This influence comes mainly from the first few group members, and increases as a function of source uniformity. Together with a lack of evidence that more credible or expert members have more influence, these findings suggest that influence in this setting is normative rather than informational. Results have implications for widespread effects of social influence on consumer and other websites where we are subject to the power of others' opinions.

"I can certainly see that you know your wine. Most of the guests who stay here wouldn't know the difference between Bordeaux and Claret." *Basil Fawlty, "Fawlty Towers"*

*This article originally appeared in *American Association of Wine Economists* (2014), AAWE Working Paper No. 153.

1. Introduction

Evaluations of wine, like many other forms of evaluation, might sensibly be based on the views of others, especially if one is as ignorant as Basil Fawlty. Wine drinkers typically pay attention not only to prices but also to others', especially experts', ratings to determine the quality of a wine (Schamel, 2000). Yet, several studies (e.g., Ashenfelter, 1990; Hodgson, 2008) have shown that an expert's opinion regarding quality can be seriously flawed. Moreover, as Reuter (2009) explains, due to conflict of interest, a wine expert's reviews might be biased (e.g., where a magazine, such as *Wine Spectator*, is an influential rating agency, and its reliance on advertising revenues may be associated with an inflation of ratings for advertisers' wines).

While economists have studied how signals from *unfamiliar others* — wine experts and price setters — play an important role in shaping wine drinkers' opinion regarding the quality of a bottle of wine, social psychologists have extensively documented how and why people are influenced by actions and beliefs of *similar others* (Asch, 1956; Cialdini *et al.*, 1990; Cialdini and Goldstein, 2004; Sherif, 1936). This research typically distinguishes influence that is "normative" ("to conform with the positive expectations of another"; Deutsch and Gerard, 1955, p. 629) versus "informational" ("to accept information obtained from another as *evidence* about reality"; *ibid.*). Social-psychological research has also shown that social influence has a significant effect even when the actions of the other people are not directly observed (Nolan *et al.*, 2008). An obvious, if relatively ignored, source of wider influence is provided by the wide reach and easy access recently provided by the internet, with consumers having even started "...abandoning traditional expert sources in favor of the perspectives of their peers" (Griskevicius *et al.*, 2008, p. 84) over a wide range of issues (see Chevalier and Mayzlin, 2006; Iyengar *et al.*, 2009).

In this chapter, we analyze the ratings posted by regular wine drinkers belonging to a webbased wine network, where wine evaluations and ratings become available to members once they are posted. Using this naturalistic data we conduct an archival analysis to ascertain the extent of the influence that prior ratings have in shaping other group members' opinions. The analysis focuses, in particular, on individuals' and the group's average ratings of a bottle of wine. By doing so, it effectively tests the validity of the argument that wine drinkers belonging to a group form their opinion, and thereafter assign a particular rating either to conform to the positive expectations of the others in their group or by accepting information obtained from the other members of the group as evidence about reality (see Festinger, 1950).

Wine ratings appear sequentially on the website we studied (i.e., after each new rating is added), allowing us to assess both the importance of "group size" and the uniformity of opinions in this form of social influence. Asch's (1951, 1956) early studies of the numerical size of the majority showed that conformity increased quite dramatically as the number of majority members increased from one to three, but the influence of additional members was minimal. Later studies by Gerard *et al.* (1968) and by Latané and Wolf (1981) suggested, however, that adding more members to the majority will, in effect, lead to more conformity but with diminishing increments per added member (see Bond and Smith, 1996). The exact nature of the function relating majority size to conformity remains an issue of debate between those who posit a linear relationship versus those who favor one or another form of non-linear relationship (Bond and Smith, 1996). Classic studies of social influence also showed that conformity is dramatically weakened when the unanimity of the majority is broken (Asch, 1951; Allen and Levine, 1971); this would lead us to expect greater impact of prior wine ratings when they were uniform. Finally, source credibility is a key determinant of persuasion (e.g., Maheswaran and 4 Chaiken, 1991), and conformity is increased by factors that increase the credibility of a majority as a valid source of reality (e.g., status and expertise) (Kiesler and Kiesler, 1969), and decreased by factors that weaken its credibility (e.g., Allen and Levine, 1971). Hence we would expect more credible, expert group members to have greater influence.

2. A Wine Social Networking Site

Cellartracker.com is the world's largest wine social networking site, in both number of catalogued bottles and number of listed tasting notes. For instance, as of November 7th, 2012, there were 233,316 users who owned 36,445,657 bottles; and Cellartracker.com's database contained 1,369,914 different wines with 2,951,070 free wine reviews from real users, and more than 404,271 professional reviews from 23 publications. While the reviews from real users are freely available at the site, professional reviews require paid subscription to the relevant publications.

The real users of the site, i.e., social group members, are allowed to freely post their reviews either by using their iPhone app cor.kz or visiting the internet site. That is to say, group members post their evaluations *in private*. However, when a group member decides to post his or her note on a particular wine, three categories of information about this wine are available for their perusal (see Supplemental Online Materials). The first section contains information on various wine classification categories such as vintage, type, producer, variety, region, sub-region, appellation, and label. The second section is about the optimum time interval within which one should drink the wine. Finally, the third section, of most interest to the scholar of social influence, contains the community tasting history (i.e., information posted by previous drinkers from within the wine network); as the site is set up, it is not possible to avoid seeing this 5 information before posting an evaluation. After a summary of the previous posts, i.e., (a) number of already posted notes, (b) mean, and (c) median score from these notes, each individual note (except the ones with no text) is listed. By clicking on the username of a community member who posted a note with a text, you would learn five different things about that member: (a) how many bottles of wine are in their inventory, (b) how many bottles they had consumed over time, (c) how many tasting notes they wrote, (d) how many members of cellartracker.com follow them, and (e) how many group members they follow.

3. Hypotheses

We tested five hypotheses:

Hypothesis 1a: There will be a direct relationship between the wine evaluations to which visitors to the website (hereafter, respondents) are exposed and their own subsequent wine evaluations; and Hypothesis 1b: this association could be even stronger than the one between respondents' evaluations and professionals' (experts') evaluations and prices.

Hypothesis 2: There will be a direct, positive relationship between the uniformity of wine evaluations to which respondents are exposed and their own subsequent wine evaluations.

Hypothesis 3: The impact of the first 3–4 evaluations will be greatest, with diminishing increments per added wine rater.

Hypothesis 4: The respondents' wine evaluations will be more in agreement with the prior evaluations, when the prior evaluations are made by more "credible" group members.

4. Method

4.1. *Data base: Wines and respondents*

To control for the effects of numerous other factors on individual evaluations, we assembled a homogeneous sample of wines. We chose wines (a) of a particular vintage (2008); (b) of a specific variety (cabernet sauvignon), and, (c) from a specific wine region, i.e., county-regionsubregion-appellation (U.S., California, Napa, Napa AVA) to yield a sufficient sample on which to test our hypotheses. From all of the available 2008 Napa Cabernet Sauvignon wines listed at Cellartracker.com, we chose 106 with at least 10 or more notes on November 17th, 2011.

In addition to collecting data on November 17th, 2011, for these 106 wines, we collected data three more times within the following year to assess stability of ratings (February 11th, 2012; April 11th, 2012; November 7th, 2012). For each wine, we tabulated the scores from community tasting history, experts' rating scores, average U.S. retail prices, and characteristics of each group member who posted a note with a score.

Table 1 presents the summary statistics for 106 wines in our sample. On November 17th, 2011, the average score (out of 100 points) was 89.60, and average price was \$55.38. There were 3,227 notes submitted, in other words there were 30 notes per wine. The retail prices and experts' ratings were not subject to change over time. However, the number of notes almost doubled within a year: As of November 7th, 2012, there were 6,157 notes, 58 notes per wine. Within the same time period, however, the average community score stayed pretty much unchanged (within the range 89.52–89.60).

5. Results

To test Hypothesis 1a, that there is a direct relationship between the wine evaluations to which respondents are exposed and their own subsequent wine evaluations; we estimated the following regression model:

$$\text{Group score}_{\text{i}} = \alpha + \beta^{*}\text{First} - \text{j score}_{\text{i}} + \nu_{\text{i}}. \qquad (1)$$

Group score_{i} is the average score for wine i, excluding the first four group members' scores; First-j score_{i} is the average score for the first j group members for wine i; α and β are scalars; and ν_{i} is a random disturbance term.

Table 2 reports the regression results; from column (1) to column (4) it shows the estimated coefficients (α and β) and their standard errors for First-1 score, First-2 score, First-3 score, First-4 score, and, as a goodness-of-fit

Table 1. Summary Data for Number of Notes, Average Score, Experts' Score, and Average Price

	Number of notes				Average score								Experts' score	Average price
	Nov. '11	Feb. '12	April '12	Nov '12	Nov. '11	Feb. '12	April '12	Nov. '12	First-1 score	First-2 score	First-3 score	First-4 score	Nov. '11	Nov. '11
Average	30	39	44	58	89.60	89.52	89.53	89.52	89.62	89.49	89.58	89.62	90.96	$55.38
Std. Dev.	30	32	39	51	3.05	3.06	3.05	3.01	3.57	3.57	3.48	3.57	3.33	$70.24
Minimum	10	11	11	12	78.20	78.20	78.20	78.20	79.00	77.00	76.67	75.50	82.00	$3.00
Maximum	239	239	304	365	97.20	97.20	97.00	97.00	98.00	98.00	98.00	98.25	100.00	$479.00
Total	3,227	4,095	4,684	6,157									36	

Source: Data is from cellartracker.com; except for experts' score, i.e., professional ratings, that are from wineaccess.com, winebid.com, and hdwine.com (accessed on November 17, 2011).

Table 2. OLS Regression Results: Average Wine Scores (Minus First Four Group Members) as Dependent Variable

Explanatory variable	(1)	(2)	(3)	(4)	(5) (WLS)	(6)	(7)	(8)	(9)	(10)
First-1 score	0.637 (0.05)*									
First-2 score		0.670 (0.05)*								
First-3 score			0.712 (0.05)*							
First-4 score				0.712 (0.04)*	0.710 (0.04)*	0.742 (0.06)*			0.540 (0.07)*	0.662 (0.05)*
Experts' score							0.632 (0.08)*	0.543 (0.10)*	0.294 (0.08)*	
Price								0.004 (0.003)	0.001 (0.002)	
Inventory*First-4 score										0.003 (0.001)*
Tasting notes*First-4 score										0.000 (0.001)
Members they follow*First-4 score										−0.129 (0.41)
Their followers*First-4 score										−0.041 (0.42)
Constant	32.442	29.452	25.745	25.687	25.958	23.548	33.838	41.562	15.193	29.585
F-statistic	144.045	187.268	228.025	276.223	264.976	144.112	64.595	34.091	74.874	61.265
R^2	0.581	0.643	0.687	0.726	0.718	0.809	0.655	0.674	0.875	0.756
Adjusted R^2	0.577	0.640	0.684	0.724	0.715	0.803	0.654	0.654	0.864	0.743
No. of observation	106	106	106	106	106	36	36	36	36	106

Note: Numbers in parentheses are standard deviations; *indicates that the estimated coefficients are statistically significant at 0.01 level.

measure, it presents F-statistic, R^2 and adjusted-R^2. All of the estimated coefficients were statistically significant at 0.01 level. Moreover, variations in First-1 score explained 58% of the variations in Group score; First-2 score 64%; First-3 score 69%; and First-4 score 73%.[1]

We next tested Hypothesis 1b, whether this association could be even stronger than the one between respondents' evaluations and experts' (opinion leaders') evaluations and prices. To do so, first, we estimated the model above, with 36 observation points, by utilizing all 36/106 wines in our sample that experts had evaluated. The regression result is reported in Column (6) of Table 2: Estimated coefficients were statistically significant at the 0.01 level; and variations in First-4 score explained 81% of the variations in the Group score. Second, we modeled the Group score as a function of (a) experts' score and (b) experts' score and price. As is reported in Column (7) the estimated coefficient for the experts' score was statistically significant at 0.01 level; and variations in the experts' score explained 66% of the variations in the Group score. When we utilized both the experts' score and the price as explanatory variables, Column (8) shows that while the estimated coefficient for the experts' score was statistically significant at 0.01 level, the coefficient for the price was not; and variations in the experts' score and the prices together explained 67% of the variations in the Group score. Consequently, these results show that variations in the scores of the first four group members did a better job by 14–15% points in explaining the variations in the Group score than either variations in the experts' score or the experts' score and the price together. To further compare experts and First-4 group members' opinion effects, we estimated the model including First-4 score, Experts' score and Price. As shown in Column (9), the estimated coefficient for First-4 score (0.540, $p < 0.01$) was almost twice as big as the coefficient for Experts' score (0.294, $p < 0.01$).

Next, we tested Hypothesis 2, that there is a direct relationship between the uniformity of wine evaluations to which respondents are exposed and their own subsequent wine evaluations. We assessed the strength of the linkage between the Group score (the average score per wine, excluding the first four group members' scores) and the First-4 score. In particular, we assessed whether a lack of uniformity among the First-four group members' scores, by sending mixed signals regarding the consensus among these first

[1]To deal with a potential heteroscedasticity problem, we estimated the model with Weighted Least Squares method and report the results in Column (5). The similarity between coulmns 4 and 5 indicates that using the OLS was appropriate.

four members, made subsequent group members' wine ratings less likely to conform with the first four members' wine evaluations (because of a lack of a clear, consensus score to conform to). To do so, we first calculated the deviations between the Group score and the First-4 score, for each wine separately. In particular, to treat upward and downward differences of the similar magnitude in the same way, we calculated, $|\text{Group score}_i - \text{First} - 4\ \text{score}_i|$. Second, we calculated the standard deviations between the first four scores, (STD-4), as our proxy for uniformity. Accordingly, the larger the standard deviation, the less uniform the wine evaluations to which respondents are exposed. Then we estimated the following model:

$$|\text{Group score}_i - \text{First} - 4\ \text{score}_i| = \delta_0 + \delta_1^*(\text{STD} - 4_i) + \upsilon_i, \qquad (2)$$

where δ_0 and δ_1 are scalars, and υ_i is a random disturbance term. According to the regression results, $\delta_0 = 0.716$ and $\delta_1 = 0.311$, and they are statistically significant at 0.01 level. Thus, there was a direct relationship between the "uniformity" of wine evaluations to which respondents were exposed and their own subsequent wine evaluations.

To test Hypothesis 3 we ran three more regressions, with First-5, First-6 and First-7 raters, respectively, as the source of potential influence. The regression results clearly supported this hypothesis; the change in R^2 diminished with each subsequent addition of a member to the source (member 2: +0.062; member 3: +0.051; member 4: +0.042; member 5: +0.031; member 6: +0.026; and member 7: +0.013). It might not seem surprising that, e.g., adding one observation to a group of four does not change the mean by much. However, even when we look at the % change in R^2 divided by % change in group size, results are similar: each (percentagewise normalized) additional group member adds more, first with an increasing and then with a decreasing rate (group size 2: 0.107; 3: 0.159; 4: 0.183; 5: 0.171; 6: 0.172; 7: 0.100).

Finally, we tested Hypothesis 4, that the respondents' wine evaluations would be more in agreement with the prior evaluations, when the prior evaluations came from more "credible" group members, and therefore would be seen as more informative. First, to capture the interaction effect of "credibility," we multiplied the First-4 score by different characteristics of the group members who posted the first four notes, namely (a) number of bottles of wine in their inventory, (b) number of tasting notes they wrote, (c) number of Cellartracker.com members who follow them, and (d) number of group members they follow, respectively. Second, we estimated the Group score as a function of the First-4 score and these four interaction effects. Estimation results are summarized in Column (10) in Table 2. These results do not yield support for hypothesis 4; there was no statistically significant interaction between First-4 score and three of the credibility indicators; the exception was the interaction effect of number of bottles in inventory ($p < 0.01$); yet the estimated magnitude of this interaction effect was very small, 0.003.

6. Discussion

We used real data from a wine networking site to test five hypotheses about social influences on wine evaluations. The results are largely in line with the hypotheses, confirming that wine evaluations are subject to social influence that appears to be normative rather than informational in nature.

In support of Hypothesis 1a we found a significant direct relationship between the wine evaluations to which respondents were exposed and their own subsequent wine evaluations. Variations in the first four group members' ratings explained 73% of the variation in subsequent wine evaluations. Consistent with Hypothesis 1b, the first four group members' ratings, regardless of the variations among these ratings, explained the rest of the group's average rating better (by some 14–15%) than expert ratings and price combined.[2]

Confirming Hypothesis 2, we found that the more uniform the earlier evaluations were, the closer the subsequent wine evaluations were to the average rating of the earlier evaluations. This result is consistent with the idea that, for normative social influence to occur, there needs to be a clear consensus score to conform to.

As predicted by Hypothesis 3, the first 3–4 evaluations by other raters had the greatest impact, with diminishing increments for each added wine rater. Adding further raters to the first four did not greatly increase the percentage of variance explained. These findings concerning the 11 major impact of the first few members are consistent with Asch's (1951, 1956) classic studies of conformity, but the finding of additional (albeit diminishing)

[2]It might be argued that if some wines were so good or so bad, the truth really would be in the wine, with no need for social influence. However, even though, as noted above, the average quality of wines was high, it was not maximal, and if there were no social influence, we would have detected no effect of especially the first few group members, which we did. Moreover, most of the ratings were within a narrow range: When we checked the first ten ratings for each of our 106 wines, 23 were within a range of $+/-2$ points, and 91 were within a range of $+/-5$ points, of the group mean.

influence with added members is more in line with earlier findings of Gerard *et al.* (1968) and Latane and Wolf (1981).

Results did not, however, support Hypothesis 4, that wine evaluations would be more in agreement with prior evaluations, when those ratings were made by more "credible" group members. Notwithstanding prior evidence for source credibility (e.g., Maheswaran and Chaiken, 1991) and expertise (Kiesler and Kiesler, 1969) as determinants of influence, it appears that informational social influence was not operative in group members' wine evaluations, or that despite using four possible indicators of credibility or expertise in the wine domain, we failed to detect greater impact of more credible group members because the construct validity of our measures of expertise was low.

Taken together, these findings suggest that there is social influence on private wine evaluations; its magnitude is larger and more significant than the effect of experts and prices combined; and it is normative rather than informational influence. As was the case in earlier studies of social influence in other domains (e.g., Goldstein *et al.*, 2008; Park *et al.*, 2001; Schultz, 1999), even without direct observation, social influence occurred by communicating a descriptive norm via written information.

We acknowledge some limitations of the study, which arise from how this networking site operates. First, we cannot be sure that members of the network do consult others' views before making their own ratings. However, that information is physically present, and would be hard to ignore; and the results are entirely consistent with them being influenced by the views of others. Second, raters only rate wines once; they do not first give their own ratings, then consult others' ratings, and then re-rate the wines. Thus we can only infer the workings of social influence in what is, in effect, a post-test only design. However, we were studying an actual wine networking site, and so this is how it works, and how presumably many people's views of wines are formed and changed. Far from reducing social influence, the internet (whether we are buying wine or books, or reserving hotels) may increase a particular, normative form of influence.

Overall, the findings may surprise some readers, especially the stronger evidence for normative than informational influence in this setting. Two plausible explanations may shed light on this observation. First, it is possible that people in wine evaluation situations do not use the ratings of others as evidence about the true nature of the product, i.e., they don't view the others as mediators of fact. After all, wine is not only an experience good'; wine evaluations may vary depending on cultural, personal biases and differences in sense of taste (Bartoshuk, 1978) and preferences of drinkers. For instance, as Amerine and Roessler (1983, pp. 57–64) explain, both physiological and psychological factors play a role in sensory performance. Second, we should consider the nature of the setting in which wine evaluations in our study were shared. Although group members in this wine networking site wrote their notes in private, once a group member writes their note it becomes visible by the rest of the group members. There is no anonymity within the group. In particular, those members who are following you, group members who are in your inner circle, will be automatically informed about your rating. This fact about perfect visibility, combined with (a) the significant direct relationship between the wine evaluations to which respondents are exposed and their own subsequent wine evaluations, and (b) the direct relationship between the uniformity of wine evaluations to which respondents are exposed and their own subsequent wine evaluations, further supports the idea that compliance, i.e., normative influence is a significant determinant of wine evaluation in this setting.

Finally, the results of our study have clear implications for marketers and managers in the wine business. In particular, marketers need to pay attention to how wine drinkers shape their views and opinions regarding the quality of a bottle of wine, because wine drinkers' opinions in return determine which wine people will be interested in buying and how much they will be willing to pay in the future. After all, wine is a non-durable consumption good, and it is purchased frequently and on a regular basis. If indeed, as our findings suggest, social influence is more important than experts' views, and social influence is not informational but normative, then it would be wise for communicators to utilize appropriate channels for their persuasive appeal to wine drinkers.

Acknowledgments

We would like to thank the following for their help and suggestions: Orley Ashenfelter, William D. Crano, Charles Judd, Robin Martin, Edward Tower, Willmetta Warholyk, and the participants of the Session #4A: Judges, Experts and Consumers of the AAWE's 6th Annual Conference in Princeton, NJ, USA, June 8th, 2012.

Declaration of Conflicting Interests

The authors declared no potential conflicts of interest with respect to the research, authorship, and/or publication of this article.

Authorship Information

O. Gokcekus developed the study concept and design, and collected and analyzed the data. O. Gokcekus and M. Hewstone performed data interpretation and drafted the chapter. All authors provided critical revisions and approved the final version of the chapter for submission.

References

Allen, V.L., and Levine, J.M. (1971). Social support and conformity: The effect of response order and differentiation from the group. *British Journal of Social and Clinical Psychology*, 10, 181–184.

Amerine, M.A., and Roessle, E.B. (1983). *Wines: Their sensory evaluation* (2nd ed.). New York, NY: W.H. Freeman and Company.

Asch, S.E. (1951). Effects of group pressure on the modification and distortion of judgments. *Groups, Leadership and Men*, edited by H. Guetzkow. Pittsburgh, PA: Carnegie Press' pp. 177–190.

Asch, S.E. (1956). Studies of independence and conformity: A minority of one against unanimous majority. *Psychological Monographs: General and Applied*, 7, 1–70. doi:10.1037/h0093718.

Ashenfelter, O. (1990). Just how good are wine writers' predictions? (Surprise! The recent vintages are rated highest!). *Liquid Assets*, 7, 1–9.

Bartoshuk, L. (1978). The psychophysics of taste. *The American Journal of Clinical Nutrition*, 31, 1068–1077.

Bond, R., and Smith, P. (1996). Culture and conformity: A meta-analysis of studies using Asch's (1952b, 1956) line judgment task. *Psychological Bulletin*, 119, 111–137.

Chevalier, J., and Mayzlin, D. (2006). The effect of word of mouth on sales: Online book reviews. *Journal of Marketing Research*, 43, 345–354.

Cialdini, R.B., and Goldstein, N.J. (2004). Social influence: Compliance and conformity. *Annual Review of Psychology*, 55, 591–621.

Cialdini, R.B., Reno, R., and Kallgren, C. (1990). A focus theory of normative conduct: Recycling the concept of norms to reduce littering in public places. *Journal of Personality and Social Psychology*, 58, 1015–1026.

Deutsch, M., and Gerard, H.B. (1955). A study of normative and informational social influences upon individual judgment. *Journal of Abnormal and Social Psychology*, 51, 629–636.

Festinger, L. (1950). Informal social communication. *Psychological Review*, 57, 271–282.

Gerard, H.B., Wilhelmy, R.A., and Conelly, E.S. (1968). Conformity and group size. *Journal of Personality and Social Psychlogy*, 8, 79–82.

Goldstein, N.J., Cialdini, R.B., and Griskevicius, V. (2008). A room with a viewpoint: Using social norms to motivate environmental conservation in hotels. *Journal of Consumer Research*, 35, 472–482.

Griskevicius, V., Cialdini, R.B., and Goldstein, N.J. (2008). Applying (and resisting) peer influence. *MIT/Sloan Management Review*, 49, 84–88.

Hodgson, R.T. (2008). An examination of judge reliability at a major U.S. wine competition. *Journal of Wine Economics*, 3, 105–113.

Iyengar, R., Han, S., and Gupta, S. (2009). Do friends influence purchases in a social network? Harvard Business School Working Paper 09–123. Harvard University.

Kiesler, C.A., and Kiesler, S.B. (1969). *Conformity*. Reading, MA: Addison Wesley.
Latane, B., and Wolf, S. (1981). The social impact of majorities and minorities. *Psychological Review*, 88, 438–453.
Maheswaran, D., and Chaiken, S. (1991). Promoting systematic processing in low motivation settings: The effect of incongruent information on processing and judgment. *Journal of Personality and Social Psychology*, 61, 13–25.
Nolan, J.M., Schultz, P.W., Cialdini, R.B., Goldstein, N.J., and Griskevicius, V. (2008). Normative social influence is underdetected. *Personality and Social Psychology Bulletin*, 34, 913–923.
Parks, C.D., Sanna, L.J., and Berel, S.R. (2001). Actions of similar others as inducements to cooperate in social dilemmas. *Personality and Social Psychology Bulletin*, 27, 345–354.
Reuter, J. (2009). Does advertising bias product reviews? An analysis of wine ratings. *Journal of Wine Economics*, 4, 125–151.
Schamel, G. (2000). Individual and collective reputation indicators of wine quality. CIES Discussion Paper 9. University of Adelaide: Centre for International Economic Studies.
Schultz, P.W. (1999). Changing behavior with normative feedback interventions: A field experiment on curbside recycling. *Basic and Applied Social Psychology*, 21, 25–36.
Sherif, M. (1936). *The psychology of social norms*. New York, NY: Harper.

Supplemental Online Material

An example cellartracker.com entry for a 2008 Napa Cabernet Sauvignon

2008 ZD Wines Cabernet Sauvignon (*USA, California, Napa Valley*)

Vintage	2008
Type	Red
Producer	ZD Wines (web)
Variety	Cabernet Sauvignon
Designation	n/a
Vineyard	n/a
Country	USA
Region	California
SubRegion	Napa Valley
Appellation	Napa Valley
UPC Code	044956001155

(NOTE: Label borrowed from 2005 vintage.)

Drinking Windows and Values

Drinking window: Drink between 2011 and 2018 *(based on 1 user opinion)*

Community Tasting History

Community Tasting Notes *(average 90.7 pts. and median of 90 pts. in 14 notes)* — hiding notes with no text

(*Continued*)

(*Continued*)

Community Tasting History

Tasted by Mezzomorto on 10/16/2011 and rated 89 points: Mint on the nose, a hint of wood tannins. Blueberry and mild currant notes up front. Clear vanilla mid palate. Smooth tannins overshadow medium acidity. A reasonable contender, perhaps more complex than 07. *(1631 views)*

Tasted by wineglas on 10/1/2011 and rated 87 points: Oak, cherry, spice and vanilla. Not real complex but drinkable. Taste like a $15/$20 Cabernet from California. *(1620 views)*

Tasted by christophee on 8/28/2011 and rated 88 points: Garnet and ruby with medium viscosity in the glass. Plum, blueberry, cassis and peppermint (Ricola) on the nose. Medium/full body with mouth coating blueberry, cherry and earth on the palate. Secondary bacon and wet tobacco. Soft tannin. Long finish, which becomes oak dominated. *(1697 views)*

Tasted by cashflow on 8/6/2011 and rated 90 points: Soft tannins and smooth. *(1693 views)*

Tasted by jdesimone4 on 6/30/2011 and rated 88 points: tried at the vineyard; very nice. smooth and not too tannic *(1758 views)*

Tasted by SipsnTips on 4/29/2011 and rated 91 points: Nice fruit notes. Tobacco on the mid palate smooth tannins. *(1860 views)*

Tasted by Anonymous on 4/3/2011: This was better than anticipated. Fruit forward, but still dry and solidly balanced. 90ish? Not my favorite style typically, but a crowd pleaser. *(1844 views)*

User Profile for "SipsnTips" (User #68,047, signed up 12/17/2008)

Bottles in inventory: 482
Bottles consumed: 238
Tasting notes written: 109 *(by time, by region, by producer, by varietal)*
Favorite tasters of SipsnTips: Anthony28rx, Istaples, yellowbird
These tasters list SipsnTips among THEIR favorites: flydcjets, Istaples

Source: www.cellartracker.com/wine.asp?iWine=1075044 (accessed on November 7, 2012.)

Index